THE PAPERS OF

THOMAS JEFFERSON

RETIREMENT SERIES

THE PAPERS OF

Thomas Jefferson

RETIREMENT SERIES

Volume 11

19 January to 31 August 1817

J. JEFFERSON LOONEY, EDITOR

ROBERT F. HAGGARD, SENIOR ASSOCIATE EDITOR

JULIE L. LAUTENSCHLAGER, ASSOCIATE EDITOR

ELLEN C. HICKMAN AND ANDREA R. GRAY, ASSISTANT EDITORS

LISA A. FRANCAVILLA, MANAGING EDITOR

ALLISON N. MADAR AND PAULA VITERBO,
EDITORIAL ASSISTANTS

CATHERINE CLARKE COINER AND SUSAN SPENGLER,
SENIOR DIGITAL TECHNICIANS

PRINCETON AND OXFORD

PRINCETON UNIVERSITY PRESS

2014

Published by Princeton University Press, 41 William Street,
Princeton, New Jersey 08540
In the United Kingdom:
Princeton University Press, 6 Oxford Street,
Woodstock, Oxfordshire OX20 1TW

Library of Congress Cataloging-in-Publication Data

Jefferson, Thomas, 1743–1826
The papers of Thomas Jefferson. Retirement series / J. Jefferson Looney, editor ...
[et al.] p. cm.
Includes bibliographical references and index.
Contents: v. 1. 4 March to 15 November 1809—[etc.]—
v. 11. 19 January to 31 August 1817
ISBN 978-0-691-16411-3 (cloth: v. 11: alk. paper)
1. Jefferson, Thomas, 1743–1826—Archives. 2. Jefferson, Thomas, 1743–1826—
Correspondence. 3. Presidents—United States—Archives.
4. Presidents—United States—Correspondence. 5. United States—
Politics and government—1809–1817—Sources. 6. United States—Politics and
government—1817–1825—Sources. I. Looney, J. Jefferson.
II. Title. III. Title: Retirement series.
E302.J442 2004b
973.4'6'092—dc22 2004048327

This book has been composed in Monticello

Princeton University Press books are printed on
acid-free paper and meet the guidelines for permanence
and durability of the Committee on Production
Guidelines for Book Longevity of the
Council on Library Resources

Printed in the United States of America

DEDICATED TO THE MEMORY OF

ADOLPH S. OCHS

PUBLISHER OF THE NEW YORK TIMES

1896–1935

WHO BY THE EXAMPLE OF A RESPONSIBLE

PRESS ENLARGED AND FORTIFIED

THE JEFFERSONIAN CONCEPT

OF A FREE PRESS

THIS EDITION was made possible by a founding grant from The New York Times Company to Princeton University.

The Retirement Series is sponsored by the Thomas Jefferson Foundation, Inc., of Charlottesville, Virginia. It was created with a six-year founding grant from The Pew Charitable Trusts to the Foundation and to Princeton University, enabling the former to take over responsibility for the volumes associated with this period. Leading gifts from Richard Gilder, Mrs. Martin S. Davis, Thomas A. Saunders III, Janemarie D. and Donald A. King, Jr., Alice Handy and Peter Stoudt, and Harlan Crow have assured the continuation of the Retirement Series. For these essential donations, and for other indispensable aid generously given by librarians, archivists, scholars, and collectors of manuscripts, the Editors record their sincere gratitude.

FOREWORD

THE 584 DOCUMENTS in this volume cover the period from 19 January to 31 August 1817, during which Jefferson devoted much of his time and attention to efforts to transform his educational vision into reality. In May 1817 at its first official meeting, the Central College Board of Visitors authorized land purchases and the launch of a subscription campaign that would eventually raise more than $44,000. Jefferson solicited architectural advice for the college from his friends William Thornton and Benjamin Henry Latrobe. Thornton's detailed response included a sketch for the central pavilion and his thoughts on the most effective academic organization, while Latrobe and Jefferson exchanged multiple letters on the subject. Late in August, Jefferson went so far as to write an anonymous letter in support of the endeavor, which Thomas Ritchie published in the *Richmond Enquirer* at his request. Jefferson also spent a great deal of time late in 1816 and early in 1817 preparing a legal brief for his chancery suit against the directors of the Rivanna Company. After years of disagreements and failed negotiations, Jefferson first composed and heavily revised a draft of a lengthy legal statement of his claim to the property rights in dispute. Later he copied the material out clean and added a series of supporting documents to bolster his argument. Although the complaint was submitted to the court in May 1817, the case was not settled until December 1819.

In March 1817 Jefferson's friend James Monroe began his first term as United States president. During the summer Jefferson learned of the death of two European friends, Madame de Staël Holstein and Pierre Samuel Du Pont de Nemours. He encouraged his friend Tadeusz Kosciuszko to leave Switzerland and relocate to or at least near Monticello, enjoining him to "close a life of liberty in a land of liberty. come and lay your bones with mine in the Cemetery of Monticello." Jefferson continued to enjoy the companionship of his own family, and in August he and his granddaughters Ellen W. Randolph (Coolidge) and Cornelia J. Randolph set out on a visit to Poplar Forest that included a trip to Natural Bridge. He wrote to his "dearest daughter & friend" Martha Jefferson Randolph from Poplar Forest that "the sun, moon and stars move here so much like what they do at Monticello, and every thing else so much in the same order, not omitting even the floods of rain, that they afford nothing new for observation."

Jefferson's mail arrived from a wide variety of correspondents both domestic and international. Lynchburg resident Thomas Humphreys provided him with a detailed plan for emancipating American slaves and colonizing them in Africa, while Jean Mourer wrote from Switzerland questioning the institution of slavery in the United States. Francis Hall followed up a visit with Jefferson and his family earlier in the winter of 1816–17 by sending a laudatory poem entitled simply "To Monticello." Richard Peters commented on the state of agriculture locally and nationally, provided his opinions on the study and writing of history, and remarked that at age seventy-three he generally enjoyed a "better State of Health, than falls to the Lot of old Bipeds." Jefferson also received large numbers of books, pamphlets, and orations sent by eager authors and political allies. The items sent to him during the months covered in this volume included a novel by Horatio G. Spafford, a series of printed circulars from various committees of the New-York Historical Society, a map of Louisiana from William Darby, a publication prospectus for another map of that state from Maxfield Ludlow, and a work by Barbé Marbois on the conspiracy of Benedict Arnold. The young Bostonian George Ticknor was in Paris helping to orchestrate Jefferson's book purchases abroad. At home, John Laval took over for the Philadelphia book merchant Nicolas G. Dufief when the latter left for Europe himself. Jefferson built a new business relationship with the bookseller Fernagus De Gelone, who operated shops in several locations, including New York and Philadelphia. In addition to replenishing his library, Jefferson restocked his wine cellar and pantry with the assistance of Stephen Cathalan in Marseille. Closer to home, he looked for a reliable supply of scuppernong wine from North Carolina and found his middleman in Hutchins G. Burton.

Correspondents continued to appeal to Jefferson's reputation as an enthusiastic supporter of innovation. Richard Claiborne and James Clarke sent letters about their respective improvements in the design of steamboat paddles and measurement of travel by carriage, and Robert H. Saunders sought his advice on the proper placement of lightning rods. Jefferson provided his correspondent George Washington Jeffreys with a catalogue of books for a newly formed agricultural society. Having long thought that reliable weather data was a boon to scientists as well as farmers, Jefferson sent his recently retired friend James Madison a digested version of his weather memorandum book, drawing on Madison's records as well as his own and covering the years since Jefferson left the presidency in 1809. Although Jefferson answered his voluminous correspondence selectively, he still chafed under the burden and remarked to William A. Burwell that "I have been obliged for many months past to rise from table & write from dinner to dark: insomuch that no office I ever was in has been so laborious as my supposed state of retirement at Monticello."

ACKNOWLEDGMENTS

MANY INDIVIDUALS and institutions provided aid and encouragement during the preparation of this volume. Those who helped us to locate and acquire primary and secondary sources and answered our research questions include our colleagues at the Thomas Jefferson Foundation, especially Anna Berkes, Jack Robertson, and Endrina Tay of the Jefferson Library, and architectural historian Gardiner Hallock; Roy E. Goodman and Keith Thomson at the American Philosophical Society; Hervé Chabanne at the Archives Municipales du Havre; Paule Hochuli Dubuis at the Bibliothèque de Genève; Jean-Jacques Eggler at the Bibliothèque et Archives de la Ville de Lausanne; Bibliothèque Nationale de France; Teresa Yoder at the Chicago Public Library; Marianne Martin at the Colonial Williamsburg Foundation; Elizabeth Dunn at Duke University's David M. Rubenstein Rare Book & Manuscript Library; Samuel K. Fore at the Harlan Crow Library in Dallas; Marita Enderl at the Herzogin Anna Amalia Bibliothek, Weimar; Steven Smith at the Historical Society of Pennsylvania; Helen LaCroix, Lisa Hasson, and Amy Cocuzza of Washington, D.C.; Leiden Universiteitsbibliotheek; Bruce Kirby, Julie Miller, and Julia Schifini at the Library of Congress's Manuscript Division and Mark Dimunation and Eric Frazier in Rare Books; Brent Tarter, Minor T. Weisiger, and their colleagues at the Library of Virginia; Debbie Harner at the Maryland Historical Society; Sarah Minegar at the Morristown National Historical Park Archives; Kim Wilson May at the Museum of Early Southern Decorative Arts in Winston-Salem, North Carolina; Margarita Logutova at the National Library of Russia in Saint Petersburg; Tal Nadan at the New York Public Library; Philip L. Hartling at the Nova Scotia Archives; Jayne E. Blair at the Orange County Historical Society; Irene Axelrod at the Phillips Library, Peabody Essex Museum; Carolyn Vega at the Pierpont Morgan Library; Lisa Jacobsen at the Presbyterian Historical Society in Philadelphia; Gabriel Swift and Don C. Skemer at Princeton University Library's Rare Books and Special Collections Department; Alexey Levukin, Anna Mikhaylova, and Natalia Zhukova at the Russian State Historical Museum in Moscow; Alison Foley at the Saint Mary's Seminary and University Archives in Baltimore; Stéphanie Genand at the Société des Études Staëliennes, Blaru, France; Andreas Frankhauser at the Staatsarchiv Solothurn, Switzerland; Ira Rezak, emeritus professor of clinical medicine, Stony Brook University; the Taylor-Kudrolli family of Newton, Mass.; Ann B. Miller at the Virginia Center for Transportation Innovation and Research; Anne

Causey, Margaret Hrabe, Regina Rush, and Ellen Welch at the Albert and Shirley Small Special Collections Library, University of Virginia; Heather Beattie at the Virginia Historical Society; and Caryl Burtner at the Virginia Museum of Fine Arts. As always, we received advice, assistance, and encouragement from many of our fellow documentary editors, including Sara Georgini, Amanda A. Mathews, and Sara Sikes at the Adams Papers; Alysia Cain from the Papers of Benjamin Franklin; Linda Monaco and Bland Whitley at the Papers of Thomas Jefferson at Princeton University; Mary A. Hackett, Angela Kreider, and David B. Mattern of the Papers of James Madison; and Cassandra Good and Daniel Preston from the Papers of James Monroe. Genevieve Moene and Roland H. Simon transcribed and translated the French letters included in this volume; Andreas Broscheid helped with German; Coulter George assisted us with passages in Greek; Rosanna M. Giammanco Frongia and Jonathan T. Hine provided aid with Italian; and John F. Miller lent his aid with Latin quotations. Kevin B. Jones helped us to understand Jefferson's calculations. The maps of Jefferson's Virginia and Albemarle County were created by Rick Britton. The other illustrations that appear in this volume were assembled with the assistance of John Benicewicz and Michael Slade of Art Resource, Inc., for the National Portrait Gallery, Smithsonian Institution; Tom Mullusky at the Gilder Lehrman Collection; Audrey McElhinney at the Library of Virginia; Anna Clutterbuck-Cook and Elaine Heavey at the Massachusetts Historical Society; Jaime Bourassa at the Missouri History Museum; Leah Stearns and Melanie Lower at the Thomas Jefferson Foundation; Christina Deane and Edward Gaynor at the University of Virginia; and Jamison Davis at the Virginia Historical Society. We thankfully acknowledge the efforts of the able staff at Princeton University Press, including Dimitri Karetnikov and Jan Lilly, and our production editor and special friend, Linny Schenck. Stephen Perkins of IDM USA assisted us in all things digital, and the volume's complex typesetting needs were ably addressed by Bob Bartleson and his associates at Integrated Publishing Solutions.

As General Editor of the Papers of Thomas Jefferson and a founding member of the Retirement Series Advisory Committee, Barbara B. Oberg has provided sound advice, steadfast support, and unfailing encouragement to us from the outset, even as she helped the edition as a whole embark on an ambitious digital publication program and directed the editing of thirteen volumes that brought the first chronological series well into Jefferson's presidency. Everyone at the Retirement Series joins in a fond farewell to Barbara and best wishes for a happy and productive future.

EDITORIAL METHOD AND APPARATUS

1. RENDERING THE TEXT

From its inception *The Papers of Thomas Jefferson* has insisted on high standards of accuracy in rendering text, but modifications in textual policy and editorial apparatus have been implemented as different approaches have become accepted in the field or as a more faithful rendering has become technically feasible. Prior discussions of textual policy appeared in Vols. 1:xxix–xxxiv, 22:vii–xi, 24:vii–viii, and 30:xiii–xiv of the First Series.

The textual method of the Retirement Series will adhere to the more literal approach adopted in Volume 30 of the parent edition. Original spelling, capitalization, and punctuation are retained as written. Such idiosyncrasies as Jefferson's failure to capitalize the beginnings of most of his sentences and abbreviations like "mr" are preserved, as are his preference for "it's" to "its" and his characteristic spellings of "knolege," "paiment," and "recieve." Modern usage is adopted in cases where intent is impossible to determine, an issue that arises most often in the context of capitalization. Some so-called slips of the pen are corrected, but the original reading is recorded in a subjoined textual note. Jefferson and others sometimes signaled a change in thought within a paragraph with extra horizontal space, and this is rendered by a three-em space. Blanks left for words and not subsequently filled by the authors are represented by a space approximating the length of the blank. Gaps, doubtful readings of illegible or damaged text, and wording supplied from other versions or by editorial conjecture are explained in the source note or in numbered textual notes. Foreign-language documents, the vast majority of which are in French during the retirement period, are transcribed in full as faithfully as possible and followed by a full translation.

Two modifications from past practice bring this series still closer to the original manuscripts. Underscored text is presented as such rather than being converted to italics. Superscripts are also preserved rather than being lowered to the baseline. In most cases of superscripting, the punctuation that is below or next to the superscripted letters is dropped, since it is virtually impossible to determine what is a period or dash as opposed to a flourish under, over, or adjacent to superscripted letters.

Limits to the more literal method are still recognized, however, and readability and consistency with past volumes are prime considerations. In keeping with the basic design implemented in the first volume of the Papers, salutations and signatures continue to display in large and small capitals rather than upper- and lowercase letters. Expansion marks over abbreviations are silently omitted. With very rare exceptions, deleted text and information on which words were added during the process of composition is not displayed within the document transcription. Based on the Editors' judgment of their significance, such emendations are either described in numbered textual notes or ignored. Datelines for letters are consistently printed at the head of the text, with a comment in the descriptive note when they have been moved. Address information, endorsements, and dockets are quoted or described in the source note rather than reproduced in the document proper.

2. *TEXTUAL DEVICES*

The following devices are employed throughout the work to clarify the presentation of the text.

[...]	Text missing and not conjecturable. The size of gaps longer than a word or two is estimated in annotation.
[ ]	Number or part of number missing or illegible.
[roman]	Conjectural reading for missing or illegible matter. A question mark follows when the reading is doubtful.
[*italic*]	Editorial comment inserted in the text.
<*italic*>	Matter deleted in the manuscript but restored in our text.

3. *DESCRIPTIVE SYMBOLS*

The following symbols are employed throughout the work to describe the various kinds of manuscript originals. When a series of versions is included, the first to be recorded is the version used for the printed text.

Dft	draft (usually a composition or rough draft; multiple drafts, when identifiable as such, are designated "2d Dft," etc.)
Dupl	duplicate
MS	manuscript (arbitrarily applied to most documents other than letters)
PoC	polygraph copy

PrC	press copy
RC	recipient's copy
SC	stylograph copy

All manuscripts of the above types are assumed to be in the hand of the author of the document to which the descriptive symbol pertains. If not, that fact is stated. On the other hand, the following types of manuscripts are assumed not to be in the hand of the author, and exceptions will be noted:

FC	file copy (applied to all contemporary copies retained by the author or his agents)
Tr	transcript (applied to all contemporary and later copies except file copies; period of transcription, unless clear by implication, will be given when known)

4. LOCATION SYMBOLS

The locations of documents printed in this edition from originals in private hands and from printed sources are recorded in self-explanatory form in the descriptive note following each document. The locations of documents printed or referenced from originals held by public and private institutions in the United States are recorded by means of the symbols used in the *MARC Code List for Organizations* (2000) maintained by the Library of Congress. The symbols DLC and MHi by themselves stand for the collections of Jefferson Papers proper in these repositories. When texts are drawn from other collections held by these two institutions, the names of those collections are added. Location symbols for documents held by institutions outside the United States are given in a subjoined list. The lists of symbols are limited to the institutions represented by documents printed or referred to in this volume.

CSmH	Huntington Library, San Marino, California	
	JF	Jefferson File
	JF-BA	Jefferson File, Bixby Acquisition
CtY	Yale University, New Haven, Connecticut	
DLC	Library of Congress, Washington, D.C.	
	TJ Papers	Thomas Jefferson Papers (this is assumed if not stated, but also given as indicated to furnish the precise location of an undated, misdated, or otherwise problematic document, thus "DLC: TJ Papers, 213:38071–2"

represents volume 213, folios 38071 and 38072 as the collection was arranged at the time the first microfilm edition was made in 1944–45. Access to the microfilm edition of the collection as it was rearranged under the Library's Presidential Papers Program is provided by the *Index to the Thomas Jefferson Papers* [1976])

DNA	National Archives, Washington, D.C., with identifications of series (preceded by record group number) as follows:
	CS — Census Schedules
	CTSLO — Central Treasury and State Loan Office Records Relating to the 6-Percent Converted Stock of 1807
	LAR — Letters of Application and Recommendation
	NPEDP — Naturalization Petitions to the United States Circuit and District Courts for the Eastern District of Pennsylvania
	PMSC — Petitions and Memorials to the Senate: Claims
	SRRWPBLW — Selected Records from Revolutionary War Pension and Bounty-Land Warrant Application Collection Files
DSI	Smithsonian Institution, Washington, D.C.
ICN	Newberry Library, Chicago, Illinois
InU	Indiana University, Bloomington
LNT	Tulane University, New Orleans, Louisiana
MaSaPEM	Peabody Essex Museum, Salem, Massachusetts
MBPLi	Boston Public Library, Boston, Massachusetts
MdBS	Saint Mary's Seminary and University, Baltimore, Maryland
MdHi	Maryland Historical Society, Baltimore
MH	Harvard University, Cambridge, Massachusetts
MHi	Massachusetts Historical Society, Boston
MoSHi	Missouri History Museum, Saint Louis
	TJC-BC — Thomas Jefferson Collection, text formerly in Bixby Collection

MoSW	Washington University, Saint Louis, Missouri
MsSM	Mississippi State University
MWA	American Antiquarian Society, Worcester, Massachusetts
N	New York State Library, Albany
NBuHi	Buffalo History Museum, Buffalo, New York
NcD	Duke University, Durham, North Carolina
NcU	University of North Carolina, Chapel Hill
	NPT — Southern Historical Collection, Nicholas Philip Trist Papers
NHi	New-York Historical Society, New York City
NjMoHP	Morristown National Historical Park, Morristown, New Jersey
NjP	Princeton University, Princeton, New Jersey
NN	New York Public Library, New York City
NNC	Columbia University, New York City
NNGL	Gilder Lehrman Collection, New York City
NNPM	Pierpont Morgan Library, New York City
OClWHi	Western Reserve Historical Society, Cleveland, Ohio
PBm	Bryn Mawr College, Bryn Mawr, Pennsylvania
PHi	Historical Society of Pennsylvania, Philadelphia
PPAmP	American Philosophical Society, Philadelphia, Pennsylvania
PPGi	Girard College, Philadelphia, Pennsylvania
PPRF	Rosenbach Foundation, Philadelphia, Pennsylvania
PWacD	David Library of the American Revolution, Washington Crossing, Pennsylvania
ScU	University of South Carolina, Columbia
TxDaHCL	Harlan Crow Library, Dallas, Texas
	JDRC — Complaint and related documents in *Jefferson v. Directors of the Rivanna Company*
TxU	University of Texas, Austin
Vi	Library of Virginia, Richmond
ViCMRL	Thomas Jefferson Library, Thomas Jefferson Foundation, Inc., Charlottesville, Virginia
ViHi	Virginia Historical Society, Richmond
ViU	University of Virginia, Charlottesville
	JCC — Joseph C. Cabell Papers
	JHC — John Hartwell Cocke Papers

PP	Papers from the Office of the Proctor and Papers of the Proctors of the University of Virginia
TJP	Thomas Jefferson Papers
TJP-CC	Thomas Jefferson Papers, text formerly in Carr-Cary Papers
TJP-Co	Thomas Jefferson Papers, text formerly in Cocke Papers
TJP-ER	Thomas Jefferson Papers, text formerly in Edgehill-Randolph Papers
TJP-LBJRC	Thomas Jefferson Papers, Thomas Jefferson's Legal Brief in *Jefferson v. Rivanna Company*, with related documents, 1817–18
TJP-PC	Thomas Jefferson Papers, text formerly in Philip B. Campbell Deposit
TJP-VMJB	Thomas Jefferson Papers, Visitors Minutes, University of Virginia and its predecessors, copy prepared after 7 October 1826 for James Breckenridge
TJP-VMJCC	Thomas Jefferson Papers, Visitors Minutes, University of Virginia and its predecessors, copy prepared after 7 October 1826 for Joseph C. Cabell
TJP-VMJHC	Thomas Jefferson Papers, Visitors Minutes, University of Virginia and its predecessors, copy prepared after 7 October 1826 for John H. Cocke
TJP-VMJLC	Thomas Jefferson Papers, Visitors Minutes, University of Virginia and its predecessors, copy prepared after

7 October 1826 for John Lewis Cochran

	TJP-VMTJ	Thomas Jefferson Papers, Visitors Minutes, University of Virginia and its predecessors, original manuscript largely in Thomas Jefferson's hand during the period of his service
ViW	College of William and Mary, Williamsburg, Virginia	
	TC-JP	Jefferson Papers, Tucker-Coleman Collection
	TJP	Thomas Jefferson Papers
ViWC	Colonial Williamsburg Foundation, Williamsburg, Virginia	
VtHi	Vermont Historical Society, Barre	
VtNN	Norwich University, Northfield, Vermont	
WHi	Wisconsin Historical Society, Madison	

The following symbols represent repositories located outside of the United States:

FrM	Archives Municipales de Marseille, France
FrNiADAM	Archives Départmentales des Alpes Maritimes, Nice, France
ItPiAFM	Archivio Filippo Mazzei, privately owned, Pisa, Italy
RuMoGIM	Gosudarstvenny Istoricheskiy Muzyey, Moscow, Russia
SwSKB	Kungliga biblioteket, Stockholm, Sweden
SzGeBGE	Bibliothèque de Genève, Geneva, Switzerland (formerly Bibliothèque Publique et Universitaire de Genève)
SzSoSt	Staatsarchiv, Solothurn, Switzerland

5. *OTHER ABBREVIATIONS AND SYMBOLS*

The following abbreviations and symbols are commonly employed in the annotation throughout the work.

Lb Letterbook (used to indicate texts copied or assembled into bound volumes)

RG Record Group (used in designating the location of documents in the Library of Virginia and the National Archives)

SJL Jefferson's "Summary Journal of Letters" written and received for the period 11 Nov. 1783 to 25 June 1826 (in DLC: TJ Papers). This epistolary record, kept in Jefferson's hand, has been checked against the TJ Editorial Files. It is to be assumed that all outgoing letters are recorded in SJL unless there is a note to the contrary. When the date of receipt of an incoming letter is recorded in SJL, it is incorporated in the notes. Information and discrepancies revealed in SJL but not found in the letter itself are also noted. Missing letters recorded in SJL are accounted for in the notes to documents mentioning them, in related documents, or in an appendix

TJ Thomas Jefferson

TJ Editorial Files Photoduplicates and other editorial materials in the office of the Papers of Thomas Jefferson: Retirement Series, Jefferson Library, Thomas Jefferson Foundation, Inc., Charlottesville

d Penny or denier

f Florin or franc

£ Pound sterling or livre, depending on context (in doubtful cases, a clarifying note will be given)

s Shilling or sou (also expressed as /)

tt Livre Tournois

℔ Per (occasionally used for pro, pre)

„ Old-style guillemet (European quotation mark)

6. *SHORT TITLES*

The following list includes short titles of works cited frequently in this edition. Since it is impossible to anticipate all the works to be cited in abbreviated form, the list is revised from volume to volume.

Acts of Assembly *Acts of the General Assembly of Virginia* (cited by session; title varies over time)

ANB John A. Garraty and Mark C. Carnes, eds., *American National Biography*, 1999, 24 vols.

Annals *Annals of the Congress of the United States: The Debates and Proceedings in the Congress of the United States ... Compiled from Authentic Materials*, Washington, D.C., Gales & Seaton, 1834–56, 42 vols. (All editions are undependable and pagination varies from one printing to another. Citations given below are to the edition mounted on the American Memory website of the Library of Congress and give the date of the debate as well as page numbers.)

APS American Philosophical Society

ASP *American State Papers: Documents, Legislative and Executive, of the Congress of the United States*, 1832–61, 38 vols.

Axelson, *Virginia Postmasters* Edith F. Axelson, *Virginia Postmasters and Post Offices, 1789–1832*, 1991

BDSCHR Walter B. Edgar and others, eds., *Biographical Directory of the South Carolina House of Representatives,* 1974– , 5 vols.

Betts, *Farm Book* Edwin M. Betts, ed., *Thomas Jefferson's Farm Book*, 1953 (in two separately paginated sections; unless otherwise specified, references are to the second section)

Betts, *Garden Book* Edwin M. Betts, ed., *Thomas Jefferson's Garden Book, 1766–1824*, 1944

Biog. Dir. Cong. *Biographical Directory of the United States Congress, 1774–Present*, online resource, Office of the Clerk, United States House of Representatives

Biographie universelle *Biographie universelle, ancienne et moderne*, new ed., 1843–65, 45 vols.

Black's Law Dictionary Bryan A. Garner and others, eds., *Black's Law Dictionary*, 7th ed., 1999

Brigham, *American Newspapers* Clarence S. Brigham, *History and Bibliography of American Newspapers, 1690–1820*, 1947, 2 vols.

Bruce, *University* Philip Alexander Bruce, *History of the University of Virginia 1819–1919: The Lengthened Shadow of One Man*, 1920–22, 5 vols.

Bush, *Life Portraits* Alfred L. Bush, *The Life Portraits of Thomas Jefferson*, rev. ed., 1987

Callahan, *U.S. Navy* Edward W. Callahan, *List of Officers of the Navy of the United States and of the Marine Corps from 1775 to 1900*, 1901, repr. 1969

Chambers, *Poplar Forest* S. Allen Chambers, *Poplar Forest & Thomas Jefferson*, 1993

Clay, *Papers* James F. Hopkins and others, eds., *The Papers of Henry Clay*, 1959–92, 11 vols.

CVSP William P. Palmer and others, eds., *Calendar of Virginia State Papers … Preserved in the Capitol at Richmond*, 1875–93, 11 vols.

DAB Allen Johnson and Dumas Malone, eds., *Dictionary of American Biography*, 1928–36, 20 vols.

DBF *Dictionnaire de biographie française*, 1933– , 19 vols.

Delaplaine's Repository Joseph Delaplaine, *Delaplaine's Repository of the Lives and Portraits of Distinguished Americans*, Philadelphia, 1816–18, 2 vols.; Poor, *Jefferson's Library*, 4 (no. 139)

Destutt de Tracy, *Treatise on Political Economy* Destutt de Tracy, *A Treatise on Political Economy; to which is prefixed a supplement to a preceding work on the understanding, or Elements of Ideology*, Georgetown, 1817; Poor, *Jefferson's Library*, 11 (no. 700)

DNCB William S. Powell, ed., *Dictionary of North Carolina Biography*, 1979–96, 6 vols.

DSB Charles C. Gillispie, ed., *Dictionary of Scientific Biography*, 1970–80, 16 vols.

DVB John T. Kneebone, Sara B. Bearss, and others, eds., *Dictionary of Virginia Biography*, 1998– , 3 vols.

EG Dickinson W. Adams and Ruth W. Lester, eds., *Jefferson's Extracts from the Gospels*, 1983, *The Papers of Thomas Jefferson*, Second Series

Fairclough, *Horace: Satires, Epistles and Ars Poetica* H. Rushton Fairclough, trans., *Horace: Satires, Epistles and Ars Poetica*, Loeb Classical Library, 1926, repr. 2005

Fairclough, *Virgil* H. Rushton Fairclough, trans., *Virgil*, Loeb Classical Library, 1916–18, rev. by G. P. Goold, 1999–2000, repr. 2002–06, 2 vols.

Ford Paul Leicester Ford, ed., *The Writings of Thomas Jefferson*, Letterpress Edition, 1892–99, 10 vols.

HAW Henry A. Washington, ed., *The Writings of Thomas Jefferson*, 1853–54, 9 vols.

Heitman, *Continental Army* Francis B. Heitman, comp., *Historical Register of Officers of the Continental Army during the War of the Revolution, April, 1775, to December, 1783*, rev. ed., 1914

Heitman, *U.S. Army* Francis B. Heitman, comp., *Historical Register and Dictionary of the United States Army*, 1903, repr. 1994, 2 vols.

Hening William Waller Hening, ed., *The Statutes at Large; being a Collection of all the Laws of Virginia*, Richmond, 1809–23, 13 vols.; Sowerby, no. 1863; Poor, *Jefferson's Library*, 10 (no. 573)

Hoefer, *Nouv. biog. générale* J. C. F. Hoefer, *Nouvelle biographie générale depuis les temps les plus reculés jusqu'a nos jours*, 1852–83, 46 vols.

Hortus Third Liberty Hyde Bailey, Ethel Zoe Bailey, and the staff of the Liberty Hyde Bailey Hortorium, Cornell University, *Hortus Third: A Concise Dictionary of Plants Cultivated in the United States and Canada*, 1976

Jackson, *Papers* Sam B. Smith, Harold D. Moser, Daniel Feller, and others, eds., *The Papers of Andrew Jackson*, 1980– , 9 vols.

Jefferson Correspondence, Bixby Worthington C. Ford, ed., *Thomas Jefferson Correspondence Printed from the Originals in the Collections of William K. Bixby*, 1916

JEP *Journal of the Executive Proceedings of the Senate of the United States*

JHD *Journal of the House of Delegates of the Commonwealth of Virginia*

JHR *Journal of the House of Representatives of the United States*

JS *Journal of the Senate of the United States*

JSV *Journal of the Senate of Virginia*

Kimball, *Jefferson, Architect* Fiske Kimball, *Thomas Jefferson, Architect*, 1916

L & B Andrew A. Lipscomb and Albert E. Bergh, eds., *The Writings of Thomas Jefferson*, Library Edition, 1903–04, 20 vols.

Latrobe, *Papers* John C. Van Horne and others, eds., *The Correspondence and Miscellaneous Papers of Benjamin Henry Latrobe*, 1984–88, 3 vols.

LCB Douglas L. Wilson, ed., *Jefferson's Literary Commonplace Book*, 1989, *The Papers of Thomas Jefferson*, Second Series

Leavitt, *Poplar Forest* Messrs. Leavitt, *Catalogue of a Private Library ... Also, The Remaining Portion of the Library of the Late Thomas Jefferson ... offered by his grandson, Francis Eppes, of Poplar Forest, Va.*, 1873

Leonard, *General Assembly* Cynthia Miller Leonard, comp., *The General Assembly of Virginia, July 30, 1619–January 11, 1978: A Bicentennial Register of Members*, 1978

List of Patents *A List of Patents granted by the United States from April 10, 1790, to December 31, 1836*, 1872

Longworth's New York Directory *Longworth's American Almanac, New-York Register, and City Directory*, New York, 1796–1842 (title varies; cited by year of publication)

MACH *Magazine of Albemarle County History*, 1940– (title varies; issued until 1951 as *Papers of the Albemarle County Historical Society*)

Madison, *Papers* William T. Hutchinson, Robert A. Rutland, John C. A. Stagg, and others, eds., *The Papers of James Madison*, 1962– , 35 vols.

Congress. Ser., 17 vols.

Pres. Ser., 7 vols.

Retirement Ser., 2 vols.

Sec. of State Ser., 9 vols.

Malone, *Jefferson* Dumas Malone, *Jefferson and his Time*, 1948–81, 6 vols.

Marshall, *Papers* Herbert A. Johnson, Charles T. Cullen, Charles F. Hobson, and others, eds., *The Papers of John Marshall*, 1974–2006, 12 vols.

MB James A. Bear Jr. and Lucia C. Stanton, eds., *Jefferson's Memorandum Books: Accounts, with Legal Records and Miscellany, 1767–1826*, 1997, *The Papers of Thomas Jefferson*, Second Series

Miller, *Treaties* Hunter Miller, ed., *Treaties and other International Acts of the United States of America*, 1931–48, 8 vols.

Notes, ed. Peden Thomas Jefferson, *Notes on the State of Virginia*, ed. William Peden, 1955

OCD Simon Hornblower and Antony Spawforth, eds., *The Oxford Classical Dictionary*, 2003

ODNB H. C. G. Matthew and Brian Harrison, eds., *Oxford Dictionary of National Biography*, 2004, 60 vols.

OED James A. H. Murray, J. A. Simpson, E. S. C. Weiner, and others, eds., *The Oxford English Dictionary*, 2d ed., 1989, 20 vols.

O'Neall, *Bench and Bar of South Carolina* John Belton O'Neall, *Biographical Sketches of the Bench and Bar of South Carolina*, 1859, 2 vols.

Peale, *Papers* Lillian B. Miller and others, eds., *The Selected Papers of Charles Willson Peale and His Family*, 1983– , 5 vols. in 6

Pierson, *Jefferson at Monticello* Hamilton W. Pierson, *Jefferson at Monticello: The Private Life of Thomas Jefferson, From Entirely New Materials*, 1862

Poor, *Jefferson's Library* Nathaniel P. Poor, *Catalogue. President Jefferson's Library*, 1829

Princetonians James McLachlan and others, eds., *Princetonians: A Biographical Dictionary*, 1976–90, 5 vols.

PTJ Julian P. Boyd, Charles T. Cullen, John Catanzariti, Barbara B. Oberg, and others, eds., *The Papers of Thomas Jefferson*, 1950– , 40 vols.

PW Wilbur S. Howell, ed., *Jefferson's Parliamentary Writings*, 1988, *The Papers of Thomas Jefferson*, Second Series

Randall, *Life* Henry S. Randall, *The Life of Thomas Jefferson*, 1858, 3 vols.

Randolph, *Domestic Life* Sarah N. Randolph, *The Domestic Life of Thomas Jefferson, Compiled from Family Letters and Reminiscences by His Great-Granddaughter*, 1871

Ristow, *American Maps and Mapmakers* Walter W. Ristow, *American Maps and Mapmakers: Commercial Cartography in the Nineteenth Century*, 1985, repr. 1986

Scoville, *New York Merchants* "Walter Barrett" [Joseph Alfred Scoville], *The Old Merchants of New York City*, 1863–69, repr. 1968, 5 vols.

Shackelford, *Descendants* George Green Shackelford, ed., *Collected Papers ... of the Monticello Association of the Descendants of Thomas Jefferson*, 1965–84, 2 vols.

Sibley's Harvard Graduates John L. Sibley and others, eds., *Sibley's Harvard Graduates*, 1873– , 18 vols.

Sowerby E. Millicent Sowerby, comp., *Catalogue of the Library of Thomas Jefferson*, 1952–59, 5 vols.

Terr. Papers Clarence E. Carter and John Porter Bloom, eds., *The Territorial Papers of the United States*, 1934–75, 28 vols.

TJR Thomas Jefferson Randolph, ed., *Memoir, Correspondence, and Miscellanies, from the Papers of Thomas Jefferson*, 1829, 4 vols.

True, "Agricultural Society" Rodney H. True, "Minute Book of the Agricultural Society of Albemarle," *Annual Report of the American Historical Association for the Year 1918* (1921), 1:261–349

U.S. Reports *Cases Argued and Decided in the Supreme Court of the United States*, 1790– (title varies; originally issued in distinct editions of separately numbered volumes with *U.S. Reports* volume numbers retroactively assigned; original volume numbers here given parenthetically)

U.S. Statutes at Large Richard Peters, ed., *The Public Statutes at Large of the United States ... 1789 to March 3, 1845*, 1845–67, 8 vols.

Va. Reports *Reports of Cases Argued and Adjudged in the Court of Appeals of Virginia*, 1798– (title varies; originally issued in distinct editions of separately numbered volumes with *Va. Reports* volume numbers retroactively assigned; original volume numbers here given parenthetically)

VMHB *Virginia Magazine of History and Biography*, 1893–

Washington, *Papers* W. W. Abbot and others, eds., *The Papers of George Washington*, 1983– , 59 vols.

Colonial Ser., 10 vols.
Confederation Ser., 6 vols.
Pres. Ser., 17 vols.
Retirement Ser., 4 vols.
Rev. War Ser., 22 vols.

William and Mary Provisional List *A Provisional List of Alumni, Grammar School Students, Members of the Faculty, and Members of the Board of Visitors of the College of William and Mary in Virginia. From 1693 to 1888*, 1941

WMQ *William and Mary Quarterly*, 1892–

Woods, *Albemarle* Edgar Woods, *Albemarle County in Virginia*, 1901, repr. 1991

CONTENTS

Foreword vii
Acknowledgments ix
Editorial Method and Apparatus xi
Maps xli
Illustrations xlv
Jefferson Chronology 2

1817

To James Barbour, *19 January* 3
To Thomas T. Barr, *19 January* 4
To David Hosack, *19 January* 4
To Hezekiah Niles, *19 January* 5
From Craven Peyton, *20 January* 5
From Horatio G. Spafford, *21 January* 5
From William A. Burwell, *22 January* 6
From Thomas Humphreys, [*ca.* 23] *January*, enclosing Plan for Emancipating and Colonizing American Slaves, *1 January*, with his Note, *23 January* 7
To William Duane, *24 January* 13
To Nicolas G. Dufief, *24 January* 13
To John Wayles Eppes, *24 January* 14
To Dabney Minor and Peter Minor, *24 January* 15
Notes on the Rent of the Henderson Lands, [*by 24 January*] 16
To Jerman Baker, *25 January* 18
Rent Settlement with Henderson Heirs, *25 January* 19
To Peter Derieux, *26 January* 21
To Peter S. Du Ponceau, *26 January* 21
To William Sampson, *26 January* 23
From Josephus B. Stuart, *26 January* 25
To Joseph Milligan, *27 January* 26
To John Barnes, *28 January* 27
To James Eastburn, *28 January* 27
From John F. Oliveira Fernandes, *29 January* 27
To Charles Thomson, *29 January* 29
From Nicolas G. Dufief, enclosing Account with Nicolas G. Dufief, *30 January* 30

From Nicolas G. Dufief, *30 January* 31
From Hugh Nelson, *30 January* 32
Analysis of Weather Memorandum Book, *January* 33
Notes by Thomas Jefferson Randolph and Thomas Jefferson on a Land Purchase, [*ca. January*] 42
From William Clark, *1 February* 43
From Lancelot Minor, *1 February* 44
Statement of Taxable Property in Albemarle County, *1 February* 44
From John Adams, *2 February* 45
From Francis Adrian Van der Kemp, *2 February* 47
From John Wood, *2 February* 49
From Hutchins G. Burton, *4 February* 50
From Alden Partridge, *4 February*, enclosing Alden Partridge to Jonathan Williams, *19 January 1812*, and Alden Partridge's Notes on Projectile Velocities, *February 1815* 51
To William A. Burwell, *6 February* 56
To Craven Peyton, *6 February* 56
From John Barnes, *7 February* 57
From Craven Peyton, *7 February* 58
From Craven Peyton, *7 February* 58
From Jerman Baker, *8 February* 59
To Nathaniel Cutting, *8 February* 60
To Thomas Humphreys, *8 February* 60
From Thomas Law, *8 February* 61
To James Madison, *8 February* 62
To John F. Oliveira Fernandes, *8 February* 63
To John H. Peyton, *8 February* 64
To Josephus B. Stuart, *8 February* 65
To John L. Sullivan, *8 February* 65
To James Baker, *9 February* 66
From Joseph C. Cabell, *9 February* 66
To Nicolas G. Dufief, *9 February* 67
To Patrick Gibson, *9 February* 67
To Chapman Johnson, *9 February* 68
Jefferson's Lawsuit against the Rivanna Company 69
I. Thomas Jefferson's Bill of Complaint against the Directors of the Rivanna Company, [*by 9 February*] 72
II. Extract from Minutes of the Directors of the Rivanna Company, *12 September 1810* 99
III. From Peter Minor, *10 November 1810* 99
IV. Extract from Minutes of the Directors of the Rivanna Company, *8 January 1811* 101

V. From Peter Minor, [*15*] *January 1811* 102
VI. Statement of the Dispute by the Directors of the Rivanna Company, [*ca. 15 January 1811*] 103
VII. Thomas Jefferson's Notes on Virginia Statutes for Clearing the Rivanna River, *27 December 1816* 104
From Joseph Milligan, *9 February* 109
To Hugh Nelson, *9 February* 111
From William Sampson, *9 February* 111
To Smith & Riddle, *9 February* 112
To John Wood, *9 February* 112
From Francis Hall, *10 February* 113
From Samuel L. Mitchill, *10 February* 114
From William Canby, *11 February* 115
From Madame de Staël Holstein, *12 February* 116
From Patrick Gibson, *13 February* 118
From Charles Yancey, *13 February* 119
From Philip I. Barziza, *14 February* 120
From John H. Peyton, *14 February* 121
From James Madison, *15 February* 121
To James Madison, *16 February* 124
To John Barnes, *17 February* 124
From Peter S. Du Ponceau, *17 February* 125
To Fernagus De Gelone, *17 February* 127
To Patrick Gibson, *17 February* 128
From George Washington Jeffreys, *17 February* 129
To Mr. Logan (of Staunton), *17 February* 130
From Charles K. Mallory, *17 February* 131
To Simeon Theus, *17 February* 131
From Jerman Baker, *19 February* 132
From Joseph C. Cabell, *19 February* 133
From Richard Rush, *19 February* 134
From William Thornton, *19 February* 135
To Samuel L. Mitchill, *20 February* 136
From Smith & Riddle, *20 February* 137
To Edwin Stark, *20 February* 137
To Simeon Theus, *20 February* 137
From Francis Adrian Van der Kemp, *20 February* 138
From Charles Yancey, *20 February* 139
From Simon Bernard, *21 February* 139
From Joseph Milligan, *21 February* 140
From José Corrêa da Serra, *22 February* 141
From Hendrick W. Gordon, *22 February* 141

From David Higginbotham, *22 February* 142
From Richard C. Derby, *23 February* 142
From Thomas Law, [*received 23 February*] 143
To Charles K. Mallory, *23 February* 144
From James Monroe, *23 February* 145
To Philip I. Barziza, *24 February* 146
From Joseph Delaplaine, *24 February* 148
To Thomas Law, *24 February* 148
From Wilson Cary Nicholas, *24 February* 149
From Robert B. Sthreshly, *24 February* 151
From Caspar Wistar, *24 February* 151
From Fernagus De Gelone, *25 February* 152
From William A. Burwell, *26 February* 153
From George M. Dallas, *27 February* 153
From Chapman Johnson, *27 February* 154
From John Barnes, *28 February*, enclosing Draft Power of Attorney to John Barnes for United States Stock Interest, *26 February* 155
To Hutchins G. Burton, *28 February* 156
From John W. Maury, *28 February* 156
From Charles Willson Peale, *28 February* 157
From Peter H. Wendover, *1 March* 159
To Madame de Corny, *2 March* 160
From Nicolas G. Dufief, *3 March* 161
To George Washington Jeffreys, enclosing Catalogue of Books on Agriculture, *3 March* 162
From Thomas Law, *3 March* 165
From John Trumbull, *3 March* 166
From William Johnson, *4 March* 167
From Thomas Eston Randolph, *4 March* 168
From Joshua Stow, *4 March* 169
From Thomas Appleton, enclosing Notes on Lupinella Grass Seed, *5 March* 170
To Thomas Mann Randolph, *5 March* 172
From Valentine W. Southall, *5 March* 172
To Richard C. Derby, *6 March* 173
To John Wayles Eppes, *6 March* 174
To Fernagus De Gelone, *6 March* 175
Instructions for Setting a Sundial, [*ca. 6 March*] 176
From William Pelham, *6 March* 177
From Robert Walsh, *6 March* 178
To Joel Yancey, *6 March* 178

To Fernagus De Gelone, *7 March* 179
To Simon Bernard, *8 March* 180
To George M. Dallas, *8 March* 180
To John H. Cocke and David Watson, *10 March* 181
From Joseph Dougherty, *10 March* 182
To James Madison, *10 March* 183
From Bernard Peyton, *10 March* 183
From John Pope, *10 March* 184
From Thomas Eston Randolph, *10 March* 185
To John Barnes, *11 March* 187
From George Gibbs, enclosing Statement of the Mineralogical Committee of the New-York Historical Society, *11 March* 187
To Joseph Miller, *11 March* 189
From Samuel L. Mitchill, enclosing Statement of the Committee on Zoology of the New-York Historical Society, *11 March* 190
To Bernard Peyton, *11 March* 193
From Fernagus De Gelone, *15 March* 193
To Thomas Eston Randolph, *15 March* 194
From Edwin Stark, *15 March* 195
To Thomas Appleton, *16 March* 196
To Stephen Cathalan, *16 March* 196
To Albert Gallatin, *16 March* 197
To David Higginbotham, *16 March* 197
To Lucy Marks, *16 March* 198
To Charles Willson Peale, *16 March* 198
To Bernard Peyton, *16 March* 199
To Archibald Thweatt, *16 March* 200
To Francis Adrian Van der Kemp, *16 March* 201
From Joseph Delaplaine, *17 March* 202
From Bernard Peyton, *17 March* 204
From Edwin Stark, *17 March* 204
To Fitzwhylsonn & Potter, *19 March* 205
To Joseph Milligan, *19 March* 205
To Wilson Cary Nicholas, *19 March* 206
To Joel Yancey, *19 March* 207
From Patrick Gibson, *20 March* 208
From David Michie, *20 March* 208
From Thomas Eston Randolph, *20 March* 210
From Edmund Bacon, *22 March* 211
To David Michie, *22 March* 212
To Thomas Eston Randolph, *22 March* 213
To Joseph Dougherty, *23 March* 214

To Craven Peyton, *23 March* 214
From Craven Peyton, *23 March* 214
To Joshua Stow, *23 March* 215
To Robert Walsh, *23 March* 215
To Jethro Wood, *23 March* 216
From Joseph Miller, *24 March* 216
From Alden Partridge, *24 March* 217
From John Barnes, *26 March* 217
From John H. Cocke, *26 March* 218
From DeWitt Clinton, *27 March* 218
To John H. Cocke, *27 March* 219
To George Divers, *27 March* 220
From George Divers, *27 March* 221
From Richard Flower, *28 March* 221
Notes and Drawings for Barboursville, [*before 29 March*] 223
From James Barbour, *29 March* 227
From Joseph C. Cabell, *30 March* 228
To Peter Minor, *30 March* 228
From Peter Minor, *30 March* 229
From Francis Adrian Van der Kemp, *30 March* 229
To David Watson, *30 March* 232
To Nicolas G. Dufief, *31 March* 233
To John Wayles Eppes, *31 March* 233
To Fernagus De Gelone, *31 March* 234
From James Eastburn, John W. Francis, and James Smith (of New York), *March* 234
To Patrick Gibson, *1 April* 236
To William D. Taylor, *1 April* 237
From Hutchins G. Burton, *2 April* 238
From Wilson Cary Nicholas, *2 April* 239
From Thomas Wells, *2 April* 240
From Nicolas G. Dufief, *4 April* 241
From Josephus B. Stuart, *5 April* 242
From David Watson, *6 April* 242
Albemarle County Court Order Concerning a Proposed Road, *8 April* 243
Notes on a Proposed Albemarle County Road, [*ca. 8 April*] 244
From David Higginbotham, *8 April* 245
From George Washington Jeffreys, *8 April* 245
To James Monroe, *8 April* 246
From Nicolas G. Dufief, *9 April* 247
From Joseph Milligan, *9 April* 248

From James Madison, *10 April* 248
From Giovanni Carmignani, *11 April* 249
To Nicolas G. Dufief, *11 April* 250
From Michael H. Walsh, [*11 April*] 251
To Joseph Delaplaine, *12 April* 251
From Alexander Garrett, *12 April* 253
From Valentine Gill, *12 April* 253
From Horatio G. Spafford, *12 April* 254
From David Bailie Warden, *12 April* 255
To James Dinsmore, *13 April* 256
To James Madison, *13 April* 257
To James Monroe, *13 April* 257
To DeWitt Clinton, *14 April* 259
To Chapman Johnson, *14 April* 259
To John W. Maury, *14 April* 260
From Bernard Peyton, *14 April* 260
To John Wood, *14 April* 261
To James Madison, *15 April* 262
To James Monroe, *15 April* 262
To Craven Peyton, *15 April* 263
From André Thoüin, *15 April* 263
From Horatio G. Spafford, *18 April* 266
From William Thornton, *18 April* 266
From John Adams, *19 April* 267
From Tristram Dalton, *22 April* 270
From James Dinsmore, *22 April* 273
From James Baker, *23 April* 274
From Joseph C. Cabell, *23 April* 275
From James Monroe, *23 April* 276
From Elkanah Watson, *24 April* 277
From Christopher Clark, *25 April* 280
From DeWitt Clinton, *25 April* 280
From Lafayette, *25 April* 281
From John Laval, *25 April* 283
To Archibald Robertson, *25 April* 284
From Josephus B. Stuart, *25 April* 285
To Patrick Gibson, *26 April* 290
From Chapman Johnson, *26 April* 291
From James Monroe, *27 April* 291
From John Wayles Eppes, *28 April* 292
To LeRoy, Bayard & Company, *28 April* 293
From Abigail Adams, *29 April* 294

To James Baker, *29 April* 295
To Fernagus De Gelone, *29 April* 295
Memorandum to James Monroe on Scuppernong Wine, [*ca. 29 April?*] 295
To Louis H. Girardin, *30 April* 296
Account with William Mitchell, [*April*] 298
To Hutchins G. Burton, *1 May* 300
To George Cabell, *1 May* 300
To John H. Cocke, *1 May* 301
From Henry A. S. Dearborn, *1 May* 302
To John Wayles Eppes, *1 May* 302
To Fitzwhylsonn & Potter, *1 May* 303
From Patrick Gibson, *1 May* 304
From Jean Mourer, *1 May* 305
To James Oldham, *1 May* 307
To Francis Adrian Van der Kemp, *1 May* 307
To Tristram Dalton, enclosing Paper Model of Thomas Mann Randolph's Plow, *2 May* 308
To John Adams, *5 May* 311
The Founding of the University of Virginia: Central College, 1816–1819 314
I. Minutes of Central College Board of Visitors, *5 May* 316
II. John H. Cocke's Description of Central College Board of Visitors Meeting, [*5 May*] 318
III. Anonymous Description of Central College Board of Visitors Meeting, [*5 May*] 320
IV. Central College Subscription List, [*ca. 7 May*] 322
V. Master List of Subscribers to Central College, [*after 7 May*] 328
To Fernagus De Gelone, *6 May* 335
To John Wood, *6 May* 335
To Isaac A. Coles, *7 May* 336
To Joseph Darmsdatt, *7 May* 336
From Isaac A. Coles, *8 May* 337
From Fernagus De Gelone, *8 May* 338
To Elkanah Watson, *8 May* 338
From Isaac Briggs, *9 May* 339
From Frank Carr, *9 May* 340
From Robert H. Saunders, *9 May* 341
To William Thornton, *9 May* 342
From Alexander Garrett, *10 May* 344
To William Johnson, *10 May* 344

To Josephus B. Stuart, *10 May* 345
From George Washington Jeffreys, *11 May* 347
Notes on the Canal Locks and Manufacturing Mill at Shadwell, *11 May* 348
From John Barnes, *12 May* 350
From Daniel Lescallier, *12 May* 351
To Fernagus De Gelone, *13 May* 352
To Fitzwhylsonn & Potter, *13 May* 352
To James Gibbon, *13 May* 353
To Lafayette, *14 May* 353
To Jean Baptiste Say, *14 May* 355
To Abigail Adams, *15 May* 357
From Isaac Briggs, *15 May* 357
To Destutt de Tracy, *15 May* 359
From Thomas Eddy, *16 May* 360
To John Barnes, *17 May* 361
From Patrick Gibson, *17 May* 362
From John Adams, *18 May* 362
To Isaac Briggs, *18 May* 364
To Louis A. Leschot, *18 May* 365
From David Higginbotham, *20 May* 366
From LeRoy, Bayard & Company, *20 May* 366
From John Manners, *20 May* 367
From Charles Willson Peale, *20 May* 371
From Caspar Wistar, *20 May* 375
From Isaac Briggs, *21 May* 376
From Luis de Onís, *21 May* 377
From James Gibbon, *22 May* 378
Notes on Value of Lots in Beverley Town (Westham), [*ca. 22 May*] 378
To Craven Peyton, *23 May* 379
To Patrick Gibson, *24 May* 379
To Patrick Gibson, *25 May* 380
To LeRoy, Bayard & Company, *25 May* 381
From Sir John Sinclair, *25 May* 381
From John Adams, *26 May* 382
To David Higginbotham, *26 May* 385
From John Barnes, *27 May* 385
From Tristram Dalton, *27 May* 386
From William Thornton, enclosing Sketches for a Corinthian Pavilion, *27 May* 387
From Aaron Clark, *28 May* 393

To Fitzwhylsonn & Potter, *28 May* 394
From Patrick Gibson, *28 May* 395
From John Wood, *29 May* 395
From Fernagus De Gelone, *31 May* 396
From William Caruthers, *2 June* 397
From John Vaughan, *2 June* 398
From Tadeusz Kosciuszko, *3 June* 398
To Lancelot Minor, *3 June* 400
From John M. Perry, *3* [*June*] 400
To John M. Perry, *3 June* 401
From John Barnes, *4 June* 402
From Mr. Durot, *4 June* 402
To Stephen Cathalan, enclosing List of Wine and Food Ordered by Thomas Jefferson and Thomas Jefferson Randolph, [*before 6 June*] 404
To de Bure Frères, *6 June* 408
To John Wayles Eppes, *6 June* 409
To Albert Gallatin, [*before 6 June*] 410
To William Lee, *6 June* 413
To George Ticknor, [*before 6 June*] 414
To David Bailie Warden, *6 June* 417
To Stephen Girard, *7 June* 418
From LeRoy, Bayard & Company, *7 June* 419
To Elisha Ticknor, *7 June* 419
To John Vaughan, *7 June* 420
From Edmund Bacon, *8 June* 421
To Daniel Brent, *8 June* 421
From Francis Adrian Van der Kemp, enclosing Translated Extract from Isaak Iselin, *Uber die Geschichte der Menschheit*, *9 June* 422
To John Barnes, *10 June* 425
To Wilson Cary Nicholas, *10 June* 426
To Caspar Wistar, *10 June* 426
To William Caruthers, *11 June* 428
To Luis de Onís, *11 June* 428
From William Darby, *12 June* 429
To George Washington Jeffreys, *12 June* 430
To Benjamin Henry Latrobe, *12 June* 431
To John Manners, *12 June* 432
To Alexander von Humboldt, *13 June* 434
To Louis Pio, *13 June* 435
To Barbé Marbois, *14 June* 436
To John Barnes, *14 June* 438

To José Corrêa da Serra, *14 June* 439
To George Divers, *14 June* 440
To Daniel Lescallier, *14 June* 441
From Dominick Lynch, *14 June* 441
From Marc Auguste Pictet, *14 June* 443
To Robert Simington, *14 June* 447
To Tadeusz Kosciuszko, *15 June* 447
From William Lee, *16 June* 449
From Wilson Cary Nicholas, *16 June* 450
Account with Mary Bacon, [*ca. 17 June*] 451
To Louis H. Girardin, *17 June* 452
From Benjamin Henry Latrobe, *17 June* 453
From Valentine W. Southall, *18 June* 453
From William Thornton, *18 June* 454
From John Vaughan, *18 June*, enclosing Account with Stephen Girard, *21 September 1816* 454
To William Duane, *19 June* 455
To Fernagus De Gelone, *19 June* 456
To Joseph Gales (1761–1841), *19 June* 456
To William Short, *19 June* 457
From Daniel Brent, *20 June* 458
To Thomas Eston Randolph, *21 June* 459
From Thomas Eston Randolph, *21 June* 459
To William Darby, *22 June* 459
To James Madison, *22 June* 460
To Thomas Eston Randolph, *22 June* 461
To Daniel Brent, *23 June* 462
From Thomas Freeborn, *23 June* 462
To Albert Gallatin, *23 June* 463
To Alexander Garrett, *23 June* 463
To Patrick Gibson, *23 June* 464
To Jeremiah A. Goodman, *23 June* 465
Conveyance of Lands for Central College from John M. Perry and Frances T. Perry to Alexander Garrett, *23 June* 465
Agreement between John M. Perry and Central College, *23 June* 468
To Robert H. Saunders, *23 June* 469
From James Leitch, *24 June* 470
To James Dinsmore, *25 June* 471
To William Lee, *25 June* 471
From Peter Poinsot, *25 June* 472
To Joel Yancey, *25 June* 475
From Joseph Gales (1761–1841), *26 June* 476

From Patrick Gibson, *26 June* 476
To Benjamin Harrison, *26 June* 477
To Dominick Lynch, *26 June* 478
From Craven Peyton, *26 June* 478
From Craven Peyton, *26 June* 479
From Benjamin Henry Latrobe, *28 June* 479
From Richard Peters, *28 June* 482
To Craven Peyton, *28 June* 485
From Craven Peyton, *28* [*June*] 486
To John Vaughan, *28 June* 486
From George Crowninshield, *30 June* 487
From Donald Fraser, *30 June* 489
From Horatio G. Spafford, *30 June* 495
To Patrick Gibson, *1 July* 496
From Thomas Humphreys, *2 July* 497
From Richard Claiborne, *4 July* 497
From William Short, *4 July* 500
From Solomon Henkel, *5 July* 503
From James Clarke, *6 July* 504
From William Lee, *6 July* 506
From John Barnes, *8 July* 507
From Stephen Cathalan, *8 July* 508
To Craven Peyton, *8 July* 514
From James Rawlings, *9 July* 521
From John Barnes, *11 July*, enclosing Account with Thomas Jefferson, [*ca. 11 July*], and Joseph Milligan to John Barnes, *18 June*, with John Barnes's Note to Thomas Jefferson, *11 July* 522
From Benjamin Harrison, *11 July* 524
To Charles Clay, *12 July* 524
To Paul A. Clay, [*ca. 12 July*] 525
From José Corrêa da Serra, *12 July* 526
From John Adams, *15 July* 527
From Mark L. Descaves, *15 July* 528
From the Seventy-Six Association, *15 July* 528
From Stephen Cathalan, *16 July* 531
To Benjamin Henry Latrobe, *16 July* 534
From John Love, *16 July* 536
From Joseph Milligan, *16 July* 537
To Craven Peyton, *16 July* 538
From Craven Peyton, *16 July* 538
From John Barnes, *17 July* 539

From Albert Gallatin, *17 July* 539
From Harrison Hall, *17 July* 541
To Craven Peyton, *17 July* 542
From P. de Valltone, *17 July* 542
Notes on the Siting of Central College, *18 July* 544
From P. de Valltone, *18 July* 545
To John H. Cocke, *19 July* 545
From Jeremiah A. Goodman, *19 July* 546
From John H. Cocke, *20 July* 546
To Jeremiah A. Goodman, *20 July* 547
To Fernagus De Gelone, *21 July* 547
To James Oldham, *21 July* 548
To John Le Tellier, *22 July* 548
From George Divers, *23 July* 549
George Divers's Answer to Interrogatories in *Jefferson v. Rivanna Company*, [*ca. 23 July*] 550
Thomas Mann Randolph's Notes on George Divers's Answer to Interrogatories in *Jefferson v. Rivanna Company*, [*after 23 July*] 555
Notes on George Divers's Answer to Interrogatories in *Jefferson v. Rivanna Company*, [*after 23 July*] 556
From David Knight, *23 July* 558
To James Madison, *23 July* 559
From Craven Peyton, *23 July* 560
From Hiram Storrs, *23 July* 560
To David Watson, *23 July* 561
From Levett Harris, *24 July* 562
From Benjamin Henry Latrobe, *24 July* 563
John H. Cocke's Description of Central College Board of Visitors Meeting, 25[*–28 July*] 565
From Peter Derieux, *25 July* 566
From Lancelot Minor, *25 July* 567
From James Monroe, *27 July* 568
Minutes of Central College Board of Visitors, *28 July* 570
From Benjamin Henry Latrobe, *28 July* 571
From Samuel L. Osborn, *28 July* 572
Agreement with Jeremiah A. Goodman, *30 July* 573
From Joseph Milligan, *30 July* 573
From John Vaughan, *30 July* 574
From A. F. De Laage, *31 July* 575
To James Rawlings, *31 July* 576
To Thomas Appleton, *1 August* 577

To James Clarke, *1 August* 581
To Mark L. Descaves, *1 August* 581
To the Seventy-Six Association, *1 August* 582
From Tanner, Vallance, Kearny, & Company, *1 August* 582
To Stephen Cathalan, *2 August* 584
To John Vaughan, *2 August* 585
To Levett Harris, *3 August* 585
To Benjamin Henry Latrobe, *3 August* 586
To John Love, *3 August* 588
From James Oldham, *3 August* 588
From Andrew Alexander, *4 August* 589
Circular to Prospective Donors to Central College, *4 August* 590
From Fernagus De Gelone, *5 August* 592
To Patrick Gibson, *5 August* 593
From Hezekiah Niles, *5 August*, enclosing Circular to Prominent Subscribers, *31 July* 594
To John Wayles Eppes, *6 August* 596
From John Goodman, Joseph Reed, Isaac Boyer, and William J. Duane, *6 August* 597
To Harrison Hall, *6 August* 599
From Quinette de Rochemont, *6 August* 600
To Benjamin Henry Latrobe, *7 August* 602
To William Lee, *7 August* 602
To Daniel Colclaser, *8 August* 603
From Hugh Chisholm, *10 August* 603
From Victor du Pont and Eleuthère I. du Pont de Nemours, *11 August* 604
From John Le Tellier, *11 August* 604
From James Ligon (for Patrick Gibson), *11 August* 605
From John Patterson, *11 August* 606
From David Whitehead, *11 August*, enclosing Abraham Clark's Recommendation of David Whitehead, *30 December 1793* 607
From George Flower, *12 August* 609
To David Knight, [*12*] *August* 610
From Benjamin Henry Latrobe, *12 August* 610
From Maxfield Ludlow, *12 August* 615
To Archibald Robertson, [*12*] *August* 617
From Archibald Robertson, *12 August* 618
From David Bailie Warden, [*ca. 12–22 August*] 618
To A. F. De Laage, [*13*] *August* 619
From A. F. De Laage, [*13*] *August* 620

To Samuel J. Harrison, Charles Johnston, and Archibald Robertson, [*13*] *August* 620
Trip to Natural Bridge, [*ca. 13–17 August*] 621
I. Extract of Cornelia J. Randolph to Virginia J. Randolph (Trist), *17 August* 622
II. Extract of Ellen W. Randolph (Coolidge) to Martha Jefferson Randolph, *18 August* 625
III. Extract of Ellen W. Randolph (Coolidge) to Martha Jefferson Randolph, [*after 29 August*] 626
IV. Cornelia J. Randolph to Virginia J. Randolph (Trist), *30 August* 628
V. Extract of Cornelia J. Randolph to Virginia J. Randolph (Trist) and Mary Elizabeth Randolph (Eppes), *24 September* 631
From George Ticknor, *14 August* 632
From James Maury, *15 August* 635
From Robert Walsh, *15 August* 635
From Joseph C. Cabell, *18 August* 636
To Patrick Gibson, [*18*] *August* 638
From Francis W. Gilmer, *18 August* 638
From Randolph Harrison, *18 August* 640
To Chapman Johnson, [*18*] *August* 641
To Martha Jefferson Randolph, *18 August* 641
To Philip Thornton, [*18*] *August* 642
To Thomas Appleton, [*20*] *August* 642
To Giovanni Carmignani, [*20*] *August* 643
To Fernagus De Gelone, [*20*] *August* 646
To John Goodman, Joseph Reed, Isaac Boyer, and William J. Duane, [*22*] *August* 647
From Hugh Chisholm, *23 August* 648
Notes on Newspaper Subscriptions, [*ca. 23 August*] 648
To Hezekiah Niles, [*23*] *August* 649
To Benjamin Henry Latrobe, [*25*] *August* 649
From James Pleasants, *25 August* 650
From James Rawlings, *25 August* 651
From Stephen Cathalan, *27 August*, enclosing Victor Adolphus Sasserno to Stephen Cathalan, *14 August*, Amant Spreafico (for Pierre Mages & Compagnie) to Stephen Cathalan, *15 August*, and Amant Spreafico to Stephen Cathalan, *19 August* 652
From Absalom Townsend, [*ca. 28*] *August* 659

CONTENTS

From John Martin Baker, *29 August*, enclosing John Martin Baker to Richard Rush, *18 August* 659
To Samuel L. Osborn, [*29*] *August* 663
Anonymous (Thomas Jefferson) to the *Richmond Enquirer*, [*ca. 29*] *August* 664
To Thomas Ritchie, [*29*] *August* 667
From Daniel Brent, *30 August* 667
From Chapman Johnson, *30 August* 668
To Hugh Chisholm, *31 August* 669
To Martha Jefferson Randolph, *31 August* 669

APPENDIX: Supplemental List of Documents Not Found 671

INDEX 673

MAPS

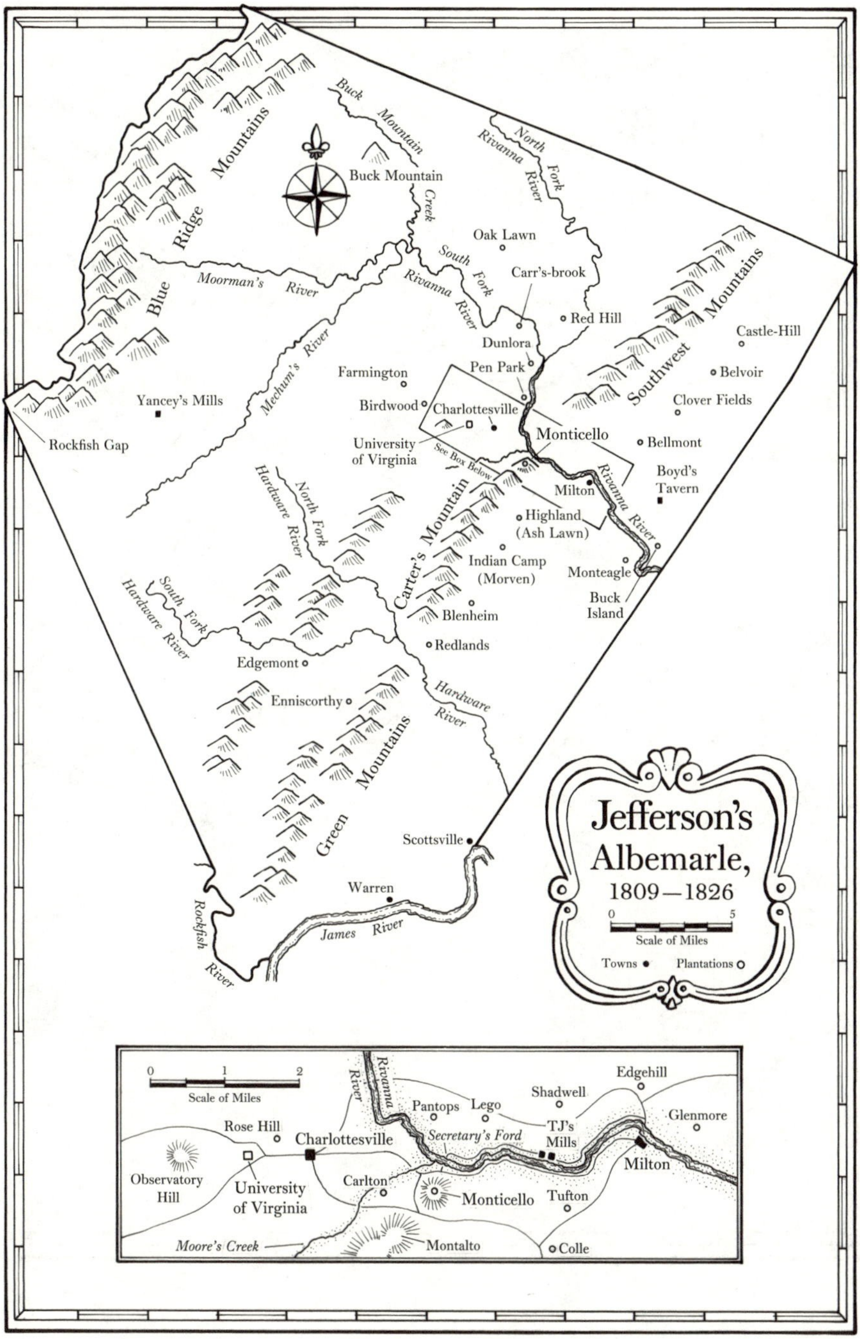
Jefferson's Albemarle, 1809—1826
0 5
Scale of Miles
Towns
Plantations
Blue Ridge Mountains
Buck Mountain Creek
Buck Mountain
North Fork Rivanna River
Oak Lawn
South Fork Rivanna River
Carr's-brook
Red Hill
Southwest Mountains
Castle-Hill
Belvoir
Clover Fields
Bellmont
Boyd's Tavern
Moorman's River
Mechum's River
Dunlora
Pen Park
Farmington
Birdwood
Charlottesville
University of Virginia
See Box Below
Monticello
Milton
Rivanna River
Highland (Ash Lawn)
Indian Camp (Morven)
Monteagle
Buck Island
Yancey's Mills
Rockfish Gap
Hardware River
North Fork Hardware River
South Fork Hardware River
Carter's Mountain
Blenheim
Redlands
Edgemont
Enniscorthy
Green Mountains
Scottsville
Warren
James River
Rockfish River
0 1 2
Scale of Miles
Rivanna River
Edgehill
Shadwell
Glenmore
Pantops
Lego
TJ's Mills
Rose Hill
Secretary's Ford
Observatory Hill
Carlton
Tufton
Montalto
Moore's Creek
Colle

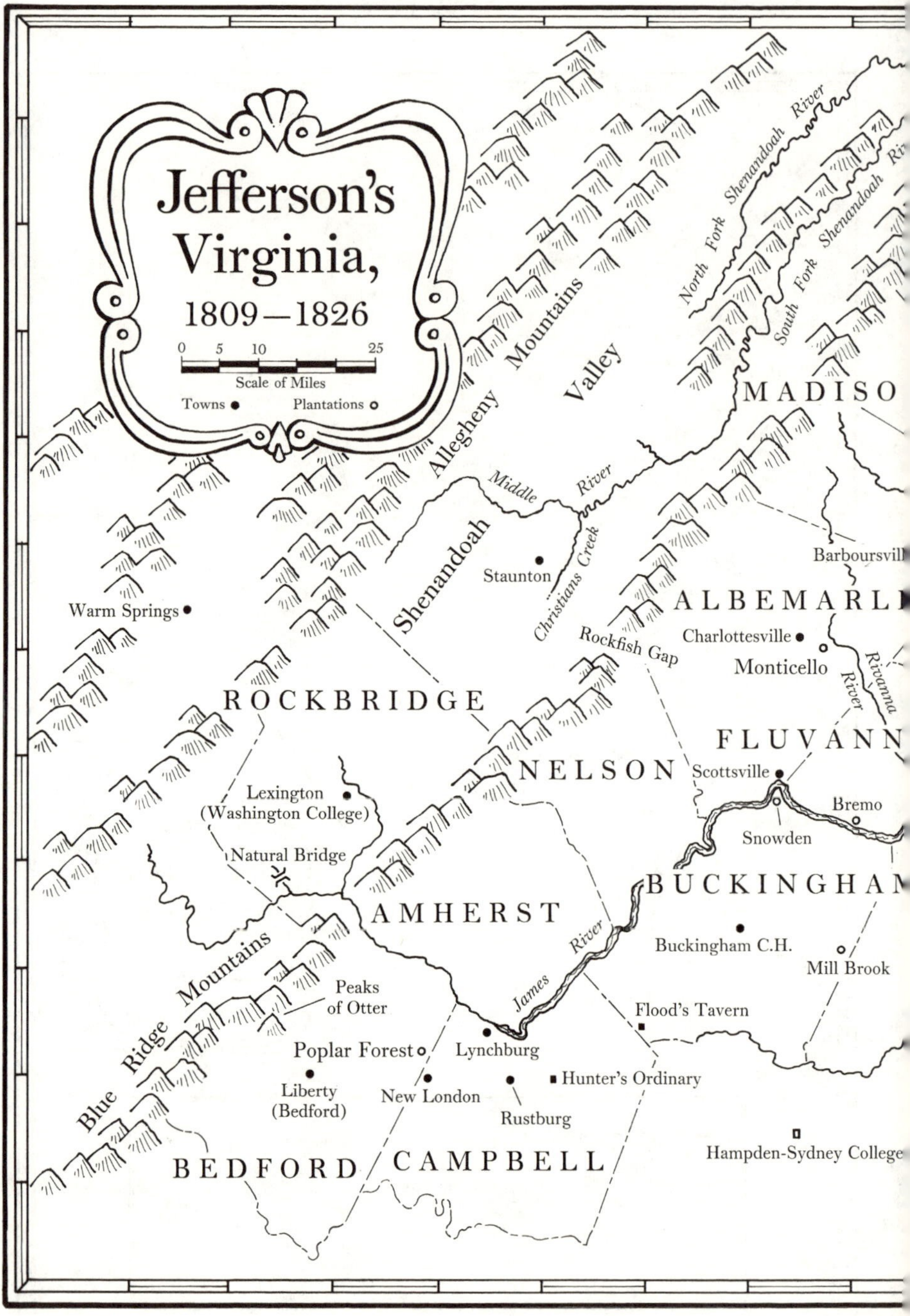
Jefferson's Virginia, 1809–1826
0 5 10 25
Scale of Miles
Towns
Plantations
Allegheny Mountains
Valley
North Fork Shenandoah River
South Fork Shenandoah River
MADISO
Middle River
Shenandoah
Staunton
Christians Creek
Barboursvill
ALBEMARL
Warm Springs
Rockfish Gap
Charlottesville
Monticello
Rivanna River
ROCKBRIDGE
FLUVANN
NELSON
Scottsville
Lexington
(Washington College)
Bremo
Snowden
Natural Bridge
BUCKINGHA
AMHERST
Buckingham C.H.
Mill Brook
James River
Blue Ridge Mountains
Peaks of Otter
Flood's Tavern
Poplar Forest
Lynchburg
Hunter's Ordinary
Liberty (Bedford)
New London
Rustburg
Hampden-Sydney College
BEDFORD
CAMPBELL

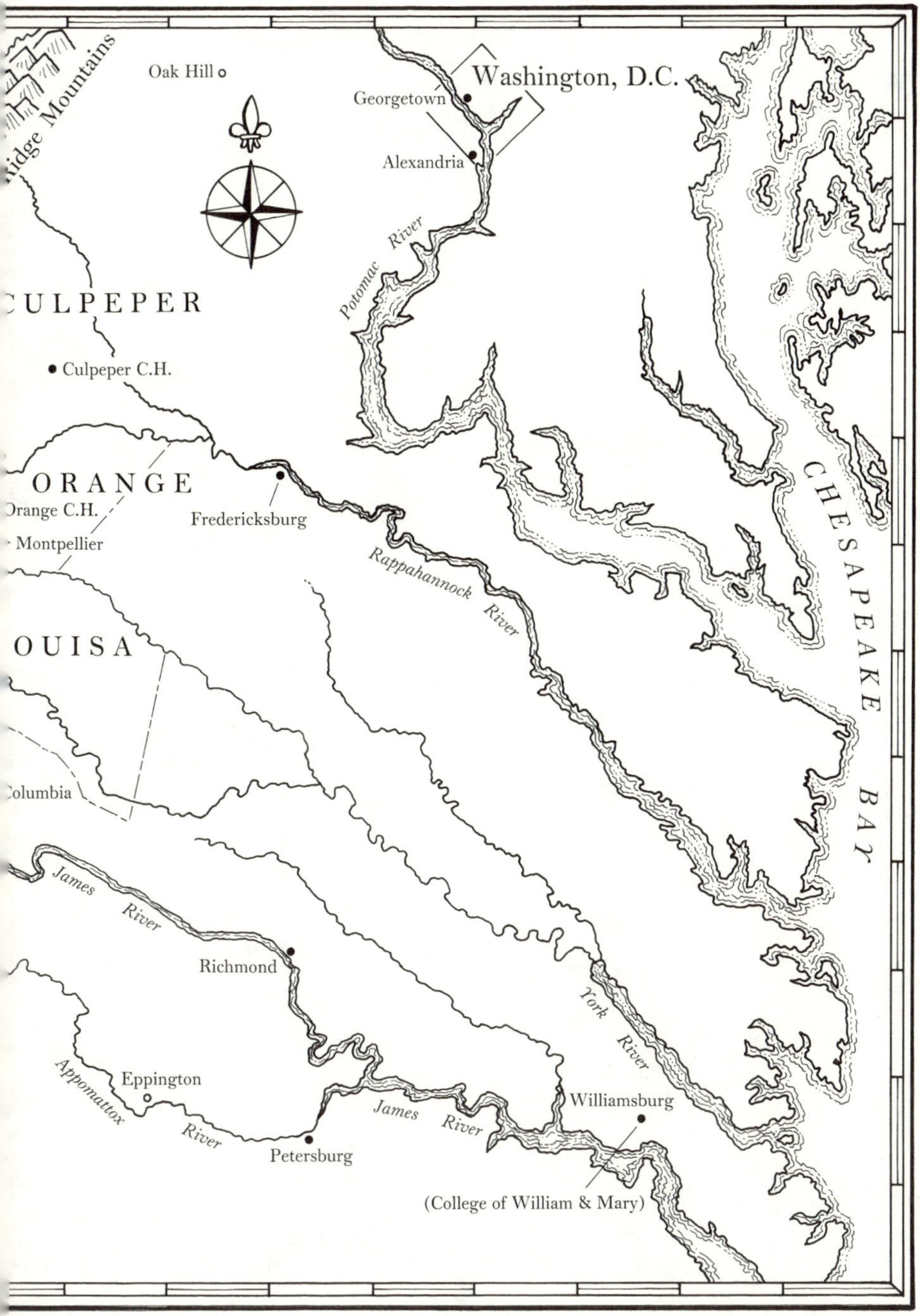

Ridge Mountains
Oak Hill
Washington, D.C.
Georgetown
Alexandria
Potomac River
CULPEPER
Culpeper C.H.
ORANGE
Orange C.H.
Montpellier
Fredericksburg
Rappahannock River
LOUISA
Columbia
James River
Richmond
York River
CHESAPEAKE BAY
Eppington
Appomattox River
Petersburg
James River
Williamsburg
(College of William & Mary)

ILLUSTRATIONS

Following page 232

JAMES MONROE BY JOHN VANDERLYN

Jefferson's old friend and political associate James Monroe (1758–1831) became the fifth president of the United States on 4 Mar. 1817. When Jefferson's granddaughter Ellen W. Randolph (Coolidge) visited Washington in the winter of 1816, she noted the presence of the portrait painter John Vanderlyn and commented that he had "taken excellent likenesses" of Monroe and other leading members of the capital city's society. During another sojourn to Washington, in 1822 Ellen purchased for her grandfather an 1817 engraving by Thomas Gimbrede based on Vanderlyn's portrait of Monroe (Ellen W. Randolph [Coolidge] to Martha Jefferson Randolph, 17 Feb. [1816] [ViU: Ellen Wayles Randolph Coolidge Correspondence]; Ellen W. Randolph [Coolidge] to TJ, 22 Mar. 1822; Stein, *Worlds*, 172).

Courtesy of the National Portrait Gallery, Smithsonian Institution.

THOMAS JEFFERSON'S PLAT OF CENTRAL COLLEGE LANDS

Jefferson likely began this plat of the "Lands of Central College" in 1817, when he orchestrated the purchase on 23 June of two pieces of land from John M. Perry and Frances T. Perry, labeled here as parcels of 153 and $43\frac{3}{4}$ acres. Not included on this plat is a $6\frac{1}{4}$-acre property that Central College purchased from Jesse Winston Garth on 7 Aug. 1817. This triangular tract adjoined the Perrys' smaller parcel along the line surveyed with bearings S. 34°, W. $48\frac{1}{2}$°, with the other two sides bounded by Three Notched Road and Wheeler's Road. Jefferson continued to update this plat until at least 1820, when the school, by then the University of Virginia, purchased the $48\frac{3}{4}$-acre parcel also included here. The 101-acre tract penciled in the center was purchased in 1825, part of a further 132-acre acquisition. The original grounds of the University of Virginia, including the Rotunda, pavilions, and student dormitories, were built in the $43\frac{3}{4}$-acre segment purchased from the Perrys in 1817 (Conveyance of Lands for Central College from John M. Perry and Frances T. Perry to Alexander Garrett, 23 June 1817).

Courtesy of the Albert and Shirley Small Special Collections Library, University of Virginia.

TOBACCO-LEAF CAPITAL BY BENJAMIN HENRY LATROBE

This was the second of two models of column capitals that Latrobe gave to Jefferson during the latter's retirement. In 1809 Latrobe had sent him one decorated with ears of maize, and in 1817 he sent this one, which echoed the decorative style of the Corinthian order. Latrobe had designed the tobacco-leaf capital by 1816, when a model was executed by the Italian carver Francisco Iardella. The capitals were completed by 1817, and the design was incorporated into columns arranged in a circular colonnade in the north wing of the United States Capitol. Latrobe recommended that Jefferson have the model painted, with the leaves of the upper tier to be colored a faint brown or umber to give the carving greater definition. Latrobe intended for those installed in the Capitol to get the same treatment, but they were instead eventually painted in bright colors and gilded. The tobacco-leaf capital pictured here has remained at Monticello since Jefferson's day (Stein, *Worlds*, 159–60; Latrobe to TJ, 5 Nov. 1816, 28 Oct. 1817; Jeffrey A. Cohen and Charles E. Brownell, eds., *The Architectural Drawings of Benjamin Henry Latrobe* [1994], vol. 2, pt. 2, pp. 588, 592).

Courtesy of the Thomas Jefferson Foundation, Inc., photograph by Edward Owen.

JAMES BARBOUR BY CHESTER HARDING

James Barbour (1775–1842), Speaker of the Virginia House of Delegates, governor of Virginia, and United States Senator, was Jefferson's friend and political ally. Chester Harding (1792–1866), a native of Massachusetts, had no formal artistic training, but discovered a talent for art after working as a sign painter. He gained experience painting portraits in Kentucky, Philadelphia, and Washington, D.C., followed by three years in Scotland and England. Harding most likely completed this oil-on-canvas portrait shortly after his 1826 return to the United States, during Barbour's tenure as secretary of war under President John Quincy Adams (*ANB*; *DAB*; *DVB*).

Courtesy of the Virginia Historical Society (1991.75).

BARBOURSVILLE

In 1817 Jefferson designed Barboursville, James Barbour's Orange County residence. Like Monticello, it featured a two-story design that gave the illusion of one. Jefferson's plans for the house included a dome that was never constructed. The photograph here shows the house as it stood before it burned on Christmas Day, 1884. The ruins, which are on the grounds of a Virginia winery, remain a tourist attraction (Bryan Clark Green, Calder Loth, and William M. S. Rasmussen, *Lost Virginia: Vanished Architecture of the Old Dominion* [2001], 57; TJ's Notes and Drawings for Barboursville, [before 29 Mar. 1817]; Barbour to TJ, 29 Mar. 1817).

Courtesy of the Virginia Historical Society (1999.172.54).

DOME ROOM AND STAIRS AT MONTICELLO

The octagonal Dome Room on the third floor of Monticello was under construction by 1800. In the early stages of planning and construction, Jefferson referred to the space as the "sky room." The narrow stairs to the upper floors of the house may have limited use of the room, the function of which changed over time. After his marriage in 1815, Jefferson's eldest grandson Thomas Jefferson Randolph lived in the Dome Room with his wife Jane H. Nicholas Randolph and, eventually, their daughter Margaret Smith Randolph (Randolph). In June 1817 the young family moved to Tufton a month ahead of the birth of their second child, Martha Jefferson Randolph (Taylor). The Dome Room seems to have been used thereafter mainly by Jefferson's grandchildren, especially the so-called "cuddy" space created when Jefferson completed work on the west portico and put down a floor in the pediment, creating a small unfinished area that could be accessed from the Dome Room. Up to and after Jefferson's death, the Dome Room was also used intermittently for storage. Jefferson descendant Sarah N. Randolph reported in an 1871 publication on Jefferson and Monticello that the room had originally been intended as a billiards venue, but no contemporary evidence supports this claim (William L. Beiswanger, *Monticello in Measured Drawings* [1998], 36–7, 64–5; Stein, *Worlds*, 116; Jack McLaughlin, *Jefferson and Monticello: The Biography of a Builder* [1988; repr. 1990], 36, 219, 250, 252–3, 271; Shackelford, *Descendants*, 1:208, 212; Margaret Bayard Smith's Account of a Visit to Monticello, [29 July–2 Aug. 1809]; Cornelia J. Randolph to Virginia J. Randolph [Trist], 18 July, 28 [July] 1819, and Nicholas P. Trist to Virginia J. Randolph [Trist], 24 Feb. 1822 [all in NcU: NPT]; Virginia J. Randolph [Trist] to Nicholas P. Trist, 5 June 1823 [DLC: Trist Papers]; Cornelia J. Randolph to Virginia J. Randolph Trist, 21 Nov. 1826, 4 Dec. 1827 [both in NcU: NPT]; Randolph, *Domestic Life*, 286).

Courtesy of Thomas Jefferson Foundation, Inc., photograph by Robert C. Lautman.

LUCY MARKS BY JOHN TOOLE

Albemarle County native Lucy Marks (1752–1837), mother of the explorer Meriwether Lewis, was known among her neighbors for her talent with herbal medicines. The artist John Toole (O'Toole) (1815–60) was born in Dublin but moved to Charlottesville in 1827 to live with an older brother after his father's death. Although he lacked formal training, late in the 1830s Toole was making a living as an itinerant portrait painter and miniaturist, working throughout central Virginia and Richmond. His oil-on-canvas portrait of Lucy Marks is undated (Charlottesville *Virginia Advocate*, 16 Mar. 1860; William B. O'Neal, *Primitive into Painter: Life and Letters of John Toole* [1960]).

Courtesy of the Missouri History Museum, Saint Louis.

NATURAL BRIDGE

Jefferson had a great appreciation for Natural Bridge and remarked in 1815 that he viewed it "in some degree as a public trust, and would on no consideration permit the bridge to be injured, defaced or masked from the public view." Despite having owned it since 1774, however, he only made a handful of visits to the Rockbridge County geological formation. Jefferson had first seen it in 1767, may have visited from Poplar Forest in 1781, and made three trips to Natural Bridge during his retirement, the first in 1815 with José Corrêa da Serra and Francis W. Gilmer, and the final two in 1817 and 1821. On his August 1817 trip he traveled from Poplar Forest with his granddaughters Ellen W. Randolph (Coolidge) and Cornelia J. Randolph to inspect his property and meet with his new tenant, a former slave named Patrick Henry. Jefferson was introduced to the Virginia painter William Roberts in London by J. Hector St. John de Crèvecoeur. Roberts renewed their acquaintance with an 1803 visit to Monticello and again contacted Jefferson the following year in Washington, D.C., where he presented him with paintings of Harpers Ferry and Natural Bridge. In 1808 Roberts gave the president prints of both paintings. During Jefferson's lifetime Roberts's painting of Natural Bridge (now lost) hung in the Dining Room at Monticello. A copy of the 1808 print by Joseph Constantine Stadler, depicted here, hangs there today (Stein, *Worlds*, 37, 83, 190; Barbara C. Batson, "Virginia Landscapes by William Roberts," *Journal of Early Southern Decorative Arts* 10 [1984]: 34–48; Roberts to TJ, 24 July 1803, [undated, received 18 July 1804], 26 Feb. 1808 [all in MHi]; TJ to William Caruthers, 15 Mar. 1815; *MB*, esp. 1:38).

Courtesy of the Thomas Jefferson Foundation, Inc.

DRAFT AND FAIR COPY OF THOMAS JEFFERSON'S BILL OF COMPLAINT AGAINST THE DIRECTORS OF THE RIVANNA COMPANY

In 1817, after several years of compromises and disagreements between Jefferson and the directors of the Rivanna Company over the use of his property along the Rivanna River, Jefferson believed his rights were at risk, and he filed a chancery case against the directors in an effort to protect his interests. He drafted his complaint late in 1816 and early in 1817. Jefferson's drafts are characterized by wide margins so as to allow for additions and reworkings. The extensive revisions to this one show the great pains Jefferson took to ready the brief for his counsel, Chapman Johnson and John H. Peyton. On some pages Jefferson inserted new material on small slips of paper, which he then adhered with red sealing wax to their proper locations. He most likely recopied the text clean using the polygraph, thus creating two copies of the final version, one intended for his counsel and another that he originally kept for himself. Sample pages from the draft and a recently discovered manuscript of one of the fair copies are reproduced here (TJ's Bill of Complaint against the Directors of the Rivanna Company, [by 9 Feb. 1817], document 1 in a group of documents on Jefferson's Lawsuit against the Rivanna Company, 9 Feb. 1817).

Courtesy of the Library of Congress and the Harlan Crow Library, Dallas, Texas.

Volume 11

19 January to 31 August 1817

JEFFERSON CHRONOLOGY

1743 • 1826

1743	Born at Shadwell, 13 April (New Style).
1760–1762	Studies at the College of William and Mary.
1762–1767	Self-education and preparation for law.
1769–1774	Albemarle delegate to House of Burgesses.
1772	Marries Martha Wayles Skelton, 1 January.
1775–1776	In Continental Congress.
1776	Drafts Declaration of Independence.
1776–1779	In Virginia House of Delegates.
1779	Submits Bill for Establishing Religious Freedom.
1779–1781	Governor of Virginia.
1782	Martha Wayles Skelton Jefferson dies, 6 September.
1783–1784	In Continental Congress.
1784–1789	In France on commission to negotiate commercial treaties and then as minister plenipotentiary at Versailles.
1790–1793	Secretary of State of the United States.
1797–1801	Vice President of the United States.
1801–1809	President of the United States.

RETIREMENT

1809	Attends James Madison's inauguration, 4 March.
	Arrives at Monticello, 15 March.
1810	Completes legal brief on New Orleans batture case, 31 July.
1811	Batture case dismissed, 5 December.
1812	Correspondence with John Adams resumed, 1 January.
	Batture pamphlet preface completed, 25 February; printed by 21 March.
1814	Named a trustee of Albemarle Academy, 25 March.
	Resigns presidency of American Philosophical Society, 23 November.
1815	Sells personal library to Congress.
1816	Writes introduction and revises translation of Destutt de Tracy, *A Treatise on Political Economy* [1818].
	Named a visitor of Central College, 18 October.
1818	Attends Rockfish Gap conference to choose location of proposed University of Virginia, 1–4 August.
	Visits Warm Springs, 7–27 August.
1819	University of Virginia chartered, 25 January; named to Board of Visitors, 13 February; elected rector, 29 March.
	Debts greatly increased by bankruptcy of Wilson Cary Nicholas.
1820	Likens debate over slavery and Missouri statehood to "a fire bell in the night," 22 April.
1821	Writes memoirs, 6 January–29 July.
1823	Visits Poplar Forest for last time, 16–25 May.
1824	Lafayette visits Monticello, 4–15 November.
1825	University of Virginia opens, 7 March.
1826	Writes will, 16–17 March.
	Last recorded letter, 25 June.
	Dies at Monticello, 4 July.

THE PAPERS OF
THOMAS JEFFERSON

To James Barbour

DEAR SIR Monticello Jan. 19. 17.

Your favor of the 9th is recieved by our last mail. I have been very long and intimately acquainted with Col° Trumbull, have had the best opportunities of knowing him thoroughly, and can therefore bear witness of my own knolege to his high degree of worth as a man. for his merit as a painter I can quote higher authorities, and assure you that on the continent of Europe, when I was there, he was considered as superior to West. Baron Grimm, who was the oracle of taste at Paris, in sculpture, painting and the other fine arts generally, gave him the decided preference, and came often to my house in Paris, while Col° Trumbull was with me, to see his paintings. I pretend not to be a Connoisseur in the art myself, but comparing him with others of that day I thought him superior to any historical painter of the time except David: it is in the historical line only that I am acquainted with his painting. in England West was preferred by the king, to whom all others followed suit. the subjects on which Col° Trumbull has employed his pencil are honorable to us, and it would be extremely desirable that they should be retained in this country as monuments of the taste, as well as of the great revolutionary scenes of our country.

You know how averse I am to be quoted on any occasion. yet as far as my testimony to Col° Trumbull's worth & talent can be of any avail, by using it in private circles, you are entirely free to do so, as a just tribute to truth and worth. Accept my friendly and respectful salutations TH: JEFFERSON

RC (NN: Barbour Papers); addressed: "The honble James Barbour of the Senate of the US. now at Washington"; franked; postmarked Milton, 22 Jan. PoC (DLC); on recto of reused address cover of John Payne Todd to TJ, 19 Sept. 1816; endorsed by TJ.

To Thomas T. Barr

Sir Monticello Jan. 19. 17.

I am very sensible of the honor done me by the Kentucky Agricultural society, in appointing me one of their honorary members. distance will be one great obstacle to my being of use to them; but a much greater and growing one will be the increasing torpor of age, now sensibly felt in body and mind. should any occasion arise however in which I can serve their institution, I shall do it with all the zeal which this mark of their kind attention entitles them to expect. in praying you to become the channel of my acknolegements to them, I beg leave to assure you of my high respect and consideration for yourself. Th: Jefferson

PoC (DLC); on verso of reused address cover to TJ; at foot of text: "Mr Thomas T. Barr"; endorsed by TJ.

To David Hosack

Monticello Jan. 19. 17.

I thank you, Sir, for the books you have been so kind as to send me. they will afford me amusement as well as instruction. from a general view I have taken of Thomas's work, it appears, with your aid, to be valuable for family use. without science in Medecine, I am yet fond of it's philosophical speculations. with these I observe your Medical Register[1] mingles disquisitions in all it's kindred branches of knolege. I am the more gratified in executing the duty of rendering you my thanks by the occasion it affords me of expressing my sense of your eminence in useful science and of assuring you of my high respect and consideration. Th: Jefferson

RC (PBm); fragment consisting of lower half of a single sheet, with missing text supplied from PoC; at foot of text: "Dr Hosack." PoC (DLC); on verso of reused address cover of John Prout to TJ, 17 Nov. 1816; endorsed by TJ.

Hosack supplied an appendix to Robert thomas's work, *The Modern Practice of Physic, exhibiting the Characters, Causes, Symptoms, Prognostics, Morbid Appearances, and Improved Method of Treating the Diseases of all Climates* (4th American ed. from 5th London ed.; New York, 1817; Poor, *Jefferson's Library*, 5 [no. 184]; TJ's copy in ViU, inscribed "Thomas Jefferson Esqr with the respects of the Editor D Hosack New york Decr 1816"). Hosack's medical journal was the *American Medical and Philosophical Register: or, Annals of Medicine, Natural History, Agriculture, and the Arts*, 4 vols. (1811–14; Poor, *Jefferson's Library*, 5 [no. 190]).

[1]Recoverable text in RC begins with this word.

To Hezekiah Niles

SIR Monticello Jan. 19. 17.

Accept my thanks for the specimen you have been so kind as to send me of the new preparation of mucilaginous substances for clarifying liquors. it is in the neatness of the manner of preparation, and equality of distribution on catgut, I suppose, that what there is of invention in it consists; as the clarifying powers of the mucilages, animal and vegetable, have been always known.

I am sorry it is not in my power to assist you with any thi[ng] towards the collection of revolutionary speeches proposed by your correspondent in the Register [of] Nov. 23. I did not even know of the existence in print of thos[e h]e mentions. if I ever possessed any they have all gone with my li[bra]ry to Congress, and my memory does not enable me even to ref[er] to them. if such a collection can be made to any extent, there can be no doubt of it's value; but where the materials are to be f[o]und I am entirely ignorant. Accept my friendly and re[s]pectful salutations TH: JEFFERSON

PoC (DLC); on verso of reused address cover to TJ; edge chipped; torn at crease; at foot of text: "Mr Niles"; endorsed by TJ.

For the COLLECTION OF REVOLUTIONARY SPEECHES, see Niles to TJ, 23 Dec. 1816.

From Craven Peyton

D. SIR. Monteagle Jany. 20. 17.

Nothing shall prevent my attending in Milton the day aftar tomorrow agreeable to Your request. please send John Hendersons—quit Claim to refresh my Memory—with great Esteem C. PEYTON

RC (MHi); addressed: "Thomas Jefferson Esqre Monticello" by "Boy"; endorsed by TJ as received 20 Jan. 1817 and so recorded in SJL.

For the QUIT CLAIM, see TJ to Peyton, 30 Dec. 1816, and note. A letter of 20 Jan. 1817 from TJ to Peyton, not found, is recorded in SJL with the additional notation: "Peyton Craven (no copy) to attend arbitrn."

From Horatio G. Spafford

ESTEEMED FRIEND— Albany, 1 Mo. 21, 1817.

I am obliged by thy kind attention. Thy Letter of Dec. 20, was duly received, & I shall avail myself of the Suggestion contained in it.

By this day's Mail, I Send No. 9 of the Magazine, with the conclusion of the Essay of 'Franklin,' to which I invite thy particular attention.

Looking over Some old Papers, I have, just now, accidentally taken up the Letter enclosed, which I Send for thy perusal. The writer is a Doctor of Divinity, & was lately President of the University of Vermont. For the opinions that Franklin advances concerning the Clergy, he has ample evidences that they are not too Severe. Shouldest thou think it can answer any good purpose, or even gratify a little curiosity, please Send the enclosed to President Madison, for perusal, & request him to transmit the original to me. I should be quite unwilling to lose this.[1] Concerning the School, & the Patent System of Franklin, I am very anxious to get thy opinion. It is the same Essay, (with some additions,) that I sent thee in M.S.—I have an invention, which I dare not entrust to the guardianship of our present Patent department, or the laws of the Patent System, which would be worth 1 million per Annum, to the United States. This is the cause of my great anxiety on this subject—& I despair of ever living to see it legally patronised in these States:—& still I feel anxious to cherish some hopes! Should not Congress do something for the benefit of Inventors, at the present Session, I expect to seek foreign aid, & appeal to the justice & policy of the Autocrat of all the Russias. I have many reasons for my dislike of the administration of the present Patent System & the conduct of the Patent Officer, which, in due time, I design to state to the public.

With great esteem, thy friend, H. G. SPAFFORD.

RC (MHi); at foot of text: "Hon. Thomas Jefferson"; endorsed by TJ as received 5 Feb. 1817 and so recorded in SJL.

For the ESSAY OF 'FRANKLIN,' see note to Spafford to TJ, 15 Dec. 1816. The LETTER ENCLOSED, not found, may have been from Daniel Clarke Sanders, a Congregational clergyman and educator who had been the first president of the University of Vermont, serving 1800–14 (*ANB*).

[1] Sentence interlined.

From William A. Burwell

MY DR SIR Washington January 22d 1817

Colo Waller Taylor Senator from Indiana has requested me to enclose the papers of Mr Graham for your examination; Mr Graham he informs me is very respectable & attatches considerable importance to the discovery he thinks he has made, But such is the confidence he places in your opinion that it will be abandon'd upon a suggestion from you—I am aware that this will give you trouble, but to gratify a worthy, man, to arrest his labors if useless or stimulate them if useful will be sufficient motives to encounter it;

please remember me to the family and accept yourself my Sincere wishes for your happiness W. A BURWELL

RC (DLC); addressed: "Thomas Jefferson Esquire Milton Virginia"; endorsed by TJ as received 5 Feb. 1817 and so recorded in SJL. Enclosures not found.

From Thomas Humphreys

SIR, Lynchburg 2 [ca. 23] January 1817

The unbounded expansion of your mind, leaves me no doubt, of an excuse being extended, for the unpresidented Liberty, I have here taken, in addressing to you, the subject matter embraced in the Envelope.

In submitting to a gentleman of your eminently high, & Commanding Station, in the literary world, together with your vast, & extensive experience in life; the enclosed plan; having for its object; the Libration from chains of slavery, (& permit me to add too,) and the princely settlement, of upwards of a million of the Human Race: I derive a satisfaction, far beyond the power of language to express. The plan is vast, it is worthy of such a great free, and magnanimous People, as constitute the great American republic;

The enjoyment of 20 years peace, & prosperity, would completely repay, & refund the Government; the money expended; in the purchasing, transportation, & settling of the Coloured People.

The principle number of the Male slaves; Understand Farming, & Planting; Or are well versant, in the various mechanical branches of business.

Many also of the females; having been brought up in genteel families, would prove greatly instrumental, in producing industry, Taste, & neatness; & in manufacturing, & making, a vast deal of their necessary clothing.

This republic of coloured people; would be greatly instrumental, in civilizing & planting the christian religion, as also the principles of Liberty, & independence; in that degraded Country of Africa: and Again, If they exercised the principles; that would be put within their grasp; they would with the advantages, & experience they possess; in 50 years, be in as high a national state of advancment; as many of the nations of the Earth, have arrived at, in the space of 200 years.

Whether you will approve of the principle, embraced in the enclosed statement: Or out of the vast & inexaustible store, of your own expanded mind; produced a plan; vastly superior: nothing would have so great a tendency to ensure its adoption, as your personal recommendation of it, to Congress; & to the assemblies of the several slave states. At the request of M[r] John Kerr, member of congress from this district, I lately forwarded him a copy of the Enclosed: & also one to M[r] William J Lewis, & Christopher Anthony, the present delagates, from the County of Campbell to the General Assembly of Virginia.

A few lines embracing your sentiments, of this momentuous subject, when your convenience will admit, will be considered a very great favor confered on me.

With Sentiments of Respect & Esteem I Remain

THOMAS HUMPHREYS—

RC (DLC: TJ Papers, 209:37223); misdated, with correct date conjectured from second date on enclosure; composed in two sittings, with some revisions and signature in a different ink; between dateline and salutation: "The Hon[ble] Thomas Jefferson"; endorsed by TJ as a letter of 2 Jan. 1817 received 5 Feb. 1817 and so recorded in SJL. RC (DLC); address cover only; with PoC of TJ to Humphreys, 8 Feb. 1817, on verso; addressed (torn): "The Hon[ble] [...]"; postmarked Lynchburg, 1 Feb.

Thomas Humphreys (ca. 1748–1825), druggist and physician, opened his Lynchburg shop in 1789. He served variously thereafter as a justice of the peace, magistrate, and sheriff for Campbell County (Campbell Co. Order Book, 3:206, 10:1, and in vol. 7 preceding p. 1; *MB*, 2:1340; Margaret Anthony Cabell, *Sketches and Recollections of Lynchburg by the Oldest Inhabitant (Mrs. Cabell) 1858* [1858; repr. with additional material by Louise A. Blunt, 1974], 298–301; Samuel J. Harrison's Answer to Bill of Complaint in *Scott v. Jefferson and Harrison*, [by 1 Aug. 1812]; *Lynchburg Press*, 4 Apr. 1817; *JHD* [1823–24 sess.], 99 [1 Jan. 1824]; Lynchburg Hustings and Corporation Court Will Book, A:179–80, B:235–8; Lynchburg *Virginian*, 2 Jan. 1826).

ENCLOSURE

Thomas Humphreys's Plan for Emancipating and Colonizing American Slaves, with his Note to Thomas Jefferson

Lynchburg 1st January 1817

The following plan, for emancipating the whole Race of the people of Colour, from United America: Is respectfully submitted, to the honorable the House of Representatives, of the United States; for their Consideration:

Of all the extraordinary, and Rare phenomenon, exibited by any nation on the theatre of existence; that of the southern parts of the United States of America, is most surprising. We observe to our astonishment, an enlightened, and polished people, richly versant in every political, Literary, agricultural, Commercial, Mechanical, and Manufactural improvement, Renowned for their skill in Milatary, and naval tactics; proudly eminent for their courage, in the Feilds of Fame; and high in Their profession of, and attachments to the most pure, and rational republican principles. The guarantee of genuine

Liberty, equality, and the rights of Man. Retaining Confined in Chains of abject slavery, in the very bosom of their Country; 1,000,000 of their unfortunate African Brethren; many of whom, or their forefathers, were draged from their native Shores, in the fetters of despotism, and Tyranically traded, and traficed for, like the beasts of the Feild; and what renders the continuation of this degrading principle the more unaccountable to Mankind, is, its being at direct War, with the Bill of Rights, or charter of Liberty; and Independence, of the several states that permit it, and in immediate opposition, to the Fundamental principles of the Government:

When we contemplate, the United States of America, in the high and commanding station they at present occupy, in the existing scale of nations; Basking themselves, in the full meridian Blaze of Liberty, and Independence;[1] we are obliged to turn away from the horrid scene of Cruelty and Injustice before us; can it be possible, that any of us, in this degraded part of the country, can have the assumptive effrontery, to boast, and talk about our patriotism, our republicanism, about Liberty equality, Rights of Man, Independence &c &c: and not blush; and what relation do we stand in, with respect to candour and truth, we must know, that we are political hypocrites, and greater Tyrants, than the Dey of Algiers, Tripoly, or any other eastern Despote.

The effects which slavery has, on the Morals, the Manners, the virtue, the Industry, and Economy, of the Inhabitants of the Country, in which it is tolerated; merits the highest consideration; But to do Justice to this subject, would require a volume, in which, to discuss it; suffice it for the present, merely to state, that in those states and parts of the country, where there are no slaves, the Inhabitants are generally more virtuous, more sober, more industrious & more attentive to their professional pursuits; have in general, a greater command of money, are not generally speaking, half so much involved in debt, enjoy a greater share of domestic happiness, and peace of mind. Again were there no slaves in the United States: the proprietors of Lands, and particularly of large Tracks would either lease the said Lands out, to the poorer classes of honest Industrious citizens; or employ them as Labourers: in the one Case, he would receive in compensation by way of Rent; such an amount in produce; or money, as would render him Indepen[d]ent, in his Circumstances: his Lands in place of being worn out, as by the former manner of culture, in the reign of slavery: would be every year improved, & in place of wild uncultivated woods, and old worn out fields, rotten fences &c &c, he would behold a number of valuable, well improved Farms; with good orchards, and Buildings, Spring up on his Estate; on the one hand, and on the Other, he would have the felicity of giving bread, employment, and happiness, to Hundreds of people, and of being conducive to the glory and strength of his country; in being instrumental to the Raising of a Number of usefull citizens, on Lands, which before, were neither to him, nor his Country, of any immediate benefit.—Again should the farmer wish, to Cultivate his Lands, by hired servants in place of leasing the custom would probably be, as in Europe, to pay off the Labourers every saturday night, in this case whatever necesseries of Life, the labourer wanted for his family, if the farmer in whose employ he then was, had the same to dispose of; the Labourer would no doubt, Lay out part of the money, he received, by way of wages, this would be a mutual Convenience to all, and would do away the necessity of Credit;

then would this country enjoy the substance of Independence, and not as at present, the Shadow.—

This situation of the country, would when once known produce vast emigrations of the poorer and industrious Classes of People, from Europe, to the United States and would add to the safety, and strength of the country.— The people would be generally clear of debt, and the supernumerary productions of the farm, in place of being laid out in the purchase of Slaves, and supporting the same; will be expended in enriching, and aggrandizing Farms; in the hire and support of a virtuous race, of usefull, Labourious Citizen[s?] who will greatly add to the strength and riches of country.—
So much for a preliminary, to the introduction of the main subject of discussion Vizt The emancipation, final disposal of; & transportation of the whole race of the Coloured people, from amongst the Citizens of these States.
And in the first place permit the Writer hereof, finally to suggest.
1st That the emancipation &c of the Coloured people, be made a national Act and to commence on the   day of   , in the year of
2ed That one tenth of the whole number of coloured people in the United States; shall be emancipated, and sent off yearly: untill the whole number, bond & free, shall be disposed of, in the Manner, to be hereafter Mentioned.
3d That the slaves be brought to a certain seaport Town; to be hereafter named: and there delivered to Commissioners, appointed for the special purpose, of Receiving, (and paying the holders for the same); at a certain given time in each year, as before stated or as soon after, as convenience will admit.—
4th That all slaves be valued by disinterested Men, to be appointed by the general Government; from the recommendation of Members of Congress, from each congressional district, a slave of the first grade, to be valued at $; and so in proportion to a child: All the free people of colour, shall also in like manner be sent off, and that in the course of the first, and second years, at furtherest; & shall be paid, each, the sum of $20.$\frac{00}{100}$ and shall participate in all the Benefits, and emoluments, in transportation, and settlement, as the slaves themselves; also in provision Tools &c.
5th That six months, previous to the assemblage of the first divission of the coloured people: one of the most healthy situations on the Continent of Africa, shall have been selected out, by Commissioners, appointed for that special purpose, and such a situation, may either be found, Embraced
From   15° to 20°   North Latitude
& from   0° to 15°   West Longitude from London
Or Embraced
From   10° to 23°   South Latitude
& from 15° to 30°   East Longitude from London
Or Embraced
From   12° North Latitude, to 12° South Latitude;
& from 30°, to 40°, & from that to 50° East Longitude from London,
Having the equinoctial Line for its centre, and although this is the furtherest off, yet it is by far, the most eligible situation, and probably at present the least inhabited
6thly That Suitable Shipping, and provisions for the voyage, be provided to transport them to their places of destination, with 1 years provisions for them: 2 Hoes, & 1 ax to each family, also 100 Common Work Horses, with as many plows, and Gear, &c, for the whole Decade:[2] accompanied by a Guard

of 1000 Soldiers, with their officers: to protect them from the incursions, & Molestations, of the Natives; as also to preserve Order, enforce obedience to the Law, to be passed for their regulation, by Congress; preserve peace, enforce Industry, and attention to the Culture of the Earth, and the various Mechanic Branches of Business, which may be prosecuted amongst them, either for their own private advantage, or the benefit of their Government, and also to see, that Justice be duly administered: that to each 1000, shall be furnished One Ton of Barr Iron, a sett of Blacksmiths, Carpenters, Coopers, sadlers, & shoemakers, Tools; also the necessary implements, for Manufactoring Flax, and Cotton Cloths; also, all necessary stationary, together with such school, & Religious books, as shall be deemed necessary, both for their instruction, as also the laying the Foundation, of Moral, and religious lives among them,

7th That the Commanding officer, shall under the direction of the President of the United States, act as Governor, or President, of the Republic: that he shall have the direction, of the internal regulations of the Establishment; such as surveying, and parcelling out to each family, their respective share of Land, the direction of its culture; The Establishment of a cotton, and flax, or Linen Manufactory, an Iron Foundery, for the purpose of manufactoring such Tools; as are necessary for the Culture of their Farms, Erecting Mills, and other public Buildings, such as a State House, to transact the public Business in, Houses for Public Worship, Academies, and Court Houses, for the administration of Justice; Planning their Towns, and establishing Markets, and distributing rewards, and inflicting punishments; under such regulations, as Congress shall from Time, to Time, point out; That it shall be the Business of the United States, to establish one Large Seminary in the settlement, where all the usefull sciences shall be taught, and that this establishment shall be conducted by 3 able professors[3] Vizt One of Divinity, the Mathemattics, and the several Branches of science, thereon dependent; One of Law, One of the Practice of phisic and surgery, in conjunction with 10 Inferior Teachers, whose Salaries are to be paid by the United States;

8th That at the end, and expiration of three Years, the whole of the then existing Army of 1000 Men, Except 50 who shall be retained as a Guard to the Governor, shall be sent back to the United States; that a Body of 600 Men of the Blacks, which shall have been previously trained, and armed for that purpose, shall be substituted in their places. That at the expiration of one year after the whole coloured people, shall have arrived at their place of destination, from the United States; which will be about the Eleventh year from the arrival, and settlement of the first division; The President of the United States, shall Transmit to the Governor, the draft of such a Constitution, as from the best Information, of the state of the Coloured Republic, he with the advice of the councill of State, Shall Judge, will best suit them; with directions, to lay the same, before a Chosen Body of their principle Men, and if approved of, to put it in Complete Operation.—

That the United States, shall continue to exercise the necessary Sovereighnty, in, and over this Colony or republic of Blacks, for the space of 21 years; from the time the 1st division, or decade landed in Africa, in which process of time, there may, it is presumable, be established such a constitution, Laws, & Regulations, as will nearly resemble, that of the United States itself. After which all the duties of the United States, shall be considered as discharged; Its Governor, Teachers, officers, & Soldiers, shall withdraw; & return to their native Country; & from that time, all further Connection shall cease, except such, as is between Freindly nations, through the Medium of Commerce, and at which time, too, it may be presumed, there will be a sufficient number, of their own colour, completely qualified, to Conduct, preserve, and perpetuate, the happy institution, which may be, by that time, established amongst them.

The whole aggregate amount, necessary to effect the purchase, the Equipment, the transportation, and Establishment of these people, on the coast of Africa; will not exceed $82.000.000 of dollars, which agreeable to the last Census; will not exceed $12. each free white person, in the United States.

Thus will the United States be freed, from one of the greatest of all earthly dangers, an Internal Enemy.

Slavery!!! This Blot; on the fairest page, of the Charter of freedom; being thus expunged, by a single Legislative Act: and the once victims of despotic power, not only Liberated, but Settled, supported, & protected, untill they are taught how to Live, be happy, and enjoy that very Liberty, Which they so often, sighed after the possession of; and that too; by their former[4] Masters.

This magnanimous display of Justice, and humanity, in the American people; would be received, with universal bursts of Applause, and Inscribed High on the Majastic Front, of the sacred Temple of Gratitude, by all the Nations of the earth, who should hear of the God like Act.—

Lynchburg 23rd January 1817

The Foregoing sentiments on the subject of Emancipation, & Transportation of the whole race of Coloured People, Bond & free, from among the Citizens of the United States of America, is Subjected to the Honorable Thomas Jefferson; former President of the United States; for his Consideration by his Freind

MS (DLC: TJ Papers, 209:37220–2); entirely in Humphreys's hand; edge trimmed.

The LAST CENSUS of 1810 enumerated 5,862,093 free white persons in the United States and its territories, plus 186,446 nonwhite free persons and 1,191,364 slaves. According to these figures, Humphreys's estimated maximum cost of $82 million for his plan would cost each free white individual nearly $14. Even if one excludes free blacks from the calculation altogether, the plan allows an average of just under $69 for the purchase, transportation, and equipment of each slave (*Aggregate amount of each description of Persons within the United States of America, and the Territories thereof, agreeably to actual enumeration made according to law, in the year 1810* [Washington, 1811]).

[1] Manuscript: "Indepence."

[2] Preceding four words interlined.

[3] Manuscript: "professions."

[4] Manuscript: "formers."

To William Duane

DEAR SIR Monticello Jan. 24. 17.

I am sincerely concerned and mortified at the failure of the remittance I had supposed made to you as long ago as March last. I received an account signed 'John B. Smyth for W[m] Duane' in Feb. consisting of 2 articles to wit the translation 60.D. a year's subscription for the Aurora to become due May 1st 16. and on the 18th of Mar. I desired my correspondents Gibson & Jefferson of Richmond to remit you 65.D. and never doubted it had been done until the receipt of your letter of the 9th inst. it must have been accidentally overlooked by them, as it is the first omission of the kind on their part which has happened in the course of a 20. years correspondence. however in a great mass of business, such things must sometimes happen. to avoid delay & the possibility of another failure I have thought it best to make the remittance to yourself directly in bills of a Richmond bank which I understand are negociable with you without loss. however if there be any loss, place it to my debit. to the former account of 65.D. I add for the present year ending May 1. 17. and therefore inclose 70.D. as transmissions of money by post sometimes fail, a line of information that it is recieved will put my mind at rest.

A great decay of bodily powers has not been without effect on the mind also, which is become sensibly sluggish, averse to the labors of the writing table, and almost incurious and insouciant as to the affairs of the world. I have scarcely the curiosity to read the newspapers, and resign myself willingly to the care of those on whom that trust has devolved in the due course of nature. I salute you with continued esteem and respect TH: JEFFERSON

PoC (DLC); on verso of reused address cover of Fitzwhylsonn & Potter to TJ, 6 Jan. 1817; at foot of text: "Genl. Duane"; endorsed by TJ.

To Nicolas G. Dufief

DEAR SIR Monticello Jan. 24. 17.

I have duly recieved the Connoissance des tems for 1817. & 1818. two copies* of Blunt's Nautical almanac for 1817. and Graglia's Italian dictionary. I presume Blunt has not yet published his Almanac for 1818.

*I find on reexamn that it is a single copy of Blunt for each of the years 1817.18. that I have rec[d]

At the time I recieved your favor of Dec. 16. my account with mess[rs] Gibson & Jefferson to the end of the year had not come to hand. I recieved it a few days ago, and on examination find charged in it as of Aug. 4. the remittance of the 31.D. to you which I had ordered in June. unless you may have omitted to enter it therefore or overlooked it, mr Gibson's correspondent must have failed either to execute his order or to inform him that he had not done so. I have thought it safest to ask your re-examination of your own books before I ask mr Gibson's enquiry into [...] failure, which I will withold until I have recieved your assurance that the error is not with you. I salute you with great esteem and respect. TH: JEFFERSON

PoC (DLC); on verso of a reused address cover from James Barbour to TJ; torn at seal; adjacent to signature: "M. Dufief"; endorsed by TJ.

TJ's ACCOUNT WITH MESS[RS] GIBSON & JEFFERSON (not found) was enclosed in James Ligon (for Patrick Gibson) to TJ, 16 Jan. 1817. TJ ordered the REMITTANCE from Gibson on 8 June 1816.

To John Wayles Eppes

DEAR SIR Monticello Jan. 24. 17.

Francis arrived here in good health the day before Yesterday. I think he cannot do better than to take this occasion of learning Spanish, because it is a language rarely taught in this country, and will be of great importance within his day. it is that too in which all the early history of America is written. I suppose he may acquire so much of it in 2. or 3. months as to pursue it easily himself afterwards.

Martin begins to turn tolerably. I send some specimens of his turning by your servant, and one of them is of the head proposed to your garden posts. I added a neck to the ball, which however nearly doubles the work. about 20. are made, and the stuff all ready for the whole. but I do not think he can do two aday. still he had better go on with them here as long as you can let him stay; however this must be as is convenient to yourself. I shall give him a pass to go home the first week in February, unless you inform me in the mean time that you can conveniently spare him. had Francis come in a gig I should have sent mrs Eppes some shrubs which she has not; but shall not fail to avail myself of some other opportunity.

I rejoice that your health permits you to return into public life, and that you are returning; nor is there any place where an honest disinterested patriot can be more useful than in the Senate of the US. I suppose you will hardly go to the call of the 4th of March, which I presume is a matter of ceremony. Patsy is absent with mrs Bankhead who is in the straw and very poorly. the rest of the family join in affectionate remembrances to mrs Eppes & yourself; be assured always of my sincere esteem & respect TH: JEFFERSON

RC (ViU: TJP); addressed: "John W. Eppes esq. Millbrook." PoC (MHi); on verso of reused address cover of Micajah Davis to TJ, 3 Sept. 1816; mutilated at seal; endorsed by TJ.

The Senate convened briefly on the 4TH OF MARCH 1817 for the inauguration of President James Monroe. PATSY: Martha Jefferson Randolph. IN THE STRAW: "in childbed, lying-in" (*OED*).

Eppes's reply of 30 Jan. 1817, not found, is recorded in SJL as received 6 Feb. 1817 from Mill Brook.

To Dabney Minor and Peter Minor

GENTLEMEN Monticello Jan. 24.

On the subject of the rents claimed from me by the representatives of Bennet Henderson, my grandson desires me to put into your hands what information I have as to the rents for what are called the lower and upper field. I had given him a statement of those recieved after[1] 1807. when returning home to live[2] I had taken the business into my own hands, and for the period before that while transacted by mr Peyton I had requested mr Peyton to attend you, as I knew nothing on the subject but through him. on examining my papers I find statements of those rents as I made them out from his information, and according to which I believe I settled them with him. be pleased to observe that the rents paid by mr T. E. Randolph were for Henderson's upper field, the Dower lands and house, and a small peice of my own land adjoining the upper field. his account mentions a Thorpe's fiel[d] [I do] not know what ground that was: for indeed these lots, [...] claimants and tenants were so numerous and complicated that I do not retain them in my memory, and sometimes without understanding them, rested them entirely on mr Peyton. I am very thankful for your kindness in undertaking to settle them, and shall recieve your judgment whatever it is with the most implicit satisfaction and conviction that it is right. I pray you to be assured of my thankfulness and friendly esteem & respect TH: JEFFERSON

PoC (MHi); on verso of reused address cover to TJ; partially dated; mutilated at seal; at foot of text: "Messrs D. & P. Minor"; endorsed by TJ as a letter of 24 Jan. 1817 to Dabney Minor and Peter Minor and so recorded in SJL.

Dabney Minor (1774–1824), planter and public official, represented Albemarle County in the Virginia House of Delegates, 1817–18. Appointed a county magistrate in 1806, he was also a founder of the Agricultural Society of Albemarle in 1817, a director of the Rivanna Company, and an officer in the county militia. Minor's second marriage was to TJ's great-niece Martha Jefferson Terrell. In 1819 he purchased Carr's-brook from the widow of his cousin, TJ's nephew Peter Carr. Minor subscribed $400 toward the establishment of Central College. At his death his personal estate included more than fifty slaves and a library containing some two hundred volumes (John B. Minor, *The Minor Family of Virginia* [1923], 14–5; Leonard, *General Assembly*, 289; Woods, *Albemarle*, 84, 373, 377; True, "Agricultural Society," 263, 269–71; Master List of Subscribers to Central College, [after 7 May 1817], document 5 in a group of documents on The Founding of the University of Virginia: Central College, 1816–1819, printed at 5 May 1817; Albemarle Co. Deed Book, 21:397; Albemarle Co. Will Book, 7:412, 8:138–50; TJ to Minor, 28 Sept. 1806 [NjMoHP: Lloyd W. Smith Collection]; Fredericksburg *Virginia Herald*, 20 Oct. 1824).

MY GRANDSON: Thomas Jefferson Randolph. The STATEMENT, a version of which may have been enclosed here, was TJ's Notes on the Rent of the Henderson Lands, [by 24 Jan. 1817].

[1] Word interlined in place of "from."
[2] Preceding four words interlined.

Notes on the Rent of the Henderson Lands

[by 24 Jan. 1817]

Notes for the clear rents of the Upper & Lower fields of Henderson's lands

1807. Nov. 17.[1] possession was delivered by John Henderson.

		D
1808.9.	T. E. Randolph pd rent for the Dower house & lands & the upper field	90
	he then gave up the lands & paid for the house & garden	60.
	consequently the lands had been rated @	30.
	deduct for the Dower lands 15. a^{s} $\frac{15}{65} = \frac{3}{13}$ of 30.D.	7
	rent for the upper field for 2. years by T. E. R. & 3. y. to wit 1813. 14. 16.[2] by myself	23
1808.	Johnson paid for the Lower field 34.D. it is believed he pd no rent for 1809.10. in considern of the house E^{t}c he built & repaired.[3] the rents remitted may be supposed @ 34.D. for 2. years to wit 1809.10.	
1811.	the rent for the house & lands was settled @ 60.D. and so has continued I suppose the rent of the house may be considered as $\frac{1}{3}$ and consequently the lands @ 40.D. for 5. years. to wit 1811–15	
	fencing. the circumference of the Upper field by the plat is about 323. po. or 1776. yds @ 5. rails to the yard	

is 8882.[4] rails; put up in spring 1813. the side on the river was carried away the following winter & the lower end entirely burnt by the people of Milton, being one half. the remaining half, after 3. years service may be reckoned at half price say therefore 6661. rails lost. cutting & mauling is worth 5.D. the 1000. hauling 40. new rails at a load, & at a mile or $1\frac{1}{2}$ mile a day 5 loads would be 200. rails costing 4.D. or 20.D. the thousand, [bu]t say 20.D. for cutting, mauling, & hauling, is 133.22 D for the whole

taxes. th[ey] appear by Peyton's acc^t to have been from 1804. to 1809 at 10.58 D the year. about 1813.14 as well as I remember they were somewhat raised, but I do not know how much. set them then @ 10.58 for 7. years (to 1814.) 74.06

---

in 1815 the state taxes of my whole land were 113.11 D what part of this was for Henderson's land I never knew, but suppose $\frac{1}{5}$ = 22.62

---

but the Congress taxes were immensely higher. the whole assessed to me here was 301.D. how much of this was for land, I know not; but certainly not less than half, say 150.D. of which $\frac{1}{5}$ for Henderson's land 30. D

Rent of Upper field @	23. Dollars	5. years			115
Lower d^o	34.	3. years =	102	}	
	40.	5	200	}	302
whole rents					417

		D	
Cr.	expence of inclosing	133.22	
	taxes for 7. years @ 10.58	74.06	
	state d^o for 1815.	22.62	
	Congress d^o for d^o	30.	
		259.90	259.90
	Balance of rents after deducting taxes & inclosure		157.10
		$\frac{1}{5}$ is	31.42

James L. Henderson's deed for the lands of t[he] 4. younger children was dated 1802. Sep. 18. but John Henderson the legal guardian was in possession of their lands, and refused to deliver possession until 1807. Nov. 17. when he did it.[5] but the upper & lower fields alone &

the dower were occupied by me or by any body.[6] the river lots & back lots laid open and unoccupied. I gave written leases to cut wood on my[7] part of the back lots. if the lessees cut any where else it was not by authority from me. they were trespassers and answerable to the owners. I rec^d rent from them for my own part only, and consequently am answerable for none.

James L. Henderson died June 9. 1813.

	Frances	Lucy.	Nancy
Upper field	N° 5	N° 6	N° 7.
Lower d°	N° 8.	N° 4	N° 3.

the lower field has been constantly occupied by Johnson, & consequently no intermission[8] of rents.

the upper field was occupied as follows

1808. 1809	by T. E. Randolph
1810 1811 1812	uninclosed and unoccupied
1813 1814	occupied by Th:J.
1815.	the fresh having carr^d away the river fence it was unoccupied
1816.	occupied by Th:J.

MS (ViU: TJP); on reused address cover to TJ; entirely in TJ's hand; undated; mutilated at seal and top edge chipped; endorsed by TJ: "Arbitration." Possibly enclosed in TJ to Dabney Minor and Peter Minor, 24 Jan. [1817].

[1] Manuscript: "27."

[2] Text from "to wit" to this point interlined.

[3] Preceding two words interlined.

[4] Correct figure is 8,880.

[5] TJ here canceled "by deed."

[6] Preceding four words interlined.

[7] TJ here canceled "lands."

[8] Manuscript: "intemission."

To Jerman Baker

Dear Sir Monticello Jan. 25. 17.

Your favor of the 13th was recieved by our last mail. Francis is now here engaged in learning Spanish. I thought he could not employ the winter better. but he has lost much of it at home. I think in a couple of months he may make such progress as that he will be able afterwards to pursue it by himself. I would then rather have him with mr Wood than any other teacher I know, but would much rather it should have been at Lynchburg [th]an[1] Richmond in point of climate. mr Eppes seems also to approve of his going to mr Wood, so that in the spring we shall ask a place for him in his school, and that he and Wayles may join again according to their mutual wishes.

I am sorry to see the report of a committee unfavorable [to] Barziza.[2] I was in hopes that making himself a citizen might have capacitated him to recieve the inheritance. I salu[te] you now & always with affectionate friendship and respect. TH: JEFFERSON

PoC (MHi); on verso of reused address cover of Thomas Appleton to TJ, 27 Sept. 1816; torn at seal, with some text rewritten by TJ; at foot of text: "German Baker esq."; endorsed by TJ.

For the REPORT OF A COMMITTEE of the Virginia House of Delegates against Philip I. Barziza's petition claiming his grandmother's estate, see note to Joseph C. Cabell to TJ, 12 Jan. 1817.

[1] Word faint.
[2] Manuscript: "Baziza."

Rent Settlement with Henderson Heirs

The undersigned to whom was refered a matter in controversy between the minor Legatees of Bennett Henderson dec^{d} & Th^{s} Jefferson, after hearing the case & the testimony offered on both sides have come to the following decision—

It appears from the testimony of sundry witnesses, that Thomas Jefferson has been in possession of the lands of Frances, Lucy, & Nancy C. Henderson since the year 1802—Of course he is Responsible to them for the rent of their part from that time untill the 1st of Jany 1817. when he gave up the possession—

As to the question made by the said Thomas, 'Have not these rents been paid?'

It appears that he became possessed of these Lands by a deed from James L Henderson to Craven Peyton bearing date the 18th Sept 1802 & by a further deed from John Henderson, 17th Novr 1807 who signs as Guardian for the three above named Legatees—But it is manifest that neither of these persons had a right to convey the lands in question;—which also seems to have been the opinion of the Purchaser; for an obligation is taken from each to make the title good, as the legatees shall respectively marry or come of age. The money therefore paid by Mr Jefferson for these lands cannot be claimed by him as an offset against the Rents. His Redress is against those of whom he purchased. It appears to us that the Sum of Seven Hundred & sixty six dollars & eighty cents is due from Mr Jefferson to the three above named Frances, Lucy & Nancy C. Henderson, as will appear by the following statement.—[1]

Th. Jefferson. D^{r} To. Frances. Lucy, & Nancy C Henderson.

To rent of the field below Milton from the year—1802. to 1816 (both inclusive) at 40$ ℔ year say 15 years	$600	
Int. on do to Jan 1st 1817 14 y^{rs}	252	
	$\frac{3}{10}$ 852 =	$255.60
To rent of the field above Milton for the same time settled at the same sum ℔ annum	600	
Int on do—for 14 years	252	
	$\frac{3}{10}$. 852 =	255.60
To rent of forest land for fire wood, (which seemed to be variable in its yearly value, we have however taken the lowest estimate) say 40$ ℔ year for 15 years	600	
Int on do. 14 years	252	
	$\frac{3}{10}$ 852 =	255.60
Ball. due Hendersons Legatees		$766 80.

We have estimated the value of these three parcels of Land from the year 1802 to 1816 both inclusive with the interest to be $2556. three tenths of which sums due to the above named Frances. Lucy & Nancy C. Henderson which amounts to $766.80 & this estimate is made under the idea that the Taxes &c. has been, & should be paid by Mr Jefferson

Given under our hands this 25th of Jan 1817

P. Minor.
Dabney Minor

Received in full for the above award of 766\frac{80}{100}$ a draft on Bernard Peyton for this amount when paid

W D Meriwether
Attorney in fact for the three younge[r] legatees of Bennet Henderson Dec

MS (ViU: TJP); in Peter Minor's hand, signed by Peter Minor and Dabney Minor, with subjoined receipt in William D. Meriwether's hand; edge trimmed; addressed: "Th: J. Randolph Esqr"; endorsed by TJ: "Hendersons. Frances, Lucy & Nancy C. Award."

have not these rents been paid was a question TJ posed in his Notes on the Rent Claims of the Heirs of Bennett Henderson, [by 30 Dec. 1816].

[1] Recto ends here.

To Peter Derieux

Dear Sir Monticello Jan. 26. 17.

On my return from Bedford I found here such a mass of letters and other business accumulated during my absence, that this is the first moment it has been in my power to turn to mr Mazzei's will. this occupies 4. sheets of paper, in a difficult hand. it is beyond my leisure to copy entirely, nor is there any one else in the neighborhood who could understand and decypher it. after some charitable legacies to the poor, to servants, and the bequest to his widow of one half of his house, gardens & other property, he adds the following residuary clause. 'in tutti gli altri suoi beni, mobili, immobili, semoventi, diritti, azioni, e generalmente in tutto quello e quanto detto Signor testatore si troverá avere, e possedere alla epoca[1] della sua morte, sua eredé universale istitui, e istituisce, e di sua propria bocca nomino e nomina la Signora Elisabetta Mazzei sua dilettissima figlia e qualora la detta sua figlia non volesse, o non potesse a[dire] la di lui eredita, sostitui, e sostituisce volgarmente e pupill[arm]enté alla medesima la prenominata signora Antonia Mazzei sua consorte; e nel caso che neppur questa volesse, o potesse adire la detta eredita, sostitui e sostituisce volgarmente alla medesima i poveri di questa citta di Pisa.' dated 1814. Dec. 3. neither yourself, nor mrs Derieux, nor any one of either of your families or friends is named or alluded to in the will either directly or indirectly. I had on a former occasion, as you had requested, stated to him the situation of mrs Derieux & yourself, and recommended his attention & beneficence to you. his answer was only to remit to you the sum which I did, and in no subsequent letter has he ever mentioned you. with my regrets on the failure of your hopes in this resource I tender to mrs Derieux and yourself the assurance of my great esteem and respect. Th: Jefferson

PoC (DLC); on verso of a reused address cover from Nicolas G. Dufief to TJ; damaged at seal, with missing text supplied from Philip Mazzei's will, 3 Dec. 1814, printed above at Thomas Appleton to TJ, 15 Apr. 1816; at foot of text: "Mr Derieux"; endorsed by TJ.

[1] Instead of preceding two words, will reads: "all'Epoca."

To Peter S. Du Ponceau

Dear Sir Monticello Jan. 26. 17.

I promised you in my letter of Jan. 22. 16. to make enquiry on the subject of the MS. journal of the boundary between Virginia and North Carolina, run in 1728. of which you have a defective transcript.

I have since been able to obtain the original for perusal, and now have it in my possession. I call it original, because it is that which has been preserved in the Westover family, having probably been copied fair[1] by the Amanuensis of Dr Byrd from his rough draught. that it was written by him is proved as well by the family tradition, as by passages in the work where the author speaks of other Commissioners calling on him at Westover, of his return to his family at Westover E^tc. in one place the writer identifies himself with the person whom he calls Steddy, and from other passages it is sufficiently evident that

Meanwell is Fitzwilliams
Firebrand Dandridge
Astrolabe Irving
Orion Mayo
Dr Humdrum. non constat.

the work shews too that Steddy, Meanwell and Firebrand were all members of the king's Council. the N. Carolina commissioners, John Lovich, Christopher Gale, Edward Moseley, and Wm Little, are designated in the Journal by 'judge Jumble, Shoebrush, Plausible, and Puzzle cause,' and the two surveyors by 'Plausible and Bo-otes.' but nothing in the journal enables us to ascribe to each his respective fictitious appellation. the MS. is of 162. pages small 8vo is entitled 'the secret history of the line,' begins with the words 'the Governor and Council of Virginia in 1727. recieved' E^tc. and ends it's narration with the words 'for which blessings may we all be sincerely thankful,' and then subjoins a list of the Commissioners and Surveyors under feigned names, the Virginia attendants by their real names, and a statement of expences and distances. this MS. wants pages 155. & 156. the 154th page ending with the words 'our Landlord who,' and the 157th beginning with the words 'fortify'd ourselves with a meat breakfast.' you say that your copy wants the first 24. pages, and about a dozen more pages in the middle of the work. let us concur then in making both compleat. send me from your's a copy of the two pages this wants, as before described, and designate to me those you want, by quoting the final & initial words of the text, between which your chasms are, and I will supply them from the original. I shall thus be able to restore to the Westover family their original made perfect, and your copy compleated will give double security against the loss of the work by accident. I salute you with great esteem & respect.

TH: JEFFERSON

RC (PPAmP: Thomas Jefferson Papers); addressed: "Peter S. Du Ponçeau esq. Philadelphia"; franked; postmarked Charlottesville, 29 Jan.; endorsed by Du Ponceau and an unidentified hand; with related notes in pencil, possibly by Du

Ponceau, on address cover. PoC (DLC); endorsed by TJ.

For the variant versions of the MS. JOURNAL, see note to TJ to Wilson Cary Nicholas, 16 Oct. 1816. In William Byrd's second description of his expedition to survey Virginia's southern boundary, he gave the major participants aliases. Despite TJ's conjectures, more recent scholarship has identified MEANWELL as William Dandridge, FIREBRAND as Richard Fitzwilliam, ASTROLABE as William Mayo, ORION as Alexander Irvine, and DR HUMDRUM as Peter Fontaine (Louis B. Wright, ed., *The Prose Works of William Byrd of Westover: Narratives of a Colonial Virginian* [1966], 27, 41, 49).

NON CONSTAT: "it is not settled" (*Black's Law Dictionary*). JUDGE JUMBLE was Christopher Gale, SHOEBRUSH was John Lovick, "Plausible" was Edward Moseley, and PUZZLE CAUSE was William Little. TJ mistakenly listed "Plausible" a second time, as a surveyor, but Alexander Irvine ("Orion") joined Mayo as Virginia's second surveyor, while Samuel Swann (BO-OTES) represented North Carolina in this capacity (Wright, *Prose Works of William Byrd*, 28, 41–3, 49, 55).

[1] Word interlined.

To William Sampson

DEAR SIR Monticello Jan. 26. 17.

I have read with great satisfaction the eloquent pamphlet you were so kind as to send me, and sympathise with every line of it. I was once a doubter Whether the labor of the Cultivator, aided by the creative powers of the earth itself, would not produce more value than that of the manufacturer, alone and unassisted by the dead subject on which he acted? in other words, Whether the more we could bring into action of the energies of our boundless territory, in addition to the labor of our citizens, the more would not be our gain? but the inventions of latter times, by labor-saving machines, do as much now for the manufacturer, as the earth for the cultivator. experience too has proved that mine was but half the question. the other half is Whether Dollars & Cents are to be weighed in the scale against real independance? the whole question then is solved; at least so far as respects our own wants.

I much fear the effect, on our infant establishments, of the policy avowed by mr Brougham, and quoted in the pamphlet. individual British merchants may lose by the late immense importations; but British commerce & manufactures, in the mass, will gain, by beating down the competition of ours, in our own markets.[1] against this policy, our protecting duties are as nothing, our patriotism less. I turn however, with some confidence, to a different auxiliary, a revolution in England, now, I believe, unavoidable. the crisis, so long expected, inevitable as death, altho' uncertain like that in it's date, is at length arrived. their government has acted over again the fable of the frog and the ox; and their bloated system has burst. they have spent the feesimple of the island in their inflated enterprises on the peace and happiness of the rest of mankind. their debts have consequently accumulated by their follies & frauds, until the interest is equal to the aggregate rents of all the farms in their country. all these rents must go to pay interest, and nothing remains to carry on the government. the possession alone of their lands is now in the nominal owner; the usufruct in the public creditors. their people too taxed up to 14. or 15. out of 16. hours of daily labor, dying of hunger in the streets & fields, the survivors can see for themselves the alternative only of following them, or of abolishing their present government of king, lords & borough-Commons, and establishing one in some other form, which will let them live in peace with the world. it is not easy to foresee the details of such a revolution; but I should not wonder to see the deportation of their king to Indostan, and of their Prince Regent to Botany bay. there, imbecility might be governed by imbecility, and vice by vice; all in suit. our wish for the good of the people of England, as well as for our own peace, should be that they may be able to form for themselves such a constitution & government as may permit them to enjoy the fruits of their own labors in peace, instead of squandering them in fomenting and paying the wars of the world. but during these struggles, their artists are to become soldiers, their manufactures to cease, their commerce sink, and our intercourse with them be suspended. this interval of suspension may revive and fix our manufactures, wean us from British aperies, and give us a national & independant character of our own. I cannot say that all this will be, but that it may be; and it ought to be supplicated from heaven by the prayers of the whole world, that at length there may be 'on earth peace, and good will towards men.' no country, more than your native one, ought to pray & be prepared for this. I wish them success, and to yourself health and prosperity. TH: JEFFERSON

RC (Mrs. Livingston T. Dickason, Short Hills, N.J., 1944); torn at seal and faint, with missing text supplied from PoC; addressed: "William Sampson esquire New York"; redirected by an unidentified hand to "Washington"; franked; postmarked (faint) [Charlottesville, 29 Jan.?], and New York, 4 Feb.; endorsed by Sampson. PoC (DLC). Undated extract printed in Washington *Daily National Intelligencer*, 10 Feb. 1817; at head of text: "ON MANUFACTURES. The following extract of a letter from the venerable JEFFERSON to WILLIAM SAMPSON, Esq acknowledging the receipt of the Address from the American Society for the encouragement of Manufactures, we have been permitted to copy for publication."

The ELOQUENT PAMPHLET quotes Henry Peter BROUGHAM: "'that it is well worth while to incur a loss on the first exportation, in order, by the glut, to stifle in the cradle those rising manufactures in the United States, which the war had forced into premature existence, contrary,' as he is pleased to assert, 'to the natural course of things'" (*Address of the American Society for the encouragement of Domestic Manufactures, to the People of the United*

States [New York, 1817; Poor, *Jefferson's Library*, 6 (no. 223); TJ's copy in DLC: Rare Book and Special Collections], 17).

In Aesop's fable of the FROG AND THE OX, a frog bursts while attempting to inflate itself to the size of an ox. A British penal settlement was located in Australia at BOTANY BAY. The phrase ON EARTH PEACE, AND GOOD WILL TOWARDS MEN is from the Bible (Luke 2.14).

[1] Extract in *Daily National Intelligencer*, lacking dateline and salutation, ends here with "&c."

From Josephus B. Stuart

SIR. Washington, January 26th 1817

On my departure from your hospitable mansion, I proceeded to Richmond, where I devoted a few days to an examination of the natural advantages & improvements of that City.—

In my opinion, the time is not far distant, when Richmond will rank as the fourth City in our union. Her great water priviledges, particularly for mills, machinery &c together with her local situation, her vicinity to extensive coal mines, (becoming daily of more importance from the constant decrease of fuel in the Eastern states), & the enterprize, intelligence & liberal views of her citizens, must necessarily produce this result.

I enclose you the memorial of Jenkins & others, relative to the Privateer Armstrong,—& also, the memorial of the ship owners & others of the City of New York, which is a complete demonstration of the correctness of the principles which you advanced, & so far as depended on your personal exertions, supported during your unparalelled political career.

Had our Commercial men listened to those principles 10 years since, they would not now have presented such a memorial as the enclosed.—

My dates from London are up to the 25th November. They represent the sufferings of all classes as unparalelled; some acts of violence had been committed by the mob in London; & the most alarming consequences were apprehended from all quarters of the Kingdom, in the course of the winter.

With grateful recollections for your politeness during my stay with you;—an unshaken attachment to your political maxims;—and best wishes for your welfare & happiness, I have, the Honor, to be, most respectfully, your most obedient Servant.— J, B, STUART.

P.S. I shall not return to Albany 'till after the close of the present session of Congress.—

RC (DLC); between signature and postscript: "His Excellency Thos Jefferson. Monticello Va"; endorsed by TJ as received 5 Feb. 1817 and so recorded in

SJL. Enclosures: (1) *The Memorial Of Frederick Jenkins, and Rensselaer Havens, in behalf of the owners, officers, and crew of the late private armed brig General Armstrong* ([Washington, 1817]; 14th Cong., 2d sess., Senate Doc. 66, ordered printed 23 Jan. 1817), stating that on 26 Sept. 1814 the brig had been in port in Faial when it was attacked by a superior British force; that despite its crew's best efforts at defense, the vessel was destroyed; that the brig and her armament had a value of $42,000; and petitioning Congress for such indemnity or compensation to the owners, officers, and crew as "under the peculiar circumstances attending her destruction, may be deemed just and equitable." (2) *The Memorial Of Ship-owners, and others, interested in foreign commerce, convened by public notice at the Tontine Coffee House, in the city of New-York, the 17th January, 1817* ([Washington, 1817]; 14th Cong., 2d sess., Senate Doc. 65, ordered printed 23 Jan. 1817; also issued as House Doc. 49), claiming that commercial and colonial regulations adopted by foreign nations to protect and promote their trade have depressed commerce in the United States and resulted in unemployment for "our seamen and the numerous classes of mechanics connected with navigation"; citing a current bill to impose an additional duty on merchandise imported into the United States from nations that exclude American vessels; and proposing a stronger law that would prohibit the importation of all foreign products not carried in American vessels, exclude any foreign produce originating in ports that refuse to reciprocate by accepting imports, and prevent foreign vessels in United States ports from loading American produce destined for ports that deny entry to American vessels.

To Joseph Milligan

DEAR SIR Monticello Jan. 27. 17.

I am in the daily hope of recieving new proof sheets and the particular wish that we may go thro' the work before April, because I shall then go to Bedford and be absent a month. I do not know how our account stands; I mean independantly of the 60.D. for the translation; for I do not wish that reimbursement until you have made it by the sale of the book. if you will send me my account, suspending that article, it shall be remitted, as the spring is the season for my gathering up & discharging these debts. in the mean time I inclose you a 20.D. bill, having occasion for Gillies's history of Greece, which I believe is in 4. vols 8vo and also his history of the world from Alexander to Augustus of which there is a good edition printed in Philadelphia in 1809. let them be handsomely and solidly bound. our bookbinders are too apt to half press their books, leaving them spongy: I shall be glad to recieve these as soon as firm binding will permit. I salute you with esteem and respect TH: JEFFERSON

PoC (DLC); on verso of reused address cover of Charles Thomson to TJ, [by 7 Jan. 1817]; at foot of text: "Mr Millegan"; endorsed by TJ.

To John Barnes

DEAR SIR Monticello Jan. 28. 17.

I now inclose you the power of Attorney which I am in hopes fulfills all the forms of the treasury & will enable us I hope to compleat this transfer for our friend. ever & affect[ly] yours TH: JEFFERSON

PoC (DLC); at foot of text: "M[r] Barnes"; endorsed by TJ. Enclosures: enclosure to TJ to Barnes, 31 Dec. 1816, and possibly also first enclosure to TJ to Barnes, 15 Dec. 1816.

OUR FRIEND: Tadeusz Kosciuszko.

To James Eastburn

SIR Monticello Jan. 28. 17.

The republication of the antient and valuable works now out of print, will certainly be an useful undertaking. but it is time for me to withdraw my attention from all long-winded enterprises. they belong to the generation which is to carry them through, as little would I presume to prescribe to them the proper objects of their attention. these books have by their worth established their own reputation, and need recommendation from nobody. you must be so good therefore as to excuse my declining to assume the direction of the public judgment as to what should or should not recieve their patronage; and with my wishes for the success of the undertaking to be assured of my personel respect to yourself TH: JEFFERSON

PoC (MHi); on verso of reused address cover to TJ; at foot of text: "Mr Eastburn"; endorsed by TJ.

From John F. Oliveira Fernandes

DEAR SIR! Norfolk 29th January 1817

The Law of the ancient Rome „De minimis non curat Prætor„ that is, „the high Dignity of the Pretor, is not to be troubled with the common events, or small affaires of the people„ would be, to me, a reason, for not imposing on your goodness and Serious engagements with trifles; should not this kind of trifles, be of such serious caracter in its consequences, as to involve the Society at a future period, in distressing circumstances.

I presume truly philosophical the Law, permitting any person, to worship God, agreably to their own persuasion & Creed; but, in my humble opinion, something very essensial, has been ommitted in the Law viz „that the Rom. catholick clergy—no matter, Should acknowledge the Primacy of Rome—only as to the Spiritual; but as for the temporalities, they Should be altogether plain Citizens, perfe[c]tly free, Submitted and amenable to Law, in every respect without acknowledgin Superior, but the Civil Magistrate.„[1]

Nor can I see, with indiference a regular convent of Jesuits—the Perturbators of the peace of the world; fixed & stablished [n]ear the Seat of our Gouvernment, and more over, publick Preceptors; making choice of their Scholars to fill up their Noviciate with young Citizens of our Country!!

from that ommitted circumstance have, in my opinion, arrised the sad results which have taken place both in charleston S.C. as well as in this place, (in consequence of the Ecclesiastics I should Say).[2] Jesuitical Despotism of the Re Arch Bishop of Baltimore L. Neale: this, gave occasion to the enclosed printed Letter, in answer to that of the Said Rev Gentleman printed in the Documents pag 31. 37—which I beg Leave to offer for your perusal and imparcial Censure.

Please to excuse my liberty—and to permit me to continue to Subscribe my Self

Dear Sir Your mo: obt & respectfull Sert

JOHN F. OLIVEIRA FERNANDES

RC (DLC); edge chipped; between dateline and salutation: "Thomas Jefferson Esquire"; endorsed by TJ as received 5 Feb. 1817 and so recorded in SJL. Enclosure: [Oliveira Fernandes], *Letter, Addressed to the Most Reverend Leonard Neale, Arch Bishop of Baltimore. by A Member of the Roman Catholic Congregation of Norfolk, in Virginia* ([Norfolk, 1816?]); with separately paginated *Documents* (one full set at MdBS: Archdiocese of Baltimore Archives, Neale Papers); specific letter by Neale mentioned above repr. in Peter Guilday, *The Catholic Church in Virginia (1815–1822)* (1924), 23–6.

DE MINIMIS NON CURAT PRÆTOR: "The praetor does not concern himself with trifles."

The ENCLOSED PRINTED LETTER, written by Oliveira Fernandes but published anonymously, was dated 30 Nov. 1816 and directed to Leonard Neale, the Catholic archbishop of Baltimore. It responded to one of 5 July 1817 from the SAID REV GENTLEMAN advising the trustees of the congregation at Norfolk of his authority to remove and appoint their pastors without their consent. New priests unacceptable to the parish trustees had been installed in both Norfolk and Charleston by Neale, a Jesuit. Oliveira Fernandes asserted the trustees' independence to make appointments free from any religious authority not chosen by themselves, concluding that "nothing can inspire the extravagant idea of a Pastor commanding absolutely the temporal concerns of our Church, but a despotical, groundless authority, which neither suits—or can ever prosper under the Government of these United States of America" (pp. 42–3).

[1] Omitted closing guillemet editorially supplied.

[2] Omitted opening parenthesis editorially supplied.

To Charles Thomson

My very dear and
antient Friend. Monticello Jan. 29. 17.

I learnt from your last letter, with much affliction, the severe and singular attack your health has lately sustained; but it's equally singular and sudden restoration confirms my confidence in the strength of your constitution of body and mind, and my conclusion that neither has recieved hurt, and that you are still ours for a long time to come. we have both much to be thankful for in the soundness of our physical organisation, and something for self-approbation in the order and regularity of life by which it has been preserved. your preceding letter had given me no cause to doubt the continued strength of your mind; and, were it not that I am always peculiarly gratified by hearing from you, I should regret you had thought the incident with mr Delaplaine worth an explanation. he wrote to me on the subject of my letter to you of Jan. 9. 1816. and asked me questions which I answer only to one being. to himself therefore I replied 'say nothing of my religion; it is known to my god and myself alone. it's evidence before the world is to be sought in my life. if that has been honest and dutiful to society, the religion which has regulated it cannot be a bad one.' it is a singular anxiety which some people have that we should all think alike. would the world be more beautiful were all our faces alike? were our tempers, our talents, our tastes, our forms, our wishes, aversions and pursuits cast exactly in the same mould? if no varieties existed in the animal, vegetable, or mineral creation, but all were strictly uniform, catholic and orthodox, what a world of physical & moral monotony would it be! these are the absurdities into which those run who usurp the throne of god, & dictate to him what he should have done. may they, with all their metaphysical riddles, appear before that tribunal with as clean hands and hearts as you and I shall. there, suspended in the scales of eternal justice, faith and works will shew their worth by their weight. God bless you and preserve you long in life & health. Th: Jefferson

RC (DLC: Thomson Papers); addressed: "Charles Thomson esq. near Philadelphia"; franked; postmarked Milton, 29 Jan.; endorsed by Thomson. PoC (DLC).

The letter from Joseph Delaplaine to TJ was dated 23 Nov. 1816, and TJ responded to him on 25 Dec. 1816 (first letter).

From Nicolas G. Dufief

MONSIEUR, A Philadelphie ce 30. Janvier 1817

J'ai eu l'honneur de vous adresser, par le courrier d'hier matin, le dernier des livres que vous aviez demandés. Vous trouverez ci-inclus mon compte par lequel il vous est du une balance de 4.50 que je tiendrai à votre disposition.

Je regrette beaucoup de n'avoir pu réussir à vous procurer une bible convenable. L'histoire de la philosophie par Enfield ne Se trouve point du tout[1] à Philadelphie; on n'y trouve que Sa philosophie.

Agréez les vœux que je fais pour votre santé, & les assurances du plus parfait dévouement

Votre très-respectueux serviteur N. G. DUFIEF

EDITORS' TRANSLATION

SIR, Philadelphia 30. January 1817

I had the honor of sending you, by yesterday morning's post, the last of the books you requested. Enclosed you will find my account indicating that you are due a balance of $4.50, which I will hold at your disposal.

I deeply regret that I could not get you a suitable Bible. *The History of Philosophy* by Enfield is absolutely impossible to find in Philadelphia; here one finds only his *philosophy*.

Please accept my wishes for your good health and the assurances of my complete devotion

Your very respectful servant N. G. DUFIEF

RC (DLC); at foot of text: "Th: Jefferson, Esquire"; endorsed by TJ as received 8 Feb. 1817 and so recorded in SJL. Translation by Dr. Genevieve Moene.

William Enfield's more readily available work on PHILOSOPHIE was the first American edition of *Institutes of Natural Philosophy, Theoretical and Practical* (Boston, 1802).

[1] Preceding two words interlined.

ENCLOSURE

Account with Nicolas G. Dufief

Philadelphia, Jan. 30, 1817.

Tho: Jefferson Esq.		
To N. G. Dufief—		D^{r}
Per bill rendered		$31.00
One Graglia's English & Italian Dict^{y}		2.50
Review of Montesquieu, sent to Mr. Adams		2.50
Two Nautical Almanacs for	1817 at $1.50	3.00
Two d^{o} d^{o}	1818 1.50	3.00
One Connaissance de Tems	1817 a	2.00
d^{o} d^{o}	1818	2.00
		$46 00
Cr.—By a Richmond Bank Note	$50	
Premium 1 per cent	0.50	
	50.50	
	46	
In your favor—a balance of	$ 4 50	

MS (DLC); in a clerk's hand; endorsed by TJ: "Dufief N. G. Jan. 30. 17."

From Nicolas G. Dufief

MONSIEUR, A Philadelphie ce 30 Janvier. 1817

Je vous ai écrit ce matin pour vous annoncer que J'avais fini d'adresser à Monticello tous les livres demandés à l'exception de la Bible & de l'histoire de la Philosophie que je n'ai pu procurer. Je m'empresse, à présent, de répondre à votre lettre du 24. reçue cette après-midi. Je puis vous certifier n'avoir reçu aucun argent de Mr Gibson en Août dernier, deux mois après les ordres que vous lui aviez donnés, ni depuis cette époque là. Nous ne manquons jamais d'accuser reception de l'argent reçu & de le mentionner, en même temps, sur nos livres. Ainsi Si la Somme de 31. dollars nous eût été transmise, Mr Gibson aurait une lettre de nous à ce sujet, ou bien son correspondant de Philadelphie, une quittance, s'il l'eut, ainsi, adressée. Vous m'obligerez beaucoup, lorsque la chose aura été éclaircie de m'informer comment l'erreur a pu être commise.

J'ai poussé la précaution jusqu'à faire remettre par une personne sûre (qui a elle-même fait les paquets et écrit leur adresse) tous les livres mentionnés dans la lettre écrite & mise à la poste ce matin, & que vous recevrez, en même temps, que la présente

J'ai l'honneur d'être, Monsieur, votre très-respectueux & très-dévoué serviteur N. G. DUFIEF

P.S vous êtes crédite de 4dlrs 50cts balance qui vous revient

EDITORS' TRANSLATION

SIR, Philadelphia 30 January. 1817

I wrote to you this morning to advise you that I had finished sending to Monticello all the books requested except the Bible and *The History of Philosophy*, which I could not obtain. I now hasten to reply to your letter of the 24th, received this afternoon. I can assure you that I received no money from Mr. Gibson last August, two months after the orders you had given him, or since then. We never fail to acknowledge money received and, at the same time, to record it on our books. Thus, if the sum of 31 dollars had been transmitted to us, Mr. Gibson would have a letter from us regarding this matter, or his correspondent in Philadelphia would have a receipt, if Mr. Gibson had sent it to him. You will oblige me much, when this matter has been clarified, by letting me know how the error could have been committed.

As a precaution, all the books mentioned in the letter written and mailed this morning, which you will receive at the same time as the present one, have been delivered by a reliable person (who also made up the packages and wrote the address on them)

I have the honor to be, Sir, your very respectful and very devoted servant N. G. DUFIEF

P.S. You have been credited with a balance of $4.50 due to you

RC (DLC); addressed: "Th: Jefferson. Esquire Monticello Virginia"; franked; postmarked Philadelphia, 30 Jan.; endorsed by TJ as received 8 Feb. 1817 and so recorded in SJL. Translation by Dr. Genevieve Moene. Enclosed in TJ to Patrick Gibson, 9 Feb. 1817.

From Hugh Nelson

DEAR SIR, Washington Jany 30. 1817[1]

The enclosed letter came under cover to me with a request that I woud forward it to you. It is said to be from a Mr Sullivan son of the late Genl Sullivan, and relates to some improvement in steam boat navigation adapted to shoal waters. It may be an invention of some utility relative to our internal navigation—

I have the Honor to be yr o. St HUGH NELSON

RC (DLC); endorsed by TJ as received 5 Feb. 1817 and so recorded in SJL. Enclosure: John L. Sullivan to TJ, 17 Jan. 1817.

[1] Reworked from "1816."

Analysis of Weather Memorandum Book

1817. January. Having been stationary at home since Mar.[1] 1809. with opportunity and leisure to keep a meteorological diary, with a good degree of exactness, this has been done: and, extracting from it a term of seven years compleat, to wit from Jan. 1. 1810. to Dec. 31. 1816. I proceed to analyse it in the various ways, and to deduce the general results which are of principal effect in the estimate of climate. the observations (3905. in the whole) were taken before sunrise of every day; and again between[2] 3. and 4. aclock P.M. on some days of occasional absence, they were necessarily omitted. in these cases the averages are taken from the days of the same denomination in the other years only, and in such way as not sensibly to affect the average of the month, still less that of the year, and to be quite evanescent in their effect on the whole term[3] of 7. years.

The table of thermometrical observations on the next page shews[4] the particular temperature of the different seasons, and[5] different years from 1810. to 1816. inclusive. it's most interesting results however are that the range of temperature with us may be considered as within the limits of $5\frac{1}{2}$.° and $94\frac{1}{2}$°[6] of Fahrenheit's[7] thermometer; and that $55\frac{1}{2}$° is it's mean and characteristic measure. these degrees fix the laws of the animal and vegetable races which may exist with us; and the comfort also of the human inhabitant, so far as depends on his sensations of heat and cold.[8] still it must be kept in mind that this is but the temperature of Monticello; that in the Northern and Western parts of the state, the Mean and Extremes are probably something lower, and in the Southern and Eastern, higher. but this place is so nearly central to the whole state, that it may fairly be considered as the Mean of the whole.

	A Table of thermometrical observation made at Monticello from											
	1810.			1811.			1812.			1813.		
	min.[9]	mean	max.	min.	mean	max.	min.	mean	max.	min.	mean	max.
Jan.	5½	38	66	20	39	68	5½	34	53	13.	35	59
Feb.	12	43	73		✶		21	40	75	19	38	65
Mar.	20	41	61	28	44	78	31½	46	70	28	48	71
Apr.	42	55	81	36	58	86	31	56	86	40	59	80
May	43	64	88	46	62	79	39	60	86	46	62	81
June	53	70	87	58	73	89	58	74	92½	54	75	93
July	60	75	88	60	76	89½	57	75	91	61	75	94½
Aug.	55	71	90	59	75	85	61	71	87	62	74	92
Sep.	50	70	81	50	67	81	47	68	75	54	69	83
Octob.	32	57	82	35	62	85	39	55	80	32	53	70
Nov.	27	44	69	32	45	62	18	43	76	20	48	71
Dec.	14	32	62	20	38	49	13	35	63	18	37	53
mean of each year[10]		55			58			55			56	

It is a common opinion that the climates of the several states of our union have undergone a sensible change since the dates of their first settlements; that the degrees both of cold & heat are moderated. the same opinion prevails as to Europe: & facts gleaned from history give reason to believe that, since the time of Augustus Caesar, the climate of Italy, for example, has changed regularly at the rate of 1.° of Fahrenheit's thermometer for every century. may we not hope that the methods invented in latter times for measuring with accuracy the degrees of heat and cold, and the observations which have been & will be made and preserved, will at length ascertain this curious fact in physical history?

Within the same period of time, about 50. morning observations, on an average, of every winter, were below the freezing point, and about 10. observations of the afternoon. this gives us 50. freezing nights,[11] & 10. freezing days for the average of our winters.[12]

Jan. 1. 1810. to Dec. 31. 1816.									
1814.			1815.			1816.			mean of each month
min.	mean	max.	min.	mean	max.	min.	mean	max.	
$16\frac{1}{2}$	36	55	$8\frac{1}{2}$	35	60	16.	34	51	36
14	42	65	16	36	57	$15\frac{1}{2}$	41	62	40
$13\frac{1}{2}$	43	73	31	54	80	25	48	75	46
35	59	82	41	60	82	30	49	71	$56\frac{1}{2}$
47	65	91	37	58	77	43	60	79	$61\frac{1}{2}$
57	69	87	54	71	88	51	70	86	72
60	74	89	63	77	89	51	71	86	75
56	75	88	58	72	84	51	73	90	73
52	70	89	45	61	82	54	63	$90\frac{1}{2}$	67
37	58	83	$38\frac{1}{2}$	59	76	37	57	73	57
23	47	71	20	46	70	24	46	71	$45\frac{1}{2}$
18	38	59	12	36	57	23	43	69	37
	$56\frac{1}{3}$			$55\frac{1}{2}$			$54\frac{1}{2}$		$55\frac{1}{2}$

It is generally observed that when the thermometer is below 55.° we have need of fire in our apartments to be comfortable. in the course of these 7. years the number of observations below 55.° in each year were as follows.[13]

in 1810	195 mornings and	124. afternoons
11.[14]	176	102.
12.	209.	137.
13.	197	123.
14.	190.	127.
15.	189.	116.
16.	172.	116.
average	190.	120.[15]

whence we conclude that we need constant fires four months in the year, and in the mornings and evenings a little more than a month preceding & following that term.[16]

The 1st white frost in	1809.10. was	Oct. 25. the last	Apr. 11.
	10.11.	18.	Mar. 19.
	11.12.	21.	Apr. 14
	12.13.	9.	
	13.14.	22.	Apr. 13.
	14.15.	24.	May. 15.
	15.16.	26.	Apr. 3.
	16.17.	7.	Apr. 12.

but we have seen, in another period, a destructive white frost as early as September.

Our first ice in	1809.10. was	Nov. 7. the last	Apr. 10.
	10.11.	Oct. 24.	Mar. 8.
	11.12.	Nov. 15.	Apr. 12.
	12.13.	13.	Mar. 25.
	13.14.	14.	17.
	14.15.	9.	22.
	15.16.	13.	19.
	16.17.	7.	20.[17]

The quantity of water (including that of snow) which fell in every month & year of the term was as follows.

	1810.	11.	12.	13.	14.	15.	16.	average of every month
Jan.	1.873	3.694	3.300	1.735	4.179	6.025	4.86	3.666[18]
Feb.	4.275	2.351	4.060	1.763	3.760	5.90	2.205	3.473
Mar.	3.173	2.295	3.090	1.750	4.386	2.96	2.825	2.926
Apr.	4.570	4.342	2.228	3.685	5.471	1.35	3.52	3.595
May.	2.124	3.779	14.761	2.670	7.134	2.57	6.19	5.604
June	5.693	5.574	5.565	0.799	3.450	2.94	0.33	3.470
July	5.729	8.206	2.825[19]	3.319	13.654	7.59	4.63	6.565
Aug.	1.883	5.969	8.963	3.920	3.370	3.48	0.85	4.062
Sep.	4.908	2.923	0.630	14.224	6.834	2.32	9.91	5.964
Oct.	0.731	7.037	5.184	4.264	2.632	0.73	3.23	3.401
Nov.	6.741	0.781	1.187	3.932	4.794	2.09	0.96	2.926
Dec.	0.333	0.5	1.232	3.658[20]	1.259	3.55	0.36	1.556
average of a year[21]	42.033	47.451	53.025	45.719	60.923	41.505	39.87	47.218

from this table we observe that the average of the water which falls in a year is $47\frac{1}{4}$ I. the minimum $41\frac{1}{2}$ and maximum 61.I. from tables kept by the late Col° James Madison, father of the President of the US. at his seat about miles N.E. from Monticello, from the year 1794. to 1801. inclusive, the average was $43\frac{1}{4}$ I. the minimum $35\frac{3}{4}$ I. and the maximum 52.I.

During the same 7. years there fell 622. rains, which gives 89. rains for every year, or 1. for every 4. days; and the average of the water falling in the year being $47\frac{1}{4}$ I. gives .53 cents of an inch for each rain, or .93 cents for a week, on an average, being nearly an inch a week.[22] were this to fall regularly, or nearly so, thro' the summer season, it would render our agriculture most prosperous, as experience has sometimes proved.

Of the 3905 observations made in the course of the 7. years 2776. were fair; by which I mean that the greater[23] part of the sky was unclouded. this shews our proportion of fair to cloudy weather to be as 2776 : 1129 :: or as 5. to 2. equivalent to 5. fair days to the week. of the other 2. one may be more than half clouded, the other wholly so. we have then 5. of what astronomers call 'observing days' in the week; and of course a chance of 5. to 2. of observing any astronomical phaenomenon which is to happen at any fixed point of time.

The snows[24] at Monticello amounted to the depth
in 1809.10 of $16\frac{1}{4}$ I. and covered the ground 19. days.

10.11.	$31\frac{3}{4}$	31.
11.12.	11.[25]	11.
12.13.	35.	22.
13.14.	$13\frac{1}{4}$	16.
14.15.	$29\frac{3}{4}$	39.
15.16.	23.	29.
16.17.	$19\frac{1}{4}$	10.[26]
average	$22\frac{1}{2}$	22.[27]

which gives an average of $22\frac{1}{2}$ I. a year, covering the ground 22. days, and a minimum of 11.I. and 11. days, & maximum of 35.I. and 39. days. according to mr Madison's tables, the average of snow, at his seat, in the winters from 1793.4. to 1801.2. inclusive, was $23\frac{1}{2}$. the minimum $10\frac{1}{8}$ & maximum $38\frac{1}{2}$[28] I. but I once (in 1772.) saw a snow here 3.f. deep.

	N.	NE.	E.	S.E.	S.	S.W.	W.	N.W.	Total
Jan	4	1	1	1	5	7	5	7	31
Feb.	3	3	1	1	4	6	4	6	28
Mar.	5	3	2	2	6	5	3	5	31
Apr.	4	2	3	2	7	6	2	4	30
May	5	2	1	1	6	6	4	6	31
June	5	2	1	1	4	6	5	6	30
July	6	2	1	1	6	5	5	5	31
Aug.	6	3	1	2	3	6	4	6	31
Sep.	6	5	1	2	4	4	3	5	30
Oct.	5	2	1	1	5	5	5	7	31
Nov.	7	2	1	1	5	5	2[29]	7	30
Dec.	5	2	1	1	5	5	5	7	31
Total	61	29	15	16	60	66	47	71	365

The course of the wind having been one of the circumstances regularly observed. I have thought it better, from the observations of the 7. years, to deduce an average for a single year, & for every month of the year. this Table accordingly exhibits the number of days in the year, & in every month of it, during which each particular wind, according to these observations, may be expected to prevail. it will be for Physicians to observe the coincidences of the diseases of each season, with the particular winds then prevalent, the quantities of heat, rain E^{t}c.

	dry.		wet
N.	4.	:	1.
NE.	3.	:	1.
E.	3.	:	1.
SE.	$3\frac{1}{2}$	:	1.
S.	4.	:	1.
S.W.	6.	:	1.
W.	$9\frac{1}{3}$	:	1.
N.W.	$10\frac{1}{4}$	:	1.

In this separate table I state the relation which each particular wind appeared to have with rain or snow. for example, of every 5. North winds, 1. was either accompanied with rain or snow, or followed by it before the next observation, and 4. were dry. of every 4. North Easters, 1. was wet, 3. dry E^{t}c. the table consequently shews the degree in which any particular wind enters as an element into the generation of rain, in combination with the temperature of the air, state of the clouds E^{t}c.

An[30] estimate of climate may be otherwise made from the advance of the spring, as manifested by animal and vegetable subjects.[31] their first appearance[32] has been observed as follows.

	at Monticello.[33]		at Montpelier.[34]	
the Red maple comes into blossom from	Feb. 18. to	Mar. 27.		
the Almond	Mar. 6.	Apr. 5.		
the Peach	9.	4.	Mar. 14. to	Apr. 16.
the Cherry	9.	13.	17.	17.
the tick appears	15.	2.		
the House Martin	18.	9.	21.	2
Asparagus comes first[35] to table	23.	14.	31.	24
the Shad arrives	28.	18.		
the Lilac blossoms	Apr. 1.	28.		
the Red-bud	2.	19.		
the Whip-poor-will is heard	2.	21.	Apr. 12.	Apr. 24.
the Dogwood blossoms	3.	22.[36]		
the Wood-Robin is heard	20. to	May 1.		
the Locust blooms	25.	17.		
the Fringe-tree	27.	5.		
the 1st brood of houseflies	28	4	May 15.	May 18.[37]
the red clover first blossoms	May 1. to			
the garden-pea first at table	3.	25.	13.	29
strawberries first ripe	3.	25.	6.	28
fire-flies appear	8. to			
Cherries first ripe	18.	25.	10	31
Artichokes first at table	28 to	June 12		
Wheat harvest begins	June 21.	29	June 12.	July 6.
Cucumbers first at table	22. to	July 5	14.	1.
Indian corn first at table	July 4.		July 16.	30
peaches first ripe	7.	21.	9	28.
the Sawyer first heard	14.	20	15	20.

The natural season of the vegetable is here noted, & not the artificial one produced by glasses, hotbeds E^{t}c. which combining art with nature, would not be a test of the latter separately.

Another Index of climate may be sought in the temperature of the waters issuing from fountains. if the deepest of the[38] reservoirs feeding these may be supposed at like distances from the surface in every part of the globe, then the lowest[39] temperature of water flowing from them would indicate that of the earth from and through which it flows. this will probably be found highest under the equator, and lower as you recede towards either pole.[40] on an examination of 15. springs in the body of the hill of Monticello, the water of the coolest was at $54\frac{1}{2}^{\circ}$[41] the outer air being then at 75.°[42] a friend assures me that in an open well of 28. feet depth in Maine, Lat. 44°–22′ and in the month of August, the water in it being then 4.f. deep, it's temperature was 52.° of Fahrenheit's[43] thermometer, that of the water of Kennebec river being at the same time $72\frac{1}{2}^{\circ}$

Lastly to close the items which designate climate, the latitude of Monticello is to be added, which, by numerous observations, lately made, with a Borda's circle of 5.I. radius with Nonius divisions to 1.′ I have found, by averaging the whole, to be 37°–57′–51″–26.‴[44]

MS (DLC: Rives Papers, Miscellany); two sheets in TJ's hand folded to form eight pages and stitched together into a booklet; partially dated; with note at head of text in an unidentified hand: "Mr. Jefferson's Memoranda of Climate." Dft (MHi); in TJ's Weather Memorandum Book, 1802–16; incomplete and differently sequenced, with much of the commentary lacking; undated; with only the most significant variations noted below. Printed in *Virginia Literary Museum and Journal of Belles Lettres, Arts, &c.* 1 (1829): 26–9. Enclosed in TJ to James Madison, 22 June 1817.

During his five years of intermittent residence in Williamsburg as a member of the House of Burgesses, 1772–77, TJ began recording weather data. His first recorded purchase of a thermometer was in 1769, and he bought another one on 4 July 1776. The earliest extant portions of TJ's meteorological diaries are held by DLC (1776–1820), with later observations in MHi (1802–16). In a summary of his early readings printed in his *Notes on the State of Virginia*, TJ noticed a change in climate and its attendant impact on humans and nature. He regarded documenting climatic change as one very practical reason to quantify weather data. While TJ did not engage directly with theories on the environmental causes of illness, he alluded above to the potential utility of wind studies for explaining the transmission of disease (*MB*, 1:29, 420, 432–6, 771–806; *Notes*, ed., Peden, 73–81; Silvio Bedini, *Jefferson and Science* [2002], 29–34; James Rodger Fleming, *Meteorology in America, 1800–1870* [1990], 9–13).

In 1784 TJ prevailed upon future United States president James Madison to "keep a diary" that would include daily barometric and thermometric readings along with wind direction and such observations of the natural world as the emergence of plants and migrations of animals. TJ assured him that "It will be an amusement to you and may become useful." Madison, possibly one or more of his brothers, and their father, THE LATE COL° JAMES MADISON, dutifully kept a record of their readings for years. Over time TJ also received weather information from other observers, including his son-in-law Thomas Mann Randolph at Monticello in TJ's absences, Bishop James Madison in Williamsburg, David Rittenhouse in Philadelphia, and John Breck Treat in Arkansas, Louisiana Territory (*PTJ*, 6:507, 7:30–1, 231, 16:351–2, 20:327–30, 30:78–81; Madison, *Papers, Congress. Ser.*, 8:514–5, 9:420–4; Treat to TJ, 31 Mar. 1809; TJ to Madison, 22 June 1817).

TJ provided a similar but more impressionistic discussion of meteorological readings he had kept in Washington during his presidency in a letter to Nathaniel Chapman, 11 Dec. 1809. He drew heavily on the analysis printed above in his 11 Apr. 1818 letter to Jacob Bigelow.

[1] Word not in *Virginia Literary Museum.*

[2] Reworked from "before."

[3] *Virginia Literary Museum*: "tenor."

[4]Dft begins here, with "this table shews."

[5]Preceding three words not in *Virginia Literary Museum.*

[6]*Virginia Literary Museum*: "94°."

[7]Manuscript: "Farenheit's."

[8]In Dft TJ here canceled "with the ordinary serenity of sky."

[9]Here and through this entire column in MS, TJ mistakenly flipped the "max." and "min." readings. *Virginia Literary Museum* followed the MS. The headings are editorially corrected above based on the Dft.

[10]Instead of preceding two words, *Virginia Literary Museum* reads "clear weather."

[11]Preceding thirteen words not in *Virginia Literary Museum.*

[12]Dft presents data from preceding paragraph in tabular form.

[13]Paragraph not in Dft.

[14]Manuscript: "12." *Virginia Literary Museum* and Dft: "11."

[15]To the right of this table in Dft, TJ canceled a table tallying "clear or cloudy" days for the same date range and giving a total of 1,234 cloudy days out of 4,027 total observations. Dft ends here.

[16]*Virginia Literary Museum*: "time."

[17]Preceding two tables included in variant form in Dft.

[18]*Virginia Literary Museum*: "3.656."

[19]*Virginia Literary Museum*: "2.025."

[20]*Virginia Literary Museum*: "6.658."

[21]Thus in text, but only the final figure in the row is an average; those preceding it are totals for each given year.

[22]Preceding nine words not in *Virginia Literary Museum.*

[23]*Virginia Literary Museum*: "quarter."

[24]Dft resumes here.

[25]In place of numeral, *Virginia Literary Museum* substitutes a blank space.

[26]*Virginia Literary Museum*: "19."

[27]Dft ends here.

[28]*Virginia Literary Museum*: "33½."

[29]*Virginia Literary Museum*: "5."

[30]Dft resumes here.

[31]Word interlined in Dft in place of "Phaenomena."

[32]Instead of preceding three words, Dft reads "the earliest & latest days of their 1st appearance."

[33]Column heading supplied from Dft.

[34]Heading, all data in this column, and vertical rules supplied from Dft.

[35]Here and in many subsequent entries, TJ interlines "first" in Dft.

[36]Entry interlined in Dft.

[37]Entry supplied from Dft.

[38]Preceding three words interlined in Dft.

[39]Word interlined in Dft.

[40]In Dft TJ here canceled "here I found from."

[41]In Dft TJ here canceled "but the others varying from that to 66° we may suppose their reservoirs to vary in depth also."

[42]Dft ends here.

[43]Manuscript: "Farenheit's."

[44]Final number not in *Virginia Literary Museum.*

Notes by Thomas Jefferson Randolph and Thomas Jefferson on a Land Purchase

[ca. Jan. 1817]

The lots of Lucy[1] Nancy[2] & Frances[3] below the town at $25 per acre Lucys lot N° 1[4] between the town & the river at the same
The three lots[5] in the upper field at $20 per acre
The ends of lots N° 3.4.5 back lots taken by Alexander the balance to be purchased at 20 shillings per acre
$300 to be paid February court, the balance of the first half six months after, the second half in twelve months
Wood to relinquish his life estate and his part of the 2nd payment to remain in the hands of the purchaser untill his wifes conveyance is had

[*in TJ's hand at foot of text:*]

			acres		D	D
Lower field.	Nancy C. N°	3.	$5\frac{1}{2}$			
	Lucy	4.	$5\frac{3}{4}$	19. a^s^ @	25 =	475
	Frances	8.	$5\frac{3}{4}$			
between town & river	Lucy	1.	2			
Upper field	Frances	5	5			
	Lucy	6	5	15. a^s^ @	20 =	300
	Nancy C.	7	5			
back lots	Lucy	3	102			
	Frances	5	102			
	Nancy	8	102			
			306			
	– of	N° 4	[50]			
			[256] acres @ 20/			

MS (ViU: TJP); in Thomas Jefferson Randolph's hand, with notes and additions by TJ; undated; two numbers faint; with undated, apparently unrelated note from Randolph to "My dear Peyton" (Bernard Peyton or Craven Peyton) on verso (one word editorially corrected): "Since I saw you I have thou[g]ht on the subject of the sale you proposed to me. I will take them on the terms you proposed one half on the first of January 1818 and the other on the first of January 1819."

Late in January 1817, after paying the back rent on the lands belonging through inheritance to three of Bennett Henderson's children, Frances Hornsby, Lucy Wood, and Nancy C. Nelson, TJ decided once again to purchase a portion of their property, which had subsequently been procured by Eli ALEXANDER, TJ's former overseer, possibly at his behest. His actual acquisition from Alexander was a bit smaller than that proposed above, primarily because TJ only bought $68\frac{3}{4}$ and $73\frac{1}{4}$ acres of back lots 3 and 5. Among other alterations, lot 8 in the lower field totaled 6, not $5\frac{3}{4}$ acres, and the deduction for lot 4 in the back lands (property that TJ had purchased from Sarah Henderson Kerr and was now deeding to Alexander as a part of the agreement) was 25½, not 50 acres. In all, TJ obtained 252¾ acres for $1,520.18. To clear this obligation to Alexander, TJ paid him $300 in January 1817 through Thomas Jefferson Randolph, $500 in July 1817 through Martin Dawson, and $720 on 28 Mar. 1818 through Gibson & Jefferson (TJ's Notes on Purchase of Henderson Property, Jan. 1817–28 Mar. 1818 [MS in ViU: TJP; on verso of portion of reused address cover to TJ; in TJ's hand, with corrections and emendations in an unidentified hand; undated]; *MB*, 2:1330, 1336, 1342; Conveyance of Henderson Land by Alexander to TJ, 28 Mar. 1818).

[1] Above this name TJ added "N° 4. 5¾ a^s^."

[2] Above this name TJ added (damaged at crease) "N° [3]. 5½."

[3] Above this name TJ added "N° 8. 5¾."

[4] TJ here interlined "2. a^s^."

[5] Above preceding two words TJ added "N° 5.6.7. 15 a^s^."

From William Clark

DEAR SIR St Louis Feby 1st 1817.

I have taken the liberty of inclosing under cover to you, a letter to Mrs Marks, and a Copy of a letter and statement of the publication of Lewis & Clarks Journal &c from Mr N. Biddle, which I latterly received,

The population of this Territory is rapidly increasing and very widely extending itself, The Lands on the Missouri having greatly the advantage as respects fertility of soil & health, draws the greatest emigration in that direction

For the last three or four years, party spirit appeared to have almost subsided, but laterly it has been revived, and increases, by the aid of the old partizans

Accept of my best wishes for your health & happiness, with the highest respect

I have the honor to be your Ob. Hbl Servt—

RC (MHi); in Clark's hand, unsigned; endorsed by TJ as a letter from "Anon. (? Gl Wm Clarke)" received 15 Mar. 1817 and so recorded in SJL. Enclosure: Nicholas Biddle to Clark, Andalusia, near Philadelphia, 21 Oct. 1816, advising Clark to agree to a proposal whereby he would relinquish to the assignees of the insolvent printing partnership of Bradford & Inskeep his claim on the books in press but retain the copyright and control of the copperplates used in printing; embedding the text of Biddle to Charles Chauncey, Andalusia, 25 June 1816, outlining for Clark's legal counsel the account supplied by the assignees of Bradford & Inskeep, concluding that the profit owed to Clark is $395.93, suggesting that the debts due to the work are "unpromising," and advancing the plan described above; also including the text of Thomas Astley to Chauncey, Philadelphia, 18 Sept. 1816, reiterating as an assignee of Bradford & Inskeep the accounting supplied by Biddle, correcting errors, concluding that Clark is owed $170.18½, agreeing to pay the debts due in connection with the work and release the copyright and copperplates to Clark, estimating their value as $600–700, and stipulating that no new edition is to appear for at least six months (Tr in ViU: Lewis-Marks Papers [microfilm; originals privately held]; FC in DLC: Biddle Papers, with placeholders for the two embedded letters; FC of Biddle-Chauncey letter and RC of Astley-Chauncey letter in NjP: Biddle Collection; printed as separate letters in Donald Jackson, ed., *Letters of the Lewis and Clark Expedition with Related Documents* [2d ed., 1978], 2:615–7, 621–3, 627).

The enclosed letter from Clark to Lucy MARKS, the mother of Meriwether Lewis, has not been found.

From Lancelot Minor

DEAR SIR Louisa Feby 1st 17

your letter of the 14th of last month came to hand by last mail. I feel disposed to do any thing I can for Mrs Marks and particularly by so doing I shall oblige you. I will certainly try to sell Mrs. Marks land altho I think the prospect a bad one the land is poor & not in demand I will advertise it upon time in the mean time I should be glad of your advice as to the Credit upon which I shall sell

I have not paid the direct Tax upon Mrs Marks land for the last year. the collection not yet commencd it is unnecessary[1] for you to remit me any money for Taxes. I have in my hands as much as (I expect) The Tax will amount to o[r] if not I can hereafter draw for the deficit upon examining the record I find no evidence for Mr Marks paying the debt as Security for John G Winston owing to the sheriff (who is now dead) failing to make a return upon the excution I think the debt doubtfull my friend Mr Johnson promises to do the best he can for securing the debt— Accept Sir my best wishes

L MINOR

RC (MHi); one word faint; endorsed by TJ as received 8 Feb. 1817 and so recorded in SJL.

[1]Manuscript: "unnessary."

Statement of Taxable Property in Albemarle County

A list of taxable property of the subscriber in Albemarle Feb. 1. 1817.

5. white tythes.
79. slaves of 16. years old & upwards
9. d° of 12. years old & not 16.
31. horses and mules.
1. gigg
1. 4-wheeled carriage (a Landau)

TH: JEFFERSON

MS (MHi); written entirely in TJ's hand on verso of portion of a reused address cover from Joseph C. Cabell to TJ; endorsed by TJ: "Sheriff Albem. taxable property 1817."

The Virginia General Assembly passed an act on 22 Feb. 1817 keeping PROPERTY-tax rates the same as they had been in 1816 (*Acts of Assembly* [1817–18 sess.], 3). TYTHES: "tithables."

From John Adams

DEAR SIR Quincy Feb. 2d 1817

In our good old English language of Gratitude, I owe you and give you a thousand thanks, for Tracy's Review of Montesquieu which Mr Dufief has Sent me by your order. I have read an hundred[1] pages, and will read the rest. He is a Sensible Man and is easily understood. He is not an abstruse misterious incomprehensi[ble][2] Condorcet. Though I have banished the Subject from my thoughts for many years, yet if Tracy and I were thirty years younger I would ask him an hundred or two of questions. His book was written when the French Experiment was glowing in the furnace not yet blown out. He all along Supposes that Men are rational and consciencious creatures. I Say So too: but I Say at the Same time that their passions and Interests generally prevail over their Reason and their consciences: and if Society does not contrive Some means of controuling and restraining[3] the former the World will go on as it has done;

I was tollerably well informed, fifty years ago, how it had gone on, and formed Some plausible conjectures how it would go on. Grim, Dupuis and Eustace have confirmed all my former Notions and made immense Additions to them. Eustace is a Suppliment to Dupuis; and both together contain a compleat draught of the Superstition Credulity and Despotism of our terrestrial Universe. They Show how Science Litteratur, mechanic Arts, and those fine Arts of Architecture, Painting, Statuary, Poetry, Musick and Eloquence: which you Love So well, and taste So exquisitely; have been Subservient to Priests and Kings Nobles and commons Monarchies and Republicks.
For they have all used them when they could: but as the rich had them oftener than the poor, in their power, the latter have always gone to the Wall.

Eustace is inestimable to a young Schollar; and a classic Traveller: but he is a plausible insidious Roman Catholick Priest and I doubt not Jesuit: He should have read Dupuis before he comenced his Travels. Very little, of the Religions of Nations more antient than the Greeks and Romans, appears to have been known to him.

I am glad to see, that De la plane has published a part of your Letter, and I hope it will procure you Some relief. I have Suffered in the same manner, though not probably in the Same degree. Necessity has compelled me to resort to two expedients to avoid or escape excessive importunity. One has been, by totally neglecting to answer Letter, after Letter. But this Method has cost me very dear in the loss of many correspondances that had been and would have been instructive and profitable to me, as well as honourable and entertaining.[4] The other has been by giving gruff, short, unintelligible misterious, enigmatical, or pedantical answers. This resource is out of your power, because it is not in your nature to avail yourself of it.

The practice however of publishing private Letters without leave, though even as rude ones as mine, is an abuse and must be reformed.

Theodore Lyman Esq[r] Junior, will I hope, deliver you this. He is an Educated and travelled Son of one of our Richest Merchants. His Health[5] has been, and is precarious,
I have been indebted to him for the perusal of the Baron de Grim. I find that all our young Gentlemen who have any Nous, and can afford to travel, have an ardent Curiosity to visit, what Shall I Say? the Man of the Mountain? The Sage of Monticello? Or the celebrated Philosopher and Statesman of Virginia? They all apply to me for Introduction. In hopes of Softening asperities, and promoting Union, I have refused none whom I thought Men of Sense.

I forgot one thing that I intended to Say. I pitty our good Brother Madison. You and I have had Children and Grand Children and great grand Children. Though they have cost Us Grief, Anxiety often Vexation, and Some times humiliation; Yet it has been cheering to have them hovering about Us; and I verily believe they have contributed largely to keep Us alive. Books cannot always expell Ennui. I therefore pitty Brother Madison and especially his Lady. I pitty him the more, because, notwithstand[6] a thousand Faults and blunders, his Administration has acquired more glory, and established more Union, than all his three Predecessors Washington Adams and Jefferson put together.

I am, as ever JOHN ADAMS

RC (DLC); at foot of text: "President Jefferson"; endorsed by TJ as received 16 Feb. 1817 and so recorded in SJL; with TJ's notes for his 5 May 1817 reply on verso of last page beneath endorsement: "Feb. 2. Apr. 19. De la plaine's publicn of my lre √Lyman √J. M's retirem[t] √Pickerings & Gardeniers √active men must have enemies. √books from authors √religion? √Independ[t] whig. Connectic[t]." RC (DLC); address cover only; with PoC of TJ to James Madison, 13 Apr. 1817, on verso; addressed: "His Excellency Thomas Jefferson Monticello Virginia"; postmarked Quincy, 3 Feb. FC (Lb in MHi: Adams Papers).

Theodore Lyman (1792–1849), author, public official, and philanthropist, was educated at Phillips Exeter Academy and graduated from Harvard University in 1810. After several years of intermittent study and travel in Europe, he returned to Boston in 1819. Lyman's published works include *A Few Weeks in Paris, during the Residence of the Allied Sovereigns in that Metropolis* (Boston, 1814), *A Short Account of the Hartford Convention* (Boston, 1823), and *The Diplomacy Of The United States* (Boston, 1826). Initially a passionate Federalist, he supported Andrew Jackson for a time but eventually became a Whig. Lyman sat in the Massachusetts legislature from 1820–25 and served terms as mayor of Boston in 1834 and 1835. He provided financial support to various reform and farm schools during his later years and bequeathed funds to the Boston Farm School and the Horticultural Society of Boston (*DAB*; *Boston Weekly Messenger*, 18 May 1820; Boston *Columbian Centinel*, 8 June 1822; *Boston Daily Atlas*, 19 July 1849).

For the letter PUBLISHED by Joseph Delaplaine, see TJ to Delaplaine, 25 Dec. 1816 (second letter). NOTWITHSTAND: "notwithstanding" (*OED*).

[1] RC: "hudred." FC: "hundred."

[2] RC: "incomprehensi." FC: "incomprehensive."

[3] RC: "restraing." FC: "restraining."

[4] RC: "entertaing." FC: "entertaining."

[5] RC: "Heath." FC: "health."

[6] FC: "notwithstanding."

From Francis Adrian Van der Kemp

DEAR AND RESPECTED SIR! Olden barneveld 2 Febr. 1817.

Although it is not mÿ power—to make this Letter in any manner interesting, yet your courtesy and kindness towards me would prompt me to answer your favour of Nov. 24—with which I was honoured. I Should have acquitted myself of this duty at a more early period, had I not been a martyr of a wounded leg, imprudently neglected, during three months. The pains being So acute, that I was not permitted for a great while to eat or Sleep, and too often could not write or think. At length[1] I am recovered—So that I this daÿ—for the first time, could leave mÿ house. And, can I then employ the residue of this day better than by giving you my Sincerest thanks for your distinguished remembrance? I can not Saÿ, that love of praise is always a weakness—but if it is—if laudari a laudato viro is not a noble Spurr—I must plead guilty.

I fully agree—that accomplished talents of the Philosopher the critic the historian—with an ardent love of truth—unconquerable firmness and undeviating candour of more than one man would be required to animate the Skeleton, and I doubt much—the high opinion I foster of our countrymen notwithstanding—if our country can produce Such a chosen Set—I Send it—nevertheless—to N. England—and another copy to London: yet—I am apprehensive with you—we Shall not See the developement of this clue—here.

Flattered by your encouragement I had taken the resolution to try what I could effect—in one Single point—I will yet try it if my days are prolonged—but during the Summer Season my garden—and unavoidable correspondence—require imperiously all my leasure time—I do not however despair of final Success, and, if I do So in my own opinion, I Shall Submit it to your judgment—in the full persuasion—if it is crowned with your approbation—it can Stand the test of the Public; idiom of language excepted.
It Seems—at first view an easy task—but I know—it Shall not be found So, when undertaken—So many prejudices to be encountered—So many preconceived opinions—imbued from infancy—to be conquered—So many—often innocent—but with naked truth Struggling biasses to be Subdued—from more than one Side that it is far more easier to direct how—and in what manner it ought to be accomplished—as to execute it.
If at anÿ time a copy of any of your publications fall in your hands honour me with their communication—
Did you ever See a Publication of our friend J. A. on feudal Laws—before our Revolution? I have thus far been unsuccessful of obtaining it—He does not possess it. Accept my thanks for the politeness—with which you have mentioned Dr. Willoughby—I am apprehensive—how highly he was flattered with the Distinction of a man, whose regards he values above those of any one living, that his health—the distance—and roads will finally prevent his indulging his ardent wishes

If at any time I am once more honoured with line, or if you would command any Services—with which it Should be in my power to comply with—I Should request a boon—to Satisfy my curiosity on two points—The last—as I am in correspondence on that Subject—and am canvassing Some delicate traits in it—viz. what is your opinion of the Constitution of the Kingdom of the United Netherlands.

The first relating to modern Literature—which I doubt not or you can explain—having been So long in France—So deeply initiated in its language—manners—customs.
what is the meaning of „porter le ruban gris de lin„?[2] I do not understand the phraseologÿ—it must relate to Epicurean voluptuousness. „La grappe de raisin—couronné de myrthe. digne de porter le ruban gris de lin„—Le Chevalier de Parnÿ makes use of it in his charming voyage—I wish to have other examples of the use of it.

Permit me to assure you, that I am with high respect and consideration

Dear Sir! Your obliged Ser^t Fr. Adr. van der Kemp

P.S. have you Seen Boudinot's[3] Star in the west? I did receive it this instant, and hope to examine it impartiallÿ—tho I believe yet—our Star came from the N.W. and never knew—or inclined to the God of Israël.

RC (DLC); dateline adjacent to signature; endorsed by TJ as received 16 Feb. 1817 and so recorded in SJL.

LAUDARI A LAUDATO VIRO: "to be praised by a praiseworthy man."

John Adams's essay on FEUDAL LAWS, more generally known as "A Dissertation on the Canon and the Feudal Law," appeared as a series of essays in the *Boston Gazette* in 1765. It was reprinted several times in England without Adams's consent (Robert J. Taylor, Richard Alan Ryerson, C. James Taylor, and others, eds., *Papers of John Adams* [1977–], 1:103–28). Adams later included it in his *A Collection of State-Papers* (London, 1782; Sowerby, no. 3000), 83–100.

LA GRAPPE DE RAISIN ... GRIS DE LIN paraphrases a portion of Évariste de Forges de Parny's 4 Sept. 1773 letter to his brother, written from Rio de Janeiro: "Tu les reverras ces Épicuriens aimables, qui portent en écharpe le ruban gris-de-lin, & la grappe de raisin couronnée de myrte" ("You will see them, the friendly epicureans, wearing a scarf of gridelin, and a cluster of grapes crowned with myrtle") and "Cet homme-là est un charmant Épicurien; il est digne de porter le ruban gris-de-lin" ("That man there is a charming epicurean; he is worthy of wearing the gridelin") (*Opuscules de M. Le Chevalier de Parny* [4th ed., (Paris), 1784], 1:129, 137–8). Gridelin is a shade of "pale purple or grey violet; sometimes, a pale red" (*OED*).

Elias BOUDINOT'S publication, *A Star in the West; or, A Humble Attempt to Discover the long lost Ten Tribes of Israel, preparatory to their return to their beloved city, Jerusalem* (Trenton, N.J., 1816), suggested that Native Americans had Jewish ancestors.

[1] Manuscript: "lenght."

[2] Omitted closing guillemet editorially supplied.

[3] Manuscript: "Bodinot's."

From John Wood

DEAR SIR Richmond 2d February 1817

From there being little prospect of the survey of the state of Virginia, being prosecuted farther than those contracts, which the Executive had entered into previous to the meeting of the Legislature; I have opened a seminary in this place, with the intention of completing the remainder of the rivers for which I had engaged during my vacation in summer. I would have resumed my establishment in Lynchburg, if I had not been informed that another teacher had settled in that town. I have thought proper to inform you of this circumstance; in case you might be inclined to send some of your young friends to my care, which would afford me much pleasure. Mr Baker of Cumberland told me he intended to write you on the subject of Mr Eppes son; whom he understood you had not engaged at any school for this year.

Although I was much pleased with my excursion along James River; yet in a pecuniary point of view it would have been more to my benefit to have remained at Lynchburg. The expenses incurred by Boats, hands, Chain carriers &c nearly amounted to the compensation of two dollars per mile. I derived much advantage from your small sextant. It was the only instrument which I used for taking angles. The only defect of this instrument; is the want of a telescope, to observe distinctly those objects which are at a distance. I shall esteem it a favour of you to indulge me with the use of it; until I finish my survey in next August. If you thought Richmond not an improper situation for your Grandson Mr Eppes; it would give me real satisfaction to be his preceptor; as I have seen few boys of a more pleasing countenance than he possesses. Requesting my respects to Mr Jefferson Randolph[1]—I have the honour to be

your obedient and obliged Servant JOHN WOOD

RC (DLC); endorsed by TJ as received 6 Feb. 1817 and so recorded in SJL. RC (DLC); address cover only; with PoC of TJ to John Barnes, 17 Feb. 1817, on verso; addressed: "Thomas Jefferson Esqr Monticello by Milton"; stamp canceled; franked; postmarked Richmond, 4 Feb.

[1]Manuscript: "Randolp."

From Hutchins G. Burton

DEAR SIR, Halifax, 4th Feby. 1817.—

I was informed by Mrs. Eppes, that you wished an annual supply of Scoupernong Wine,—I am in the habit of purchasing for the use of my own family, and will with much pleasure undertake the Commission, as it will be no additional trouble.—Be good enough to inform me, whether it would be more convenient for you that the wine be sent to Petersburg, Richmond, or to Mr John W. Eppes's, as I can at any time forward it to either of those places.—

I am apprehensive that I shall not be able to purchase a barrel of the best quality untill next fall, as it is now late in the season,—and it is likely the Malthers have sold the greater part of the present crop.—I shall, however have an opportunity of knowing in a few weeks, and should I meet with success will follow your directions.

I am, with the highest consideration Yours.

HUTCHINS G. BURTON

RC (MHi); addressed: "Thomas Jefferson Esquire Monticello Virginia" and "post office Cartersvill"; franked; postmarked Halifax, N.C., "<*Jan*> Febry–5th"; endorsed by TJ as received 27 Feb. 1817 and so recorded in SJL.

Hutchins Gordon Burton (d. 1836), attorney and public official, was probably a native of Virginia. He moved to North Carolina at an early age, attended the University of North Carolina in 1795, later read law, and was admitted to the bar in 1806. Burton represented Mecklenburg County in the North Carolina House of Commons for one full session and part of a second, 1809–10. He resigned his seat after being elected state attorney general, a position he retained until 1816. The following year Burton returned to the lower house of the state legislature, representing the borough of Halifax. He served in the United States House of Representatives, 1819–24, and as governor of North Carolina, 1824–27. Burton allied himself politically with strict constructionists and those who opposed the extension of federal power. A proponent of education and state-funded internal improvements, during his governorship free public education in North Carolina advanced with the passage of the Literary Fund Bill. President John Quincy Adams nominated Burton as territorial governor of Arkansas in 1829, but the Senate did not confirm him. He was also a high-ranking Masonic officer (*ANB*; *DAB*; *DNCB*, 1:285–6; Daniel Lindsey Grant, *Alumni History of the University of North Carolina* [2d ed., 1924], 88; Charles L. Coon, *The Beginnings of Public Education in North Carolina* [1908], 1:xiii, xix, xxx–xxxvii; *JEP*, 3:630, 634 [6, 15 Jan. 1829]; *Raleigh Register and North-Carolina Gazette*, 26 Apr. 1836).

From Alden Partridge

SIR West Point (N.Y) Feby 4th 1817

I had the honor duly to receive your letter of the 3d of January 1816—Containing your Calculation of the Altitudes of the Peaks of Otter—for which, and for your observations relative to the Barometer be pleased, Sir, to accept my unfeigned acknowledgements. I now take the liberty, Sir, to enclose you for your examination the Copy of a letter I wrote about five years ago, to Genl Williams relative to the Method adopted by Mr Robbins, for determining[1] the initial velocities of Military Projectiles by means of the Ballistic Pendulum, but concerning which I never obtained the Genls opinion. To this I have annexed a table containing the Results of some Experiments which I made at this Place about two years ago, (on the Ice of the River) upon the principles contained in this letter. You will oblige me, Sir, by taking the trouble to examine my objections to Mr Robbins method, and also the method which I have proposed in the 2nd part of the letter, and giving me your opinion upon the Subject. Since I last wrote you I have calculated from barometrical observation the Altitudes of the high-lands of Nave-Sink near Sandy-Hook and likewise the Altitude of Hemp Stead Harbour Hill said to be the highest land on Long-Island. I have also made some observations for the purpose of testing practically, the Accuracy of the Method of measuring heights by the Barometer, by applying it to the determining of very small altitudes. The results obtained from these observations and also the Altitudes[2] of the High lands of Navesink and of Harbour-Hill, I will do myself the honor in a few days to enclose you.—

I have the honor to be with the greatest Respect and Esteem, Sir, your Obed^{t} Servt

A PARTRIDGE
Capt. of Engs

RC (MHi); at foot of text: "Thomas Jefferson Esquir late President of the U. S—"; endorsed by TJ as received 16 Feb. 1817 and so recorded in SJL.

TJ's letter to Partridge containing his CALCULATION OF THE ALTITUDES OF THE PEAKS OF OTTER was actually dated 2 Jan. 1816. Benjamin Robins (ROBBINS), a British mathematician and military engineer, used his BALLISTIC PENDULUM to measure the velocity of projectiles and the force of exploding gunpowder (*ODNB*).

[1]Manuscript: "determing."
[2]Manuscript: "Alitudes."

ENCLOSURES

I

Alden Partridge to Jonathan Williams

SIR

Norwich January 19th 1812

Reflecting a few days ago upon the manner of ascertaining the initial velocities of Military projectiles, by means of the ballistic pendulum, it struck my mind that this method[1] is not altogether accurate. I take the liberty therefore to state to you what appears objectionable in it, requesting if I am in an error you will have the goodness to rectify it.

The method above alluded to seems to be founded upon two mechanical principles; one is, that when one nonelastic body in motion[2] strikes upon another at rest, the quantity of motion after the stroke, is the same as that before it; the other is, that if two bodies of unequal quantities of matter have equal momenta, the velocity of the larger body, must be as much less than that of the smaller, as its quantity of matter is greater—
Now to apply these principles; a ball in motion strikes the ballistic pendulum (the weight of which, as well as the centres of gravity, of oscillation, and of gyration are supposed to be known) at rest, and causes it to vibrate; now if we can determine the velocity with which the pendulum vibrates it is evident from the second of the above mentioned principles that we can determine the velocity of the ball—Now when the pendulum (after the first vibration) descends down again to its vertical position, it will have acquired the same velocity with which it began to ascend, and from the laws of falling bodies, the velocity of the centre of oscillation is such as a heavy body would acquire by falling freely through the versed-sine of the arc described by the same centre. But by the nature of the circle, the versed-sine is a third proportional to the diameter and chord of its arc; knowing therefore the diameter of the circle which is twice the distance of the centre of oscillation from the point of suspension; and also the chord of the arc through which this centre vibrates we

can ascertain by a single proportion the versed-sine of the arc; and from the laws of falling bodies the velocity acquired in descending through it, that is the velocity of the centre of oscillation—

Having determined the velocity of the centre of oscillation we can from that ascertain the velocity of the point of impact (the point where the ball strikes the pendulum) for the velocities of those points will be to each other directly, as their distances from the point of suspension—Now since the ball in motion strikes upon the pendulum at rest, and thereby puts it in motion, by the first of the principles above stated; the momentum of the pendulum ought to be equal to that of the ball; and since we know the weight of the pendulum and of the ball, and have also determined the velocity with which the point of impact moves, we can (from the second principle laid down) by a single proportion ascertain the velocity of the ball—

But the query in my mind is, whether the ball striking the pendulum and penetrating it, communicates to it as great a quantity of motion as it would if it struck it with the same velocity without penetrating it, supposing them both perfectly non-elastic—
It appears to me that it would not, but that by the yeilding of the fibres of the wood before it, its force could be (as it were) deadened in such a manner, as to partake more of the nature of pressure than of percussion—There is also another consideration which appears to me to affect the accuracy of this method which is, that the motion of the ball, and of the point of impact are never in the same direction—for suppose the ball to strike the pendulum in a horizontal direction then by the vibration of the pendulum, the point of impact must describe the arc of a circle, and therefore must move between a horizontal and a perpendicular direction ... A part of the force of the ball must therefore be spent upon the axis of motion of the Pendulum—From these considerations it appears to me that this method gives the velocity of Military projectiles less than the true velocity—

I will now Sir, take the liberty of proposing for your consideration a method by which I am induced to believe that the initial velocities of cannon balls of any size may be accurately determined. It is found by experiment, (and the same conclusion is also deducible from theory) that bodies descending freely by the force of gravity fall through $16\frac{1}{12}$[3] feet during the first second of time. we also know that if a body continues to descend for any number of seconds by the force of gravity, that the spaces through which it would fall during each of those seconds would be as the odd numbers 1, 3, 5, 7, and also that the whole spaces through which it would have fallen at the end of each of those seconds would be as the squares of the times,[4] that is as the squares of the numbers 1, 2, 3, 4, 8 &c. Now from what has been said, it is evident that if a second be divided into four equal parts, that a body falling freely by the force of gravity, would fall through spaces during each of those parts, that would be to each other as the odd numbers 1, 3, 5, 7, and also that the spaces fallen through at the end of each of those parts would be as the squares of the numbers 1, 2, 3, 4, that is as the numbers 1, 4, 9, 16. consequently at the end of the first part it would have fallen $1\frac{1}{192}$ feet; at the end of the second part $4\frac{1}{48}$ feet, at the end of the third $9\frac{3}{64}$ feet, and at the end 4th $16\frac{1}{12}$ feet—Now to apply what has been said to determining the initial velocity of cannon balls; suppose a cannon was placed and accurately levelled on a plain sand beach at the different altitudes,[5] $1\frac{1}{192}$, $4\frac{1}{48}$, $9\frac{3}{64}$ & $16\frac{1}{12}$[6] feet above the surface of the ground; then if it were fired at those heights[7] it is evident that the ball ought to come to the ground in the same time it would if it were to drop from the muzzle of the gun; for the force of the powder acting in a horizontal direction does not counteract the force of gravity upon the ball, which therefore by the composition and resolution of forces must come to the ground in the same time that it would if it were not acted upon by the powder at all; the ball therefore when fired from the first elevation would fly before striking the ground $\frac{1}{4}^{th}$ of a second; when fired from the second, $\frac{1}{2}$ a second—when fired from the third $\frac{3}{4}$ of a second, and when fired from the fourth 1 second. and if the distance over which it passed during each of those times were accurately measured we should obtain the velocities required—

By this method I am inclined to think may be determined with a considerable degree of accuracy the ratio of the resistance of the air upon cannon balls of the same diameter moving with different degrees of velocity; for suppose we have ascertained from experiment the charges of Powder that will give initial velocities that are as the numbers 1. 2, 3. & so on; and suppose the charge of N° 1, to give a velocity of 600[8] feet per second then it is evident Nos. 2 & 3 would give velocities of 1200 & 1800 feet per second respectively supposing they met with no more resistance from the air than the first one—as much therefore as they fell short of those velocities, so much more must they be resisted by the air than the first one—

I will thank you Sir to examine what I have written, and if I am in an error I hope you will have the goodness to rectify it and give me notice—

Tr (DLC: TJ Papers, 194:34597–9, 34600); with second enclosure subjoined; ellipsis in original; endorsed by TJ as a letter of 19 Jan. 1817 from Partridge to himself received 16 Feb. 1817 and so recorded in SJL. FC (VtNN: Partridge Papers); in a bound volume of Partridge manuscripts; at head of text: "Copy of a Letter from captain Alden Partridge to colonel Jonathan Williams, Late commandant of the U.S. corps of Engineers upon the Ballastic Pendulum, and determining the velocities of cannon Balls." Tr (InU: Williams Papers); dated 20 Jan. 1812, with slight variations in wording. Tr (InU: Williams Papers); dated 20 Jan. 1812, with slight variations in wording.

[1] FC: "the manner." 2d InU Tr: "the method."

[2] Preceding two words interlined by Partridge.

[3] Manuscript: "$16\frac{1}{2}$." FC and both InU Trs: "$16\frac{1}{12}$."

[4] Repeated phrase "that is, as the squares of the times," not in FC or InU Trs, is editorially omitted.

[5] FC: "elevations." 2d InU Tr: "heights."

[6] Manuscript: "$16\frac{1}{2}$." FC and both InU Trs: "$16\frac{1}{12}$."

[7] FC: "elevations." 1st InU Tr: "altitudes."

[8] Preceding sixteen words supplied from FC and also included in both InU Trs.

II

Alden Partridge's Notes on Projectile Velocities

A Table

Containing the results of some experiments made at the Military Academy at West Point, for the purpose of ascertaining the velocities of cannon balls fired with different charges of powder. February 1815.

	Calibre of the Gun	Height above the ground in feet	Charge in powder	N° of shots fired	Greatest distance before the ball struck in feet—	Least distance in ft.	Mean distance in ft.	Difference of mean distances in feet	Time of flight in seconds[1]	
	12	$4\frac{1}{48}$	$1\frac{1}{4}$	3	538	464	491	—	$\frac{1}{2}$	
	do.	do.	$1\frac{1}{2}$	3	609	557	599	108	$\frac{1}{2}$	
	do.	do.	$2\frac{1}{2}$	3	784	723	749	150	$\frac{1}{2}$	
	do.	do.	3	2	1032	1025	1028	279.	$\frac{1}{2}$	
	do.	do.	4	1	1032	1025[2]	1083	55.	$\frac{1}{2}$	

Note.[3]

In the foregoing experiments it is to be observed that the Gun was each time levelled by means of a spirit-level which had been previously corrected and determined to be accurate—The powder for the different charges was not weighed, but measured as accurately as possible, in copper measures which had the weight they would contain marked on them—

The balls used were not good, being old with too[4] much windage, and apparently not well made in the first place—better ones however could not be obtained—

Under these circumstances I do not consider that these results are to be relied on as entirely accurate—I am however strongly induced to believe that under different circumstances (when materials proper for making experiments can be obtained) the method here followed, will be found, not only more general, but also more accurate, for determining the velocities of cannon balls, than any hitherto practiced. The principles upon which it is founded I have explained in another place. Should circumstances permit I shall endeavour at some future time, to make a complete course of experiments upon those principles, for the purpose of determining not only the velocities of cannon balls during different parts of a second, but also to ascertain the different resistance of the air to them when fired with degrees of velocity—

A. Partridge
Captain of Engineers

MS (DLC: TJ Papers, 194:34599–600); subjoined to preceding enclosure; in an unidentified hand; partially dated; with Table and Note on separate pages. FC (VtNN: Partridge Papers); in a bound volume of Partridge manuscripts; partially dated.

[1] FC adds an additional blank column for "Remarks."

[2] Thus in MS, but this and figure to left should have the same value. Both numbers may mistakenly repeat those in the row above. FC leaves these cells blank.

[3] Word not in FC.

[4] MS: "to." FC: "too."

To William A. Burwell

DEAR SIR Monticello Feb. 6. 17.

Your favor of Jan. 22. came to hand last night, with the papers of mr Graham inclosed. of all mechanical machines existing, the steam engine is that which I have the least studied. the principle we all understand; and the structure of the original one I understood when at College. but have never since paid the least attention to the multiplied improvements which have changed nearly every thing but the principle. this is a special reason for returning mr Graham's papers without any opinion on them. but a general reason, and one which, if I give any answer at all, I now give to all such applications, and to all men on every subject, except to my personal friends, or on affairs of duty, is that I am grown old, and worn down by the drudgery of the writing table. repose and tranquility are become necessaries of life for me. nor will you think me unreasonable when I assure you that from the moment of my retirement from Washington, I have labored dayly from sunrise to XII. or I. aclock, say from [7] to 8. hours a day, answering letters, few of which are of the least concern to myself; and that instead of their decreasing as I had long had the hope, I have been obliged for many months past to rise from table & write from dinner to dark: insomuch that no office I ever was in has been so laborious as my supposed state of retirement at Monticello. unable to bear up longer against it, either in body or mind, I am obliged to declare myself in a state of insurgency, and to assume my right to live out thc drcgs of life at least, without being under the whip & spur from morning to night. I hope you will explain all this, with my best respects to Col° Taylor, that you will call on us on your return, and be assured of my constant & affectionate attachment & respect.

TH: JEFFERSON

PoC (DLC); on verso of a reused address cover from Hezekiah Niles to TJ; torn at seal; at foot of text: "William A. Burwell esq."; endorsed by TJ. Enclosures not found.

To Craven Peyton

DEAR SIR Monticello Feb. 6. 17.

I am infinitely obliged by the kind offer of the sum mentioned in your letter, and any further one you will be able to spare: an award is given against me for between 7. & 800.D. for rent to the Hendersons, to be paid instantly. I have also to pay 1600.D. more for the 3. shares of the daughters. this, with purchase of corn, and two years failure of crops embarrasses me beyond my expectations. I will send tomorrow and ask you for an order on Richmond for the present sum which will answer as well as the cash. with much thankfulness therefore I am Dr Sir

Your friend & ser^{t} TH: JEFFERSON

P.S. old mrs Henderson has sworn that Bennet was not of age when he signed the deed of confirmation. I must pray you to enquire among the old women of your neighborhood who best remember these things. it is on our testimony here alone I am to depend.

PoC (MHi); on verso of a reused address cover from John Adams or Abigail Adams to TJ; endorsed by TJ.

From John Barnes

DEAR SIR George Town 7^{h} Feby 1817.

In pursuance of your late fav^{r} of the 28 Ult^{o} Recd the 1st Ins^{t} I have at length effected a Transfer—of your two Certificates of 6 pCt of U States Amo^{t} \$12,499.99—in the like sums

viz N° 90 for \$ 11.363 $^{\underline{63}}$

and 37 $\underline{1\,136.^{36}}$ \$12,499.99—

and dated the 3^{d} Ins^{t} which I now inclose you—

together with J Mason, President of the Bank of Columbia at George Town in the Dist of Columbia & dated 10th Jany 1817—N° 1314. for forty Six Shares of said Bank Stock & also in the Name of Thaddeus Kosciusko—you likewise receive[1] herewith the Gen^{ls} original power of Attorney to you—

you will please to observe this transfer of yrs of the 6 pCt, is for the Principal only—and do not Authorize me to receive the Interest.—for which a seperate Genl power—from you is Necessary rather, than a Quarterly Order—

The Bank I flatter my self is perfectly satisfied—as to paying me the half yearly Dividends—

I have already lodged duplicate—Under the Notarial Seal of the Generals Original power—to you—

As no Notice has been taken of my statem^{t} of the good Generals Acco^{t} Curr^{t} with me—up to the 26 Novr last App^{t}[2] Balance in my fav^{r} \$812. I have to beg you will inform me, least any Accident or Miscarriage may have prevented your receiving it, in which case I should tender you duplicates thereof—

with sentiments of Esteem and perfect Regard—I am Dear Sir—
Your most Obed[t] and very hum[l] servant JOHN BARNES,

RC (ViU: TJP-ER); at foot of text: "Thomas Jefferson Esq[r] Monticello—Virginia"; endorsed by TJ as received 16 Feb. 1817 and so recorded in SJL.

The TWO CERTIFICATES enclosed here have not been found, but the ledger of the United States Treasury records the transfer of the sums listed above on 3 Feb. 1817 (DNA: RG 53, CTSLO, Central Treasury Records Ledger, 65:65). For the ORIGINAL POWER OF ATTORNEY, see first enclosure to TJ to Barnes, 12 Oct. 1816. The ACCO[T] CURR[T] WITH ME—UP TO THE 26 NOV[R] LAST was enclosed in Barnes to TJ, 7 Jan. 1817.

[1] Manuscript: "recive."
[2] Abbreviation for "Apparent."

From Craven Peyton

D. SIR Monteagle Feb[y] 7–1817.

Agreeable to my promise, I send my Son, with this lettar to inform You, I have Fifteen hundred Dollars Now in Richm[d] I wish to be informed if You wish it braught up or a Draft at Sight. You can be Accomodated in eathar way, this with Othar Money I shall soon have will enable You I hope to keep back Your produce untill the hight of the Markett. it depends entirely On Circumstances at what time I may wish the Money refunded it shall lay in Your hands As long as I possibly can do without it. if a draft is wished I will come up at Any hour You may wish & give it. Very Sincerely Yr. Fr[d] & Servt

C. PEYTON

RC (MHi); inconsistently endorsed by TJ as a letter of 7 Feb. received 6 Feb. 1817 and so recorded in SJL.

From Craven Peyton

DEAR SIR Monteagle Feby 7[th1] 17.

I am compelled to be in Charlotesville early tomorrow, And will most certainly call, And give You the Drafts time enough, to send it by this weeks Mail, if I supposed it cou[d] possibly make the smallest difference with You I wou[d] with pleasure send it by the boy

with Sincere esteem C. PEYTON

RC (MHi); addressed: "Thomas Jefferson esqr Monticello"; inconsistently endorsed by TJ as a letter of 7 Feb. received 6 Feb. 1817 and so recorded in SJL.

[1] Reworked from "8th."

From Jerman Baker

D[R] Sir, Richmond 8 Feb[y] 1817

Yours of the 26 Ult[o] came to hand yesterday After an absence of several weeks from my Seat in the house in consequence of indisposition, I returned on Monday last & found to my very great surprise that Co[l] Yancey availing himself of the absence of M[r] Maury M[r] Thweatt & myself, had reported a bill incorporating a Company to turnpike the road from Rock Fish Gap to Moores ford. At my motion the Bill was recommitted, & I added to the Com[ee] a day was then fixed on by M[r] Y— and myself when the subject was to be taken up, yet strange to tell M[r] Y— without giving me any Notice, convened the Committee at an earlier day, and reported the bill without amendment; At this stage of the business M[r] Maury resumed his seat in the House yesterday and anticipated me in a motion to lay the bill on the Table, which prevailed, & it will probably not be called up again this Session; However I shall be very watchful and should it be called up think I shall be able to postpone it indefinitely.

The petition of Count Barziza was rejected by the Com[ee] on the ground that it was a Judicial & not a Legislative question, there being other claimants, viz The daughters of the late M[r] Lee of Green Spring. One of whom married M[r] John Hopkins late Com[er] of Loans.

Wayles is with M[r] Wood & I am much pleased to hear that you will shortly send Francis, like yourself I should have prefered Lynchburg to this place, but M[r] Wood objected to the former for the want of Society and a Library.

I return the plat sent M[r] Thweatt & myself M[r] Yancey never gave us an opportunity of using it. Be pleased, Sir, to present my affectionate regards to M[rs] R. and family. And for yourself accept assurances of my most sincere friendship and profound respect—

Jerman Baker

RC (MHi); endorsed by TJ as received 16 Feb. 1817 and so recorded in SJL. RC (MHi); address cover only; with PoC of TJ to David Higginbotham, 16 Mar. 1817, on verso; addressed: "Thomas Jefferson Esquire Monticello"; franked; postmarked Richmond, 11 Feb.

TJ's previous letter was dated 25 Jan. 1817, not the 26 ult[o]. Charles Yancey presented a bill incorporating a company to turnpike the road from rock fish gap to moores ford in the Virginia House of Delegates on 3 Feb. 1817 and reported it without amendment two days later. A motion to table the bill by Thomas W. Maury, his fellow delegate from Albemarle County, was carried on 7 Feb. 1817 (*JHD* [1816–17 sess.], 187, 194, 200).

The daughters of William Lee were Portia Hodgson and Cornelia Hopkins (*U.S. Reports*, 17 [4 Wheaton]: 453–65). wayles: John Wayles Baker. francis: Francis Eppes. For the enclosed plat sent m[r] thweatt & myself, not found, see TJ to Archibald Thweatt, 14 Jan. 1817, and note.

To Nathaniel Cutting

DEAR SIR Monticello Feb. 8. 17.

Your favor of Jan. 18. was long on the road, as happens often with our winter mails; and altho' it has been some days at hand, incessant occupations have put it out of my power sooner to answer it. I look back with great pleasure to the times of our early acquaintance, now nearly 30. years past, and I bear fully in mind the services you rendered our country in the Consulate at Havre; and afterwards those with which you were charged with Col° Humphreys in the mission to the Barbary states. the latter I recollect were so performed as to give entire satisfaction to Gen[l] Washington then president, and to myself as Secretary of state, and to recieve our marked approbation. your endeavors to avail our Navy yard of a method of establishing a Ropery, with a great economy of space, were still in progress when I left Washington and I only learnt afterwards that it proved a losing enterprise to yourself. the talents and integrity manifested in these services, might, I am conscious, have been usefully engaged for the public in higher grades than that to which they have been applied; and if the testimony I bear to them can avail either the public or yourself of their employment in more interesting stations, it will add pleasure to the duty of giving this assurance of them.

Accept that also of my continued friendship good wi[shes & respect.] [TH: JEFFERSON]

PoC (DLC); closing, signature, and internal address faint, with missing text supplied from Trs; at foot of text: "Capt. [Nat]haniel Cutting"; endorsed by TJ. Tr (DNA: RG 46, PMSC, 15th Cong., 1st sess.); entirely in Cutting's hand; at head of text: "Copy." Tr (DNA: RG 46, PMSC, 15th Cong., 1st sess.); entirely in Cutting's hand; at head of text: "Copy."

To Thomas Humphreys

[D]EAR SIR Monticello Feb. 8. 17.

Your favor of Jan. 2. did not come to my hands until the 5th instant. I concur entirely in your leading principles of gradual emancipation, of establishment on the coast of Africa, and the patronage of our nation until the emigrants shall be able to protect themselves. the subordinate details might be easily arranged. but the bare proposition of purchase by the United states generally would excite infinite indignation in all the states North of Maryland. the sacrifice must fall on the States alone which hold them; and the difficult question will be how to lessen this so as to reconcile our fellow citizens to it. personally I am ready and desirous to make any sacrifice which shall ensure their gradual but compleat retirement from the state, and effectually at the same time establish them elsewhere in freedom and safety. but I have not percieved the growth of this disposition in the rising generation, of which I once had sanguine hopes. no symptoms inform me that it will take place in my day. I leave it therefore to time, and not at all without hope, that the day will come, equally desirable and welcome to us as to them: perhaps the proposition now on the carpet at Washington, to provide an establishment on the coast of Africa for voluntary emigrations of people of colour may be the corner stone of this future edifice. praying for it's completion as early as may most promote the good of all, I salute you with great esteem and respect.

TH: JEFFERSON

PoC (DLC); on verso of portion of reused address cover of Humphreys to TJ, [ca. 23] Jan. 1817; salutation faint; at foot of text: "Dr Thomas Humphreys."

Humphreys's FAVOR is printed above at 23 Jan. 1817. The PROPOSITION NOW ON THE CARPET was made by the newly formed American Colonization Society. At its inaugural meeting in Washington on 1 Jan. 1817, the society resolved that its president, Bushrod Washington, and its Board of Managers should petition Congress concerning colonization. A memorial was accordingly presented by John Randolph of Roanoke on 14 Jan. 1817. Timothy Pickering, a member of the House committee on the African slave trade, reported on the petition on 11 Feb. 1817 and proposed a joint resolution urging the United States president to negotiate with other nations regarding abolition of the slave trade, ask Great Britain to admit to Sierra Leone free American blacks who were emigrating voluntarily, and, barring that, seek agreement from Britain and other maritime powers for the United States to establish a permanently neutral colony for free blacks on the African coast. The proposal was read twice and committed to a committee of the whole House, but was not considered further (Washington *Daily National Intelligencer*, 3 Jan. 1817; *JHR*, 10:199, 380; *Annals*, 14th Cong., 2d sess., 939–41).

From Thomas Law

DEAR SIR— Washington Feby 8th 1817.

Permit me to request your attention to the enclosed—I have endeavored to convey my sentiments with perspicuity & energy—The subject is a most important one, & I obeyed the impulse of duty—Conscious how much prejudice I have to encounter, I hope that some abler pen, will strengthen what is weak & enlighten what may be obscure—

I remain With sincere esteem THOS LAW—

RC (DLC); endorsed by TJ as received 16 Feb. 1817 and so recorded in SJL. RC (DLC); address cover only; with PoC of TJ to James Monroe, 13 Apr. 1817, on verso; addressed: "To Thomas Jefferson Esq Monte Cello"; franked; postmarked

Washington City, 10 Feb. Enclosure: Law, *Homo's Letters on a National Currency, addressed to the People of the United States* (Washington, 1817; possibly Poor, *Jefferson's Library*, 9 [no. 491]).

To James Madison

Dear Sir Monticello Feb. 8. 17.

In a late letter from mr Spafford of Albany I received the inclosed with a request that after perusal I would forward it to you, adding a desire that, when read, you would address it under cover to him, as he sets some value on the possession of it. his object in[1] making the communication to either of us is not explained, but perhaps it may be understood by you. your frank on a blank cover will let him see that I have complied with his request. We have at length received commissions for the Visitors of our Central college; but as we may expect the pleasure of your return among us with the returning spring, I defer asking a meeting until it shall be convenient to you to join us. As you are at the fountain head of political news, I shall give you that only which is agricultural. we have had a most severe spell of cold, which commenced on the 11th of Jan. on the 19th of that month the thermometer was at 6°, that is 26° below freezing. on the 5th of this month it was at $9\frac{1}{2}$° has been twice at 13° and only three mornings of the last 3. weeks above freezing. within that time it has been 7. days below freezing thro' the day. $6\frac{1}{2}$ I. only of snow have fallen at different times, and I think the winter has been as remarkably dry as the summer was. apprehensions are entertained for our wheat, which looks wretchedly. but the fine autumn and month of Dec. may have enabled it to push it's roots beyond the reach of frost. the tobacco fever is over, and little preparation making for that plant. corn is at 5. 6. & 7.D. according to it's position, and the apprehension of want continues. this may serve as a little preparation for your return to these contemplations, and especially as furnishing an opportunity of assuring you of my constant and affectionate friendship and respect

Th: Jefferson

RC (DLC: Madison Papers); endorsed by Madison. PoC (DLC); on verso of reused address cover of John Trumbull to TJ, 26 Dec. 1816; endorsed by TJ. Enclosure not found.

A missing letter from Madison to TJ of 7 Feb. 1817 is recorded in SJL as received 5 Mar. 1817.

[1] TJ here canceled "desiring."

To John F. Oliveira Fernandes

Dear Sir Monticello Feb. 8. 17.

I have read with pleasure and edification the pamphlet and documents you were so kind as to send me. the attempt seems really extraordinary, in this age and country, to sieze on private and voluntary funds under spiritual authority. and it is a novelty in any country to impose a teacher against the will of the employers. I have always supposed it a principle of every church that endowment entitles to collation. in England, whose church government is in structure the same with that of Rome, the lay proprietor of a benefice has the never-questioned right of Collation. he must, to be sure, take a regularly ordained clergyman; but he has free choice among all these. in this state, while we had a regularly established church, the parishes furnished a glebe, paid the salaries, and built the churches; and their vestrymen, chosen by themselves, collated to the parish the clergyman of their choice. but here you have an advantage which we had not. our contributions being required by law, we could not withold them, so as to get rid of an incumbent who proved himself not to have merited our choice. yours being voluntary, may be withdrawn, and the incumbent in [th]at way got rid of. for it is the money which is the inspiring principle of the priesthood. this is the essential object of all their impositions, duperies & usurpations.

I believe still that our law is wise in restraining it's legitimate cognisance to the <u>actions</u> of men. if we permitted the civil authority to cross that only-definable line, I doubt we should experience more evil than at present. I suspect that the reverend bishop has already found that 'the tail' is as learned as 'the head,' and I am sure that a congregation of which you are a member, must have the benefit of too much light to bow the neck implicitly to the yoke of barbarism and ignorance with the offer of which they are now insulted. Accept the assurance of my friendly & respectful esteem & respect. Th: Jefferson

PoC (DLC); on verso of a reused address cover from Josephus B. Stuart to TJ; mutilated at seal, with some of the missing text rewritten by TJ; at foot of text: "Doct[r] Fernandes"; endorsed by TJ.

TJ's ironic reference to the tail and the head alludes to Archbishop Leonard Neale's letter to the trustees of the Catholic congregation at Norfolk. Neale argued that when lay trustees assume the power to conduct all temporal concerns of a congregation, they acquire the ability to "*frustrate the most genuine views of the pastor on all occasions.* This appears to me *unjust, and a fair inversion of the order of nature, which forbids the head to become the tail*" (quote from separately paginated *Documents*, 32–3 [copy at MdBS: Archdiocese of Baltimore Archives, Neale Papers], supplement to [Oliveira Fernandes], *Letter, Addressed to the Most Reverend Leonard Neale, Arch Bishop of Baltimore. by A Member of the Roman Catholic*

Congregation of Norfolk, in Virginia ([Norfolk, 1816?]); repr. in Peter Guilday, *The Catholic Church in Virginia (1815–1822)* [1924], 23).

To John H. Peyton

DEAR SIR M[o]nticello Feb. 8. 17.

I have built, [as] you perhaps know, very expensive manufacturing and grist mills on the Rivanna river, near this place, the canal to which alone has cost me 20,000. Dollars. the Rivanna company claim a right to use this canal for navigation, independently of my permission, and of the regulations necessary to prevent obstruction to the operation of my mills. this obliges me to bring a suit in Chancery against them to quiet my title in which I ask the benefit of your aid, as I have done that of mr Johnson. at present I must request you to inclose me by return of mail a subpoena in Chancery against George Divers, William D. Meriwether, Nimrod Bramham, Dabney Minor and John Kelly of Albemarle[1] subscribers, members, and Directors of the Rivanna company. be so good as to send this by return of mail, as I learn that three of these gentlemen are about to resign, and I would rather make them parties than any new hands. Accept the assurance of my great esteem and respect. TH: JEFFERSON

PoC (MHi); on verso of reused address cover of James Maury to TJ, 7 Nov. 1816; damaged at seal; at foot of text: "Howe Peyton esq."; endorsed by TJ.

John Howe Peyton (1778–1847), attorney and public official, graduated from the College of New Jersey (later Princeton University) in 1797, studied law, and entered into practice by 1800. He represented Prince William County in the Virginia House of Delegates, 1808–10, after which he moved to Staunton and accepted appointment as commonwealth's attorney for the district comprising Albemarle, Augusta, and Rockbridge counties. Peyton was the brother of TJ's Richmond agent Bernard Peyton and a leader of the local bar who acted as one of TJ's attorneys in his dispute with the Rivanna Company. He returned to politics in 1839 as a state senator for the Augusta and Rockbridge district and held the position for nearly two terms before resigning in 1845 due to poor health. A great proponent of education in Virginia, Peyton was a trustee of Washington College (later Washington and Lee University) and the Staunton Academy, a founder of the Virginia Female Institute (later Stuart Hall School) at Staunton, and a visitor of the United States Military Academy. He also helped establish the Virginia Military Institute. Peyton died near Staunton at his estate, Montgomery Hall, leaving property valued in excess of $30,000, including at least eighty-six slaves (J. Lewis Peyton, *Memoir of John Howe Peyton, in sketches by his Contemporaries* [1894]; John T. L. Preston, "Sketch of the Hon. John Howe Peyton," *New-England Historical and Genealogical Register* 35 [1881]: 9–20; *General Catalogue of Princeton University 1746–1906* [1908], 111; Leonard, *General Assembly*; *MB*, 2:1373; Augusta Co. Will Book, 27:398–400, 28:415–30, 30:326–7, 488–96; *Staunton Spectator, and General Advertiser*, 8 Apr. 1847; Washington *Daily National Intelligencer*, 3 May 1847).

[1] Preceding two words interlined.

To Josephus B. Stuart

Dear Sir Monticello Feb. 8. 17.

Your favor of Jan. 26. reached me two days ago, and I am glad to see that our merchants, as well as our rulers, are at length looking to principles of navigation which, as Secretary of state, I submitted to them in a Report of Dec. 1793.—the crew of the Armstrong have also my sincere prayers for indemnification either thro' our government or from it: for a more gallant conduct than theirs never honored any nation.—I am entirely of opinion with you as to the future prospects of Richmond. the advantages of water, coal and iron united there, with the easy communication which may be opened with the Western country, are second to those of none of our Atlantic[1] states, and time and circumstances may at some future day, give them all their developement. but these things are for your day, not for mine; and I am made happy when I see a young citizen coming into life with the energy of youth and the observation and information of age. the prospect to our dear country, and, I trust, to all the human race, is transcendantly animating; but an old man has nothing but prayers to offer in it's behalf. these are sincere for the general good, as also for your particular health & prosperity. Th: Jefferson

RC (NjP: Andre deCoppet Collection); at foot of text: "J. B Stuart esq"; endorsed by Stuart as received 13 Feb. 1817 and with his further notation: "N° 2." PoC (DLC); on verso of a reused address cover from Stuart to TJ; torn at seal, with some words rewritten by TJ; endorsed by TJ.

For TJ's REPORT OF DEC. 1793 on commerce, see *PTJ*, 27:532–81.

[1] Manuscript: "Antlantic."

To John L. Sullivan

Dear Sir Monticello Feb. 8. 17.

Your favor of Jan. 17. is just now recieved. I readily see how desirable it is that the steam-boat, hitherto confined to ti[de]waters, should extend it's benefits to the river navigation of the upper country; and I shall with pleasure communicate the prospect of it which the letter you have favored me with gives, to the circle of society around me. but, dear Sir, this is small; I [am?] grown old, go little from home, and am desirous to retire from every thing public and to give to repose and tranquility the feeble existence which remains to me. the discoveries daily made, and vast amelioration of the condition of man resulting from them, might i[n]spire a curiosity to live to see them in action. sed hoc non f[atum?] datum est. to this necessity I resign myself willingly, and to the guardianship of my younger fellow citizens, for whom, in th[e?] day of weakness I have endeavored to perform the same good offi[ces.?] Accept my best wishes for the success of your inventions, and assurances of my great esteem and respect.

Th: Jefferson

PoC (MHi); edge chipped and trimmed; at foot of text: "John L. Sullivan esq."; endorsed by TJ.

sed hoc non f[atum?] datum est: "but this is not a fate given to me."

To James Baker

Sir Monticello Feb. 9.

Understanding that you keep supplies of Codfish and of Tongues and sounds, I have to ask the favor of you to furnish me with a Kental of good dumbfish, and a keg of tongues and sounds. mr Gibson my correspondent in Richmond, will be so good as to recieve & forward them and to pay you the amount on presenting him this letter Accept the tender of my respect Th: Jefferson

PoC (MHi); on verso of portion of reused address cover to TJ; partially dated, but endorsed by TJ as a letter of 9 Feb. 1817 and so recorded in SJL; at foot of text: "Mr James Baker."

kental: quintal. dumbfish: dunfish, salted New England cod that turns a dun or brownish gray color when cured (*OED*).

From Joseph C. Cabell

Dear Sir, Richmond 9. Feb: 1817.

The petition of Count Barziza was rejected some time past in the House of Delegates

I have kept a watchful eye on the Turnpike Bill to which you desired me to attend. Mr Thweat has shewn a very friendly anxiety on the occasion. I spoke to several of my friends in the[1] House of Delegates, to cooperate with him. Mr Maury has been ill nearly the whole of the session. But an agreement has been entered into by all the members of the House of Delegates who feel an interest in this subject, that when the Bill shall have been read a second or third time, it shall be laid on the table in that House, and there remain. The object is to let the matter lie over till another session. This I believe will be agreeable to you.

I had some part in hewing down the mammoth Bank bill sent us from the House of Delegates. In the share I bore in the discussion in the Senate, I took occasion to state the saving to the nation by the substitution of bank paper for specie, and used your own calculation, referring to anonymous authority. It appeared to make a considerable impression.

Mr Rives lately came on from Washington, & brings me the agreeable information that Mr Milligan will have Tracy's Political economy ready for delivery in a month from this time.

I am, Dr Sir, most respectfully & truly yours

JOSEPH C. CABELL

RC (ViU: TJP-PC); at foot of text: "Mr Jefferson"; endorsed by TJ as received 16 Feb. 1817 and so recorded in SJL.

TJ included his CALCULATION on the substitution of bank paper for specie in a 23 Sept. 1814 letter to Cabell.

[1] Cabell here canceled "low."

To Nicolas G. Dufief

DEAR SIR Monticello Feb. 9. 1817.

I recieved last night your two favors of Jan. 30. and all the books have been received as stated in your account. I have now to request you to send me a copy of your dictionary; let the 1st vol. come first as being most immediately wanting.

I have no doubt you are correct as to the 31.D. and that mr Gibson is so also. he has probably charged me on ordering payment, and his correspondent in Philadelphia has by some inadvertence overlooked it. I shall write to mr Gibson, and you shall know the result. I salute you with esteem & respect TH: JEFFERSON

PoC (DLC); on verso of portion of reused address cover to TJ; at foot of text: "Mr Dufief"; endorsed by TJ.

To Patrick Gibson

DEAR SIR Monticello Feb. 9. 17.

I recieved in December from Mr Dufief of Philadelphia a letter of the 16th of that month informing me he had not recieved a sum of 31.D. which I had notified to him that you would be so kind as to remit him. I immediately inclosed him the sum in bank notes. a short time[1] after this, say Jan. 19. your favor of the 16th came to hand inclosing my account, in which I found the remittance charged as of Aug. 4. I thereupon wrote to mr Dufief to ask whether he had not been mistaken, and I inclose you his answer in the negative. I now presume that you have charged the remittance when you ordered it, and that your correspondent in Philadelphia has by oversight omitted the paiment This however you will readily learn and set to rights. yours with great esteem & respect TH: JEFFERSON

PoC (MHi); on verso of reused address cover of John L. Sullivan to TJ, 17 Jan. 1817; at foot of text: "Mr Gibson"; endorsed by TJ. Enclosure: Nicolas G. Dufief to TJ, 30 Jan. 1817 (second letter).

[1]Preceding two words interlined in place of "few days."

To Chapman Johnson

DEAR SIR Monticello Feb. 9. 17.

I now send you a copy of my bill and of the documents which I have been longer getting ready than I expected. there is still a document N° 6. wanting. this copy of both bill & documents is prepared for your use and that of mr Peyton also engaged in the cause, but when that is done I will ask the return of both, as I ought to preserve them among my papers. the bill is long, and perhaps too argumentative. this is easier accounted for than justified. for two or three years the subject has been constantly forced on my attention & reflection, and in drawing the bill the facts & principles spontaneously and constantly forced themselves on my pen. I do not see however any thing in it which does not give some pertinent information to the judge. but any omissions, alterations or additions which you may think necessary shall be made to the original which I retain, before it shall be forwarded to be filed. if you could do me the favor on your return to make this instead of Charlottesville your stage for an evening, it would give me an opportunity of recieving your advice as to any necessary alterations. in the mean time I shall shew the bill to four of the five directors, and correct, in concert with them any error of fact which they may point out to me. I salute you with great friendship and respect. TH: JEFFERSON

PoC (MHi); on verso of portion of reused address cover containing only a wax seal; at foot of text: "Chapman Johnson esq."; endorsed by TJ. Enclosure: TJ's Bill of Complaint against the Rivanna Company, [by 9 Feb. 1817], document 1 in a group of documents on Jefferson's Lawsuit against the Rivanna Company, 9 Feb. 1817.

The DOCUMENTS that accompanied this letter and its enclosure are described in the list of numbered exhibits in the note to the latter. In indicating that he would obtain comments on the enclosure from FOUR OF THE FIVE DIRECTORS of the Rivanna Company, TJ was presumably excluding his antagonist William D. Meriwether.

Jefferson's Lawsuit against the Rivanna Company

I. THOMAS JEFFERSON'S BILL OF COMPLAINT AGAINST THE DIRECTORS OF THE RIVANNA COMPANY, [BY 9 FEB. 1817]

II. EXTRACT FROM MINUTES OF THE DIRECTORS OF THE RIVANNA COMPANY, 12 SEPT. 1810

III. PETER MINOR TO THOMAS JEFFERSON, 10 NOV. 1810

IV. EXTRACT FROM MINUTES OF THE DIRECTORS OF THE RIVANNA COMPANY, 8 JAN. 1811

V. PETER MINOR TO THOMAS JEFFERSON, [15] JAN. 1811

VI. STATEMENT OF THE DISPUTE BY THE DIRECTORS OF THE RIVANNA COMPANY, [CA. 15 JAN. 1811]

VII. THOMAS JEFFERSON'S NOTES ON VIRGINIA STATUTES FOR CLEARING THE RIVANNA RIVER, 27 DEC. 1816

EDITORIAL NOTE

In 1806 an act of the Virginia General Assembly established the Rivanna Company in order to improve the navigation of the Rivanna River between Milton and Charlottesville. This section of the river included property owned by Jefferson. After receiving title to this tract under his father's will, he spent many years and thousands of dollars building a canal, mills, and a dam along the Rivanna's edge. Owing to flooding and general maintenance costs, Jefferson regularly poured funds into these structures. When the Rivanna Company was established, he initially accommodated the requirements and requests of its directors. Jefferson agreed to cut his dam wherever they chose to create a passage through it, and he allowed them to use his canal to improve navigation. His one caveat was that nothing should damage his mills. Contention arose, however, over the placement of locks and the company's management of them as well as its insistence that Jefferson raise his dam and give the navigation priority access during times of low water.

By 1812, when the company petitioned the General Assembly for an expansion of its powers, Jefferson had become increasingly defensive over what he perceived as a violation of his property rights. In a 5 Jan. 1813 letter to Joseph C. Cabell he expressed his frustration: "I learn by the newspapers that a petition has been presented to the legislature by the Rivanna company praying an enlargement of their powers. as these are to be executed wholly within my lands, and almost solely over my property, and have not hitherto been exercised with much forbearance as to the injury to which they expose me, it becomes necessary while they ask for power, for me to ask protection from it."

Although Jefferson and the company directors compromised in the bill that eventually passed into law on 31 Jan. 1814, by the autumn of 1816 the two sides again found themselves at odds. Jefferson's September 1816 meeting with the directors to seek a solution apparently failed, for on 26 Dec. of that year he wrote of the Rivanna Company to his legal counsel Chapman Johnson that "certain claims of right, equal, & even paramount to my own, which they set up to my canal, a work which has cost me 30,000.D. and which would render it's value almost null to me, oblige me to bring a suit in chancery to quiet my title."

Debates over the legalities of riparian rights were not new to Jefferson. He had been beset by litigation with the Henderson family and its representatives since the latter part of the 1790s stemming from Jefferson's assertion that the Henderson's milldam on the Rivanna was unauthorized and threatened the security of his own mill. His experience as United States president also included entanglements of this kind. Even after retiring to Monticello, Jefferson found himself defending his 1807 decision to remove Edward Livingston from batture lands near New Orleans long viewed as commons. Livingston sued him in 1810 for $100,000 in damages, and although the United States Circuit Court for the Virginia District dismissed the case on jurisdictional grounds in 1811, Jefferson published a lengthy defense the following year. He concluded that Livingston, "having taken possession of the beach of the river Missisipi adjacent to the city of New-Orleans, in defiance of the general right of the nation to the property and use of the beaches and beds of their rivers, it became my duty, as charged with the preservation of the public property, to remove the intrusion, and to maintain the citizens of the United States in their right to a common use of that beach."

In contrast, as a private citizen responding to the claims of the Rivanna Company, and in a case involving English rather than European legal precedents, Jefferson emphatically denied "that any law, natural or civil, gives to one individual a right to enter another's land, to dig a canal thro' it for the purposes of navigation, or to take possession of one dug by the proprietor himself for his own purposes, and much less so to use it by making locks or other constructions of his own, as to destroy or endanger the constructions or uses for which the proprietor made it." He described his primary goal as the establishment of "his clear and undivided right in his property."

Between 26 Dec. 1816, when he advised Johnson that a draft was substantially ready, and 9 Feb. 1817, when he sent him a copy, Jefferson completed his bill of complaint against the Rivanna Company. During this period he may also have drawn up his "Notes on Legal Processes" (MS in DLC: TJ Papers, 194:34547; written entirely in TJ's hand on a small scrap; undated), in which he outlined the basic course of chancery cases and cited two legal authorities, John Fonblanque and John Freeman Mitford, both of whose works he had sold to the Library of Congress in 1815.

Jefferson's draft of his complaint, held by the Library of Congress, is entirely in his hand and heavily reworked. He penned it in his usual style for such documents, leaving a wide margin on one side of the paper so as to allow ample space for rewriting and additions. Despite those allowances, several pages were so heavily reworked or supplemented that he had to attach separate slips of paper to the draft sheet in order to position his further revisions in their appropriate locations.

Jefferson most likely used his polygraph to create two clean copies, with one to be submitted to his legal counsel and the other kept for his own reference. At some point he may have found it necessary to send out his retained copy as well. Presumably it was then that he returned to the draft and inserted numbers and vertical lines corresponding to the pagination of the clean text so that, even without one of the fair copies in front of him, he could easily point to specific sections of his argument.

During the spring of 1817 Jefferson sent the complaint to Chapman Johnson and John H. Peyton, his legal representatives. He also circulated it to his friend Peter Minor. The following spring the directors filed their answer. The Superior Court of Chancery did not pronounce its decision until December 1819, when it supported the public right to use Jefferson's canal but ruled that he had no responsibility to construct additional locks. The court also emphasized that, public use notwithstanding, Jefferson's property rights were first and foremost to be respected.

The master texts for documents I–V and VII below were unknown until a copy of the case file, containing material dating as late as 1819, was sold by private owners in 2012. For that reason, documents II–VII are printed here rather than in their chronological place in earlier volumes. Jefferson appears to have revised his plans for the exhibits included with this file. Initially he numbered several texts not referenced in his final composition, including Minor to TJ, 10 Oct. 1810, 15 Nov. 1813, and TJ to Minor, 31 Oct. 1810 and its enclosure, 18, 20 Nov. 1810, and 18 Nov. 1813. Jefferson's final list of numbered exhibits is provided below in the annotation to the Bill of Complaint (Peter Jefferson's will, proved 13 Oct. 1757, Albemarle Co. Will Book, 2:32–4; Robert F. Haggard, "Thomas Jefferson v. The Heirs of Bennett Henderson, 1795–1818: A Case Study in Caveat Emptor," *MACH* 63 [2005]: 1–29; *Acts of Assembly* [1806–07 sess.], 24–5 [30 Dec. 1806], [1813–14 sess.], 91–2 [31 Jan. 1814]; *U.S. Statutes at Large*, 2:445–6 [3 Mar. 1807]; Edward Livingston's Bill of Complaint against TJ, [ca. July 1810], enclosed in George Hay to TJ, 20 July 1810; Jefferson, *The Proceedings of the Government of the United States, in maintaining The Public Right to the Beach of the Missisipi, Adjacent to New-Orleans, against the Intrusion of Edward Livingston* [New York, 1812; Sowerby, nos. 3501, 3508; Poor, *Jefferson's Library*, 10 (no. 604)], esp. p. iii; *MB*, 2:1098–9, 1373; TJ to Minor, 30 Sept. 1810, 25 Aug. 1816; Petition of the Rivanna Company to the Virginia General Assembly, [ca. 5 Oct. 1812]; TJ to Philip P. Barbour, 4 Jan. 1813; TJ to Nicholas H. Lewis, 5 Sept. 1816; TJ to Johnson, 26 Dec. 1816; Sowerby, nos. 1720, 1738; Answer of the President and Directors of the Rivanna Company to TJ's Bill of Complaint, [by 7 Apr. 1818]; Judgment by Virginia Superior Court of Chancery in *Jefferson v. Directors of the Rivanna Company*, 8 Dec. 1819).

I. Thomas Jefferson's Bill of Complaint against the Directors of the Rivanna Company

[by 9 Feb. 1817]

To the honorable John Brown, Judge of the Superior court of[1] Chancery holden at Staunton.[2]

Humbly complaining sheweth unto your Honor your Orator Thomas Jefferson of the county of Albemarle[3] that Peter Jefferson father of your orator was in his lifetime seised and possessed as in feesimple of a certain tract of land called Shadwell, on the North side of the Rivanna river, and adjacent thereto in the county of Albemarle whereon he had erected, according to the prescriptions[4] of the law, a water grist mill, the water to which was deduced from the river by a canal from a dam across the same about half a mile above the s^{d} mill; which tract of land, with others on both sides of the river adjacent thereto, together with the bed of the river (granted to the said Peter Jefferson by letters patent bearing date the 10th day of Sep. 1755. herewith exhibited N° 1.) became the property of your orator,[5] on the death of his sd father, which happened in 1757. and by the provisions of his will: that by the great flood, which happened in the year 1771. the sd mill-house was carried away, and it's dam demolished; and your orator, believing that by a new canal extended $\frac{3}{4}$ of a mile above the millsite he could draw his supply of water from above a natural ridge[6] of rocks, which would render a dam unnecessary, accordingly undertook a new canal, applying to the court for authority for the same, and to rebuild his mill, and getting their order renewed from time to time, during the work: that the undertaking proved to be exceedingly laborious and expensive, immense bodies of rock discovering themselves in the bed of the canal on digging into the same, which required to be removed by the force of gunpowder, sometimes to the depth of fourteen feet: that to these causes of delay were added interruptions by the revolutionary war, almost perpetual absences of your orator, in the public service,[7] from home, from the state, and from the continent, during the sd war, and during the period also which succeeded it; & a suit in Chancery which he was obliged to institute to remove a dam newly[8] erected below, which overflowed his site; insomuch that altho' your orator kept employed from 8. or 10. to 15. men, except in the winter months, for more than 20. of the years intervening between the demolition of the old, and completion of the new mill, and consumed additionally immense quantities of gunpowder, iron[9] and steel, the sd canal was not completed (and then to the breadth of 5. feet only at bottom) till the year 1807. which quantity of labor and the attendant expences your orator is convinced, from the best calculation he is now able to make, could not have been employed for less than twenty thousand dollars, for the accomplishment of the canal alone, & exclusive of the buildings which have cost him not less than ten thousand Dollars more: that in the year 1795. your orator, flattering himself that he was not very distant from the consummation of his work, had an inquest taken by order of court, which found that,[10] your orator not proposing to make a dam, but only to stop some small sluices in the natural ridge of rocks, no lands whatever would be overflowed, nor injurious stagnation of waters produced; that dams below that prevented fish of passage from reaching it; and, from natural obstructions no navigation was practised; 'but that, if the river be opened for navigation hereafter, the interests of your orator ought to be postponed to that object, and those authorised to open the river should be free to make their opening in any part they think best, either of the said natural ridge of rocks, or of any stoppage which he should have made.' as by the sd inquest, to this bill annexed with the order of court thereon,[11] as an Exhibit N° 2.[12] will more particularly appear: that, in the prosecution of the work however, difficulties multiplied, by the increasing quantity of rock, and altho' your orator enlarged his force, and admitted no intermissions of labor, but during the winter months, ten years more were consumed on it, and the work appeared not yet within any assignable term of accomplishment: concluding therefore that it would be easier to raise a dam 3. or 4. feet high than to sink his canal that much deeper, he applied to the court of Albemarle, in the year 1805[13] & obtained an order for another Inquest, who attending accordingly, were charged, agreeably to law, to enquire and say on their oaths whether a dam of the height desired would cause the lands of others, or their mansion-house, offices, curtilage, gardens or orchards to be overflowed? whether the health of the neighbors would be annoyed by the stagnation of the waters? in what degree fish of passage & ordinary navigation would be obstructed, & whether by any and[14] what means such obstruction might be prevented: but they were neither charged nor authorised by law, nor by their oath, to make any bargains as to these particulars, to bind the public by any stipulations, or to impose any conditions on your orator, but simply to state with truth the facts referred to their enquiry by law: that they accordingly found and stated, as had been done by the Inquest which had acted before them, that no injury would be produced to the property or health of others, that few or no fish of passage were taken as high as this mill, 'that no navigation was then practised thro' this part of the said river, natural obstructions preventing the same, that if the river be opened for navigation hereafter, if it be found best to pass thro' the canal of the proprietor, this dam would be necessary to enable vessels to pass, and, if it be found best to open the bed of the river, then a lock would be necessary at this dam': that in the course of the examination one or more individuals of the jury[15] suggested the opinion that the most practicable channel of future[16] navigation for this part of the river would be the canal of your orator, and expressed a wish that this might be permitted, which was answered on the part of your orator generally and in substance (for at this distance of time he does not pretend to recollect the very words which past, but his general impression only)[17] by expressions of his willingness to accomodate the public on this, as on all other occasions, not too injurious; but that no words passed constituting or importing an actual contract, or any contemplation of making a present one; for your orator well knew that, besides the want of authority in the jury to make or to exact any contract on the subject, before such general permission could be given, many preliminary articles and arrangements must be stipulated, and that the settlement of these[18] would require something more of consideration and solemnity than mere conversations in the field with a jury, whose formal stipulations even would oblige nobody, because authorised by nobody: that nevertheless when the jury retired in secret to close their inquisition, these individuals persisted, (on what motives will perhaps appear in the evidence)[19] in inserting what has been considered as importing an agreement[20] on the part of your orator, while others opposed it as none of their business, being[21] no part of the duties or authorities committed to them; but these finally acquiesced,[22] and these words were entered at the close of their inquisition, to wit, 'it is further understood by the jury, and agreed to on the part of the sd Thomas [your orator meaning][23] that the canal shall be used as an improvement in extending the navigation from Milton upwards, if that shall be adjudged the best course for the sd navigation,' and the jurors enlarged the height of the dam proposed to six feet, instead of 3. or 4. intended by your orator, who[24] took no avail however from this enlargement,[25] & raised his dam three feet only on the upper side;[26] and that in this form the sd inquisition N° 3. was returned and placed on the records of the court and the order given which is thereto subjoined;[27] but on inspection of the original, now on the files in the clerk's office it will be seen that the whole of the inquest preceding those words 'it is further understood by the jury and agreed to on the part of the sd Thomas'[28] E^t^c is in the handwriting of this Complainant, but that those words, and what follow are in the handwriting of another; whereas, having written the rest of the inquisition for them, and being on the spot and a few paces distant only, it would seem a thing of course that they should have requested him to write this passage also, were it only as a proof of his knolege and agreement to it; and the omission to do this may naturally excite a suspicion that what he knew, he wrote; and what he did not write was either not known, or not agreed to by him: that two years still of labor and expence were incurred[29] before the final completion of your orator's mills, which did not get into operation until the year 1807. thirty six years after the destruction of the original mill; during which whole time their reestablishment was pursued, with no considerable intermissions except a part of the 6. years of your orator's absence in Europe.

And your orator further states that several acts of assembly having been previously passed from the year 1764. to 1805. inclusive; authorising various schemes and propositions for opening & improving the navigation of the sd river, some by voluntary subscriptions, others by associated companies, all of which had failed in their execution, and become abortive, certain individuals in 1806 proposed that another company and capital should be made up and an undertaking entered into for opening the navigation of the sd Rivanna river from Moore's ford opposite Charlottesville to Milton,[30] a distance of about five miles (from whence downwards navigation was already habitually practised) with the privilege of taking tolls as a reimbursement and profit for the capital to be employed: that for this purpose they petitioned the legislature who accordingly passed 'an Act incorporating a company to open and improve the navigation of the Rivanna river from Milton to Moore's ford opposite the town of Charlottesville in the county of Albemarle.' bearing date Dec. 30. 1806. authorising subscriptions to be recieved for the purpose, incorporating the subscribers by the style & title[31] of 'the Rivanna company,' giving them power to chuse five Directors 'to manage the business of the association,' and giving to the Directors powers to appoint a treasurer, to order payment of the subscriptions, 'to contract and agree with any person or persons for clearing and improving the navigation of the said river in such manner as they shall think proper' and to recieve specified tolls; in which act, and a subsequent amendatory act, and in the general principles of law resulting from them, and in no other source, are contained all the rights and powers of this company: that the company from slow progress in the subscriptions of capital, and delays of organisation, did not commence it's operations[32] until the year 1810: that Directors having been then appointed, to wit, George Divers, William D. Meriwether, Nimrod Bramham,[33] Dabney Minor and John Kelly esquires, all of them of the same county of Albemarle, and as subscribers, members and Directors of the sd Rivanna company,[34] named defendants in this bill, a meeting of the four last named of the sd Directors was had on the[35] 12th of Sep. 1810. at the sd Shadwell mills, at which they came to resolutions declaring that, if they should chuse to carry the navigation along the bed of the river, your orator must, at his own expence, erect a lock in the sd dam, and keep the same in perpetual repair, and, if they should chuse to carry the navigation thro' his canal, they proposed that he should appropriate as much money and labor to further improvements of his canal as would be equal to the erection and perpetual repairs of the locks in former case: on which resolutions, claiming right to the labors of the life of your orator, & to the fruits of his heavy and oppressive expenditures before stated, your orator begs leave to observe, that between Moore's ford and Milton, the limits permitted to the sd company, the obstructions to navigation are so inconsiderable that they would have been easily and voluntarily removed by the neighbors themselves, rather than be subject to a toll,[36] excepting only the passage of the river thro' the South West ridge of mountains, from it's entrance into them at the Secretary's ford to it's last issue from them at the foot of the Sandy falls; thro' which space of two miles and a quarter, the river exhibits a perpetual succession of rocks and rapids, all of which are compleatly gotten over by the dead sheet of water effected by your orator's pond, heading at the Secretary's ford and his canal ending 28. poles below the Sandy falls; for the use of which accomodation,[37] very great as it was, and such as the funds of the company could never have effected, your orator asked of them neither compensation nor reimbursement, but such reasonable cautions only as experience might prove necessary to guard his works against interruption or destruction; yet[38] these resolutions proposed that in addition to this accomodation,[39] your orator should give a still further sum equal to the cost and perpetual maintenance[40] of the locks which should let the boats down from his canal into the river; thus requiring the whole difficulties of the navigation to be surmounted[41] at his individual expence, while the tolls permitted to be levied to defray the expences of these works would go into the pockets of the company to reimburse monies which they had never expended on them:[42] that the authority or legality of[43] these resolutions, communicated to your orator by the Secretary of the Directors, in the copy of the same annexed to this bill as an Exhibit N° 4. being absolutely denied by your orator,[44] a conference with him was requested in a letter from their Secretary of Oct. 10. 1810.[45] at which conference the conflicting claims & opinions were discussed, a desire of friendly compromise was manifested[46] on both sides, many propositions were exchanged in that spirit, & they separated with a view to commit to writing in due form such articles as their conversation had induced them to hope might be mutually acceded to: that with this view your orator prepared the draught of an indenture, and communicated it to their Secretary, who answered the same by his letter of Nov. 10. 1810. N° 5.[47] now exhibited, and inclosing the counter draught N° 6.[48] that while your orator was under expectation that the points of difference were now so nearly approximated as to give hopes they would lead to a conclusion, which altho' not entirely satisfactory to either party,[49] might be preferred by both as a compromise for the sake of peace, he recieved from the Secretary of the Directors, a letter of January 18. 1811. covering[50] their resolutions of Jan. 8. 1811. N° 7. with a Statement N° 8. informing your orator that they had abandoned altogether[51] the plan of carrying the navigation thro' the canal of your orator, and had resolved to open[52] the bed of the river; and, still thinking that your orator would be bound to erect and maintain the lock, which would be necessary at his dam, proposed to refer that question to arbitrators learned in the law to be mutually agreed on: that your orator, without delay, in a letter to the Secretary of January 24. N° 9.[53] expressed his great satisfaction at this abandonment of their views on his Canal, and their adoption of the bed of the river, and that he would chearfully concur in referring to arbitration the decision of the question of his liability to erect and maintain the lock: that being then near his departure on a journey, he would be ready on his return to do what was further[54] requisite; and that on his return, he further offered, in a letter to the Secretary of Mar. 3. 1811. N° 10.[55] to save them[56] even the trouble of an arbitration, by removing his dam to it's foundation in such place, and of such width as the Directors should deem necessary; that thus restoring a sufficient width of[57] the bed of the river to the state of nature, in which it was before he built his dam, the residue of his dam[58] would be an aid, instead of an obstacle to navigation, by making a deeper sluice, and thus the ground of the proposed arbitration be entirely done away;[59] which several papers N°s 7. 8. 9. 10. he annexes to this bill & prays that they may be recieved as Exhibits:

That your orator thus liberated from the embarrasments which had threatened his Canal and mills, and from pretensions which tended to poison his title to his own property, determined immediately to carry into execution and at his own expence[60] what he had always intended sooner or later to do, that is to say, to widen his canal so as to enable those above who should chuse to have their grain manufactured at his mills, to bring it in boats to the mill-door, which he accordingly undertook, and, with a strong force accomplished without much delay,[61] taking down also[62] a massive work of stone which constituted his pierhead at the entrance of the Canal, with an arch & bridge over it of stone, because the gate was too narrow, and the arch too low to admit a boat loaded with grain, blowing the opening of the rock to it's necessary width, and rebuilding the pierhead in the same massive form, with an arch high enough to admit loaded vessels;[63] and thus gave to his customers from above, and to himself for what wheat he should purchase,[64] a safe navigation from the Secretary's ford to his mill: and, still to increase it's conveniences, being now become proprietor of the land adjacent to the Milton falls on the South side of the river and about three quarters of a mile below his mill, while the lands adjacent to the sd falls on the North side were the property of Thomas Mann Randolph esq. he in conjunction with the sd Thomas M. opened a practicable and safe sluice through the sd Milton falls to the sheet of water adjacent to the town, so that a safe navigation was now compleated for whatever should come to his mill, as well as what should issue from it,[65] to the town of Milton from whence the navigation downwards had been long in use.[66]

And your orator further shews that the sd act of assembly establishing the sd Rivanna company had authorised them to place their toll-house at Milton, and to exact toll from whatever should pass that toll-house; that this was[67] nearly a mile below the locks of the great falls if established at their lower end[68] at your orator's mill, and a mile and three quarters below them if established[69] at your orator's dam; that it consequently subjected to toll all the produce of the adjacent country, above & below, which should be brought in waggons to your orator's mills, or to any other landing within that space, and be water-borne from thence, all the produce of the farmers above, which, without entering their locks, should be sent to your orator's mill to be manufactured on account of the owner, and all your orator's own grain, whether raised or purchased, which, in like manner, without entering their locks, should pass along his own pond and canal, to and from his own mills: which toll might as reasonably have been levied on whatever passed along roads, or other rivers, thro' the whole state: that a bill being introduced into the House of Delegates[70] at the ensuing session of 1812–13[71] to amend the former law in other particulars, your orator wished that this flagrant injustice, of which the legislature could not have been aware, should also be amended, and he applied to the Delegates[72] of the county, and Senator of the district to have it done; that the sd Directors, on behalf of the sd company being opposed to this (as is declared in the letter of their secretary of Nov. 10. 1810. N° 5. in these words 'an exception is next made to any produce, other than of your own lands adjacent, passing by water to your mill toll free') the bill passed the lower house without this correction, and an amendment inserting it being proposed[73] from the Senate, it was suffered to lie over[74] unacted on; that in the course of the ensuing year the sd Directors taking the subject into more mature[75] consideration, agreed that the legislature should be requested to pass the sd bill as amended by the Senate, restraining their right of toll to what only should pass thro' their locks, and saving moreover all private rights; and the bill was accordingly so passed.[76]

And your orator further states that all the propositions which had been formerly exchanged between the parties as preparatory to a contract for yielding to the sd company a qualified right of using his canal, having fallen to the ground by the abandonment of that negociation, and become null and unobligatory as if never made; and a more careful reexamination, and trials of the bed of the river having convinced the Directors that to effect a passage along that was beyond the competence of the company's funds, and induced an abandonment of that measure also, & of the arbitration proposed;[77] and your orator having now moreover widened his canal[78] so as to make it compleatly navigable for loaded boats, for the benefit of his customers and himself, the Directors[79] returned to the wish of being permitted to avail the Company of it for their navigation also, for which nothing was now necessary but to[80] make the locks, and a short cut into them from your orator's canal: that your orator being sincerely disposed to accomodate the Company by any sacrifices not too injurious to the works to which he had devoted so much time, labor and expence, readily concurred with them in a new effort to devise means of effecting this: that in proceeding to details, the spot in which[81] the locks should be placed produced some difference of opinion, among the Directors themselves, as well as with your orator: that your orator was very anxious that they should be placed below his mill, where a capacious hollow formed by a spring branch offered a reservoir,[82] which being filled by the water running in waste thro' the night, and that also which was furnished by the spring,[83] might have gone far towards, and perhaps sufficed for,[84] discharging the boats of the day, and threatened[85] so little danger to the mills, that your orator offered to release them from all responsibility for any damage which might be produced by the destruction of the locks, if placed there: that a majority of the Directors, and he believes all of them, except the defendant William D. Meriwether,[86] concurred in these views, and ordered the locks to be placed there accordingly; but that the defendant William D. Meriwether, to whom the plan and[87] execution of the work was to be confided, insisted with strenuousness that they should be placed above the mill, in the narrow spit of land between the canal & river, composed of a loose sandy mould of little resistance against water; and pressed it so perseveringly, that the other Directors, yielding to his urgencies, rescinded their order: that the business between your orator and them was thenceforward[88] carried on by verbal conference only,[89] and without writing: that your orator had become sensible that time and actual experience would be necessary to develope the inconveniencies and injuries actually produced[90] by the navigation of his canal, and which should be guarded against by specific contract; and the Directors, as he supposed, were willing to avoid a definite and formal explanation of their liabilities; but that it was perfectly[91] expressed and understood that your orator was to let them have the use of the canal and surplus water only; that in times of low water, when there should not be enough for both the mills & locks, the mills were to have the preference, and to continue uninterrupted in their operations; and that for this purpose it was agreed that the bottom of the upper lock gate should be made two feet above the level of[92] the forebays of the mills; or, instead of that, that a bason should be dug below the opening to the locks, of such capacity[93] that it's contents should be sufficient to keep the mills going during the passage of boats;[94] and on this general understanding the Directors went on building their locks, and your orator acquiesced in their doing so, and gave the greater part of the timber for their construction, without any specification in writing[95] of conditions in detail, or any mention, even in conversation,[96] of the term of time they should continue, each party trusting to a reasonable conduct in the other: that the bason which was made was found in experience to suffice for the mills but a few minutes only, that the bottom of the upper lock gate, instead of being made two feet higher than that of the forebays, is in fact twenty two inches lower: that the bottom of the third or lowest chamber, which should have been below the level of the river water at it's tail, so that boats might float out or in on the dead water of that level at all times, was made considerably higher, thereby forming, at low tides, a dry shoal between the tail of the lock, and the dead water of the river, insomuch that for a boat which has descended into the 3^{d} lock, a great re-supply of water from above is necessary to form a wave sufficient to float it over the shoal into the water of the river below, thereby occasioning a great waste of water, and a much greater with the return-boats, for which the gates of all the chambers must be thrown open, & the whole current of the canal drawn thro them to furnish a stream on which the ascending boat may ride up into the lowest lock, a most unreasonable abuse certainly of the use of the water indulged to them, and at times when least to be spared:[97] that the works were so leaky as to let as much water pass thro' them habitually as would turn a pair of mill stones; and moreover there being no keeper to the locks, the boatmen often opened them without consulting[98] the miller, whose first notice would be a cessation of the motion of his mill:[99] that this state of things being considered as merely probationary, and leading to a[100] developement of the provisions which would be necessary in future and[101] formal contracts for a fixed term, it was submitted to with little complaint and the miller, in dry seasons, when applied to by the boatmen, generally stopped his mill, and gave them the benefit of the water for the passage of their boat: that the locks commenced operation in   and continued until the summer of 1816. when, having been built of green timber, they had so far gone to decay that the sides of the chambers had bulged inwardly from the pressure of the earth in which they were incased, and the uppermost particularly[102] so much as not to admit a boat: that their condition being now such as that no partial repairs could probably continue them practicable more than another year, when their entire rebuilding would become necessary and perhaps[103] of more permanent materials;[104] and as the company would by that time have had the whole benefit of their expenditures by the entire rotting and disappearance of the subject on which they had been employed so as[105] (in the absence of all valuable consideration of the part of your orator as the price of his permission) to remove all claim founded on[106] any expences which that permission had led them to incur, your orator thought it a fit occasion to bring to a pause the loose and indefinite course hitherto pursued, and to come to a[107] written and formal agreement of the specific interests, powers and obligations of each party in future:[108] that he therefore wrote the letter of Aug. 25. 1816. N° 11. requesting a meeting and conference with the Directors: that a meeting was accordingly had,[109] at which the defendants George Divers, William D. Meriwether, Dabney Minor and John Kelly attended: that your orator stated to them the inconveniencies and injuries with which the use of his canal for the purposes of navigation had been attended,[110] the entire inefficacy of the bason constructed, the want of a proper[111] difference of level between the entrance of the upper lock, and of the forebays, the irregularities of the boatmen in drawing off the water in dry seasons for their boats, and leaving the mills in inaction, the great addition to the expenditure of water, in low tides, & when least to be spared, occasioned by the error in the level of the lowest chamber, the habitual waste of water from the leakiness of the works, their present ruinous state of endangering their being broken up, and with them the spit of land separating the canal from the river, and, without expressing or entertaining an idea of refusing to continue to them the use of the canal under just regulations, he requested to know what they would propose[112] to do? that this question was answered by the def. William D. Meriwether, by asking in return what he (your orator) meant to do? would he repair the locks? would he rebuild them? would he raise and maintain his dam so high as to give at all times a sufficient volume of water for both the locks and mills? all of which interrogatories[113] being answered negatively the sd William D. Meriwether declared peremptorily that your orator was bound to erect and permanently maintain the locks, that he had granted to them the use of his canal, which implied a grant of the water also, without which it would be useless, and that when there was water sufficient for the locks only,[114] or for the mills, the locks were entitled to the preference, and the mills were to stand still. your orator could not but be astonished and confounded[115] at the high & peremptory tone and compass[116] of this assumption over his property; and altho' the other defs present did not confirm the dogmas[117] of their colleague, but acknoleged the preference of the mills in the right to water, and that the surplus alone was what they had understood to be yielded to them, yet considering that the said William D. Meriwether was to be, as he had been, their Executive agent, fearing the efficaciousness of his perseverances, and expecting an uneasy time under his hands, and the more so as he would deem himself in the exercise of rights, and your orator as recieving water by indulgence only, your orator retired from the meeting, in the persuasion that he ought no longer to trust the condition of his title to the fugitive remembrance of verbal conversations, and indefinite understandings; and much less that, on such ground and with such a prospect, he ought to enter on a new term of undefined indulgence in the use of his canal; and the Directors, as he learnt afterwards, proceeded[118] to resolutions for temporary repairs only, and such as may perhaps continue[119] the sd locks practicable another year: and he takes occasion here to do justice to the conduct and dispositions of the other directors in these transactions, and to declare that they have[120] been on every occasion moderate, candid, and friendly;[121] he charges them with no frauds, no combinations or confederacies, which the usual style of application to this honorable court[122] seems to have supposed necessary to give it jurisdiction; he is persuaded[123] that their proceedings have been the result of opinions honestly entertained, and pursued from a sense of duty to the company for which they act; and believing the assertion of no falsehood necessary to authorize this honorable court to interpose between the conflicting[124] claims of it's suitors, he charges only that these claims and proceedings of the sd Directors and company[125] are contrary to equity and good conscience, that they are injurious to your orator, and[126] properly, and only relievable in this honorable[127] court, which alone hath power to quiet the title of those whose property is menaced and clouded[128] by adverse pretensions, to be brought forwards perhaps at a future day, when[129] the death of parties and witnesses, or other circumstances, may have occurred unfavorable to right and truth, and injuring, by doubt, in the mean time, the sale or other disposition of the property.[130]

And your Orator[131] says therefore that **So it is**, may it please your honor that[132] the sd Directors, sometimes pretend[133] that the upper inhabitants have by the principles of law, both natural and civil,[134] a right of passage along all navigable waters; whereas, your orator, without appealing to strictness of law, because as willing as they are desirous that the upper inhabitants should have the benefit of an innocent passage along the river, asserts that when streams, not naturally navigable, are proposed to be made so, it is to be at the expence of those to be benefited by it, and not by the prostration of the rights of the riparian proprietors,[135] no law, natural or civil, imposing on these[136] the burthen of making navigable the watercourses in or adjacent to their lands:[137] that the portion of the Rivanna which passes thro' the base of the South West mountains neither was, nor is yet, naturally navigable, that part of it only being even now navigable which is made so by your orator's mill dam; that, owning the bed of the river, and the lands adjacent on both sides by purchase and grant from the king, the organ of that time for the exercise of this national function,[138] (with no other reservation but of certain mines, if any, and of a quitrent) your orator did what he had a lawful right to do, in laying down a dam on the bed of the river, observing at the same time all the preliminary requisitions of the law, and that no ex post facto burthen or[139] condition can be imposed on him; but that those whose interest it is to make that part of the river navigable, and especially those who are to recieve a toll for doing it,[140] must do it at their own expence of locks, sluices, or other means, doing to your orator's dam the least injury possible; and for the soundness of this doctrine he appeals to the law of Feb. 13. 1816. c. 46. entitled 'an act to prevent obstructions in the navigable watercourses within the Commonwealth,' which, altho' it takes away Common-law rights in running waters, grantable by the law, and granted by the king (tidewaters alone being unsusceptible of grant) and altho' it declares itself prospective only, yet your orator is willing that it shall act retrospectively on his case, because he thinks it's restrictions salutary for the public, and such as ought to have been provided at a much earlier date. by this act, whose object is to reduce to uniformity and sound principle a practice which had been various unsettled, and not always strict in right, as to[141] streams not naturally navigable, but capable of being made so, it is declared that whenever dams are made across such, they shall not impair the public right to the use of the water for the purpose of navigation, but that it shall be lawful for the public to insert locks in the dams, and to use the water necessary for navigation without making any compensation for it to the owner of the dam; plainly shewing that the locks are to be inserted at the expence of the public, or of those individuals, few or many, acting as if they were the public:[142] but your orator denies that any law, natural or civil, gives to one individual a right to enter another's land, to dig a canal thro' it for the purposes of navigation, or to take possession of one dug by the proprietor himself for his own purposes, and much less so to use it by making locks or other constructions of his own, as to destroy or endanger the constructions or uses for which the proprietor made it; and he adds that if instances of authorising[143] canals thro' the private freehold of a citizen can be quoted within this commonwealth they are extremely few, on occasions of the first magnitude, by authority of a law made in each special case, providing ample indemnification to the proprietor, and generally indeed presenting to him some advantage which procures his consent to this violation of his property.*[144]

[*] I kn[ow o]f b[ut] three instances, to wit the acts for [c]learing the Potomak, James river, and the Rappahanoc. the two former were too wide to have had any dams erected across them; the Rappahanoc had many: and to shew the sentiments of the legislature on the rights of the owners of dams and canals on navigable waters, I will place here an Abstract from the Act of 1811. Feb. 9. c. 74. for opening the navigation of Rappahanoc. this provides expressly that where it shall be absolutely necessary to make canals or improvements on private property, if private negociation shall fail, a jury shall be summoned, and shall describe and value the land, property and privileges requisite for the company, and the damages which they shall pay to the owner; and where it shall be necessary to affix locks to any mill dam, if private negociation with the owner fails, a jury shall be summoned and proceed to state in a report the disadvantages that the sd locks and water for their purposes will produce to the owner, the benefit he may derive from them, the value of the earth, stone and gravel which may be taken for building them, and shall fix an annual rent to be paid by the company for liberty of affixing their locks to such dam, and using such quantity of water as may be absolutely necessary for navigating: and that if any further damage shall arise to the proprietor in

But the Directors further pretend that they have acquired a right to the use of your orator's canal by contract between one of the juries and himself, alledging in express words 'that[146] the jury granted him the right to build a dam, and that the right of improving & using the canal was one consideration with the jury in granting him the right to make a dam.' but 1st[147] your orator utterly denies that he held or derived the right to make a dam from any jury, any court, or any other existing functionary: he affirms that the original purchase and grant from the crown gave him that right, that the exercise of it has been so far only laid under restraint by the law as that he was not permitted to overflow the property or annoy the health of others, or to obstruct ordinary navigation, that is to say, navigation ordinarily practised at the time; but these facts being previously & negatively ascertained by the oath of a jury, and their correctness satisfactorily reported to a court, (for which the law had made provision) the restriction was thereby ipso facto removed, and he became free to exercise his original right, in virtue of the grant from the crown and not from that of the court or jury: that the only authority given to the jury was to speak the truth as to these facts, to enquire and report if, by the dam proposed, the property of neighbors would be overflowed, or their health annoyed, if there was any ordinary existing navigation practised which would be obstructed, and by what means it might be prevented; and, when they had found these facts, they had fulfilled all they were sworn or authorised to do, they were functi officio, and if they found anything further, it was beyond the limits of their commission and authority, impertinent and nugatory; that the sd jurors were not charged or empowered to say whether a navigation could be accomplished hereafter, or by what project or means it could be accomplished; they were not made brokers or parties as well as jurors,[148] to make bargains for the ground thro' which it would pass; for the materials to be employed, or with workmen to do it, all of which were equally beyond their competency, and that if they took on themselves these offices, it did not bind the public, nor consequently the other

consequence of the works of the sd company, or if they lavishly use the water, or carelessly or wantonly impede any mill or works, the further damage is to be assessed and paid in like manner, and so toties quoties; that the water shall not be used by the company but for the purpose of navigation, and that without wilfully or negligently wasting at their locks, or any where else, more than is absolutely necessary: that in extraordinary dry seasons it shall not be lawful for the company to navigate the same at all, so as to impede in any degree, more or less, the grinding of grain.—the provisions of this law shew how materially different are the opinions of the legislature who act and feel[145] equally for us all, from the claims of the Rivanna company, who act and feel for themselves alone, as these claims are advanced in their resolutions N° 4. the letter N° 5. and the declarations of the defendant William D. Meriwether of Aug. 1816.

party, as the law admits of no unilateral contract, the obligation on one side being the consideration which constitutes obligation on the other; in fine that the condition they are alledged to have made[149] was as nugatory as any other they could have exacted,[150] however foreign to their charge, or irrelative to it's subject.

And your Orator 2dly denies that the Inquisition[151] relied on furnishes any legal testimony of the contract alledged; because the jurors were sworn to speak the truth as to particular facts only, specially stated in their oath, to wit, whether property, health, or ordinary navigation would be injured? and this contract imputed to the jury, and the consent to it,[152] not being among the facts to which they were specifically sworn, it stands as a mere voluntary declaration, not made under the obligation of an oath, never sworn to in any way, and is therefore legal proof of nothing.[153]

3dly your orator insists that had the jury been authorised to make a contract for the public, that which is imputed to them[154] would have been merely nude, and[155] void, for want of consideration; for if the enlargement of the canal was to be the consideration, then the contract has failed by non-performance on their part, and their absolutely declining to close the contract into which that stipulation might have entered;[156] and that element of the bargain withdrawn, he defies ingenuity itself to point out one cent of advantage he was ever to recieve in consideration of the great inconveniencies and injuries to which he was to be exposed: that the freedom to build a dam which was your orator's right, and no grant from the jury, was not viewed by themselves[157] as a valuable consideration to your orator, but for the interest of the navigation[158] more than for his, appears by their proposing and taking the extraordinary[159] height of 6. feet instead of 3. or 4. which was all your orator desired, needed, or used: and[160] would it be said that the mere finding the truth of facts by the jury could be a valuable consideration to your orator? would the jury say (as the Exhibit N° 5. says for them)[161] that they made that finding the condition of your orator's consent? would they, if interrogated, say that without that consent, they would have sworn that the property of the neighbors would be overflowed, their health annoyed, or that there was then a navigation ordinarily practised which would be obstructed? in other words, that they would have perjured themselves if this consent had been refused? or, would they not have found the truth, such refusal notwithstanding? and if so, how could this finding of what they could not deny or withold, be a consideration or condition as urged in the sd Exhibit?[162] or, if it could be so, and were it true that so corrupt a sale of their oath was made by the jury, or so corrupt a purchase of it by your orator, would not the turpitude of such a contract have been such as that this court would not sustain,[163] much less inforce or protect it?[164] but this corruptness of the transaction, had it been intended as a bargain, proves it not so intended; as does the character of the jury, most of them known at this day as men of truth, probity, and pure honor, incapable of a bargain of which their oath was the price, and acquiescing under the earnestness of others for this insertion solely from viewing it as a conversation, manifesting indeed the wishes of some of the jury; and general willingness of your Orator but not as an actual grant on his part, in barter for an oath on theirs; an imputation which ought not to be presumed or believed on words susceptible of a different and an innocent meaning.

Your Orator 4thly[165] insists that had such a contract been intended,[166] which he expressly denies, it would have been so unconscionable, that on that ground alone no[167] court of equity would have given it countenance or effect; for that if ever there were a case in which a[168] locus penitentiae should be indulged to the frailty of human nature, it would have been in the case of an exaction so unwarrantable, of[169] a contract so unguarded, so contrary to what a reasonable man should make, or a just one accept, and much less what the public would exact, to the oppression and ruin of a single individual for the benefit of a company; their rule of action being that benefit and burthen must go together, and not that all the burthen shall be thrown on one, and all the benefit go to others.

And your Orator 5thly insists that had a contract been intended by these loose conversations, and informal transactions, it could have been but inchoate[170] and preparatory, and was never so far matured and particularly detailed in it's specific and necessary articles,[171] as to be capable of being carried into execution, or of having the deficient articles supplied by any rules of law, or necessary inferences from the general[172] article agreed on; that it would have been as if two persons had formally agreed on the building of a house, the one for the other, without settling the articles of materials, size, form, time or price, an agreement which no court would undertake to supply or carry into execution, but would dismiss the parties to finish their[173] bargain for themselves, and not trouble a court to do it for them:[174] and had that understanding and agreement, which the jury loosely express, been meant by them as a serious assertion that they had actually made a bargain[175] 'that the sd canal should be used as an improvement in extending the navigation,' which your orator, in vindication of their character insists is a misinterpretation of their words and meaning,[176] how loose, how indefinite, imperfect and inexecutable[177] such a contract would have been, your honor has seen by the repeated and ineffectual, altho' earnest efforts made between the Directors and your orator to supply and compleat the articles so as to reduce them to a perfect, from being merely an inchoate, incipient contract; such as, for example, who should give the 2. or 3. feet additional width to the canal, then wanting,[178] to enable boats to enter and pass it? (which your orator's experience had proved would be a serious undertaking) what indemnification was to follow on[179] the suspension of the mills during that operation, and during other interruptions?[180] who, on the introduction of a greater volume of water, than was necessary for the mills, was to maintain the bank of the canal next to the river, which was low and weak thro' a considerable extent? who was to fix the spot where the locks should be located, so as not to endanger the destruction of the narrow spit of land between the canal and river, and it's being carried off entirely, should the locks be broken up by high waters? how was the burthen of repairing & tightening the dam, and of cleansing the canal, from time to time whenever necessary,[181] to be divided between the two parties sharing the benefit of the waters? which party was to have a preference, during the dry season of the year, when there would not be water enough for both the mills and the locks? and at all seasons of the year, when the increased population and produce may perhaps[182] occupy the locks thro' the whole year? what were to be the attendance and regulations at the locks to prevent contraventions of right by disorderly assemblages of watermen? and what was to be the term of these stipulations? were they to be at will? for years? or in fee simple? could these deficient articles be supplied by any rule of law, by any inference from the general stipulation alledged, or by the maxims or functions of any court? and does not the want of these essential provisions sufficiently evince that no present contract could be under contemplation, where all the articles[183] which were to compose it were omitted, and prove also the wisdom and carefulness of the law which, for the passing of property, or exchange of covenants, requires[184] apt words, and certain ceremonies, to prevent impositions, misunderstandings, and unintentional, from being construed into, intentional acts?[185] and for the conveyance of an interest in real estate particularly, requires that it shall be by deed in writing, naming both parties with their particular designations, using fit words of conveyance, expressing the duration of the interest, whether for term of years, for[186] life, or perpetual inheritance or succession, that it shall be indented, signed, sealed and delivered by the party granting, acknoleged by himself in court, or proved by witnesses sworn to the very acts of signing and delivery, and recorded within a limited time; the absence of every single one of which unequivocal evidences of intention, so familiarly known as requisites to all the parties, is unequivocal evidence of the absence of all intention to convey a real interest, which, whether it should be a tenancy in common, or whatever other estate, known or unknown to the law, would still be a realty, requiring the forms of real conveyance.[187]

6thly your orator insists that had a real contract been contemplated by the jury, on behalf of the public, it would not have devolved, either by inheritance or purchase, on this Rivanna company, who are not the public, but a mere company of private individuals, incorporated by law on the turnpike principle of furnishing capital, and making a good highway, in consideration of a toll to be levied for their reimbursement and profit: and if their prospects are in the event disappointed, if their highway accomodates too few to justify their too sanguine calculations of reimbursement and profit, then they have made a bad speculation; but should this be made good out of the lands of others which lie in their way? if their funds were originally inadequate, should they be allowed to use the property of others as a supplement? the law has only authorised them to open the bed of the river, and this too, in express words, by private and voluntary contracts; but not by impressment, or[188] seisure, without voluntary agreement: in compensation for their labor and expences, it gives them a right to a toll to be added to their inheritance, but not to take the inheritance of another, and add it to theirs; for such the channel of their navigation, and your orator's canal if made a part of it, will become by law:[189] and if the officiousness of a jury could have given a colour of claim, or a ground of action to the public,[190] the legislature has not assigned this right of action to this Rivanna company; it has not transferred to them as private prosecutors, a litigious bargain, pretended to have been made on one part, but denied on the other: on the contrary, it has scrupulously, & by express words restrained them to such contracts as themselves should make, neither binding nor benefiting them by those alledged to have been made by others. if this right to an Use in the Canal became the property of a company on it's establishment[191] by law, is it of the company of 1805? of that of 1806.? or of that which is to succeed them[192] on their failure? is the Use in that case to be sold, as their private property, for their private benefit, & liable to be suppressed at the caprice of the purchaser? what is the law regulating it's transmission? and is it for these uncertainties that your orator is to be despoiled of his property?[193]

And lastly it has been pretended on the part of the Directors that your orator 'granted to them the use of his canal, which implied a grant of the water also, without which, it has been said, it would be[194] useless' and thus gave them an exclusive use of the water; as if permission to another to enter our house implied a permission to[195] turn us out of it; a pretension self-convicted by it's own absurdity.

So that, on the whole, with respect to this pretended contract, your orator denies that it was ever made, or intended by the parties; and insists that had it been made in the form pretended, it would have been void, as without authority, without proof, without consideration, unconscionable, imperfect, absurd, and untransferred to this company.[196]

In tender consideration of which proceedings, pretensions, and claims of the sd Directors, and to the end that they and every of them may, on their corporal oath true and perfect answer make to all & singular the premisses as specifically and fully as if the same were here again repeated by way of interrogatory, and more especially that they and each of them may, in their separate and distinct answer, separately & distinctly say, each for himself, whether the Rivanna river, in it's passage thro' the base of the South West ridge of mountains, that is to say, from the Secretary's ford to the foot of the Sandy falls, or of the falls next above the mills of the Complainant is navigable along it's bed for loaded boats or batteaux? whether it does not present thro' that whole passage a continual succession of rocks & rapids, except where the same are covered by your orator's mill pond? whether such navigation was ordinarily practised, or in what degree, before the erection of the Complainant's mill-dam, and particularly at the times when the two inquests of 1795. and 1805. found that it was not? if it would be practicable were the sd mill dam away, as affirmed in the document[197] called a Statement N° 8. why was it not practised, and why did not the sd Directors persevere in their purpose of using it? that they may state what was the condition of the river, and what the amount of loading at the times when the sd document affirms that loaded boats of flour and tobacco passed down in safety? how many passed within their knolege or belief, and[198] did they pass without unlading, and did the boats return that way[199] either loaded or empty? that they may say whether, in their opinion, the expence of removing obstructions in the remaining parts of the river, within their limits, would not be very trifling in comparison with that between the Secretary's ford, & foot of the Sandy falls? whether the pond and canal[200] of your orator do not furnish a dead sheet of water, and safe, and sufficient navigation from the Secretary's ford to his mills, and are not the mills below the Sandy falls? were not the sd dam and canal made by your orator, and at his sole expence? did the Directors or their agents employ any, and what labor on the dam or canal, which could be of any advantage to the sd mills? did not they the Directors agree at one time to fix the bottom of their upper lock-gate two feet, or how much, above the level of the[201] bottom of the entrance into the forebays of the sd mills, and afterwards to make a bason of such capacity as that it's contents should supply working water to the mills while boats were passing thro' the locks? was the bottom of the said gate fixed in the level agreed on, or was a bason, adequate to the purpose agreed on, ever made? that they may declare whether, after abandoning the first negociation with the Complainant for the use of his canal, and their second purpose of using the bed of the river, they entered into any contract with him, written or verbal, for the use of his canal? what was that contract? and for what term of time? whether the Complainant granted them the water in preference to the wants of his mills?[202] that the def. William D. Meriwether may say whether he did not, at the meeting of the Directors of Aug. 1816. declare the paramount right of the locks over the mills in times of scarcity, substantially as herein before stated? and the sd defendants George Divers, Dabney Minor, and John Kelly may say whether he did not make that declaration in their presence and hearing? that the sd defendants may declare whether the Complainant ever recieved any and what compensation or consideration from them for the use of his canal? that they may state when the locks came into operation, what is their present condition, how long they suppose they will continue practicable without fundamental repairs, or entire rebuilding? and whether their funds are adequate to that rebuilding? that they may say whether if the locks should be torn away by high waters, or fall in by decay they will not be likely to extend the chasm they will leave to the canal itself, and endanger the entire destruction of much of it's bank?[203] that they may declare whether the sd Peter Minor in the bill named was not their Secretary, and authorised to attest transmit and recieve communications on their behalf? and that they may set forth the[204] names of the individuals who[205] are legal members of the sd Rivanna company, entitled to it's emoluments and liable to it's responsibilities.

And for these purposes your Orator prays that this honorable court will grant to him a writ or writs of subpoena, to be directed to the sd Rivanna company, and especially to[206] the sd George Divers, William D. Meriwether, Nimrod Bramham, Dabney Minor and John Kelly, subscribers members, and Directors of the same,[207] and to each of them commanding them to be and appear in this court on a certain day and under a certain penalty therein to be named, then and there to answer the premisses, and to abide such decree as shall be therein made; and further that it may be decreed that the claim of the sd Rivanna company, their Directors, agents and all others to hold and exercise any right of navigation, or other use in the canal of your orator, under the authority or finding of the Inquest of Aug. 10. 1805. or under any other authority whatsoever, is without foundation in law or equity: that in consideration nevertheless of the expence the sd company have incurred in building and keeping the sd locks in repair, & of the consent of this complainant, they be permitted to continue the use of the same for navigation, as far as the surplus water, not wanting for the mills of the Complainant may be competent thereto until the 1st day of July 1818. or such other day as this court shall think reasonable, from which time the sd Complainant and his heirs shall stand seised in their exclusive right to the sd Canal, and it's water, and their title to the same be for ever quieted against all claims of the sd company, their Directors, agents, or other persons whatsoever, which have arisen previous to the date of the decree, and that the sd claims shall thenceforward be perpetually enjoined. And so far as your orator's consent may be deemed necessary, he does hereby expressly[208] consent that they shall continue to use his canal on the same grounds as heretofore during the limited term which this court shall think reasonable as aforesaid; feeling every disposition, even thereafter, to yield the same accomodation, [for] the tran[spor]tation of produce, under reasonable regulations;[209] his object in the present bill of complaint being to establish his clear and undivided right in his property, that the indulgences to others in a participation of the use of it may be voluntary on his part[210] and subject to the regulations he shall find necessary to prevent injury and destruction to his mills, and that in the disposal of the same to his family hereafter he may be assured that he will be giving them lands and not lawsuits for their future subsistence: and further to manifest that he has no wish to embarras the defendants in their duties,[211] or to impair their funds, which he supposes have nothing to spare, by expences foreign to their primary object, he takes on himself to defray the legal costs which shall be incurred by them in the present suit in this honorable court: and, asking such further and other relief as to this honorable court shall seem agreeable to equity and good conscience, he will, as in duty bound, ever pray Etc

TH: JEFFERSON

MS (TxDaHCL: JDRC); in TJ's hand; undated; last page mutilated, with some missing text supplied from Dft and Tr; docketed in an unidentified hand: "Thos Jefferson vs The Rivanna Coy} Bill," and in a different hand (one word illegible): "Filed 2nd May 1817 Augt Rules 1817 ans of G. Divers filed Septr 12 1817 [...]

Defts except Divers & could depo as to him." Dft (DLC: TJ Papers, 211:37573–84); with wide margins characteristic of TJ's drafts and texts on which he invited the comments of others; undated; heavily reworked and with slips of paper with further revisions added, with only the most significant differences noted below. Tr (ViU: TJP-LBJRC); undated; with some variations and copying errors, only the most significant of which are noted below. Enclosed in TJ to Chapman Johnson, 9 Feb. and 14 Apr. 1817, TJ to George Divers, 27 Mar. 1817, and TJ to Peter Minor, 30 Mar. 1817.

The exhibits accompanying this document and numbered by TJ are as follows: (1) Letters Patent to Peter Jefferson, 10 Sept. 1755, issued during the administration of Lieutenant Governor Robert Dinwiddie and documenting payment of 15 shillings for 1,900 acres on the south side of the Rivanna River above Secretary's Ford (FC in Vi: RG 4, Land Office Patents [1751–56], 718–9). (2) 18 Sept. 1795 Inquest on Shadwell Mill (*PTJ*, 28:471–4; a newly discovered Tr with a hitherto unknown map related to TJ's 1795 Bill in Chancery on the Henderson Milldam [*PTJ*, 28:480–5] is in TxDaHCL: JDRC, entirely in TJ's hand, at head of text: "N° 2."). (3) 10 Aug. 1805 Inquest on Shadwell Mill and Dam (DLC; TxDaHCL: JDRC). (4) Extract from Minutes of a Meeting of the Directors of the Rivanna Company, 12 Sept. 1810 (printed below as document no. II). (5) Peter Minor to TJ, 10 Nov. 1810 (printed below as document no. III). (6) Agreement as Proposed by the Directors of the Rivanna Company, [ca. 10 Nov. 1810] (not found, but largely recoverable from preceding document and from TJ's Proposed Agreement with the Directors of the Rivanna Company, [ca. 31 Oct. 1810], printed above as an enclosure to TJ to Minor, 31 Oct. 1810; see also TJ to Chapman Johnson, 9 June 1819). (7) Extract from Minutes of the Directors of the Rivanna Company, 8 Jan. 1811 (printed below as document no. IV). (8) Statement of the Dispute by the Directors of the Rivanna Company, [ca. 15 Jan. 1811] (printed below as document no. VI). (9) TJ to Minor, 24 Jan. 1811 (not found; previously accounted for at TJ to Minor, 3 Mar. 1811). (10) TJ to Minor, 3 Mar. 1811 (printed above at that date). (11) TJ to Minor, 25 Aug. 1816 (printed above at that date).

DEDUCED: "brought or drawn from" (*OED*). For the SUIT IN CHANCERY on the Henderson milldam, see exhibit no. 2 above and *PTJ*, 28:480–5. For the Virginia statutes PASSED FROM THE YEAR 1764. TO 1805. INCLUSIVE as well as those of 1806, 1814, and 1816, see TJ's Notes on Virginia Statutes for Clearing the Rivanna River, 27 Dec. 1816, printed below as document no. VII. For the ACT OF 1811, see *Acts of Assembly* (1810–11 sess.), 31–42 (9 Feb. 1811).

TOTIES QUOTIES: "as occasion demands" (*OED*). After completing the duties and functions of their original commission, officials are FUNCTI OFFICIO, no longer in possession of legal authority. At the LOCUS PENITENTIAE it is not yet too late to withdraw from a contract (*Black's Law Dictionary*).

[1] Preceding six words interlined in Dft.

[2] In Dft TJ here added "for that district."

[3] Preceding five words interlined in Dft.

[4] Word interlined in Dft in place of "order."

[5] Text from "of the river" to this point interlined and added in margin of Dft in place of "thereof granted by patents from the crown, became the property of your orator."

[6] Tr: "bridge."

[7] Preceding four words interlined in Dft.

[8] Word interlined in Dft. In MS TJ here canceled "constructed."

[9] Word interlined in Dft.

[10] In Dft TJ here canceled "no lands would be."

[11] Preceding six words interlined in MS and Dft.

[12] Preceding five words interlined in Dft in place of "as a part thereof."

[13] Preceding four words interlined in Dft.

[14] Tr: "or."

[15] Word interlined in Dft in place of "Inquest."

[16] Word interlined in Dft.

[17] Preceding five words interlined in Dft.

[18] Preceding six words interlined in Dft in place of "such as, who should give the 2. or 3.f. additional width to the canal to enable boats to enter & pass it, which your orator's experience had proved would be a serious undertaking? what was to indemnify the suspension of the mills during that operation? who, on the introduction of a greater volume of water than was necessary for the mills, was to maintain the bank of the canal next to the river, which was low and weak thro' a considerable space? who was to fix the spot where the locks should be located so as not to endanger the destruction of the narrow spit of land beween the canal & river and it's being carried off entirely should the locks be broken up by high waters? how was the burthen of repairing and tightening the dam & cleansing the canal to be divided between the two parties sharing the benefit of the waters? <*what was to be the atten*> which party was to have a preference during the dry season of the year when there would not be water enough for both the mills & locks? what were to be the attendce and regulations at the locks to prevent contraventions of right by licentious assemblages of watermen? and what was to be the term of these stipulns? were they to be at will, for years or in feesimple? <*surely*> and that the settlement of articles these so difficult and so indispensable as preliminaries to a general grant."

[19] Parenthetical phrase interlined in Dft.

[20] Preceding eight words interlined in Dft in place of "something like an acquiescence if not a contract."

[21] Preceding five words interlined in Dft.

[22] Word interlined in Dft in place of "yielded."

[23] Brackets in original.

[24] In Dft TJ here canceled "in fact."

[25] Reworked in Dft from "from it however."

[26] Dft here adds "as fully sufficient for the supplies needed by his mills."

[27] Preceding eight words interlined in MS and Dft.

[28] Omitted closing quotation mark editorially supplied.

[29] Text from "sd Inquisition N° 3." through first syllable of this word added in Dft on both sides of a slip of paper sealed down and folded along top edge. Canceled text under flap not currently recoverable. Remaining portion of word to end of paragraph added in left margin.

[30] Preceding two words interlined in Dft.

[31] Preceding three words interlined in Dft in place of "name."

[32] Text from beginning of paragraph to this point added in Dft on both sides of a slip of paper sealed down and folded along top edge. Canceled text under flap not currently recoverable.

[33] MS: "Branham." Dft: "Bramham."

[34] Sentence from "as subscribers" to this point interlined in Dft.

[35] In Dft TJ here canceled "8th of Jany 1810 at Charlottesville."

[36] Preceding seven words interlined in Dft.

[37] Preceding six words interlined in Dft in place of "that in addition to this accomodation which."

[38] Word added in Dft in place of a section the final version of which reads "& canal, for due regulations of the conduct of boatmen in opening & shutting the locks and a right to revise and correct, from term to term these compacts of arrangement, as experience should develope their insufficiencies & inconveniencies."

[39] Preceding five words interlined in Dft.

[40] Preceding three words interlined in Dft.

[41] Preceding three words interlined in Dft.

[42] Text from "on which resolutions" to this point added in margin of Dft in place of twenty canceled and largely illegible lines.

[43] Preceding four words interlined in Dft.

[44] In Dft TJ here canceled "of Sep [30] 1810 a copy of which <*your*> he begs leave also to annex to this bill as a part thereof that this produced the invitation to."

[45] In Dft TJ here canceled "also now exhibited N° 5."

[46] Word interlined in Dft in place of "exercised."

[47] Preceding three words interlined in Dft.

[48] In Dft TJ here canceled "<*but it's*> the variations of which from that of your orator are explained in the same letter of Nov. 10. & his replies of Nov. the 18th & 20th [. . .]," with section beginning "& his replies" deleted in ink and the initial portion subsequently struck through in pencil.

[49] In Dft TJ here canceled "would."

[50] Preceding seven words interlined in Dft.

[51] Word interlined in Dft.

[52] Dft here adds "it thro'."

[53] Preceding two words interlined in Dft.

[54] Word interlined in Dft.

[55] Preceding three words interlined in Dft.

[56] In Dft TJ here canceled "still."

[57] Preceding four words interlined in Dft.

[58] Preceding five words interlined in Dft in place of "it."

[59] Remainder of sentence interlined in Dft.

[60] In Dft TJ here canceled "so as to give to others no claim on the ground of their contributions."

[61] Reworked in Dft from "and accomplished with a strong force."

[62] Preceding three words interlined in Dft in place of "took."

[63] Preceding nine words interlined in Dft.

[64] Preceding nine words interlined in Dft.

[65] Preceding eight words interlined in Dft.

[66] In Dft TJ here canceled "And your Orator further states that the sd Directors having more carefully re-examined the bed of the river, and tried experiments of the practicability of making a passage along it, became convinced that the undertaking was beyond the competence of their funds; and returned to the wish, if it could be obtained, of passing thro' your Orator's Canal, as the only one within the limits of their means, and now made and without any expence of theirs compleatly capable of admitting loaded boats; but all the propositions which had been formerly exchanged between the parties as preparatory to a contract having, by the abandonment of that contract fallen to the ground, become null and unobligatory, the business would be to be taken up de novo, both parties standing on ground perfectly new & clear of obligation. that in this state of things a bill was introduced on their part into the Legislature, <*which proposed*> to amend the former acts which among other things had authorised them to locate their toll house at the town of Milton, and consequently to take toll for every thing which should pass that, insomuch that."

[67] Preceding four words interlined in Dft.

[68] Preceding four words interlined in Dft.

[69] In Dft TJ here canceled "at their beginning."

[70] Word interlined in Dft in place of "Representatives."

[71] Dates interlined in Dft in place of "1811–12."

[72] Word interlined in Dft in place of "representatives."

[73] Word interlined in Dft in place of "sent down."

[74] Word interlined in Dft.

[75] Preceding two words interlined in Dft.

[76] In Dft TJ here used asterisks to key a note in the left margin reading "1814. Jan. 31." Following key in text of Dft he canceled "as will be seen by the letter of the Secretary of Nov. 15. 1813. N° 15 and your orator's answer of Nov. 18. 1813. N° 16 confirmed by the public records, which letters your orator exhibits annexed to this bill."

[77] Preceding thirteen words interlined in Dft.

[78] Preceding six words interlined in Dft in place of "and moreover having been now, without any expence to them been widened."

[79] Preceding ten words interlined in Dft in place of "they."

[80] In Dft TJ here canceled "build."

[81] In right margin of Dft adjacent to this word TJ wrote "May 1811."

[82] Word interlined in Dft in place of "bason."

[83] Preceding nine words interlined in Dft.

[84] Preceding four words interlined in Dft.

[85] Word interlined in Dft in place of "produced."

[86] Preceding twelve words interlined in Dft.

[87] Preceding two words interlined in Dft.

[88] Word interlined in Dft.

[89] In Dft TJ here canceled "nothing."

[90] Reworked in Dft from "injuries which would be produced to him."

[91] Reworked in Dft from "liabilities, it being perfectly however."

[92] In Dft TJ here canceled "that of the entrances into."

[93] Preceding three words interlined in Dft in place of "so large."

[94] Section from "and that for this purpose" to this point added in right margin of Dft, followed by "& that as a more certain caution [still?] the bottom of the upper lock gate should be made 2. feet above the level of that of the entrances into the forebays of ye mills: or, instead of it that," canceled.

[95] Preceding two words interlined in Dft.

[96] Preceding three words interlined in Dft.

[97] Text from last syllable of "insomuch" to this point added in left margin of Dft.

[98] In Dft TJ here canceled "or notifying."

[99] Preceding eight words interlined in Dft in place of "the <*stopping of*> ceasing of his stones to turn."

[100] In Dft TJ here canceled "knolege."

[101] Preceding two words interlined in Dft.

[102] Word interlined in Dft.

[103] Word interlined in Dft.

[104] In Dft TJ here canceled "might."

[105] In Dft TJ here canceled "to furnish."

[106] Preceding two words interlined in Dft in place of "from the."

[107] In Dft TJ here canceled "specific."

[108] Reworked in Dft from "obligations which each party should in future be entitled to claim and have observed."

[109] Word interlined in Dft in place of "convened."

[110] Word interlined in Dft in place of "accompanied."

[111] Word interlined in Dft.

[112] Reworked in Dft from "they proposed."

[113] Word interlined in Dft.

[114] Word interlined in Dft and deleted four words later following "mills."

[115] Reworked in Dft from "but shew astonishment."

[116] Preceding two words interlined in Dft.

[117] Word interlined in Dft in place of "assumptions."

[118] Word interlined in Dft in place of "came."

[119] Word interlined in Dft in place of "render."

[120] Section from "and altho' the other defs present" to this point interlined and added in right margin of Dft in place of "but does the other defendants present the justice to say that they acknoleged the preference of right to the water, & that the surplus water alone, over & above what was wanting for the mills was all that had ever been granted to them, and further he asks permission here to bear witness that the conduct of the other directors in these transactions has ever."

[121] Reworked in Dft from "been reasonable, moderate, fair, and friendly on every occasion."

[122] Preceding four words interlined in Dft.

[123] Preceding three words interlined in Dft in place of "but believes."

[124] Word interlined in Dft in place of "opposing."

[125] Preceding six words interlined in Dft.

[126] Preceding five words interlined in Dft.

[127] Word interlined in Dft.

[128] Word interlined in Dft in place of "<*overshadowed*> beclouded."

[129] Preceding ten words interlined in Dft in place of "and kept under suspence until."

[130] Preceding sixteen words interlined in Dft.

[131] Preceding two words interlined in Dft in place of "he."

[132] MS: "that that." Dft: "that."

[133] In Dft TJ here used asterisks to key a note in the left margin reading "Statement N° 8."

[134] Reworked in Dft from "by the law of nature."

[135] Preceding seventeen words interlined in Dft in place of "interested."

[136] Reworked in Dft from "on the riparian proprietor."

[137] Section from "your orator, without appealing to strictness of law" to this point added in Dft on a slip of paper sealed down on all four corners. Canceled text beneath is not currently recoverable.

[138] Preceding thirteen words interlined in Dft in place of "crown."

[139] Preceding two words interlined in Dft.

[140] Preceding twelve words interlined in Dft.

[141] Section from "entitled" to this point added in right margin of Dft in place of "wherein, to settle definitively by a general law the rights of the public in."

[142] In Dft TJ here canceled "and altho' this act speaks of the future only (retrospective laws being against our usage) yet being declaratory of the public right, what is it's right to-day, must have been so yesterday, and, by the maxim of 'like reason like law,' must apply to dams which had been made, as well as to those made thereafter, of which right the declaration of the legislature is evidence, altho' it does not verbally legislate on the antecedent case."

[143] Word interlined in Dft in place of "permitting."

[144] In both MS and Dft, the following author footnote is added on both sides of slips of paper sealed down along top edges and folded. Top edge of note in MS is frayed.

[145] Preceding two words interlined in Dft, here and again further on in sentence.

[146] In Dft TJ here used asterisks to key a note in the right margin reading "exhibit N° 5."

[147] Word interlined in Dft.

[148] Preceding eleven words interlined in Dft, reworked from "they were not brokers as well as jurors."

[149] Preceding five words interlined in Dft in place of "have reported."

[150] Word interlined in Dft in place of "<*pre*>assumed."

[151] Reworked in Dft from "Inquest."

[152] Text from "and the" to this point interlined in Dft, with "the" omitted.

[153] Paragraph added in left margin of Dft.

[154] Preceding four words interlined in Dft in place of "they say they have made."

[155] Preceding three words interlined in Dft.

[156] Preceding eighteen words interlined in Dft in place of "by the other party of the consideration stipulated."

[157] Preceding two words interlined in Dft.

[158] Word interlined in Dft in place of "public."

[159] Word subsequently added in Dft.

[160] Section from "that the freedom" to this point interlined and added in right margin of Dft.

[161] Parenthetical phrase interlined in Dft.

[162] Preceding six words interlined in Dft.

[163] Preceding ten words reworked in Dft from "one which this court would sustain."

[164] In Dft, remainder of paragraph added on separate scrap, originally affixed to but now separated from page. The canceled text now exposed in right margin reads "[...] [yo]ur orator acquits the jury of all preten[sion] or supposition that they were making a bargain. many of them were personally known to him, m[en] of truth, probity and pure honor, high in his estimation, and incapable of proposing a bargain in which they had no consideration to offer but the abusive use of their <*own*> oath; and that they considered themselves as making a bargain is an unjust imputation on them, and such as ought not to be voluntarily advanced, presumed or believed. 1. Harrison's Ch. pr. 8."

[165] In Dft TJ here canceled "and finally."

[166] Reworked in Dft from "entered into."

[167] Reworked in Dft from "would have been unauthoritative voluntary, imperfect, unwarrantable & unconscionable and that on those grounds no."

[168] In Dft TJ here used asterisks to key a note at foot of page reading "1. Harrison's Ch. pr. 8."

[169] Reworked in Dft from "have been on."

[170] Next to this word in right margin of Dft TJ noted "Fonblanque. 1.3.6."

[171]Preceding four words interlined in Dft in place of "component parts."

[172]Word interlined in Dft.

[173]Preceding two words interlined in Dft in place of "make a."

[174]Reworked in Dft from "and not apply to a court to make it."

[175]Text from "and agreement" to this point interlined in Dft in place of "of the jury of an actual bargain made between them and the sd Thomas."

[176]Preceding seventeen words interlined in Dft in place of "been the understanding of all instead of some of them only."

[177]Tr: "inexcusable."

[178]Preceding two words interlined in Dft.

[179]Preceding five words interlined in Dft in place of "was to indemnify."

[180]Preceding four words interlined in Dft.

[181]Preceding six words interlined in Dft.

[182]Word added in margins of Dft.

[183]Word interlined in place of "essentials" in MS and Dft.

[184]In Dft TJ here used daggers to key a note in the right margin reading "Fonblanque 1.3.1."

[185]In Dft TJ here used double daggers to key a note in the right margin reading "ib. [i.e., Fonblanque] 1.3.8."

[186]Dft: "of."

[187]In Dft text from "into, intentional acts?" to this point interlined and added in right margin and on both sides of partially sealed-down flap also in margin.

[188]In Dft TJ here canceled "laying hands."

[189]Preceding twenty-one words interlined in Dft at the bottom of a flap.

[190]Tr: "Company."

[191]Tr: "reestablishment."

[192]Preceding four words interlined in Dft in place of "shall follow."

[193]Paragraph added in Dft on both sides of a slip of paper sealed down along top edge and folded.

[194]Reworked in Dft from "without which it would have been."

[195]Word interlined in Dft in place of "that he should."

[196]Text from "a pretension" to this point added in right margin and on both sides of a partially pasted-down slip in Dft.

[197]Dft inserts "N° 8" here, rather than later in the sentence.

[198]Preceding nine words interlined in Dft.

[199]Preceding two words interlined in MS and Dft.

[200]Text from "that they may say" to this point interlined and added in margins of Dft in place of "whether the pond and canal."

[201]Preceding three words added in margin of Dft.

[202]Dft here adds "or only the surplus over & above what should be requisite for his mills?"

[203]Reworked in Dft from "the destruction of much of that."

[204]Remainder of paragraph interlined and added in right margin of Dft.

[205]In Dft TJ here canceled "having regularly subscribed since the date of the act incorporating them."

[206]Preceding seven words interlined in Dft.

[207]Preceding seven words interlined in Dft.

[208]Word interlined in Dft.

[209]Preceding three words interlined in Dft.

[210]Preceding three words interlined in MS and Dft.

[211]Preceding three words interlined in Dft.

II. Extract from Minutes of the Directors of the Rivanna Company

At a meeting of the Directors of the Rivanna company at Shadwell mills on Wednesday the 12th Sep. 1810. present Wm D. Meriwether, Nimrod Bramham, John Kelly and Dabney Minor.

Upon taking a view of mr Jefferson's mill dam, it is the unanimous opinion of the Directors in case they make choice of the bed of the river to effect the navigation contemplated that mr Jefferson must at his own expence erect a lock at the aforesaid dam, and keep the same in perpetual repair; and this opinion is founded as well on the principles of Natural law as on the verdict of the jury which was impanelled in the case of the said dam, in which the right of free navigation is expressly reserved.

It is ordered that the Secretary do forthwith acquaint mr Jefferson with the opinion above expressed, and ascertain his sentiments respecting the same.

It is further ordered by the Directors in case mr Jefferson's opinion on this subject coincides with their own and in case they finally make choice of his mill canal as the most safe and effectual course for the navigation contemplated, that the Secretary do request him to state whether he will be willing to appropriate as much money or labor in improving the navigation of the canal aforesd as will be equal to the erection of the lock, and the repairs abovementioned; which money or labor shall be fairly ascertained between the Directors & himself.

Extract from the minutes

teste P. Minor Sec^{y}

Tr (TxDaHCL: JDRC); entirely in TJ's hand; at head of text: "N° 4."

III. Peter Minor to Thomas Jefferson

Dear Sir Ridgway Nov. 10. 1810.

I submitted the Indenture I recieved from you to the Directors at a meeting which they held a few days since, when all were present. tho' none of them had attempted a similar instrument, it was generally determined that yours, in several parts, was exceptionable. I was instructed to draw up one from yours, according to their ideas of what would be right; which I now inclose together with your own, that you may observe the alterations. as they differ materially in some points,

I am instructed to state to you the reasons by which the Directors are governed.

1st you are every where omitted being mentioned as proprietor of the bed of the river; the directors think the omission or insertion of this no ways material to the instrument; they are more over unwilling to acknowledge that of which they do not feel themselves entirely convinced, or to relinquish what their successors might hereafter claim as a right. 2d your deed says 'the company shall have the use & benefit of the mill dam and pond, for the purposes of navigation, so long as for your own use you shall chuse to maintain the same, [or suffer them to remain.'] the words in brackets I have omitted. it is clear that you have a right to discontinue your works, or suffer them to go down; but it is also clear that after the company have bestowed labour, and made them competent to their uses, that you will have no right to remove the dam, or to fill up the canal. 3. an exception is next made to any produce other than of your own lands adjacent, passing by water to your mills toll-free. such produce on it's passage would recieve the benefit of all the works above, and certainly could not be exempted from toll with any degree of justice. besides the Directors do not feel themselves authorised by their powers to make such a stipulation. the same consideration will also impel them to make no distinction at the Milton falls, provided they build a lock there, or otherwise improve it so as to admit the easy passage of boats. 4. the obligations imposed on the company should extend no further than the making & maintaining the canal & the dam (in case they raise it) in a state of sufficiency for their (the company's) purposes, and that only during the continuance of their incorporation. the admission of more water into the canal will certainly benefit all your works. the company will also take care to make the canal (and the dam in case they raise it) more secure than they find it; but, because they do this, must they be liable for every fresh that may come and tear it to pieces?

It will also occur to you at once that an obligation of this sort cannot be perpetual on a company incorporated for a particular purpose, to be dissolved as soon as that purpose is effected. it must cease when the company ceases to exist. 5. upon the last point, which is certainly the most material, we are directly at issue. to pay in damages what the two mills might be worth, or in other words what they would be able to make in the course of 6. or 8. weeks, would be to surrender our subscription paper at once. the directors (and a majority of them are millers of experience) all think, your works would be greatly benefited by the additional water which they will admit into the canal; on this consideration they can think of no terms so fair and equitable as those expressed in the deed, to wit, that you shall only be indemnified for such suspensions E[t]c. as shall exceed the time of 30. days. they weigh the advantages of their works to you as a full equivalent for all stopages during that length of time. if they are rightly informed too, there exists a stipulation between your tenant & yourself providing for this very case; so that the loss cannot be great to either of you. it will also be done at a time of the year when your interests will be least affected. 'It is further understood by the jury, and agreed to on the part of the sd Thomas, that the canal shall be used as an improvement in extending the navigation from Milton upwards, if that shall be adjudged the best course for the navigation.' this is a contract between yourself & the jury who granted you the right to build a dam in 1805. there is no stipulation about indemnity for stoppages, from which it would appear that the right of improving & using sd canal, without paying for such suspensions, was one consideration with the jury in granting you the right to make a dam. this was the understanding of the jury at any rate, if not the interpretation of that part of the Inquest.   I think upon a calm consideration of the Indenture as amended, you will find it to contain such a composition of mutual interests & obligations as ought to be admitted. the Directors are anxious to come to a definitive conclusion on this subject as early as possible. I must therefore request you to signify your assent or dissent to the inclosed by December court. the matter has been maturely considered by the Directors, who think that they cannot accede to any instrument which differs materially from the one inclosed.

Your friend & hble serv[t] P. Minor

Tr (TxDaHCL: JDRC); entirely in TJ's hand; brackets in original; at head of text: "N[o] 5."; at foot of text: "M[r] Jefferson." Previously accounted for by the Editors as a missing document at TJ to James Monroe, 8 Jan. 1811.

The INDENTURE was TJ's Proposed Agreement with the Directors of the Rivanna Company, [ca. 31 Oct. 1810] (printed above at TJ to Minor, 31 Oct. 1810), enclosed herein along with a missing counterproposal.

IV. Extract from Minutes of the Directors of the Rivanna Company

At a meeting of the Directors of the Rivanna company at Charlottesville on Tuesday 8th of January 1811. present William D. Meriwether, Nimrod Branham, Dabney Minor and John Kelly.

Upon further consideration the Directors resolve to carry the navigation thro the bed of the river, and not through mr Jefferson's millrace, as was first contemplated, and they are still unanimously of opinion that mr Jefferson should build and maintain the lock which will be necessary at his dam. Ordered that the Secretary do acquaint him therewith, and, if he still dissents from the opinion of the Directors, propose to submit the decision of the question to such gentlemen of the bench or bar as may be agreed on, in order to avoid the delay, and other disagreeable consequences incident to a legal controversy. Extract from the minutes. test. P. Minor. Sec[y]

Tr (TxDaHCL: JDRC); with covering letter subjoined; entirely in TJ's hand; at head of text: "N° 7." Enclosed in the following document.

V. Peter Minor to Thomas Jefferson

Dear Sir Ridgway Jan. 18. [15] 1811.

By the above extract you will see the course which the Directors have determined finally to pursue. this may surprise you perhaps after the last conference which you held together, as they then thought the canal would afford the best course, and seemed to accede to the propositions you made. but upon further consideration of all the circumstances, the responsability which would attach to them in case they made use of your works, the delay which might occur to boats in passing the locks, particularly at low water (and probably, at those times, the entire stoppage of your mills) the limited extent of their funds, and lastly the bed of the river itself, which upon another view they consider more practicable for the purposes of navigation than they expected, they have determined to adopt the safest course, viz, to carry it through the river itself. this resolve then places them and yourself upon the same footing, as it respects a lock at your dam, as when our correspondence commenced. I am therefore instructed (in case you adhere to your original opinion respecting the erection of the lock at the dam) to propose to refer the decision of the question, upon such a statement of facts as shall be agreed on, together with the Inquests taken in the case of your dam, and the general and particular laws respecting navigation, either to three judges of any of the Superior courts or to any three eminent lawyers, as you may think proper, & for their decision to bind the parties, in the acts they are to perform.

The Directors acting as the representatives of others, do not concieve themselves at liberty to concede any point in which the rights of their constituents may be involved; and they feel assured that you will view this proposition in it's true light, as in no wise tending to produce embarrassment, but to procure a speedy decision of the question where the rights of both parties will be impartially considered.

Enclosed is a statement of the question, such as the Directors propose to be submitted to the referees, subject to your correction. the documents referred to may be procured whenever wanted; and, if you think proper, perhaps it would facilitate the decision to submit the question, with all the laws and documents connected with it, upon it's own merits, without any argument on either side.

Your friend & hble serv^t P. MINOR.

P.S. this communication has been delayed by my endeavoring to procure the law of 1794. but my enquiries for it throughout the neighborhood have been fruitless, no person having preserved a copy. the mention of it in the statement of facts is only from verbal authority. you probably have the act of 94. and can see if my statement is correct.

P.M.

Tr (TxDaHCL: JDRC); subjoined to Tr of preceding document; entirely in TJ's hand; dateline, corrected based on SJL, beneath signature; between signature and postscript: "Mr Jefferson." Recorded in SJL as a letter of 15 Jan. 1811 received 22 Jan. 1811 from Ridgway. Previously accounted for by the Editors as a missing document at TJ to Minor, 3 Mar. 1811. Enclosures: the two documents printed immediately above and below this one.

For the INQUESTS TAKEN, see exhibits nos. 2 and 3 described in annotation to first numbered document above. For the LAW OF 1794, see TJ's Notes on Virginia Statutes for Clearing the Rivanna River, 27 Dec. 1816, printed below as document no. VII.

VI. Statement of the Dispute by the Directors of the Rivanna Company

[ca. 15 Jan. 1811]

Statement.

ee sion of 4. | ee acts 305. | cts of 6.

The legislature passed an act[1] in <u>1794</u>. authorising those who would subscribe money for that purpose, to open the navigation of the Rivanna river, from the highest point capable of being made navigable to the town of Milton. under this act subscriptions to a large amount were obtained, and commissioners chosen to ascertain the highest point of navigation, which they did. this law was amended by an act[2] passed in <u>1805</u>. and subsequently by an act passed Dec. 30. 1806.[3] 'Incorporating a company to open & extend the navigation of the Rivanna river from Milton to Moore's ford opposite the town of Charlottesville.' this company, from not being completely organised, never began it's operations till 1810. but now propose to comply with all the provisions of the act. across this river Thomas Jefferson has erected a mill dam, he owning the lands on both sides of the river, both above and below the dam; in erecting which the sd Thomas complied with every legal requisite, two Inquests being taken on it, one in 1795. and one in 1805. both Inquests however contemplating and taking into view the future navigation of the river.[4] It will be necessary now to erect a lock at this dam to enable boats to pass, whereas if the dam was away no lock would be necessary, as before it's erection, several boats loaded with flour passed down in safety; and during the last winter or spring, a boat loaded with tobacco passed down to the dam, and was there obliged to unload. upon consideration then of the above facts, and of the inquests that have been taken, and of the principles of law both natural and civil, that bear upon the subject, the question to be decided is Whether the sd Thomas is bound to erect and maintain the lock at his dam, which will be necessary to enable vessels to pass?

4. see Inquests.

Tr (ViU: TJP); entirely in TJ's hand; undated; torn at upper left corner, with apparent loss of an endorsement or notation. Enclosed in preceding document.

For the acts of the LEGISLATURE, see following document. For the TWO INQUESTS, see exhibits nos. 2 and 3 described in annotation to first numbered document above.

VII. Thomas Jefferson's Notes on Virginia Statutes for Clearing the Rivanna River

1816. Dec. 27. The act of 1816. Feb. 13. c. 46. having been passed since the date of the preceding[1] letter, it may not be amiss to bestow some thoughts on the present state of the subject.

What is the line of discrimination between the waters which may be exclusively private property, and those on which the public may have some claim? by the common law of England it is that at which the running, and the tidewaters meet. the latter cannot be granted by the king; the former may; and this was the law transplanted here. to them it was not an inconvenient one; because their tide waters penetrate deep[2] into the island, while their running streams are short and small, offering little or no navigation. but here it was ill adapted to our running rivers, large, long, extending to the distant mountains, and even through them; and carrying practicable navigation to, or near, every man's door. while these rivers continue broad, nobody, I believe, has thought their exclusive property worth the original purchase money, and perpetual payment of quitrents & taxes. but where they have become narrow, individuals taking grants of lands on both sides of a river, often preferred running the chain across at their upper & lower lines to meandring it with the margin of the stream on both sides. it is under this practice and this principle that we hold, as exclusive property, the springs we drink from, the branches which water our cattle, those which irrigate our meadows, the creeks and incipient rivers working the mills which grind our corn. the advantages of retaining for the public in this country the right of navigation in such of these streams as were navigable, or capable of being made so, were so obvious & so important, that the change of the English law in this particular was among the first which it was incumbent on the legislature to have made. the first step however towards it, which seems to have been taken, was after the change in our government, and by the act of 1780. c. 2. [repeated in 1792. c. 86.] which provides that 'no grants issued for the beds of rivers & creeks,[3] in the Eastern part of the Commonwealth, which have remained ungranted[4] by the former government, and which have been used as a Common to all the good people thereof, shall be valid.' acknoleging thus the validity of those already granted. the use of these was never reached by any act until the commencement of the present year, 1816. in the mean while they had interposed occasionally to authorise the opening particular rivers; governed however by no general principle, but moulding each law to the local circumstances, interests and passions mingled in the case; so that their practices have been sometimes contradictory, sometimes unjust. when at length they proceeded to adjust the limits between private & public right in watercourses, and to settle by a general law the future claims of each, it was impossible that a wiser or juster ground could have been taken. they do not resume the beds of the streams which have been granted, but only a right of navigating them; and as it would have been difficult to define the precise volume of water which should fix the point at which each stream should be declared to be exclusively & permanently private, they have given a substantial, & perfectly practicable definition. 'wherever a watercourse is navigable, or whenever it may be made so, the right to use the water for navigation is retained to the public.' until it is made navigable, or put under the process of being made so, it is private & exclusive; but after that the public have in it the specific right of navigation. this is a line therefore, not fixed by a demarcation, but varying with the varying state of society, advancing with the advance of our population & wealth, and penetrating further & further up our private streams, as the means increase of rendering them still further & further navigable. at present then the beds of the tide-waters are public property, those of running streams, where granted, are private property as yet, but subject to a possible, springing use in the public. but no part of either of these laws of 1780. & 1816.[5] takes from the riparian proprietor any thing more than a joint use in the water. neither of them interferes with the works he has lawfully erected; neither imposes on him any ex-post facto burthen, or requires him to make locks, slopes, or canals to effect a navigation, where it did not before exist. that is left to be done by those who want it, & who are to be benefited by it; and, under the general principle of law, they are so to do it as to produce the least injury possible to those who have conflicting or joint rights. and in this spirit were formed the two laws of 1805. & 1806. which consign the effecting the navigation to a company, who purchase, at that price, the right to take a toll. neither that of 1805. which created a company, & gave a toll, nor that of 1806. which created another company, or[6] toll likewise, imposes any burthen or obligation whatever on the owner of any dam already erected, but leaves the company to make their way as they can by private contract.

On the subject of[7] these laws, to dispel the confusion in which the Statement N° 8. involves them, representing them as being all now in force, and the benefit of all vested in the Rivanna company, I will give a view of them.

1764. 'An act for clearing the great falls of James river, the river Chickahominy and the North branch of James river.' In 1763. (I was then not quite of age) learning that a canoe with a family in it had passed and repassed several times between Buckisland creek in Albemarle & the Byrd creek in Goochland, and that there were no serious obstacles below Adams's falls (now Magruder's) I went in a canoe from the Mountain falls (now Milton[8]) to Adams's, and found that that section of the river could be made navigable for loaded boats by removing loose rock only. I set on foot a subscription, and obtained £200. Doct^r Walker, our representative, got inserted in the act here cited a nomination of 11. trustees with authority to do what was necessary for effecting the navigation of this river from the mouth upwards. Roger & George Thompson then living on the river, undertook and executed the work; & on what was then done, the river was navigated habitually for[9] 40. years.

1794. c. 51. 'An act concerning the clearing of the North fork of James river.' the desire to extend the navigation from the Mountain or Milton falls upwards, produced in 1791. a new subscription; and in 1794. the act here cited, which it has not been in my power to see.

but the rough draught of the subscription paper, still in my possession, informs me that the object was to name trustees, with power to receive subscriptions, & to 'extend the navigation from the sd Mountain falls upwards as far as may be.' but the subscriptions in this case, as in the former, were voluntary. no incorporation was asked, no toll. as in the course of 10. years following it was found that sufficient funds could not be raised as a free gift, a plan was adopted of forming by subscription a company, who should undertake the work, & receive a toll for reimbursement & profit. this produced the act of

1805. Jan. 30. c. 25. 'An act to amend an act entitled an act concerning the clearing the North fork of James river.' it appointed 42. commissioners to recieve subscriptions; authorised the subscribers to chuse 5. Directors 'to manage the business of the association,' and the Directors to call for the money subscribed, 'to contract & agree with any persons for clearing & improving the navigation' from Milton upwards[10] <u>indefinitely</u>, to recieve certain tolls; and it repealed all acts within the <u>purview</u> of that, to wit,[11] all acts providing for the same objects <u>purviewed</u>[12] or provided for in this act. and as this act provided expressly for clearing the river from the Mountain or Milton falls upwards, that of 1794. providing exactly for the same thing, was hereby repealed, & the enterprise left to stand on this act alone. Money was subscribed; but when the subscribers met, they differed as to the place of beginning the work. the lower subscribers insisted on beginning at the lower end, the upper at the upper end from a fear that their subscriptions would be exhausted at the lower end, and the burthen of extending upwards would be left on their shoulders alone, the purposes of the lower subscribers being once fully answered. this schism produced an abortion of the act. the lower subscribers withdrew, formed a new company, & obtained a new and independant law, confined to the navigation of the definite section of the river from Milton to Moore's ford, a distance of about 5. miles. this was the act of

1806. Dec. 30 c. 55.[13] and in order to exclude the subscribers of the upper schism from all interference, they dropped the term of 'amending'[14] in the title of the act and entitled it as a new & substantive 'Act, incorporating a company to open and improve the navigation of the Rivanna river from Milton to Moore's ford, opposite the town of Charlottesville in the county of Albemarle.' it names 15. Commissioners only; in other respects is nearly a verbal copy of the preceding, but, further, incorporates the subscribers into a body politic, by the style & title of 'the Rivanna company,' enables them to sue and be sued, restrains them to the section from Milton to Moore's ford, and repeals all acts within the purview of that. so that the whole of the preceding act, except the names and stations of the Commissioners, being verbatim included in this, was of course repealed. consequently it is not correct in the Statement to say that the acts of 1794. & 1805. were amended[15] by that of 1806. they fell to the ground, were abandoned & extinguished by non execution, in the first place, and were moreover expressly repealed by that of 1806. the Rivanna company then have no existence as such, can claim no rights, nor authorities under any prior acts, but stand solely on that of 1806. which gave them their first existence, and on a subsequent amendatory act of

1813.14.[16] 'an act to amend the act intituled an act incorporating a company to open and improve the navigation of the Rivanna river from Milton to Moore's ford opposite the town of Charlottesville in the county of Albemarle & for other purposes.' changing the tolls restraining them to objects which pass thro' their locks,[17] and limiting the term of their continuance to Feb. 1. 1840. these two acts therefore of 1806. and 1813.14. constitute the charter, & the sole charter of the Rivanna company, notwithstanding the claims of the Statement to the benefit of the whole range of the laws which have been past for clearing this river.

It has been thought unnecessary here to notice the act of 1811. Jan. 29. c. 26.[18] incorporating another company, by the name of 'the Rivanna river[19] company' because that company was confined to the section from Milton downwards: nor, but to point out an inconsistency, another operation on the same section of the river. a sum of money[20] was borrowed from the James river company to improve that lower section, and was repaid by donative subscriptions. Capt Meriwether was one of two or three trustees[21] to employ it.[22] Magruder did not own the bed of the river,[23] and had erected a dam across it 20. or 30. years after the public were in full possession and daily use of the navigation. yet Capt Meriwether[24] did not require him to cede the use of his Canal, to raise his dam, to build a lock, or to pay a sum equivalent to that and it's perpetual maintenance; but, as a trustee,[25] gave him[26] 500.D. for which Magruder undertook to build the lock; forgetting afterwards, as a Director,[27] the homely, but moral adage that 'what was sauce for the goose should have been sauce for the gander.'[28]

MS (TxDaHCL: JDRC); subjoined to Tr of extract of TJ to Peter Minor, 30 Sept. 1810; entirely in TJ's hand; brackets in original. FC (DLC: TJ Papers, 211:37587–9); entirely in TJ's hand; undated; containing the same text in a different order; at head of text: "Notes on the several acts of assembly for clearing the Rivanna river."

The Virginia ACT OF 1816 was "An Act to prevent obstructions in the navigable water courses within the Commonwealth" (*Acts of Assembly* [1815–16 sess.], 67–9

[13 Feb. 1816]). The ACT OF 1780 was "An Act to secure to the Publick certain Lands heretofore held as a Common" (*Acts of Assembly* [1780 sess.], 6). The provisions of that statute were repeated in section 6 of "An Act for reducing into one, the several Acts concerning the Land-Office; ascertaining the Terms and manner of granting waste and unappropriated Lands; for settling the Titles and Bounds of Lands; directing the mode of Processioning, and prescribing the Duty of Surveyors" (*Acts of Assembly* [1792–93 sess.], 37–44 [17 Dec. 1792]). For the TWO LAWS OF 1805. & 1806, passed 30 Jan. 1805 and 30 Dec. 1806, respectively, see *Acts of Assembly* (1804–05 sess.), 26–8; (1805–06 sess.), 24–5.

For THE STATEMENT N° 8, see preceding document. For the statute of 1764, see *The Acts of Assembly Now in Force, in the Colony of Virginia* (Williamsburg, 1769), 455–6. The act of 1794 was passed 22 Dec. (*Acts of Assembly* [1794 sess.], 30–1). For the ROUGH DRAUGHT OF THE SUBSCRIPTION PAPER, see *PTJ*, 18:39–41. For the law of 1813.14, see *Acts of Assembly* (1813–14 sess.), 91–2 (31 Jan. 1814). For the ACT OF 1811, see *Acts of Assembly* (1810–11 sess.), 42–9 (29 Jan. 1811).

[1] Instead of preceding two words, FC reads "this."

[2] FC: "deeply."

[3] Preceding three words underscored in FC.

[4] Word underscored in FC.

[5] Preceding four words not in FC.

[6] MS: "on." FC: "or."

[7] FC begins here, with preceding four words replaced by "With respect to."

[8] FC here adds "falls."

[9] Remainder of sentence in FC reads "<*40.*> 35. years before any thing more was done to it."

[10] Word in FC in single quotes and underscored, with following word not underscored.

[11] Instead of preceding two words, FC reads "i.e."

[12] Word not underscored in FC.

[13] FC places the title of the act directly after the citation.

[14] FC: "amendment."

[15] Word underscored in FC.

[16] Reworked from "1812.13." FC: "1814. Jan. 31. c. 39."

[17] Preceding four words underscored in FC.

[18] FC here interlines "c. 75?"

[19] Word not underscored in FC.

[20] FC: "900.D."

[21] FC: "Capt W. D. Meriwether and Francis Walker dec^{d} were trustees."

[22] FC here adds "Altho'."

[23] Remainder of sentence in FC reads "and the public had been in full possession & daily use of this navigation 35. years, which the dam he was about to erect would compleatly obstruct."

[24] Instead of preceding two words, FC reads "mr Meriwether & his colleague."

[25] Preceding three words not in FC.

[26] Text in FC from this point to "build the lock" instead reads "700. of the 900 D. of the subscribers towards these objects."

[27] Instead of preceding two words, FC reads "a Director of the Rivanna river."

[28] FC concludes here with first two paragraphs of MS.

From Joseph Milligan

DEAR SIR Georgetown February 9th 1817

Yours of the 27th ult has been with me three or four days the 20 Dollars which it Contained are at your Credit for which accept my thanks

this day fortnight I sent you the third proof which has not yet been returned and it is ten days since the fourth proof was sent off and it has not returned I delayed answering two or three days in hopes that they might be with me in that time and that I might send you the 5th with my answer to yours of the 27th ult I now enclose you the prospectus as published in the National Intelligencer it is Corrected now by your original manuscript I send it for your inspection as I propose to make Six pages of the Book out of it to immediatly follow the title page there must be some neglect in the post office either at Georgetown or Milton as it never could be thus long to have a proof from you will you have the goodness to state the matter to the post master of Milton as I have done to the post master of Georgetown and if the fault is not found out may be obviate in future

I have a copy of Gillies Greece 4 vols 8vo Boards which I will have bound in a fortnight and Send you and if it is possible in that time to get his history of the world I will bind it and Send it also

the first moment I have I will state your account but it will not be until the end of the present session of Congress as it will take at least ten days to wait on them and other public Characters of Washington which I must do in person to obtain their names as Subscribers to Tracy^s Political Economy[1] already three or four have sent in their names from the House of Representatives to have them put to the list of Subscribers and as the book will be well printed and Elegantly bound at a cheap rate I think I shall get the whole Edition of one thousand Copies Subscribed for particularly as I will make the book very Scarce to nonsubscribers I am engaged night and day & Sundays in preparing the account books for the[2] Office of Discount and Deposit of the Bank of the United States which will be opened on the 17th instant in the Treasury office in Washington

With respect yours JOSEPH MILLIGAN

RC (DLC); endorsed by TJ as received 16 Feb. 1817 and so recorded in SJL. Enclosure: TJ's Title and Prospectus for Destutt de Tracy's *Treatise on Political Economy*, [ca. 6 Apr. 1816], as printed in the Washington *Daily National Intelligencer*, 7 Feb. 1817, with minor variations and the addition of Milligan's specification that the book will run to about four hundred octavo pages, and that it will be printed on fine wove paper using a new pica type, bound in gilt calf, sold for $3 per copy, and that only as many copies as are subscribed for will be printed.

[1] Manuscript: "Eonomy."
[2] Manuscript: "the the."

To Hugh Nelson

DEAR SIR Monticello Feb. 9. 17.

I have duly recieved your favor covering the letter from mr Sullivan and have addressed the answer to himself directly. if his plan of applying the steamboat to the upper navigation succeeds it will be of great advantage to us.

For political news we look to your quarter, and our neighborhood offers nothing worth communicating. we have had near a month of very hard weather, the thermometer having been one morning as low as 6.° say 26.° below ice. very little snow has fallen, that now on the ground having made up only 8.I. for the whole winter. much is apprehended for our wheat, and I never saw it look worse. corn is at 5. 6. 7.D. according to it's position, and considerable fear of want. we are all rejoicing at the near prospect of seeing once more in circulation the good old metallic money which may give us a measure of the value of our property, instead of being to be measured itself by the indefinite standard of property. I salute you with great friendship and respect. TH: JEFFERSON

PoC (MHi); on verso of a reused address cover from Horatio G. Spafford to TJ; at foot of text: "The honble Hugh Nelson"; endorsed by TJ.

From William Sampson

DEAR SIR Washington Feby 9 1817

Your very obliging and interesting letter was sent after me from New York. I cannot thank you enough for so great a favor. I hope I have not transgressed in Suffering a part of it to be published in the national intelligencer where it will appear tomorrow. It was done at the desire and upon Consultation with some that respect you most, The time pressed and the accession of force to what I may under your sanction now call the public interest called for it. I know how frank and free you bear yourself towards your Country and those who take its part and that you have little reason to mask your sentiments. I write this to deprecate your displeasure and do not pretend to trouble you with any claim of a further answer Your ease and leisure after a long life of patriotism is sacred to me and all your friends. I shall hold your silence to be assent and shall remain[1]

Yours with all deference and respect Your obged & obed^{t} Servant

WILLIAM SAMPSON

RC (MHi); endorsed by TJ as received 16 Feb. 1817 and so recorded in SJL. RC (DLC); address cover only; with PoC of TJ to Charles Willson Peale, 16 Mar. 1817, on recto; addressed: "Mr Jefferson Monticello"; franked; postmarked Washington, 10 Feb.

[1]Manuscript: "remained."

To Smith & Riddle

MESSRS SMITH AND RIDDLE Monticello Feb. 9. 17.

I have to ask the favor of you to procure for me from your correspondents in Boston the following window glass of the best quality

50. panes 12. I. square.
50. do 12. by 18. I.
10. do 24. by 18. I.

Mr Gibson my correspondent in Richmond will do me the favor to pay the amount on delivery, and presenting to him this letter. Accept the tender of my respect. TH: JEFFERSON

PoC (MHi); on verso of portion of reused address cover to TJ; endorsed by TJ.

Smith & Riddle was a Richmond mercantile firm. Its principal partners, Andrew Smith and Joseph Riddle, began business on 1 May 1815. Their stock initially included plaster of paris, window glass and tumblers from Boston, spermaceti candles, lard, refined Peruvian bark (*cinchona*), and school Bibles. Later that year the firm added Madeira and other wines to its inventory and offered to supply drafts on New York and Boston. In April 1816 it purchased some of TJ's flour through Patrick Gibson. The firm dissolved in the spring of 1819, but TJ transacted business with Smith as late as 1821 (Richmond *Enquirer*, 13 May 1815; *Richmond Enquirer*, 12 Dec. 1815; John Barnes to TJ, 2 Dec. 1816; Gibson to TJ, 10 May 1816, and enclosure; TJ to Smith & Riddle, 15 June 1819; Smith to TJ, 18 June 1819, 31 July 1821).

To John Wood

DEAR SIR Monticello Feb. 9. 17.

Your favor of the 2d is recieved, and you are welcome to the use of my sextant for the rest of your survey.

My grandson Francis Eppes is now here, learning Spanish. we expect he will be so far advanced in a couple of months as to be able to go on by himself. he will then be to go to some school, to carry him on in his Latin & Greek, in the former of which he has still much to learn, in the latter all but the grammar. I had intended to propose to his father that he should go to you, as he ultimately decides where to send him. Lynchburg would have been greatly preferred for healthiness, altho I suppose by his withdrawing from Richmond during the months of August and September, he might escape the effects of the climate. I have little doubt that mr Eppes will approve his going to you. there was no teacher in Lynchburg in the beginning of December, and whether there be one or not, I am confident you may command as many pupils there at all times as you would chuse to undertake. I am not without a hope therefore that the healthiness of the place will again invite you to it. I salute you with esteem and respect.

TH: JEFFERSON

PoC (MHi); on verso of a reused address cover from Horatio G. Spafford to TJ; at foot of text: "Mr John Wood"; endorsed by TJ.

From Francis Hall

MY DEAR SIR Charleston. Feby 10th

From the best Information I can procure here The Composition for lining Cisterns consists of $\frac{1}{5}$ German Terrace or Cement (an imported Article) mixed with $\frac{4}{5}$ of Lime. This mixture is said to be perfectly insoluble, and even to harden in water.

I regret that this trifling piece of Information is the only method I have of evincing[1] my grateful sense of your kind hospitality, and of the essential aid I received from your Servants when waggon-wrecked on your shore.

I remain, my dear Sir—

With great sincerity & Respect Your very obliged Servant

F HALL

P.S. The following Lines came accidentally in my way: I should not have troubled you with them, had I had no sounder excuse for writing

To Monticello

From Monticello's verdant Brow,
What Eye hath scann'd Th' Expanse below
Where glebe and farm, & forest-shade
Alternately in distance fade;
The red hill's crest of spiry Pines;
And Mountain Ridge, whose long blue Lines
Seem pencill'd on the cloudless Sky;
And Village glist'ning white, and nigh;
What eye hath gaz'd on Scene so fair,
In the pure light, and Mountain air,
Nor felt it was a thought of pain

Never to gaze on it again?
From Monticello's classic seat
What Pilgrim e'er bent willing feet:
Turn'd from its hospitable door,
Nor sigh'd he ne'er should pass it more?
For there doth Wisdom sit retir'd,
Whom hoary years have nigh inspir'd:
There Science holds Communion high
With the bright Wand'rers of the Sky,
or bends attentive to peruse
The Tablets of th' Historic Muse;
And there the Doves of Peace are found,
And Freedom loves to tread the mound,
And drink upon the mossy Lawn
The Gale of Eve, and breath of Dawn;
Not the mad Nymph by Gaul ador'd
Grasping the bloody Axe, and sword;
But such as Phidias had design'd;
An Image of th' immortal mind,
And sculptur'd into breathing stone
To si[t] [beside?] th' Olympian Throne—

RC (DLC: TJ Papers, 209:37278–9); partially dated; mutilated at seal; addressed: "Thomas Jefferson Esqr Monticello Virginia"; stamped; postmarked Charleston, 12 Feb.; endorsed by TJ as a letter from "Hall J." received 27 Feb. 1817 and so recorded in SJL.

Tarras (TERRACE) is a mortar or cement made from pulverized German pumice (*OED*). For the WAGGON-WRECKED departure from Monticello, see Hall's Account of a Visit to Monticello, 7–8 Jan. 1817. A MAD NYMPH appears in line 47 of William Collins's poem, "Ode to Fear" (Roger Lonsdale, ed., *The Poems of Thomas Gray, William Collins, Oliver Goldsmith* [1969], 421). PHIDIAS was an ancient Athenian famed for his sculpture of an enthroned Zeus in the god's temple at Olympia (*OCD*, 1158).

[1]Manuscript: "evining."

From Samuel L. Mitchill

SIR

New york feb^{y} 10. 1817

I forwarded to you a few days ago by the mail, a print of the characters distinguishable on the Chaldean bricks, lately brought to New york.

It did not seem likely at that time, I should trouble you so soon again. But the request of Richard C. Derby Esq. to carry a note of introduction to you, determines me to put pen to paper sooner than I expected. This gentleman informs me he intends to make a voyage to Europe, and to travel through several of its most important States. He is desirous of becoming the medium of intercourse between the Sçavans of his own Country & those of the Regions he [m]ay visit. He will feel himself honoured by [y]our commands & dispatches to your learn[e]d friends & correspondents beyond the Atl[an]tic:

So many things are reported [to] me from the North & Northwest, that I [i]nfinitely regret that the President of the US. has not imitated the example you set, of exploring the physical geography & natural history of the Land. Can you not induce him to attach to the Commission for settling boundaries with Great Britain, one or more persons who can report to him the geology, zoology, and statistics of the places they shall visit?

I have the honour of renewing Sir assurance of my respect

SAM[L] L MITCHILL

RC (DLC); edge torn; endorsed by TJ as received 27 Feb. 1817 and so recorded (with letter mistakenly dated 21 Feb.) in SJL. RC (MHi); address cover only; with PoC of TJ to Thomas Eston Randolph, 22 Mar. 1817, on verso; addressed: "The hon[ble] Thomas Jefferson Monticello (to introduce R. C. Derby of Boston Esq)." Enclosed in Richard C. Derby to TJ, 23 Feb. 1817.

The PRINT OF THE CHARACTERS DISTINGUISHABLE ON THE CHALDEAN BRICKS was *Antiquities from Asia, brought to New-York in Jan. 1817, by Capt. Henry Austin, and now at Dr. Mitchill's* (broadside in PPAmP). Drawn by C. H. Smith and engraved by Alexander Anderson for Henry Meigs, it contained two illustrations of cuneiform characters in "the actual size." The first depicted "the Inscription on a Fragment of Brick taken from the Mosque at the Tomb of Daniel the Prophet, situated in the Desert, forty miles N.W. of Basra." The second represented "the Characters distinguishable on the Bricks, nearly thirteen inches square and three inches thick, from the ruins of ancient Babylon."

SÇAVANS: an obsolete variant of "savants" (*OED*).

From William Canby

ESTEEMED FRIEND THOMAS JEFFERSON, 11th 2mo 1817.—

an Accurrence took place som time past, w[h] caused a desire to write to thee, hoping som imbecility of a mind frequently weak, need not always separate friends, to wit Reading our friend Ch[s] Thomsons Synopsis on the Evangelists, a thing New to me. & agreeable, particularly a Note appearing to Reconcile the apparently different genealogies, of the Lord Jesus, given in Matt[w] & Luke.—for th'o that, & other apparent imperfections in the letter of Scripture, have given me but little trouble, having long when serious or [levitily?] Reading them felt somthing like a spirit of Interpretation w[h] I think wil ever attend the mind seeking after an Acquaintance with the living God, yet correct Scripture is desirable—I have met but the one copy, & propos'd to the owner to send it thee, but he supposed it quite likely C. Thomson had sent it thee, & his had been mostly out on loan, if thou art desirous, & hast not perus'd it—its like it may be procured in Philad[a]

W^M^ CANBY.

RC (MHi); one word illegible; dateline at foot of text; endorsed by TJ as received 19 Feb. 1817 and so recorded in SJL. RC (DLC); address cover only; with PoC of TJ to Fitzwhylsonn & Potter, 19 Mar. 1817, on verso; addressed: "Thomas Jefferson Esquire Monticello.—Virginia"; franked; postmarked Wilmington, Del., 12 Feb. 1817.

Charles Thomson reconciled seemingly variant genealogies of JESUS in note 3 (pp. 4–7 of separately paginated notes) to *A Synopsis of the Four Evangelists: or, A Regular History of the Conception, Birth, Doctrine, Miracles, Death, Resurrection, and Ascension of Jesus Christ, in the Words of the Evangelists* (Philadelphia, 1815; Poor, *Jefferson's Library*, 9 [no. 509]).

From Madame de Staël Holstein

paris—ce 12 fevrier—1817—

je ne Saurai vous dire my dear Sir, combien une lettre de vous me cause d'émotion il me Semble que c'est vraiment d'un autre monde qu'il m'arrive une voix Si pure et qui parle de Si haut—Souvent les larmes me viennent aux yeux je ne Sais pourquoi, Seulement parce que notre pauvre france est Si loin de tout ce que vous rèpandez de lumieres autour de vous—Serons nous libres une fois dans ce pays? où vingt Scpt ans d'efforts ne nous ont amené que la tyrannie et la conquete? il y a pourtant au fonds de cette grande masse un désir de recueillir quelques fruits de ce qu'elle a souffert une idée confuse de liberté qui plane Sur toutes les tétes mais nos privilegiés Sont incorrigibles, et le mot de legitimité consacrant tout le passé on ne Sait à quoi Sert le tems dans un pays où l'on voudrait le faire passer lui méme pour un usurpateur—vous avez ici un ministre Si èclairé qu'il doit vous dire l'état du pays mieux que personne moi je passe tour à tour de l'esperance au désespoir—tantot le cours des choses me parait pour nous, tantot les hommes me paraissent lutter contre avec une telle force qu'ils se transmettent de génération en génération un amour invincible pour leurs privilèges—vous n'avez point eu de passé chez vous c'est un bien grand avantage mais peut être aussi vous Sera t'il difficile d'y introduire cette Sorte de littérature et de gout de Société dont nous jouissions jadis—en vérité cela même aussi nous passe et je crains que nous ne perdions notre esprit avec le reste—je vais publier un ouvrage que je recommande à votre intérêt il est intitulé considérations sur les faits principaux de la revolution de france c'est à la fin de l'annèe qu'il paraitra—vous y verrez votre nom avec le Sentiment qu'il m'inspire—je vous demande votre bonté pour un autre de mes ouvrages mon fils qui doit partir au printems prochain il vous peindra la france mieux que personne car il a vraiment de l'esprit et de la vivacité mais je ne Sais trop qu'en faire dans ce pays et cependant il n'en aime aucun autre vous me peignez à merveille cet asyle universel que vous accordez à tous ceux qui Sont bannis de leur patri[e] je vous l'avoue ceux que j'aime le moins ce Sont les purs bonapartistes il n'y a point là d'opinion tout est interet et rien ne peut donner l'idée du mal que ce grand egoïste a fait à la france—je vois Souvent Mr de la fayette qui reste le mème malgrè la vie—votre nom est prononcé par nous comme celui d'un des Saints de l'humanité—mr et Mad. de broglie vous présentent leurs hommages car toute ma famille Se vante de votre bienveillance pour moi—

NECKER DE STAËL

EDITORS' TRANSLATION

Paris—12 February—1817—

I could not tell you, my dear Sir, how moved I was to get your letter. I have the impression that a voice so pure, speaking from such heights, really comes to me from another world. Tears often come to my eyes, I do not know why, just because our unfortunate France is so far from all the enlightenment you spread around you. Will we ever be free in this country, where twenty-seven years of effort have brought us only tyranny and conquest? Nevertheless, at the heart of this great mass of people lies a desire to harvest a few fruits from what it has suffered, a vague idea of liberty hovering over every head. But our privileged class is incorrigible and uses the word legitimacy to anoint all the ways of the past. One does not know what value the passage of time affords in a country where one prefers to treat it as a usurper. You have here a minister so enlightened that he, better than anyone, must tell you about the state of the country. As for me, I waver between hope and despair. On some occasions things seem to move in our favor, on others it seems to me that men fight against us with such force that they transmit from generation to generation an invincible love of their privileges. You have no past in your country, which is a great advantage, but it may also make it difficult to introduce there the kind of literature and taste for society that we used to enjoy. In truth, the same happens here, and I fear that we will lose our minds with the rest. I am publishing a book that I recommend to you; it is entitled reflections on the principal events of the French Revolution. It will come out at the end of the year. In it you will see your name together with the sentiment it inspires in me. I ask for your indulgence for another one of my works: my son, who is supposed to leave next spring. He will describe France to you better than anyone, because he really has wit and vivacity; but I do not know what to do with him in this country, and yet he loves no other. You describe marvelously well the universal asylum that you grant to all those who are banned from their homeland. I confess that the ones I like the least are the pure Bonapartists; they have no beliefs; to them all is self-interest, and you can have no idea the evil this selfish man has done to France. I often see Mr. Lafayette, who remains the same despite the passage of time. We invoke your name as one of the saints of humanity. Mr. and Mrs. de Broglie send their regards because all my family takes pride in your goodwill toward me—

NECKER DE STAËL

RC (NNPM); with a number of words rewritten by TJ for clarity; edge chipped; endorsed by TJ as received 8 May 1817 and so recorded (with mistaken composition date of 2 Feb.) in SJL. Translation by Dr. Genevieve Moene. Enclosed in Richard Rush to TJ, 3 May 1817, a brief note from Washington reading "Received, today, under cover at the department of state, and forwarded with R. Rush's respectful compliments" (RC in MHi, dateline at foot of text, endorsed by TJ as a letter received 8 May 1817 from <*Robert*> Richard Rush and recorded with that date of receipt in SJL; RC in DLC, address cover only, with PoC of TJ to John Vaughan, 28 June 1817, on verso, addressed: "Mr Jefferson Monticello," franked, postmarked Washington, 4 May).

The MINISTRE SI ÈCLAIRÉ was Albert Gallatin. The concluding remarks of Madame de Staël Holstein's posthumously published OUVRAGE, *Considérations sur les principaux événemens de La Révolution Françoise*, 3 vols. (Paris, 1818; Poor, *Jefferson's Library*, 4 [no. 91]), praised TJ: "S'agit-il de l'abolition de la traite des nègres, de la liberté de la presse, de la tolérance religieuse, Jefferson pense comme La Fayette, La Fayette comme Wilberforce; et ceux qui ne sont plus comptent aussi dans la sainte ligue. . . . Tout un ordre de vertus, aussi-bien que d'idées, semble former cette chaîne d'or décrite par Homère, qui, en rattachant l'homme au ciel, l'affranchit de tous les fers de la tyrannie" ("With regard to abolition of the slave trade, freedom of the press, and religious toleration, Jefferson thinks like Lafayette, Lafayette like Wilberforce; and those no longer living are also counted as members of the holy alliance. . . . A whole array of virtues, as well as ideas, seems to form the golden chain described by Homer which, connecting man to the heavens, liberates everyone from the shackles of tyranny") (3:390–1).

From Patrick Gibson

SIR Richmond 13th Feby 1817—

I have received your favor of the 9th Inst and am sorry to find that Mr Dufief had not received the money you directed to be paid to him thro' the agency I had directed, and more particularly so, as I apprehend that another small sum, which was to have been paid to the Collector is in the same situation—Not having myself any transactions with Philada I applied, on the receipt of your letter, to Mr Fisher, and requested him to make the payment of both these sums, thro' the medium of his friend Mr Howell, who in reply to his letter (in June) stated that it should be done, and under the fullest impression that he would comply with the terms of his letter the money was paid to Mr F

I have requested this Gent[n] to write to M[r] Howell, not however doubting M[r] Dufief's correctness, but with the view of ascertaining if the small sum has been paid to the Collector With great respect

Your ob[t] Serv PATRICK GIBSON

RC (MHi); between dateline and salutation: "Thomas Jefferson Esq[re]"; endorsed by TJ as received 16 Feb. 1817 and so recorded in SJL.

John Steele was THE COLLECTOR in Philadelphia.

From Charles Yancey

D[R] SIR Richmond 13th of February 1817

we are yet in Session & I am truly tired of debating I have waited thus long before I have acted on the Contemplated turnpike from Rockfish Gap to Lewis's ferry the people of Charlottesville have directed me to fix a Deposit at Lewis's ferry for them as a place lower down would Subject them to additional expence we have talked of turnpiking to each ford but as the Road to Secretaries ford is not an established one I do not know whether the[1] assemley will do it or not. I however dispair of either this Session I am however very Critically Situated as the people of Charlottesville[2] & north & west of that Seem Anxious to fix a place of deposit at Lewis's ferry alledging that this would not prevent the road from being turned down the River which I believe to be the nearest Road & Shall Certainly State it So to the house the people or Members of the west Seem to be for the ferry. Messrs Thweat & Baker have often asked of me to postpone this affair & Said they wished to attend the Com[ee] which have been Summoned five or Six times but they never attended but once & the Com[ee] being all personally Acquainted Seem to be in favor of the ferry for a Deposit & accordingly directed a report to the house which is now before them. I had never heard of Your application to the Court to turn the Road untill the petition to establish the turn pike had been presented. the convention bill has been rejected by the Senate 12 to 9. I am respectfully Your mo ob Hble Ser[t] CHARLES YANCEY

RC (DLC); addressed: "Tho[s] Jefferson Esq[r] Monticello"; stamp canceled; franked; postmarked Richmond, 14 Feb.; endorsed by TJ as received 16 Feb. 1817 and so recorded in SJL.

The bill "Requiring the Sheriffs of the different Counties and Corporations within this Commonwealth to take the sense of the People upon the propriety of calling a Convention" was REJECTED in the Senate on 11 Feb. 1817 (*JSV* [1816–17 sess.], 55).

[1] Yancey here canceled "Court."
[2] Manuscript: "Charlottesvill."

From Philip I. Barziza

MOST HONORABLE SIR February 14th Williamsburg

Your Kind Letter was sent to me at Richmond where I was gone with my guardian Mr McCandlish, in hope of hearing a favourable decision of my cause from the General assembly and for the purpose of endeavouring to make fall the thick veil under which my affairs Lay conceald.

In the first place, Sir, I render you my most sincer and greatful thanks for the goodness which you had to recommend me to the Gentlemen your friends whose names you expressed in your graciouse Letter, and in the next I beg you would forgive me the tardiness of my answering, and to attributud it to the eagerness which I had of acquainting with my success. but alas! … all in vaine, the decision of the General assembly, the different atvises of the Counsellors, and friends, all has Left me in the same darkness in which I was when I first came in to this Country, so that I am at Lost for not Knowing what to do, nor what to think. Therefore, Sir, have the Generosity to pardon me in this critical Circumstance, if I humbly dare beg you[r] advise and opinion, upon my claimes to the Real estate of the deceased my Grandmother Mrs Paradise. I acknowledge honourable Sir, that it is to much daring on my part, but conscious of your wisdom and profound knowledge in all branches of Litterature, but specialy in the Laws of your Country, and urged by my distressed incertitude, I have sufferd myself to be mislead. However great as might be my misbehavior, I put all my trust in the benevolent and generous feeling of your heart, for hoping that you will forgive me; and that for the future I shall not be deprived, no mor than at present, to have the honor to be

Your most humble, & obt Servt PHILIP I. BARZIZA

P.S. Agreable to your[1] horders I have sent instruction to my agent in Italy to forward the books to the Counsul of the U. S. of America at Leghorne, and I hope that in a short time you will receive theme—

RC (DLC: TJ Papers, 209:37282–3); partially dated; dateline adjacent to signature; edge chipped; ellipsis in original; postscript on verso of address leaf; addressed: "To the Most Honorable Thomas Jefferson Charlotteville Monticello"; franked; postmarked Williamsburg, 15 Feb.; endorsed by TJ as received 23 Feb. 1817 and so recorded in SJL; with additional notation by TJ related to his 24 Feb. 1817 response: "Acts. Ass. 1. 207. chdr of citizens wherever born are citizens.
169. descent thro' an alien no bar
2. Herty 104. §. 4. relates to citizens naturalized, not natural."

The American consul (COUNSUL) at Leghorn was Thomas Appleton.

[1]Manuscript: "yuor."

From John H. Peyton

D[R] SIR — Staunton Feby 14th 1817

Your letter post marked the 8th of Feby did not arrive here till last evening which will account to you for the delay in my reply.—I hasten now, to comply with your request by enclosing a Spa in chy[1] vs the directors of the Rivanna company—As you appear to be anxious that this Spa Should be immediately served I have caused it to be directed to the Sheriff of Albemarle to be executed.—Such execution will be equally valid as tho' it had been served by the Marshall—Our Marshall owing to other pressing engagements could not attend to this business as soon as you wished—It will give me pleasure to serve you professionally in obtaining the object you have in view by this Suit, & to be associated with Mr Johnson is every way agreeable to me—

As you are much better acquainted with the history of your own case & the gradual encroachments which this company have made upon you than either of your counsel we should be much gratified with your notes upon this Subject either thrown into the form of a bill in equity, or otherwise—

I am with the sincerest respect
Yr obt Hble Sert — JOHN H. PEYTON

RC (MHi); endorsed by TJ as received 19 Feb. 1817 and so recorded in SJL. RC (MHi); address cover only; with PoC of TJ to Joel Yancey, 19 Mar. 1817, on verso; addressed: "Thomas Jefferson Esqr late President of the U States Monticello Albemarle"; franked; postmarked Staunton, 17 Feb. Enclosure not found.

[1] Abbreviation for "Subpoena in chancery."

From James Madison

DEAR SIR — Washington Feby 15. 1817

I recd yesterday yours covering the letter of Mr Spafford, which was forwarded to him as you suggested: His object in communicating it I collect only from its contents. He probably exhibited it as a proof of the spirit and views of the Eastern States during the late war.

As with you the weather here has of late been remarkable both for the degree & continuance of Cold, and the winter throughout for its dryness. The Earth has however had the advantage of a cover of snow during the period most needing it. The Wheat fields still have a slight protection from it. This morning is the coldest we have yet had. The Thermometer, on the N. side of the House under an open shed, was at 8 OC. 4.°[1] above 0. at this moment half after 9 OC. it stands at $6\frac{1}{2}$.° Yesterday morning about the same hour it was at 8.° and at 3 OC. between 10° & 11.°

Our information from abroad has been very scanty for a long time, and we are without any of late date. From S[t] Petersburg nothing has been rec[d] shewing the effect of M[r] Coles' communications on the Emperor. M[r] Pinkney left Naples re infecta. He had to contend with pride poverty and want of principle. M[r] Gallatin's demands of indemnity are not rec[d] with the same insensibility, but will have a very diminutive success, if any at all. The Gov[t] of Spain, with its habitual mean cunning, after drawing the negociations to Madrid, has now sent them back to Onis, with powers, without instructions. They foolishly forget that, with respect to the territorial questions at least, we are in possession of that portion of our claims, which is immediately wanted, and that delay is our ally, and even Guarantee for every thing. The British Cabinet seems as well disposed as is consistent with its jealousies, and the prejudices it has worked up in the nation ag[st] us. We are anxious to learn the result of our answer to the Dey of Algiers. It is nearly 3 months since a line was rec[d] from Chauncy or Shaler; nor has even a rumor reached us since their return to Algiers.

All the latest acc[ts] from Europe turn principally[2] on the failure of the harvests, and the prospects of scarcity. If they are not greatly exaggerated the distress must be severe in many districts, and considerable every where. When the failure in this Country comes to be known, which was not the case at the latest dates, the prospect will doubtless be more gloomy.

You will see that Cong[s] have spent their time chiefly on the Compensation law, which has finally taken the most exceptionable of all turns; and on the Claims law as it is called relating to horses & houses destroyed by the Enemy, which is still undecided in the Senate. They shrink from a struggle for reciprocity in the W.I. trade; but the H. of R. have sent to the Senate a navigation Act, reciprocating the great principle of the British Acts, which if passed by the Senate, will be felt deeply in G.B. in its example, if not in its operation.[3] Another Bill has gone to the Senate which I have not seen; and of a very extraordinary character, if it has been rightly stated to me. The object of it is, to compass by law only an authority over roads & Canals. It is said the Senate are not likely to concur in the project;[4] whether from an objection to the principle or the expediency of it, is uncertain—I shall hasten my departure from this place as much as possible; but I fear I shall be detained longer after the 4th of March, than I wish. The severe weather, unites with the winding up of my public business, in retarding the preparations during the Session of Congress, and they will from their multiplicity[5] be a little tedious after we can devote ourselves exclusively thereto. On my reach[g] home, I shall recollect your notice of the call which will afford me the pleasure of assuring you in person of my sincere & constant affection JAMES MADISON

RC (DLC: Madison Papers); endorsed by TJ as received 19 Feb. 1817 and so recorded (with mistaken composition date of 11 Feb.) in SJL. RC (DLC); address cover only; with PoC of TJ to Wilson Cary Nicholas, 19 Mar. 1817, on verso; addressed: "Thomas Jefferson Esqr near Milton Albemarle County Virginia"; franked; postmarked Washington City, 16 Feb.

To ease tensions with Russia strained by the Kosloff affair (see note to James Monroe to TJ, 22 Oct. 1816), Madison and Monroe sent Edward Coles to S[T] PETERSBURG as a special envoy in support of Levett Harris, the United States chargé d'affaires there (Monroe to Madison, 29 June 1816 [DLC: Madison Papers, Rives Collection]; Elihu Benjamin Washburne, *Sketch of Edward Coles, second governor of Illinois, and of the Slavery Struggle of 1823–4* [1882], 39–43). In addition to his duties as United States minister plenipotentiary to Russia, William PINKNEY was given the same posting for Naples after Madison suggested to the Senate the "importance and expediency of a mission to Naples, for the purpose of negotiating indemnities to our citizens for spoliations committed by the Neapolitan government" (*JEP*, 3:32, 35, 45, 46 [28 Feb., 7 Mar., 20, 23 Apr. 1816]). Madison charged Commodore Isaac Chauncey and United States consul William Shaler with renewing the peace treaty with the DEY OF ALGIERS. The treaty was signed on 22 and 23 Dec. 1816 but not ratified by the Senate until February 1822 (Miller, *Treaties*, 2:617–44).

The COMPENSATION LAW established an annual salary in place of daily pay for senators, representatives, and territorial delegates. It was passed on 19 Mar. 1816 and repealed on 6 Feb. 1817 (*U.S. Statutes at Large*, 3:257–8, 345). A CLAIMS LAW authorizing payments for various types of property lost in the War of 1812 was approved on 3 Mar. 1817 (*U.S. Statutes at Large*, 3:397–8). W.I.: West Indies. "An Act concerning the NAVIGATION of the United States" passed on 1 Mar. 1817. Its first section restricted imports into the United States from "any foreign port or place, except in vessels of the United States" or in foreign vessels belonging to the citizens or subjects of the country in which the goods originated or were first shipped for transportation. The provision did not, however, "extend to the vessels of any foreign nation which has not adopted, and which shall not adopt, a similar regulation" (*U.S. Statutes at Large*, 3:351–2).

The measure OF A VERY EXTRAORDINARY CHARACTER was the so-called Bonus Bill, which authorized payments for internal improvements with the public share of dividends paid by the Second Bank of the United States. The House of Representatives and the Senate approved it on 8 and 28 Feb., respectively, but Madison vetoed it on 3 Mar. 1817 as his presidency ended. He explained that "the permanent success of the Constitution depends on the definite partition of powers between the General and the State Governments, and that no adequate landmarks would be left by the constructive extension of the powers of Congress, as proposed in this bill" (*JHR*, 10:369; *JS*, 6:339–41; *Annals*, 14th Cong., 2d sess., 211–2).

[1] Unmatched opening parenthesis preceding this word editorially omitted.

[2] Word interlined.

[3] Preceding eight words interlined in place of "in its operation & example."

[4] Word interlined in place of "Effort."

[5] Manuscript: "muliplicity."

To James Madison

DEAR SIR Monticello Feb. 16. 17.

The bearer hereof, mr George Flower, is an English gentleman farmer, was the companion of mr Burkbeck in his journey through France, and is the person to whom the dedication of that book is addressed, he came over on behalf of his own family and that of mr Burkbeck, to chuse a settlement for them. having made the tour of the temperate latitudes of the US. he has purchased a settlement near Lynchburg. he came recommended to me from M. de la Fayette and M. de Lasteyrie, and is indeed worthy of all recommendation. he is well informed of men and things in England, without prejudice in their favor, and communicative. believing you will find satisfaction & information from his conversation, I ask permission for him to make his bow to you as he passes through Washington where he proposes to rest a day or two in his progress Northwardly to embark for England. ever affectionately & respectfully yours

TH: JEFFERSON

RC (CtY: Franklin Collection); addressed: "James Madison President of the US Washington" and "favored by Mr Flower." PoC (DLC); on verso of a reused address cover from Nicolas G. Dufief to TJ; endorsed by TJ.

Morris Birkbeck dedicated his BOOK, *Notes on a Journey through France … in July, August, and September, 1814, Describing the Habits of the People, and the Agriculture of the Country* (1st American ed., Philadelphia, 1815; Poor, *Jefferson's Library*, 7 [no. 324]), to George Flower, his "agreeable and intelligent fellow-traveller," offering him "this little volume as the result of our joint observations."

To John Barnes

DEAR SIR M[o]n[ticell]o Feb. 17. 17.

I recieved last night your fav[or] of the 7th and in it the following certificates of stock in the name of Genl Kosciuzko, to wit,

	D C		
US. Certificate N° 90. for	11,363. 63	six per cents	of loan of May 2. 1814.
N° 37. for	1,136. 36	supplemental d°	of d°

Bank of Columbia certificate N° 1314. for 46 shares in that bank @ 100. D Jan. 10. 1817.

As you think a special power will be necessary for you to recieve the interest of the US. stock, I will ask the favor of you to send me the proper instrument to enable you to recieve it, which I will sign. I give you this trouble, because the peculiar forms of the treasury are unknown to me. I recieved in due time your account with Gen[l] Kosciuzko to Nov. last; balance in your favor 812.D. and omitted to acknolege it, because I am little familiar with these things, and have so unbounded confidence in your exactness & integrity as to be entirely satisfied all is right. I salute you with affectionate esteem & respect. TH: JEFFERSON

PoC (DLC); on verso of reused address cover of John Wood to TJ, 2 Feb. 1817; two words faint; at foot of text: "M[r] Barnes"; endorsed by TJ.

From Peter S. Du Ponceau

DEAR SIR Philad[a] 17th Feb[y] 1817

I have received the letter which you have done me the honor to write to me on the 26th ult[o]. It would have done great pleasure to the Historical Committee to have contributed to the restoration of the interesting MS. of which your letter gives an account; but the one in their possession, and which, by their order, I have the honor to enclose, is entirely different from that which you mention. There are in it no feigned names, but, on the contrary, those of Fitzwilliam, Mayo, Moseley & Little are given at full length. I am not Sufficiently acquainted with the "history of the line," to judge of the relation which the two MSS. bear to each other, or to Say whether both are the work of the Same hand. I find in our MS. p. 32. that an ineffectual attempt had been made before to Survey the boundary line between the two provinces. But as it speaks of "the present Commissioners," it would seem as if the first Commission had been trusted to other persons, & would lead us to believe that both MSS. relate to the Same operation—Ours also does not appear to have been written at the time, but to have been composed at leisure from notes several Years afterwards. For you will find, page 166, that it speaks of a thunder storm which happened in 1736; & page 157, of the trade of the people of the then infant colony of Georgia, with the Indians, which began to be pretty considerable about the Year 1739. These Circumstances made M[r] Correa believe that this was not the Journal of the Commissioners appointed in the Year 1728 (I mean of one of the Commissioners) & that it related to a Subsequent operation. I see no reason, as yet to join with him in this opinion, but the sentiments of M[r] Correa are entitled to so much respect, that I have thought it my duty to Submit this to you.

The Historical Committee request that you will be So good as to peruse the Enclosed MS. & compare it with the one in your hands, & to assure you that they will concur with you in any measure that you may Suggest to make either or both a benefit to the literature of our Country. When you have done with it, they will be obliged to you for returning it to them. Their intention, unless you Should Suggest Something better, is to publish it in their Historical Collections. You will find a number of passages Struck out with a pencil, & others attempted to be amended in the same manner. This is presumed to have been done by Mr Denny, in whose hands the MS. once was. A few lively passages, perhaps, will want to be a little softened, before the work goes to the press.

The pages wanting in this MS. are 1 to 24—and 124. 125. 126. 127. 128. 129. 139 & 140—The appendix also is not complete.

You will be pleased to hear, that our Committee have particularly turned their attention to the languages of our Indian nations, & that many Curious & interesting facts have been the result of their enquiries—For instance, it has been observed, that no nations elsewhere can combine so many ideas together in one word, by means of a most admirable combination of Grammatical forms, by which they can unite almost all the parts of Speech into one, which is the verb, & with them may be Very properly denominated Verbum κατα ἐξοχὴν. For it is truly the "word of words," What would not Anacreon or Tibullus have given to have been able in their amatory poems to Say in one Single word "O thou who makest me happy!" This is done in the language of the Delawares by means of the Vocative inflexion of the participle of a compound verb. The word is Wulamalessohalian! from Wulamalsin to be happy, from which are formed a variety of verbs, including by means of slight alterations & inflexions, the ideas of the pronouns both governing & governed, & all the other accessory ideas which are found in the participle above mentioned, which is regularly declined thro' all its Cases as the verbs are Conjugated thro' their moods & Tenses—Those multiform, compound parts of Speech, in which there are fewer irregularities than in any other language, are peculiar to the Indian nations, are found with few variations in all their idioms thro' the Continent from North to South, & disappear in the adjacent Countries of Asia & Europe. I am preparing a Communication to the Society on this interesting Subject; the study of languages has been too long confined to mere "word hunting" for the sake of finding affinities of Sound. Perhaps a comparison of the grammatical forms of the different nations may produce more Successful Results. The Committee, & myself in particular, would be much obliged to you for any hints that might throw further lights upon this Subject

I have the honor to be with the greatest respect

Sir Your most obedient humble servant

PETER S, DU PONCEAU

RC (DLC); at head of text: "Thomas Jefferson, Esq[r]"; endorsed by TJ (with mistaken 1816 year of composition) as received 23 Feb. 1817 and so recorded (with correct composition date) in SJL. FC (PPAmP: APS Historical and Literary Committee Letterbook). Enclosure: William Byrd, "The History of the Dividing Line" (MS in PPAmP; printed in Louis B. Wright, ed., *The Prose Works of William Byrd of Westover: Narratives of a Colonial Virginian* [1966], 155–336).

VERBUM κατα ἐξοχὴν: "the word par excellence."

To Fernagus De Gelone

SIR Montice[l]lo Feb. 17. 17.

I have recieved a copy of a catalogue of books which you announce for sale, and ask the favor of you to send me a little note of information as to the following.

Column 1[st] Papers found in Robespierre's house. in what language size[1] & price?

3[d] Peyrard's Archimedes. in what language? what size, & price?

5th Correspondence of Cortez with Charles V. what language, size & price?

6th Hippocrates's works. in what language, size & price? and are they all his works, or only particular parts?

8th Mounier on the causes which have kept the French from being free. language? size & price?

on receiving this information, I can decide which of them I will ask for, remit the price, and direct how they shall be sent. Accept my respectful salutations. TH: JEFFERSON

PoC (MHi); on verso of reused address cover to TJ; dateline faint; at foot of text: "M[r] J. L. Fernagus de Gelone New York. 113. Pearl street. Hanover square"; endorsed by TJ.

Jean Louis Fernagus De Gelone (b. ca. 1783), a French royalist, was exiled in 1802 during Napoleon's consulate. After being imprisoned in Saint Domingue, he was sent with former officers of the revolutionary leader Toussaint L'Overture to a labor camp in Guiana, from which he escaped in 1804 following a severe illness. Fernagus De Gelone later settled in Philadelphia as a bookseller specializing in foreign works. Late in 1816 he had opened a shop in New York City, and in addition by 1819 he had stores in Washington, D.C., and Paris. He also published a travel guide to the United States, *Manuel-Guide des Voyageurs aux États-Unis* (Paris, 1818).

Beginning in 1820 Fernagus De Gelone added to his retail establishment a coeducational boarding and day school in New York City. The curriculum included languages, natural philosophy, surveying, fencing, music, and carpentry, as well as education for deaf and mute students. After encountering financial difficulties in 1821, Fernagus De Gelone moved by early the following year to Port au Prince, Haiti, where he found government employment (Fernagus De Gelone, *Relation de la déportation et de l'exil a Cayenne d'un Jeune Français, sous le Consulat de Buonaparte, en 1802. En Sept Lettres* [Paris, 1816]; New York *Columbian*, 7 Dec. 1816; Fernagus De Gelone to TJ, 15 Dec. 1818, 5 Oct. 1820, 10 Jan. 1822; Washington *Daily National Intelligencer*, 25 Feb. 1819; New York *Commercial Advertiser*, 17 Apr., 23 May, 16 June 1820).

[1] Word interlined.

To Patrick Gibson

Dear Sir Mon[t]icel[lo] Feb. 17. 17.

Your favor of the 13th came to hand last night, and confirms what I had not doubted that the error stated by mr Dufief had happened at Philadelphia. if the same has taken place with mr Steele the collector I shall be happy that it be corrected; because I feel much obligation to the Collectors for their kindness respecting these parcels. I should not have troubled you with this but that I feel how much I owe to you an apology for the repeated troubles you have had with these numerous little consignments, which have been so uselessly multiplied by my correspondents mr Cathalan at Marseilles and Appleton at Leghorn. instead of keeping the articles together & shipping all together, they have sent them off one by one as they collected them, and by any vessel which happened to be in their place bound to any port of the US. this has produced transactions with the Custom houses of Boston, New York, Philadelphia, Baltimore, Norfolk [an]d Charleston, and multiplied your trouble still more than mine. I have now some parcels at Charleston, for which I fear a conveyance will not be readily found. as I shall annually recieve things from mr Cathalan, I shall desire him to send them all together so as to give us but a single transaction with one collector in the year, and to guard you from being so much harrassed again. I salute you with affection and respect

Th: Jefferson

PoC (MHi); on verso of a reused address cover from Craven Peyton to TJ; dateline faint; mutilated at seal; at foot of text: "Mr Gibson"; endorsed by TJ as a letter of 16 Feb. 1817 and so recorded in SJL.

From George Washington Jeffreys

Dear Sir Red House N° C Feby 17th 1817.

A Society has been established at this place for the promotion of Agriculture and rural affairs

A Book entitled the 'Arator' by Col° Taylor of Caroline Va has awakened us to a sense of the importance of the subject and has shown us how little we knew of a pursuit on[1] which not only our own individual comfort depends, but also the prosperity and independence of our country. A few spirited gentlemen in our neighbourhood have organized themselves into a Society for the laudable purpose of awakening the attention of the people[2] of our county to the important subject of husbandry and of convincing them of the necessity of making some improvements therein—

We have resolved to establish a Library to consist of Books treating exclusively on the subject of Agriculture & rural affairs—Will you be so good as to lend us your assistance in making out a catalouge of Books—of such books as will constitute a valuable agricultural library not only for our own instruction and improvement, but also for that of our rising generation—In addressing you this letter I am aware of the oppressive correspondence which you have to attend to,—I will not insist upon an answer—but should you find leisure, I can assure you that the society would feel grateful and happy in receiving your aid & information in our laudable efforts of advancing the[3] interest of agriculture—To whom can we apply more properly than to yourself—who ardently wishes for the prosperity, happiness and independence of your country and who is qualified to give us the requested information, not only from an extensive knowledge of the subject, but from the practical attention which you have given it.

In your communication, to me, a few remarks on horizontal ploughing would be received with much pleasure—This is a subject in which we are much interested as our lands are very hilly and broken—Can hilly land be ploughed horizontally in such a manner as to retain the water and prevent it from washing the soil to the bottoms?—We have understood that you have turned your attention to the practice of horizontal ploughing—We should therefore be happy to avail ourselves of such remarks and such information as you may give us on the subject—Such a catalouge of Books as you may set down for us we will endeavour to procure—

A letter addressed to me at the post office Red House N° C. will be received and duly laid before the Society—

Yours very Respectfully George W. Jeffreys Secy
to Red House Agrl Society—

RC (DLC); addressed: "Thomas Jefferson Esqr Milton Albemarle cty Va" by "mail"; franked; endorsed by TJ as received 1 Mar. 1817 and so recorded in SJL.

George Washington Jeffreys (ca. 1793–1848), agriculturist, writer, and public official, served as a postmaster in Caswell County, North Carolina, from 1811 to at least 1820, and he was a clerk and later secretary to the trustees for Hyco Academy in that county. He studied at the University of North Carolina in 1813 and served as a trustee of that institution from 1842 until his death. Writing under the pseudonym "Agricola," Jeffreys published *A Series of Essays on Agriculture & Rural Affairs* (Raleigh, 1819), in which he promoted experimentation and innovation in agriculture. He was a resident of Person County when he sat on the North Carolina Council of State, 1824–34. Jeffreys was a corresponding secretary for the American Bible Society from at least 1824 to 1826. Under the pen name "An Advocate of the Blood Horse," he authored a series of articles on the breeding of fine horses, first published in the *Petersburg Intelligencer* in 1826 and later reprinted elsewhere (*DNCB*, 3:276; *Table of Post Offices in the United States* [Washington, 1811], 50; Robert J. Stets, *Postmasters & Postoffices of the United States, 1782–1811* [1994], 200; John L. Cheney Jr., ed., *North Carolina Government, 1585–1979* [1981], 173–5; American Bible Society, *Report* 8 [1824]: 186; 9 [1825]: 124; 10 [1826]: 128; Charles L. Coon, *North Carolina Schools and Academies 1790–1840* [1915], 24, 26, 809; Daniel Lindsey Grant, *Alumni History of the University of North Carolina* [2d ed., 1924], 317, 943; Alexander Mackay-Smith, *The Colonial Quarter Race Horse* [1983], 97; *Weekly Raleigh Register, and North Carolina Gazette*, 28 June 1848).

On 15 July 1817 Jeffreys requested similar ASSISTANCE IN MAKING OUT A CATALOUGE OF BOOKS from John Adams, describing agriculture in the South as in "the lowest state of degradation" and asserting that "Massachusetts, with the rest of the northern states, is far before us in agricultural improvements, and would our farmers attend, she could give us volumes of useful information on this subject—I am happy to observe that the people about here begin to be convinced of their imperfect and deteriorating state of agriculture and to evince a disposition to make improvements" (RC in MHi: Adams Papers).

[1]Word interlined in place of an uncanceled "in."

[2]Manuscript: "poeple."

[3]Jeffreys here canceled "cause."

To Mr. Logan (of Staunton)

DEAR SIR Monticello Feb. 17. 17.

I have transcribed and send you according to promise a copy of my Equation of time adapted to the present state of the heavens, and which will not be sensibly variant for a great many years to come. this will enable you to ascertain the defaced figures in the round one I gave you, suited to the form & size of a watch paper. when engraved, a half dozen copies for the use of our family will oblige me. accept my best wishes for your health and success and assurances of my esteem & respect.

TH: JEFFERSON

PoC (CSmH: JF-BA); on verso of a reused address cover from John Wayles Eppes to TJ; at foot of text: "Mr Logan"; endorsed by TJ as a letter to Logan at "Staunton" and so recorded in SJL.

For an earlier version of TJ's EQUATION OF TIME, see his 15 Nov. 1811 letter to Melatiah Nash.

From Charles K. Mallory

SIR Norfolk Feby 17th 1817

In compliance with the request contained in your letter of the 1st of Septr last I do myself the pleasure to inform you that there have arrived here, via Charleston, consigned to my care, two cases of Tuscan wine sent to you by our Consul at Leghorn in the Brig Saucy Jack, which, according to your directions, I shall have forwarded by the first good opportunity to Messrs Gibson & Jefferson of Richmond. Assuring you that I shall at all times take pleasure in attending to your commands, I have the honor to be with very high respect & regard

Your ob^{t} serv^{t} CHA^{S} K. MALLORY

RC (MHi); endorsed by TJ as received 23 Feb. 1817 and so recorded in SJL. RC (DLC); address cover only; with PoC of TJ to Thomas Appleton, 16 Mar. 1817, on verso; addressed: "The Honb^{le} Thomas Jefferson Monticello"; franked; postmarked Norfolk, 18 Feb.

To Simeon Theus

SIR M[ont]ic[ello] [in] Virginia Feb. 17. 1[7].

By a letter of Oct. 20. from mr Appleton our Consul at Leghorn I am informed that he had shipped on board the brig Saucy-Jack, Capt Humphreys for Charleston S.C. 2. cases containing together 87. bottles of Florence wine, consigned to the[1] Collector of Charleston. being in the practice of importing my wines & some other articles annually from Marseiles & Leghorn, at which places vessels to any particular port of the US. cannot always be found, I have been obliged to take the liberty of desiring mr Ca[tha]llan & mr Appleton our Consuls at those places, to put them on board any vessel bound to any port between Cape Cod & Cape Henry; and (not having correspondents at these places) to consign them to the Collector of the port, on whose kindness I would throw myself to recieve & forward them. it is from necessity I suppose that mr Appleton has sent the above cases to your port, and rendered[2] it necessary for me, with this apology, to ask the favor of your information whether they are arrived, and what is the amount of duties & charges which shall be immediately remitted you thro' Messrs Gibson & Jefferson my correspondents in Richmond by a bill, or by myself in bills of the US. bank if they shall have reached us by that time: on reciept of which I will request you to forward them by any vessel bound to Norfolk or Richmond to my sd correspondents in Richmond who will pay freight and other charges from your port. excuse, if you please, this trouble which, being extraofficial,

I had no right, nor indeed intention, to have brought on you, and accept the assurance of my great respect. Th: Jefferson

PoC (MHi); on verso of reused address cover of otherwise unlocated letter from Archibald Thweatt to TJ, 2 Feb. 1817 (addressed: "Thomas Jefferson esq: Monticello Albemarle county V[a]"; franked; postmarked Richmond, 4 Feb.; recorded in SJL as received 6 Feb. 1817 from Richmond); portions faint, with date of composition confirmed by endorsement and SJL; at foot of text: "The Collector of Charleston"; endorsed by TJ as a letter to "Theus Simon" and so recorded in SJL.

Simeon Theus (d. 1821), merchant and public official, served in the Continental army, 1775–83, rising from second lieutenant to captain and enduring British captivity after the fall of Charleston in 1780. He was awarded the brevet rank of major in 1783 and later joined the Society of the Cincinnati. Following the war Theus was a partner in a Charleston factorage firm. He served as a South Carolina commissioner for settling the state's Revolutionary War claims against the United States, and he was also a state treasurer and cashier of the state bank. In 1800 President John Adams nominated Theus as commissioner of valuations for the direct tax in South Carolina. He accepted the position but resigned less than a year later. In 1802 Theus declined TJ's nomination as commissioner of bankruptcy for South Carolina, but he accepted appointment as collector at Charleston in 1806 and held that post until 1819. As collector, Theus helped enforce the Embargo of 1807 and was sued in this capacity in the prominent case of *Gilchrist v. Collector of Charleston.* A circuit court decision in the plaintiff's favor the following year circumscribed the power of TJ's administration to detain ships until stronger legislation was obtained (Heitman, *Continental Army*, 538; Charleston *South-Carolina Gazette, and Public Advertiser*, 11/15 Dec. 1784; Charleston *City-Gazette & Daily Advertiser*, 22 May, 24 Dec. 1794, 30 Aug. 1800, 24 Dec. 1802; Harold C. Syrett and others, eds., *The Papers of Alexander Hamilton* [1961–87], 14:295, 16:42; *PTJ*, 34:136n, 37:152–3, 512–3, 699, 711; *JEP*, 1:337, 338, 350, 2:16, 17, 3:170 [5, 7 Feb., 28 Apr. 1800, 20, 21 Jan. 1806, 26 Jan. 1819]; TJ to Theus, 10 Sept. 1808 [DLC]; *ANB*, 12:142 [William Johnson]; *The Federal Cases: Comprising Cases Argued and Determined in the Circuit and District Courts of the United States* [1894–97], 10:355–66; Charleston *City Gazette and Commercial Daily Advertiser*, 7 July 1818, 11 Apr. 1821; gravestone inscription in Circular Congregational Church Burying Ground, Charleston).

[1] Reworked from "you."

[2] Edge chipped, with ending of this word rewritten by TJ.

From Jerman Baker

D[r] Sir, House of Delegates 19 Feb[y] 1817

I take pleasure in communicating to you the fate of the Bill incorporating a Company to Turnpike the Road from Rock Fish Gap to Moore's Ford, A motion was made by M[r] Thweatt this morning to postpone it indefinitely which succeeded, a similar motion was made by me some days since but was lost by a small majority

Be pleased Sir, to present my affectionate regards to M[rs] R— & family—& be assured of the sincere affection & profound respect of

Y[rs] Jerman Baker

RC (MHi); endorsed by TJ as received 23 Feb. 1817 and so recorded in SJL. RC (MHi); address cover only; with PoC of TJ to Bernard Peyton, 16 Mar. 1817, on verso; addressed: "Thomas Jefferson Esquire Monticello"; franked; postmarked Richmond, 20 Feb.

From Joseph C. Cabell

DEAR SIR, Richmond 19th Feb: 1817.

The Bill respecting the Turnpike from Rockfish Gap was this day postponed indefinitely in the House of Delegates. Col: yancey, as I am informed by Mr Thweat, did every thing in his power to push the Bill thro' the House, after having consented to lay it on the table for the Balance of the session.

The Bill for taking the sense of the people as to the expediency of calling a convention was rejected in the Senate. The Bill for equalizing the Senatorial districts & the Land tax has since passed. I was an advocate for this last bill, and used the first Bill reported by yourself Mr Pendleton & Mr Wythe in the year 1779. to prove that we had the constitutional power to alter the classes.

The University Bill is now under consideration in the Senate. I cannot predict its fate. It comes to us, however, at a most inauspicious period, when the members are impatient to break up & go home.

I am, Dr sir, very truly yours JOSEPH C. CABELL

RC (ViU: TJP-PC); endorsed by TJ as received 23 Feb. 1817 and so recorded in SJL. RC (DLC); address cover only; with PoC of TJ to Francis Adrian Van der Kemp, 16 Mar. 1817, on verso; addressed: "Thomas Jefferson esq. Monticello"; franked; postmarked Richmond, 21 Feb.

Cabell was an ADVOCATE of "An Act for arranging the Counties into Districts for the election of Senators, and for equalizing the Land Tax," which passed into law on 18 Feb. 1817 (*Acts of Assembly* [1816–17 sess.], 7–15). For the FIRST BILL REPORTED by TJ, Edmund Pendleton, and George Wythe, see *PTJ*, 2:336–7.

The UNIVERSITY BILL, "Providing for the establishment of Primary Schools, Academies, Colleges, and an University," outlined a new plan for public education in Virginia, proposing that a ten-member Board of Public Instruction be elected annually by joint ballot of the Senate and House of Delegates; specifying that the governor serve as president of the Board and that its geographical composition be balanced among different regions of the state; calling for an annual meeting in Charlottesville or another location until the University of Virginia is complete, after which all meetings shall be held there; empowering the Board to establish the University of Virginia, decide on its professorships and curriculum, and recommend laws related to public education to the General Assembly; calling for the appointment of three commissioners in each county or corporation court with the authority to divide their jurisdictions into townships and wards for the purpose of establishing primary schools; prescribing the method for designating schoolhouse property and mandating the election of five trustees for each township or ward; describing the roles of the trustees and the arrangements for tuition payments, teacher salaries, and funding of educational supplies; authorizing the Board to divide the state into forty-eight academic districts of reasonably equal population based on the last census; establishing rules for the integration of schools already in existence into the new public education system; describing the procedure for the founding and operation of a new academy in an academical district; recognizing the Ann Smith Academy for female education as acceptable to the Board and limiting the number of such institutions in the state to a total of three; giving the Board authority to establish four new colleges to be named Pendleton, Wythe, Henry, and Jefferson; outlining the geographical distribution of the colleges and the responsibilities of twenty-five trustees for each, who will be appointed by the Board; providing that with the consent of the trustees or visitors of the existing colleges, William and Mary, Hampden-Sydney, and Washington, these institutions can be integrated into the new system of public education; instructing the Board to determine the site of the new University of Virginia as soon as possible; authorizing each county or corporation court to appoint three or more commissioners at its next meeting charged with collecting subscriptions from the residents in support of the educational institutions described in the bill; requiring the trustees of the primary schools, academies, and colleges to submit an annual report to the Board from which it will compile a statement on the condition of public education for presentation to the General Assembly; reiterating the responsibilities of the president and directors of the Literary Fund; repealing all existing acts and sections of acts falling within the purview of the new statute and detailing the process for its coming into effect; and appending a list of four amendments made by the Senate, including one explicitly subjecting the Board to the control of the General Assembly; another terminating the act at the end of the next legislative session unless it is reauthorized then and suspending the expenditure of money from the Literary Fund until such reauthorization; and a third requiring each commissioner of revenue to report on the institutions in his district to the Board and the governor and Council of State by 1 Dec. 1818 and stipulating that each county, city, corporate town, and the borough of Norfolk be required to appoint not less than five and not more than ten commissioners of the Literary Fund and listing their responsibilities (printed in *Sundry Documents on the Subject of a System Of Public Education, for the State Of Virginia* [Richmond, 1817], 35–52; Poor, *Jefferson's Library*, 5 [no. 211]).

A Senate committee chaired by Chapman Johnson amended the University Bill and reported it out on 20 Feb. 1817. Cabell noted that Johnson invoked the "Patronage of Mr Jefferson" for the legislation while urging the advantages of Staunton as the new institution's home (MS in ViU: JCC; entirely in Cabell's hand; undated; endorsed by Cabell: "Notes of Heads of Johnson's argument on the University Bill"). The first two amendments described above, designed to aid passage by increasing legislative control, may have been drafted by Cabell (MS in ViU: JCC; entirely in Cabell's hand; undated; endorsed by Cabell: "Amendments to the University Bill of Sess^n^ 1816–17"). The Senate rejected the measure the same day on a tie seven-to-seven vote (*JSV* [1816–17 sess.], 67 [20 Feb. 1817]).

From Richard Rush

Dear sir. Washington February 19. 1817

There are so many motives for visiting Monticello, that it is no wonder all are ambitious to do so. Mr Derby, a gentleman of Boston and greatly in esteem among those who have the pleasure of his acquaintance, desires to pay his respects to you, and I know how largely I shall promote his gratification in thus affording him an opportunity.

Inducements more than common, operate with Mr Derby. He contemplates going to Europe soon, with his accomplished lady, and he well appreciates the disadvantage it would be to leave his country without the honor of being known to you.

I beg you, sir, to pardon the freedom upon which I venture; and, together with my prayers for the continuance of every blessing to you, to accept the assurances of my sincere and profound respect.

RICHARD RUSH.

RC (MHi); endorsed by TJ as received 27 Feb. 1817 and so recorded in SJL. RC (DLC); address cover only; with PoC of TJ to Joseph Dougherty, 23 Mar. 1817, on verso; addressed: "Mr Jefferson. Monticello" by "Mr Derby." Enclosed in Richard C. Derby to TJ, 23 Feb. 1817.

From William Thornton

DEAR SIR City of Washington 19th Feby 1817

I have been waiting till this Day to obtain a Copy of the List of Patents, and lose not a moment in writing to you.—

Colonel Trumbull has been here some time, & has expressed satisfaction on viewing the Copy I made of your Portrait. I have placed it in the Congressional Library, in a very superb gilt Frame, that when the members view the works by wch the inside of your head was so well stored, they might also have a good Idea of the outside of the Head.—I mean to send the original (put up with care, along with Mr West's Sketch) by your worthy & highly esteemed Successor Mr Madison—

Col: Trumbull wishes to paint some large Pictures for the Congress, and I am pleased to find a general impression in fav^r of this important undertaking.—

The affairs of South America progress with great rapidity to the compleat emancipation of that extensive rich & beautiful Country.

We have had very severe weather for some time past, but the Thermometer was never lower than six Degrees above 0 of Farenheit, in the open air, at 6 o'Clock in the morning.—

Mr Whitlow, whom you may perhaps remember as the discoverer of a species of the Urtica, in the back parts of the State of N. York, & called the Urtica Whitlowi has lately found a species of the Asclepias, or milk weed, which produces a flax or vegetable Silk, from its fineness of texture, that promises to produce a revolution in fabricks: for it is not only very fine but long & strong—and is easily raised in large quantity.—The Urtica grows ab^{t} 5 feet high, & an acre will produce ab^{t} from 800 to a thousand W^{t}—It is peren^{l} & requires not rotting—The texture is fine, & stronger than hemp. These Plants are produced in the back Countries in abundance—The Asclepias—in Canada in great quantities. If we had here a botanic Garden, we could send various valuable Seeds to all parts of our Country—and render incalculable benefits. Mr Whitlow is here.—My respectful Compl^{ts} to every member of y^{r} worthy Family—

I am dear Sir wth the highest Consid^{n} &c W. THORNTON

Mr Sampson of New York presents to you his most respectful Compl^{ts} & begs your acceptance of the Pamphlet on Domestic Manuf^{g} which I have the pleasure of inclosing—

RC (DLC); with postscript on verso of address leaf; addressed: "Honorable Thomas Jefferson"; endorsed by TJ as received 27 Feb. 1817 and so recorded in SJL. Enclosure: *Letter from the Secretary of State, transmitting A List of the Names of Persons to whom Patents have been Issued, for the invention of any new or useful art, or machine, manufacture, or composition of matter, or any improvement thereon, from January 1st, 1816, to January 1st, 1817* (Washington, 1817).

The enclosed PAMPHLET may have been an additional copy of the enclosure to William Sampson to TJ, 9 Jan. 1817.

To Samuel L. Mitchill

Monticello Feb. 20. 17.

Th: Jefferson returns his thanks to Dr Mitchell for the print of Asiatic antiquities he has been so kind as to send him, which, however unintelligible to him, is still a curiosity. he is happy in the occasion it has presented of a mutual recognition of former fellowship in service, and of renewing to him the assurance of his constant esteem & respect.

RC (Christie's, New York City, 1992); dateline at foot of text; addressed: "The honble Doctor Mitchell of Congress now at Washington"; franked; postmarked Charlottesville, 21 Feb.; redirected in an unidentified hand to "New York"; endorsed by Mitchill as received 28 Feb. 1817. PoC (DLC); on verso of portion of reused address cover to TJ; endorsed by TJ.

From Smith & Riddle

SIR Richmond 20th Febry 1817

In Compliance with your request, we have transmitted to the manager of the Boston Glass manufactory, the order you favor'd us with, under date the 9th Inst, for One Hundred and ten panes of best quality Window Glass, which we have requested to be pack'd with special Care, in order to ensure its safe transportation—

On its arrival here, we shall deliver it to your Correspondent Mr Gibson, agreeable to your instructions

We are with Respect Yr Obedt Servts SMITH & RIDDLE

RC (MHi); in Andrew Smith's hand; endorsed by TJ as received 23 Feb. 1817 and so recorded in SJL. RC (MHi); address cover only; with PoC of TJ to Peter Minor, 30 Mar. 1817, on verso; addressed: "Thomas Jefferson Esqr Monticello"; franked; postmarked Richmond, 20 Feb.

To Edwin Stark

SIR Monticello Feb. 20. 17.

A letter just recieved from mr Theus Collector of Charleston informs me he had forwarded to Norfolk two cases of wine addressed to your care. they contain 83. bottles of Florence wine. I do not know what duties or expences they may come charged with to your hands; but if you will have the goodness to forward them to messrs Gibson & Jefferson my correspondents at Richmond, and to draw on them for reimbursement, they will pay it on sight. and I will take the liberty of making the same request as to any articles which may in future come to your office for me, which those gentlemen will always recieve for me and pay all charges on demand. accept my thanks for the trouble this gives you and the assurances of my esteem & respect

TH: JEFFERSON

PoC (MHi); on verso of portion of reused address cover to TJ; at foot of text: "Mr Edwin Starke"; endorsed by TJ.

To Simeon Theus

SIR Monticello Feb. 20. 17.

I recieved yesterday only your favor of Jan. 22. and two days before had written a letter on the subject of the wine mentioned in your letter addressed to 'The Collector for the district of Charleston.' after so long a retirement from the knolege of what is passing, I did not know who might be now in office there. your letter was therefore the more acceptable as evidence that you were still in life and function. it has not informed me however what duties are to be paid for the wine, and the freight & other charges which you have probably advanced for me. the object of the present therefore is to ask that information. if an occasion occurs of your drawing for it at once on mess^{rs} Gibson & Jefferson, my correspondents at Richmond, they will pay it at sight; if no such occasion I will remit it by mail in banknotes recievable with you, as soon as made known to me. accept my thanks for your obliging attentions on this occasion & the assurance of my great respect and esteem. TH: JEFFERSON

PoC (MHi); at foot of text: "Simeon Theus esq."; endorsed by TJ.

Theus's FAVOR OF JAN. 22, not found, is recorded in SJL as received 19 Feb. 1817 from Charleston.

From Francis Adrian Van der Kemp

DEAR SIR! Olden barneveld[1] 20 Febr. 1817.

Mrs A.A had the kindness to Send me inclosed N° of the Month Rep—to convey it, after its perusal, to Monticello. I expect, it is the only one on our continent. That excellent Lady received it from her Son at the court of St. James.

Although I regret, that there has not been complied with my injunctions—Still I rejoyce at the publication, and can find reasons to palliate this appearing neglect. My friend the Rev. J. joyce died—Suddenly and unexpected in June last before he could have received my Letter—One of his Executors as I Suppose Rev. Aspland—may not have Seen my Letter or may not have considered—my requests of that moment, to require a punctual compliance, as mr joyce might have found himself obliged to. I had Signed O...d—he puts Olden barneveld—he insinuates Sincerus is the Same with the [...] writer on Servetus although I then used the Signature of Candidus—and gives the Syllabus to an American Statesman—I question—if another number Shall reach this country—but if So—it must be among your friends—otherwise a clue was given, to guess at the author—as one man only could be the Father of that production.

Continue to honour me with your remembrance[2]—and believe me to remain with the highest consideration and respect

Dear Sir! Your most obed. and obliged S^{t}

FR. ADR. VAN DER KEMP

RC (DLC); dateline at foot of text; first ellipsis in original; edge chipped; endorsed by TJ as received 5 Mar. 1817 and so recorded in SJL. Enclosure: *Monthly Repository of Theology and General Literature* 11 (Oct. 1816).

In a letter dated 7 Feb. 1817, Abigail Adams (MRS A.A) explained to Van der Kemp that John Quincy Adams had "inclosed to me the Monthly Repository, saying that, A mr Aspland an Unitarian Clergyman called upon him, and gave him two copies of a late periodical publication, one of which he inclosed, as he thought it would be particularly interesting to his Father, and to me; as containing a Letter from mr Van der Kemp and one to him—as he supposed from mr Jefferson, with a Syllabus for a comparison between the doctrine of Jesus and that of the Grecian phylosophers and that of the Jews before the Time of Jesus—you know I presume by what Authority they appear in public" (PHi: Van der Kemp Collection). In his 24 Feb. 1817 reply, Van der Kemp noted that TJ's letter was written not to him but to Benjamin Rush and reported that he had "conveyed the Repos. this week to Montecello—and hope it may there be as acceptable as it was to me" (MHi: Adams Papers).

Writing as CANDIDUS, Van der Kemp penned eight letters on the life of the sixteenth-century Spanish theologian and physician Miguel Serveto (Servetus) in the *Monthly Repository of Theology and General Literature* 5 (1810).

[1] Manuscript: "Olden barneved."
[2] Manuscript: "rememenbrance."

From Charles Yancey

DR SIR Richmond 20th February 1817

we have postponed the Consideration of the turnpike[1] Contemplated from Rockfish Gap to Lewis' ferry. my Colleague proposed to turn pike each road to the River to this I objected & prefered postponing I have been Some embarrassed in this Case on Acct of So many applications. we Shall be up tomorrow

Yours respectfully C' YANCEY.

RC (DLC); addressed: "Thomas Jefferson Esqr Montecello"; franked; postmarked Richmond, 20 Feb.; endorsed by TJ as received 23 Feb. 1817 and so recorded in SJL.

[1] Manuscript: "turnpke."

From Simon Bernard

MONSIEUR Washington 21 Fevrier 1817.

Monsieur le Général Lafayette m'avait fait la faveur de me donner une lettre pour me présenter devant vous; le désir de jouir de l'honneur d'approcher de votre personne m'avait fait différer jusqu'ici de vous remettre cette lettre, espérant toujours qu'une occasion heureuse me procurerait cet avantage Si précieux pour moi.

Mais de nouveaux ordres éloignant à cet égard mes espérances, je ne dois plus différer de vous envoyer ce présent que m'avait fait Monsieur le Général Lafayette.

Je vous Supplie, Monsieur, de daigner me permettre de vous offrir ici tous les Sentimens de l'admiration la plus respectueuse qui m'a été inspirée en Europe pour vos vertus et votre carriere élevée.

BERNARD
Brigadier-Général du Génie.

EDITORS' TRANSLATION

SIR Washington 21 February 1817.

General Lafayette favored me with a letter of introduction to you; the desire to meet you in person made me postpone sending you this letter until now, always hoping that a fortunate opportunity would procure me this benefit so precious to me.

But new orders render my hope more distant, and I must no longer postpone sending you this favor that General Lafayette gave me.

Sir, I beg you to allow me to offer you here the expression of the most respectful admiration of your virtues and lofty career, which have inspired me in Europe.

BERNARD
Brigadier General of Engineers.

RC (DLC); endorsed by TJ as received 27 Feb. 1817 and so recorded in SJL. Translation by Dr. Genevieve Moene. Enclosure: Lafayette to TJ, 16 Sept. 1816.

From Joseph Milligan

DEAR SIR Georgetown February 21st 1817

I wrote on the 9th instant enclosing you the prospectus it has not yet been returned I have received the 3rd & 4th proofs in the due course of the mail from the date of your returning[1] them

yours with respect JOSEPH MILLIGAN

RC (DLC); endorsed by TJ as received 27 Feb. 1817 and so recorded in SJL; with notation by TJ beneath endorsement: "his 9th recd 16th dispatchd 17th
21st recd 27."

[1] Manuscript: "returnng."

From José Corrêa da Serra

Sir Washington 22 Febr[y] 1817

Mr Derby a well known gentleman of Boston, has told me how he desired to pay a visit to Virginia, and to have the honor of being presented to you. Though his known caracter be a competent passport every where, still he is persuaded that decency requires that he be presented by some one of your acquaintances, and wishes me to perform this function. I am very glad to have this occasion of presenting to you my respects, and of testifying to you once more the sentiments of attachment and respect with which i am and allways will be

Sir Your most obedient serv[t] and friend

J. Corrèa de Serra

RC (NNPM); endorsed by TJ as received 27 Feb. 1817 and so recorded in SJL. Enclosed in Richard C. Derby to TJ, 23 Feb. 1817.

From Hendrick W. Gordon

Sir Merrimack, N, Hampshire, February 22nd 1817.

The interest you have taken in the manufactures of our Country, has induced me to offer for your examination the scraps of cloth herewith enclosed; they are from peices spun & wove in my own family, and dressed in this neighbourhood by a native born American. Either of the peices would afford a profit at $3 dolls a yard, single width. Let the enemies of American manufactures say what they will, we are not an independent people without them.

With great consideration of Respect & Esteem, I am, Sir, Your most Obedient Servant, Hendrick W Gordon.

RC (MHi); endorsed by TJ as a letter of 2 Feb. 1817 received 15 Mar. 1817 and so recorded in SJL. RC (DLC); address cover only; with PoC of TJ to John Barnes, 17 May 1817, on verso; addressed: "Honourable Thomas Jefferson, Esquire, Late President of the U States. Monticello"; franked.

Hendrick W. Gordon (ca. 1782–1819), merchant, operated a hotel near Boston in 1804 and by 1806 was the proprietor of a mercantile firm in that city. In 1814 President James Madison followed up his recess appointment of Gordon as federal tax collector for the 10th Collection District in Massachusetts by nominating him for the same position, but the Senate declined to confirm him. Although Gordon applied for federal offices multiple times between 1813 and 1817 and was recommended by John Adams, he secured no other post. Secretary of the Navy William Jones described him to Madison in 1813 as "not long since a Federalist and unfit." By July 1815 Gordon had relocated permanently to Merrimack, New Hampshire, where he acted as a justice of the peace (Gordon to John Quincy Adams, 13 Sept. 1817, and other material in his files in DNA: RG 59, LAR, 1809–25; Madison, *Papers, Pres. Ser.*, 5:635–6, 6:54, 693;

Boston Gazette, 21 May 1804, 23 Oct. 1806; *JEP*, 2:455, 468 [18 Jan., 4 Feb. 1814]; *The New-Hampshire Register, and Pocket Almanack, for the year 1817* [Exeter and Concord, N.H., 1816], 52; *Portsmouth Oracle*, 3 Apr. 1819).

From David Higginbotham

Dear Sir Richmond 22nd Feby 1817

Some time ago you Said you had Some idea of painting your house again, we have now on hand the best English white Lead and Spanish brown ground in oil in quarter kegs, the price will be $4½ ⅌ keg for the former and $3 ⅌ keg for the latter, should you want any you can write me, our markets are Steady Flour $14 and dull Tob^{o} from $7. to 12 in demand.

I am Dear Sir Your mo obt David Higginbotham

RC (MHi); endorsed by TJ as received <*6*> 5 Mar. 1817. Recorded in SJL as received 5 Mar. 1817. RC (MHi); address cover only; with PoC of TJ to William D. Taylor, 1 Apr. 1817, on verso; addressed: "Thomas Jefferson Esquire Monticello"; franked; postmarked Richmond, 25 Feb.

From Richard C. Derby

Respected Sir Washington 23^{d} Febru^{y} 1817

The enclos'd letters were given me by my friends knowing that it was my intention (before Mrs Derbys and my departure for Europe) to visit you at your seat in Virginia. but circumstances preventing I take the liberty to enclose them to you at the same time observing that Mrs Derby and myself should feel doubly delighted should you be inclind to forward us Letters to Boston. Our friends Ticknor and Everett are making great progress in Germany and the President of Cambridge College looks forward with great hopes for their aid and assistance at that seminary. Mrs Peter Cruger informd me that you had given letters occasionally to a Madame Corny, she has given us one, but one from so high a source as yourself will be of more consequence to us.

Should it be your wish I shall feel proud and honourd to execute any orders that you may have for Europe, and united with the taste of Madame Derby, and some of our friends in Paris there is no doubt but that they will be executed as you wish.

M^{rs} D and myself about 12 years ago spent 3 years in Europe having visited England France Germany Holland Switzerland, & Italy at present it is our intention to visit Scotland Ireland Sweden Denmark, Russia Prussia, Germany (vienna) Switzerland & France

After my return from Europe should God spare my life, I shall then pay you a visit and if I should learn any thing from the Literary or Scientific men in that Country, I shall respected Sir be pleasd to communicate it

I am with profound respect Your obed[t] Humble S[t]

RICHARD C DERBY

RC (DLC); endorsed by TJ as received 27 Feb. 1817 and so recorded in SJL. Enclosures: (1) Samuel L. Mitchill to TJ, 10 Feb. 1817. (2) Richard Rush to TJ, 19 Feb. 1817. (3) José Corrêa da Serra to TJ, 22 Feb. 1817.

Richard Crowninshield Derby (1777–1854) descended from a line of wealthy merchants and shipmasters in Salem, Massachusetts. Following his father's death the family began to experience a reversal of fortune. In 1817 Derby unsuccessfully sought a diplomatic appointment from James Monroe. At his death he left at least $12,500 to charities in the Boston area (Robert Safford Hale, *Genealogy of Descendants of Thomas Hale of Watton, England, and of Newbury, Mass.* [1889], 246; MaSaPEM: Derby Family Papers; David L. Ferguson, *Cleopatra's Barge: The Crowninshield Story* [1976], 46, 48–9; *ANB*, 6:465–7 [Elias Hasket Derby]; Derby to Monroe, partially dated 1817 [NN: Monroe Papers, filed at 9 Nov. 1817]; *Boston Daily Atlas*, 13 Apr. 1854).

John Thornton Kirkland was the PRESIDENT of Harvard University (CAMBRIDGE COLLEGE) (*DAB*).

From Thomas Law

DEAR SIR. [received 23 Feb. 1817]

Our Society will be highly gratified if you will permit us to insert your name amongst the Members who are desirous of promoting the objects we have in view—

I remain With sincere esteem and regard THO[S] LAW

RC (DLC: TJ Papers, 209:37298); undated; endorsed by TJ as received 23 Feb. Recorded in SJL as received 23 Feb. 1817.

With this letter Law may have enclosed two works related to the Columbian Institute for the Promotion of Arts and Sciences (the SOCIETY). An oration by Edward Cutbush, *An Address, delivered before the Columbian Institute, for the Promotion of Arts and Sciences, at the City of Washington, on the 11th January, 1817* (Washington, 1817; Poor, *Jefferson's Library*, 6 [no. 223]; TJ's copy in DLC: Rare Book and Special Collections), urged the organization to establish a library, a museum, and a national botanical garden where valuable seeds and plants could be cultivated for distribution to other parts of the nation; recommended that it print circulars "containing the necessary questions for the information of the Institute, so arranged, and divested of technical terms, that those persons, who have not been engaged in scientific pursuits, may be enabled to comprehend and answer them with promptness" (p. 22); articulated the hope that "the members of our national government, to whom has been confided the guardianship of the District of Columbia, will extend their fostering care to this establishment, and, if no constitutional restrictions forbid it, that a part of the public ground, reserved for national purposes, may be vested in the 'Columbian Institute for the promotion of Arts and Sciences,' for the purpose of carrying into effect the leading objects of the association"; and noted that "a small pecuniary aid would enable the Institute, at an earlier period, to extend its benefits to all parts of the United States" (pp. 27–8). A printed circular from Benjamin Henry Latrobe, William W. Seaton, and Edmund Law, Washington, 1 Feb. 1817, writing as the corresponding committee of the Columbian Institute (Poor, *Jefferson's Library*, 6 [no. 223]; TJ's copy in DLC: Rare Book and Special Collections, bound with the Cutbush *Address*), requested respondents to supply data, including geographical, meteorological, infrastructural, botanical, mineralogical, and manufacturing facts relative to their region; called for the submission of such grains as "may be useful as food for man or animals, or which produce oils, &c. that the seeds may be sown in our garden, and if they multiply, that they may be disseminated throughout the United States"; promised to repay contributions with vegetables and plants from the institute's collection; and concluded by asserting that "By the reciprocation of knowledge acquired by the exchange of useful productions and by the co-operation of the philosopher and philanthropist, we indulge the pleasing expectation of rendering our Institute at this Metropolis by assiduity and zeal a public benefit, increasing and improving with the growth of this Republican Government."

The Columbian Institute's minutes for its 11 Jan. 1817 meeting record that it was "ordered that Thomas Jefferson, John Adams and James Madison be entered as honorary members of the Institute" (MS in DSI: Columbian Institute Records).

To Charles K. Mallory

SIR Monticello Feb. 23. 17.

Your favor of the 17th came to hand yesterday. I had, two days before, addressed a letter, on the subject of these packages of wine to mr Starke of your office, with whom I had had occasion to exchange a letter in Oct. on another article. I learn from yours now before me, that you had been so kind as to anticipate my request to him, and to forward the cases to messrs Gibson & Jefferson according to the former request in mine of Sep. 1. to yourself. for this be pleased to accept my thanks, and especially for the kind assurances in your letter of a like future attention to these small consignments of mine. it is the more my duty to be thankful to you, as this trouble may possibly fall on you once or twice a year, from the circum[stances] explained in my former letter. on this, as on any fu[t]ure occasion, if you will have the goodness to send a statement of duties and charges, either to Messrs Gibson & Jefferson or myself they will be instantly remitted by either of us. Accept the Assurance of my great esteem & respect.

TH: JEFFERSON

PoC (MHi); on verso of a reused address cover from John Wayles Eppes to TJ; mutilated at seal; at foot of text: "Charles K. Mallory esq."; endorsed by TJ.

From James Monroe

Dear Sir washington Feby 23. 1817

I had the pleasure to receive the letter which you forwarded to me through Col: Trumbull, & to apply it, with the best effect, to the purpose for which it was intended. Congress passed a law, under which a contract has been concluded with him, for the painting of four pieces; the declaration of Independance; the surrender of Burgoyne, that of Cornwallis; & the resignation of Gen[l] washington. For these he is to receive 32.000. dolr[s], 8000. in advance, and 6. on the completion of each picture. I am satisfied that he owes this tribute of respect, principally, to your favorable opinion of his merit.

To your friendship, & good wishes in my favor, I have always had the greatest sensibility, and shall continue to have. The time is approaching, when I shall commence the duties of the trust suggested in your last, the difficulties of which, have been felt, in a certain degree, even in the present stage; particularly in the formation of the administration with which I am to act. On full consideration of all circumstances, I have thought that it would produce a bad effect, to place any one from this quarter of the union, in the dep[t] of state, or from the south or west. You know how much has been said to impress a belief, on the country, north, & East of this, that the citizens from Virg[a], holding the Presidency, have made appointments to that dep[t], to secure the sucession, from it, to the Presidency, of the person who happend to be from that state. my opinion is, that those of that state, who have been elected to the Presidency, would have obtain'd that proof of the public confidence, had they not previously filled the dep[t] of state, except myself, & that my service in another dep[t], contributed more to overcome prejudices against my election, than that in the dep[t] of state. It is however, not sufficient, that this allegation is unfounded. much effect has been produc'd by it; so much, indeed, that I am inclind, to believe, that if I nominated any one from this quarter [including the south & west, which in relation to such a nomination at this time, would be view[ed] in the same light][1] I should embody against the [ap]proaching adm[n], principally, to defeat, the suspected arrangment for the sucession, the whole of the country, north, of the Delaware, immediately, and that, the rest, to the Potow[k], would be likely to follow it My wish is to prevent such a combination, the ill effect of which, would be so sensibly felt, on so many important public interests, among which, the just claims, according to the relative merit of the parties, of persons, in this quarter, ought not to be disregarded. With this view, I have thought it adviseable, to select a person for the dep[t] of state, from the Eastern States, in consequence of which my attention has been turnd to M[r] Adams, who by his age, long experience in our foreign affairs, and adop[ti]on into the republican party, seems to have superior pretentions to any there. To Mr Crawford I have intimated my sincere desire that he will remain where he is. To Mr Clay, the dep[t] of war was offer'd, which he declind. It is offerd to Gov Shelby, who will be nominated to it before his answer is recd.[2] M[r] Crowninshield it is understood will remain in the navy dep[t]. I can hardly hope, that our southern gentlemen, who have good pretentions, will enter fully into this view of the subject, but having formd my opinion, on great consideration, I shall probably adhere to it.

On our affairs, generally, I will take some opportunity, soon, of writing you, if, indeed, I cannot, make a visit to our neighborhood, which I have wished & intended. I beg you to be assurd of my constant and affectionate regard & great respect

JA[S] MONROE

RC (DLC); edge chipped; endorsed by TJ as received 27 Feb. 1817 and so recorded in SJL.

The Senate confirmed Isaac SHELBY, Monroe's nominee as secretary of war, but he declined the appointment. Monroe then appointed John C. Calhoun, who accepted the office and won Senate confirmation (*JEP*, 3:89, 91, 95, 98 [5 Mar., 12, 15 Dec. 1817]).

[1] Outer pair of brackets in original.
[2] Preceding five words interlined.

To Philip I. Barziza

DEAR SIR Monticello Feb. 24.[1] 17.

Your favor of the 14th came to hand last night. letters from mr Thweatt and mr Baker of the House of Representatives, and mr Cabell of the Senate (whose attention I had asked to see justice done you) had informed me that the legislature had declined acting on your case, as one which belonged to the courts of justice. my hope had been that they would give to you any right which might have resulted to the state by escheat: and it seems their opinion that there has been no escheat. the courts of justice will therefore have to decide on it, and I would advise you to prefer those of the state to the US. courts.

On the question of legal right, I really am not qualified to give you advice worth your notice. upwards of 40. years withdrawn from the practice of the law & from all familiarity with legal questions have rendered me entirely rusty on those subjects. the general view I have had was this. your grandmother, mrs Paradise, was a native citizen of Virginia, and did not lose that character by her residence in England. our laws Ch. 110. § 1. makes children, wheresoever born, of citizens, to be citizens themselves. your mother then, the countess Barziza was a citizen. but even were she not, the same laws Ch. 93. §. 18. makes descent thro' an alien no bar, and the law of Congress 1802 c. 28. §. 4. respects not natural citizens, but those formally naturalized. the only doubt which occurs to me is, there being collateral heirs capable of recieving the descent at the moment it was cast by the death of mrs Paradise, whether it could be divested by your becoming subsequently a citizen. on this question, and on that whether the marriage settlement of mrs Paradise is entirely out of the question, the lawyers of the day are much better qualified to decide than I am. our courts being, as they should be, inaccessible to all private influence or application, I can only offer my good wishes for your success, because I believe it just in natural law, and assure you of my great esteem and respect.

TH: JEFFERSON

PoC (DLC); on verso of a reused address cover from John Barnes to TJ; at foot of text: "Viscount Philip S. Barziza"; endorsed by TJ.

The letter from Archibald THWEATT is accounted for above at the note to TJ to Simeon Theus, 17 Feb. 1817.

By section 1 of "An Act declaring who shall be deemed Citizens of this Commonwealth, and pointing out the mode by which the Right of Citizenship may be acquired or relinquished," passed 23 Dec. 1792, CHILDREN "wheresoever born, whose fathers or mothers are or were citizens at the time of the birth of such children, shall be deemed citizens of this commonwealth, until they relinquish that character in manner hereinafter mentioned." Section 18 of "An Act to reduce into one the several Acts directing the course of Descents," passed 8 Dec. 1792, confirmed descent THRO' AN ALIEN: "it shall be no bar to a party that any ancestor through whom he derives his descent from the intestate, is, or hath been an alien" (*A Collection of All Such Acts of the General Assembly of Virginia, of a public & permanent nature, as are now in force* [2d ed., Richmond, 1814], 235, 237, 290–1).

The LAW OF CONGRESS passed 14 Apr. 1802 was "An Act to establish an uniform rule of Naturalization, and to repeal the acts heretofore passed on that subject." Section 4 established conditions under which children of naturalized citizens could be considered citizens (*U.S. Statutes at Large*, 2:153, 155; Thomas Herty, *A Digest of the Laws of the United States of America* [Baltimore, 1800–02; Poor, *Jefferson's Library*, 10 (no. 589)], 2:104). For the 1769 MARRIAGE SETTLEMENT, see TJ's Abstract of Marriage Settlement of John Paradise and Lucy Ludwell Paradise and Sir William Jones's notes on the same, both printed above at TJ's 24 Dec. 1815 letter to Barziza.

[1] Above date TJ interlined and then deleted "for 23."

From Joseph Delaplaine

Dear sir, Philad^{a} Feby 24^{h} 1817.

I received, duly, your very obliging favour with an accompanying recommendation of the Repository, which I caused to be published in six or seven Newspapers. It was all I could have wished.—I thank you for it most sincerely. It shall be given with a future n^{o} of the Work.—

Your life & Portrait are preparing for the second half volume.—Mr Madison's will be given in the 3^{d}—

I should, I must confess, have liked to have said something of your religious belief in your life, but as you have enjoined it upon me not to touch the subject, & as I know I have your confidence, I shall certainly never incur your displeasure.

I trust, dear sir, my life of you will be a just one, and if it is a just one, it ought to give satisfaction to all.

Best respects to Mrs Randolph & the Col^{o}—[1]

Whenever you will do me the honour to drop me a line, it will be receivd with great happiness.

May God bless you

yours with esteem Joseph Delaplaine

RC (DLC); endorsed by TJ as received 5 Mar. 1817 and so recorded in SJL. RC (MHi); address cover only; with PoC of TJ to de Bure Frères, 6 June 1817, on recto and verso; addressed: "Thomas Jefferson Esqr Monticello Virginia"; stamp canceled; franked; postmarked Philadelphia, 24 Feb.

For TJ's very obliging favour and recommendation of the repository, see TJ to Delaplaine, 25 Dec. 1816, first and second letters, respectively. James madison's biography was not ultimately included in *Delaplaine's Repository*.

[1] Paragraph interlined.

To Thomas Law

Dear Sir Monticello Feb. 24. 17.

The enrolment of my name among those of the members of the Columbian Institute is an honor which I recieve with the acknolegements it so justly calls for. I place it to the account of their kindness, and not of any services I can now render them. age and it's effects forbid me that expectation, and teach me that it is not among the ruins of memory that new materials for science are to be sought. the institution of your society adds another to the views of futurity which fill with delight our contemplations on the future destinies of our beloved country, and of the advancement it is to produce in the character and condition of man. with prayers for it's prosperity, I tender to the Institute and yourself the assurance of my high respect and consideration.

TH: JEFFERSON

RC (DSI: Columbian Institute Records); addressed: "Thomas Law esquire Washington Col."; franked; postmarked (faint) Charlottesville, 2[5?] Feb.; endorsement in an unidentified hand reads, in part, "Th: Jefferson—to Thos Law, relative to his election as an honorary member of the Columbian Institute." PoC (DLC); endorsed by TJ.

From Wilson Cary Nicholas

MY DEAR SIR Richmond Feby 24. 1817

The situation that I have been in for some time past has prevented my answering your last letter and making my acknowledgements for your friendly attention to Mr Armistead. I have the pleasure to inform you, your application procured Mr A. an appointment that if he is prudent will enable him to support his family.

A long and intimate acquaintance with you has given me a thorough knowledge of the excellence of your heart and how little effect that sort of intercourse with the world which usually blunts the feelings of others has had upon you. Your effort to revive the cordiality that formerly subsisted between Col. Monroe & myself is a strong[1] proof of this. To you I believe I may appeal for the sincerity of my attachment to him, and the delicacy of my course at the time he chose to take offence.[2] My personal attachment to Col M. &. Mr Madison were equal, with the former I had been longest acquainted & most familiar, for the talents of the latter I had the greatest respect & believed he was able to render my country most service. My confidence in the disinterestedness & patriotism of the two gentn was equal. With these feelings I gave my support to Mr M. when they were competitors for the presidency, but in a manner that wou'd have been justifiable in a brother of Col. M. For this I had many motives, my long friendship, my unwillingness to be instrumental in seperating[3] any man from the party, & I will say from self respect. I persevered to the last, even after I thought I saw the course Col. Monroe was pursuing was calculated[4] to sacrifice his old & best friends, some of them men to whom I had the strongest attachment from personal & public considerations,[5] to whom he owed every thing, and what was less excusable the interes[t] of his country. However these might & I confess did lessen my confidence in Col M, they were not grounds for a persona[l] difference, nor did I ever make them so, there was no act of mine that cou'd have justified any thing of the sort on his part. Nothing however occurred (to my knowledge) that ought to prevent my considering the visit he made me & his explanation given to you as satisfactory. I have seen too much of the world & have met with too few men able to resist temptation to look for any thing like perfection in many public men. Nor am I of opinion that Col Monroe's aberrations shou'd prevent his ever being forgiven. He[6] soon will be in a situation where he may entitle himself to the confidence of every man and obliterate the recollection of every thing unpleasant that is past. The welfare of my country is so intimately connected with his doing so that I sincerely hope he may. As to my feelings I can assure you I have none that partake of resentment or the slightest ill will towards Col. M. on the contrary I am perfectly willing to consider "that this clou'd has passed away."[7] I trust my Dear Sir I need give no assurance of my high respect & attachment to you, nor the deference I pay to your opinions upon every subject. The friendship with which you have honored me has ever been a source of my highest gratification.[8] I expect my future residence will be in this city. If you can make me useful to you in any way; I beg you to command my services without the least reserve. I have been confined for several days with a very severe cold.

I am with greatest respect & regard Dear Sir your hum. Serv.

W. C. NICHOLAS

RC (DLC); edge trimmed; endorsed by TJ as received 1 Mar. 1817 and so recorded in SJL. RC (DLC); address cover only; with PoC of TJ to David Bailie Warden, 6 June 1817, on recto and verso; addressed: "Thomas Jefferson Esqr Monticello Milton"; franked; postmarked Richmond, 27 Feb. Dft (ViU: TJP-ER); lacking dateline, salutation, and first paragraph; with emendations in ink and pencil.

THAT THIS CLOU'D HAS PASSED AWAY quotes from TJ's 13 Nov. 1816 letter to Nicholas.

1 Dft: "is another."

2 Dft here strikes through in pencil "I considered frankness to you as to men & measures, a duty I owed you & the public."

3 Dft: "driving."

4 Dft: "I saw in Col M. a determination," not canceled when Nicholas interlined in pencil the substitute language of the RC.

5 Preceding twelve words interlined in Dft.

6 Dft: "He has been and."

7 At this point in Dft Nicholas canceled "and mutual good will has resumed its place with both," a continuation of the quotation from TJ's 13 Nov. 1816 letter to him.

8 Dft ends here with "I am &c W.C.N."

From Robert B. Sthreshly

DEAR SIR Henderson Kentuckey Feb[y] 24. 1817

M[r] Larkin Towles the bearer of this a Gentleman of respectability who has been living in the Neighbourhood being pleased with the Country returns for the purpose of Moving out in the spring & it being a good oportunity M[rs] Sthreshly has written to the Ladies to collect & send her out Some Garden Seed Flower Roots & shrubs[1] & in addition to which will you be good enough to send me some sprout Kale Seed any attention you may shew M[r] Towles will be an obligation[2] on myself

I stoped here November last in consiquence of the cold weather seting in being much pleased with the country I have purchased land within three Miles of the Town of Henderson in a healthy part of the Country at 3 Dollars ℔ acree which had you such in Albermarle would be worth from $60 to $100 ℔ acree but the Labor of opening them is Very great

I am Dear Sir with the highest Esteem your Friend

ROBERT B STHRESHLY

RC (MHi); endorsed by TJ as received 29 Aug. 1817 and so recorded in SJL.

Larkin Smith Towles (1796–1829) was the son of Thomas Towles. The father represented Spotsylvania County in the Virginia House of Delegates, 1782–85. The younger Towles died in Bourbon County, Kentucky ("The Towles Family," *VMHB* 8 [1901]: 428; Leonard, *General Assembly*, 147, 151, 155).

[1] Manuscript: "srubs."
[2] Manuscript: "oblition."

From Caspar Wistar

DEAR SIR Philad[a] Feb[y] 24–1817—

Permit me to present to you the Bearer D[r] Stevenson, a very interesting young gentleman of New York, who is about to embark for Europe but makes a previous visit to the Southward. He has lately returned from Lake Superior & can give you a good account of what he has seen on his Journey, & also of the present state of public sentiment in New York. I hope to receive by his return an agreeable account of the continuance of your health & happiness, & with the warmest wishes for the welfare of your numerous family, am

Your affectionate friend C WISTAR—

RC (DLC); dateline adjacent to signature; at foot of text: "M[r] Jefferson"; endorsed by TJ as received 10 Apr. 1817 and so recorded in SJL, which has the additional notation: "D[r] Stevenson."

John B. Stevenson (1795–1863), physician, graduated from Columbia College (later Columbia University) in 1811, although he was denied his A.B. diploma for years in a dispute over his refusal to accept faculty-ordered revisions to his commencement address. He received a medical degree from the College of Physicians and Surgeons (later part of Columbia University) in 1816. Stevenson served as a militia officer during the War of 1812. After traveling in Europe, he practiced medicine in New York City and was a founding member of the New York Academy of Sciences under its original name of the Lyceum of Natural History (William M. Macbean, *Biographical Register of Saint Andrew's Society of the State of New York* [1922–25], 2:132–4; New York *Columbian*, 20 Aug. 1811, 6 June 1812; Milton Halsey Thomas, *Columbia University Officers and Alumni 1754–1857* [1936], 128, 195; Stevenson to John W. Francis, Paris, 8 Nov. 1818 [NN: Francis Papers]; Herman Le Roy Fairchild, *A History of the New York Academy of Sciences formerly the Lyceum of Natural History* [1887], 21; *New York Herald*, 26 Aug. 1863).

From Fernagus De Gelone

SIR New York 25. february 1817.

I have received the honour of your letter and I take the liberty to forward you a copy of the catalogue of my books and Maps.—here are the documents You desire to have.

Rapport fait par Courtois, de l'examen des papiers trouvés chez Robespierre & Ses complices, Paris. 1. 8vo Sewed. coarse paper. $1.75.

Œuvres d'Archimède, traduites littéralement, avec commentaire par Peyrard; ouvrage approuvé par l'Institut. &[a] 2. 8vo Sewed. 1808. figures and plates 4.50.

Correspondance de fernand Cortez avec Charles Quint out of print in france. I have Sold my two copies.

hippocrate, toutes Ses œuvres, traduites Sur le texte Grec, d'après l'edition de foesuis, par Gardeil, avec la vie d'hippocrate par Dacier. Toulouse. 1801. 4. 8vo Sewed. 8.00

Recherches sur les causes qui ont empêché les français de devenir libres et Sur les moyens qui leur restent pour acquerir la liberté, par Mounier. Genève. 1792. 2. 8vo Sewed. coarse paper 2.75.

17.D.

I am most respectfully Sir Your most humble obedient servant

J. LOUIS FERNAGUS DE GELONE

RC (MHi); at head of text: "Thomas Jefferson Esqre Monticello"; endorsed by TJ as received 5 Mar. 1817 and so recorded in SJL. Enclosure: Fernagus De Gelone, *Catalogue of Latin, English, French, Spanish, and Italian Books, Maps, &c. for sale by J. L. Fernagus de Gelone, Agent, for the United States, Canada, New-Orleans, Spanish America, and Isles* (New York, [1817?]; described as catalogue "No. 2" on p. 1).

From William A. Burwell

My dr Sir. Baltimore feby 26th 1817

Colo Taylor & myself, equally regret having troubled you with Mr Graham's papers, & feel Satisfied that you have expressed no opinion—I expected you would receive many letters in your retirement from those who have your happiness at heart, or wish the Sanction of your name to Support favorite opinions, but I had no idea that your labors were So great; I am only Surprised that you have Submitted for Such a length of time—If I am not compelled to pass thro Richmond it will give me great pleasure to See you once more—please remember me kindly to the family, & accept yourself my best wishes for your happiness W. A Burwell

RC (DLC); endorsed by TJ as received 5 Mar. 1817 and so recorded in SJL. RC (MHi); address cover only; with PoC of TJ to John Wayles Eppes, 31 Mar. 1817, on verso; addressed: "Thomas Jefferson Esq Milton Virginia"; stamp canceled; postmarked.

From George M. Dallas

Sir, Philadelphia 27. February 1817.

The inclosed proposals have been issued, after receiving the repeated solicitations of my late father's friends. I am, however, unwilling to effectuate them, unless sanctioned and encouraged by those for whom he often expressed the highest admiration and respect.

Though fearful of obtruding myself upon your notice, I cannot refrain from soliciting your sentiments as to the propriety and utility of the contemplated publication. My motive for so doing, if fairly appreciated, must, I am sure, constitute an ample apology.

With great veneration I have the honor to be Sir Y[r] mo: obed: Ser[t]

Geo: M: Dallas.

RC (DLC); at foot of text: "Thomas Jefferson Esq[r] Monticello Virg[a]"; endorsed by TJ as received 5 Mar. 1817 and so recorded in SJL. Enclosure: Dallas, *Proposals for publishing, by subscription, The Works of Alexander James Dallas, with His Biography Prefixed, and accompanied by portions of his correspondence, both public and private* (undated broadside in DLC: TJ Papers, 209:37310), stating "the author's aim to make a select compilation of such productions as may be most acceptable to his country, and of those principally on which the lasting reputation of the deceased must be founded"; indicating that the selection of materials for the personal narrative will be made with "greater latitude," such that "whatever detail or scrutiny may tend to develope the incidents of a life hitherto but partially known, or accurately to determine the character of an individual so long conspicuous, will be freely and candidly resorted to"; and noting that the three volumes will cost $3 apiece for subscribers and $10 per volume after publication, that subscriptions will be accepted by M. Thomas in Philadelphia and by agents of the *Analectic Magazine*, that persons obtaining six subscribers and accepting responsibility for payment will receive a complimentary copy for their trouble, and that booksellers will be allowed the "usual commission."

George Mifflin Dallas (1792–1864), attorney, public official, and diplomat, was born in Philadelphia and graduated from the College of New Jersey (later Princeton University) in 1810. After studying law under his father, Alexander J. Dallas, he was admitted to the Philadelphia bar in 1813. That same year Albert Gallatin selected the younger Dallas as his private secretary on a peace mission to Russia. Returning to the United States in 1814, Dallas secured a post in the Treasury Department under his father, who was then treasury secretary. From 1817 to 1820 Dallas was deputy attorney general for Philadelphia, and he was mayor of that city, 1828–29. He completed the final two years of an unexpired United States Senate term, 1831–33. Resuming his private law practice when he was not in office, Dallas held various local and federal positions, including state attorney general and United States envoy extraordinary and minister plenipotentiary to Russia, before he was elected vice president on the Democratic ticket with James K. Polk, serving from 1845 to 1849. He ended his public career with an appointment as envoy extraordinary and minister plenipotentiary to Great Britain, 1856–61 (*ANB*; *DAB*; John M. Belohlavek, *George Mifflin Dallas: Jacksonian Patrician* [1977]; Julia Dallas, ed., *A Series of Letters from London written During the Years 1856, '57, '58, '59, and '60* [1869]; Susan Dallas, ed., *Diary of George Mifflin Dallas While United States Minister to Russia 1837 to 1839, and to England 1856 to 1861* [1892]; *Philadelphia Inquirer*, 2 Jan. 1865).

From Chapman Johnson

DEAR SIR, Richmond 27. February 1817.

I had the pleasure of receiving your letter, enclosing your bill in Equity, with the accompanying documents—with which, however, I have not yet had an opportunity to make myself acquainted.

I expect to be detained here, until some day next week, and then to set out, with my family, on my return home. I shall pass through Louisa to see my friends there, where it is probable I may be detained a day or two—When I leave Louisa, I will do myself the pleasure to accept your invitation, and spend a night at Monticello—

In the mean time, I will examine your bill and documents, so as to enable me to ask such explanations as may be necessary to my understanding of the cause—

very respectfully your most obt Sv^{t} C. JOHNSON

RC (MHi); endorsed by TJ as received 1 Mar. 1817 and so recorded in SJL. RC (MHi); address cover only; with PoC of TJ to Patrick Gibson, 1 Apr. 1817, on recto and verso; addressed: "Thomas Jefferson Esquire Monticello"; franked; postmarked Richmond, 27 Feb.

From John Barnes

Dear Sir George Town 28th feby 1817.

Your Esteemed favr 17th Acknowledgs Recpt of the Certificates of Genl Kosciusko's 6 ℔Ct as well Bank Stock of Columbia—as specified—And now inclose you Copy of the form required—for you to Execute—in Order—to my receiving[1] the quarterly Interest, on the former—for the dividend on the Bank Stock—I trust is already satisfactory—adjusted—with Referance to the Genls a/c—I purpose soon as the Navigation & Opportunity presents, to forward Duplicates thereof to the good Genl—lest yours—may not have reached him—

most Respectfully. Dear Sir—your very Obedt servt

John Barnes,

RC (ViU: TJP-ER); endorsed by TJ as received 5 Mar. 1817 and so recorded in SJL. RC (MHi); address cover only; with PoC of TJ to Fernagus De Gelone, 31 Mar. 1817, on verso; addressed: "Thomas Jefferson, Esqr Monticello—Virginia"; franked; postmarked Georgetown, 1 Mar.

[1] Manuscript: "reciving."

ENCLOSURE

Draft Power of Attorney to John Barnes for United States Stock Interest

Know all Men, by these presents That I, Thomas Jefferson, of Monticello in Virginia do subsitute—and Appoint—John Barnes, of George Town in the Territory of Columbia my Attorney in Fact for the purpose of Receiving from the Treasury of the United States—all Sums of Interest, due or to become due on any public Stock standing in the Name of Thaddeus Kosciusko. Now of Soleure in Swiserland—for whom, I am in fact Attorney as per Copy thereof Deposited in the Treasury of the U States. Referance thereto, will fully Appear

witness my hand & seal this day of 1817.

(Seal)

Witness—

Whether the above form—executed by Mr Jefferson & acknowledged by a Magistrate or Notarey—will admit JB. to receive[1] the Int. Quarterly—if not. be pleased to Correct it. for JB. to forward it Agreable to Mr Jeffersons request— Geo Town 26 feby 1817

MS (ViU: TJP-ER); entirely in Barnes's hand; at head of text: "Copy"; at foot of text: "To Richd Smith Esqr." Executed version enclosed in TJ to Barnes, 11 Mar. 1817.

[1] Manuscript: "recive."

To Hutchins G. Burton

Dear Sir Monticello Feb. 28. 17.

Your favor of the 4th was recieved yesterday evening only; and I hasten to return my thanks for the trouble you have in endeavoring to procure me some of the Scupernong wine. a quarter cask of it would be very desirable; and to be sent to the address of Messrs Gibson and Jefferson my correspondents at Richmond, which is my only convenient deposit. from thence we have water carriage direct to this place. the difficulty is thro' what channel to make the payment, and, the amount being unknown to me, I see no other than that of adding to your trouble that of your drawing on my account on Gibson and Jefferson in favor of the person who furnishes & forwards the wine. I will immediately write to them to honor your draught. this as to the present. but that I may be enabled to procure supplies hereafte[r I m]ust pray you to have the goodness to place me in correspondence with the person who makes the best crop of the wine. if you will be so good as to send me his name and address, and prepare him by letter for hearing from me, he and I can settle the channel of conveying the wines, and making payment to our mutual convenience. I understand the wine is made in the neighborhood of Albemarle sound, in which case he has possibly a correspondent at Norfolk, who with mine at Richmond can transact between us whatever is necessary. this will shorten the business and relieve you from the trouble of a more circuitous communication. I pray you to be assured of my due sense of your kindness and of my great respect & esteem.

Th: Jefferson

PoC (MHi); on verso of reused address cover of Joseph C. Cabell to TJ, 12 Jan. 1817; mutilated at seal; at foot of text: "Hutchins G. Burton esq."; endorsed by TJ.

From John W. Maury

Sir Frankfort Ky Feb. 28th 1817

It must be a source of consolation to one like yourself approaching the close of a long & illustrious life, to see by anticipation, the praise which a grateful country will bestow on your memory, by reading what is unanimously accorded to the only one whose services can claim a preference to yours, in our struggle for freedom. That you may long live to enjoy these anticipations and that freedom is Sir the sincere wish of your admirer John W Maury

RC (DLC); endorsed by TJ as received 1 Apr. 1817 and so recorded (with mistaken date of composition of 8 Feb.) in SJL. RC (MHi); address cover only; with PoC of TJ to Elisha Ticknor, 7 June 1817, on verso; addressed: "Thomas Jefferson Esquire Near Charlottesville Albemarle Virginia Via Washington City"; franked; postmarked Frankfort, 3 Mar., and Charlottesville, 1 Apr. Enclosure: Maury, "An Oration In commemoration of the birth of General Washington, delivered at the request of a committee appointed for that purpose, on the 22d of February 1817, in Frankfort, Ky.," recalling Washington's leadership and heroism; encouraging the audience to "Examine from time to time your own conduct, and compare it with his, to know whether you be likely to attain that excellence, which will make his memory as durable as letters, and as blessed as it will be brilliant"; and entreating "young countrymen" to pay tribute to Washington by demonstrating "some similitude to him, that the admiration, which we now offer up, is something more than vain panegyric, or empty fiction" (clipping from Frankfort *Commentator*, 28 Feb. 1817, in DLC: TJ Papers, 209:37312; at head of text: "The Commentator. Friday, February 28, 1817").

From Charles Willson Peale

DEAR SIR, Belfield Feb[y] 28. 1817.

In several visits I made to Philad[a] after receiving your statement concerning young M[c]elhany, my inquiries about him was fruitless, at last I meet with him at a Watch-makers who had promised me notice when he should be found in the City. M[r] M[c]elhany seemed much confused when he spoke to me, on my asking him why he did not call on you before he left Charlotteville—he told me that he wrote a letter to you, I told him that you had not received any letter from him before you wrote to me, and therefore you could not account for his leaving that place in so hasty a manner—He acqnowledged that you had been kind to him. I presumed to ask him, why he left Charloteville,[1] was it not a good place to get imployment? he said that several persons there informed him that he could not get business. I believe he is doing journey work in the Shop where I found him. If you wish me to make any further inquiries for another artist, please to inform me.

I find by a paragraph in some of our news-papers, that your numerous corrispondance is very burdensome to you; and prevent your enjoyment of reading &c sutable to your time of life. I sensebly feel for you, as I have felt that in having too much to do, that much time is mispent,—I see much of my past follies; in trying to do every thing I wanted done in mechanic arts—and also by my attempts in agriculture—which is most certainly the most honorable and salubrious employment; and my health has been much improved since I purchased this farm, but I have not mended my pecuniary affairs; In my first setting out, I hired too[2] many hands, and then on building a

Mill, I spent my time and money in Making Machinery, now totally lost, as I have given a part of said mill to my sons to carry on Cotton spinning—as my dust would spoil their work—my desire to aid sundry friends who had lost their teeth, also engrossed too much of my time—The Affairs of the Museum called for my attention. The envy of some men at the prosperity of the Museum has made them active to take from me the profits, to encrease the public treasury—By resuming my pensil to add as many valuable characters as I can obtain, & in my leisure moments to attend to a foreign corrispondance—and if I have hours to spare, to do something in the historical line, I believe will be the most profitable mode to serve the public, & my family will be most benefited thereby. you will propably think as many others have thought, that I am too far advanced in the vale of life to succeed well. I cannot be mistaken, at least I hope not, since my labours of one year has given Many proofs of my improvement in colouring, as well as correctniss of semblance. I ramble into tales of Igotism, one of the objects of this letter, is to ask your permission to give for publication, some of the many hints, which in our correspondance you have so obligingly communicated, for improovements on farming, as may be advantagous to farmers—either to the Agricultral Society, or elsewere as you may approve with, or without your Name—I mean simply only extracts of what I conceive are of much importance; the proper plowing of hilly grounds for corn; the simplicity of implements for cuting straw; and other machinery which I can select by looking over your letters.

I do not at this moment recollect any object that I deem worthy of engrossing your time, except that of cutting up corn stalks into small food for cattle—I attempted that work with a machine which I had at the mill, it was an English cutting machine with a heavy Wheel on which was fixed a curved cutting knife—My band, so you have observed in one of your letters, was too falacious—It was troublesome & so I gave it up—but I have lately heard of some Man in the City, having invented a machine that cuts corn Stocks with facility—I am inclined to beleive that the best method must be in the manner of a Guilotine with some means for feeding it, perhaps by rollers—but simplicity of moovements is all important—

If on seeing his machine I find it good, I mean to trouble you with another letter, The sweetness I taste in Corn stalks induces me to beleive it[3] must make a valuable addition to other food for Cattle.

accept my best wishes for your health and happiness and beleive me with much esteem your friend C W Peale

RC (DLC); damaged at seal, with two words supplied from PoC; addressed: "Thomas Jefferson Esq[r] Monticella Virginia"; stamped; postmarked Philadelphia, 1 Mar.; endorsed by TJ as received 15 Mar. 1817 and so recorded in SJL; with TJ's notation on address leaf relating to his 16 Mar. 1817 reply: "M[c]Ilheny variety of vocns extracts of my lres cutting & using cornstalks." PoC (PPAmP: Peale Letterbook).

The STATEMENT was in TJ to Peale, 24 Dec. 1816. Joseph E. McIlhenny wrote to TJ on 21 Dec. [1816], just before his HASTY departure from Charlottesville. Peale may have seen a newspaper version of TJ's second letter to Joseph Delaplaine of 25 Dec. 1816, which complained of his NUMEROUS CORRISPONDANCE. For the BAND deemed FALACIOUS by TJ, see Peale to TJ, 28 Dec. 1813, and TJ to Peale, 21 Mar. 1815.

[1]Manuscript: "Chartoleville."
[2]RC: "to." PoC: "too."
[3]Manuscript: "is."

From Peter H. Wendover

RESPECTED SIR— Washington City 1st March 1817

In January 1815 I had the honor to forward you from New York, a small volume[1] of Sermons delivered in that City, by the Rev Dr M[c]Leod, in the preceding Summer, adapted to the then reasonable expectation that an attack would be made on that part of our beloved Country by the British—To those Sermons you were pleased to give the testimony of your high approbation.

That worthy Divine having during the present Session of Congress made a visit to this City, presented me a volume[2] of some of his Sermons since preached, and recently published; I beg leave to enclose it to you Sir, in care of my worthy friend, the hon. Judge Nelson of Virginia who has kindly promised to deliver it to you.

With my best wishes that the remnant of your days may be as happy, as the past have been useful, permit me to subscribe myself

Sir, Most Respectfully Your Ob[t] & Hum[l] Serv[t]

P[R] H: WENDOVER

RC (MoSHi: TJC-BC); in an unidentified hand, signed by Wendover; endorsed by TJ as received 8 May 1817 and so recorded in SJL. RC (MoSHi: TJC-BC); address cover only; with PoC of TJ to John Le Tellier, 22 July 1817, on verso; addressed: "Thomas Jefferson Esquire Montecello Virginia." Enclosure: Alexander McLeod, *The Life and Power of True Godliness; described in a Series of Discourses* (New York, 1816; Poor, *Jefferson's Library*, 9 [no. 536]).

Wendover's earlier letter to TJ was dated 30 JANUARY 1815.

[1]Manuscript: "volumn."
[2]Manuscript: "volumn."

To Madame de Corny

Monticello Mar. 2. 1817.

It had been so long, my very dear and antient friend, since I had heard any thing of you thro' any channel, that I had become uncertain whether you might still be among the living. I have been relieved from that incertitude by the request of mr and mrs Derby to give them a letter to you, informing me at the same time that they had one for you from mrs Cruger. I give it therefore readily in return for the happiness they have procured me by this information, as well as to oblige them. I am not personally acquainted with them, but their reputation authorises me to assure you of their worth, and of the esteem in which they are held in the United States. they visited France and the Southern countries of Europe about a dozen years ago, and now propose to visit France and the Northern regions. permit them then, en passant, to pay their respects to you, & favor them with a portion of that partial attention which you have ever so kindly shown to us Americans. I claim it particularly for mrs Derby as a sample of our American fair.

Thro' what scenes, my dear friend, have we passed since those endeared to us by the society of mrs Church, Cosway, Trumbul E^{t}c. what transitions from those to the tyrannies of Robespierre, of the Directories, of Bonaparte, and now of the allies! these cannot have failed by their sweeping afflictions, to have overshadowed even your life with gloom, if not with suffering. and when are these to end? and how are they to end? but let us[1] not hoist the curtain which separates our time from those horrors. let us live out our little day without sympathising, if we can, with miseries which are to belong to another age. my country has been prosperous and happy: but, in endeavoring to make it so, my life has been worn down with cares and anxieties. twenty years of labor and solicitude, after parting with you, during which the whole of my time and attention was absorbed by incessant occupations, which cut me off from intercourse and correspondence with my friends, brought me to that period of life which it ceases to be enjoyment. altho' I have had good health, yet the hand of time presses heavily on me. I am become feeble in body, inert in mind, and much retired from the society of the world to that of my own fire-side. my eldest daughter, who was just old enough to be a little known to you, has rendered that a circle of no small compass. among ten grandchildren, and four great grandchildren, we are in no solitude. to another than yourself these would be uninteresting egotisms but the same friendship will render them acceptable to you, which makes me wish to hear from you, to know if you enjoy good health, if your spirits are lively, if they still derive nourishment from society, & above all if you have recovered from the effects of your unfortunate fall, so as to walk out and cheer yourself with the enlivening variety of the fields and public walks. give me another letter, my friend, and tell me all this, and a great deal more about yourself, and be assured of my unabated sentiments of affection and respect. Th: Jefferson

PoC (DLC); at foot of first page: "M[de] de Corny"; endorsed by TJ. Enclosed in TJ to Richard C. Derby, 6 Mar. 1817.

TJ's eldest daughter was Martha Jefferson Randolph.

[1]TJ here canceled "draw."

From Nicolas G. Dufief

Monsieur, A Philad[e] ce 3e de Mars. 1817

Je vous ai adressé, ce matin, par la poste, le dernier volume de mon dictionnaire. J'espère que les 3 volumes seront arrivés Sans accident. Il me Semble que Mr Gibson aurait été beaucoup plus régulier commercialement parlant de ne débiter votre compte des 31 d[lls] qu'autant que son correspondant de Philadelphie lui eût envoyé un reçu de Moi, que certainement il eût éxigé si l'on m'eût payé cette Somme.

J'ai l'honneur d'être avec le plus profond respect Votre très dévoué serviteur N. G. Dufief

P.S. Nous vous avons débité de 12 d[lls]: prix du dictionnaire & crédite de. 4[dl] $\frac{50}{100}$: balance qui vous était due

EDITORS' TRANSLATION

Sir, Philadelphia 3 March. 1817

This morning I sent you through the mail the last volume of my dictionary. I hope that the three volumes have arrived without incident. It seems to me that it would have been much more correct, commercially speaking, if Mr. Gibson had not debited the 31 dollars from your account until his correspondent in Philadelphia sent him a receipt from me. One would certainly have been demanded of me if I had been paid this sum.

I have the honor to be, with the most profound respect, your very devoted servant N. G. Dufief

P.S. We have debited you 12 dollars, the price of the dictionary, and credited you with $4.50, the balance due to you

RC (DLC); at foot of text: "Th: Jefferson. Esqre"; endorsed by TJ as received 15 Mar. 1817 and so recorded in SJL. Translation by Dr. Genevieve Moene.

Patrick Gibson's Philadelphia CORRESPONDANT was a Mr. Fisher.

To George Washington Jeffreys

SIR Montic[el]lo Mar. 3. 17.

Your favor of Feb. 17. came to hand two days ago. I wish it were more in my power to fulfill the request of furnishing you with a full and compleat catalogue for an Agricultural library. for this first and most useful of all human arts and sciences I have had from earliest life the strongest partiality. yet such have been the circumstances of the times in which I have happened to live that it has never been in my power to indulge it. my reading in that line therefore has been necessarily restrained. and for practice I have had still less leisure and opportunity until age had deprived me of the activity it called for. the catalogue therefore now inclosed, is sent rather in proof of my readiness, than of my competence to serve your society. there is probably no better husbandry known at present than that of England. but that is for the climate & productions of England. their books lay for us a foundation of good general principles: but we ought, for their application, to look more than we have done into the practices of countries and climates more homogeneous with our own. I speak as a Southern man. the agriculture of France and Italy is good, and has been better than at this time; the former in the age of De Serres, the latter in the time of Cato, Varro E^{t}c. lessons useful to us may also be derived from Greece and Asia Minor, in the times of their eminence in science and population. I wish I could have been more copious in that part of my catalogue; but my acquaintance with their agricultural writings has not enabled me to be so.

The horizontal ploughing, after which you enquire, has been practised here by Col^{o} Randolph, my son in law, who first introduced it, about a dozen or fifteen years.[1] it's advantages were so soon observed that it has already become very general, and has entirely changed & renovated the face of our country. every rain before that, while it did a temporary good, did greater permanent evil, by carrying off our soil; and fields were no sooner cleared than wasted. at present we may say that we lose none of our soil, the rain not absorbed in the moment of it's fall being retained in the hollows of the beds until it can be absorbed. our practice is when we first enter on this process, with a rafter level of 10.f. span, to lay off guide-lines, conducted horizontally from one end to the other of the field, and about 30. yards apart. the steps of the level on the ground are marked by a stroke of a hoe, and immediately followed by a plough to preserve the trace. a man, or a boy of 12. or 15. years old, with the level, and two smaller boys to mark the steps, the one with sticks, the other with the hoe, will do an acre of this an hour, and when once done, it is forever done. we generally level a field the year it is put into corn, until all have been once levelled. the intermediate furrows are run by the eye of the ploughman, governed by these guide lines, and is so done as to lay the earth in horizontal beds of 6.f. wide with deep hollows or water furrows between them, to hold superfluous rain. the inequalities of declivity in the hill will vary in places the distance of the guide lines, and occasion gores, which are thrown into short beds. As in ploughing very steep hillsides horizontally the common plough can scarcely throw the furrow up-hill, Col° Randolph has contrived a very simple alteration of the share which throws the furrow down-hill both going and coming. it is as if two shares were welded together at their strait side, and at a right angle with each other. this turns on it's bar as a pivot, so as to lay either share horizontal and the other vertical, & is done by the ploughman in an instant by a single motion of the hand, at the end of every furrow. I inclose a bit of paper cut into the form of the double share, which being opened, at the fold, to a right angle, will give an idea of it's general principle. I have transferred this method of ploughing to a possession I have near Lynchburg 90. miles to the S.W. from this place, where it is spreading rapidly, and will be the salvation of that, as it confessedly has been of this part of the country. horizontal and deep ploughing, with the use of plaister & clover, which are but beginning to be used here, we believe will restore this part of our country to it's original fertility which was exceeded by no upland in the state. This is the best account I am able to give you of the horizontal ploughing. poor, as I am, in the practice of agriculture, and not rich in it's theory, I can do no more than prove my wishes to be useful, adding those for the success of your institution, and assurances of my great respect & consideration.

TH: JEFFERSON

PoC (DLC); dateline faint; one word in body of text rewritten by TJ due to polygraph misalignment; at foot of first page: "M[r] George M. Jeffreys." Printed in *American Farmer* 2 (1820): 93–4.

Jeffreys addressed similar inquiries regarding an agricultural library to John Taylor and John Adams, and they responded on 16 Aug. 1816 and 29 July 1817, respectively (*American Farmer* 2 [1820]: 93, 94).

An engraving depicting the RAFTER LEVEL, along with excerpts from the letter above, appeared in *American Farmer* 1 (1820): 357–8, 358 (two editions of same date with variant pagination). The enclosed BIT OF PAPER folded to demonstrate the principle of Thomas Mann Randolph's plowshare has not been found, but for a similar example see TJ to Tristram Dalton, 2 May 1817, and enclosure. The POSSESSION I HAVE NEAR LYNCHBURG was Poplar Forest.

[1] *American Farmer* here adds "since."

E N C L O S U R E

Catalogue of Books on Agriculture

[ca. 3 Mar. 1817]

Geoponica Bassi. Niclasii. Lipsiae. 1781. Gr. Lat. 2. v. 8vo
Owen's translation of the Geoponics. Eng. 2. v. 8vo
Scriptores rei rusticae veteres. [Cato, Varro,[1] Columella, Palladius.] the edition published at Leipsic by Schneider about 1790–9. 8vo
Oeconomie rurale de Saboureux. 6. v. 8vo [a transln of Cato, Varro, Columella, Palladius][2]
Dickson's Husbandry of the antients. 2. v. 8vo

Dizzionario d'Agricultura dal Ronconi. 2. v. 8vo
L'Agricoltore del Trinci. 2. v. 12mo or 1. v. 8vo
Reflexions sur l'agriculture de Naples par Tupputi. 8vo
Corso di Agricultura dal Proposito Lastri. 5. v. 12mo
Istruzzione elementari di Agricultura, del Fabbroni. 8vo
Della Coltivazione degli Ulivi del Vettori, é degli Agrumi.[3] 8vo

Theatre d'agriculture de De Serres. 2. v. 4to the late edition with modern learned notes
Duhamel's husbandry.
Rozier. there is a body of French husbandry published by the Abbé Rozier and others, of high reputation, in 10. or 12. vols 4to title not recollected.
Traité de la Vigne de Bidet et Duhamel. 2. v. 12mo
Maupin sur la vigne. 8vo
Traité sur la vigne, par Chaptal, Rozier, Parmentier et Dussieux. 2. v. 8vo
Lasteyrie du Cotonnier et de sa culture. 8vo
Daubenton's advice to shepherds. 8vo [translated & published in Boston]
Lasteyrie sur les betes à laine d'Espagne. 8vo

Home's principles of agriculture and vegetation. 8vo
Mills's chemical elements of agriculture. 12mo
Kirwan on manures. 12mo
Hale's statical essays. 2. v. 8vo
Tull's horse-hoeing husbandry 8vo
Evelyn's Terra. by Hunter. 4to
Hale's body of husbandry 4. v. 8vo
Home' gentleman farmer. 8vo

Young's rural economy. 8vo Young's farmer's guide. 8vo Young's experimental agriculture. 3. v. 8vo Young's travels in France.	Young's Annals of agriculture and many other works, written merely for money, are scarcely worth buying. those here named contain whatever of his is worth having

Brown's rural affairs.
the Rural Socrates.

Boardley's Essays and Notes on husbandry 8vo
Taylor's Arator. 12mo
Peters's agricultural enquiries on Gypsum. 8vo
Livingston's essay on sheep. 8vo
Memoirs of the Philadelphia agricultural society 2. v. 8vo
Transactions of the agricultural society of N. York, 4to
[there are some good works published in the Eastern states. titles unknown.]

Millar's gardener's dictionary. fol.
Millar's gardener's Calendar. 8vo
Abercrombie's gardener's pocket dictionary. 3. v. 12mo
Every man his own gardener. by Mawe. 12mo
McMahon's American gardener's Calendar 8vo [Philadelphia.]
American gardener by Gardiner & Hepburn. 12mo [Washington]
a Treatise on gardening by John Randolph. 16[°][4] [Richmond]
Culture de la grosse Asperge de Hollande par Filassier 12mo
De la Brosse de la culture du figuier. 12mo
Langley's Pomona. fol.
Knight on the apple and pear, on cyder and perry. 12mo
Forsyth on the culture and management of fruit trees. 8vo
Evelyn's Sylva.
Traité sur les Abeilles[5] par della Rocca. 3. v. 8vo

PoC (DLC: TJ Papers, 209:37317); entirely in TJ's hand; undated; brackets in original except as explained in notes 2 and 4 below. Printed in *American Farmer* 2 (1820): 94.

This list of recommended books on agriculture may have been based in part on a similar one that TJ prepared for Wilson Cary Nicholas in 1809 (see TJ to Nicholas, 16 Dec. 1809, and enclosure).

[1] *American Farmer*: "Barro," here and in next entry.
[2] Omitted closing bracket editorially supplied.
[3] *American Farmer*: "agrunic."
[4] Superscript illegible.
[5] *American Farmer*: "Abeitles."

From Thomas Law

Dear Sir, Washington March 3rd 1817

I enclose to you what I deem a sine quâ non in finance—Mr Monroe is in favor of it & Mr Crawford desired the Com^{ee} on a national Currency to write to him that he might introduce it to a limited amount of five or ten Million—Mr Calhoun the Chairman promised to write, Mr Crawford replied he would be very glad of it—But Mr Calhoun never summoned the Com[ee] on the subject—

I remain With sincere esteem Yr mt Ob[t] st T LAW—

RC (DLC); endorsed by TJ as received 15 Mar. 1817 and so recorded in SJL. Enclosure not found.

John C. Calhoun chaired the United States House of Representatives Committee on a Uniform NATIONAL CURRENCY.

From John Trumbull

DEAR SIR Washington March 3[d] 1817.

I trust you will forgive my having so long delayed to answer your very kind letter of January 10th—the reason has been[1] that I could write nothing with certainty, until by passing the appropriation bill, the House of Representatives had sanctioned the agreement which was made with me by the President

I have now the pleasure to say that[2] I am authorized to paint four of the great Events of the Revolution:—the Declaration of Independance:—the Surrender of Burgoyne:—the Surrender of Cornwallis:—& the Resignation of Washington:—the pictures are to be 12 feet high by 18 feet long, which will give to the principal figures the Size of Life.—I shall begin with the Declaration of Independance, & shall exert all my Talent to produce a work worthy of the Event, and of the high patronage with which I am honored;[3]—The kind approbation of my object,[4] which you was so good as to express, contributed[5] powerfully to my very unexpected[6] Success;—and I beg you to accept my cordial thanks.[7]

My mind recurs with delight to the days which I formerly passed in your house at Paris, but time has not failed to exert his accustomed talent at Destruction;—M[rs] Church is gone:—He is ruined in fortune, & returned to England: Kitty is now M[rs] Cruger. & the mother of five or Six fine Children:—M[rs] Cosway, I believe is living in Milan with a Sister,[8] but I have no correct information of her for some time: even her brother M[r] Ge[o] Hatfield the architect here, has not heard lately.—I learn from Madame De Neuville, the French Minister's lady here,[9] that Madame de Corny is her particular friend, & was very lately in perfect health.

I beg to be mentioned with affectionate remembrance to your Daughter, and request you to accept my best wishes for your health, & for a long and happy Life.

I am D[r] Sir faithfully & gratefully your's JN[O] TRUMBULL

RC (DLC); at head of text: "Thos Jefferson Esqr"; endorsed by TJ as received 15 Mar. 1817 and so recorded in SJL. Dft (CtY: Franklin Collection); first page only; evidently removed from a letterbook and now tipped into an extra-illustrated copy of *Autobiography, Reminiscences and Letters of John Trumbull, from 1756 to 1841* (1841); only the most significant variations are noted below.

For the APPROPRIATION BILL, see note to Trumbull to TJ, 26 Dec. 1816. Anne Marguerite Joséphine Henriette Rouillé de Marigny Hyde DE NEUVILLE was the wife of Jean Guillaume Hyde de Neuville, the French ambassador to the United States.

[1] Dft here adds "that I did not feel."

[2] Dft here adds "unexpected Success has attended me."

[3] Dft: "high patronage which I enjoy."

[4] Preceding three words not in Dft.

[5] Word interlined in Dft in place of "weighed."

[6] Preceeding two words not in Dft.

[7] Dft here cancels "—in truth."

[8] Preceding three words not in Dft.

[9] Dft ends here with "that Madame de Corny is living, & well, & an intimate friend of hers."

From William Johnson

MY DEAR SIR Washington March 4. 1817

I have committed to the Care of my young Friend Mr Todd a small Present of which I must solicit your Acceptance not from any intrinsic Value in the thing itself, but as an Expression of my grateful, respectful and affectionate Recollection.

It is a walking-Stick which appears to be of Tortoise shell but it is in Fact only that Substance moulded over a hickory Rod by a simple but ingenious Process which will immediately occur to you. I hope you will find it somewhat of a Rarity.

But Sir the Head of it is in my Eye & I hope it will be in yours more an Object of Interest. It is taken from the Root of an Oak under which your venerable Friend Gadsden assembled the first little Band of Conspirators that convened in our Country. The Place where it stood was remote and retired from Observation. About thirty of them met of whom but one is now living. After solemnly deliberating on the interesting Subject which brought them together, with Hands crossd and united round the Tree, they took the dangerous Resolution which you will read on the Scroll which encircles the Oak engraven on the Head of this walking Stick. "We will resist" I believe it to be a Fact that not an Individual Swerved from this Resolution;—With regard to their Leader no one knows better than yourself with what Energy & Firmness he adhered to it. The Tree was cut down by the British, but I took up the Root and have made use of it in various Ways to keep alive the Sacred Flame of —76.

I have also taken the Liberty to send you a Copy of an Essay which I delivered not long Since to a Society which we have established in Charleston for the Purpose of drawing together the little Science that our Country can boast of. I must solicit much Indulgence for this humble Effort not to satisfy Enquiry but only to excite it. On the Subject of the Olive our Prospects begin to brighten, and I had some of my own raising cured which I intended to send on to you, had I been able to obtain an Opportunity. I have a great Wish that you should eat of the Trees introduced by yourself.

With the sincerest Wishes for your Happiness I subscribe myself
With the profoundest Respect & Esteem
Your very hle S[t] WILL[M] JOHNSON JR

P.S. Since the Commencement of the severe Cold of this Winter the Tortoise-Shell has shrunk from the Head exhibiting a neat little Instance of relative contractibility or perhaps of relative [Speci]fic Heat. I expect it will return in the Summer & force [out] the Wax

RC (DLC); edge chipped; postscript written perpendicularly along left margin of final page; beneath signature: "Thomas Jefferson Esqr"; endorsed by TJ as a letter received 4 May 1817 from "Johnson W[m] (judge)." Recorded in SJL as received 3 May 1817. Enclosure: Johnson, *Nugæ Georgicæ; An Essay, delivered to the Literary and Philosophical Society of Charleston, South-Carolina, October 14, 1815* (Charleston, 1815; Poor, *Jefferson's Library*, 7 [no. 303]; TJ's copy in MBPLi, inscribed on title page (trimmed): "To Thomas Jefferson Esqr With a Tender of the Venerati[on] of the Author").

Christopher GADSDEN organized the Sons of Liberty in Charleston (*ANB*).

In the enclosure Johnson quoted from TJ's observations on European OLIVE cultivation in his letter to William Drayton of 30 July 1787 (*PTJ*, 11:644–50, esp. 648) and asserted that TJ had erred in stating that a tree produces a good crop of fruit at twenty years old, contending instead that "This may be true when raised from the seed; and it may also be true that it is continually improving until that age. But I have eaten olives from my own trees in six years after I commenced to propagate them, and by raising them from scions, cuttings and root-grafting, the production is materially expedited" (pp. 28–9).

From Thomas Eston Randolph

DEAR SIR Ashton 4th March 1817

M[r] Colclaser, the Miller at Shadwell, who is equally concern'd with me in that business, has received an advantageous offer from M[r] Philip Payne to superintend a Mill which he has lately erected on the waters of Roanoke, and wishes to be inform'd immediately, if he will accept it.—In consequence thereof he applied to me yesterday to know my intentions respecting Shadwell Mill; but as the Lease under which I occupy it expires the 1st July next, it is necessary that I should previously consult with you on the subject, for which purpose I will do myself the pleasure to call at MºCello in a day or two—It may not be amiss that I state to you, that we wish to rent the Mill for 3 years for a certain mony rent, to be paid quarterly—and to have the priviledge of extending the lease to 5 years—in which case we shall immediately engage a Millwright to commence a complete repair of the machinery the instant we have finish'd grinding—the contemplated repairs are estimated to cost 500 to $550.—

We shall expect that you will do such repairs as are indispensable in consequence of the Mill walls leaving the Floors, and thereby causing a serious loss of wheat &c—We propose also that you remove the Head block walls, so that by lengthening the Shafts the water wheels may not rub as they now do, nor cast the water against the Mill walls, the former frequently causes them to be stop'd in the winter, and to the latter circumstance I am disposed to attribute the settling of that corner of the Mill, the rock was originally soft, and being constantly, wet, it has yielded to the great pressure above—The end wall (that next the wheels) has settled considerably during the last year, and I think a prop or props may be so placed as to assist it very materially—we also wish to know whether we can have access to your Land to get Timber for the necessary repairs of the Mill, and on what terms?—

I am with great respect & Afft regards Yrs

THOS ESTON RANDOLPH

RC (MHi); dateline at foot of text; addressed: "Thomas Jefferson Esqe MºCello"; endorsed by TJ as received 5 Mar. 1817 and so recorded in SJL.

From Joshua Stow

SIR, Middletown Ct March 4–1817.

Permit me, in the name of the Connecticut Society for the encouragement of American Manufactures, to enclose to you their Address and Constitution.

I am, very respectfully Your Obedient Servant J STOW

RC (CSmH: JF-BA); addressed: "The Hon, Thomas Jefferson, Monticello, Virginia"; franked; postmarked; endorsed by TJ as received 20 Mar. 1817 and so recorded in SJL. Enclosure: *Address of the Connecticut Society for the Encouragement of American Manufactures* (Middletown, 1817; Poor, *Jefferson's Library*, 6 [no. 223]; TJ's copy in DLC: Rare Book and Special Collections), asserting that the encouragement of American manufactures should not be a partisan issue; calling for impartial support of agriculture, manufacturing, and commerce; arguing that the protection and encouragement of these domestic endeavors is the best defense against dependence on Europe; demonstrating that domestic manufacturing will strengthen the bonds between the northern and southern states; warning that New England risks depopulation unless it acts; noting that the society will encourage Americans to "*compare American fabrics with foreign, and when the former, of equal worth, are offered at equal price, let them be purchased in preference to the latter*" (p. 22); observing that although Connecticut has an advantage in manufacturing and a comparatively numerous population, its produce is "barely sufficient for its own consumption," and adding that while "*carrying* and *foreign* commerce are permanently impaired," the "Coasting trade will derive its principal aid from the manufactures of our country. They are the *last*, *best hope* of Connecticut" (p. 22); and concluding with the society's constitution and slate of officers as adopted at Middletown, 18 Feb. 1817.

Joshua Stow (1762–1842), public official, served as commissary agent on Moses Cleaveland's survey of the Connecticut Western Reserve in 1796. Stow purchased an Ohio township within that land claim and named it after himself. In 1813 he was a director of the Middletown Bank, and he became a federal tax collector in Middletown that same year. Stow served in 1818 as a delegate to a Connecticut constitutional convention, where he was among those selected to frame and draft the constitution. A strong anti-Federalist, he lobbied for protection of religious freedom, and he eventually won an award for damages when he sued the editor of the New Haven *Connecticut Journal* for libel after it published incendiary remarks on that subject attributed to him. Stow was a state senator in 1820, and he served as postmaster for Middletown from at least 1817 until 1841 (OClWHi: Stow Papers; Henry Howe, *Historical Collections of Ohio* [1890–91], 3:337–8; Richard J. Purcell, *Connecticut in Transition, 1775–1818* [1918], 376, 379, 380; J. Hammond Trumbull, *Historical Notes on The Constitutions of Connecticut, 1639–1818* [1901], 52, 54, 56, 57; *Report of the case of Joshua Stow vs. Sherman Converse, for a Libel* [New Haven, 1822]; *The Connecticut Register, for the Year of our Lord, 1813* [New London, (1812)], 134; *The Connecticut Register, and United States Calendar, for the Year of our Lord 1817* [New London, (1816)], 150, 174; *The Connecticut Register, and United States Calendar, for the Year of our Lord 1820* [New London, (1819)], 49; *JEP*, 2:438, 440, 4:610, 615, 5:335 [13, 20 Dec. 1813, 16, 20 Feb. 1837, 3 Feb. 1841]; Middletown *Constitution*, 12 Oct. 1842; gravestone inscription in Middlefield Cemetery, Middlesex Co., Conn.).

From Thomas Appleton

Sir — Leghorn 5th march 1817—

By the ship Heroine Capt Smith for Boston, I have address'd to the care of mr. Dearborn, the collector, a bag containing about half a bushel of Lupinella grass-seed; requesting he would give it, the earliest conveyance to you.—it was my intention, to have sent it by a vessel bound to one of the southern ports, but having chang'd her destination for another part of Europe, I am compell'd to improve the present opportunity for Boston; and which departs in the course of the day.—of all the grass of Italy, no one approaches the numerous qualities of the Lupinella. I have taken the liberty then, to send you this little parcel of the Seed, with the inclos'd directions, as to its cultivation, knowing as I well do how great will be the acquisition to our country, if it can be Successfully introduc'd; a circumstance of which I cannot have the Smallest doubt.—I have, likewise, sent some of these Seed to m[r] Crawford, as he wrote me, how desirous he was, to obtain some Valuable grass, to make a trial in Georgia.—I have also Sent another parcel, to M[r] John Prince of Boston, who, I understand, is distinguish'd for his experiments and improvements in grass.—I mention their names, that you may be able to learn from them, their success.—Since my letter of the 20th of march of the last year, informing you of the death of m[r] mazzei, I am totally depriv'd of any of your favors: a circumstance I greatly regret, in a special manner, as it prevents me from being able to give any satisfactory reply to the very pressing inquiries of mad[me] mazzei, as to the period, when she can receive the amount of her property in the united States.—my last respects, Sir, were in date of the 27th of September, by the brig Saucy-Jack, Capt[n] Richard Humphries for charleston-Carolina. at the same time, I shipp'd for you, and to the care of the Collector, two cases of Ama-wine—this letter contain'd some observations on the Statue and piedestal of Washington, intended for the senate hall of north-Carolina—as I, likewise, wrote Governor Miller, very fully on this subject, I am, therefore, anxiously waiting his reply, for m[r] Canova of Rome, accepted the commission.—

Accept, Sir, the very Sincere expressions of my great esteem & respect—
TH: APPLETON

RC (DLC); addressed: "Thomas Jefferson, esquire Monticello Virginia," with additional notation: "favor'd by Capt Smith Ship Heroine Via Boston"; franked; postmarked Boston, 22 Apr.; endorsed by TJ.

Appleton's most recent letter was that of 20 Oct. 1816, not the one he sent on the 27TH OF SEPTEMBER.

ENCLOSURE

Thomas Appleton's Notes on Lupinella Grass Seed

[ca. 5 Mar. 1817]

Lupinella-grass-seed

The Lupinella grass is unquestionably, the most prolific & most nutricious, known in Italy. and preferr'd by horses, oxen, sheep &[c] to every other species.—It should be planted in grounds, not Subject to inundations, or wet soils—it is commonly planted here, on small elevations.—It should be cut with a Sickle, as is grain, and bound in Small bundles of about 7# each, to prevent the flowers from wasting; and a short time before they are perfectly mature—The Cattle fed on this hay, require no oats or brans; indeed, it should be given with moderation to horses of luxury: to hard-labouring horses, it may be freely given.—In addition to these qualities, the ground in which it has been planted, three successive years, on the fourth, you may plant wheat, from which you will reap a most abundant harvest, without the aid of any species of manure—the leanest grounds by this cultivation, become rich & fertile.—It produces here about six thousand american pounds of hay, on a field which would require two bushels of wheat.—

MS (DLC: TJ Papers, 209:37125); entirely in Appleton's hand; undated.

To Thomas Mann Randolph

DEAR SIR Montic[el]lo Mar. 5. 17.

I inclose you a letter from Judge Peters, president of the board of agriculture at Philadelphia, solliciting either a drawing or a model of your hill-side plough. I prefer sending it to you while at Varina, because as you have Isaac there you may find it as easy to have the plough made there as a model, and from Varina you can give it a ready passage to Philadelphia. this however as is convenient to yourself.

Anne continued mending and was able to be taken up out of her bed and to sit up two or three days, until she was taken with a bowel complaint which has checked her course of convalescence. Dr Bankhead had gone down before this came on her. every body else is well here. At court the day before Yesterday, Yancey declined offering himself for any thing; and Maury[1] having declined also, Dabney Minor & Capt Clarke became sole candidates. no opposition to Cabell. ever and affectionately yours. TH: JEFFERSON

PoC (ViU: TJP-ER); on verso of reused address cover of William Sampson to TJ, 9 Jan. 1817; dateline faint; at foot of text: "Col^o^ T. M. Randolph"; endorsed by TJ. For the enclosed letter from Richard Peters to TJ, 15 Feb. 1817, not found, see note to TJ to Joshua Stow, 23 Mar. 1817. Enclosed in TJ to Bernard Peyton, 5 Mar. 1817 (not found) (see Peyton to TJ, 10 Mar. 1817, and note).

ANNE: Ann C. Bankhead.

[1] TJ here canceled "& mr Clarke."

From Valentine W. Southall

DEAR SIR, March 5. '17

By referance to the acts concerning roads I find, that an application to the County Court to discontinue a road must be preceded by one month's notice in some public paper and an advertisement at the door of the courthouse. See 1 Vol. R. Code p. 423.

Jeff. tells me this has not been done. I, therefore, thought it best to delay the application,

respectfully V. W. SOUTHALL

RC (MHi); endorsed by TJ as received 6 Mar. 1817 and so recorded in SJL.

Valentine Wood Southall (d. 1861), attorney and public official, was a family friend and frequent visitor to Monticello in his youth. He was admitted to the Albemarle bar in 1813 and succeeded Thomas Jefferson Randolph four years later as collector of the federal direct tax and internal duties for Virginia's 19th Collection District. Southall was the first secretary for the Board of Visitors of Central College and presided over a dinner held at the Rotunda of the University of Virginia during Lafayette's visit in November 1824. He represented Albemarle County in nine sessions of the House of Delegates, 1833–34, 1835–36, 1839–42, and 1843–46, and served as Speaker, 1840–42 and 1844–45. Southall was also a member of his county's delegations to the state's constitutional convention of 1850–51 and the state convention of 1861, in the latter of which he joined the majorities that first rejected and then approved secession (*Speakers and Clerks of the Virginia House of Delegates, 1776–1976* [1976], 63; Woods, *Albemarle*, 317–8; Pierson, *Jefferson at Monticello*, 90–1; *JEP*, 3:68 [2, 3 Jan. 1817]; Meeting Minutes of the Central College Board of Visitors, 5 May 1817; *Richmond Enquirer*, 16 Nov. 1824; Leonard, *General Assembly*; Albemarle Co. Will Book, 26:240–4; Washington *Daily National Intelligencer*, 4 Sept. 1861).

"An Act to amend and explain the act concerning Public Roads" appeared on P. 423 of the first volume of *A Collection of all such Acts of the General Assembly of Virginia, of a public and permanent nature, as are now in force* (Richmond, 1803–8). JEFF.: Thomas Jefferson Randolph.

To Richard C. Derby

SIR Monticello Mar. 6. 17.

Your letter of Feb. 27. from Washington is just now recieved. mrs Randolph and family, as well as myself, would have been much gratified by the visit which mrs Derby and yourself had proposed to make us at Monticello, had the state of the roads, the weather, & other circumstances permitted it. but 'tout ce qui est differé n'est pas perdu,' as the French say, and as I am by your letter encouraged to expect after your return. after travelling over so much foreign country a more extended knolege of our own may offer you interesting contrasts, and not all of them to our disadvantage.

It had been so long since I had heard of Madame de Corny that I had begun to be uncertain whether she was still living, and on that doubt had been afraid to write to her. but mrs Cruger being good authority for that fact I now write with pleasure, and am indebted to mrs Derby and yourself for the opportunity of doing it. my last information was that she had become decrepid by a fall and much retired from the world. twenty seven years of revolutions & counterevolutions, aided by the ordinary course of mortality have swept off the whole of my friends & acquaintances in Paris, Madame de Corny & Mons[r] de la Fayette excepted. to this last you need no letter, & I recollect no other now living to whom a letter would be either useful or agreeable to you. I have some literary correspondents there, not personally known to me, nor as to their habits of society. I thank you for your kind offers of service in Europe: but I am so far withdrawn from my relations with that hemisphere, as to leave me nothing wherewith to trouble you. with the Indian wish therefore of clear skies, smooth waters, and propitious spirits, I tender to mrs Darby and yourself the assurance of my high respect & consideration

TH: JEFFERSON

PoC (DLC); on verso of a reused address cover from Nicolas G. Dufief to TJ; edge torn, with missing text rewritten by TJ; at foot of text: "Richard C. Derby esq."; endorsed by TJ. Enclosure: TJ to Madame de Corny, 2 Mar. 1817.

Derby's letter FROM WASHINGTON was dated 23 Feb. 1817. TOUT CE QUI EST DIFFERÉ N'EST PAS PERDU: "not all that is postponed is lost."

To John Wayles Eppes

DEAR SIR Monticello Mar. 6. 17.

I have detained Martin a little longer than you intended because my waggons were to set off this day for Bedford[1] and I concluded to send him with the work he had done by one of them. it was but one day's journey of their way, and saves your waggon a trip of 5. days to come for them. by Martin's count there are 129. knobs. their tops will require to be kept well painted, as they present the end of the grain to the weather.

I send you also the dial I promised to make you. I calculated the hourlines, and adapted the gnomon to the latitude of Willis's mountain, as I found it by the last observation & with the best instrument, which latitude is marked on the dial. I inclose directions for setting it.

M[rs] Eppes will recieve herewith a box containing some calycanthuses, prickly locusts (Robinia hispida) a Snowberry bush and the sweet-scented curran. the two last were brought from the Pacific ocean by Lewis & Clarke. the snowberry is beautiful in autumn & winter by it's bunches of snow white berries. I send in a paper some sprout kale to be sowed and transplanted as cabbage. it is to remain in it's place during winter, and will give 2. or 3. successive crops of sprouts from the beginning of December to April, and is a fine, tender, sweet winter vegetable. a letter from mr Burton informs me he has been so kind as to take measures to procure me a cask of Scupernong. Francis has gone on diligently with his Spanish, and in a month more will be sufficiently master of it not to lose it. he will then return to you. mr Wood wishes very much to have him, having been greatly pleased with him at Poplar forest. he is undoubtedly our best Grecian,[2] and will pay particular attention to Francis. on account of health I much wish he had opened his school at Lynchburg. however his vacation is during the sickly months. present me respectfully to mrs Eppes and be assured of my constant & affectionate attachment & respect TH: JEFFERSON[3]

P. S. I have just recollected that mrs Eppes asked for some figs. I have therefore had put into the box some of a purple fig deemed very fine, but some also of a white fig which I brought from Marseilles superior to any thing of the kind I have ever seen. we have also found a single Halesia plant, the only one I have except the mother bush. it is the most magnificent flowering shrub I have ever seen. mine is 15. or 20.f. high and 30.f. diameter

RC (PPAmP: Thomas Jefferson Papers); edge torn, with missing text supplied from PoC; postscript on verso; addressed: "John W. Eppes esquire Millbrook." PoC (CSmH: JF); on verso of reused address cover of Robert Patterson to TJ, 13 Dec. 1816; mutilated at seal; endorsed by TJ. Enclosure: TJ's Instructions for Setting a Sundial, [ca. 6 Mar. 1817].

[1] Preceding two words interlined.

[2] RC: "Graecian." PoC: "Grecian."

[3] In place of full postscript, verso of PoC reads "P. S. a Halesia sent. also purple & white figs."

To Fernagus De Gelone

SIR Monticello Mar. 6. 17.

I recieved last night your's of Feb. 25. and now ask the favor of you to send me the Archimede de Peyrard 2. v. 8vo 4. D 50 [C] and Hippocrate de Gardeil. 4. v. 8vo 8.D. for which I inclose you 12. D 50 C in bills of the Richmond banks which I presume can be exchanged at par with you, as they are 1. or 2. p.c. above par at Philadelphia. if any person who is coming on by the stage to Washington would deliver them there to mr Millegan bookseller, or coming on to Richmond would deliver them there to messrs Gibson & Jefferson merchants, it would be the quickest conveyance. otherwise they may come by water from New York, whence coal vessels, flour vessels Etc sail daily for Richmond where, if delivered to Gibson & Jefferson they will pay charges & forward them. drop me a line of information if you please, when dispatched and by what conveyance, and accept the assurance of my respect. TH: JEFFERSON

PoC (MHi); on verso of reused address cover of Jerman Baker to TJ, 13 Jan. 1817; edge trimmed; mutilated at seal, with missing text rewritten by TJ; at foot of text: "M. Fernagus de Gelone"; endorsed by TJ.

Instructions for Setting a Sundial

[ca. 6 Mar. 1817]

To set the Dial.

The first and all-important object is to have the top of the dial post perfectly horizontal. without this it never can be true one moment. to this end, after the post is immoveably fixed in the ground, the top should be tried with a level and planed to the true horizontal level in every direction. it will take a butt of a tree 28. or 29.I. diameter. when planed, place the dial on it concentrically with the post. fix the gnomon of the dial in it's groove truly, the toe at the 6. aclock mark, the heel on the 12. aclock or meridian line.[1] test the perpendicularity of the gnomon by the walnut square sent; (which square had better be kept to rectify the perpendicularity occasionally when, by any accident it gets bent.) set the dial then as nearly right as you can, by a watch, or by guess. about 9. aclock in the forenoon stick a bit of wax, of the size & form of a Bristol-drop shot on the upper edge of the gnomon, sliding it up or down on the edge until[2] it's shadow shall fall exactly on the outer circle of the dial. mark that point in the circle slightly with the point of a pin. let the wax stay on exactly in the same place,[3] and, in the afternoon, watch when it's shadow shall be crossing the same circle on the other side, and mark the circle there again with the point of a pin. if these two points are equidistant from the 12. aclock, or meridian line, the dial is right: if not, take half the difference between their two distances from the meridian line, and twist the dial plate round on the block exactly that much from the nearest point. do the same the next day, & so the 3^{d} 4th E^{t}c. days until the shadow of the wax pellet shall cross the circle exactly equidistantly from the meridian. your dial will then be accurately true. have 2. nails ready entered in the North and South nail holes in the margin and tap them alternately that they may fix the dial firmly[4] to the block without jostling it out of place, and when driven home secure it by screws thro' the other holes. the gnomon being of sheet lead and liable to be bent is made to take out easily to be straitened again between two boards.

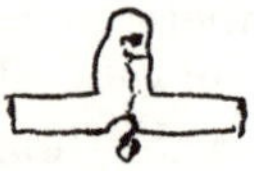

MS (MHi); written entirely in TJ's hand on verso of portion of a reused address cover to him; undated. Enclosed in TJ to John Wayles Eppes, 6 Mar. 1817.

In 1782 William Watts of Bristol, England, patented a method of dropping hot lead from different heights to produce small round SHOT of varying sizes (*Repertory of Arts and Manufactures* 3 [1795]: 313–5).

[1] Reworked from "the heel where the 12. aclock or meridian line intersects the inner circle."

[2] Preceding nine words interlined in place of "so that."

[3] Preceding five words interlined.

[4] Word interlined.

From William Pelham

SIR, Zanesville Ohio Mar. 6. 1817

I had some years ago the pleasure of submitting to your inspection an humble attempt to note the sounds of the English Language which was favorably received. Since that period I have removed from Boston and become an inhabitant of Ohio.

The perusal of an editorial article in our republican paper of this day prompts me to request that I may be permitted to lay before you (with the utmost deference and respect) the paper which contains it, as a specimen not only of the state of the typographic art in this town, but of the prevailing sentiments of the people, as expressed by the intelligent editor who is also from Boston.

If the liberty I thus take of a few moments intrusion should be deemed impertinent and unseasonable I shall sincerely regret my error, if otherwise, I shall feel gratified in my attempt to afford you a few minutes relaxation from more important concerns.

I am, Sir,
with true respect, Your humble Serv[t] W[M] PELHAM

RC (MHi); endorsed by TJ as received 31 Mar. 1817 and so recorded in SJL. RC (MHi); address cover only; with PoC of TJ to Stephen Girard, 7 June 1817, on verso; addressed: "Honourable Tho[s] Jefferson Monticello Virginia."

The enclosed REPUBLICAN PAPER was the Zanesville *Muskingum Messenger*. Josiah Heard, formerly of Wayland, Massachusetts, joined the paper in 1816 and was sole publisher by November of that year (Brigham, *American Newspapers*, 2:822; John H. Edwards, *A History of the Heard Family, of Wayland, Mass.* [1880], 12). The main editorial in the 6 Mar. 1817 issue, "The Fourth of March," concerned the United States Constitution. Calling on citizens to remain watchful of government, it warned of "less danger of our constitution being subverted by the governments of Europe, than of its being undermined by domestic traitors," and concluded with a reminder that officers of both the national and state governments should be so monitored that, if legislators' conduct did not comport with the "principles of republicanism and justice which are recognized by our state constitution," the next election might supply a "corrective" measure.

From Robert Walsh

Balt^r^ 6^h^ March 1817

M^r^ Ro Walsh J^r^ has the honor to present to Mr Jefferson the volume sent herewith, presuming that the scientific and literary intelligence which it Contains, may be of interest to one, who embraces so large a portion of human knowledge in the range of his enquiry.

RC (DLC); dateline at foot of text; addressed: "Thomas Jefferson Esqre"; endorsed by TJ as received 15 Mar. 1817 and so recorded in SJL.

Robert Walsh (1784–1859), author, educator, and diplomat, was a native of Baltimore who studied at Saint Mary's Seminary (Saint Mary's College from 1805 and later Saint Mary's Seminary and University) and Georgetown College (later Georgetown University). He read law with Robert Goodloe Harper. After completing his education, Walsh traveled in Europe and spent some time as secretary to William Pinkney at the American legation in London. When Walsh returned to the United States in 1809, he settled in Philadelphia, where he edited a succession of short-lived publications. In 1817 he joined José Corrêa da Serra in a visit to Monticello. Walsh founded the *American Quarterly Review* in 1827 and headed it until at least 1835. He also contributed articles to the *Encyclopædia Americana*, supplied the biography of Benjamin Franklin for *Delaplaine's Repository*, edited several literary works, and published his own monographs, including *An Appeal from the Judgments of Great Britain respecting the United States of America* (Philadelphia, 1819; Poor, *Jefferson's Library*, 11 [no. 685]), a work that garnered praise from TJ. Walsh was elected to the American Philosophical Society in 1812, served as professor of general literature at the University of Pennsylvania, 1818–28, and became a trustee of that institution in the latter year. In 1844 President John Tyler appointed him United States consul at Paris, a position from which he resigned in 1851. Walsh remained in France and died in Paris (*DAB*; Madison, *Papers, Retirement Ser.*, 1:170; Mary Frederick Lochemes, *Robert Walsh: His Story* [1941]; APS, Minutes, 17 Jan. 1812 [MS in PPAmP]; *Catalogue of the Alumni of the University of Pennsylvania* [1877], 9, 11; TJ to Francis W. Gilmer, 14 Oct. 1817, and note; TJ to Walsh, 6 Feb. 1820; *JEP*, 6:361, 370, 8:296 [18, 31 Dec. 1844, 27 Feb. 1851]; Philadelphia *North American and United States Gazette*, 28 Feb. 1859; Washington *Daily National Intelligencer*, 5 Aug. 1859).

The VOLUME SENT HEREWITH was the *American Register; or Summary Review of History, Politics, and Literature* (1817; Poor, *Jefferson's Library*, 14 [no. 926]), vol. 1. Walsh edited both volumes of this semiannual serial. In 1810 and 1811 he had also edited vols. 6–7, the concluding numbers, of the *American Register, or General Repository of History, Politics and Science* (Lochemes, *Robert Walsh*, 49, 60, 68, 82–8, 229).

To Joel Yancey

[DE]AR SIR Montic[e]ll[o] Mar. 6. 17.

During the unexampled spell of hard weather which we had [in] Jan. & Feb.,[1] I thought it better not to send the waggoners on the road, and especially as Milly and her two young children were to come back with them. but it has been with inexpressible regret that I have been obliged to retain them latterly while these fine ploughing days were passing. but the necessity of bringing corn from a distance to save us from starving, obliged me to keep them till this day. I thought it better to add a 6th mule and carry your waggon as well as ours, and prevent Dick's having two trips. the quantity of corn I have been obliged to buy here and it's high price will take all the money of the year nearly; for the June as well as August drought, of which you had only the latter reduced us below the third of an ordinary crop. I have not heard yet whether the flour from Bedford is gone down. the tob° has of course been retarded by the bad weather for handling it. I inclose a bill of scantling which I hope mr Martin will be so good as to saw immediately, as it is what is to employ John Hemings in the autumn. I send by the waggon a box which may be set any where in the house. I expect to be with you about the middle of April, and I believe I left directions for Nace as to the garden. some artichoke roots are sent by the waggon which he must plant in the locks of the fence within the large garden. those we got from mr Clay are not the true kind. they will carry some Pride of China plants which may be planted[2] somewhere near the mounds. if we can conveniently fix some Guinea shoats to breed from[3] the waggon shall carry a male and two or three females. Accept the assurance of my great friendship and respect TH: JEFFERSON

PoC (MHi); on verso of portion of a reused address cover from John Adams or Abigail Adams to TJ; dateline, salutation, and one additional word faint; at foot of text: "Mr Yancey"; endorsed by TJ. Enclosure not found.

Milly's TWO YOUNG CHILDREN were Sandy (b. 1813) and Jane (b. 1816) (Betts, *Farm Book*, pt. 1, 131). TJ first grew PRIDE OF CHINA PLANTS, also called the chinaberry tree, at Monticello in 1778 (Betts, *Garden Book*, 76, 79, 83).

[1] Reworked from "Feb. and March."
[2] TJ here canceled "any."
[3] TJ here canceled "a pair shall go for each place."

To Fernagus De Gelone

SIR Monticello Mar. 7. 17.

After dispatching my letter of yesterday in answer to your's of Feb. 25. I looked over the catalogue you had inclosed me and found 2. or 3. other books which I will pray you to send me with those ordered in my letter, to wit.

La Conquista de Mexico, De Solis 3. v. 8vo I take for granted it is in Spanish.
Borda. usage du Cercle 4to
Tragedies d'Euripides. 4. v. 12mo if in <u>prose</u>; but not if in <u>verse</u>.

the prices not being mentioned, if you will note them to me I will remit them in the same way I did for the others. I salute you with respect. TH: JEFFERSON

PoC (MHi); on verso of reused address cover of Thomas Appleton to TJ, 20 Oct. 1816; at foot of text: "M. Fernagus de Gelone"; endorsed by TJ.

To Simon Bernard

SIR Monticello Mar. 8. 17.

I am honored with your letter of Feb. 21. covering one from my friend the General la Fayette. I sincerely congratulate you on your arrival in this land of peace and safety, and still more I congratulate my country on the acquisition of your talents, which, directing our preparations for war, are most likely to continue it a land of peace and safety. I wish that in any circumstances of your new situation, you may find a compensation for the great change of society and habits you must experience. I should certainly have been happy to have recieved you at Monticello: but yield, as I ought to the claims of the public on you, as well as to your personal convenience, to which the season, the state of the roads and length of journey would not have been propitious. should your future duties or curiosity lead you at any time into this region of country, I shall always be proud to prove to you in person my high sense of your worth, and of the obligations we shall owe you, and I salute you with assurances of my great esteem and respect. TH: JEFFERSON

PoC (DLC); on verso of reused address cover to TJ; at foot of text: "Gen[l] Bernard"; endorsed by TJ.

To George M. Dallas

SIR Monticello Mar. 8. 17.

Condoling sincerely, as I have done, with the family of the late mr Dallas, as well as with the public, for the great loss sustained in him, it is a satisfaction to learn that we are likely to have the benefit of whatever he has left in writing. what this may be I am not informed, except so far as already published: but besides the benefit of a republication, I am sure he has written nothing which will not be instructive to the public, and honorable to himself. his mind was of that character which could produce nothing incorrect. I have no hesitation therefore in adding mine to the suffrage of those friends who have recommended the publication, and to ask permission to become a subscriber.

I pray you to present to his family my sincerest sympathies and respects; to which I am desired to add particularly those of my grandaughter Ellen Randolph, whose affections for them, engaged by so many civilities and kindnesses, interested her deeply in their afflictions. these she would have expressed herself to her friend Miss Dallas, but for my advice not to re-open wounds which time and silence, the only medicines of grief, can alone heal.

Accept my salutations and assurances of esteem & respect.

TH: JEFFERSON

PoC (DLC); on verso of a reused address cover from John Adams or Abigail Adams to TJ; at foot of text: "Mr George M. Dallas"; endorsed by TJ.

To John H. Cocke and David Watson

DEAR[1] SIR — Monticello Mar. 10. 17.

It has been in contemplation for some time to establish a College some where near Charlottesville, of which I presume you have been apprised by the reciept of a Commission from the Governor appointing you one of the 6. Visitors. a first meeting of the Visitors is extremely urgent, to recieve from our predecessors what belongs to the institution, and to set it in motion. no person being particularly authorised to call the first meeting, I have presumed, as being nearest the place of meeting, to request the other visitors, as I now do yourself, to meet at Charlottesville on Tuesday the 8th of April. if to this favor you will add that of making this place your headquarters, I shall be happy to recieve you, and if it could be the day or evening preceding, we could in an evening's conversation[2] come to a common understanding with each other, so that our attendance[3] at Charlottesville the next day would be short and merely of form. I tender you the assurance of my great respect and esteem. TH: JEFFERSON

RC (Sotheby's, New York City, 1987); addressed: "General Cocke Bremo near New Canton Fluvanna"; franked; postmarked; endorsed by Cocke. FC (DLC); entirely in TJ's hand; at foot of text: "Majr Augustus Watson <*esq.*> Genl J. H. Cocke"; endorsed by TJ as a letter to "Watson <*Augustus*> David" and to Cocke and recorded in SJL as separate letters of the same date to both recipients, without correction of Watson's given name. Enclosed in TJ to Watson and to Peter Minor, both 30 Mar. 1817.

David Watson (1773–1830), attorney and public official, graduated from the College of William and Mary in 1797 and then began a career in law. During the War of 1812 he served in the militia as a major and commander of a troop of cavalry from Louisa County. Watson represented that county for seven sessions in the Virginia House of Delegates, 1801–02, 1806–09, 1814–15, and 1820–22. He was elected to a state constitutional convention in 1829 but was unable to attend due to ill health. Watson contributed literary compositions to the Richmond *Enquirer*, was a founding member of the Agricultural Society of Albemarle, and sat on the first board of visitors of Central College and its successor, the University of Virginia. At his death he left sizable landholdings and a personal estate valued in excess of $20,000, including more than sixty slaves (ViU: Watson Family Papers; Fillmore Norfleet, *Saint-Mémin in Virginia: Portraits and Biographies* [1942], 85, 220; *William and Mary Provisional List*, 43; Stuart Lee Butler, *A Guide to Virginia Militia Units in the War of 1812* [1988], 129, 259, 290; Leonard, *General Assembly*; *MB*, 2:1282; True, "Agricultural Society," 247, 263, 269; *Richmond Enquirer*, 17 June 1828, 7 Apr. 1829, 10 Aug. 1830; *Farmers' Register* 2 [1834]: 216; Louisa Co. Will Book, 8:177–9, 252–4, 307–8).

The 18 Oct. 1816 COMMISSION FROM THE GOVERNOR is printed above as an enclosure to Wilson Cary Nicholas's letter to TJ of that date.

[1] Word not in FC.
[2] FC: "conversa-."
[3] FC: "attending."

From Joseph Dougherty

DEAR SIR Washington City Mar. 10th 1817

During the late session of congress Mr Timms, the assistant doorkeeper to the Senate became so frequently intoxicated that the Senate came to a resolution to elect another in his place.[1] the resolution however, was laid on the table, and kept as a rod over him the remaining part of the session.

I was an applicant for his place, and put my papers in the hands of Gov. Barbour where they remained till near the close of the session.

I requested of Gov. B. by note to send them to me. He inclosed them, directed them to me, and gave them to Timms, Timms gave them to the messenger—who also was an applicant. They are lost, and have reason to blive, wilfully destroyd

As these documents were of infinite value to me, particularly the letter from you, recommending me to the office of Sergeant at arms. That letter, in your hand writing, directed to the Honble Mr Lambert of N. J. is lost, or, destroyd

You will verry much oblige me sir, by renewing[2] it. inclosed is a copy of one sent to J. B. V. which you left open for my perusal.

Your Humble Servt JOS DOUGHERTY

RC (DLC); endorsed by TJ as received 20 Mar. 1817 and so recorded in SJL. RC (MHi); address cover only; with PoC of TJ to Patrick Gibson, 25 May 1817, on verso; addressed: "Thos Jefferson Esqr Late President of the U States Monticello Va"; franked; postmarked.

The United States Senate passed a resolution to appoint an ASSISTANT DOORKEEPER on 30 Dec. 1816. It voted on 25 Feb. 1817 to allow Charles Tims (TIMMS) "one hundred dollars for his attendance during the present session" (*JEP*, 6:71, 304). In TJ's Circular to Certain Republican Senators, 19 Sept. 1811, enclosed in his letter to Dougherty of the same date, he recommended Dougherty for the OFFICE OF SERGEANT AT ARMS. Enclosed above was a copy of the text TJ sent to Joseph Bradley Varnum (J. B. V.).

[1]Manuscript: "plac."
[2]Manuscript: "rewewing."

To James Madison

DEAR SIR Monticello Mar. 10. 17.

Besey calling on me for some seed allows me just time to write a line, to await your arrival at home, requesting your attendance as a visitor of our proposed college on Tuesday the 8th of April, being the day after our election. you will of course, I am in hopes come here the day or evening before, that we may have some previous consultation on the subject. I shall also request Genl Cocke & mr Watson to make this their head quarters, as I have done mr Cabell. Colo Monroe I suppose will not be in the neighborhood. congratulating you on the riddance of your burthens, I salute you affectionately and respectfully.

TH: JEFFERSON

RC (ViU: TJP); on one sheet folded to form four pages, including address leaf; addressed: "James Madison late President of the US. Montpelier by mr Besey"; with unrelated notation on verso of letter in an unidentified hand (one word editorially corrected): "Suppose a House Whose roof is 3000 Square feet in surface what space would it be necessary to contain all the Water which might fall during a rain of one Inch dep[t]h?," and further calculations and diagrams in the same unidentified hand on recto and verso of address leaf. PoC (DLC); on verso of portion of reused address cover to TJ; endorsed by TJ.

BESEY: Charles Bizet.

From Bernard Peyton

DEAR SIR, Richmond 10th: March "17

I had the pleasure to receive your esteemed favor of the 5th current, this morning, enclosing one to Colo Randolph—upon enquiry I find from the time he left here, he must have reached Monticello the day after the date of your letter, I will therefore preserve this communication until I receive your farther instruction.—

I have a particular friend and companion about to set out on a Tour of Europe for his improvement, who is anxious to obtain some letters of introduction to persons in the different parts of it, which he contemplates visiting, &. knowing no person who can confer this favor with so much effect as yourself, I take the liberty to solicit it, in his, and my own name—I feel great reluctance at doing this, knowing as

I do the excessive labour, and inconvenience you are exposed too, by the frequency of such applications—I trust tho' you will pardon me, and attribute it to my great regard for this young Gentleman, & my anxiety that every facility should be afforded him in this laudable persuit, convinced as I am, that he will one day become an ornament to his native state— I alude to M[r] William C. Preston, son to Gen[l] Francis Preston of Washington County V[a]—he is now in his twenty-fourth year & is universally considered a young man of most extraordinary acquirement & promise, his probity I can vouch for—

Should this request be not inconsistent with any resolution you may have made, I shall feel extremely obliged by your compliance—be so good in that event, as to forward them under cover to me at your convenience.—

Very respectfully sir Your Obd: Hub: Sert:

BERNARD PEYTON

RC (MHi); at foot of text: "Thomas Jefferson Esq[r] Monticello"; endorsed by TJ as received 15 Mar. 1817 and so recorded in SJL.

William Campbell Preston (1794–1860), attorney, public official, and educator, was born in Philadelphia, the son of Francis Preston, a congressman from Abingdon. He began his studies at Washington College (later Washington and Lee University) in Lexington, received an A.B. in 1812 from South Carolina College (later the University of South Carolina) in Columbia, read law in Richmond under William Wirt, and completed his legal education at the University of Edinburgh. Licensed to practice in Virginia in 1820, Preston moved back to Columbia by 1824, where he continued to practice law and became involved in politics. He was a member of the lower house of the South Carolina legislature, 1828–33, and in the latter year he was elected to fill a vacant United States Senate seat. Preston entered the Senate as a Democrat and resigned in 1842 as a Whig. An eloquent orator, he was a stalwart defender of slavery, states' rights, and Nullification, and a bitter opponent of Andrew Jackson. Preston served as president of South Carolina College and taught classics there from 1846 until a stroke caused him to retire in 1851. He was a trustee of the college until 1857. Preston donated his extensive personal library to found the Columbia Lyceum and died in that city (*ANB*; *DAB*; O'Neall, *Bench and Bar of South Carolina*, 2:531–5; Minnie Clare Yarborough, ed., *The Reminiscences of William C. Preston* [1933]; ScU: Preston Papers; *Charleston Tri-Weekly Courier*, 24, 26 May, 16 June 1860).

TJ'S FAVOR OF THE 5TH CURRENT, covering his letter of that date to Thomas Mann Randolph, has not been found and is not recorded in SJL.

From John Pope

DR SIR   Lexington March 10th 1817

I beg leave to make known to you my freind Doctor Watkins of Tennessee who has purchased a farm near you & is about to become your neighbour—He is a gentleman of fine talents & high respectability & worthy of your attention—I shall be obliged by any services you may render him—Please to accept assurances of the respect & esteem of your most ob[t] Hble Ser JOHN POPE

RC (MHi); dateline at foot of text; endorsed by TJ as received 23 Dec. 1817 and so recorded in SJL. Enclosed in Thomas G. Watkins to TJ, 21 Dec. 1817.

John Pope (1770–1845), attorney and public official, was a native of Prince William County, Virginia, who moved to Kentucky by 1780 with his parents. He studied for one year at the College of William and Mary in 1790. Pope then read for the bar in Kentucky and began a law practice in Shelbyville. In 1798, 1802, and 1806 he was elected to the Kentucky General Assembly, and he cast his vote for TJ as a presidential elector in 1800. Pope sat in the United States Senate, 1807–13, with service as president pro tempore, 1809–11. He lost his bid for reelection due in part to his opposition to the American declaration of war on Great Britain in 1812, and his political views brought him into conflict with Henry Clay. Pope taught law at Transylvania University, 1813–16, after which he moved to Frankfort and became Kentucky's secretary of state. By 1819 he had become an ally of Andrew Jackson, who rewarded him with the governorship of Arkansas Territory, 1829–35. Pope then resumed the practice of law in Springfield, Kentucky, and he served three terms as a Whig in the United States House of Representatives, 1837–43 (Orval Walker Baylor, *John Pope, Kentuckian: His Life and Times, 1770–1845* [1943]; *William and Mary Provisional List*, 33; Clay, *Papers*; George T. Blakey, "Rendezvous with Republicanism: John Pope vs. Henry Clay in 1816," *Indiana Magazine of History* 62 [1966]: 233–50; *Biog. Dir. Cong.*; *JEP*, 4:8, 9 [9 Mar. 1829]; Jackson, *Papers*, esp. 7:28–9; *Terr. Papers*, 19:100–1 and vol. 21; *Boston Daily Atlas*, 29 July 1845).

From Thomas Eston Randolph

DEAR SIR Ashton 10th March 1817

Since I had the pleasure of seeing you, I have communicated with M[r] Colclaser on the subject of paying a Flour Rent for the Mill, for a new Lease—he says—no Miller can afford to give the Rent which we are now paying, and declines a concern in it on the terms of the present year—I wish however to continue the business, and as I shall be satisfied with a moderate profit, I will take the liberty to submit some remarks to your attention—

The season of 1815/16 M[r] Divers' Mill was not in operation his wheat (two crops I believe) was ground at Pen Park Mill, that, and the Shadwell Mill together, did not grind over 21,000 bushels, nor do I believe any wheat was sent down the River—the loss at Shadwell Mill was considerable—the Rent was paid in money—had it been a Flour rent, the loss would have been much greater—

The prevailing opinion among Farmers, Merchants & Millers since the return of Peace, is, that wheat cannot be lower than 6 shillings—which will be $6 doll: ℔ barrel for Flour—and it may be much higher—it is therefore evident that the Tenant can derive no possible advantage by a change from a money to a Flour rent, when rated at its lowest value, but he may be a very serious loser—For instance—the season of 15/16 we did not receive wheat enough to have paid a Rent of 213 bar[s] of Flour there would have been a deficiency of 25 or 30 barrels which we must have purchasd, suppose at a medium price of $7—it would have been an additional loss of $210.— to the Miller or Tenant—while the Proprietor at same time gains a dollar on 213⅓ barrels—

When the Shadwell Mill was built, $1,200,— was consider'd by very competent judges, as a very sufficient Rent for it—since that period Craven's Mill is built which will always command a very respectable custom—Capt: Meriwether is building a manufacturing Mill, still nearer to Shadwell—and below—is Campbell's (late Wood's) which will be compleated the ensuing autumn—with all this competition, it appears to me only reasonable that the rent of Shadwell Mill should rather be reduced, than increasd—I do not however ask for an abatement—I am willing to give $1280.— as formerly, and if you have any doubt about the regular payment of it, quarter yearly, I will give you any security to insure it that you may require—

Or, if you insist on a flour rent, let the price be fix'd at a medium value—say $6.— the lowest—and $8.— the highest (and it must often be higher) gives $7— ℔ barrel—

I will make another proposition—If you will furnish the barrels, and receive the flour at the Mill, I will continue to pay the present[1] Rent, say 213⅓ barrels—and as you seem'd to intimate that 40 thousand bushels of wheat, or even a larger quantity, may be received at the Mill, I will agree to pay an additional rent of 12½ cents for every Five bushels and 20[lb] of wheat deliver'd at the Mill over Thirty thousand bushels for each year during the Lease—

If I had been bless'd with the happy faculty of condensing my ideas in fewer words, I would not have imposed so long on your patience—I will only add, that I do not wish for any advantage, but shall be willing to engage the Mill on terms offering mutual benefits—

I am with sincere esteem, Yrs THO[S] ESTON RANDOLPH

RC (MHi); dateline beneath signature; addressed: "Thomas Jefferson Esq[re] M[o]Cello"; endorsed by TJ as received 14 Mar. 1817 and so recorded in SJL.

[1] Word interlined in place of "former."

To John Barnes

DEAR SIR Monticello Mar. 11. 17.

Yours of Feb. 28. was recieved on the 5th instant and I now inclose you a power of Attorney copied from th[e] form you sent me. it has been detained by the difficulty of access to a justice of peace in a county of 60. miles length over which they are sparsely scattered, and difficult to be found at home. I hope the form is such as not to require periodical renewals, which if the certificate of a magistrate be required would become excessively oppressive. ever and affectionately yours

TH: JEFFERSON

PoC (DLC); on verso of portion of a reused address cover from John Barnes to TJ; one word faint; at foot of text: "Mr Barnes"; endorsed by TJ. Enclosure: an executed version, not found, of enclosure to Barnes to TJ, 28 Feb. 1817.

From George Gibbs

SIR, *New-York Institution,* March 11. *1817.*

By request of the Mineralogical Committee of the New-York Historical Society, I have the honour to forward to you a notice of their intention to form a collection of the minerals and fossils of the United States. The object of this undertaking being of great public utility, they trust that it will meet with general encouragement. Allow me, Sir, in their behalf, to request of you such donations of minerals and petrefactions of the United States as you may have it in your power to procure for us, and such information as yourself or friends may possess of the mineralogy of any part of the United States.

I have the honour to be, Sir, very respectfully, Your obedient servant,

GEORGE GIBBS *Chairman.*

RC (ViW: TC-JP); printed circular, with month, day, final digit of year, and Gibbs's signature in his hand; with enclosure subjoined; at head of text: "(CIRCULAR.)." RC (MHi); address cover only; with PoC of TJ to Lancelot Minor, 3 June 1817, on verso; addressed in Gibbs's hand: "Thomas Jefferson Esqr Monticello Virginia"; franked; postmarked New York, 15 Mar.

George Gibbs (1776–1833), mineralogist and patron of science, was born in Newport, Rhode Island. His father, expecting him to follow in the merchant-shipping business from which the family derived its wealth, sent him to China in 1796. The younger Gibbs, however, preferred travel and mineralogy. He toured, studied, and amassed a mineral collection in Europe, 1801–05. When Gibbs returned to the United States, his holdings of mineral specimens were the largest in North America, and he opened them to scholars for study. By 1812 his friendship with Professor Benjamin Silliman led him to place a portion of the collection on deposit at Yale College (later Yale University), and in 1825 the school purchased it in its entirety for $20,000. Gibbs also funded student prizes at Yale and encouraged Silliman to found the *American Journal of Science and Arts*. He died at his estate on Long Island and was buried in Portsmouth, Rhode Island. The mineral gibbsite is named in his honor (*ANB*; *DAB*; WHi: Gibbs Family Papers; *OED*; *Newport Mercury*, 10 Aug. 1833; *American Journal of Science and Arts* 25 [1834]: 214–5).

ENCLOSURE

Statement of the Mineralogical Committee of the New-York Historical Society

THE Mineralogical Committee of the New-York Historical Society, having by their order prepared an apartment for the purpose of receiving and displaying a collection of the minerals and fossils of the United States, beg leave to communicate to the public the arrangements that have been made, and the further claims of the Society to the patronage of the friends of science.

The progress of the science of mineralogy in the United States has been very satisfactory to its friends in this country, and the labours of American mineralogists have met with great applause in Europe. Several new species, and many varieties of minerals have been discovered here, and the increasing attention to this science promises many interesting and valuable discoveries. But in a country so vast and so recently settled as the United States, we can hardly expect to find many who have visited, for mineralogical objects, any very large portion of its territory. The researches of most of them have been limited to their own state or the district in which they live. A great number of valuable specimens remain in the hands of persons, who, either ignorant of their value, preserve them only for temporary gratification, or, who having no object in making a collection, would be very happy to place them where they would become useful, in a public Institution. To collect these scattered materials of our natural history, to display the riches of the mineral kingdom of each of our states; to inform the scientific traveller and citizen; to encourage the growing taste of this science in our country; to communicate discoveries and invite researches; are objects so useful, so important, that it would be impossible to doubt of the public favour being shown to this undertaking.

The Corporation of the city of New-York having, with characteristic liberality, accommodated the Historical Society with a suite of apartments for this purpose, they have now been fitted up with cases with glass doors, one case being devoted to each state, after the manner adopted in the national collection at the Ecole des Mines at Paris.

The Committee beg leave, therefore, to request donations of minerals and fossils for their collection, from the scientific and patriotic in every part of the Union. They will be received with grateful acknowledgments, and displayed to the best advantage.

They beg leave also to state, that it would be extremely useful to the Society to have the exact localities of the minerals determined, and such further information of the neighbouring country, as the donor can procure.[1]

By order of the Mineralogical Committee,

GEORGE GIBBS, *Chairman.*

Minerals and fossils intended for the Society, it is desired may be forwarded to John Pintard. N° 52. Wall Street[2]—If from a distance, they should be packed up with great care, to prevent their being broken or injured in the transportation.

New-York, 11. March–1817.[3]

Printed circular (ViW: TC-JP); subjoined to covering letter; with portions in John Pintard's hand as noted below; at head of text: "NEW-YORK HISTORICAL SOCIETY"; endorsed by TJ as a letter from Pintard received 28 Mar. 1817 and so recorded in SJL.

In SJL TJ recorded receipt from New York on 28 Apr. 1817 of an undated letter from Pintard, not found, with the additional notation "N.Y. circular. Minerals." This may have been a second copy of the above letter and enclosure.

[1] Manuscript: "procrue."

[2] Pintard's name and address added in his hand.

[3] Day, month, and final digit of year added in Pintard's hand.

To Joseph Miller

DEAR CAPTAIN Monticello Mar. 11. 17.

The season calling for corks has come upon me before I had thought of it, and it being difficult to get them good but from a person who understands them, I must pray you to send me as many gross of the best as the inclosed bill of 5.D. will pay for. I understand that a steam packet now plies between Norfolk and Richmond so that I am in hopes they can come certainly and speedily addressed to mr Gibson. if you will be so good as to drop me a linc of information when you send them off, I will take measures to have them called for at mr Gibson's, lest they should be delayed there. Peter's brewing of the last season I am in hopes will prove excellent. at least the only cask of it we have tried proves so. altho' our hopes of your settling among us are damped by your long absence, yet we do not despair altogether. in the mean time Charlottesville is improving much both in buildings and society. I salute you with great friendship.

TH: JEFFERSON

PoC (DLC); at foot of text: "Capt Miller"; endorsed by TJ.

Peter Hemmings had done the BREWING OF THE LAST SEASON.

From Samuel L. Mitchill

SIR, *New-York Institution, March* 11, 1817.

In behalf of the New-York Historical Society, I beg leave to solicit your assistance toward the formation of a Zoological Museum. For the purpose of becoming more extensively and intimately acquainted with the animal creation, a plan has been digested for collecting specimens and productions from the different tribes. These it is intended to preserve and arrange in an apartment allotted for their reception. The document annexed to this letter, contains some of the leading subjects of inquiry. Every fact and article relative to this exalted Department of Natural History will be thankfully accepted and duly estimated. I beg you to accept the assurance of my good will and respect,

SAMUEL L. MITCHILL, Chairman.

RC (DLC); printed text; with enclosure subjoined; at head of text: "(CIRCULAR.) AMERICAN ZOOLOGY AND GEOLOGY"; at foot of text: "*To* "; endorsed by TJ as a letter from Mitchill received 5 Apr. 1817, with additional notation: "(circular. Zoology)," and so recorded (out of sequence at end of 1816) in SJL.

ENCLOSURE

Statement of the Committee on Zoology of the New-York Historical Society

Pursuant to a resolve of the Historical Society, at the meeting held in the New-York Institution, on the 11*th day of March,* 1817, *the Committee on Zoology offered a Report concerning the means of promoting that Department of Natural Science.*

FOR carrying into effect the design of the Society, measures ought to be adopted to form a Cabinet of Zoology. Some of the leading objects are comprehended in the following summary; from which it will appear, that the collection of facts, specimens, drawings, and books, may be commenced immediately; that all the citizens may be solicited to exert themselves, and that much may be accomplished with very little cost.

From the class of *Polypes*, inhabiting the depths of the ocean, are derived the productions called Zoophytes and Lithophytes. Every article belonging to the Gorgonias and Corals, to the Madrepores and Flustras, and to each of the kindred families, is worthy of a place in the Museum.

The *Radiary* animals furnish productions no less interesting. In particular, the Asterias with its constellation of sea-stars, and the Echinus with its brood of sea-urchins, will furnish many species, easy to be gathered, transmitted, and preserved.

So little has hitherto been done in relation to our *Insects*, that almost the whole field of ENTOMOLOGY remains to be cultivated. In an effort to form a collection of these numerous swarms, all hands may be employed. There being no particular difficulty either in procuring or preserving these creatures, it may be expected, that in a few years, all the larger animals of this class may be possessed by the Society, and disposed according to the most approved of the modern systems.

The *Crustaceous* class will also furnish specimens, easy to be preserved and transported. From the extensive families of Crabs, Lobsters, and their congeners, a becoming diligence will gather abundant supplies.

Molluscous animals make important and elegant contributions to Naturalists. Their univalve, bivalve, and multivalve shells, commonly survive their authors. Their arrangement into genera and species, forms the science of CONCHOLOGY. It is recommended that early and persevering pains be bestowed upon this subject, and that these beautiful productions be methodized after the most excellent of the plans that have been proposed.

Considering the facility with which *fishes* may be preserved, by drying their half skins on a board, it is desirable that at least all new species should be brought forward for examination and description. Important additions may thus be made to our ICHTHYOLOGY. To a people, who already consider their FISHERIES of the utmost importance, both to the States and to the nation, no additional recommendation is necessary, further than to ask of our fellow-citizens all manner of communications.

Among the *amphibious* orders, tortoises, frogs, serpents, and lizards, are so easily preserved, that individuals of these kinds are solicited from such persons as feel a generous ardour to favour the views of the Society.

Contributions towards the history of the *Mammalia*, may be expected from the fur merchants, furriers, and hunters. Almost every thing, known under the titles of FURS and PELTRIES, passes through our city, or is contained within it. By application to the proper sources of intelligence, there is a confident expectation of a rich return of all the matters comprised in their respective provinces. It is not generally understood,[1] what extensive and important knowledge, on these subjects is in store within a great city, ready to be imparted to those who will seek it.

Anatomy is the basis of improved Zoology. The classification of animals is founded upon their organization. This can be ascertained only by *dissection.* The use of the knife is recommended for the purpose of acquiring an acquaintance with the structure of animals. It is proposed, that the members avail themselves of all opportunities to cultivate COMPARATIVE ANATOMY, and to communicate the result of their labours and researches to the Society. There is, perhaps, no department of the science more replete with novelty and instruction, and with the means of conferring wide and lasting reputation to those who skilfully engage in it.

To exhibit and perpetuate the researches of the gentlemen who undertake the arduous task of anatomical examination, the accomplishment of SKETCHING and DRAWING is an indispensable qualification. Beyond the representation of internal appearances, whether healthy or morbid, this art applies to all outward forms that stand in need of delineation. It is recommended to the members to procure plates and pictures of natural objects, and bring them for safe keeping and popular utility, to be placed in the portfolios of the Society.

There would be an inexcusable omission in passing over unnoticed, the VETERINARY ART or PROFESSION. The diseases of domestic animals are deeply and intimately connected with the property and comfort of man. Every thing that can illustrate or cure the distempers of sheep, neat cattle, horses, swine, dogs, poultry, and of quadrupeds and birds generally, will be highly acceptable. This valuable branch of knowledge, known by the name of *Epizootic*, deserves more particular cultivation than it has hitherto received among us.

BOOKS on the various branches of Natural History, are eminently desirable. They will constitute the *Library* which the Society intends to form. There can be no doubt that many important volumes, from Aristotle up to Lamarck, might be collected from their scattered sources, if proper pains were taken. It is recommended, that every exertion be made to effectuate this object. Proprietors and authors may be frequently found, willing to be liberal, as soon as they are satisfied that a worthy occasion presents.

FOSSILS ought to be collected with particular care. The organic remains of vegetables and animals, imbedded in stone, or buried in the other strata of the earth, are frequent in our region. Some of them resemble living species; while others are not known, at present, to be inhabitants of this globe. From the Ocean to the Lakes, they present themselves to the eye of the Geologist. Let them be gathered into one body. Let the Mastodons, Crocodiles, Encrinites, Pectinites, Ammonites, Belemnites, and other reliques of the extinct races, be assembled and classed; and then let the philosopher survey the whole, and draw wise and pious conclusions. The city of New-York may be considered as a center surrounded by wonders of this sort; and the great Lakes, with their tributary streams, exhibit testimonials no less surprising and characteristic.

Zoological research is promoted in several ways by foreign commerce. Living animals are frequently imported; and these, whenever circumstances are favourable, ought to be examined, and if necessary to be described and figured. Cargoes, and even ballast, often contain excellent specimens, both of the animal and fossil kind. Peculiar creatures are known to inhabit the outer bottoms of vessels, where they may be seen before they are disturbed for the purpose of cleaning and repairing. Sometimes too, fishes, not usually visitors of our harbours, follow the track of ships from the Ocean, and offer themselves to the curiosity of the Naturalist. All these sources of knowledge deserve to be carefully explored.

Persons who favour the Society with donations, will be honourably noticed and remembered: their offerings shall be duly registered and labelled. As, from its act of incorporation, it possesses succession and perpetuity, the contributions of public-spirited individuals are exempted from the fate too often incidental to private establishments. They will endure for a great length of years, and descend to future generations.

Remarks on the more elaborate and expensive preparations of Zoology, are reserved for a future report. In the mean time, it is supposed the matters herein suggested, will, for a season, occupy all the industry of the members and their friends.

The Committee, however, cannot close, without an earnest recommendation to the study of MAN. The migration of human beings from Tatary, Scandinavia, and Polynesia, to the north-western, north-eastern, and south-western regions of America, merit extraordinary attention. There is nothing extravagant in the belief, that colonies, or bands of adventurers by the way of the Aleutian Islands, the shores of Greenland, and the Pacific Ocean, penetrated our Continent at an early day; and that their descendants settled, by bloodshed and exterminating wars, their respective claims to the country situated south of the middle Lakes, four or five hundred years before the voyage of Columbus.

All which is respectfully submitted.

SAMUEL L. MITCHILL, *Chairman.*

New-York, 11*th March*, 1817.

Printed circular (DLC); subjoined to covering letter.

[1] Manuscript: "undrestood."

To Bernard Peyton

DEAR SIR Monticello Mar. 11. 17.

I must ask the favor of you to purchase for me 6 gross of the best corks to be had in Richmond, and to send them by the stage to Milton to the address of mr Vest postmaster, the season for using them being now actually upon us. mr Gibson as usual will be so good as to pay the bill. affectionately and respectfully yours TH: JEFFERSON

PoC (MHi); on verso of reused address cover to TJ; at foot of text: "Capt Bernard Peyton"; endorsed by TJ.

From Fernagus De Gelone

SIR New York March 15th 1817.

In answer to your orders, I direct to you this day, per schooner Astrea, bound to Richmond, as will appear to you in the herein inclosed bill of lading, a box the direction of which is: Thomas Jefferson, Esqre Monticello, Milton Va, Care of Mess. Gibson & Jefferson, Richmond Va it contains

1. Copy of hippocrate. 4 8vo Sewed	$8.00
1— Archimède de Peyrard. 2. 8vo do	4.50
	$12.50

(these 12 dollars 50 cents, I have received.)

It contains, according to your order, also—

1 Conquista de Mexico, Solis, 3. 8vo Sewed Spanish	$6.50
1. tragedies d'Euripide, par Prevost. 4. 12mo Sewed in prose	3.00
1. Description et usage du Cercle de refléxion—par Borda. 1 Small 4to tables of logarithms—and plates	3.50
	$13.00

I am most respectfully Sir Your humble obedient Servant

J. LOUIS FERNAGUS DE GELONE.

RC (MHi); endorsed by TJ as received 23 Mar. 1817 and so recorded in SJL; with additional notation by TJ beneath endorsement: "13.D." RC (MHi); address cover only; with PoC of TJ to Patrick Gibson, 24 May 1817, on verso; addressed: "Thomas Jefferson Esq[re] Monticello. Milton V[a]"; franked; postmarked New York, 15 Mar. Enclosure not found.

To Thomas Eston Randolph

Dear Sir Monticello Mar. 15. 17.

Your letter of the 10th was handed to me yesterday afternoon only when the Shadwell mills were built, the rent was settled on great enquiry made in this state as well as in those North of us, at one out of every 24. Barrels of flour expected to be manufactured, and to be taken at the place of sale. we supposed the Shadwell mills would manufacture 5000. Barrels of which, according to this proportion, $208\frac{1}{3}$ would go to the landlord, and $4791\frac{2}{3}$ remain to the miller and his customers, if he worked on commission, or to the miller himself, if he purchased. you say in your letter 'the prevailing opinion among farmers, merchants, and millers, since the return of peace is that wheat cannot be lower than 6/. which will be 6.D. p[r] barrel, for flour, and it may be much higher.' suppose this to be correct. when flour is at its lowest price of 6.D. the landlord recieves 6. times $208\frac{1}{3}$, or 1250. D the miller 6. times $4791\frac{2}{3}$ or 28,750.D if flour rises 1.D. say to 7.D. the landlord recieves $208\frac{1}{3}$ D more, the miller $4791\frac{2}{3}$ D more [if it ris]es 2.D. say to 8.D. the landlord recieves twice $208\frac{1}{3}$ more, the miller twice $4791\frac{2}{3}$ more if it rises 3.D. say to 9.D. the landlord recieves three times $208\frac{1}{3}$ more, the miller 3. times $4791\frac{2}{3}$ more thus, for every dollar more recieved by the landlord, the miller gets 23. additional, gaining always by a rise in price 23. times as much as the landlord does.

the rent is properly fixed in flour, because it is safest and right that the landlord and tenant should share the loss as well as gain proportionably, and[1] to guard both against the fluctuations of market and money. our money is no longer to be trusted as a measure of value, but from day to day. and it seems it is to become less so, as I am assured it is a general sentiment of the legislature to permit, at their next session, every one who will, to set up a bank. the deluge of paper then is to be without limits. when the Shadwell mills were built, 13. or 14. years ago, 1250.D. would have procured more capital, say of land or negroes, than the double of that sum now. this shews how unjust it would be to pay me now a rent of only 1250.D. but the half in value of what was then correctly settled. 5. Barrels were afterwards added to the 208$\frac{1}{3}$ by particular stipulation as interest on the cost of the store house, subsequently built. I cannot therefore agree to hav[e an]y thing to do with a money rent. I assure you at the same time, that I sincerely wish you to retain the mill. it is neither my interest or desire to be frequently changing tenants. but still a rent, once established on sound principles, must be stable, and cannot be permitted to fluctuate with the momentary ups and downs of circumstances. I might perhaps agree to a part of the sacrifice suggested in your last proposition, that of finding barrels for the rent-flour, which I can do within myself, while from you they require cash; this will be a reduction of near 100.D. but further than this I cannot change the established terms.

As to the competition of new mills, they cannot increase as fast as the production of wheat: and, if business be as well done at the Shadwell mills, these will be preferred to those off from the river, because being at the landing from whence the produce is to be water-borne, they save the farmer the trouble of [a?] 2^{d} trip with his teams to move it to the waterside, often distant from him. the lower mills on the river certainly have the natural advantage of a shorter water carriage to market. but the difference is added to their land carriage, by their being that much further from the rich producing country. the farmer will gladly save this additional labor to his teams, by stopping at the nearest mill from which his produce can be water-borne.

These views, which I believe to be sound, will, I hope, have their weight with you, and I pray you to accept the assurance of my affectionate and respectful attachment. TH: JEFFERSON

PoC (MHi); on verso of a reused address cover from Joseph C. Cabell to TJ; mutilated at seal and ink stained, with some words rewritten by TJ; at foot of text: "Thomas E. Randolph esq."; endorsed by TJ.

[1]Manuscript: "and and."

From Edwin Stark

SIR Ass^{t} Comm^{ys} Office Norfolk 15th March 1817

On my[1] arrival from Washington I found your favor of the 20th Feb^{y}

I am sorry to inform you the two boxes of Wine have not as yet come to hand perhaps they have taken a rong direction as I cannot get any tidings of them in this place If you know the name of the Vessel they were shipt in, from Charleston, be so good as to acquaint me or if you think it necessary I will advertise them as missing

It will at all times afford me great pleasure to attend to your commands in this place

I have the Honor to be Sir with g Respect your hbl Servt

EDWIN STARK

RC (MHi); at foot of text: "Thomas Jefferson Esquire Monticello"; endorsed by TJ as received 20 Mar. 1817 and so recorded in SJL.

[1]Manuscript: "Omy my."

To Thomas Appleton

DEAR SIR Monticello M[ar.] 16. 17.

This will be handed you by mr William C. Preston, son of Genl Francis Preston of this state, who in the course of his travels in Europe, may probably find occasion to call on you. he is not personally known to me, but I am assured of his worth and distinguished talents by those who know him and command my entire confidence. his standing in this state is high, and I believe I render you service when I make known to you, among those of my countrymen who present themselves to you, such of them as are worthy of your attentions and patronage. this gentleman is certainly so, and I bear witness to it the more willingly as it adds to the occasions which I am always happy to embrace of renewing to you the assurances of my affectionate friendship & respect. TH: JEFFERSON

PoC (DLC); on verso of reused address cover of Charles K. Mallory to TJ, 17 Feb. 1817; dateline faint; at foot of text: "Mr Appleton"; endorsed by TJ as a letter of 16 Mar. 1817 and so recorded in SJL, which adds that it was to be carried by Preston. Enclosed in TJ to Bernard Peyton, 16 Mar. 1817.

To Stephen Cathalan

DEAR SIR Monticello Mar. 16. 17.

This will be handed you by mr William C. Preston, son of Genl Francis Preston of this state, who in the course of his travels in Europe may probably have it in his power to call on you. he is not personally known to me; but I am assured of his distinguished talents and personal worth by those who know him and command my entire confidence. his standing in this state is high, and I believe I render you service when I make know[n] to you, among those of my countrymen who present themselve[s] to you, such of them as are worthy of your attentions and patronage. this gentleman is certainly so, and I bear witness to it the more willingly as it adds to the occasions which I am always happy to embrace, of renewing to you the assurance of my affectionate friendship and respect.

Th: Jefferson

PoC (DLC); on verso of a reused address cover from Joseph Milligan to TJ; torn at seal; at foot of text: "M. Cathalan"; endorsed by TJ. Recorded in SJL as carried by Preston. Enclosed in TJ to Bernard Peyton, 16 Mar. 1817.

To Albert Gallatin

Dear Sir Monticello Mar. 16. 17.

This will be handed to you by mr William C. Preston a young gentleman of this state, either son, or nephew (I know not which) to the gentleman of that name with whom you served in Congress about 1792. I do not know him personelly, but learn from those who do, and in whom I have confidence, that he is of excellent talents, and perfect integrity. his standing in this state is high, and he will probably become prominent. judging from my own experience when in your situation, I think I serve you in making known to you when those who present themselves to you are worthy of your notice and patronage. I believe this gentleman to be so. I am glad by him to repeat to you the assurances of my constant friendship and respect.

Th: Jefferson

RC (ViW: Robert Morton Hughes Collection); addressed (one word editorially corrected): "His Excellency Albert Gallatin Min. Plen[y] of the US. of Ameri[c]a Paris favored by mr Preston." PoC (MHi); on verso of reused address cover to TJ; endorsed by TJ. Recorded in SJL as carried by Preston. Enclosed in TJ to Bernard Peyton, 16 Mar. 1817.

Francis Preston, the father of William C. Preston, served in the United States House of Representatives, 1793–97. Gallatin sat in the House from 1795 until 1801.

To David Higginbotham

Dear Sir Monti[cell]o Mar. 16. 17

I recieved duly your favor of Feb. 22. on the subject of paints. I shall certainly want a very great quantity in the course of the present year, as I have to renew the whole outer painting of this house and the terrasses, and to paint that in Bedford which has never been done. but I did not make more of any thing scarcely last year than would pay for the corn we did not make. I must therefore delay my demand till towards autumn so as to bring the time of payment within reach of the growing crop. ever and with great friendship Yours

TH: JEFFERSON

PoC (MHi); on verso of reused address cover of Jerman Baker to TJ, 8 Feb. 1817; dateline faint; at foot of text: "Mr Higgenbotham"; endorsed by TJ.

To Lucy Marks

DEAR MADAM Monticello Mar. 16. 17.

In a letter which came to me by mail yesterday and to which the writer had forgotten to subscribe his name, I received those I now send you, the one sealed, the other open as it now is. observing the name of General Clarke on one of them[1] and my letter being dated at Louisville induces me to suppose it is from him. I tender you the assurance of my great esteem and respect. TH: JEFFERSON

PoC (MHi); on verso of a reused address cover from Samuel L. Mitchill to TJ, with unrelated address cover to Mitchill on recto; at foot of text: "Mrs Marks"; endorsed by TJ as a letter to "Marks mrs. of Ivy cr." Enclosures: enclosures to William Clark to TJ, 1 Feb. 1817.

Lucy Meriwether Lewis Marks (1752–1837), a native of Albemarle County, married first William Lewis, of Locust Hill. Their son Meriwether Lewis was joint leader of the Lewis and Clark Expedition. After the death of her first husband, she married John Marks. Among her neighbors Marks was known for her aptitude with herbal medicines. At her death she owned at least forty-eight slaves (Louisa H. A. Minor, *The Meriwethers and Their Connections* [1892], 23, 61–2, 163; National Society of the Daughters of the American Revolution, *DAR Patriot Index* [2003], 2:1646; Mary Rawlings, *The Albemarle of Other Days* [1925], 58–65; Sarah Travers Lewis Anderson, *Lewises, Meriwethers and their Kin* [1938], 180–2; Albemarle Co. Will Book, 13:36–8, 341–2). A likeness of Marks is reproduced elsewhere in this volume.

[1] Preceding four words interlined.

To Charles Willson Peale

DEAR SIR Monticello Mar. 16. 17.

Your favor of Feb. 28. came to hand yesterday evening only. mr McIlhenny is right in saying he left a letter for me; but I did not get it till a month after he went away. however all is well. we have had the good fortune to get a Swiss from Neufchatel, inferior, I think, to no watchmaker I have ever known. sober, industrious, and moderate. he brought me recommendations from Doctr Patterson & mr Haslaer. he compleatly knocks down the opposition-bungler who came from Stanton to contest the ground with mr McIlhenny, gets more work than he can do, and sells more watches than he could have done in Philadelphia. brought up among the mountains of Switzerland, he is delighted with ours.—I admire you in the variety of vocations to which you can give your attention. I cannot do this. I wish to be always reading, and am vexed with every thing which takes me from it. with respect to my letters to you mentioning some agricultural practices E^{t}c make what use you please of them, only not giving my name. this would draw letters upon me, which are the affliction of my life by the drudgery they subject me to in writing answers. we have sometimes practised the feeding with our corn-stocks. we chop them in a trough with a hatchet, which is a guillotine, you know, worked by hand. I doubt if the descending force added by the arm to the gravity of the hatchet is[1] as laborious as would be the lifting power exercised to raise a guillotine of such weight as that it's gravity alone should produce the same effect. but trial alone can[2] prove this, as every thing else in life, and as it has proved to me the value of your friendship and produced for it the sincere return of mine.

TH: JEFFERSON

RC (TxU: Thomas Jefferson Collection); at foot of text: "C. W. Peale esq." PoC (DLC); on recto of reused address cover of William Sampson to TJ, 9 Feb. 1817; torn at seal, with some words rewritten by TJ; endorsed by TJ.

The LETTER Joseph E. McIlhenney wrote TJ before leaving Charlottesville was dated 21 Dec. [1816]. The SWISS FROM NEUFCHATEL was Louis A. Leschot, who was recommended along with his family in Ferdinand R. Hassler to Robert Patterson, 2 Dec. 1816, enclosed in Patterson to TJ, 13 Dec. 1816.

[1] Reworked from "to it's own gravity is."

[2] TJ here canceled "decide this."

To Bernard Peyton

DEAR SIR Monticello Mar. 16. 17.

During an absence of 27. years from Europe, the ordinary course of mortality, aided by a bloody revolution & active guillotine has swept off nearly every personel acquaintance on that side of the Atlantic. with some literary characters I have since had correspondence, but not knowing them personally or their habits of society, I do not take the liberty of giving letters of introduction to them. the letter which I inclose to mr Gallatin will give to mr Preston the benefit of his introduction to living characters unknown to me; and supposing he may visit the Southern countries I add letters to mr Cathalan of Marseilles and mr Appleton of Leghorn, the [two?] sea ports he will be most likely to visit. when you have rea[d them?], be so good as to stick wafers in them, as my friends will distinguish, favorably for him, sealed from open letters of introduction. I salute you with constant friendship and respect. TH: JEFFERSON

PoC (MHi); on verso of reused address cover of Jerman Baker to TJ, 19 Feb. 1817; torn at seal, with one word rewritten by TJ; at foot of text: "Capt Bernard Peyton"; endorsed by TJ. Enclosures: TJ to Thomas Appleton, to Stephen Cathalan, and to Albert Gallatin, all of 16 Mar. 1817.

To Archibald Thweatt

DEAR SIR Monticello Mar. 16. 17.

your favor of the 2[d] was recieved yesterday. I am much indebted to you for your attention to our turn-pike road, which was an electioneering maneuver of the scoundrel Yancey. the day the bill was postponed in spite of him he had the base hypocrisy to write to me and insinuate he had had it postponed. he attended our last court with a view of feeling the pulse of the people, but so many of his tricks were become known, that he shrunk from all contest, and declared himself no longer a candidate.

You make enquiry about the level of the river at Eppington, supposing it to have been taken by me for mr Eppes. it is like a dream to me that some examination of it was made by me, but so little do I remember about it that I am not quite sure of the fact. you ask the cost of a mill carrying 3. or 4. pair of stones. mine carries 2. pr. of burrs, the one of 5.f. the other of 6.f. and a pr. of rubbers for cleaning the grain, with all the modern labor saving machinery, the house very roomly, & walls of stone. it cost me 10,000.D. but good judges say it ought to have cost but 8000. this is exclusive of the canal which alone cost me 20,000.D. and of the dam. the best handmill is that which has least machinery, so that the labor of him who works it is not wasted by friction. a pair of small stones about 2.f. diam. fixed under

a gallows, with a handspike working loose in a hole in the runner going half thro' it, and another in the top of the gallows, is the best I have known. for a horse mill, the best is a horisontal spur wheel fixed exactly as what we call the horsewheel of a threshing machine. these spurs drive a vertical trundle, on the[1] spindle of which the running stone is fixed.

Our family all join in affectionate attachment to mrs Thweatt and yourself and I add assurances of sincere friendship & respect for both.

TH: JEFFERSON

PoC (DLC); on verso of a reused address cover from Jerman Baker to TJ; mutilated at seal, with missing text rewritten by TJ; at foot of text: "Archibald Thweatt esq."; endorsed by TJ.

Thweatt's FAVOR OF THE 2D, not found, is recorded in SJL as received 15 Mar. 1817 from Eppington. ROOMLY: "spacious; capacious" (*OED*).

[1] TJ here canceled "axis."

To Francis Adrian Van der Kemp

DEAR SIR Monticello Mar. 16. 17.

I learn with real concern that the editor of the Theological Repository possesses the name of the author of the Syllabus. altho he coyly witholds it for the present, he will need but a little coaxing to give it out and to let loose upon him the genus irritabile vatum, there and here. be it so. I shall recieve with folded arms all their hacking & hewing. I shall not ask their passport to a country, which they claim indeed as theirs, but which was made, I trust, for moral man, and not for dogmatising venal jugglers. should they however, instead of abuse, appeal to the tribunal of reason and fact, I shall really be glad to see on what point they will begin their attack. for it expressly excludes all question of supernatural character or endowment. I am in hopes it may find advocates as well as opposers, and produce for us a temperate & full developement. as to myself I shall be a silent Auditor.

Mr Adams's book on Feudal law, mentioned in your letter of Feb: 2. I possessed, and it is now in the library at Washington which I ceded to Congress. in the same letter you ask if I can explain the phrase 'il est digne de porter le ruban gris de lin.' I do not know that I can. gris de lin is the French designation of the colour which the English call grizzle. the ruban gris de lin may be the badge of some association, unknown, I acknolege, to me, but to which the author from whom you quote it may have some allusion. I shall be happy to learn that you pursue your purpose as to the life of the great reformer, and more so in seeing it accomplished. I return the Repository[1] with thanks for the opportunity of seeing it, and I pray you to accept my friendly and respectful salutations.

TH: JEFFERSON

RC (NBuHi: Van der Kemp Papers). PoC (DLC); on verso of reused address cover of Joseph C. Cabell to TJ, 19 Feb. 1817; mutilated at seal, with missing words rewritten by TJ; beneath signature: "Mr Vanderkemp"; endorsed by TJ. Enclosure:

Monthly Repository of Theology and General Literature 11 (Oct. 1816).

Robert Aspland was the EDITOR of the *Monthly Repository of Theology and General Literature.* GENUS IRRITABILE VATUM: "the fretful tribe of bards" (Horace, *Epistles*, 2.2.102, in Fairclough, *Horace: Satires, Epistles and Ars Poetica*, 432–3). Jesus was the GREAT REFORMER.

[1]Before this word in PoC, TJ placed an asterisk keyed to a note at foot of text: "N° 130. Oct. 1816."

From Joseph Delaplaine

DEAR SIR, Philadelphia March 17th 1817

I have already acknowledged the receipt of your last obliging favours.—

I beg you to inform me whether you ever had any children besides Mrs Eppes & Mrs Randolph—what are the ages of these ladies—and how many children they have and all their names?—

What Literary and other societies you may be a member of in this & other countries? or what societies you have been a member of?

Where were you educated? How many brothers & sisters living?

What languages are you conversant with?

What Literary productions have you given?

When did Mrs Jefferson die? And what age were your daughters at the time of her death? & any thing else that you may think proper to communicate with regard to your family.[1]

When were you first a member of the house of Burgesses?

Dear sir, when I was with you in June last, I omitted to ask you thc above questions, & I beg you to have the goodness to furnish answers as soon as possible, as your life is nearly completed. It is withheld from the press in order to add the above named information. It will appear with your portrait in the 2d half vol, with those of Peyton Randolph—Jay—King—Clinton & Robert Fulton.—I am sensible that justice will be done to it. I have had every assistance in it, to make it satisfactory, & I trust that posterity will admire it, as I am sure that the people of our time, will believe it true

Mr Madison's life & Portrait will be given in the third half vol:. He was kind enough to furnish me a number of leading facts & dates. To complete his life, however, I must resort to pamphlets, Books, & friends. I will do it as much justice as I possibly can.—

When I was with you my Notes in my memorandum book ran thus, after you showed me the original draft of the Declaration of Independence—"The Legislature of Virginia instructed Richard Henry Lee to move in Congress for the declaration—a committee of five were appointed to draft a declaration—Committee desired M[r] Jefferson to pen it. M[r] Adams & D[r] Franklin looked at it.—M[r] Adams inserted "time after such dissolutions," in lieu of the "invasions of the rights of the people" Here my Notes appear confused, & I think I am not correct.—

D[r] Franklin "but Scotch & foreign mercenaries to invade & deluge us in blood," & inserted "destroy us," in lieu.

M[r] Adams defended it with all his might throughout.—

Except the corrections above stated, M[r] Jefferson penned every word of the orig[l] draft of the[2] Dec: of Independence."—

Thus far my Notes. I beg you to set me right, If I am wrong. & I believe I am with regard to the alteration made by M[r] Adams. But I believe I am correct as to the alteration made by D[r] Franklin.

I have seen M[r] Leiper; he has kindly offered to give me what information I want that is in his power.—

Hoping to have the honour of receiving a letter by return of the mail, for I am much hurried, I remain

with perfect esteem yours ob J DELAPLAINE

If any thing else strikes you, I do wish you would oblige me with it.—

When I was at Monticello, I think you expressed a desire to have the portrait of the late president M[r] Adams. I have just had it painted for me by M[r] Morse who studied in London for many years & who brought with him to Boston a high reputation. M[r] Morse was born in Boston, & is son to Geographer Morse.

I received a letter from a Gentleman in Boston who in speaking of the portrait of M[r] Adams, observes, "M[r] Adams's portrait is pronounced by his family and friends, the best likeness that has ever been taken of him."—I should suppose that on this recommendation I may rely, & of course the portrait must be very valuable. If you desire a copy of his portrait still, I will with pleasure cause it to be immediately taken by one of our best Artists in Philad[a]. I think I shall employ M[r] Otis; It will cost exactly Thirty dollars, & considering how well I shall have it painted; the price may be considered cheap. Please to let me know.—M[r] Madison also requested me to procure a portrait for him of M[r] Adams; of course I shall send him one.—

RC (DLC); postscript on verso of address leaf; addressed: "Thomas Jefferson Esq[r] Monticello V[a]"; endorsed by TJ as received 28 Mar. 1817 and so recorded in SJL.

[1] Preceding sixteen words interlined.
[2] Preceding four words interlined.

From Bernard Peyton

Dear sir Rich[d] 17 March 1817.

I am favord this morning with yours of the 11th Current—

I have searched the City for the best Velvet Corks, & have succeeded in procuring the six Gross wished of excellent quality, which shall be forwarded by tomorrow's stage, to the address of M[r] Vest Milton—

I wrote you a few days since on the subject of M[r] Preston—I hope you may find it convenient to comply with my request—

I have delivered to Co[l] Randolph your letter enclosed to me—in haste—Very respectfully sir

Your Obd: Servt: B. Peyton

6 Gross Velvet Corks at—125 Cts $7.50

RC (MHi); endorsed by TJ as received 20 Mar. 1817 and so recorded in SJL. RC (DLC); address cover only; with PoC of TJ to Fitzwhylsonn & Potter, 28 May 1817, on verso; addressed: "Thomas Jefferson Esq[r] Monticello near Milton"; stamped; postmarked Richmond, 17 Mar.

Corks of the highest quality were classified superfine, or velvet (*OED*). your letter enclosed to me: TJ to Thomas Mann Randolph, 5 Mar. 1817.

From Edwin Stark

Sir Comms[ys] office Norfolk 17th March 1817

I did myself the pleasure to address you a few days since on the subject of your wine from Charleston

I was then under the impression they were missing but I have this morning had the satisfaction to learn from our Collector that the two boxes in question was put on board of the sloop Antelope Capt Laurence for Richmond on the 22[d] Feb[y], to be deliverd to your friends Mess[rs] G & Jefferson to whom a receipt for the same was forwarded

I again assure you it will be highly gratifying to my feelings to act, as your agent or correspondent in this place

I am Sir with very gt respect your hb[l] Serv[t] Edwin Stark

RC (MHi); at foot of text: "Thomas Jefferson Esq[r] Monticello"; endorsed by TJ as received 23 Mar. 1817 and so recorded in SJL.

The collector at Norfolk was Charles K. Mallory.

By some unidentified channel after this date, Alexander Pyke conveyed to TJ his pamphlet, *An Oration, delivered on the 17th March, 1817, before the Shamrock Friendly Association of New-York, and a numerous concourse of citizens and strangers assembled to celebrate the anniversary of St. Patrick* (New York, 1817; Poor, *Jefferson's Library*, 13 [no. 826]; TJ's copy in ViU, with Pyke's MS inscription [trimmed]: "Respectfully presented to Thomas [Jef]ferson Esq, by The Author").

To Fitzwhylsonn & Potter

MESSRS FITZWHYLSON AND POTTER [Mo]nticello Mar. 19. 17.

Mr Vest, postmaster of Milton, who committed the volumes of Edinburg review to the stage, which I sent you, thinks he shall be able to recover them. the difficulty has arisen by a change of the driver. he says they were left by the former driver at the old stage office. perhaps you can find them there. I have generally had a good deal of bookbinding to do, and am likely still to need it occasionally. I have hitherto sent it to Georgetown to mr Millegan on account of the superiority of his work. our American bindings are faulty in execution as well as materials. they are so springy that when once a book has been opened, it will never shut close again. a book well bound is as heavy as a piece of lead, with solid pasteboard for it's cover. I now send you a small box containing Virgil 4. vols. Tacitus[1] 4. vols, Botta 1. vol. and the Clavis Homerica to be bound into 2. vols. I should be glad to have them bound in the best manner of the Richmond binders (not however in Marocco) as it would be more convenient to me to send there than to Georgetown. I would wish all the dispatch consistent with good work. when done they may be sent by the Milton stage addressed to me to the [c]are of mr Vest postmaster, who will pay the carriage. Accept the tender of my respect.

TH: JEFFERSON

PoC (DLC); on verso of reused address cover of William Canby to TJ, 11 Feb. 1817; dateline faint; damaged at seal; endorsed by TJ.

[1] Word interlined in place of "Juvenal."

To Joseph Milligan

DEAR SIR Monticello [Mar]. 19. 17.

The last proof sheet I recieved from you was to pa. 48. Mar. 1. and dispatched it Mar. 2. I am anxious to get as forward as possible, as 4. weeks hence I go to Bedford, & shall be absent 4. weeks.

I send thro' the care of mr Gray a small box, containing Homer 9. vols, Juvenal 4. vols, & Horace 2. vols, to be bound as they are tied up. I wish them to be done in your handsomest & solidest manner (but not in Marocco.) well pressed, and substantial pasteboard. the backs particularly well gilt. I shall be very impatient to recieve these works as quickly as good work will admit. I am in daily expectation of recieving Gibbons's two works. yours with friendship & esteem TH: JEFFERSON

PoC (DLC); on verso of portion of reused address cover to TJ; dateline faint; at foot of text: "Mr Millegan"; endorsed by TJ as a letter of 19 Mar. 1817 and so recorded in SJL.

To Wilson Cary Nicholas

DEAR SIR Monticello Mar. 19. 17.

A considerable time ago I recieved from the Historical committee of the Philosophical society of Philada a letter informing me they were in possession of a MS. volume, which from their description I concluded must be a copy of Colo Byrd's journal of the Carolina boundary. it was on that occasion I asked the favor of you to procure me the reading that work. as they meant to print theirs and there was no author's name, they asked me to make enquiry concerning it and sent me their copy. on comparing them, the handwriting is the same, the subject the same, and unquestionably the author the same. yet they are different compositions, often mentioning the same circumstances, but more frequently supplementory each to the other, so that neither is compleat of itself. I think therefore that if one is printed the other should be also. as I do not know from what member of the Westover family you obtained the one you sent me, I must again avail myself of your kind mediation to know whether we may be permitted the use of this one to print it. I will undertake for the return of a printed copy of both instead of this; for manuscripts get so cut up and dirtied in the process of printing as to be in fact destroyed. I reserve both these works in my hands until I can obtain an answer, but ready to return this one whenever required. I salute you with constant affection and respect. TH: JEF[FER]SON

PoC (DLC); on verso of reused address cover of James Madison to TJ, 15 Feb. 1817; signature faint; torn at seal, with missing text rewritten by TJ; at foot of text: "Wilson C. Nicholas esq."; endorsed by TJ.

The letter from the HISTORICAL and Literary Committee of the American PHILOSOPHICAL SOCIETY was Peter S. Du Ponceau to TJ, 14 Nov. 1815.

To Joel Yancey

Dear Sir Monticell[o] Mar. 19. 17.

The waggons arrived yesterday forenoon with every thing safe except that Jerry left one of his mules dying[1] on the road. this I dare say was the effect of poverty, which is the stamp of all our animals here. they have no forage short or long but what I buy, and people are now talking of 8. and 10.D. a barrel for corn. I hope, if there is to be such another year, I shall not live to see it. I shall be anxious to learn that your flour is gone off, as I have heavy payments for corn[2] to make at our next court (April 7.) for which I must draw on that fund. I think it would be well to send off your tobacco one or two hogsheads at a time as you can get it ready. I see no reason to expect any rise of price by keeping that back. the bill of scantling I sent you will not be above a day's work for mr Martin's mill, so I hope he will do it for me. if you have had the rain with you which we have had, Dick has lost as yet no ploughing days. the earth may be dry enough tomorrow, but is not as yet, which will reduce the loss of ploughing to three days. 2. years of embargo, 3. of war, and 2. of drought have made me anxious for one good crop, to be well sold, which would set me quite afloat. I have entire confidence in your efforts and in your friendship and that every thing will be done under your care which the seasons permit. I shall be able to set out for Poplar Forest about the 15th or 16th of April. Dick will leave this about noon to-day, and will carry some packages, chiefly of liquors, which should be put into the cellar immediately. I am in hopes you will mention in the letter which you promise by mail, how much wheat went to the mill, or how much flour it yields, clear, that I may know the extent of that fund. I salute you with sincere friendship & respect. Th: Jefferson

PoC (MHi); on verso of reused address cover of John H. Peyton to TJ, 14 Feb. 1817; dateline faint; mutilated at seal, with missing text rewritten by TJ; at foot of text: "Mr Yancey"; endorsed by TJ.

Yancey's previous letter to TJ of 12 Mar., recorded in SJL as received 18 Mar. 1817 from Poplar Forest, as well as the letter which you promise by mail, dated 27 Mar. and recorded in SJL as received 1 Apr. 1817 from Lynchburg, have not been found.

[1] Manuscript: "deying."

[2] Preceding two words interlined.

From Patrick Gibson

SIR Richmond 20th March 1817.

Your note in bank for $2000. falling due the 4th of next month I send you the inclosed for your signature—With great respect I am

Your obt Servt PATRICK GIBSON

RC (MHi); between dateline and salutation: "Thomas Jefferson Esqre"; endorsed by TJ as received 31 Mar. 1817 and so recorded in SJL; with TJ's notes (one word illegible) for his 1 Apr. 1817 reply on verso: "note wine molasses boo[k?]s. sell flour." Enclosure not found.

From David Michie

SIR, Buck Island March 20th 1817

Some recent reports, not correct, as they respect myself, in relation to my pretensions to the mill scite at Milton, have induced me again to address you on that subject. It is not a fact, that I have determined to postpone the prosecution, of what I consider a legal & just claim, untill your death. It is not a fact, that I either dread you, as an opposing litigant, or fear the severest scrutiny on legal grounds into the validity of my title. Other motives might have been ascribed to me, with less injury to myself, & with equal honor to you. For instance, it might have been presumed, that I felt in common with my fellow citizens, a very high respect for your character, as a friend of free government, & as a benefactor to my country. That foreseeing the results, which must enevitably ensue, from a rigid prosecution of my claim, I waited for the moment, when the feelings already excited might subside, & when reason alone would be our umpire. The avocations sir, of the war, the distress of sickness, & the requisite attention to more important concernments, might have shielded me from imputations, with the liberal & enlightened as unmerited, as they are unjust. Whatever opinion you may have unfortunately formed of me, permit me to assure you, that I am not personally your enemy, & that it would be no gratification to me, to be instrumental in tearing a single laurel from your brow. With such dispositions towards you personally, I cannot otherwise than be sensibly affected by insinuations, which go vitally to wound my integrity as a man, & my honor as a gentleman—Outraged in this respect, as well as others, & still more vitally outraged by the unparelelled, decision in the case of the certiorari—a decision, for the grounds of which, we in vain refer to the copious & perspicuous authorities of the dead—or to the living sages of the Law:

& the causes which have heretofore restrained me from the execution of my fixed & immutable purpose, as to the property in question ceasing, in part, to exist, I shall in a short time, adopt legal measures, to bring before a proper tribunal, my title, fortified by every evidence, I can possibly collect, either in immediate reference to it, or which may have a tendency to dissipate prejudice, & place me in a fair point of view before the Judiciary of my country. Before I enter upon this arduous task I think it indispensably necessary to lay before the public, in a form to ensure to it general notoriety, every circumstance which has heretofore transpired, which will embrace our correspondence & a faithful report of the case of the Certiorari, with the arguments of counsel, & the obiter opinion of the judge, as to the power of transfering the subject before the general court, if his view of it was not satisfactory—

To evince however to you Sir, the respect I am bound to entertain, even after what has transpired, for venerable age, and services in many instances highly meritorious, I propose to you, that on my motion, I may be permitted, to take a few depositions, with notice to you of the time & place, which shall not be committed to record, unless after a view of their contents, you should determine to stand a legal investigation. As however the evidence already[1] taken by yourself has not corresponded as I believe with your expectations of its nature, & as that to be taken by me, will shed much light on the validity of my claim, I flatter myself, that on a view of it, you will perceive the inutility of further litigation—

This I offer with a prospect of an extrajudicial adjustment which seemed to have met your concurrence in the earliest stage, of our controversy—That you may not be at a loss, for the object I contemplate to attain by this evidence, I have no hesitation in intimating to you, that I expect to nullify Col° James Lewis's sale as trustee, by a complete developement, of every circumstance, the most minute & palpable, which led to that conveyance, as well as those, which attended its execution. Effecting satisfactorily this end, I presume no question can arise, under the decision of the court of appeals, of J Hendersons right to establish a mill under the original order of the court of this county, the benefit of which has already been legally conveyed to me.

I have the honor to be with due respect Y[r] Ob[t] Hble Serv[t]

David Michie

P.S.

I had intended to have postponed any communication to you untill my family were perfectly restored to health—But having received from your agent Mr Peyton yesterday, a note of a nature rather surprizing, particularly in the present state of the controversy between us, I could but consider it honorable & fair to apprize you of the course I shall have emediately to take, especially as you yourself may be affected, in some measure thereby. D.M.

RC (MHi); addressed: "Thos Jefferson Esqr Monticello"; endorsed by TJ as received 20 Mar. 1817 and so recorded in SJL.

For the DECISION IN THE CASE OF THE CERTIORARI, see Archibald Stuart's Decision in *Jefferson v. Michie*, [15 Oct. 1813]. OBITER is short for "obiter dictum," an incidental judicial observation not forming part of the decision and thus lacking the force of precedent (*Black's Law Dictionary*).

[1] Word interlined.

From Thomas Eston Randolph

DEAR SIR Ashton 20th March 1817

I have maturely consider'd the contents of your letter of the 15th instant, which I received on the day of its date—

I do not hesitate to acknowledge that I am very desirous to retain the Mill, and, far from wishing you to make any sacrifice of Rent, I feel most sincerely disposed to pay a Rent fully adequate to all the advantages which its situation offers—From the former amount of mony Rent, although it is generally consider'd to be very high, I should not have ask'd for any abatement, and the only difficulty which I feel in paying a Flour Rent, is, that it undeniably offers great profit, and no loss whatever to the Landlord; while on the contrary—to the Tenant it admits some risk without a probable advantage—I therefore did, and do still think, if the rent be paid in Flour, the Flour should be rated at a medium price—it seems to be the general opinion that it cannot for many years be less than $6.— valuing it then, at $7.— would reduce the rent to 182$\frac{6}{7}$ barrels of Flour—That quantity I am willing to give; and in addition thereto, I will pay 12$\frac{1}{2}$ cents for every 5. bush 20 ℔ of Wheat received in the Mill over 25,000 bushels—(in my former letter I said 30,000)—or, I will give 190 barrels of Flour—

Permit me to make some remarks on the calculations contain'd in your letter—as they apply to the Landlord, they are perfectly correct, but certainly incorrect as to the Tenant, whether he be consider'd a purchaser of wheat, or merely grinding on commission—because, in the former case, the price of wheat is generally proportion'd to the price of Flour, consequently the Tenants profit can only be calculated on the advantage of grinding—in other words—on the difference between the quantity of wheat received at the Mill for a barrel of Flour, and the quantity which it actually takes to make a barrel of Flour—The Tenant's purchasing wheat is a matter of speculation, by which he may make a profit, or he may very possibly sustain a loss—You say (on a supposition that 5000 barrels are manufactured)—"When Flour is at its lowest price of \$6.— the Landlord receives 6 times $208\frac{1}{3}$ or \$1250.— the Tenant 6 times $4791\frac{2}{3}$ or \$28,750.— dollars" and you further observe, that "For every dollar more received by the Landlord, the Tenant gets 23 additional, gaining always by a rise in price 23 times as much as the Landlord does" I think I can prove to your satisfaction that the Tenants profit on 5000 barrels is not the double of the Landlord—For every 5. bush 20 ℔ of wheat received at Shadwell Mill, we return a barrel of Flour, and insure $\frac{5}{6}^{ths}$ to be S.[1] fine—we make a barrel of Flour out of 4. bush 40 ℔ of wheat, some times more, or less, according to the quality of the wheat—thus, the Mill profit appears to be $\frac{1}{8}^{th}$—accordingly, $\frac{1}{8}^{th}$ of 5000 barrels will be 625 barrels, deduct therefrom $213\frac{1}{3}$ barrels, the rent now paid, will leave to the Tenant a profit of, only $411\frac{2}{3}$ barrels—I believe I may vouch for the correctness of this statement, and when you consider all the risk which the Tenant is subject to, you will not think the double of the amount of Rent more than he ought to calculate on, it is more however than has ever yet been made at that Mill—The only apology which I can offer for troubling you with this letter, is my conviction of your being much mistaken in regard to the profits of the Mill—with affectionate regards I am Dr sir Yours sincerely

THOs ESTON RANDOLPH

RC (MHi); dateline at foot of text; addressed: "Thomas Jefferson Esqe"; endorsed by TJ as received 20 Mar. 1817 and so recorded in SJL.

[1] Abbreviation for "Super."

From Edmund Bacon

DEAR SIR. 22nd March 1817—

The time has at length arrive when the situation of my family requires that I should indeavour to get a home my three sons haveing now arrive to an age and size necessary to commence the maner of labour by which they must get their living I must really declare that nothing but necessaty induceis me to Proceede in the undertaking which I now think of ingageing with my intention is to indeavour to moove to the western Part of the country this comeing fall to inable me to get good land considering that the Principal Object now before me to get such land in this part of the country is a matter beyond my reach of course my misfortin is like that of the rest of Persons here without land and money suffishient to Purchase consequently I am compelled to incounter with that disagreable circumstance to my feelings as well as to expence to leave my native Part of the world. to do this I am dependant upon you for every dollar that I can Possoplely command in this case is required. The time I propose to set of is the 10th of sepr next. my Yeare with You does not end untill the 22d of that month but it would be very important to my interst to set of by the 1st day of the sd month as I have a long Journey before me upon this subjec I must if You Please require an answer soon as convenient to You as I should like to commence my arraingments even at this Present time

I must state that having so long done your business in Peace this eleventh Yeare during which time I have recieved all good and Kind treatment that can be due from an imployer to a hireling which has permantly fixed my real $\frac{2}{5}$ which never can end but with my life

Your Ob St. E: Bacon

RC (MHi); dateline at foot of text; superfluous punctuation editorially omitted; addressed: "Mr. Thomas Jefferson Monticello"; endorsed by TJ as received 22 Mar. 1817.

To David Michie

Sir Monticello Mar. 22. 17.

Your's of the 20th was recieved on the day of it's date. I do not know why that part of it is addressed to me which complains of insinuations against your integrity as a man, and honor as a gentleman. I am not aware of having uttered such myself, and cannot be answerable for what may have been uttered by others. As little do I percieve why 'a note which you say is of a nature a little surprising recieved by you from mr Peyton' you chuse to consider coming from him as my agent. I know of no such note, nor is mr Peyton my agent. while I was living out of the state, he was so kind as to act for me in the purchase which has produced a collision of interests between you & myself. this he did voluntarily and faithfully. but that trouble, I had no right to continue on him after I returned home to live and to act for myself. during the 8. years elapsed since that time, I have been my own sole agent in this business, as should be known to no one better than to yourself, because whatever has been transacted in it with you, has been always by myself. I understand your letter as proposing an extrajudicial determination of this controversy. you know how much I wished this in the beginning: that you also agreed to it, but that after taking a single deposition, you retracted your agreement, and in a letter informed me that you declined all further extrajudicial proceeding. I was consequently obliged to return to the regular forms of the law for whatever I deemed necessary for my further security, and seeing no reason for changing the course a second time, I prefer continuing it in that line, and leaving to our lawyers it's future direction. The transfer your letter contemplates of a judiciary litigation before the tribunal of the public will be your act, not mine. with what object they will judge, and whether the appeal is proper to themselves, or respectful to the authorities to whom they have confided it's decision. I salute you with respect.

TH: JEFFERSON

PoC (MHi); on verso of portion of a reused address cover from William Thornton to TJ; at foot of text: "M[r] David Michie"; endorsed by TJ.

Michie declined FURTHER EXTRAJUDICIAL PROCEEDING in his 30 May 1813 letter to TJ.

To Thomas Eston Randolph

DEAR SIR Monticello Mar. 22. 17.

I sincerely regret that we happen to see the same subject in lights so very different, with respect to the mill. but the rent of a real property must, you know, be a fixt thing. as it's original cost cannot be varied, so the interest or rent on that cannot vary with daily and transient occurrences, and especially on a lease for time. it is easy to reduce a rent, but impossible to raise it again. the reduction is a permanent annihilation of so much of the capital. In order to approximate nearer to the offer in your letter of the 20th I will change the form of mine, and, retracting the proposition to find the barrels, I will take 200. Barrels of **S. F.** flour, say 50. Barrels a quarter, delivered at Richmond and of that inspection for the mill and it's appurtenances including the storehouse. this I fix in future for the permanent rent, never to be departed from. In my former letter I omitted to answer your enquiry as to timber for the repairs of the mill. they may be taken from my lands without charge. ever & affectionately

Yours TH: JEFFERSON

PoC (MHi); on verso of reused address cover of Samuel L. Mitchill to TJ, 10 Feb. 1817; at foot of text: "Thomas E. Randolph esq."; endorsed by TJ.

To Joseph Dougherty

Dear Sir Monticello Mar. 23. 17.

your letter of the 10th did not come to hand until the 20th instant. on examining my files I find that the letter to mr Lambert was an exact copy of that to Genl Varnum and all the others to whom I wrote on that occasion. I have therefore recopied it and addressed it to mr Lambert, which I now inclose, and return you the copy of that to Genl Varnum. wishing you success in your application I salute you with friendship & attachment. Th: Jefferson

PoC (DLC); on verso of reused address cover of Richard Rush to TJ, 19 Feb. 1817; at foot of text: "Mr Joseph Dougherty"; endorsed by TJ. Enclosure: two copies of TJ's Circular to Certain Republican Senators, 19 Sept. 1811.

To Craven Peyton

Dear Sir Monticello Mar. 23. 17.

You sometime ago had corn for sale which you were so kind as to offer me. if you have still any to spare, I will be glad to take it at the price at which you are selling. be so good as to inform me by the bearer, and as to the quantity and price.

I salute you with esteem and respect. Th: Jefferson

PoC (MHi); on verso of reused address cover to TJ; at foot of text: "Craven Peyton esq."; endorsed by TJ.

From Craven Peyton

Dear Sir Monteagle Mch 23d 17.

I am raeley sorry to inform You, I fear I have sold my corn two close, I regret very much I had not of kept for You, the eighty Barrells You named to me but M. Bacon informed me, You was fully supplied,

With great esteem C. Peyton

RC (ViU: TJP-ER); addressed: "Thomas Jefferson esqr Monticello"; endorsed by TJ as received 23 Mar. 1817 and so recorded in SJL.

To Joshua Stow

SIR Monticello Mar. 23. 17.

I have recieved the copy you have been so kind as to send me of the Address and Constitution of the Connecticut society for the encouragement of American manufactures, and beg leave thro' you to return thanks to the Society for this mark of their attention. no one more zealously wishes success to their views, from a very thorough conviction of their importance to the Cement, as well as Independance of the union. I offer to them and yourself the assurance of my high consideration. TH: JEFFERSON

PoC (CSmH: JF-BA); on verso of address cover of otherwise unlocated letter from Richard Peters to TJ, 15 Feb. 1817 (addressed: "Thomas Jefferson Esqr Monticello Virginia"; franked; postmarked; recorded in SJL as received 27 Feb. 1817 from Philadelphia); at foot of text: "Mr Joshua Stow"; endorsed by TJ.

To Robert Walsh

Monticello Mar. 23. 17.

I thank you, kind Sir, for the favor of sending me a copy of the American Register of the present year. I had not before an opportunity of witnessing it's merit. a first view of it's matter and manner now assures me that I shall read it with interest and satisfaction. altho' at my age[1] more is forgotten than newly learnt, yet I am still glad to know what is going forward in the literary world, what others are learning, and see with pleasure young coursers taking lead in the race of science, the goal of which, altho' not at infinite, is yet at an indefinite distance. I shall ask leave to become a subscriber and, hoping there may be an agent for the work within our state, I shall take care to furnish him the standing means of recieving the price always at his convenience. I avail my self with pleasure of the occasion now furnished of assuring you of my great esteem and respect.

TH: JEFFERSON

PoC (DLC); on verso of a reused address cover from James Monroe to TJ; at foot of text: "R. Walsh esq."; endorsed by TJ.

[1] TJ here canceled "little."

To Jethro Wood

Sir Monticello Mar. 23. 17.

I recieved on the 7th of Nov. your favor of Oct. 1. and delayed it's acknolegement until the arrival, within this week past, of the plough you have been so kind as to send me on the part of the firm of which you are a member. for this mark of their attention I pray them to accept my thanks. I have examined it with care, and think it promises well in all it's parts; and shall exhibit it with pleasure to the notice of our practical, as well as our theoretical farmers. I have no doubt it would produce many calls, were there a deposit within the state from which they could be furnished; as at Richmond, for example. the water communications from thence would place them within the reach of a great part of the state. with the tender of my great respect to your firm, I pray you to accept the same for yourself personally.

Th: Jefferson

RC (CtY: Franklin Collection); addressed: "Mr Jethro Wood Aurora. Cayuga New York"; franked; postmarked Milton, 25 Mar.; with unrelated calculations in an unidentified hand on recto and verso. PoC (MoSHi: TJC-BC); on verso of reused address cover of Lafayette to TJ, 16 Sept. 1816; mutilated at seal, with some missing text rewritten by TJ; endorsed by TJ.

From Joseph Miller

Honrod Frind Norfolk March 24th 1817—

yours of the 11th Came to hand on the 22th and I am hapey to heare from you this Day I have Shiped on Board of the Slope Hope Capt Lawrance a Small Baill of Corks Which hopes Will Come Safe and Please you[1] Did Say whether them that I Sent in Decmr Came or not I have Been Very Lame all thes Winter but now the Warm Weather Coming on I am in Hopes of Getting Better I intend Vissiting Charloteville thes Spring and as Soone as I Dare Travell

Times heare is Dull but [hpg] for Better Should Eany Thing Be Wanting from heare I will Do it with Pleasur My Best Respts to you and all the Famuly I Rem yours Humb Set Joseph Miller

My Repects to old Peter I am Glad he has Dun so well

RC (DLC); one word illegible; at head of text: "Mr Jefferson"; endorsed by TJ as received 2 Apr. 1817 and so recorded in SJL.

old peter was Peter Hemmings.

[1] Uncanceled "D" before this word editorially omitted.

From Alden Partridge

SIR West Point March 24th 1817.

Although I have not the honor of a personal Acquaintance with you, yet I trust you will excuse the liberty I take in introducing to your Acquaintance the Bearer Mr Benjamin O. Tyler. Mr Tyler resided at this Place a considerable part of last year in the Capacity of Professor of Penmanship. The improvements which he has made in the Art of writing, and the success which has attended him as an Instructor speak much in favor of his talents and Acquirements.[1] He is a Gentleman of respectability and integrity and in visiting you, Sir, is actuated purely by a desire of paying his respects to a Personage so justly entitled as yourself, to the respect, Esteem, and Gratitude of every American—

I have the honor to be with the greatest respect and Esteem, Sir, your Obedient Servant

A PARTRIDGE
Capt. of Engineers

RC (MHi); at foot of text: "Thomas Jefferson Esquir late President of the United States"; endorsed by TJ as a letter of 24 Mar. 1818 received that same day and so recorded in SJL. Enclosed in Benjamin O. Tyler to TJ, 14 Mar. 1818.

[1]Manuscript: "Acquiements."

From John Barnes

DEAR SIR— George Town Coa 26 March 1817.

I take the liberty of inclosing—the Messenger of this Town, 24th as it contains,—two—interesting—Prothetic letters, of the late President Adams in 1756.—to the late Judge Cushing (—then Brother school master,)—will, I am sure please you—his friend Dalton was I presume—a Branch—if not the very man—the good & worthy—but unfortunate T: Dalton[1] late of the City of washington whose former Residence in abt 1786. was I think—at Boston or Salem—Mr Dalton had a seat in the Senate of Congress at New York before the present Constitution—was formed—at which time I was personaly known to him—

most respectfully & very sincerely—Your Obedt servant.

JOHN BARNES,

RC (ViU: TJP-ER); endorsed by TJ as received 31 Mar. 1817 and so recorded in SJL. RC (MHi); address cover only; with PoC of TJ to John Vaughan, 7 June 1817, on recto and verso; addressed: "Thomas Jefferson Esqr Monticello Virginia"; franked; postmarked Georgetown, 26 Mar. Enclosure: Georgetown *Messenger*, 24 Mar. 1817.

PROTHETIC: "antecedent" (*OED*), in this context presumably meaning prior to attaining renown. The enclosed newspaper contained two letters, dated 1 Apr. and 19 Oct. 1756, from John ADAMS to Charles CUSHING, Adams's former classmate at Harvard and fellow schoolmaster. In the first Adams leaned toward becoming a clergyman (and spoke in passing of his fondness for his friend and classmate Tristram DALTON), and in the second he explained his decision to begin studying law instead. The letters are reprinted in Robert J. Taylor, Richard Alan Ryerson, C. James Taylor, and others, eds., *Papers of John Adams* (1977–), 1:12–5, 21–3.

[1]Manuscript: "Dalto."

From John H. Cocke

DEAR SIR, Bremo March 26. 1817

I have received your letter of the 10th March and shall not fail, without some unforeseen obstacle to attend the meeting, you propose, of the Visitors for the establishment of the College in the neighbourhood of Charlottesville.

I accept your polite invitation—and will be at Monticello on Monday the 7 of April.

I have been long desirous to obtain some of your Marseilles fig—and send the Bearer hereof to get a few plants—You will oblige me, in sending also, some of the paper mulberry—and half a dozen cuttings of your lombardy poplar, which I think you told me, was of a distinct species from the common lombardy poplar.—

I send you half a dozen bottles of the Carolina scuppernong, wine—which I hope you will do me the favor to accept as some testimony of the high respect & Esteem with which I am Your obedt Servant

J. H. COCKE

RC (CSmH: JF); endorsed by TJ as received 27 Mar. 1817 and so recorded in SJL. RC (DLC); address cover only; with PoC of TJ to Isaac Briggs, 18 May 1817, on verso; addressed: "Mr Jefferson Monticello" via "Jesse."

From DeWitt Clinton

DEAR SIR Albany 27 March 1817.

Some days ago I sent to you a treatise on Canals compiled at the request of the Canal Commissioners of this State. I now forward all the reports &c. which relate to the contemplated Erie & Champlain Canals & which will give you a full & commanding[1] view of the whole field of enquiry,[2] with the addition of a map of this State in order to supply the want of a topographical map in the case of the Champlain Canal.

The high respect which I entertain for your opinion and the enlarged & public-spirited views which are cherished[3] by you, must render a communication from you on this subject peculiarly gratifying & interesting but I dare not solicit it, lest it might interfere too much with more important avocations

I am with sincere respect & regard Your most obed^t servant

DEWITT CLINTON

RC (DLC); endorsed by TJ as received 8 Apr. 1817 and so recorded in SJL. RC (ViW: TC-JP); address cover only; with PoC of TJ to Louis Pio, 13 June 1817, on verso; addressed: "Thomas Jefferson Esqr Monticello Virginia"; stamp canceled; franked; postmarked (faint) Albany, 2[8?] Mar., and Monticello, N.Y., 5 Apr., with note in unidentified hand to "fow^d." Dft (Lb in NNC: Clinton Papers); lacking closing and signature.

The TREATISE ON CANALS was "Atticus" [Clinton], *Remarks on the Proposed Canal, from Lake Erie to the Hudson River* (New York, 1816). The enclosed REPORTS &C. probably included *Memorial of the Citizens of New-York, in favour of a Canal Navigation between the Great Western Lakes and the Tide-Waters of the Hudson* (New York, 1816; Poor, *Jefferson's Library*, 5 [no. 217]; TJ's copy in PPAmP); *Report of the Joint Committee of the Legislature of New-York, on the Subject of the Canals, from Lake Erie to the Hudson River, and from Lake Champlain to the Same. In Assembly, March 19, 1817. Read, and ordered to be printed* (Albany, 1817; Poor, *Jefferson's Library*, 5 [no. 217]; TJ's copy in PPAmP); *Report of the Commissioners of the State of New-York, on the Canals from Lake Erie to the Hudson River, and from Lake Champlain to the Same. Presented to the Legislature, 17th February, 1817* (Albany, 1817; Poor, *Jefferson's Library*, 5 [no. 217]; TJ's copy in PPAmP); and Gideon Granger, *Speech of Gideon Granger, Esq. delivered before a Convention of the People of Ontario County, N.Y. Jan. 8, 1817, on the subject of a Canal from Lake Erie to Hudson's River* ([New York, 1817]; Poor, *Jefferson's Library*, 5 [no. 217]; TJ's copy in PPAmP). On p. 13 of Granger's speech, he summarized Spain's efforts to claim the Mississippi River following the American Revolution and the resulting contention between the northern and southern states of the Union and concluded that "The western waters were then saved by the northern states refusing to accede to the demands of Spain." On his copy TJ penciled a notation that "this is exactly the reverse of the truth." The MAP OF THIS STATE (New York) has not been identified.

[1] Preceding two words interlined in Dft.

[2] Preceding four words interlined in Dft in place of "interesting subject."

[3] Manuscript: "cheished."

To John H. Cocke

Monticello Mar. 27. 17

Th: Jefferson is very thankful to Genl Cocke for the sample of Scuppernong wine which he has been so kind as to send him, and which he considers to be as fine, as it is a singular wine. he sends him plants of the Marseilles fig & of the Paper or Otaheite mulberry, & cuttings of the Lombardy[1] poplar which he brought from France, very different from the common one, being a tree of some shade. he adds a couple of plants of the prickly locust (Robinia hispida) a rich blossoming shrub, rarely to be met with; and some cuttings of the Snow-berry bush, brought from the Pacific by Cap[t] Lewis. it's beauty is the snow white bunches of berries which it retains after the leaf has fallen; it is of the size of a goose-berry bush. he does not know certainly that it will grow from a cutting but believes it will & is sorry he has not a bush to spare with roots. he will expect the pleasure of seeing Gen[l] Cocke on the court day, & salutes him with friendship & respect.

RC (ViU: TJP); dateline at foot of text; addressed: "General Cocke Bremo"; endorsed by Cocke; with additional notation on verso in Nathaniel Francis Cabell's hand in two different inks: "M[r] Jefferson to Gen. Cocke March 27th 1817. (Presented by Gen C. to N.F.C. [Nathaniel Francis Cabell] Nov 1855" and "& now given to my daughter S.F.C. [Sallie Faulcon Cabell] as an Autograph. June 1879.)." Tr (Vi: Nathaniel Francis Cabell Papers); in Nathaniel Francis Cabell's hand; misdated 22 Mar. 1817; at head of text: "(Copy)"; notation on verso reading, in part: "(I only sent a Copy, as the original has been given away as an Autograph. N.F.C.)." Not recorded in SJL.

In his diary entry for 28 Mar. 1817 (MS in ViU: JHC), Cocke recorded that "Jesse returned from Monticello" with the MARSEILLES FIG and the other plants and cuttings listed above.

[1]Tr: "Lombard."

To George Divers

DEAR SIR Monticello Mar. 27. 17.

I write to you because you are a Director of the Rivanna company, yet not as a Director, but as an individual and friend for consultation. the present condition of the locks is such as to call ere long for an entire new rebuilding. before this is proposed, it is certainly desirable, both for the company and myself, that we should know of a certainty on what ground we stand in point of right: and this can only be settled by a judiciary decision. I propose therefore to bring a friendly bill[1] in Chancery, on which, with the separate answers of the Directors, the Chancellor will, on motion, and without a day's delay decide this point authoritatively. with this view I have prepared a bill; and as I am anxious to state in it no fact which is not exact, I inclose it and ask the favor of you to peruse it with attention, and to take notice of any fact you think not correct. I will not give you the trouble of making notes, or writing letters on the subject, to which there is no end. but I will ride up the day after tomorrow if you will be at home,[2] & ask a dinner of you, and exchange explanations verbally as to any thing which may need correction. there are some facts, which being unknown to the Directors themselves, will of course require depositions: particularly with respects to the Inquest of 1805.

but for those which are within their knolege, their answers will of course save the time and trouble of calling on witnesses: ever and affectionately yours Th: Jefferson

PoC (MHi); on verso of a note in Joseph Milligan's hand possibly related to his 21 Feb. 1817 letter to TJ: "Despatched Georgetown Feby 22nd 1817 regular day of the post going to Milton"; at foot of text: "George Divers esq."; endorsed by TJ. Enclosure: TJ's Bill of Complaint against the Rivanna Company, [by 9 Feb. 1817].

[1] Word interlined in place of "suit."
[2] Preceding six words interlined.

From George Divers

Dr sir Farmington 27th Mar. 1817

I have receiv'd your note together with the Bill mentiond, to which I will give the attention you require, & shall be glad to see you here to dinner the day after tomorrow, I have been in a bad state of Health for some time past, but am rather better today than usual—The large potatoes you gave me turn'd out very well, I send you in return seven that was produced from seed that came from the eastward, I also send you a few of a very forward kind that came from Liverpool last spring, I have divided with you a few peach stones & some cabbage seed which I lately recd from Mr Thos Cropper which I send by your servant with sincere respect

I am yr: friend George Divers

RC (MHi); endorsed by TJ as received 27 Mar. 1817 and so recorded in SJL.

From Richard Flower

Dear Sir Mar. 28–1817 Marden near Hertford

The Familiarity of this address you will readily excuse as you are aware that without personal acquaintce one can esteem in the highest degree from a knowledge of Character Talent & virtues. and altho distance has prevented any personal Interview with you I assure you of my high esteem for you, from an intimate knowledge of your Character as president your public Speeches to Congress and many epistles of a more private Nature wh have fallen into my hands but what has made you really dear to me is the hospitality and kindness you have shewn my amiable & much esteem'd Son for wh you will accept my most sincere thanks—

In my last Letter receiv'd from him he informs me he has purchased an Estate of about 750 Acres of Land in the western part of

Virginia and it is natural that I should feel deeply interested in his Welfare not only on Account of my affection for him. but on Account of the consequences of his well being w^{h} will draw in his Train numbers of farmers as settlers also Labourers of the most industrious Class, who are unhappily become of little Value to the Government under w^{h} they live and are become sensible of their Situation in this respect, and ready to a considerable extent to rely on the report my son gives of America—

It is also stated in his last Letter that he intended sailing for England in the middle of April w^{h} I hope has been prevented by Letters dispatchd to him by various persons informing him of Mr Birkbeck & a party of Friends coming out to him immediately and praying him to stay till they arrived—If it should happen that my Son should have saild from America before he has seen Mr Birkbeck you will confer a great obligation on me if you will inform Mr Birkbeck of the situation of his purchase and if it could in any way be of any advantage to M^{r} B— as a temporary Residence for himself or any of their party. it will give both him & myself great pleasure—Mr Birkbeck has brought out with him a most valuable Cargo of Intellect information industry & Virtue[1]—and are a good specimen of the Circle of an extensive acquaintance, who are tremblingly alive to the Calamities w^{h} await their Country and looking towards America as an assylum from the troubles occasion'd by an overwhelming Taxation & severe oppression its constant Attendant—It is far from my Intention to be drawn into any thing like an Essay of our political Situation but to thank you most sincerely for your Favours shewn to my Son and assure you nothing would give me greater pleasure than having an opportunity of making some grateful Return—

I remain Yours respectfully RICHARD FLOWER

RC (MHi); addressed: "Thos Jefferson Esqr Monticello America favourd by Mr Birkbeck"; endorsed by TJ as received 19 May 1817.

Richard Flower (ca. 1761–1829), brewer, farmer, and reformer, was a native of England. He began his career in brewing and was drawn into politics and pamphleteering, authoring *Observations on Beer and Brewers, in which the Inequality, Injustice, and Impolicy, of the Malt and Beer Tax, are Demonstrated* (Cambridge, Eng., 1802). After the British government failed to address the concerns thus expressed, Flower shifted his business interests to sheep breeding and agriculture. When his Marden estate suffered from the impact of taxation and low crop prices, he published *Abolition of Tithe Recommended, in an Address to the Agriculturists of Great Britain* (Harlow, Eng., 1809). In 1818 he sold the estate and followed his eldest son, George Flower, to the United States. Flower settled initially in Lexington, Kentucky. The following year he moved to Albion, Illinois, where the younger Flower had established an agricultural community composed primarily of English immigrants. Flower authored two more pamphlets, *Letters from Lexington and the Illinois* (London, 1819) and *Letters from the Illinois, 1820. 1821.* (London, 1822), in which he defended the Albion settlement against attacks by the political writer and critic William Cobbett. He was a leader of the successful movement to keep slavery out of Illinois, built a tavern and founded a library in Albion, and led weekly religious services there. After one trip back to England in 1824, during which he helped to negotiate Robert Owen's purchase of land for his utopian colony at New Harmony, Indiana, Flower returned to his adopted home and died in Albion (*ANB*; *DAB*; Vandalia *Illinois Intelligencer*, 12 [misdated 13] Sept. 1829).

[1]Manuscript: "Vitue."

Notes and Drawings for Barboursville

[before 29 Mar. 1817]

		f. running measure
2 walls $1\frac{1}{2}$ brick thick	41.f long =	82
6. d^o	19. =	114
1 d^o	22 =	22
2. d^o	30 =	60
		278
2. d^o 2. bricks thick	$42\frac{1}{2}$ =	85 f. run^g measure.

			f
a column of wall 1.f. running measure	9 f. pitch below & 2. bricks thick	will take 24. bricks ×	9 = 216
	18 f. pitch above & $1\frac{1}{2}$ brick thick	18. bricks ×	18 = 324
			540. bricks
a column of wall 1.f. running measure	9 f. pitch below[1] & $2\frac{1}{2}$ brick thick	30. bricks ×	9 = 270
	18.f pitch above & 2. bricks thick	24. bricks ×	18 = 432
			702.

	bricks
278. f. running measure at 540. bricks to every foot will be =	150,120
85. f at 702	59,670
4. fireplaces & 2. shafts on the top	2,784
2. porticos, underpinning 4. bricks thick, $5\frac{1}{2}$ f high, 62.f run^g measure	16,368
	228,842 bricks in the whole.

the 2. walls dividing the middle rooms from the side rooms are made 2. bricks, or 18 I. thick that all the flues of the 8 fire places may run

up in their thickness, each flue being[2] 9.I. wide one way, and 16.I. or 18 I. the other way, being 144 or 162. square inches and experience has abundantly proved that 144. square I. or 1. square foot is sufficient to vent the smoke.

these flues must be brought together at the top of the wall over the points a.b. where the cross walls of the bed rooms join, and[3] being 4. in number each, they will form a square shaft 3.f. square, containing 4. flues of 12.I. square separated by a lath of 4.I.

the fire places below are of brick, projecting into the room, but stopping at the height of 5 or $5\frac{1}{2}$ f. by which time the flue may be gathered back into the thickness of the wall. this saves abundance of bricks and prevents breaking the cornice into angles.

---

the public rooms to wit the 2. middle rooms and the Dining room are 18 f pitch. in the clear.

the private rooms are the lower one [ ]$\frac{1}{2}$ f. pitch in the clear

$8\frac{1}{2}$	joists & floors	
1		1.f
$7\frac{1}{2}$	upper room	7[ ] f pitch in the clear[4]
1	joists	
18.f		18.f

the house being 41.f. wide and the cornice projecting 18.I. on each side makes the joists 44.f. long from point to point.

the height of the roof must be $\frac{2}{9}$ of it's span, consequently 8. f 8 I high.

the windows of the upper rooms admit only of a cornice running round the body of the house, but for the porticoes there must be an architrave & frize also, making a compleat entablature.

the external order may be Tuscan. and the floor of the porticos 6.I. lower than that of the house

in that case the order entire will be 19 f–6 I

	f I
the cornice	1–6
frize	1–
architrave	1
entablature	3–6
the capital	1. 0
fust	14.
base	1.
column entire	16.

the diameter of the column below is 2 f it's diminished diameter above is 18.I.

I would recommend the octagon room to have an Ionic modillion cornice and the Dining room an Ionic dentil cornice; these being easily made and yielding to none in beauty the architraves of the doors and windows must be $\frac{1}{6}$ of their clear opening

Rumford fireplaces adapted to wood, should be 18.I. deep 2.f wide in the back and 4.f. in front, or 1 f. 9 I. in back & 3 f 6.I. in front. 3. f to 3. f 3 I high

the upper rooms should have stoves, to save stacks[5]

the windows of the two middle rooms should go down to the floor.

the 3. center doors are 5.f. wide &[5] as high as the windows, and the Southern one should be a sash door. the other doors should be 7.f. high and $3\frac{1}{2}$ or 3. feet wide.

3 f. 3.I. by 6 f. 6 I. is a good width and height for windows below, & suits glass of 12. by 18 I. the windows above, for glass of the same size must be 3 f 3.I. by 4.f. 9.I. opening on a swivel joint[6] being restrained in their height by the outer cornice & the low pitch of the rooms.

the stairs leading from the lower to the upper rooms can occupy but 10 f by $3\frac{1}{2}$ on the floor & therefore will have 14 treads of $8\frac{1}{2}$ I. and 15 rises of $7\frac{3}{4}$ I. under each are steps down to the cellars, and from the upper floor of one should be steps up into the loft and a trap door in the roof to get out on that.

the Dome is to be on posts from the top of the wall to the plate the top of which is 18.I. above the ridge pole. the radius of the dome is 17 f 8. I it's arc is of 120.° it's plinths are 10.I. high each. the shingling of the roof of the house should go a foot or more under the sides of the dome, to prevent leaking at the junctures. this renders a support of framed work for the dome better than to raise the brick walls. the ribs of the roof are made of 4 thicknesses of inch plank 12.I. wide, breaking joists the dome may be omitted altogether if desired. the cornice of the dome is a mere surbase moulding of 6.I

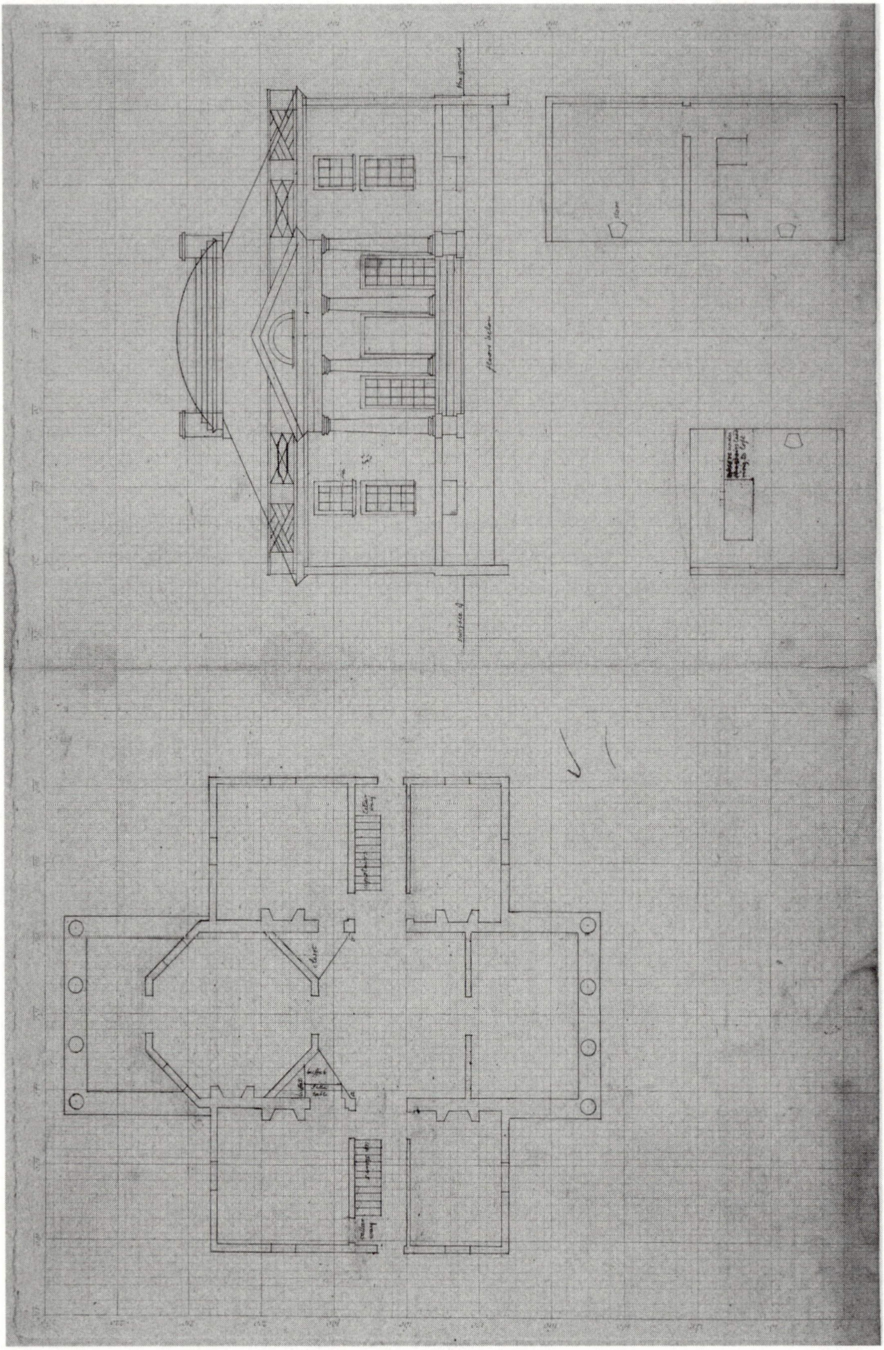

MS (MHi); written entirely in TJ's hand on $13\frac{5}{16}$-by-$20\frac{3}{4}$-inch sheet of brown, single-sided, engraved, coordinate paper folded in half to form four pages, with notes on p. 1 and drawings on pp. 2–3; undated; two numbers reworked and illegible.

These notes were evidently composed prior to 29 Mar. 1817, when James Barbour thanked TJ for his plan for this building. TJ also prepared a drawing of the rear elevation (PrC in MHi, entirely in TJ's hand, undated; reproduced in Kimball, *Jefferson, Architect*, fig. 205).

A FUST is the shaft of a column (*OED*).

Barbour followed TJ's design for his Barboursville estate fairly closely, although he did take advantage of the latter's concession that THE DOME MAY BE OMITTED ALTOGETHER IF DESIRED (Kimball, *Jefferson, Architect*, 185–6, fig. 206). A photograph of the structure as it stood prior to a devastating 1884 fire is reproduced elsewhere in this volume, as is a likeness of Barbour.

[1] Reworked from "above."

[2] TJ here canceled "10."

[3] Preceding eight words interlined.

[4] To the right of this brace TJ canceled "the joists of all the rooms lay on the top of the wall, and are sloped at their ends thus so as to make a part of the roof, & not of the body of the house the top

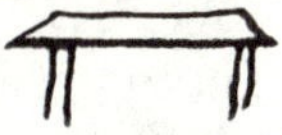

of the cornice outside being even with the bottom of the joist is nailed to brackets suspended from the joists."

[5] Sentence interlined.

[6] TJ here canceled "10.f. high in the clear."

[7] Preceding five words interlined.

From James Barbour

DEAR SIR Barboursville March 29th 17

The bearers of this, James Bradley and Edward Ancel are the undertakers of my building—the former a Carpenter—the latter a bricklayer—I have resolved on the plan you were good enough to present me and for which I return you my Sincere thanks—You were kind enough to accompany the plan with a Suggestion that it would be well for my workmen to See your building and receive such verbal explanations as might facilitate their labors. To that end I have directed them to repair to Monticello. I trust you will excuse the trouble I give you tho I am conscious I tax your kindness very heavily—If you have anything in the Seed way which you would recommend and which is not common you will oblige me by sending it

I tender you my best respects JAS BARBOUR

RC (MHi); endorsed by TJ as received 30 Mar. 1817 and so recorded in SJL; with unrelated calculation by TJ on verso. RC (MHi); address cover only; with PoC of TJ to John Wayles Eppes, 6 June 1817, on verso; addressed: "Thomas Jefferson Esqr Monticello."

Edward Ancell (1748–1832), bricklayer, was a native of England who settled first in Calvert County, Maryland. He purchased land in Orange County in 1779 and lived there subsequently (Benjamin Lucius Ancell, *Descendants of Edward Ancell of Virginia* [1933], 1–2; Orange Co. Deed Book, 17:164–6, 21:358–9; Orange Co. Will Book, 7:451–2).

From Joseph C. Cabell

Dear Sir, Edgewood. 30th march. 1817.

I have had a good hunt among my papers for Main's recipe for the preparation of Haws: and at length, after almost despairing, have found it in the midst of a small volume of extracts from Brown's Rural Affairs. I now send it to you, agreeably to your desire. I am, dear sir, very respectfully & truly yours

Joseph C. Cabell

RC (ViU: TJP-PC); endorsed by TJ as received 8 Apr. 1817 and so recorded in SJL. Enclosure not found.

To Peter Minor

Dear Sir Monticello Mar. 30. 17.

The inclosed letter to Majr Watson is to request him to meet the visitors of our proposed college here on the day or evening before our next court (Monday) that by an evening's conference together we may come to an understanding of what should be done at our formal meeting which is to be at Charlottesville the next day Tuesday. Can you contrive it in time, or give it such a direction as, being left by the bearer, on his return, at the Charlottesville post office, will ensure Majr Watson's getting it in time.

I ask the favor of you to read the inclosed, addressed to mr Dabney Minor. it's length being too much for the stay of the bearer I will count on your being so good as to send it to mr Minor as soon as you have read it, that he may have time to do the same before Jefferson shall have called. Your's with great esteem and respect

Th: Jefferson

PoC (MHi); on verso of reused address cover of Smith & Riddle to TJ, 20 Feb. 1817; mutilated at seal, with missing text rewritten by TJ; at foot of text: "Peter Minor esq."; endorsed by TJ. Enclosures: (1) TJ to David Watson, 30 Mar. 1817, and enclosure. (2) TJ's Bill of Complaint against the Rivanna Company, [by 9 Feb. 1817].

jefferson: Thomas Jefferson Randolph.

From Peter Minor

Dr. Sir Ridgeway Mar. 30: 17

I have rec^d your packet enclosing a letter to Maj^r Watson, & a communication to Mr D. Minor. I will take care to send the letter to Maj^r Watson by a special messenger, as I feel greatly interested in the success of the central college, & if his health will permit I know he will attend: but I hear that he has been a good deal confined of late by the Rheumatism—

I shall as you request peruse your bill in chancery, & will deliver it to Mr Minor early tomorrow. I highly commend the resolution you express to have the footing upon which yourself & the Directors stand as it respects your respective rights, fixd upon a certain basis, & perhaps the mode you propose is finally the best; tho: with the exception of one of the board, I believe the matter could be satisfactorily adjusted without the odium of a law suit, which however freindly it may be called, is apt to leave an asperity behind it, & a great degree of prejudice among those who feel themselves interested; I mean those who use the navigation.

with high Esteem yrs P Minor

RC (MHi); endorsed by TJ as received 30 Mar. 1817 and so recorded in SJL.

The one of the board of the Rivanna Company hostile to TJ was probably William D. Meriwether.

From Francis Adrian Van der Kemp

Dear and respected Sir! Olden Barneveld 30 March. 1817.

As I have nothing—deserving your attention—to communicate, I rather Should deem it improper to answer Your favour of the 16 with which I was honoured, was it not—that your courtesy imposed upon me a duty—to free you from an error which caused you some concern—not that I am apprehensive—that you had any thing to fear from a clamorous rabble of ignorant—bitter bigots—as I would do you the justice to Suppose, that you Scorn their revilings—and laught at their threatnings too cordially—than that they could decompose your quiet, or disturb your Serenity of mind—I See you rather unmoved—with a Smile at their restless vain endeavours—

Biancheggia in mar lo Scoglio
Par che vacilli, e pare
che lo Sommerga il mare
Fatto maggior di Se.

Ma dura a tanto orgoglio
Quel combattuto Sasso:
E'l mar tranquillo, e basso
Poi gli lambisce il piè

But I Should have been guilty of indiscretion, was your apprehension founded—No Sir! I never yet abused confidence. The Editor of the Theol. Rep—does not—did never possess the name of the author of the Syllabus—The Original, as I informed you, remains me—I Send a copy in my handwriting did not even hint to mr joÿce—the author—but requested him, as I foresaw that hints may be thrown out, not to permit himself a Surmise—and I doubt not, or mr joÿce, had he remained alive, till the arrival of my Letter—would not have allowed himself a Liberty, which might give any umbrage or offence to the Author. I presume the Present Editor, whom I guess to be the Rev. Aspland—did not See the Letter—and permitted himself a Surmise, on ground—what he had Seen in Belsham's Memoirs. I have directly written to mr Aspland—requesting him—to indulge not further in this conjecture—and I doubt not, or he Shall comply with my wishes—and—although I am pretty indifferent, what a certain class may Say about me—yet I took it for a rule—Since long—noli irritare crabrones. I know by experience how unmercifully the Stings of these hornets and wasps, are intruded—to court their attack—when yet a youth I Stept forward in defence of my master—Prof. at Law—against this Pharisaical phalanx and raised their rage in proportion I blunted their weapons and my friend A— warned me when yet in Europe—„do not meddle with the clergÿ—when you cross the Atlantic„.

I ardently hope with you, and I expect it—that the Subject of the Syllabus Shall be eventually fairly discussed—Truth does not want meretricial ornaments—and must be immoveable. As Soon I receive Lett. from England—and have opened again a correspondence with any one deserving my confidence—I shall be informed—what well-come this Stranger met in England.

I made Some attempts to range and digest materials—but as the Summer-Labour is approaching—I may not vacate to mÿ amusements before winter—if my days are So far prolonged. This Spring many avocations prevented me—to make a beginning. One requested my opini[on] on capital punishments—another on Boudinot's Star in the west—another on Agriculture—and lately what I taught on the lawfulness of marrying two Sisters one after the other. This is here, ex cathedra, called an incestuous marriage, on futile grounds—whereas it is permitted by the Law of nature—and never—as was prohibited—

by Mozaic institutions—allowed, for arguments sake, that these were yet obligatorÿ—

You See in the Month. Rep. a wish—to know Something more of Dr. Balth. Bekker, a Dutch clergyman—a man for his age of vast learning—great Liberality—and acute mind—He actually conquered and destroy'd the kingdom of the Devil—in his work the enchanted world—hinc ella lacrymæ!—the good Soul might not longer preach the gospel—because he did not believe in the Devil—It was good for him—that the Magistracy of Amsterdam—would not intermeddle—that he Should not be Suspended in office—but they resolved, „that he Should be paid during life—and remain invested with the outward honours of his dignity„.

I drew few rough outlines of his Character—and give a concise content of his Book—for the Month. Rep—

I did not intend—that you Should have returned the Repository—My friend A. and mine opinion was that it Should have remained at Monticello—I am happy in possessing the original—

Examining this winter a part of the hist. of Italy—I fell on that Singular Character Nic. Rienzi—Nearly at the Same epoch one Jacopo Bossalaro—an Augustin monk at Pavia—had nearly Succeeded in revolutionising that part of Italÿ—It Should be acceptable—could you—at any convenient time—as once for all—I request—never to drop one Single line—which Should cause the least inconvenience—and when of this point assured—I Shall write freelÿ, and accept with Sincere gratitude, the Smallest favour, I am honoured with:—could you then at any convenient time impart Something, or inform me of the Sources—to become more acquainted with these two, I Shall be highly gratified.

I cannot disguise, that the distinguished attention, with which you continue to honour me, gives me an exquisite pleasure—more So—as mÿ friend Adams Stands not alone in his warm attachment and generous protection towards a Western cottager—

I doubt not, or you too will cordially permit me, to assure you, that I am with high respect and consideration

Dear and respected Sir! Your most obed. & obliged S[t]

FR. ADR. VAN DER KEMP

RC (DLC); dateline at foot of text; edge chipped; endorsed by TJ as received 15 Apr. 1817 and so recorded in SJL.

BIANCHEGGIA IN MAR LO SCOGLIO ... POI GLI LAMBISCE IL PIÈ: "The rock, with foamy billows white, Seems sinking down the tumbling tide, While soaring o'er its topmost height, The waters gain on every side. But proudly batter'd round in vain Its stately head the tempest braves, Till smooth'd to calms, the placid main

Creeps round its foot with lambent waves." John Hoole, *Dramas and Other Poems; of the Abbé Pietro Metastasio. Translated from the Italian* (London, 1800), 1:414, thus renders an excerpt from Pietro Metastasio's 1735 poem *Il Sogno di Scipione*. Metastasio based his work in turn on Cicero's *Somnium Scipionis* in the latter's *De Re Publica* (Clinton Walker Keyes, ed. and trans., *Cicero De Re Publica De Legibus*, Loeb Classical Library [1928; repr. 1952], 260–83). Wolfgang Amadeus Mozart used the Metastasio text as the libretto for his short opera of 1772 also called *Il sogno di Scipione* (John W. Warrack and Ewan West, *Concise Oxford Dictionary of Opera* [3d ed., 1996], 349, 483).

NOLI IRRITARE CRABRONES: "do not provoke the hornets." Van der Kemp's MASTER was Frederik Adolph van der Marck. John Adams WARNED Van der Kemp not to interfere with the clergy.

A query regarding Balthasar BEKKER appeared in the *Monthly Repository of Theology and General Literature* 11 (1816): 594. In his book entitled *De Betoverde Weereld* (THE ENCHANTED WORLD) (Amsterdam, 1691), Bekker expressed his doubts of the reality of witchcraft and the existence of the Devil. Van der Kemp gave the ROUGH OUTLINES OF HIS CHARACTER in the *Monthly Repository of Theology and Literature* 12 (1817): 449–54.

Abigail Adams agreed that the copy of the REPOSITORY containing TJ's syllabus of the doctrines of Jesus need not be returned by TJ. The fourteenth-century Italian popular leader Nicola di Lorenzo (NIC. RIENZI) is more commonly referred to as Cola di Rienzo.

To David Watson

SIR Monticello Mar. 30.[1] 17.

A letter, of which the inclosed is a copy, was addressed to you on the day of it's date, but misdirected both as to your Christian name and post office by the mistake of a friend who happened to be here. I send a duplicate therefore and renew urgently my request that you will be so good as to come here the day or evening before; as you will meet mr Madison, General Cocke, & mr Cabell here, and we can arrange much more satisfactorily in the evening's conversation what may be proper to be done at Charlottesville the next day. I repeat to you the assurance of my great esteem and respect.

TH: JEFFERSON

PoC (DLC); on verso of a reused address cover from José Corrêa da Serra to TJ; at foot of text: "Maj^{r} David Watson"; endorsed by TJ as a letter to David Watson and so recorded in SJL. Enclosed in TJ to Peter Minor, 30 Mar. 1817.

The enclosed DUPLICATE was a correctly addressed copy of TJ to John H. Cocke and David Watson, 10 Mar. 1817, recorded under that date in SJL as separate letters to Cocke and "Augustus" Watson.

[1] First digit reworked from "2."

James Monroe by John Vanderlyn

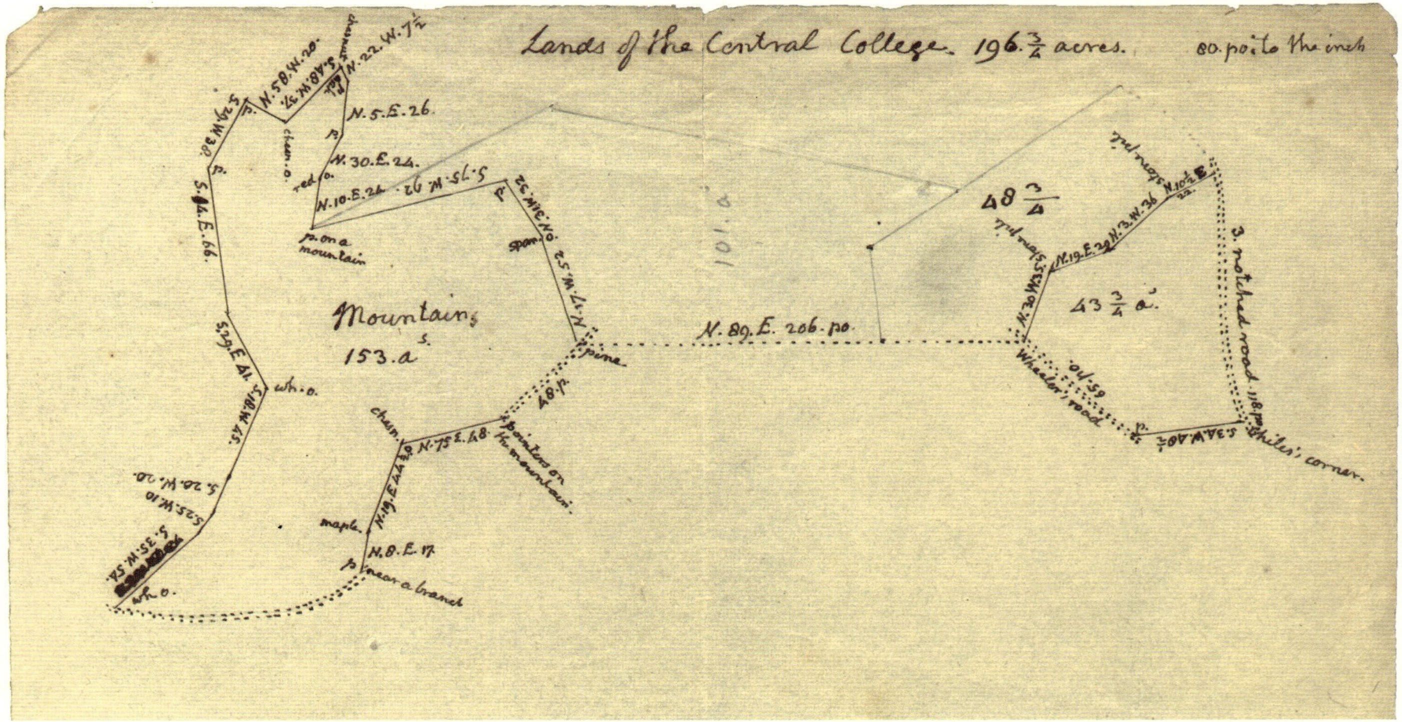

Thomas Jefferson's Plat of Central College Lands

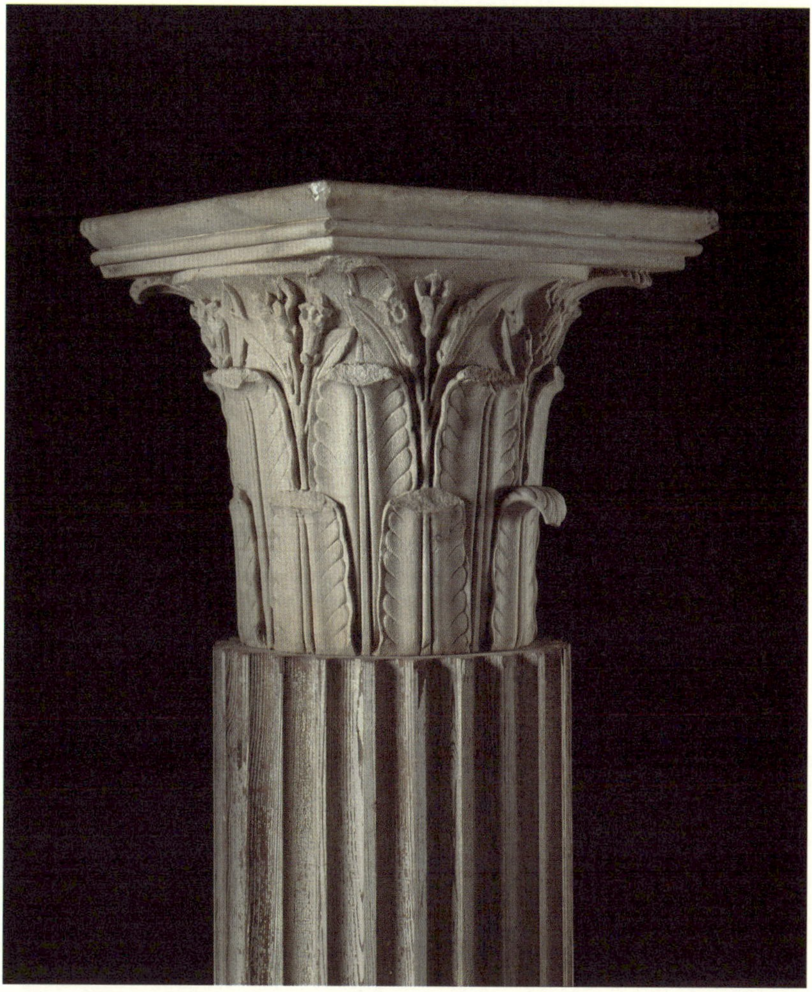

Tobacco-Leaf Capital by Benjamin Henry Latrobe

James Barbour, by Chester Harding, and Barboursville

Dome Room and Stairs at Monticello

Lucy Marks by John Toole

Natural Bridge

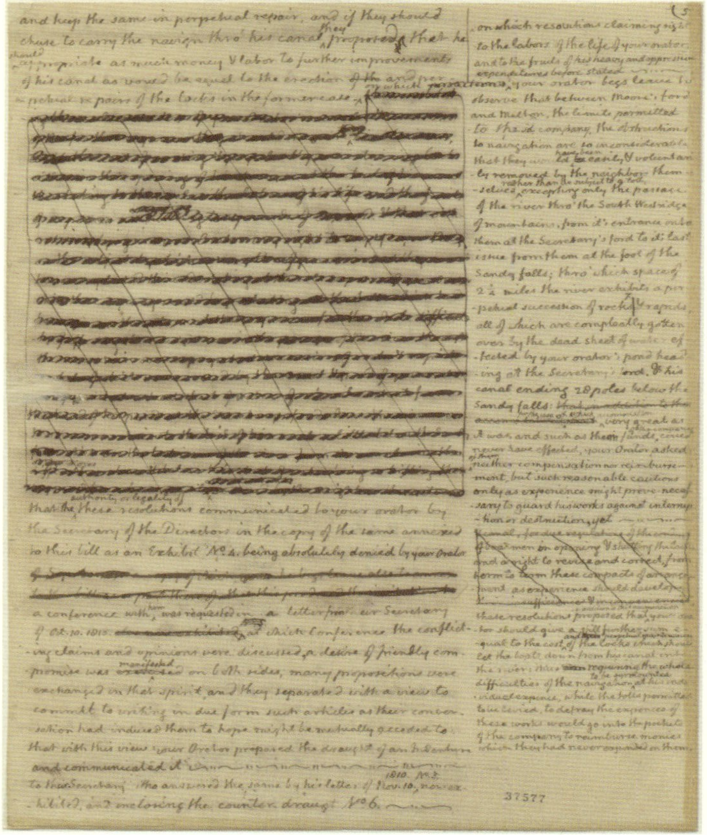

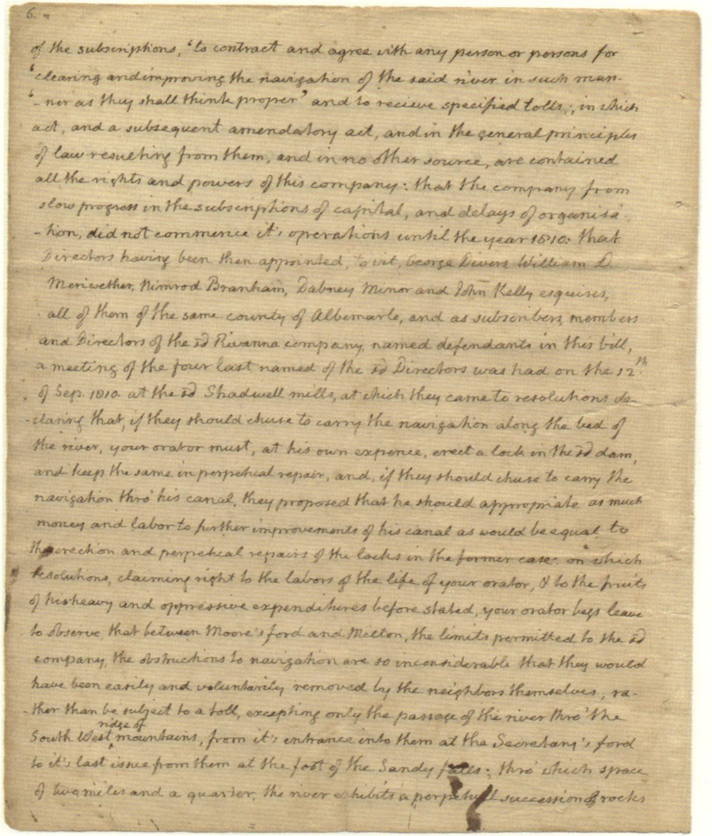

6.

of the subscriptions, 'to contract and agree with any person or persons for 'cleaning and improving the navigation of the said river in such man-'-ner as they shall think proper' and to recieve specified tolls; in which act, and a subsequent amendatory act, and in the general principles of law resulting from them, and in no other source, are contained all the rights and powers of this company: that the company from slow progress in the subscriptions of capital, and delays of organisa-tion, did not commence it's operations until the year 1810: that Directors having been then appointed, to wit, George Divers William D. Meriwether, Nimrod Bramham, Dabney Minor and John Kelly esquires, all of them of the same county of Albemarle, and as subscribers, members and Directors of the sd Rivanna company, named defendants in this bill, a meeting of the four last named of the sd Directors was had on the 12th of Sep. 1810. at the sd Shadwell mills, at which they came to resolutions de-claring that, if they should chuse to carry the navigation along the bed of the river, your orator must, at his own expence, erect a lock in the sd dam, and keep the same in perpetual repair, and, if they should chuse to carry the navigation thro' his canal, they proposed that he should appropriate as much money and labor to further improvements of his canal as would be equal to the erection and perpetual repairs of the locks in the former case: on which resolutions, claiming right to the labors of the life of your orator, & to the fruits of his heavy and oppressive expenditures before stated, your orator begs leave to observe, that between Moore's ford and Milton, the limits permitted to the sd company, the obstructions to navigation are so inconsiderable that they would have been easily and voluntarily removed by the neighbors themselves, ra-ther than be subject to a toll, excepting only the passage of the river thro' the South West ridge of mountains, from it's entrance into them at the Secretary's ford to it's last issue from them at the foot of the Sandy falls; thro' which space of two miles and a quarter, the river exhibits a perpetual succession of rocks

Draft and Fair Copy of Thomas Jefferson's Bill of Complaint against the Directors of the Rivanna Company

To Nicolas G. Dufief

DEAR SIR Monticello Mar. 31. 17.

I am unlucky in the dictionaries I recieve from you, this being the 2[d] time I believe that I have recieved them with a false half sheet, from the carelessness of the binder. the 1st volume of the set last recieved had the 6. leaves now returned instead of the 6. from 'Notopede—to Onglee' inclusive, which I shall be glad to recieve from you in exchange for those inclosed.

I salute you with friendship and respect. TH: JEFFERSON

RC (ViU: TJP); at foot of text: "M. Dufief." PoC (DLC); on verso of reused address cover of otherwise unlocated letter from Archibald Thweatt to TJ, 19 Feb. 1817 (addressed: "Thomas Jefferson esq: Monticello Albemarle county V[a]"; franked; postmarked Richmond, 21 Feb.; recorded in SJL as received 23 Feb. 1817 from Richmond); endorsed by TJ.

For TJ's earlier problems with defects in DICTIONARIES from Dufief, see TJ to Dufief, 22 Aug. 1813, and Dufief to TJ, 6, 29 Sept. 1813. The LEAVES NOW RETURNED from Dufief, *A New Universal and Pronouncing Dictionary of the French and English Languages*, 3 vols. (Philadelphia, 1810; Sowerby, no. 4822; Poor, *Jefferson's Library*, 14 [no. 881]), have not been identified. TJ was missing vol. 1, pp. 541–52.

To John Wayles Eppes

DEAR SIR Monticello Mar. 31. 17.

Francis will set out tomorrow for Mill-brook. he has his constant health, and has applied himself assiduously & solely to Spanish. he now possesses this so well that reading a little in it every day, he will be in no danger of losing it. in the French he is well established; and the possession of these two languages is well worth the little check he has recieved in his Latin, I think he should now apply his shoulder mainly to the Greek. in learning that his Latin necessarily goes on with equal pace; because the lexicons are all in Greek and Latin. I have no doubt that Wood is the best Grecian we can find, and from the attachment he has taken to Francis I think he will be very particularly attentive to him. there will be this farther advantage with him, that when he is sufficiently advanced in Latin and Greek, he can enter on the Mathematics with Wood, whom I consider as the best Mathematician in the state. if you should conclude to send him to Wood I will write to him and state to him the course I think most advantageous to be pursued. I have great hope and confidence he will return to Lynchburg, altho' he does not yet think so himself. it is much to be desired for the security of health. present me respectfully to mrs Eppes, and be assured of my constant and affectionate attachment.

TH: JEFFERSON

PoC (MHi); on verso of reused address cover of William A. Burwell to TJ, 26 Feb. 1817; torn at seal, with missing text rewritten by TJ; at foot of text: "J. W. Eppes esq."; endorsed by TJ.

To Fernagus De Gelone

SIR Monticello Mar. 31. 17.

Your favor of the 15th is at hand, covering an account of the books forwarded, balance due you 13.D. which I now inclose you in Virginia bank bills. I hope shortly to hear of the safe arrival of the books at Richmond, and tender you my salutations and assurances of respect.

TH: JEFFERSON

PoC (MHi); on verso of reused address cover of John Barnes to TJ, 28 Feb. 1817; at foot of text: "M. J. Louis Fernagus de Gelone"; endorsed by TJ.

From James Eastburn, John W. Francis, and James Smith (of New York)

SIR, *New-York*, *March*, 1817.

Being appointed a committee of the NEW-YORK HISTORICAL SOCIETY (instituted in the year 1804) for the collection of Manuscripts and scarce Books, relating to the History of this Country, and hoping that it may be in your power to aid our researches, and to contribute to our collection, we beg leave to subjoin an extract from the first Report of the Society, which will explain the object. It is as follows:

"Manuscripts, Records, Pamphlets, and Books relative to the History of this Country, and particularly to the points of inquiry subjoined;

Orations, Sermons, Essays, Discourses, Poems and Tracts; delivered, written, or published on any public occasion, or which concern any public transaction or remarkable character or event;

Laws, Journals, Copies of Records, and Proceedings of Congresses, Legislatures, General Assemblies, Conventions, Committees of Safety, Secret Committees for General Objects, Treaties and Negotiations with any Indian Tribes, or with any State or Nation;

Proceedings of Ecclesiastical Conventions, Synods, General Assemblies, Presbyteries, and Societies of all denominations of Christians;

Narratives of Missionaries, and Proceedings of Missionary Societies;

Narratives of Indian Wars, Battles and Exploits; of the Adventures and Sufferings of Captives, Voyagers, and Travellers;

Minutes and Proceedings of Societies for the Abolition of Slavery, and the Transactions of Societies for Political, Literary, and Scientific Purposes;

Accounts of Universities, Colleges, Academies and Schools; their origin, progress and present state;

Topographical descriptions of Cities, Towns, Counties, and Districts, at various periods, with Maps and whatever relates to the progressive Geography of the Country;

Statistical Tables; Tables of Diseases, Births and Deaths, and of Population; of Meteorological Observations, and Facts relating to Climate;

Accounts of Exports and Imports at various periods, and of the progress of Manufactures and Commerce;

Magazines, Reviews, Newspapers, and other Periodical Publications, particularly such as appeared antecedent to the year 1783;

Biographical Memoirs and Anecdotes of eminent and remarkable Persons in America, or who have been connected with its settlement or history;

Original Essays and Disquisitions on the Natural, Civil, Literary or Ecclesiastical History of any State, City, Town or District."

As the object recommends itself to the attention of every gentleman who sees the importance of preserving, by such means as are now adopted, the otherwise perishing records of his country, we forbear any other remarks. Whatever information you can give, or Manuscripts and scarce Books you can contribute, be pleased to address to the care of Mr. JAMES EASTBURN, in this city, and your communications will be thankfully acknowledged by the Society.

We are, Sir, very respectfully, Your most obedient servants,

JAMES EASTBURN,
JOHN W. FRANCIS,
JAMES SMITH,
Committee of the N. Y. Historical Society, for collecting Manuscripts and scarce Books.

RC (DLC: Rare Book and Special Collections); printed circular; partially dated; addressed: "His Excelly Thos Jefferson Monticello"; franked; postmarked New York, 30 May, and Nashville, 18 June; endorsed by TJ (torn) as a letter from "[Eastburn] James et. al." received 15 July 1817. Recorded in SJL as a letter received from Eastburn on that date, with additional bracketed notation: "circulr for Histor. soc."

John Wakefield Francis (1789–1861), physician, received an A.B. from Columbia

College (later Columbia University) in 1809 and completed his medical degree at New York City's College of Physicians and Surgeons two years later. After graduation he coedited the *American Medical and Philosophical Register* with his former teacher and mentor, David Hosack. In 1813 Francis joined the faculty of the College of Physicians and Surgeons (which later merged with Columbia University), serving there until 1826. He also sat on the board of trustees of that college, 1814–26. In the latter year Francis was among a small group of leading physicians who established and taught at Rutgers Medical College, but the school was open only four years. He retired from medical education thereafter but remained an active practitioner, with special prominence in obstetrics. Francis also devoted his time and resources to the promotion of numerous societies. He served the New-York Historical Society as librarian, domestic corresponding secretary, and member of the standing committee; became a member of the American Philosophical Society in 1844; and was elected to two terms as president of the New York Academy of Medicine beginning in 1847. The 1857 anniversary discourse Francis delivered to the New-York Historical Society was enlarged and published the following year as *Old New York; or, Reminiscences of the Past Sixty Years* (*DAB*; Valentine Mott, *Eulogy on the late John W. Francis, M.D. LL.D* [1861]; Milton Halsey Thomas, *Columbia University Officers and Alumni 1754–1857* [1936], 60, 126, 193; Robert W. G. Vail, *Knickerbocker Birthday: A Sesqui-Centennial History of the New-York Historical Society, 1804–1954* [1954], esp. 395, 480; *New York Herald*, 9 Feb. 1861).

To Patrick Gibson

DEAR SIR Monticello Apr. 1. 17.

I am really afflicted at having suffered the renewal of my note to have escaped attention; and the more so as yours of Mar. 28 did not reach me till after the departure of our post yesterday, Monday and our next Richmond mail is not till Friday, 4th the very day on which my note becomes due; and it will not reach you till the morning of the 6th. but regret is useless, however sincerely felt. I now inclose the renewal.

Mr Yancey informs me the Bedford flour is delivered, but dreadfully short of expectation in quantity. I do not understand this miscalculation of his. he writes me the tobacco was all nearly ready, and I have pressed him to send it immediately, so that it may soon be with you. we have here about 80. barrels of flour, which Johnson promises to take down at his next trip. I consider this as the best month generally for selling flour, & therefore wish you to dispose of it as soon as you please for the price of the day. so also of the tobacco as soon as recieved. but all this will not make both ends meet with me for the present year. the drought of the last was so disastrous that the scanty wheat crop it yielded scarcely buys the corn which it failed to yield almost entirely. unless the bank & yourself can indulge me in one or two thousand Dollars additional for the year to come, I shall be much distressed. on this subject I can be more precise when my flour and tobacco shall all be sold, and the amount known to me. in the mean time, and perhaps within a few days, I may be obliged to make 2. or 3. draughts on you for about 150.D. each: and I will request you to send me by Johnson a keg of 25. ℔ of powder, and a hogshead of the best molasses. I think there is a kind called sugar-house molasses deemed the best. and I must further request you, as soon as the sale will justify it, to remit 400.D. for me to mr John Vaughan of Philada. I authorised mr Hutchins G. Burton of North Carolina to draw on you for the amount of a 30. gallon cask of Carolina wine, which I suppose will be about 40.D. be pleased to honor his draught. I shall set out for Bedford about a week hence, and be absent between 2. & 3. weeks. I salute you with affectionate respect.

TH: JEFFERSON

PoC (MHi); on verso of reused address cover of Chapman Johnson to TJ, 27 Feb. 1817; at foot of first page: "Mr Gibson"; endorsed by TJ.

Gibson's letter OF MAR. 28 was actually dated 20 Mar. 1817.

In SJL, TJ recorded Gibson's 8 Apr. response to the above letter, not found, as received 10 Apr. 1817 from Richmond.

To William D. Taylor

SIR — Monticello Apr. 1. 17.

A friend informs me he has seen in the Enquirer a tract of land of mine in Rockbridge, of 157. acres including the Natural bridge advertized for sale for the taxes. I suppose this must have been in that paper of Mar. 21. which has failed to come to me and therefore not seen by myself. the lands being under lease I had relied on the tenant for the payment of the taxes. I must now ask the favor of you to apply to mr Gibson of the firm of Gibson & Jefferson of Richmond, who, on presenting this letter will pay the amount due. you will further oblige me by committing the reciept to the mail, that I may be at ease as to the payment. Accept the assurance of my respect.

TH: JEFFERSON

PoC (MHi); on verso of reused address cover of David Higginbotham to TJ, 22 Feb. 1817; at foot of text: "William D. Taylor esq."; endorsed by TJ.

William D. Taylor (1781–1858) was appointed tax collector in 1814 for the 18th Collection District of Virginia, which consisted of Goochland, Hanover, Henrico, and Charles City counties. Taylor was postmaster for Taylorsville, Hanover County, 1819–25, followed by service at Goochland Court House, 1825–28, and then a return to his former position at Taylorsville from 1828 until at least 1856. His business interests also included milling, the proprietorship of the Taylorsville horse races, horse breeding, and tavern keeping. In 1850 Taylor owned forty-eight slaves (*Virginia Genealogical Society Quarterly*

Bulletin 6 [1968]: 61; *JEP*, 2:455–6, 468 [18 Jan., 4 Feb. 1814]; *U.S. Statutes at Large*, 3:22–34, esp. 24; *Acts of Assembly* [1814–15 sess.], 102 [13 Dec. 1814]; [1841–42 sess.], 29 [17 Feb. 1842]; Axelson, *Virginia Postmasters*, 76, 90; Daniel D. T. Leech, *Post Office Directory; or, Business Man's Guide to the Post Offices in the United States* [1856], 183; *Richmond Enquirer*, 5 Apr. 1836; *American Turf Register and Sporting Magazine* 2 [1830]: 151–2; DNA: RG 29, CS, Hanover Co., 1850 slave schedules; gravestone inscription in Taylor Cemetery, Doswell).

Although Taylor's collection district did not include Rockbridge County, where TJ's TRACT OF LAND was located, as the collector in Richmond he orchestrated the sale of lands on which taxes were overdue. An advertisement he placed in the 21 Mar. 1817 issue of the *Richmond Enquirer* listed the properties in Augusta and Rockbridge on which the direct tax of 1815 had gone unpaid for a year, stating that these tracts, "or so much thereof, as may be necessary to satisfy the said Tax due thereon, with an addition of twenty per cent.," would be "sold, at public sale, at the Bell-Tavern, in the City of Richmond, in the County of Henrico, on Friday, the 16th day of May, 1817, at 10 o'clock, A.M. and continue from day to day, until sold." One of the Rockbridge properties was "Thos. Jefferson, 157 acres of land, on both sides of Cedar creek; and includes the Natural bridge, improved," which owed $6.21 in taxes. In the same notice Taylor requested the editors of the *Lynchburg Press* and the Winchester *Republican Constellation* to run the advertisement "once a week for eight weeks" and send him the bill.

TJ's TENANT at Natural Bridge was Philip Thornton.

From Hutchins G. Burton

DEAR SIR, Halifax, April 2. 1817.—

I have purchased for you, a barrel of Wine two years old.—I think it much better than the barrel I sent Mr Eppes—I shall forward it by the first opportunity to Richmond—I hope it may not be adulterated, as the Waggonners sometimes take the liberty of playing tricks with articles of this kind, confided to their care,—It will not be necessary to give Mr Gibson any instructions about a draft on my account, as Mr Eppes & myself have considerable dealing, we can adjust the matter at any time—I gave $26 for the barrel—I will make arrangements with Mr Pettigrew an old schoolmate of mine, in the course of the present summer, to furnish you with a regular supply, by the way of Norfolk.—I had written to him, but he is now at Newyork.—I shall be on the seaboard in June or July,—the Legislature have appointed Commissioners for the purpose of ascertaining if it is possible to effect a direct passage to sea.—Accept of my Sincere wishes for your health & happiness—

I am, with respect your obt. sevt— H G. BURTON

RC (MHi); endorsed by TJ as received 29 Apr. 1817 and so recorded in SJL. RC (MHi); address cover only; with PoC of TJ to Robert Simington, 14 June 1817, on verso; addressed: "Thos. Jefferson Esquire Monticello Virginia Post office Cartersville"; stamped; postmarked Halifax Court House, 5 Apr.

From Wilson Cary Nicholas

My Dear Sir Richmond Ap[l] 2. 1817

I have written to M[r] Harrison for his permission to print the work of Col. Byrd, that I Sent you, I have no doubt he will consent to it, I am satisfied your wishes will be conclusive, & that the family of Col. Byrd will be highly gratified. When I received your answer to my application about the consulate at Leghorn for my son, I at once abandoned all thoughts of it, as nothing can induce me to wish for a moment, that any man you patronized shou'd be removed from office. I wou'd not[1] renew the subject but upon the belief that M[r] Appleton, is not now the man you suppose him to be; previous to my former letter to you I had reason to believe this was the case, but I am now convinced of it, & I am equally sure if the same impression is made upon your mind, it will not be your wish he shou'd be continued in office. I have seen enough of the world to make me receive with great caution reports to the prejudice of any man & in most cases to reject all information coming from a source, where there is a possible bias. The channel through which I get my information is subject to this objection, by all who do not know its author & my near connexion with him, wou'd prevent my stating it to any person, but one who I am sure wou'd give us both credit for believing the information communicated.

The character that I trust you have heard of my son will I hope justify me in saying to you, that the most perfect confidence may be reposed in his honor justice & liberality. & your knowledge of me & the friendship with which you have honored will be some justification of this communication. In a letter of the 26th of Jan[y] my son speaking of M[r] Appleton, says, "If he were worthy of his office, or if he were not viewed with most undisguised contempt, as well by his own country men, as by every one here; I am sure I shou'd be among the last to ask for a preference which is certainly due to services, which without being over rated, must be considered as stronger than the claims of a man who has been a stranger to his country for the last thirty years. He was known to M[r] Crawford when at paris, and to his opinion of him, without knowing what it is, I wou'd most confidently appeal in support of my pretensions. I am sure if M[r] Jefferson knew him now, he wou'd withdraw his support; as I am convinced he wou'd never continue in office, a man who is no less insensible to the respect due to his station & to his country men, Than he is destitute of the energy & spirit necessary to ensure it. a life spent for the most part in the low debaucheries & filthy intrigues of paris, is not suited to the attainment of a knowledge of our country or its people, nor is it likely to have that degree of respectability, which americans of the present day, have a right to look for in their agents abroad." I am very far from wishing or expecting you to take any part against Mr Appleton, and I shou'd be equally unwilling to have any agency in procuring the removal of a man who you had a wish shou'd be continued in office, even if it cou'd be affected. When I first received my sons letter out of respect to you & from motives of delicacy I determined to say nothing upon the subject, upon more reflection, I decided to submit its contents to you, and if you did not disapprove of it, to get some friend of Robert to recommend him. Col Randolph who has lately been here, will give you correct information of the state of the market. I fear tobacco unless of the best quality will be very low.

I am with the greatest respect & regard Dear Sir most sincerely yours

W. C. NICHOLAS

RC (DLC); addressed: "Thomas Jefferson Esqr Monticello Milton"; franked; postmarked Richmond, 3 Apr.; endorsed by TJ as received 5 Apr. 1817 and so recorded (out of sequence at the end of 1816) in SJL.

In 1815 Nicholas had unsuccessfully sought the CONSULATE AT LEGHORN for his son Robert Carter Nicholas (Wilson Cary Nicholas to TJ, 14 July, 3 Aug. 1815; TJ to Nicholas, 15 July, 9 Aug. 1815).

[1] Nicholas here canceled "now."

From Thomas Wells

SIR April 2d 1817.

I have the pleasure to inform you that Mr G. Divers has several prime Muttons but no Veal, I shall send out this morning else where, should I succeede it will give me infinite pleasure to furnish you—

Suffer me also to inform you that thire is a Machine come to this place yesterday that shaves a Side of leather with greate virility say Half a Minute which there is a patton for, the Stranger wishes very much you should see it in opperation—should it be pleasing to you he will at any hour to day be Ready to shew you the Operation excuse this liberty with greate Respect

Yo & THO WELLS

RC (MHi); dateline beneath signature; addressed: "Thos Jeffeson Esqr Present"; endorsed by TJ: "Wells Thos."

Thomas Wells (1771–1822), tavern keeper, was born in Hackettstown, New Jersey. He moved with his family to Virginia following the Revolutionary War. Wells operated the Eagle Tavern in Charlottesville and the Franklin Hotel in Lynchburg, and TJ purchased land from him in 1802. He was an officer in the Albemarle County militia and a member of the local Masonic lodge. Wells was appointed to the revived Albemarle Academy Board of Trustees in 1814 and subscribed $200 toward the establishment of Central College three years later. At his death in Richmond he left a personal estate valued at $1,974 (Lottie Wright Davis, *Records of Lewis, Meriwether and Kindred Families* [1951], 127–8; K. Edward Lay, *The Architecture of Jefferson Country: Charlottesville and Albemarle County, Virginia* [2000], 87, 168, 303, 318; *PTJ*, 38:354–6, 359–60, 396–8; *MB*, 2:1082, 1083; *Lynchburg Press*, 31 Oct. 1817; Woods, *Albemarle*, 372; *Proceedings of a Grand Annual Communication of the Grand Lodge of Virginia* [Richmond, 1806], 31; Minutes of the Albemarle Academy Board of Trustees, 25 Mar. 1814; Master List of Subscribers to Central College, [after 7 May 1817], document 5 in a group of documents on The Founding of the University of Virginia: Central College, 1816–1819, printed at 5 May 1817; Albemarle Co. Will Book, 7:301–5; *Richmond Enquirer*, 27 Aug. 1822).

From Nicolas G. Dufief

Monsieur, A Philad[e] ce 4 Avril 1817

Dans 2 ou 3 semaines je dois partir pour l'Europe, où je compte rester plusieurs mois. si je puis vous y être utile à quelque chose vous pouvez compter sur mon zèle et mon exactitude. Mes affaires seront continuées pendant mon absence par mon ami Mr. J. Laval qui a bien voulu s'en charger. Vous pouvez, en toute confiance, vous adresser à lui pour toutes les mêmes choses pour lesquelles vous m'avez honoré de votre correspondance.

J'ai l'honneur d'être avec tous les sentimens qui vous sont dus, et en faisant les vœux les plus ardens pour votre prospérité. Votre très-dévoué serviteur N. G. Dufief

P.S. si pendant mon absence vous vouliez faire venir quelque chose d'Europe, vos demandes me seraient transmises par mon ami partout où je serais.

EDITORS' TRANSLATION

Sir, Philadelphia 4 April 1817

In two or three weeks I must leave for Europe, where I intend to stay for several months. If, while there, I can be useful to you in any way, you may count on my zeal and punctuality. My business will be carried on during my absence by my friend Mr. J. Laval, who is good enough to take care of it. You can, with complete confidence, turn to him for all the same matters with which you have honored me in your correspondence.

I have the honor to be, with all respect due to you and the most ardent wishes for your prosperity, your very devoted servant N. G. Dufief

P.S. If, during my absence, you would like to have anything sent from Europe, my friend can convey your requests to me no matter where I am.

RC (DLC); adjacent to signature: "Th: Jefferson, Esquire"; endorsed by TJ as received 10 Apr. 1817 and so recorded in SJL. Translation by Dr. Genevieve Moene.

From Josephus B. Stuart

SIR. New York, 5th April 1817.

I take the liberty to send you the inclosed paper, by which you will see, the portentious state of the British Government & Nation. My letters from London, speak confidently of an approaching crisis.—

Most respectfully Yours, J. B. STUART

P.S. You know the influence & connections of the Marquis of Wellesly—note his speech.—

RC (DLC); endorsed by TJ as received 14 Apr. 1817 and so recorded in SJL. RC (MHi); address cover only; with PoC of TJ to Fernagus De Gelone, 29 Apr. 1817, on verso; addressed: "Honorable Thomas Jefferson. Monticello. Virginia"; franked; postmarked New York, 5 Apr.

The INCLOSED PAPER may have been the 4 Apr. 1817 issue of the New York *Commercial Advertiser*, which contained extracts from recently arrived London newspapers that included a message from the Prince Regent delivered 28 Jan. 1817 following an assault on him by a mob outside Parliament, two other messages from him of 3 and 4 Feb. 1817, and proceedings of both houses of Parliament relative to the Regent's communications regarding the distressed state of the nation. On 29 Jan. 1817 Richard Wellesley (WELLESLY), Marquess Wellesley, spoke in the House of Lords against any idea of universal suffrage and annual parliaments, which might "make the House of Commons the tool of democracy." Agreeing, however, that the British people were in need of relief, he supported "entering immediately into an inquiry into their distresses and their causes."

From David Watson

SIR, Louisa 6th Apl 1817

Your communication of March the 10th concerning a meeting of the visitors of a College to be established near Charlottesville, came duly to hand; as also a duplicate, with your note of March the 30th. It would give me very great pleasure to meet the other visitors at Monticello, agreeably to your polite invitation; & I hoped, till very lately, that I should be able to do so. But my health has been bad for some time; & I have been frequently unable to ride as far as Charlottesville, without much inconvenience, & even danger to my health; which happens unfortunately to be the case at present.

As I presume a meeting of all the visitors is not necessary to enable them to act, I hope no inconvenience will arise from my unavoidable absence.

With the greatest respect for yourself, and the other visitors, Yr Obt DAVID WATSON

RC (DLC); endorsed by TJ as received 7 Apr. 1817 and so recorded in SJL.

Albemarle County Court Order Concerning a Proposed Road

At A court held for Albemarle county the 8th day of April 1817.[1]

On the motion of Thomas J Randolph and Thomas Jefferson to alter the road leading from the Orange fork near Lewis's ferry downwards thro the lands of Richard Sampson, Thomas J Randolph and Thomas Jefferson to the mouth of the chapel branch, and instead thereof to substitute the road already opened, on the lands of Charles L Bankhead, from the corner of his fence nearest Charlottesville to the secretarys ford, thence across the river and down its northern side to the mouth of the same chapel branch, It is ordered[2] that Joseph Coleman, Benjamin Childress, Andrew Hart, Robert McCullock jr John Slaughter, Brightberry Brown, and Horsley Goodman, or any three of them being first sworn before a justice of the peace, do view the ground along which such substitute road is proposed to be conducted and make report to this court truly and impartially the conveniencies and inconveniencies which will result as well to individuals as to the publick, if such way shall be established[3] and that they also view the present established road and report in like manner the comparative conveniencies and inconveniencies thereof.[4] And on the like motion to alter also the road from Moores creek where the said Charles L Bankheads fence corners on it thro' the thoro'-fare of the mountain to the fork of the same road at Colle, and instead thereof to establish[5] the road before mentioned from the corner of his fence nearest Charlottesville to the secretarys ford and thence down the southern side of the river to Milton with a fork from the same near the mouth of the Indian branch up to the said branch to the said fork at Colle, It is Ordered that the same persons or any three of them being first sworn before a justice of the peace, do view the ground along which such substitute road is proposed to be conducted and make report to this court truly & impartially the conveniencies and inconveniencies which will result as well to individuals as to the publick if such way shall be established[6] and that they also view the present established road and report in like manner the comparative conveniencies and inconveniencies thereof

A Copy
teste

Alex Garrett C.C

Tr (ViU: TJP-ER); in Alexander Garrett's hand, with marginal note by TJ. FC (Albemarle Co. Order Book [1816–18], 238–9); dated 8 Apr. 1817 at head of day's proceedings; at foot of day's proceedings: "Signed David J. Lewis." Dft (ViU: TJP-ER); with TJ's Notes on a Proposed Albemarle County Road, [ca. 8

Apr. 1817], on verso; undated, variant version entirely in TJ's hand: "On motion to <*put down*> discontinue the road from Moore's creek where Charles L. Bankhead's fence corner's on it to the fork of the same road at Colle, and to establish instead thereof the road already opened on the lands of Charles L. Bankhead's from the corner of his fence nearest Charlottesville to the Secretary's ford and down the South side of the river to Milton; and the road also already opened from Colle down the Indian branch into the proposed road between Charlottesville & Milton. And to <*put down*> discontinue the road leading from the Orange fork downwards thro the lands of <*John W. Eppes*> Richard Sampson T. J. Randolph Thomas Jefferson & Thomas <*J*> M. Randolph to the mouth of the Chapel branch, and establish instead thereof the road before proposed to the Secretary's ford and across the same along the road also already opened on the North side of the river to the mouth of the Chapel branch. Whereupon it is ordered that do view the comparative conveniences & inconveniences of the roads so proposed to be established and of those proposed to be discontinued & report the same to this court." Enclosed in Circular from TJ to Joseph Coleman and Others, 1 Oct. 1817.

In SJL TJ recorded two missing letters from Charles L. Bankhead, one inconsistently recorded as dated 12 Apr. 1817 and received 11 Apr. from Carlton, and another, undated and lacking place of origin, received 15 Apr.

[1] Dateline not in FC.

[2] FC here adds "by the Court."

[3] FC: "substituted."

[4] In left margin, perpendicular to text to this point, TJ inserted a note reading "so far only is to be viewed now."

[5] FC: "substitute."

[6] FC: "substituted."

Notes on a Proposed Albemarle County Road

[ca. 8 Apr. 1817]

Present roads		Proposed roads			
from the Mainstreet of Charlottesville	Miles		po	miles	
to Moore's creek	0.98	to Secretary's ford	614.	= 1.92.	by Smith
the Thoro'fare	1.25	Mouth of Meadow br.	532	= 1.66	by protraction
Colle fork	1.32	Milton 8403. feet		= 1.59	by the level
Milton ford	2.94			5.17	
	6.49				

from the Mainstreet of Charlottesville			
to the Colle fork	3.55	to mouth of Meadow br.	3.58
		mouth of Indian br.	.37
		Colle fork	

	from the Courthouse						
by Moore's ford	poles	miles			po		
to Shadwell branch	1133 =	3.54	by Smith	to Clermont fork	154.		by Smith
mouth of Chapel br.	349 =	1.09	by Th: J. R	Sec's ford	460		
		4.63			614		miles
		4.52		mill dam	462	=	1.44
		.11 = 192½ yds		Mill	244	=	.76
				Chapel br.	129	=	.40
							4.52

MS (ViU: TJP-ER); entirely in TJ's hand; undated; with Dft of Albemarle County Court Order Concerning a Proposed Road, 8 Apr. 1817, on verso.

From David Higginbotham

Dear Sir Morven 8th April 1817.

I now enclose you a copy of the morgage, to m[r] Short, from which you can be so good as to draw the deed of release from m[r] Short to me and at same time enclose it to him for him to do the needful and return to you, to be recorded in Court, I am raily sorry to give you so much trouble about this business

I am Dear Sir Your mo ob St David Higginbotham

RC (MHi); endorsed by TJ as received 14 Apr. 1817 and so recorded in SJL. RC (MHi); address cover only; with PoC of TJ to Craven Peyton, 15 Apr. 1817, on verso; addressed: "Thomas Jefferson Esq Monticello"; franked; postmarked Lindsays Store, 12 Apr. For the enclosed mortgage, see note to TJ to William Short, 10 Feb. 1813.

From George Washington Jeffreys

Venerable Sir Red House N.C April 8th 1817.

Your letter of 3rd ultimo, with an inclosed catalouge of Books, together with a model of a plough was duly received—Permit me in behalf of our agricultural Society to return you their sincere thanks and most grateful acknowledgments for your politeness and attention to them—Your letter was read to the Society and it was unanimously ordered to be inscribed into the books of the society—The information which it contained on horizontal ploughing was entirely satisfactory—Some parts of the catalouge will also be useful to us—I cannot conclude without tendering to you in my own individual capacity the feelings of the high respect and consideration which I entertain towards you—

Yours Sincerely GEORGE WASHINGTON JEFFREYS Sec[y]

RC (DLC); endorsed by TJ as received 25 May 1817 and so recorded in SJL. RC (DLC); address cover only; with PoC of TJ to William Lee, 25 June 1817, on verso; addressed: "Thomas Jefferson Esqr Milton V[a]" by "Mail"; franked; postmarked Red House, 7 Apr. 1817.

To James Monroe

DEAR SIR Monticello Apr. 8. 17.

I shall not waste your time in idle congratulations. you know my joy on the commitment of the helm of our government to your hands.

I promised you, when I should have recieved and tried the wines I had ordered from France and Italy, to give you a note of the kinds which I should think worthy of your procurement: and this being the season for ordering them, so that they may come in the mild temperature of autumn, I now fulfill my promise—they are the following.

Vin blanc liqoureux d'Hermitage de M. Jourdan à Tains. this costs about 82½ cents a bottle put on ship-board.

Vin de Ledanon (in Languedoc) something of the Port character, but higher flavored, more delicate, less rough. I do not know it's price, but probably about 25. cents a bottle.

Vin de Roussillon. the best is that of Perpignan or Rivesalte of the crop of M. Durand. it costs 74. cents a gallon, bears bringing in the cask. if put into bottles there it costs 11. cents a bottle more than if bottled here by an inexplicable & pernicious arrangement of our Tariff.

Vin de Nice. the crop called Bellet, of mr Sasserno is best. this is the most elegant every day wine in the world and costs 31. cents the bottle. not much being made it is little known at the gen[l] market.

M[r] Cathalan of Marseilles is the best channel for getting the three first of these wines, and a good one for the Nice, being in their neighborhood, and knowing well who makes the crops of best quality. the Nice being a wine foreign to France, occasions some troublesome forms. if you could get that direct from Sasserno himself at Nice, it would be better. and, by the bye, he is very anxious for the appointment of Consul for the US. at that place. I knew his father well; one of the most respectable merchants and men of the place. I hear a good character of the son, who has succeeded to his business. he understands English well, having past some time in a Counting house in

London for improvement. I believe we have not many vessels going to that port annually; yet as the appointment brings no expence to the US. and is sometimes salutary to our merchants and seamen, I see no objection to naming one there.

There is still another wine to be named to you, which is the wine of Florence called Montepulciano, with which Appleton can best furnish you. there is a particular very best crop of it known to him, and which he has usually sent to me. this costs 25. cents per bottle. he knows too from experience how to have it so bottled and packed as to ensure it's bearing the passage, which in the ordinary way it does not. I have imported it thro him annually 10. or 12. years and do not think I have lost 1. bottle in 100.

I salute you with all my wishes for a prosperous & splendid voyage over the ocean on which you are embarked, and with sincere prayers for the continuance of your life and health. TH: JEFFERSON

RC (DLC: Monroe Papers); addressed: "James Monroe President of the US."; franked; postmarked Milton, 12 Apr.; endorsed by Monroe, with additional endorsement and summary notes in an unidentified hand. PoC (DLC); on reused address cover to TJ; endorsed by TJ.

From Nicolas G. Dufief

MONSIEUR A Philadelphie ce 9. Avril 1817

Je suis désolé de la négligence de mon relieur, et pour la réparer complètement, je vous prie de me renvoyer le volume afin que j'en fasse relier un exactement de la même manière. En attendant vous pourrez vous servir de celui que je vous adresse et qui ne sera rendu que lorsque le vôtre vous sera parvenu. Les autres méprises seront réparées de même, si vous voulez avoir la bonté de le mettre en notre pouvoir. Je crains bien de partir avant d'apprendre de vos nouvelles. Mr J. Laval N. 118 Chesnut Street qui a bien voulu se charger de mes affaires pendant mon absence se fera un plaisir d'exécuter tous vos ordres avec le même empressement que j'ai toujours manifesté.

Agréez les assurances de mon respectueux dévouement

N. G. DUFIEF

EDITORS' TRANSLATION

SIR Philadelphia 9. April 1817

I deeply regret the negligence of my bookbinder, and in order to compensate for it completely, please return the volume to me so that I can have one bound in exactly the same manner. In the meantime you can use the one I am sending you, which you should return to me only when your replacement reaches you. Other mistakes will be similarly redressed, if you are kind enough to allow us to do so.

I fear that I will depart before hearing from you. Mr. J. Laval N. 118 Chestnut Street, who is willing to take care of my business during my absence, will be delighted to execute your orders with the same eagerness I have always shown.

Please accept the assurance of my respectful devotion

N. G. DUFIEF

RC (DLC); endorsed by TJ as received 15 Apr. 1817 and so recorded in SJL. Translation by Dr. Genevieve Moene. Enclosure: Dufief, *A New Universal and Pronouncing Dictionary of the French and English Languages* (Philadelphia, 1810; Sowerby, no. 4822; Poor, *Jefferson's Library*, 14 [no. 881]), vol. 1.

From Joseph Milligan

April 9th 1817

The proof herewith Sent is taken in a rough manner as there was not time to have it properly Chased up and leaded without delaying to an other post day but as it can be leaded and justified after it is corrected I trust you will excuse the haste

yours JOSEPH MILLIGAN

RC (DLC); dateline at foot of text, with "Thos: Jefferson Esqr" above that; endorsed by TJ as received 14 Apr. 1817 and so recorded in SJL. Enclosure: proof sheets, not found, of Destutt de Tracy, *Treatise on Political Economy*.

From James Madison

DEAR SIR Montpellier Ap[l] 10. 1817

Having been detained in Washington untill the 6th inst. I did not reach home till Tuesday night, and of course too late to comply with the arrangement notified in yours of the 10th March by Bizet. I take for granted that the other Visitors met, and that for the present at least my attendance will not be needed. As it has always been our purpose to pay a visit to Monticello at no distant day after our final return from Washington, I could wish it to coincide with the time that may be fixt for the next meeting for the business of the College, and that this if discretionary may not be required for some time. Besides the effect of a fatiguing journey, our presence will for some time be necessary at home in order to attend to a thousand little preparations & some important ones, which will not admit of delay.

Your affectionate friend JAMES MADISON

RC (ViU: TJP); at foot of text: "Mr Jefferson"; endorsed by TJ as received 14 Apr. 1817 and so recorded in SJL.

From Giovanni Carmignani

Chiarissimo Signore Pisa li 11. Aprile 1817.

Con altra mia del decorso anno le annunziai la morte dell'ottimo, e bravo Sig. Filippo Mazzei della di cui ultime volontà fui nominato io Esecutore nel suo testamento; Presi nel tempo stesso la libertà di farle presente la situazione poco felice in cui quell'Uomo troppo amico degli Uomini aveva lasciate le cose sue economiche, e la necessità in cui trovavasi la sua unica Figlia, ed Erede di ritirare il prezzo de' fondi di sua proprietà che Ella vendè per suo conto in codeste Contrade.

Privo di risposta a quella mia lettera, e nascendo fondato sospetto che il Capitale proveniente da quel prezzo sebbene giunto in Europa sia ritenuto da mani poco fedeli, [io][1] mi rivolgo nuovamente a Lei, Chiarissimo Signore, onde pregarlo a compiacersi di darmi notizia se quel prezzo fù realizzato, e se fù spedito quà ℘ conto della Erede Mazzei alla mia direzione.

Consapevole dell'amicizia di cui [E]lla[2] degnava onorare il defunto Mazzei, e dell'interesse che prendeva al ben'essere della sua famiglia, oso lusingarmi che vorra accogliere co' sentimenti medesimi questa mia Lettera, e degnarsi d'interporre la efficace sua mediazione ℘ L'oggetto che la somma di cui si tratta giunga al più presto possibile nelle mie mani.

Io feci annettere alla mia prima lettera la Copia autentica del testamento, e de' Codicilli del fù Sigr Mazzei. qualora questi Documenti fossero smarriti; Ella potrebbe ciò nonostante far pervenire la somma indicata a qualche Banchiere, o Negoziante di Livorno colla ingiunzione di non pagarla se non ai legittimi rappresentanti la Eredità di detto fù Sigr Filippo Mazzei

Colgo questa occasione ℘ rinnovare a Lei la espressione sincera de' sentimenti di Venerazione, e di altissima stima co' quali ho L'onore di essere.

Di Lei Chiariss° Signore
Divotismo obdmo Servitore Giovanni Carmignani—

EDITORS' TRANSLATION

Dear Sir Pisa 11. April 1817.

With my other letter of last year, I announced to you the death of the excellent and worthy Mr. Philip Mazzei, by whose last wishes I was nominated executor in his testament; at the same time, I took the liberty of alerting you to the less than happy situation in which that man, who was too much the friend of mankind, left his economic affairs, and the necessity under which his only daughter and heiress finds herself to withdraw the price of her land, which you sold on her behalf in those parts.

Lacking a response to my letter and having a growing, well-founded suspicion that the capital from that sale, although having reached Europe, may be held by less than trustworthy hands, I am turning again to you, dear Sir, to request of you the favor to advise me whether that price was realized and if it was sent here to my address on behalf of the heiress Mazzei.

Well aware of the friendship with which you deigned to honor the deceased Mazzei, and of the interest that you took in his family's well-being, I dare flatter myself that you will receive this letter of mine with the same feelings and deign to interpose your effective mediation in order that the sum in question may reach my hands as soon as possible.

I attached an authenticated copy of the testament and the codicils of the late Mr. Mazzei to my first letter. Should these documents have been lost, you could still send the sum in question to any banker or merchant of Leghorn, with the injunction to pay it only to the legitimate representatives of the estate of the said late Mr. Philip Mazzei

I take this occasion to renew to you the sincere expression of sentiments of veneration and of very high esteem with which I have the honor of being, Dear Sir

Your very devoted obedient servant Giovanni Carmignani—

RC (DLC); in a clerk's hand, signed by Carmignani; dateline at foot of text; endorsed by TJ as received 2 Aug. 1817 and so recorded in SJL. Tr (facsimile in Margherita Marchione, Barbara B. Oberg, and S. Eugene Scalia, eds., *Philip Mazzei: The Comprehensive Microform Edition of His Papers, 1730–1816*); mutilated; includes additional endorsement: "Copia di due lettere spedite al Sig[r] Jeferson Scritte dal Professore Carmignani e spedite il 17. Aprile 1817" ("Copy of two letters sent to Mr. Jefferson written by Professor Carmignani and sent on 17 April 1817"). Translation by Dr. Jonathan T. Hine.

[1] Edge chipped, with missing word supplied from Tr.

[2] Edge chipped.

To Nicolas G. Dufief

Dear Sir Monticello Apr. 11. 17.

I have just recieved your favor of the 4th informing me you are about departing for Europe, and kindly offering your service there. I will avail myself of it for a small purpose. there is at Paris a learned Greek D[r] Coray[1] who writes the antient Greek in all it's purity, and has published some very fine editions of Greek authors, particularly

Hippocrates & Plutarch. for the last I have written thro' another Channel. but he has published also some smaller works, to wit A specimen of an edition of Homer, a Hierocles, and two or three other small Greek works with Greek prefaces & notes, and a selection of Scholia. if you will have the goodness to procure and send me these you will oblige me, handsomely bound. with every wish for a pleasant voyage, health, and a happy meeting with your friends I salute you with great esteem and respect. TH: JEFFERSON

PoC (DLC); at foot of text: "M. Dufief"; endorsed by TJ. Engraved facsimile of RC in SzGeBGE; with minor variations, only the most significant of which is noted below.

TJ eventually acquired a copy of Adamantios Coray's edition of HIPPOCRATES, *Τὸ Περὶ Ἀέρων, Ὑδάτων, Τόπων* ... (2d ed., Paris, 1816; Poor, *Jefferson's Library*, 5 [no. 200]; TJ's copy in MoSW). This publication included the Greek originals and French translations of works by Hippocrates on *Airs, Waters, Places* and on *Law*, as well as a Greek text of Galen's essay, *The Best Doctor is Also a Philosopher*.

[1] PoC: "Caray." Engraved facsimile: "Coray."

From Michael H. Walsh

TO HIS EXCELLENCY
THOS JEFFERSON Friday Morng [11 Apr. 1817] Monticello—

To impress a feature of recollection, that cannot be blotted from existance, a stranger, and a foreigner begs leave to realize this feeling, by being admitted to your presence

independant of The high admiration, that republicans reject, your Excellency will permit me to Join in the homage the world pays you—

I have the honour to be your Excellencys devoted humble St

MICHAEL. H. WALSH—

RC (MHi); partially dated at foot of text; addressed: "To his Excellency—Thos Jefferson Monticello"; endorsed by TJ as a letter of 11 Apr. 1817 from Michael A. Walsh received that day and so recorded in SJL.

To Joseph Delaplaine

DEAR SIR Monticello Apr. 12. 17.

My repugnance is so invincible to be saying any thing of my own history, as if worthy to occupy the public attention, that I have suffered your letter of Mar. 17. but not recieved till Mar. 28. to lie thus long, without resolution enough to take it up. I indulged myself at some length on a former occasion, because it was to repel a calumny still sometimes repeated, after the death of it's numerous brethren, by which a party at one time thought they could write me down, deeming even science itself, as well as my affection for it, a fit object of ridicule and a disqualification for the affairs of government. I still think that many of the objects of your enquiry are too minute for public notice. the number, names, and ages of my children, grandchildren, great grandchildren E^{t}c would produce fatigue and disgust to your readers, of which I would be an unwilling instrument. it will certainly be enough to say that from one daughter living and another deceased[1] I have a numerous family of grandchildren, and an increasing one of great grandchildren.—I was married on new year's day of 1772. and mrs Jefferson died in the autumn of 1782.—I was educated at William and Mary college in Williamsburg. I read Greek, Latin, French, Italian, Spanish, and English of course, with something of it's radix the Anglo-Saxon. I became a member of the legislature of Virginia in 1769. at the accession of Lord Botetourt to our government. I could not readily make a statement of the literary societies of which I am a member. they are many and would be long to enumerate, and would savour too much of vanity and pedantry. would it not be better to say merely that I am a member of many literary societies in Europe and America? your statements of the corrections of the Declaration of Independance by Dr Franklin and mr Adams, are neither of them at all exact. I should think it better to say generally that the rough draught was communicated to those two gentlemen, who, each of them made 2. or 3. short and verbal alterations only. but even this is laying more stress on mere composition than it merits; for that alone was mine; the sentiments were of all America.   I already possess a portrait of mr Adams, done by our countryman[2] Brown, when we were both in England, and have no occasion therefore for the copy you propose to me. accept my apologies for not going more fully into the minutiae of your letter, with my friendly & respectful salutations.

TH: JEFFERSON

RC (LNT: George H. and Katherine M. Davis Collection); addressed: "Mr Joseph Delaplaine Philadelphia"; franked; postmarked; endorsed by Delaplaine; with additional notation in an unidentified hand: "Hair to retreat from the top from the lid of the eye to eyebrow right Eye Left cheek & eye more in shadow." PoC (DLC); on verso of reused address cover to TJ; torn at seal; endorsed by TJ.

[1] Preceding seven words interlined.
[2] Manuscript: "countrymen."

From Alexander Garrett

D[R] SIR 12th April—17

In consequence of M[r] Perrys absence from home, I was not able to see him untill yesterday at sun set, when I closed the contract with him in behalf of the college, he has promised to survey it as soon as possible say Wednessday or thursday next; I understand from M[r] Winn, that the Glebe money in his hands except about 6. or 700$ is in Virginia bank stock, should not some arrangements be immediately made to dispose of so much of this stock as will enable the Visitors to meet the payment for this purchase of Perry. M[r] Winn says the stock is now at about $105–

Very Respectfully Yours ALEX GARRETT

RC (CSmH: JF); addressed: "M[r] Jefferson Monticello"; endorsed by TJ as received 12 Apr. 1817.

From Valentine Gill

SIR Blue bell House N.S. Halifax April 12th 1817

The eminence of your character, your philosophic and scientific genius[1] and your ability to promote and reward merit, has prompted me to seek at Monticello, the retreat of its bountiful donor, that patronage,[2] for want of which oft times fair science droops, and ability remains unnoticed and unrewarded;

"And many's the flower thats doom'd to bloom unseen,
And waste its fragrance on the desert air."[3]

Your universal knowledge and love of science will plead the excuse for the intrusion of an adventurer, an exile of Erin, whose hopes there once flattering, is now without pain to be rememberd no more, I have been regularly bred to the Engineer department, Surveying in its fullest extent, leveling and conducting Canals &c. My drawings of Maps Plans &c, will be found not inferior.

I was brought in here while on my way to your enviting shores, where I have been employ'd but not to the extent of my wishes

the first desire of my heart, is to become a resident of your land of liberty! as a friend to science and humanity, say can I hope for employment there; I have a small family companions of my adventurous fate, prudence forbids my leaving this without a Knowledge of where I should take them; with diffidence I humbly solicit this mark of your condescension, which should I be so fortunate to attain, my gratitude shall ever remain unabated, Your general knowledge of the country, and intimacy with its conducters might point out employment for me, at some of its public works, or your extensive domain would perhaps afford a field sufficient to found my entroduction.

I have the Honor to be Sir, with every mark of Respect & esteem your most Obed^t Hble Servt &c VALENTINE GILL

RC (MHi); dateline at foot of text; endorsed by TJ as received 4 May 1817 and so recorded in SJL.

Valentine Gill, surveyor and cartographer, lived in Enniscorthy, County Wexford, Ireland. In 1811 he published a map of that county based on his surveys. By 1814 Gill was in Halifax, Nova Scotia, where he helped to complete surveying work for the Shubenacadie Canal. From 1817–21 he worked for the New York State Canal Commission as an engineer surveying the route for the Champlain and Erie canals. Gill settled by 1819 in Herkimer, New York, and by 1827 he worked in a surveyor's office in Rochester. He lived there for the next decade and was among the incorporating members of the Rochester Hibernian Benevolent Society. By 1840 Gill was the proprietor of a mathematical and drawing school in Columbus, Ohio (*List of Persons who have suffered Losses in their Property in the County of Wexford* [(Dublin, 1799)], 9; "Valentine Gill's map of Co. Wexford," *Past* 20 [1997]: 90–1; Barbara Grantmyre, "Two Peripatetic Gentlemen," *Nova Scotia Historical Quarterly* 6 [1976]: 375–89; Madison, *Papers, Retirement Ser.*, 1:23–4, 53–5, 58–9, 74; Cooperstown, N.Y., *Otsego Herald*, 22 Nov. 1819; DNA: RG 29, CS, N.Y., Herkimer, 1820, Ohio, Columbus, 1840; Sylvanus H. Sweet, *Documentary Sketch of New York State Canals* [1863], 111, 468; *Laws of the State of New York, in relation to the Erie and Champlain Canals* [Albany, 1825], 1:452–3; *A Directory for the Village of Rochester* [1827], 147; *Laws of the State of New-York, passed at the Fifty-Fourth Session of the Legislature* [1831], 239–40 [21 Apr. 1831]; Columbus *Ohio Statesman*, 5 Jan. 1841).

AND MANY'S THE FLOWER ... DESERT AIR paraphrases Thomas Gray, "Elegy Written in a Country Churchyard," lines 55–6 of which read "Full many a flower is born to blush unseen / And waste its sweetness on the desert air" (Roger Lonsdale, ed., *The Poems of Thomas Gray, William Collins, Oliver Goldsmith* [1969], 127).

[1] Manuscript: "genuis."

[2] Manuscript: "paronage."

[3] Omitted closing quotation mark editorially supplied.

From Horatio G. Spafford

RESPECTED FRIEND— Albany, 4 Mo. 12, 1817.

I enclose, herewith; a Small Novel, of which I ask thy acceptance. It is the first thing of the kind that I have written, & I do not wish to be known as the writer. If it do but amuse thee, I shall be glad, & should gladly learn that the composition is approved. I hope thou wilt find time to read it, & that many years of health & enjoyment may be indulged to thee by that dread Being who guides events. Very respectfully, thy friend, H. G. SPAFFORD.

RC (MHi); at foot of text: "Hon. Thomas Jefferson"; endorsed by TJ as received 28 Apr. 1817 and so recorded in SJL. Enclosure: "Maria-Ann Burlingham" [Spafford], *The Mother-In-Law: or Memoirs of Madam de Morville* (Boston, 1817).

From David Bailie Warden

DEAR SIR, Paris, 12 april, 1817.

mr. Ticknor arrived here yesterday and handed me your letter of the 7th february 1815, for which I am greatly indebted. I wrote to you on the 14th of July last inclosing the invoice of your Books, which were forwarded from Havre to new york by the ship united states, and addressed to the collector of that port. I should be glad to hear of their safe arrival. If you wish for others it will give me great pleasure to procure and forward them to you

The correspondence of Franklin has at last made its appearance at London, and a Translation at Paris; but it is not well ascertained whether any part has been suppressed—Perhaps you are the only person who can decide this point. Some of the french Journals, from political motives, have commenced a very unjust critique of this patriotic and truly philosophical correspondence.

Your friend the abbé Rochon died a few days ago, after a fortnights illness, and preserved his faculties to the last moment. His daughter left this world a few hours before him—The present minister of marine, who was greatly attached to him, will no doubt obtain a pension for his widow. He was occupied for some time in writing the history of steam Boats, which he has left unfinished. In him I have lost an excellent friend; whom I had the pleasure of seeing frequently during several years.

our minister has not been able to obtain an answer on the subject of claims; and proposes to spend a part of the summer in switzerland.

The migration of frenchmen to the united states still continues—the views of the military class are directed towards South america—

A society has been lately organised here for the purpose of establishing an agricultural and Commercial Colony on the coast of Senegal. Two vessels with emigrants have already sailed for that destination and another is preparing.—I pray you, to present my respects to mr. and mrs. Randolph

I am, dear sir, with great respect
your very obliged servt, D B. WARDEN

RC (DLC); at foot of text: "Thomas Jefferson Esquire"; endorsed by TJ as received 18 June 1817 and so recorded in SJL.

TJ's letter to Warden was dated 27 Feb., not 7TH FEBRUARY 1815. The COLLECTOR of the port of New York was David Gelston. William Temple Franklin issued a second edition of THE CORRESPONDENCE of his grandfather, *The Private Correspondence of Benjamin Franklin, LL.D. F.R.S. &c.*, 2 vols. (London, 1817). The one-volume French TRANSLATION was *Correspondance Choisie de Benjamin Franklin* (Paris, 1817). The French MINISTER OF MARINE was François Joseph de Gratet, vicomte Dubouchage.

Originally founded in 1814, the Société Coloniale Philanthropique de la Sénégambie suspended its activities following Napoleon's 1815 return to Paris. It was revived in 1816 for the PURPOSE of completing "the discovery of the whole interior of the continent of Africa, and to carry the torch of religion, with all the benefits of civilization, agriculture, and the useful arts, among the nations that inhabit that vast continent, which is, as yet, so little known, but which, notwithstanding, is one of the finest, richest, and most fertile parts of the globe. To accomplish these great objects, the Colonial Society proposes to establish, upon the coast of French Africa, in Senegambia, near Cape Verd and on the continent, an Agricultural Colony, which, in a few years, may prove a substitute to France for a part of those she has lost, and which may open, at the same time, a vast asylum for the countless number of unfortunate French citizens, who, tossed about by political convulsions, have been exposed for five-and-twenty years to the outrages and inconstancy of Fortune" ("French Colonial Society," *Colonial Journal* 5 [1817]: 409–10).

To James Dinsmore

DEAR SIR Monticello Apr. 13. 17.

We are about to establish a College near Charlottesville on the lands formerly Col° Monroe's, a mile above the town. we do not propose to erect a single grand building, but to form a square of perhaps 200 yards, and to arrange around that pavilions of about 24. by 36.f. one for every professorship & his school. they are to be of various forms, models of chaste architecture, as examples for the school of architecure to be formed on. we shall build one only in the latter end of this year, and go on with others year after year, as our funds increase. indeed we believe that our establishment will draw to it the great state university which is to be located at the next meeting of the legislature. the College, the immediate subject of this letter, is under the direction of 6. visitors, mr Madison, Col° Monroe, Genl Cocke mr Cabell, mr Watson of Louisa, & myself, and we are to meet on the 6th of May to put it into motion. I suppose the superintendance of the buildings will rest chiefly on myself as most convenient. so far as it does I should wish to commit it to yourself and mr Nelson, and while little is called for this year which might disturb your present engagements, it will open a great field of future employment for you. will you undertake it? if you will, be so good as to let me hear from you as soon as you can, and I would rather wish it to be before the 6th of May. there is a person here who wishes to offer you two very fine boys, his sons, as apprentices; but on this nothing need be said until you determine to come. tender my esteem to mr Nelson & be assured of it respectfully yourself. TH: JEFFERSON

PoC (ViU: TJP); on verso of reused address cover to TJ; at foot of text: "Mr James Dinsmore"; endorsed by TJ.

MR NELSON: John Neilson.

To James Madison

DEAR SIR Monticello Apr. 13. 17.

Your letter of Feb. 15. having given me the hope you would attend the meeting of the Visitors of the Central college near Charlottesville I lodged one for you at Montpelier notifying that our meeting would be on the day after our April court. a detention at Washington I presume prevented your attendance, and mr Watson being sick, only Gen[l] Cocke, mr Cabell and myself met. altho' not a majority, the urgency of some circumstances obliged us to take some provisional steps, in which we hope the approbation of our colleagues at a future meeting, which we agreed to call for on the 6th of May, being the day after our court. circumstances which will be explained to you make us believe that a full meeting of all the visitors, on the first occasion at least, will decide a great object in the state system of general education; and I have accordingly so pressed the subject on Col[o] Monroe as will I think ensure his attendance, and I hope we shall not fail in yours. the people of this section of our country, look to a full meeting of all with unusual anxiety, all believing it will decide the location of the State University for this place in opposition to the pretentions of Stanton, which unites the tramontane interest. the location will be decided on at the next session of the legislature. I set out for Bedford within 2. or 3. days, but shall make a point of returning in time, in the hope of seeing you. constant & affectionate respect.

TH: JEFFERSON

RC (DLC: Madison Papers, Rives Collection); at foot of text: "M[r] Madison"; endorsed by Madison. PoC (DLC); on verso of reused address cover of John Adams to TJ, 2 Feb. 1817; mutilated at seal, with some words rewritten by TJ; endorsed by TJ.

To James Monroe

DEAR SIR Monticello Apr. 13. 17.

The reciept of a commission as Visitor, will have informed you, if you did not know it before, that we have in contemplation to establish a College near Charlottesville. by the act of assembly which fixes our constitution, it is to be under the direction of 6. visitors. your commission has informed you you were one of these, & your colleagues are mr Madison, Gen[l] Cocke, mr Joseph C. Cabell, mr Watson of Louisa and myself. a meeting, and immediately, is indispensable to fix the site, purchase the grounds, begin building E[t]c. we endeavored to have one the day of our last court, but mr Madison was not returned home, & mr Watson was sick, so that only Mess[rs] Cocke Cabell & myself attended. we agreed to call one on the day succeeding our May court, to wit, Tuesday the 6th of May. a still more important object than the College itself makes this meeting interesting. the legislature, at their next meeting will locate the University they propose, on a truly great scale, & with ample funds. Staunton claims it, & will have the tramontane interest. yet $\frac{2}{3}$ of the population is below the mountains; and if schism among them can be prevented, it will be placed below. the centrality of Charlottesville & other favorable circumstances places it on the highest ground of competition: and it is important to lift it up to the public view. the site is fixed at your former residence above Charlottesville. 200 acres of land provisionally agreed for. the commencement of the buildings immediately will draw the public attention to it. but what every one believes will bring it the most into notice, is a full meeting of the Visitors. the attendance of yourself there, mr Madison and the others will be a spectacle which will vividly strike the public eye, will be talked of, put into the papers, coupled with the purpose, and give preeminence to the place. a site marked out by such a visitation, for the Central college, for that is the title the law has given it, will be respected, it will silence cis-montane competition unite suffrages, and ensure us against schism. your attendance for this once is looked for with great desire & anxiety by the people of this section of country, and you can never do an act so gratifying to them, as by joining this meeting. as a visit to your farm however short must be desirable to you, I am in hopes you will so time it as to meet us on the occasion. the other gentlemen will be at Monticello the overnight, that is to say the evening or to dinner on the 5th which is court day. I do suppose there can be nothing nationally important, in the present state of general quiet, to oppose such a visit, and I will allow myself to hope we shall see you accordingly. I salute you with perfect affection and respect Th: Jefferson

RC (DLC: Monroe Papers); addressed: "James Monroe President of the US. Washington"; franked; postmarked Charlottesville, 13 Apr.; endorsed by Monroe, with additional endorsement and summary notes in an unidentified hand. PoC (DLC); on reused address cover of Thomas Law to TJ, 8 Feb. 1817; endorsed by TJ.

"An Act for establishing a College in the county of Albemarle," WHICH FIXES OUR CONSTITUTION, passed on 14 Feb. 1816. Its third provision provided for six visitors "who shall hold their offices each for the term of three years" (*Acts of Assembly* [1815–16 sess.], 191–3).

To DeWitt Clinton

Dear Sir Monticello Apr. 14. 17.

I have to acknolege the receipt of your favor of Mar. 27. of the very valuable Treatise on Inland navigation, and of the several reports on the junction of the waters of lakes Erie and Champlain with those of the Hudson. the conception is bold and great, and the accomplishment will be equally useful. the works of Europe in that line shrink into insignificance in comparison with these. having no facts to go on but those reported by the Commissioners we cannot but concur in their conclusions of practicability, and with a confidence proportioned to their known abilities, & accuracy. the question of expence is perhaps less certain, as well from the hidden obstacles, not known until the earth is opened, as from other circumstances which cannot be foreseen. but no probable degree of expence can transcend that of it's utility. the prospect of the future face of America is magnificent indeed: but for the revolutionary generation it is to be enjoyed in contemplation only.

With my thanks for these communications, and every wish for the success of these great and honorable enterprises accept the assurance of my great respect & esteem Th: Jefferson

RC (NNC: Clinton Papers); addressed: "Dewitt Clinton esquire New York"; franked; postmarked Milton, 15 Apr.; endorsed by Clinton. PoC (DLC); on verso of a reused address cover from Archibald Robertson to TJ; torn at seal; endorsed by TJ. Printed in the *New-York Columbian*, 21 Apr. 1817, and elsewhere.

To Chapman Johnson

Dear Sir Monticello Apr. 14. 17.

I now inclose my bill in Chancery for the file of the court. it has been read by all the defs. four of them acknolege the facts, within their own knolege, to be correct. they are glad the suit is brought, that they may know their rightful ground, and will answer without delay, and consent to it's being brought on by motion as soon as ready. some depositions will be necessary. the suit will be entirely friendly as to them. what the fifth gentleman will do can only be conjectured from what he has done. the others I believe are perfectly convinced by the bill that the right is against them on both the grounds, of claim under the jury and of the expence incurred by my permission, that this cannot go beyond the full enjoyment of all their expences when the whole of what they were employed on will have perished. the matter of right being once settled, we shall without difficulty agree on the future course. I return you the subpoena, to be renewed, which will give you an opportunity of correcting the additions to the names of the defendants if necessary. be so good as to return me a new one without delay, and accept my friendly & respectful salutations.

TH: JEFFERSON

PoC (MHi); on verso of a reused address cover from James Monroe to TJ; at foot of text: "Chapman Johnson esq."; endorsed by TJ. Enclosure: TJ's Bill of Complaint against the Rivanna Company, [by 9 Feb. 1817]. Other enclosure not found.

THE DEFS, the directors of the Rivanna Company, were Nimrod Bramham, George Divers, John Kelly, Dabney Minor, and the FIFTH GENTLEMAN, William D. Meriwether.

To John W. Maury

Monticello Apr. 14. 17.

Th: Jefferson presents his compliments to mr John W. Maury, and his thanks for the eloquent Eulogium on General Washington which he has been so kind as to send him. the subject merits all the praise which man can bestow, and the terms in which it has been bestowed are worthy of the subject. nothing can be so pleasing to one retiring from the business of his country, as to see [t]hat those on whom they devolve are worthy and capable of them. he hopes that the talents manifested in the composition recieved will not remain long unemployed for the public benefit; and he salutes mr Maury with great esteem & respect.

PoC (DLC); on verso of a reused address cover from Martha Jefferson Randolph to TJ; dateline at foot of text; edge trimmed; endorsed by TJ.

From Bernard Peyton

D^R SIR Rich^d 14th April 1817

I was favord this morning with your note of the 8th Current by Mr Gilmore & have now the pleasure to subjoin rect for the 100 ℔s Rice you wished, sent by the return of the Boat—I searched the City for the best, and latest arrivals from the South of this article & send you what is <u>warranted</u> of the <u>new crop</u>, & said to be of very superior quality, I am not myself a judge of the article—I hope you may find it to answer the description—

I take this opportunity to return you my sincere thanks as well as those of M[r] Preston for the letters you were good enough to enclose me—he has taken his departure some time since—

By an arrival at New York from Liverpool we have letters of a late date, which has caused Flour to advance considerably in price—it is held this morning at $13.50 ad 14 but no sales yet—the holders are aprehensive of a still farther advance—the price on saturday was $12.50 ad 12.75— Tobacco dull at $6 a $11— in haste—
Very respectfully sir

Your assured friend & Obd: Sert: B. PEYTON

RC (MHi); endorsed by TJ as received 28 Apr. 1817 and so recorded (with a mistaken composition date of 23 Apr.) in SJL; subjoined to Joseph Gilmore's receipt to Peyton, Richmond, 14 Apr. 1817: "Rec[d] in good order one $\frac{1}{2}$ Barrel Rice to be delivered in like good order to Tho[s] Jefferson Esq[r] Monticello—he paying freight as customary" (MS in MHi; in Gilmore's hand and signed by him).

TJ's NOTE OF THE 8TH CURRENT is not recorded in SJL and has not been found.

To John Wood

DEAR SIR Monticello Apr. 14. 17.

My grandson Francis Eppes left us a fortnight ago, and carried from me strong recommendations to his father to take advantage of your kind offer to recieve him in your school. he has past the two last winters with us, the preceding one in learning French, the last Spanish. in French he is a tolerable proficient: but of Spanish he will need to read a little every day to keep it up & improve it. he has both pronunciations tolerably well. these two languages amply remunerate the check given to his progress in Latin. to that and the Greek he has now to apply his shoulder, and especially the latter, as it necessarily exercises him in Latin also. I wish him to be substantially grounded in them before he commences the Mathematics. I still entertain a hope that you will find inducements to return to Lynchburg where you can always have as many pupils as you please. I dread the foundations of future disease, the consequence of a residence for any time in any part of the lower country. I salute you with esteem and respect.

TH: JEFFERSON

PoC (MHi); on verso of reused address cover of Joseph Miller to TJ, 6 Dec. 1816; at foot of text: "M[r] Wood"; endorsed by TJ.

To James Madison

Dear Sir Monticello Apr. 15. 17.

I sincerely congratulate you on your release from incessant labors, corroding anxieties, active enemies & interested friends, & on your return to your books & farm, to tranquility & independance. a day of these is worth ages of the former. but all this you know. yours of the 10th was delivered to me yesterday. mine of the 13th had been sent off the moment it was written. we are made happy by mrs Madison's proposing to join you in the visit. I wish you could come a day or two before our meeting that we might have time to talk over the measures we ought to take. the first day of the spring & fall terms of our circuit court is what the law has appointed for our semi-annual meetings. we did not think of that when we appointed the 2d day. the 1st being the day of our County as well as District court, there will be a great collection of people, and so far one end of our meeting would be better promoted. and I have no doubt the other gentlemen will be at court, in which case, if you are here, it will be a legal meeting notwithstanding our appointing another day. I hope therefore you will be with us. I set out for Bedford tomorrow morning and shall be back here the 29th. all join me in affectionate respects to mrs Madison and yourself.

Th: Jefferson

RC (DLC: Madison Papers, Rives Collection); at foot of text: "Mr Madison"; endorsed by Madison. PoC (DLC); on verso of reused address cover to TJ; endorsed by TJ.

To James Monroe

Th: Jefferson to the
President of the US. Monticello Apr. 15. 17.

Finding subsequently, what had not been before attended to that the law had appointed the 1st day of our Spring & Autumn District court for the stated meetings of the Visitors of the Central College, it is concluded that our meeting should be on the 5th instead of the 6th of May (noted in my letter of the 13th) and that being the 1st day of both our County & District courts, the collection of the people will be great, and so far give a wider spread to our object. we shall hope therefore to see you on that day. mr Madison will join us the day before. ever & affectly yours.

RC (CtY: Franklin Collection); dateline at foot of text; addressed: "James Monroe President of the US. Washington"; endorsed by Monroe. PoC (DLC); on verso of reused address cover to TJ; edge chipped; endorsed by TJ.

To Craven Peyton

Sir Monticello Apr. 15. 17.

I have secured the return of the 1500.D. you were so kind as to lend me, by a sale of part of the land to mr Dawson, the price payable July 1. this will enable your negociator in Kentucky to ask a shorter day of payment. should you fail in that negociation, I can still find use for the money according to your own convenience. I set out for Bedford tomorrow morning to be back on the 29th. I salute you with esteem & respect.

Th: Jefferson

PoC (MHi); on verso of reused address cover of David Higginbotham to TJ, 8 Apr. 1817; at foot of text: "Mr Peyton"; endorsed by TJ.

TJ sold Martin dawson 256 acres of land near Milton that had been a part of the tract he purchased from the heirs of Bennett Henderson (*MB*, 2:1336, 1342; TJ's Conveyance of Milton Lands to Martin Dawson, 28 Mar. 1818).

From André Thoüin

Monsieur et l'un des Patriarches de La liberté Americaine, Paris le 15 Avril 1817.

J'ai l'honneur de vous anoncer que j'ai remis mon faible tribut annuel au Capitaine Chazal, de Charleston, dont le navire etait en chargement au havre de grace et Se proposait d'en partir pour retourner dans Sa patrie vers la fin de février dernier. Il est composé d'une centaine d'especes de graines de vegetaux utiles et agréables renfermées dans une petite caisse à votre adresse. Je desire que cet assortiment vous Soit parvenu et qu'il vous reusisse bien.

Il me parait que les Etablissemens Scientifiques ainsi que les Societes liberales Se multiplient dans votre chere Patrie et que les Sciences y font de rapides progrès. C'est vous, Monsieur, qu'il y avéz donné cette Salutaire impulsion. Ne Serait-il pas tems de S'occuper, actuellement, que l'amerique Se peuple considerablement, d'Etablir de bonnes Ecoles d'Economie rurale et domestique, à l'Instar[1] de celle formée par M. de fellemberg, en Suisse; les quelles en presentant des modeles de toutes les cultures utiles à etablir en amerique, offriraient encore des fabriques, des Usines perfectionees ainsi que des outils, ustenciles, machines et Substances propres à l'exploitation des fermes, Metairies et autres biens ruraux? Il me Semble que le moment est favorable pour mêttre un tel projet en execution et que Si l'on attend plus tard il Sera plus difficile de l'executer. Mais ce n'est pas a moi a dire ce qui convient le mieux à votre patrie. elle a en vous,

Monsieur, un Juge bien plus éclairé Sur Ses veritables interêts et Sur les moyens de les remplir.

J'ai appris avec une vive Satisfaction qu'on etait enfin parvenu à cultiver la vigne avec Succès, Sur les côteaux bordés par l'ohio. C'est vraiment un tresor pour L'amerique qui vaut beaucoup plus que les mines d'or du Perou. En occupant a Sa culture une population nombreuse elle retiendra dans le pays les Sommes considerables qui en Sortes pour L'acquisition de cette utile liqueur. Mais il faudrait trouver les moyen d'empecher ce qui arrive en Europe dans tous les pays de Vignoble. C'est que les habitans y Sont pauvres et presque tous malheureux deformés dans leur physique et affectés pour la plupart de maladies qui abregent leur carière, comparativement aux Cultivateurs de grains. Ses accidens Sont occasionnés par L'Irregularite des recoltes, par la nature du Travail et plus encore par la forme des outils dont ils Se Servent pour cultiver la vigne. Il est je crois des moyens de remedier en grande partie à tous ces malheurs. l'Etablissement de caisses d'assurances, d'une part ensuite l'emploi d'outils a long manche d'un autre part ou même celui de petites charrues Substituée[2] a la houe remplirait ces buts, en beaucoup de circonstances. Quelques essais qui été faits ici Semblent prouver la verite de ces assertions.[3]

Pardon, Monsieur, de vous entretenir Si long tems, mais je n'ai pû resister au plaisir de vous parler de votre chere Patrie; Sur la quel la plupart des habitans de cette vieille Europe ont les yeux fixés, les uns par Jalousie les autres par L'envie de S'y rendre et de L'habiter. Aussi les gouvernants ne manquent-ils pas d'en faire dire beaucoup de mal par leurs journeaux mais cela ne fait rien aux personnes qui Savent les entendre; au contraire parce que Sachans qu'ils disent toujours l'opposé de la verite, ils n'ont pas de peine de la reconnoître aux Soins qu'ils prenent pour la cacher.

Veuillèz je vous prie me Permettre de vous renouveller, l'expression des Sentimens de vénération que vous voue depuis longtems et pour toujours

Monsieur et Vénérable Collegue Et avec les quels je vous prie de recevoir Mon tres respectueux hommage THOÜIN

EDITORS' TRANSLATION

SIR AND ONE OF THE PATRIARCHS OF AMERICAN LIBERTY, Paris 15 April 1817.

I have the honor to notify you that I have delivered my feeble annual tribute to Captain Chazal, of Charleston, whose ship was being loaded in Le Havre-de-Grâce and who planned on leaving there to return to his country about the end of this past February. It consists of the seeds of about a hundred species of useful and agreeable plants enclosed in a little crate addressed to you. I hope this assortment has reached you and that it will succeed with you.

I understand that scientific establishments as well as liberal societies are multiplying in your dear nation, and that the sciences are making rapid progress there. You, Sir, have given them this beneficial impulse. Would it not be time, now that America is becoming considerably populated, to establish good schools of rural and domestic economy, in accord with the example of the one created by Mr. von Fellenberg in Switzerland? These schools, while displaying samples of all the useful crops to be established in America, would also offer models of manufactures and improved factories, as well as tools, utensils, machines, and substances specific to the cultivation of farms, tenant farms, and other rural properties. It seems to me that the time is right to implement such a project and that, if we wait until later, its execution will be more difficult. But it is not for me to say what best suits your country. In you, Sir, it has a much more enlightened judge of its true interests and the means of achieving them.

I learned with much satisfaction that vineyards havc finally been successfully cultivated on the banks of the Ohio River. They are really a treasure for America, and are worth much more than the gold mines of Peru. By keeping a large population busy with their cultivation, the country will retain the considerable sums of money that are now leaving it as a result of importing that useful liqueur. But we will need to find ways to prevent what is happening in all the wine-producing countries of Europe. That is, the inhabitants there are poor; almost all of them are miserable and deformed in their physical appearance; and the majority are suffering from diseases that shorten their careers compared to people who grow grains. Their mishaps are caused by the irregularity of the crops, by the nature of the work, and even more by the shape of the tools they use to cultivate vineyards. I believe that, for the most part, means can be found to remedy these misfortunes. The establishment of insurance funds on the one hand, the use of tools equipped with long handles on the other, or even the substitution of small plows for the hoe, will in many circumstances fulfill these goals. Some attempts that have been made here seem to verify these assertions.

Forgive me, Sir, for being so long-winded, but I could not resist the pleasure of talking to you about your dear country, on which most of the inhabitants of this old Europe have fixed their eyes, some out of jealousy, others because they desire to go and live there. Those in the government are thus wont to malign it through their newspapers, but this does not matter to people who know how to interpret them. On the contrary, knowing that they always say the opposite of the truth, people have no trouble recognizing it by the pains taken to hide it.

Please allow me to renew the expression of the feelings of veneration I have for a long time, and will forever, devote to you

Sir and venerable colleague, and with which I ask you to receive my very respectful homage

THOÜIN

RC (DLC: TJ Papers, 209:37377); on printed letterhead of the "Administration du Muséum d'Histoire Naturelle, au Jardin du Roi"; at foot of first page: "M. Th. Jefferson, Citoyen des Etats-unis Correspondant de L'Institut de france &c. En Amerique"; endorsed by TJ as a letter of 11 Apr. 1817 received 2 Aug. 1817 and so recorded in SJL. Translation by Dr. Genevieve Moene.

The ECOLES D'ECONOMIE RURALE ET DOMESTIQUE of the Swiss educator and agriculturist Philipp Emanuel von Fellenberg were located on his estate of Hofwyl, near Bern. Influenced by the ideas of the educational reformer Johann Heinrich Pestalozzi, Fellenberg encouraged interaction among students from varying economic and social backgrounds and combined classroom education with practical training. He infused his institutions with philanthropic ideals and sought to improve the condition of all people by minimizing class conflict (John S. Doskey, ed., *The European Journals of William Maclure* [1988], 177, 179, 622–3; Will S. Monroe, *History of the Pestalozzian Movement in the United States* [1907], 11–2).

[1] Manuscript: "l'Istar."
[2] Manuscript: "Subtituée."
[3] Manuscript: "assetions."

From Horatio G. Spafford

Albany, 4 Mo. 18, 1817.

If, from more important duties, & reading of greater interest, thou canst spare time to read my little Novel, I should be glad to learn how it is approved. THE AUTHOR.

RC (MHi); dateline adjacent to signature; addressed: "Hon. Thomas Jefferson, LL.D."; endorsed by TJ as a letter from Spafford received 29 Apr. 1817 and so recorded in SJL.

From William Thornton

DEAR SIR City of Washington 18th of April 1817

Mr & Mrs Madison left this City for Orange County on the 6th Inst. and were so kind as to take the Drawing by Mr West and the Painting by Mr Stewart which you were so very obliging as to lend to me, and for which I return you my sincere thanks.—I copied Mr West's Drawing & many thought I surpassed the original; but I know that in many parts I could not equal it, though I laboured much to effect what he did with very great ease. It is a beautiful Drawing—It was a little injured before you sent it, I think it must have been done by a damp Situation. I took care to keep it dry, and pasted a moist paper over it to prevent any thing from touching it, which by being stretched over the straining frame effectually preserves the Drawing—The fine Head which Mr Stewart painted of you, I have copied a second time, & have imitated it very exactly in water colours; but it is I find almost impossible to give the force, the expression, the firmness of character, at the same time the softness, and beauty of the original. I have however succeeded better than I expected to have done, & am pleased that I made the second Drawing, for I think it more like the Painting than the first, & I admire the painting more than any head done in this antique Stile that I ever beheld. It is one of the finest & most exquisite pieces I know, and is truly invaluable.—If any thing should happen to either of them I should never forgive myself for having taken the liberty of requesting the loan of them.—I hope however they are so safely packed, and in such careful hands, that no injury will be sustained. If any unforeseen accident should happen, all the compensation I can make will be to send my Copies, but I own they would poorly compensate such a loss.—I again thank you very sincerely for your kindness.—I have often wished it were possible to get a Cast of that unrivalled Bust that Ceracchi made of you; for though I have seen many Busts—by Houdon & others, I know of none that I admire so much as that.—If you should have no objection I would endeavour to engage a good Sculptor who can execute it well, to take the materials to Monticello, and cast it. I believe there is no danger of injury in doing it. M[r] Angelucci the Secretary of M[r] Deneuville the French Minister is just going to France (in ab[t] a week) & will return in 15 Days after his arrival in Paris. If you have any Commands there, it would be an opportunity that would fulfil every wish; and M[r] Angelucci I know would think himself honored by any commission from one so highly respected.—

I am dear Sir with the highest respect & consideration y[r] obliged Fr[d] &c

WILLIAM THORNTON—

RC (MHi); addressed: "Honorable Thomas Jefferson Monticello"; franked; postmarked Washington City, 19 Apr.; endorsed by TJ as received 28 Apr. 1817 and so recorded in SJL.

Thornton copied Gilbert Stuart's portrait of TJ A SECOND TIME after 29 Mar. 1817, when he wrote John Payne Todd that "I have a small Box in which the Pictures may be packed that I wish to send back to M[r] Jefferson—and as I wish to take another Sketch of his Head, I beg to know when you intend to send off yours, that I may know how long I may keep them unpacked, and that I can judge of the time requisite" (RC in PHi: Simon Gratz Autograph Collection; addressed: "John Payne Todd Esq[re]").

DENEUVILLE: Jean Guillaume Hyde de Neuville.

From John Adams

DEAR SIR Quincy April 19 1817

My loving and beloved Friend, Pickering, has been pleased to inform the World that I have "few Friends." I wanted to whip the rogue, and I had it in my Power, if it had been in my Will to do it, till the blood come. But all my real Friends as I thought them, with Dexter and Grey at their Head insisted "that I Should not Say a Word." "That nothing that Such a Person could write would do me the least

Injury." That it "would betray the Constitution and the Government, if a President out or in Should enter into a Newspaper controversy, with one of his Ministers whom he had removed from his office, in Justification of himself for that removal or any thing else." And they talked a great deal about "The Dignity" of the Office of President, which I do not find that any other Persons, public or private regard very much.

Nevertheless, I fear that Mr Pickerings Information is too true. It is impossible that any Man Should run Such a Gauntlet as I have been driven through, and have many Friends at last. This "all who know me know" though I cannot Say "who love me tell."

I have, however, either Friends who wish to amuse and Solace my old age; or Ennemies who mean to heap coals of fire on my head and kill me with kindness: for they overwhelm me with Books from all quarters, enough to offuscate all Eyes, and Smother and Stifle all human Understanding. Chateaubriand, Grim, Tucker, Dupuis, La Harpe, Simondi, Eustace A new Translation of Herodotus by Belloe with more Notes than Text. What Should I do, with all this lumber? I make my "Woman kind" as the Antiquary expresses it, read to me, all the English: but as they will not read the French, I am obliged to excruciate my Eyes to read it myself. And all to what purpose? I verily believe I was as wise and good, Seventy Years ago, as I am now.

At that Period Lemuel Bryant was my Parish Priest; and Joseph Cleverly my Latin School Master. Lemuel was a jolly[1] jocular and liberal Schollar and Divine. Joseph a Scollar and Gentleman; but a biggoted episcopalian of the School of Bishop Saunders and Dr Hicks, a down right conscientious passive Obedience Man in Church and State The Parson and the Pedagogue lived much together, but were eternally disputing about Government and Religion. One day, when the Schoolmaster had been more than commonly fanatical, and declared "if he were a Monark, He would have but one Religion in his Dominions" The Parson coolly replied "Cleverly! You would be the best Man in the World, if you had no Religion."

Twenty times, in the course of my late Reading, have I been upon the point of breaking out, "This would be the best of all possible Worlds, if there were no Religion in it"!!! But in this exclamati[on] I Should have been as fanatical as Bryant or Cleverly. Without Religion this World would be Something not fit to be mentioned in polite Company, I mean Hell. So far from believing in the total and universal depravity of human Nature; I believe there is no Individual totally depraved. The most abandoned Scoundrel that ever existed, never yet Wholly extinguished his Conscience, and while Conscience remains

there is Some Religion. Popes, Jesuits and Sorbonists and Inquisitors have Some Conscience and Some Religion.
So had Marius and Sylla, Cæsar Cataline and Anthony, and Augustus had not much more, let Virgil and Horace Say what they will.

What Shall We think of Virgil and Horace, Sallust Quintillian, Pliny and even Tacitus? and even Cicero, Brutus and Seneca? Pompey I leave out of the question, as a mere politician and Soldier. Every One of these great Creatures has left indelible marks of Conscience and consequently of Religion, tho' every one of them has left abundant proofs of profligate violations of their Consciences by their little and great Passions and paltry Interests.

The vast prospect of Mankind, which these Books have passed in Review before me, from the most ancient records, histories, traditions and Fables that remain to Us, to the present day, has Sickened my very Soul; and almost reconciled me to Swifts Travels among The Yahoo's. Yet I never can be a Misanthrope. Homo Sum. I must hate myself before I can hate my Fellow Men: and that I cannot and will not do, No! I will not hate any of them, base, brutal and devilish as Some of them have been to me.

From the bottom of my Soul, I pitty my Fellow Men. Fears and Terrors appear to have produced an universal[2] Credulity. Fears of Calamities in Life and punishments after death, Seem to have possessed to[3] Souls of all Men. But fear of Pain and death, here, do not Seem to have been So unconquerable as fear of what is to come hereafter. Priests, Hierophants, Popes, Despots Emperors, Kings, Princes Nobles, have been as credulous as Shoeblacks, Boots, and Kitchen Scullions. The former Seem to have believed in their divine Rights as Sincerely as the latter. Auto de fee's in Spain and Portugal have been celebrated with as good Faith as Excommunications have been practiced in Connecticutt or as Baptisms have been[4] refused in Phyladelphia,
How it is possible that[5] Mankind Should Submit to be governed as they have been is to me an inscrutable Mystery. How they could bear to be taxed to build the Temple of Diana at Ephesus, the Pyramids of Egypt, Saint Peters at Rome, Notre Dame at Paris, St. Pauls in London, with a million Etceteras; when my Navy Yards, and my quasi Army made Such a popular Clamour, I know not. Yet all my Peccadillos, never excited[6] such a rage as the late Compensation Law!!!

I congratulate you, on the late Election in Connecticutt. It is a kind of Epocha. Several causes have conspired. One which you would not Suspect. Some one, no doubt instigated by the Devil, has taken it into his head to print a new Edition of "The independent Whig" even in

Connecticut, and has Scattered the Volumes through the State. These Volumes it is Said, have produced a Burst of Indignation against Priestcraft Bigotry and Intollerance, and in conjunction with other causes have produced the late Election. When writing to you I never know when to

Subscribe JOHN ADAMS

RC (DLC); edge chipped, with missing text supplied from FC; at foot of text: "President Jefferson"; endorsed by TJ as received 30 Apr. 1817 and so recorded in SJL. FC (Lb in MHi: Adams Papers). TJ made notes for his 5 May 1817 response to this and Adams's preceding letter of 2 Feb. 1817 on verso of last page of the February document.

In the fifth of a series of newspaper essays, in 1811 Timothy PICKERING discussed Adams's rationale for removing him as secretary of state in 1800, stating that Adams had "few, a very few friends in the U. States, *of any sort*." He quoted as evidence a passage from a letter Adams wrote to Daniel Wright and Erastus Lyman, 13 Mar. 1809, which had found its way into the newspapers at that time: "I always consider the WHOLE NATION as my CHILDREN: but they have almost all been UNDUTIFUL to me. You two gentlemen are almost the only ones, out of my own house, who have for a long time, and I thank you for it, expressed a filial affection for JOHN ADAMS" (Baltimore *Federal Republican & Commercial Gazette*, 15 Mar. 1811; Springfield, Mass., *Hampshire Federalist*, 11 May 1809; Charles W. Upham, *The Life of Timothy Pickering* [1867–73], 4:190–1).

Adams quotes Alexander Pope's translation of Horace's comment that ALL WHO KNOW ME KNOW of my virtues and that those WHO LOVE ME TELL ("The First Satire of the Second Book of Horace," line 138 [*The Works of Alexander Pope, Esq.* (Edinburgh, printed for J. Balfour, 1764); Adams's copy in MBPLi], 2:174). OFFUSCATE: "bewilder, confuse" (*OED*). BISHOP SAUNDERS AND DR HICKS: probably Nicholas Sander and George Hickes (*ODNB*). The mathematician and philosopher Gottfried Wilhelm Leibniz argued that this is THE BEST OF ALL POSSIBLE WORLDS.

For the COMPENSATION LAW, see James Madison to TJ, 15 Feb. 1817, and note. The LATE ELECTION in Connecticut resulted in a Republican majority in the state House of Representatives and victory by Oliver Wolcott, the Toleration Party candidate for governor (Middletown, Conn., *Middlesex Gazette*, 17 Apr. 1817). The NEW EDITION of *The Independent Whig: or, a Defence of Primitive Christianity, and of our Ecclesiastical Establishment, against the exorbitant claims and encroachments of fanatical and disaffected clergymen* (4 vols. in 1, Hartford, 1816) reprinted a British weekly periodical from 1720–21.

1 Word not in FC.

2 RC: "univeral." FC: "universal."

3 Thus in manuscript; Adams probably intended "the."

4 Preceding eight words not in FC.

5 RC: "than." FC: "<*than*> that."

6 Word interlined in place of "Said" by the same hand that wrote the FC.

From Tristram Dalton

SIR. Boston 22nd April 1817

I have the honour to send You, herewith, another number of "The Massachusetts Agricultural Repository and Journal"[1]—

By this it appears that the growing of Wheat is becoming an object worthy attention, in this section of the Union: which, for many years, has been deemed impracticable. The causes assigned were various: by the friends in Pennsylvania, to the persecution of the Quakers, so called; and to the hanging a number of persons for witchcraft—Some attributed the cause to Barbara Bushes, however distant from the Wheat: and other like ridiculous ones—. If Experiments on this crop have heretofore been fairly made & failed, which I doubt, the great alteration of the Weather in this climate may be the real cause—The summers of former years were fully long and hot enough to ripen the favourite crop, Indian Corn, of the slowest growth; whereas for several years past they have not been long enough to bring the quickest growth to perfection—. A Gentleman living in Newbury, told me, thirty years ago, that he sowed annually one acre with Wheat, for his family use in extras; Rye & Indian being their common bread; and that he had on an average annually, fifteen bushels, without any particular culture. Very few instances of this occurred at the time: farmers remaining satisfied with bread, $\frac{2}{3}$d Indian $\frac{1}{3}$d Rye.—The last mentioned having, for a few years, been also uncertain, may be another inducement to turn their attention to wheat. On my return from Washington, after an absence of twenty years, I was informed that many had raised wheat with great success. In Essex, my Native County, the soil of which is in general very good, I found, on critical[2] enquiry, that the culture of this grain was becoming familiar, and approved of—Eighteen bushels ℔ acre was esteemed an average crop—some reached to twenty five bushels—Necessity—and profit may open the eyes of our common farmers, and drive them to adopt this system. Their farms being from 80 to 150 acres only, the obtaining bread stuff for the use of their own families is all that can be expected.

In this pamphlet I see a communication[3] from Mr Quincy to the Society, recommending the field culture of vegetables, for the food of Cattle in winter. In this I join him fully—having proved the usefulness, even the necesity of it. During the Revolutionary War, I took the management of a farm, on the banks of the Merimac, into my own hands—It consisted of less than two hundred acres of land—and short of thirty acres of saltmarsh ten miles distant. I superintended it for three years, and kept thirty six Cows, which were milked every day—changing them as they became dry—and other cattle fully equal to ten such Cows; Knowing that the former, to be profitable, must have succulent food, and that such a stock could not be kept during our long and cold winters, on the Production of the farm, obtained by the usual mode of farming, I adopted the crop of potatoes—which I found successful. Reading in the Encyclopedia an account of, what was thought an extraordinary, produce of an Acre of Carrotts, I paid attention to this valuable root—. The soil of the farm being rich, but stiff, I tried the first year only one acre, ploughing & harrowing well; and had two hundred & fifty bushels, measured after the tops were taken off. This I followed the next years with better success.

Leaving a garden, in Newburyport, I had measured two thirds of an Acre—and sowed it with carrott seed, in beds, with alleys or paths sufficient[4] only for the man to weed them—. The soil was sandy loam,[5] the most proper for this root, and as highly cultivated as possible.—From this $\frac{2}{3}^{ds}$ of an acre were taken five hundred bushels of Carrots, after the tops were taken off—weighing on an average sixty pounds—This year I put into my farm cellar three hundred bushels of Carrots, some being taken from the garden attached to the farm—and fifteen hundred bushels of potatoes, which, with the hay out on the farm, carried the Stock through a long tedious winter, and turned them out in good order when the pastures were ready to feed them—Beside the thirty six milch cows, I had nine, which became dry in the winter,—fatted on the potatoes and hay, giving them no water—My Horses, with one or two exceptions, preferred the carrots to Oats.—I fed them however with Oats—The hogs preferred them to Indian Corn: which latter was given them a few weeks before killing, to harden the fat. It was usual to give our Oxen Corn, beside hay, when about their spring work—I worked mine on Carrots & hay, and found it equally good, if not better—I published, as a stimulous to our farmers, an account of the extraordinary crop of Carrots from the Garden[6]—The apparent labour in weading them, which once almost discouraged me, prevented, for a time, the least attempt to try it—It was not so with the potatoes—for although my neighbors sneered at my raising so many roots for my cattle, they were soon convinced of the benefit, and silently, but partially, followed my example—and from putting into their cellars about eight or ten bushels of potatoes for family use, they were seen to put in from 100 to 500—which, however they send mostly to Market—For some Years there did not appear any increase in the Culture of Carrots—On my return, after so long absence, I was surprized to see, in the Salem Market, many cart loads of Carrots, at ten dollars ℔ Ton weight—half the price of the best herds grass, or timothy Hay, which could not be bought under twenty dollars ℔ Ton. On enquiry I was told that my account of the quantity of this root taken from $\frac{2}{3}^{d}$ of an Acre had led farmers to Try—and finding it profitable, the culture of it had become common

Taking every thing into view I am of opinion that Potatoes are preferable to any other root; but lament that spirits can be extracted from them—The back settlers in N Hampshire & Vermont rob their families of this necessary food—carry it to the Distilleries—exchange it for the most detestible of Whiskey—and become Sots—

Whatever may be the issue of these experiments, I confess I would not choose this climate as a farmer.

your observations on a choice to be preferred are fresh in my mind. Viz[t] that from the Equater you would travel North, untill you came where Sleds and Sleighs were used, then retreat to a proper distance from them.

The length of this letter requires an apology, especially as it is on a subject more familiar to you than myself—and on which I have paid very little attention for many years, tho' not an idle observer—

Pardoning this, I pray you, Sir, to be assured of the highest respect & esteem of

Your obliged and most obed Servant TRISTRAM DALTON

RC (DLC); at foot of text: "The Honorable Thomas Jefferson"; endorsed by TJ as received 30 Apr. 1817 from "<*Timothy*> Tristram" Dalton and recorded with that date of receipt in SJL. Enclosure: *Massachusetts Agricultural Journal* (Poor, *Jefferson's Library*, 6 [no. 270]), 4 (Jan. 1817).

Barbarea (BARBARA) is also called winter cress (*Hortus Third*, 138). An article by Josiah QUINCY, "On the Field Culture of Vegetables, as Food for Cattle in Winter," appeared on pp. 211–7 of the above enclosure. Dalton read about the PRODUCE OF AN ACRE OF CARROTTS in the *Encyclopædia Britannica* (2d ed., Edinburgh, 1777–84), 1:135–6. He PUBLISHED an account of his carrot crop in two installments in the *Salem Mercury*, 8, 15 Apr. 1788. The article was in the form of a letter from Dalton to Benjamin Lincoln, the chairman of the Agriculture Committee for the American Academy of Arts and Sciences.

1 Omitted closing quotation mark editorially supplied.
2 Manuscript: "crtical."
3 Manuscript: "communiation."
4 Preceding three words interlined.
5 Manuscript: "loom."
6 Preceding three words interlined.

From James Dinsmore

SIR Petersburg April 22. 1817

your favour of the 13th Ins[t] was duly received, and I beg leave to return you my most Sincere thanks for your Continued attention to my Interests—the proposition you make is most agreeable to me and I with pleasure accept of it, as I prefer that Neighbourhood to any I have yet lived in—tho in a pecuniary point of view this is the preferable place—we expect to finish our present engagements here in about two months but if it is Necessary I Should have no objection to make a trip up there at any time Called on—it is probable m[r] Neilson will also move up the Country when we finish here—I forwarded Some time Since to Co^{lnl} Monroe (at his request) a plan & estimate of a House to be Built in Albemarle but have not heard from him Since—& have had it Stated in a letter from Charlottesville that he now purposes—Building in Loudon—I have forwarded to m^{r} Austin in Charlottesvill two Books (Bakers Chronicle & the History of the Holy Wars. printed in 1684)[1]—which were entrusted to my Care when in Norfolk last winter—By Cap^{tn} Robert Simington with a request that I would present them to <u>you</u> in his Name as a tribute of his Respect for your person & Charecter—

with great Respt yours JA^{S} DINSMORE

NB mr Neilson[2] Sends his best wishes

RC (ViU: TJP); endorsed by TJ as received 29 Apr. 1817 and so recorded in SJL; with additional notation by TJ on verso: "Capt Robert Simington. Norfolk." RC (CSmH: JF-BA); address cover only; with PoC of TJ to Daniel Lescallier, 14 June 1817, on verso; addressed: "Thomas Jefferson Esqr Monticello"; stamped; postmarked Petersburg, 22 Apr.

On 29 Apr. 1817 Dinsmore informed John H. Cocke from Petersburg that either himself or John NEILSON would "do your work, as I have promised mr Jefferson to execute a Job in the Neighbou[r]hood of Charlottesville this fall—of which he mentions you as one of the visitors & in Consequence have made arrangements to quit here So Soon as we finish our present Engagements which will be in about two months" (RC in ViU: JHC; one word editorially corrected). That work was at Cocke's Bremo estate, while the proposed BUILDING IN LOUDON County was subsequently constructed as James Monroe's Oak Hill plantation.

The TWO BOOKS were Sir Richard Baker, *A Chronicle of the Kings of England* (London, 1684; Poor, *Jefferson's Library*, 4 [no. 100]; for an earlier ed. see Sowerby, no. 357), and an unidentified edition of Louis Maimbourg, *The History of the Crusade; or, the Expeditions of the Christian Princes for the Conquest of the Holy Land*, trans. John Nalson (London, 1685; Poor, *Jefferson's Library*, 5 [no. 161]). TJ had previously owned the latter work in the original French (*Histoire des Croisades pour la delivrance de la Terre Sainte*, 4 vols. [2d ed., Paris, 1682; Sowerby, no. 619]).

[1] Omitted closing parenthesis editorially supplied.

[2] Manuscript: "Nelson."

From James Baker

SIR— Richmond April 23. 1817—

Immediately on receipt of your order of Feby 9th I requested my friend in Boston to forward me a quintal of best Dun Fish (there being none in this city) the receipt of which has been prevented 'till this time—mr Gibson will forward it to you—Should any other article peculiar to the northern market be wanted it will afford me pleasure to receive your order—

Respectfully Your Humble Servt JAMES BAKER

RC (MHi); endorsed by TJ as received 28 Apr. 1817 and so recorded in SJL. RC (DLC); address cover only; with PoC of TJ to George Washington Jeffreys, 12 June 1817, on verso; addressed: "Thomas Jefferson Esqr Montecello Virginia"; franked; postmarked (faint) Richmond, [2]4 Apr.

From Joseph C. Cabell

DEAR SIR, Bremo. 23^{d} April. 1817.

I arrived at this place yesterday evening on my return home from the election in Goochland. Genl Cocke informs me that he met you at Enniscorthy as you were going to Bedford, and that he learned from you that the meeting which you proposed of the Visitors of the Central College was intended to be on the day fixed in the Law for the Genl meeting in the Spring, viz, on the first day of the Albemarle Superior Court, which will be on 13th of may. At the time of our last conversation on this subject at monticello, I understood that our meeting would take place on the day after the next Albemarle inferior Court, which would be the 6th of may. I remember that Genl Cocke observed that the proposed meeting would occur on the very day fixed by the law for the first general meeting: and supposing he was accurate I did not refer to the act. Having made arrangements to go to Williamsburg and Lancaster County immediately after the last election in the Senatorial district, which will be on the 28th ins^{t} it was very inconvenient for me to postpone my departure till 6th of may, but as you seemed desirous for me to remain I reluctantly consented. I then made my arrangements for going down the country on 6th may. It is with sincere regret that I inform you that it will be out of my power to attend on 13th. I will not trouble you with the various reasons which will prevent my attendance; but will content myself with observing, that Genl Cocke, considers me as entirely excusable; & under these circumstances I hope you will excuse my absence. The only case in which my presence could be of any importance would be to secure a meeting. But of the attendance of four members I hope there can be no doubt. Genl Cocke will see maj^{r} Watson between this and the day of meeting, and correct the information I lately gave him as to the 6th may. And as m^{r} madison is now at home, and has promised to perform the duties of a Visitor, I presume there can be no doubt of his attendance. I beg you to be assured that no ordinary state of affairs should prevent my faithful attention to this business: and of this assurance, I hope to furnish a proof in my future punctuality.

I remain, Dr Sir, most respectfully & faithfully y^{rs}

JOSEPH C. CABELL

RC (ViU: TJP-PC); endorsed by TJ as received 30 Apr. 1817 and so recorded in SJL. RC (MHi); address cover only; with PoC of TJ to James Rawlings, 31 July 1817, on verso; addressed: "Thomas Jefferson Esq. Poplar Forest Bedford"; with additional note in Cabell's hand (damaged at seal): "If there Should be a post-office nearer to Poplar Forest than Lynchburg, the post mast[er a]t the latter place will confer a favor by forwarding this letter."

From James Monroe

Dear Sir washington april 23. 1817

I have to acknowledge three letters from you, of the 8th 13th & 15th of this month. The note, in the first, of the different kinds of wines, to be procur'd in France & Italy, and of the persons to be applied to for them, will be of great service to me. I shall immediately profit of it, and shall be very glad, to be able, to render you, any service by extending the order, to such as you may want, of which be so good as to inform me.

It would give me sincere pleasure, to attend the meeting of Visitors to be held on the 5th of may, for establishing the site of the central college, in our county, and I will do it, if in my power. In a few days, I will decide the question, and inform you of the result. Soon after my election to the present office, I determind to make a tour along our coast, & to the westward, to enable me to execute with the greatest advantage, the duties assigned me, relative to public defense, as to fortifications dock yards &a, and to set out about the middle of may. arrangments are mad[e] for my departure about that time, and indeed, it is the best season, for such a journey, especially as I hope, from it, much advantage to my heal[th] which is however, now, in a good state. How s[oon] the trip to Albemarle, will be practicable; paying due regard to intermediate duties here, forms the difficulty, which I shall be happy to surmount, if in my power. To the wishes of the county, I have due sensibility, and should be highly gratified to meet so many friends, as would be present there. There are no very important duties, pressing here, at this time, but you well know, that there never is a moment, whe[n] there is not something, of interest, and often of an embarrassing kind. Such exist now, relative to which, if I cannot make you the visit in contemplation, I will write you soon; and if I come, I shall have a better opportunity of communicating in person. For the interest which you take in my success, which is always very gratifying & consoling to me, I am truly thankful—

with great respect very sincerely your friend

James Monroe

RC (DLC); edge chipped and trimmed; endorsed by TJ as received 29 Apr. 1817 and so recorded in SJL. RC (DLC); address cover only; with PoC of TJ to Barbé Marbois, 14 June 1817, on recto and verso; addressed: "Thomas Jefferson Monticello"; franked; postmarked (faint) Washington City, 2[3] Apr.

From Elkanah Watson

SIR Albany. 24th Ap 1817

Knowing You are already Sufficiently oppress'd with numerous correspondence—and probably Some unprofitable Ones, It is Sir with No Small diffidence I presume to intrude myself: I Stand pledg'd however to confine myself to a Specific object, in which I am well convinc'd, we have congenial feelings, and views.

You have doubtless been informed of[1] the Successfull efforts, & progress of the Berkshire Agricultural Society—its objects—its practical usefullness, & extending a Salutary example throughout the Union. It was my good fortune to originate, and conduct the whole machinery for Several years; I therefore make free to introduce myself to your Notice, as the late President of that institution—and author of a Tour in Holland in 1784, which I am told is hon'd with a place in your library.

Haveing Sold my estate in Pittsfield and returned again to my former residence in this dignified State and being principally absorbed in promoting the Great Canals, and the progress of the territory of Michigan where I have purchased all the estates formerly Govr Hull's, I have taken my Leave forever of Berkshire, and the persuits of Agriculture as a practical[2] farmer. Thus much premis'd—I will Now Sir come to the express object of this communication

Being for many Years deeply impress'd with the Salutary effects of well organiz'd Agricultural Societies, I had often witnessd by a long residence in Europe, especially in England, and the wonderful effects of our experiment in Berkshire even without Means I suggestd to Our Mutual friend Genl Mason of[3] Georgetown (who did Me the honor to Spend a week at my house in Pittsfield, with his charming Lady & daughter in attending Our cattle Show in 1814) the importance of the institution of a National bord of Agriculture—he fully accorded with Me, and Knowing that my mind had been absorbed in these Views for Several years, he requested I would digest, and bring forth a project he would Support. The Result of the outlines of a System, for that great National Object are published in Niles Register the 19th Instant page 126—to which I beg leave to refer with all its crude imperfections together with the annex'd remarks also pen'd by Me.

Haveing recently indirectly learn't that your patriotic mind had Also taken a direction in the Same channel and that the public were about being benefitted by the result of your reflections in publication, which would[4] have appeard in a periodical work in this City conducted by an eccentric Quaker—who has recently been compel'd to Suspend that work; under these circumstances, If I am correctly informed, I rejoice to find a Gentleman of your preeminent Standing in the great American family, So usefully, and in the evening of your invaluable Life, So patriotically imployed.

To conclude, and to relieve you from this long letter, I beg Sir you will accept my Services in co'operating zealously with you in these Northern States to diffuse as far as my limitted influence May extend, a deep impression on the public Mind, preparatory to the next Meeting of Congress.—So as to bring the great object into immediate View—that we May before we leave the theâtre of Our beloved Country enjoy the Satisfaction of Seeing Some of its usefull effects realiz'd before we depart hence and thus Also, holding into View a prominent link in the great Chain leading to the high destinies which a'wait our blessed Country & posterity.

Permit Me respected Sir to add One more Suggestion—Should Mr Munro fortunately be fully impress'd with the important object—& thus be induced to Make it a prominent feature in his first communication to Congress I have No doubt under your transcendant influence, & example—aided by the labours of Genl Mason—& my utmost efforts—the establishment of a National bord of Agriculture—liberally endowed, would be the certain result. I am Sir—with profound respect and esteeme. Your Obt St

ELKANAH WATSON

RC (DLC); at foot of text: "The Honbl Thos Jefferson"; endorsed by TJ as received 4 May 1817 and so recorded in SJL.

Elkanah Watson (1758–1842), merchant and agriculturist, was born and educated in Plymouth, Massachusetts. Following a six-year apprenticeship with a prosperous merchant in Providence, Rhode Island, he sailed for Europe in 1779. Watson there entered into a business partnership in Nantes, France, and traveled widely in England, France, and the Netherlands. Returning to the United States late in 1784, he visited George Washington at Mount Vernon and settled for a time in North Carolina. Watson relocated in 1789 to Albany, New York, where he helped found several banks, supported the construction of turnpike roads and canals, and fought for free public education. In 1807 he retired to a farm near Pittsfield, Massachusetts, and devoted himself to scientific agriculture. One of the founders of the Berkshire Agricultural Society, he served as its first president, 1811–15. Watson returned to Albany in 1816 and moved in 1825 to Essex County, New York, where he died. Watson was an early supporter of the construction of the Erie Canal and the movement to establish local fairs and agricultural societies (*ANB*; *DAB*; N: Watson Papers; Boston *Independent Ledger, and the American Advertiser*, 29 May 1780; Sowerby, no. 3872; Washington, *Papers, Confederation Ser.*, 2:456–8; *PTJ*, 37:526–7; *New-York Journal, & Patriotic Register*, 20 June 1792; New York *Daily Advertiser*, 14 July 1792; *Albany Gazette*, 6 May, 6 June 1805; Watson, *History of the Rise, Progress, and Existing State of the Berkshire Agricultural Society, in Massachusetts* [Albany, 1819], esp. 9, 14, 29; Pittsfield *Berkshire Reporter*, 20 July 1811; *Pittsfield Sun*, 8 Feb. 1816; *New-York Spectator*, 14 Dec. 1842).

Watson drafted an earlier version of this letter dated Albany, 2 Jan. 1817, expressing as his object the establishment of a national board of agriculture; seeking the support of TJ and President James Monroe for such an institution; noting that George Washington "recommended the measure in his inaugural Speech" and that Watson himself, as president of the Berkshire Agricultural Society, had petitioned Congress on the subject in 1814; stating that he has communicated with James Madison, who "highly approves of the plan"; fearing that constitutional difficulties will be a barrier to success; noting that when Representative John Hulbert spoke in favor of the petition in Congress he was "ridiculed, & laugh'd at for urging the Matter especially by southern Members"; noting that John Mason, of Georgetown, "has promis'd me to bring all his influ[e]nce to bare—to promote the object"; and concluding by expressing his pleasure at learning that TJ also intends "to Sustain it with zeal—and to furnish the public with your views on the Subject" (FC in Lb in N: Watson Papers; entirely in Watson's hand; one word editorially corrected; at head of text: "Letter to Thomas Jefferson"; at top of second page: "National bord of Agriculture"; adjacent to signature in parentheses: "Vide his answer page 79"; date reworked to 24 Apr. 1817 in an unidentified hand; this version not recorded in SJL and probably never received by TJ).

Watson's book, *A Tour in Holland, in MDCCLXXXIV* (Worcester, 1790; Sowerby, no. 3872) was in the LIBRARY TJ sold to Congress.

The OUTLINES OF A SYSTEM appeared in an article entitled "A Board of Agriculture proposed," which laid out a twelve-point organizational plan that accompanied the petition of the Berkshire Agricultural Society to Congress and concluded with the "Remarks of a Correspondent" [Watson], who asserted that such a society would "tend as a cement to the union, by assimilating our agricultural habits, by uniform excitements and competitions; thus rousing and bringing into activity a laudable and useful spirit of emulation in every section of this great republic" (reprinted from the *Albany Argus* in the Baltimore *Niles' Weekly Register*, 19 Apr. 1817).

The ECCENTRIC QUAKER was Horatio G. Spafford. MR MUNRO: James Monroe.

A missing letter from Thomas Melvill dated 10 Jan. 1816 is recorded in SJL as received 27 Jan. 1816 from Pittsfield, with the additional notation "Pr. agr. soc. Berkshire." This may have been the covering letter for TJ's 24 Oct. 1815 membership diploma in the Berkshire Agricultural Society (MS in MHi; printed diploma, with TJ's name, location, appointment as "Honorary Member," and the date filled in by Melvill; signed by Melvill as president and William C. Jarvis as recording secretary). TJ's 6 Feb. 1816 response to Melvill, also not found, is recorded in SJL as written from Monticello.

1 Manuscript: "off."
2 Watson here canceled "man."
3 Manuscript: "off."
4 Word reworked from "Should."

From Christopher Clark

Dear Sir, Academy 25 April 17

Agreeably to my expectation met Capt Irvine at this place and we have had a little conversation on the Subject of the Roads he seems not to have formed a correct estimate of the Relative goodness of the two and will again travel the new one with a View to a further examination he is satisfied with the old one and appears unwilling to abandon it on a mere conjecture of obtaining an other that shall be nearly as good his opposition is however founded on correct principles and will be withdrawn on a conviction that the private injury is in an over proportion to the public good in the old Roads continuing

We find great defficulties in obtaining a proven person to take charge of this Seminary and are casting our eyes on mr John Wood of whom you spoke so favorably this morning we feel great anxiety for the prosperity of the place and if he can be obtained would be glad to employ him my own wishes as well as the desire of the Gentlemen present are directed to your friendly assistance in obtaining his services if it shall comport with your View of the Subject we shall write to him at Richmond and if not puting you to too much trouble will be much obliged by you droping him a line in our behalf

Accept my best wishes for a pleasant Journey and good weather home Chris Clark

RC (MHi); endorsed by TJ as received 26 Apr. 1817 and so recorded in SJL, which indicates that it was received at Poplar Forest.

The seminary was the New London Academy.

From DeWitt Clinton

Dear Sir New York 25 April 1817

I had the pleasure of receiving Your interesting letter respecting the contemplated communications between the great Lakes and the Atlantic Ocean; and I now send to You the laws of the State on this subject. The work will be undertaken this season and will be prosecuted with order and with rapidity.

I thank you most cordially for the communication—And I assure you that it always affords me the greatest pleasure to see the powerful weight of your opinion and the high authority of your name, operating in favor of institutions and undertakings associated with the honor and the prosperity of our beloved Country with the greatest respect and the most sincere attachment.[1]

I am Your most Obed^{t} ser^{t} DeWitt Clinton

RC (DLC); at foot of text: "Thomas Jefferson Esqr"; endorsed by TJ as received 30 Apr. 1817 and so recorded in SJL. Dft (Lb in NNC: Clinton Papers). Enclosure: *Laws of the State of New-York, respecting Navigable Communications between The Great Western and Northern Lakes and the Atlantic Ocean* (New York, 1817; Poor, *Jefferson's Library*, 5 [no. 217]; TJ's copy in PPAmP); including texts of "An Act to provide for the improvement of the internal navigation of this State," passed 17 Apr. 1816, and "An Act, respecting Navigable Communications between the Great Western and Northern Lakes and the Atlantic Ocean," passed 15 Apr. 1817.

[1] Reworked in Dft from "Accept the assurances of my respect & attachment."

From Lafayette

My dear friend La grange April 25^{h} 1817

I Was a few days Ago in paris when Mr G. Ticknor Left a Card and a Letter from You which I Hastened, with Affectionate Eagerness, to peruse. not a little perplexed Was I to Understand Some parts of it, when I perceived that Since it Had been writen two Revolutions and two dynasties Had Successively Reigned in france. m^{r} Ticknor whom I Had the pleasure to See the Next day Confirmed by His own Account the date of the Letter the General Contents of which, However, are fit for Any time And afforded me much Gratification.

You Justly did observe the Situation in which the patriots, at the first Restoration, found themselves Entangled. an Arrant despot and Conqueror, after Having Spent out abroad all Material and Moral Means of Resistance, was Subdued, and dethroned, the Bourbons Had Been Replaced, Before an opportunity was Given, or wished for By Either of the Belligerent parties, Bonaparte less than Any of them, to Call out the Exertions of National liberality and patriotism. at the Second period an oppening Had Been left. an insurrection, the produce of discontent of the Bourbons more than Attachment to Bonaparte Had Restored Him to the tuileries, But Under a Necessity to acknowledge, and with a possibility for us to Reassume our old doctrines. I was one of those who would Have Rid the Country of all pretentions Both Royal and imperial, and trusted for it's defense to a Revolution wholly National, a System which Bonaparte Himself Has Since Confessed was the only one Equal to our dangers. But the Majority of the patriots, and their Representatives Had Rather leave our fate to the Heroïsm Of two Hundred thousand Regulars Headed By an Emperor, the greatest Captain living. this was Better than Submission, Conquest, and Counter Revolution—Better than a division of the defensive forces. we Joined them and Gave Unreserved Support. taking Care to Exact Every Concession, to Reinstate ourselves into Every institution of freedom, to watch Every bad trick and to provide Against Every bad intention of despotism, Untill the desertion of the Emperor, after the Battle of waterloo, and His attempt to dissolve the National Representation and Usurp a dictatorship, United all the patriots in the defensive measures which produced His abdication.

our affairs were then very Low. our time very short. twelve Hundred thousand Enraged Ennemies were near at Hand. Yet a national movement might Have Saved Us, when a fatal but too Common Mistake prompted the Assembly to Seek a Guarantee more in the[1] interests than in the Sentiments of their Elective Executive. the next morning fouché Sent An Emissary to Lewis the 18 and Wellington, and persuaded the best intentionned people of the Great Services I Could Render in an Embassy to the foreign powers. when we Returned, my Companions and myself, the Capitulation of paris Had been Signed, and the Army were on their Way to the Loire.

How the wishes of an Ultimate Stand on that River Have been defeated it would be too long to Explain. nor shall I this time Enter into particulars of our Situation Since the Second Restoration to this day. The Royal party are divided into Ultras and Ministeriels the former Adhering to the princes, the Second to the king. these ones are chiefly Conducted By a Committee of place men Educated at the Bonapartian School, and Having learned from their abjured master more Art and prudence than the violent Ultras Can Ever possess. in the Last Session the Ultras Have affected a liberality which very Akwardly Sits Upon them. their ministerial adversaries did oppose to them a System of Election, which altho it Admits only Hundred and twenty thousand Electors for the whole kingdom, viz[2] those who pay 300 francs of taxes, Seems already popular Enough to Excite not only the fears of the Ultra, but also the Repentance of the ministerials,—they are Masters of the press, individual liberty is at their disposal, the means of the police, of the administrations, of the Civil list, of the foreign Courts are immense. Yet they are afraid Lest the Next Returns, for the 5h to be elected this Year, may add Some more decided patriots to the few independents who, in the last Session, Have Been neither Ultra, or ministerial, but Merely National.

This Letter is Entrusted to my friend mr descaves, a Gallo American merchant, whom I Beg leave to present to you if it is His Happy lot to Call at monticello. our friend mde de Staël Has been very ill—now she is in A State of Languor which Gives me still great fears of

Her Health. Her charming daughter is married to A young peer, Victor Broglie, step Son to m[r] d'argenson, both my intimate friends, and Among the Best patriots of france. I Have Communicated your Letter to m. de tracy, but Have no time to Receive His Answer. He most gratefully feels your friendship[3] and approbation. His blindness is almost Complete, but He Hopes from the Operation of the Cataracts Which will be made this Summer.

I wish I Had Some weecks before me to Answer Your demand Respecting the Campaign of 81. but Have Got the Copy of a precis made by a french officer in my family which may in a great measure answer your purpose. I Send it With a few notes. I think m[r] Marshall Has in His possession a map of virginia, with all the marches and Encampements of that Campaign which I Have Some years ago Sent to him. Those documents, with your official, and your friendly Remembrances may assist the author of the work, as far as I Have been Concerned in the transactions of that Happy Epoch of my life.

Adieu, my Excellent friend, you well know my Cordial Respect and Grateful affection LAFAYETTE

RC (DLC); endorsed by TJ as received 22 July 1817 and so recorded in SJL. Enclosure not found. Enclosed in Mark L. Descaves to TJ, 15 July 1817.

The LETTER FROM YOU was TJ to Lafayette, 14 Feb. 1815. The 5[H] TO BE ELECTED THIS YEAR: under article 37 of Louis XVIII's constitutional charter of 1814, one-fifth of the French Chamber of Deputies was to be renewed each year (Henry C. Lockwood, *Constitutional History of France* [1890], 365). The AUTHOR OF THE WORK was Louis H. Girardin.

[1]Thus in manuscript, but "their" may have been intended.
[2]Manuscript: "wiz."
[3]Manuscript: "frienship."

From John Laval

SIR, Philadelphia April 25th 1817

Your Letter of the 11th inst[t] came to hand, a few hours after M[r] Dufief's departure from Philadelphia. I have forwarded it to him, yesterday, by Ship Andrew, bound to Liverpool.

According to your previous request, I have, at length, Succeeded in procuring, for you, a copy of Enfield's History of Philosophy; the work is not to be had in any Bookstore, & it is only by accident that it has been obtained. I Send the first volume by this day's mail, & the Second will follow next week, according to usage. the Price is $7—

I daily expect a large importation from Paris, in the various departments of Literature, of which, when received, you will be early advised.

in the absence of my friend, I tender you my Services for your Commands, here or in any part of Europe.—

I am with the greatest respect Sir, Your very humble Servant

JOHN LAVAL

P.S. there appears on Dufief's Books a Balance of $\$4\frac{50}{100}$ in your favor—

RC (DLC); dateline beneath postscript; at foot of text: "Thomas Jefferson Esq[re]"; endorsed by TJ as received 30 Apr. 1817 from Laval writing for Nicolas G. Dufief and so recorded in SJL. RC (MHi); address cover only; with first two pages of PoC of TJ to Tadeusz Kosciuszko, 15 June 1817, on recto and verso; addressed: "Thomas Jefferson Esq[re] late Presid[t] of the United States Monticello—V[a]"; franked; postmarked Philadelphia, 25 Apr.

John Laval (ca. 1769–1839), merchant and bookseller, was a native of Strasbourg, France. When he became a naturalized American citizen in 1798 he had been in the United States for five years, having emigrated from Saint Domingue. In 1804 Laval became the first president of the Société de Bienfaisance de Philadelphia (French Benevolent Society of Philadelphia), a charity devoted to providing aid to émigrés of French descent. Laval took over Nicolas G. Dufief's book business in Philadelphia when the latter departed for Europe in 1817. TJ ordered titles from Laval as late as 1824, and Laval continued in the book trade until his own death (Laval's naturalization record, 7 Dec. 1798 [DNA: RG 21, NPEDP]; Cornelius William Stafford, *The Philadelphia Directory, for 1800* [Philadelphia, 1800], 75; French Benevolent Society of Philadelphia Records [PHi]; *MB*; Dufief to TJ, 4 Apr. 1817; TJ to Laval, 12 Sept. 1824; Laval to TJ, 24 Sept. 1824; *A. M'Elroy's Philadelphia Directory for 1839* [1839], 142; Philadelphia *Poulson's American Daily Advertiser*, 13 July 1839; Philadelphia *Public Ledger*, 15 July 1839; Philadelphia *Pennsylvania Inquirer and Daily Courier*, 13 Nov. 1839).

To Archibald Robertson

DEAR SIR — Poplar Forest Apr. 25. 17.

This being the season in which the farmer recieves the fruits of his year's labor, it is that also in which he is to pay attention to his debts. no debt of mine gives me more anxiety than that to yourself, in which I have had great indulgen[c]e. two years of embargo and non-intercourse, 3 of war, and 2. of disastrous drought have successively baffled my wishes to be reducing it. the failure of our corn crop, which with myself in Albemarle was almost total, and great here also, has absorbed so much of my other produce of the last year as, with the taxes and current expences of the plantations to leave me very little indeed for antecedent debts. on a view of these, my hope is that I may perhaps be able, when all is at market and sold to pay you about 1000.D. to keep down the increasing amount until the better management under which my plantations now are, and better crops may enable me to do what I so much wish. one or two full crops would place me compleatly at ease. so far that of the present year looks well. in the course of the ensuing month my wheat and tobacco will all have been sold, and you shall then hear from me with all the effect in my power. I salute you with great friendship and respect.

TH: JEFFERSON

P.S. Apr. 26. I have drawn on you in favor of Nimrod Darnell for 130.96 William Miller 50.D. Robert Miller 50.D. not to be called for by them until you should have received 230.96 D on the draught on Gibson & Jefferson now inclosed.

PoC (ViU: TJP); one word faint; adjacent to signature: "M[r] Robertson"; endorsed by TJ. Enclosure not found.

From Josephus B. Stuart

DEAR SIR. Albany 25th April, 1817.

On the eve of my departure from the City of Washington, I had the Honor to receive yours of the 8th of February last. From that time to the present, Journies & business have denied me leisure; & even now I should possibly, forbear obtruding myself upon your verry precious time, were it not that certain considerations constrain me, in common with many of our fellow citizens whose opinions are entitled to respect, to differ with you in one opinion expressed in your letter;—that having become "an old man you have nothing but prayers to offer for the welfare of your Country, & all the human race." The American People, Sir, are daily refuting the doctrine that Republicks are ungratefull. It is a gross libel on their character: they are well informed, & faithfull to those who are faithfull to them.

They will never cease to regard your prayers as they do your works;—with gratitude;—& the only question is, at what period they will be satisfied with the former, & cease to desire the latter. They are sensible how sweet & desireable repose & quiet are to any man who has numbered his three score & ten; & more especially to one, whose whole life has been one continued scene of effort for the interest & welfare of his Country, & for promoting the general happiness of the human race.

They are sensible your Sun is drawing towards the horizon, & there wish is, that its last rays may beam in serenest splendour,—& that it may set without a cloud or a spot,—& that twilight may long be reflected from the mirror of its history, to guide Freemen in the path of Liberty & happiness. But, Sir, the same great principle of Justice on which rests the gratitude of the American People, prompts them to vigilance in guarding for their posterity the inheritance they have receivd from the Fathers. Duty to the Republic, often rising above their own delicate feelings, constrains them to put in requisition the talents of the great men when they know the task must be irksome.—In this, they adopt the language of Cicero that, "We are not born for our selves only, but partly for our Country, partly for our friends." They know that much may be required where much has been given,—& are so governed by interest as to exact the last mite. In applying this principle to yourself, Sir, it is difficult to say what bounds the American People will prescribe to their exactions. The bounty of Heaven has extended to you such length of days, & height of fame, that your fellow Citizens will venture to draw for a surpluss dividend of service & counsel, from a fund so rich & inexhaustable. Your existence, Sir, has fallen on a period more eventfull perhaps, than any one of the same length, that was ever carved between the bourns of time.—America your scene of action.—Your physical & moral powers were fortunably moulded & formed, by an education as well adapted to them, as they were for the distinguished part assigned you in the grand drama of the world.

At an early period of your political life, you had secured a fame which must pass as safely down the tide of time as our Declaration of Independence.

Through the Revolution & succeeding 18 years you reapt, in every field of glory, your ample share of the harvest. Being then called to the administration of the Government, your situation became delicate in the extreme. Before you the precepts, principles, practice & example of the great Father of his Country: all sanctified in the love which the nation bore to him.—At that time & under such circumstances, it certainly required a bold stretch of political sagacity, to discern what might be the result of any measures varying from those which had been adopted,—or the application of principles not recognized in, & sanctioned by, the political chart before you. Such novel course might Justly have been considered the more perilous, as it was to affect the deepest interests of a Country, too vast both in extent & resources to be measured by any scale which had been applied to the European world. The general maxims which had been then settled by a long course of experience for the government of all concerns of peace[1] or war, finance, commerce, agriculture, or polity, fell far short of ascertaining any correct & practical calculations relative to the affairs of the United States. The concerns of this Country were advancing with strides so rapid, as apparently to baffle calculation; so gigantic as to outstrip the wisdom of the wisest. The scene was so vast, so novel, so unparallelled, that modern politicians, generally, could only gaze in admiration, & seemed rather lost in astonishment than drawing any practical conclusions. In short, it seemed rather an age of Miracles, than philosophy; & men were more inclined to adore an invisible hand, than to trace effects to their causes.—Fortunate for the United States, fortunate for the human race, there happened then to live a political philosopher whose eye undazzeled by the blaze of glory, could survey the whole ground: whose profound sagacity could fathom the deep & rapid current of events; & who by a dexterity peculiar to himself, could direct & controul the whole for the permanent interests of his Country. There was another & not less Herculaen task to be performed by the Ruler of the American People. He had to analyze their minds,—their whole moral system: to acquaint himself intimately with all the elements of their character; their manners, their morals, their religious tenets as they might ramify under a mild & tolerant government: their prejudices, their partialities, their predeliction for pursuits, & every trait of character which might be expected to develope itself in a young & enterprizeing nation, spread over a vast teritory, & only controuled by a new & experimental government.

All this was to be accomplished before prudence would permit you, Sir, to attempt the great object of your administration, as I understand it, which was to recast the character of the American People, by gradually changing their radical pursuits from excessive & extravagant Commerce, to more safe & rational agriculture. This great change although much opposed, especially by commercial men, would have been much sooner & more easily effected, had not the convulsed state of Europe, sharpened the too keen commercial appetite of the American People, by throwing almost the whole trade of the world into their hands. But this effect has expired almost simultaneous with the cause.—All extremes are attended with unpleasant consequences, & excessive excitement no less in the political than in the Animal system, produces an indirect debility. Hence, those sufferings which now affect the Commercial part of community, & through them the whole body, for one member cannot suffer alone.—But the strongest spasm is over, & a year of scarcity has rendered the people thoughtfull, & prepared their minds to look to the Land for more sure subsistence. Thus, Sir, in the short period of 16 years (& one half of that behind the scene), have you been able to read that which was but prediction, now prophesy fulfilled:—to see the grand system of policy crayoned out by your own sagacity, so nearly accomplished, that no doubt can now remain as to the opinion that your Biographer, or the Historian of our Country, must express to posterity on the subject. Sensible men of both political parties agree, that you have accomplished your object; although, some still doubt as to the result: that is, whether checking the mania for Commerce, & the consequent & far more injurious Bank Mania,—& giving broader scope to agriculture, with fostering of manufactures, will render our government most stable & permanent; the people most happy, & the glory of the nation most substantial? As our government is founded on public opinion, & public opinion is but the aggregate of individual opinions, I can have no doubt on which we can most safely rely; that formed by the yeomanry of the Country,—or of Commercial men.—The latter cooped up in Cities, seldom extend their views beyond the smoke which surrounds them, or their calculations farther than the projected voyage, & the profits which will reward it.—Such men are extremely capricious, & likely to fall with all their monied interest, influence & dependents under the management of demagogues, who can more easily marshal for mischievious purposes 100,000 Inhabitants of a City, than they could rouse to action for any purposes the population of a County consisting of 10.000.—

The yeomanry of the Country from the nature of their pursuits, from their mode of thinking & acting, are accustomed to decide for themselves. Born upon their own fee simple, owing neither rent, tribute or homage, to any man, nurtured in the lap of Independence, & taught by their Fathers neither to bow the neck or bend the knee to any, on earth, but the government of their Country, or any above, but the God of the universe; they know their rights, & knowing will maintain them.

In short, I consider the yeomanry of this Country, in Peace the safe supporters of the government, in War the bulwark of the realm. Such, Sir, do I consider the hastily drawn, but true character of that class of the American People, most deservedly the highest favord by the general policy of your administration.

And, now, Sir, permit me to draw a short conclusion from, I fear, too tedious premises, & that is, that the American People, after all you have done for them, wish one more last & lasting favor from you: that is, that not withstanding your advanced age, your extensive correspondence, your numerous & important duties, you will yet favor them & the world with such history of your own life & times, as your leisure may permit you to compile. For such a work the voice of the nation, as far as I can ascertain it, seems to be loud & united.

It is verry natural for the people to suppose, that he who could while young in years, & in the infancy of this government, with an intuitive view look through all the vast & complicated concerns of the nation; who by his wisdom could shape them thus far to the happiest result, can, at the mature & honorable age of three score & 14 years, with a mind unmarred by time, & aided by the powerfull auxilliares of observation & experience, point out their safest[2] course for years to come, & guide them by his counsels in the right way to prosperity & happiness, to greatness & glory.—Let me pray you, Sir, to ponder on this request:—You can put in requisition any talents you please for the drudgery of the undertaking, & spare yourself any farther labor than furnishing dockuments & dictating[3] the order.—

I learn, Sir, from the papers, that M[r] Monroe contemplates taking a Journey to the north this season. Cannot the wishes of your fellow Citizens prevail upon you to do the same. Be assured, Sir, it would afford infinite gratification to the northern & Eastern States. I have ever considered it one great misfortune of the Republic that her distinguished Citizens commingle so little. Unfortunately, the spirit of party has of late years, too much either prevented or marred social intercourse. It has now, at least for a time subsided: & while all seem anxious to unite in counsels calculated to promote the public welfare, is the time for the Fathers of the nation to brighten the chain.—Should you determine to visit the north, it would afford me great pleasure to discharge the duty of meeting you at Washington, at any time you may name, & to minister to the ease, safety & comfort of your Journey wherever you may wish to travel. Pardon, Dear Sir, the length & imperfections of my tedious letter, & accept the perfect

respect & gratitude, of your much obliged friend, & very Humble Servant. JOSEPHUS BRADNER STUART.

P.S. I have made an arrangement with M[r] Duane for the immediate publication of the "Franklin Manuscripts." Our mutual friend D[r] Wistar was well a few days since.

Permit me to present my best respects to M[rs] & Miss Randolph.

Yours &c. J, B, STUART.

RC (DLC); endorsed by TJ as received 4 May 1817 and so recorded in SJL. RC (MHi); address cover only; with PoC of TJ to James Oldham, 21 July 1817, on verso; addressed: "The Honorable Thomas Jefferson. Monticello. Virginia"; stamp canceled; franked; postmarked.

AN OLD MAN ... HUMAN RACE paraphrases the closing of TJ's letter to Stuart of 8 Feb. 1817. WE ARE NOT BORN FOR OUR SELVES ONLY, BUT PARTLY FOR OUR COUNTRY, PARTLY FOR OUR FRIENDS comes from Cicero, *De Officiis*, 1.7.22 (*Cicero De Officiis*, trans. Walter Miller,

Loeb Classical Library [1913; repr. 1990], 22, 23). The GREAT FATHER OF HIS COUNTRY was George Washington.

Stuart was the New York agent for William Temple Franklin, who was in the process of publishing his grandfather Benjamin Franklin's MANUSCRIPTS in London. For the relationship between William Duane and the younger Franklin, see Francis S. Philbrick, "Notes on Early Editions and Editors of Franklin," APS, *Proceedings* 97 (1953): 551–64.

[1] Manuscript: "peacee."
[2] Manuscript: "safeest."
[3] Manuscript: "ditating."

To Patrick Gibson

DEAR SIR Poplar Forest Apr. 26. 17.

I am this day setting out on my return to Monticello and have drawn on you in favor of mr Robertson for 230.96 D

in my last letter from that place I mentioned that there were about 80. barrels of flour still to go from Albemarle. it turned out to be 96. of which 45. were sent off before I came away, and mr Tho[s] Eston Randolph (tenant of my mill) promised to send off the remaining 51. without delay, which I trust has been done. from this place 7. hhds of tob[o] are this day laden on the boats of D[r] Cabell, the general carrier of my produce here, which will be in Richmond about this day week, and 3. hhds more will go on the return of the same boats. I would wish this tob[o] to be sold immediately, as I had before requested as to the flour. this is the more pressing as I have to pay a sum of 2000.D. to mess[rs] Leroy and Bayard of New York as soon after the 7th of May as practicable, and certainly within that month. this is towards the balance of an old account with the bankers of the US. in Amsterdam, left unsettled when I left Europe, & too carelessly neglected from that time. it was settled the last year, & the balance originally something upwards of 2000.D. only had, with twenty odd years interest got up to about 6000.D. I promised to pay it in 3. years by equal instalments, one of which is now becoming due. this money must be paid in preference to all other demands, as no delay will be admitted, and therefore I must pray you as soon as the flour & tobacco is sold, to remit the 2000.D. to mess[rs] Leroy & Bayard. had it not been for this payment, I could have made both ends of the year meet, notwithstanding the disastrous drought, which, by the destruction of our corn crop, absorbed so much of our other produce for that article. but this payment leaves me so destitute that unless the bank will indulge me with a couple of thousand Dollars additional to my existing note, I shall be in a state of distress which will afflict me beyond measure. I will not ask it indefinitely, so as to place it under the denomination of standing or permanent paper; but only to bring it within the reach of the growing crop. in this way I hope it may not be within the restrictions of their rule, and that they may relieve me consistently with that. I should need it in the course of the Month of May, and therefore inclose you a blank note to be used if it can be obtained.

I shall be glad to learn from you when the remittance is made to mr Vaughan according to a former request, that I may instruct him as to the application of it. I salute you with friendship and respect.

TH: JEFFERSON

PoC (MHi); at foot of first page: "M[r] Gibson"; endorsed by TJ. Enclosure not found.

From Chapman Johnson

DEAR SIR, Staunton 26th April 1817.

Your letter dated the 14th of this month, was not received by me, until a few days since, on my return from an absence of a fortnight—Since that time, I have been very busily engaged in court every day, and must beg you to accept this fact as some apology for my permitting one or two post days to pass, without sending you the subpoena, you desired me to enclose—I hope the delay will produce no inconvenience—The process you will receive enclosed, returnable to the next term, which commences it's session, on the 15th of June.

Your bill for the court accompanied your letter, and will be duly filed—

With very great respect Your most obt. Svt. C JOHNSON

RC (MHi); endorsed by TJ as received 1 May 1817 and so recorded in SJL. RC (DLC); address cover only; with PoC of TJ to James Clarke, 1 Aug. 1817, on verso; addressed: "Thomas Jefferson Esquire Monticello"; franked; postmarked Staunton, 30 Apr. Enclosure not found.

From James Monroe

DEAR SIR washington april 27. 1817

I have decided to comply with your summons, and shall be with you at the time appointed.

with great respect your friend & servt— JAMES MONROE

RC (MHi); endorsed by TJ as received 30 Apr. 1817 and so recorded in SJL.

From John Wayles Eppes

Dear Sir, Mill Brook april 28th 1817.

I regret that I was not at home when your servant returned with Francis—It was so late when my servant returned from North Carolina with the grape slips that I thought it best to set them out at once and put the part designed for you into a very rich bed in my garden—Martha sent part of them to you—The others still remain and shall be particularly attended to—By sending down at the proper season next year you will be certain of a good stock if they live through summer.

Francis has gone to Richmond—I requested him on his arrival there to write to you—and hope he has done so—I would prefer greatly his being fixed in the upper or middle country—I think from a conversation I had with Wood he might be easily prevailed on to locate himself at Lynchburg—I do not think he would be satisfied in a country situation or I would have proposed to him fixing in my neighbourhood—His great objection to Lynchburg appears to be the want of Books and of persons of science—He speaks of the inhabitants as a race devoted solely to gain and having no ideas unconnected with money—From his habits however I do not consider Society as very important to him & I suppose he might find books at Lynchburg—

I enclose a letter from General Calvin Jones of North Carolina to Colo: Burton on the subject of the scuppernon grape—It does not correspond exactly with the account which I had previously received of the grape—

In a letter from Colo: Burton he informs me that he has procured for you a cask of the scuppernon wine two years old—He says it is greatly superior to what you tasted at my house and that he has made arrangements for forwarding it to Mr Gibson at Richmond—He begs that you will give yourself no trouble on the subject of the payment which can at any time be made through me after the wine is received—

Our election in this District will close today—The course pursued by Mr Randolph is a new one—He has gone round to the different courts & addressed the people at considerable length—He declares himself to be no candidate but those who have heard him Speak particularly at the Prince Edward election Seem to think him as anxious as usual [a]bout the election—A poll has been held for him in all th[e] counties and his opponent Austin will probably be elected by a majority of 200 votes—

Jefferson was here two days since—The family at Monticello were all well except Mrs Randolph who felt something of the Rheumatism—I have recovered my strength but still feel occasionally severe pain about my head & stomach—It will I hope gradually wear off—I have been obliged to quit the use both of wine & spirit & to confine myself principally to water and at Dinner a glass of Porter and water or sometimes porter alone—But even in the use of this I am compelled to be very moderate—

accept for your health & happiness my warm wishes.

Yours sincerely JNO: W: EPPES

RC (ViU: TJP-ER); damaged at seal; endorsed by TJ as received 23 June 1817 and so recorded in SJL. Enclosure not found, but see TJ to John S. Skinner, 4 Oct. 1820.

Archibald AUSTIN defeated John Randolph of Roanoke, who had not formally declared his candidacy, in the spring 1817 election for the United States House of Representatives district that included Buckingham, Charlotte, Cumberland, and Prince Edward counties (*DVB*, 1:250–1). JEFFERSON: Thomas Jefferson Randolph.

To LeRoy, Bayard & Company

MESS[RS] LEROY BAYARD & CO. Monticello Apr. 28. 17.

A journey of considerable absence, from which I am just now returned has prevented my earlier informing you that I am not unmindful of the approaching term for paying the 1st instalment of the debt which the indulgence of Mess[rs] Vanstaphorst and Hubard has so long left in my hands. on a view of the time necessary to get our produce to market in the spring season, for selling it, and recieving payment, which is sometimes at 30, at 60, & even at 90. days, I had in my letter to you stated that all the months of April and May might be necessary for the remittance; and altho' the day fixed in your answer was the 7th of May, yet I trust that when the circumstances of sale call for it, a delay of some days will be added to the other indulgences experienced, indemnifying that delay by the usual interest. I shall be able in the course of that month to make the remittance becoming due, and salute you with perfect esteem & respect

TH: JEFFERSON

RC (Christie's, New York City, 1996); addressed: "Mess[rs] Leroy Bayard & co New York"; franked; incorrectly postmarked Charlottesville, 31 Apr.; endorsed by an unidentified hand as received 5 May and answered 20 May. PoC (DLC); endorsed by TJ.

LeRoy, Bayard & Company set THE 7TH OF MAY annually as the date for TJ's remittances in its letter to him of 7 Aug. 1816. TJ had responded on 15 Aug. 1816 that those payments might be delayed.

From Abigail Adams

Dear Sir Quincy April 29th 1817

what right have I to be one of your tormentors? and amongst the numerous applicants for introductory Letters?

why I will plead, old acquaintance, old Friendship and your well known Benevolence— but to the Subject of my present address. Mr Theodore Lyman, who possesses an ardent thirst for Literature, and whose Father, is one of our most respectable Characters for probity, honour, & wealth, this young Gentleman has been much out of health, occasiond by too close application to his Studies. He is now going abroad with the hopes of regaining it—He is desirious of getting an introduction to some Gentlemen of Letters in France—my good Husband has furnishd him, with one to the Marquis Le Fayette, one to mr Marbois, and one to mr Gallatin, But as your acquaintance with men of Letters in France is of a more recent date, I thought it probable that you might give him a Letter or two, which might be of much Service to him, from the weight and respectability of your Character, He understands the French language, and is a young Gentleman of most estimable Character, and acquirements, whom I am not asshamed to recommend

he is a Nephew of mr Williams late consul of the US in England.—he has been once in England and in France before, and knows full well that to Men of Letters he cannot be easily admitted, without honorable introduction— He has been So attentive in Supplying us with rare, and valuable Books that I feel indebted to him for his kindness, and as I am not able myself to repay his civility,—like other debtors—I am drawing upon my Friends—any Letter you may think proper to forward you will please to Send under cover to my Husband. and they will be gratefully acknowledgd, by your old and Steady Friend

Abigail Adams

RC (DLC); endorsed by TJ as received 12 May 1817 and so recorded in SJL.

THEODORE LYMAN was the namesake of his father, a Boston merchant (*DAB*). John Adams wrote a letter of introduction for Lyman to Madame de Staël Holstein on 8 Apr. 1817. Three days later he penned similar letters to Lafayette and Albert GALLATIN (Lb in MHi: Adams Papers).

To James Baker

Sir Monticello Apr. 29. 17.

I recieved yesterday your favor of the 23^d^, informing me of the deposit of Dum-fish with mr Gibson which I shall direct the first boat from this place to call for; & I shall be glad to recieve by the same conveyance 4. kegs of tongues & sounds, such as the one you sent me some time ago, to be lodged also with mr Gibson who will pay this in addition to the amount of the fish. I thank you for your kind offer of furnishing me with the articles peculiar to the Northern market, and will take the liberty of availing myself of it from time to time as my wants may require, & tender you the assurance of my esteem & respect Th: Jefferson

PoC (MHi); on verso of a reused address cover from Joseph Milligan to TJ; at foot of text: "Mr James Baker"; endorsed by TJ.

To Fernagus De Gelone

Sir Monticello Apr. 29. 17.

The possession of Peyrard's translation of Archimedes makes me now wish to have that by him of Euclid, which I see noted in your Catalogue page. 23. be so good as to send me this, which being a single volume may come by the ordinary mail, only noting on the envelope that it is so many sheets of printed paper, in order to regulate the charge of postage. the price being noted shall be remitted in the usual way. I tender you my respectful salutations.

Th: Jefferson

PoC (MHi); on verso of reused address cover of Josephus B. Stuart to TJ, 5 Apr. 1817; at foot of text: "Mr Fernagus de Gelone"; endorsed by TJ.

Memorandum to James Monroe on Scuppernong Wine

[ca. 29 Apr. 1817?]

The wine called Scuppernon (or some name like that) is made as I am informed on the South side of Albemarle Sound, on & near a creek of that name. it is easily procured by a correspondent in Norfolk with which place Scuppernon has a short and direct communication by water. I had asked the favor of mr H. G. Burton of N. Carolina to procure me a correspondent from whom I could get regular supplies of that wine in future; he named to me his friend mr Pettigrew with whom he would make arrangements for that purpose. a strict charge is necessary not to put a drop of brandy in it. of three samples which I have seen, two were totally destroyed by doses of brandy, the 3[d] had some, but not so much as to drown entirely the flavor of the wine, which I am persuaded is fine if left pure & native unadulterated by any kind of cookery.

MS (DLC: Monroe Papers); entirely in TJ's hand; undated, with date conjectured from date of receipt of Hutchins G. Burton to TJ, 2 Apr. 1817; at foot of text: "Th: Jefferson for President Monroe."

To Louis H. Girardin

Dear Sir Monticello Apr. 30. 17.

M. De Laage did me the favor to call on me with your's of Mar. 2. I was happy to recieve him, and, as a commencement of intercourse I requested him to dine with us; but he was on his departure on a journey to Buckingham, and soon after his return, I sat out for Bedford from whence I am but just now returned. I shall soon now I hope find occasion to shew my respect for M. De Laage and for your recommendation of him. your letter is the only information I have recieved of the printing of your history. it is strange that the newspapers have not announced it. I conjecture from this that it is not yet ready for delivery.

I have recieved from Germany and France the books I wrote for. the editions from the former country have all the extraordinary value which produced the recommendation of mr Ticknor. Heyne's Iliad stands foremost. in editorial merit it is far beyond any thing I have ever seen. his Virgil is equally distinguished; altho, as we do not need so much aid with him as with Homer, we deem it secondary to that in value. Ruperti's illustrations of Juvenal are equally admirable. they give a new degree of understanding to that difficult satyrist. Oberling's Tacitus too is valuable. the books from Paris were faithfully furnished by Debure; vastly dearer however than I had known them; while those from Germany, Greek, & Latin cost but about a dollar a volume unbound. I am just now making out another catalogue for Paris, in which will be the celebrated edition of Plutarch by the learned Greek Karay at Paris. you promise a catalogue of some valuable books you have recieved from France. I shall be glad to recieve a list of such as you propose to dispose of, if any, with their prices, & sizes. I have lately got some rare things from a mr Fernagus de Gelone of N. York; particularly literal French translations of Hippocrates, Archimedes & Euclid. he seems to have imported some of the new and valuable publications from France. I am in hopes that your Hermitage will not make of you a mere recluse: that you will sometimes wander into the world, and if into this part of it that you will give us the pleasure of a visit; and I salute you with great esteem & respect.

TH: JEFFERSON

RC (PPAmP: Thomas Jefferson Papers); addressed: "Mr L. H. Girardin at the Hermitage near Staunton"; franked; postmarked Milton, 3 May.

Girardin's letter of MAR. 2., not found, is recorded in SJL as received 7 Mar. 1817 from his "Hermitage" estate.

Account with William Mitchell

[Apr. 1817]

Wm Mitchell in Account Dr	Bar. flour	D.C	with Th: Jefferson Cr.	Bar. flour	D. C.
b ℔					
To wheat of			By 2. Bar. **SF.**		
1815. 174– 36 @ 6/		174.59	flour @ 6.D.		12.
a balance. 2– 50 @ 5/		2.38	1. do @ 12.D.		12.
b ℔					
To wheat of 1816.			86. Bar.		
to wit 191–51 @ 2. D to pay cash bale		383.03	midlings @ 5.D.		430.
462– @ 5½. b for **F.** flour	84.		16. do 6.D.		96.
2–54 a balance due			60. ℔ bacon 1/		10.
656.05			By **F.** flour in excha. for		
			462.b. wheat @ 5½	84.	
	84–	560.		84.	560.[1]

Wm Mitchell in Account Dr	Bar. flour	D.C	with Th: Jefferson Cr		
			By 2. Bar. **S.F.**		
b ℔			flour. @ 6.D.		12.
To wheat of 1815. 174–36 } 177.26[2] in **F.** flour			1. do @ 12.D.		12.
a balance 2–50 } @ 5½	32–		86. Bar.		
			midlings @ 5.D.		430.

b						
To wheat of 1816. to wit	280. @ 2.D. to pay cash balance 376.05 in **F.** flour @ $5\frac{1}{2}$ 656.05	68–72	560.	16. d° @ 6.D.		96.
				60. ℔ bacon @ 1/		10.
				By **F.** flour in exchange for wheat @ $5\frac{1}{2}$	84.	
				Balance of d° still due	16–72	
		100–72	560.		100–72	560.

MS (ViU: TJP-ER); entirely in TJ's hand; undated; endorsed by TJ: "Mitchell Wm Apr. 1817."

TJ here prepared his ACCOUNT with Mitchell by two variant methods and, evidently preferring the results of the first, canceled the one beneath.

[1] Both sides of table from this point are struck through with separate diagonal lines.

[2] Reworked from "176.86."

To Hutchins G. Burton

Dear Sir Monticello May 1. 17.

Your favor of Apr. 2. came to hand two days ago only. I thank you for the kind office of procuring me the cask of wine, and still more for the purpose of placing me in correspondence with mr Pettigrew, thro' whom I may draw future supplies directly. I have this day inclosed to mr Eppes a draught on mr Gibson for 26.D. I observe the makers of this wine have fallen into the barbarous practice of dosing their wine with brandy. that you sent mr Eppes had but little, but it was sensible. the next sample I saw was Gen[l] Cocke's, in which there was so much as to drown the flavor of the wine, and I have seen a third sample which absolutely cannot be distinguished from strong brandy toddy. this will destroy the reputation of the wine. this unhappy taste is peculiar to the English, and we derive it by imitation from them. every person in a wine country knows that a single glass of brandy will adulterate the fine flavor of a whole cask of wine, and that a little [m]ore will destroy the vinous flavor entirely, and give to a sensible palate that of brandy only. the truth is that there should not be a single drop of brandy put into it. no money will tempt a European vigneron to put a single drop of brandy into his wine, because it would destroy it's reputation. this is done by the merchant, and only for an English or American customer, who always requires it expressly. the merchants of Bordeaux expressed to me their astonishment at this singular coarseness of taste. I hope I shall be able to prevail on the Scuppernon vigneron to furnish mine at least without a drop of brandy. with my thanks for your kind attention in ordering this supply, be pleased to accept the assurance of my great esteem and respect. Th: Jefferson

PoC (MHi); on verso of reused address cover of Pierre Samuel Du Pont de Nemours to TJ, 18 Aug. 1816; torn at seal; at foot of text: "H. G. Burton esq."; endorsed by TJ.

To George Cabell

Sir Monticello May 1. 17.

It was intimated to me while in Bedford that you wished to know something more particularly of mr Flower for whom you had done some kind offices, and entered into some engagements. of this he expressed a grateful sense here, and I believe you may be assured he is entirely worthy of the services you rendered him. he is the person who was with mr Burkbeck on the tour through France which has been in all our bookstores for two or three years, and to whom that book is dedicated. he is the son of an English gentleman landholder, of large family connections, and the particular friend of Burkbeck. these, considering a revolution in England as inevitable, sent him over to this country to examine it and find out an eligible situation for them. after the purchase made thro' you, which I believe was for himself, he came here & staid some weeks with us, having originally brought me letters of recommendation from some friends in Europe. he left us the last of February, intending to go to N. York and take passage in the first vessel bound for England; but in Philadelphia met letters from mr Burkbeck[1] informing him he should embark in early spring. Flower is therefore now awaiting his arrival in or near Philadelphia. his father, who was doubtful about coming, when he left England, has decided to come as soon as he can dispose of his estate, and this will probably bring most of the family, and I am in hopes the purchase you made for him will fix the location of the family. from what I have seen of mr Flower I have the most unqualified reliance on his worth & perfect good faith. on the supposition that this account of him might satisfy your mind that the services you have rendered him have been worthily bestowed, I have thought it a duty to give it with assurances of my great esteem & respect. TH: JEFFERSON

PoC (MHi); on verso of reused address cover of David Gelston to TJ, 31 Aug. 1816; at foot of text: "Dr George Cabell"; endorsed by TJ.

MR BURKBECK: Morris Birkbeck.

[1]Manuscript: "Burbeck."

To John H. Cocke

DEAR SIR Monticello May 1. 17.

The present express is sent to remove all uncertainty as to the day of our meeting, which, for the reasons mentioned when I had the pleasure of seeing you at Enniscorthy, is to be on Monday next, our county court day, instead of the next day Tuesday. I have a letter from the President Monroe assuring me I may rely on his attendance. I expect mr Madison & his family the day after tomorrow. your attendance will ensure a meeting. mr Cabell will not be here, nor probably mr Watson. should we fail of a meeting, I fear I should be obliged to give up the purchase of the land: I hope you will be here on Sunday, & if to dinner so much the more pleasing.

yours with friendship & respect TH: JEFFERSON

RC (ViU: TJP-Co); addressed: "General Cocke Bremo"; endorsed by Cocke. PoC (DLC); on verso of reused address cover of Joseph Delaplaine to TJ, 26 Oct. 1816; endorsed by TJ.

For the PURCHASE OF THE LAND, see Conveyance of Lands for Central College from John M. Perry and Frances T. Perry to Alexander Garrett, 23 June 1817.

From Henry A. S. Dearborn

RESPECTED SIR, Custom House Boston May 1. 1817.—

I received a letter from the U.S. Consul Th. Appleton Esqr at Leghorn & a package containing he says some valuable grass seeds for you by the ship Heroine, which I shall send to the Collector at Richmond by the first coaster which will be in a few[1] days.

I shall write the Collector to hold the package subject to your order.

With the highest respect I have the honor to be Sir your obt. St.

H, A, S, DEARBORN

I have this day sent the within mentioned package to the Col^{r} of Richmond by the Schooner Little William J. Gage.

May 1. 1817. D.

RC (DLC); lacking postscript; endorsed by TJ as a letter from "Dearborn ? Boston" received 12 May 1817 and so recorded in SJL. RC (MHi); address cover and postscript only; with PoC of TJ to Craven Peyton, 28 June 1817, on verso; addressed: "Thomas Jefferson Esqr Monticello Virginia"; franked; postmarked Boston, 2 May.

The COLLECTOR AT RICHMOND was James Gibbon.

[1]Manuscript: "fiew."

To John Wayles Eppes

DEAR SIR Monticello May 1. 17.

I have recieved a letter from mr Burton, informing me he had purchased for me a barrel of Scuppernon wine. I had before informed him that I would desire mr Gibson of Richmond to pay his draught for it, and I had accordingly so done, but mr Burton prefers settling it with you. I therefore now inclose you a draught on Gibson, the most convenient channel of remittance to myself, and I am in hopes it will answer your purpose. You have seen the report of the two committees of parliament. private letters from England say that matters are much worse there than these state, or the public papers. I believe a revolution there to be absolutely unavoidable. a bankruptcy must take place, and that must produce revolution.

We are endeavoring to establish a college near Charlottesville called the central college, under the direction of 6. visitors. these are mr Madison, Col^{o} Monroe, Genl Cocke, Joseph C. Cabell, mr Watson of Louisa & myself. we are to meet on Monday next to set it agoing. mr Madison & Col^{o} Monroe both promise me to be here, as will the other gentlemen. we have purchased the land, and shall immediately build the pavilion for one professorship, that of languages, to be ready to recieve pupils early in the spring. I think to propose it to Wood, and that he will come. I am in hopes you will approve of Francis's coming also. present us all respectfully to mrs Eppes and accept the assurance of my affectionate attachment. TH: JEFFERSON

RC (ViU: TJP); at foot of text: "J. W. Eppes esq." PoC (CSmH: JF); endorsed by TJ. Enclosure not found.

The REPORT of the "Committee of Secresy" of the British House of Commons appeared in the Washington *Daily National Intelligencer*, 20 Apr. 1817, and elsewhere, along with comments summarizing a similar report from the House of Lords. These documents described clubs of revolutionary political insurgents in London and its surrounding areas, leading Prime Minister Robert Banks Jenkinson, 2d Earl of Liverpool, to authorize a temporary suspension of the writ of habeas corpus in all cases of alleged treason (*ODNB*).

To Fitzwhylsonn & Potter

MESS^{RS} FITZWHYLSON AND POTTER Monticello May 1. 17.

I suppose I must consider the N^{os} of the Edinburg Review sent you by the stage as irrecoverably lost, and proceed to get my N^{os} compleated. I have the 14. vols republished bringing the work down to N° 28. and I now inclose you N°s 51. 52. consequently I want from N° 29. to 50. inclusive which will make 11. vols, and the two N^{os} I send will make a 12th to be half bound and lettered, which I must pray you to furnish me. I have N° 53. but do not send it till I get 54.

I wrote to you some time ago for a copy of Josephus in English. I have lately seen an edition in 3. v. 8vo printed at Springfield in Connecticut for Johnson and Warner. it is on mean paper, and indifferent type. yet if no better can be got in 8vo I must be contented with that; but am in hopes you can get it better bound than the spungy copy I saw.

There are two boatmen, Johnson & Gilmore belonging to Milton who will bring articles for me safely, and are more to be trusted than the stage. I am in hopes the books sent to you, to be bound as stated in my letter of Mar. 19. are ready by this time, and I would prefer their being committed to either Johnson or Gilmore rather than to the stage. Accept my respectful salutations. TH: JEFFERSON

RC (NN: Thomas Jefferson Papers). PoC (DLC); on verso of reused address cover to TJ; endorsed by TJ.

From Patrick Gibson

SIR Richmond 1st May 1817—

I yesterday received your favor of the 26th Ulto inclosing a note for $2000. with a view to having it discounted and that amount remitted to Messrs LeRoy & Bayard of New York as soon after the 7th Inst as practicable—I shall offer it this day week, and as I entertain very little doubt of its being discounted, you may inform these Gentlemen that the remittance shall leave this the 9th—however as I know that we cannot expect a renewal in this bank even for another 60d/– it will be necessary to try it elsewhere, and as I presume the US. branch will be in operation by that time, we must endeavour to renew it there I am not informed of the principle upon which that institution proposes to lend money, you can however ascertain through its President, whether or not the money can be obtained for the time you propose, if not some other means must be resorted to—
Your draft in favor of Mr Robertson for $230.96 is paid—
46 barrels of your flour received by Wm Johnson 14th Ulto were condemned as unmerchantable, having been made (so says the Inspr) of smutte[d] wheat, these have been sold at 11½$ on 60d/–. Int added[1] there remains yet on hand 84 bls: fine and 53 Sr[2] fine, so soon as I shall have disposed of this I shall make the remittance to Mr Vaughan, which I hope will be in a few days—With great respect I am

Your obt Servt PATRICK GIBSON

RC (MHi); edge trimmed; betweeen dateline and salutation: "Thomas Jefferson Esqre"; endorsed by TJ as received 8 May 1817 and so recorded in SJL.

Wilson Cary Nicholas was the PRESIDENT of the Richmond branch of the Second Bank of the United States.

[1] Preceding two words interlined.
[2] Abbreviation for "Super."

From Jean Mourer

Isle St Pierre, au Lac de Bienne,
Canton de Berne, en Suisse,
le 1 Mai 1817, & l'an 40 de la Liberté
de l'Amérique Septentrionale

Monsieur le Président!

Un homme, ami de la Liberté, vient, depuis une petite Isle de l'Europe, vous présenter l'hommage de Ses respects, & celle de Son admiration pour la Sagesse avec laquelle vous conduisez votre grande & florissante République.

Dans le courant du mois de Mars, & dans les premiers jours de celui d'Avril, il est parti, tant de la Suisse, que de l'allemagne, au dela de 3000 personnes pour l'Amérique; Dieu veuille les protéger dans leur voyage & leur faire trouver le bonheur dans la nouvelle pâtrie qu'ils se choisissent.

Mais, Monsieur le Président! Serait-il vrai, comme l'annoncent nos gazettes, que de votre territoire, Sort des Spéculateurs d'hommes? qu'ils les achètent a leur arrivèe en Amérique? qu'ils les revendent a des proprietaires agricoles, pour leur Servir d'Esclaves pendant 6, 12, & même Vingt années?

J'aime à croire & ma conscience m'assure que cette nouvelle est fausse; que je serais heureux, Monsieur le Président, si vous aviez la bonté de me mettre dans la possibilité de la démentir publiquement, pour le plus grand honneur de votre pâtrie, sur la terre de laqu'elle j'aimerais finir mes jours … Veuillez m'y appeler.

Veuille la Providence veiller Sur vos jours, afin que les habitans du nouveau monde puissent vous bénir pendant une longue Suite d'Années

J'ai l'honneur de me dire avec Estime & Considération
Monsieur le Président
Votre très humble & Obéiss[t] Serviteur Jean Mourer

L'Isle St Pierre est devenue célèbre par le Séjour qu'y a fait J[n] Jacques Rousseau.

Messieurs Charles Ellis de Richmond
Pierson de New York
Anthony Moris, de Philadelphie
Packman
Howard
Maclure
Ont visités ce beau Séjour.—

EDITORS' TRANSLATION

Saint-Pierre Island, on Lake of Bienne, Canton of Bern, Switzerland, 1 May 1817, and in year 40 of North American freedom

Mr. President!

A man, a friend of liberty, comes from a little island in Europe to present to you his respects and his admiration for the wisdom with which you lead your great and prosperous republic.

During the month of March and the first days of April of the current year, more than 3,000 people from Switzerland and Germany left for America; may God protect them in their voyage and help them find happiness in the new homeland they are choosing for themselves.

But, Mr. President! Can it be true, as our gazettes report, that speculators in men come from your territory? Is it true that they buy men when they arrive in America? That they resell them to plantation owners, to serve as slaves for 6, 12, and even twenty years?

I would like to believe that this piece of news is false, and my conscience assures me so. How happy I would be, Mr. President, if you would be good enough to enable me to deny it publicly, for the greatest honor of your country, on which soil I would like to end my days … May you call me there.

May Providence protect you, so that the inhabitants of the New World can bless you for many more years

I have the honor to be, with respect and consideration
Mr. President
Your very humble and obedient servant Jean Mourer

Saint-Pierre Island became famous for Jean Jacques Rousseau's stay here.
Messrs. Charles Ellis from Richmond
Pierson from New York
Anthony Morris from Philadelphia
Packman
Howard
Maclure
have visited this beautiful place.—

RC (MoSHi: TJC-BC); dateline beneath signature; ellipsis in original; postscript on verso of address leaf; addressed: "A Monsieur Monsieur Jefferson Président du Conseil des Etats unis de l'Amérique Septentrionale à Wasington"; stamped "SHIP"; redirected in an unidentified hand to "Monticello"; franked; postmarked New York, 29 July; endorsed by TJ as received 5 Aug. 1817 and so recorded in SJL. Translation by Dr. Genevieve Moene.

Jean Jacques ROUSSEAU spent two months on Saint-Pierre Island in 1765 (Albert Metzger, *Jean-Jacques Rousseau a l'Ile Saint-Pierre [Lac de Bienne], 1765* [1877], 8).

To James Oldham

DEAR SIR Monticello May 1. 17.

I have occasion for 100. feet of Mahogany to work up into commodes or chests of drawers, one half to be fine, the other half of second rate. your kindness heretofore in executing these little commissions for me encourages me to ask the favor of you to procure this for me. mr Gibson, on sight of this letter will be so kind as to pay the amount, and I will direct a boatman to call on you for it. I believe the stuff for these purposes should be inch thick. I have recieved my supply of glass from Boston. with my apologies for this trouble accept the assurance of my great esteem and respect.

TH JEFFERSON

PoC (MHi); at foot of text: "Cap[t] James Oldham"; endorsed by TJ; with unrelated notes by TJ on verso: "Garth & Mousley. their acct for 1773. settled & signed May. 4. 1774" (see *MB*, 1:373).

To Francis Adrian Van der Kemp

DEAR SIR Monticello May 1. 17.

I thank you for your letter of Mar. 30. my mind is entirely relieved by your assurance that my name did not cross the Atlantic in connection with the Syllabus. the suggestion then of the Editor of the Theological Repository was like those of our newspaper editors who pretend they know every thing, but in discretion will not tell us, while we see that they give us all they know and a great deal more. I am now at the age of quietism, and wish not to be kicked by the asses of hierophantism. I hope you will find time to take up this subject. there are some new publications in Germany which would greatly aid it. to wit,

Augusti's translation & Commentary on the 7. Catholic epistles, in which he has thrown great light on the opinions of the primitive Christians & on the innovations of S[t] Paul printed at Lemgo 1808. in 2. vols. 8[vo]

Palmer's Paul and Gamaliel. Giessen. 1806.

Munter's history of dogmas. Gottingen 1806. shewing the formation of the dogmatical system of Christianity.

Augusti's Manual of the history of Christian dogmas. Leipsic 1805.

Marheinacke's Manual of Ecclesiastical history. Erlangen 1806. developing the simple ideas of the first Christians, and the causes & progress of the subsequent changes.

I have not written for these books, because I suppose they are in German which I do not read; but I expect they are profoundly learned on their subjects

In answer to your enquiries respecting Rienzi, the best account I have met with[1] of this poor counterfiet of the Gracchi, who seems to have had enthusiasm & eloquence, without either wisdom or firmness, is in the 5th & 6th vols of Sigismondi. he quotes for his authority chiefly the Frammenti di Storia Romana d'anonimo contemporaneo. of the monk Borselaro I know nothing, and my books are all gone to where they will be more useful, & my memory waning under the hand of time.—I think Bekker might have demanded a truce from his antagonists, on the question of a Hell, by desiring them first to fix it's geography. but wherever it be, it is certainly the best patrimony of the church, and procures them in exchange the solid acres of this world. I salute you with entire esteem and respect.

TH: JEFFERSON

RC (NBuHi: Van der Kemp Papers); addressed: "Mr Fr. Adr. Vanderkemp Oldenbarnevelt near Trenton, New York"; franked; postmarked Charlottesville, 3 May; with additional notation by Van der Kemp: "Longbane hist: of Plagiarism." PoC (DLC); endorsed by TJ.

The EDITOR OF THE THEOLOGICAL REPOSITORY was Robert Aspland. SIGISMONDI: Jean Charles Léonard Simonde de Sismondi. BORSELARO: Jacopo Bussolari.

[1] Preceding four words interlined.

To Tristram Dalton

DEAR SIR Monticello May 2. 17.

I am indebted for your favor of Apr. 22. and for the copy of the Agricultural magazine it covered, which is indeed a very useful work. while I was an amateur in Agricultural science (for practical knolege my course of life never permitted me) I was very partial to the drilled husbandry of Tull, and thought still better of it when reformed by Young to 12.I. rows. but I had not time to try it while young, and now grown old I have not the requisite activity either of body or mind.

With respect to the field culture of vegetables for cattle, instead of the carrot and potato recommended by yourself and the magazine, & the beet by others, we find the Jerusalem artichoke best for winter, & the Succory for Summer use. this last was brought over from France to England by Arthur Young, as you will see in his travels thro' France, & some of the seed sent by him to Genl Washington, who spared me a part of it. it is as productive as the Lucerne, without it's laborious culture, & indeed without any culture except the keeping it clean the first year. the Jerusalem artichoke far exceeds the potato in produce, and remains in the ground thro' the winter to be dug as wanted. A method of ploughing our hill sides horizontally, introduced into this most hilly part of our country, by Col° T. M.[1] Randolph, my son in law, may be worth mentioning to you. he has practised it a dozen or 15. years, and it's advantages were so immediately observed that it has already become very general, and has entirely changed and renovated the face of our country. every rain, before that, while it gave a temporary refreshment, did permanent evil by carrying off our soil: and fields were no sooner cleared than wasted. at present we may say that we lose none of our soil, the rain not absorbed in the moment of it's fall being retained in the hollows between the beds until it can be absorbed. our practice is when we first enter on this process, with a rafter level of 10.f. span, to lay off guide lines conducted horizontally around the hill or valley from one end to the other of the field, and about 30. yards apart. the steps of the level on the ground are marked by a stroke of a hoe, and immediately followed by a plough to preserve the trace. a man or a lad, with the level, and two small boys, the one with sticks, the other with the hoe, will do an acre of this in an hour, and when once done it is forever done.[2] we generally level a field the year it is put into Indian corn, laying it into beds of 6.f. wide with a large water furrow between the beds, until all the fields have been once levelled. the intermediate furrows are run by the eye of the ploughman governed by these guide lines. the inequalities of declivity in the hill will vary in places the distance of the guide lines, & occasion gores which are thrown into short beds. As in ploughing very steep hill sides horizontally the common plough can scarcely throw the furrow uphill, Col° Randolph has contrived a very simple alteration of the share, which throws the furrow downhill both going and coming. it is as if two shares were welded together at their strait side, and at a right angle with each other. this turns on it's bar as on a pivot, so as to lay either share horizontal, when[3] the other becoming vertical acts as a mould board. this is done by the ploughman in an instant by a single motion of the hand, at the end of every furrow. I inclose a bit of paper cut into the form of the double share, which being opened at the fold to a right angle, will give an idea of it's general principle. horizontal and deep ploughing, with the use of plaister and clover, which are but beginning to be used here will, as we believe, restore this part of our country to it's original fertility, which was exceeded by no upland in the state. believing that some of these things might be acceptable to you I have hazarded them as testimonies of my great esteem & respect.

TH: JEFFERSON

RC (NNGL, on deposit NHi); mutilated at fold, with missing letters supplied from PoC; filed with this text is a note from Chester S. Stoddard to Paul Leicester Ford, 18 Oct. 1890: "I herewith hand you for perusal my Jefferson letter—I regret that a few years ago I tore off the address—which bore the frank of Thos Jefferson—at request of a friend who desired the autograph—The letter was addressed to Tristram Dalton, and to me an interesting feature is the paper pattern of the plough share—The writer of the Declaration of Independence may himself have secured this 'bit of paper' with the old fashioned pin— You Can readily understand the value of this document to one who has been a Collector of such things." PoC (DLC); on a reused address cover from Archibald Robertson to TJ; torn at seal, with some missing text rewritten by TJ; at foot of first page: "Tristram Dalton esq." Printed in *Massachusetts Agricultural Journal* 4 (1817): 328–31.

In January 1791 Arthur Young sent SUCCORY seed to George Washington, who shared it with TJ by 1794. In reporting his success to the president, TJ described the crop as "one of the greatest acquisitions a farmer can have" (Washington, *Papers, Pres. Ser.*, 7:284, 286n, 8:431; *PTJ*, 28:232–3, 464, 498).

[1] *Massachusetts Agricultural Journal*: "J. M."

[2] *Massachusetts Agricultural Journal*: "when done, it remains forever."

[3] Instead of preceding two words, *Massachusetts Agricultural Journal* reads "horizontally; then."

ENCLOSURE

Paper Model of Thomas Mann Randolph's Plow

[ca. 2 May 1817]

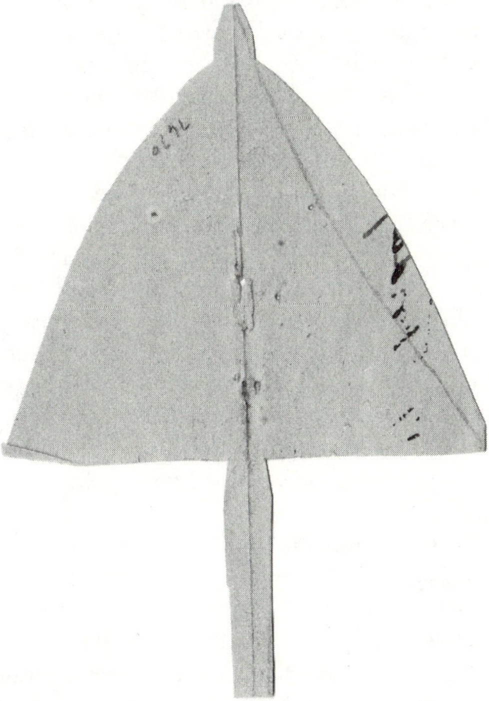

MS (NNGL, on deposit NHi); cut and folded by TJ.

To John Adams

DEAR SIR Monticello. May 5. 17.

Absences and avocations had prevented my acknoleging your favor of Feb. 2. when that of Apr. 19. arrived. I had not the pleasure of recieving the former by the hands of mr Lyman. his business probably carried him in another direction; for I am far inland, & distant from the great line of communication between the trading cities. your recommendations are always welcome, for indeed the subjects of them always merit that welcome, and some of them in an extraordinary degree. they make us acquainted with what there is of excellent in our ancient sister state of Massachusets, once venerated and beloved, and still hanging on our hopes, for what need we despair of after the resurrection of Connecticut to light and liberality. I had believed that, the last retreat of Monkish darkness, bigotry, and abhorrence of those advances[1] of the mind which had carried the other states a century ahead of them. they seemed still to be exactly where their forefathers were when they schismatised from the Covenant of works, and to consider, as dangerous heresies, all innovations good or bad. I join you therefore in sincere congratulations that this den of the priesthood is at length broken up, and that a protestant popedom is no longer to disgrace the American history and character. if, by religion, we are to understand Sectarian dogmas, in which no two of them agree, then your exclamation on that hypothesis is just, 'that this would be the best of all possible worlds, if there were no religion in it':[2] but if the moral precepts, innate in man, and made a part of his physical constitution, as necessary for a social being, if the sublime doctrines of philanthropism, and deism taught us by Jesus of Nazareth in which all agree, constitute true religion, then, without it, this would be, as you again say, 'something not fit to be named, even indeed a Hell.'[3]

You certainly acted wisely in taking no notice of what the malice of Pickering could say of you. were such things to be answered, our lives would be wasted in the filth of findings and provings, instead of being employed in promoting the happiness and prosperity of our fellow citizens. the tenor of your life is the proper and sufficient answer. it is fortunate for those in public trust that posterity will judge them by their works, and not by the malignant vituperations and invectives of the Pickerings and Gardeniers of their age. after all, men of energy of character must have enemies: because there are two sides to every question, and taking one with decision, and acting on it with effect, those who take the other will of course be hostile in proportion as they feel that effect. thus in the revolution, Hancock and the Adamses were the raw-head and bloody bones of tories and traitors; who yet knew nothing of you personally but what was good.—I do not entertain your apprehensions for the happiness of our brother Madison in a state of retirement. such a mind as his, fraught with information, and with matter for reflection, can never know ennui. besides, there will always be work enough cut out for him to continue his active usefulness to his country. for example, he and Monroe (the president,) are now here on the work of a collegiate institution to be established in our neighborhood, of which they and myself are three of six Visitors.

this, if it succeeds, will raise up children for mr Madison to employ his attentions[4] thro' life. I say, if it succeeds; for we have two very essential wants in our way 1. means to compass our views & 2dly men qualified to fulfill them. and these you will agree are essential wants indeed.

I am glad to find you have a copy of Sismondi, because his is a field familiar to you, and on which you can judge him. his work is highly praised, but I have not yet read it. I have been occupied and delighted with reading another work, the title of which did not promise much useful information or amusement, l'Italia avanti il dominio dei Romani dal Micali. it has often you know been a subject of regret that Carthage had no writer to give her side of her own history, while her wealth, power, and splendor prove she must have had a very distinguished policy and government. Micali has given the counterpart of the Roman history for[5] the nations over which they extended their domination. for this he has gleaned up matter from every quarter, and furnished materials for reflection and digestion to those who, thinking as they read have percieved there was a great deal of matter behind the curtain, could that be fully withdrawn. he certainly gives new views of a nation whose splendor has masked and palliated their barbarous ambition.   I am now reading Botta's history of our own revolution. bating the antient practice, which he has adopted, of putting speeches into mouths which never made them, and fancying motives of action which we never felt, he has given that history with more detail, precision and candor than any writer I have yet met with. it is to be sure compiled from those writers; but it is a good secretion of their matter, the pure from the impure, and presented in a just sense of right in opposition to usurpation.—Accept assurances for mrs Adams and yourself of my affectionate esteem and respect.

TH: JEFFERSON

RC (MHi: Adams Papers); at foot of first page: "President Adams"; endorsed by Adams as answered 18 May 1817. PoC (DLC). TJ made notes for this letter on the verso of the last page of Adams to TJ, 2 Feb. 1817.

RAW-HEAD AND BLOODY BONES: nursery bugbears used to terrify children (*OED*).

[1] Manuscript: "advancces."
[2] Omitted quotation marks supplied from PoC, with quote taken from Adams to TJ, 19 Apr. 1817.
[3] Omitted closing quotation mark supplied from PoC, with quote adapted from Adams to TJ, 19 Apr. 1817.
[4] PoC: "attention."
[5] TJ here canceled "all."

The Founding of the University of Virginia: Central College, 1816–1819

I. MINUTES OF CENTRAL COLLEGE BOARD OF VISITORS, 5 MAY 1817

II. JOHN H. COCKE'S DESCRIPTION OF CENTRAL COLLEGE BOARD OF VISITORS MEETING, [5 MAY 1817]

III. ANONYMOUS DESCRIPTION OF CENTRAL COLLEGE BOARD OF VISITORS MEETING, [5 MAY 1817]

IV. CENTRAL COLLEGE SUBSCRIPTION LIST, [CA. 7 MAY 1817]

V. MASTER LIST OF SUBSCRIBERS TO CENTRAL COLLEGE, [AFTER 7 MAY 1817]

EDITORIAL NOTE

The bill establishing Central College became law on 14 Feb. 1816, and on 25 Mar. of that year Frank Carr, who had served as secretary for the trustees of the Albemarle Academy, submitted recommendations to Virginia governor Wilson Cary Nicholas for appointments to the new college's Board of Visitors. Carr told Nicholas that several former Albemarle Academy trustees had drawn up the list, which consisted of Jefferson, Joseph C. Cabell, John H. Cocke, James Madison, James Monroe, and David Watson. The governor duly appointed all six men.

Jefferson arranged for a meeting of the new Board of Visitors on 8 Apr. 1817, but with only Cabell and Cocke in attendance, he postponed the transaction of business to 5 May 1817. He believed that a full meeting of the visitors was of the utmost importance if Central College were to become Virginia's public university. Jefferson wrote to both Madison and Monroe on 13 Apr. stressing that their presence would play a crucial role in strengthening the new institution's claim to preeminence, undercutting competition from localities farther west, and gratifying the local populace. His efforts were largely successful, and on 5 May 1817 the visitors gathered for their first formal meeting, with only Cabell and Watson absent.

During the Central College phase, Jefferson's vision for his university began to be realized. At the 5 May meeting the members agreed to initiate a subscription campaign to promote the college. Two days later Cocke reported picking up the subscription papers that Jefferson had been preparing. Five of the visitors subscribed $1,000 each, while Watson pledged $200. Cocke and Cabell argued that the visitors should jointly ask several prominent citizens from each county to promote the subscription, but at its July meeting the board adopted a less ambitious scheme urged by Jefferson and Madison under which each visitor would contact only his own particular acquaintances. They circulated the printed forms, and as subscriptions came in names and pledges were copied onto subsequent forms to demonstrate the campaign's success to other potential donors, with Jefferson's name and amount subscribed at the top of each. Although he was unwilling to risk alienating the citizens of Virginia with as aggressive a fund-raising effort as that advocated by Cocke and Cabell, Jefferson did promote Central College and the subscription in an anonymous article he wrote for the *Richmond Enquirer* at the end of August 1817. Subscription lists were returned with pledges through the winter of 1817 and into 1818, with the first of four annual installments scheduled for payment on 1 Apr. 1818. Past-due pledges were still being collected after Jefferson's death, but long before that the subscription funds had proved to be an important source of revenue for Central College. In August 1818 a group of subscribers authorized the fledgling institution to transfer its funds to a proposed University of Virginia.

By the autumn of 1817 the Board had approved the purchase of two tracts of land from John M. Perry and Frances T. Perry, and Jefferson had advanced to the architectural planning stage, with both William Thornton and Benjamin Henry Latrobe contributing ideas and opinions. The cornerstone of what would become Pavilion VII was laid with full Masonic honors on 6 Oct. 1817. While Jefferson and the other visitors began courting potential faculty and continued to establish the financial and physical foundations for Central College, they found themselves in the midst of a battle to secure its status as the state university of Virginia. Jefferson and Cabell collaborated in the autumn of 1817 to draft a bill regarding allocations from the state literary fund. The measure that passed into law on 21 Feb. 1818 stipulated that a twenty-four person board comprised of one appointee from each state senatorial district meet "at the tavern in Rockfish gap on the Blue Ridge" on 1 Aug. 1818 and report back to the legislature on several matters, including "a proper scite for the University" and a "plan for the buildings thereof." Based on this report, on 25 Jan. 1819 the legislature passed "An Act for establishing an University," thereby transforming Central College into the University of Virginia (*Acts of Assembly* [1815–16 sess.], 191–3; [1817–18 sess.], 11–5; [1818–19 sess.], 15–8; Carr to Nicholas, 25 Mar. 1816 [Vi: RG 3, Nicholas Executive Papers]; Jennings L. Wagoner Jr., *Jefferson and Education* [2004], 91–2, 104–10; Nicholas to TJ, 18 Oct. 1816, and enclosure; TJ to Madison, 13 Apr. 1817; TJ to Monroe, 13 Apr. 1817; Thornton to TJ, 27 May 1817; Agreement between John M. Perry and Central College, 23 June 1817; Conveyance of Lands for Central College from John M. Perry and Frances T. Perry to Alexander Garrett, 23 June 1817; Latrobe to TJ, 24 July 1817; Cocke's Description of a Central College Board of Visitors Meeting, 25[–28 July 1817]; Cabell to TJ, 18 Aug. 1817; Anonymous [TJ] to the *Richmond Enquirer*, [ca. 29] Aug. 1817; Cocke's Account of the Laying of the Cornerstone at Central College, 5–6 Oct. 1817; Central College Donors and Founders to University of Virginia Commissioners, [before 1 Aug. 1818]; John L. Thomas's Report as Collector for the University of Virginia, 30 Sept. 1826 [ViU]).

I. Minutes of Central College Board of Visitors

At a meeting of the Visitors of the Central college held at Charlottesville on the 5th day of May[1] 1817. on a call by three members, to wit, John Hartwell Cocke, Joseph C. Cabell & Th Jefferson, present James Monroe, James Madison, John H. Cocke,[2] and Th: Jefferson

The[3] records of the trustees of the Albemarle academy, in lieu of which the Central college is established, were recieved from their Secretary by the hands of Alexr Garrett one of the sd trustees,[4] Resolved that Valentine W. Southall be appointed Secretary to the board, and, that the sd records be delivered to him.

The board proceeded to the appointment of a Proctor and the said Alexander Garrett was appointed, with a request that he will act as Treasurer also until a special appointment can be made.[5]

The board being informed that at a meeting which had been proposed for the 8th day of April last at Charlottesville and at which the three members only who called this present meeting had attended, the sd members had visited & examined the different sites for the College within a convenient distance around Charlottesville had deemed the one offered them by John Perry about a mile above the town, to be the most suitable, and offered on the most reasonable terms, and had provisionally authorised a purchase of certain parcels thereof for the site of the sd college & it's appendages, and the members now present having themselves proceeded to the sd grounds, examined them, and considered the terms of the sd provisional purchase, do now approve of the sd grounds as a site for the sd college & it's appendages and of the terms of purchase, which they hereby confirm & ratify, and they accordingly authorize their Proctor above named to proceed to obtain a regular conveyance thereof to himself & his successors in trust for the sd College.

The act establishing the Central college having transferred to the same all the rights and claims existing in the Albemarle academy & its trustees, and having in aid of the subscriptions & donations obtained or to be obtained & of the proceeds of the lottery authorised by law specially empowered[6] this college by it's proper officers to demand and recieve the monies which arose from the sales of the Glebe lands of the parishes of Saint Ann & Fredericksville,[7] or such part thereof as belongs to the county of Albemarle or it's citizens, in whatever hands they may be, to be employed for the purposes of this college, Ordered that the Proctor enquire into the state of the said property &

report the same to this board; and that in the mean time he be authorised to demand and recieve so much of the said monies as may be requisite to pay for the lands purchased from the sd John Perry, and to make payment accordingly.

On view of a plan presented to the trustees of the Albemarle academy for erecting a distinct pavilion or building for each separate professorship, and for arranging these around a square, each pavilion containing a schoolroom & two apartments for the accomodation of the Professor with other reasonable conveniences[8] the board determines that one of those pavilions shall now be erected; and they request the Proctor, so soon as the funds are at his command to agree with proper workmen for the building of one, of stone or brick below ground, & of brick above, of substantial work, of regular architecture, well executed, and to be compleated if possible during the ensuing summer & winter: that the lot for the sd pavilions be delineated on the ground of the breadth of feet with two parallel sides of indefinite length, and that the pavilion first to be erected be placed on one of the lines so delineated, with it's floor in such degree of elevation from the ground as may[9] corrrespond with the regular inclined plane to which it may admit of being reduced hereafter.

And it is further resolved that so far as the funds may admit, the Proctor be requested to proceed to the erection of dormitories for the students adjacent to the said pavilion, not exceeding ten on each side, of brick, & of regular architecture according to the same plan proposed.

The board proceeding to consider the plan of a lottery prepared by the trustees of the Albemarle academy approve of the same, and resolve that it be carried into execution and without delay by the Proctor and by such agents as he shall appoint, and that the monies to be recieved for tickets by those entrusted with the sale of them, be from time to time & at short periods paid into the hands of the proctor and by him deposited in the bank of Virginia in Richmond, with which bank it is thought expedient that an account should be opened with him in trust for the Central College.

Resolved that a subscription paper be prepared, and placed in such hands as the Proctor shall deem will be most likely to promote it with energy and success in which shall be different[10] columns, to wit one for those who may prefer giving a donation in gross, another for those who may be willing to give a certain sum annually for the term of four years; and a third for donations in any other form; and that the monies subscribed be disposed of as they are recieved by the Proctor, in the manner above prescribed for those received on the lottery.

Resolved that Thomas Jefferson and John H. Cocke be a Committee on the part of the Visitors with authority jointly or severally[11] to advise and sanction all plans and the application of monies for executing them, which may be within the purview and functions of the Proctor for the time being.[12]

May 5. 1817.

TH: JEFFERSON
JAMES MONROE
JAMES MADISON
J. H. COCKE[13]

MS (ViU: TJP-VMTJ); in TJ's hand except for final paragraph in James Madison's hand, signed by TJ, James Monroe, Madison, and John H. Cocke; edge chipped and damaged at crease, with some missing text supplied from Tr in ViU: TJP-VMJCC. Tr (ViU: TJP-VMJCC). Tr (ViU: TJP-VMJHC). Tr (ViU: TJP-VMJB). Tr (ViU: VMJLC).

For the plan FOR ERECTING A DISTINCT PAVILION, see Estimate and Plans for Albemarle Academy/Central College, [ca. 18 Nov. 1814]. The PLAN OF A LOTTERY is described in Minutes of the Albemarle Academy Board of Trustees, 3 May 1814.

1 Word interlined in place of "April."

2 TJ here canceled "David Watson."

3 TJ here canceled "papers <*of*> and."

4 Remainder of paragraph interlined in place of "and were recommitted to the said Alexander Garrett with a request that he will keep them under his charge, and act as Secretary to this board until one shall be regularly appointed."

5 TJ here canceled a paragraph reading "On reading the rules of proceeding of the trustees of the Albemarle academy established at their meeting of the   day of   the same are approved and adopted for the ordinary government of this board; Except."

6 Word interlined in place of "authorised."

7 VMJCC and VMJHC Trs: "Frederickville."

8 Preceding four words interlined.

9 TJ here canceled "be adapted."

10 Word interlined in place of "two."

11 Preceding three words interlined.

12 Paragraph in Madison's hand.

13 All Trs here add Valentine W. Southall's name as secretary.

II. John H. Cocke's Description of Central College Board of Visitors Meeting

[5 May 1817]

5. A Cloudy Morng. Left home at $\frac{1}{4}$ before 4 O'Clock, and reached Monticello at $\frac{1}{4}$ after 8—Found the Family just up from Breakfast and the three illustrious Gentlemen with whom I was to act waiting for my arrival.—After getting Breakfast—rode again over the grounds offer'd as a site for the College by Mr Perry & already approved of by—Mr Cabell, Mr Jefferson & myself—Mr Madison & the President fully accorded in our views—Rode to the top of the small mountain which is to be embraced in the purchase from whence by taking some

object on the ridge of Carters Mountain Southward, Mr Jefferson observed a meridional line cou'd be established of 8 or 10 miles in length—a grand desideratum in the site of an observatory which he proposes this spot for—Mr Madison playfully remarked that this point shou'd be denominated the Apex of Science—Found Mr Madison, cheerful, communicative and very fond of conversing on agricultural subjects—fortunately for me that being the only subject upon which I had any chance of rendering myself at all interesting to a man of his superior acquirements & extensive knowledge—The President was serious and carried the marks of much care upon his brow—Mr Jefferson as usual was Easy & communicative—and under the full influence of his characteristic zeal for the success of the scheme for the establishment of the College—of which he may be fairly said to be the Father—May it prosper & bring forth the fruits of Science. After viewing the land which lies about 1 mile to the west of Charlottesville we returned and retiring to one of the jury rooms in the C^{t} Ho: committed our proceedings to writing elected Alexander Garret Esqre Proctor & Treasurer. & V. M. Southal Secretary to the board of Visitors—Mr Jefferson & myself were appointed a committee to aid, assist, & direct the Proctor in the execution of the buildings And the Proctor was order'd to proceed to conclude the purchase of the Land and obtain possession of the funds transfer'd to the Institution from the Albemarle Academy by act of the Legislature—Session 1815 & 1816—

Declined dining at Monticello that I might assist my friends Peter Minor, Col^{o} I A Coles, W^{m} F, Gordon, Capt. Jno Coles—& others who had been long anxious to make the effort, to establish an agricultural Society at Charlottesville—We according formed a meeting consisting of the following Gentlemen either present or by proxey—Mr Jefferson, I A Coles John Coles, Frank Carr, John Campbell Wm Woods—Wm F. Gordon Doctor Chas Cocke—Peter Minor Tucker Coles, Dabney Minor, Danl F. Carr, John Gilmer, George Gilmer, Thos M. Randolph, Thos Jefferson Randolph, Doctor Mann Page, John Patterson, Saml Carr & Alexander Garret of Albemarle.

Jos: C. Cabell, Robt Rives & W^{m} C Rives of Nelson—

J. H. Cocke & Wilson J. Cary of Fluvanna—

James Barbour, P. P. Barbour & Dabney Minor of Orange.

David Watson, & Frederick Harris of Louisa.—

A committee consisting of the following Gentlemen was appointed to prepare a system of Rules & Regulations for the Society to be submitted to the next meeting to be held on the first day of the Fall Circuit Court at Charlottesville—to wit Mr Jefferson, James Barbour, John Patterson, Jos: C. Cabell, & J. H. Cocke.—

Went to Monticello in the Eveng. but finding much company in y[e] House went home with Tho[s] J. Randolph accompanied by my friend J Patterson—

MS (ViU: JHC); diary entry entirely in Cocke's hand; partially dated.

III. Anonymous Description of Central College Board of Visitors Meeting

[5 May 1817]

"On Monday last, our court day in Charlottesville, we were gratified in seeing together, Mr. Jefferson, Mr. Madison and Mr. Monroe, the three most illustrious men of Virginia, and successive Presidents of the U. States. The presence of these gentlemen, two of whom have filled with distinguished ability and success, the first office in the gift of a free people, and have successively retired from their high stations, crowned with the gratitude and cheered by the applause of their country, and the other just elevated to the same distinction, and justifying the hopes and anticipations of his countrymen, by a life of ardent and sucessful devotion to the public good, excited feelings of grateful triumph. It was indeed a gratifying spectacle to the friends of free government—a practical commentary on our republican institutions, well calculated to refute the sophisters of arbitrary power, to silence the slanderers of popular government, and to correct the honest apprehensions and timid misgivings of its friends. Contrasted with the tremendous vicissitudes by which power has been usurped and lost during thirty years in Europe, with the gloomy tragedies which have been acted, or are still acting, on that theatre of blood—the state of our happy country is a subject of just triumph and grateful acknowledgement—A view of our happy condition, and the feelings of gratitude rising in my bosom, in contemplating the miseries of other nations, and comparing our fortunate allotment with their's, has hurried me beyond my usual moderation. These reflections are not, however, altogether misplaced—much of our prosperity and happiness, under heaven, is owing to the freedom of our government, and the just and liberal policy of our administrations.—The presence of the three illustrious Citizens who have had for many years past an important concern in the management of the public affairs of our country, naturally excites panegyric on that popular form of government which enables the public to command such talents and virtues.

"You may judge that our feelings of gratitude and pleasure, were encreased, when it was known that motives still directed to their country's good, had brought them together—They are visitors of the "Central College," lately established in this county—and, together with General Cocke, another of the visitors, met on Monday, for the first time, to commence its organization. They proceeded to purchase two hundred acres of land, upon which they have fixed the scite for the College, upon a beautiful and commanding eminence, about one mile from the town, and to determine upon the erection of a building, which tho' comparatively small, is intended hereafter as their funds increase, to form a part of a more extensive establishment upon a plan which may be enlarged or curtailed without deranging its order or beauty—It is contemplated to increase the funds, in the first place, by a lottery already authorised by law, and secondly, by subscriptions throughout the middle section of the state. From the central position of the College, from the remarkable healthiness of the country around it, and especially from the character of its visitors who seem to have espoused its interest with a zeal and enthusiasm that nothing can baffle—great reliance I think may be placed upon this scheme for its advancement. It is hoped too that the Legislature in its contemplated scheme of public seminaries will not overlook this rising institution, which if properly endowed, and under the auspices of its present visitors, would bid fair to rival the first establishment of the kind in the Union."

Printed in *Richmond Enquirer*, 23 May 1817; at head of text: "*Extract of a letter to a gentleman in this City, from his Correspondent, dated*—CHARLOTTESVILLE, May 7th, 1817."

An earlier report in the *Richmond Enquirer* of 13 May 1817 stated that on MONDAY 5 May 1817, "three men were seen together at Charlottesville (county of Albemarle) each of whom alone is calculated to attract the eager gaze of their Fellow-Citizens—We mean, Thomas Jefferson, James Madison, and James Monroe, two of them, ex-presidents, and the last the present President of the U. States. They have been friends for years, and are as sincere friends at this moment.—Messrs. Madison and Monroe had attended Mr. J. on horseback, from Monticello to Charlottesville; to assist in fixing a scite for a 'Central College'—under the Act of the General Assembly.* The appearance of three such men together at a village where the citizens of the county had met to attend their court, is an event, which for its singularity, deserves the notice of a passing paragraph.
*The Trustees are the three gentlemen already named, Gen. Cocke (who attended.) and Messrs. Cabell and Watson. On this day, the scite of the College was fixed upon, and the ground purchased."

IV. Central College Subscription List

[ca. 7 May 1817]

CENTRAL COLLEGE.

Considering the right of self-government among the greatest political blessings, that this cannot be maintained but by an intelligent and instructed people, that to disseminate instruction, institutions for the purpose must be multiplied and made convenient, that the College proposed to be established near Charlottesville, under the name of the CENTRAL COLLEGE, will facilitate the means of education to a considerable extent of country round about it, and that the salubrity of its climate and other local advantages will present it favourably to the notice of parents and guardians:

WE, the subscribers, do hereby promise to pay to the visitors of the said Central College, or their authorised officer or agent, in trust, for the purposes of the said College, the sums severally and respectively herein affixed to our several names; that is to say, all single sums in gross annexed to our names to be paid on the first day of April 1818, and all sums noted to be annual for the term of four years to be paid annually on the first day of April 1818, and of the three following years.

Subscribers Names[1]	Residence[2]	Sum subscribed.	Terms sub-scripturd[3]	Total $[s]
THOMAS JEFFERSON	Albemarle.	one thousand dollars	4 annual Instal[ts]	$1000.00
GEORGE DIVERS	"	one thousand dollars	ditto	1000.
JOHN H COCKE	Fluvanna	one thousand dollars	ditto	1000.
JOSEPH C CABELL	Nelson	one thousand dollars	ditto	1000[4]
NIMROD BRAMHAM	Albemarle	Five hundred dollars	ditto	500
JAMES LEITCH	Charlottesville	Five hundred dollars	ditto	500
ALEX GARRETT	"	Five hundred dollars	ditto	500
DAVID ISAACS	"	two hundred dollars	ditto	200
THOMAS WELLS	"	two hundred dollars	ditto	200
JOHN POLLOCK	"	two hundred dollars	ditto	200
JOSEPH BISHOP	"	two hundred dollars	ditto	200
SAMUEL CARR	Albemarle	Five hundred dollars	ditto	500

Thomas J Randolph	"	Five hundred dollars	ditto	500
John C Ragland	Charlottesville	two hundred dollars	ditto	200
Robert Gentry	Albemarle	one hundred dollars	ditto	100
Ira Garrett	"	one hundred dollars	ditto	100
Jesse W Garth	Charlottesville	two hundred dollars	ditto	200
John M Perry	Albemarle	two hundred dollars	ditto	200
Benjamin Austin	Charlottesville	One hundred dollars	ditto	100
Allen Dawson	"	One hundred dollars	ditto	100
Hugh Chisholm[5]	"	One hundred dollars	ditto	100
William Watson	"	one hundred dollars	ditto	100[6]
William Dunkum	Albemarle	one hundred dollars	ditto	100
Clifton Harris	"	one hundred dollars	ditto	100
John Winn	Charlottesville	three hundred dollars	ditto	300
William H Merewether	Albemarle	two hundred dollars	ditto	200
John Scott jr	"	Five hundred dollars	ditto	500
Cash[7]	"	twenty dollars	ditto	20
Daniel Mayo Railey	"	one hundred dollars	ditto	100
Nicholas H Lewis	"	three hundred dollars	ditto	300.
Jesse Garth	"	One hundred & fifty dollars	ditto	150
Micajah Woods	"	two hundred dollars	ditto	200
Tucker Coles	"	Five hundred dollars	ditto	500
Isaac A Coles	"	two hundred dollars	ditto	200
Walter Coles	"	two hundred dollars	ditto	200
John Coles	"	Five hundred dollars	ditto	500
Mann Page	"	Four hundred dollars	ditto	400
Charles Cocke	"	Five hundred dollars	ditto	500[8]

John Patterson	"	One thousand dollars	ditto	1000
Wilson C Nicholas	"	one thousand dollars	ditto	1000[9]
James Minor	Albemarle	three hundred dollars	ditto	300
Drury Wood	Albemarle	one hundred dollars	ditto	100
James H Terrel	"	two hundred dollars	ditto	200
Dabney Minor	"	four hundred dollars	ditto	400
Frank Carr	"	four hundred dollars	ditto	400
Martin Thacker	"	Sixty dollars	ditto	60
Charles Brown	Charlottesville	One hundred dollars	ditto	100
Jeremiah A Goodman[10]	"	fifty dollars	ditto	50
John Dunkum	"	One hundred dollars	ditto	100
James Lindsay	"	one hundred dollars	ditto	100
Ira Harris	"	One hundred dollars	ditto	100
Opie Norris	Charlottesville	three hundred dollars	ditto	300
William Leitch		One hundred dollars	ditto	100
William Garth	Albemarle	One hundred & fifty dollars	ditto	150
John H Craven	"	Five hundred dollars	ditto	500
Henry Chiles	"	One hundred dollars	ditto	100
John Fagg	"	one hundred dollars	ditto	100
W^m F Gordon	"	four hundred dollars	ditto	400
Reuben Maury	"	One hundred dollars	ditto	100
John H. Marks[11]	"	one hundred dollars	ditto	100
Garland Garth	"	three hundred dollars	ditto	300
James W Saunders	Charlottesville	Fifty dollars	ditto	50
Willis D Garth	Albemarle	Eighty dollars	ditto	80

Thomas Draffen	"	Sixty dollars	ditto	60
Benjamin Harden	"	One hundred dollars	ditto	100
John Slaughter	"	Fifty dollars	ditto	50
Charles Harper	"	two hundred dollars	ditto	200
Daniel F Carr	"	two hundred dollars	ditto	200
John Minor	"	two hundred dollars	ditto	200
James Garnett	"	Fifty dollars	ditto	50.
[*Signatures on ViU: JHC MS:*]				
Charles A Scott		five hundred dollars	ditto[12]	500
Wilson J. Cary		two hundred dollars	ditto	200.
Horatio Wills		forty Dollar	ditt°	40
John R Perkins		Forty Dollars	"	40
Wm B. Johnson		one hundred	ditto	100
Josa Key		Forty Dollars	ditto	40
Miles Cary		one hundred dollars	do	100
William Pasteur		Eighty dolls	do	80
John Fuqua		Forty dollars	4 Annual Instalmts	$40
John Winn jr		Fifty dollars	ditto	50
George Holeman		two hundred	D°	200
Jacob Myers		one hundred	D°	100
[*Entries specific to CSmH MS:*]				
Norborne K. Thomas	"[13]	One Hund^d^ & Seventy five	"[14]	175
Howel Lewis	"	Two Hundred dollars	"	200
. L. Thomas	"	One Hundred dollars	"	100
John Thomas	"	Forty dollars	"	40

Edmund Anderson	Richmond	Two hundred dollars	"	200
Peter Minor	Albemarle	Five Hundred dollars	"	500
Charles Day	Charlottesville	Fifty dollars	"	50
Dixon Dedman	Albemarle	Fifty dollars	"	50
Zachariah Shackleford	"	Two Hundred dollars	"	200
John Watson L.M.	"	One Hundred & fifty d[ls]	"	150
Nelson Barksdale	"	Two Hundred dollars	"	200
John Fretwell	"	One Hundred dollars	"	100
William Brown	"	Twenty dollars	"	20
William J. Robertson	"	One Hundred dollars	"	100
Nathaniel Anderson	"	One Hundred dollars	"	100
Nelson T. Shelton	"	One Hundred dollars	"	100
Robert L. Coleman	"	One Hundred dollars	"	100
William A. Shelton	"	One Hundred dolls	"	100
William Morris	"	Twenty dollars	"	20
				$22325
Elijah Brown	"	One hundred dollars		100

MS (ViU: JHC); printed form, with bulk of entries in a clerk's hand, but ending with twelve entries in the hands of Fluvanna County subscribers that are specific to this text; undated; lacking column headings and column of subscribers' residences. MS (CSmH: Robert Alonzo Brock Collection); printed form, with all entries in a clerk's hand; following the order of names in preceding text except as noted, but ending with twenty entries listing subscribers from Albemarle County, Charlottesville, and Richmond, in the same clerk's hand, which are specific to this text; undated. Tr (ViU); typescript; largely following the order of names in preceding texts; lacking column headings and column of subscribers' residences; undated; at head of text: "a copy Taken from a copy of John Coles, Esq., donated by the Rev. Isaac Coles for copying, May 20, 1929"; with 21 May 1929 certification that it is "A true copy" signed by Luther Greene and Wesley Greene.

Although no manuscript version of the introductory text at the head of the subscription list survives in TJ's hand, he probably drafted it. In his diary entry for 7 May 1817, John H. Cocke wrote that he "Returned to Charlottesville about mid day Accompanied Mr Garret, the Proctor, & Southall the Secretary to Monticello to dinner to get the subscription papers which M^r^ J— had been preparing for promoting the college & that I might have an opportunity to subscribe before I left the County—Mr Jefferson head[s] the list of subscribers with a thousand dollars—followed his Example to the same amo^t^ for myself & also for my friend Jos: C. Cabell who had authorized me to subscribe for him what the other visitors did—Mr Madison had left Monticello & the President had proceed'd also to Washington— Was detained all night by rain at Monticello" (MS in ViU: JHC; in Cocke's hand; one word editorially corrected).

TJ enclosed blank subscription forms to Craven Peyton on 28 June 1817 and to William A. Burwell, John Wayles Eppes, William B. Giles, Randolph Harrison, Thomas Newton, James Pleasants, and Archibald Thweatt on 4 Aug. 1817.

The name of JOHN MINOR, of Albemarle County, is not on the Master List of Subscribers to Central College printed immediately below. L.M.: Little Mountain.

[1] Column headings supplied from CSmH MS.

[2] Column for place of residence supplied from CSmH MS.

[3] Order of final two columns reversed in CSmH MS.

[4] Order of preceding three names given in ViU Tr as Cocke, Cabell, and Divers.

[5] ViU MS: "Chisholmn." Both other texts: "Chisholm."

[6] Entry for Watson not in ViU Tr.

[7] CSmH MS here adds "rec^d^ by J.L." and leaves column for term of subscription blank.

[8] ViU Tr here adds "a Copy" and indicates that at this point the intermediate sum of $12,670 was added in pencil.

[9] ViU Tr ends here, with entries for Patterson and Nicholas reversed, followed by "a Copy."

[10] Preceding seven names in a different order in CSmH MS (Minor, Carr, Thacker, Brown, Wood, Terrell, and Goodman), with ditto marks following Goodman's name correctly indicating that his place of residence was Albemarle County rather than Charlottesville.

[11] Middle initial supplied from CSmH MS.

[12] That is, four annual installments, here and below.

[13] That is, Albemarle County, here and below.

[14] That is, four annual installments, here and below.

V. Master List of Subscribers to Central College

[after 7 May 1817]

Subscriptions to the Central College from persons residing in the county of Albemarle and in other counties and places.

Names.	Sum subscribed.	No. of installments.
Albemarle county.		
Nathaniel Anderson,	$100 00	4 installments.
Benjamin Austin,	100 00	"
Nelson Barksdale,	200 00	"
Joseph Bishop,	200 00	"
Nimrod Bramham,	500 00	"
Achillis Broadhead,	75 00	"
Charles Brown,	100 00	"
William Brown,	20 00	"
Elijah Brown,	100 00	"
William Brown,	25 00	"
Samuel Carr,	500 00	
Frank Carr,	400 00	
Daniel F. Carr,	200 00	
James O. Carr,	300 00	
John F. Carr,	50 00	
Henry Chiles,	100 00	
Hugh Chisholm,	100 00	
James Clarke,	200 00	
Joseph Coffman,	50 00	
Charles Cocke,	500 00	
Robert L. Coleman,	100 00	
Tucker Coles,	500 00	
John Coles,	500 00	
Isaac A. Coles,	200 00	
Walter Coles,	200 00	
John H. Craven,	500 00	
Isaac Curd,	100 00	
Cash,	20 00	
Allen Dawson,	100 00	
Martin Dawson,	200 00	
James Dinsmore,	200 00	
Dixon Deadman,	50 00	
George Divers,	1,000 00	

Charles Day,	50 00	
William Dunkum,	100 00	
John Dunkum,	100 00	
Thomas Draffen,	60 00	
Samuel Dyer, sr.,	400 00	
Samuel Dyer, jr.,	200 00	
Francis B. Dyer,	100 00	
Archibald B. Duke,	50 00	
Richard Duke,	200 00	
Charles Everitte,	333 33	
John Fagg,	100 00	
John Fretwell,	100 00	
Jesse W. Garth,	200 00	
Jesse Garth, sr.,	150 00	
William Garth,	150 00	
Garland Garth,	300 00	
Willis D. Garth,	80 00	
Alexander Garrett,	500 00	4 installments
Ira Garrett,	100 00	
James Garnett,	50 00	
Robert Gentry,	100 00	
Jeremiah A. Goodman,	50 00	
William F. Gordon,	200 00	
John Goss,	200 00	
Clifton Harris,	100 00	
Ira Harris,	100 00	
John Harris,	1,000 00	
Benjamin Harden,	100 00	
Charles Harper,	200 00	
William Hamner,	20 00	
Andrew Hart,	100 00	
Samuel L. Hart,	100 00	
John Hudson,	100 00	
Thomas Jefferson,	1,000 00	
John Jones,	75 00	
David Isaacs,	200 00	
James Kinsolving, sr.,	50 00	
George W. Kinsolving,	50 00	
James Leitch,	500 00	
William Leitch,	100 00	
Nicholas H. Lewis,	300 00	
Howell Lewis,	200 00	

Jesse Lewis,	100 00	4 installments.
Reuben Lindsay, sr.,	1,000 00	
James Lindsay,	100 00	
Reuben Maury,	100 00	
Thomas W. Maury,	100 00	
John H. Marks,	100 00	
Francis McGehee,	40 00	
William H. Merewether,	200 00	
James Minor,	300 00	
Dabney Minor,	400 00	
Peter Minor,	500 00	5 installments.
James Monroe,	1,000 00	4 "
William Morris,	20 00	
Wilson C. Nicholas,	1,000 00	
Opie Norris,	300 00	
Mann Page,	400 00	
John Patterson,	1,000 00	
John M. Perry,	200 00	
Moses Perrygory,	25 00	
John Pollock,	200 00	
Peter Porter,	20 00	
Thomas J. Randolph,	500 00	4 installments.
Thomas E. Randolph,	200 00	
John C. Ragland,	200 00	
Daniel M. Railey,	100 00	
William J. Robertson,	100 00	
John Rogers,	200 00	
William Ragland,	25 00	1 installment.
James[1] W. Saunders,	50 00	
John Scott, jr.,	500 00	
Zachariah Shackleford,	200 00	
Nelson T. Shelton,	100 00	
William A. Shelton,	100 00	
John Slaughter,	50 00	
Valentine W. Southall,	200 00	
Lewis Teel,	100 00	
James H. Terrell,	200 00	
Martin Thacker,	60 00	
John L. Thomas,	100 00	
John Thomas, jr.,	40 00	
William Watson,	100 00	
John Watson, L. M.,	150 00	

John Walker,	20 00		
James G. Waddle,	160 00		
Christian Wertenbaker,	25 00		
John Winn,	300 00		
Arthur Whitehurst,	50 00		
Micajah Woods,	200 00		
Drury Wood,	100 00		
William Woods, S.,	200 00		
Richard Woods,	100 00		
James Wood,	50 00		
George M. Woods,	100 00		
Thomas Wood,	100 00		
		$27,443 33	
Amherst county.			
Richard S. Ellis,	100 00		
		100 00	
Buckingham county.			
John W. Eppes,	200 00		
		200 00	
Cumberland county.			
William Bondurant,	100 00		
George W. Bondurant,	50 00		
Jerman Baker,	100 00		
Alex. Cheatwood,	60 00		
F. B. Deane,	100 00		4 installments.
William Daniel,	100 00		
G. H. Fitzgerald,	40 00		
Randolph Harrison,	500 00		
Carter E. Harrison,	100 00		
Thomas H. Harrison,	200 00		
Jesse Hughes,	50 00		
James Jennings,	40 00		
Richard P. James,	50 00		
John Miller,	80 00		
John Page,	100 00		
William Skipwith,	50 00		
George N. Skipwith,	100 00		
Stephen W. Trent,	100 00		
Wm. M. Thornton,	100 00		
Thomas N. Walton,	10 00		
Hugh Watson,	50 00		
William H. Watkins,	40 00		

D. A. Wilson,	20 00		
J. B. Woodson,	20 00		
Charles Woodson,	30 00		
		2,190 00	
Fluvanna county.			
Wilson J. Cary,	200 00		
Miles Cary,	100 00		
John H. Cocke,	1,000 00		
John Dyer,	100 00		
John Fuqua,	40 00		
George Holeman,	200 00		
Wm. B. Johnson,	100 00		
Joshua Key,	40 00		
Jacob Myers,	100 00		
John R. Perkins,	40 00		
Wm. Pasture,	80 00		
Charles A. Scott,	500 00		
Horatio Wills,	40 00		
John Winn,	50 00		
		2,590 00	
Goochland county.			
Benjamin Anderson,	100 00		4 installments.
William Bolling,	100 00		
Archibald Bryce, jr.	50 00		
William F. Carter,	5 00		
John G. Crouch,	20 00		
W. Campbell,	25 00		
Edward Garland,	100 00		
Thomas Miller,	100 00		
Thomas Pemberton,	100 00		
George C. Pickett,	50 00		
James Pleasants, jr.	100 00		
Wm. G. Pendleton,	100 00		
Thomas M. Randolph,	100 00		
Wm. Salmon,	5 00		
Richard Sampson,	50 00		
George S. Smith,	20 00		
Joseph S. Watkins,	100 00		
Thomas B. Watkins,	20 00		
Benjamin P. Watkins,	20 00		
Tarlton Woodson,	20 00		
		1,185 00	

Loudoun county.		
Armstead T. Mason,	200 00	
		200 00
Louisa county.		
Frederick Harris,	400 00	
William Morris, jr.	200 00	
James Minor,	200 00	
George W. Trueheart,	200 00	
James Watson,	200 00	
David Watson,	200 00	
		1,400 00
Lynchburg.		
S. J. Harrison,	200 00	
Charles Johnston,	200 00	
William Mitchell,	200 00	
Robert Morris,	200 00	
Richard Pollard,	100 00	
Thomas Wells,	200 00	
Joel Yancey,	200 00	
		1,300 00
Nelson county.		
Joseph C. Cabell,	1,000 00	
William Cabell, sen'r,	100 00	
Landon Cabell,	200 00	
George Calloway,	100 00	
John P. Cobbs,	200 00	
John Digges,	50 00	
Henry Dawson,	24 00	
Spottswood Garland,	100 00	
William B. Hare,	100 00	
Robert J. Kincaid,	50 00	
Samuel Loving,	50 00	
Thomas S. McClelland,	100 00	
John Mosby,	28 00	
Zachariah Nevil,	50 00	
Robert Rives,	500 00	
William C. Rives,	200 00	
Joseph Shelton,	50 00	
Michael Woods,	50 00	
		2,952 00
Orange county.		
Samuel Hardesty,	30 00	

James Madison,	1,000 00		
		1,030 00	
Richmond city.			
Edmund Anderson,	200 00		
William Carter,	500 00		
John Coalter,	100 00		
F. W. Gilmer,	100 00		
Jacqueline B. Harvie,	500 00		
Jesse B. Key,	200 00		
Hall Neilson,	30 00		
Bernard Peyton,	200 00		
B. Roddy,	20 00		
Norborne K. Thomas,	175 00		
St. George Tucker,	200 00		
		2,225 00	
Spottsylvania county.			
Francis W. Taliaferro,	400 00		
		400 00	
Stafford county.			
William Brent, Jr.	100 00		
		100 00	
Winchester.			
Dabney Carr,	100 00		
Hugh Holmes,	300 00		
Henry Lee, Jr.	200 00		
Henry St. George Tucker,	200 00		
		800 00	
Albemarle,			27,443 33
Amherst,			100 00
Buckingham,			200 00
Cumberland,			2,190 00
Fluvanna,			2,590 00
Goochland,			1,185 00
Loudoun,			200 00
Louisa,			1,400 00
Lynchburg,			1,300 00
Nelson,			2,952 00
Orange,			1,030 00
Richmond city,			2,225 00
Spottsylvania,			400 00
Stafford,			100 00
Winchester,			800 00
			$44,115 33

Printed in *Early History of the University of Virginia, as contained in the letters of Thomas Jefferson and Joseph C. Cabell, hitherto unpublished*, ed. Nathaniel F. Cabell (1856), 404–12; undated; with internal running totals at breaks of printed pages editorially omitted.

This cumulative list was compiled from pledges made after the printed subscription forms were prepared, about 7 May 1817.

L. M.: Little Mountain. THOMAS WELLS resided in Charlottesville, not Lynchburg.

[1] Printed text: "John."

To Fernagus De Gelone

SIR Monticello May 6. 17.

Casting my eye again over your catalogue, I find two other books I should be glad to possess

Architecture de Vitruve. 12mo pa. 5.

Cormon Dictionnaire François & Espagnol 2. v. 8vo

these may also come by the mail only sending them separately a volume at a time, and a week apart to avoid loading our weekly mail. send first, if you please, the Vol. of Cormon Span. & French. a note of the cost being sent, the sum shall be remitted. I salute you with esteem and respect TH: JEFFERSON

PoC (MHi); on verso of reused address cover to TJ; at foot of text: "Fernagus de Gelone"; endorsed by TJ.

To John Wood

DEAR SIR Monti[cello] May. 6. 17.

You mentioned once to me at Poplar Forest that there was about 5. years ago noted in the Edinburg Review a Greek and English Lexicon, a general one, & not merely of the N. testament. I am just sending off a catalogue to be brought from London, and should be glad to get this, if you can with as little delay as convenient furnish me the title. I have not the Edinburg Review of that period, or I would not give you this trouble.

The trustees of the N. London academy are without a teacher, and would be very glad to employ you, and desired me to mention it to you. you know the place and it's circumstances as well as myself, so I need not repeat them.

We had a meeting yesterday at Charlottesville of the Visitors of the Central College proposed to be established near that place. mr Madison, Col^{o} Monroe General Cocke and myself attended. mr Cabell & mr Watson, the other two visitors were not there. we fixed on a scite, on the road above the town 1. mile, purchased the land, and shall instantly begin a pavilion for one professor, containing a schoolroom, below & 2. chambers for the Professor above, which we count on finishing by Spring, when we propose to engage a Professor for the Classics and begin. the next summer we shall erect another pavilion for another professorship and so on as our funds come in. speaking for myself, as 1. of 6. I should ask your undertaking the first, which I mention now for your consideration. there are ulterior views, but they are uncertain. Accept the assurance of my esteem & respect.

Th: Jefferson

PoC (DLC); on verso of reused address cover of Joseph C. Cabell to TJ, 4 Aug. 1816; dateline faint; at foot of text: "M[r] John Wood"; endorsed by TJ.

To Isaac A. Coles

[Dea]r Sir Monticello May 7. 17.

Have you any orchard grass seed left? or have your brothers any? I want about a bushel to finish a grass lot now prepared for it, [an]d should be very thankful for that much.—I looked for you at court [to] invite you to come and see mrs Madison & mr Madison, but could not [fin]d you. I thought too you ought not to need an invitation to come here or to see them. Appleton of Leghorn has sent me some grass seed (arrived [at?] Boston) which he calls Lupinella, of which he gives a very high account as to produce 6000 ℔ in the ground which requires 2. bushels of wheat when sown in wheat. when I recieve it I shall wish to distribute it among careful farmers, in which number I count you. ever & affectionately yours

Th: Jefferson

PoC (MHi); on verso of portion of reused address cover to TJ; some text lost along left margin due to polygraph misalignment, with one word rewritten by TJ; at foot of text: "Col[o] Coles"; endorsed by TJ.

To Joseph Darmsdatt

Dear Sir Monticello May 7. 17.

The advance of the season having reminded me that the supposed arrival of fresh herrings made it time to ask for the annual supply, a doubt arose in my mind whether I had paid you for the last, and proceeding to examine my papers, I find I have not. I cannot account for this lapse of attention, unless it be (as I find no note of the amount from you) that I have waited to recieve that until it escaped my memory altogether. still uninformed of it I must ask the favor of you to call on mr Gibson for it, whatever it may be, and adding to it the amount of what I now write for, he will be so good as to pay both on presenting this letter.

The supply now to be asked for is of 6. barrels of herrings & 1. of shad to be sent to Milton by Johnson's boat who will call for it in about ten days, and 6. barrels of herrings to be sent to Lynchburg to the address of mr Archibald Robertson, who will pay the freight. if on enquiry for the Lynchburg boats D[r] Cabell's should happen to be there, they would be preferred, if not, then by such as you shall think best. I salute you with great esteem and respect.

TH: JEFFERSON

PoC (MHi); on verso of reused address cover to TJ; at foot of text: "M[r] Joseph Darmsdat"; endorsed by TJ.

In his records for the previous day, TJ indicated that he "Wrote to Joseph Darmsdat for 12. bar. herrings & 1. of shad and desired him to call on Mr. Gibson for the amount of these & of the last year's like supply, not paid for" (*MB*, 2:1333).

From Isaac A. Coles

DEAR SIR, Enniscorthy may 8th 1817.

I have not an Orchard Grass seed left, but as I think it possible that my Brother may still have some on hand, I have directed your servant to go there—I fear however, as it is now so much later than we are in the habit of sowing it, that you will be disappointed in getting any—.

I only got a glimpse of you on monday as you ascended to the Jury room, and was called off to dine before you came down again—. I would have come up with Gen[l] Cocke in the evening to see you, & pay my respects to M[r] & M[rs] Madison, if I had not apprehended from the size of the party I heard were with you, that your House was entirely full.

I shall be very thankful for a few seed of the Lupinella when you receive it, & will certainly give it a fair experiment—In haste I am ever

faithfully & devotedly y[rs] I. A. COLES

RC (DLC); at foot of text: "Tho[s] Jefferson"; endorsed by TJ as received 9 May 1817 and so recorded in SJL.

From Fernagus De Gelone

SIR New York 8. May 1817.

I directed to you per mail accordingly to your order, two days ago, a copy of Euclide par Peyrard. the price is two dollars—and fifty cents. I enclosed my late catalogues.

I am most respectfully Sir Your most obedient humble Servant

J: LOUIS FERNAGUS DE GELONE

RC (MHi); at head of text: "Thomas Jefferson. Monticelo"; endorsed by TJ as received 14 May 1817 and so recorded in SJL.

To Elkanah Watson

SIR Monticello May 8. 17.

I have duly recieved your favor of Apr. 24. and had long remarked the course and labors of the Berkshire[1] society, of which you were president. we have been indebted to them for much useful information, and for the example they have set of zeal in the most important of all human arts, agriculture. about a dozen years ago an effort was made at Washington for the establishment there of a general board of agriculture, to which were proposed to be affiliated a secondary board in each state, and to this again subordinary boards in every county. the person most active in producing this institution was Isaac Briggs of that neighborhood, who was made Secretary of it,[2] and mr Madison, while Secretary of state, was it's[3] president. he still I believe possesses the skeleton of the organisation;[4] but whether they ever published any thing, or not, I do not know. with respect to myself, you have been quite misinformed[5] as to my having any intention to take part[6] in any periodical publication, agricultural or of any other character. I know, with the Preacher, that there is a time for all things, a time to labor, as well as to cease from labor, and that this last time has fallen on me. dayly and hourly admonitions, physical and moral warn me to leave to other and younger citizens, the management of what are to be their own concerns, and to be contented with the share I have had in those of my own day. I submit to these monitions the more willingly as they favor that rest & quiet which the increasing debility of age calls for; & have therefore to offer only my prayers for success to the efforts of others, and praise to those engaged in them, among whom I distinguish yourself, and to whom I particularly address the assurance of my great respect. TH: JEFFERSON

RC (NjMoHP: Lloyd W. Smith Collection); holes in manuscript, with missing text supplied from PoC; at foot of text: "M[r] Elkanah Watson"; docketed by Watson: "Vide–President's Maddisons Letter on the Subject of a Nat[l] bord Agriculture this book p[g] 164." PoC (DLC). Tr (Lb in N: Watson Papers).

The GENERAL BOARD OF AGRICULTURE organized by Isaac Briggs was the American Board of Agriculture. At its founding meeting on 22 Feb. 1803, Briggs and James Madison were elected secretary and president, respectively (*PTJ*, 37:339–40). The biblical reference to A TIME FOR ALL THINGS is from Ecclesiastes 3.1–8.

[1] Tr here interlines "ag[l]."
[2] Instead of preceding nine words, Tr reads "who was Sec[y]."
[3] Preceding six words not in Tr.
[4] Remainder of sentence not in Tr.
[5] Reworked from "uninformed."
[6] Remainder of sentence not in Tr.

From Isaac Briggs

MY DEAR FRIEND, Philadelphia 5 mo. 9.–1817

I feel myself treading on sacred ground when I approach the scenes illuminated and made glorious by the mild lights of a long life uniformly dedicated to usefulness and to virtue. With veneration I approach the Wisdom of age—with love I approach my friend—yet with these delightful feelings is mixed some reluctance, when, for an object quite selfish, I invade the tranquility of thy retirement and disturb the repose of thy evening, by asking, for myself, a favor.

I was informed yesterday, that my name had been mentioned to DeWitt Clinton, as a person proper to be employed in ascertaining the direction and level of some important lines relating to the grand Canal proposed to be made from Lake Erie. DeWitt Clinton, who is President of the Board of Commissioners, suggested the propriety of my making an application for the appointment, aided by the testimonials of those who know my qualifications. My friends here are quite willing to say all they know, but it is supposed a line from thee would have more weight than all the rest, as I was engaged in some important works, under thy administration as President, and much within thy view. The Board will meet in New York on the 15 instant, but 6 days hence—will it be too great a task for thee to address a line on this subject to DeWitt Clinton? if it should not reach him precisely by the 15, perhaps it may still be of service.

Until yesterday morning, all my expectations of advantageous business seemed to have been disappointed in succession, and almost every door of hope seemed closed in anguish,—as an anchor to a mind tossed on the waves of affliction, there remained a little Faith in the merciful Providence of God. I had often remembered with the consolation of hope the beautiful passage, quoted, in thy letter to my Daughter, Mary, "I have been young, now I am old, yet never have I known the righteous to suffer, or his seed begging their bread." Yesterday afternoon, when almost every hope had fled, the information of this prospect in New York, broke suddenly and unexpectedly upon me like a light from Heaven.

If my prayers will avail aught, they are always offered up for thy happiness, here and hereafter.

With sentiments of Love, Veneration and Gratitude,

I salute thee. ISAAC BRIGGS.

N.B. I expect to be in New York from the 13 instant, until the business as it respects me, shall be decided. I. B.

RC (DLC); endorsed by TJ as received 17 May 1817 and so recorded in SJL. RC (Forbes Magazine Collection, New York City, 2003); address cover only; with PoC of TJ to James Dinsmore, 25 June 1817, on verso; addressed by Briggs: "Thomas Jefferson, Monticello, near Charlottesville, Albemarle Cy Va," with his additional notation: "To be forwarded with Speed"; franked; postmarked Philadelphia, 9 May. FC (MdHi: Briggs-Stabler Papers); entirely in Briggs's hand; lacking postscript; endorsed by Briggs.

I HAVE BEEN YOUNG . . . BEGGING THEIR BREAD alludes to TJ's quotation of Psalms 37.25 in his 17 Apr. 1816 letter to Mary B. Briggs.

From Frank Carr

DEAR SIR, Bentivar May 9th 1817

We have received a letter from Mr Terrell in which he complains that letters under date of April 11th 1816 were the only letters he had received from his friends in this country. These were the first letters written to him, & his anxiety is very great. All others have fail'd to reach him—It was thro' your friendly aid that they were forwarded; and that the enclosed may more certainly arrive at it's destination, for which his state of anxiety makes us all solicitous, you will add to the numerous obligations under which you have laid all his friends, by putting it into the channel of your communications with Europe, & giving us directions how future letters may reach him.

With sincere respect &c I am &c FRANK CARR

RC (ViU: TJP-CC); endorsed by TJ as received 14 May 1817 and so recorded in SJL.

THE ENCLOSED probably included a letter written at Bentivar on 5 May 1817 from Martha J. Terrell (Minor) to her brother Dabney C. Terrell in Geneva, in which she assured him that although he had received no letters, many had been sent to him; informed him of the birth of their nephew, Peter Carr, and the subsequent death on 22 June 1816 of the baby's mother, their sister Virginia Terrell

Carr; and announced her intention to "enclose mine in a polite note to M[r] Jefferson, begging him to forward this, and inform me how to direct in future" (RC in ViU: Papers of the Carr and Terrell Families; addressed: "Mr: Dabney C. Terrell," with "at Geneva" added in a different hand).

From Robert H. Saunders

Dear Sir, Short pump May 9th 1817

Having met with considerable losses from the fall of lightning upon several species of[1] property at my plantation in the County of Goochland and to guard as much as possible against such an occurrance at this place have come to a resolution of Erecting one or more Franklins as I Shall be advised by You, to my present dwelling,—After giving you a description of the house you perhaps may be the better able to Judge correctly.—my house is 32 feet long two stories high and Twenty feet wide, the whole Altitude 34. feet, it has a wing at each end, one of which is thirty two feet long the other 16 makeing the whole length of the building 80 feet.

There stands at the west end of the house three oak trees one a little N. of west,—from, the chimney 39 feet, one west 40 feet, the other s. west 39 feet all of which projects one or two feet above the top of the Chimney and none of which exceeds the distance of 24 feet from the end of the wing.—At the E. end there stands about 12 or thirteen lofty trees; all of which are several feet higher than the chimney which is at that end.—one of which stands about 15 feet from the chimney & three others in different directions not exceeding thirty feet.—Having now given you the length, breadth, & height; of the house, and the contiguity of a number of trees;—You will be so good as to answer the following questions, First is it necessary for the safety of a house that there should be a Franklin or Franklins attached to it

2[ly] If necessary; will my house require one or more if the latter where ought they to be put.

3[ly] will not the trees above spoken of in some measure superceed the necessity of a Franklin by the aptitude the Lightning has of striking the most elivated objects.

4[ly] If necessary to set up one or more conductors, shall I make them fast to polls set up for that purpose or shall I fix them to some of the trees nearest to the house.

5[ly] Shall I use any precaution where the conductor passes through the iron boults, to prevent its flying off from the Franklin

6ly Is it necessary that the rod should go to any debth in the Earth, or is it material that it Should be inclosed with plank or otherwise.—

You will be so good as to pardon me for giving you so much trouble, nothing but the necessity of the case would have made me presume so much upon your Goodness. Be pleased to accept of a sincear tender of my best wishes, for your health, happiness, & prosperity while you are permited to stay in this World.

I am with great respect your most Obt Hble Sert

Ro. H. Saunders

RC (MHi); addressed: "Thomas Jefferson Esqure Monticller To the particular care of Mr Wells"; endorsed by TJ as received 15 June 1817 and so recorded in SJL.

Robert Hyde Saunders (ca. 1758–1833), innkeeper and farmer, enlisted in 1775 in a militia company from Cumberland (later Powhatan) County and became a sergeant in the 7th Virginia Regiment the following year. He was appointed an ensign in the 1st Virginia Regiment in 1777, rose to lieutenant later that same year, and resigned in 1778. Saunders afterwards served as an adjutant in 1781. By 1814 he was living at his Henrico County property called Short Pump, where he operated a tavern that catered to traffic between Richmond and Charlottesville and functioned as a health resort. Saunders also owned coal-producing land on Tuckahoe Creek and property in Goochland County. He was postmaster at Short Pump from 1819 until about 1826 and was appointed again in 1828. When Saunders died in Henrico County, his Short Pump property consisted of 741 acres (James Edmonds Saunders and Elizabeth Saunders Blair Stubbs, *Early Settlers of Alabama* [1899], 461; Petition by Saunders, 12 Nov. 1791 [Vi: RG 78, Legislative Petitions, Miscellaneous]; DNA: RG 15, SRRWPBLW; Vi: RG 3, Revolutionary War Bounty Warrants; *ASP*, *Public Lands*, 7:360; *The Pension Roll of 1835* [1835; indexed ed., 1992], 3:791; Vi: Business Records Collection, Mutual Assurance Society Declarations, nos. 476, 1322, 1323, 1327; *Richmond Enquirer*, 20 Nov. 1821, 28 May 1830, 12 Nov. 1833; Axelson, *Virginia Postmasters*, 94; *VMHB* 35 [1927]: 450; Henrico Co. Will Book, 8:377–9).

Saunders owned a PLANTATION called Bradford in Goochland County (Mutual Assurance Society Declarations, no. 1323). Lightning rods were called FRANKLINS in honor of Benjamin Franklin, their inventor (*OED*).

[1] Preceding three words interlined.

To William Thornton

Dear Sir Monticello May 9. 17

Your favor of Apr. 18. was duly recieved, and the two drawings were delivered here by mr & mrs Madison in perfect good order. with respect to Ciracchi's bust, any artist whom you may dispose to do so shall be welcome to come and make a cast of plaister from it. we have always plaister at hand.

We are commencing here the establishment of a college, and instead of building a magnificent house which would exhaust all our funds, we propose to lay off a square of about 7. or 800.f. on the outside of which we shall arrange separate pavilions, one for each professor and his scholars. each pavilion will have a schoolroom below, and 2 rooms for the Professor above and between pavilion and pavilion a range of dormitories for the boys, one story high, giving to each a room 10.f. wide & 14.f. deep. the pavilions about 36. wide in front and 24.f. in depth. this sketch will give you an idea of it

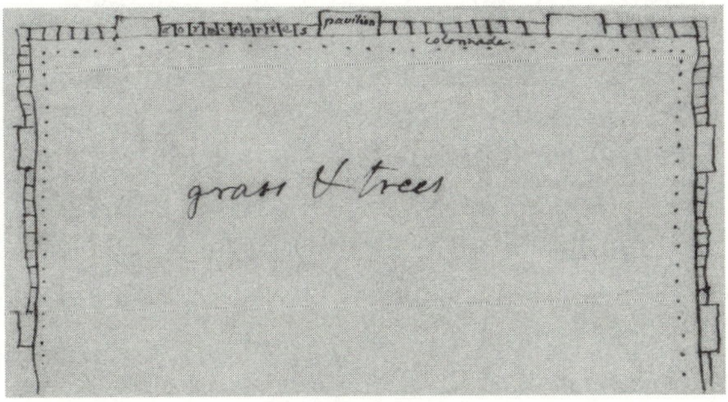

the whole of the pavilions and dormitories to be united by a colonnade in front of the height of the lower story of the pavilions, under which they may go dry from school to school. the colonnade will be of square brick pilasters (at first) with a Tuscan entablature. now what we wish is that these pavilions as they will shew themselves above the dormitories, shall be models of taste & good architecture, & of a variety of appearance, no two alike, so as to serve as specimens for the Architectural lectures. will you set your imagination to work and[1] sketch some designs for us. no matter how loosely with the pen, without the trouble of referring to scale or rule; for we want nothing but the outline of the architecture, as the internal must be arranged according to local convenience. a few sketches, such as need not take you a moment, will greatly oblige us. the visitors of the college are President Monroe, mr Madison, 3 others whom you do not know & myself. we have to struggle against two important wants, money, and men for professors, capable of fulfilling our views. they may come in time for all Europe seems to be breaking up. in the mean time help us to provide snug and handsome lodges for them. I salute you with friendship and respect.

TH: JEFFERSON

RC (DLC: Thornton Papers); addressed: "Dr William Thornton Washington. Col."; franked; postmarked Milton, 13 May; endorsed by Thornton: "Hon: Th: Jefferson—respecting a College in Virga—Ansd 27th May 1817." PoC (ViU: TJP); on portion of reused sheet with wax seal fragments; some sections faint; endorsed by TJ.

[1] PoC: "&."

From Alexander Garrett

ALEX: GARRETT TO M[R] JEFFERSON 10th May. 17.

A.G. had an interview with M[r] Perry on yesterday in which M[r] P. disclaimed all intentions of insisting upon any conditions being annexed to his conveyance of the land to the Central College, M[r] P. is to meet AG. in town to day, A.G. now hopes that the deed: as drawn will be signed by M[r] P. if not to day at some short period hereafter, in the mean time AG. thinks a silence and apparent indifference on his part best calculated to ensure his success— Alex Garrett presents M[r] Jefferson with a couple of shad which he hopes M[r] J will find good. A.G. was with M[r] Divers yesterday. he is better than he was a few days ago tho yet much indisposed.

RC (CSmH: JF); dateline at foot of text; addressed: "M[r] Jefferson Monticello"; endorsed by TJ.

To William Johnson

DEAR SIR Monticello May 10. 17.

I recieved from the hands of mr Madison your favor of Mar. 4. and it's elegant accompaniment the tortoise shell walking staff, for which, as in duty bound, I render many thanks. however singular it's merit, from the ingenious process by which the staff is formed, the claim of the head is more singular and important, as part of the tree which yielded cover to the incipient counsels which have changed and will change the face of the habitable globe, which have planted, and will plant freedom & happiness in soils never witnessing before but the wretchedness of savage life, or the oppressions of despotism. nor will I forget the merit it derives from the person of the giver. we have been associated in times and labors covered with awful gloom and painful anxieties for the destinies of our country, and we have lived to see those our labors and anxieties issue in the happiest forms and principles of administration which man has ever yet seen: and acquire, thro' a course of 24. years, past, or certain of passing, a force of habit which will protect them from change. these scenes, which we have witnessed, leave endearing impressions on fellow-laborers, which I can assure you with sincerity have lost none of their strength with me, and which I am happy in this occasion of expressing.

The pamphlet you were so kind as to send me manifests a zeal, which cannot be too much praised, for the interests of agriculture, the employment of our first parents in Eden, the happiest we can follow, and the most important to our country. while it displays the happy capabilities of that portion of it which you inhabit, it shews how much is yet to be done to develop them fully. I am not without hope that thro' your efforts and example, we shall yet see it a country abounding in wine and oil. North Carolina has the merit of taking the lead in the former culture, of giving the first specimen of an exquisite wine, produced in quantity, and established in it's culture beyond the danger of being discontinued. her Scuppernon wine, made on the South side of the Sound, would be distinguished on the best tables of Europe, for it's fine aroma, and chrystalline transparence. unhappily that aroma, in most of the samples I have seen, has been entirely submerged in brandy. this coarse taste and practice is the peculiarity of Englishmen, and of their apes Americans. I hope it will be discontinued, and that this fortunate example will encourage our country to go forward in this culture. the olive, the Sesamus, the Cane & Coffee offer field enough for the efforts of your's and the other states South & West of you. we, of this state, must make bread, and be contented with so much of that as a miserable insect will leave us. this remnant will scarcely feed us the present year, for such swarms of the Wheat-fly were never before seen in this country.—I salute you, dear Sir, with constant and undiminished affection and respect.

TH: JEFFERSON

PoC (DLC); at foot of first page: "Judge Wm Johnson."

To Josephus B. Stuart

DEAR SIR Monticello May 10. 17.

Your favor of Apr. 25th[1] is duly recieved. I am very sensible of the partiality with which you are so good as to review the course I have held in public life; and I have also to be thankful to my fellow citizens for a like indulgence generally shewn to my endeavors to be useful to them. they give quite as much credit as is merited to the difficulties supposed to attend the public administration. there are no mysteries in it. difficulties indeed sometimes arise; but common sense and honest intentions will generally steer thro' them, and, where they cannot be surmounted, I have ever seen the well-intentioned part of our fellow citizens sufficiently disposed not to look for impossibilities. we all know that a farm however large is not more difficult to direct than a garden, and does not call for more attention or skill.

I hope with you that the policy of our country will settle down with as much navigation and commerce only as our own exchanges will require, and that the disadvantage will be seen of our undertaking to carry on that of other nations. this indeed may bring gain to a few individuals, and enable them to call off from our farms more laborers to be converted into lackies & grooms for them; but it will bring nothing to our country but wars, debt, & dilapidation. this has been the course of England, and her examples have fearful influence on us. in copying her we do not seem to consider that like premisses induce like consequences. the bank-mania is one of the most threatening of these imitations. it is raising up a monied aristocracy in our country which has already set the government at defiance, and altho' forced at length to yield a little on this first essay of their strength, their principles are unyielded and unyielding. these have taken deep root in the hearts of that class from which our legislators are drawn, and the sop to Cerberus from fable, has become history. their principles lay hold of the good, their pelf of the bad, and thus those whom the constitution had placed as guards to it's portals, are sophisticated or suborned from their duties. that paper money has some advantages is admitted. but that it's abuses also are inevitable and, by breaking up the measure of value, makes a lottery of all private property, cannot be denied. shall we ever be able to put a constitutional veto on it? You say I must go to writing history. while in public life, I had not time: and now that I am retired, I am past the time. to write history requires a whole life of observation, of enquiry, of labor and correction. it's materials are not to be found among the ruins of a decayed memory. at this day I should begin where I ought to have left off. the 'solve senescentem equum' is a precept we learn in youth, but for the practice of age; and were I to disregard it it would be but a proof the more of it's soundness. if any thing has ever merited to me the respect of my fellow-citizens, themselves, I hope, would wish me not to lose it by exposing the decay of faculties of which it was the reward. I must then, dear Sir, leave to yourself and your brethren of the rising generation to arraign at your tribunal the actions of your predecessors, and to pronounce the sentence they may have merited or incurred. if the sacrifices of that age have resulted in the good of this, then all is well, and we shall be rewarded by their approbation, and shall be authorised to say 'go ye, and do likewise.' to yourself I tender personally the assurance of great esteem & respect Th: Jefferson

RC (MH: Schaffner Collection); addressed: "Doct[r] Josephus B. Stuart Albany"; franked; postmarked Milton, 13 May; endorsed by Stuart as received 18 May, with his additional notation: "N[o] 4." PoC (DLC).

Aeneas gives a drugged SOP TO CERBERUS in order to pass into the underworld in Virgil, *Aeneid*, 6.417–25 (Fairclough, *Virgil*, 1:560–3). SOLVE SENESCENTEM EQUUM paraphrases Horace, *Epistles*, 1.1.8, which reads "solve senescentem mature sanus equum": "Be wise in time, and turn loose the ageing horse" (Fairclough, *Horace: Satires, Epistles and Ars Poetica*, 250–1). After telling the story of the Good Samaritan, Jesus advises his listeners to GO YE, AND DO LIKEWISE (Luke 10.37).

[1]Date reworked from "2" by an unidentified hand. PoC: "2."

From George Washington Jeffreys

D[R] SIR Red House N[o] C May 11th 1817.

Having read an account of the Tunis-Broad-tail mountain sheep in the 2 vol Memoirs Phil[a] Society, I was much pleased with the many good qualities of this breed, and am therefore induced to get into the stock of them—Judge Peters observes page (211) that he obtained the original stock from Colo. Pickering then secretary of state, to whom they were sent by William Eeaton Esqr when Consul of the U S. at Tunis—

There are some broad tailed sheep in my neighbourhood, which are called by the owner Barbary sheep—He informed me a few days ago that he brought them from Caroline county or perhaps off the Rappahanock river Virginia, and that he obtained the ram from a M[r] Battle living on that river—He further observed, that he was informed that the original stock of this breed, were imported into this country by you—The object of this letter is to ascertain this fact—Those that I saw the other day, of my neighbours, appeared to coincide with the description given of the genuine breed by Judge Peters—

They have remarkably broad tails, flap ears, no horns and yellow and black spots on the wool—As I intend to obtain this breed of my neighbour, I should be gratified to know, and therefore should esteem it as a particular favour, if you would inform me whether you have ever imported any of this breed, where they originally came from, and whether they are the same of those sent to Colo. Pickering by William Eeaton Esqr—

Any observations respecting the value of this breed, the manner of raising or crossing them profitably && would also be thankfully received— Permit me to assure you of my high respects and that I remain yours very sincerely—

GEORGE WASHINGTON JEFFREYS.

NB. Your communication enclosing a catalouge of Books and some remarks on horizontal ploughing was duly received—for this politeness and goodness of yours you have not only mine, but the Societies warmest & most grateful aknowledgements—

G. W. JEFFREYS—

RC (DLC); between signature and postscript: "Hon^{le} Thos Jefferson Esqr"; endorsed by TJ as received 25 May 1817 and so recorded in SJL.

The 1810 ACCOUNT of the Tunis broad-tail sheep by Richard Peters can be found in Philadelphia Society for Promoting Agriculture, *Memoirs* 2 (1811): 211–33.

Notes on the Canal Locks and Manufacturing Mill at Shadwell

Measures taken at the locks & large mill, by myself May 11. 17.

the water was running $4\frac{1}{2}$ I. deep over the waste.
surface of water in canal above that in upper chamber $8\frac{1}{4}$ I   0–$8\frac{1}{2}$
depth of water in upper chamber, from it's surface to

		it's floor	6 f. 6 I.	6–6
	middle d^{o}	d^{o}	1–4	
	lowest d^{o}	d^{o}	1–8	
clear lift of	middle lock	7.f. 6 I.		7–6
	Lowest d^{o}	7 f 8 I	deduct depth of water—leaves	6–0
clear width of the chambers		8.f.		20–$4\frac{1}{2}$
each recess is 9.I.			deduct depth on waste	$4\frac{1}{2}$
clear width at recesses		9 f. 6		20–0

clear length of each chamber inside 68.f. 6.I.
the floor of the lowest chamber being 1.f. too high, call the whole   f 21–0
then 3. lifts of 7.f. each accomplishes it

Mill

from surface of water in the canal to bottom of forebay or top of wheel	2f 9I.
diam. of wheel 14.f.	14–0
bottom of wheel above surface of river at the tail 2.f.	2
	18–9
deduct depth of water on the waste	$4\frac{1}{2}$
leaves height of waste above the surface of the river at the tail	18–$4\frac{1}{2}$
height of waste above surface of river at the tail of the lock as above	20–0
this diff^{ce} may be the fall in the river from tail of lock to tail of mill.	1–$7\frac{1}{2}$′[1]

Stone work for locks of 3. chambers of 7.f. lift each. exclusive of foundations.

	f	
3. chambers of 70.f. length clear, for both sides	420	
38. abutments @ 11 f–8. I apart, 8.f. long at bottom 4.f. at top say 6.f.	228	perch
running measure	648 =	40.
thickness 4.f. at bottom, 2.f. at top. say 3.f. × 40 =		120.
height above foundation, or floor 10 f. × 120.		1200.
4. breast walls 16.f. long. make 64.f. running measure =	3.75 perch.	
4. f. thick	15.	
7. f. high. say for round numbers		100.
		1300. perch.

	D	
Stone mason for laying @ .75	975.	
lime & planter's work @ 1.75	2275.	by myself.
Carpenter's & Smith's work & digging		

Suppose the foundation of the lower lock sufficient, & the others going down to that

foundation of middle chamber 7 f below it's floor is	140 f = $8\frac{1}{2}$ perch × 4 × 7 =	238. perch.
it's breast 1. perch long, 4.f. thick, 7.f. to the floor		28
foundation of upper chamber 14.f below it's floor is	140 f = $8\frac{1}{2}$ perch × 4 × 14 =	476
it's 2. breasts, 1. perch long, 4 f. thick 14.f. high is	140 f = $8\frac{1}{2}$ × 4 × 14 =	112
		854.

	D	
Mason @ .75	640	
lime and planter's work @ 1.75	1494.	by myself
	2134	

	D			
All together work done by the mason	975 + 640.	= 1615		
by myself	2275 + 1494	= 3769		D
		5384	} =	4385. by myself
suppose Carpenter's & smith's work & digging worth		616		
		6000		

MS (MHi); written entirely in TJ's hand on both sides of a single sheet; paper watermarked 1794.

[1] Recto ends here, with last line of text trimmed but legible.

From John Barnes

DEAR SIR— George Town 12th May. 1817.

I have the pleasure to hand you the several inclosiers—viz Genl Kosciusko's 6th Novr Baring Brothers & Co to Buckley & Abbatt 31st Decr together with Baring & Co 10th feb^{y}. the Contents of the latter, recd yesterday very satisfactory.—presume you have ere this—or will soon receive[1] advices to confirm these late remittances—whereby the good Genl will be at ease from his late embarrism^{ts}—

I have long since flattered my self the gratification of paying you (for the last time) my personal respects—in Course of the present summer—although a very unfit subject for the undertaken the many inconveniency's Attend^{g} such a distant Tour at my time of Life so ill suited to the Accustomed regular hours of ease &^{a} &^{a} together with the very unpleasant Circumstance I labour under—in point of not hearing so well as to join in a general conversation—

At this Instance however my 2^{d} G. Son—Mr J. Ab^{m} Duryee a promising Young Man of ab^{t} 22 years—Educated at Yale College Under the Revered President the late Revd Tim^{y} Dwight—and this last Season Attending—The Medical Lectures, under Professor Husac and others in New York—Accompanied with his Amiable Sister Maria not in perfect Health whom I had not seen for 15 yrs passed are now present with me—on a Visit for a M^{o} or two. I am so taken up with—that I cannot at present fix on a day—or M^{o}—it must however be at a time most suitable to your not be^{g} absent from Monticello—

Mr Saml Milligan a Nephew—of <u>Joseph</u>—M—a Deserving Young Man, and Trust Worthy—who has been my Deputy these 3 y^{s} and gives general satisfaction, so that I can savely confide on his performing the several Duties of the Office in my Absence—same as if I was present.

with the greatest Respect I am Dear Sir—Your very Obed^{t} servant

JOHN BARNES.

RC (ViU: TJP-ER); at foot of text: "Thomas Jefferson Esqr Monticello"; endorsed by TJ as received 14 May 1817 and so recorded in SJL. RC (DLC); partial address cover only; with PoC of TJ to Daniel Brent, 23 June 1817, on verso; addressed: "Th[...]"; postmarked Georgetown, 12 May. Enclosures not found.

Barnes's grandson Abraham Jacob DURYEE graduated from Yale College (later Yale University) in 1815 and earned a medical degree from the College of Physicians and Surgeons (later part of Columbia University) in 1819 (*Catalogue of the Officers and Graduates of Yale University ... 1701–1910* [1910], 89). PROFESSOR HUSAC: David Hosack.

[1]Manuscript: "recive."

From Daniel Lescallier

HONOURED SIR New York May 12th 1817

Altho' I can hardly flatter myself of your remembering my having had the honour to be received by you, in the year 1803, when returning from Guadeloupe, I have taken the liberty to write to you this letter, in order to present and introduce to you, one of our very interesting exiled citizens Mr Le Baron Quinette de Rochemont, who entertains a very great desire, in visiting Virginia, and some of the Southern States, to enjoy the satisfaction of your conversation and acquaintance.

For my part, I would have been much gratified in making the same tour, and being favoured some hours by your company and conversation, but I am forced by my limited means and my situation, Since I left the consulate genl of France, at the changes of our government, to keep quiet, and wait patiently for the return of tranquillity and wisdom in our desolated country, and I may say all Europe, which more or less partakes of the same unsteady situation.

I mean to occupy my time mean while in a publication, from the oriental languages, of which I take this opportunity to offer you the preface and beginning, with the Scheme of it, recommending it to your attention and patronage.

I am very respectfully, Sir, Your most obt h. Servt

LESCALLIER

RC (CSmH: JF-BA); endorsed by TJ as received 7 June 1817 and so recorded in SJL, which has TJ's additional note that it was delivered "by Baron Quinette."

The PREFACE AND BEGINNING that Lescallier enclosed here was probably his pamphlet entitled *The Enchanted Throne, An Indian Story translated from the Persian Language* (New York, 1817). It consisted of Lescallier's preface discussing his translation experience, a summary of the narrative, and a brief description of his editorial practices. Lescallier later published the full work in French as *Le Trône Enchanté, Conte Indien traduit du Persan* (New York, 1817).

On this date Lescallier also wrote Quinette de Rochemont an introduction to James Madison, but that letter was never delivered (Madison, *Papers, Retirement Ser.*, 1:155).

To Fernagus De Gelone

SIR Monticello May 13.

I recieved yesterday the Euclid I had requested, and in the leaf of a catalogue accompanying it, I observe 'le Theatre d'Aristophane par Poinsinet. 4. v. 8vo.' I presume from the generality of the title that it contains the whole of his works, and in that case I would be glad if you will send it to me. I wish this may get to your hands in time to come with the Cormon & Vitruve asked for in a letter of May 6, as they can come safely by water only, and by a vessel bound to Richmond direct, addressed to $Mess^{rs}$ Gibson & Jefferson my correspondents there. I salute you with respect. TH: JEFFERSON

PoC (MHi); on verso of portion of reused sheet reading "[...]ging to the [...] Thermometre" in an unidentified hand; partially dated; at foot of text: "Mr Fernagus de Gelone"; endorsed by TJ as a letter of 13 May 1817 and so recorded in SJL.

To Fitzwhylsonn & Potter

$MESS^{RS}$ FITZWHYLSON & POTTER Monticello May 13. 17.

Within a very few days a trusty boatman will go from Milton to Richmond, whom I will direct to call on you in the hope that the books I sent you for binding will be ready; as also the Edinburgh reviews. be pleased to send with them

Oliver Evans's Mill-book

McMahon's gardening

the laws of the last session of our legislature (in boards) if ready or whenever they shall come out. Accept the assurance of my respect.

TH: JEFFERSON

RC (NcD: Thomas Nelson Page Papers). PoC (DLC); on verso of reused address cover to TJ; endorsed by TJ.

To James Gibbon

Dear Sir Monticello May 13. 17.

Mr Dearborn Collector of Boston writes me that he had recieved for me a small parcel of grass seeds (Lupinella) sent me by mr Appleton our Consul at Leghorn, which he should forward to you by a Coaster in a few days. I will ask the favor of you to deliver them when recieved to Messrs Gibson & Jefferson who will pay whatever is due on them, and will forward them to me. Accept the assurance of my great esteem & respect. Th: Jefferson

PoC (DLC); on verso of a reused address cover from Bernard Peyton to TJ; at foot of text: "Majr Gibbons"; endorsed by TJ.

To Lafayette

Monticello May 14. 17.

Altho', dear Sir, much retired from the world, and medling little in it's concerns, yet I think it almost a religious duty to salute, at times, my old friends, were it only to say, and to know that 'all's well.' our hobby has been politics; but all here is so quiet, and with you so desperate, that little matter is furnished us for active attention. with you too it has long been forbidden ground, and therefore imprudent for a foreign friend to tread, in writing to you. but, altho' our speculations might be intrusive, our prayers cannot but be acceptable, and mine are sincerely offered for the well-being of France. what government she can bear, depends not on the state of science, however exalted, in a select band of enlightened men, but on the condition of the general mind. that, I am sure, is advanced, and will advance; and the last change of government was fortunate, inasmuch as the new will be less obstructive to the effects of that advancement. for I consider your foreign military oppression as an ephemeral obstacle only. here all is quiet. the British war has left us in debt; but that is a cheap price for the good it has done us. the establishment of the necessary manufactures among ourselves, the proof that our government is solid, can stand the shock of war, and is superior even to civil schism, are precious facts for us: and of these the strongest proofs were furnished when, with four Eastern states tied to us, as dead to living bodies, all doubt was removed as to the atchievements of the war, had it continued. but it's best effect has been the compleat suppression of party. the federalists who were truly American, and their great mass was so, have separated from their brethren who were mere Anglomen, and are recieved with cordiality into the republican ranks. even Connecticut, as a state, and the last one expected to yield it's steady habits (which were essentially bigotted in politics as well as religion) has chosen a republican governor, and republican legislature. Massachusets indeed still lags; because most deeply involved in the parricide crimes and treasons of the war. but her gangrene is contracting, the sound flesh advancing on it, and all there will be well. I mentioned Connecticut as the most hopeless of our states. little Delaware had escaped my attention. that is essentially a quaker state, the fragment of a religious sect which, there, in the other states, in England, are a homogeneous mass, acting with one mind, and that directed by the mother-society in England. dispersed, as the Jews, they still form, as those do, one nation, foreign to the land they live in. they are protestant Jesuits, implicitly devoted to the will of their Superior, and forgetting all duties to their country in the execution of the policy of their order. when war is proposed with England, they have religious scruples, but when with France, these are laid by, and they become clamorous for it. they are however silent, passive, and give no other trouble than of whipping them along. nor is the election of Monroe an inefficient circumstance in our felicities. four and twenty years, which he will accomplish, of administration in republican forms and principles, will so consecrate them in the eyes of the people as to secure them against the danger of change. the evanition of party dissensions has harmonised intercourse, & sweetened society beyond imagination. the war then has done us all this good, and the further one of assuring the world that, altho' attached to peace from a sense of it's blessings, we will meet war when it is made necessary.

I wish I could give better hopes of our Southern brethren. the atchievement of their independance of Spain is no longer a question. but it is a very serious one what will then become of them? ignorance & bigotry, like other insanities, are incapable of self-government. they will fall under military despotisms, and become the murderous tools of the ambition of their respective Bonapartes, and whether this will be for their greater happiness the rule of one only has taught you to judge. no one, I hope, can doubt my wish to see them and all mankind exercising self-government, & capable of exercising it. but the question is not what we wish, but what is practicable? as their sincere friend and brother then, I do believe the best thing for them would be for themselves to come to an accord with Spain under the guarantee of France, Russia, Holland & the US. allowing to Spain a nominal supremacy with authority only to keep the peace among them, leaving them otherwise all the powers of self-government, until their experience in them, their emancipation from their priests, and advancement in information shall prepare them for compleat independance. I exclude England from this confederacy because her selfish principles render her incapable of honorable patronage or disinterested co-operation: unless indeed, what seems now probable, a revolution should restore to her an honest government, one which will permit the world to live in peace. Portugal grasping at an extension of her dominion in the South has lost her great Northern province of Pernambuco, and I shall not wonder if Brazil should revolt in mass, and send their royal family back to Portugal. Brazil is more populous, more wealthy, more energetic, and as wise as Portugal.—I have been insensibly led, my dear friend, while writing to you, to indulge in that line of sentiment in which we have been always associated, forgetting that these are matters not belonging to my time. not so with you, who have still many years to be a spectator of these events. that these years may indeed be many and happy is the sincere prayer of your affectionate friend TH: JEFFERSON

P.S. I need not add my recommendations of mr Lyman, the bearer of this letter, to those of mr Adams, because his are sufficient to procure all your attentions; and it is thro' him alone that I know mr Lyman, having never had the pleasure of seeing him.

RC (NjMoHP: Park Collection). PoC (DLC); edge trimmed and corner torn; at foot of first page: "M. de la Fayette." Enclosed in TJ to Abigail Adams, 15 May 1817.

Five EASTERN STATES participated in the Hartford Convention (see notes to TJ to John Melish, 10 Dec. 1814, and TJ to John Holmes, 23 Sept. 1815). The REPUBLICAN GOVERNOR of Connecticut was Oliver Wolcott. EVANITION: "disappearance" (*OED*). For the ROYAL FAMILY of Portugal, see note to Pierre Samuel Du Pont de Nemours to TJ, 26 May 1815.

To Jean Baptiste Say

DEAR SIR Monticello May 14. 17.

Your letter of June 15. 1814. came to my hands on the 9th of Dec. following, and that of Aug. 22. of the same year was recieved on the 11th of May 15. in the mean time I had answered the former on the 2d of March, & had gone fully into all details in the line of information to which your enquiries had led, stating every thing on the subject of prices, articles of culture, climate society Etc which I thought would aid your determination on the question of removal. this letter was committed to the care of a mr Ticknor, a young gentleman of Boston, who was on the point of embarking for France; but before actual embarcation, peace taking place with England, he went first to that country, and thence to Gottingen, where I expect he has continued to about this time. how this letter was conveyed to you, or whether you ever recieved it, I am uninformed; but a fear that it might have miscarried has led me to this recapitulation, that, in that case, you might know the truth, and be assured I was incapable of omitting to comply with your request of information on points so interesting to you. the only change, since occurring, as to any particulars of that information, has been in our circulating medium, which, from the wretched state it was then in, has become much worse by the great increase of bank-paper in circulation, and the consequent advance of nominal prices; and that advance of such uncertainty as that nothing can now be estimated in that medium. I add this to the information formerly given on the possibility that you may still contemplate a removal; and can assure you that your arrival here would be hailed with universal welcome, & by none with more than by myself. I rejoice that the book of which you were so kind as to send me a copy is becoming known here, begins to be much read; and I really see in that circumstance chiefly, a prospect, however distant, that our rulers will come in time to understand the subject, and to apply the remedy which is in their power only. a shorter work of mr Tracy's on the same subject is in a course of publication, and will cooperate with yours to the same end.

For the conveyance of this letter I avail myself of the kindness of it's bearer mr Lyman, a young gentleman of Boston, who proposes to visit France for his health. he is not personally known to me; but is much recommended on the part of mr Adams, former President of the United States. he speaks of him as a young man of great worth and promise, and whose ardor in pursuit of science has produced that derangement of health which occasions his visit to Europe. in proposing to him to be the bearer of a letter to you, he naturally wished an introduction to a character of such advantageous standing in the literary world, and to place the honor of being made known to you among the rewards of his voyage. be so good then as to recieve him into your notice and to indulge a desire on his part produced by motives of veneration for your character, and accept the assurance of my great respect and esteem. TH: JEFFERSON

RC (RuMoGIM). PoC (DLC); at foot of first page: "M. Say"; endorsed by TJ. Enclosed in TJ to Abigail Adams, 15 May 1817.

Say had sent TJ his BOOK entitled *Traité d'Économie Politique*, 2 vols. (2d ed., Paris, 1814; Poor, *Jefferson's Library*, 11 [no. 697]). Destutt de TRACY's work on the same subject was his *Treatise on Political Economy*.

To Abigail Adams

Monticello May 15. 17.

Your letters, dear Madam, are always welcome, and your requests are commands to me. I only regret that I can do so little towards obeying them. but eight and twenty years since I left France would, in the ordinary course of mortality, have swept off seven eighths of my acquaintances, and when to this lapse of time are added the knife of the Guillotine & scythe of constant and sanguinary wars, I am left without a single personal acquaintance there of the literary family; for Dupont, the only one of that day still living, is in the US. a correspondence however has since taken place with some literati not known to me personally, nor their habits of society, or situations in life. among these I have chosen M. destutt-Tracy & Say; the former great in the moral sciences, the latter particularly in that of Political economy. Mr Tracy's connection too with M. de la Fayette will facilitate mr Lyman's acquaintance with him. I have selected these two the rather because, in the course of our correspondence, I owe a letter to each, and am glad to avail myself of the opportunity by mr Lyman of paying the debt, adding to my letters the recommendations of him which your information authorises. should therefore any circumstance prevent mr Lyman's visit to France direct, I will pray him to forward the letters by the first entirely safe conveyance, under cover to mr Gallatin. in the letter to M. de la Fayette I have associated my sollicitations with those of mr Adams for the courtesies to mr Lyman, which he so willingly extends to all Americans. wishing a pleasant voyage and tour to him, and to yourself and mr Adams long years of health and happiness, I tender you the homage of my constant respect and attachment.

TH: JEFFERSON

RC (MHi: Adams Papers); addressed: "Mrs Adams Quincy"; endorsed by Adams. PoC (DLC); on verso of a reused address cover from Bernard Peyton to TJ; mutilated at seal, with missing text rewritten by TJ; endorsed by TJ. Enclosures: (1) TJ to Lafayette, 14 May 1817. (2) TJ to Jean Baptiste Say, 14 May 1817. (3) TJ to Destutt de Tracy, 15 May 1817.

From Isaac Briggs

MY DEAR FRIEND, New York, 5 mo 15–1817

I arrived here the day before yesterday—and I have this day received the appointment of surveyor for the contemplated grand Canal. My friend Thomas Eddy of this City, has generally been in the first rank amongst his fellow citizens as an active and efficient promoter of useful and benevolent works, has long been one of the commissioners for this particular object, and, though he is not now one, still retains all his wishes for its success, and the energies of his mind are still in full activity for its accomplishment. He has mentioned in conversation with me his views that the task of the ascertainment of lines, and the superintendence of the work of making the Canal would be too burdensome for one man—that the magnitude of the object would not only render expedient but necessary the employment of two Superintendents, an Engineer and a Mathematician, each in his appropriate department. I perfectly accord with him in these views—I mentioned to him Thomas Moore, a man whom I knew to be eminently qualified for such an undertaking, of a sound and discriminating mind, a judicious and practical civil Engineer, and one with whom I should be glad to act—I remarked that thou wast well acquainted with his qualifications and talents, and suggested the propriety[1] of his addressing thee on the subject and requesting thy opinion. He alleged he had no acquaintance with thee, but if I would write he would enclose my letter in a few lines from himself.

I know not whether Thomas Moore would accept such an appointment, but I am induced to believe the Commissioners would be liberal in their offers, and I also believe his correctness and economy to be such in the application of public money, that more would be saved by giving him a salary of $10,000 a year than by employing one less qualified for nothing.

Accept, dear friend, my love and affectionate salutations.

ISAAC BRIGGS.

RC (DLC); at foot of text: "Thomas Jefferson"; endorsed by TJ as received 22 May 1817 and so recorded in SJL. Enclosed in Thomas Eddy to TJ, 16 May 1817.

Soon after his appointment as SURVEYOR of a section of the Erie Canal, Briggs began work between Rome and Utica, New York (*Report of the Commissioners of the State of New-York, on the Canals from Lake Erie to the Hudson River, and from Lake Champlain to the same* [Albany, 1818], 7). In 1811 Thomas Eddy had been appointed one of nine COMMISSIONERS to oversee the improvement of internal navigation in the state of New York. Although he was active in the effort to get the Erie and Champlain canal projects started, Eddy was not one of the commissioners chosen in 1817 (*Laws of the State of New-York*, 34th sess. [1811]: 334–5 [8 Apr. 1811]; 39th–41st sess. [1818]: 295, 301–2 [17 Apr. 1816, 15 Apr. 1817]; David Hosack, *Memoir of De Witt Clinton* [1829], 374–8).

In the spring of 1817 Benjamin Wright was appointed ENGINEER for the Erie Canal while James Geddes was appointed for the Champlain Canal (Noble E. Whitford, *History of the Canal System of the State of New York* [1906], 1:86). Briggs's brother-in-law THOMAS MOORE became principal engineer of Virginia's Board of Public Works the following year (*Alexandria Gazette & Daily Advertiser*, 28 Nov. 1818; Anna Briggs Bentley, *American Grit: A Woman's Letters from the Ohio Frontier*, ed. Emily Foster [2002], 13).

[1] Manuscript: "propropriety."

To Destutt de Tracy

Dear Sir Monticello May 15. 17.

I have to acknolege the reciept of your two letters of Feb. 4. & Dec. 24. 16. and, with the last, your Principes logiques, and a 2[d] copy of your 4th vol. of which I had before recieved a printed one as well as the MS. the Analysis of Dupuy and the luminous tract on public instruction I had possessed some time before, and had availed myself of some of the leading ideas of the latter in the scheme of an institution here on a much smaller scale, and obliged to adapt it's details to the localities, the ideas, character & circumstances of our country. I sincerely sympathise with the misfortunes of your health and loss of sight, and equally condole with the world on their loss in the curtailment of the valuable instruction they were in the course of recieving from your continued labors. the completion of your circle of the moral sciences would have formed an epoch in the history of the human mind, much of which indeed you have effected; but while something more can be done, we never think we have enough. the unfinished part too 'de la Morale' is of the first degree of interest. but are we in the condition of those who grieve without hope? I am indeed not without hope that in the occupation of your mind with these studies you will find a refuge from the sense of your physical sufferings, and forget, for a time, your own evils, while indicating to others the road to their good. perhaps we owe to the blindness of Homer and Milton the three great epic works they have left us; and the English professor Saunderson under the same disability, lost nothing of his acumen in Mathematical pursuits. why then should we despair of a similar phaenomenon in the moral sciences? this, I believe, is the country which will profit most from your lessons, because here we are free to rally to, and realize all sound principles; and those of your Commentaries on Montesquieu, will, I am persuaded, have much and lasting effect in reclaiming us from his errors, ridding us of his artificial principles, and fixing our government on the basis of reason and right. nor have I less hope from the effect of the 4th part of your work on Political economy. it is this hope which has supported my perseverance in it's publication here, thro' all the difficulties and delays it has experienced. the translation is now in the press, and the proof sheets are regularly transmitted to me by mail, for correction. the last sheet reached the 123[d] page of the French edition; and, from the time the printer takes for every sheet, I suspect he does not wish to compleat it until the next meeting of Congress. perhaps this will be an advantage; as it's novelty may more readily attract the notice of the members, and they may become the instruments of carrying it back to their respective states, and of it's general dissemination. there is no branch of science on which information is more wanted here, and, under the want of which, we are suffering more. as soon as the translation is out, you may rely on recieving copies from me.

I am furnished with an opportunity of conveying you this letter by the intention of a mr Lyman, a young American, to visit France: and in proposing to him to be the bearer of a letter to you, he naturally wished an introduction to a character of such eminence in the literary world. he is not personally known to me, but is highly recommended on the part of mr Adams, former President of the United States, who speaks of him as a young man of great worth and promise, and whose ardor in pursuit of science has produced that derangement of health which travelling it is hoped will relieve.

be so good then as to permit him to present himself to you, & to place that honor among the rewards of his voyage to Europe. he carries a letter from Mr Adams to M. de la Fayette to whom I write also. I pray you to accept my friendly salutations, and the assurance of my great and respectful esteem and consideration. TH: JEFFERSON

PoC (DLC); at foot of first page: "M. le Comte Des-Tutt de Tracy de l'Institut de France"; endorsed by TJ. Enclosed in TJ to Abigail Adams, 15 May 1817.

From Thomas Eddy

RESPECTED FRIEND New york 5th mo. 16th 1817

The Commissioners to connect the Navigable Waters of Lake Erie and the Hudson River have not yet appointed an Engineer, and it is very[1] difficult to select a person for so important and responsible a situation—The appointment will be a very honorable one, and it is desirable it should be conferred on a Man fully competent, and deserving intire confidence—To direct the manner in which the various parts of the work should be executed, to make contracts with the workmen &c &c requires a combination of talents, industry, and intelligence, that is rarely to be found in an individual—

I have been long acquainted with the general character of Thomas Moore of Maryland, and it occured to me, that he would answer the views of the Commissioners, but having no personal acquaintance with him, and not being possessed of a sufficient knowledge of his abilities, to justify me in recommending him to the Commissioners, I am induced by the recommendation of my Friend Isaac Briggs,[2] to take the liberty of making application to thee for information.—

Not having the pleasure of an acquaintance, I must confide in thy well known public character, and disposition to aid every improvement interesting to our common country, to excuse the liberty of addressing thee on the above subject, and am with sentiments of[3] great Respect and Esteem

Thy Assured Friend THOMAS EDDY

RC (DLC); endorsed by TJ as received 22 May 1817 and so recorded in SJL. Printed in Samuel L. Knapp, *The Life of Thomas Eddy* (1834), 268. Enclosure: Isaac Briggs to TJ, 15 May 1817.

Thomas Eddy (1758–1827), merchant and reformer, was a native of Philadelphia. Apprenticed about 1771–73 to a tanner in Burlington, New Jersey, by 1777 he had taken up mercantile pursuits in Philadelphia. Eddy was a Quaker and a Loyalist who moved in 1779 to New York City, where he partnered for a time with his brother Charles Eddy and later with him and Benjamin Sykes as Eddy, Sykes, & Company. Between 1784 and 1790 he ran a mercantile firm with another brother, George Eddy, in Philadelphia, leaving that city for an interval to run a store in Fredericksburg on behalf of the partnership. Eddy went bankrupt in 1790 and settled permanently in New York City about 1791, prospering as an insurance broker and underwriter and speculating in the public debt. He was appointed in 1810 to a New York state canal commission. Becoming involved in numerous areas of reform, Eddy sought to improve the city's schools, hospitals, and insane asylums, and he promoted the abolition of slavery and the colonization abroad of former slaves. He had a particular interest in prison reform, working to build penitentiaries and end imprisonment for debt. Eddy died in New York City (*ANB*; *DAB*; Knapp, *Thomas Eddy*; *PTJ*, 36:553–4; Scoville, *New York Merchants*, 2:342–6; *Pennsylvania Ledger: or the Philadelphia Market-Day Advertiser*, 13 Dec. 1777; New York *Royal Gazette*, 30 June 1781, 25 May 1782; Philadelphia *Pennsylvania Packet, and Daily Advertiser*, 22 Sept. 1784; *Federal Gazette and Philadelphia Daily Advertiser*, 29 Apr. 1790; *New-York Daily Gazette*, 9 Oct. 1790; *The New-York Directory, and Register, for the year 1791* [New York, 1791], 39; *Delaplaine's Repository*, 1:195; Madison, *Papers, Pres. Ser.*, 3:480–1; *New-York Evening Post*, 17 Sept. 1827).

1 Word not in Knapp, *Thomas Eddy*.

2 Instead of preceding two words, Knapp, *Thomas Eddy*, reads "J. B., who has just been appointed to the mathematical department, as surveyor."

3 Instead of preceding four words, Knapp, *Thomas Eddy*, reads "beg thee to believe me, with."

To John Barnes

DEAR SIR May 17. 17. Monticello

Yours of the 12th is received [a]nd I am happy to find that the General's distresses have been so happily relieved. I am in hopes the regular course of commerce now will enable us to prevent any such recurrence of want to him. I am equally gratified by the prospect of seeing you here once more: and as I pass much of the temperate seasons at Poplar Forest, to prevent the danger of my losing the satisfaction of your visit, I will state to you my expected movements. I shall set out for that place about the 20th of June and be back about the

10th of July; set out again for Poplar Forest about Aug 10. and not return till the last of Sep. should any change in these movements occur, I will take care to advise you, and shall continue to expect you at your convenience. I should be glad mr Millegan could be informed of these epochs that he might push mr Tracy's work while I am here; and in the mean time send me the books he was to bind for me. indeed if you should come in the first interval before stated I should be glad they should come under your care as they are book[s] recieved from Germany, which could not be replaced if lost.
eve[r] and affectionately [yours?]

I return the Gen's & Baring's lette[rs.] [Th: Jefferson]

PoC (DLC); on verso of reused address cover of Hendrick W. Gordon to TJ, 22 Feb. 1817; faint; torn at seal, with missing words rewrittten by TJ; at foot of text: "Mr Barnes"; endorsed by TJ. Enclosures not found.

From Patrick Gibson

Sir Richmond 17th May 1817

I have received seven Hhds of your Tobo which I have sold to J Mutter & Co on 60d/. credit at $8\frac{1}{4}$ no part of it was fine, and 1 Hhd. so indifft as to cause some hesitation in passing it—Our flour market is excessively dull, indeed it is impossible to say what price could now be obtained, as none seem willing to purchase, I do not know that 12$ could be obtained—I have not been able to make any further sale of yours—I have advice from Le Roy Bayard & Co of the receipt of a dft at 3d/s for $2000. remitted them on your accot for which I had to pay a prem: of 1 pCt—I inclose a note for your signature to renew the one due 3/6th of next month With much respect

Your obt Servt Patrick Gibson

RC (MHi); between dateline and salutation: "Thomas Jefferson Esqre"; endorsed by TJ as a letter of 20 May received 22 May 1817 and so recorded in SJL. Enclosure not found.

From John Adams

Dear Sir Quincy May 18. 1817

Lyman was mortified that he could not visit Monticello. He is gone to Europe a Second time. I regret that he did not See you, He would have executed any commision for you in the litterary line, at any pain or any expence. I have many apprehensions for his health, which is very delicate and precarious. But he is Seized with the Mania of all our young etherial Spirits, for foreign travel. I fear they will loose more than they will acquire. They will loose that unadulterated Enthusiasm for their native Country which has produced the greatest Characters among Us.

Oh! Lord! Do you think that a Protestant Popedom is annihilated in America.? Do you recollect, or have you ever attended to the ecclesiastical Strifes in Maryland Pensilvania, New York, and every part of New England? What a mercy it is, that these People cannot whip and crop, and pillory and roast, as yet in the U.S.? If they could they would.

Do you know that The General of the Jesuits and consequently all his Host have their Eyes on this Country? Do you know that the Church of England is employing more means and more Art, to propagate their demipopery among Us, than ever? Quakers, Anabaptists Moravians Swedenborgians, Methodists, Unitarians, Nothingarians in all Europe are employing underhand means to propagate their Sectarian Systems in these States.

The multitude and diversity of them, you will Say, is our Security against them all. God grant it. But if We consider that the Presbyterians and Methodists are far the most numerous; and the most likely to unite[1] let a George Whitefield arise, with a military cast, like Mahomet, or Loyola, and what will become of all the other Sects who can never unite?

My Friends or Enemies continue to overwhelm me with Books, Whatever may be their intension, charitable or otherwise, they certainly contribute, to continue me to vegetate, much as I have done for the Sixteen years last past.

Sir John Malcoms History of Persia, and Sir William Jones's Works are now poured out upon me and a little cargo is coming from Europe. What can I do with all this learned lumber? Is it necessary to Salvation to investigate all these Cosmogonies and Mythologies? Is Bryant Gebelin, Dupuis, or Sir William Jones, right.?

What a frown upon Man kind, was the premature death of Sir William Jones? Why could not Jones and Dupuis have conversed or corresponded with each other? Had Jones read Dupuis, or Dupuis Jones, the Works of both would be immensely improved though each would probably have adhered to his System.

I Should admire to See a Counsel, composed of Gebelin, Bryant Jones and Dupuis. Let them live together and compare Notes. The human race ought to contribute to furnish them with all the Books in the Universe, and the means of Subsistence.

I am not expert enough in Italien to read Botta, and I know not that he has been translated. Indeed I have been So little Satisfied with Histories of the American Revolution, that I have long Since, ceased to read them. The Truth is lost, in adulatory Panegyricks, and in vituperary Insolence.

I wish you, Mr Madison and Mr Monroe Success, in your Collegiate institution. And I wish that Superstition in Religion exciting[2] Superstition in Politicks, and both united in directing military Force, alias glory may never blow up all your benevolent and phylanthropic Lucubrations. But the History of all ages is against you.

It is said, that no Effort in favour of Virtue, is ever lost. I doubt whether it was ever true; whether it is now true; but hope it will be true. In the moral Government of the World, no doubt it was, is, and ever will be true: but it has not yet appeared to be true on this Earth.

I am Sir, Sincerely your friend JOHN ADAMS

P.S. Have you Seen the Phylosophy of human Nature, and the History of the War, in the Western States, from Kentucky[?] How vigorously Science and Litterature Spring up, as well as Patriotism and Heroism in transalleganian Regions? Have You Seen Wilkinsons History? &c. &c. &c. J. A.

RC (DLC); edge trimmed; endorsed by TJ as received 2 June 1817 and so recorded in SJL. RC (DLC); address cover only; with PoC of TJ to David Knight, [12] Aug. 1817, on verso; addressed in an unidentified hand: "His Excellency Thomas Jefferson. Monticello. Virginia"; postmarked Quincy, 21 May. FC (Lb in MHi: Adams Papers).

The superior GENERAL of the Jesuits was Tadeusz Brzozowski. NOTHINGARIANS lack religious beliefs (*OED*).

[1] Preceding six words interlined.
[2] FC: "excelling."

To Isaac Briggs

DEAR SIR May 18. 17.

Your favor of the 9th never came to hand till the last night, viz. two days after the meeting of the board at New York who were to decide on the persons to be employed in the direction of their grand canal: and as the arrangements of our mail render it impossible to get a letter to N. York before the last of the month, the certainty that the decision will be over, prevents my doing more than to acknolege your letter. I have thought it the less important, as my opinion of your high talents as a Mathematician and Astronomer was sufficiently proved by my having appointed you Surveyor General of the South Western department, and again by my employing you to designate the direction of the nearest[1] road from Washington to N. Orleans which should not cross the mountains by observations of Latitude and Longitude only, and my well known[2] approbation of what you did. this work required Mathematical talents of a high order. my solicitations to you too to undertake the astronomical observations & calculations for the map of our state, had that proceeded on the scale at first contemplated, was a proof that I continued my confidence in you. still, had your letter arrived in time I should with great pleasure and as an act of duty, have given testimony direct of my confidence in your qualifications, industry & integrity. as it is I can only tender my regrets that your application came so late, with the assurance of my constant friendship & respect. TH: JEFFERSON

PoC (DLC); on verso of reused address cover of John H. Cocke to TJ, 26 Mar. 1817; at foot of text: "Mr Isaac Briggs"; endorsed by TJ.

[1]Preceding two words interlined in place of "a."

[2]Manuscript: "know."

To Louis A. Leschot

TH: JEFFERSON TO MR LESCHOT. Monticello May 18. 17.

Mr Girardin, a French literary gentleman, & friend of mine, living near Staunton, called on me on his way to Richmond. having a repeating watch which he valued much, but which had been mu[ch] injured by ignorant workmen, he left her with me, on my advice; to get the favor of you to repair her, for which purpose I send her by the bearer. he will call on you about Saturday or Sunday next, in the hope you will be able by that time to have repaired her. he is a gentleman of great worth, and his acquaintance in Staunton will enable him to serve you there.

I salute mrs Leschot and yourself with friendship, and with assurances that we shall be much gratified by your visits whenever you can spare the time. our wishes are that you will come at your own convenience, without the ceremony of particular invitations which might not suit your convenience.

RC (ViU: TJP); torn at folds; addressed: "Mr Leschot." Not recorded in SJL.

Louis A. Leschot (1779–1838), watchmaker, was born in the village of Les Brenets in the Swiss canton of Neuchâtel. He married into the Montandon family of watchmakers and immigrated to the United States with them about 1815. Leschot and his wife settled in Charlottesville early in 1817 as a result of a multiyear effort by TJ to secure a watchmaker for the town. TJ frequently patronized Leschot, purchasing watches and watch parts and paying him for watch and clock repair. He also bought spoons and spectacles from him. In 1837 Leschot became a naturalized United States citizen. He was buried at Monticello (Catherine B. Hollan, *Virginia Silversmiths, Jewelers, Watch- and Clockmakers, 1607–1860, Their Lives and Marks* [2010], 458–9, 949; *MB*; DNA: RG 29, CS, Albemarle Co., 1820, 1830; Albemarle Co. Law Order Book [1831–37], 263, 410–1; Albemarle Co. Will Book, 13:151; Shackelford, *Descendants*, 1:261).

From David Higginbotham

DEAR SIR, Richmond 20th May 1817.

If you have not yet sold your westham lots and are still disposed to sell them, be pleased to say the number you have and the size and the price you ask for them, I will perhaps purchase them if the price is not two high, I may perhaps be able to turn them into Cash in some way or other to suit us both, be pleased to say what is the loss we shall all sustain this year by the Hessian fly, shall we make half crops or not, I have so many different reports that it is hard to get a correct opinion

I am Dear Sir Your Mo^{t} Obt DAVID HIGGINBOTHAM

RC (MHi); endorsed by TJ as received 22 May 1817 and so recorded in SJL. RC (MHi); address cover only; with PoC of TJ to Albert Gallatin, 23 June 1817, on verso; addressed: "Thomas Jefferson Esq Monticello"; stamped; postmarked.

From LeRoy, Bayard & Company

SIR Newyork the 20^{t} May 1817.

We were in course favor'd with the Letters you did us the honor of addressing to us on the 15 Aug & 28 April last and yesterday we received payment of a remittance made to us on your account

by Mr Patrick Gibson of Richmond		$2000.
which we credit against the first bond due by you to Mess. N. & J & R Van Staphorst		
$1000. with Interest to 31 Decr 1815	$2083.20	
add interest to this day $16\frac{2}{3}$ m^{o} @ 6%	173.59.	2256.79
leaving due on the 1^{t} bond value this day		$ 256.79.

and on the 7 May 1818 $2083.20
7 May 1819 $2083.20 } with Interest

@ 6% ℘ annum from 1 Jany 1816 Till discharged being in conformity with what agreed ℘ our respect of 7 Aug. last. We have the honor to Salute with high consideration Sir Your h^{b} S^{t}

LEROY BAYARD & Co

RC (DLC); in the hand of a representative of LeRoy, Bayard, & Company; between dateline and salutation: "The Honble Th^o^ Jefferson, Monticello"; endorsed by TJ as received 28 May 1817 and so recorded in SJL.

From John Manners

DEAR SIR, Flemington May 20th 1817

On a former occasion I took the liberty of consulting you on an interesting and important subject of Natural Science, and feel myself much honoured by the attention you were pleased to show my letter, in giving it a reply so ample, so instructing, & so satisfactory. I only regret that I did not apply for permission to publish it.

I am fully convinced of the correctness of the observation contained in your letter respecting the Unity of the operations of Nature, & of the advantage to be derived to our memories by an artificial classification of her productions.

I am myself emphatically an Unitarian. I believe in the Unity of the Deity with my friends Cooper Priestley and other theologians, in opposition to the polytheism of the Athanasian creed. I believe in the Unity of Disease, in opposition to the nosological systems of Sauvages[1] Sydenham Linnæus Cullen & other pathologists, with my truely worthy friend & preceptor in medicine the immortal Rush, for whom I shall ever feel a lively sense of gratitude for the innumerable instances of kindness & attention with which he honoured me, both during my pupilage, & after I graduated & practiced in that metropolis. But I must not permit my love for my departed master to carry me from my subject. And further, I believe with you and the learned M. Buffon the great advocate of individualism, in the Unity of the operations of Nature. Yet I cannot join M. Buffon in condemning all classification as injudicious.

Certainly the division of natural productions into Classes orders genera Species tribes sects & societies tho' strictly artificial, facilitates the acquisition of a knowledge of the science of Nature. But among all the authors who have classified the productions of nature, I do not know that any one is intrinsically much better than another. Thus the classifications of Ray Klein Brisson Linnæus Cuvier Blumenbach[2] Jussieu Hauy &c. have each of them their respective merits. But for the reason contained in your letter, I think that the systema Naturæ must ever remain the grand Book of Record among naturalists. This is the opinion of my worthy & learned friend Dr Saml L. Mitchill of N. York.

Our late departed friend Dr Benj. Smith Barton, whose death must long be deplored by every naturalist, to whom I took the liberty of showing your letter, requested me to state to you, that the observations of the Cheval[r] d'Abboville respecting the mammæ of the opposum being only discoverable during pregnancy or suckling her young is incorrect. He said he had fully proved that they were discoverable at all times.

I was not before aware that it had been ascertained that the ornithorynchus of New Holland was viviparous. But notwithstanding this fact, has it not in the aggregate as many characteristics of the Aves, as of the Mammalia & does it not want some of the most essential of the latter.

I should do an injustice to my feelings, on the present occasion, were I not to acknowledge that I have derived more instruction from reading your letter than from all the books which I have seen upon the subject of which it treats.

I formerly devoted much time & attention to the study of the natural sciences, but the pursuit of two professions, and the attention which I must necessarily bestow to the instruction of my pupils of both law & medicine, leave me little time to cultivate my former more favorite studies.

On the present occasion I wish your instruction on an important subject of national jurisprudence. I should be much gratified to know your opinion of the right of expatriation. The authorities on both sides of the question are so numerous & respectable as to render it difficult to decide. From my own view of the subject I should conclude that the ne exuere ligeantiam was not founded in law, & certainly not in reason

It cannot be founded in the law of Nature. For in a state of Nature, all ethical writers agree that every person has a right to emigrate to whatever place his convenience or his inclinations may lead him, & to occupy what ever lands he pleases: as all men are equal he owes allegiance to none.

It is not founded in the revealed Law. Numerous instances of expatriation are mentioned in both the old and New Testaments.

It is not founded in the law of Nations For altho' Sir Edward Coke, Sir Mathew Hale, Sir William Blackstone, and other English jurists contend that it is the law of Nations, yet, in my humble opinion, the better authoriti[es] deny this position. Puffendorf Cicero[3] Grotius Burlamaqui Locke Vattel &c. all admit the right of expatriation.

If it exist then in the United states it must be sought for in the Municipal Law. No such law, however, is expressed in either the constitution of the United states or their legislative acts.

It has been contended that we have adopted it by implication with the common law, & that it is founded in our lex non Scripta or unwritten Codes. But I should like to be informed how & at what time the United States in their federal & national capacity adopted a common law. If we have a common law, is it that of England? If that of England, whether intire or in part? & what part?

In the course of my researches in the science of Jurisprudence I have found so much difference of opinion of authors, so much contrariety of decision of courts, & so much difficulty on the subject, that I have determined to appeal to you for satisfactory information. Thus while Judge Chase, Judge Tucker, & Mr Madison, are of opinion that the common law of England has no binding authority in our national government, Judge Ellsworth Judge Washington & Judge Peters contend that the federal courts are invested with common law jurisdiction. Of the latter opinion is my father-in-law Judge Cooper, under whose direction my legal studies were conducted, & to whom I am indebted for whatever talents, as a lawyer, I may be thought to possess, as expressed in his edition of Justinian (p 405). altho he seems to have expressed a different opinion in Cooper's Bankrupt Law (p 230 & 283).

I must confess, that independent of any authorities upon the subject, considering the constitution as the warrant of attorney to the agents of the general government by their principals the several individual & independent states, which must be construed strictly, I cannot see how they are invested with any common law authority legislative executive or judiciary not expressly delegated to them—The federal government therefore, deriving all their powers from the states could not have adopted a Common law in their federal capacity.

But it has been said, that the states had granted it to the federal government by implication[.] The strict construction, however, which the constitution must receive would forbid such a conclusion. Add to this the twelfth article of the amendments to the constitution of the United States which expressly declares that "the powers not delegated to the United States by the constitution nor prohibited by it to the states, are reserved to the states respectively or to the people" Which according to Vattel & all writers on national law is a mere recognition of the law of nations.

The common law of England therefore, can have no more binding authority in our federal government than the Institutes of Justinian, or the Code Napoleon. It may be referred to as a known law but it is lex sub graviori lege, & has no binding authority. Otherwise we might boast our written constitution in vain.

It is admitted that the individual states may prohibit the emigration of their subjects. And admitting that every state in the Union had made such prohibition, which however is not the fact, yet it would not become the law of the United States unless expressly made so by constitutional or legislative regulation.

I am aware I stand in need of an apology for the liberty I have taken, but the interest I feel in the subject, the polite attention you were pleased to show my former letter, & your preeminent abilitie[s] to instruct, must plead my excuse.

I remain D^r sir Very Respectfully Yours &c.

JNO. MANNERS

RC (DLC); edge trimmed; addressed: "Thomas Jefferson L.L.D. Monticello, Virginia"; franked; postmarked Ringoes, 20 May; endorsed by TJ as received 28 May 1817 and so recorded in SJL.

In his *Additional Facts, Observations, and Conjectures relative to the Generation of the Opossum of North-America* (Philadelphia, 1813), Benjamin Smith Barton refuted assertions regarding the opossum (OPPOSUM) by François Marie, chevalier (later comte) d'Aboville, which had been published in François Jean, marquis de Chastellux, *Travels in North America in the Years 1780, 1781 and 1782*, trans. and ed. Howard C. Rice Jr. (1963; see also Sowerby, nos. 4021, 4023), 2:465–8.

The ornithorhynchus (ORNITHORYNCHUS) is the duck-billed platypus (*OED*). AVES: the taxonomic class to which birds belong. NE EXUERE LIGEANTIAM: "your allegiance is not to be renounced," a reference to the British principle that citizenship was inalienable and could not be relinquished of one's own volition.

Thomas Cooper remarked in his EDITION of *The Institutes of Justinian. With Notes* (Philadelphia, 1812; Sowerby, no. 2192; Poor, *Jefferson's Library*, 10 [no. 613]), 405, that "even in this country, we adopt in every state, all our legal maxims and institutions not contained in constitutional or legislative acts, as the common law of the state. Nor can common law be entirely dispensed with even in the code of the United States, notwithstanding the very able opinions of Mr. Madison and Judge Chase."

Conversely, in *The Bankrupt Law of America compared with The Bankrupt Law of England* (Philadelphia, 1801; Sowerby, no. 1994), 230, Cooper EXPRESSED A DIFFERENT OPINION, asserting that, while precedents of the English courts might inform judicial decisions, "I do not know that they have ever been considered with us as absolutely binding." Later in that work he was even more definitive in stating that "English cases are not *binding* in our courts" (p. 283).

LEX SUB GRAVIORI LEGE: "laws subject to a weightier law."

[1] Manuscript: "Savanges."
[2] Manuscript: "Bleumenbach."
[3] Manuscript: "Cecero."

From Charles Willson Peale

MY DEAR SIR   Belfield May 20th 1817.

Although very unwilling to give you the least trouble in the epistolary line, yet I feel a desire to communicate what I consider a cricis of my labours on the Museum—beleiving that you esteem it a work of importance to the enlightning of the Public mind. Envy of some men and self-interest in others have made them active, to get the Museum remooved from the State-House, and the City being indebt and without funds, and limited in their powers to raise money—The Corporation by one set of men were urged to put a high rent, and some others advised them to let me be rent free. Yet all acknowledge the importance that the Museum is to the City, Nay, even the men who are the most active to fix a high rent, but they say that the income can afford it, without considering that taking away its funds is robing it of the means of improvement—and also my means of supporting 4 families, besides a support to the labouring hands in it.

I made to the Corporation a specific proposition, which I conceived was so much the interest of the City to accept, that was I to publish it, they would be compelled to ascent through the Voice of the People—I proposed to make over to the City all my right and title to the Museum for ever, and to give an annual rent of 800$, and also to appropriate 400$ annually for its increase & support under their approbation of its application, on condition that they would allow the Museum to remain in perpetuity in the upper part of the State-house, and allow me or my heirs to extend it over the fireproof Offices, east & West, the building to be made at my expence, and after paying all the incidental expences, and that I and my heirs should also be bound to take all suitable care of the articles and the regulation of the Establishment, then the surplus revenue we would receive as the proper reward for exertion and the right of inheritance, and as the most certain means of insuring its prosperity. By this Plan the City would reap all the benefit of such an Establishment without a single cent expence—But I have good reason to believe that a number of Attornies at Law are desireous to get the rooms we occupy—and there are a number of that Profession in the Councils, whose influence as men of Words will swerve the Councils from their duty.

The question is not yet finally determined, but I am prepaired to send them my determination, which will be to this purpose, Vizt that I conceived my Plan would have secured to the City of Philada an Institution of immence Value to the Citizens in a Political, moral and religious point of View. Not only contributing to the general Wealth, by its inducements of Straingers to visit and Stay with us, but also by enlarging the Public minds in Arts and Science by various Lectures on Subjects furnished by the Museum.—By harmonising jaring Sentiments in assembling company promiscuously togather viewing the immence varieties of the works of an alwise Creator.—And in the cheapest mode to amuse at the same moment to instruct in a forcible manner, the vain, the Idle, and the profligate, to win them from haunt of Vice and disapation.—And lastly, that the Museum would furnish food for the minds of wise and good Men, Women & Children of the present day, and to rising generations by its perpetuity. I say, "By the enlargement and increase of the Institution on the proposed Plan, I beleived I was serving the City at the least possible expence to it, with Riches, Virtue & honour.—But if your honorable boards think it is not of such interest to the City, I must doubt my opinion as being premature, and submit to your superior judgement. And as there has been surmises that I had endeavored by my address, in July 1816, to the Corporation and the Public, to stir up an opposition to them, I declare that my object was to give the support of Public opinion to an act, which I vainly thought, that the Corporation wished to adopt. To avoid such censure in future, it is not my intention to publish in Newspapers any thing on the Subject, except an advertizement for the Sale of the Museum, which I hope will not give offence to your honorable boards, when you consider that at my time of life, it is prudent to provide for a change, and as far as possible to prevent all cause of strife amongst my Children.

Therefore I pray your honorable boards to suffer the Museum to remain in its present situation at a Moderate rent, untill I can provide for some other disposition of it, of which I will not fail to give you due notice according to custom & common usage.

I am" &c &c.

I have acquainted some members of the Councils with my intentions of presenting an address to the above purport. they say that perhaps the business may take a differant turn—I tell them that I shall wait, and not do any thing hastily. Many friends to the Museum advise me to get a lot and build, There is great difficulty to obtain a lott in such a situation as would be Advantagous—besides I am fearful of the perplexities attending the erecting a building sufficiently large for an encreasing Museum. quietness at my time of life is very desireable, and I wish only to amuse myself with my Pencils and take care of my health. If I can[1] sell the Museum at 120,000$ it will releive me from all future trouble—and in Philad[a] it will give the Purchasers a good interest for their money and be an encreasing fund to them.

To give you what I think a striking trait of the importance of the museum to the City by its attraction of Straingers—on thursday night last week I went to the Museum alone, there were upwards of 150 persons there—I walked from Room to Room looking for some Person of my acquaintance; I sat down to view them passing before me while they were viewing various articles in the Museum & to my surprize I could not find a single person that to my knowledge I had seen before, except my own family.

The orderly behavour, the harmony, & the pleasure that prevails in every countenance, is truly greatful to my feelings—And also the chemical & Phylosophical experiments made by my Son Rubens, diffusing important knowledge to numerous people who otherways would never have the chance of acquiring any thing in that way—surely those things which enlighten, and make the multitude happy, ought to meet with liberal encouragement. a well organised Museum on a permanent foundation, from its Usefulness, would receive valuable donations & bequests. this was my view in my offer of it to the City of Philad[a]. And in the plan of regulations I intended to give it a nominal Value divided into 100 Shares, each share to have a Vote in the appointment of a President a Treasurer & Secretary, the Secretary to be keeper and manager of the Museum—The accounts to be settled every 6 months, and after all incidental expences are paid, each Stockholder to receive his dividend—

This is but an imperfect sketch of what will be arranged for the completing the establishment—should it succeed, (which I can scarcely think it will, as I believe a combination of Lawyers are oppossing it,) I will give you the detail.

Before I close my Scrole, I will in addition say—that suppose a lot and a building may be obtained for 40,000$ which added to the above moderate valuation, makes 160,000$. In a good situation in Philad[a] the income with very little trouble and proper attention to its Visitors, will pay 6 ℘[r] C[t] on that sum—and by the common increase of Inhabitants with an accumulation of interesting articles, in a few years it undoubtedly would give 10 ℘[r] C[ts]. In my view, a suitable Building need not be a costly one, Walls of sufficient extent with only one Coat of plastering—No Carpenters work except floors, windows, Roof & some doors, And a respectable intrance from the Street. I intend a journey to N. York in a few days, in order to obtain a settlement of property due me by a former Marriage—Doct[r] Mitchel and some others fond of Natural History will doubtless inform me what encouragemint to those Studies in that City, can be obtained of the Corporation—information of this kind will be desirable[.] Not that I have a wish of sending the Museum to N. York, unless I am compel'd to do so, by dire necessity. Enough on this subject. I am much pleased to hear that you have at last obtained a good artist in Clock & watch work—I have nothing in the Mechanical line worth notice, except the construction of a fire Engine envented by M[r] Perkins, which appears to me the most simple and yet powerful that I have seen—my Son in Law, Coleman Sellers (who is an excellent Mechanick) is engaged with M[r] Perkins in the establishment of a manufactory of them—Scarcely a day passes, if any of the Engines are seen but they have applicants for either Small or large Engines—some made for Gardens, mooved on wheel Barrows, at 30$—Villiage Engines at 200$ & large of great power to 1000$—The manner of working is by a horizontal motion, and is greatly preferable to the perpendicular working—and an important advantage in the horizontal working, is, that men can work to any extent by means of Ropes.

Accept my best wishes for your health and beleive me with much esteem your friend C W PEALE

RC (DLC); edge trimmed; endorsed by TJ as received 28 May 1817 and so recorded in SJL. RC (MHi); address cover only; with PoC of TJ to Joel Yancey, 25 June 1817, on verso; addressed: "Thomas Jefferson Esq[r] Monticlla Virginea"; franked; postmarked Philadelphia, 22 May. PoC (PPAmP: Peale Letterbook).

On 10 Apr. 1817 Peale made his SPECIFIC PROPOSITION to the Select and Common councils of Philadelphia that that city acquire the title to his museum under the terms described here (Peale, *Papers*, 3:477–8). For his ADDRESS of July 1816, see Peale to TJ, 9 Aug. 1816. Peale traveled to New York City between 23 May and 24 Nov. 1817 in an unsuccessful effort to obtain a SETTLEMENT on his children's behalf from the estate of his late wife, Elizabeth DePeyster Peale (Peale, *Papers*, 3:487). The GOOD ARTIST IN CLOCK & WATCH WORK was Louis A. Leschot.

Jacob PERKINS received patents for improvements to fire engines on 6 Aug. 1812 and 23 Mar. 1813. He and Coleman Sellers partnered to sell such apparatus based on his designs from about 1817 to 1818 (*List of Patents*, 116, 124; Eugene S. Ferguson, ed., *Early Engineering Reminiscences (1815–40) of George Escol Sellers* [1965], 12, 15–6).

[1] Peale here canceled "dispose."

From Caspar Wistar

My Dear Sir Philad[a] May 20th 1817—

Since I have understood the oppressive extent of your Correspondence, I have felt the greatest reluctance at addressing a letter to you; but the long interval has become painful to my self, & I am delighted with an opportunity of reviving your recollection of me. Inclosed is an account of the publication of D[r] Franklin's letters & some small specimens of them. I believe this publication will evince that the writer was fairly entitled, not only to all the reputation he enjoyed, but a great deal more; & for the excellence of his heart as well as the clearness of his head. D[r] Priestley informed me that he spent with D[r] Franklin several hours of the last day which the Doctor passed in England. They were principally occupied in reading news Papers which had just arrived from America, & contained the first accounts of the Battle of Lexington. Franklin Several times shed tears, Said that the contest would be very bloody, & he should not live to See the end of it, but that his Country men would be successful. When this publication is read our great Countryman will be judged by what he really said, & thought, & did, & will need no Vindication. You see there are Subjects not political treated in these letters; I indulge the hope of Seeing you again, & when I have that pleasure Shall certainly not forget to enquire of you respecting some of them. I regret that I did not attempt 20 years ago[1] to collect materials for forming a description of the life & manners of Franklin, as they were before the Commencement of the revolution. It could have been done then very easily from the accounts of his associates; but the opportunity has passed away—It ought to be remembered that he embraced every proper occasion of being merry.

I believe that he was fond of the pleasures of the table. An old Lady whose husband was one of his intimate friends, & had a very florid face, enquired of the Doctor how he preserved his face of Such a proper colour—"Madam, when my irons grow too hot, I draw them out of the fire," was the reply—

When D[r] Stewart passed through Philad[a] I took the liberty of Sending by him the New Map of Mellish which I did not then know you had Seen. You can make a very good use of two copies & I beg your acceptance of it—

Please to assure M[rs] Randolph & the rest of your family of my grateful recollection of them & believe me with Sincerity & affection

your obliged friend C. Wistar

P.S. We are about commencing the publication of another volume of the A P. Transactions and hope for a Communication from you.

RC (DLC); dateline adjacent to signature; addressed: "His Excellency Tho[s] Jefferson"; endorsed by TJ as received 25 May 1817 and so recorded in SJL. Enclosure not found.

William Duane published four volumes (numbered 2–5) of *The Works of Dr. Benjamin Franklin, in Philosophy, Politics, and Morals: containing* ... (Philadelphia, 1808–09; Sowerby, no. 4931). He published vols. 6 and 1 in 1817 and 1818, respectively, drawing heavily on new examples of FRANKLIN's writings in an edition of his papers recently published in London by William Temple Franklin (Francis S. Philbrick, "Notes on Early Editions and Editors of Franklin," APS, *Proceedings* 97 [1953]: 551–3). The new subtitle for Duane's 1817 volume emphasized its inclusion of private letters: *containing his Diplomatic Correspondence, as minister of the United States, at the court of Versailles; his Private Epistolary Correspondence, miscellaneous, literary, and philosophical subjects, between the years 1753 and 1790, developing the Secret History of his Political Transactions and Negotiations*.

The map sent by Wistar and delivered by Josephus B. Stuart (STEWART) when the latter visited Monticello in December 1816 was probably John Melish's *Map of the United States with the contiguous British & Spanish Possessions* (Philadelphia, 1816). A P.: American Philosophical Society.

[1] Preceding three words interlined.

From Isaac Briggs

MY DEAR FRIEND, Washington City, 5 mo 21–1817

On the 15 or 16 instant I wrote to thee from New York, informing thee that I had received an appointment from the Canal commissioners for employment in the mathematical department for making the grand Canal between the Western and Northern Lakes and the Atlantic Ocean. In that letter I expressed my decided opinion that if the Commissioners could avail the public of the talents and services, as civil Engineer, of our friend Thomas Moore, even by a very liberal compensation, the result would be a great saving of expense in the end, as well as probably shortening the period and encreasing the chances of its final accomplishment. I wish very much to be associated with Thomas Moore in this great work. I could say much for his qualifications and to urge the propriety of employing him, but delicacy forbids, as we are nearly alied in marriage. I think a great point would be gained, if we could obtain his company and services in exploring <u>during the present season</u> the different proposed routes, examining the circumstances connected with them, and assisting in the selection of the most proper. If, in this thing, I have thy concurrence, of which I feel a strong belief, I indulge the expectation that thou wilt address DeWitt Clinton or Thomas Eddy (N° 220 William Street New-York) on the subject. I hope it will be done soon—notwithstanding it is with real reluctance I invade, and with veneration I approach, the sacred tranquility of the evening of a life of virtue.

Accept my most affectionate salutations. ISAAC BRIGGS.

I expect to be in New York on this day week (28)

RC (DLC); endorsed by TJ as received 28 May 1817 and so recorded in SJL. RC (DLC); address cover only; with PoC of TJ to Samuel L. Osborn, [29] Aug. 1817, on verso; addressed: "Thomas Jefferson Monticello, near Charlottesville, V[a]"; franked; postmarked Washington City, 21 May. FC (MdHi: Briggs-Stabler Papers); entirely in Briggs's hand; lacking postscript; at head of text: "Copy"; endorsed by Briggs.

From Luis de Onís

SIR, Washington 21st May 1817.

Not doubting that it will be gratifying to you to be informed of the respect paid at the Havana to the memory of the late Dr Valli, whose death was occasioned by a dangerous experiment which he tryed on himself, which was announced some time ago in the Public Papers of this Country, I take the liberty to send to you inclosed, the Funeral Oration that was pronounced at an extra meeting of the Royal Patriotic Society of said city, and which was transmitted to me by Don Alexandro Ramirez, Intendent General of the Island of Cuba, a Member and Director of said Royal Patriotic Society, together with the resolution of that Board that "the Memory of D[r] Valli, be perpetuated by a neat & plain monument, to be erected as a testimonial of the gratitude which is due to those illustrious men who sacrifice themselves in the cause of humanity."[1]

In addressing you, Sir, I cannot forbear the opportunity of expressing to you the sentiments of great regard and high consideration, with which I have the honor to remain,

Sir, Your most obedient humble Servant.

THE CHEVALIER DE ONIS

RC (DLC); at foot of first page: "His Excellency Thomas Jefferson"; endorsed by TJ as received 5 June 1817 and so recorded in SJL. Enclosure: Tomás Romay y Chacón, *Elogio del Dr. D. Eusebio Valli ... Leído en junta ordinaria de la Sociedad económica de esta ciudad el 22 de noviembre de 1816* (Havana, 1816; Poor, *Jefferson's Library*, 5 [no. 163]).

Eusebio Valli's MONUMENT was to read "Epitafio. Aqui Yace el Dr. Eusebio

Valli, victima de su amor a la humanidad; La Sociedad Economica de La Habana recomienda su memoria. Año de 1816" ("Epitaph. Here lies Dr. Eusebio Valli, victim of his love of humanity. The Economic Society of Havana commends his memory. In the year 1816") (Romay y Chacón, *Elogio del Dr. D. Eusebio Valli*, 11).

[1] Omitted closing quotation mark editorially supplied.

From James Gibbon

D^R^ SIR — Richmond May 22^d^ 1817

It happen'd very opportunely, that at the moment I rec^d^ y^r^ letter, a Capt from Boston appeard at my office with your parcell of seeds of which I had been apprizd by Mr Dearborne; they have been sent on by Mr Gibson in charge of a boat man who usually takes parcells for you under an injunction to keep it dry as Mr D. directed[1]
I hope you will receive[2] it in good order

I have the honor to be with perfect respect Yr M^o^ Ob

J GIBBON

There has been no charge made—

RC (DLC); endorsed by TJ as received 28 May 1817 and so recorded in SJL. RC (DLC); address cover only; with PoC of TJ to Thomas Ritchie, [29] Aug. 1817, on verso; addressed: "Th^o^ Jefferson Esqr Monte Cello near Milton"; franked; postmarked Richmond, 25 May.

[1] Manuscript: "dircted."
[2] Manuscript: "recive."

Notes on Value of Lots in Beverley Town (Westham)

[ca. 22 May 1817]

my lots in Beverly town N°s 57. 107. 108. 151[1]
1751. June 5. cost 86/ each
what worth at 6. p.c. comp^d^ int. 1817. June 3
formula $l = ar^{n-1}$

Log. 1.06 = r	0.0253059
Log. 1.06 × 65 (= n – 1)	1.6448835
Log. 86. = a	1.9344985
N° 3796.5 s = Log.	3.5793820
D.632.7[2]	

the same at 5. p.c. comp. int. to 1797. May 1.
and then at 6. p.c. to 1817. May 1.

Log. 1.05 = r		0.0211893
Log. 1.05 × 45 (= n - 1)		0.9535185
Log. 86 = a		1.9344985
N° 772.71 s =	Log.	2.8880170
D 128.80		

2^d opern from 1797. to 1817. 20.y. @ 6. p.c.

Log. 1.06 = r	0.0253059
Log. 1.06 × 19 (n - 1)	0.4808121
Log. 128.80 = a	2.8880170
N° 2337.9 = Log.	3.3688291

Dol. 390.

128.80 D + 390 D = 518. D 80 c for each lot

the lots generally are 2 ch–24 l = 215.84 f square
containing half an acre each.[3]
streets 3. po. wide = $49\frac{1}{2}$ f
but N° 151. the ferry lot is 431.68 f[4] = 431 f–8 I extent on the river.

MS (DLC: TJ Papers, 232:41549); written entirely in TJ's hand on one side of a narrow scrap; undated.

TJ presumably calculated these values for his lots in Beverley Town (Westham) after receipt on 22 May 1817 of David Higginbotham's letter of 20 May 1817. The maximum allowable interest rate in Virginia was increased from 5. P.C. to 6 percent in November 1796. The change took effect on 1 May 1797 (*Acts of Assembly* [1796 sess.], 16–7).

[1] Lot numbers added in a different ink from remainder of manuscript.
[2] Reworked from "D.622.7."
[3] Preceding five words interlined.
[4] Reworked from "331.68 f."

To Craven Peyton

Monticello May 23. 17.

Th: Jefferson asks the favor of mr Peyton to come and take a pea-dinner with him the day after tomorrow (Sunday)

RC (Mrs. Charles W. Biggs, Lewisburg, W.Va., 1950; photocopy in MsSM); dateline at foot of text; addressed: "Mr Peyton Monteagle." Not recorded in SJL.

To Patrick Gibson

DEAR SIR Monticello May 24. 17.

I return by our first mail the note for renewal inclosed in your's of the 20th inst. and I am very thankful for the accomodation obtained, and payment remitted to Leroy and Bayard. if the Virginia bank cannot consistently with their rules renew it, I am in hopes that of the US. may come to my aid, as I understand it begins business this week. I observe a stamp on the paper you inclosed me; but I presume that can be added whenever I send you my notes on ordinary paper. should that bank not give me an accomodation for some months say, till the next crop comes in, I shall be infinitely distressed.

I am in hopes you will be able to sell my flour in time to meet a draught I have given Th: J. Randolph for 500.D. and one which I must give to mr Southall (our present Collector) whenever he calls for it for upwards of 600.D. besides 3. or 4. others for from 1. to 200. which I must soon make. at the close of the ensuing month I shall have 53.[1] Barrels of flour forwarded, being a quarter's mill rent, and I am in hopes that before this you will have recieved 3. more hhds of tobacco from Poplar Forest.

[I] salute you with constant friendship and respect.

TH: JEFFERSON

P. S. I wait your notice of the remittance to mr Vaughan.

PoC (MHi); on verso of reused address cover of Fernagus De Gelone to TJ, 15 Mar. 1817; torn at seal; adjacent to signature: "Mr Gibson"; endorsed by TJ. Enclosure not found. Enclosed in TJ to Gibson, 25 May 1817.

Gibson's letter OF THE 20TH INST. was actually dated 17 May 1817.

On this date TJ recorded that he had renewed his standing note for $2,000 with the Bank of Virginia and that Gibson had remitted an additional note for $2,000 on his behalf from the bank to LeRoy, Bayard & Company in partial PAYMENT of his debt to the firm of N. & J. & R. van Staphorst (*MB*, 2:1333).

The Richmond branch of the Second Bank OF THE US. had commenced discounting notes and issuing paper on 21 May 1817 (*Alexandria Gazette & Daily Advertiser*, 2 June 1817). TJ had given his grandson Thomas Jefferson Randolph a DRAUGHT on Gibson & Jefferson for $500 on 17 May 1817.

[1] In left margin, keyed to this point with an asterisk, TJ noted that "these had been sent by T. E. R. [Thomas Eston Randolph] May 3."

To Patrick Gibson

DEAR SIR Monticello May 25. 17.

It was not till I had sealed the inclosed that I turned to the settlement of my debt to the Van Staphorsts, which my memory had supposed a little under 2000. D each instalment, whereas I find it was a little over that sum, to wit 2083.20 D with interest @ 6. p.c. from Jan. 1. 1816. there is still therefore a balance of 83.20 principal[1] due to them with interest on the whole from Jan. 1. 1816 this I must pray you to remit in order to close that instalment. I repeat assurances of esteem & respect. TH: JEFFERSON

PoC (MHi); on verso of reused address cover of Joseph Dougherty to TJ, 10 Mar. 1817; at foot of text: "M[r] Gibson"; endorsed by TJ. Enclosure: TJ to Gibson, 24 May 1817.

In his financial records for this date, TJ estimated the BALANCE of principal and interest due on the 1817 installment of his debt payments to N. & J. & R. van Staphorst to be around $260 (*MB*, 2:1333).

[1]Word interlined.

To LeRoy, Bayard & Company

MESS[RS] LEROY AND BAYARD Monticello May 25. 17.

A lapse of memory, never discovered till this moment calls for immediate apology and correction. my memory had represented to me the annual instalments of my debt to the mess[rs] Van Staphorsts as something under 2000.D. and I had therefore desired mr Gibson to remit that round sum. on just now recieving his information that he had done so, I turned to your letter of Aug. 7. 16. and find it was 2083.20 D with interest also from Jan. 1. 16. I have therefore this day desired mr Gibson to remit you the additional 83.20 D with interest on the whole sum till you shall recieve it, to compleat the payment of that instalment, and I repeat to you the assurances of my great esteem and respect. TH: JEFFERSON

RC (SwSKB, 1947); addressed: "Mess[rs] LeRoy & Bayard New York"; franked; postmarked Milton, 27 May; endorsed by a representative of the firm as answered 7 June 1817. PoC (DLC); on verso of a reused address cover from Edwin Stark to TJ; endorsed by TJ.

From Sir John Sinclair

MY DEAR SIR, 32. Sackville Street. 25th May–1817.

I perused, with much satisfaction, and real interest, the important communication with which you favoured me; and took care that some of those, who have weight in the councils of this country, should be aware of its contents.—I trust that it will materially tend, to remove the remains of any jealousy which may still subsist between the governments of the two countries.—on that head, (the repression of jealousy), I am happy to find, that there is not a shade of difference between us.

I must now revert to our favourite topic, that of agriculture.—after above thirty years labour, I am anxious to communicate to the world, the result of both my practical experience, and literary research.—It is now printing, under the title of, "The Code of agriculture." My intention is, to condense, into one volume octavo, the substance of all the information I have collected in that long period of time. The inclosed printed paper will explain the nature of the undertaking.—I have written to your new President on the subject, offering to send over to america, some copies of the work, the instant it is completed, in the hopes, that a new edition of it will be published, under the auspices of the government of that rising Empire; by means of which, with the assistance of the agricultural societies established in america, much useful information might be collected in that country, by which the work might afterwards be essentially improved.

I hope that this plan will meet with your approbation; and with my best wishes for your health and happiness,—I remain, with much esteem and regard

very faithfully yours JOHN SINCLAIR

N. B. I have not neglected to mention, in the Section on Implements of Husbandry, your ingenious improvement on the construction of the plough. I inclose a proof sheet, just received from the Printers containing the notes (see p. 105), in which that subject is mentioned.

RC (MHi); dateline between signature and postscript; addressed: "Thomas Jefferson Esqr America"; franked; endorsed by TJ as received <*28*> 29 Aug. 1817 and so recorded in SJL. Enclosures not found.

Sinclair had written to PRESIDENT James Monroe on 27 Mar. 1817 (PPRF).

In a footnote on page 105 of *The Code of Agriculture* (London, 1817), Sinclair wrote that "An improvement in the plough-ear, or mould-board, of swing ploughs, has been recommended by the celebrated Jefferson, formerly President of the United States of America, who has cultivated the mechanical branches of agriculture with much success."

From John Adams

DEAR SIR Quincy May 26. 1817

Mr Leslie Combs of Kentucky has Sent me a "History of the late War, in the Western Country, by Mr Robert B. McAffee" and "The Phylosophy of Human Nature by Joseph Buchanan."

"The[1] History," I am glad to See:[2] because it will preserve facts, to the honour, and immortal glory of the Western people. Indeed I am not Sorry that "the Phylosophy" has been published, because it has been a Maxim with me for Sixty years at least, Never to be afraid of a Book.

Nevertheless I cannot foresee much Utility in reviving, in this Country, the controversy between the Spiritualists and the Material-

ists. Why Should time be wasted in disputing about two Substances when both parties agree that neither knows any thing about either. If Spirit is an abstraction, a conjecture, a Chimera: Matter is an abstraction, a conjecture, a Chimera; for We know as much, or rather as little of one as of the other. We may read Cudworth Clerk Leibnitz, Berkley Hume Bolinbroke and Priestley and a million other Volumes in all Ages, and be obliged at last to confess that We have learned nothing. Spirit and matter Still remain a Riddle.[3] Define the terms however, and the controversy is Soon Settld. If Spirit is an active Something and matter an inactive Something, it is certain that one is not the other. We can no more conceive that Extension or Solidity can think or feel, or See, or hear, or taste or Smell: than We can conceive that Perception Memory Imagination or Reason can remove a mountain or blow a rock. This Enigma has puzzled Mankind from the beginning, and probably will to the End. Œconomy of time requires that We Should waste no more in So idle an Amusement.
In the 11th discourse of Sir William Jones before The Asiatic Society Vol. 3. p. 229. of his works, We find that Materialists and Immaterialists existed in India and that they accused each other of Atheism, before Berkly or Priestley, or Dupuis, or Plato, or Pythagoras were born. Indeed Neuton himself, appears to have discovered nothing that was not known to the Antient Indians: He has only furnished more ample demonstrations of the doctrines they taught. Sir John Malcomb agrees with Jones and Dupuis in the Astrological origin of Heathen Mithologies.[4]

Vain Man! Mind your own Business! Do no Wrong! Do all the good you can! Eat your Canvas back ducks, drink your burgundy, Sleep your Siesta,[5] when necessary, And Trust in God.!

What a mighty bubble? What a tremendous Waterspout has Napolion been according to his Life, written by himself? He Says he was the Creature of the Principles and manners[6] of the Age. By which no doubt, he means the Age of Reason; the progress of Manilius's Ratio; of Plato's Logos &c. I believe him. A Whirlwind raised him and a Whirlwind blowed him a Way to St Helena. He is very confident that the Age of Reason is not past; and So am I; but I hope that Reason will never again rashly and hastily create Such Creatures as him. Liberty, Equality, Fraternity, and Humanity will never again, I hope blindly Surrender themselves to an[7] unbounded ambition for national conquests, nor implicitly commit themselves to the custody and guardianship of Arms and Heroes. If they do, they will again End in St. Helena, Inquisitions Jesuits and Sacre Ligues.

Poor Laureate Southey, is writhing in Torments under the Laugh of the three kingdoms all Europe and America, upon the publication of his Wat Tyler. I wonder whether he, or Bona Suffers most.

I congratulate You and Madison and Monroe, on your noble Employment in founding a University. From Such a noble Tryumvirate, the World will expect Something very great and very new. But if it contains anything quite original, and very excellent, I fear the prejudices are too deeply rooted to Suffer it to last long, though it may be accepted at first. It will not always have three Such colossal reputations to Support it.

The Pernambuco Ambassador, his Secretary of Legation and private Secretary, respectable People, have made me a Visit. Having been Some year or two in a Similar Situation I could not but Sympathize with him. As Bona Says the Age of Reason is not ended. Nothing can tottally extinguish or eclipse the Light which has been Shed abroad by the press.

I am, Sir, with hearty wishes for your health and hapiness your Friend and humble Servant JOHN ADAMS

RC (DLC); addressed in an unidentified hand: "President Jefferson Monticello"; endorsed by TJ as received 11 June 1817 and so recorded in SJL. FC (Lb in MHi: Adams Papers). A possible additional address cover to this letter (addressed in same unidentified hand: "His Excellency Thomas Jefferson Monticello—Virginia"; postmarked Quincy, 26 May) was reused, with PoC of TJ to Joseph Gales (1761–1841), 19 June 1817, on verso.

LESLIE COMBS sent Adams the books mentioned with a letter of 8 Apr. 1817 (MHi: Adams Papers). Sir William Jones delivered his 11TH DISCOURSE to the Asiatick Society on 20 Feb. 1794 on the topic of "The Philosophy of the Asiaticks" (John Shore, Baron Teignmouth, ed., *The Works of Sir William Jones* [London, 1807], 3:229–52). The recently published *Manuscrit venu de St. Hélène, d'une manière inconnue* (London, 1817), purportedly an account of Napoloeon's LIFE, WRITTEN BY HIMSELF (Boston *Independent Chronicle*, 19 May 1817), has subsequently been attributed to Jacob Frédéric Lullin de Châteauvieux. SACRE LIGUES: "Holy Alliances."

In February 1817 *Wat Tyler*, a poem written decades earlier by the British poet laureate Robert SOUTHEY, was published in London without his consent. A juvenile effort generally regarded as possessing little literary merit, its appearance led to criticism of Southey for his perceived departure from the radical politics of his younger days (Frank Taliaferro Hoadley, "The Controversy over Southey's Wat Tyler," *Studies in Philology* 38 [1941]: 81–96).

Antônio Gonçalves da Cruz was the minister to the United States from the Republic of PERNAMBUCO, a Brazilian province that had recently declared its independence from Portugal. He and his colleagues arrived in Boston on 14 May 1817 (Boston *Independent Chronicle*, 15 May 1817). The revolt was soon suppressed. As an American diplomat during the Revolutionary War, Adams had been in the SIMILAR SITUATION of an emissary from a country whose independence had not been recognized abroad.

[1] Omitted opening quotation mark editorially supplied.

[2] Remainder of sentence interlined.

[3] RC: "a Riddles," with "a" interlined. FC: "a Riddle."

[4] Sentence interlined.
[5] RC and FC: "sesta."
[6] RC: "manrers." FC: "manners."
[7] RC: "and." FC: "an."

To David Higginbotham

DEAR SIR Monticello May 26. 17.

Yours of the 20th is recieved. I had never thought of selling my lots in Beverly town, but to pay a debt, I will do it, on terms rigorously just, that is to say, for first cost and compound interest on it to this day; rating interest at 5. p.c. till 1797. when it was raised by law, and at 6. p.c. for the then amount to the present day. mine are the lots No 57. 107. 108. and 151. they are generally 215. f 10 I square, but 151. is the ferry lot and extends on the river 431 f–8. I it's depth from the bank being small. my father paid for each of them June 5. 1751. a doubloon or £4–6[1] equal to $14\frac{1}{3}$ Dollars. the titles to all these lots depend I believe on an authenticated plan of the town, with the names of the proprietors written in their respective lots, now in my possession. I have heard that the record of it was destroyed by the British while in possession of Richmond. the present amount of the prices of the lots to be paid by a credit in your account against me.

The destruction of the wheat in this neighborhood by the fly is entirely unparalleled. Burnley says that some of yours will lose only one third, other parts of it two thirds, & one the whole. you will make about half a crop. this is about the expectation as to mine. but much depends on the weather. we have just had a fine rain, which has cleared up warm. if good growing weather continues it will help us much. I salute you with friendship & respect.

TH: JEFFERSON

PoC (MHi); on verso of a reused address cover from Edwin Stark to TJ; at foot of text: "Mr Higginbotham"; endorsed by TJ.

For the AUTHENTICATED PLAN OF THE TOWN, see note to TJ to Thomas Taylor, 28 Dec. 1814.

[1] £ is a symbol for "lira."

From John Barnes

DEAR SIR— George Town Coa 27th May 1817.

I am Hond by your favr 17th and Notice the particular dates of your Movemts the most suitable to my offices—will be, to embrace—the interval between this, and 20th June. of course[1] I purpose leaving G. T. 31st—the want of a friend—(in Case of Accidt) has induced me in taking the Liberty of engaging—the Young Studint Mentioned—in my last—with whom, I flatter my self you will not be displeased—

M[r] Milligan has promised—to hand me—whatever of the Books—he is able to compleat—

Yrs most Respectfully, with great Esteem—

Yr most Obed[t] servant JOHN BARNES.

RC (ViU: TJP-ER); at foot of text: "Thomas Jefferson Esq[r] Monticello"; endorsed by TJ as received 31 May 1817 and so recorded in SJL.

[1]Manuscript: "coure."

From Tristram Dalton

DEAR SIR. Boston May 27th 1817

I have to acknowledge & thank you for your favour of the 2nd Inst: which I communicated to my friend Aaron Dexter Esq[r] President of the Mass[as] Agricultural Society. He and his friends are highly gratified by your account of Co[l] Randolph's success in ploughing hill sides horizontally—a desideratum long sought for, in vain, in this quarter. Several Gentlemen are anxious to begin the system—but lest there should be a difect in a plow that might be made under their direction for this purpose, the President has requested me to ask the favour of you, which as it is for general utility, I flatter myself you will excuse this liberty, to order a plow made according to Co[l] Randolph's plan, complete, and forwarded to Richmond, to the care of M[r] James Baker Merchant there, who will pay the cost and every charge attending it—

Doctor Dexter desires me to present to you, Sir, his respectful compliments with the enclosed inaugural address of Doctor Gorham, his successor, as professor of chymistry in Harvard University. It is said to be ingenious, and as affording a few minutes amusement.

Pardon my intrusion on your time—the object I trust will procure it.

I pray my respectful regards may be presented to Co[l] Randolph, and that you will accept the assurances of high esteem and regards of

your most obed[t] Servant TRISTRAM DALTON

RC (DLC); at foot of text: "Hnble Tho[s] Jefferson"; endorsed by TJ as received 15 July 1817 and so recorded in SJL. Enclosure: John Gorham, *Inaugural Address, delivered in the Chapel of the University at Cambridge, December 11, 1816* (Boston, 1817; Poor, *Jefferson's Library*, 13 [no. 826]; TJ's copy in ViU).

From William Thornton

My dear Sir City of Washington May 27th 1817

I was very much gratified by hearing that the two Drawings arrived safe, and am highly obligated to[1] Mr & mrs Madison for their kind attention to them. I return my particular thanks for your kindness in lending them to me, and I am also under great obligation for your further favour in granting me permission to employ an Artist to take a Cast of that superb Bust, which I think one of the finest I ever beheld. I shall not fail to seek for one that I hope will do justice to it,—without injuring so invaluable a Specimen of the highest genius.—

It gives me great pleasure to find Virginia disposed to erect an extensive[2] College, which must produce great effects by Example. I was also pleased to see an Acct of the meeting of such distinguished[3] Characters, as the three Presidents of the United States on so praise-worthy an Occasion. How different to the[4] meeting of the three Emperors on the Continent of Europe, after a bloody Battle!—[5] In asking my Sketches you flatter me highly, but[6] I fear all I can do will fall very far short of what you expect: I will however freely communicate my Ideas; because the most learned & ingenious may sometimes obtain hints from those of very inferior Capacity, that may be deemed worthy of attention.—I shall not confine myself merely to the Buildings, but will take the liberty of suggesting whatever may strike my mind as I proceed. It is first necessary to consider the extent of the learning intended to be inculcated by this Institution;[7] because the Masters, or Professors of the Sciences, & the high grades of learning[8] would require proportionate Accommodation. Great & learned men would necessarily be considered as Gentlemen of high Character & Consideration, &[9] would expect to be provided for accordingly. I therefore should consider two rooms for each as inadequate, especially if men of Family:—but the two rooms are perhaps only intended as the College-rooms, & that each will have a Family-house, distinct from the College.—If so I proceed.—The Halls would require to be large, if intended for lecturing Rooms, & the upper Story would be in better proportion as to height: they[10] would also require to have Accommodations for the Apparatus, Chymical, Philosophical, Mechanical &c[11]—However such Accommodations as an University would require, would not be necessary for a College.—I have drawn only two Specimens of the Orders. You wish the Halls or Pavilions to contain the different Orders of Architecture, that they might serve hereafter as models.—I admire every thing that would tend to give chaste[12] Ideas of elegance[13] & grandeur. Accustomed to pure Architecture, the mind would relish in time no other, & therefore the more pure the better.—I have drawn a Pavilion for the Centre, with Corinthian Columns, & a Pediment. I would advise only the three orders: for I consider the Composite as only a mixture of the Corinthian & Ionic; & the Tuscan as only a very clumsy Doric.—Your general Arrangement I admire, but would take the liberty of advising that the two buildings next the Angles[14] be joined together, & be placed in the angles.[15]

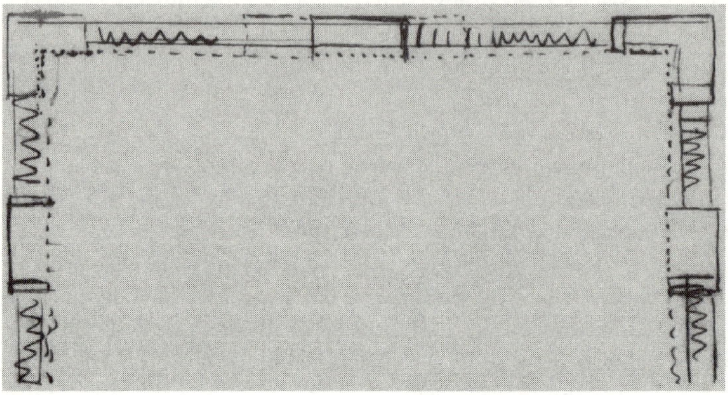

They would, of[16] course, be in the ancient Ionic, that beautiful and chaste order.—I thought it unnecessary to draw it, because you have only to convert the Sketches[17] already given, into the Ionic, to have the effect.—I would only have one Pediment, and that in the Centre. If at any time it would be thought necessary to extend[18] these Buildings, they may very easily have additions at each side, without extending the Colonnade, and the Entablature would only have to be carried round. This would give a variety, and the side Buildings would serve as a back ground or base to the projecting[19] central parts of each.—It is of great importance in Buildings, the extent of which cannot be foreseen, to provide for such additions as may correspond, & finally tend rather to beautify and perfect, than to disfigure or[20] deform the whole; and this plan of yours I think admirably calculated for almost indefinite extension.[21]—The Entablature of the Doric Pavilion may be enriched, and that to the Dormitories may be plain.[22] I have drawn Columns in front of the Dormitories, & also square Pillars, but the Columns are not only handsomer but cheaper,—being also more easily built, and less subject to accidental as well as wilful[23] injury.—I have omitted the plinths, as they not only tend to shorten the Column, but increase the expense, interrupt the walk, and add not much[24] to the beauty.[25]—I would make the Dormitories with Shed roofs, that should commence at the top of the parapet. This would[26] carry all the water to the outside, which would take away all appearance of a roof, & thereby add greatly to the beauty of the Build^g^. I advise that it be built of Brick in the roughest manner,[27] & plastered over in imitation of freestone.[28] Columns can be made in this way most beautifully, as I have seen them done at m^r^ Lewis's, near mount Vernon,[29] where they have stood above 12 years, & I did not find a single crack or fissure. The Bricks were made expressly for columnar work, and when they were to be plastered, the Brick-work was perfectly saturated with water[30] which prevented the plaister from drying too rapidly.—The mortar was not laid on fresh. It was composed of two thirds sharp well washed fine white[31] sand, & one third well slaked lime. I would mix these with Smiths' Forge-water. I would also dissolve some Vitriol of Iron in the water for the ashlar Plaister,[32] not only to increase the binding quality of the mortar, but also to give a fine yellow Colour—which on Experiment you will find beautiful and cheap.[33]—All the plaistering should be tinctured in the same manner, for the plain ashlar work,[34] or yellow Sand may be used with the lime, or yellow okre,[35] which will give the same appearance; and the Columns and Entablatures being white will produce a beautiful and delicate contrast.—I prefer a pale yellow to white for the general ground Colour of a building, as it assimilates beautifully with the Trees, and general Tint of nature; while white looks cold & glaring, and destroys the keeping.[36]—The Caps & Bases of the Columns ought to be of freestone; or they may be of artificial Stone. This is to be had very cheap from Coade's manufactory, in the Borough of London;[37] or they may be made of pipe clay, with a little fine white[38] sand, & a Solution of Alkaline Salt; which will give a mat, but firm Surface, when well burnt in a Potter's Kiln. I have tried this, & made very good artificial Stone.—By this mode the Caps of the Columns may be made as durable as Stone, and cheaper than wood.—Pateras modillions &c may be made in the same manner, if thought necessary hereafter, to enrich any particular part.[39]—I admire the general disposition and plan of this Establishment, and, to obtain[40] in perfection what is wanted, I would advise that the Site be chosen in the woods, and clear out whatever is not wanted, clumping the most beautiful and thriving of the forest Trees,[41] in handsome Groves, and leaving straggling ones occasionally, by wch Nature may be so artfully[42] imitated, as to produce a perfect Picture and above all things let such a place be selected, as, though it be a high & healthy Table Ground,[43] will afford by a Tube from a higher Source[44] a grand Fountain in the centre of the College Square.[45]—This will be not only highly ornamental, but it will supply water in case of Fire.—If a rivulet could also be brought near, by digging a Conduit, it might[46] furnish a large basin or Pond, which could be made of any required[47] depth & size. This would do for the Students to swim and dive in, during Summer, and to skait on during Winter[.—]There ought also to be a botanic Garden, as well as a culinary one.—There ought to be extra grounds for the great Exercises; such as running, riding, Archery[,][48] Shooting with Pistols, rifles, Cannon,—The military Exercises on horseback & foot.—In the Roman Catholic Academy, in George Town, C[a], they have erected a Ball Alley, but I would allow no Child's-play. Let all the Exercises be such as would tend to make great and useful men, and the military Exercises, fencing with the broad and smal[l] Sword, boxing with mufflers, playing the single Stick, jumping, wrestling, throwing the Javelin and whatever tends to render men more athletic, at the same time that it tends to perfect them in what may eventually be of use, ought only[49] to be permitted, as sports in their leisure hours. Thus would I make men of active[50] Bodies, as well as of extraordinary Minds.[51]—I have written a general System of Education, which your great Predecessor Washington was pleased to approve. The outline I have before often mentioned. I recommended the Establishment of primary Schools, admitting all the Children capable of learning, & to have[52] a hundred Students in each, at the public Expense.—After a few Years study they would be subject to examination in public, by the Trustees—ninety would be dropt, and ten out of the hundred should be taken at the public expense to the High Schools. These would also contain a hundred each, at the public expense; and if the Parents of any of the ninety should incline at their own expense, to continue them, they would undergo a public Examination with the adopted[53] Children of the republic, & some of them might be elected on the succeeding Examinations; for sometimes the Faculties of the greatest Geniuses are slow in development. On the 2[d] Examination ten would again be chose[n] out of the hundred, and sent at the public Expense to the Colleges, and in like manner ten out of the hundred chosen to be perfected in the great national University, in all that it is possible for man to teach; by which we might draw Newtons & Bacons from the Back woods; & produce, in one Age, by this sifting of Genius, Ability, & Learning, more great Characters, than the world ever possessed at any one time.—[54]

I fear I shall tire your patience—I remain with the highest respect and consideration Y[rs] &c WILLIAM THORNTON

RC (DLC); edge chipped and trimmed; at foot of text: "Honble Thomas Jefferson"; endorsed by TJ as received 11 June 1817 and so recorded in SJL. Dft (DLC: Thornton Papers); heavily reworked, with only the most significant alterations noted below; unsigned and lacking name of addressee.

A published ACC^{T} OF THE MEETING in May 1817 of the Central College Board of Visitors, attended by past and present United States presidents TJ, James Madison, and James Monroe, is printed above at 5 May. The design of Woodlawn, Lawrence LEWIS's Fairfax County plantation located near Mount Vernon and completed in 1806, has been attributed to Thornton (Calder Loth, ed., *The Virginia Landmarks Register* [1999], 161).

FORGE-WATER has had heated iron immersed in it (*OED*). Eleanor Coade operated a MANUFACTORY in London at which she perfected a weather-resistant type of stoneware that mimicked stone (*ODNB*). PATERAS are architectural ornaments resembling shallow, round dishes (*OED*).

In 1814 Georgetown College (later Georgetown University) built a brick BALL ALLEY at which students could play handball (James S. Easby-Smith, *Georgetown University in the District of Columbia 1789–1907* [1907], 1:48). In this context, MUFFLERS are boxing gloves (*OED*).

Between 1795 and 1797 Thornton outlined a GENERAL SYSTEM OF EDUCATION in which he envisioned elementary through university education supported by either a direct or import tax. President George Washington had been especially interested in the national university proposed thereby (Charles M. Harris and Daniel Preston, eds., *Papers of William Thornton* [1995–], 1:l, 346–66).

[1] Preceding five words interlined in Dft in place of "for which I have to return thanks to."

[2] Word interlined in Dft.

[3] Word interlined in Dft in place of "respectable."

[4] Preceding five words interlined in Dft in place of "object—greater in its consequence than the result of the."

[5] Preceding two sentences interlined and added in margin of Dft.

[6] Preceding two words interlined in Dft in place of "and."

[7] Reworked in Dft from "extent of the intended Institution."

[8] Preceding nine words interlined in Dft.

[9] Reworked in Dft from "of Character, and."

[10] Preceding thirteen words interlined in Dft in place of "and."

[11] Preceding four words interlined in Dft.

[12] Word interlined in Dft.

[13] In Dft Thornton here canceled "mixed with neatness."

[14] Instead of preceding three words, Dft reads "marked 2 & 3."

[15] The following sketch is less extensive in Dft: 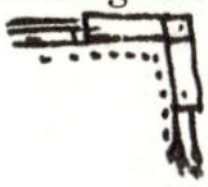

[16] Preceding three words, with "which" instead of "They," interlined in Dft in place of "and the 4th & 5th on each side to be placed in the centre of the Flanks—The Building in the Angle would of."

[17] Reworked in Dft from "suppose the Drawings."

[18] Word interlined in Dft in place of "increase the size of."

[19] Preceding seven words interlined in Dft in place of "base to the."

[20] Preceding two words interlined in Dft.

[21] Sentence interlined and added in left margin and at base of page of Dft, with marginal addition keyed by a ⊕ symbol.

[22] Bulk of sentence interlined in Dft, incorporating "The Dormitories" from beginning of a reworked sentence.

[23] Preceding five words interlined in Dft.

[24] Word interlined in Dft.

[25] Text from "I have drawn" to this point added at top margin of Dft and keyed to this point with a ⊙ symbol.

[26] Preceding nine words interlined in Dft.

[27] Preceding four words interlined in Dft.

[28] Preceding four words interlined in Dft.

[29] Remainder of sentence interlined in Dft.

[30] Reworked in Dft from "the Brick is made perfectly wet." Remainder of sentence interlined in RC and lacking in Dft.

[31] Preceding two words interlined in Dft.

[32] Preceding seven words interlined in Dft.

[33] Preceding three words interlined in Dft in place of "good."

[34] Text from here to semicolon added in left margin of Dft and keyed to this point with a # symbol.

[35] Preceding three words interlined in RC and lacking in Dft.

[36] Sentence interlined in Dft.

[37] Preceding four words interlined in Dft in place of "England."

[38] Word not in Dft.

[39] In Dft Thornton here interlined "I would rough cast all the outside of the Building. It may be coloured with a little yellow oaker, or a Solution of the vitriol of iron."

[40] In Dft Thornton here interlined "more easily what is wanted" and then replaced the phrase with the following five words.

[41] Text from "the most" to this point interlined in Dft, with "and thriving" omitted.

[42] Preceding nine words interlined in Dft in place of "Trees which may by a Person of Taste be made."

[43] Preceding nine words interlined in Dft.

[44] Preceding seven words interlined in Dft in place of "to bring a brook or Rivulet near."

[45] Word interlined in Dft in place of "grounds."

[46] Preceding six words interlined in Dft in place of "it would."

[47] Word interlined in Dft.

[48] Word interlined in Dft.

[49] Word interlined in Dft.

[50] Word interlined in Dft in place of "great."

[51] Sentence interlined in Dft.

[52] Preceding ten words interlined in Dft in place of "of."

[53] Word interlined in Dft.

[54] Dft ends here.

ENCLOSURE

William Thornton's Sketches for a Corinthian Pavilion

[ca. 27 May 1817]

MS (ViU: TJP); in Thornton's hand; undated.

From Aaron Clark

RESPECTED SIR. Albany N.Y. May 28. 1817.

Allow me the pleasure of presenting you with the Enclosed Copy of my Oration on the Subject of the Savages—

I Shall be extremely gratified to learn you rec^{d} them &^{c}

Ever truly your Republican fellow Citizen and admirer

AARON CLARK

RC (MHi); dateline beneath signature; endorsed by TJ as received 11 June 1817 and so recorded in SJL. RC: left half of address cover only (CSmH: JF-BA), with

PoC of TJ to Dominick Lynch, 26 June 1817, on verso; right half of address cover only (DLC), with PoC of TJ to William Short, 19 June 1817, on verso; addressed (damaged at crease): "Hon[...] Thomas Jefferson Esqr late President of the U.S.A. Monticello Virginia"; franked; postmarked Albany, 29 May.

Aaron Clark (d. 1861), attorney, banker, and public official, was born in Worthington, Hampshire County, Massachusetts, and studied at Hamilton Oneida Academy (later Hamilton College) in Clinton, New York, before graduating in 1808 from Union College in Schenectady. He then studied law, served as private secretary to Governor Daniel D. Tompkins in 1810, and was clerk of the New York state assembly between 1814 and 1820. In the last capacity Clark authored several works on legislative procedure. He moved to New York City about 1821, became a teller at the North River Bank, and prospered as a lottery agent between 1825 and 1833. Clark was elected mayor of New York City on the Whig ticket in 1837 and served two terms before losing his bid for a third in 1839. He was president of the Merchants' Insurance Company, 1851–52. Clark acquired extensive property holdings in New York City and Brooklyn. He died at his home in Brooklyn (*Memorial Biographics of the New England Historic Genealogical Society* [1880–1908], 4:293–6; Melvin G. Holli and Peter d'Alroy Jones, eds., *Biographical Dictionary of American Mayors, 1820–1980: Big City Mayors* [1981], 66–7; Melvin Gilbert Dodge and Daniel Wyette Burke, eds., *The Clark Prize Book* [1894], 9–14; Hugh Hastings, ed., *Public Papers of Daniel D. Tompkins* [1898–1902], 2:286–7, 541–2; *Longworth's New York Directory* [1821]: 118; [1825]: 118; [1833]: 177; Clay, *Papers*, 9:477, 595–6; *The New-York City and Co-Partnership Directory, for 1843 & 1844* [1843], 70; *The New York City Directory, for 1851–1852* [1851], 108; *The New-York City Directory, for 1853–1854* [1853], 133; New York *Evening Post*, 3 Aug. 1861).

The enclosed ORATION was probably a newspaper version of a 22 July 1816 speech by Clark to the Pi Beta Phi Society in Schenectady, which he later had printed in pamphlet form as *An Oration. A Project For the Civilization of the Indians of North America* (Albany, 1819) (New York *Columbian*, 20 Feb. 1817). In this address Clark argued that Native Americans could be "civilized" through instruction in agriculture, the establishment of schools conducted in their native languages and, only after that, by the work of Christian missionaries (Clark, *Oration*, 6, 9, 11–3, 16).

To Fitzwhylsonn & Potter

MESS^{RS} FITZWHYLSON AND POTTER Monticello May 28. 17

The books which you bound for me are safely recieved and I this day send another parcel by Col^{o} Randolph, who will have delivered them to you probably before your receipt of this. the bindings already recieved are good, and particularly in the article I value of their solid pressure. varieties in the bindings are also useful as well as pleasing to distinguish them on the shelf, and particularly the richness and variegation of the back. I shall be glad to recieve these as soon as is consistent with their being well-bound. another parcel is in a course of collection to go some time hence. I have written on the different covers the words for lettering their backs, and give a list below. I salute you with respect. TH: JEFFERSON

[Hi]ppocrate de Gardeil. 4. vols
Mexico de De Solis. 3. v.
Euclide de Peyrard.
Archimede de Peyrard. 2. v.
Geographia plantarum. Humboldt.

PoC (DLC); on verso of reused address cover of Bernard Peyton to TJ, 17 Mar. 1817; torn at seal; endorsed by TJ.

Some time before this Alexander von HUMBOLDT had sent TJ his work *De Distributione Geographica Plantarum*, with the inscription "à Mr. Jefferson hommage d'admiration de respect et de reconnaissance L'auteur" ("To Mr. Jefferson, a tribute of admiration, respect, and gratitude from the author") (Paris, 1817; Poor, *Jefferson's Library*, 6 [no. 281]; TJ's copy in DLC: Rare Book and Special Collections).

From Patrick Gibson

SIR — Richmond 28th May 1817

I have received your favors of the 24 & 25th Inst with a note for renewal in the Virga bank—I am sorry to say it has not been in my power to sell a barrel of your flour nor can I meet with any one to make me an offer for it—a few hundred barrels were sold yesterday at $11—but I know of no one willing to give even that price I have remitted to Mr Vaughan of Philada a check for $400. and to LeRoy Bayard & Co the further sum of $255.6 by a check on Philada not being able to obtain one on New York

With great respect
Your ob Servt — PATRICK GIBSON

RC (MHi); between dateline and salutation: "Thomas Jefferson Esqre"; endorsed by TJ as a letter of 26 May received 5 June 1817 and so recorded in SJL.

From John Wood

DEAR SIR — Richmond 29th May 1817

I received your favour of the 6t instant, and would have answered it immediately, could I have procured the volume of the Edinburg Review which contains an account of the Greek and English Lexicon that I mentioned. I requested Colonel Randolph to state this circumstance to you. I regret it has not been in my power yet to obtain that volume of the review. I spoke to M. Campbell the keeper of the Richmond Library who is a gentleman of universal acquaintance with classical authors. He says it was published in London seven or eight years ago but does not recollect the name. he thinks however no mistake can be made in procuring it, or writing for it, as it is the only general Lexicon in Greek & English that ever was published. M. Campbell is brother to the author of the pleasures of hope, and possesses more correct information than any person in this place in regard to London Publications.

I return you my grateful thanks, for your obliging attention in communicating to me the information respecting the contemplated college at Charlottesville[.] If my state of health permit me superintending a public seminary, when it goes into operation, I would prefer the situation to any other I know; but finding that nothing is so beneficial to my rhumatic complaint, as continued exercise and that long confinement or sitting much always causes it, I am apprehensive that in a few years I may be prevented from teaching a public school; where close attention is required.

I am sorry that from arrangements respecting the survey of the rivers, I have been compelled to break up my school in this place a month sooner than I intended. I set out on Saturday to survey the Piankitank, Rappahannock & Chickehomony & shall return sometime in July, when I again commence up the York river & the Bay shore from the Cape Henry to Potomac. I shall have the whole certainly completed before October.—

I have been much pleased with the progress of your Grandson Mr Francis Eppes—He read with me the two first books of the Odes of Horace and in Greek Œsops Fables—His disposition is equal to that of any boy I ever saw.

I remain with respect & esteem your obedient Servant

John Wood

RC (DLC); edge chipped; addressed: "Thomas Jefferson Esqr Monticello near Milton"; franked; postmarked Richmond, 29 May; endorsed by TJ as received 31 May 1817 and so recorded in SJL.

S. Campbell operated the RICHMOND LIBRARY on the corner of Bank and 10th streets (*The Richmond Directory, Register and Almanac, for the Year 1819* [Richmond, 1819], 39).

From Fernagus De Gelone

Sir New York 31^rst May 1817.

I was establishing a dépôt for foreign Books in Philadelphia when your letter came to my hands. I Sent you then according to your directions the 1^rst and Second volumes of Cormon's french and spanish Dictionary by mail, in two different days. the Architecture of Vitruvius had been Sold.

To day I direct to Messrs Gibson & Jefferson, a copy of Théâtre d'Aristophane, 4 vol. in 8vo by one of the trading Sloops playing from New York to Richmond.

Your bill then Stands thus:

Géometrie d'Euclide, par Peyrard. 1. 8vo	2.50
Cormon, Dictionnaire français & Espagnol. 2. 8vo	4 87½
Théâtre d'Aristophane. 4. 8vo	7.00
	$14.37½

I am most respectfully Sir Your most humble obed[t] Servant

J LOUIS FERNAGUS DE GELONE

RC (MHi); endorsed by TJ as received 11 June 1817 and so recorded in SJL; with additional notation by TJ beneath endorsement: "June 19. inclosed 15.D." RC (MHi); address cover only; with PoC of TJ to Fernagus De Gelone, 19 June 1817, on verso; addressed: "Thomas Jefferson Monticello. Milton V[a]"; franked; postmarked New York, 31 May.

With this letter Fernagus De Gelone probably enclosed a receipt to himself from Henry Butler, New York, 31 May 1817, in which Butler, describing himself as master of the schooner *Sea Lion*, accepts "a bundle of paper directed to Thomas Jefferson, Monticello, Milton, V[a] Care of Mess[rs] Gibson & Jefferson, Richmond, V[a] which I engage to deliver to the Said Gentlemen in Richmond, on their paying me for freight, twenty-five-cents" (MS in MHi; in Butler's hand; endorsed by TJ: "Fernagus de Gelone").

From William Caruthers

SIR   Lexington 2nd June 1817

Patrick Henry a free Man of Coular requested me to Write You that he Will Rent What land is Cultivatable On the Bridge Tract—Which is perhaps about 10 Acres all of Which is to Clear off & Enclose & for Which he is Willing to pay a fair Value—

Patrick is a Man of Good Behavior and as the Neighbours are Destroying Your Timber Verry much it Might not be Amiss to Authorise him—to Take care of it in Order to Which it Might be Well to have the lines Run by the Surveyor of the County

Accept My Best Respects   W[M] CARUTHERS

RC (MHi); addressed (trimmed): "[...] J[e]fferson Esqr Monticello Milton PO"; endorsed by TJ as received 10 June 1817 and so recorded in SJL.

Patrick Henry (d. 1829) purchased his freedom in 1811 in Westmoreland County. He bought his enslaved wife from a resident of Lexington in 1815 and freed her the following year. By then Henry was living in Rockbridge County, where for a time he was employed by TJ's Natural Bridge tenant Philip Thornton. In 1817 Henry entered into an agreement with TJ to rent and farm the latter's land at Natural Bridge in return for paying the annual taxes on the property. He lived near the bridge itself, acted as a guide for visitors to it, and looked after TJ's interests there generally (Marie Tyler-McGraw,

An African Republic: Black & White Virginians in the Making of Liberia [2007], 146; Westmoreland Co. Deeds and Wills, 22:217; Vi: RG 48, Personal Property Tax Returns, Rockbridge Co., 1816–23, 1825, 1827–29; *MB*, 2:1337, 1380; Cornelia J. Randolph to Virginia J. Randolph [Trist], 30 Aug. 1817, document 4 in a group of documents on Jefferson's Trip to Natural Bridge, [ca. 13–17 Aug. 1817]; TJ to Philip Thornton, 10 Mar. 1818; DNA: RG 29, CS, Rockbridge Co., 1820, 1830; Rockbridge Co. Will Book, 4:191–2, 6:340–1).

From John Vaughan

D SIR Philad. June 2. 1817

By the Hamlet; Pearson, I have Sent a box & enclosed bill of Lading to Gibson & Jefferson—It contains Agricultural books from France—

I have this day recieved 400 from M Patrick Gibson of Richmond on your acco. & subject to your orders—

We commence printing our Volume in a few days. Vol 1. of a new series—should you be inclind to faver us with any Communication, it would be highly acceptable to us, & should be here in three or four Weeks—perhaps later would do—

I remain Yours Sincerly JN VAUGHAN

Would it be agreeable to you that I should in Your name subscribe for one or More Copies of the Volume—The sale is limited & we find it difficult to get a printer to undertake it, unless the members exert themselves to procure subscribers, & that must generally be amongst themselves

RC (MHi); endorsed by TJ as received 11 June 1817 and so recorded in SJL; with notes by TJ for his 28 June 1817 reply beneath endorsement: "70.D. for $66\frac{2}{3}$ subscribe transns contribns Lewis's vocab. Hist^{l} commee duplicate y^{ro} Sec. state." RC (DLC); address cover only; with PoC of TJ to William Duane, 19 June 1817, on verso; addressed: "Thomas Jefferson Monticello"; franked; postmarked Philadelphia, 2 June.

The first volume of a NEW SERIES of APS, *Transactions*, was published in Philadelphia in 1818 following a nine-year hiatus (APS, Minutes, 16 May 1817 [MS in PPAmP]).

From Tadeusz Kosciuszko

MON CHER AMI— Soleure le 3 Juin 1817.

Comme vous vous réposéz tranquilement sur vos l'Auriers si justement acquis et sur la Réputation Générale et tant chérie encore par vos Concytoyens. Il ne faut pas pour cela oublier vos Amis en Europe, qui vous aiment tout autant que vos Compatriotes. Vous me dévez

deux ou trois lettres. Apresat[1] il s'agit de rendre un service éssentiel à une personne de mes Connoissances Mr Poinsot démeurant en Amerique à acheté à Richmond 1.200. Acres de terre dans le Comté de Monongalia et que Mr Patrick Henry Gouverneur alors de l'Etat de Virginie lui à delivré le 23 Mai 1785 avec le Contrat, elles sont situees près de vos terres appéllées le Peek of Otter il payoit déja land taxes et il a aussi le Plan et le titre dont il vous envoit une Copie. Mais révenu en Europe la révolution Francaise et les autres evénéments l'ont empeché de réclamer sa Proprieté.
Ayéz la bonté de charger quelqu'un de votre part, afin qu'il puisse revandiquer cette terre et Vous témoigner avec moi sa parfaite réconnoissance,

Agréez l'assurance de ma haute Consideration

T Kosciuszko

EDITORS' TRANSLATION

My Dear Friend— Solothurn 3 June 1817.
You are quietly resting on the laurels you so justly acquired and on the public reputation that is still so dear to your fellow citizens. Yet you must not forget your friends in Europe, who love you as much as your countrymen do. You owe me two or three letters. In addition, my acquaintance Mr. Poinsot needs an essential favor. While living in America, in Richmond he bought 1,200 acres of land in Monongalia County. Mr. Patrick Henry, then governor of the state of Virginia, gave him the land grant on 23 May 1785. The tract is located near your land called the Peaks of Otter. He has already paid land taxes, and he also has the map and the title, of which he is sending you a copy. But having returned to Europe, the French Revolution and other events prevented him from claiming his property.
Please be so kind as to assign someone to this matter, so that he can claim this land and express with me his complete gratitude to you.

Please accept the assurance of my high consideration

T Kosciuszko

RC (MHi); dateline at foot of text; endorsed by TJ as received 24 Sept. 1817 and so recorded in SJL. Translation by Dr. Genevieve Moene. Enclosed in Peter Poinsot to TJ, 25 June 1817. A Dupl of this letter, not found, is recorded in SJL as received 29 Sept. 1817 from Solothurn. It was enclosed in a Dupl (dated 10 July 1817) of Poinsot to TJ, 25 June 1817.

[1]Thus in manuscript; "après ça" was presumably intended.

To Lancelot Minor

Dear Sir Monticello June 3. 17.

I am 2. or 3. days later than my promise in sending you the inclosed order on Messrs Gibson & Jefferson for 160. D 08 c for Col[o] Callis's estate[1] to refund what Hastings Marks had recieved for the 150. acres of land in Fluvanna sold by him to Col[o] Callis and recovered by David Ross. I must refer you to my letters of 1812. May 29. & Oct. 29. 1813. May 26. and 1816. July 14. for the principles on which the amount is estimated. the principal being 69.D. due since 1795. I have added 22. years interest at 6. per cent. 91. D 08 c making in the whole 160. D 08 c the amount of the order. this I believe settles almost the last article of that administration, and the chief pleasure I recieve from it is in the relief it brings to you. the sale of the land, if it [cou]ld be effected would close all. I salute you with great thankfulness, esteem & respect Th: Jefferson

PoC (MHi); on verso of reused address cover of George Gibbs to TJ, 11 Mar. 1817; torn at seal, with some missing text rewritten by TJ; at foot of text: "Col[o] Lancelot Minor"; endorsed by TJ. Enclosure not found.

TJ wrote to Minor on 30 May 1812, not may 29.

[1]TJ here canceled "to discharge."

From John M. Perry

Dear Sir Albemarle may [Junc] 3rd 1817

I had hoped that from the verry pressing solicitations to you through Capt Garrett that you would of Concented for me to have undertaken the buildings for the College—and I assure you that nothing is more desireous—I no that I Could please you in the execution of the work haveing it in my power to obtain the verry best mechanics—it is a fact well known to you, that many of the best buildings in the Country are undertaken by men that never executed work with their own hands—and should you now think proper to intrust the Care of this work to me it will not only be executed in all the forms of architecture. but will be Considered by me one among the many favors which I have received from your hands. thus I have taken the liberty to address you with a hope that it will meet your approbation

Respectfully your o,b, St. John M. Perry

RC (CSmH: JF); misdated; endorsed by TJ as a letter of 3 May 1817 received the same day. Recorded in SJL as a letter of 3 June 1817 received that same day, with the later date confirmed by TJ's 3 June response.

To John M. Perry

SIR Monticello June 3. 17.

In the purchase of the site of the College from you, there are two questions entirely distinct; 1. as to the title, which it is our duty to have conveyed to the institution clear, & unembarrassed by any conditions other than the usual one of the payment of the price stipulated.[1] the 2^d^ who shall do all the various works which the prosecution of the object may require? these must be left free to be disposed of as they arise, in the best manner we can. you wish us to be bound in the same or a concurrent contract to employ you to do the wooden work. but does our duty permit us thus to bind the instn hand & foot, to employ any particular person, who may do the work well or ill, and leave us to law suits for indemnification? you acknolege, and we all know that your skill does not go either to the execution of the work yourself properly, or to the knowing when it is properly executed[2] our daily inspection cannot be expected. age, as to myself, and long absences, put that out of the question. yet the constant inspection of a competent eye is necessary, with the power to dismiss the workman found incompetent or unfaithful. otherwise we should be at the mercy of those you employ whom we do not know[3] & who may go on to the completion of the work, under your own eye, & be going amiss[4] the whole time without your knowing it. you might, with equal justice, insist on a covenant that you should do the stone work; brick work, iron work and every thing else that is to be done. but could we be justifiable in such a covenant? in a competn between two undertakers, the one acknoleging himself entirely ignorant how the work is to be done, the other a perfect master of it, can there be a doubt which it is our duty to prefer? it will certainly be my wish that every thing should be turned thro' your hands, which you could do as well as another; and there will be much which you could do, and would, I have no doubt, be employed to do: but these would be in details to be provided for as they arise. this subject would take too much time[5] & would be too laborious to be treated in writing: I can only add therefore that so far as would depend on me, my friendly disposns to you, would always make me wish you should have a preference in work against equal competitors, entertaining for you sentiments of sincere good will & esteem.[6]

TH:J

Dft (DLC); on verso of reused address cover to TJ; endorsed by TJ.

[1]Word interlined.

[2]Text from this point to "otherwise we should" interlined in place of "we shall then" and rewritten by TJ at foot of first page for clarity, with latter version,

exhibiting minor variations in punctuation and word order, used above.

[3] Preceding five words interlined.

[4] Word interlined in place of "wrong."

[5] Preceding five words interlined in place of "however is too long."

[6] Reworked from "sincere esteem & friendship."

From John Barnes

Dear Sir Milton Wednesd^{y} Even^{g} 4 June

We are here, at the foot of your Mountain, but for the Want of horses—or Carriage dare not Approach Monticello—

yrs most respectfully J Barnes.

the fatigue of the Journey—I wish—to tarry here this Even^{g}—

RC (ViU: TJP-ER); partially dated; dateline beneath signature; addressed: "Thomas Jefferson Esqr"; endorsed by TJ as received 5 June 1817 and so recorded in SJL.

From Mr. Durot

Monsieur 4. Juin Mrs Metzler's House Main street Richmond

permettez à un français connu de la famille Noailles qui arrive en cette ville et qui peut S'y fixer pour quelque temps, de reclamer de Vous des Sentiments de bienveillance dont il se croit digne et qu'il Se flatte de justifier à L'avenir auprès de Vous.

L'etat actuel de ma fortune me fait aviser à tous les moiens honnetes d'ameliorer mon Sort et j'invoque le Secours de l'influence que vous devez avoir sous tous les raports, et en ce moment Comme homme de Lettres, pour engager vos amis à L'achat de plusieurs objets d'un merite intrinseque, dont La Note Suit:

plusieurs Collections de Medailles d'après L'Antique chacune de 150. faites par l'homme le plus habile en Europe.

1. Serie de 23. Estampes en feuilles, des Animaux du Museum de Paris, dans Leur Couleurs Naturelles, dessinés en Vie.

1. Livre in folio, Intitulé: Tableaux historiques des Campagnes des français en Italie, Jusques à la Bataille de Marengo, Suivis des operations de L'Armée d'Orient, et des Bulletins Officiels de la Grande Armée, et de L'Armée d'Italie

Les Vues prises Sur Les Lieux, et Gravées d'après Les dessins de Vernet.

Je me propose de faire une Vente publique du 10. au 15. de Ce mois d'Estampes, Enquadrées, parmi lesquelles On voit

1. Serie de 12. habitations Champetres, Baties dans les Jardins du Museum, à Paris, d'un gout exquis
1. Elegante Collection de fleurs
1. d° fruits
4. Sujets de la Bible, traités en grand
&ª &ª &ª
Henri IV. & Gabrielle, d'une parfaite Ressemblance
Louis XIV & La Valliere, avec nombre de figurs

Un autre que vous Monsieur, pourrais trouver de l'indiscretion dans ma demarche vis-àvis de vous, mais j'ai la noble assurance de trouver dans vos genereuses habitudes, un motif d'excuse qui leve tout Scrupule à cet egard.

Agreez Monsieur, les sentiments de la haute consideration avec laquelle Jai lhonneur d'etre Votre très humble serviteur

DUROT

EDITORS' TRANSLATION

SIR 4. June Mrs Metzler's House Main street Richmond
Allow a Frenchman who is known to the Noailles family, who arrives in this city, and may settle here for some time, to ask for your kindness, of which he believes himself worthy, and of which he hopes he will prove himself to you in the future.

The current state of my finances makes me look into every honest means of improving my situation, and I ask for help through the influence you must have in every aspect, and in your capacity as a man of letters, to encourage your friends to buy several objects of intrinsic value, listed as follows:

Several collections of medals copied from antiquity, each numbering 150, made by the most skilled man in Europe.
1. A series of 23 prints of the animals in the Muséum National d'Histoire Naturelle in Paris, in their natural colors, drawn from live models.
1. A folio book entitled *Tableaux historiques des campagnes d'Italie … jusqu'à la bataille de Marengo, suivis … des operations de l'armée d'Orient, … des bulletins officiels de la grande Armée et de l'armée d'Italie*
Views taken on the spot, and engraved after Vernet's drawings.

From the 10th to the 15th of this month, I propose to hold a public sale of framed prints, including:
1. A series of 12 rustic dwellings built in the Jardin des plantes at the museum in Paris, done in exquisite taste
1. An elegant collection of flowers
1. ditto fruits
4. Scenes from the Bible, in large format
etc. etc. etc.
Henry IV and Gabrielle, a perfect likeness
Louis XIV and La Vallière, with many other figures

Anyone other than you, Sir, might find my request tactless, but I have great confidence that your generous nature will find grounds for an excuse, which removes every scruple in this regard.

Please accept, Sir, the feelings of high consideration with which I have the honor to be your very humble servant DUROT

RC (DLC); dateline at foot of text; endorsed by TJ as received 10 June 1817 and so recorded in SJL. Translation by Dr. Genevieve Moene.

An unidentified "French gentleman" put his collection of prints and medals up for auction on 31 Oct. 1817 in Georgetown, D.C., with the stated purpose of raising money in order to join the French settlement along the Tombigbee River in Alabama. The sale included "two most superb copies of Bonaparte's Campaign in Italy, with an historical description of his campaign in Egypt and Germany," and "a collection of small Medals, cast in sulphur, representing an exact likeness of celebrated Antique personages," which was copied from Napoleon's collection "by one of the most eminent artists in France" (Georgetown *National Messenger*, 27 Oct. 1817).

To Stephen Cathalan

DEAR SIR Monticello[1] [before 6 June 1817]

My last to you was of Feb. 1. 16. since which I have recieved your several favors of Feb. 15. Mar. 19. June 1. 4. 19. & July 12. & the several parcels of wine & Maccaroni, came safe to hand. all of them were good; but those particularly esteemed for daily use are the Nice, Ledanon & Roussillon. the Nice de Bellet is superlatively fine, for which I am particularly obliged to M. Spreafico. the vin de Ledanon too is excellent, and the Roussillon of M. Durand very good. this last will be most sought for from this quarter, as being lower priced, & more adapted to the taste of this country, artificially created by our long restraint under the English government to the strong wines of Portugal and Spain. the Ledanon recalled to my memory what I had drunk at your table 30. years ago, and I am as partial to it now as then. the return of the first swallow, just now seen, reminds me that the season is now arrived when the provision of another year should be attended to. I therefore am now directing a remittance to mr Vaughan, my friend and correspondent at Philadelphia, requesting him to transmit 200. Dollars of it for myself and 65. Dollars for my grandson Thomas Jefferson Randolph, either to yourself directly, or to place it at Paris at your command. when you shall have recieved it, I will pray you to procure for me the wines and other articles stated in the invoice inclosed, and to extend your kindness to my grandson also, who is this day leaving us with his wife and child to commence separate housekeeping, and prays me to present him to your good offices. I do it with the greater satisfaction, because I can conscientiously assure you of his most solid integrity honor and diligence. when I shall be no more, all my affairs will be left in his hands. I state his invoice separately, and will pray you to have his parcels separately packed, that we may each know our own. in your letter of June 19. you remind me of mr Bergasse's former establishment at Marseilles, and that his son continues the business of compounding the wines of the country in imitation of others, and particularly that he can furnish the quality of Bordeaux claret at a franc per bottle, box included, and 3. years old. it is this which my grandson asks for, on my assurance to him that mr Bergasse's imitations were perfect, of which I had tasted several, and that they contained not a drop of any thing but the pure juice of the grape. if you R will have the goodness to have my parcels marked T.I. & his T.I. they will be taken care of by the way as if they were all mine, and will still be easily separated when they come to our hands. Address them to the Collector of the Customs of any port from Boston to the Chesapeake, but be so good as to send them all together, in the same vessel, that I may have occasion to transact with a single collector only. our distance from the sea-port towns, and little communication with them, renders the multiplication of transactions with them very troublesome, tedious & uncertain. Not knowing exactly what these articles may cost, should they exceed the remittance, dock the excess off of my invoice; and should they cost less than the remittance, carry the balance on to the next year's account. there is a number of my friends who have tasted these wines at my table, and are so much pleased with their qualities and prices that they are about forming a company, and engaging an agent in Richmond, to import for them once a year what each shall direct. I have promised, when their association is made up, to recommend their agent to you, & to warrant them faithful supplies. Our new President, Col° Monroe, has asked from me some information as to the wines I would recommend for his table and how to get them. I recommended to him the vin blanc liqoureux d'Hermitage de M. Jourdans, the Ledanon, the Roussillon de M. Durand; and the Nice de Bellet of M. Sasserno, and that he should get them thro' you, as best knowing the particular qualities to which I refer. I am anxious to introduce here these fine wines in place of the alcoholic wines of Spain and Portugal; and the universal approbation of all who taste them at my table will, I am persuaded, turn by degrees the current of demand from this part of our country, [an]d that it will continue to spread de proche en proche. the delicacy and innocence of these wines will change the habit from the coarse & inebriating kinds hitherto only known here. my own annual demand will generally be about what it is this year; the President's probably the double or treble. the wine of M. Jourdan being chiefly for a bonne bouche, I shall still ask for it occasionally.

In my letter recommending wines to the President, I propose to him the naming young mr Sasserno our Consul at Nice. the fear is that he may consider our commerce with that port as too inconsiderable to justify the placing a consul there. I wish I were able to state to him the nature of that commerce, & how many of our vessels may touch there of a year.

On the arrival of the Nice wine at Alexandria I wrote to request the Collector to get your Acquit à Caution discharged by the signature of the French Consul there, and to inclose it to me. he informed me there was no French Consul there then, but that there would soon be one and that I might rely on his sending you a due discharge of[2] the Acquit a Caution. I hope this has been done, and that on discontinuing the freedom of your port, the reciept and reshipment of foreign articles hereafter will be put on the easy footing it is in England & in this country. it is much easier to insulate the few foreign goods arriving for re-exportation, than the whole city from the country to which it belongs.[3]

The immortal flowers arrived safe, and we placed the garland on the head of Genl Washington's bust, in our Dining-room. we thank you for them, and for the offer to send the living plant. but this is all but impossible. it would have three distinct water-voyages to get to this place, besides waiting for opportunities in the custom house & warehouses, and, passing thro' so many hands, it could not be expected that all would use the necessary diligence for preserving them in life: and when arrived, they could not stand our winter, the cold of which, descends sometimes to 14.° below zero of Reaumur. it would therefore be taking and giving a great deal of trouble, to result certainly in disappointment & regret. I hope you will be able to make up and dispatch the wines Etc. by the 1st of September, that they may be sure to get to us before winter commences. earlier than that they might suffer by heat on the passage or in the warehouses:[4] and if you can drop me a line of information on your reciept of this and of mr Vaughan's remittance, it will place my mind at ease under the assurance of recieving my supplies. Wishing all possible happiness to yourself & family, I salute you with unchanging friendship and respect. TH: JEFFERSON

P.S. June 6. 17. since writing the preceding, which has laid by me some time, the President has called on me at Monticello; and I took that occasion of pressing on him the appointment of young[5] mr Sasserno Consul at Nice: he consented, and asked me to give him his Christian name. on looking for it thro' all your letters and those of mr Spreafico, it is never once mentioned. if you will be so good as to send it to me as soon as you recieve this, it may be here before the next meeting of the Senate, and so no time lost.

PoC (DLC: TJ Papers, 210:37451–2); on a reused address cover from TJ to George Divers; undated, with dated postscript; torn at seal, with some words rewritten by TJ; at foot of first page: "M. Cathalan"; endorsed by TJ as a letter of 6 June 1817 and so recorded in SJL; notation by TJ at foot of text: "sent by duplicates the one thro' mr Vaughan, the other under cover to mr Gallatin thro the state office." Enclosed in TJ to Albert Gallatin, [before 6 June], TJ to John Vaughan, 7 June, and TJ to Daniel Brent, 8 June 1817.

TJ acknowledges as distinct documents, dated 1 and 4 JUNE 1816, a Cathalan letter printed above at 4 June 1816 but also sent by him to TJ as an additional text with the earlier date. Thomas Jefferson Randolph, his wife Jane H. Nicholas Randolph, and their daughter Margaret Smith Randolph were moving from the Dome Room at Monticello (illustrated elsewhere in this volume) to TJ's Tufton estate to begin SEPARATE HOUSEKEEPING (Shackelford, *Descendants*, 1:77). DE PROCHE EN PROCHE: "little by little." BONNE BOUCHE: "special treat."

TJ's letter to the collector of Alexandria regarding the ACQUIT À CAUTION (French customhouse bond) was TJ to Charles Simms, 5 June 1816. The reply, which came instead from the deputy collector, was William D. Simms to TJ, 1 July 1816.

[1] TJ here canceled "June 6. 17."
[2] Preceding four words interlined.
[3] Sentence interlined.
[4] Sentence to this point interlined.
[5] Manuscript: "youn."

ENCLOSURE

List of Wine and Food Ordered from Stephen Cathalan by Thomas Jefferson and Thomas Jefferson Randolph

[ca. 6 June 1817]

Vin de Perpignan de M. Durand. 100. gallons, en double futaille.
Vin de Ledanon. 100. bottles. say, one hundred.
Vin de Nice de Bellet. 200. bottles. say, two hundred.
best Olive oil. 5. gallons in bottles.
Maccaroni 100. ℔.
Raisins. 50. ℔. those of Smyrna, sans pepins, would be preferred.
Anchovies. 1. doz. bottles.
the above are for Th: Jefferson

The following articles are for Thomas J. Randolph.

60. gallons of Vin de Perpignan of M. Durand, in double casks.
100. bottles vin de M. Bergasse of the quality of Bordeaux claret.
50. ℔ Maccaroni.

PoC (DLC: TJ Papers, 210:37453); entirely in TJ's hand; undated.

EN DOUBLE FUTAILLE: "in double casks." SANS PEPINS: "seedless."

To de Bure Frères

MESSIEURS
DEBURES FRERES Monticello in Virginia. June 6. 1817.

I addressed, the last year, a catalogue of some books I wanted, [to?] mr Ticknor, an American gentleman, and the best bibliograph of my [ac]quaintance, whom I expected the letter would have found in Paris. but not being there, he was so good as to forward it to the friendly care of mr Warden, to whom I am indebted for the delivery of it to you. the books all arrived safely, and I take this occasion of expressing to you my satisfaction with the care and exactitude with which they were selected & forwarded. their bindings too were mostly in the handsome style I like. I now take the liberty of considering this as having placed me in correspondence with you, and as authorising the addresses I shall annually have occasion to make to you for articles in the same line. I am now taking measures to have a sum of 135. Dollars placed in your hands by my correspondent in Philadelphia; but not knowing thro' what channel he will be able to do this, I desire him to communicate that to you himself. when you shall have recieved it, I have to request you to employ it in furnishing me as far as it will go, with the books named in the catalogue now inclosed, giving a preference in the order in which they are named, and curtailing the list from the bottom upwards to where it begins to exceed the sum remitted. I expect mr Ticknor is arriving at Paris about this time. he is so perfectly acquainted with the best editions of Classics, & especially those lately of the German sçavans, that I pray you to consult him, & consider his advice as absolutely controuling my own choice, & giving me the benefit of his knolege, so much more recent & extensive than mine. I inclose him a copy of the catalogue, and ask the favor of his advice to you which I am sure he will give, on your application. either mr Gallatin our Ambassador at Paris, or mr Warden will advise you of the opportunities offered at Havre for their conveyance, when you shall let them know that the package is ready. I think it is better they should be packed in a trunk; and it is very important that they be shipped as soon as ready, and especially by the month of September, that they may not be exposed to the certain damage of a winter passage. I salute you with assurances of great respect. TH: JEFFERSON

P.S. if any volumes of Sismondi, subsequent to the 11. you sent me, have since appeared, be so good as to send them unbound.

PoC (MHi); on reused address cover of Joseph Delaplaine to TJ, 24 Feb. 1817; with loss of text at left margin, possibly due to polygraph misalignment; at foot of first page: "sent by duplicates under cover to mr Gallatin"; endorsed by TJ. Enclosed in TJ to Albert Gallatin, [before 6 June 1817], TJ to John Vaughan, 7 June 1817, and TJ to Daniel Brent, 8 June 1817. Enclosure not found.

Vaughan was TJ's CORRESPONDENT in Philadelphia.

To John Wayles Eppes

DEAR SIR Monticello June 6. 17.

By a letter from mr Wood recieved a few days ago, I learned with great regret that he was obliged to suspend his school for four months (till the last of September) in order to compleat the public survey he had undertaken. regret being unavailing, the question is how Francis may best employ those 4. months. I observe he has made no progress in Arithmetic, and think therefore he could not do better than lay his shoulder to that during this vacation. if an instructor is necessary, I presume you have them in your neighborhood, who besides the 4. elementary rules, including the rule of three, can teach the extraction of the roots, vulgar and decimal fractions, Progressions & even the use of Logarithms. but with Bezout (which you possess) I do not think he will need the aid of an instructor. that author is so remarkably plain that any one may teach himself by his aid. nothing could give me more pleasure than to have him here, and to give him any little aid to the understanding of that author which he might need, should it be agreeable to yourself and him. I say this merely to express my own dispositions, without urging yours or his. he should give one half the day to Arithmetic, & the other to his Latin and Greek; and in the course of the 4. months he may have a sufficient foundation to begin the study of mathematics. mr Wood writes me very encouragingly both as to his capacity and dispositions, which cannot but add to our natural excitements to his improvement. my anxiety on this occasion will, I am sure, be an apology to you for my troubling you on a subject where your own will must be supreme. mrs Randolph and the girls join me in affectionate respects to mrs Eppes and yourself, to which I add my particular salutations

TH: JEFFERSON

RC (ViU: TJP); at foot of text: "J. W. Eppes esq." PoC (MHi); on verso of reused address cover of James Barbour to TJ, 29 Mar. 1817; endorsed by TJ.

To Albert Gallatin

Dear Sir Monticello. [before 6 June 1817]

The importance that the inclosed letters should safely reach their destination impels me to avail my self of the protection of your cover. this is an inconvenience to which your situation exposes you, while it adds to the opportunities of exercising yourself in works of charity.

According to the opinion I hazarded to you, a little before your departure, we have had almost an entire change in the body of Congress. the unpopularity of the Compensation law was compleated by the manner of repealing it, as to all the world, except themselves. in some states, it is said, every member is changed: in all many. what opposition there was to the original law was chiefly from Southern members. yet many of those,[1] have been left out, because they recieved the advanced wages. I have never known so unanimous a sentiment of disapprobation: and what is remarkable, is that it was spontaneous. the newspapers were almost entirely silent, and the people, not only unled by their leaders, but in opposition to them. I confess I was highly pleased with this proof of the innate good sense, the vigilance, and the determination of the people to act for themselves. Among the laws of the late Congress, some were of note. a navigation act, particularly, applicable to those nations only who have navigation acts; pinching one of them especially, not only in the general way, but in the intercourse with her foreign possessions. this part may re-act on us, and it remains for trial which may bear longest. A law respecting our conduct as a Neutral between Spain and her contending colonies was past by a majority of 1. only I believe, and against the very general sentiment of our country. it is thought to strain our complaisance to Spain beyond her right or merit, and almost against the right of the other party, and certainly against the claims they have to our good wishes and neighborly relations. that we should wish to see the people of other countries free, is as natural and at least as justifiable, as that one king should wish to see the kings of other countries maintained in their despotism. right to both parties, innocent favor to the juster cause, is our proper sentiment.

you will have learnt that an act for internal improvement, after passing both houses, was negatived by the President. the act was founded avowedly on the principle that the phrase in the constitution which authorises Congress 'to lay taxes to pay the debts and provide for the general welfare' was an extension of the powers specifically enumerated to whatever would promote the general welfare;[2] and this, you know, was the federal doctrine: whereas our tenet ever was, and indeed it is almost the only landmark which now divides the federalists from the republicans, that Congress had not unlimited powers to provide for the general welfare, but were restrained to those specifically enumerated; and that, as it was never meant they should provide for that welfare but by the exercise of the enumerated powers, so it could not have been meant they should raise money for purposes which the enumeration did not place under their action: consequently that the specification of powers is a limitation of the purposes for which they may raise money. I think the passage and rejection of this bill a fortunate incident. every state will certainly concede the power; and this will be a national confirmation of the grounds of appeal to them, & will settle for ever the meaning of this phrase, which by a mere grammatical quibble, has countenanced the General government in a claim of universal power. for in the phrase 'to lay taxes to pay the debts & provide for the general welfare' it is a mere question of Syntax whether the two last infinitives are governed by the first, or are distinct & coordinate powers; a question unequivocally decided by the exact definition of powers immediately following. it is fortunate for another reason, as the states in conceding the power, will modify it, either by requiring the federal ratio of expence in each state, or otherwise, so as to secure us against it's partial exercise. without this caution, intrigue, negociation and the barter of votes might become as habitual in Congress as they are in those legislatures which have the appointment of officers, and which with us is called 'logging,' the term of the farmers for their exchanges of aid in rolling together the logs of their newly cleared grounds.

three of our papers have presented us the copy of an act of the legislature of New York which, if it has really past, will carry us back to the times of the darkest bigotry and barbarism to find a parallel. it's purport is that all those who shall <u>hereafter</u> join in communion with the religious sect of Shaking Quakers shall be deemed civilly dead, their marriages dissolved, and all their children and property taken out of their hands. this act being published nakedly in the papers, without the usual signatures, or any history of the circumstances of it's passage, I am not without a hope it may have been a mere abortive attempt. it contrasts singularly with a cotemporary vote of the Pensylvania legislature, who on a proposition to make the belief in a god a necessary qualification for office, rejected it by a great majority, altho' assuredly there was not a single Atheist in their body. and you remember to have heard that when the act for religious freedom was before the Virginia assembly, a motion to insert the name of Jesus Christ before the phrase 'the author of our holy religion' which stood in the bill, was rejected, altho' that was the creed of a great majority of them.

I have been charmed to see that a presidential election now produces scarcely any agitation. on mr Madison's election there was little, on Monroe's all but none. in mr Adams's time and mine parties were so nearly balanced as to make the struggle fearful for our peace. but, since the decided ascendancy of the republican body, federalism has looked on with silent, but unresisting anguish. in the middle Southern and Western states, it is as low as it ever can be; for nature has made some men monarchists and tories by their constitution, and some of course there always will be. I took the liberty of introducing to you a mr Terril, son of a neice of mine, who was going to the College of Geneva. this makes it a duty for me to say to you in confidence that his friends apprehend he is going on in a style of expence above his means; on which subject they are, I believe, giving him some admonitions which they think necessary.

We have had a remarkably cold winter. at Hallowell in Maine, the mercury was at 34.° below Zero, of Farenheit, which is 16.° lower than it was in Paris in 1788.9. here it was at 6.° above zero, which is our greatest degree of cold.

Present me respectfully to mrs Gallatin, and be assured of my constant and affectionate friendship. TH: JEFFERSON

P.S. June 6. 17. this letter written some time ago, is now only dispatched, & covers a letter to mr Terril recieved recently.

RC (NHi: Gallatin Papers); undated, with dated postscript added separately to RC and PoC; at foot of first page: "Mr Gallatin." PoC (DLC: TJ Papers, 210:37478–9); notation by TJ at foot of text: "sent by duplicates, the one thro' mr Vaughan the other thro the state office." Enclosures: (1) TJ to Stephen Cathalan, [before 6 June 1817]. (2) TJ to de Bure Frères, 6 June 1817. (3) TJ to George Ticknor, [before 6 June 1817]. (4) TJ to David Bailie Warden, 6 June 1817. (5) Enclosure to Frank Carr to TJ, 9 May 1817. Enclosed in TJ to John Vaughan, 7 June 1817, and TJ to Daniel Brent, 8 June 1817.

"An Act more effectually to preserve the neutral relations of the United States," passed 3 Mar. 1817, was designed to prevent Americans from providing armed ships to revolutionaries in the Latin American colonies of SPAIN (*U.S. Statutes at Large*, 3:370–1; Charles G. Fenwick, *The Neutrality Laws of the United States* [1912], 35–40). During the divorce and custody case of Eunice Chapman, the legislature of New York rejected a proposal to declare Chapman's estranged husband, James Chapman, and all other Shakers CIVILLY DEAD (Washington *Daily National Intelligencer*, 31 Mar. 1817; Nelson M. Blake, "Eunice Against the Shakers," *New York History* 41 [1960]: 359–78). A temperature reading of minus 34° in HALLOWELL, District of Maine, was published in the Washington *Daily National Intelligencer*, 25 Jan. 1817, and elsewhere. TJ had previously reported that the coldest temperature in Paris in the winter of 1788–89 was minus 9.5° Fahrenheit (*PTJ*, 14:358).

[1] TJ here canceled "who opposed it too."
[2] Preceding seven words interlined.

To William Lee

Dear Sir Monticello June 6. 17.

The National Intelligencer informs us there is a numerous party of Swiss stocking weavers arrived at Washington, and mr Barnes of Georgetown, now here, tells me he thinks they are under your patronage. believing it for their interest to distribute themselves to good posts in the country, I take the liberty of stating that I think there is no better stand for one or two of them than the town of Charlottesville, 3 miles distant from me. it is a mountainous country, of course healthy, inhabited by an industrious, thriving & independant yeomanry, whose wives & daughters would furnish much of the spun material, and all would buy that ready-woven. I have enquired and found they can be accomodated with comfortable quarters, paying from 20. to 30.D. a year for a good room. European goods are dear, but the necessaries of life very cheap. I have the promise of the merchants of the village that they will do every thing in their power to prosper them. if a family or families should come with bulky baggage, they had better come round by water to Richmond in the vessels constantly passing from your district to that place, where they will always find open batteaux coming up the river to Charlottesville. single persons may come direct in the stage from Washington to Charlottesville.

a silversmith, if any among them, would find great employment at the same place & would be particularly well recieved. we have there a fine watchmaker; a Swiss from Neufchatel, finding much more work than he can do, and taking in money as fast as he can earn it. he finds himself peculiarly happy and delighted with the country & his own situation. if you can encourage good subjects from among these emigrants you will ensure their success, accomodate this vicinage and do an acceptable favor to your friend & serv[t]

Th: Jefferson

PoC (DLC); on verso of reused address cover to TJ; at foot of text: "William Lee esq."; endorsed by TJ.

The Washington *Daily National Intelligencer* of 24 May 1817 included a pseudonymous article by "*A friend to manufactures and the District*." It reported that a group of swiss stocking weavers had set up a workshop there that employed "the new machinery of England, with the additional improvements of France," and it touted the benefits of the enterprise for the local advancement of domestic manufactures. Charlottesville's Swiss watchmaker was Louis A. Leschot.

To George Ticknor

DEAR SIR Monticello [before 6 June 1817]

My last to you was of Feb. 8. 16. since which I have recieved yours of Mar. 15. Apr. 23. & July 10. 16. in this last you mentioned that you should be in Paris this spring, till which time therefore I have deferred acknoleging them; and also because winter passages for letters to Europe are rare, slow, and uncertain.

The German editions of Homer, Virgil, Juvenal, Aeschylus and Tacitus, which you were so kind as to forward to me thro' your father, came all safe, and it was a great convenience to me to be permitted to remit the amount to him at Boston, rather than to Europe. the editions of Heyne, Ruperti, Oberlin, are indeed of the first order; but especially Heyne's of the Iliad. it exceeds any thing I had ever conceived in editorial merit. how much it makes us wish he had done the same with the Odyssey. in his Iliad I observe he had the benefit of Villeoison's Venetian edition. this style of editing has all the superiority your former letters have ascribed to it, and urges us to read again the authors we have formerly read to obtain a new and higher understanding of them.

The other part of my catalogue was committed by mr Warden to the Debures freres, booksellers of Paris, who under his directions, executed it entirely to my satisfaction, as far as the sum would go which I remitted; and I had desired that to be considered as the limit of my demand. prices had so much risen above what I had known them, and what they were stated at in the old Catalogue, that altho' I had made considerable allowance, they were still far beyond that. I am now remitting a further sum to the Debures directly, to furnish so much of a catalogue inclosed to them as it will procure; and I direct them, if you are in Paris, to trouble you for your advice, and to take it implicitly. having stated to you in my letter of Feb. 8. the general circumstances which guide my preference in the choice of editions I will ask the favor of you to give me the benefit of your more recent and particular knolege of them: for which purpose I inclose you a copy of the catalogue sent to the Debures. from Villers' Coup d'oeil of German literature, published by Treuttell & Wurtz. Paris 1809. I collect notices of some editions: but he is not particular in his descriptions. for example, he mentions a Livy by Ruperti. is this in the superior style of his Juvenal, and of manageable size, say in 8vo? if it is, I shall send for it hereafter.[1] if not, I shall content myself with the edition Clerici, sent me by the Debures the last year. is the Herodotus of Reitz and Schaeffer or that of Schweighaeuser, or the German edition mentioned in your letter of Nov. 25. 15. best? he mentions the Euripides of Zimmerman published at Frankfort 1808. is this in 8vo? also a Dion Cassius, published in 1807. without describing it. is it a good one, and of manageable size? I do not see Lucian among the Greek Classics, which have employed the attention of the German Sçavans.—but I should never be done with the interrogatories suggested even by the single publication of Villers, were I to indulge myself in them. many original works also are there mentioned, well worth procuring; but that he does not say in what language written; and, if in German, they would be useless to me.

I suppose that your friends of Boston furnish you with our domestic news. Improvement is now the general word with us. canals, roads, education occupy principal attention. a bill which had passed both houses of Congress for beginning these works, was negatived by the President, on constitutional, and I believe, sound grounds; that instrument not having placed this among the enumerated objects to which they are authorised to apply the public contributions. he recommended an application to the states for an extension of their powers to this object, which will I believe be unanimously conceded, & will be a better way of obtaining the end, than by strained constructions, which would loosen all the bands of the constitution. in the mean time the states separately are going on with this work. New York is undertaking the most gigantic enterprise of uniting the waters of L. Erie and the Hudson; Jersey those of the Delaware & Rariton. this state proposes several such works; but most particularly has applied itself to establishments for education, by taking up the plan I proposed to them 40. years ago, which you will see explained in the Notes on Virginia. they have provided for this special object an ample fund, and a growing one. they propose an elementary school in every ward or township, for reading, writing and common arithmetic; a college in every district, suppose of 80. or 100. miles square, for laying the foundations of the sciences in general, to wit, languages geography & the higher branches of Arithmetic; and a single University embracing every science deemed useful in the present state of the world. this last may very possibly be placed near Charlottesville, which you know is under view from Monticello.

Amid these enlarged measures, the papers tell us of one by the legislature of New York so much in the opposite direction that it would puzzle us to say in what, the darkest, age of the history of bigotry and barbarism, we should find an apt place for it. <u>it is said</u> they have declared by law that all those who hereafter shall join in communion with the religious sect of Shaking quakers, shall be deemed civilly dead, their marriage vows dissolved, and all their children and property taken from them; without any provision for rehabilitation in case of resipiscence. to prove that this departure from the spirit of our institutions is local, and I hope merely momentary, Pensylvania about the same time, rejected a proposition to make the belief in a god a necessary qualification for office, altho' I presume there was not an Atheist in their body.: and I dare say you have heard that when the law for freedom of religion was before the Virginia legislature, in which the phrase 'the author of our holy religion' happened to be they rejected a proposition to prefix to it the name of 'Jesus Christ,' altho certainly a great majority of them considered him as such. yet they would not undertake to say that for every one. the New York law is so recent that nothing has yet been said about it; & I do imagine, if it has been past, their next legislature will repeal it, and make an amende honorable to the general spirit of their confederates. nothing having yet appeared but the naked act, without signature, or a word of the history of it's passage, there is room to hope it has been merely an abortive attempt.

Of the Volcanic state of Europe I know little, and will say nothing; and add to the length of this, for myself & the individuals of my family, who remember you with particular friendship, the assurances of the highest esteem and respect. TH: JEFFERSON

June 6. 1817. P.S. the preceding written some time ago, is now only dispatched.

PoC (DLC: TJ Papers, 210:37455–6); undated, with dated postscript; at foot of first page: "Mr Ticknor"; endorsed by TJ as a letter of 6 June 1817 and so recorded in SJL; with additional notation by TJ beneath postscript: "send by duplicates, the one thro' his father, the other under cover to mr Gallatin yro State office." Enclosed in TJ to Albert Gallatin, [before 6 June 1817], TJ to Elisha Ticknor, 7 June 1817, and TJ to Daniel Brent, 8 June 1817. Enclosure not found.

For TJ's educational PLAN for Virginia, see *Notes*, ed., Peden, 146–9, and "A Bill for the More General Diffusion of Knowledge" (*PTJ*, 2:526–35). RESIPISCENCE: the act of coming to one's senses (*OED*). AMENDE HONORABLE: an open apology made to redress an offense (*Black's Law Dictionary*).

[1]Preceding five words interlined in place of "wish to have it."

To David Bailie Warden

DEAR SIR Monticello June 6. 17.

Your several favors of July 12. 14. & Aug. 9. with the invoices of the books, in the purchase and dispatch of which you were so kind as to take a part, and the books themselves have been all safely recieved. I am under great obligations to you for your aid in this supply to the amusements of my old age; and for the satisfactory manner in which the Messrs Debures freres[1] have executed my commission. by placing me too in correspondence with them it enables me at this time to address a commission for another supply to themselves directly without troubling you with it, and of continuing to do the same thing annually as I shall probably do. I am sure you will always be so good as to advise them of the best opportunities of conveyance on their application. I hope that in your new undertaking as agent for the settlement of claims you find success & compensation, towards which, in that or any other line, my good wishes & offices should certainly never be wanting or spared.

On the Volcanic situation of Europe perhaps it is best to say nothing; and the rather as we can foresee nothing certain & may compromit the safe transmission of our letters by useless speculations. on the subject of England only I will permit myself to express my belief that the great crisis so long foretold by the political prophets is now at length arrived, and, by putting her hors de combat, will give the world some respite from war, some leisure for the pursuits of peace, industry and happiness. with us, three main objects occupy our attention. the payment of our public debt, establishment of manufactures, & internal improvement by canals, roads and public education. I thank you for your kind attention to mr Terril. he is a worthy young man. but his friends here are apprehensive he is indulging in a style of expence to which his means are not competent, and they are giving him admonitions which they think necessary on that subject.

Winter passages for letters to Europe being rare, slow & uncertain I have got into the habit of taking up my pen, cum hirundine primâ, to recall myself to the recollection of my friends there. the opening spring will soon therefore convey my friendly salutations to Baron Humboldt, to whom, altho' our country offers nothing worthy of communication, I shall certainly take occasion to convey the expressions of my very affectionate & respectful attachment. I salute you on the part of my family as well as myself[2] with the same assurances of esteem & friendship. TH: JEFFERSON

RC (MdHi: Warden Papers); edge damaged, with missing punctuation supplied from PoC; addressed: "Mr David B. Warden à Paris," with "Rue Pot de Fer St Sulpice N° 12" added in an unidentified hand; endorsed by Warden as received 12 Aug. PoC (DLC); on reused address cover of Wilson Cary Nicholas to TJ, 24 Feb. 1817; endorsed by TJ; additional notation by TJ at foot of text: "sent under cover to mr Gallatin." Dupl (MdHi: Warden Papers); endorsed by Warden. Enclosed in TJ to Albert Gallatin, [before 6 June 1817], TJ to John Vaughan, 7 June 1817, and TJ to Daniel Brent, 8 June 1817.

For Warden's NEW UNDERTAKING, see the third enclosure to his 9 Aug. 1816 letter to TJ. COMPROMIT: "compromise" (*OED*). CUM HIRUNDINE PRIMÂ references Horace, *Epistles*, 1.7.12–3, which reads "te, dulcis amice, reviset cum Zephyris, si concedes, et hirundine prima": "you, dear friend, he will—if you permit—revisit along with the zephyrs and the first swallow" (Fairclough, *Horace: Satires, Epistles and Ars Poetica*, 294–5).

[1] Word not in Dupl.
[2] Preceding ten words not in Dupl.

To Stephen Girard

DEAR SIR Monticello June 7. 17.

I was much gratified on a former occasion by having the security of your bill that in the books and wines I ordered from France I should not be disappointed. there is probably some balance still due to you on that score; as, after placing 200. of the 550.D. in Marseilles, there remained for Paris 350.D. of the employment of this last sum I have no other account from my correspondent than that he paid 1900 *f*–25 c for the books; and to this must have been added their transportation to Havre, of which I have no account. but the 1900 *f*–25 c alone at par would have been 356.29 D and the real exchange may have made it more, besides the transportation to Havre. these articles being unknown to me, I must ask the favor of you to give a note of the balance due you to my friend mr Vaughan who will discharge it on my account. I have now requested him to remit for me a sum of 400 D to Paris for similar objects with the last. not knowing how far it might be within the line of your convenience, we dare not ask a like accomodation of credit from you, however desirable on account of certainty against disappointment. with my thanks for the past favor, I pray you to accept the assurance of my great personal esteem and respect.

TH: JEFFERSON

RC (PPGi: Girard Papers [microfilm at PPAmP]); addressed: "M[r] Stephen Girard Philadelphia"; stamp canceled; franked; endorsed in an unidentified hand as received 13 June 1817. PoC (MHi); on verso of reused address cover of William Pelham to TJ, 6 Mar. 1817; torn at seal, with several words rewritten by TJ; endorsed by TJ.

David Bailie Warden, TJ's CORRESPONDENT in Paris, had taken charge of his orders for books from the firm of de Bure Frères.

From LeRoy, Bayard & Company

SIR Newyork the 7 June 1817.

M. P. Gibson having further remitted us on your account $255.6. to meet the $256.79.—mention'd & in respect of the 20^t ult^o whereby the first of your Bonds to Mess. N. & J. & R Van Staphorst for $1000. with Interest, becomes cancelled we have the honor of Sending you Said bond, here enclosed, with our receipt thereon and acknowledging your favr of 25: ult^o we Salute[1] with great respect

Sir Yr m H Serv LEROY BAYARD & Co

RC (DLC); in the hand of a representative of LeRoy, Bayard & Company; at head of text: "The Honob^le Thomas Jefferson, Monticello"; endorsed by TJ as received 17 June 1817 and so recorded in SJL. Enclosure: bond of TJ to van Staphorst & Hubbard, 26 Mar. 1797, for a $1,000 installment on a $2,000 loan, to be paid before 1 Oct. 1800, with 6 percent interest due at that time (MS in DLC: TJ Papers, 101:17333–4, in TJ's hand and signed by him, with signature mutilated to cancel bond, witnessed by David Watson, with attestation in TJ's hand signed by justice of the peace Thomas Bell and certified by signature of Albemarle County clerk John Nicholas on 3 Apr. 1797, endorsed at foot of text in same hand as covering letter [trimmed]: "Received Payment of the within Bond pr One thous[and] Dollars with Interest Newyork June 7^h 1817 LeRoy Bayard & Co pr N & J & R Van Staphorst of Amst[erdam]," docketed in an unidentified hand: "Thos Jefferson. Obl^e groot $1,000—vervalt 1 October 1800. a 6 p.c.—van 1 October 1796 af" ["Thos Jefferson. bond for $1,000 due 1 October 1800 at 6 percent from 1 October 1796 onwards"], with additional calculations by TJ:

	"D
1796. Oct 1.	1000.
1817. June 7. Int. @ 6 p.c.	
20 y–8 m–7 D	1240.1/
	2240.1/";

PrC in DLC: TJ Papers, 101:17336–7, lacking signatures of witness, justice, and county clerk, with unfilled blanks for names and date in attestation, lacking docket and TJ's calculations).

The bond returned here was one of two TJ enclosed to van Staphorst & Hubbard in a letter of 27 Mar. 1797 (*PTJ*, 29:329–31; *MB*, 2:957).

[1] Manuscript: "Saluute."

To Elisha Ticknor

DEAR SIR Monticello June 7. 17.

Expecting that mr George Tickner, your son, would be at Paris about this time, I have deferred till now the acknolegement of his favors: and believing the inclosed will reach him more safely and speedily thro' the favor of your transmission, I take the liberty, according to his request, and your permission of putting it under cover to you. it is fortunate for him that the quiet of Europe still continues, and is likely to continue long enough for the peaceable indulgence of his travels and stay in it. I pray you to be assured of my great esteem & respect. TH: JEFFERSON

RC (InU); endorsed by Ticknor. PoC (MHi); on verso of reused address cover of John W. Maury to TJ, 28 Feb. 1817; at foot of text: "Elisha Tickner esq."; endorsed by TJ. Enclosure: TJ to George Ticknor, [before 6 June 1817].

To John Vaughan

DEAR SIR Monticello June 7. 17.

The season for my annual call for books and wines from France now recurring, I had desired my correspondent mr Gibson of Richmond to remit you a sum of 400.D. which he writes me he has done. this I must request you, according to your usual goodness, to dispose of for me by investing it in a safe bill on Paris, where I wish 135.D of it made payable to Mess[rs] Debures, freres, libraires de Paris, and 265 D. to the order of M. Cathalan our Consul at Marseilles. I would ask all the dispatch in this which your convenience will admit, because it is so important to get both articles safe arrived, before the commencement of winter. mr Girard's credit is so sure, that the same channel would be very desirable. but it may be out of the line of his convenience. on the former occasion he was so kind as to extend his credit beyond the exact sum of 350.D. payable in Paris. I find that the books cost 1900 *f*–25 c which, at par, would have been 356. D 29 c and the actual exchange may have made it more. there must also have been some expences of transportation to Havre, of which I have no account. so that on the whole there may be a balance of some Dollars due him. I do not know how your and my account stands: but be this as it may, I must pray you to enquire into, and pay to mr Girard the balance which may be due him (without encroaching on the 400.D. which I would wish to go entire to France) and the moment you inform me how I shall then stand on your books, I will remit to you whatever I may be deficient. I inclose a letter to mr Cathalan, and one to mr Gallatin covering one to the Debures, which I ask the favor of you to forward by a safe conveyance. they direct the employment of the money, remitted. Your habitual kindness encourages me to trouble you with these petty affairs, which I do not know how otherwise to manage for myself. they give me however always the acceptable occasion of renewing to you the assurances of my great esteem and respect. TH: JEFFERSON

RC (PPAmP: Vaughan Papers); at foot of first page: "mr Vaughan"; endorsed by Vaughan as "rec[d] 12th ans[d] 18th." PoC (MHi); on reused address cover of John Barnes to TJ, 26 Mar. 1817; endorsed by TJ. Enclosures: (1) TJ to Stephen Cathalan, [before 6 June 1817]. (2) TJ to de Bure Frères, 6 June 1817. (3) TJ to Albert Gallatin, [before 6 June 1817]. (4) TJ to David Bailie Warden, 6 June 1817.

From Edmund Bacon

Sir. 8th June 1817—

Mr York says he had no instructions to recieve the money for the mules and that Mr. Munroe had never authorised him to recieve his money. shall I write to Mr Munroe informing him I have the money ready to pay to any Person he will direct or mention to recieve it. we have been cuting clover too days. it is not a very good chance to save hay as the land is very rough and the clover very low.

My mother has met with an unexpected call for money and has requested me to pay her forty dollars. that is so nigh all that is in your hands I expect we had as well pay it all to her. I have the order in favour of Rogers for 84 D and drew the money from Mr. Southall for Yorks order. paid to Rogers $84 leaveing a balance in hand of $36 so that will still count a part of the $120 for the mules.

Yours sincerly E Bacon

RC (DLC); dateline adjacent to signature; superfluous punctuation editorially omitted; with MS of TJ's Account with Mary Bacon, [ca. 17 June 1817], on verso; addressed: "Mr Jefferson Monticello."

On 2 June 1817 TJ indicated that he had given Mr. York, overseer for James Monroe (munroe), an "order on V. W. Southall for 120.D. price of 2. mules bot. last year," but he then canceled the entry and wrote "Not pd. to York." On the date of this letter Bacon used that order to make payments on TJ's behalf to John Rogers and to his own mother, Mary Bacon. TJ paid Monroe on 3 Oct. 1817 (*MB*, 2:1334, 1339).

To Daniel Brent

Dear Sir Monticello June 8. 17.

Long indulgence by your predecessors in the direction of the department of State in the privilege of getting my letters to Europe put under the same cover with the official dispatches of the department has encoraged me to ask the same favor of you. my increasing aversion to writing will be a security against any abuse of this favor. on this ground I take the liberty of inclosing a letter to mr Gallatin, and requesting of your goodness to give it a <u>safe</u> passage with the[1] dispatches of your office to that legation, and pray you to accept the assurance of my great esteem and respect. Th: Jefferson

PoC (DLC); at foot of text: "Mr <*William*> Brent," with first name presumably canceled by TJ after receipt of Brent's letter of 20 June 1817. Recorded in SJL as a letter to Daniel Brent. Enclosures: (1) TJ to Albert Gallatin, [before 6 June 1817]. (2) TJ to Stephen Cathalan, [before 6 June 1817]. (3) TJ to de Bure Frères, 6 June 1817. (4) TJ to George Ticknor, [before 6 June 1817]. (5) TJ to

David Bailie Warden, 6 June 1817. (6) Enclosure to Frank Carr to TJ, 9 May 1817.

[1]Manuscript: "withe."

From Francis Adrian Van der Kemp

DEAR AND RESPECTED SIR! Oldenbarneveld 9 Jun. 1817.

I was highly gratified with your favour of the 1 of maÿ—as I am now convinced—that no doubt remains with you, if I could abuse the confidence, with which I was honoured—It is with me a Sacred principle—never to make use—in any manner—of a trust—as upon an explicit permission—under no pretext whatever—not even to oblige the friend of my bosom—not even to hurt a rancourous enemÿ—And now I proceed with the Same unlimited confidence.

I wrote to Germany for the books recommended—with the proviso that the expences were not too high—when it would be improper in one—cui curta Suppellex.

If I receive them—and they contain remarks—deserving your notice I Shall communicate them.

on the Skeleton—in your possession—following additions may be justly added—

Religion of the Jews
Sects—Pharisees—Sadducees—Essenes.
Part. ii
Concise views of &c
Apparition of Angels—Development of this System
Consequences:
Examination of the preaching of Jezus and his Disciples
Part. iii
Perfect morality—&c
Simplicity
Part. iv
Prejudices &c
Priest-craft. Examination of its existence—extent.

I lately received a present of German Literature—among which Iselin's geschichte der menschheit or history of mankind—I was delighted, I was Surprised and the profound investigations of that man—and do not recollect—to have met with in any language—So many luminous observations—encompassed—in two Such Small vols. Mine edition is the fifth published in 1786. He was from Zurick—and employd in his country in State-Employ as well as in Literature.

I requested my friend Mappa, who remembers yet with pleasure, the politeness which he received from you in France—during your Embassy in that countrÿ; to translate it for me—as I wanted time.—

Permit me to renew the assurance that I remain—with Sincere respect—

Dear & respected Sir! Your most obed. & obliged

FR. ADR. VAN DR KEMP

RC (DLC); dateline at foot of text; endorsed by TJ as received 18 June 1817 and so recorded in SJL. RC (MHi); address cover only; with PoC of TJ to Alexander Garrett and Valentine W. Southall, 23 Sept. 1817, on verso; addressed: "Thomas Jefferson LLD. Monticello Virginia"; franked; postmarked Trenton, N.Y., 10 June.

CUI CURTA SUPPELLEX: "who has modest resources." The SKELETON in TJ's possession to which Van der Kemp adds here is his Synopsis of a Proposed Book, printed above at 1 Nov. 1816.

ENCLOSURE

Translated Extract from Isaak Iselin, *Über die Geschichte der Menschheit*

[ca. 9 June 1817]

Isaak Iselin geschichte der menschheit vol. ii Lib. 7—HauptSt. 23 pag 217.[1]

the Christian Religion.

During the period that the monstrous Edifice of Roman grandeur tottered under its own weight; when its Political body wasted itself, by its own internal corruption, arose in the most abandonned province, the Christian Religion.

This Divine doctrine distinguished itself at its first promulgation from all other Religions by a Sublime Simplicity, and the purest clearness. with these excellent attributes it became Suitable for every Condition, for every calling or vocation, for every Situation.

It encompassed all what was lofty, great, and elevated, which in every other Religion was destroyed, not being polluted with absurdities which disgraced it. It comprehended that excellent observance of morality, and was also the Surest guide to happiness, tempering and mollifying the human mind.

The Philosophers have observed that a Nation of true Christians, never could be warlike. They judged rightly. A Philosophizing People would find themselves in a defenceless Situation. Sound Sense reproves War as much as Christianity reprobates it. To its barbarous origin it owes all, and with its annihilation it must disappear. It is no blame on, but the greatest Commendation of the Christian Religion, when it is Said that it disapproves war.

The Christian Religion disgusted, and displeased barbarous and vain Men, even on account of its purity, its meekness, and its venerable pre-eminence.

The Priest discovered early that it did not engage the Senses Sufficiently, and that the imagination was not enough captivated, therefore he borrowed of a false Philosophy fanatical dreams, and from the dominant Religion delusive Ceremonies.(*)

He thereby increased his Consequence with the ignorant, who had already embraced his doctrine, and gained many more to whom Christianity in its true Sincerity would never have been pleasing. The more he stifled the true Spirit of Religion; The more he added thereunto fascinating outworks: The more he oppressed the genius of the People. By these means he extended his powers, of which he cunningly availed himself, Sometimes to Strengthen Princely despotism, at other times mitigating it, but in the end to devour and annihilate all by his own Despotism.

The Christian Religion must also be viewed and considered in two points. The true, the inward Christianity is an immediate operation of the Deity. No Man, no Philosophy, no reason can give true faith and Sanctification. These are powerful gifts, which are the property of the Elect, and those Elect, constitute alone the true Church, which is dispersed throughout all visible Congregations. These no human resistance can Scan, or meddle with. They are not Subjected to any human Law. Upon them no Pope, no King, or Prince has power. It is no Exteriour Form, and no outward constitution is her own.

On the contrary, the External[2] Christianity is no immediate operation of the Divinity. It consists in usages, Ceremonies, Forms, which, under the name of the Christian Religion, from the first Century unto our days, have been prescribed to the Nations with numerous alterations. It is the Shape, it is the dress which Men gave to[3] the Sublimest doctrine. It is the opinion of the Pope, of Luther, of Zwinglius.(†)

It may, and can Philosophically be examined. Its influence in Morals, in Laws, in the Sciences itself, has made it for ever a powerful engine[4] in Politics. Under the Roman Emperors, the adulterated Christianity had already corrupted the taste, stifled the light of knowledge, and with its ignorance and darkness introduced the Ecclesiastical Slavery, which caused more Ruin to the Empire, than the Barbarian incursions. Through[5] the true knowledge, even these Should[6] have been reformed into reasonable Men, whereas bigotry and Superstition made them yet more inhuman.

By this unnatural christianity has the Spirit, and the Minds of all the European Nations, received and adopted a very particular Strain, giving to this part of the world throughout, a altered[7] Situation.

(*) Christianam religionem absolutam & Simplicem anili Superstitione Confundens; in qua Scrutanda perplexius, quam componenda gravius, excitavit discidia plurima; quæ progressa fusius alit convertatione verborum, ut catervis antistitum jumentis publicis ultro citroque discurrentibus per Sinodos, quos appellant, dum ritum omnem ad fuum trahere conantur arbitrium, rei vehiculariæ Succideret nervos, Says of the Emperour Constantin, Ammianus Marcellinus, 21. 16. From this we can form an Idea of the Spirit of this Emperour, and of the Spirit of his Priesthood.

(†) Now I say this, that among you one saith: I am of Paul; the other: I am of Apollos; the third: I am of Peter; the fourth: I am of Christ. 1 Cor. 1. v. 12. &c. See also v. 4. 5. & 6. of the 3d chapter of the Same Epistle.[8]

T. ii. pag. 206

† In this manner lived the Essener (Jos. B. J. vi. 2) among the corrupted Jews—a Society—which in many respects Seemed to have been the model of the first Christians.

MS (DLC: TJ Papers, 210:37462); extract probably translated by Adam Gerard Mappa; in an unidentified hand, with notes and revisions by Francis Adrian Van der Kemp as indicated; undated; extract based on Isaak Iselin, *über die Geschichte der Menschheit* (Basel, 1786; repr. 1976), 2:217–22; authorial footnotes retained; with final excerpt added by Van der Kemp from 2:206.

CHRISTIANAM RELIGIONEM ABSOLUTAM ... NERVOS ("The plain and simple religion of the Christians he obscured by a dotard's superstition, and by subtle and involved discussions about dogma, rather than by seriously trying to make them agree, he aroused many controversies; and as these spread more and more, he fed them with contentious words. And since throngs of bishops hastened hither and thither on the public post-horses to the various synods, as they call them, while he sought to make the whole ritual conform to his own will, he cut the sinews of the courier-service"). This description of the faith of the Roman emperor Constantius II is in a history by Ammianus Marcellinus, 21.16.18 (*Ammianus Marcellinus*, trans. John C. Rolfe, Loeb Classical Library [1935–39; repr. 1972], 2:182–5).

Iselin referred on page 206 of his work to the second main section of book six of the ancient historian Josephus's work, *The Jewish War.*

[1] Text to this point in Van der Kemp's hand.

[2] Here is canceled "or Superficial."

[3] Reworked by Van der Kemp from "which gave Men."

[4] Word interlined by Van der Kemp in place of an illegible deletion.

[5] Word interlined by Van der Kemp in place of "With."

[6] Reordered by Van der Kemp from "should even these."

[7] Word interlined by Van der Kemp in place of "variable."

[8] Remainder of text in Van der Kemp's hand, at foot of page and rotated 180° from preceding text.

To John Barnes

DEAR SIR Monticello June 10. 17.

This is written a few minutes after your departure from this place; for on returning into my room, and recollecting your question of yesterday, whether I had no remittance to make to your quarter, it occurred that I was indebted for the National Intelligencer for some years back; for indeed on examination I do not find that I have paid it later than to Oct. 31. 13. as it will give you less trouble to put the little sum I furnished you into the hands of the editor of that paper, than to remit it to me, I will pray you to pay it to him to be credited to me on his books. I should be glad if he would then let me know how my account will stand.

I comfort myself on your departure by persuading myself to hope that you may find the exercise & amusement of the journey so favorable to your health as to encourage you to repeat your acceptable visits from year to year. wishing this may find you arrived at home and in good health I salute you a[ffecti]onately

TH: JEFFERSON

PoC (DLC); on verso of reused address cover to TJ; hole in manuscript; at foot of text: "M[r] Barnes"; endorsed by TJ.

On 9 June 1817 TJ borrowed the LITTLE SUM of $25 from James Leitch to loan to Barnes. He repaid Leitch on 16 June (*MB*, 2:1334).

To Wilson Cary Nicholas

DEAR SIR Monticello June 10. 17.

I am detaining from the Philosophical society their copy of Col° Byrd's journal, until I can learn whether I may be permitted to send with it also the supplementary one of which I obtained the loan thro' your favor. will you be so good as to favor me with the name of the person to whom it belongs, that I may sollicit the permission without troubling you?

Does your new bank propose to do any business with country people? I have been in the habit of asking small accomodations occasionally from the Virginia bank where I had for some time past a note of 2000.D. the disastrous corn-crop of the last year & the excessive price of that article obliged me to apply to them lately for an additional 2000.D. to be indulged until the present crop should furnish new resources. they readily furnished the sum, but said [that?] the rules established for some time to come would forbid them to renew it at the expiration of the 60 days. mr Gibson, my correspondent & endorser advised me to enquire in time whether I could be enabled by the US. bank to take up the note when due, under a prospect of it's renewal for some months. will you be so good as to inform me on this subject? your friends in our vicinity are all well. I salute you with friendship and respect. TH: JEFFERSON

PoC (DLC); on verso of reused address cover to TJ; mutilated at seal; at foot of text: "Col° W. C. Nicholas"; endorsed by TJ.

Nicholas's NEW BANK was the Richmond branch of the Second Bank of the United States, of which he had been elected president in February 1817 (*ANB*; *Richmond Enquirer*, 20 Feb. 1817).

To Caspar Wistar

DEAR SIR Monticello June 10. 17.

Your favor of May 20. has been recieved, and with it the specimen of the letters of Doct[r] Franklin which we are likely to have published. I wish we may have <u>all</u>; but I am not yet relieved from the fear of suppressions. the anecdotes of his life would also be pleasing and instructive, and would place him in still another, and more amiable attitude before us. I shall be glad indeed if you think of collecting & publishing them. some two or three I could furnish, and with the more pleasure if personally to yourself on the occasion of the visit with which you flatter us. I hope I shall not lose it's benefit, as I have that of some other friends, by my occasional visits to Poplar Forest; at which place I shall be the latter part of this, & beginning of the next month; and again thro' the months of August & September.

I shall be glad to see another volume of the transactions of the Philosophical society; but have no contributions for it. in earlier life, when I might have done something on subjects analogous to their pursuits, I was constantly engaged in public affairs; and now that I am retired from them, without books, and without memory, I can hazard nothing which would do credit either to them or myself. the truth is that I have been drawn by the history of the times from Physical & mathematical sciences, which were my passion, to those of politics & government towards which I had naturally no inclination.

I take this occasion of thanking you for Mellish's map, which ought to have been the subject of an earlier and special acknolegement. it was not forgotten, but reserved only, for some other occasion of addressing you. for a correspondence with my friends has never been, and never can be a burthen to me. I have suffered heavily under that of persons at large, distributed all over the US. consulting me on subjects of no concern to myself, and yet, if answered at all, to be answered with some care, because of the frequent breaches of confidence by the publication of my letters. against this I have been obliged to revolt; and for a principal, among other reasons, that it occupied time which I wished to employ in correspondence with my friends. in this number I hold yourself most cordially, and shall never be happier than when your letters give me occasion of repeating to you the assurances of my affectionate friendship and respect.

TH: JEFFERSON

PoC (DLC); on a reused address cover from DeWitt Clinton to TJ; at foot of first page: "Doct[r] Wistar"; endorsed by TJ.

To William Caruthers

SIR Monticello June 11. 17.

I recieved yesterday your favor of the 2^d^ inst. and I readily consent that Patrick Henry, the freeman of colour whom you recommend, should live on my land at the Natural bridge, and cultivate the cultivable lands on it, on the sole conditions of paying the taxes annually as they arise, and of preventing trespasses. I some time since saw the tract advertized for sale by the US. Collector, and immediately sent him the taxes. but I do not know how it is with the state taxes. I cannot find that I have paid them myself since 1813. nor do I know if Dr Thornton has paid them. I requested him verbally to pay up any arrears due and place it in account between us,[1] which he promised to do, but I am uninformed whether it is done or not. should it be at all jeopardised as to the state taxes, I would hope your kindness would drop me a line of information. if they are unpaid now, on recieving a line of information, I would immediately remit them to you by mail. I expect to be at the bridge in September, and probably in that season every year as it is but 28. miles from my place in Bedford where I pass at different times about three months in the year. I salute you with great esteem and [resp]ect TH: JEFFERSON

PoC (DLC); on verso of reused address cover to TJ; mutilated at seal, with two words rewritten by TJ; at foot of text: "William Caruthers esq."; endorsed by TJ.

[1] Preceding seven words interlined.

To Luis de Onís

Monticello June 11. 17.

I thank you, Sir, for the Eulogy on Dr Valli which you have been so kind as to send me. his devotion to the good of his fellow-men merited all which the Orator has said of him, and entitles him to a distinguished niche in our Martyrology. how far his experiments may contribute to the preservation of human life I am not qualified to judge; but it is much to be regretted that his last one was not tried on a less valuable subject. the expression of sentiments so just towards him is the more pleasing to me, as it furnishes me the occasion of renewing to you the assurances of my high consideration and regard.

TH: JEFFERSON

PoC (DLC); on verso of a reused address cover from DeWitt Clinton to TJ; at foot of text: "H. E. The Cheval^r^ de Onis"; endorsed by TJ. Tr (TJ Editorial Files); 1955 typescript by an Onís descendant.

From William Darby

SIR. New York, June 12th 1817.

Being uncertain whether you have received a Copy of my Map and Statistical tracts of Louisiana, I am under considerable embarrassment in addressing, to you, this note. From your character, as the head of the Literature of your country, I should deem no apology necessary in soliciting your opinion of a work, upon a country towards the incorporation of which, into the U.S. your personal exertions contributed so much;—but not having myself remitted you a copy, I am at a loss to know whether the production has met your eye or not. When at Richmond in April last I sold a copy to Col. Lindsay, who informed me that, he expected Mr Melish sent you a copy of mine with some of his own. I would have done myself the honor of sending one, but the first Edition was hurried, and published under many very serious disadvantages; I was therefore anxious to give the work more perfection before giving you the trouble of perusal.

I am now on the eve of entering upon a second edition, wherin I hope to retrench many of the defects, and add much useful matter respecting the regions contiguous to Louisiana, not embraced in the present work.

I met in this City Mr Isaac Briggs, to whom I exhibited the map and Book, and red a very flattering certificate expressing his opinion of its correctness; an opinion the more gratifying because rd from a man whose personal knowledge of the country, and whose respectability of character, will give weight to any work, to which his name is attached

I have taken the liberty to enclose you a copy of the Book, with a reduced Map; a copy of the second Edition and Large Map I hope in a few months to have the pleasure of presenting in person.

Should you deem it worthy your attention to give the work a perusal and remit your opinion in reply to this, the favor will be very gratefully received by

Sir. Very respectfully Your Obt sert WILLIAM DARBY

RC (DLC); at foot of text: "Thomas Jefferson Esq."; endorsed by TJ as received 18 June 1817 and so recorded in SJL. Enclosure: Darby, *A Geographical Description of the State of Louisiana ... being an accompaniment to the Map of Louisiana* (Philadelphia, 1816; Poor, *Jefferson's Library*, 7 [no. 369]).

William Darby (1775–1854), surveyor and geographer, was born in Hanover Township in what is now Dauphin County, Pennsylvania. He moved with his family to Ohio in 1781, and after educating himself he began teaching school at the age of eighteen. About 1799 Darby took up cotton farming in Natchez, and he served as a United States deputy surveyor from about 1804 to 1809. Soon thereafter he began working on his map and statistical account of Louisiana. Darby served as a topographer for Andrew Jackson during the War of 1812, after which he went to Philadelphia. There, with the aid of John Melish, he published the first edition of *A Geographical Description of the State of Louisiana* in 1816. Melish incorporated Darby's work into his own map of the United States, which was used by the federal government in setting boundary lines with Spain under the 1819 Adams-Onís Treaty. Darby spent many years attempting to procure government compensation for his mapping of Louisiana, finally succeeding in 1854. He was also one of the surveyors of the United States border with Canada in 1818, and he wrote numerous geographical publications. Later in life Darby lived in Harrisburg, Pennsylvania, and Montgomery County, Maryland, before moving to Washington, D.C., where he worked as a clerk in the General Land Office. He died in Washington (*DAB*; "Autobiographical Letter of William Darby," in William Henry Egle, ed., *Notes and Queries Historical and Genealogical chiefly relating to Interior Pennsylvania*, 1st and 2d ser. [1894–95], 1:33–41; Ristow, *American Maps and Mapmakers*, 142–5; Darby to James Monroe, 27 Feb. 1819 [DNA: RG 59, LAR, 1817–25]; DNA: RG 29, CS, Washington, D.C., 1850; *JHR*, esp. 49:1246 [1 Aug. 1854]; *JS*, esp. 45:613 [1 Aug. 1854]; *U.S. Statutes at Large*, 10:805; Washington *Daily National Intelligencer*, 10 Oct. 1854).

Darby published a letter from ISAAC BRIGGS praising the accuracy of his map in the second edition of *A Geographical Description of the State of Louisiana* (New York, 1817), 335–6.

To George Washington Jeffreys

SIR Monticello. June 12. 17.

I have to acknolege your two letters of Apr. 8. & May 11. on the subject of the broad-tailed sheep. it is to be observed that there are different races of them, very distinct, & very different in merit, three of these have fallen under my observation. 1. those from the Cape of good hope with broad tails turned up like that of a nicked horse, long legs, light bodies & slight fleeces. 2. those from Algiers, of somewhat less stature and better form & size. and 3. those from Tunis, of low stature, round bodies, full fleeces of good quality, hardy, thrifty, always fat, and of high-flavored flesh. it must have been of these last that Gen[l] Eaton brought to this country. I recieved myself a ram and ewe, brought in one of our vessels from Tunis direct. but the ewe would never breed, her massive tail never admitting the commerce of the ram. I have bred from the ram, in and in for ten years past with a different race, and have found that when a ewe gets to be about $\frac{7}{8}$ pure blood, the same obstacle becomes so enlarged as to prevent further procreation. I continue this breed for the use of the table, and because the wool is as good as that of our ordinary sheep. I have Merinos in a separate situation: but their wool cannot be used for coarse purposes, and there is no demand for it here, which renders them less profitable than others. I have in still a distinct & distant situation, another Spanish breed, which, yielding to the broad-tail as to the table, is in other respects the most valuable of all. hardy, heavy-bodied, heavy-fleeced, and of a good staple for country service. it is the best cross for the broad-tailed breed.—this information, slight as it is, is all I am enabled to give you, and pretends to no other merit than that of proving to you the sentiments of respect & esteem of which I beg leave to assure you. TH: JEFFERSON

PoC (DLC); on verso of reused address cover of James Baker to TJ, 23 Apr. 1817; mutilated at seal, with two words rewritten by TJ; at foot of text: "M[r] George Washington Jeffreys"; endorsed by TJ.

TJ received a RAM AND EWE of the broadtail Barbary or Tunis variety in 1806 from Commodore John Rodgers on the latter's return from Tripoli (Rodgers to TJ, 30 July 1806 [MHi]).

To Benjamin Henry Latrobe

DEAR SIR Monticello June 12. 17.

This letter is that of a friendly beggar. I will explain to you the case & then it's object. we are commencing here the establishment of a College, and instead of building a magnificent house which would exhaust all our funds, we propose to lay off[1] a square or rather 3. sides of a square about 7. or 800.f. wide, leaving it open at one end to be extended indefinitely. on the closed end, and on the two sides we propose to arrange separate pavilions for each professor & his school. each Pavilion is to have a school-room below, and 2. rooms for the Professor above; and between pavilion & pavilion a range of Dormitories for the students, one story high, giving to each a room 10 f. wide & 14.f. deep. the Pavilions about 36.f. wide in front, & 24.f. in depth. this sketch will gi[ve] you an idea of the general plan.

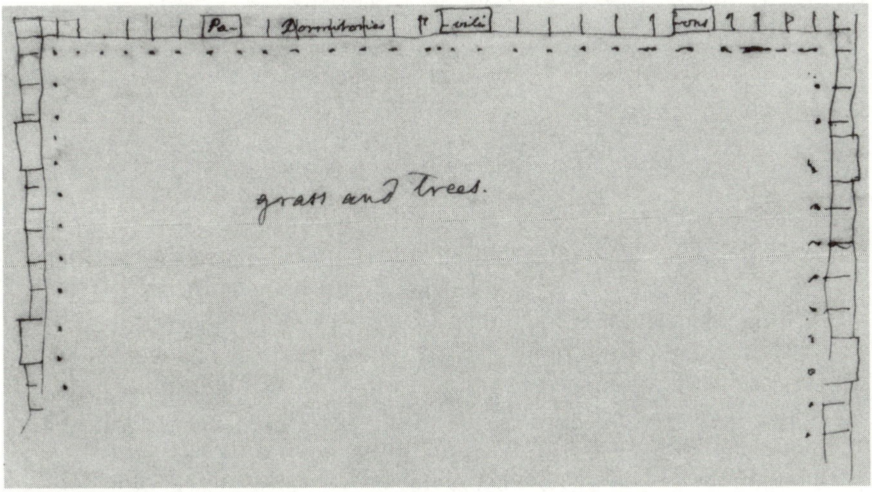

the whole of the pavilions and dormitories to be united by a colonnade in front, of the height of the lower story of the pavilions & about 8.f. wide[2] under which they may go dry from school to school. the top of the dormitories to be flat as was that of the offices of the President's house at Washington. now what we wish is that these pavilions, as they will shew themselves above the Dormitories, should be models of taste and correct architecture, and of a variety of appearance, no two alike, so as to serve as specimens of [the?] orders for the architectural lectures. and we come to you in eleemosinary form, to take up your pencil, and sketch for us some general outlines of designs no matter how loose, and rough, without the trouble of referring to scale or rule; for we want nothing but the general idea of[3] the external, as the internal must be arranged in detail according to local convenience. a few sketches, such as shall take you not more than a minute apiece, mere expressions of a first trait of imagination, will greatly oblige us. the Visitors of the College are President Monroe, mr Madison, 3 others whom you do not know, and myself. but we have to struggle with beggarly funds, and the want of professors capable of fulfilling our views. these however may perhaps come in time, for all Europe seems to be breaking up. in the mean time help us to provide snug and handsome lodges for them, and you will greatly[4] oblige one who entertains for you sentiments of great esteem & respect

TH: JEFFERSON

P.S. my dial captivates every body foreign as well as home-bred, as a handsome object & accurate measurer of time.

PoC (DLC); on reused address cover to TJ; two words faint; at foot of first page: "Mr Latrobe"; endorsed by TJ.

[1] Manuscript: "of."
[2] Preceding five words interlined.
[3] Preceding four words interlined.
[4] Manuscript: "great."

To John Manners

SIR — Monticello June 12. 17.

Your favor of May 20. has been recieved some time since: but the increasing inertness of age renders me slow in obeying the calls of the writing table, and less equal than I have been to it's labors.

My opinion on the right of Expatriation has been so long ago as the year 1776. consigned to record in the Act of the Virginia code, drawn by myself recognising the right expressly, & prescribing the mode of exercising it. the evidence of this natural right, like that of our right to life, liberty, the use of our faculties, the pursuit of happiness, is not left to the feeble and sophistical investigations of reason but is impressed on the sense of every man. we do not claim these under the Charter of kings or legislators; but under the king of kings[.] if he has made it a law in the nature of man to pursue his own happiness, he has left him free in the choice of place as well as mode: and we may safely call on the whole body of English Jurists to produce the map on which Nature has traced, for each individual, the geographical line which she forbids him to cross in pursuit of happiness. it certainly does not exist in his mind. where then is it? I believe too I might safely affirm that there is not another nation, civilized or savage which has ever denied this natural right. I doubt if there is another which refuses it's exercise. I know it is allowed in some of the most respectable countries of continental Europe; nor have I ever heard of one in which it was not. how it is among our savage neighbors, who have no law but that of Nature, we all know.

Tho long estranged from legal reading and reasoning, & little familiar with the decisions of particular judges, I have considered that respecting the obligation of the Common law in this country as a very plain one, and merely a question of document. if we are under that law, the document which made us so can surely be produced; and as far as this can be produced, so far we are subject to it, and farther we are not. most of the states did, I believe, at an early period of their legislation, adopt the English law, Common and Statute, more or less in a body, as far as localities admitted of their application. in these states then the common law, so far as adopted is the lex loci. then comes the law of Congress declaring that what is law in any state shall be the rule of decision in their courts, as to matters arising within that state, except when controuled by their own statutes. but this law of Congress has been considered as extending to civil cases only; and that no such provision has been made for criminal ones. a similar provision then for criminal offences would, in like manner, be an adoption of more or less of the Common law, as part of the lex loci, where the offence is committed; and would cover the whole field of legislation for the general government. I have turned to the passage you refer to in Judge Cooper's Justinian, and should suppose the general expressions there used would admit of modification conformable to this doctrine. it would alarm me indeed, in any case, to find myself entertaining an opinion different from that of a judgment so accurately organised as his. but I am quite persuaded that whenever Judge Cooper shall be led to consider that question simply and nakedly, it is so much within his course of thinking, as liberal as logical, that, rejecting all blind and undefined obligation, he will hold to the positive and

explicit precepts of the law alone. Accept these hasty sentiments on the subjects you propose as hasarded in proof of my great esteem & respect.
TH: JEFFERSON

PoC (DLC); edge trimmed; at foot of first page: "Doct[r] John Manners."

For TJ's OPINION ON THE RIGHT OF EXPATRIATION, see bill numbered 55 in a grouping of documents on "The Revisal of the Laws 1776–1786" (*PTJ*, 2:476–9).

TJ's invocation of natural rights to LIFE, LIBERTY and THE PURSUIT OF HAPPINESS recalls the Declaration of Independence (*PTJ*, 1:423, 429). LEX LOCI: "the law of the place" (*Black's Law Dictionary*).

To Alexander von Humboldt

DEAR SIR Monticello June 13. 17.

The reciept of your Distributio geographica plantarum, with the duty of thanking you for a work which sheds so much new and valuable light on botanical science, excites the desire also of presenting myself to your recollection, and of expressing to you those sentiments of high admiration and esteem, which, altho' long silent, have never slept. the physical information you have given us of a country hitherto so shamefully unknown, has come exactly in time to guide our understandings in the great political revolution now bringing it into prominence on the stage of the world. the issue of it's struggles, as they respect Spain, is no longer matter of doubt. as it respects their own liberty, peace & happiness we cannot be quite so certain. whether the blinds of bigotry, the shackles of the priesthood, and the fascinating glare of rank and wealth give fair play to the common sense of the mass of their people, so far as to qualify them for self government, is what we do not know. perhaps our wishes may be stronger than our hopes.[1] the first principle of republicanism is that the lex majoris partis is the fundamental law of every society of individuals of equal rights: to consider the will of the society enounced by the majority of a single vote as sacred as if unanimous, is the first of all lessons in importance, yet the last which is thoroughly learnt. this law once disregarded, no other remains but that of force, which ends necessarily in military despotism. this has been the history of the French revolution; and I wish the understanding of our Southern brethren[2] may be sufficiently enlarged and firm to see that their fate depends on it's sacred observance.

In our America, we are turning to public improvements. schools, roads and canals are every where either in operation or contemplation. the most gigantic undertaking yet proposed is that of New York for drawing[3] the waters of Lake Erie into the Hudson. the distance is 353. miles, and the height to be surmounted 691. feet. the expence will be great; but it's effect incalculably powerful in favor of the Atlantic states. internal navigation by steam boats is rapidly spreading thro all our states, and that by sails and oars will ere long be looked back to as among the curiosities of antiquity. we count much too on it's efficacy in harbor defence; and it will soon be tried for navigation by sea. we consider this employment of the contributions which our citizens can spare, after feeding, and clothing, and lodging themselves comfortably, as more useful, more moral, and even more splendid, than that preferred by Europe, of destroying human life, labor and happiness.

I write this letter without knowing where it will find you. but wherever that may be, I am sure it will find you engaged in something instructive for man. if at Paris, you are of course in habits of society with mr Gallatin our worthy, our able and excellent minister, who will give you, from time to time, the details of the progress of a country in whose prosperity you are so good as to feel an interest, and in which your name is revered among those of the great worthies of the world. god bless you, and preserve you, long to enjoy the gratitude of your fellow men, and to be blessed with honors, health, and happiness.

TH: JEFFERSON

PoC (DLC); at foot of first page: "Baron Humboldt." Tr (ViU: TJP); posthumous extract in Nicholas P. Trist's hand. Enclosed in TJ to Daniel Brent and TJ to Albert Gallatin, both 23 June 1817.

LEX MAJORIS PARTIS: "law of the majority."

[1]Tr consists of remainder of paragraph.
[2]Tr here adds "(Spanish Americans)."
[3]Word interlined in place of "joining."

To Louis Pio

Monticello June 13. 17.

I have recieved, my dear Sir, your letter of Aug. 29. with great sensibility. it recalls to my memory scenes in earlier life which were very interesting, and many of them past with you. I have not forgotten either them or you, altho' so much of time and space has intervened, and events of so great and different characters have occupied our attention. you have seen the horrors of Robespierre, the tracasseries of the Directory, the unprincipled aggressions of Bonaparte on every human right. my destiny has been smoother, among a people loving peace, observing justice, pursuing industry, and asking of the world only to let them alone. yet this inoffensive request has been refused, and they have been forced to shew that, preferring the plough, they can yet handle the sword. the inextinguishable hatred and hostility of England has interrupted for a while our peaceable course, and she is now about to pay the forfiet of all her crimes. the demolition of Bonaparte was but half the work of liberation for the world from tyranny. the great pyrate of the ocean remained but happily to sink under the effects of his own vices and follies. these are concerns however in which neither you nor I need take part. I am glad you have made an acquaintance with M[r] Gallatin. you will find him an able, honest and friendly man, of plain habits, & above ceremony.—I am now feeling the effects of age; enfeebled in body & less active in mind. my daughter, whom you knew, has provided for my old age a numerous family of grand children, and these again begin to add to our society another generation of descendants. I shall die therefore in the midst of those I love, and shall retain while I live the strong sentiments I have ever entertained for you of sincere esteem & respect.

TH: JEFFERSON

PoC (ViW: TC-JP); on verso of reused address cover of DeWitt Clinton to TJ, 27 Mar. 1817; at foot of text: "The Chevalier Pio. rue Ste Honoré N° 284. prés St Roch. á Paris"; endorsed by TJ. Enclosed in TJ to Daniel Brent and TJ to Albert Gallatin, both 23 June 1817.

TRACASSERIES: "bickerings."

To Barbé Marbois

Monticello in Virginia June 14. 17.

I thank you, dear Sir, for the copy of the interesting narrative of the Complot d'Arnold which you have been so kind as to send me. it throws lights on that incident of history which we did not possess before an incident which merits to be known, as a lesson to mankind, in all it's details. this mark of your attention recalls to my mind the earlier period of life at which I had the pleasure of your personal acquaintance and renews the sentiments of high respect and esteem with which that acquaintance inspired me. I had not failed to accompany your personal sufferings during the civil convulsions of your country, and had sincerely sympathised with them. An awful period indeed has past in Europe since our first acquaintance. when I left France at the close of 89. your revolution was, as I thought, under the direction of able & honest men. but the madness of some of their successors, the vices of others, the malicious intrigues of an envious and corrupting neighbor, the tracasseri[es] of the Directory, the usurpations, the havoc, and devastations of your Attila, and the equal usurpations, depredations and oppressions of your hypocritical deliverers, will form a mournful period in the history of man, a period of which the last chapter will not be seen in your day or mine, and one which I still fear is to be written in characters of blood. had Bonaparte reflected that such is the moral construction of the world, that no national crime passes unpunished in the long run, he would not now be in the cage of St Helena: and were your present oppressors to reflect on the same truth, they would spare to their own countries the penalties on their present wrongs which will be inflicted on them in future times. the seeds of hatred and revenge which they are now sowing with a large hand will not fail to produce their fruits in time. like their brother robbers on the high way, they suppose the escape of the moment a final escape, and deem infamy and future risk countervailed by present gain.[1] Our lot has been happier. when you witnessed our first struggles in the war of independance, you little calculated, more than we did, on the rapid growth and prosperity of this country; on the practical demonstration it was about to exhibit, of the happy truth that Man is capable of self-government, and only rendered otherwise by the moral degradation designedly superinduced on him by the wicked arts of his tyrants.

I have much confidence that we shall proceed successfully for ages to come; and that, contrary to the principle of Montesquieu, it will be seen that the larger the extent of country, the more firm it's republican structure, if founded, not on conquest, but in principles of compact & equality.[2] my hope of it's duration is built much on the enlargement of the resources of life going hand in hand with the enlargement of territory, and the belief [that] men are disposed to live honestly, if the means of doing so are open [to the]m. with the consolation of this belief in the future result of our labors, I have that of other prophets who foretell distant events, that I shall not live to see it falsified. my theory has always been that if we are to dream, the flatteries of hope are as cheap, and pleasanter than the gloom of despair. I wish to yourself a long life of honors, health and happiness.

TH: JEFFERSON

PoC (DLC); on reused address cover of James Monroe to TJ, 23 Apr. 1817; torn at seal; at foot of first page: "M. de Marbois." Tr (ViU: TJP); posthumous extract in Nicholas P. Trist's hand. Enclosed in TJ to Daniel Brent and TJ to Albert Gallatin, both 23 June 1817.

François, comte de Barbé Marbois (1745–1837), diplomat, was born in Metz, France, where he was educated before studying law in Paris. In 1768 he obtained his first position in the foreign office, and thereafter he enjoyed a long career in France and abroad as a diplomat and politician, including service in the United States as secretary to the French legation beginning in 1779 and as chargé d'affaires, 1784–85. During his time in America, Barbé Marbois circulated a questionnaire on behalf of the French government that sought information about the individual American states. TJ's 1780–81 response was eventually published as *Notes on the State of Virginia*. They corresponded only rarely, but in 1783 Barbé Marbois helped TJ find a French tutor in Philadelphia for his daughter Martha Jefferson (Randolph). As minister of the public treasury, Barbé Marbois negotiated the Louisiana Purchase Treaty in 1803. He was elected to the American Philosophical Society in 1780, serving as councillor, 1781–85, and he became a member of the Institut de France in 1816. Barbé Marbois authored works on subjects that included agriculture, geography, and history. He died in Paris (*DBF*; Hoefer, *Nouv. biog. générale*, 4:428–31; E. Wilson Lyon, *The Man Who Sold Louisiana: The Career of Francois Barbe-Marbois* [1942; repr. 1974]; *PTJ*, esp. 4:166–7, 6:373–4, 34:xli–xlii, 423–4n; *Notes*, ed. Peden, xii–xv; Philadelphia *Pennsylvania Packet or the General Advertiser*, 27 Jan. 1780; APS, Minutes, 5 Jan. 1781, 2 Jan. 1784 [MS in PPAmP]; Miller, *Treaties*, 2:498–528).

The INTERESTING NARRATIVE of Benedict Arnold's plot was Barbé Marbois, *Complot d'Arnold et de Sir Henry Clinton contre les États-Unis d'Amérique et contre le Général Washington. Septembre 1780* (Paris, 1816; Poor, *Jefferson's Library*, 4 [no. 138]). TJ's copy in MoSW includes a handwritten, signed inscription by Barbé Marbois dated Paris, 30 Dec. 1816: "L'auteur aime à croire que Monsieur Jepherson a gardé de lui quelque Souvenir, Il, lui offre cet opuscule et l'hommage de Son respect" ("The author, liking to believe that Mr. Jefferson has retained some memory of him, offers him this opuscule and the tribute of his respect"). Barbé Marbois also sent a copy of this work to James Madison some time before October 1817 (Madison, *Papers, Retirement Ser.*, 1:139–40).

The PERSONAL SUFFERINGS Barbé Marbois experienced during the French Revolution included exile to French Guiana by the Directory in 1797 (Lyon, *Man Who Sold Louisiana*, 95–112). Montesquieu stated his PRINCIPLE that large republics could not survive in book eight, chapter sixteen of his *Esprit des Lois* (*De l'Esprit des Loix* [Geneva, 1748], 1:195–7).

[1] Tr begins here.
[2] Tr ends here.

To John Barnes

DEAR SIR Monticello June 14. 17.

A young negro man, named Thruston, brother to Edy, who while I was in Washington, was in the kitchen under the instruction of Mr Julien, has escaped from my grandson to whom I had given him. he is supposed to have gone to Washington and to be there lurking under the connivance of some of his sister's old friends. the bearer, mr Wheat, my grandson's overseer, who is acquainted in that vicinity, goes on in quest of him. my grandson has furnished him with what is thought sufficient for all his expences. yet as unforeseen circumstances may render his stay longer than is expected to accomplish his purpose, my grandson has desired me to request of you, should he become in want, to furnish any reasonable sum which he may further want, rather than his mission should be abortive, which I will see remitted as soon as made known. I inclose you a letter recieved on the day of your departure, and felt sincerely the disappointment and delay which the misinformation of the postmaster brou[ght] [...]

TH: JEFFERSON

P.S. it is thought best that the mission of the bearer should be known to no mortal but yourself & him, and that not the least intimation of it should get out.

PoC (DLC); on verso of reused address cover to TJ; mutilated at seal, with words rewritten by TJ but still illegible; adjacent to signature: "Mr John Barnes"; endorsed by TJ. Enclosure not found.

Rezin Wheat (d. 1846) moved by 1805 to Albemarle County from Prince Georges County, Maryland. He served as Thomas Jefferson Randolph's overseer from at least 1817 until 1820. In 1840 he owned five slaves (Arliss Shaffer Monk, "Undocumented Genealogies: To Trust or Not to Trust? Lessons from Several Strains of Wheat," *National Genealogical Society Quarterly* 86 [1998]: 48–9; *MB*, 2:1275, 1312; DNA: RG 29, CS, Albemarle Co., 1810–40; Woods, *Albemarle County*, 403; Albemarle Co. Will Book, 17:215–6, 20:473).

TJ had given Thruston Hern to his GRANDSON Thomas Jefferson Randolph in 1813 (TJ's Conveyance of Slaves to Thomas Jefferson Randolph, 26 Mar. 1813). Hern, who had apparently escaped by posing as one of James Madison's slaves during the latter's May 1817 visit to Monticello, was not recaptured (Lucia Stanton, *"Those Who Labor for My Happiness": Slavery at Thomas Jefferson's Monticello* [2012], 139; Pierson, *Jefferson at Monticello*, 110–1).

To José Corrêa da Serra

DEAR SIR Monticello June 14. 17.

No one could recieve greater pleasure than I did at the proof that your sovereign set a due value on your merit, as manifested by the honorable duties assigned to you with us. but into this sentiment a little spice of egoism also thrust itself. as the appointment was to fix your residence almost in our vicinity, it gave me the hope of more frequently seeing you here. I trust that this hope will be verified at the ensuing season, when health as well as leisure will recommend a visit to us. and that I may not, as before, lose the advantage of it by my frequent and long visits to Poplar Forest, I will take the precaution of mentioning to you that I shall be at that place during the latter part of this, and the beginning of the next month, say to the 10th and again thro' the months of August & September in the last of which I shall visit the Natural bridge: for being but 28. miles from Poplar Forest, which may be rode in 8. hours, I think I shall be disposed to make it an annual visit while strength enough remains. the President expected to be about two months on his Northern tour, and will then find it prudent to exchange Washington for Albemarle, until the arrival of frost. I am in hopes you will take measures to have a meeting here with mr Gilmer, whose visit will be equally welcome and desirable to us all. that you may have many and long years of honors, health & happiness is the prayer of yours affectionately.

TH: JEFFERSON

RC (PWacD: Sol Feinstone Collection, on deposit PPAmP). PoC (DLC); on verso of reused address cover to TJ; mutilated at seal, with some words rewritten by TJ; at foot of text: "M. Correa de Serra"; endorsed by TJ.

To George Divers

DEAR SIR Monticello June 14. 17.

In the present state of your health, I am very unwilling that any trouble which can be avoided should be thrown on you on my part; and to lessen this as much as possible is the object of the present letter. my bill in Chancery on the subject of the Canal would regularly require your answer in due form, on oath E[t]c. which would oblige you to call on a lawyer to draw it, a justice of the peace to administer the oath E[t]c. I desire nothing of this. if you will have the goodness then, with the interrogatories of the bill before you to write me a letter giving answers to these interrogatories, without form, affidavit or other ceremony, I will subscribe to the letter an admission that it shall be taken as your answer, and, as such, made a part of the record, as your formal answ[e]r would have been. lest you should not have the bill in your possesion I send you a copy of the interrogatories. some of these are not within your knolege, as being intended for others of the Directors, or to be matter of examination by witnesses. where this is the case, you can say that the circumstance is not within your knolege. I wish to bring this matter to an early close, because the condition of the locks will shortly require entire renovation, or the navigation will be suspended. but before any thing new can be done, it is indispensable that each party should know their legal rights, for which purpose it is that a decree of the Chancery has been applied for. I meant this process as merely friendly; as what was as much desired by the Directors as by myself, in which there is no wish any where to stand on formalities or to practise delays. ever & affectionately your's.

TH: JEFFERSON

PoC (MHi); on verso of reused address cover to TJ; mutilated at seal and crease, with several words rewritten by TJ; at foot of text: "George Divers esq."; endorsed by TJ.

The exact COPY OF THE INTERROGATORIES enclosed here has not been found, but these queries can be found above in TJ's Bill of Complaint against the Rivanna Company, [by 9 Feb. 1817], the first in a group of documents on Jefferson's Lawsuit against the Rivanna Company printed above at 9 Feb. 1817, and below in Divers's Answer to Interrogatories in *Jefferson v. Rivanna Company*, [ca. 23 July 1817].

To Daniel Lescallier

Monticello June 14. 17.

I thank you, Sir, for the Persian tale of the Enchanted throne which you have been so kind as to send me. I have read it with satisfaction and with the more as a piece of natural history, presenting to us, as in a map, the mind of the man of Persia, and the means of measuring it. it shews us too the value of our art of printing, the facility it affords us of cultivating a good taste, and the superiority it gives to our compositions over theirs. I return you the Prospectus with my name, which I inscribe on it with pleasure.

I thank you also for the valuable acquaintance you have enabled me to make with the Baron de Quenelle. his visit has been a source to me of much information and satisfaction. after a stay of some days I parted with him with regret.

I recollect with pleasure the favor of your call on me at Washington, and am happy in the present occasion of expressing to you the assurance of my high consideration and respect.

TH: JEFFERSON

PoC (CSmH: JF-BA); on verso of reused address cover of James Dinsmore to TJ, 22 Apr. 1817; torn at seal, with two words rewritten by TJ; at foot of text: "M. le Baron Lescallier"; endorsed by TJ.

For the enclosed PROSPECTUS, not found, see Lescallier to TJ, 12 May 1817. BARON DE QUENELLE: Quinette de Rochemont.

From Dominick Lynch

SIR, New york 14th June 1817

"The American Society for the Encouragement of Domestic manufactures," instituted in this city, sensible of the zeal you have uniformly displayed in the promotion of every object, connected with the Welfare and Independence of our country, had the honor to elect you a member, at their last meeting, convened,[1] for the purpose of initiating into the Society James Monroe, President of the United States—

It would afford me the highest gratification, to announce to the Society, your assent to become one of its members—

I have the honor to remain With respect & consideration Sir, your Obe[t] Serv[t]

D. Lynch Jun[R]
Secretary[2]

RC (CSmH: JF); at foot of text: "M[r] Jefferson"; endorsed by TJ as a letter from "Lynch D. (Sec[y] Amer. soc. f[r] ncorgm[t] domest. manuf.)" received 24 June 1817 and so recorded in SJL. Printed in *New-York Evening Post*, 4 Aug. 1817, and elsewhere.

Dominick Lynch (ca. 1787–1837), wine merchant, was born in New York City. He attended Georgetown College (later Georgetown University) late in the 1790s and by 1809 had returned to his native city and started a firm that eventually specialized in wine. Lynch was secretary of the American Society for the Encouragement of Domestic Manufactures from its founding in 1816 until about 1820. He served as secretary of the North River Steamboat Company and as a director of the North River Insurance Company and the New York branch of the Second Bank of the United States. In 1825 Lynch arranged what was reputedly the first Italian opera performance in New York. He died in Paris (John Gilmary Shea, *Memorial of the First Centenary of Georgetown College, D. C.* [1891], 26–8; Thomas F. Meehan, "Catholic Literary New York, 1800–1840," *Catholic Historical Review* 4 [1919]: 407–8; Scoville, *New York Merchants*, 1:169–71; *Longworth's New York Directory* [1809]: 248; [1827]: 314; *New-York Gazette & General Advertiser*, 11 May 1810; New York *Commercial Advertiser*, 6 Dec. 1816; *New-York Columbian*, 20 Jan. 1818, 23 May 1821; New York *National Advocate*, 24 Nov. 1819, 28 Jan. 1820; New York *National Advocate* [country edition], 10 Dec. 1822, 2 Dec. 1823; *New-York Spectator*, 11 Sept. 1837).

The American Society for the Encouragement of Domestic Manufactures was organized in New York City late in 1816, with Daniel D. Tompkins as its first president. It frequently petitioned the government for protection of domestic manufactures by means of tariffs on imports and increased duties on imported goods sold at auction (New York *Commercial Advertiser*, 6 Dec. 1816; New York *Columbian*, 10 Dec. 1816; note to William Sampson to TJ, 9 Jan. 1817; *JHR*, 10:304–5, 11:130, 13:447, 14:24–5, 15:163 [29 Jan. 1817, 10 Jan. 1818, 24 Apr., 21 Nov. 1820, 21 Jan. 1822]; New York *Mercantile Advertiser*, 2 Mar. 1818; *New-York Columbian*, 22 Nov. 1819; Murray N. Rothbard, *The Panic of 1819: Reactions and Policies* [1962; repr. 2007], 210; *JS*, 9:50 [27 Dec. 1819]; *Memorial of the American Society for the Encouragement of Domestic Manufactures* [Washington, 1822]).

President JAMES MONROE attended the 13 June 1817 meeting of the American Society for the Encouragement of Domestic Manufactures while in New York City on a tour of the northeastern states. In a speech after being made a member, he stated that "he duly appreciated the objects of the Institution, which were particularly dear to him, from their being intimately connected with the *real* Independence of our Country." Monroe assured his audience "that he would use his efforts as far as the general interest of the country would permit, to promote the patriotic and laudable objects of the society." James Madison, TJ, and John Adams were then unanimously admitted as members, and copies of the above letter were sent to all three (*New-York Evening Post*, 14 June, 4 Aug. 1817; Madison, *Papers, Retirement Ser.*, 1:57–8, 74–6; Adams to Lynch, 23 June 1817 [Lb in MHi: Adams Papers]).

[1] *New-York Evening Post* here adds "on the 13th inst."

[2] Word not in *New-York Evening Post*.

From Marc Auguste Pictet

MONSIEUR   Geneve 14 Juin 1817

Répondre à la lettre la plus obligeante[1] au bout d'une année Seulement, est une négligence apparente que la distance de l'amerique Seroit loin de justifier, Si je ne pouvois au moins répliquer par les motifs dont je vais avoir lhonneur de vous rendre compte.

Dès que Mr Terrel m'eut remis la lettre dont il etoit le porteur, je m'emprèssai de chercher à répondre à la confiance dont vous m'honoriez, en cherchant pour lui une maison, ou plutôt une famille, dans laquelle il pût Se trouver bien, à tous égards. J'eus le bonheur de réussir en la personne de Mr Maurice, Ex-maire de Geneve pendant plus de dix ans; mon ami d'enfance, et l'un de mes collaborateurs dans le Recueil intitulé Bibliotheque universelle; c'est un homme fort considéré à Genève; Son fils ainé est maître des Requêtes au Conseil d'Etat à Paris, et le cadet, à peu près de l'age de Mr Terrel, fait les mêmes études auxquelles celui ci alloit être appelé; Mad^e Maurice, Dame aimable et bonne, complettoit fort agréablement le ménage dans lequel j'eus le bonheur de l'introduire (Seul étranger) et dans lequel il a eté constamment traité comme l'un des fils de la maison, et où il Se trouvoit très heureusement placé pour apprendre le francais, parce qu'on n'y parloit point d'autre langue.[2]

Il chercha d'abord à Se mettre (à l'aide de leçons particulieres) en etat de Subir l'examen preâlable de belles lettres et de mathematiques nécessaire pour être admis dans l'auditoire de Philosophie, au 1er aout, (commencement de l'année academique) Il S'en tira moins mal qu'on n'auroit du l'attendre d'un jeune homme à qui Son peu de connoissance de la langue francaise avoit dû rendre le travail particulièrement difficile. Il intéressa les Professeurs[3] par Sa persévérance à vaincre les difficultés, disposition qui l'a animé pendant tout le cours de l'année académique. Il l'a terminée au milieu de mai, par un examen très Satisfaisant, et qui lui a fait un véritable honneur,[4] Sur les quatre parties de l'enseignement qu'il a recu, Savoir la Philos^e Morale, la Physique,[5] la Botanique, et les mathematiques.

Sa Santé n'a pas été aussi constamment bonne que nous l'aurions desiré; il etoît Souvent attaqué de maux de tête; et la pénible nouvelle de la mort d'une Sœur chérie, nouvelle qui ne lui est parvenue qu'au commencement du printems, l'a affligé au point de le forcer à interrompre Ses études pendant quelque tems

Son Séjour chez Mr Maurice l'a mis a portée de frequenter la meilleure Societé, et de S'y former aux usages dont l'habitude est le Signe d'une education bonne et liberale. Il a pu y modifier utilement certaines idées politico-morales, dont il etoit imbu, qui peuvent etre bonnes et justes dans certaines limites, mais, que l'exagération peut rendre fausses, et quelquefois ridicules. Il n'est pas devenu un homme du monde, mais bien plus Social quil ne l'étoit; et il est revenu de quelques préventions fortes qu'il avoit apportées de Son pays, et qui n'etoient bonnes à rien qu'à diminuer le nombre de Ses amis.

J'ignore quelles Sont Ses intentions et quelles Seront les vôtres à Son égard, monsieur; je crois qu'une Seconde année des etudes de philosophie (et c'est leur etendue ordinaire) ne pourroit que lui être fort utile; et qu'en restant placé comme il l'est il achéveroit de Se former, Sous d'autres rapports. Il a de l'esprit, de la Sagacité; mais une teinte de Singularité,[6] qui disparaitra peutêtre avec le tems et le frottement Social.

Vous voyez Monsieur, que Si j'avois pris la plume plutôt, je n'aurois pu vous offrir qu'une espérance, ce qui devient aujourdhui pour vous une réalité agréable, d'après l'interet que vous voulez bien prendre à ce jeune homme qui me Semble le mériter à tous égards. Je Saisis l'occasion que veut bien m'offrir Mr Gallatin votre ambassadeur (qui va quitter Geneve, où nous l'avons possédé quelques tems) pour vous faire passer avec Sureté cette lettre.

Mr Gallatin veut bien aussi me promettre de S'intéresser à faire connaitre en amérique le Recueil[7] publié à Geneve pendant vingt ans (1796–1815) Sous le titre de Bibliothéque Britannique et continué depuis 18 mois Sur un plan plus etendu, Sous le titre de Bibliothéque universelle. Il ne m'appartient pas d'en faire l'eloge, vû la part considerable que je prends à Sa redaction; mais je puis avec vérité l'indiquer aux amateurs des lettres des Sciences, et des arts (y compris l'agriculture) en amerique, comme l'ouvrage francais qui pourroit le mieux les mettre, et les entretenir, au courant des progrès des connaissances en Europe; et, actuellement que les communications Sont r'ouvertes avec elle, et avec la France, en particulier, rien ne Seroit plus facile que d'etablir un mode régulier d'envoi tous les mois aux Abonnés d'amerique. Mr Warden votre ancien Consul, et encore résidant à Paris a bien voulu m'offrir d'etre l'intermediaire de ces communications, et elles Seroient en bonnes mains.[8] Si vous daigniez Monsieur honorer de quelque intérêt une entreprise litteraire dont plus de 20 ans d'existence au travers des circonstances les plus difficiles[9] ont assez bien prouvé l'utilité, rien ne pourroit contribuer plus efficacement à la recommander dans les Etats unis. J'y ai inséré plusieurs articles d'amérique puisés dans les Transactions de vos Societés Savantes.[10]

Veuillez Monsieur agréer l'expression de la haute consideration et du dévouement respectueux avec lesquels j'ai lhonneur d'etre

Monsieur Votre très humble & très obeïssant Serviteur

M. A. Pictet Prof[r]
Présid. de la Soc. des Arts de Geneve,
Correspond[t] de l'Institut de france;
des Soc. Roy. de Londres et d'Edinbourg

EDITORS' TRANSLATION

Sir Geneva 14 June 1817

Answering a most obliging letter after a year has passed is an apparent negligence that distance from America would be far from justifying, if I were unable to respond with reasons that I will have the honor to recount.

As soon as Mr. Terrell gave me the letter he bore, I eagerly sought to fulfill the trust with which you honored me, by finding him a house, or rather a family, in which he could be comfortable in every respect. I was fortunate to succeed by finding Mr. Maurice, formerly mayor of Geneva for more than ten years, my childhood friend, and one of my collaborators in the compilation entitled the *Bibliothèque Universelle*. He is highly regarded in Geneva. His eldest son is the master of requests to the Council of State in Paris, and the youngest one, who is about the same age as Mr. Terrell, is pursuing the same line of studies as he is. Mrs. Maurice, a pleasant and good lady, very agreeably completed the household into which I had the pleasure to introduce him (and in which he was the only foreigner). In this household he was always treated as one of the sons of the family, and he was very well placed to learn French, as no other language was spoken there.

He tried, first of all (with the help of private lessons), to prepare himself for the preliminary examinations in the humanities and mathematics that are necessary to be admitted into the philosophy lectures on 1 August (the beginning of the academic year). He did better than could have been expected of a young man whose scant knowledge of the French language must have made the work particularly difficult. The professors took an interest in him because of his perseverance in overcoming difficulties, a quality that has animated him throughout the academic year. He finished in the middle of May with a very satisfactory examination (which was a real honor) on the four parts of the curriculum, that is to say moral philosophy, physics, botany, and mathematics.

His health has not been as consistently good as we would have wished. He has often suffered from headaches, and the painful news of the death of a beloved sister, which reached him only at the beginning of spring, so afflicted him as to force him to interrupt his studies for some time

His stay at Mr. Maurice's house has allowed him to frequent the best society and become trained in the customs that are the hallmark of a good and liberal education. In this company he has been able to modify some of his deeply ingrained ideas about political morality, notions that can be good and just within certain limits, but which, when exaggerated, become wrong and sometimes ridiculous. He has not become a man of the world, but he is much more sociable than he used to be, and he has overcome a few strong prejudices that he had brought from his country, which could only serve to diminish the number of his friends.

I do not know, Sir, what his plans are or what yours will be regarding him. I believe a second year studying philosophy (the customary length of these studies) could only be most useful to him, and that remaining where he is will allow him to complete his education in other respects. He is witty and wise, but with a touch of peculiarity that will perhaps disappear with time and through social contact.

You see, Sir, that had I written earlier I would have been able to offer you only a hope, which has today become a pleasant reality for you, since you take such an interest in this young man, who seems to me to be deserving in every respect. I seize the opportunity of a safe conveyance of this letter through your ambassador, Mr. Gallatin (who is leaving Geneva, where we have had him for some time).

Mr. Gallatin also willingly promises to help make known in America the compilation that has been published in Geneva for twenty years (1796–1815) as the *Bibliothèque Britannique* and which has continued to be published for eighteen months on a broader basis as the *Bibliothèque Universelle*. It is not for me to praise it, given the considerable part I have taken in its editing, but I can truthfully commend it to American lovers of the humanities, sciences, and arts (including agriculture) as the French publication that might best keep them informed of the progress of knowledge in Europe. Now that communications are reopened with Europe, and with France in particular, nothing could be easier than to establish regular monthly deliveries to American subscribers. Mr. Warden, your former consul, who is still residing in Paris, has kindly offered himself as an intermediary for these communications, and they will be in good hands. If you deigned, Sir, to honor with some interest a literary enterprise that has proven to be useful for more than twenty years, under the most difficult circumstances, nothing could contribute more effectively to recommend it in the United States. I have included in it several articles from America, taken from the transactions of your learned societies.

Please accept, Sir, the high consideration and respectful devotion with which I have the honor to be

Sir, your very humble and very obedient servant

M. A. PICTET Professor
President of the Société des Arts de Genève,
Correspondent of the Institut de France,
and of the royal societies of London and Edinburgh

RC (DLC); endorsed by TJ as received 25 Sept. 1817 and so recorded in SJL. Dft (Fréderic Rilliet, Geneva, Switzerland, 1947); unsigned. Translation by Dr. Genevieve Moene. Enclosed in Albert Gallatin to TJ, 17 July 1817, Frank Carr to TJ, [received 23 Dec. 1817], and probably also in a missing letter from TJ to Carr of 29 Sept. 1817.

From 1796 to 1815 Pictet, Charles Pictet de Rochemont, and Frédéric Guillaume MAURICE published the *Bibliothèque Britannique*, which consisted primarily of reprinted British scientific articles. Thereafter the journal broadened its scope and changed its name to the *Bibliothèque Universelle* (*DSB*, 10:603). Maurice's son Jean Frédéric Théodore Maurice had been named a MAÎTRE DES REQUÊTES in 1814 (*Biographie des Hommes Vivants* [Paris, 1816–19], 4:385). Dabney C. Terrell's recently deceased SŒUR was Virginia Terrell Carr, the wife of TJ's correspondent Frank Carr.

[1] Preceding three words not in Dft.
[2] Instead of "d'autre langue," Dft reads "anglais" ("English").
[3] Preceding two words not in Dft.
[4] Preceding eight words not in Dft.
[5] Instead of preceding two words, Dft reads "Philo nat." ("natural philosophy").
[6] Dft here adds "et un excès de timidité" ("and an excess of shyness").
[7] Dft here adds "periodique" ("periodical").
[8] Sentence added at foot of text in Dft and keyed to this point with a  symbol.
[9] Preceding seven words not in Dft.
[10] Dft ends here.

To Robert Simington

Monticello. June 14. 17.

Th: Jefferson presents his compliments to Capt Simington and his thanks for the two books he has been so kind as to send him through mr Dinsmore, which he has safely recieved. they are rare, and of merit in themselves; and derive additional value as evidences of good will on the part of Capt Simington, of which Th:J. is duly sensible. he salutes him with the same sentiments of good will and respect.

PoC (MHi); on verso of reused address cover of Hutchins G. Burton to TJ, 2 Apr. 1817; dateline at foot of text; endorsed by TJ as a letter to "Simington Robert" and so recorded in SJL.

Robert Simington (ca. 1770–1826), sea captain, was a grocer and commission merchant in Norfolk in 1806. His schooner, the *Rising States*, was captured in 1812 by a British brig (*The Norfolk Directory* [Norfolk, 1806], 29; DNA: RG 29, CS, Norfolk, 1810; Baltimore *Federal Republican*, 28 Nov. 1810, 18 July 1811; *Alexandria Daily Gazette, Commercial & Political*, 16 Sept. 1812; Norfolk *American Beacon and Commercial Diary*, 12 Oct. 1816, 24 Feb. 1817, 20 May 1818; *American Commercial Beacon and Norfolk & Portsmouth Daily Advertiser*, 13 Sept. 1819, 20 Mar., 26 June 1820, 30 Dec. 1826; *Norfolk and Portsmouth Herald*, 1 Jan. 1827).

To Tadeusz Kosciuszko

Monticello June 15. 17.

I have been much distressed, my dear friend & General at the embarrasments you have experienced from the want of punctuality in your remittances; but with equal satisfaction I have learnt from your letter to mr Barnes that they were at length recieved. my inland situation, withdrawn far from all the commercial cities, has obliged me to leave to mr Barnes altogether the reciept and remittance of your funds. to a more honest or punctual man this care could not be committed. but it is impossible to be always guarded against bad bills. the merchants keep their affairs so secret to themselves that it is difficult to know always who are good; and if either drawer or drawee is in default, disappointment ensues. it was lucky he was able to recover the protested bill, so as to avoid it's total loss. these considerations, joined to the great age of mr Barnes, now 87. and my own age, now 74. make it worthy of consideration whether you might not be less exposed to delays, if your funds were now transferred to Europe. neither mr Barnes nor myself have much more of life to expect. and should we recieve the order of 'March' nearly together, your affairs here would be without superintendance, until you could learn their situation, and send over new powers. your funds could be now sold without loss. the only danger is that of bad bills in remitting them, and whether you can find an equally safe and advantageous deposit there. the rotten and bankrupt state of the merchants of England renders that channel too unsafe. the surest would be Amsterdam. but bills on that place are sometimes difficult to be had, and interest there is very low. take all this, my dear friend into consideration, and whatever you wish shall be executed with all the caution practicable. the good bill sent you in lieu of the protested one, and then the protested one additionally place mr Barnes considerably in advance for you, and will occasion a longer interval before another remittance.

We are going on so smoothly and quietly here that I have little more to say to you of our affairs than that all is well. our new President is now on a tour to cxamine our places of defence, and have them made what they should be. we are building ships of the line & frigates, paying off our debts, and putting ourselves into as safe a military posture as we can. internal improvements too are in great activity. schools, roads and canals are become objects of occupation in all the states. the most gigantic undertaking is that of New York, to bring the waters of Lake Erie into the Hudson, thro' a length of 353. miles, and over a height of 661. feet. steam boats are now introducing into every river of size, and we count much on the efficacy of steam frigates, and floating batteries moved by steam, for harbor defence. some permanent defence for the Chesapeak bay, thro' which more than half our produce is exported, is anxiously sought for, but not yet satisfactorily devised. we recieve immense emigrations from Europe. those from France are the least valuable, being mostly men of high military rank, knowing nothing but war, and nothing at all of the sort of war which the peculiarities of our country require. still they are welcome, and recieved in our bosom as strangers needing asylum. from Switzerland

and Great Britain we get valuable people, especially the last who bring us good agriculture as well as the manufacturing arts. for happily their emigrants are of these classes, who are breaking up there, and leaving their nobility to work for themselves.

Would you not, my dear friend, be now better here than at Soleure? that the society of Paris is better than ours we admitted: but we shall not[1] yield that point to every European location. if you like a city life, fix in the Quaker city of Philadelphia. if the country, I would say come to Monticello, and be one of our family. but you formerly protested against that as incroaching on your independance; altho' it would have been ourselves who would have been dependant on you for the happiness of your society. but if this is still scrupled, come and build a house, or rent a house so near as to dine with us every day. we have a healthy country and excellent neighborly society. or fix yourself in Charlottesville, a country village of 500. inhabitants, good people, 2½ miles from me, and where I am inviting some of the Swiss artists to come & establish themselves. think seriously of this, my dear friend, close a life of liberty in a land of liberty. come and lay your bones with mine in the Cemetery of Monticello. this too will be the best way of placing your funds and yourself together; and will enable me to give you in person those assurances of affectionate friendship and respect which must now be committed to the hazard of this letter.

TH: JEFFERSON

RC (ICN: Thomas Jefferson Letters); with partial Dft of Kosciuszko to TJ, 15 Sept. 1817, on verso of final page. PoC (MHi); with first two pages on reused address cover of John Laval to TJ, 25 Apr. 1817, and final page on verso of a different reused address cover to TJ; torn at seal, with missing text rewritten by TJ; endorsed by TJ as a letter to "Kosciuzko Thaddeus." Enclosed in TJ to Daniel Brent and TJ to Albert Gallatin, both 23 June 1817.

[1] In enhancing the preceding three words in PoC, TJ changed them to "we do not."

From William Lee

RESPECTED SIR/. Washington June 16 1817.

The little Swiss colony of Stocking weavers to which the letter you honored me with refers is composed of three heads of families their children and four workmen with twenty four choice Looms many of which are after the English model with the newest french improvements. I am half concerned in this factory the whole of which has cost me in the purchase of the Looms and the passage & sustenance of the workmen a considerable sum— It would give me great pleasure to meet your wishes but having but four good workmen and the Looms being assorted for the weaving of hose pantaloons petticoats drawers &c I cannot seperate them at present without injuring the establishment the few workmen I have being necessary to instruct the apprentices I am about taking.—An intelligent lad of twelve or fourteen years of age becomes a good weaver in the course of a few months and as I have with me mechanicks to make as many looms as I want my plan is to take twenty apprentices and while they are learning the art of weaving to make a number of looms for sale and on selling them allow my apprentices to engage with the purchasers, by this means I shall distribute them about the country and do much good—A Loom or two in a country town would employ the yarn Spun by the women and supply the neighbourhood with Stockings and coarse pantaloons drawers under vests &c—Charlottesville shall be the first town I will supply and if you know of a smart boy or two in that place that would like to learn the trade I will thank you to send them to me and next year they shall return to their own village good workmen—one Loom can turn off a pair of pantaloons in a day without the help of a tailor except for the button holes and running up the seams half way up the legs which can be done by a woman—we can board our apprentices here at 2$ per week and our hired workman finds all sorts of yarn here better than in Europe the woolen in particular he says is far superior—I have been very anxious about this factory but I now think our success will be complete our work is so much superior to that imported—one pair of our Cotton silk or worsted stockings will wear as long as four pair of those imported from England.

I am Sir with great respect & attachment your obliged & obedient

Wm Lee

RC (DLC); addressed: "Thomas Jefferson Monticello"; franked; postmarked Washington City, 17 June; endorsed by TJ as received 21 June 1817 and so recorded in SJL. Enclosed in TJ to Alexander Garrett, 23 June 1817, and James Leitch to TJ, 24 June 1817.

From Wilson Cary Nicholas

My Dear Sir Richmond June 16. 1817

As soon as I came to Richmond, after receiving your letter of the 19th of march, in which you express a wish to have that part of Col Byrd's journal printed that I sent to you, I applied to Mr Thomas Taylor, the agent & friend of the family, to obtain the permission, he promised to do so and there was no doubt it wou'd be readily given. In consequence of your letter of the 10th instant I went in search of Mr Taylor this morning, but he was in the country. I will certainly see him tomorrow. I received the book from Mr Harrison of Berkeley. We are restrained by the regulations of the mother Bank from discounting accommodation paper, but our power to discount the same sum or a larger amount for the same parties, is unlimitted but by our discretion. I have no doubt the directors of the U.S. Bank will discount your paper from time to time, as you may wish to have it done. My seeming inattention to your request about the journal, will not I hope prevent your employing me in future in any way I can serve you.

I am with the greatest respect & attachment your friend & humble servant W. C. NICHOLAS

RC (DLC); endorsed by TJ as received 22 June 1817 and so recorded in SJL. RC (DLC); address cover only; with PoC of TJ to Thomas Appleton, 29 Sept. 1817, on verso; addressed: "Thomas Jefferson Esqr Monticello Milton"; franked; postmarked Richmond, 17 June.

Account with Mary Bacon

[ca. 17 June 1817]

		D C
1817. Jan. 6. recd		95.48
June 6. 5. mo. int.		2.49
		97.97
pd money from Fitz.	20.	
May 15. ord. Southall	25.	45.
		52.97
June 8. pd		36
		16.97
17 pd		16.97
		0– 0

MS (DLC: TJ Papers, 210:37460); on verso of Edmund Bacon to TJ, 8 June 1817; entirely in TJ's hand; undated; endorsed by TJ: "Bacon Mary."

Mary Anne Williamson Bacon (d. 1833) was the mother of TJ's overseer Edmund Bacon. By 1794 she was occasionally selling TJ turkeys and mutton. She inherited three slaves and 500 acres in Albemarle County from her husband, Harwood Bacon, in 1807. Bacon remained in the county until at least 1822. She died in Saint Louis County, Missouri (*MB*; Eurie Pearl Wilford Neel, *The Wilford-Williford Family Treks into America* [1959], 434; Albemarle Co. Will Book, 4:292–3, 315–8; DNA: RG 29, CS, Albemarle Co., 1810; Memoranda Book of Edmund Bacon, 1802–22 [ViU]).

On JAN. 6. 1817 TJ had borrowed $145 from Edmund Bacon, $95.48 of which had come from Mary Bacon. Edmund Bacon paid his mother $20 on TJ's behalf on 15 May 1817, using funds received from William D. Fitch (FITZ) as a payment on the latter's account with TJ (*MB*, 2:1330, 1333–5).

To Louis H. Girardin

DEAR SIR Monticello June 17. 17.

Your favors of May 30. and June 5. are recieved with the article respecting J. Q. Adams which I am glad to possess. of the works you think of translating, Botta would sell best; next to this Dumeril. Bezout altho of very high value would probably find purchasers only in the higher schools, and would be slow in extending even to them. but it is very desirable it should be introduced there. when there shall be a Secretary at war appointed, if I am so far acquainted with him as to have a right to take the liberty, I will certainly propose it to him. but I take for granted he will expect the proposition as to price to come from you

I will ask the favor of you to send me the following books

Erasmus. Elzevir.	1.50
Historiae Byzantinae scriptores.	3.75.
Heliodorus.	3.
Theodoretus	2.
Conciones et Orationes	1.
Lipsius	.50
to which adding for the Bible	2.25
the amount will be	14.D.

which I now inclose you. the books may either come by the stage to mr Wells who will do me the favor to pay the portage, or by a safe waggoner addressed to the care of mr James[1] Leitch who will do the same. I expect within a week to set out for Bedford, and to be absent three weeks. I salute you with great esteem & respect. TH: JEFFERSON

RC (PPAmP: Thomas Jefferson Papers); addressed: "Mr L. H. Girardin at the Hermitage near Staunton"; franked; postmarked Charlottesville, 19 June.

Girardin's FAVORS of 30 May and 5 June and an additional letter from him of 22 June, none of which have been found, are recorded in SJL as received from the Hermitage on 5, 6, and 27 June 1817, respectively. For the appointment late this year of John C. Calhoun as SECRETARY AT WAR, see note to James Monroe to TJ, 23 Feb. 1817. LIPSIUS: Joest Lips.

[1] Word interlined.

From Benjamin Henry Latrobe

Dear Sir   Washington June 17th 1817

Your letter of the 12th curr^t (P.M.[1] 14th June) I have just now received, and am, more than I can express, flattered and gratified by the request it contains.—And not only is it pleasing to me, to find that after so many Years knowledge of my character & talents, while employed in the public service under your eye & direction, I still retain your esteem and friendship, but I have derived important professional improvement from the entirely novel plan of an Academy suggested by you. At this moment I have only time to thank you for all your letter contains; but by the 1st of July, I will transmit to You all that my professional knowledge enables me to suggest & design towards the execution of Your plan, of which I shall ask leave to retain a Copy. I have long considered the common plan of a College as most radically defective.—In your design the principal evils of the usual barrack arrangement appear to be avoided. But I have only had time to read your letter, and now can only assure You of that respect & attachment with which I always have been & am

Your,   B H Latrobe

RC (DLC); at head of text: "Thos Jefferson Esqr Monticello"; endorsed by TJ as received 24 June 1817 and so recorded in SJL.

[1] Abbreviation for "postmarked."

From Valentine W. Southall

Charlottesville, June 18. 17.

V W southall encloses Mr Jefferson $100—the amount advanced is $910, exclusive of $250 for which Mr J. has already draughted. Should Mr J. contemplate an abscence from Albemarle beyond the 10th or 11th of July, VWs. would beg a draught before he starts—otherwise, it will answer after he rcturns—wishing him a pleasant trip, VWs. begs him to accept the assurance of his respect & esteem.

RC (MHi); dateline at foot of text; endorsed by TJ: "Southall Valentine W."

Between 8 May 1817 and this date TJ borrowed $910 from Southall to cover various plantation expenses. On 27 June, before his departure for Poplar Forest, TJ obtained a further $80 from him in cash, and he repaid Southall for the entire sum on that date with a draft on Gibson & Jefferson for $990. On 7 Apr. 1817 TJ had borrowed $250, for which he reimbursed Southall by a draft on Gibson & Jefferson on 15 Apr. (*MB*, 2:1331–5).

From William Thornton

City of Washington 18th June 1817

W: Thornton's respectful Complim^{ts} to his highly esteemed Friend m^{r} Jefferson, and begs leave to present the Bearer Mr Thomas Freeborn, as a very respectable Inhabitant of New York, who is desirous of paying his respects to one of whom he has heard so much, and whose Principles he has long admired.—

RC (MHi); dateline at foot of text; endorsed by TJ as received 28 June 1817 and so recorded in SJL. Enclosed in Thomas Freeborn to TJ, 23 June 1817.

On this date Thornton wrote a similar letter to James Madison (Madison, *Papers, Retirement Ser.*, 1:67).

From John Vaughan

D^{R} SIR Philad. June 18th 1817

Your favor of 7. is recieved & agreeably to your request I have Settled with M^{r} s: Girard & have paid ballance of his account $\$66\frac{66}{100}$—at your Debit acco^{t} is enclosed—as desired I have purchased
of him for 265\$ a $5^{\underline{15}}$ f^{r} producing $1364^{\underline{75}}$ f^{r} order Stephen Cathalan
& for <u>135</u>\$ " " <u>695.25</u>[1] " Debures Freres—
\$400 f^{s} 2060—
I have sent one of each under cover to them via N York & the letters you sent are gone with them—I send seconds from home, but want Copies of your orders, to forward.—I adressed a line to each of the houses.—I advised that we had commenced printing a Volume, & that any Communication from you would be highly acceptable—D: B. S Barton left all his Indian Vocabularies to the Antiq^{n} Soc^{y} Massachussets—can you Send me a list of those sent by you of Lewis & Clarkes that I may try to get them before the other goes—Your letter to M Correa mentions them, but does not describe them or give the number

I remain Yours &c JN VAUGHAN

PS

a few Books hence sent by M Warden they were in a box left at Ghent when our Consul was there—The box was adressed to M Short

RC (MHi); endorsed by TJ as received 24 June 1817 and so recorded in SJL. RC (DLC); address cover only; with PoC of TJ to David Knight, 5 Oct. 1817, on verso;

addressed: "Thomas Jefferson Monticello V[a]"; franked; postmarked Philadelphia, 18 June.

YOUR LETTER TO M CORREA: TJ to José Corrêa da Serra, 26 Apr. 1816.

[1] Reworked from "692.25."

ENCLOSURE

Account with Stephen Girard

Philad[a] 21st Septr 1816.

Thomas Jefferson Esqre
To Stephen Girard

For Premium on the cost of $550, in Specie which were paid on his account in Paris by Messrs Perregeaux Lafitte & Co as p[r] their Letter dated 14[th] May 1816 in virtue of my Letters of Credit to the following Persons.

Stephen Chatalon of Marseilles			
for $200—paid with	F[cs]	1056.—	
Brokerage $\frac{1}{8}$%		1.30	
George Thicknor at Paris			
for $350.—paid with		1837.50	
Perregaux & Lafitte Commission			
on F[cs] 2894.80	a $\frac{1}{2}$ p[r]c[t]	14.47	
	Francs	2909.27	
	at 18$\frac{3}{4}$. cents for 1 Franc	$555.48.[1]	
	Premium at 12 p[r]c[t]		66.66.

MS (MHi); in an unidentified hand; endorsed in a different unidentified hand: "Girard stephen."

[1] The correct figure is $545.48.

To William Duane

Monticello June 19. 17.

Th: Jefferson with his compliments to Gen[l] Duane incloses him 5 Dollars to be placed to his Aurora account, which he believ[es] has been heretofore paid up to May 1. 1817. he salutes him with continued esteem and respect.

PoC (DLC); on verso of reused address cover of John Vaughan to TJ, 2 June 1817; dateline at foot of text; with one word faint and one number rewritten by TJ for clarity; endorsed by TJ, with his additional notation: "newspapers."

To Fernagus De Gelone

Monticello June 19. 17.

Th: Jefferson presents his compliments to m^{r} Fernagus de Gelone and incloses[1] 15. Dollars in discharge of his account under date of May 31. 1817. the Aristophane is expected; all the other books have come safely to hand. he regrets that the Vitruve had been disposed of, as being a small & probably cheap edition of that author.

PoC (MHi); on verso of reused address cover of Fernagus De Gelone to TJ, 31 May 1817; dateline at foot of text; endorsed by TJ.

[1] Preceding two words interlined.

To Joseph Gales (1761–1841)

SIR Monticello June 19. 17.

Your favor of May 23. came to hand a few days ago, with a statement of my account for your paper from Jan. 1809. to Jan. 1817. a term of 8. years. I now inclose you 24.D. the amount: but some apology is due for the prodigious delay, for justification there could be none had I considered myself a subscriber. but the truth is that on winding up my affairs in Washington in the beginning of 1809. I scrupulously paid up every newspaper account I had in the world, and thought I had been, as I meant to be, equally exact in desiring every paper to be discontinued, except the Nat^{l} Intelligencer and Aurora, the only papers, out of my own state, I meant to read. I find that it was thro' a servant I paid yours to your son Feb. 9. 09 being 5. D 25 c. either the servant or your son must have forgotten the notice of discontinuance. still many of the editors have now & then when they had something curious in their papers addressed one to me occasionally. yours came to me [...] now and then, so irregularly as not to excite a suspicion that they [were?] constantly sent as to a subscriber, and I assure you I had no suspicion, that the notice of discontinuance had failed being given to you as to others. but all this is merely to place on it's true ground the apparent negligence & injustice of which I should seem to have been guilty towards you. it is enough for me that you thought me a subscriber, and that the paper was sent from your office, whether it came to me or not. and I hope that this prompt attention to the first notice I have recieved in the eight years will satisfy you that this extraordinary delay has proceeded merely from misapprehension, with a request now to discontinue my subscription accept my acknolegements for the long indulgence intended really on your part, and the assurance of my great esteem & respect.

TH: JEFFERSON

PoC (DLC); on verso of a reused address cover from John Adams to TJ, possibly a duplicate of that from his letter of 26 May 1817; torn at seal; at foot of text: "Mr Joseph Gale"; endorsed by TJ.

Joseph Gales (1761–1841), printer and journalist, was born in Eckington, Derbyshire, England, and apprenticed with printers in Manchester and Newark-on-Trent before starting the *Sheffield Register* in 1787. His publication of reformist articles brought him unfavorable attention from the British government, and in 1794 he fled from England to Hamburg. Gales immigrated to Philadelphia with his family the following year. He worked for the publishers of the Philadelphia *American Daily Advertiser* before taking over that city's *Independent Gazetteer* in 1796. Gales settled in 1799 in Raleigh, North Carolina, where he established the *Raleigh Register*. His son Weston R. Gales became a partner in the paper in 1822 and assumed control in 1839. TJ subscribed to both the Philadelphia *Independent Gazetteer* and the *Raleigh Register*. Gales also served as North Carolina's state printer for several decades beginning in 1800 and was mayor of Raleigh, 1819–33 and 1840–41. He was a lifelong advocate of such reform causes as education, internal improvements, religious toleration, and an end to imprisonment for debt. Gales served as secretary of the Raleigh chapter of the American Colonization Society beginning in 1819 and as treasurer of the national organization during a sojourn in Washington, D.C., 1834–39. He died in Raleigh (*DAB*; *DNCB*, 2:265–7; *ODNB*; Seth Cotlar, "Joseph Gales and the Making of the Jeffersonian Middle Class," in *The Revolution of 1800: Democracy, Race, and the New Republic*, ed. James Horn, Jan Ellen Lewis, and Peter S. Onuf [2002], 331–59; Brigham, *American Newspapers*, 2:774–5, 910; *PTJ*, 37:312; *MB*, 2:963, 1019, 1199, 1335; *Raleigh Register, and North Carolina Gazette*, 4 Jan. 1822, 21, 28 Sept. 1839, 27 Aug. 1841; Washington *Daily National Intelligencer*, 28 Aug. 1841).

Gales's missing FAVOR OF MAY 23 is noted at TJ to Samuel J. Harrison, Charles Johnston, and Archibald Robertson, [13] Aug. 1817. On 9 Feb. 1809 TJ gave his SERVANT Joseph Dougherty $5.25 to pay Gales's SON Joseph Gales (1786–1860) for his subscription to the *Raleigh Register* (*MB*, 2:1241).

To William Short

DEAR SIR Monticello June 19. 17.

Mr Higginbotham having mortgaged to you the lands he purchased as a security for the paiments stipulated, & those payments being made, he thinks there should be a release of the mortgage on your part, for which purpose I inclose you an instrument with a note of the manner of acknolegement.

My letters from France inform me of the death of the Abbé Rochon, and that of his daughter a few hours before him. he left an unfinished history of steam-boats. a company is formed there to settle an agricultural and commercial colony on the coast of Senegal. two vessels with emigrants for that destination had already sailed & a third was ready to sail. the tide of military emigrants was setting chiefly to S. America; whether to increase the happiness of that people or not, is still a problem. I have lately had a visit from Baron Quenette, from whom I have recieved much interesting information as to the proceedings while the emperor of Russia and K. of Prussia were there. he appears to me a very sensible, well informed and able man, neither a friend to their late military tyrant nor to the ancien regime, but wishing and hoping for a limited monarchy and representative legislature. I hear of a critique commenced in some of the French journals on Franklin's letters on political grounds.

We have nothing here worth communicating to you. we are endeavoring to establish a college in Albemarle, if we can get sufficient funds; but our chief hope is to draw to it the University which the state proposes, and for which liberal funds are provided. I set out for Bedford in a few days to be absent 3. weeks, and propose also to pass the months of August & September there. ever and affectionately yours

TH: JEFFERSON

RC (ViW: TJP); at foot of text: "W. Short esq."; addressed (cut): "William [...]"; franked; postmarked Milton, 21 Ju[ne]. PoC (DLC); on verso of right half of reused address cover of Aaron Clark to TJ, 28 May 1817; endorsed by TJ. Enclosure not found.

The king of PRUSSIA was Frederick William III.

From Daniel Brent

DEAR SIR, Washington, Department of State, June 20. 1817.

I have just recd the letter (addressed, thro' mistake, to my Brother William) which you did me the Honor to write to me on the 8th of this month, and I have the satisfaction to inform you that the one which came enclosed for Mr Gallatin is already forwarded from this Department to New york, to be transmitted thence by some safe opportunity to France.

It will at all times afford me the highest gratification to forward your letters, or in any other way to contribute to your accommodation and Convenience, by executing such other Commands as you may please to honor me with. I am, Dear Sir, with sentiments of the greatest Respect and Esteem, your very obed^t^ serv^t^

DANIEL BRENT.

RC (DLC); at foot of first page: "Mr Jefferson"; endorsed by TJ as received 25 June 1817 and so recorded in SJL.

To Thomas Eston Randolph

Dear Sir Monticello June 21 17

On casting my eye over your account I observed that I should have to ask the favor of you to have me furnished with the details of the flour delivered, to wit, a statement of the dates, quantities & persons to whom delivered, without which I cannot settle either with the boat men, or mr Gibson. I imagine you take the boatmen's receipts by which th[ey] stand charged to their employer. a distinction necessary to be obser[ved] is between the crop & rent flour.

I have taken for granted there would be a quarter's rent due to me and payable on the 1st day of July. am I not right in this? I am to write to mr Gibson tomorrow, and lest I should misinform him, I send the bearer on purpose that I may write with certainty. I had hoped to have overtaken you at the mill, but you had passed on before I got there. your's affectionately Th: Jefferson

PoC (MHi); on verso of portion of reused address cover containing only a wax seal; edge torn; at foot of text: "T. E. Randolph esq."; endorsed by TJ.

From Thomas Eston Randolph

Dear Sir Ashton 21st June 1817

I cannot furnish the account you require without the use of the Day book, which is always kept at the Mill—but I will endeavour to send it in time for you to write tomorrow— The flour is paid in full, except a balance of 1 bar—9 ℔ which is in the Mill, subject to your order

very Afftly Yours Thos Eston Randolph

RC (MHi); at foot of text: "Thomas Jefferson Esqre"; endorsed by TJ as received 21 June 1817 and so recorded in SJL.

In SJL TJ recorded an additional letter from Randolph, not found and evidently undated but received 22 June 1817.

To William Darby

Monticello June 22. 17.

I thank you, Sir, for the copy of your Description of Louisiana which you have been so kind as to send me. it arrives in the moment of my departure on a journey of considerable absence. I shall avail myself of the first moments of leisure after my return to read it, &

doubt not I shall recieve from it both pleasure and information. the labors of an oppressive correspondence reduce almost to nothing the moments I can devote to reading. Accept the assurance of my great respect & consideration. TH: JEFFERSON

P.S. the Rio Norte is unquestionably the Western limit of Louisiana, and is so claimed by us.

PoC (DLC); on verso of reused address cover to TJ; at foot of text: "Mr William Darby"; endorsed by TJ. Printed in Darby, *A Geographical Description of the State of Louisiana* (2d ed., New York, 1817), 336.

In the 1816 first edition of his *Geographical Description of the State of Louisiana*, which he had recently sent TJ, Darby asserted that the southwestern boundary of the Louisiana Purchase was based on the place on the Gulf of Mexico where René Robert Cavelier de La Salle had landed in the 1680s (p. 11). For TJ's explanation of his belief that the Rio Grande (also called the Río Bravo del NORTE) was the correct WESTERN boundary, see TJ to John Melish, 31 Dec. 1816.

To James Madison

DEAR SIR Monticello June 22. 17.

In two packages, distinct from this letter, I return you your father's meteorological diaries, which you were so kind as to lend me, and a piece on paper money recieved from you some time ago. from the former I have made out tables of rain and snow, and a calendar of animal and vegetable matters announcing the advance of seasons. having now compleated 7. years of observations since my return home, I have drawn such general results from them in the form of tables and otherwise, as may be comprehended[1] by the mind, & retained by the memory. they constitute an estimate of our climate, the only useful object to which they can be applied. I inclose you a copy of both.[2] I have for some time been very anxious to pay you a visit: but mrs Randolph wishing to join in it, and detained by the daily expectation of the measles appearing among her children, it has been put off until I am now within 2 or 3. days of setting out for my harvest in Bedford to be absent 3. weeks; and as I shall pass the months of Aug. & Sep. there, we must pay our visit in July, after the harvest is over. when here an observation fell from you once or twice which did not strike me at the time, but reflection afterwards led me to hope it had meaning; and that you thought of applying your retirement to the best use possible, to a work which we have both long wished to see well done, and which we thought at one time would have been done. my printed materials are all gone to Washington, but those in letters & notes & memm[s] remain with me, are very voluminous, very full, and shall be entirely at your command. but this subject can be fathomed only in conversation, and must therefore await the visit.—we just learn the desperate situation of young Eston Randolph son of T. E. Randolph our neighbor; the two families being in their intercourse and relations almost as one, fills that of Monticello with affliction. he had just landed at Baltimore from an East India voyage. ever & affectionately yours. TH: JEFFERSON

RC (DLC: Madison Papers, Rives Collection); at foot of text: "James Madison"; endorsed by Madison. PoC (DLC); on verso of portion of reused address cover to TJ; damaged at seal and several words faint; endorsed by TJ. Enclosure: TJ's Analysis of his Weather Memorandum Book, Jan. 1817.

For the Madison family METEOROLOGICAL DIARIES returned here, see note to TJ's Analysis of his Weather Memorandum Book, Jan. 1817. The PIECE ON PAPER MONEY was probably Madison's 1779–80 essay on "Money," described above at James Monroe to TJ, 26 Apr. 1815, where it was enclosed to TJ at Madison's request. The WORK that TJ and Madison had long wished to see completed was probably a history of the United States from a Republican perspective. They had fruitlessly proposed such a project to Joel Barlow in 1802 (*PTJ*, 37:400–1). William ESTON RANDOLPH, son of Thomas Eston Randolph, died 16 June 1817 in Baltimore (*Baltimore Patriot & Mercantile Advertiser*, 17 June 1817).

[1]Word interlined in place of "understood."

[2]Preceding seven words interlined.

To Thomas Eston Randolph

DEAR SIR Monticello June 22. 1817.

You need not hurry yourself at all as to the extracts from your Daybook. a letter from George Stevenson to mr Randolph just recieved gives the uneasy information that your son Eston is very ill at Baltimore. indeed he says that he is in imminent danger. his case is an inflammatory fever. having given this cause of alarm, mr Stevenson will undoubtedly write by every mail while the crisis continues. with hopes therefore that the next mail will bring a more favorable account, and an assurance that if directed to us it shall be sent to you in the very instant I am ever and affectionately yours

TH: JEFFERSON

PoC (MHi); on verso of portion of reused address cover to TJ; at foot of text: "T. E. Randolph esq."; endorsed by TJ.

To Daniel Brent

Dear Sir Monticello June 23. 17.

I very lately took the liberty of requesting you to give a safe passage with your official dispatches to a part of my European correspondence. I have now to ask the same for the residue not then ready, and hope this will close the trouble imposed on you for the present year for which I pray you to accept my apologies, with the assurance of my great esteem and respect. Th: Jefferson

PoC (DLC); on verso of portion of reused address cover of John Barnes to TJ, 12 May 1817; at foot of text: "Mr Brent"; endorsed by TJ, with his additional notation: "lre to Gallatin, cover^{g} Kosciuzko E^{t}c." Enclosures: (1) TJ to Alexander von Humboldt, 13 June 1817. (2) TJ to Louis Pio, 13 June 1817. (3) TJ to Barbé Marbois, 14 June 1817. (4) TJ to Tadeusz Kosciuszko, 15 June 1817. (5) TJ to Albert Gallatin, 23 June 1817.

From Thomas Freeborn

Respected Friend Alexandria 6 m^{o} 23 1817

I have been trying to make an excuse for severall years to pay thee a vissit—have for a few days past antiscipated the pleasure I Should have in seeing mine & my countrys Friend, but alas I have been disapointed I tried two days to get a Carriage in Fredericks town, to take me out to thy place, but could not succeed—however I hope to see thee & it may be in the fall—I have a letter of Introduction from my Friend doctor Thornton of Wasshington City enclosed I hand it thee, with my card on which thou may see Jethro Woods plough which I have the vending of in the southern States on the atlantic, the one thou hast—I forwarded to Philadelphia & it was by mistake sent thee—I forwarded one at the same time to Alexandria for thee in particular, however as thou hast it it is all well

I am deeply interested in the afore said plough & any communication thou should make to me on the subject would be Gratefully recd at 210 Front St N. York by thy

Friend Thos Freeborn

RC (MHi); endorsed by TJ as received 28 June 1817 and so recorded in SJL. RC (ViWC: Mrs. George P. Coleman Collection, 1945); address cover only; with PoC of TJ to Quinette de Rochemont, 30 Sept. 1817, on verso; addressed: "Thomas Jefferson Montacello Varginia"; franked; postmarked Orange Court House, 28 June. Enclosure: William Thornton to TJ, 18 June 1817. Other enclosure not found.

Thomas Freeborn (ca. 1774–1846), merchant and manufacturer, was working as a cooper in New York City by 1800. In 1815, while continuing his cooperage at Crane Wharf, he also operated as a merchant at 210 Front Street. Beginning about 1817 Freeborn manufactured and sold cast-iron plows based on the designs of Jethro Wood. In addition, he operated a foundry until at least 1831. Freeborn served as an officer of the Mercantile Insurance Company and as a director of both the Franklin Bank and the Bank of Washington and Warren (William Wade Hinshaw and others, *Encyclopedia of American Quaker Genealogy* [1936–50; repr. 1969–77], 3:127; *Longworth's New York Directory* [1800]: 205; [1815]: 215; [1816]: 213; [1820]: 189; [1823]: 183; [1831]: 284; Peter D. McClelland, *Sowing Modernity: America's First Agricultural Revolution* [1997], 251; New York *Mercantile Advertiser*, 30 Jan., 29 Apr. 1818; Scoville, *New York Merchants*, 1:241; Washington *Daily National Intelligencer*, 3 Apr. 1820; New York *National Advocate*, 5 Feb. 1822 [country ed.], 26 June 1824; New York *Evening Post*, 9 Dec. 1846).

To Albert Gallatin

DEAR SIR Monticello June 23. 17.

In a letter of the 6th inst. I took the liberty of troubling you with a part of my annual correspondence at Paris. the remainder, not then ready, I now take the liberty of putting under your cover as a supplement to the trouble then given. not knowing where Baron Humboldt is I must ask the favor of you to add the necessary address. nothing new having occurred since my last, I can only repeat the assurances of my affectionate esteem and respect. TH: JEFFERSON

RC (NHi: Gallatin Papers); endorsed by Gallatin. PoC (MHi); on verso of reused address cover of David Higginbotham to TJ, 20 May 1817; beneath signature: "Mr Gallatin"; endorsed by TJ, with his additional notation at foot of text: "lres to Kosciuzko, Humboldt, Marbois, Pio." Enclosures: (1) TJ to Alexander von Humboldt, 13 June 1817. (2) TJ to Louis Pio, 13 June 1817. (3) TJ to Barbé Marbois, 14 June 1817. (4) TJ to Tadeusz Kosciuszko, 15 June 1817. Enclosed in TJ to Daniel Brent, 23 June 1817.

To Alexander Garrett

DEAR SIR Monticello June 23. 17.

I thought it so important to close with mr Perry & especially to get a clause for the conveyance of the land put into writing that I undertook to sign the inclosed paper in your name. we have agreed that 2. copies of this shall be made, the one for him the other for you, leaving out the clause for conveying the land, and that the deed for the land shall be signed at the same time with the 2. copies of the articles. these you will of course sign for yourself, when the one I inclose may be destroyed.

I inclose you also a letter from mr Lee, from which you will see on what ground stands our chance for a stocking weaver. be so good as to shew it to mr Leitch & any others of the gentlemen who take an interest in promoting the town. the question is whether a good young man of 18. or 20. can be found who will go and learn the art. We have now the Carnation cherries in perfection if you think them worth sending for, for our little messenger & his mule are constantly on the go somewhere or other. perhaps mr Leitch also would think the cherries worth sending for, & if so, they are at his service. I salute you with friendship and respect. TH: JEFFERSON

RC (ViW: Small Collections, Jefferson Papers); addressed: "Mr Garrett"; endorsed by Garrett. Enclosure: William Lee to TJ, 16 June 1817.

The INCLOSED PAPER, not found, was apparently a preliminary version of the Agreement between John M. Perry and Central College of this date.

In Charlottesville on this date Garrett wrote to John H. Cocke that "Knowing your anxiety to learn the state of the controversey with Perry about the title to the land purchased of him for the use of the Central collage, I hasten to communicate to you that all difficulties have been removed by an agreement between Messrs Jefferson & Perry by which Mr Perry is to build one Pavilion, and the deed from Perry for the land was this day signed and acknowledged and is now of record. the friends to the Collage may now therefore proceed with their subscriptions being enabled to say with certainty where the collage is to be erected" (ViU: JHC).

To Patrick Gibson

DEAR SIR Monticello June 23. 17.

Anxious to be on a sure footing as to provision for my additional note at the bank of Virginia, in the event of it's not being within th[e] rule to renew it, I wrote to mr Nicholas President of the National branch bank of Richmond to know if I could be accomodated there with 2000.D. to be renewed for some months. his answer recieved yesterday is in thes[e] words. 'we are restrained by the regulations of the mother bank from discoun[t]ing accommodation paper; but our power to discount the same sum, or a larger amount for the same parties, is unlimited but by our discretion. I hav[e] no doubt the Directors of this bank[1] will discount your paper from time to time, as you may wish to have it done.' I am in hopes therefore there will be no danger of failing to pay it up at the Virginia bank when due if their rule forbids it's renewal; and for this purpose, not knowing the form of the Note at the National bank, I inclose a blank, signed, to be filled up according to their form. at the same time I send another to be used at the Virginia bank, if the additional note can be renewed there, as I prefer a steady connection to a desultory one. I hope all my flour is sold for whatever price it would bring. on general grounds I think April the best month for selling, but never to pass over May, because of the competition of the new crop. accidental circumstances may however sometimes controul the general course. I am the more anxious that a sale should have been made on account of the draught in favor of our Collector mr Southall, which in my letter of May 24. I informed you would b[e] upwards of 600.D. but which subsequent furnitures of money for calls here will make upwards of 900.D. this is exclusive of the 250.D. for which I drew in his favor early in April, and which I do not know if he has yet presented. being to make his deposit in Richmond about the 10th of July he will call on you about that time. I set out for Bedford in 2. or 3. days to be absent 3. weeks. I salute you with great esteem & respec[t] TH: JEFFERSON

PoC (MHi); on verso of reused address cover; edge trimmed; at foot of text: "Mr Gibson"; endorsed by TJ. Enclosures not found.

[1] Wilson Cary Nicholas to TJ, 16 June 1817: "of the U.S. Bank."

To Jeremiah A. Goodman

SIR Monticello June 23. 17.

I am sorry it will not be in my power to furnish you the money you desire, nor any further sum whatever until next April, and it would be but deception to engage it. indeed when I paid the last sum, this was stated to you, and distinctly agreed to. all my resources are exhausted by the failure of my crops, until another comes in. it will then give me as great pleasure to pay this debt, as to you to recieve it, and I am sorry it is not in power to do it sooner. for the present I can only tender you my best wishes and respects. TH: JEFFERSON

PoC (MHi); on verso of portion of a reused address cover from John Barnes to TJ; at foot of text: "Mr Jeremiah A. Goodman"; endorsed by TJ.

On 10 Apr. 1817 TJ had PAID THE LAST SUM of $50 toward the amount he owed Goodman for his service as overseer (*MB*, 2:1333).

Conveyance of Lands for Central College from John M. Perry and Frances T. Perry to Alexander Garrett

This indenture made on the 23d[1] day of June[2] 1817. between John Perry & Frances T Perry his wife[3] of the county of Albemarle on the one part and Alexander Garrett proctor of the Central college acting in trust for the sd college on the other part witnesseth that the sd John & Frances[4] in consideration of the sum of fourteen hundred and twenty one dollars twenty five cents, the payment whereof is sufficiently secured, doth hereby bargain & sell to the sd Alexander two parcels of land in the sd county of Albemarle, the one containing forty three acres & three fourths about a mile above Charlottesville on the public road to Staunton, the other about five eighths of a mile from the former, containing one hundred & fifty three acres, comprehending the top and part of a mountain, which tract first mentioned is bounded as follows to wit beginning at a stake on Wheeler's road & running N. 30.° W. 35. poles to a stone pile, thence N. 19.° E. 29. po. to a stake near the garden of the sd John, thence N. 3.° W. 36. po. to a stone pile and persimmon, thence N. $10\frac{1}{2}$° E. 22. po. to a stake on the three notched road, thence down & along the sd road 118. po. to a pine stump in the road, corner to Henry Chiles & Jesse W. Garth, thence S. 34. W. $48\frac{1}{2}$ po. to pointers on Wheeler's road, thence along the sd Wheeler's road 65. poles to the beginning: and the other tract mentioned in the second place begins at a Pine tree on the Mountain road (which pine tree bears S 89.° W. 206. po. from the point of beginning and ending of the first mentioned tract, in Wheeler's road) and runs from the sd pine tree N. 17. W. 52. po. to a Spanish oak, N. 31. W. 32. po. to pointers, S. 75. W. 92. po. to pointers on the mountain, N. 10. E. 24. po. to a red oak, N. 30. E. 24. po. to pointers, N. 5. E. 26. po. to pointers, N. 22. W. $7\frac{1}{2}$ po. to a Chesnut oak, S 48. W. 37. po. to a chesnut oak, N. 58. W. 20. po. to pointers, S. 29. W. 38. po. to pointers, S. 14. E. 66. po. to a stake, S. 29. E. 41. po. to a white oak, S. 18. W. 45. po. to a stake, S. 20. W.[5] 20. po. to a stake, S. 25. W. 10. po. to a stake, S. 35. W. 54. po. to a white oak on Wheeler's road, thence down the sd Wheeler's road 118. po. to pointers near a branch, thence N. 8. E. 17. po. to a maple, N. 19. E. $44\frac{1}{2}$ po. to a chesnut oak, N. 75. E. 48. po. to pointers on the Mountain road aforesaid, & along the sd road 48. po. to the pine at the beginning. to have and to hold the sd two parcels of land with their appurtenances to him the said Alexander, and his successors proctors of the sd Central college, to and for the use of the said college for ever. and the sd John Perry & Frances T Perry[6] for themselves[7] his heirs, executors and administrators the said[8] two parcels of land with their appurtenances to the sd Alexander and his successors proctors of the sd College, and for the use of the sd College, doth covenant that he will warrant, and doth warrant and will for ever defend. Witness the hand & name of the sd John, and his seal hereto set on the day and year above named.

signed, sealed & delivered in presence of }

John M. Perry
Frances T. Perry

MS (ViU: TJP); on indented paper; in TJ's hand except as noted below; signed and sealed by John M. Perry and Frances T. Perry; with signed attestation by Albemarle County deputy clerk William Wertenbaker at foot of text: "In the Office of the County Court of Albemarle the 23rd day of June 1817. This Indenture of bargain and sale from John M Perry to Alexander Garrett Proctor for the central College was produced to me in the said Office and Acknowledged by the said John M Perry party thereto and thereupon the same is admitted to record"; endorsed by Wertenbaker: "Perry To Garrett Proctor of the Central College} Deed 23^{d} June 1817 Acknow^{d} before me by Jno M Perry & admitted to record Wm Wertenbaker DC"; with additional endorsements in two different unidentified hands: "Recorded Page 356" and "Commission & recorded Page 407 Examined." Tr (Albemarle Co. Deed Book, 20:356–7); edge trimmed; in Wertenbaker's hand and including his 23 June 1817 attestation; with additional notations in two different hands: "Exam^{d}" and "Deliv^{d} Pr Order to P U V^{a} [Proctor, University of Virginia, i.e., Arthur S. Brockenbrough] the 13 Oct 1825."

Frances T. Perry (ca. 1780–1837) was the wife of the builder John M. Perry. About 1835 the Perrys left Albemarle County and spent time in Louisiana and Missouri. Frances Perry died in Saint Louis (Woods, *Albemarle*, 295, 393; *Lynchburg Virginian*, 25 Sept. 1837).

This transaction represents the first purchase of land for Central College (later the University of Virginia). A plat of these two parcels drawn by TJ is reproduced elsewhere in this volume.

On 7 July 1817 Micajah Woods and William Woods, justices of the Albemarle County Court, examined Frances T. Perry, who acknowledged that she consented to this conveyance of land freely and without coercion (MS in ViU: TJP, printed form, with blanks filled in by Garrett, signed by Micajah Woods and William Woods, with signed attestation by Garrett on verso: "In the Office of the County Court of Albemarle the seventh day of August 1817 This Commission & certificate of the relinquishment of dower of Mrs Frances T Perry wife of John M Perry were returned to me in said Office and annexed to record"; Tr in Albemarle Co. Deed Book, 20:407–8, with identical endorsement by Garrett).

On 7 Aug. 1817 Nelson Barksdale, the newly appointed proctor, acquired a third tract for Central College from Jesse Winston Garth for the sum of $1 and a credit of $30 an acre toward Garth's pledge of $200 to the Central College subscription. This land measured 6.25 acres and adjoined the eastern border of the smaller of two parcels conveyed by the Perrys. It was described as "lying and being in the county of Albemarle on the main road leading from Charlottesville to Staunton the same being a part of that tract of land conveyed to the said Jesse W Garth by Henry West Alberly alias Henry Chiles and bounded as follows. to wit Begining at a pine stump in the said Staunton road formerly the corner of said Jesse W Garth and John M Perry now the corner of the Central College tract, thence down the said Staunton road to where Wheelers road empties into the said main Staunton road, thence up and with the said Wheelers road to the Corner of the Central college tract on said Wheelers road on John M Perry thence with the line of the said Central College to the begining" (MS in ViU, in Garrett's hand, signed by Garth, with signed attestation by Garrett at foot of text: "At a Court continued and held for Albemarle County the 7th day of August 1817. This Indenture was produced into Court and Acknowledged by Jesse W Garth party thereto and Ordered to be recorded," endorsed by Garrett: "Garth to Barksdale. Proctor to C.C} Deed," and with note by Garrett beneath endorsement: "7th August 1817 Acknow^{d} & ordered to be recorded Exam^{d} Recorded 406"; Tr in Albemarle Co. Deed Book, 20:406–7, in Garrett's hand and including his 7 Aug. 1817 attestation, with additional notations in two different hands: "Examined" and "Deliv^{d} Proctor U V^{a} 13 Oct 1825 p^{r} Order").

[1] Number added in an unidentified hand.

[2] Month added in an unidentified hand.

[3]Preceding six words interlined in an unidentified hand in MS and Tr.

[4]Preceding two words interlined in an unidentified hand in MS and Tr.

[5]Tr: "E."

[6]Preceding four words interlined in an unidentified hand.

[7]Word reworked from "himself" in same hand as interlineations.

[8]Sentence from "John Perry" to this point interlined in Tr by original transcriber, with "Frances T. Perry" further interlined in the different hand noted above.

Agreement between John M. Perry and Central College

Articles of Agreement made and concluded this twenty third day of June one thousand eight hundred and seventeen between Alexander Garrett as Proctor of the Central College in Albemarle on the one part and John M. Perry on the other part, Witness, First, that a Pavilion or Schoolhouse being to be built for the said College on one of the lots of land purchased for the s^{d} College of the said John M Perry, the body of which pavilion is to be built of brick and to contain one room below and two above stairs with cellars & offices below the said John undertakes and hereby covenants to and with the said Proctor and his successors in office, to do all the Carpenter's and House joiner's work of the said pavilion as shall be prescribed to him, that he will provide all the meterials of wood and iron mongery which shall be required, that the meterials shall be of sound and durable quality, the Carpenters work shall be done solidly, neatly, and well fitted, and the house joinery in the best manner, and strictly according to such forms and orders of Architecture as the said Proctor or his successors shall prescribe; that all the work necessary to be put up or in, as the brick layer proceeds, shall allways be ready by the time the brick layer is ready for it, and all the residue to be done by him shall be compleated and put up within five months after the brick layer shall have so far done the walls as that they shall be capable of recieveing it; and the said John M Perry doth further agree and covenant, that if any part of the Carpenters work or house joinery shall not be done in the most perfect good manner, or not strictly according to the forms and orders of Architecture which shall be prescribed to him as aforesaid, the said Proctor or his successors shall have a right to have the same altered or taken down and rebuilt according to the forms prescribed, by any person he shall employ at the expence of the said John, and the parties to these presents further agree, that if any part of the work shall be objected to as insufficient or inconformable to what is herein before stipulated that its sufficiency or non conformity shall be finally decided on by three competent persons one chosen by each party and the[1] two persons chosen are hereby empower'd to choose a third equally competent And the said John doth further agree that if the work shall not be done at the respective times stipulated that the said Proctor or his successors shall be free to have it done by such person as he shall employ at the expence of the said John, and be entitled to damages for all wrongful delay to be paid by the said John—

And the said Alexander, covenants in the name of the said College and on its behalf, that for all meterials furnished by the said John, the reasonable price they shall have cost him, or which they shall be worth if furnished by himself, shall be paid him, and for all Carpenter's work or house-joinery done, he shall be paid the prices which were paid by James Madison late President of the United States to James Dinsmore for similar work done at Montpelier,[2] which payments shall be made to him as follows towit Five hundred dollars in hand, five hundred dollars more, when the roof shall be raised, and the ballance when it shall be compleated, In Witness whereof the parties hereto subscribe their names the day & year first within written

In presence of, } Approved[3] ALEX GARRETT
WM WERTENBAKER } TH: JEFFERSON Proctor to Central College (seal)
JOHN M. PERRY (seal)

MS (ViU: TJP); in Garrett's hand, signed by Garrett, Perry, TJ, and Wertenbaker; with additional note on following page in Garrett's hand and signed by Perry: "Charlottesville 16th September 1817. Recieved of Alexander Garrett late Proctor to the Central College five hundred dollars it being the sum mentioned in this agreeement as the first payment for the building herein before-named"; docketed in an unidentified hand: "No 3—Perry with Central College} Agreement."

A preliminary version of this agreement, not found, was apparently enclosed in TJ's letter to Alexander Garrett of this date.

[1] Reworked from "and in case of disagreement the."

[2] Manuscript: "Montplier."

[3] Word in TJ's hand.

To Robert H. Saunders

SIR Monticello June 23. 17.

Your letter of May 9. did not get to hand until the 15th instant, and your post office not being named in your letter I must direct this to Goochland courthouse where it mentions that you have a plantation. having trees so near as you describe to your house, and higher than the chimnies, I should certainly prefer fixing the Conductor to a tree, as a higher object, and because should the rod be at any time overcharged, the tree itself is a good conductor for the surplus matter. it saves also all connection with the house by the supporting staples. the rod should have it's point tipped with gold or silver leaf to prevent rusting, and should rise 6. or 8. feet above the top of the tree. if the rod is not all in one piece it is better the pieces should be socketed into one another than linked. where it enters the ground it should bend off from the foundation of the house 5. or 6. feet, and no coating in the ground is material as it there delivers it's charge to the body of the earth where it [is] dissipated at once Accept the assurance of my respect. TH: JEFFERSON

PoC (MHi); on verso of reused address cover of otherwise unlocated letter from David Higginbotham to TJ, 22 May 1817 (addressed: "Thomas Jefferson Esquire Monticello"; franked; postmarked Richmond, 2 June; recorded in SJL as received 5 June 1817 from Richmond); mutilated at seal; at foot of text: "M[r] R[o] H. Saunders"; endorsed by TJ.

From James Leitch

SIR, Charlottesville June 24th 1817

Enclosed is M[r] Lees Letter to you respecting the Stocking Weaver which I detained from M[r] Garrett in Order to shew some of the Citizens who I am glad to find are anxious for the establishment

I would propose sending two apprentices but think better to send from the age of 18 to 20 of known[1] Stability as younger would not be Capable of managing the Business on their return, & as it is not presumable they would have Funds to purchase the Machinary that a Company should be formed for that purpose & in that Case it would be necessary to ascertain what the machinery would cost to carry on every part of the Business (Silk excepted); that Sum with an Addition of a few Hundred Dollars to purchase Materials to be divided into Shares of 50 or $100 & Sold—by that means it would give a more general interest in its welfare & be less Burthensome on an Individual should it fail—It would also be necessary to know whether the apprentices are to pay for their own Board &[c]
should these Idea's meet your approbation be good enough to make the enquiries so as the necessary steps may be taken towards raising the Funds

respectfully your Obed[t] Serv[t] JA[S] LEITCH

RC (MHi); endorsed by TJ as received 24 June 1817 and so recorded in SJL. Enclosure: William Lee to TJ, 16 June 1817.

[1]Manuscript: "know."

To James Dinsmore

DEAR SIR Monticello June 25. 17.

On examining the sites for our college we found not one comparable to Perry's, and prices beyond our means; and as Perry persisted positively in refusing a deed but on condition of doing the wooden work of the building now proposed, it was concluded we ought not to lose the permanent advantages to the institution, on a question about the execution of this single building, and especially as he has agreed that if any part of the work is done insufficiently, or not exactly in the forms or order of architecture we shall prescribe, it may be taken down & put up by any other person at his expence. as this leaves us perfectly free as to all the other buildings we concluded with him. he has accordingly conveyed the land; and Chisolm meets me in Lynchburg a few days hence to engage a bricklayer, master of the business there. our future operations will depend much on the success of our subscriptions, of which we entertain good hope, and of which yourself and mr Nelson shall be advised. I salute you both with friendship and respect. TH: JEFFERSON

RC (ViU: TJP); hole in manuscript, with missing word supplied from PoC; addressed: "M[r] James Dinsmore Petersburg Virg[a]"; franked; postmarked Milton, 28 June. PoC (Forbes Magazine Collection, New York City, 2003); on verso of reused address cover of Isaac Briggs to TJ, 9 May 1817; endorsed by TJ.

To William Lee

DEAR SIR Monticello June 25. 17.

Your favor of the 16th has been duly recieved, and on communicating it to some of the inhabitants of Charlottesville they find an excellent young man of 20. years of age who has been brought up a linen-weaver, and who is willing to devote a year to learn the stocking weaving business, which is more likely to succeed here than his first trade. supposing he is to be discharged at the end of a year, he wishes to know whether he is to pay his board, whether at the end of a year he can be sure of having a loom and how much it will cost him. if you will be so kind as to drop me a line of answer to these enquiries for his satisfaction, he will go on immediately on it's reciept. I sincerely wish you success and full indemnification for your patriotic efforts, and am anxious myself to see our own little village furnish the neighborhood with the comforts we have too long depended on others for, and eat along side of our farms the bread we have had to send 1000 leagues to him who worked for us at that distance. I salute you with great esteem and respect Th: Jefferson

PoC (DLC); on verso of reused address cover of George Washington Jeffreys to TJ, 8 Apr. 1817; at foot of text: "Wm Lee esq."; endorsed by TJ.

The young man was Michael Graham.

From Peter Poinsot

Monsieur Cette, Département de l'Hérault 25 Juin 1817:

Je viens sous la recommandation de mon bon & digne ami, le Général kosciuzsko, reclamer de votre bienveillance[1] vos soins & votre protection. voici ce dont il Sagit.

J'achetai en 1784 à Richmond, 1200 Acres de terre situées dans le Comté de Monongalia, à la tête de la rivière du petit kenhawai.[2] Le 23 mai 1785 Son Excellence Patrick Henry Gouverneur de l'Ètat de Virginie m'en délivra le Contrat: des affaires de famille m'aïant appellé en France, me contraignerent de quitter ce beau pays avec le plus grand regret et les honnetetés que J'en ai reçües ne S'effaceront jamais de ma mémoire, de retour, & n'ayant aucun espoir de retourner en Amérique, J'essayai d'envoyer ma procuration en 1791 à Mr Adrien Walck consul hollandais à Baltimore, ce dernier me répondit que les terres[3] qui se vendaient étaient des Parcelles de 20 à 30,000 Acres, que lobjet étant trop petit qu'il ne pouvait les placer. Le notaire qui me fit la procuration, ne pouvant instrumenter qu'en français fut obligé[4] de faire traduire mon Contrat (Deed) en cette langue. l'original fut laissé en dépot chez mon ami, Pierre Siau, Président, alors, du Tribunal du Commerce de Marseille, où je me trouvais à cette époque,[5] ce dernier, comme beaucoup d'honnètes gens obligé de fuir, et quitter précipitament sa maison pour aller chercher une asile tranquile, Sa maison, Ses magazins,[6] furent de suitte mise au pillage, mon Contrat Subit le meme Sort de ses effets (Evènement de la Révolution) heureusement pour moi, que je gardai une Copie litérale, traduite, de mon Contrat avec le plan, dont je Joins ici copie, vous observant que je payai l'année Suivante à Samuel Craw £3. argent courrant de Virginie pour Land taxes à raison de 5*f* par 100 Acres. Je pense quil serait nécessaire de se procurer du Bureau des terres à Richmond un Duplicata du Contrat, et ensuite de prendre les renseignements convenables Sur la Situation des terres, leur valeur approximative, les impositions qu'elles pourraient devoir, afin que je pusse indiquer une maison pour satisfaire aux depenses & fraix qu'elles pourraient nécessiter. Je viens, au nom de mon ami, Vous prier, de charger qu'elqu'un intimément connu de vous pour les lumieres et la probité de reclamer en mon nom les dittes terres, & d'aprés la lettre quil vous plaira m'honorer, (comme je tiens beaucoup a ce Continent que j'ai habité avec tant de Satisfacion), Je verrai à décider mon fils ainé pour aller en prendre possession & s'y établir, il me convient d'avoir les renseignements les plus précis pour ne pas l'exposer à faire un voyage infructueux. Vous parlerai je de reconnaissance? helas, J'enporte deja dans mon coeur l'expression la plus vive. Agréez Monsieur l'Assurance de ma considération la plus distinguée et le respect avec lesquels Jai lhonneur d'être, Monsieur,

Votre trés humble & trés obéissant serviteur POINSOT

Je Joins inclus la lettre du Général Kosciuzsko
ma Seconde, par Bordeaux, Vous emportera le duplicata—La presente vous parviendra par les soins de Monsr I C Barnet consul à Paris[7]

[*Additional postscript in Dupl, on verso of endorsement leaf:*]
D'après la carte il parait que ces terres Sont situées au 38 & 39 degrés latitude. Longitude de Paris 84 degrés dans la belle vallée de la riviere du Kenhawai—il serait bien de Savoir leur vrai Situation léloignement des villes—aussi que les communications des routes &c

EDITORS' TRANSLATION

SIR Cette, Department of Hérault 25 June 1817:

Recommended by my good and worthy friend, General Kosciuszko, I ask for your kindness, aid, and protection concerning the following.
In 1784 I bought in Richmond 1,200 acres of land located in Monongalia County, at the head of the Little Kanawha River. On 23 May 1785 His Excellency Patrick Henry, governor of the state of Virginia, delivered the contract to me. Family matters recalled me to France and forced me to leave this beautiful country with great regret, and its kindness to me will never be erased from my memory. Back in France, and with no hope of returning to America, I tried in 1791 to send my power of attorney to Mr. Adriaan Valck, the Dutch consul at Baltimore. He replied that the land was being sold in parcels of 20 to 30,000 acres, and that he could not sell my property because it was too small. Because the notary who made out the power of attorney for me knew only French, he needed to have my contract (deed) translated into

that language. The original was deposited at the house of my friend Pierre Siau, then president of the tribunal of commerce of Marseille, where I then resided. Siau, who like a lot of honest people was forced to flee, hurriedly left his home to seek a tranquil asylum. His house and stores were immediately looted. My contract suffered the same fate as his belongings (a result of the Revolution). Luckily for me, I had kept a literal copy of my contract, translated, with the map, a copy of which I enclose here. Note that the following year I paid Samuel McCraw £3. in current Virginia money for land taxes at the rate of 5 francs per 100 acres. I think it would be necessary to obtain a duplicate of the contract from the land bureau in Richmond, and then to get the proper information about the location of the land, its approximate value, and the taxes it might incur, so that I can select a firm to pay the necessary expenses and fees. In the name of my friend, I ask you to entrust someone whose expertise and integrity you know well to claim the said land in my name; and according to the letter with which you will honor me (as I greatly value this continent in which I have lived with such satisfaction), I will decide whether to send my eldest son to take possession of the land and establish himself there. It would suit me to have the most precise information so that my son might not undertake a trip in vain. Will I speak of gratitude? Alas, I already carry its most vivid expression in my heart. Please accept, Sir, the assurance of my most distinguished consideration and the respect with which I have the honor to be, Sir,

Your very humble and very obedient servant POINSOT

I enclose here General Kosciuszko's letter
My next letter, via Bordeaux, will bring you the duplicate—The present letter will be delivered to you care of Mr. Isaac Cox Barnet, consul at Paris

[*Additional postscript in Dupl, on verso of endorsement leaf:*]
According to the map, these lands seem to be situated between 38 and 39 degrees of latitude. The longitude from Paris is 84 degrees, in the beautiful valley of the Kanawha River—it would be good to know their precise location, their distance from villages—as well as road communications, etc.

RC (DLC); at foot of first page: "Monsieur Thomas Jefferson Esq[r]"; endorsed by TJ as received 24 Sept. 1817 and so recorded in SJL; with TJ's additional notation (torn) beneath endorsement: "1817. Dec. 30. duplicate [encl]osed to Jos. C. Cabell." Dupl (DLC); dated 10 July 1817; endorsed by TJ as received 29 Sept. 1817 and so recorded in SJL. Enclosures: (1) Land grant by Governor Patrick Henry to "Peter Poinsot Des-Essart," Richmond, 23 May 1785, stating that by virtue of Land Office Treasury Warrant 10,518, issued 7 Dec. 1781 (20 Dec. 1781 in French Trs), Poinsot, as assignee of Honoré Giround, Hedgman Triplett, and Champion Travis, is granted 1,200 acres of land in Monongalia County on the headwaters of the west fork of the Little Kanawha River as described in a survey dated 4 Aug. 1784 (4 May in French Trs) (FC in Lb in Vi: RG 4, Land Office Grants, O:621; Tr in DLC: TJ Papers, 212:37825–6, in the hands of two clerks, with signed attestation by William G. Pendleton, Richmond, 24 Jan. 1818, docketed as a copy made for Joseph C. Cabell for a fee of $1, and with Governor James P. Preston's appended certification that Pendleton is register of the Virginia Land Office, in a clerk's hand and signed by Preston, Richmond, 26 Jan. 1818, enclosed in Cabell to TJ, 6 Feb. 1818; Tr in DLC: TJ Papers, 213:38085, in French, entirely in Poinsot's hand and certified by him in Cette, 18 June 1817, with plat at head of text and including notation that on 23 May 1786 he paid Samuel McCraw land taxes of £3 in Virginia currency at a rate of five francs per acre, and ending with an explanation of the loss of the original land-grant document and the circumstances of its translation into French, enclosed in RC of covering letter; Tr in DLC: TJ Papers, 210:37517, in French, entirely in Poinsot's hand and certified by him at Cette, 10 July 1817, with plat at head of text and including same notation on payment to McCraw and same observation at the end, enclosed in Dupl of covering letter). (2) Tadeusz Kosciuszko to TJ, 3 June 1817. Enclosed with first enclosure in TJ to Cabell, 31 Dec. 1817, and Cabell to TJ, 6, 13 Feb. 1818.

Peter Poinsot swore an oath of allegiance and fidelity (as "Peter Poinsot des Essarts") to the United States in Philadelphia in 1784. By 1805 he had returned to France, where his landholdings included a vineyard in Gigean, near Cette. Poinsot served as a tax collector in Cette and in 1815 became a chancellor for the British consulate at that port. Between 1817 and 1819 he unsuccessfuly sought an American consular position at Cette, enlisting the assistance of Tadeusz Kosciuszko, whom he had befriended while both were in the United States (Harry H. Pierson, ed., "Excerpts from the Consular Register in the American Consulate General, Paris, France," *New England Historical and Genealogical Register* 110 [1956]: 133; Poinsot file in DNA: RG 59, LAR, 1817–25; Poinsot to Kosciuszko, 12 Feb. 1817 [SzSoSt]).

[1] Preceding two words not in Dupl.

[2] Preceding nine words not in Dupl.

[3] Manuscript: "que les terres que les terres."

[4] Manuscript: "obliger."

[5] Preceding seven words not in Dupl.

[6] Preceding two words not in Dupl.

[7] Text from "ma Seconde" to this point not in Dupl.

To Joel Yancey

DEAR SIR Monticello June 25. 17.

I send off Nace and Philip this morning to assist in your harvest, and intended to have set out myself, but am prevented by the lameness of one of my horses. I am in hopes he will be fit for the road in 2. or 3. days more, and that I shall be close on the heels of the bearers. we begin to cut rye this day and on Monday our wheat will be in order. it is recovered from the fly more than we ever expected. I salute you with friendship & respect TH: JEFFERSON

PoC (MHi); on verso of reused address cover of Charles Willson Peale to TJ, 20 May 1817; at foot of text: "Mr Yancey"; endorsed by TJ.

NACE and PHILIP remained in Bedford County until at least 13 July 1817, when TJ recorded giving them $12\frac{1}{2}$ cents to pay the bridge toll at Lynchburg on the day that he departed Poplar Forest for Monticello (*MB*, 2:1335).

From Joseph Gales (1761–1841)

Sir, Raleigh, June 26, 1817.

Your favor of the 19th inst. inclosing to me $24 for the Register during the last eight years, came duly to hand, and is thankfully acknowledged.

Your Apology for suffering the Acct to run so long is very satisfactory. No order having been recd to discontinue the Paper, it was of course sent on; tho' whenever I have thought on the subject, I thought it probable you might wish to discontinue it, and at length determined to ascertain the fact by forwarding you the Acct

When the Register contains any thing which I think will be interesting to you (which, of course, can seldom happen) a copy shall be forwarded.

I am, very respectfy Your obt Servt Jo. Gales.

RC (MHi); dateline at foot of text; endorsed by TJ as received 15 July 1817 and so recorded in SJL. RC (DLC); address cover only; with PoC of TJ to Jeremiah A. Goodman, 20 July 1817, on verso; addressed: "Hon Thos Jefferson Monticello, Virga"; franked; postmarked Raleigh, 26 June.

From Patrick Gibson

Sir Richmond 26th June 1817

I have received your favor of the 23d inclosing two notes for renewal, which I am sorry to say will not answer, not being written upon stamp'd paper and this is the only manner in which the US: bank will receive it, the other banks have of late also adopted a similar resolution, to have them stamp'd at the Office would cost $10 each—I therefore send you inclosed two stamps for your signature—from the state of your account with me, (a copy of which shall be forwarded to the end of this month) and from the drafts advised, I find the proceeds of your sales will fall much short of your demands, and as $3000 may be obtain'd from the US. bank with as much facility as 2000 I have sent you one of the stamps for the former sum, which I doubt not will meet with your approbation, I have sold the remainder of your flour say 97 bls. S1 fine & 87 fine at $11 Cash it is now offering at $10 on 90d/s2—With great respect I am

Your ob Servt Patrick Gibson

RC (MHi); endorsed by TJ as received 1 July 1817 and so recorded in SJL. RC (MHi); address cover only; with PoC of TJ to Archibald Robertson, [12] Aug. 1817, on verso; addressed: "Thomas Jefferson Esqre Monticello now at Poplar Forest Care of Mr saml J. Harrison Lynchburg"; stamp canceled; postmarked Richmond, 28 June; with additional notation by Gibson: "Mr Harrison will be pleas'd to have this deliver'd as soon as possible." Enclosures not found.

[1]Abbreviation for "Super."

[2]Abbreviation for "days' sight." Manuscript: "^{d}/$_{s}$."

To Benjamin Harrison

Dear Sir Monticello June 26. 17.

The American Philosophical society (at Philadelphia) are in possession of a MS. journal of Col^{o} Byrd, father of the late Col^{o} Wm Byrd, while he was on the line of Virginia & Carolina. I suppose it went with the Westover library & thro' that channel has come to them. it was evidently written by the author for publication, and they mean to print it. the one which, thro' the channel of Col^{o} Nicholas, I have had your permission to read, is a diary of the same survey, yet by no means a copy. each of these contains many and interesting facts & observations which the other has not, each is important as a supplement to the other, and both equally worthy of the good sense of the writer, and of possession by the public. both go to the same object of pourtraying the state of society & manners of that time. I am sure the Philosophical society would be glad to print both at the same time; and the object of this letter is to ask your permission to me to send on to them the copy I hold as yet under your indulgence, with a view to it's being printed? your answer shall determine it's being forwarded to them or returned to yourself without further delay. Accept the assurance of my esteem and respect. Th: Jefferson

PoC (DLC); on verso of reused address cover to TJ; at foot of text: "Benjamin Harrison esq."; endorsed by TJ.

Benjamin Harrison (1787–1842), grandson of Virginia governor Benjamin Harrison (d. 1791), was born at Berkeley plantation in Charles City County. He graduated from the College of William and Mary in 1806. Two years later TJ nominated Harrison to be commissioner of loans for Virginia, but the Senate rejected the appointment. Harrison represented Charles City County in the House of Delegates, 1814–15, and in a state convention opposed to Andrew Jackson's presidential aspirations in 1828. The 1840 census listed him in possession of sixty-eight slaves. The following year he was present at the death of his uncle, United States president William Henry Harrison (Fillmore Norfleet, *Saint-Mémin in Virginia: Portraits and Biographies* [1942], 73, 171–2; Louise Pecquet du Bellet, *Some Prominent Virginia Families* [1907; repr. 1976], 2:519; ViHi: Byrd Family Papers; Richmond *Enquirer*, 11 July 1806; Margaret Page to TJ, 30 Sept. 1808 [MHi]; TJ to Albert Gallatin, 10 Oct. 1808 [NHi: Gallatin Papers]; *JEP*, 2:84, 88 [14 Nov., 6 Dec. 1808]; DNA: RG 29, CS, Charles City Co., 1810–40; Leonard, *General Assembly*, 277; *Richmond Enquirer*, 10 Jan. 1828; Baltimore *Niles' National Register*, 17 Apr. 1841; Washington *Daily National Intelligencer*, 3 Feb. 1842).

To Dominick Lynch

SIR Monticello June 26. 17.

I am very[1] thankful for the honor done me by an association with the American society for the encouragement of domestic manufactures instituted in New York. the history of the last 20. years has been a sufficient lesson for us all to depend for necessaries on ourselves alone: and I hope that 20. years more will place the American hemisphere under a system of it's own, essentially peaceable and industrious, and not needing to extract it's comforts out of the eternal fires raging in the old world. the efforts of the members of your institution being necessarily engaged in their respective vicinages, I consider myself, by their choice, as but a link of union between the promoters there and here of the same patriotic objects. praying you to present to the society my just acknolegements for this mark of attention, I tender to yourself the assurance of my great respect & consideration

TH: JEFFERSON

PoC (CSmH: JF-BA); on verso of left half of reused address cover of Aaron Clark to TJ, 28 May 1817; at foot of text: "Mr Lynch"; endorsed by TJ. Printed in *New-York Evening Post*, 4 Aug. 1817, and elsewhere.

[1] Word not in *New-York Evening Post*.

From Craven Peyton

DEAR SIR Monteagle June 26—17

You was so good as to say You woud give me Your Opinion, On the Deed from Lewis to Lewis, I have therefore sent a Coppy by my Son with the Opinion of Messrs Wickham & Wirt they appear to entartain no doubt, indeed if the case was a doubtfull One I woud endeavour to Compomise, Your goodness in Complying with my wishes in this case, will lay me, Undar the greatest Obligations to You, with Sincere

Esteem Yrs C. PEYTON

RC (ViU: TJP); with TJ's draft notes for his 8 July 1817 response on verso; endorsed by TJ as received 26 June 1817 and so recorded in SJL.

For the DEED from Charles L. Lewis to Charles Lewis and the OPINION by John Wickham and William Wirt, see note to Peyton's second letter of this date.

From Craven Peyton

D. Sir. Monteagle June, 26—17

My Son informs me, You propose makeing up An Opinion in a few days, to give You a More Correct Idea of the case I hear inclose a Coppy of all, the proceeding Testimony &c I assure You it gives me pain to trouble You, it is of such importance to me, & I feal such confidence, in Your Opinion, from that Opinion, my future calculations will be made, from the Maney transactions which has taken place between Us. I feal Confident You will place no Confidence, in C., L., Lewis Deposition, in deed his lettars filed, prove, positively the reverse, togethar with his Deed, I shall always feal the greates pleasure in rendaring You service in Any way within my power, for the trouble I give in this case

with the greatest Esteem C. Peyton

RC (MHi); addressed: "Thomas Jefferson esq Monticello"; endorsed by TJ as received 26 June 1817 and so recorded in SJL.

The proceeding testimony &c probably included the following deeds, as well as a legal opinion that Peyton had solicited from John Wickham and William Wirt, not found, and other unidentified court documents: (1) Deed of 30 July 1802 between Charles L. Lewis and his wife Lucy on one part and their son Charles Lewis on the other, all of Albemarle County, in which Charles L. Lewis deeded 650 acres along the Rivanna River, bounded by the Milton road and Buck Island Creek, to his son for five shillings, the land to be held by Charles Lewis for "the term of his natural life"; specifying that, should the younger Lewis marry, the land would become his in fee simple to pass on to his heirs; but adding that, should he never marry or die without heirs, the land would revert to his sisters; proved by two witnesses at the August 1802 court, and fully proved with a third witness on 2 July 1804 (Albemarle Co. Deed Book, 14:506–7). (2) Deed of 18 July 1804 between Charles Lewis and Craven Peyton, both of Albemarle County, conveying Lewis's interest in the same 650 acres to Peyton for 1,500 pounds; proved at the October 1804 court (Albemarle Co. Deed Book, 15:33–4). (3) Deed of 29 Sept. 1804 between Charles L. Lewis and his wife Lucy on one part and Peyton on the other, all of Albemarle County, conveying the same 650 acres to Peyton for 1,500 pounds; describing the land as having been "conditionally conveyed to Charles L. Lewis Jr and which the sd Peyton has since bought of the said Lewis Jr."; proved at the October 1804 court (Albemarle Co. Deed Book, 15:30–1).

From Benjamin Henry Latrobe

Dear Sir, Washington, June 28th 1817

I have found so much pleasure in studying the plan of your College, that the drawings have grown into a larger bulk than can be conveniently sent by the Mail. If you can point out to me any convenient mode of conveyance within a few days, I should gladly avail myself of it. I have put the whole upon one very large sheet, which I am very unwilling to double; and to roll it on a stick will make it inconvenient for the Mail bag. Colonels M[c]Crae & M[c]Craw of Richmond are now here, & in a week will return. If the conveyance from Richmond is more convenient, they will cheerfully take it thither.

The Capitol is growing into a more intelligible form & arrangement, than it had since its destruction by the British.—If the permanence of the seat of the Government at Washington would not have been endangered by it,—it would have been better in every point of view that the wish of Adm. Cockburn had prevailed over the humanity of Gen[l] Ross, & the whole building had been destroyed by Gunpowder. At a less expense to the U States, a much more convenient, & magnificient building could have been erected, than will be made of the ruins of the former.

Many alterations have been made in the interior. The form of the house of Representatives is changed so as to admit the members to the South windows & the Gallery is of course on the E. N. & West sides.—The Senate Chamber is enlarged to the utmost possible extent which the Walls would permit. The staircase the construction of which you may remember to have been rather singular & the execution uncommonly excellent, is now converted into a Large Vestibule with a rotunda to admit light into the lower story, and a more easy ascent is made by a new Staircase on the S.E. side where a Court was intended by the plan of 1806–7. The President has taken a very strong interest in the completion of the Capitol, & the work is going on as rapidly as Men & money can execute it.

In the National Intelligencer of January 18th 1817 I gave some account of the beautiful Marble of which most of the Columns of the Capitol are to be made.—There are now 9 blocks here, from 6 to 8 feet long each. Three of them make one Column. They are rounded, but not yet polished.—Nothing can exceed the beauty of the Stone when polished, & as the Cement which unites the pebbles does not receive quite so high a polish as the pebbles themselves, the Mass acquires a spangled appearance, which adds greatly to the brilliancy of its effect.

The remark I have made on the difficulty of introducing this marble is not one of those tirades, in which disappointed men are apt to indulge. The opposition of so respectable a Man as M[r] Blagden was to be encountered, & of many others. He reported in writing, that the stone would not bear its own weight, when lewis'ed. I immediately suspended by a small Lewis, a block of 2 Ton weight in the Capitol. He then doubted whether it could be wrought,—& to try the experiment, a small Column 3 inches in diameter which had been wrought & polished, & had been placed in the temporary house of Representatives the whole Session, was knocked to pieces by the Sandstone cutters, & the fragments produced to prove that it could not be wrought or polished. But the President soon decided the contest & there are now 100 Men, laborers & Stonecutters at work in the Quarry.—I presume, that below Your mountain the same stone must be found. It crosses the Rappahannoc in Orange County, in very large Masses.—

I need not assure you, that any opportunity which may occur, to prove to you how sincere is the respect & attachment, which as an individual and as a citizen I feel towards you, will be eagerly seized by me & improved.

Most respectfully Y[rs] B Henry Latrobe.

P.S. I have a rough Stone Model of the Capital of a Column composed of Tobacco leaves & flowers which I wish to send to you. I can easily get it to Richmond by a Coal Vessel returning thither[.] If you will please to let me know to whom I shall direct it, I shall be obliged to You. I will enclose in the box some specimens of the Pebble Marble.— The Capital has too weak an effect, & I intend to cut the relief of the leaves deeper. But it never will equal the Corn capital.

In the printed account of the Marble there are many typographical Errors.—Bedding stone is printed for Pudding stone &c

I write still with Peale's or rather Hawkin's, polygraph,—the same which I have had since 1803.—It is a little crazy, & has lost its spring which I have not been able to replace so that I write a somewhat different hand with the polygraph, from that which I write without it. You had adopted Bolton's manifold Writer when I last saw You, but as your letter is written with common ink I presume you have returned to the Polygraph.

RC (DLC); edge trimmed; at head of text: "Tho[s] Jefferson Esq[r] Monticello"; endorsed by TJ as received 15 July 1817 and so recorded in SJL; with TJ's notes for his 16 July 1817 reply beneath postscript: "has taken too much trouble with
drawings
send by mail
the new marble
send capital to G. & J. Richm[d]
Polygraph."

Latrobe's letter to the editors describing the discovery and character of marble used in the United States Capitol was dated JANUARY 18TH 1817 and published in the Washington *Daily National Intelligencer* of 24 Jan. 1817 (Latrobe, *Papers*, 3:851–6). An image of Latrobe's capital for a column decorated with TOBACCO LEAVES & FLOWERS is reproduced elsewhere in this volume (see also his 5 Nov. 1816 letter to TJ).

From Richard Peters

Dear Sir Belmont June 28th 1817.

I waited for a monthly Meeting of our agricultural Society, before acknowledging the Receipt of your kind & polite Attention to my Request, in sending the Hill-side plough. I had it placed in the Society's Ware-room; where it will be viewed by those who will take Advantage of it, as a Pattern. The Society were much pleased with the Present, & very thankful to you for the Donation; which evinces your Disposition to promote all Objects calculated to forward the public Prosperity; whereof Agriculture is, most assuredly, the Foundation. Our Farmers live comfortably with indifferent Husbandry; our public Burthens being light, & our Country affording a Retreat from impoverished Soils, to those fertile, & easily attainable. A few Implements suffice, in the present State of Things; but Necessity will multiply the Kinds & Numbers of farming Utensils & Implements; & we shall perceive more than we now do, that the Tools of a Farmer should be calculated for his local Situation, as well as the different Operations his Art requires. Your Account of the Hill-side plough, & its profitable Application to the Tillage of Surfaces whereon the common Plough is very defective, both in its immediate Uses & their Consequences, should convince all concerned in Husbandry, that their Stock of Tools should be composed of every Instrument required in the different Branches of their Business, as necessarily as those of an Artisan. The Adaptation of Ploughs to the Nature & Attributes of the Soils on which they are to operate, is all essential. Aration being the most indispensable of all other Branches of Husbandry, should be performed with Tools the most perfect & appropriate. And yet, in some of the best cultivated Countries in Europe, the Ploughs arc among the worst Instruments they possess; & the Ploughing far short of Perfection.

I received & communicated to the Society, Col Randolph's Explanation of the Parts of the Plough. He has great Merit in bringing so valuable an Instrument into Use; & is entitled to our best Thanks for diffusing a Knowledge of it. We will have it rendered perfect, by supplying the Parts mentioned by him as being necessary in its Operation, & will have a Trial made of its Application to the Grounds for which it is calculated.

Our Accounts from different Parts of Pennsylvania, Jersey, & New York, as[1] to the State of Crops, are very flattering. The Indian Corn has fared the worst; owing to the Ravages of the Cutworm. The Hessian Fly has been destructive, in some Fields; but, in general, the Crops both of Grain & Grass, promise great Abundance. I never had better Winter Grain; tho' the Fly is among it. My Straw is strong; & resists the Impression [m]ade by the Flaxseed-like Tegument, containing the Progeny of the Fly; & this is the great Cause of its Injuries; & not as many suppose, its consuming the Plants or the Grain. In many Parts of Maryland, & the Seaboard Country of Virginia, the Intelligence we receive is gloomy enough. But from the upper Country of both those States, we have pleasing Accounts; not, however, unmixed with some Alloy.

I hope you enjoy good Health, the Cordial of advanced Life. In the Commencement of my 74th Year, I have Reason to be grateful to the Almighty, that he has favoured me with Blessing of Health, whilst most People so far on their Journey to a better World, are afflicted with some chronic Disease. Some temporary Complaints, of no long Continuance, I have occasionally; but in general I enjoy a better State of Health, than falls to the Lot of old Bipeds.

We have lost our old Governor & Chief Justice, McKean; who lived to a good old Age. With all his Failings, he was respectable in our public Affairs; & "has done the State some Service." Yet his Faults will be remembered by many, who will either forget, or want the Candour to acknowledge, his good Deeds. Such is the Fate of too many who have appeared on the public Stage; not only in this our Day, but in past times. And there is little Difference in human Nature, be the Form of Government under which Men live, what it may. The Art of writing History is difficult, & its Productions seldom correct. We who live in times the most remarkable for uncommon & almost incredible Events, do not easily arrive at the Truth of Facts passing in a Manner before our Eyes; yet we suppose that those who write an hundred Years hence, will impartially & truly represent them. Having myself been intimately acquainted with very many of[2] the Transactions of an important Period of our national Existence, I read History with no implicit Faith; because my Knowledge of many things does not accord with the public Account of them. Biographers are led away by personal Attachments, or Antipathies. Yet there is enough of Truth, both in History & Biography, to make Individuals less selfish, & Governments more wise. I therefore take them both for better or worse; & jog on contented with the Instruction & Entertainment they afford. We have exhibited a brilliant Phœnomenon in the History of Nations; about which Historians will differ, as much as Philosophers now do as to the Spots in the Sun. We have arrived to such an Eminence of Wealth & Prosperity, with the Capacity to defend them, with any tolerable Management, against all Assailants, (except, probably, ourselves,) as none of us who laboured in our Revolution, could have anticipated; tho' our Predictions did not want Enthusiasm or Confidence. These Predictions, or rather zealous Hopes, were the Stimuli which urged us on, thro' many a dreary Day. Few of us expected to see them realized; & indeed there are but few who have lived to witness them. Yet if some Seer had truly foretold them, we should have set him down as a false Prophet, or a Madman. Recollecting the many Vicissitudes & dangerous Passages we went through; I often wonder not only at our providential Escapes, but at the Magnitude of the Enjoyments our Labours have afforded, to those who neither then toiled or spun. I always feel an Impulse of Affection when I see one of our old Coadjutors, let his Rank or Condition in Life be what it may; nor do I experience the least Degree of Envy, when I see those who profit by our Toils. There is Nothing selfish in my Pleasures on this Score; for I have gained as little by my Share in our revolutionary Struggle, as any Individual engaged in it. I enjoy, in common with others of this Day, the Light of our political Constellation; & tho' there may be Spots in our Luminary; yet I anticipate its shining brightly, when I can no longer enjoy its Beams. You must excuse this rhapsodical Effusion; for my Mind has a Kind of annual Visitation of such Ideas, when the 4th of July approaches. The Fall of an old revolutionary Companion, too, brings forward such recollections & it seem[s] weakening an old Arch, sufficiently wrecked by the Dilapidations of Time. There are but few of the Bricks left; & the whole will shortly tumble; & mix with the Clay from which they sprang. New Structures rise on its Ruins; & long may <u>they</u> defy the Tooth of Time!

Under the Influence of revolutionary Sympathies, & long personal Esteem, accept of my best Wishes, & Assurances of the respectful Consideration with which I am

truly yours RICHARD PETERS

RC (DLC); edge chipped; endorsed by TJ as received 15 July 1817 and so recorded in SJL. RC (DLC); address cover only; with PoC of TJ to James Madison, 23 July 1817, on verso; addressed: "Thomas Jefferson Esqr Monticello Virginia"; stamp canceled; franked; postmarked Philadelphia, 30 June.

Thomas Mann RANDOLPH'S EXPLANATION and an engraving of his hillside plow were published in the Philadelphia Society for Promoting Agriculture's *Memoirs* 4 (1818): 18 (p. misnumbered "81"). HAS DONE THE STATE SOME SERVICE comes from William Shakespeare, *Othello*, act 5, scene 2. In the Bible, the lilies of the field NEITHER THEN TOILED OR SPUN (Matthew 7.28; Luke 12.27).

[1] Reworked from "Pennsylvania & Jersey, as."

[2] Preceding three words interlined.

To Craven Peyton

DEAR SIR Monticello June 28. 17.

I have your papers under consideration, and altho' I think myself tolerably satisfied on the subject, yet, as I am about setting out to Bedford and too much pressed with preparations for that journey, I would rather keep them till my return (a fortnight hence) as both there as well as on the road I can consider it more uninterruptedly. if the letters of Col^{o} Lewis[1] N° 1. to 26. referred to in Hening's depn are in your hands I should like to see them. but above all there is a matter of evidence, which I doubt not is in your favor, is important, and yet wholly passed over in the answer and depositions. the deed of 1802. was not[2] proved by the 3^{d} witness till July 2. 1804. your deed was executed 16. days after[3] but when was your bargain with Charles Lewis concluded, because the constructive notice arising from the record of the deed could not operate till July 2. & altho your deed is 16. days later, yet I have no doubt your bargain <u>verbally</u>, if not <u>written</u> was concluded before July 2. Hening can probably say when he was applied to to value the lands, and draw the deed. very likely the application to him was on that very court day, July 2. if not before. the bargain must have been concluded before he was applied to.[4] state this fact to me by memory if you can. I inclose you the subscription paper of our [col]lege; if this succeeds our neighborhood will become the central object of the state. and it's importance to yourself as the father of sons to be educated will be of immediate consequence; for if we can raise enough to effect the establishment we mean to begin with a grammar school in April next, and in the course of the next summer to build for 3. other professors. the payments are made quite easy. be so good as to subscribe your name and contributions, which I am sure will be as liberal as they ought to be. I salute you with friendship and esteem. TH: JEFFERSON

P.S. return the paper by the bearer if you please.

PoC (MHi); on verso of reused address cover and postscript to Henry A. S. Dearborn to TJ, 1 May 1817; mutilated at seal, with some text rewritten by TJ; at foot of text: "Mr Peyton"; endorsed by TJ.

For examples of the enclosed SUBSCRIPTION PAPER, see document 4 in a group of documents on The Founding of the University of Virginia: Central College, 1816–1819, printed above at 5 May 1817.

[1] Word interlined.
[2] Word interlined.
[3] Word interlined.
[4] Sentence interlined.

From Craven Peyton

DEAR SIR. Monteagle July [June] 28–1817.

In Answar to Yours of today, the bargain was made with C. Lewis several weeks before the Deed was executed & it was several weeks before, that M Henning was spoken to, to make the valuation, I held a lien,[1] on the Land from C. Lewis dated some little time aftar the deed from his Farthar & the Land nevar was in the possession of C. Lewis. this point nevar was named by Any of my Councel, Col^{o} Lewis Lettars are all filed,[2] I will have Coppies of them by Your return, if You wish, will you do me the favour to Inclose Wickhams & Wirts Opinion & I will send for the papar tomorrow, Undar my presant situation, & state of suspence, I feal loth to put my name to the Subscription papar, my Family is very large, & if I am Cast in this suite, my funds may fall short, it is my intention & wish to subscribe liberally—if my funds will permit.

with sincere Esteem C. PEYTON

RC (MHi); misdated; endorsed by TJ as a letter of 28 "<*July*> June" 1817 received 28 June 1817. Recorded in SJL as a letter of 28 June 1817 received the same day.

CAST: "to defeat in an action at law" (*OED*).

[1] Manuscript: "lion."
[2] Manuscript: "filled."

To John Vaughan

DEAR SIR Monticello June 28. 17.

Your two letters of the 2^{d} and 18th have been recieved in due time. mine of the 7th had partly anticipated your requests of the 2^{d}

I thank you for the advance to mr Girard, and now inclose 70.D. to cover it in bills of the Virginia bank which I understand pass with you. the duplicates you advise for Cathalan & Debures, I had sent thro' the Secretary of State's office. I shall be glad to subscribe for the volume of transactions now in the press, and ask the favor of you to have my name placed on the subscription paper. but I have nothing to offer for insertion in it. in earlier life when I should from inclination have devoted myself to pursuits analogous to those of our society, my time was all engrossed by public duties, and now without either books or memory I could offer nothing which would do credit either to the society or myself. you enquire for the Indian vocabularies of Messrs Lewis and Clarke. all their papers are at present under a kind of embargo. they consist of 1. Lewis's MS. pocket journals of the journey. 2. his Indian Vocabularies. 3. his astronomical observations, particularly for the longitudes. 4. his map, and drawings. a part of these papers were deposited with Dr Barton; some with mr Biddle, others I know not where. of the pocket journals Mr Correa got 4. out of 11. or 12. from mrs Barton & sent them to me. he informed me that mr Biddle would not think himself authorised to deliver the portion of the papers he recieved from Genl Clarke without his order; whereon I wrote to Genl Clarke, & recieved his order for the whole some time ago. but I have held it up until a Secretary at War[1] is appointed, that office having some rights to these papers. as soon as that appointment is made, I shall endeavor to collect the whole, to deposite the MS. journals & Vocabularies with the Philosophical society, adding a collection of some vocabularies made by myself, and to get the Sec^y at War to employ some person to whom I may deliver the Astronomical papers for calculation, and the geographical ones for the correct execution of a map; for in that published with his journal, altho' the latitudes may be correct, the longitudes cannot be. I wait therefore only for this appointment to begin my endeavors for a compleat collection and distribution of these papers. the historical committee were so kind as to send me Col^o Byrd's MS. journal of the survey of the boundary between N. Carolina & Virginia. I am in negociation with the family to obtain his private journal of the same expedition containing much matter not in the public one, equally curious, and equally worthy of being printed. as soon as I obtain a definitive answer I shall return them theirs, and the other also if I can obtain leave. Accept my friendly and respectful salutations. TH: JEFFERSON

RC (PPAmP: Thomas Jefferson Papers); addressed: "John Vaughan esquire Philadelphia"; franked; postmarked Charlottesville, 1 July; endorsed in an unidentified hand as received 4 July, with additional notation in Vaughan's hand that it "remits 70$" and an unrelated sketch in an unidentified hand. PoC (DLC); on verso of reused address cover of Richard Rush to TJ, 3 May 1817 (noted above at Madame de Staël Holstein to TJ, 12 Feb. 1817); endorsed by TJ.

[1] Word interlined, with "was" left uncanceled on the line.

From George Crowninshield

MUCH RESPECTED SIR Marseilles 30th June 1817

Stephen Cathalan Esq^e the United States Consul for this place, having accumulated an ample fortune, and being desirous of retiring from active life, has resigned his Office to Mr Joshua Dodge an established Commission Merchant at this place, and is very highly esteemed and beloved; this Gentleman is in my opinion every way qualified for the Office, and should he obtain the appointment from our government, I am persuaded he would do honor to the United States.—

At this place are many Commission Merchants, and I am very possitive that no new establishment from the United States could obtain a living, as the Commerce from the United States to this port is not sufficient to support more than those already established: and it requires an acquaintance with the business and the language, which Mr Dodge is perfectly acquainted with, having resided here for some time.—Mr Dodge is related to our family, and was educated in the Counting house of the late firm of George Crowninshield & Sons of which I was a Partner, I know him to be correct, capable & very active; And respected Sir, permit me to refer you for further information respecting Mr Dodge to my Brother the Honble Secretary of the Navy of the United States.—Any assistance you may please to offer to obtain Mr Dodge the appointment of Consul for Marceilles will infinitely oblige one, who has the Honor to be with every sentiment of Respect and Esteem,

Sir,

Your most obedient, Humble and devoted servant

George Crowninshield

RC (DLC); in a clerk's hand, signed by Crowninshield; between dateline and salutation: "Thomas Jefferson Esq^e^"; endorsed by TJ as received 27 Oct. 1817 and so recorded in SJL. Enclosed in Stephen Cathalan to TJ, 8 July 1817, and probably in Benjamin W. Crowninshield to TJ, 26 Dec. 1817.

George Crowninshield (1766–1817), merchant and yacht traveler, was born into a wealthy merchant family in Salem, Massachusetts. At an early age he was sent to sea as a captain's clerk. Crowninshield went on to captain ships in the West and East Indies before returning to Salem in about 1800 to assist his father in the countinghouse of the family firm, George Crowninshield & Sons, which was reorganized in 1809 as George Crowninshield & Company. In August 1813 Crowninshield sailed one of his family's ships to Canada to retrieve the bodies of American naval officers killed in the capture of the USS *Chesapeake*. The family firm dissolved following the death of his father in 1815. Crowninshield retired at that point as a wealthy man and began constructing *Cleopatra's Barge*, reportedly the first American yacht built solely for pleasure. He set sail for the Mediterranean on the vessel in March 1817. After attracting large crowds but none of the royalty he hoped to entertain, Crowninshield returned to Salem and died on board his yacht (*ANB*; *DAB*; David L. Ferguson, *Cleopatra's Barge: The Crowninshield Story* [1976], 83–118; Madison, *Papers, Pres. Ser.*, 4:337, 6:450–2, 544–5; Salem *Essex Register*, 21 June 1809; *Salem Gazette*, 28 Nov. 1817).

Joshua Dodge (1791–1872), merchant and diplomat, was born in Salem, Massachusetts, attended Phillips Academy in Andover about 1802, and trained in the countinghouse of George Crowninshield & Sons. Dodge arrived in France about 1809. By 1815 he was a commission merchant in Marseille working with several Massachusetts firms, and that same year he began to solicit appointment as the port's consul. In 1817 Dodge made an agreement with the incumbent consul, Stephen Cathalan, that allowed Cathalan to remain in the position while Dodge took over the duties. Cathalan retained the title of consul and a portion of the accompanying remuneration but agreed to help Dodge obtain the position officially when he did resign, with this assistance to come, in part through Cathalan's friendship with TJ. Following Cathalan's death in May 1819, Dodge was appointed temporary consul at Marseille by Albert Gallatin, the United States minister plenipotentiary to France. President James Monroe gave Dodge the permanent appointment later in the year. He served until President Andrew Jackson removed him about 1830. From 1820 onwards Dodge helped TJ procure wines from Europe, both as an individual and after 1821 through his firm, Dodge & Oxnard. In 1823 he spent a week visiting TJ at Monticello. President Jackson appointed Dodge consul at Bremen in 1834. He held this post until 1839 and ended his diplomatic service shortly thereafter as a special agent attending to the interests of the American tobacco trade with Europe (*Biographical Catalogue of the Trustees, Teachers and Students of Phillips Academy, Andover, 1778–1830* [1903], 47; Benjamin W. Crowninshield to TJ, 20 Sept. 1817; Dodge to TJ, 26 May 1819, with enclosures, and 7 July 1823; Ellen W. Randolph [Coolidge] to Nicholas P. Trist, 28 Mar. 1823 [DLC: Nicholas P. Trist Papers]; DNA: RG 59, LAR, 1809–25; *MB*; *JEP*, 3:186, 197, 4:52, 344, 348, 5:241 [3, 31 Jan. 1820, 3 Feb. 1830, 21 Jan., 10 Feb. 1834, 14 Jan. 1840]; Washington *Daily National Intelligencer*, 1 Feb. 1842; *Boston Daily Advertiser*, 5 Oct. 1872; gravestone inscription in Mount Auburn Cemetery, Cambridge, Mass.).

Dodge was RELATED to the Crowninshields through his mother, Elizabeth Crowninshield Dodge, who was a cousin to George and Benjamin W. Crowninshield (*Sibley's Harvard Graduates*, 17:505; Joseph Thompson Dodge, *Genealogy of the Dodge Family of Essex County, Mass 1629–1894* [1894], 143; *The Diary of William Bentley, D.D. Pastor of the East Church Salem, Massachusetts* [1905–14], 4:335–6).

From Donald Fraser

VENERABLE SIR. New York June 30th 1817.

Knowing that your useful life, for upwards of Fifty Years past has been Devoted to the promotion of the best Interest of your beloved country, in various important stations; As a member of the Legislature of your native State; Governor of the Same; as an Ambassador to a foreign Court; Secretary of State; & lastly President of these U. States—The Duties of all which offices, you have, as History will record; performed with Integrity and great ability.

Two cogent reasons induced me to intrude upon your avowed & desired privacy; at your advanced age:

First, to evince, that I had not forgotten, your liberality towards me, some Years ago; when I had lost, the fruits of many Years' Industry, by misplaced confidence.

Secondly—I frequently ruminate of the three Corinthian Pillars, of the American Revolution—George Washington, Thomas Jefferson & Benjn Franklin: whose names, will doubtless, be held in high veneration, by the American Nation, for many Centuries to come; & revered,

& admired, by all the lovers of rational Liberty, throughout the civilized world.

The Idea Struck me, that, if I could convey anything that might, in the smallest degree, amuse, the only survivor of those three eminent Patriots, a small portion of my time, could not be Employed to a better purpose. But, I have not the vanity to suppose, that the present communication, can convey much Novelty, to a person of your extensive reading; yet, triffles, light as air, may at times, afford some amusement to a Philosopher, after profound reflection; and I've Somewhere read, that the celebrated Logiccion, John Locke, used to read Romances for his amusement, occasionally. I have, occasionally, for these Sixteen Years past wrote some pieces in Defence of the General Government. When that malignant caluminator; William Coleman the Editor of the "Evening-Post" Printed here; carpt & Distorted every Speech & Message, Delivered by Presidents Jefferson and Madison to Congress.

The two following pieces, which You may not have Seen, I wrote in Defence of my friend, the present V. President,

To the Editor of the "National Advocate."

Sir—Upon perusing m^r Coleman's Strictures of friday last, relative to a certain pecuniary transaction, in which Govr Tompkins was an Agent; I was Struck, with m^r Coleman's attempts to hold forth, one of our most incorruptible[1] & Excellent Patriots, (a man of irreproachible character, in every Stage of his public life) as a Swindler! I am an old man, & remember, many adages; I'll give you a common one—"Not to estimate any man's character, from the applause of his friends, nor the calumination of his enemies." If my memory serves me, the following sentiments are contained in letters, which I received, from two Great and good men, now no more!—"I have read your remarks on Party-Spirit; they are well-founded. It is greatly to be lamented, that Party politicians are so little inclined to do justice to their opponents[2] merits. Benjn Rush."

"A thorough-paced party politician, censures, that he approves of: he confides in men whom he heartily despises; He opposes the measures of his antagonist, tho, his reason tells him, they are proper[3]

Robt R. Livingston."

Wm Coleman's remarks on the foregoing piece.

"A writer, in the National Advocate, under the Signature of an old Citizen; Quotes, with great form & ceremony the sayings of Dr Rush & Chancellor Livingston; in order to assist Governor Tompkins, on the present occasion; whom, he calls, an incorruptible & excellent

Patriot.—I tell these people again, the Advocate its Editor & correspondents, that I will not be diverted from my object."
[Novr 8th 1815.[4]]—My Second piece.
Mr Philips—I have read a number of Anecdotes. The following one, in my opinion, is very applicable to the present state of Parties, in this Country:—A certain wealthy English Baronet, had an only Son, a mere Dolt.—His father Sent him to several eminent Teachers; none of whom, could make a Scholar of this heir to an ancient[5] family#—. The Father therefore, applied to the late accomplished Earl of Chesterfield, to recommend him a proper Tutor for his Darling Son; Chesterfield, pointed out to him Dr Bushby:—"What, exclaimed the Baronet, with Surprize, Dont Your Lordship know? that Dr B. is a Whig, & a warm opposer of our Party?—I can't think of entrusting him with my Son; as he might poison his mind with his own principles." Chesterfield, replied—Dr B. is a very honest and a learned man; he'll do justice bye Your Son: he has adhered to his Party in the worst as well as the best of times; & never changed Sides: When in office, I endeavored to retain it, by every method I could think of; when turned out, I tried hard to get in again: wrote and spoke against my opponents.—Now, the Erudite Editor of the Evening-Post, has certainly, followed Chesterfields maxim, in Politics:—As he has uniformly, for these fifteen years past, caluminated a Jefferson, a Madison, & now a Tompkins: From what motive is best Known to himself; whether from selfish or Patriotic motives.—I am, conscious, that their are Some genuine Patriots on the Federal Side; Such as John Jay &c. whom, I Should be sorry to see any Republican Editor, treat with personal abuse; as Wm Coleman has Some of the most reputable characters in the Republican Side.

A friend to the People.[6]

Novr 11. 1816. or, 15.'—
[William Coleman, did not think proper to make any reply to my Second piece]

Anecdotes: Some of which probably Sir, you may have previously met with.

#The foregoing anecdote, reminded me of the following remark, which I'd read some years ago:—A wealthy Roman Citizen, had an only Son, whom no Teacher could learn. His father heard of Socrate's fame, went to Athens with him, offered, Socrates one half of his fortune if he'd make his Son a Schollar. The Philosopher, replied—"My Mother, was a mid-wife; but She could never Deliver a woman, unless She was first with Child;—If Nature, has given Your Son a capacity, I'll try to make him a Schollar; but, not otherwise"

N° 1. In 1784. A Capt. Blake, a Sturdy-Irish man, who served with Credit, in our Revolutionary war, went to London, where he was informed, that a certain Cockney Shop-keeper, there, was in the habit of Burlesquing every Irish man, that came in his way: Capt B. went to his Shop, & enquired for some Red-Scarlet!! with the full Brogue accent. The Shop-Keeper Shewed him some Green blue &c—Paddy, did[7] not like his conduct, & resolved to be revenged of him—Hence, he pointed at a piece of White Casimere which lay under some other pieces; whilst the Cockney was pulling it out Capt. B— gave him a violent blow on the nose, which made the blood gush out freely, upon the Cloth.—Paddy said "now my honey—Thats the ting I want by my Shoul. cut me off two yards of it here's the mony; & for the future, take care how you Burlesque Irish folks."

N° 2. Jemmy[8] Boswel, one day, Said to Saml Johnson, when I used to sit with you & drink wine, it used to make my head ache—Johnson, Sir, it is not the wine, that you drank, which made[9] your head ache, Boswell[10]—Indeed! Doctor, you don't tell me So! Indeed Sir, I do tell You So. Boswell, then D^r^ what was it that made my head ache?—Johnson, in his usual Surly manner, Said—The Sense that I put into it. Boswel, What Dr Does Sense, make the head ache? Johnson, yes, Sir, when the head is not used to it!—

N° 3. When this learned English big Brute travelled into the Highlands of Scotland; he put up Some Days, at the Castle of the Laird of M^c^Leod of Rassae: whose Lady, was a very accomplished woman; She passed sometime in London & Paris:—They one night, had Green pease at Supper, in the month of November, being raised in a hot-house: Lady M^c^Leod, asked him how[11] he liked their Highland pease?—Johnson, O! Madam, they might serve well enough for Hogs in England; Then Sir, Says She, help youself!!

N° 4. A Gent^man^ Knowing Dr Johnson's aversion to Scotsmen, laid another; of five Guineas, that Johnson, would not Speake well of any Caledonian.—They both went together to the Doctor's lodging: when one of them asked him, what he thought of Lord Mansfield? "What do I think of him; that he is a truly great & good man." "But, D^r^ he's a Scochman" I Know that; but he came[12] to Westminster School, at the age of seven years; I never Said, that a Scotsman, might not turn out to be a clever fellow, if they were caught when[13] young: For, the very cattle of Scotland, will get larger & better when Brought to England!!

N° 5. Soon after the peace, or rather, truce of Amïens, was concluded, between the French, & the English, the Fashion was, of wearing long whiskers declining; among the Gent, of[14] England; a Young Nobleman, made one, in a Dinner party; which, mr Curran,[15] the celebratd Irish advocate, graced with his presence; my Lord, says Curran, who seeing the young officer's cheeks were Shaded with an enormous grove of hair, my Lord, when do you put your whiskers upon the peace establishment? When you put your tongue, upon the Civil list!—

I can Rhyme readily, but I'm no Poet.

As the following verses will fully evince.

[Halls' History of the late war—page,[16] 278th]

... "Among others, the numerous Society of Free-Masons, joined in a body, headed by their Grand-Master: Proceeded to Brooklyne heights (opposite to New York) & assisted, very Spiritedly in the Defence of the City—: on this occasion, an elderly Gent one of the order, who had two Sons officers in the army one of whom had Distinguished himself highly, during the war, for his wounds & Bravery; sung the following Stanzas, in his own Character, of Mason & Father, whilst the Lodge was at refreshment.

Hail Children of light, whom the Charities Send,
Where the blood-hounds of Britain, are shortly expect'd:
Who, Your Country, Your wives & firesides to defend,
On the Summit of Brooklyne, have ramparts erect'd.
Firm and true to the trade, continue your aid,
'Till the topstone, with Shouting triumphantlys laid:
The Free & accepted, will never despair;
Led on by their worthy Grand-master & Mayor.
For me, whose dismissal must shortly arrive,
To Heaven, I prefer this my fervent Petition,
May I never America's freedom Survive;
Nor, behold her disgrac'd by a Slavish Submission:
And, tho, righteously Steel'd, if at last She must Yield;
May my Sons do their duty, or die in the field!"[17]

Lines Spoken on Brooklyne heights, Septr 2d 1815:
... When working with the Teachers, Being formerly one.

1. Well, when our daily work is done,
   Which will be at the setting sun:
   Molasses, Pork, & pumpkin pie,
   I vow we'll eat before we die:

2d You must not think us barren fools—
   Because we are pent up in Schools:
   And, shou'd the foe, but make a breach,
   We shall to them good-manners teach:

3d Our Country Shall continue free,
As long as we teach, A— B. C.
And, if a foe Should tread our Sod,
They'll find, how we can use the rod.

Lines Spoken when working with the Caledonian Society; my countrymen; many of whom are Tories.[18] Such Sentiments as I, could wish them to entertain

Our Native-land, & friends respect,
All foreign influence reject:
The works we are raising, we firmly intend,
With our lives & our Fortunes, 'till Death to defend:
And, he that won't fight, when his country's in Danger;
He's unworthy our notice, like a Dog in a menger

My Son Donalds toast at a public Dinner on the 28th Novr 1814—on the Frontiers.—"The county of Ontario, The army of the U.S. when in great Jeopardy at Erie; her young men flew to their aid; & Sunk all party distinctions, of Feds & Demos. into that of American-free men."

The person who has taken the liberty of addressing you at present has not the honor of a personal acquaintance; yet, he trusts, that the well-known Suavity, of your manners, will induce you to pardon the length & freedom of this Communication—: Im a Native of the Highlands of Scotland—In my 67th—44. of which, I've been in America—My father, Col. Thos Fraser, was wounded in the Decissive battle of Culodon, April 1745; where, their were 240 Frasers present—He never liked the Hanoverian Kings, nor myself,—nor my eldest Son Donald, neither:—He has been four times wounded, in as many hard fought battles—The Capture of "York"[19] & Fort George, the bloody battle of Chepawa, & lastly at the famous Sortie from Erie; where he was Shot through the Leg, in the act of Spiking one of the Enemy's Cannon; as Genl Porters letter to Government mentions: Thank God, he can still walk & ride—: The Government has been very liberal towards him, being twice Brevetted; lastly from a first Lieut. to a Major—He's now Secy to Genl Porter, one of the commissioners for Settling the Boundary line, agreeably to the Treaty of Ghent. Has been Aide camp to Generals Pike Porter & Brown.—The name of[20] that able Statesman, & amiable character James Madison, Shall be ever held in high estimation by me, for his Liberality towards my Son, by giving a full Majors Pension: which he has transferred to me, to soothe my declining age—: May he be, not only temporally rewarded here, but eternally hereafter.—Your being a Parent Yourself, will induce you to pardon the partiality of a father.

That your health may be preserved for some years, here, & be eternally happy in the next world, Is the Sincere wish of Sir, Your Obd[t] humble Servant. DONALD FRASER SEN[R]

RC (MHi); brackets and ellipses in original; dateline at foot of text; numbered at head of each page in Fraser's hand; sent in two sections, with pp. 1–3 enclosed in an address cover labeled by Fraser as "N° 1" and addressed: "Thomas Jefferson Esq[r] Late President of the U. States Monticella Virginia"; franked; postmarked New York, 30 June, and pp. 4–6 enclosed in an address cover labeled by Fraser as "N° 2" and similarly addressed, franked, and postmarked; endorsed by TJ (on second address cover) as a letter of 3 June 1817 received 15 July 1817 and so recorded (with correct date of composition) in SJL.

Fraser also quoted his NOV[R] 8TH 1815 New York *National Advocate* article in his letter to TJ of 2 June 1816, and he repeated his NOV[R] 11 1815 article from the same newspaper in his letters to TJ of 2 and 27 June 1816. Anecdote N° 2 can be found in James Boswell, *The Life of Samuel Johnson LL.D.* (London, 1791), 2:286. A version of anecdote N° 4 is in Boswell, *Life of Johnson*, 1:381. Fraser's 1 Sept. 1814 verses on the construction of Fort Masonic were published beginning on the 278TH page of Gilbert J. Hunt, *The Late War, between the United States and Great Britain … written in the ancient historical style* (New York, 1816; Poor, *Jefferson's Library*, 5 [no. 144]), and were included, along with the succeeding verses SPOKEN ON BROOKLYNE HEIGHTS, in Fraser to TJ, 27 June 1816.

The Battle of Culloden (CULODON) actually took place on 16 Apr. 1746. Fraser wrote to JAMES MADISON on 8 June 1817 to thank the latter for the pension awarded to Fraser's namesake son (Madison, *Papers, Retirement Ser.*, 1:56–7).

[1] Manuscript: "incorrupible."
[2] Preceding two words interlined in place of "each others."
[3] Superfluous closing quotation mark editorially omitted.
[4] Reworked from "1816."
[5] Manuscript: "ancint."
[6] Unmatched closing quotation mark editorially omitted.
[7] Manuscript: "did did."
[8] Manuscript: "Jemny."
[9] Manuscript: "mad."
[10] First three-page section ends here with the catch word "Boswell," spelled "Bosewel" in the continuation.
[11] Manuscript: "asked the how."
[12] Manuscript: "he came he came."
[13] Manuscript: "whn."
[14] Manuscript: "of of."
[15] Manuscript: "Currurran."
[16] Manuscript: "page, page."
[17] Omitted closing quotation mark editorially supplied.
[18] Fraser here inserted a # sign. No matching author footnote keyed to this symbol has been found.
[19] Inconsistent closing single quotation mark editorially changed to a closing double quotation mark.
[20] Manuscript: "of of."

From Horatio G. Spafford

RESPECTED FRIEND— Albany, 6 Mo. 30, 1817.

Although I have not any thing to communicate that might Seem to excuse this Letter, yet, being about to remove from this State, & to abandon, for years, my late pursuits, I feel a desire to apprize thee of my intention & prospects. Weary of literary labors, I am Soon going to my farm, with an intention to devote 10 years to settling & improving my land, & my fortune. I own Some good land, in Venango Co., Pennsylvania, near Franklin, where is a Post Office, & where I spend the present Summer. By autumn, or certainly by next Spring, I hope to have my own log-house ready for my family. If I have tolerable success, I hope to be able to sell some of my land, which is entirely wild, & make this pay in part for improving the rest—& thus provide a competency for old age.

I am here to put in operation the invention of which I spoke, in a letter, written near 2 years' since. Nothing will prevent success, but want of capital. With 10,000 dolls., I could make 20,000, in 1 year. It is my main object, in seeking to acquire money, that I may have Some to operate with in this way.

Thy old age is unclouded; & none more rejoice at it than myself. May it long continue, & thy example add lustre to America & this age, is the Sincere & fervent prayer, of, thy grateful friend,

HORATIO G. SPAFFORD.

RC (MHi); at foot of text: "Hon. Thomas Jefferson"; endorsed by TJ as received 15 July 1817 and so recorded in SJL.

To Patrick Gibson

DEAR SIR Poplar Forest July 1. 17.

This moment arrived here, I find your favor of June 26 and lest the notes should be wanting, I sign them without loss of time and inclose them with assurances of my great esteem & respect

TH: JEFFERSON

PoC (Mrs. T. Wilber Chelf, Mrs. Virginius Dabney, and Mrs. Alexander W. Parker, Richmond, 1944; photocopy in ViU: TJP); on verso of portion of reused address cover; at foot of text: "Mr Gibson"; endorsed by TJ. Enclosures not found.

On 2 July 1817 TJ recorded that the NOTES returned here included a renewal of his standing loan of $2,000 from the Bank of Virginia and a $3,000 note on the Richmond branch of the Second Bank of the United States, with the latter intended to cover his current expenses and pay off another $2,000 note that had been drawn on the Bank of Virginia on 24 May 1817 (*MB*, 2:1333, 1335).

From Thomas Humphreys

Lynchburg—2nd July 1817

Thomas Humphreys, has the pleasure of Informing the Honble Thomas Jefferson; that in consequence of a general note of his, having been presented to T. H., by Nace; not having any common Trusses, that would fitt said Nace; he has sent one that precisely suits the servant; & which with care, will last him his life time; the price of which is Eight Dollars; but should it not be approved of; Mr Jefferson will in that case, direct it to be returned.

RC (MHi); dateline at foot of text; endorsed by TJ as received 2 July 1817 and so recorded in SJL. RC (DLC: TJ Papers, ser. 10); address cover only; with PoC of TJ to Patrick Gibson, [18] Aug. 1817, on verso; addressed: "The Honble Thomas Jefferson Poplar Forest ℘ Sevt Nace."

From Richard Claiborne

Very dear Sir New Orleans July 4th 1817.

I greet you on this memorable day. Rejoicing cannon are roaring like peals of thunder, and patriot citizens singing Tedeum in all the churches. I wish the author of the declaration of Independence, and the political father of Louisiana were here to enjoy the Scene. But he rests from his labors, and receives the praises of mankind.

Steam Boats, Sir, which have been my dreams and my thoughts for 30 years, have become the pride of America, and the wonder of the world! With Eagle Wings they give to internal navigation a facility unknown and unexpected to mankind; yet they must go further and cross the Ocean! I am vain enough indeed to pursuade myself that an Essay I am preparing for the Press, on Steam Navigation, will give a Spur to the attempt. my work is a development of the Water wheel, and of the Web-foot, and shows that the wheel is terreneal, and the Web-foot aquatic, and ought to be preferred. My datum is, that "Nature made a Web-foot, but never made a Paddle, or an Oar, or a wheel." My Duckfoot paddle, which name, Sir, you pronounced as soon as you saw it, will give to us Duck Boats—and if a Duck could act at Sea, why could not a Duck Boat act at Sea also? The Duck could swim across the Ocean, were it not that she could not carry sufficient food for her passage. A Duck Boat could carry enough and to spare. Give a Duck Boat all the properties of a Duck—that is, give her impenetrability to water, and limbs, and force, and let all the sceptics in the world tell me if they can why it could not cross the ocean? Objections in some persons would be, that sufficient fresh water and fuel, could not be carried—but I think I have quieted, in my book, those difficulties far enough to justify a trial. my pamphlet will contain the following plates:

Plate 1. Shewing how to apply two Duckfoot paddles to a Barge to be rowed by one man or more, with the partial stroke, as with the Oar:

Plate 2. How to apply four Duckfoot paddles to a boat to be worked by steam, with the successive stroke, or uniform force, by means of the upright steam Engine, with semicircles applied to horizontal levers.

Plate 3. How to apply four duckfoot paddles to a Steam boat, to be worked by reversed cranks, connected with horizontal pitmans, so as to give to the paddles, the horse motion.

Plate 4. How to apply the common paddle to Steam boats, to be worked by reversed Cranks, and operate vertically in and out of the water.

Plate 5. The construction and operation of a marine planetary Battery, to be worked by the force of Steam and the Duckfoot Paddle.

The last plate starts a novel idea in maritime Science—but it is no less true that the battery possesses all the properties of a Planet, being circular in form, and while it circinates in its orbit, turns on its own Center, and exposes different Ordnances as luminous bodies emit rays of light. Happening to have a rough Sketch by me, I enclose it for your perusal. One or two of these Batteries in each of the lakes of Canada, would send every foreign ship of war about their business—two would clear the Gulf of Mexico of Pirates and put down monarchical maritime insolence—One at each port of the United States would enable us to bid defiance to invasion—and I wish from the bottom of my heart I could send one [as][1] an Argo to St Helena!

You see, Sir, my head is still full of nautical pursuits, particularly of the Duckfoot paddle, and if I live, I have no doubt of seeing it supercede the Wheel, and abolishing the Sail universally. But I have some right to complain; for this, that, notwithstanding a petition I forwarded to Congress two Sessions ago, and before my patent expired, to extend my patent, or provide by Law for the renewal of patents—tho' inventions become public property after the expiration of Patents, the government, I fear, has been surprised into a patent granted to a person in New York for a "Goose Foot"—for so I see he advertises it; so that, notwithstanding my improvements, for I have made many Sir Since the date of my patent granted under your administration as President—that is, simplified the machinery, and given to the paddle a double effect,—notwithstanding I say these improvements, and my researches, labors, and expenses of twenty years duration, I dare not now use my own invention! nor can the public use it, tho' they were entitled to it on the expiration of my patent. I believe, as much as I am sitting in my chair, that what the inventor calls his Goose Foot is a plagiarism to all intents and purposes—for my Duckfoot has been known for upwards of 20 years, and the goose foot has but just now made its appearance! In truth, it is a plagiarism, unless the author of the invention can convince me that he never saw or heard of my discovery, and convince me more particularly of the difference, in principle between[2] a Goose's foot and a Duck's foot. But if government has been surprised—they will perceive it—and I have no doubt that Congress will, at their next Session set all things right as to patent controversies.

Have patience with me Sir, one moment longer, and then I have done. I will make it a question, that, if this Duckfoot of mine be thus meritorious as I have represented it to be, why is it that it has not been carred[3] into public use before now? Two reasons are obvious answers. Before Fulton succeeded with Steam Boats, I and others who had advocated the practicability of the institution for years before m[r] Fulton came out with his plan, were denounced as Idiots—and after Fulton did succeed, then all doubts ceased, and all speculation ran into his vortex.

I have done Sir, and I offer the respect and affection I bear for you, as an apology for this intrusion. R Claiborne

RC (DLC); in a clerk's hand, signed by Claiborne; at foot of text: "Tho. Jefferson Esq[r] Monticello"; endorsed by TJ as received 16 Oct. 1817 and so recorded in SJL. Enclosure not found.

Richard Claiborne (ca. 1752–1819), public official and inventor, was a native of Virginia. He served in the Revolutionary War beginning in 1777, eventually rising to the rank of deputy quartermaster for Virginia. At the close of the war Claiborne worked to reconcile accounts with the state's assistant deputy quartermasters. By 1787 he was living in London, where he authored a treatise on the cultivation of tobacco that was translated into Polish. Claiborne returned to the United States at the end of 1794 and took up residence in Philadelphia. He subsequently moved to Washington, D.C., in hopes of finding work and furthering his inventing, and in 1802 he received a patent for an "Improvement in paddles for propelling boats." Finding little success in the nation's capital, Claiborne sought an appointment in Mississippi Territory from TJ. Although his request failed, he still moved at the end of 1803 to that territory, where he served as postmaster of the town of Washington and, beginning about 1804, as clerk to the territorial Board of Land Commissioners. By 1806 Claiborne was the private secretary of his younger cousin William C. C. Claiborne, the governor of Orleans Territory, and the following year he was appointed clerk of the Superior Court for the First District of Orleans Territory. He served as judge of Rapides Parish from 1808 until about

1812. Claiborne then practiced law in New Orleans and continued to work on his design for a ship's paddle shaped like a duck's foot. TJ corresponded frequently with Claiborne in 1781 when he was governor and the latter was deputy quartermaster, and in 1802 he attended a demonstration of Claiborne's paddle on the Anacostia River and gave him fifty dollars "in charity." Claiborne died in New Orleans (Jared William Bradley, ed., *Interim Appointment: W. C. C. Claiborne Letter Book, 1804–1805* [2002], 546–52; *VMHB* 1 [1894]: 320, 323; *CVSP*; *PTJ*, esp. 4:340–2, 38:271–2; Heitman, *Continental Army*, 155–6; Curtis Carroll Davis, "'A National Property': Richard Claiborne's Tobacco Treatise for Poland," *WMQ*, 3d ser., 21 [1964]: 93–117; *List of Patents*, 26; DNA: RG 59, LAR, 1801–09; *MB*, 2:1083; *Terr. Papers*; Dunbar Rowland, ed., *Official Letter Books of W. C. C. Claiborne, 1801–1816* [1917], esp. 6:251; *New-York Evening Post*, 3 Oct. 1818; Natchez *Mississippi State Gazette*, 24 Mar. 1819; Washington *Daily National Intelligencer*, 27 Apr. 1819).

CIRCINATES: "rotates" (*OED*). Napoleon was in exile at S^T^ HELENA. Claiborne's PETITION for the extension of his patent was presented to the United States House of Representatives on 15 Feb. 1816 and rejected on 6 Jan. 1817. He was granted permission to withdraw it on 13 Mar. 1818 (*JHR*, 14th Cong., 1st sess., 347; 2d sess., 144; 15th Cong., 1st sess., 326).

[1] Omitted word editorially supplied.
[2] Manuscript: "been."
[3] Thus in manuscript.

From William Short

DEAR SIR Philad[a] July 4. —17

I have not hastened to reply to your letter of June 19. because I saw that your departure for Bedford would prevent your recieving it until your return; & the present will reach Monticello at your debotter.

I am sorry that M[r] H. should think any thing further, to be necessary for his safety; not, assuredly, that I am not willing to give him every satisfaction his caution can devise, but because this would require my attending in the Mayor's office; of all places the most disagreeable, & in this hot season not without inconvenience. It is, as you know, the police office, as well as a court of record. And whenever it is open, it is crowded by all the miserable, filthy, & pestilent people that can be gathered together. The instrument which M[r] H. requires is mere surplusage; & as surplusage does not vitiate, I should without hesitation have executed it, but for the reason mentioned. If however he shall persist in wishing it, this inconvenience shall not prevent my complying. It cannot be however until my return to the City in the fall, as I am now leaving it for the summer. The Mayor's office will then also be less objectionable.

My reason for thinking this instrument not necessary to the security of M[r] H. is, that it has not been judged necessary, in several cases of a similar kind in which I have been concerned in the State of N.

York. When the mortgage which I held was paid off, the papers were returned & full satisfaction was indorsed on them; & that was all that was done. Mr H. has paid me in full, the papers are returned &, as well as I remember, with a similar indorsement. I hold no evidence of any claim against him, & he on the contrary, holds evidence of his debt having been paid off. On further reflexion therefore on the part of Mr H. I take for granted, he will be satisfied with things as they stand at present—but if perchance it be not so, I shall consider myself bound to comply with his wishes.

I had heard through different chanels of the death of the worthy Abbé, & I regret it most sincerely. He is a loss to the useful arts. In his letters to me he claimed, & I think with reason, the merit of having suggested to sir H. Davy (by what he had effected many years ago & placed on record) the idea of his late valuable discovery as to safety lamps. His mind remained active & zealous to the last.

I have very lately received a trunk of books which Mr Warden had forwarded to Ghent for me, during the negotiations there, & where it has remained lost for several years. In that collection were some from M. Rochon, of which a part were for you. I have put the trunk into Mr Vaughan's hands, requested him to dispose of those for you as you might direct, & take the others for the use of the Philo. society.

It will be a very happy event if the colony on the coast of Africa, which you mention, should succeed—It would aid towards civilizing & ameliorating the state of that unhappy region. I had never heard of this project before—it is difficult to be sanguine in such matters, where the French are the authors.

I fear we shall not be more successful as to our projected Colony of free blacks. Those that are not yet free their masters will prevent from going, & those that are free will not consent to go. And if this were not so, the expense of a new establishment would not be hazarded by Congress. Why could not some arrangement be made with the Government of Haiti for incorporating these people into that political family of free people of color?

A man who has been situated as Quinette in these late years, must have of course much interesting information to communicate, & I do not doubt proved a very agreeable inmate. One of his compeers, Fouché, has published I observed a work on the subject of these times, that is said to be highly interesting. It is so difficult to establish an early & rapid communication as to new works from France direct, that we must probably[1] be content in the first instance, to read the English translation, & to this I feel always a great repugnance.

The critique on Franklin's works, on political grounds, I had not heard of, but I think it probable it will be with much severity & asperity—Almost all the most able & piquant reviewers who write at present, are of the ultra cast.

I shall be very glad to learn that you have drawn the University to your neighborhood. It is unquestionably the most eligible situation in the State. I have always retained a great partiality for that quarter from the purity & elasticity of the air, & the pleasurable sensations which it excited in me, when first I breathed it, in ascending from the flat & low part of the country. To this moment I have a perfect recollection of the impression which the first view of a mountain made on me in approaching Monticello from Elk island. A place of education should always be in a mountainous region in my opinion. I think it will have a tendency to elevate the young ideas as they start. Correa says if ever there be an epic poem composed in the U.S. it will be in Virginia—& I say, if it should be so, it will be by some man who has been educated in or near the mountainous region.

The papers told us some time ago that you & Monroe were occupied in selecting a site near Charlottesville for a college. I did not know at that time, the nature or origin of this business.

Monroe seems to have now his hands full of other matters. His voyage Royal (this was the denomination he gave to the visit which G[l] Washington made to the southward soon after being made President, when he spoke to me of it in France) is producing a favorable effect as to himself & is doing away the virulence of party spirit. His kind & unassuming demeanor, with those who make the first advances to him—And so prone are men, even the fullest blooded Republicans, to idolatry, that he will meet with crowds every where not only disposed to make the first advances, but to worship if he pleases, as long as he shall present himself clothed with the purple. It will be at Boston, I do not doubt, where the greatest demonstrations will be made. I am pleased with the cordial manner in which he has been recieved every where—first because I am glad to see a base party spirit subsiding, & secondly because I have great good will towards Monroe. I did not see him here; & I was sorry for it. When I went to wait on him at his lodgings he was out; & I left my card. I did not return again parcequ'il ne m'a rien fait dire, & because I knew I should only find myself in a vulgar herd of idolaters; for which I feel now less disposition than I ever did.

The long experience of public affairs which Monroe has had, must have matured his judgment—his heart was always good—he begins his administration under most favorable auspices, & I hope therefore that both his country & himself will derive advantage & satisfaction from his Presidency—

With best wishes for your health & happiness I remain my dear sir ever & faithfully yours W: SHORT

I succeeded in procuring at Dallas's sale, a copy of your Notes on Virginia—It was the Philad. edition of 1801.—published by Rawle—I also found there a copy of the Debates of the Virginia Convention— Among some books wch I have lately rec[d] from France I find a work by Barbé Marbois, wch is entitled Complot d'Arnold. It is highly flattering to the American character & seems to be made a vehicle for giving some lessons to his countrymen at the present day.

RC (MHi); endorsed by TJ as received 15 July 1817 and so recorded in SJL. RC (DLC); address cover only; with PoC of TJ to David Watson, 23 July 1817, on verso; addressed: "Thomas Jefferson Monticello mail to Milton V[a]"; franked; postmarked Philadelphia, 4 July.

YOUR DEBOTTER: "the moment of your arrival"; literally, "the removal of your boots." MR H.: David Higginbotham. The ABBÉ was Alexis Marie Rochon. President James Monroe's VOYAGE ROYAL took him to Philadelphia, 5–7 June, and Boston, 2–7 July 1817 (Daniel Preston and Marlena C. DeLong, *The Papers of James Monroe* [2003–], 1:7). PARCEQU'IL NE M'A RIEN FAIT DIRE: "because he did not respond." The deceased Alexander J. DALLAS's library was sold in Philadelphia on 16 Apr. 1817 (Philadelphia *Poulson's American Daily Advertiser*, 11 Apr. 1817).

[1]Manuscript: "probally."

From Solomon Henkel

RESPECTED FRIEND New Market Shenandoah County
THOMAS JEFFERSON virginia July 5th 1817.

By M[r] Thomas Tausy I Send you a glass tumbler full of Hony which I obtained from my Bees according to the Plan laid down by M[r] Morgan of Prince Town of New Jersy. Finding the Methode so pleasing a one I thought it my duty to publish the Success I have had with it which I did as you will find in the gazette printed at Winchester accompaning this glass out of that publication you will find how I have managed the Boxes &c. Knowing you to be a Friend to all usefull improvements and Scients I have (by the request of M[r] Tausy) taken the Liberty to Send you a present as above in hopes you will comunicate the Improvement to your Neighbours. (If you think it worthy of comunicating). Should you have discovered a better Plan then this or Some additional Improvements I would receive them with Pleasure as Some Gentlemen have requested me to have handbills Struck which will give a full account of the Management of Bees &c which I could have done at my printing office.

I remain your humble Servant Solomon Henkel.—

RC (MHi); endorsed by TJ as received 5 Oct. 1817 and so recorded in SJL. Enclosed in Alexander Garrett to TJ, 5 Oct. 1817.

Solomon Henkel (1777–1847), physician, pharmacist, and printer, studied medicine in Philadelphia before returning to Virginia in 1793 and later opening a drugstore in New Market. He expanded his business to sell books, and in 1806 his family started a prolific printing business in New Market that specialized in German-language and Lutheran texts and operated a weekly German newspaper. Henkel took over the press in 1814. He served as postmaster of New Market, 1801–14, and he practiced medicine in addition to his work as a printer (Charles W. Cassell, William J. Finck, and Elon O. Henkel, eds., *History of The Lutheran Church in Virginia and East Tennessee* [1930], 14, 309–12; Albert Sydney Edmonds, "The Henkels, Early Printers in New Market, Virginia, with a Bibliography," *WMQ*, 2d ser., 18 [1938]: 174–95; Brigham, *American Newspapers*, 2:1122; Axelson, *Virginia Postmasters*, 173; DNA: RG 29, CS, Shenandoah Co., 1810–40; *American Medical Reporter* 1 [1818]: 398–9; *Cultivator* 8 [1841]: 97; *American Farmer, and Spirit of the Agricultural Journals of the Day*, new ser., 6 [1844]: 109; ViU: Henkel-Miller Family Papers; Vi: Henkel Family Papers; Shenandoah Co. Will Book, Y:184–9; gravestone in Emmanuel Lutheran Church Cemetery, New Market).

Henkel's enclosed piece from an unidentified issue of the Winchester GAZETTE was reprinted in the *Alexandria Gazette & Daily Advertiser*, 19 July 1817. It included instructions from an encyclopedia article written by George Morgan of Princeton, New Jersey, on how to extract honey from a hive without harming the bees, along with Henkel's 6 June 1816 covering letter and his own observations on the method (Anthony F. M. Willich, *The Domestic Encyclopædia; or, A Dictionary of Facts, and Useful Knowledge*, ed. James Mease [Philadelphia, 1803–04], 1:239–40).

From James Clarke

Dear Sir— Powhatan County, July 6th 1817

Fearing that you have many intrusive correspondants, and that I may be rank'd among the number, it is with great deference I make this little communication; which I hope you will excuse.

When I had the pleasure of being in your company (about 8. or 9 years ago, at Monteceloe) conversing on the subject of the Odomater, you asked me, if I thought it practicable to construct a machine that could lay down the platt of a road by the traveling of a carriage over it? I answered, I had thought but little on the subject; but from the few thoughts I had spent on it, I was of opinion it could be done. You replyed, you thought diferently. Since then, having been engaged in many other persuits, I thought but little more on the subject. Untill this spring, having entirely recovered from a long and dangerous indisposition acquired in the army of Norfolk in 1813; and being more at leasure to try experiments, I turn'd my attention a little more on the subject; and have at length reduced the theory to practice.—With very temporary materials I made a machine with which (being attached to the carriage wheel) I made a survey of a triangle of road, about 12 mile in Circimference, which completely answered my expectation. If it will not intrude too much on your attention, I will give a few of the out lines.

The chart is placed on a horizontal plane on the floor of the carriage The part of the machine which marks off the platt, progresses on the chart as the carriage moves. A rod, or index, placed convenient to the eye, and moved by the hand, is kept constantly pointing to the North-Star. This index being connected with the machine, and changing its angle with the carriage, at every turn of the road, produces on the chart, all the turns and angles which there is in the road.

But, altho this machine is perfect in principle, it is not so in practice; for want of a perfect index. The objections to this index are, 1st It can be used only in the night, 2d It can be used only in fair weather, 3d It can be used only in latitudes, neither too high, nor too low, 4th The North-Star is too often eclipsed by trees and other objects; perticularly in summer.

I have tryed several experiments to make the magnetick needle answer as an index; but have not been able to succeed; in consequence of the vibration of the needle produced by the agitation of the carriage. If this difficulty could be removed, I have no doubt it would be a very valuable acquisition. And what would add still more to its convenience—the ascent, and descent, of unlevel ground could be taken upon the same principle, and at the same time.

To take the ascent & descent, a pendulum would be a very good index. Altho the pendulum would be constantly vibrating, it[s] general direction would be perpendicular to the horizon. And as the plane of the chart varies from the plane of the horizon, by the ascending or descending of the carriage, so will the pendulum vary from its right angle with the plane of the chart; and mark off a track thereon, above, or below, a right line on the chart, representing the horizon

In surveying water courses, navigable by boats, or even canoes the magnetick needle would answer exceedingly well as an index to this machine if the water was still; but as the machine would receive its motion from the surface of the water, the current would defeat the object, and render it impracticable.

In surveying publick roads, with this instrument, the magnetick needle will answer very well, by the addition of one person more, to go before with a white pole; and stoping the carriage at each turn of the road, long enough for the needle to rest, and to set the index.

And this I think will be a great improvement on the common way of surveying roads; as it will be more expeditious, less expensive, and less subject to error: as the surveyor will not have to keep a reckoning—to enter his notes—and to plott from those notes. all of which are subject [to][1] error. But I have already drawn your attention too long I am affraid, from subjects more interesting—

Please Sir, accept the highest esteem, and venerati[on,] of your most obedient and very humble Servan[t] JAMES CLARKE

RC (DLC); damaged at seal; addressed: "Mr Thomas Jefferson Monteceloe Albemarle county" by "mail"; franked; endorsed by TJ as received 15 July 1817 and so recorded in SJL.

James Clarke (ca. 1759–1830), planter and inventor, was a Revolutionary War veteran who became a lieutenant colonel of the Powhatan County militia in 1803 and led the county's militia regiment during the War of 1812. He lived for many years at Belnemus, his 530-acre estate in Powhatan County. During a visit to Monticello in 1807, Clarke gave TJ an odometer of his own invention. TJ used the device, which rang a bell every mile traveled, on his carriage until at least 1821. In 1818 Clarke obtained a patent for this invention. He served as president of the Powhatan auxiliary of the American Colonization Society in the 1820s. At the time of his death Clarke owned personal property valued at $6,010.62, including sixteen slaves as well as a number of odometers (G. Brown Goode, *Virginia Cousins: A Study of the Ancestry and Posterity of John Goode of Whitby* [1887], 229–30; TJ to Clarke, 22 May, 5 June 1807 [both in DLC], 5 Sept. 1820; Clarke to TJ, 27 May 1807 [MHi]; DNA: RG 29, CS, Powhatan Co., 1810–30; Stuart Lee Butler, *A Guide to Virginia Militia Units in the War of 1812* [1988], 172, 227; *List of Patents*, 196; Leesburg *Genius of Liberty*, 8 Aug. 1820; *MB*, 2:1374; American Society for Colonizing the Free People of Colour of the United States [later the American Colonization Society], *Annual Reports* 9 [1826]: 61; 10 [1827]: 88; 11 [1828]: 50–9 [all repr. 1969]; *Daily Richmond Whig* and *Richmond Commercial Compiler*, both 3 Jan. 1831; Powhatan Co. Will Book, 8:390–2, 419–24; *Richmond Enquirer*, 13 May 1831).

[1] Omitted word editorially supplied.

From William Lee

RESPECTED & VERY DEAR SIR, Washington July 6th 1817.

Your favor of the 25th of last month was duly recd and I should have replied to it before now but that a slight indisposition arising from the pain of a neglected dislocation prevented it—I have conversed with my principal Swiss who thinks that the young man you mention ought to pay his own board as he comes simply to learn the trade for his own benefit—our apprentices after the first year become good workmen and therefore yield us a profit during the remainder of their service but this is a different case—He can board in the family or where he pleases and when he has learnt the art of weaving stocking knit he shall have a loom but what the price will be I cannot fix at this moment as we have not yet begun to make them—We shall be liberal with him—Mr Duane sent me last week an Englishman who was brought up at the stocking looms & a young man from German town—I have engaged them both—they say they never saw such beautiful looms—I am confident we shall succeed but any benefit I may reap will never repay me for the trouble I have been out and the anxiety I experience—There is a noted prejudice against our manufactures with the capitalists and our Banks are not liberal—

With the highest veneration I have the honor to be your obliged & obedient Servant Wm Lee

RC (DLC); at foot of text: "Mr Jefferson"; endorsed by TJ as received 15 July 1817 and so recorded in SJL. Enclosed in James Leitch to TJ, 25 Dec. 1817.

From John Barnes

Dear Sir— George Town Coa 8th July 1817.

with referance to Mr L. Leschuts 7 watches

say 5 Single Capt a	$40	is 200	is 320	say $2 Each for
— 2 double d	60	120	of 14	regulating $306 nt

in order then to try their real merit, and worth—I placed one of the five said to be No 486. on inspection—had no Number—but Morris Tobias London—Mr Eckles—one of the first watch makers—or rather menders—in George Town and man of good Character—at very 1st sight pronounced it of Genevian make—and made—for sale only—like onto Peter Pindars—Raisors—not for Use—inquiring[1] the price—I told him for the present, was a secret. all I wishd of him was to put the Contents in the best order and time. and withal to furnish me particular Minute of its, imperfections and to say what its real worth was—between the Seller & buyer—in a day or two I expect his Candid Report—Under this mode of proceeding I purpose to treat with him, on each watch—at present he doesnt know I am possessed of any other—and lest I may have bought the Rabit—I intend to dispose of them seperately. in order to avoid a flemish Accot in Speculating in an Article I am no judge[2] of—I am still pursuaded Mr Leschuts has not charged an extra profit, but to prove—he is neither the maker—nor the finisher—but the Vender Only

or rather as Mr Eckles—a watch mender—the charge here for regulating a new watch $2.50 or $3—

In course of 10 or 12 days I purpose purchasing a Cash draft here—on a Bank at New York—in my fav[r] for said $306. and endorse it payable to Louis Leschut—or Order and transmit it to Charlottesville under Cover to you thro fear of Accident.—

excuse my troubling you with these particulars

very Respectfully—your most obed servant JOHN BARNES,

PS. I do think after all M[r] Leschut ought to allow me the diffn of half a doll[r] on each but I do not insist upon it—ie, his books are not favorable for complying with any such requests—

July 11th M[r] Eckles has just now handed me his report and opinion (what was to be expected—) that these kind of watches are very ordinary and not worth more than $40.—so far I think—he is correct—and that I will not be able to dispose of it for more—perhaps I may add—his expences for regulating it say $2.50 and glad to be let off so easy in so adventrous a speculation—

RC (ViU: TJP-ER); with first postscript adjacent to and beneath signature, and dated postscript on verso of address leaf; addressed: "Thomas Jefferson Esq[r] Monticello"; endorsed by TJ as received 15 July 1817 and so recorded in SJL.

M[R] ECKLES: Charles E. Eckel (Catherine B. Hollan, *Virginia Silversmiths, Jewelers, Watch- and Clockmakers, 1607–1860, Their Lives and Marks* [2010], 246). A humorous poem by "PETER Pindar" [John Wolcot] tells the story of a peddler who sells cheap razors. When confronted on their apparent inability to do what they were designed to do, he retorts that the razors were designed not to shave, but to sell ([Wolcot], *Farewell Odes. for the year 1786. by Peter Pindar, Esq.* [London, 1786], 16–20). BOUGHT THE RABIT (rabbit): gotten a bad deal. A FLEMISH account has a negative balance (*OED*).

[1]Manuscript: "inquring."
[2]Manuscript: "jude."

From Stephen Cathalan

MY DEAR SIR & MOST RESPECTED FRIEND!

Marseilles the 8th July 1817—

I have the honor to Represent to you that tho' I may, under your Good and Fatherly Protection (whereof I have So Long had Convincing & Continued Proofs, till this Day) deservedly Expect, that as Long as I will Live, or I Shall be able to Continue to fill the Duties of the Consul & agent of the navy of the united States in this Consular District, with the Same zeal, assiduity & Integrity and to hold it to the honor of the nation & Government I am Representing[1] here, as I have done hitherto;—however Considering that Such Commissions are not granted for Life During, being removeables, as it is Stated therein, that they are =During the Pleasure of the President, for the Time being=; that the President is himself Removeable every four years; that hitherto and Since the Constitution of the united States is in Force, no Presidents[2] have ever Passed the Term of Eight years, or of Two Presidencies, it may be Possible that, a Day, it may no more be the Pleasure of the President to Let me Continue to hold that office, as Several other Consuls of the U.S. have already Experienced, they having been Revoked or Superceded, which I humbly confess it, would hurt my Feelings if Such Event Should happen Some Day to me!—when I observe the number of citizens native of the U.S. applicants for it, Long Since tho' hitherto, unsuccessfully,!—but I am also apprehensive that there is now amongst them, Some Envious, Jealous Restless Cunning Fellows, who from Hunger or under Speculations, are Employing the most Low &[3] base means, or Calumnious Denunciations,[4] anonimous Letters &ª &ª—who may by Insidious hypocrisy & with unremitted Perseverance, if not timely unmasked, at Last Succeed, by & Thro' Prejudiced Protections, against me, to obtain over me this Consulate;—There is one here of this kind, already known for Such actions, whom I Think it my Duty to Point out, who is Mr A Fitch Junior of the House of Montgomerys Fitch & Co merchts in this City, who has already Prejudiced against me Commore Isaac Chauncey—Commanding in chief the Naval Forces[5] in the Mediteranean, who arived in this Road on the 11th June ulto and Sailed on the 16th dto witht Ending the 40ne[6];—I am making an official Detailled Report of the whole Transaction to the Hble Secretary of the Navy;—

it has been Reported to me, Since, that Mr Fitch has been, Previously & even Since the Commodore Sailed out, in Boats, without taking in any Guard of the health office, or their Leave (as I do) Several Times, long Side of the U.S. Ship Washington to Speak with Comre I. Chauncey, Long Side also of the U.s. Frigates united states & Constellation, the U.S. Brig Spark & the U.s. Corvette Erie, Spreading amongst their Capns & officers, Specialy to those of the Frigate united States, where Last year, while in this Road, he had already Intrigued towards Comre John Shaw, but Specialy towards[7] Mr Jes Hry Clarke, a Gentleman of a Dissimulated complexion, as it has appeared to me and to others, & Circulating thus =the Consul of the U.s. in this City has no Influence over the Local authorities, that he was not Respected in this Place &ª &ª that it would be better of Course for the Americans Resorting[8] here that there Should not be any consul of the U.s. than Such a one as Mr Cathalan; that any other in his Stead, Should have forced the Board of Health to Report their

Resolve of 15 Days 40[ne] & to be Satisfied with 7 Days only, &[a] &[a] &[a]=[9]

in Such Circumstances, I Find myself arived at a Period of Life (being Born on the 10th June 1757—Tho', Thank God, in a Good State of Health and Spirits) to Follow the Shade of the Great Examples, Given by the Immortal George Washington, by your Self & James Madison,! who after having Employed the Best Part of their Lives in the Service of their Country, in the highest & most honorable Stations =Retired to the Bosom of their Families, Friends, Books and Farms, felicity which the Times in which your Existence has happened to be Placed has never Permitted you to know= (as p[r] your kind letter to me of the 29th June 07—)[10] and I Think that the best now I have to do, is to ask to the Actual most honorable President, James (the 2[d]) Monroe[11] for my Resignation, But—Provided I may be allowed Thro' your Self, to Render a Last & the best Service, which may Lay in my Power, to the united States, in offering to him a candidate for & as my Successor, Joshua Dodge of Salem, aged 26 years, as the only native Citizen Merchant in Marseilles (without Pretending to Injure any others also Established here) who reunite in himself all the good Requisite qualities, to fullfill this office, I am So Long honored with;

when I am Considering, as I have Experienced it! that the Emoluments attached to this office, mere Casuelties, with[t] any Fixed Salary, nor even any Compensation Granted for Chancelor & Secretary, Stationary, nor any Extraordinary Expences, to make the Due honors in the Representation here of the American Nation & Government; Should Such a Consulate in Marseilles, be a Day Granted to officers in the navy or the army of the U.s. Retired from the active Service, as a Reward for their past one, or to any other Citizen native of the U.s. not already established here, who Should Come here on the Purpose of Exercising it, not being already Possessor of an Independant Fortune, he would Soon find, this Consulate of Marseilles, as a Burden too heavy to be able to support it Longer; and Soon after he would ask for his Resignation!,[12]—the above Considerations will not opperate against M[r] Joshua Dodge, he having already a good Run of Busisness on hand, Respectable Merchants & Friends in the united States, with means & Good will to Support with Dignity and honor this office.

however this Consulate, tho' it may appear at first Sight of a very Little Importance, (as it may be thought,) by it's Profits, as it does not Procure Consignments, it Requires however a Constant aptitude and over Looking, a great deal of Experience and knowledge, in the best way for applying with Success towards the Several authorities in this Consular District, when applications are to be made, to avoid a Positive Refusal, when uncertain of Success, which is then very disagreable in Deed! while when Personaly & verbaly made, (verba volant Sed Scripta manent) or Properly Couched, in writing, there is but Little Doubt that they will be Granted; I Could State you Thousands Instances in which I have thus Succeed & not Three in which I have not;[13] but in this Respect I must Gratefully acknowledge, that I am owing this good method, and I will never forget[14] it! to your wise and Experienced Instructions, when Secretary of State, you Sent me, the Letters Patent of George Washington the first President of the united States, appointing me their Consul for this city &ca;—but this is not the whole,! Following those So well dictated Principles! I have So well Succeeded with So many kind of Subversed & Inversed authorities, which one over the other Superceded in France Since 27 years, that I have by my Franckness, openly, & not other wise, Succeeded here & even in Paris,[15] in Influencing over their Contrary opinions;

I hope that our Present Minister Pleny and Envoy Extraordinary[16] Albert Gallatin at Paris, not a native of the U. States as I am not, In following your Example, when you was in Paris in that Same Capacity, will as near as you as well Succeed[17] in his Embassy; in acting[18] as you have Tought to us, how in this Corner of the world,!—

but there Remain Still, my Dear Sir, a[19] Painfull and Disagreable Task to Fill & to void as Cups of vinegar & many I have thus Drunk, tho' I was not Thirsty!!! & I hope that my Successor, who it may be, one Day, will have a better Beverage!!!—it is to avoid (which is very Difficult)[20] or not meet with the Fault Finders, the Censure & the Tiresome arguments of the american Citizens already Stablished[21] here or of Part thereof, and of these Resorting in this District, for the First time, unaccustomed with the Customs & manners, the Laws, the Formalities or even the Shackles, they are here Surrounded with, which the other Foreigners and the French Nationals, are Supporting without any Exceptions in their Favour! This is not an Easy matter to make them understand by their American[22] Consul!

as to Mr Joshua Dodge, whom I dare to be Presented by you to the President, I have Strictly and in Silence Examined, even Scrutinised his Conduct Since he is here; and it is now my Duty to Confess that he is one amongst So many American[23] Citizens, whom I have had occasion to be acquainted with in this City, who is generally acknowledged to be Invested with upright Probity, Integrity, Good Breading (Speaking & writing well the French Language) knowledge, abilities, and Something better and very Scarce in this =Iron Age,= to be Found! Short Ambition and Sound Disinterested Patriotism for his Country; to which is to be added, not only the Support or the Protection of his own Friends, in the Several States of the union; but also the general Esteem he has already acquired from the Sundry Classes of the Inhabitants of this Populous City with whom he has had occasion to be acquainted with, and above all my Fatherly esteem and Friendship; and in order he may be (meantime the Pleasure of the President may be known to me) Au Fait, of the Details of this Chancery, I am appointing him on this Day as my Chancelor & I Shall appoint him Shortly after as my Proconsul or attorney, to act in my stead in this Consular District, under my own Responsibility.

I now, my Dear Sir, Inclose you my Resignation addressed to the President, with my Letter to the Honble Secry of State accompaning it,[24] but Respectfully Request from you that Said Resignation may not be given in, untill you have Positive Promise of the President, that Mr Dodge Shall be appointed in my Place;—I hope & Feel Confident that your good Influence with the Government will obtain for me the nomination of my Friend Mr Dodge, I ask it, from you, my much Respected Friend! as one of the greatest obligations you can Confer upon me; For nothing will give me more Pleasure than to be the means through your Self and your good Influence in Placing Mr Dodge in this Consulate, because I candidly Think he is worthy to honor it;

I have Informed him that it is my wish, he Should thro' you, me & his Friends, Cooperating in Concert, with you, get this Place and in Consequence, he is writing to his Relation & Friend & Protector, the Hble Benjin Willm Crowninshield[25] Secretary of the Navy, Requesting his assistance & Cooperation with you;

Permit me my Dear Respected Friend to beg of you to be So kind, as to write him a few lines, as Soon as after the Receipt of this as Possible, Informing the Said Secretary of the Navy, the Course you wish to have Pursued in order to obtain Mr Joshua Dodge this Consulate, that you will also write to the President respecting the Same,

Should you, unfortunately, Find that Government will not appoint Mr Dodge; I Beg you will not Give in my Resignation, as I Should Prefer[26] Remaining, to have any other Person than Mr Dodge, appointed;—I hope that the foregoing Arrangment and Resignation in Favor of Mr Joshua Dodge, will meet with your Fatherly approbation, and that it will be Through your Influence, I may have the Pleasure of Introducing Mr Dodge to the Public officers, within this Consular District as my Successor, but also as your Protegé! the more as I herein Inclose a Letter of Recommendation in his Favor, addressed to you by George Crowninshield Esqr a Brother to the Secretary of the U.s. Navy, who has Lately visited this Place & Toulon in his Beautifull Brig Cleopatra's Barge and told me that his Intention being to Return into the Mediteranean next winter, Probably with his Said Brother, has assured me he will Join with me, to Prevail on you, to Embrace that fair opportunity to Revisit Marseilles, Paris, Italy &[a] &[a]

what Pleasure then, when Retired, as you are already,[27] for me, to Receive you in my house and probably to be able to accompany you & assist you in visiting Some other Places, you, nor I have not Seen!

May the Allmighty Preserve you in good health! & I too! in order that =mes Chateaux en Espagne= may be thus Executed; in the mean time, I beg you to accept the most Sanguine assurances of my Gratitude and Great Respect which will Last as Long as I will be able to Say and Subscribe my Self!

My Dear Sir & Protector!

Your most obedient & Faithfull Servant & Sincere Friend

STEPHEN CATHALAN.

P.S. Be pleased to observe that my Resign[on] to the President with my Letter to the Sec[ry] of State, are dated in Blanck to be filled by you.[28]

Dupl (DLC); addressed: "Thomas Jefferson Esquire Monticello"; between dateline and salutation: "Duplicata The orig[al] by Havre"; endorsed by TJ as received 29 Sept. 1817 and so recorded in SJL. RC (MHi); only the most significant variations are noted below; addressed: "Thomas Jefferson Esq[r] &[a] &[a] &[a] Monticello"; endorsed by TJ as received 27 Oct. 1817 and so recorded in SJL. Enclosure: George Crowninshield to TJ, 30 June 1817. Other enclosures not found. Enclosed in Cathalan to TJ, 16 July 1817.

According to their commissions, consuls served DURING THE PLEASURE OF THE PRESIDENT, FOR THE TIME BEING (for an example, see *PTJ*, 27:857, 864). Asa FITCH JUNIOR sought for years to replace Cathalan as United States consul at Marseille (DNA: RG 59, LAR, 1809–25). The American commodore ISAAC CHAUNCEY complained to Cathalan in a letter of 14 June 1817 that it was a "national insult" that his squadron and other American naval vessels were subjected to extended quarantines in the port of Marseille (RC in FrM: Cathalan-Samatan Collection). ROAD: "roadstead" (*OED*). TJ's letter of 29TH JUNE 1807 is in DLC.

VERBA VOLANT SED SCRIPTA MANENT: "spoken words fly but written words stay." The INSTRUCTIONS that TJ sent to Cathalan in 1790 as a newly appointed vice-consul can be found in *PTJ*, 17:423–5. The reference to the present as a debased or IRON AGE is from TJ to Cathalan, 3 July 1815. MES CHATEAUX EN ESPAGNE: "my castles in Spain" or "my castles in the air" (*OED*).

1 Dupl: "Reprensenting." RC: "Representing."

2 Dupl: "President." RC: "Presidents."

3 Preceding two words not in RC.

4 Dupl: "Denonciations." RC: "Denunciations."

5 RC here adds "of the U.S."

6 Preceding four words not in RC. Here and below, "40[ne]" is an abbreviation for "quarantine."

7 RC here adds "the Purser."

[8] Dupl: "Ressorting." RC: "Resorting."
[9] Omitted closing quotation mark supplied from RC.
[10] Text from "felicity" to this point not in RC.
[11] Word not in RC.
[12] Preceding nine words not in RC.
[13] Preceding fourteen words not in RC.
[14] Dupl: "forgett." RC: "Forget."
[15] Preceding five words not in RC.
[16] Instead of preceding three words, RC reads "of the U.S."
[17] Instead of text from "In following" to this point, RC reads "but Knowing pretty much as you did & following your Example, will as well Succeed."
[18] Dupl: "if or in acting." RC: "in acting."
[19] Dupl: "an." RC: "a."
[20] Parenthetical phrase not in RC.
[21] RC: "established."
[22] Word not in RC.
[23] Dupl: "Americans." RC: "American."
[24] Preceding eleven words not in RC.
[25] Dupl: "Chrowninshield." RC: "Crowninshield."
[26] Dupl: "Preffer." RC: "Prefer."
[27] Dupl: "allready." RC: "already."
[28] Postscript in RC reads "P.S. Please to observe that the Dates in the Inclosed are Left in Blanck."

To Craven Peyton

DEAR SIR Poplar Forest. July 8. 17.

It is now five and forty years since I have withdrawn from the practice of the law: I have but occasionally, within that period, read any thing on it's subjects, have rarely reflected on them with any attention, or permitted myself to form opinions with any degree of confidence, still less to oppose these opinions to those of gentlemen now of that faculty, and in dayly familiarity with the decisions of latter, as well as former times. at your request however I have considered the papers you sent me, and will give you my thoughts because you request, and seem to set value on them. still I must warn you against giving them weight where opposed to the opinions of gentlemen in actual practice.

I will state the case as it is presented to my mind by the bill, the answer, the deeds and depositions of Hening and Anderson, putting Lewis's out of view for reasons which will appear.

In 1802. Charles Lewis dec[d] informed mr Peyton that his father Cha[s] Lilburne Lewis proposed to give him a life-estate in the lands in question, and requested him to draw a deed to that effect. mr Peyton drew, & gave him such a deed; and, without particular enquiry, always supposed it was the one which was used. but, instead of it, another was substituted, which, in addition to the estate for life to Charles, gave him the remainder in fee, on the contingency of his marriage; but, on failure of that contingency, gave it over to his sisters the complainants, and the defend[t] mrs Peyton. this was dated July 30. 1802. Charles Lewis having entered into the military life, offered the lands for sale, first to others for the sum of 3000 Dollars, and afterwards to mr Peyton. mr Peyton entered into treaty with him, and at the same time with his father for the remainder in fee, which he supposed still in him, as his draught of a deed had left it. the purchase is agreed on, but not at the price offered to others, mr Peyton insisting that he would pay the full value, according to a valuation to be made by some person of their mutual choice. mr Hening, one of the deponents, was chosen, who went over & examined the land, and, on the understanding that the feesimple was to be conveyed, valued it at 5000.D. on the 18th of July 1804. Charles Lewis executed a deed conveying to mr Peyton all his right in the land, and on the 29th of Sep. following, Charles Lilburne Lewis executed his separate deed for the same lands, describing them as the land he had conditionally (meaning contingently) conveyed to the sd Charles Lewis junior, and which the sd Peyton had bought of him, and conveying to the said Peyton the reversion or remainder therein; and binds himself and his heirs to warrant the sd parcel of lands to the sd Peyton and his heirs 'against the claim of all and every other person whatsoever.' each deed acknoleged payment of the entire sum at which the feesimple was valued, but the whole price seems to have been[1] relinquished to the son, the father viewing it probably as an advancement on his entering into the world, and dispensing therefore with the contingency of marriage. the precise time at which Charles Lewis and mr Peyton began to treat for the land, or concluded that treaty, does not appear in the papers; but it is said to have been many weeks before the execution of the deed. sixteen days however before the execution of that deed, to wit, on the 2d of July 1804. the deed of 1802 having been proved in legal time by 2. witnesses only, the 3d witness is procured to go into court & prove it also. by whom was the procurement of the 3d witness made, so opportunely in point of time? we are left to conjecture; and, in charity to all others, we must fix it on him who was, at the same time, deliberately committing the solemn fraud of conveying the same feesimple to mr Peyton. the answer explicitly abjures all notice of that deed, all suspicion that any other than the one drawn by the respondent had been used, and denies that he had ever heard a suggestion of any remainder, or other interest whatever, conveyed to the daughters. it appears that during all[2] the time of these transactions one of these daughters was living in the house with him, and three others with their father in sight of it; that they were all supported by mr Peyton, that the land in question was spread under their sight, so that they could not go to their doors without seeing it, and if any of them were infants in law, they were all at the age of discretion, of marrigeable years, and yet never suggested either to Peyton himself, or to his wife their sister & coparcener that he was buying what was theirs. Charles Lewis died in 1806. having never been married, and in 1814. this title which had slept a dozen years, unthought of by the complainants, and unknown to others, is raked up, a suit commenced, and the father is brought from Tennissee to support by his oath that one of the opposing claims created by himself for which he had practised so much contrivance.

Thus stands the case then, according to the testimony adduced, unless the deposition of Charles Lilburne Lewis be considered as testimony. but it would be against all the laws of human confidence to give any credit to such a witness. in 1802. by deed solemnly executed, he conveys away the whole feesimple of his land to volunteers who pay nothing for it, and in 1804. he again as solemnly conveys the same whole feesimple to another, who pays it's full value, thus defrauding his son in law and one daughter out of 5000.D. the feesimple value, to give it gratis to others, and then offers himself as a witness to prove his own palpable and recorded fraud; a fraud the more revolting as coupled with the act of hunting up a 3d witness to rivet rights under his 1st deed, while he was deliberately treating to convey the same rights, and did convey them to another by a 2d deed. if it be urged that this witness came in of his own accord, and on a sense of duty, it must be admitted that this tardy impulse of conscience in the witness came very à propos, and at the eleventh hour. but when we consider that 16. days more, added to the 2. years he had held off would have made his aid too late, can we avoid suspecting that he was sought and brought to the book at this critical moment by some one who knew intimately what was going forward?   but by whom? when we take a survey of all the parties interested in the fraud, who could it be? Peyton? impossible. the daughters? their situation, habits, and opportunities of life clear them of this active operation. was it Charles Lewis? or Charles Lilburne Lewis? the wish to help sisters might be a motive, but that to help daughters is a stronger one; and falling on one convicted of fraud by his own acts, exposes, without a doubt, the unseen hand by which this witness was beckoned in. these considerations leave the answer of the defendants without impeachment by this deposition, and the more so as two unexceptionable witnesses are requisite to invalidate the peremptory denial of notice in the answer.

Some questions, of more or less difficulty, have been raised in this case, which are however but collateral to what is important. e.g. the answer questions whether the Contingent remainder limited to the daughters is not too remote to be sustained by law? the Counsel will consequently enquire whether the law will not await a contingency which is certainly to happen at or before the end of a life in being?

2. Whether persons, not parties to the deed, can claim under it? here the difference must be shewn between this and every family settlement whereto it is rare to make any other party but him who takes the first estate.

3. Under the law which declares that no deed shall be good against a purchaser without notice, unless proved by 3. witnesses, and recorded within 8. months, the Answer questions whether the deed of 1802. is not a mere nullity as to a purchaser? a question well worthy of being tried. I know indeed that in former times, sound lawyers were of opinion that a deed whose proof was compleated after the 8 months, was, from the time of completion, good in Equity against those who purchased <u>after</u> that completion. but I have been told that some latter decisions have contradicted that opinion. with these decisions I am not acquainted. but certainly the late act of assembly declaring that the deed shall be good from the time of such completion raises a presumption that it was not so before, and consequently not when this deed was executed.

But, independently of this last question, the following, in my view, are the strong points in this case.

1. Mr Peyton is a purchaser for <u>valuable</u> consideration, actually paid. this is uncontrovertibly established by the answer and depositions, and is not even questioned in the bill.

2. he is a purchaser bonâ fide, <u>without notice</u>. Altho' the record of a deed, the pendency of a suit, the enactment of a law, are considered as notice of the thing to every body, and that this is a salutary construction generally, and for the safety of titles, yet we all know that these things may all take place, and an individual have no knolege of them. altho' the deed of 1802 was lodged in court for proof, yet bystanders rarely notice a deed at the time it is produced in court, and more rarely know it's contents, and that this was a secret transaction there is every reason to believe. Hening & Anderson knew nothing of any claim of the daughters, altho' they were intimate with the affairs of the family. it is more probable then that it should have been unknown in the neighborhood; and the more so as no proof is produced that it was known to any mortal except to Charles Lilburne Lewis the principal agent in the deception of the defendants. they, by their answer fully purge themselves of <u>actual</u> notice, declaring that they never heard, or suspected that such a claim existed until 1814, a dozen years after the date of the deed. Charles L. Lewis, to be sure, swears

he mentioned it to Peyton; but his recorded deed attests the reverse of his oath, when it warrants a feesimple title to Peyton against all persons whatsoever; and this pointed testimony only fills up the measure of the fraud he has practised. the evidence of a witness thus palpably convicting himself, cannot be recieved; and even could it be, it is still but of a single witness, where two are requisite to overweigh the testimony of the answer. the fact of no actual notice then is established. nay more, it is established that the actual notice was the reverse: for the deed of 1804, as has already been observed, was a solemn declaration, and actual notice that he had never, by any other, conveyed away the same remainder, that it still continued in him, and would pass to mr Peyton by the deed he was signing. common sense too testifies that if mr Peyton had had actual notice that the remainder was no longer in the father, he would not have treated for an useless conveyance[3] from him, and still less would have paid the full feesimple value, when he was to obtain but a life estate.

As to constructive notice from the proof of the deed in court, if the deed, according to an opinion before noticed, be not an absolute nullity, because not proved within 8. months, it is Equity only which can interpose, and make it's subsequent proof good; and Equity will withold it's interposition, if other cause, good in equity also, can be shewn to the contrary. now, altho' the 2[d] deed was not executed till the 18th of July 1804. 16. days after the probat of the other by the 3[d] witness, yet it seems, and may still be proved that the contract was concluded absolutely, between the parties, several weeks before mr Hening was called on to value the lands, and to prepare the deed, and that it was still several weeks more, after he was called on, before the deed was executed. the purchase then was made, and the land (which had been long in possession of the def. under a former lien) was become the defendant's in equity several weeks before this tardy completion of the other probat. the actual conveyance was, in conscience but a ceremony, due from the instant the bargain was concluded; and Equity considering always that as already done, which ought to be done, will make the deed look back to the date of the contract. it will not interpose to set aside a law, or to make good an imperfect act, in favor of the one party, when, according to it's own principles, the other has the equitable right, united with the possession. as the probat of the 3[d] witness then was a nullity in law, no constructive notice arises in law; and if equity would in any case supply a constructive notice (a thing unjust in itself) where there was none actually, yet it will not do it where there is a prior and greater equity in the other party, and proof of the absence of actual notice. the defendant then is a purchaser for valuable consideration, bonâ fide paid, & without notice actual or constructive.

3. the Complainants are mere volunteers. the deed as to them expresses no consideration whatever, not even that of natural affection. but had this been expressed, altho' it is a good consideration, it is not a valuable one, but merely voluntary, and would be set aside, in favor of a plaintiff, a bonâ fide purchaser, for valuable consideration. a fortiori then a court of equity will not enforce a deed, in favor of a mere volunteer, against a defendant, a bonâ fide purchaser, for valuable consideration. and for greater reason, still, will it not avail mere volunteers of the fraud of their donor against such a purchaser. surely a court of equity can never lend it's power to enforce a fraud, whether in favor of him who commits it, or of any other claiming under it.

And if it will not come in aid of persons against whom nothing can be said but that they are mere volunteers, who have paid nothing for the lands they claim, much less will it do so, where the volunteers themselves have connived at the fraud, & participated in it. living, as these complainants did, either in the house of the def^{s} or in sight of it, the two families, father, brothers & sisters in habits of daily and family intercourse, a treaty going on for the sale of the lands almost[4] under their feet, it was impossible it should have been unknown to any of them, that it should not at some time have been mentioned in conversations in their presence; & the smallest hint would have been sufficient to give alarm to these complainants, to put them on the alert for the safety of their own title. yet, witnesses as they must have been of the fraud practising on their sister & brother in law, they see it go on in silence, give no hint of their title, never drop a caution even in conversations with their sister, but suffer their rights to be conveyed away, and the full price to be paid for them, by an innocent purchaser, without giving him any notice or caveat as to their prior claim. I have no books to turn to from which to cite cases, but I know that the books abound with decisions that the mere silence of a person while their rights, even of the most valid character, are bargaining away to a purchaser without notice of them, implies either assent, or participation in the fraud, and for ever bars any future claim on their part; and it has the same effect in the present case as if they had joined in the deed conveying the lands to the defendants.

If then the deed of 1802. was not a nullity for want of timely probat, which is to be enquired into, it was Null by the want of notice to the def. either actual or constructive, by the active fraud of the father, and the passive fraud of the sisters, by the valuable basis of the one claim, and the voluntary one of the other, and secured by the sacred character of equity, which will never lend it's authority to enforce fraud against innocence.—Such, dear Sir, are the views of your case which present themselves to my mind. the stress I lay on the conclusion of your purchase before the final probat of the adversary deed may so far merit notice as to consult your counsel on the expediency of taking measures for opening again the pleadings so as to procure the establishmt of that fact, either by your own amendatory answer, or by the reexamination of mr Hening, & in this no time is to be lost. but I claim no confidence in these opinions, conscious as I am of a long-lost familiarity with subjects of this nature. the better information of your counsel must be your guide, and what I offer is but in proof of my attention to your request and of the great esteem and respect of which I now tender you the assurance.

TH: JEFFERSON

RC (Mrs. Charles W. Biggs, Lewisburg, W.Va., 1950; photocopy in MsSM); addressed: "Craven Peyton esquire Monteagle." PoC (DLC); endorsed by TJ. Dft (ViU: TJP); on verso of Peyton to TJ, 26 June 1817 (first letter); partial abstract entirely in TJ's hand reading as follows:

"Lewis v. Peyton.

Subsidiary questions. 1. can one, not a party to a deed claim under it?

2. is the wording of the deed Lewis to Lewis, such as, altho' recorded to amount to notice?

3. is the deed Lewis to Lewis to be considered as a will? & if so, was it revoked by that of Lewis to Peyton?

4. is the limn too remote? 5. Warranty

The strong points.

1. Peyton is a purchaser for valble and full considn

2. he was a bonâ fide purchaser, with constructive notice indeed (from the recording of the deed) but not actual notice

3. his actual notice was the contrary from the silence of the parties.

4. the daurs [daughters] are volunteers, and altho' the Chancellor might set aside the 2d deed in favor of creditors, he wd not in favr of volunteers. especially of volunteers, participating in a fraudulent silence.

5. not only the silence of C. L. Lewis on executing the deed to Peyton, but the import of that deed itself convicts him of gross fraud, & disqualifies him from being a witness."

Enclosed in TJ to Peyton, 16 July 1817.

This case was evidently settled or dropped, because Peyton maintained his title to the Monteagle estate until his death in 1837. The parcel was part of a tract sold by his executors in 1838 (Albemarle Co. Deed Book, 36:367–8). For a discussion of the case as it related to the larger legal issues of the Lewis family, see Boynton Merrill Jr., *Jefferson's Nephews: A Frontier Tragedy* (1976), esp. 50–4 and 314–6.

For the deeds referenced by TJ above, see note to Peyton to TJ, 26 June 1817 (second letter). In addition to MRS PEYTON (Jane Peyton), the daughters of Charles L. Lewis and TJ's sister Lucy Jefferson Lewis included Martha A. C. Lewis (Monroe), Lucy B. Lewis, and Ann M. Lewis. The Virginia LAW WHICH DECLARES THAT NO DEED SHALL BE GOOD AGAINST A PURCHASER WITHOUT NOTICE was enacted on 13 Dec. 1792, while the LATE ACT OF ASSEMBLY that amended this regulation became law on 9 Feb. 1814 (*Acts of Assembly* [1792–93 sess.], 48–50; [1813–14 sess.], 35–7). Peyton's ownership did not come into question UNTIL 1814, when the recording of a 10 Sept. 1805 deed from Charles L. Lewis to Peyton for a final portion of the Monteagle tract was challenged (Albemarle Co. Deed Book, 15:409–10; TJ to Peyton, 13 Aug. 1814).

[1] TJ here canceled what appears to be "paid."

[2] Word interlined.

[3] Reworked from "a conveyance."

[4] Word interlined.

From James Rawlings

DEAR SIR, Richmond 9 July 1817.

On the Records of the Mutual Assurance Society against Fire on Buildings of the state of Virginia I find entered for Assurance a Mill House near to the Town of Milton, in the name of, John Henderson for the legatees of Bennett Henderson decs^d which mill has been Transferred to you. Several quotas have been assessed on this building, the amount of which it will become my duty to demand of you, unless, as I am inclined to think, the House was removed or demolished at a date anterior to the assessment of the quotas.

As I am not in possession of any evidence of the time when this mill was pulled down and as the charges for Insurance necessarily cease with the destruction of the subject Insured, you will greatly oblige me by stating at what time the mill was demolished, in order that I may release the charges made subsequent thereto.

With great Respect y^r most Ob^t JAMES RAWLINGS

P. Ag^t M A S^y

RC (MHi); between dateline and salutation: "Thomas Jefferson Esqr Montecello"; endorsed by TJ as a letter from James "Rawlins" received 15 July 1817 and so recorded in SJL; with additional notation by TJ beneath endorsement relating to his response of 31 July 1817: "1795. Bill in Chancery for abating Henderson's dam 1799. Oct. 1. Decree 1804. May 1. I bought the millstones." RC (DLC); address cover only; with PoC of TJ to Benjamin Henry Latrobe, 16 July 1817, on recto and verso; addressed: "Thomas Jefferson Esqr near Milton"; stamp canceled; franked; postmarked.

James Rawlings (ca. 1788–1838) was promoted from clerk of accounts to principal agent for the Mutual Assurance Society following the death of Samuel Greenhow in 1815. In 1829 and 1833 he served as a senior alderman for the city of Richmond. Rawlings resigned from the Mutual Assurance Society in 1837 on being named president of the Farmers' Bank of Virginia, and he held the latter position until his death at his home in Richmond (John B. Danforth and Herbert A. Claiborne, *Historical Sketch of the Mutual Assurance Society of Virginia* [1879], 44, 58–9; *MB*, 2:1344, 1393; Marshall, *Papers*, 11:264–5, 12:575–6; A. Böhmer Rudd, comp., *Shockoe Hill Cemetery, Richmond, Virginia: Register of Interments, April 10, 1822–December 31, 1950* [1960–62], 1:15; *Richmond Enquirer*, 7 Apr. 1829, 9 Apr. 1833, 15, 17 Feb. 1838).

P. AG^T M A S^Y: Principal Agent Mutual Assurance Society.

From John Barnes

DEAR SIR— George Town Co[a] 11th July 1817.

since my Return, I have revised your Acco[t] & thereby corrected an error of mine in your fav[r] of $12. now adjusted—and herewith, inclose you a perfect statem[t] by which I remain your Debter $11—doll[r]—M[r] Milligans Note, bespeakes his good intention—but I dare not wait—its final issue—I shall however daily Urge the delivery—

M[r] Wheat, handed me your fav[r] of the 14[h]—the 20th Ult[o] and withal informed me he had been in Washington had met, with a decent looking man—who presumed—from M[r] Wheats discription of Thruston he could in Course of a day or two point him Out—that his Usual business was waiting on Gent[n] dressing Boots, &c—and from Appearances suspected, he wished Concealm[t]—that his Usual place was in a Cellar—I offered M[r] Wheat whatever money he might stand in need off—but assured me, he had suff[t] and promised to call on me next day.—

but nothing has transpired since, respecting either—

I beg you Sir—Accept my most gratefull thanks for your very friendly Attention as well for your Renewed Invitation—which I dare not Hope to realize a 88—My best wishes, attend to good families at and [. . .] Monticello—many very many, happy Years.—

Most Respectfully—and very sincerely your Obed[t] serv[t]

JOHN BARNES,

RC (ViU: TJP-ER); one word illegible; at foot of text: "Thomas Jefferson Esq[r] Monticello—Virg[a]"; endorsed by TJ as received 15 July 1817 and so recorded in SJL.

ENCLOSURES

I

Account with John Barnes

[ca. 11 July 1817]

John Barnes, In a/c with Thomas Jefferson Esqr—

1814				
Sep[r] 2[d]	Of Gibson & Jefferson Rich[d] recd		$380	
	for this sum to be pass'd to the C[t] of Gen[l] Kosciusko say	$360		
	for this sum to J Barnes	8		
	for do to do	12		
			$380	
	of course T.J. to have C[t] with JB		for	20

Octr 10	To an Alexandria Bank Note			5	
1815.					
Apr^{l} 26.	Mr Jeffersons Order on The Treasurer U States for		$4870		
	for so much of said Order to the Principal of Genl				
	Kosciusko ⅌	4500			
	to d^{o} for Int due this day	360			
			4860		
	the residue to T.J. credit w^{h} JB			10	
1817					
June 9^{h}	To Cash advanced J Barnes			25	60
	per Contra—				
1814.					
Apr^{l} 27	for Cash paid Genl Armstrong for 40 francs paid for you in Paris			8	
1816					
June 6	for this sum paid Mrs Madison on Miss Randolphs Acco^{t}			20	
1817					
June 17	for d^{o} paid Gales & Seaton for National Intelligencer to 31 Oct ⅌ recp^{t}			21	49
	Balance in fav^{r} of Mr Jefferson			EE	$11

George Town Co^{a} July 1817
JOHN BARNES,

MS (ViU: TJP-ER); entirely in Barnes's hand; partially dated; with top horizontal rule and all vertical rules in red ink.

With this account Barnes probably enclosed a receipt from Gales & Seaton for the payment of $21 on 17 June 1817 for TJ's subscription to the Washington NATIONAL INTELLIGENCER from 31 Oct. 1813 to 31 Oct. 1817 (MS in DLC: TJ Papers, 210:37483; printed form, with blanks filled in by an unidentified hand; edge trimmed; endorsed by TJ: "Newspapers. National Intellig^{r} rec^{t} Oct. 31. 13 to Oct. 31. 17."). EE: "errors excepted."

II

Joseph Milligan to John Barnes, with Barnes's Note to Thomas Jefferson

MR BARNES June 18th 1817

I received the Box of Books from Mr Jefferson that he Sent to be bound they are now in the hands of one of my young men and will be finished in ten days also the book of tables which you brought will be bound in the Same time I will Send them all to Fredericksburg about the 6th or 7th of July that they may meet Mr Jefferson on his return to Monticello

Yours JOSEPH MILLIGAN[1]

July. 11th yesterday Mr Milligan shewed to me the several Volumes neatly Bound & ready for Boxing—only waited—two or three to compleat the whole—and will be put on Board the Steam Boat Washington to Morrow Eveng for Fredericksburg—in Care of Mr Gray—

JB—

RC (DLC: TJ Papers, 210:37485–6); recto in Milligan's hand and verso, partially dated, in Barnes's hand; addressed by Milligan: "John Barnes Esqr Georgetown"; endorsed by Barnes; also endorsed by TJ: "Millegan Joseph to mr Barnes June 18. 17."

[1] Recto ends here.

From Benjamin Harrison

DEAR SIR, Berkley July 11th 1817,

By the last Mail, I received your letter of the 26th ult and avail myself of the first opportunity to Richmond of answering it. The Manuscript in question I have ever thought worthy of publication and am much pleased that it has fallen into such hands—I shall approve entirely of any use which you may think proper to make of it, but would recommend its not being published immediately as I have every reason to hope that I shall be able to obtain a copy of a Manuscript on the same subjects and by the same Author which is in the possession of Mrs Harrison of Brandon; From what I have heard of this work; it is much fuller on the subject of the Carolina Boundary than either of those which you have seen, and contains a great variety of Anecdotes illustrative of the manners of the Period at which it was written—Should I not be disappointed, you may expect the Copy by the first safe conveyance which is afforded me, after its completion—

With sentiments of the highest respect

I am yr hum St BEN: HARRISON

RC (DLC); at foot of text: "Thos Jefferson Esqr"; endorsed by TJ as received 16 July 1817 and so recorded in SJL. RC (MHi); address cover only; with PoC of TJ to John Vaughan, 2 Aug. 1817, on verso; addressed: "Thos Jefferson Esqr Monticello Albemarle"; stamped; postmarked Richmond, 12 July.

The MANUSCRIPT owned by Benjamin Harrison was a text of William Byrd (1674–1744), "The Secret History of the Line," while that belonging to Evelyn Taylor Byrd HARRISON, of Brandon, was a copy of "The History of the Dividing Line," Byrd's more serious history of the 1728 expedition to survey the boundary of Virginia and North Carolina (TJ to Wilson Cary Nicholas, 16 Oct. 1816, and note).

To Charles Clay

DEAR SIR Poplar forest July 12. 17.

This is the only fair day since you were here, & being to depart tomorrow, I must employ it otherwise than in paying the visit I had intended you. I shall be back however within 3. weeks and have time then to render the double.

In the mean while as your Paul is desirous of laying up useful things in the storehouse of his mind, I send him a little bundle of canons of conduct which may merit a shelf after the one occupied by the Decalogue[1] of first authority. if he will get them by heart, occasions will not be wanting for their useful application. you can furnish him also with another decad, and, regulating his life by this Code of practice, it may bring pleasure and profit to himself, and praise from others. wishing pleasure, profit, and praise to him, to you, and yours, I salute you with constant friendship and respect.

Th: Jefferson

PoC (DLC); with subjoined FC of enclosure. Enclosure: TJ to Paul A. Clay, [ca. 12 July 1817].

[1]Manuscript: "Decalouge."

To Paul A. Clay

Th: Jefferson to Paul Clay S. [ca. 12 July 1817]

1. never spend your money before you have it.
2. never buy what you don't want, because it is cheap: it will be dear to you.[1]
3. Pride costs us more than hunger, thirst and cold.
4. never put off to tomorrow what you can do to-day.
5. never trouble another for what you can do yourself.
6 think as you please and let others do so: you will then have no disputes.[2]
7. how much pain have cost us the things which have never happened![3]
8. take things always by their smooth handle[4]
9. when angry, count 10. before you speak: if very angry, 100.
10. when at table, remember that we never repent of having eaten or drunk <u>too little</u>

haec animo concipe dicta tuo. et vale Th: Jefferson

FC (DLC); entirely in TJ's hand; undated; subjoined to PoC of covering letter. Enclosed in TJ to Charles Clay, 12 July 1817. Not recorded in SJL.

Paul Aurelius Clay (1807–80), planter, was the son of TJ's longtime friend and neighbor Charles Clay. He was born in Bedford County and grew up at Petty Grove plantation. At his father's death in 1820, Clay inherited a silver can (drinking vessel) that TJ had given to the elder Clay. He attended the University of Virginia in 1826 and 1827. Clay farmed in Bedford County for many years, and by 1850 his personal estate was valued at $25,000, including twenty-seven slaves. He subsequently lived in Henrico County before moving to Charlotte County, where he died (*VMHB* 31 [1923]: 262–3; Clay family Bible record, 1745–1873 [Vi]; Bedford Co. Will Book, 5:171–2; Joseph

Van Holt Nash, *Students of the University of Virginia: A Semi-centennial Catalogue, with Brief Biographical Sketches* [1878]; TJ to Arthur S. Brockenbrough, 19 Dec. 1825; J. Staunton Moore, comp., *The Annals and History of Henrico Parish, Diocese of Virginia* [1904; repr. 1979], 242; *Richmond Enquirer*, 14 Sept. 1838; DNA: RG 29, CS, Bedford Co., 1840, 1850, 1850 slave schedules, Henrico Co., 1860, Charlotte Co., Madison Township, 1870; *Lynchburg Virginian*, 4 Oct. 1880).

TJ refined the above advice, the so-called Canons of Conduct, over the course of his retirement. Most of the maxims were not original to TJ, although his arrangement of them was. For a later version, see enclosure to TJ to Thomas Jefferson Smith, 21 Feb. 1825.

The English schoolmaster William Lily used the admonition HAEC ANIMO CONCIPE DICTA TUO ("take these words into your mind") (Lily, *A Short Introduction of Grammar* [London, 1695; Sowerby, no. 4784]). ET VALE: "and farewell."

[1]TJ here canceled "3. take care of your pence. the pounds will take care of themselves" and renumbered the subsequent three items on the list to reflect the deletion.

[2]Sentence interlined in place of "7. never do a good thing by halves."

[3]Sentence interlined in place of "<*8*> 7. think as you please, and let others do so: you will then have no disputes."

[4]Sentence interlined, with further interlineation beneath that of "how much pain h," erased.

From José Corrêa da Serra

DEAR SIR New York. 12. July. 1817.

Your very kind and esteemed Letter of the 14th of Last month was directed to Washington, which place i had left the 3d of that month for Philadelphia, and after a short stay had Left that city also to ramble through parts of the country which i had not yet visited. At Last it has reached my hands, and i hasten to thank you for all your friendly dispositions towards me which i duly prize. Every circumstance well weighed i believe the best epoch for my pilgrimage to Monticello this year will be the Latter part of september, and i will apprize Mr Gilmer of your wish of his being of the party, and concert with him the details of the journey. The summer i intend to pass in the state of New York and in New England where i can fill many chasms that remain in my kno[w]ledge of these parts of your country. If it was not contrary to my duty i would also peep into Canada but that may be done perhaps in other time if my Life and strength continue. In the mean time receive the assurances of my most cordial respect and friendship

Your most obedient servt JOSEPH CORRÈA DE SERRA

RC (MHi); hole in manuscript; endorsed by TJ as received 22 July 1817 and so recorded in SJL.

From John Adams

DEAR SIR Quincy July 15 1817

I am impatient to See your Plan of a University and new System of Education. To assist you in your contemplations, I Send you, a Pamphlet,[1] "The Politicks of Connecticut." By a federal Republican in the name of Hamilton. Was there ever Such a combination? Two Copies were Sent me from the Post on Saturday last: I know not from whence nor by whom.

Now Sir! please to hear a modest Proposal. Let me go back to twenty. Give me a million of Revenue, a Library of a Million of Volumes, and as many more as I Should want. I would devote my Life to Such an Œvrage as Condercet[2] tells us, that Turgot had in contemplation, all his Lifetime. I would digest Bryant Gebelin, Dupuis, Sir William Jones and above all the Acta Sanctorum of the Bolandists.

I know where this investigation would end. In Montesquiues 12 duodecimo[3] Pages.

Is the Biography of Democratus[4] and Heraclitus a Fable, or History? I cannot contemplate human affairs, without laughing or crying. I choose to laugh. When People talk of the Freedom of Writing Speaking or thinking, I cannot choose but laugh. No such thing ever existed, No such thing now exists: but I hope it will exist, But it must be hundreds of years after you and I Shall write and Speak no more.

JOHN ADAMS

RC (DLC); at foot of text: "Mr Jefferson"; endorsed by TJ as received 29 July 1817 and so recorded in SJL. FC (Lb in MHi: Adams Papers). Enclosure: "A Federal Republican," later signing himself "Hamilton" [George H. Richards], *The Politics of Connecticut: or, a Statement of Facts, Addressed to Honest Men of All Parties, religious and political, in the State: particularly to the mass of community, a Bold and Hardy Yeomanry, who compose the flesh and muscle, the blood and bone of the Body Politic* (Hartford, 1817).

In his biography of TURGOT, Condorcet included a chapter describing a work that his subject had contemplated writing "respecting the human soul, the order of the universe, and the Supreme Being; respecting the principles of society and the rights of man; respecting political constitutions, legislation, and executive power; respecting natural education; and respecting the means of perfecting the human race relatively to the exercise and increase of its powers" (Condorcet, *The Life of M. Turgot* [London, 1787; translation of the 1786 Paris edition of the *Vie de Monsieur Turgot*; Adams's copies of both works in MBPLi], 272). For the 12 DUODECIMO PAGES of Montesquieu, see Adams to TJ, 28 June 1812. The Greek philosophers Democritus (DEMOCRATUS) and HERACLITUS are often depicted together for contrast, with the former characterized as constantly laughing and the latter always weeping (Cora E. Lutz, "Democritus and Heraclitus," *Classical Journal* 49 [1954]: 309–14).

[1] RC: "Pamplet." FC: "Pamphlet."
[2] FC: "Condorcet."
[3] RC: "duodedimo." FC: "duodecimo."
[4] FC: "Democritus."

From Mark L. Descaves

SIR Balt^{o} July 15th 1817.

Inclosed I have the honour of forwarding to you a letter our distinguished friend Gen. Lafayette entrusted to my care with a request to deliver it in y^{r} own hands Should I be at liberty, Shortly after my arrival in this country to gratify my great & Sincere desire of paying my respects to you at y^{r} residence.—Deprived of even a faint hope that in the course of this Summer I should be so much disengaged as to be able of visiting Virginia, I send you per Mail, as in this case I have been directed to act by our worthy friend, the inclosed dispatch.—

If it were in my power to be of any Service to you Sir, either in taking care y^{r} answer to our friend should reach him safe or in any other way my services might be acceptable or usefull to you I beg you will rest assured I should consider it as a particular favour to be called upon to accomplish the offers and promises of my Sincerest & most unbounded devotion.

With great regard I have the honour to be, Sir, Y^{r} very hble obed^{t} Servt

MARK L DESCAVES

RC (MHi); at foot of text: "Thomas Jefferson Esqre"; endorsed by TJ as a letter from "<*Destaves*> Deslaves Mark L." received 22 July 1817 and so recorded in SJL. Enclosure: Lafayette to TJ, 25 Apr. 1817.

Mark L. Descaves, merchant, was a partner by 1815 in the Baltimore firm of Descaves & Mercier, which imported French furniture. The partnership was insolvent by January 1817 (Marshall, *Papers*, 8:151–2, 190; *Baltimore Price Current*, 4 Nov. 1815; *Baltimore Patriot & Evening Advertiser*, 26 Feb., 29 May 1816; *The Baltimore Directory and Register, For the Year 1816* [Baltimore, 1816], 53; Annapolis *Maryland Gazette and Political Intelligencer*, 30 Jan. 1817; *The Baltimore Directory, For 1817–18* [Baltimore, 1817], 49; *Baltimore Patriot & Mercantile Advertiser*, 29 Mar. 1822).

Descaves's ARRIVAL at New York City occurred on 30 June 1817 (*New-York Daily Advertiser*, 1 July 1817).

From the Seventy-Six Association

DEAR SIR, Charleston So. Ca 15th July 1817—

By direction of the '76 Association we [ha]ve the honor to transmit you the following Oration [de]livered before that Society and the citizens of Charles[ton], on the 4th ins^{t} by Benjamin Elliott Esqr—

The energy with which this production upholds [the] Republican cause; and the eloquence with which it [il]lustrates its principles, give it we conceive strong claims [to] your perusal. The blessings of a free people have [fo]llowed you into that retirement, which will be [ev]er hallowed by the recollection, that you have [so] essentially contributed to the welfare and hap[pi]ness of our beloved Country—That the life [of] the Father of the Republican Family may [be] long preserved, must be the sincere wish of [ev]ery friend to America, and is the fervent [pr]ayer of those who Respectfully subscribe [the]mselves.   Your Ob[d] Servt[s]—

CHRIST[R] L BLACK.
WILLIAM SINGELLTON
T. LOUGHTON SMITH
SAM[L] BURGER
THO. D CONDY
} Standing Committee '76 Association

RC (ViU); written on verso of title page of the enclosure presented to TJ; in Black's hand, signed by Black, Singellton, Smith, Burger, and Condy; edge trimmed; at foot of text: "Honb[le] Thomas Jefferson Monticello Virginia." Enclosure: Benjamin Elliott, *An Oration, delivered in St. Philip's Church, before the inhabitants of Charleston, South-Carolina; on Friday, the Fourth of July, 1817, in commemoration of American Independence; by appointment of the '76 Association, And published at the Request of that Society* (Charleston, 1817; Poor, *Jefferson's Library*, 13 [no. 826]; TJ's copy in ViU), declaring that the best way for the United States to "ensure to our posterity, the beatitude we inherit" is to study the model of "Our revolutionary ancestors" (p. 4); celebrating American victories in the War of 1812; asserting that European nations have begun emulating the United States; affirming that in TJ and Benjamin Franklin the French people saw "splendidly illustrated, how republicanism was adorned with science, patriotism, and genius" (p. 16); predicting that in the future the United States will experience rapid population growth and "more complete amalgamation of these states, into one community" (p. 19); claiming that American "Naval skill is appreciated by European statesmen as their best security" against British domination (p. 22); linking manufacturing and the arts with continued American ascendance; and concluding with a call for a national system of education. The PoC of TJ to Samuel M. Reid, 13 Oct. 1817, is written on the verso of an address cover that evidently either enclosed this letter and the pamphlet on which it was written or an otherwise unknown accompanying letter (RC in MHi; address cover only; addressed in Black's hand: "Honb[le] Thomas Jefferson Monticello Virginia" and "per Mail"; franked; postmarked Charleston, 16 July).

Christopher L. Black served as keeper of Charleston's militia arsenal from at least 1818–20. In 1831 he was elected recording secretary of the newly formed South Carolina State Rights and Free Trade Association (*The Planters' & Merchants' Almanac, for the Year of Our Lord 1818* [Charleston, (1817)]; *The Planters' & Merchants' City Almanac, for the Year of Our Lord 1820* [Charleston, (1819)]; *New-England Magazine* 1 [1831]: 258).

William Singellton, attorney, was admitted to the bar in Charleston in 1817, became an ensign in the South Carolina militia the same year, and represented Saint Bartholomew Parish in the South Carolina House of Representatives, 1818–19 and 1820–21 (O'Neall, *Bench and Bar of South Carolina*, 2:603; Charleston *City Gazette and Commercial Daily Advertiser*, 18 June 1817; *BDSCHR*, 5:249).

Thomas Loughton Smith (d. 1817), attorney, was the son of William Loughton Smith. He studied law in Philadelphia and was admitted to the bar in Charleston in 1815 (George C. Rogers Jr., *Evolution of a Federalist: William Loughton Smith of Charleston [1758–1812]* [1962],

397–8, 402; O'Neall, *Bench and Bar of South Carolina*, 2:603; Charleston *Southern Patriot, And Commercial Advertiser*, 26 Nov. 1817).

Samuel Burger (d. ca. 1846), public official, was deputy secretary of state for South Carolina from 1813 until his election in December 1816 as tax collector for Charleston's parishes of Saint Philip and Saint Michael, a position he held until his death. He became a director of the Bank of the State of South-Carolina in 1821 and served as a Charleston city warden from at least 1821–23 (Joseph Folker, *A Directory of the City and District of Charleston; and Stranger's Guide ... for the Year 1813* [Charleston, (1813)], 7; Abraham Motte, *Charleston Directory, and Strangers' Guide, for the Year 1816* [Charleston, 1816], 14; Charleston *City Gazette and Commercial Daily Advertiser*, 4 Dec. 1816, 4 Sept., 19 Dec. 1821, 9 Jan. 1823; Charleston *Southern Patriot*, 2 Apr. 1845, 2 Jan. 1846 [funeral announcement]).

Thomas Doughty Condy (ca. 1798–1858), planter, attorney, and public official, was admitted to the bar in Charleston in 1818 and won a special election that same year to fill a vacant seat representing Saint Philip and Saint Michael parishes in the South Carolina House of Representatives. In 1819 he delivered the annual oration sponsored by the Seventy-Six Association to commemorate American independence. He was reelected as a state representative for the 1822–23 session. Condy was a member of the state militia and compiled *A Digest of the Laws of the United States & the State of South-Carolina, now of force, relating to the Militia* (1830). In 1832 he was confirmed as United States marshal for South Carolina, a position he held until his death. Condy owned real estate valued at $20,000 and at least thirty-nine slaves in 1850 (O'Neall, *Bench and Bar of South Carolina*, 2:600; *BDSCHR*, 5:52–3; Condy, *An Oration, Delivered, In St. Philip's Church, before an assemblage of the inhabitants of Charleston, South-Carolina, On the 5th Day of July, 1819; [the 4th being Sunday] In Commemoration of American Independence, by appointment of the '76 Association* [Charleston, 1819]; *JS*, 22:268, 270 [19, 20 Dec. 1832]; DNA: RG 29, CS, Charleston, 1850, 1850 slave schedules; *JEP*, 10:420 [30 May 1858]).

At some point the Seventy-Six Association also sent TJ a copy of its 1816 Independence Day address by William Lance, *An Oration, delivered on the Fourth of July, 1816, In St. Michael's Church, S. C. by appointment of the '76 Association* (Charleston, [1816]; Poor, *Jefferson's Library*, 13 [no. 826]; TJ's copy in ViU, inscribed to TJ on verso of title page [edge trimmed]: "[T]he Honble Thomas Jefferson Respectfully presented by order of the '76 Association Charleston S^{o} Carolina Tho: W. Bacot Chairman Com^{ee} of Arrange^{t}"), celebrating the anniversary of American independence and the moment when an "ignominious bondage was abolished—a gallant and magnanimous people effected their deliverance from slavery.—There was an instantaneous transfiguration of British subjects into American citizens. The sun which rose upon *vassals* set upon *freemen*" (p. 5); recalling the circumstances leading to the War of 1812 and highlighting TJ, "who had devoted all his life to public service, and his transcendent talents unerringly to the promotion of republican liberty" (p. 10); summarizing the course of the war and asserting that it was a "just and necessary war, declared and conducted without any prospect or thought of foreign alliance" (p. 19); and concluding that the American "*Republic stands alone in the universe*. It exists as the bird of classical fable, the only one of its kind" (p. 21).

From Stephen Cathalan

My Dear Sir &
most Respected Friend Marseilles the 16th July 1817—

In my Letter of the 15th February 1816, I had the honor of Remiting you Bill of Lading[1] & Invoice of

1 Case cont^{ing} 50 Bottles Hermitage wine } Shipped on the Brig
1 d^{to} Maccaroni } Pilot Dixon Master

consigned to the Collector of the District of Phil^{a} Cost on Board F 248.02.

on the 19th March 16 I Remited you Bill of Lading[2] & Invoice of 4 Cases Red Wine of nice, on the Brig agenoria Cyril Martin Master Bound for Alexandria; I doubt not they Reached you as the D^{ty} Col^{or} Mr Simms, Returned me the acquits a Caution of this Customs, Proving they had been Landed, on which my Bond was Canceled, cost & charges— 346—

In mine of the 4th June 16, I Informed you, that I had Shipped on the Ship Lothair John Stone M^{er} Bound for norfolk & I had Inclosed the Bill of Loading[3] in my Letter to the Collector of the District, for 1 D^{ble} Cask Cont^{ing}[4] 120 litres wine of Roussillon, to his Consig^{on} & to be forwarded to you;—on the 19th d^{to} I advised you, that I had Shipped on the Brig ocean, Nath^{el} S. Bond Master—

2 Boxes of 12 B^{tls} Each Red wine of Paillerolle, with—
1 Basket Maccaroni; Cost of the Maccaroni 35—

F629–02[5]

& on the Brig Gen^{al} Marion Rubben Brumley M^{er} 1 Box Cont^{ing} 30 B^{tles} Red wine of Lédenon; Both those 2 vessels Bound for new-York, Remiting you the Bills of Loading, Consigned to the Coll^{or} of that District;

on the 12th July 16 by the Brig David Maffet of Phil^{a} Is^{ac} Douane Master Bound for Phil^{ia} I Sent you a Small Box, Directed to the Collector of that District, containing Fleurs Immortelles, which, by my Letter of that Day (12th July) I was begging you to offer to the Ladies, your Daughter & Grand Daughters;

and on the 3^{d} August 16 I Sent to the Collector of that District, Bill of Loading of the 2^{d} D^{ble} Cask of Roussillon[6] wine I Shipped on the Ship Prosperity of Phil^{a} S^{el} Barclay Master;

I hope that the whole has Reached you in good order & in due time, but as Since your very kind Letter of the 1st febr^{y} 1816, not any others from you have hitherto Reached me, & I hopping from one Day to another to Receive a line mentioning me,[7] that the whole had been Safely delivered to you, I have Postponed till now to address to you;

M^{r} f. Durand of Perpignan in Sending me the Roussillon wine, did not Give me it's Peculiar name or Cottage,[8] nor the quantity Contained in each Cask, he Said only that it was the Such as you wished & he was Confident that you would be satisfied of it; adding that his first Invoice Costed on the Spot *f* 145—

=to be paid by me to his Brother in this City,= which I did		
to which adding Freight, waggonage, Droits Réunis &—Custom house's Duties &^{a} till on Board		13–50–
the 2^{d} Invoice (as p^{r} his Letters) Cost	F 151–	F 158–50–
charges, as above, till on Board	14–50–	165–50–
		F 324 —

which I have charged on your Debit—

his Brother, here, whom I charged to ask him the name of this wine, in Paying it to him, Received at Last in answer, that it was old Rivesaltes;—

you will Please to observe by the Acc^{t} Cur^{t} herewith, that it Remains in my hands a Balance due to you p^{r} F 102–98—Subject to your orders, or for any future commands, to be Executed by me, from you; I wishing much to hear, if you have been Satisfied of the qualities of what I Sent you;

in my Letter of the 19th March 1816—, I took the Liberty of Inclosing a Copy of my Petition of the 15th September 1814 to James Madison Esqr, then President of the united States, in which, without your Leave, I made use in my Behalf of Some Paragraphs in your Letter to me of the 29th June 1807—;—as Since I have not been favoured with a Line from you, I am apprehensive, you may have disapproved my So Doing;—if it Should be the Case, or Should you have disapproved the Contents of my Said Petition, I beg you to accept my Excuses & Regrets!

I have neither Received hitherto, any Answer to it, from the Secretaries of State, James Monroe, nor John Quincy adams Esq^{rs}, his Successor, Since the first is President of the united States; nor from the Minister Plen^{ry} of the U.S. at Paris, who has Received not any orders hitherto, to Pay me the amount of my Claims;—

if on the Contrary you have Found that my Demand for the Balance, which I Think it to be due to me by the u.s. Government is Just

& to be Paid to me, I beg you to use your good Influence & Protection in my favour in order I may be Paid for it.

I beg your Refference to my Letter of the 8th Ins^{t} via havre de Grace, whereof I Remit you herewith the Duplicata, in which there, is Inclosed my Letter to the H^{ble} John Quincy Adams Sec^{ry} of State, Conveying my Resignation, which I offer to the most H^{ble} James Monroe President of the united States; Begging you to keep it, or to forward it when Ever you will Please, or find it Convenient; I would Even, as you are my Protector & Support, have Consulted you, before Sending to you the whole, but you will Excuse me in considering how, we are So far distant, one of the other, & the Length[9] of Time, before Your wise opinion, on that Subject could be made known to me; I beg Leave to Confirm you that I wish much Mr J^{a} Dodge Should be, one Day, my Successor, because I Think him to be worthy[10] to be Such, & I would be very sorry, that one Day Some other one might not do honor to the u.S. in Exercising,[11] after me, this office; I attach, I must Confess it to you, de L'amour Propre;—allways at your Commands

I have the honor to be with Great Respect! my Dear Sir & most Respected Friend! Your Most obedient, Devoted Servant & Sincere obliged Friend STEPHEN CATHALAN.

Received by order & for account of Thos Jefferson Esquire of Monticello State of virginia by Steph^{n} Cathalan of Marseilles

1815 october 1st by Steph^{n} Girard of Phil^{a} Credit on Perregaux, Lafitte & c^{o} of Paris p^{r} D^{ars} 200—which they Paid me at *f* 5.28 c. p^{r} D^{ar} F 1056—

1816 To Invoices Sent to him—vizt

15 Feb^{ry}	F 248–02—	as p^{r} Detail in this Letter—
19th March	346—	
19th June	35—	
1817		
July 16th	324—	
	102.98—	to Balance Brought on a new account to his credit
	F 1056—	Errors Excepted Marseilles the 16th July 1817—

STEPHEN CATHALAN.

[*Postscript supplied from Dupl:*]

I Beg your Refference to the herewith Report & printed Document &^{a} I address to the hh^{ble} Secretary of the Navy of the U. States at

Washington, which I have Left unsealed, for your Perusal, Tho' I apprehend that you will find it Rather too Long and Tedious; I Beg you after to Seal it, & forward it to him.

S. C[AN] The 25th July 17

RC (MHi); at foot of first page: "Thomas Jefferson Esquire &[a] &[a] Monticello"; lacking final postscript; endorsed by TJ as received 29 Sept. 1817 and so recorded in SJL. Dupl (MHi); only the most significant variations are noted below; at head of text: "2[ta] the original via Havre"; endorsed by TJ as a letter of 25 July 1817 received 12 Oct. 1817 and so recorded in SJL. Enclosures: (1) Cathalan to TJ, 8 July 1817. (2) Cathalan's report to Benjamin W. Crowninshield, Marseille, 21 July [1817], outlining a dispute with Commodore Isaac Chauncey and William Shaler, the United States consul general at Algiers, over the length of quarantine for a squadron of American naval vessels, consisting of the ship *Washington*, the frigates *United States* and *Constellation*, and the brig *Spark*, which arrived at Marseille on 11 June 1817 from Mahón, Spain; stating that the Marseille board of health had assigned the entire squadron a quarantine of fifteen days rather than the anticipated seven because Shaler, who had come from Algiers and was thus subject to the longer quarantine, had traveled on multiple ships of the squadron during different legs of its journey; relating that Chauncey perceived this extended quarantine to be an insult to the United States; giving evidence that the rules of quarantine applied to the American squadron were routine even for French warships and vessels carrying French dignitaries; citing correspondence with Captain Thomas Gamble of the corvette *Erie* (probably also enclosed here but not found) to refute Chauncey's charge that a previous quarantine of an American vessel had left ill feelings; accusing Asa Fitch, an American merchant in Marseille, of prejudicing Chauncey against Cathalan; reporting that Fitch had broken quarantine to pass letters to other American warships after Chauncey's early departure and that the latter had emphatically declared that neither he nor his command would return to a French port unless war with France broke out and he was coming to fight; and describing printed deliberations of the Marseille board of health (probably also enclosed here but not found) that condemned the actions of Fitch and his associates (FC in FrM; entirely in Cathalan's hand; misdated 1818).

"Acquits à caution" (ACQUITS A CAUTION) are customhouse bonds. DROITS RÉUNIS: "indirect taxes."

[1] RC: "Loading." Dupl: "Lading."
[2] RC: "Loading." Dupl: "Lading."
[3] Preceding two words, interlined in RC, are not in Dupl.
[4] Dupl here adds "38-Gallons or."
[5] Total not in Dupl.
[6] Dupl here adds "(Rivesaltes)."
[7] Instead of preceding two words, Dupl reads "from you, mentioning."
[8] Preceding two words not in Dupl.
[9] RC and Dupl: "Lenght."
[10] RC: "worth." Dupl: "worthy."
[11] RC: "Exercing." Dupl: "Exercising."

To Benjamin Henry Latrobe

DEAR SIR — Monticello July 16. 17.

I found your favor of June 28. on my return hither from my other home, about 90 miles S.W. from hence and near Lynchburg, the mos[t][1] growing place in America. they have there the new method of moulding the stock brick in oil, and execute with it the most beautiful brick work, I have ever seen. I went there to try to get a workman skilled in it to come and build our first Academical pavilion, for which they are now making the bricks. I fear you have given yourself too much trouble about the designs for us. I did not mean to give you this, but since you have been so kind as to take it it shall turn to good account. our fellow-citizens are subscribing with a liberality I had no expectation of, and the confidence this proves in the visitors is a new obligation on them to spare no pains in the execution of their trust. I am anxious to recieve your draught as soon as possible, because we must immediately lay the 1st stone, as the 1st pavilion must be finished this fall and we have few workmen. we have not, for instance a single stone cutter. I think [y]our drawings had better come in the form of a roll by the mail. any necessary doubling of the paper may be easily obliterated by the screw press which I possess. the tobacco capital you are so kind as to propose to send to me will come safely if addressed to Messrs Gibson and Jefferson my correspondents in Richmond who will pay freight & other expences. I am pleased with your account of the Columbian marble. I have no doubt it is part of the same vein which passes thro' Orange as you say; strikes James river at the mouth of Rockfish, runs up that river to near Lynchburg, there goes off South-Westwardly crossing Roanoke Etc it is accompanied thro' it's whole course by a narrow bed of limestone running near and parallel to it. the limestone passes within 6. miles of Monticello, but the marble does not shew within 30. miles. I carried samples of it to Philadelphia 40. years ago, & had them polished. they were very various, and some very fine. on a cliff of James river enough shews itself to build a city.—I still use constantly the polygraph I have used a dozen years. the pen frame has become a little rickety, but as it will still do, I am afraid to undertake tightening it up myself. the single advantage of Wedgewood's Manifold-writer is it's being so portable. it takes very little room in one's baggage, and may be resorted to in a moment on the road, for copying as well as writing a hasty letter. but fetid copying paper makes the copies a perfect nuisance on your shelves, nor can it bear any comparison in any other point of view with the Polygraph, which I consider as one of the great inventions of the age. could we get a stone cutter with you, capable of forming a Doric base & capital, the drawing being furnished him, should we apply for one, and what would be the daily wages, or monthly, of such an one, boarding himself? when we get our academical village under way, I am in hopes you will think that & Monticello worth a visit: the levelling the ground into terraces will take time and labor. we propose a distinct t[erra]s for every 2. pavilions and their adjacent dormitories, that is [...] a pavilion at each end of each terras. ever your's with [...]ship, respect & best wishes

TH: JEFFERSON

PoC (DLC); on reused address cover of James Rawlings to TJ, 9 July 1817; damaged at seal; at foot of first page: "M[r] Latrobe"; endorsed by TJ.

In his *Notes on the State of Virginia*, TJ described the vein of marble found at JAMES RIVER AT THE MOUTH OF ROCKFISH River as "very good marble, and in very great abundance" (*Notes*, ed. Peden, 29).

[1]Word faint.

From John Love

DEAR SIR Buckland July 16th 1817.

At an early period of the summer, the President passed on this road, when I had the pleasure of seeing him: He was then satisfyed from the different appearances of the common wheats, and the kind here called the Lawler that the latter was uninjured by the Hessian fly, and engaged from me 200 bush[ls] for himself, and 200 for you, to Whom He mentioned his intention to write on the subject—I have still a considerable portion of my crop to dispose of, but orders for it have been received to a considerable amount from different parts of the U. States, & will probably soon be equal to the quantity to be disposed of in this neighbourhood—It may therefore be proper that I should more certainly at this time be informed of your wishes on the subject, as I have not had the honor of hearing from you—If more should be wished I can supply it, or if less it will be a matter of no importance. I see small parcels of it have been raised this year on James river you have therefore probably seen the growth of it, or I would inclose a stalk, it is I think much hardier than that of any other kind—But as the cause of the exemption of this wheat from the ravages of the fly could not be satisfactorily agreed on by the members of the committees of this neighbourhood, it was not in our power to make any public statement on this part of the subject—

The crops in this neighbourhood of the Lawler wheat are of good quality, not quite so heavy as the last year; The growth has been very great as might be expected, my crop is entirely clear of disease, altho I am told in the neighbourhood of Fauquir C.h. the smut has appeared in considerable quantity—My farm has not yet been visited with this dreadfull disease, & I believe it has not found its way to James river, I think from what I have seen in this neighbourhood it is attributable to bad seed, as it is very much the custom here to cut wheat in a green state, & the seed does not mature so perfectly as when left to the process of nature—

By middle or 20th of August, I could be prepared to deliver wheat for seed—

Be pleased Sir to accept the assurance of my most respectfull recollections, & perfect esteem—and best wishes for your happiness—I am Sir your Ob[t] Srv[t] JN[o] LOVE

RC (CSmH: JF-BA); endorsed by TJ as received 2 Aug. 1817 and so recorded in SJL. RC (DLC); address cover only; with PoC of TJ to Benjamin Henry Latrobe, 12 Oct. 1817, on verso; addressed: "Thomas Jefferson Esquire Monticello near Charlottsville va"; franked; postmarked Buckland, 16 July.

John Love (d. 1822), attorney, planter, and public official, qualified for the bar in Alexandria in 1801. He was a states' rights Republican who represented Fauquier County in the Virginia House of Delegates, 1805–07, was a member of the United States House of Representatives, 1807–11, and sat for Fairfax and Prince William counties in the Senate of Virginia, 1816–19. Love owned Buckland, an estate of some 1,200 acres located on the border of Fauquier and Prince William counties, where he farmed and had a milling complex known as Kinsley Mills. In 1797 he successfully petitioned the General Assembly to establish the town of Buckland on his land in Prince William County (*Alexandria Advertiser*, 23 Aug. 1797; *Acts of Assembly* [1797–98 sess.], 33–4 [19 Jan. 1798]; *Alexandria Advertiser and Commercial Intelligencer*, 14 Apr. 1801; Leonard, *General Assembly*; Love to the Freeholders of Culpeper and Fauquier Counties, 28 Mar. 1807 [printed circular in PHi]; Love to TJ, 20 Apr. 1808 [DNA: RG 59, LAR, 1801–09]; Noble E. Cunningham Jr., ed., *Circular Letters of Congressmen to Their Constituents, 1789–1829* [1978], 2:776–84; *Alexandria Herald*, 22 Jan. 1817, 8 Dec. 1820, 8 June 1822; *Alexandria Gazette & Daily Advertiser*, 9 Apr. 1819; Washington *Daily National Intelligencer*, 16 Aug. 1822).

LAWLER wheat had been introduced into Fauquier County by James Lawler in 1810 from Chester County, Pennsylvania, where it was known as "Jones' white wheat." In the summer of 1817 Love and several of his neighbors made a concerted effort to promote the variety by virtue of its apparent resistance to the Hessian fly (Baltimore *Niles' Weekly Register*, 28 June 1817; Love to Roberts Vaux, 17 June 1817, printed in Philadelphia Society for Promoting Agriculture, *Memoirs* 4 [1818]: 208–10).

On 15 July 1817 Love wrote a similar letter to James Madison (Madison, *Papers, Retirement Ser.*, 1:88–9).

From Joseph Milligan

Georgetown July 16th 1817

By this days steam boat I have sent your books Homer &[c] together with the two vols mathematical in all Seventeen Volumes They are sent to the care of M[r] W[m] F Gray Bookseller of Fredericksburg with a request to have them sent on without delay

Yours With Esteem JOSEPH MILLIGAN

RC (DLC); endorsement by TJ torn. Recorded in SJL as received 21 July 1817.

To Craven Peyton

Dear Sir Monticello July 16. 17.

I returned from Poplar Forest yesterday, and now send you your papers with my opinion on them. the issue of the cause will depend mainly on the question whether you knew of the estate in remr[1] conveyed to the daughters? Col° Lewis's deposition that he informed you of it; is the only testimony against you but your answer, his deed to the contrary and other circumstances will overweigh his assertion in the mind of any man as it does in mine. I have therefore in giving a candid opinion been obliged to speak hard of him. this is intended for your satisfaction; but considering the connection which has been between him and me decency, & the desire of peace dictate that my opinion of his conduct should not be made known, nor become the subject of neighborhood conversation, as it might bring on me useless pain.

I suppose Johnson is employed against you, and therefore recommend to you by all means to employ Sheffy, lately settled in Staunton. he is very able. but think immediately of establishing by new testimony the date of the conclusion of your bargain verbally with Charles Lewis. if that is fixed and you are equally defended, you are in no danger. Yours with friendship and respect Th: Jefferson

PoC (DLC); on verso of reused address cover to TJ; at foot of text: "Mr Peyton"; endorsed by TJ. Enclosures: (1) TJ to Peyton, 8 July 1817. (2) Enclosures described at Peyton to TJ, 26 June 1817 (second letter).

The connection which has been between him and me was Charles L. Lewis's marriage to TJ's deceased sister Lucy Jefferson Lewis.

[1] Abbreviation for "remainder."

From Craven Peyton

Dear Sir Monteagle July 16–1817.

I receavd by Your Servant, the papars with Your Opinion, Shuffey Peyton and Baldwin are my Councel, they were informed of the Strong point You made respecting the recording of the Deed by the 3d witness aftar it was Out of date they replid, & said a Deed, which is not recorded in due time, is as it respects a subsequence purchaser, presisely as if it had not been recorded at all, this was the Law then, & since altared to have effect aftar being fully proven, this point being in my favour, I hope, leaves but little doubt of my success, I cant express the pleasing sensation of fealing produced by Your Opinion & remarks, On the subject & with Your permission, I woud enclose

Your Opinion, to my Council with directions to read it & enclose it to me again, & not to let it be seen by Any othar person, nor to mention it. Untill I receave Your instructions there is no Consideration On this earth, that cou[d] induce me to violate Any Confidence You might place in me, Any expressions of gratitude for this & many Othar Kindness I have receav[d] wou[d] fall very far short of my fealings for You, truely & Sincerely

Yr Fr[d] & Serv[t] C. PEYTON

RC (MHi); endorsed by TJ as received 17 July 1817 and so recorded in SJL.

SHUFFEY: Daniel Sheffy.

From John Barnes

DEAR SIR— George Town Co[a] 17th July 1817—

I now inclose you agreable to my letter of the 11th (for the Use of M[r] Louis Leschut—Charlotteville)[1] Richard Smith Cash[r] of the Office of Dist and Deposit at Washington his Order on ditto at Bank N York for $306. and by me endorsed—and Numbered 861.

with renewed Respects &c—

I am—your most Obed[t] JOHN BARNES.

PS. M[r] Milligan has this day forwarded your Box of Books Via Steam Boat to M[r] Gray Frederickb[g]

RC (ViU: TJP-ER); at foot of text: "Thomas Jefferson Esq[r] Monticello"; endorsed by TJ as received 22 July 1817 and so recorded in SJL. Enclosure not found.

Barnes's letter of 8 July 1817, not that OF THE 11TH, dealt with the issue of payment for Louis A. Leschot. A letter from TJ to Barnes, not found, is recorded in SJL as written 29 July 1817 from Monticello.

[1]Omitted closing parenthesis editorially supplied.

From Albert Gallatin

DEAR SIR Paris 17th July 1817

I enclose a letter from Professor Pictet which he gave me during a last excursion to Geneva. I saw there your nephew Terrel with whom every one is well pleased and who appears to be desirous of improving himself in every respect. He is not at all dissipated, and if his expences somewhat exceed his calculations, it is because he has fixed himself in the house of one of the most respectable citizens of Geneva, where he finds advantages of education and society, which he could not have obtained in a common boarding house, but where he could not have been received without paying a greater compensation than the common rate, as the gentleman was not in the habit of taking boarders. Mr Stephenson of Baltimore in whose hands Mr Terrell's funds were placed is said to have failed. Mr Terrell's expences are in the mean while defrayed by Mr Morton of Bordeaux to whom I wrote on the subject; and it is desirable that Mr Terrell's friends should make some other provision for him. He has written to his sister & to Mr Carr, but had not as yet received any answer.[1]

The growing prosperity of the United States is an object of admiration for all the friends of liberty in Europe, a reproach on almost all the European Governments. At no period has America stood on higher ground abroad than now; and every one who represents her may feel a just pride in the contrast between her situation & that of all other countries, and in the feeling of her perfect independence from all foreign powers. This last sentiment acquires new force here in seeing the situation of France under the guardianship of the four great Potentates. That this state of things should cease is in every respect highly desirable. Although not immediately affected by it, we cannot but wish to see the antient natural check of England resume its place in the system of the civilised world; and it can hardly be borne in the present state of knowledge that Austria or Russia should in the great scale stand before France. Indeed it is only physical power that now prevails; and as I had most sincerely wished that France when oppressing others should be driven back within her own bounds, I may be allowed to sigh for her emancipation from foreign yoke. I cannot view the arrangements made at Vienna as calculated to ensure even tranquillity. There is now a kind of torpid breathing spell; but the fire is not extinct. The political institutions do not either here, in Italy, or even Germany, harmonize with the state of knowledge, with the feelings and wishes of the people. What must be the consequence? New conflicts whenever opportunity will offer, and bloody revolutions effected or attempted, instead of that happy, peaceable & gradual improvement which philanthropists had anticipated and which seems to be exclusively the portion of our happy country.

We have lately lost Mad^e^ Staël, & she is a public loss. Her mind improved with her years, without any diminution of her fine & brilliant genius. She was a power by herself & had more influence on public opinion and even on the acts of Gov^t^ than any other person not in the ministry. I may add that she was one of your most sincere admirers.

I thirst for America, and I hope that the time is not distant when I may again see her shores, & enjoy the blessings which are found only there. There I also hope of once more meeting with you. Accept, in the mean while, the reiterated assurance[2] of my respect & of my unalterable attachment.

Your obed^t Servt ALBERT GALLATIN

RC (DLC); at foot of text: "Mr Jefferson"; endorsed by TJ as received 25 Sept. 1817 and so recorded in SJL. Tr (NHi: Gallatin Papers); posthumous copy; incomplete. Enclosure: Marc Auguste Pictet to TJ, 14 June 1817. Enclosed in Frank Carr to TJ, [received 23 Dec. 1817], and probably also in a missing letter from TJ to Carr of 29 Sept. 1817.

MR STEPHENSON: George P. Stevenson. Dabney C. Terrell had WRITTEN TO HIS SISTER Martha J. Terrell (Minor) and to Frank Carr, their brother-in-law.

The FOUR GREAT POTENTATES of Austria, Great Britain, Prussia, and Russia made key decisions about the future of France at the Congress of VIENNA, September 1814–June 1815 (Owen Connelly and others, eds., *Historical Dictionary of Napoleonic France, 1799–1815* [1985], 486–8). Madame de STAËL Holstein died 15 July 1817 (New York *Commercial Advertiser*, 3 Sept. 1817).

[1] Tr begins here.
[2] Tr ends here with "&c &c."

From Harrison Hall

SIR, Philad[a] July 17, 1817

Your Subscription to the Law Journal for Vols. 5 & 6 amounting to $10.00 being due—I have to request that you will remit the same by mail, or otherwise, as soon as may be convenient

Your's very respectfully HARRISON HALL
133 Chesnut st.

Your Subscription for the Port Folio for the present year is also due, ($6.00) You will have the goodness for the future, to remit this money direct to me instead of paying it to Mr. Cottem, as heretofore, as it is extremely troublesome for me to settle an acct with him—

RC (DLC); with "(Over)" adjacent to signature; postscript on verso; endorsed by TJ as received 2 Aug. 1817 and so recorded in SJL; notation by TJ above endorsement: "Newspapers."

Harrison Hall (1785–1866), publisher and author, spent his youth variously in Philadelphia, on the Eastern Shore of Maryland, and in Lamberton, New Jersey. He was a nongraduate member of the University of Pennsylvania class of 1803, and by 1812 he was a partner in the Philadelphia firm of Capp & Hall. In 1813 Hall authored a work on distilling. From 1816 to 1827 he and his brother John E. Hall were publisher and editor respectively of the *Port Folio* magazine in Philadelphia. During his long career in printing, Hall published the literary works of numerous members of his family. He also ran a bookstore and subsequently worked as a stationer and a surveyor. Hall moved to Cincinnati in 1865 and died there (Randolph C. Randall, *James Hall: Spokesman of the New West* [1964]; Will J. Maxwell, comp., *General Alumni Catalogue of the University of Pennsylvania* [1917], 25; Philadelphia *Poulson's American Daily Advertiser*, 22 Apr. 1812; Hall, *Hall's Distiller* [Philadelphia, 1813]; *MB*, 2:1337, 1415; John Adems Paxton, *The Philadelphia Directory and Register, for 1818* [Philadelphia, 1818]; A. M'Elroy, *A. M'Elroy's Philadelphia Directory, for 1839* [1839], 102; *M*[c]*Elroy's Philadelphia Directory for 1844* [1844], 126; DNA: RG 29, CS, Pa., Philadelphia, 1850, 1860; *Historical Magazine* 10 [1866]: 200; burial record, Spring Grove Cemetery, Cincinnati).

To Craven Peyton

TH:J. TO MR PEYTON July 17. 17.

you are quite free, my dear Sir, to make the use you propose of the opinion I gave you, and under the cautions you express. my object is to avoid giving useless offence. I salute you with friendship

P.S. your serv[t] has been detained by the interruption of a visit from a foreigner

RC (Mrs. Charles W. Biggs, Lewisburg, W.Va., 1950; photocopy in MsSM); dateline between note and postscript; addressed: "Mr Peyton Mont-eagle." Not recorded in SJL.

From P. de Valltone

RESPECTABLE MONSIEUR: Charlottesville ce 17 Juillet 1817

Veuillez je vous prie vouloir bien m'excuser sur la liberté que je prends de m'adresser a vous sans avoir l'honneur d'en être connû, mais j'ose me flatter d'avance que vous serez assez bon que de me pardonner cette demarche en faveur du motif qui me guide et m'anime;

Je me plais a croire que vous vous rappelez encore du souvenir de m[r] Etienne Cathalan à Marseille;—Etant parti de France pour me rendre en ce pays-ci, et ayant essuyé des malheurs sans nombre, qui m'ont empechés de faire mes petites affaires, a pouvoir retourner dans ma patrie; j'ai cru propre de pouvoir m'obtenir un peu de terre dans le Tombegbee River, ce que je fis, vû les circonstances malheureuses ou je me reduit en ce moment; ayant cru m'embarquer a New York pour Mobile, j'eu l'honneur de vous faire achéminer une lettre, que me donna mon Cousin Cathalan, pour vous remêttre, et que je mis à la poste, incluse dans cela que je vous ecrivis alors vous faisant part des details des circonstances de mes affaires, et que je ne doute pas que vous ayez reçu en leurs temps;—Le navire n'étant pas parti pour la dite destination, j'ai mieux faire aulieu d'attendre de m'achéminer par Christiansburgh la, ce que j'executais a pieds jusqu'ici, et ayant sçu que vous demeuriez aux environs, je prends la liberté de vous écrire ne pouvant pas marcher: afin d'obtenir de vos conseils sur le pays que je vais parcourir, n'ayant aucunes connoissance, attendant votre bonté d'acquiescer a ma demande—J'ai l'honneur d'être—

très Estim^ble^ Monsieur avec une parfaite Consideration & Respect—Votre devoué & hble Serviteur P. DE VALLTONE

EDITORS' TRANSLATION

RESPECTABLE SIR: Charlottesville 17 July 1817

Please be so kind as to forgive the liberty I take in addressing myself to you without the honor of being known by you, but I dare flatter myself in advance that you will be so good as to pardon this step on account of the motive that guides and animates me;

I believe that you still remember Mr. Stephen Cathalan of Marseille;—Having left France to come to this country and suffered innumerable misfortunes, which have prevented me from attending to my affairs and returning to my homeland, I thought it would be right, given the unhappy circumstances to which I am reduced at the moment, to acquire some land on the Tombigbee River, which I did. Thinking that I was going to embark from New York for Mobile, I had the honor of forwarding to you a letter given to me by my cousin Cathalan, which I have put in the mail, enclosed in the one I wrote to you then informing you of the detailed circumstances of my affairs, and I have no doubt that you received them at that time;—The ship not having left for the said destination, rather than wait I proceeded via Christiansburg, and have come all the way here on foot. Having learned that you live nearby, I take the liberty of writing you, being unable to walk, in order to obtain your advice regarding the country through which I am about to travel, since I have absolutely no knowledge of it. Waiting in the hope that you will kindly approve of my request—I have the honor to be—

Very estimable Sir, with full consideration and respect—Your devoted and humble servant P. DE VALLTONE

RC (MHi); between dateline and salutation: "L'Honorable Mr Thom^s^ Jefferson"; endorsed by TJ as received 17 July 1817 and so recorded in SJL. Translation by Dr. Genevieve Moene.

P. de Valltone also signed himself "Alex^r^ P. Wallona" and was known by TJ's correspondent Stephen Cathalan as "Alex Paulian Wallong." According to Valltone, he became secretary to the French minister at Madrid in about 1808 and afterwards served as a supercargo on merchant vessels. He suffered reverses when one of his ships was captured by the British in 1815 and another was subsequently wrecked off the coast of France. Valltone embarked on a third ship for New York but had to be rescued when it was lost in a storm. In 1816 Valltone was in France attempting to claim property that had been owned by his father in the latter's native city of Nîmes. He soon made the acquaintance of Cathalan, who attempted to assist the young man. The following year Valltone unsuccessfully sought a position as secretary or clerk to an American minister or consul abroad ("Alex^r^ P. Wallona" to James Monroe, 24 Apr. 1817 [DNA: RG 59, LAR, 1817–25]; Cathalan to TJ, 30 Mar. 1818).

TJ did not record receipt of a LETTRE of introduction from Cathalan or any previous letters from Valltone in SJL or elsewhere, and no such letters have been found. Cathalan later denied that he had written TJ on Valltone's behalf (TJ to Cathalan, 2 Aug. 1817; Cathalan to TJ, 30 Mar. 1818).

Notes on the Siting of Central College

1817 Operations at & for the College

July 18.

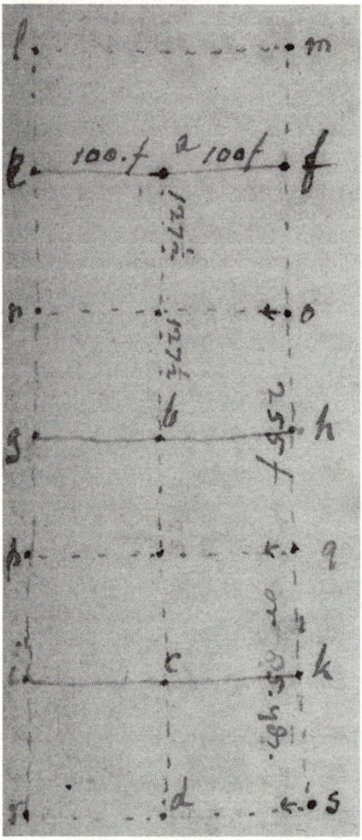

a. the place at which the theodolite was fixed being the center of the Northern square, and the point destined for some principal building in the level of the square l.m n.o.

---

the fall from a. to d. 18.f.

---

from[1] a. to d the bearing magnetically S. 21.$^{\circ}$ W
add for variation $2\frac{1}{2}$
S. $23\frac{1}{2}$ W

? the true meridian was that day $2\frac{1}{2}^{\circ}$ to left of magnetic.

b. is the center of the middle square, and at

g. we propose to erect our first pavilion.

c. is the center of the Southern square.

locust stakes were driven at l.a.f.[2]/ g.b.h./i.c.k. and

at d. is a pile of stones.

each square is to be level within itself, with a pavilion at each end to wit at ef. gh. ik. and 10. dormitories on each side of each pavilion filling up the sides of the squares

from a. to b. was measured 255.f. or 85. yds, b.c. the same, & c.d. the half.

from the points a.b.c. was measured 100.f. each way to ef. gh. ik. making thus each square 255 f. by 200.f. = .8541 of an acre or nearly $\frac{17}{20}$

MS (ViU: TJP); with TJ's Notes on Pavilions, 7 Dec. 1819, subjoined; entirely in TJ's hand; filed with TJ's Specifications for the University of Virginia.

TJ's overseer Edmund Bacon later recalled the process of laying out the grounds of Central College: "My next instruction was to get ten able-bodied hands to commence the work. I soon got them, and Mr. Jefferson started from Monticello to lay off the foundation, and see the work commenced. An Irishman named Dinsmore, and I, went along with him. As we passed through Charlottesville, I went to old Davy Isaacs' store, and got a ball of twine, and Dinsmore found some shingles and made some pegs, and we all went on to the old field together. Mr. Jefferson looked over the ground some time, and then stuck down a peg. He stuck the very first peg in that building, and then directed me where to carry the line, and I stuck the second. He carried one end of the line, and I the other, in laying off the foundation of the University. He had a little rule in his pocket that he always carried with him, and with this he measured off the ground, and laid off the entire foundation, and then set the men at work" (Pierson, *Jefferson at Monticello*, 20).

[1]To the left of this word TJ placed an asterisk keying this text to his subjoined 7 Dec. 1819 Notes on Pavilions.

[2]Thus in manuscript, but TJ probably meant "e.a.f.," with "e" being the somewhat unclear second reference point in left column in drawing reproduced here.

From P. de Valltone

HONORABLE SIR, Charlottesville July 18th 1817.

I tooke the liberty of directing a letter to you yesterday, the bearers being two young gentlemen, living with me, at Wells's Hotel, not wishing to remit the letter to proper hands, they handed it to a person, which perhapps has not transmitted the Same, to you, if he has done it I hope you will be so kind as to excuse my liberty of so doing, as I find meself better I expect to proceed to Tombegbee after tomorrow; wishing you a very good health—I beg to remain with the utmost respect

honble sir—your most obt hble Servant P. DE VALLTONE

RC (MHi); endorsed by TJ as a letter of 18 June 1817 received 19 June 1817. Recorded in SJL as a letter of 18 July 1817 received the following day.

To John H. Cocke

DEAR SIR Monticello July 19. 17.

The promptitude of subscriptions, far beyond my expectations calls for a prompt decision on some matters which I had supposed might have been in time at our fall meeting. I propose to go to mr Madison's to consult with him between the middle & last of the ensuing week, and I should be very happy if you could come, go with me to the College ground to see what is done & doing and then to mr Madison's to assist in our consultations. any day that suits you to come from Wednesday to Saturday inclusive, I will be ready to attend you. our squares are laid off, the brickyard begun, and the levilling will be begun in the course of the week. Your's with friendship & respect

TH: JEFFERSON

RC (ViU: TJP); addressed: "General Cocke Bremo Fluvanna"; endorsed by Cocke. PoC (DLC); on verso of reused address cover to TJ; endorsed by TJ.

From Jeremiah A. Goodman

DER SIR July the 19 day 1817

on mature reflecttion I wish to seel the negro girl I bought of you, and feelling anxiousley for you to have her so as for the Child & her mother not to be parted I will Let you have her very reasonable indeed, if you will give me as she stands $180 for the girl you shall have her and this to be paid the first day of August Eightteen hundread & Eightteen be so good as to Let me know by the boy and at Court I will bring the Bill of sail forward

J A GOODMAN

RC (MHi); adjacent to signature: "Mr Jfferson"; endorsed by TJ as received 20 July 1817 and so recorded in SJL; with notation by TJ in pencil at foot of text referencing his 30 Nov. 1815 sale of Sally Goodman for $150 and his probably related calculation on verso.

The NEGRO GIRL was Sally Goodman and HER MOTHER was TJ's slave Aggy, the daughter of Dinah and Dick.

From John H. Cocke

DEAR SIR Bremo July 20. 1817

I have received yours of the 19.—accompanied by a letter from Mr Garrett with a list of the subscribers to the College. I rejoice with you at the liberality of the subscriptions.

I will be at Monticello on Thursday next early enough to visit the site of the College on that day, and will accompany you the day following to Mr Madisons if necessary.—

I shall avail myself of an opportunity, which offers itself by Judge Tucker tomorrow, to request the attendance of Mr Cabell

Yours with highest respect & Esteem J. H. COCKE

RC (CSmH: JF); at foot of text: "Mr Jefferson"; endorsed by TJ as received <23> 22 July 1817 and recorded in SJL as received the earlier date.

The letter from Alexander GARRETT to Cocke, Charlottesville, 19 July 1817, enclosed a copy of the Central College Subscription List (printed above at 5 May 1817) as it then stood, indicated that pledges had so exceeded expectations that he believed TJ's plans had changed, reported that TJ intended to write Cocke soon and hoped to convene a meeting of the Board of Visitors at Montpellier, and informed Cocke that "Mr Jefferson was yesterday ingaged in assertaining the level of the College Hill & laying off the direction of the range of buildings now intended to be put up. and as the first buildings will give the direction to the entire buildings, it must be of the very first importance to commence <*right,*> it properly—I sincerely wish you could see the ground before we commence leveling, there may exist some objection to it, or some <*better*> improvement might be suggested by you to Mr Jefferson" (ViU: JHC).

To Jeremiah A. Goodman

SIR   Monticello July 20. 17.

with respect to the girl Sally, the fair thing is to consider the bargain as annulled, and for me to repay you the sum allowed for her, 150.D. with interest till repaid: but I cannot undertake the repayment but in all May 1819. I had as live pay in May 18. as in Aug. 18. but I could not do this conveniently, this with the repayment of her clothing comes to something more than you propose. I tender you my best wishes   TH: JEFFERSON

P.S. July 30. 17. the only contribution you have given to the clothing or subsistence of the child being the sum of 15.D. allowed me for corn[1] in a subsequent account, I mean that that shall also be repaid with interest.

RC (DLC); postscript added separately to RC and PoC; addressed: "Mr Jeremiah A. Goodman Albemarle"; endorsed by TJ. PoC (DLC); on verso of reused address cover of Joseph Gales (1761–1841) to TJ, 26 June 1817; endorsed by TJ.

For the SUBSEQUENT ACCOUNT, see note to TJ's Agreement with Goodman, 30 July 1817.

[1]Preceding two words interlined in RC and incorporated cleanly in PoC.

To Fernagus De Gelone

SIR   Monticello July 21. 17.

I see on your catalogue Graglia's Italian & English dictionary and Cormon's Italian & French dict. in 2. vols 8vo which I request you to send me. the conveyance by water is so slow, that I must ask these by the mail, sending each volume singly, and a week apart that no one mail may be burthen[ed] with more than a single volume. send Cormon's Italian & French volume first, as most wanted, with a note of prices. Aristophane not yet recieved, altho I doubt not it is in Richmond. I salute you with esteem and respect   TH: JEFFERSON

PoC (MHi); on verso of a reused address cover from John Barnes to TJ; text obscured at crease; at foot of text: "M[r] Fernagus de Gelone"; endorsed by TJ.

To James Oldham

DEAR SIR Monticello July 21. 17.

The mahogany you were so kind as to get for me has been recieved, and suits me perfectly. I am afraid I am troublesome to you, and yet having no other friend in Richmond who understands these things, I have no other means of having a good choice. I must therefore now trouble you for $\frac{1}{2}$ a dozen mortise doorlocks of which 2. to be plated handles for doors $1\frac{1}{2}$ I. thick, the others brass for doors $1\frac{1}{4}$ I. thick, to be sent by the Milton stage, unless there should be a Milton boat there which is the safest conveyance. mr Gibson will as usual pay the bill. I salute you with friendship & respect. TH: JEFFERSON

P.S. also 6. edge bolts or secret bolts[1] for the edges of folding doors

RC (ViCMRL, on deposit ViU: TJP); mutilated at seal and damaged at crease, with missing text supplied from PoC; postscript added separately to RC and PoC; addressed: "Cap[t] James Oldham Richmond"; franked; postmarked Milton, 22 July; with versos of letter and address leaf used for a later letter and address leaf from Samuel Ruggles Slack to Andrew J. Locke, of Boston, dated Mechum's River, Albemarle County, 19 Oct. 1848, stating that TJ's letter had been given to Slack by Oldham's widow, a parishioner of his, that "there is no doubt of its authenticity," and that Slack was now presenting it to Locke. PoC (MHi); on verso of reused address cover of Josephus B. Stuart to TJ, 25 Apr. 1817; endorsed by TJ. Filed with RC is RC of Connie L. Wentworth to Breckinridge Long, Lexington, Mass., 17 Apr. 1926, stating that on a recent visit to Monticello she had recalled inheriting the above letter from her father, Andrew J. Locke, that she was now very gladly presenting it to Monticello, and that she wondered "if it may not have been written on one of those little shelf desks in the study. Also if the mahogony referred to were used by Jefferson himself for the ladder or music stand."

[1] Preceding three words interlined in RC.

To John Le Tellier

DEAR SIR Monticello July 22. 17.

I live about three miles from a pleasant & respectable village called Charlottesville of about 500. inhabitants. the county of Albemarle in which it is, and of which it is the center of all the business, has about 20,000. inhabitants, many rich and all independant. the soil is the most fertile of any upland soil I know in the state, and a healthier climate is not in the world. we are about establishing a college a mile from the town, at which we count on seeing 2. or 300. students. provisions abound and are cheap; and rent is about 30.D. a year for good rooms, and less proportionably for indifferent. we want a good silversmith in the town, & such an one would find more work than he could do, and ready money always. I have prevented the inhabitants from engaging another until I [cou?]ld hear from you, and in giving them a true account of y[our] character & talents, they would give you a preference to [all oth?]er competitors. I know nothing of your present situation, but [have?] stated all these circumstances to enable you to decide for yourself whether an establishment here, without a single competitor, might not be better for yourself & family. perhaps before you decide, you had better come and see for yourself. the stage will deposit you at my door, where we shall be glad to keep you until you can look about you and decide. but I set out for Bedford on the 5th of August & shall be there till late in September. our court is on the 4th of August, where you would see the county assembled, and it would be well that you should be here 2. or 3. days before that. in the mean time drop me a line that I may know whether to expect you, & be assured of every service I can render you as of my continued esteem.

TH: JEFFERSON

PoC (MoSHi: TJC-BC); on verso of reused address cover of Peter H. Wendover to TJ, 1 Mar. 1817; mutilated at seal; at foot of text: "Mr Letellier"; endorsed by TJ.

From George Divers

DR SIR Farm[ington 2]3d July. 1817.

Your letter of the 14th June was recieved some time ago. in[1] making out my answer to your bill, I avail myself with great satisfaction of the very friendly offer it contains, to dispense with the legal formalities customary in Chancery proceedings. my[2] bad health and preparations for a long absence from home, with a view to recruit it deprives me almost of ability or leisure to attend to any thing else. I have therefore, in the way you propose, answered to the best of my knoledge the interrogatories in your bill, and added a few remarks upon some other points of it which I thought my duty to the company compelled me to notice. sincerely your friend GEORGE DIVERS[3]

Tr (DLC: TJ Papers, 211:37585); with Tr of enclosure subjoined; entirely in TJ's hand; mutilated, with portion of place and date of composition supplied from ViU Tr; at foot of text: "Thomas Jefferson esq." Tr (ViU: TJP-LBJRC); in a clerk's hand. Enclosure: Divers's Answer to Interrogatories in *Jefferson v. Rivanna Company*, [ca. 23 July 1817].

[1] ViU Tr: "I."
[2] ViU Tr here adds "present."
[3] DLC Tr: "Diver." ViU Tr: "Divers."

George Divers's Answer to Interrogatories in *Jefferson v. Rivanna Company*

[ca. 23 July 1817]

Interrogatories in Thos Jefferson's bill with the answers of Geo. Divers one of the Directors of the Rivanna company thereto.

1st whether the Rivanna river, in it's passage thro' the base of the S.W. ridge of[1] mountains, that is to say, from the Secretary's ford to the foot of the Sandy falls; or the falls next above the mills of the Complt is navigable along it's bed for loaded boats or batteaux?

Ans. in it's present state it certainly is not. but it is concieved, by some, that a practicable and safe navigation could be effected along it.

2. Whether it does not present, thro' that whole passage, a continual succession of rocks & rapids, except where the same are covered by your orator's millpond? Answ. it does.

3. whether such navigation was ordinarily practised, or in what degree, before the erection of the Complt's milldam, & particularly at the time when the two inquests of 1795. & 1805. found it was not? Answ. I have no knolege of the two inquests of 1795. & 1805. or of their finding: neither do I know of any navigation being practised at that time; but it is currently said & believed that two boats loaded with 4. hhds of tobo each descended[2] in safety from above Charlottesville about the year 1792. or 3.

4. if it would be practicable, were the sd mill-dam away, as affirmed in the document No 8. called 'a Statement'[3] why was it not practised? & why did not the Directors persevere in their purpose of using it? Ans. It was not practised because the natural obstructions, which made it difficult, had not been removed; & the Directors did not persevere in their purpose of using it, because they concieved the break or opening which the Complt proposed & agreed to make in his dam, would produce so rapid a current of water as to endanger perhaps the <u>descent</u> of boats, and prevent their <u>ascent</u> altogether, & th[us prove] inadequate to the purpose; but more especia[lly] they abandoned the bed of the river, because the Complt again profferd the use of his canal for their navigat[ion] which they always thought the most eligible route.

5. that they may state what was the condition of the river, & what the amount of loading at the times when the sd document affirms that loaded boats of flour & tobo passed down in safety.

6. how many passed within their knolege or belief, and did they pass without unloading, & did the boats return that way, either loaded or

empty? Answ. upon the subject of these interrogatories as well as that of the 3d I have no personal knolege. but it is believed that the river in every instance was considerably swollen.

7. that they may say whether, in their opinion, the expense of removing obstructions in the remaining parts of the river within their limits, would not be very trifling in comparison with that between the Secretary's ford and the foot of the Sandy falls? Answ. I think the expense between the Secretary's ford & Sandy falls would exceed that of the other parts of the river, but in what degree my want of experience in that kind of business makes me unable to say.

8. Whether the pond and canal of your orator do not furnish a dead sheet of water & safe & sufficient navign from the Sec's ford to his mills, & are not the mills below the Sandy falls? Answ. Yes,

9. Were not the sd dam & canal made by your orator & at his sole expence? Answr yes.

10. Did the Directors, or their agents[4] employ any and what labor, on the dam or canal, which could be of advantage to the sd mills? Answ. The directors or their agents did not employ any labor on the dam or canal, that I know of, which could be of any advantage to the sd mills: but I am informed by their agent that the hands in the employment of the directors assisted in widening the canal, which was originally too narrow to admit the passage of boats.

11. Did not the directors agree at one time to fix the bottom of their upper lock gate 2.f. or how much above the level of the bottom of the entrance into the forebays of the sd mills? and afterwards to make a bason of such capacity as that it's contents should supply working water to the mills while boats were passing[5] the locks? 12. Was the bottom of the sd gate fixed in the level agreed on, or was a bason adequate to the purposes agreed on ever made? Answ. I do not recollect to have heard of any stipulated level at which to fix the lock gate: but it was agreed on the part of the dire[ct]ors that they should make a bason of such capacity that it's contents should be sufficient to keep the mills going during the passage of boats; & that it was respectively understood and agreed to that an enlargement of the Complt's canal to double it's then width, from two points agreed on, would be sufficient to constitute the sd bason: & I am informed, but of this I have no personal knolege, that the hands then employed by the directors proceede[d immedi]ately to execute the work, and widened the canal to the extent proposed from the points agreed on, and deepened it to the surface of the water then in the canal, but the occupant of the mill at that time refusing to stop his work & suffer the water to be drawn off, the deepening to the extent proposed could not[6] be accomplished.

of the actual height or level at which the lock-gate is fixed, I have no knolege.

13. that they may declare whether, after abandoning their first negotiation with the Complt for the use of his canal, & their 2d purpose of using the bed of the river, they entered into any contract with him, written or verbal, for the use of his canal? 14. what was that contract, & for what length of time? Answ. no contract of any kind was entered into.

15. Whether the Complt granted them the water, in preference to the wants of his mills? or only the surplus water over & above what should be requisite for his mills?[7] Answ. it never was concieved by me that the mills were to be deprived of water by the passing of boats.

16. that the def Wm D. Meriwether may say whether he did not, at the meeting of the Directors of Aug. 1816. declare the paramount right of the locks over the mills in times of scarcity, substantially as herein stated? 17. that the sd George Divers, Dabney Minor, & John Kelly may say whether he did not make that declaration in their presence & hearing? Answ. he did.

18. that the sd defs may declare whether the Complt ever recieved any & what compensn or considern from them for the use of his canal? Answ. in answer to this interrogatory it must be admitted that no direct or pecuniary compensn has ever been given. but it is concieved that an ample equivelent for the use of the canal is annually recieved or saved by the Complt in consequence of the canal being used for navign; in the 1st place the opening of the river above the sd mills by the Rivanna co. I am informed brings to his mills a considerable accession of grain in consequence of the facility of water carriage which it would otherwise not recieve. 2dly a bye law of the directors admits the property of the Complt of every kind or denomination to pass their locks free of toll, a privilege which he certainly finds convenient in transporting timber & produce of various kinds to & from his[8] different farms above & below the locks. & 3dly the produce of the Complt's mill is exempted from paying toll which the company had a right to demand, they being authorised to fix their toll-house at the upper boundary line of the town of Milton, [& in]vested with the power of demanding toll upon all loading passing it. but in consideration of the great facility afforded to the navign by the use of the Complt's canal, the directors gave up that right as long as they continued to use it, & consented to the passage of the amendatory act in the bill mentd. see the 3d section of the sd act & also the commencing clause.

19. that they may state when the locks came into operati[on what is their] present condition, how long they suppose they will continue

practicable without fundamental repair[s or entire] rebuilding, & whether their funds are adequate to that rebuilding? Answ. the locks came into operation the fall of 1811. I cannot speak with certainty of their present condition, or of the length of time they will last without rebuilding, tho', from the best accounts, I should judge 2. or 3. years. the funds of the company are not adequate to their rebuilding.

20. that they may say whether, if the locks should be torn away by high water, or fall in by decay, they will not be likely to extend the chasm they will leave to the canal itself, and endanger the entire destruction of much of it's bank? Answ. I think this is probable.

21. that they may declare whether the sd Peter Minor, in the bill named, was not their Secretary & authorised to attest transmit & recieve communications on their behalf? Answ. he was.

22. And that they may set forth the names of the individuals who are legal members of the Rivanna co. entitled to it's emoluments & liable to it's responsabilities? Answ. who the actual company are, it is difficult to state, some of the subscribers are dead, some removed from the state without having ever paid, and some proved insolvent. not having any of the papers in my possession, I cannot furnish a copy of the original subscription: but this will be done by some of the other directors in their answer

There are some points in the Complt's bill not embraced by these interrogatories which I feel it my duty to notice. it says the Rivanna co. was incorporated on the turnpike principle, with a view to derive profit from the Capital invested (I quote from memory, not having the bill before me) I think the subscriptions were not made with a view to profit. they may rather be considered in the light of loans to effect a public good. it is true the principal & interest are to be returned by the slow income of tolls. but who would call this a profitable stock? or who would have loaned money towards it, if a public benefit was not to be derived? when the principal & interest are returned, the tolls are to cease, and the river to become a public highway. this is not like the turnpike principle, which looks to a permanent dividend of more than legal interest. respecting the sluice thro' the Milton falls, constructed by the Complt in conjunction with T. M. Randolph, as stated in the bill, it is thought in the 1st place that they had no right to make it. the exclusive use of the river for the purposes of navign being previously vested in the Rivanna co. and 2dly the sluice itself was stated to be inadequate to the purpose, not allowing, except with difficulty, the ascent even of an empty boat; so that the directors, in executing that part of their undertaking, could not avail themselves of any part of the sd sluice, but were obliged to stop it up, and by taking a different, and more extended route, graduated the fall, so as now to admit the ascent of boats loaded with the weight of 4. tons.

GEORGE DIVERS.

Tr (DLC: TJ Papers, 211:37585–6); subjoined to Tr of Divers to TJ, 23 July 1817; entirely in TJ's hand; undated; mutilated, with missing text supplied from ViU Tr; signed attestation by TJ at foot of text: "In the bill of complaint exhibited by myself in the Chancery court of Staunton against George Divers & others, Directors of the Rivanna co. in Albemarle, I consent that these answers to the interrogatories of the bill shall be recieved and considered as the answer of the sd George Divers to the bill, with equal effect as if given in regular form, & under oath of the usual tenor. Witness my hand this 17th day of Aug. 1817," with attestation probably composed 18 Aug. 1817 based on TJ's consistent misdating of letters written and received at Poplar Forest in August 1817. Tr (ViU: TJP-LBJRC); entirely in a clerk's hand, including TJ's attestation; undated. Enclosed in Divers to TJ, 23 July 1817, and TJ to Chapman Johnson, [18] Aug. 1817.

The two INQUESTS OF 1795. & 1805. are numbered 2 and 3 in the list of exhibits described in annotation at TJ's Bill of Complaint against the Directors of the Rivanna Company, [by 9 Feb. 1817], document 1 in a group of documents on Jefferson's Lawsuit against the Rivanna Company, printed above at 9 Feb. 1817. DOCUMENT Nº 8, the Statement of the Dispute by the Directors of the Rivanna Company, [ca. 15 Jan. 1811], is document 6 in the same group of documents.

The AGENT of the Rivanna Company referred to by Divers in his answer to query ten was Immanuel Poor. The OCCUPANT OF THE MILL mentioned in the answer to query twelve was Jonathan Shoemaker. Section eight of the 30 Dec. 1806 act establishing the Rivanna Company allowed it to place its TOLL-HOUSE "at the upper boundary line of the town of Milton, or elsewhere higher up the said river" (*Acts of Assembly* [1806–07], 24).

The AMENDATORY ACT of 31 Jan. 1814 was "An Act to amend the Act, entitled 'an Act incorporating a Company to open and improve the navigation of the Rivanna River from Milton to Moore's Ford, opposite the town of Charlottesville, in the county of Albemarle, and for other purposes.'" The third section of this later act specified that "so long as the company aforesaid shall continue to use the navigation of the canal leading to the Shadwell Mills, no toll shall be demanded or received on their behalf, unless the same shall be demanded and received at the locks which now are, or hereafter may be erected by them on said canal; and shall be demanded and received only on articles passing the said locks." Its COMMENCING CLAUSE put the statute in force only after the company's directors assented to it and had it recorded in the Albemarle County Court, and the law included a 1 Feb. 1840 expiration date (*Acts of Assembly* [1813–14], 91–2).

1 Preceding two words not in ViU Tr.

2 Instead of preceding two words, ViU Tr reads "passed."

3 Order of preceding five words follows Dft rather than MS of TJ's Bill of Complaint against the Directors of the Rivanna Company, printed above at 9 Feb. 1817.

4 Preceding three words not in ViU Tr.

5 ViU Tr: "repassing."

6 Word not in ViU Tr.

7 Preceding fifteen words are in Dft but not in MS of TJ's Bill of Complaint.

8 ViU Tr: "the."

Thomas Mann Randolph's Notes on George Divers's Answer to Interrogatories in *Jefferson v. Rivanna Company*

[after 23 July 1817]

The answer of G. Divers.

Notes by TMR. Qu. 12. 'and ×widened the canal to the extent proposed'   ×untrue.

ib. 'the ‡occupant of the mill.'   ‡Shoemaker.

qu. 18. 'a considerable accession of grain.'   causes a considble loss of grain for grist.

ib. 'transporting ‡timber & produce E^t^c to & from his farms E^t^c' ‡by, not, to the mill.

ib. 'the produce of the mill exempted from toll.' full toll for leave to go out at the lower end, of the channel. whole price for about $\frac{1}{5}$ the advantage. at last the waggonage & boatage are the same price for y^t^ part of the way.

observations. 'had no right to make the sluice.' how many years did the company remain wholly inactive? would they ever have acted if those concerned in the mills had not commenced? the first answer does for both questions.

ib. 'were obliged to ‡stop up the sluice.' ‡all the boatmen desire to have it opened again. let them be asked.

ib. 'admit the ‡ascent of boats with 4. ton.' ‡the way of ascent projected, after the abandmt of that by a chain was not executed, because the company[1] interfered. let the boatmen decide which is best.

Tr (DLC: TJ Papers, 211:37595); with TJ's Notes on George Divers's Answer to Interrogatories in *Jefferson v. Rivanna Company*, [after 23 July 1817], subjoined; entirely in TJ's hand; undated.

[1] TJ here canceled "objected to it."

Notes on George Divers's Answer to Interrogatories in *Jefferson v. Rivanna Company*

[after 23 July 1817]

Mr Divers's answer. Notes on it.

These answers of mr Divers are to be considered as if given under oath in the usual tenor,[1] that is to say that whatever facts are stated as of his own knolege, are true; he is incapable of affirming on his own knolege, any fact which is not true: but his hear-says and opinions are open to observation[2] here, as they w^d be in a regular answer

Answ. 10. 'he was informed by their agent that the hands in the employment of the directors assisted in widening the canal, which was originally too narrow to admit the passage of a boat.' This can refer to nothing except the passing place. otherwise it[3] was either a misunderstanding of mr D. or gross misinformn from the agent. the directors had a recess dug in the bank in the upper part of the canal, of the length & breadth of a batteau, for one to retire into while another should pass by, and they dug the enlargement of the canal at the lower end[4] of 2. or 3. batteau lengths for the bason of supply to this the informn of the manager must have referred, & he was misunderstood by mr Divers, or he grossly misrepresented the fact to mr D. for towards the[5] widening of the canal any where else they never struck a stroke. the canal & pierhead both were originally too narrow for a boat; & when the company concluded to use the canal, I chose[6] to widen it myself, to wit from 5 f. to 7.f. and to let them do nothing which should give them any permanent claim on the canal. I accdly took down the pierhead & built it anew & wider, and widened the canal thro' the whole[7] myself, as is stated in the bill. the passing place, the bason & the locks are all they ever did; these were solely for their own purposes & not of the smallest advantage to the mills.

Answ. to qu. 11. & 12. 'it was agreed on the part of the directors that they should make a bason of such capacity as to keep the mills going during the passage of boats.' this is the strict truth; but there is error in adding 'that it was understood and agreed that doubling the width would be sufficient.' unless he means only that it was agreed among the directors, and[8] as a matter of opinion; but the only joint[9] agreement was 'that it should be sufficient.'

And again 'that he is informed, but of this he has no personal knolege that the directors' hands widened & deepened the canal (for the bason) to the surface of the water then in the canal, & that the occupant (then a mr Shoemaker) refused to stop his work, & suffer the water to be drawn off. Etc.' this work was agreed to be done in the idle interval of June & July, & the very days were fixed within which it should be done; it would have been their fault therefore if they delayed the work until the season for grinding had recommenced. but his informn was too loose[10] and the ground itself will now shew that the widening even to[11] the surface of the water was of a very trifling extent.[12]

Qu. 18. it is his opinion that I had an ample equivalent for the use of my canal. 1. 'he is informed it brings a considble accession of grain to the mill.' but the truth is that the grain now brought by water to my mill, would have been brought in waggons to it, while it continued[13] the highest point of navigation; but that much the greatest part of what might have come for that reason is now ground at the upper mills, and water-borne from them as being now the higher points of navign. 2. 'the locks are a convenience to me for the transportation of timber and produce to & from my farms above & below them.' as to the produce of my farms, to wit, wheat, it goes to my mill direct, & from it without passing the locks. and as to timber, on one single occasion of a fence on the river below carried away by a flood, I carried rails from above but not chusing to accept of any thing from them which could give them a claim as a consideration or compensation, I had them tumbled over the bank at the mill and reladen there again & carried to the place wanting. an empty boat or canoe has on a few occns passed, but an empty vessel is not tollable, and if it were this would be but a small item of credit even[14] against the timber given them of which the locks were built.[15] 3. 'the produce of my mill is exempted from toll.'[16] and would they in conscience, if the law had permitted it, have taken toll for produce which, like that of my mills, passed by their locks, along my own canal but never thro' them? this observation shews how seriously it was intended, as it is further proved by the fact, that having applied to the legislature for an amendatory act respecting their toll, one of the Directors being then a representative of the county, got the bill thro' the lower house without any correction of this glaring[17] injustice, & when returned by the senate with an amendment restraining them from taking toll for what had not passed thro' their locks, he chose to let the bill drop rather than give up the claim. and it was not till the next year that the directors consented to take the bill with this correction. and the refraining from taking toll for my passing along my own canal, is now cited as a boon of theirs; as the wolf in the fable deemed it boon enough for the simple Crane, that in extracting the bone from his throat, he had got his own neck out in safety.

Dft (DLC: TJ Papers, 211:37595); subjoined to Thomas Mann Randolph's Notes on George Divers's Answer to Interrogatories in *Jefferson v. Rivanna Company*, [after 23 July 1817]; entirely in TJ's hand; undated. Enclosed in TJ to Chapman Johnson, [18] Aug. 1817.

A closely related text, TJ's Observations on Divers's Answer to Interrogatories in *Jefferson v. Rivanna Company*, is printed below at 9 June 1819.

The AGENT of the Rivanna Company was Immanuel Poor. Rivanna Company director Nimrod Bramham was the legislative REPRESENTATIVE OF THE COUNTY of Albemarle, 1811–13, who sought to obtain passage of the first version of a bill that was eventually enacted as "An Act to amend the Act, entitled 'an Act incorporating a Company to open and improve the navigation of the Rivanna River from Milton to Moore's Ford, opposite the town of Charlottesville, in the county of Albemarle, and for other purposes.'" The AMENDMENT successfully introduced in the Senate of Virginia became the third section of the 31 Jan. 1814 act, cited above by Divers in his Answer to Interrogatories (Petition of Rivanna Company to Virginia General Assembly, [ca. 5 Oct. 1812]; TJ to Joseph C. Cabell, 7 Nov. 1813, and enclosure). The FABLE of the wolf and the crane is attributed to Aesop.

[1] Reworked from "of the usual form."

[2] Reworked from "require some observations."

[3] Preceding ten words interlined.

[4] Preceding four words interlined.

[5] Text from "to this the informn" to this point interlined in place of "but towards the."

[6] Word interlined in place of "determined."

[7] Preceding three words interlined in place of "entirely."

[8] Preceding twelve words interlined in place of "this may have been mentioned."

[9] Word interlined.

[10] Preceding six words interlined in place of "but the whole is a fable."

[11] Reworked from "that there <*was no*> never was any widening commenced and stopp[ed] at" (torn).

[12] TJ here canceled a line reading "Additional observations by mr Divers."

[13] Preceding three words interlined in place of "because it was then."

[14] Text from "but not chusing" to this point interlined in place of "thro' the locks to replace it. <*if it has*> the toll of these boat loads of rails might have amounted to some cents or even dollars, and would be but a small item of credit."

[15] Preceding two words mistakenly canceled by TJ.

[16] Omitted closing single quotation mark editorially supplied.

[17] Word interlined.

From David Knight

SIR, Lynchburg July 23d 1817

I was applied to some 10 or 12 Days ago by Mr Joell Yancey to do some brick[1] work for you in the neighbourhood of Charlottesville & in 3 or 4 Days thereafter I started to see you but unfortunately my horse was taken sick on the way & not being able to get another on the road was compelled to return I should have made a second start before this but have a very large kiln of brick which I am compeled to burn amediately I have just put fire to it & as soon as it is finishd I will come down to see you unless some unfore seen occurrence should take place to prevent me I am anxious to do your work & for fear that something might take place to prevent me from going down I shall be glad if you will write to me as soon as you receive this & let me know if we should agree at what time you will want me to commence I can begin at any time you please as I have a partner here who can go on with the work that I have undertaken in this place

Respectfully yrs &c DAVID KNIGHT

RC (CSmH: JF); endorsed by TJ as received 2 Aug. 1817 and so recorded in SJL. RC (DLC); address cover only; with PoC of TJ to John Martin Baker, 12 Oct. 1817, on verso; addressed: "Thomas Jefferson esqr Charlottes Ville"; franked; postmarked Lynchburg, 24 July.

David Knight may have been the Maryland native (born ca. 1771) who was an apprentice in Baltimore in 1790 and was working as a bricklayer in that city by 1800. He was in Lynchburg in 1817, when he was hired to do brickwork for Central College. In October and November of that year Knight worked on Pavilion VII and three dormitories (*Maryland Journal and Baltimore Advertiser*, 13 Apr. 1790; *The New Baltimore Directory, and Annual Register; for 1800 and 1801* [Baltimore, (1800)], 58; Agreement between Knight and Central College, 11 Oct. 1817, enclosed in TJ to Nelson Barksdale, 11 Nov. 1817; University of Virginia proctor's ledgers, vol. 1 [ViU: PP]).

[1] Word interlined.

To James Madison

DEAR SIR Monticello July 23. 17.

The promptitude & success of our subscription paper, now amounting to upwards of 20,000.D. with a prospect much beyond that renders the decision immediately necessary of some important questions which I had thought might have laid over to our periodical meeting the last of September. having an opportunity of writing to Genl Cocke, I invited him to join me in a visit to you on Friday the 25th. I recd his answer last night, that he would do so and would try to bring mr Cabell with him. last night also an opportunity was offered me of sending a letter to mr Watson. I do so; and he probably will be with you also. thus the visit I had promised for my self singly to you on my return, is suddenly manufactured into a meeting of our visitors at Montpelier,[1] te inconsulto. I do not know whether mr Cabell & mr Watson will certainly come, but Genl Cocke & my self will be certainly with you on Friday, to dinner if we can get there by half after two; if not, we will dine at Gordon's & be with you afterwards, therefore do not wait a moment for us. the illness of our principal driver will disappoint mrs Randolph in the participation in the visit which she had much at heart. affectionate esteem & respect to mrs Madison & yourself.

TH: JEFFERSON

RC (NNGL, on deposit NHi); addressed: "James Madison esq. Montpelier near Orange C. H."; franked; postmarked Milton, 26 July. PoC (DLC); on verso of reused address cover of Richard Peters to TJ, 28 June 1817; endorsed by TJ.

TE INCONSULTO: "without consulting you."

[1]Manuscript: "Monpelier."

From Craven Peyton

July 23^d 17—

C. Peyton presents his respects to M. Jefferson And informs him, there is some Ladis hear, from below, who is desirous, of seeing Monticello And if a greeable, will wride up, in the fournoon Noon tomorrow.

RC (DLC: TJ Papers, 211:37615); dateline at foot of text; with Dft of TJ to Thomas Appleton, [20] Aug. 1817, on verso.

From Hiram Storrs

DEAR SIR, Milledgeville 23^d July 1817

I take the liberty of addressing you on a subject of much importance as it respects a friend of mine in this part of the country, who wishes to obtain information relative to the public Records which were carried away from Virginia by the British at the close of the Revolution. Presuming, that from your accurate knowlege of the transactions of that date, you could give the desired information, it was deemed expedient to address you relative thereto. A[1] particular friend of mine, Col. John Lewis, son of John Lewis of Albemarle County Virginia, deceased, has a claim to lands in the Mississippi Territory, granted to his father since the year '68, while East & West Florida was in the possession of the British[2] Governm^t. The grant is not to be found here, & the records of it Col. Lewis is informed by a friend of his, is somewhere among the public records carried to England. This friend, who says he saw this record of the Grant among the American papers in London, is now absent & not to be found; & our correspondent in London, to whom we have written, not being able to ascertain, where those Records were deposited, we wish Sir, that you would have the goodness, if it be in your power, to inform us, where, or in what

Office in London the pilfered Records were lodged. The Grant was for an Island at the mouth of the Mobile, called, Lewis's Island, which as the Col. informs me, was surveyed for his father of Albemarle, who imployed persons for that Express purpose. If Sir, it be in your power to throw any light on this interesting subject, you will greatly oblige the Colonel & his family, and also, your fellow Citizen, who most respectfully subscribes himself

yr friend & Ob^{t} Servt HIRAM STORRS

RC (DLC); endorsed by TJ as received <*18*> 19 Aug. 1817 and so recorded in SJL.

Hiram Storrs (1769–1821), attorney, was a native of Lebanon, New Hampshire. He graduated from Dartmouth College in 1793. Storrs practiced law in Milledgeville, Georgia, and died there (*General Catalogue of Dartmouth College and the Associated Schools, 1769–1925* [1925], 99).

[1]Manuscript: "&."
[2]Manuscript: "Brittish."

To David Watson

DEAR SIR Monticello July 23. 17.

The promptitude and success with which our subscription has advanced, render the immediate decision necessary of some questions respecting the system for our college which I had expected might have laid over to our periodical meeting in September. Genl Cocke & myself had agreed to go to mr Madison's on Friday the 25th. last night he wrote me he would bring mr Cabell also; and last night too I learned of the opportunity which brings you this letter. I avail myself of it to ask you to meet us at mr Madison's on Friday, the day after tomorrow to join us in a consultation which has been so suddenly hatched up that it has been out of my power to give you earlier notice of it. in the hope you will find it still convenient to come I salute you with great esteem & respect. TH: JEFFERSON

PoC (DLC); on verso of reused address cover of William Short to TJ, 4 July 1817; at foot of text: "Mr Watson"; endorsed by TJ.

John H. Cocke's letter, received LAST NIGHT, was dated 20 July 1817.

From Levett Harris

SIR, Philadelphia 24. July 1817.

After a residence in Russia of fourteen Years, I have returned to the United States. Permit me to consecrate the first moments of my arrival in my native City, to the paying of my respects to my great patron and protector. Tis to you Sir, that I owe the occasion of my advancement to fortune, and I hope to consideration. At the age of twenty four years, You distinguished me by the appointment of Consul Gl. to Russia. Through the indulgent protection of my Government, I was afterwards advanced to the rank of minister of third order, and I flatter myself that my conduct in every service confided to me (which in some instances has not been unimportant) has imparted no less Satisfaction to yourself and your Successor, than my long residence in a Country, now so intimately connected with my own, will have proved mutually advantageous.

The Emperor Alexander at an audience of leave, which he accorded me a few days before I left his capital, took particular occasion to speak of Mr. Jefferson, and to request me to renew to you Sir, the assurances of the great respect with which your high character had inspired him. The like sentiments were testified by the Empress Mother at the audience of leave which was afterwards assigned me by Her Imperial Majesty.

I reserve myself to entertain You more at large on what passed on these interesting Occasions, as I promise myself the honor, in the course of the ensuing Autumn, of paying a visit to monticello.

A few days previous to my leaving St Petersburg, one of your literary friends there, Professor Adelung, requested me to take charge of the accompanying volume which treats of a Subject in which I know you have taken a deep interest.

I am with profound respect and Veneration,

Sir, Your most obedient hum[le] servant LEVETT HARRIS

RC (DLC); endorsed by TJ as received 2 Aug. 1817 and so recorded in SJL. RC (Mrs. T. Wilber Chelf, Mrs. Virginius Dabney, and Mrs. Alexander W. Parker, Richmond, 1944; photocopy in ViU: TJP); address cover only; with PoC of TJ to Patrick Gibson, 30 Oct. 1817, on verso; addressed: "The Honorable Thomas Jefferson Esquire Monticello accompanied with a large packet"; franked; postmarked Philadelphia, 25 July.

The ACCOMPANYING VOLUME was probably Friedrich Adelung, *Catherinens der Grossen Verdienste um die Vergleichende Sprachenkunde* (Saint Petersburg, 1815).

From Benjamin Henry Latrobe

DEAR SIR, Washington July 24h 1817

Yesterday I had the pleasure to receive Your letter d. July 16th (P.mark 19h). I had presumed that you were from home, and also that as your institution has been so lately organized, some time could be given to the preparation of a design for the buildings.—But by your letter I find not only that I have been designing under a great misconception of your locale[1] but also have presumed upon more time for deliberation than you can give me.—I supposed from your letter, & the sketch it contains, that your ground would be tolerably level along the long & closed side of your open quadrangle, which side, I suppose would be the North side, so as to make the continued portico face to the South. But in your last letter occur these words: "The levelling the ground into Terraces will take time & labor." We propose a distinct terras for every 2 pavilions, & their dormitories, that is a pavilion at each end of each terrace.—

Thus it appears to me, that instead of a continuous line of building, you want a series of detached masses, on different levels.—I write in great haste this morning, & surrounded by interruptions, or I would send you better sketches than are below. They will explain the ideas I had.—Not having a copy of my great Sheet I will retain it, till I have again the pleasure of hearing from you when I may perhaps add Something useful.—A week will thus be lost, which I regret, but it may not be in vain.—

The locks of the Potowmac lower Canal having fallen in, beyond the power of Art to restore them, we suffer difficulty in getting down our Columbian Marble; but a great effort will be made to bring them thence by Land. Your opinion on the suggestions which I ventured to make as to the origin of this Marble, in my paper in the Nat. Intelligencer of the 18th of Jany, would be particularly acceptable to me. If they apply to the range with which you are acquainted, my opinion that these pebbles are the beach of the ancient Gulph stream, & are probably the ruins of Southern Marbles once occupying the excavation of the Gulphs of Darien & Mexico may receive more plausibility. The Abbe Roxas told me, & pointed out in the Block which I had polished, that many of the pieces were Mexican Marbles well known to him.

I am with the sincerest respect Yrs B HENRY LATROBE.

AA, will be the least expensive pavilions because the lower story will be covered by the Dormitories (one story high)[2] (which I suppose will also be study rooms) and might be built first.—BB pavilions having the same dimensions, & general Mass but exhibiting different styles or orders of Architections. CC d° d° DD d° d° Center building which ought to exhibit in Mass & details as perfect a specimen of good Architectural taste as can be divised. I should propose below, a couple or 4 rooms for Janitors or Tutors, above a room,  for Chemical or other lectures, above a circular lecture room under the dome; The pavilions to be, as proposed, habitations of Professors & lecture rooms.—But, if Professors are married, will they not require more than 2 rooms each, & a kitchen. I have exhibited such an arrangement.—

The above is the arrangement, I believe, sketched in your first letter, & might be executed on ground, falling each way East & West from the Center, & descending as much as may be N & South, because the E & West sides of the Quadrangle might be detached from the upper range.

I have now only to request of You one favor; namely, that, you will believe, that the pleasure I derive from the study & occupation which this project gives me, is much greater than any possible trouble which you might suppose, it occasioned, nor does it at all interfere with any business;—for I can without any inconvenience, & with much more satisfaction, devote to it those moments, which I devote to reading or chat.—In truth,—I pride myself much more on the power which my profession gives to me to be useful to the public & to my friends, than I should on any wealth which I might acquire in practising it.

Your very kind invitation to visit you, so often given & so impossible, I fear, to accept, has my best thanks. But with a large family to support, dependent on a Salary of 2.500 ℔ Annum, & having a heavy debt of Mr Fulton's to discharge, which it will require Years to recover from his heirs, I am obliged to shut myself up from the society of my neighbors, even, & dare not[3] indulge any hope of pleasure abroad.—Very truly Yrs B HENRY LATROBE

RC (DLC); at head of text: "Thos Jefferson Esqre Monticello"; endorsed by TJ as received 2 Aug. 1817 and so recorded in SJL.

The LOCKS operated by the Potomac Company had fallen in on 11 July 1817, preventing navigation (Washington *Daily National Intelligencer*, 22 July 1817). The HEAVY DEBT grew out of Latrobe's failed steamboat partnership with Robert Fulton (Latrobe, *Papers*, 3:337–43).

[1] Manuscript: "local."
[2] Parenthetical phrase interlined.
[3] Word interlined.

John H. Cocke's Description of Central College Board of Visitors Meeting

[25–28 July 1817]

25. Went to Monticello to Breakfast—Accompanied Mr Jefferson with Mr Southal & Mr Garrett to view the site—in which the changes proposed by Mr Jefferson as to the position of the buildings appear to be judicious in as much as they are calculated to save much labor in removing Earth—Returned with Mr Jefferson to dinner—Called in Charlottesville and found the amot of Subscriptions on Mr Leitches list between 22 & 23,000$. Mr Jefferson having written to Major Watson to meet us at Mr Madisons determines to go on in the morng.

Mr Cabell joined us at Monticello after night—This insured a quorum of the Visitors—

26. A fine day—Left Monticello at ¼ after 6 & arrived at Montpelier ¼ after 12 O'Clock—In conference upon the subject of sending subscription into the other Counties. it was in vain urged by Mr Cabell & myself that a joint address from the Visitors to four or five influential Gentlemen in each County requesting their attention & exertions for the promotion of the scheme, wou'd be productive of extensively beneficial results—We finally yielded to Mr Jeffersons suggestion of dividing the Counties among ourselves each taking those wherein he

has particular acquaintances & addressing them individually—thus loosing in a very great degree the vast influence of the Names of Jefferson & Madison in promoting the Subscription.—

Application to be made to Doctor Knox of the Balt. Col. to undertake the Professorship of Languages—And to Cooper to fill the next professorship as soon as we can be prepared to receive him—

M[r] Jefferson gave us the following history of the introduction of the Cedar into Albemarle: M[r] Hickman the fourth settler in that County carried up the first tree—M[r] Bolling the Brother in law of M[r] J— planted two near the grave of one of his Children who died at Shadwell about the year 1755 from which all in that Neighbourhood came—

MS (ViU: JHC); diary entry entirely in Cocke's hand; partially dated.

Sometime before this meeting of the Board of Visitors, Joseph C. CABELL prepared a proposed list of commissioners to aid in collecting subscriptions for Central College. He generally suggested at least three names each in his alphabetically organized survey of sixty-five counties and five municipalities (leaving Albemarle County blank and naming only George Cabell for Lynchburg), which covered eastern and central Virginia but excluded the western part of the state (undated MS in ViU: JCC; entirely in Cabell's hand and endorsed by him: "Sketch of Commissioners proposed to be appointed in all the counties east of the Blue Ridge for promoting the subscription to the Central College. M[r] Jefferson & M[r] Madison did not come into this measure, and it was declined").

From Peter Derieux

MONSIEUR Richmond 25. Juillet 1817.

Ayant ecrit en France aussitot que j'appris La mort de Mr Mazzei, a Leffet de faire des informations relatives a mes droits dans sa succession et me procurer des papiers qui m'etoient necessaires, J'ose esperer d'aprés les bontés que vous avés toujours eu pour moi, que vous aurés encore eu celle de retarder Lenvoi des remises que vous vous proposiés de faire à son executeur, J'usqua ce que Jaye recu les reponses que j'attends journellement de Paris.—

Vous m'obligerés beaucoup, Monsieur, si vous voulés bien ajouter aux services que vous mavés rendu, celui de me marquer combien de tems je puis encore esperer que vous voudrés bien differer; et de me croire dans Les sentiments de reconnaissance et du plus respectueux attachement avec Les qu'els J'ay L'honneur d'être:

Monsieur

Votre trés humble et trés obeiss[t] Serviteur P. DERIEUX

EDITORS' TRANSLATION

SIR Richmond 25. July 1817.

Having written to France as soon as I learned of Mr. Mazzei's death in order to inquire about my rights to his estate and obtain some papers I needed, I dare hope, considering the goodness you have always shown me, that you will do me the additional kindness of delaying the remittances you intended to make to his executor until I receive the replies I expect any day from Paris.—

You would greatly oblige me, Sir, if you would be willing to add to the favors you have done me, that of letting me know how long I may hope that you will postpone sending the remittances; and to believe in my feelings of gratitude and the most respectful attachment, with which I have the honor to be:

Sir

Your very humble and obedient servant P. DERIEUX

RC (DLC); dateline at foot of text; endorsed by TJ as received 2 Aug. 1817 and so recorded in SJL. RC (DLC); address cover only; with PoC of TJ to George P. Stevenson, 30 Oct. 1817, on verso; addressed: "Honble Thos Jefferson Monticello V^{a}"; franked; postmarked Richmond, 25 July. Translation by Dr. Genevieve Moene.

From Lancelot Minor

DEAR SIR Louisa. July 25 1817

I have been prevented for sometime acknowledging your letter of the 7th of last month enclosing your Draft upon Mess^{s} Gibson & Jefferson by my own Indisposition and the Illness of my Eldest son who I am glad to say is now better. I have paid the amount of the draft to the Agent of Mrs Callis (Doct Kean) which I beleive closes Mr. Marks affairs in my hands—except the claim upon John G Winston which I am doubtfull will never be come at but I will still endeavour to have it collected—the land belonging to Mrs Marks in my Nieghbourhood is poor and unsaleable If you still wish it sold I will with pleasure give my aid in the sale—you will be please to direct whether I shall forward the papers belonging Mrs Marks in my hands to you or not

Accept Dear Sir my best wishes for your Happiness.

L MINOR

RC (MHi); endorsed by TJ without date of receipt, but recorded in SJL as received 2 Aug. 1817.

TJ's LETTER OF THE 7TH OF LAST MONTH was actually dated 3 June 1817.

From James Monroe

DEAR SIR Plattsburg July 27. 1817

I arriv'd here the day before yesterday on my way to Sacketts harbour, & thence to the westward, in completion of the tour, which I advised you, that I had, in contemplation, before I left washington. I have been, Eastward, as far as Portland, and after returning to Dover in N. Hamshire, have come here, by Concord, & Hanover in that State, & windsor, Montpelier, & Burlington, in Vermont. yesterday, I visited Rouse's point, within two hundred yards of the boundary line, where we are engaged in erecting a work of some importance, as it is supposed, to command the entrance into the lake, from Canada. gen[l] Brown met me here. Tomorrow I proceed, with him, by ogdensbg, to Sacketts harbour, & thence to Detroit, unless I should be compelled, on reaching Erie, to cling to the southeastern side of that lake, & seek my way home, through the state of ohio, by circumstances I may not be able to controul.

When I undertook this tour, I expected to have executed it, as I might have done, in an inferior station, and even as a private citizen, but I found, at Bal: that it would be impracticable for me to do it. I, had, therefore, the alternative, of either returning home, or complying with the opinion of the public, & immediately, I took the latter course, relying on them, to put me forward, as fast as possible, which has been done. I have been exposed, to excessive fatigue, & labour, in my tour, by the pressure of a very crowded population, which has sought, to manifest, its respect, for our union, & republican institutions, in every step, I took, and in modes wh[ic]h made a trial of my strength, as well, phiscally, as mentally. In the principal towns, the whole population, has been in motion, and in a manner, to produce the greatest degree of excit'ment possible. In the Eastern section of our union, I have Seen, distinctly, that the great cause, which brought the people forward, was a conviction, that they had sufferd in their character, by their conduct in the late war, and a desire to show, that unfavorable opinions, and as they thought, unjust, had been formd, in regard to their views and principles. They seiz'd the opportunity, which the casual incident of my tour presented to them, of making a strong exertion, to restore themselves to the confidence, and ground which they had formerly held, in the affections of their brethern, in other quarters. I have seen enough, to satisfy me, that the great mass of our fellow citizens, in the Eastern States, are as firmly attached to the union and to republican gov[t], as I have always believd, or could desire them to be.

In all the towns thro' which I passed, there was an union between the parties, except in the case of Boston. I had supposd that that union, was particularly to be desird by the republican party, since as it would be founded, exclusively on their own principles, every thing would be gaind by them. Some of our old, and honest friends at Boston, were, however, unwilling to amalgamate, with their former opponents, even on our own ground, and in consequence presented an address of their own: This formd the principal difficulty, that I have had to meet, to guard against any injury, arising from the step taken, to the republican cause, to the republican party, or the persons individually. You will have seen this address, & my reply, & be enabled to judge, of the probable result.

I hope to see you the latter end of next month, when we will enter into details, which the few minutes I now enjoy, do not admit, however glad I sho[u^{d}] be to do it. I most ardently wish to get home, to visit my family & friends, & to enjoy in peace, some moments of repose, to which I have been an utter stranger, since I left washington. with my best wishes for your welfare, I am dear Sir respectfully & sincerely your

friend & serv^{t} JAMES MONROE

RC (DLC); edge trimmed and chipped; endorsed by TJ as received 18 Aug. 1817 but corrected in SJL to show receipt on 19 Aug.

The WORK OF SOME IMPORTANCE was a new American fort on Lake Champlain that was begun in 1816 but never completed after a subsequent survey located it on Canadian soil. After a treaty put the site back into the hands of the United States, Fort Montgomery was erected there in 1844 (*Plattsburgh Republican*, 2 Aug. 1817, 28 Feb. 1819; *Boston Commercial Gazette*, 6 Sept. 1819; Rene Chartrand and Donato Spedaliere, *Forts of the War of 1812* [2012], 56).

According to one contemporary report, during his 1817 tour Monroe hoped to travel with "as much celerity as the avowed purposes of his journey would permit: and, to do this, he was desirous to pass through the intermediate towns, with as much privacy as possible." However at Baltimore (BAL:), the first stop on his journey, "being already anticipated by the citizens of that place, they determined that he should be publicly received, and conducted, by a military escort, to his quarters. A corresponding desire to receive the President in a manner suitable to his elevated rank, and with a respect due to his eminent public services, soon evinced itself in all the principal cities, through which he would be obliged to pass, and preparations were every where making, to pay him the highest possible honors" (Samuel Putnam Waldo, *The Tour of James Monroe, President of the United States, in the year 1817* [Hartford, 1818], 14).

A committee of Boston Republicans comprised of Henry A. S. Dearborn, Benjamin Austin, Thomas Melvill, William Little, Russell Sturgis, Jacob Rhoades, John Brazer, and William Ingalls delivered an ADDRESS to Monroe on 4 July 1817. They congratulated him on his election and expressed their desire that his administration would patronize "such institutions as will extend the useful branches of science and literature, and promote the agricultural, manufacturing and commercial interests of your constituents." They also hoped "that your name will be recorded in the American annals with the same respectful veneration as distinguishes the characters of your illustrious precedessors, WASHINGTON, ADAMS, JEFFERSON and MADISON" (Boston *Columbian Centinel*, 12 July 1817; reprinted in other newspapers and Waldo, *Tour of James Monroe*, 107–9). Monroe's REPLY emphasized his commitment to republican government and desire that everyone would "unite in future in the measures necessary to secure it" (*Columbian Centinel*, 16 July 1817; reprinted in other newspapers and Waldo, *Tour of James Monroe*, 109–12).

Minutes of Central College Board of Visitors

July 28. 1817.

At a called meeting of the Visitors of the Central College, held at the House of Mr Madison in Orange, Thomas Jefferson, James Madison, John Hartwell Cocke, and Joseph C. Cabell, being present:

The plan of the first Pavilion to be erected, and the proceedings thereupon, having been stated and agreed to

It is agreed that application be made to Doctor Knox of Baltimore to accept the Professorship of Languages, Belles Lettres, Rhetoric, History and Geography, and that an independent salary of five hundred dollars, with a perquisite of twenty five dollars, from each pupil, to-gether with chambers for his accomodation, be allowed him as a compensation for his services, he finding the necessary assistant ushers.

Alexander Garritt requesting[1] to resign the office of Proctor, it is agreed that Nelson Barksdale of the county of Albemarle be appointed his successor.

It is also agreed that it be expedient to import a stone cutter from Italy, and that Mr Jefferson be authorized & requested to take the requisite measures to effect that object.

JAMES MADISON
J. H. COCKE
JOSEPH C. CABELL
TH: JEFFERSON

MS (ViU: TJP-VMTJ); in Cabell's hand, signed by Madison, Cocke, Cabell, and TJ. Tr (ViU: TJP-VMJCC). Tr (ViU: TJP-VMJHC). Tr (ViU: TJP-VMJB). FC (ViU: JCC); abstract in Cabell's hand lacking the opening list of meeting attendees and signatures; at head of text: "Meeting at Mr Madison's"; conjoined with similar FC of Minutes of Central College Board of Visitors, 7 Oct. 1817.

[1] Trs: "requested."

From Benjamin Henry Latrobe

Dr Sir Washington July 28th 1817

Since my last of the 24th I have engaged a young man of the name of Johnson, to undertake your Stone cutting, should the terms be approved. He is not only capable to cut a Doric Capital, or a Base, but to execute the common Architectural decorations, as foliage & Rosettes, with great neatness & dispatch, for, in the scarcity of Carvers, I have, for some time past, put him under Andrei, & have lately employed him to carve the rosettes in the Caissons of the cornice of the H. of Rep. which he has done quite to my Satisfaction. He also possesses that quality, so essential to the workmen, you employ, good temper, & is besides (which is not always compatible with good temper) quite sober.—His terms are 2$.50 ⅌ day, finding himself. This is what our journeymen earn here, in Summer. If he is to have the charge of more men, he will expect his wages to be encreased, and he expects constant employment while engaged, & well, & that his actual expenses to the spot, & back again (should he return to Washington) shall be paid.—He is ready to depart at a few days notice

I observe in the newspaper a letter from a Gentleman in Virginia dated July 20th, mentioning his visit to Monticello, & that you were then at Your Bedford Estate. If so I cannot expect an early answer to this letter or to my last, but I shall keep Johnson ready for You whenever I do hear from You.—

Notwithstanding the convenience, & great utility to many of my most important interests which I find from the Polygraph, it is a fact, that Peale never could dispose of more than 60, 40 of which about, as his Son tells me, were sold by my recommendation. In each of the public offices here, one was procured, but never used, & I found them in 1812, almost destroyed. For knowing them to be useless where they were, I endeavored to borrow one for a Member of Congress, & found them in a very neglected state.—I have often recommended them to Merchants, but they object, "that their Clerks are always sufficient for the copying of their letters, & would otherwise be unemployed, & moreover never write a good hand for want of practice; & that they must copy their letters into books, for safekeeping, & for production in courts of justice."—In all this there is certainly something substantial, enough to prevent innovation in a system, in which form, & uniform practice is assuredly very essential; for merchants, are generally a sort of Machines, & govern themselves as much by the practice of their business, as Lawyers do. Thus in the most writing class of men, the Polygraph has had no introduction, & is used only by a few litterary men, who will take the pains to save themselves trouble.

With the Tobacco Capital, I shall send you some polished specimens of the Potomac Marble.

I am as ever with the highest esteem yrs B H LATROBE.

RC (DLC: TJ Papers, 210:37530–1); addressed: "Thomas Jefferson Esq[r] Monticello Virg[a]"; franked; postmarked Washington, 3 Aug.; endorsed by TJ as a letter of 28 July received 7 Aug. 1817. Recorded in SJL as a letter of 18 July received 7 Aug. 1817.

A letter written by a GENTLEMAN described only as a "traveller in Virginia," dated Lynchburg, 20 July, gave an account of a brief visit to Monticello while TJ was away at Poplar Forest: "I was received by col. Randolph, whose polite attentions could not fail making the deepest impression. The building is elegant, both in the architecture and finish; the beauty and taste displayed in the internal decoration, and the sublimity of the surrounding scenery cannot be surpassed. Nature and art appear to have united in its structure and embellishment, and to have presented it to the world as a production of their joint powers" (Washington *Daily National Intelligencer*, 26 July 1817).

From Samuel L. Osborn

MUCH RESPECTED SIR, Kennebunk, July 28th 1817.

Pardon a few lines from a person so far below you in abilities and renown. They were sent with the hope of receiving an answer, barely acknowledging the receipt of mine, that I might have something to remember our **Jefferson** by. I ask for nothing more.—Forgive me, Sir, when I inform you that you have been my political Idol ever since I was twelve years of age.—I have been engaged about seven years past as an Instructor to our dear youth; and, now keep an English & W.I. Goods Store, which requires my attention so much, that I never expect to gratify my eyes with your presence on this side the grave; but I hope 'ere long to behold You with **Washington, Franklin** & many other worthies in the mansions of Everlasting Peace.—

I Subscribe myself most respectfully, Sir, your devoted friend

SAM[L] L. OSBORN

RC (DLC); at foot of text: "Hon. Thomas Jefferson"; endorsed by TJ as received <*18*> 19 Aug. 1817 and so recorded in SJL.

Samuel L. Osborn (1788–1857), teacher and merchant, operated a store in Kennebunk, District of Maine, by 1816. In 1819 he and his brother James Osborn formed the partnership of Samuel L. Osborn & Company. It dissolved in 1821, with Samuel retaining the store. Osborn was still in trade in 1850, when he possessed property valued at $4,000 (Daniel Remich, *History of Kennebunk from its Earliest Settlement to 1890* [1911], 247, 253, 412, 526–7; DNA: RG 29, CS, Me., Kennebunk, 1850).

W.I.: "West India."

Agreement with Jeremiah A. Goodman

Having at the date of a settlement of Nov. 30. 1815. with Jeremiah A. Goodman sold to him a negro girl called Sally for the sum of 150. Dollars, for which sum I was then allowed a credit in account; it is now agreed with the sd Jeremiah that that sale shall be annulled; that the said negro girl Sally shall now become my property, and that I shall repay to him the said sum of 150.D. with interest thereon from the sd 30th of November 1815. until repaid; and also that I shall repay him the sum of fifteen Dollars allowed me in account on the 16th day of December 1816. for subsistence for the sd girl with interest thereon from the sd 16th of Dec. 1816. until payment and that these payments of the sd sums of 150.D. & of 15.D. with their respective interests shall be made in the month of May eighteen hundred and nineteen. Witness my hand this 30th day of July 1817. TH: JEFFERSON

I agree to the above and have delivered up the deed for the negro girl who has always been in the possession of the sd Thomas.

JEREMIAH A GOODMAN

MS (NNGL, on deposit NHi); in TJ's hand, signed by TJ and Goodman; endorsed by TJ: "Goodman Jeremiah A. 1817. July 30."; with notation on verso in Goodman's hand, signed by Goodman and witnessed by Benjamin Whaler: "September the tenth day 1817 I Assign the benefit of the within to John L Oneal"; followed by three notations in unidentified hands, the first signed by O'Neal and witnessed by Michael Johnson: "1817 Decr 18th I assign the within to Wayt & Winn value recd," the second signed by Twyman Wayt: "1821 March 5th Recd Draft on Bernard Peyton for the within," and the third reading: "Thos Jeffersons note $1."

The account of THE 16TH DAY OF DECEMBER 1816, not found, was presumably enclosed in Goodman's missing letter to TJ of 15 Dec. 1816, accounted for above at TJ to Joel Yancey, 21 Dec. 1816. On 5 Mar. 1821 TJ settled this debt by giving Twyman Wayt, the ultimate assignee, a draft on Bernard Peyton for $219.72 (TJ to Peyton, 4 Mar. 1821; *MB*, 2:1372). The DEED for the sale of Sally Goodman has not been found.

From Joseph Milligan

Georgetown July 30th 1817

I shall send you another proof by the next mail If it would not be too much trouble I should like that you would receive and return a proof once a week whilst you are in Bedford but in this matter I do not wish you to do any thing that would not be agreeable to you only the book has been so long in hand I am desirous to progress with

Yours With Esteem JOSEPH MILLIGAN

RC (DLC); at foot of text: "Thomas Jefferson Esqr"; endorsed by TJ without date of receipt, but recorded in SJL as received 2 Aug. 1817.

Milligan was sending TJ PROOF sheets of Destutt de Tracy, *Treatise on Political Economy*.

From John Vaughan

DEAR SIR Philad. 30 July 1817

Your favor of 28 June was rcv[d], it was accidentally mislaid, until this day—I shall see M[r] Biddle & M[rs] Barton & do all in my power relative to the papers of Lewis & Clarke, & advise results—We have reason to be very thankful to you for what you are doing relative to this Subject & also relative to Birds private Journal—

We have lately recieved from the Adj. Gen. Office (D Parker) Pikes Journal Part 1st of his work—Hunter's & Dunbars Journals up the Washita & to the Hot Springs <u>all Manuscript</u>—Pikes has been published & I believe M[r] Dunbars, except the Astron[l] Survey—I do not know whether Hunters has—we are only in possession of Pikes printed Journal—We are now examining—

I hand you your a/c Ballance due You $34\frac{28}{100}$—which I hope will prove Correct

I remain Yours &c JN VAUGHAN

RC (MHi); at head of text: "Thomas Jefferson Monticello"; endorsed by TJ as a letter of 31 July 1817 received 5 Aug. 1817 and so recorded in SJL. Enclosure not found.

BIRDS PRIVATE JOURNAL was the secret account by William Byrd (1674–1744) of the 1728 expedition to survey Virginia's southern boundary.

The American Philosophical Society recorded on 18 July 1817 that they had RECEIVED from Daniel Parker some manuscript expedition journals, including two volumes in which William Dunbar documented his journey with George Hunter, "by order of the government," up the Red and Ouachita rivers to the Hot Springs of Arkansas, 1804–05, and the first part of Zebulon Montgomery Pike's journal of his voyage to the source of the Mississippi, 1805–06 (APS, Minutes [MS in PPAmP]; PPAmP: Expedition Journals). Pike was the author of *An Account of Expeditions to the Sources of the Mississippi, and through the Western Parts of Louisiana ... And a Tour through the Interior Parts of New Spain* (Philadelphia, 1810; Sowerby, no. 4169; Poor, *Jefferson's Library*, 7 [no. 371]). Dunbar published numerous articles drawn from his travel observations in APS, *Transactions* 6 (1809).

From A. F. De Laage

MONSIEUR, Charlottesville 31 J^t 1817

Je me Suis rendu ce matin à Monticello, pour vous présenter mes respects, et vous temoigner toute ma reconnoissance des Bontés que vous avez eues pour moi pendant mon Séjour à Charlottesville: Croyez, je vous prie, Monsieur, que je sens bien vivement l'extrême Distance qui existe entre Vous et moi, et qui les Politesses dont vous m'avez comblé, Sont pour moi un honneur dont je Serai toujours fier, et que je ne pourrai jamais oublier—

Je quitte votre Voisinage, et vais m'établir à Lynchburg, ou j'espere trouver les moyens de mieux combattre l'infortune. d'avoir été reçu chez vous Monsieur, d'avoir été admis à votre table, est presque le Seul titre que j'aie à la bienveillance des habitants de Lynchburg: oscrais je esperer que ce ne fut pas une indiscrétion de ma Part, de vous demander une introduction à quelques Personnes de cette Ville? Veuillez, Monsieur, Si vous m'accordez ma Demande, faire remettre le tout à M. Wells, qui me le fera parvenir: Car des affaires me forcent impérieusement a Partir demain matin: Veuillez aussi, je vous en Supplie, Monsieur, croire à toute la Reconnoissance et au profond Respect avec lesquels—

J'ai l'honneur d'être, Monsieur, Votre très humble et très obeissant Serviteur— A. F. DE LAAGE

M^de De Laage vous prie de présenter Ses respects à Madame Randolph—

EDITORS' TRANSLATION

SIR, Charlottesville 31 July 1817

I went to Monticello this morning, to pay you my respects and express all my gratitude for the kindness you have shown me during my stay in Charlottesville. Please believe, Sir, that I am acutely aware of the extreme distance that exists between you and me, and that I consider the courtesy you showered upon me as an honor of which I will always be proud, and that I will never be able to forget—

I am leaving your neighborhood and going to settle in Lynchburg, where I hope to find the means of overcoming misfortune. Having been received at your house, Sir, and admitted to your table is almost my only claim on the benevolence of the inhabitants of Lynchburg. Could I hope that I would not be committing an indiscretion in asking you for an introduction to some of the people in that town? If you grant me my request, Sir, please hand everything to Mr. Wells, who will forward it to me, because urgent business obliges me to depart tomorrow morning. I also beg you, Sir, to believe in the gratitude and profound respect with which—

I have the honor to be, Sir, your very humble and very obedient servant—

A. F. De Laage

Mrs. De Laage asks that you present her respects to Mrs. Randolph—

RC (DLC); at head of text: "Mr Th. Jefferson"; endorsed by TJ as received 2 Aug. 1817 and so recorded in SJL. Translation by Dr. Genevieve Moene.

A. F. De Laage served in the military in his native France before arriving in the United States. By March 1817 he was in the Charlottesville area and formed a brief acquaintance with TJ and his family at Monticello. In August of that year he relocated to Lynchburg, where he operated a shop before deciding early in 1818 to move to New Orleans (TJ to Louis H. Girardin, 30 Apr. 1817; TJ to Samuel J. Harrison, Charles Johnston, and Archibald Robertson, [13] Aug. 1817; Ellen W. Randolph [Coolidge] to Martha Jefferson Randolph, [after 29 Aug. 1817], extracted below at 13 Aug. 1817 as the third in a group of documents on Jefferson's Trip to Natural Bridge; De Laage to TJ, 22 Jan. 1818; Harrison to TJ, 24 Jan. 1818).

To James Rawlings

Sir Monticello July 31. 17.

Your favor of July 9. was recieved on the 15th. with respect to Henderson's mill the case is thus. Henderson the father, while I was absent in Europe, without any application to the court, or any jury, built the mill and overflowed a millseat of mine 3. feet. he died leaving ten children his heirs.[1] after my return, to wit, in 1795. I brought a bill in Chancery to oblige them to take away their dam. in 1799 Oct. 1. I obtained a decree for it's demolition, and took it down soon after. from that time it ceased to be a mill. in May 1804. I bought their millstones, and then successively purchased from the parceners their respective portions of the estate; but as they still thought their millhouse worth something & capable of reestablishment, & consequently asked something considerable for it, I, who knew it to be worth nothing, refused to give any thing for it, & there was a reservation in every deed to themselves of the mill and site, so that it was excepted out of the conveyances to me. becoming afterwards sensible that their expectations of the revival of their mill were desperate, they sold all the materials, even to the stones of the walls, which were taken down & carried away in 1808. or 1809. it has ceased therefore to be a mill about 17. years, and been out of existence entirely about 8. or 9. years. if any body can be answerable under these circumstances, it cannot be myself, being expressly excepted out of the conveyances to me; and if it is the family, they are dispersed over the Western states, and nearly all of them, I believe, bankrupt. mr David Higgenbotham of Richmond was living on the spot, and in sight of the mill; he is well acquainted with all these transactions, & remembers some, I dare say, better than I do. I will ask the favor of you therefore to enquire of him as I should be glad to have corrected any mistake I may have made & he is very capable of correcting it. Accept the assurances of my respect TH: JEFFERSON

PoC (MHi); on verso of reused address cover of Joseph C. Cabell to TJ, 23 Apr. 1817; at foot of text: "Mr James Rawlins"; endorsed by TJ, with his additional notation above endorsement: "Fire-insurance."

For the 1 Oct. 1799 DECREE in chancery ordering the destruction of the Hendersons' milldam, see *PTJ*, 31:208. TJ agreed on 1 May 1804 to purchase John Henderson's pair of five-foot burr MILLSTONES (*MB*, 2:1125).

[1] Sentence interlined.

To Thomas Appleton

DEAR SIR Monticello Aug. 1. 17.

My last to you was of July 18. 16. since which I have recieved yours of May 15. and 30. July 30. Sep. 27. & Oct. 20. of the same year, & Mar. 5. of the present, with the seed of the Lupinella. this came to hand too late to be sown this season, and is therefore reserved for the ensuing spring. mr Madison recieved what you sent him somewhat earlier, & sowed a little (not chusing to venture the whole.) I am recently returned from a visit to him and saw the plants just come up. from their appearance we judged them to be a species of Saintfoin. the next year however I shall sow the whole of mine, and be able to judge of it.

In my letter to you of July 18. and one of the same date to Mr Carmigniani, on the subject of mr Mazzei's funds I explained the situation of this country, which, after being shut up from all means of disposing of it's produce during a war of 3. years, had experienced seasons the most adverse to agriculture which had ever been known. at that moment also appearances were unfavorable for the year then current; but in the hope it might change for the better, I ventured to promise myself and mr Carmigniani that a commencement of remittance of principal and interest should be made in the present year. but the drought which was prevailing at the date of my letter, continued thro' the whole season of the growth of our crops, and produced a failure in them much greater than in the preceding year; insomuch that there has been the greatest distress for bread, which has sold generally at 5. times it's usual price. few farmers have made enough of other things to pay for their bread; and the present year has been equally afflicting for their crop of wheat, by such an inundation of Hessian fly as was never seen before. a great part of my own crop has not yielded seed. whole fields did not give an ear for every square foot, & many turned their cattle on their wheat to make something of it as pasture. after such a disaster the last year, and so gloomy a prospect for the present, following the distresses of the war, our farmers are scarcely able to meet the indispensable expences of taxes, culture & food for their families and laborers. under such difficulties & prospects, I have not only been unable to make the remittance I had promised to mr Carmigniani, of the first portion of principal and interest, but am really afraid to promise it for the next, such are the prospects of the present season; and unwilling, by renewed and precise engagements, to hazard renewed breaches of them I am constrained to sollicit the consent of the family to let the money lie awhile in my hands, and to recieve remittances of it in portions as I can make them. they may be assured they shall be made as soon and as fast as would be in my power, were I to engage for specific sums and dates. the interest I solemnly engage to send them annually, and about this season of the year. I am in hopes that the punctual reciept of the interest from hence will be the same to them, as if recieved from a depository there, while it will be a kind accomodation to me; and I hope it the more as this is really money which I recovered out of the fire for them, by lawsuits & persevering efforts, & which I am certain mr Mazzei, no more than myself had never hoped to obtain. with respect to the ultimate safety of the principal in my hands, any person from this state can satisfy them that my landed property alone is of more than fifty times the amount of this sum. flattering myself then that under these circumstances, and where the difference to them is only whether they shall recieve their interest from **A.** or from **B.** I shall be indulged with this accomodation, I have remitted to my friend John Vaughan of Philadelphia 400. Dollars to be invested in a good bill payable to yourself, with a request to you that you will pay to whoever of the family is entitled to recieve it, a year's interest, to wit 380. Dollars 52 cents. Altho' I suggest an indulgence indefinite in it's particular term, I have no idea of postponing the commencement of my remittances, by thirds, more than a year or two longer. if the seasons should, against the course of nature hitherto observed continue constantly hostile to our agriculture, I will certainly relieve myself at once by a sale of property sufficient to refund this whole debt, a measure very disagreeable while the expectation exists of doing it from the annual profits: and the family will be always free to discontinue the indulgence if the delay should be protracted unreasonably and inconveniently to them.

the nett proceeds of the sale of the ground in Richmond was 6342, say six thousand three hundred and forty two Dollars, recieved July 14. 1813. if the family consents to my proposal, I will, on being so informed, settle up the back-interest, add it to the principal, send them a specific obligation and thencef[orth] remit annually the interest of six percent, with portions of the principal as fast as I shall be able. I think there remains no other item of account between mr Mazzei and myself, except 50.D. paid to the lawyer employed in the recovery, & 20.D. to mr Derieux by particular request of mr Mazzei.

I write all this to you, because you have hitherto been the mutual channel of this business; for altho mr Carmigniani wrote me a letter which I answered July 18. as beforementioned, with a full explanation of the state of the debt, the circumstances which had occasioned it's remaining in my hands, and the remittances proposed, yet the marriage of miss Mazzei with mr Pini has, I suppose determined his agency. I shall be uneasy until I learn that the family is contented with this arrangement, and I will therefore sollicit an early line from you. We are erecting a College in my neighborhood, in which with other visitors I have a direction. we are in want of a stone-cutter, not of the very first order, but capable of cutting an Ionic capital when drawn for him, and we suppose we can be better accomodated with one from your place than here. for indeed such workmen are scarcely to be had here at all. I am authorised therefore to request you to send us such an one on the best terms you can. we will pay his passage to Norfolk or Richmond, & thence to this place, and give such annual wages as you shall agree for, in addition to our finding him lodging & subsistence, on condition he is bound, before he sails, to serve us three years from the date of his arrival at this place, and that we may withold such portions of his wages as you shall fix on, until his time is out as a security that he will stay his time out. on this subject too it is necessary I should hear from you as soon as possible, because we shall want him to commence work by April next. but he must come to Norfolk or Richmond direct, and to no other port; for he would immediately on his landing elsewhere be debauched from his contract.

The wines you were so good as to send me were all recieved exactly as you described them. the Ama wine was the best, but still not equal to the Montepulciano, and as I learn from your letter of Sep. 27. that the crop of wines for that year was desperate I have not applied to you for any this year. if however it has proved that any good Montepulciano (of the growth formerly sent me) has been produced, contrary to your expectation, the little atom of balance of the 400.D. remaining after payment of the interest, might be invested in that. it will give us a taste. unless indeed it be wanting to aid the departure of the Stone-cutter, to which use, if necessary, I would prefer it's application. my correspondents at Richmond are mess[rs] Gibson & Jefferson, to whom he may, on arrival there apply to be forwarded to this place. at Norfolk I have no particular correspondent. yet Cap[t] Joseph Miller of that place, or perhaps the Collector of the port would forward him to Richmond.

In the same letter of July 18. I informed you that mr Bracken, the administrator of mr Bellini had at length settled his account and deposited the balance of 635. Dollars 48 cents in the bank of Virginia at Richmond: that, considering the uncertain state of persons in commerce in England, the only ready channel of remittance, I was afraid to undertake it's remittance, and therefore it would lie in the bank, where it bears no interest, until called for. mr Fancelli should therefore withdraw it as soon as he can. for this purpose he may draw on me, which draught I will answer, by one at sight, in favor of the holder, on the bank of Virginia, where the money lies ready for delivery at a moment's call. or if there should be difficulty in this, and mr Fancelli directs I will get mr Vaughan, my own correspondent, to make the remittance in the safest way he can. Present, if you please the homage of my respect of Mesdames Mazzei & Pini, and to mr Pini also. their connection with my late much esteemed friend Mazzei gives me an interest in their health & happiness and places at their command any services I can render them. but there can hardly arise occasion for these, unless they should catch the general fever of emigration to America, which whether it would be for the happiness of those whose habits of society are fixed by age, may be doubted: but cannot be as to the happiness and means of prosperity of their descendants. Accept yourself assurances of my great friendship and respect.

TH: JEFFERSON

P.S. I inclose a letter for Count Barziza of Venice, from his brother, now with me on a visit, which be so good as to commit to the post office.

PoC (DLC); one word faint; at foot of first page: "M[r] Appleton"; endorsed by TJ; with TJ's notation at foot of text: "Aug. 2. sent original to mr Vaughan." Enclosed in TJ to John Vaughan, 2 Aug. 1817. Enclosure not found.

A missing Dupl of this letter was apparently conjoined with TJ to Appleton, [20] Aug. 1817, both of which were enclosed in a letter from TJ to Daniel Brent that is not recorded in SJL and has not been found. In Brent's response of 30 Aug. 1817, he gives the date of the letter from TJ as 22 Aug. 1817, but based on TJ's consistent misdating of letters written and received at Poplar Forest in August 1817, it was most likely composed a day later.

TJ's LAST to Appleton was actually dated 16 Mar. 1817. James MADISON received lupinella seed from Appleton via William H. Crawford in April 1817 (Madison, *Papers, Retirement Ser.*, 1:32–3;

Washington *Daily National Intelligencer*, 23 June 1817). Lupinella is the Italian name for sainfoin (SAINTFOIN). In October 1808 TJ paid $50 to Samuel McCraw, the LAWYER EMPLOYED IN THE RECOVERY of Philip Mazzei's house and lot in Richmond (*MB*, 2:1232).

To James Clarke

DEAR SIR Monticello Aug. 1. 17.

I have duly recieved your favor of July 6. and am glad you have turned your attention to the invention of means for surveying and platting at the same time. I have but occasionally looked at the subject as a desideratum; but never seriously aiming at it's solution myself. the basis however of what has occurred to me is a four wheeled carriage, very light, the wheels to be like cotton spinning wheels & all other parts proportionably light. just over the bolt which connects the perch with the fore axle, suppose a machine fixed, so as to remain steadily in the direction of the perch, and the fore-axle made to govern a tracer which should draw on paper all the changes of angle and direction which the fore axle should commence. but as to the wheelwork & other contrivances necessary to effect this on paper, I never aimed at them. they are much more within your competence. I am afraid you will find the magnetic needle too weak and tremulous an agent to fulfill your views. Accept the assurance of my great esteem and respect TH: JEFFERSON

PoC (DLC); on verso of reused address cover of Chapman Johnson to TJ, 26 Apr. 1817; at foot of text: "Col° James Clarke"; endorsed by TJ.

To Mark L. Descaves

Monticello Aug. 1. 17.

Th: Jefferson presents his compliments and his thanks to Mr Deslaves for his obliging attention in forwarding to him a letter from his friend M. de la Fayette; which indeed he would have recieved with more pleasure from the hand of M. Deslaves himself had his curiosity or convenience tempted him to have visited Virginia. having very lately written to Genl La Fayette, he has only to express his obligations to M. Deslaves for his kind offers of transmission, and to salute him with great consideration.

PoC (MHi); on verso of reused address cover to TJ; dateline at foot of text; endorsed by TJ as a letter to Mark L. "Deslaves" and so recorded in SJL.

To the Seventy-Six Association

Monticello Aug. 1. 17.

Th: Jefferson returns his thanks to the members of the '76 association at Charleston, as well as to their Standing Committee, for the communication of the eloquent oration of mr Elliott which he has read with great pleasure. he assures them of his sensibility on this mark of their kind attention, and salutes them with the tender of his high consideration and respect.

PoC (MoSHi: TJC-BC); on verso of reused address cover of otherwise unlocated letter from William D. Taylor to TJ, 7 Apr. 1817 (addressed: "Thomas Jefferson Esq[r] Monticello Virginia"; franked by Taylor: "Collectors office W[m] D Taylor"; postmarked Richmond, 7 Apr.; recorded in SJL as received 10 Apr. 1817 from Richmond); dateline at foot of text; endorsed by TJ.

From Tanner, Vallance, Kearny, & Company

SIR, *Philadelphia, August* 1*st,* 1817.

The publishers of the American Atlas, the prospectus and plan of which are subjoined, respectfully solicit your aid in behalf of the undertaking. The unusual expense necessary in the proposed work, which is intended to give a correct and minute geographical view of each of the United States on an extensive scale, induces them to adopt this method of obtaining the requisite encouragement for executing it in a style worthy of our country, and the flourishing state of the Arts. The publishers respectfully submit the following plan of the work to your consideration, which they confidently trust will receive your approbation and that of the American Public.

TANNER, VALLANCE, KEARNY, & CO.

Broadside (DLC: Printed Ephemera Collection); with enclosure on verso; addressed: "Tho[s] Jefferson Esq[r] Monticello V[a]"; stamp canceled; franked; postmarked Philadelphia, 4 Aug.; endorsed by TJ as a "Circular" from "Tanner & co." received 18 Aug. 1817 but recorded in SJL with date of receipt corrected to 19 Aug. 1817. Enclosure: prospectus by Tanner, Vallance, Kearny, & Company for a *New and Elegant American Atlas*, stating that the geographer John Henry Eddy, of New York, will draw the maps; describing European maps of the United States as "extremely defective and incorrect"; indicating that the work will include maps of the world and of each individual state and territory; specifying that the state maps will be engraved from original drawings when possible and will include geographic features as well as cities, towns, villages, and the principal roads; announcing that the first maps will be ready for publication the following autumn; advertising that they will be "purely American" in execution, printed on "first quality Columbier paper," and "coloured in an elegant and appropriate manner";

stipulating that the work will be completed in thirteen segments, of which the first twelve will contain three sheets and the last will have five, including "an elegant engraved title sheet"; listing the price as $5 per segment, payable on delivery, with anyone who obtains five subscriptions and makes himself responsible for their payment eligible to receive a sixth set free; requesting previously unpublished geographical information from "gentlemen residing in the interior"; and concluding with a blank subscription list (broadside in DLC: Printed Ephemera Collection; on verso of covering circular letter).

Tanner, Vallance, Kearny, & Company was an engraving firm established in Philadelphia by Benjamin Tanner, his brother Henry S. Tanner, John Vallance, and Francis Kearny. The firm, which was active by 1817 and dissolved early in 1820, issued the first two folios of the *New American Atlas* in 1819. After it dissolved, Henry S. Tanner finished the last three folios alone, 1821–23. The final total of maps had been significantly reduced in order to lower production costs, but the work was still significant for its use of a uniform and ambitious scale of fifteen geographical miles to the inch for the state maps and for its citation of the sources it employed (H. Glenn Brown and Maude O. Brown, *A Directory of the Book-Arts and Book Trade in Philadelphia to 1820, Including Painters and Engravers* [1950], 69, 116, 117, 120; John Adems Paxton, *The Philadelphia Directory and Register* [Philadelphia, 1818] and [Philadelphia, 1819]; Philadelphia *Franklin Gazette*, 27 Jan. 1820; Ristow, *American Maps and Mapmakers*, 191–3).

Benjamin Tanner (1775–1848) was a native of New York City who apprenticed to a French engraver in that city before relocating permanently to Philadelphia about 1799. Among other endeavors he partnered with Francis Kearny and Cornelius Tiebout in a banknote-engraving firm beginning in 1817. From 1835 onwards Tanner worked solely on engraving checks and banknotes. He retired in 1845 and died in Baltimore (*ANB*; *DAB*; Brown and Brown, *Directory of the Book-Arts*, 116; Washington *Daily National Intelligencer*, 23 Nov. 1848).

Henry Schenck Tanner (1786–1858) was born in New York City and moved as a youth to Philadelphia to learn engraving from his elder brother Benjamin Tanner. The younger Tanner specialized in cartography and engraved numerous maps, atlases, and other geographical works. By 1844 he moved back to New York City, where he died (*ANB*; *DAB*; Ristow, *American Maps and Mapmakers*; Brown and Brown, *Directory of the Book-Arts*, 116; *McElroy's Philadelphia Directory for 1843* [1843], 275; *The New-York City Directory for 1844 & 1845* [1844], 339; New York *Evening Post*, 18 May 1858).

John Vallance (ca. 1771–1823) was born in Glasgow, Scotland, and moved permanently in about 1791 to Philadelphia, where he worked as an engraver specializing in scrip and banknotes. He partnered early in his career with James Thackara. Vallance died in Philadelphia (Mantle Fielding, *Dictionary of American Painters, Sculptors and Engravers* [1926; repr. 1974], 380; Brown and Brown, *Directory of the Book-Arts*, 117, 120).

Francis Kearny (1785–1837) was born in Perth Amboy, New Jersey. After studying drawing in New York City, he apprenticed to an engraver there at age eighteen. Kearny opened his own engraving business in New York before moving to Philadelphia in 1810. After partnering briefly in several firms, he worked on his own, specializing in engravings for periodicals and religious works. Kearny died in Perth Amboy (*DAB*; William Dunlap, *A History of the Rise and Progress of the Arts of Design in the United States* [1834; repr. 1969], 2:211–2; Brown and Brown, *Directory of the Book-Arts*, 69; New York *Evening Post*, 2 Sept. 1837).

To Stephen Cathalan

DEAR SIR Monticello Aug. 2. 17.

In my preceding letters I have expressed to you my expectation that some of my acquaintances who taste here the wines I get from you would probably begin the introduction of them by applications to you, and that I would make them known to you as worthy of attention and good service. mr David Higginbotham, a merchant of Richmond & friend of mine proposes to apply to you for some of the wine of Rivesalte of Roussillon, such as you have sent me, and perhaps for some others. I assure him because I am sure myself, that you will have him furnished with the best and on the best terms.

I take this occasion of going into the following explanation for your satisfaction as well as my own. A few days ago a mr Valltone wrote me a line from the neighboring village of Charlottesville, calling himself your cousin, stating that he had been the bearer of a letter from you to me that he had inclosed it to me[1] in one of his own from New york by mail, and was now proceeding to Tombigbee in the South. in the course of 27. years of unceasing and extensive[2] correspondence thro' our mail, I have never had a single letter miscarry. this circumstance as well as mr Valltone's having separated himself from his letter, induced [so]me doubt, and being in the moment of setting out on a visit to mr Madison, I did not answer the letter. on my return he called on me, and soon percieved my doubt. he appeared hurt, entered into conversation respecting you, by which I percieved you were not unknown to him, & therefore I loosened myself from my first reserve. he stated that his object in calling was to obtain such information as I could give relative to the country he was going to. whether there were any other way in which I could have been useful to him, and which he might decline mentioning on percieving that the want of his credentials was felt, I do not know; but this I can assure you that a letter from you delivered by a cousin of yours, would have commanded for him all the resources of which I am master. he was in good health, and proceeded on his journey; and I have thought it a duty to explain this transaction truly to you, that you might be assured I could not be wanting in attentions or services to any one connected with you and bearing unsuspected evidence of it. I salute you with constant affection & respect.

TH: JEFFERSON

PoC (DLC); on verso of a reused address cover from P. de Valltone to TJ; torn at seal, with one word rewritten by TJ; at foot of text: "M. Cathalan"; endorsed by TJ.

[1]Preceding two words interlined. [2]Preceding two words interlined.

To John Vaughan

Dear Sir Monticello Aug. 2. 17.

I have occasion to remit a sum of 400 Dollars to mr Thomas Appleton our Consul at Leghorn, and must therefore again have recourse to your friendship to do it. for this purpose I now inclose you 400. Dollars in bills of the bank of Virginia, which I am in hopes are good with you. no bill of the US. bank has yet reached this. I know nothing of the exchanges between the US. and foreign countries, which are sometimes I suppose above par and sometimes below. however this may be, being desirous to pay that precise sum at Leghorn, I will ask the favor of you to remit the whole sum and if there be any thing additional due, it shall be replaced to you by return of the mail which brings me notice of it. I inclose a letter to mr Appleton to go with the remittance, and shall send a duplicate through the Secretary of states office,[1] supposing they have public vessels frequently going to the Mediterranean. I set out for my possessions near Lynchburg within 4. or 5. days and shall be there till about the 20th of Sep. if therefore there be a deficiency in the sum now sent, be so good as to direct your letter to me 'at Poplar Forest near Lynchburg' and I will make the remittance from thence. I salute you with great friendship & respect. Th: Jefferson

RC (NjMoHP: Lloyd W. Smith Collection); at foot of text: "John Vaughan esq." PoC (MHi); on verso of reused address cover of Benjamin Harrison to TJ, 11 July 1817; torn at seal; endorsed by TJ. Enclosure: TJ to Thomas Appleton, 1 Aug. 1817.

[1]Word interlined.

To Levett Harris

Dear Sir [Monticello] Aug. 3. 17.

Your favor of July 24. came to hand yesterday, and I sincerely congratulate you on your safe arrival in your native country. you will find it I am sure much altered from what you left it. a great but somewhat dropsical increase of wealth, with a vast progress in luxury.

I am much flattered by the notice of the Emperor. I have been acting on the humble field of promoting peace, and leaving to industry all it's earnings; the Emperor has been directing the destinies of the world and I believe has ameliorated them as much as less virtuous cooperators would permit him. he is young, able good, and has long years of action still remaining to merit from posterity their devout thanks to heaven that such a ruler has lived. your visit to Monticello will be recieved with great acknolegements and welcome, and will be to me a source of instruction as to the details of what has been passing in the world which cannot be obtained thro' the lying channels of the public. I set out in 4. or 5. days for a distant possession 30. leagues South, and shall be back by the last week in September, in time to recieve you here at the season you contemplate. in the mean while I pray you to accept the assurance of my great esteem and respect. TH: JEFFERSON

PoC (DLC); on verso of reused address cover to TJ; dateline faint; torn at seal, with one word rewritten by TJ; at foot of text: "Levitt Harris esq."; endorsed by TJ.

To Benjamin Henry Latrobe

DEAR SIR Monticello Aug. 3. 17.

Your favor of July 24. was recieved yesterday. you might well be led by my 1st letter into error as to the disposition of our grounds & buildings. the general idea of an Academical village rather than of one large building [w]as formed by me, perhaps about 15. years ago, on being consulted by mr L. W. Tazewell then a member of our legislature, which was supposed to be then disposed to go into that measure. when called upon 2. or 3. years ago by the trustees of the Albemarle academy, I recommended the same plan & drew the ichnography & elevations for them. but this was all before any actual site was acquired, consequently imaginary and formed on the idea of a plain ad libitum. the site is lately bought and on a survey it is on a narrow ridge, declining from North to South, so as to give us a width between the 2 rows of pavilions of 200.f. only from East to West, and the gentle declivity of the ridge gives us three levels of 255.f. each from N. to South, each about 3.f. lower than the one next above, thus

which presents some difficulty how we may best form the junction of the 2. different heights of the dormitories at the falls a. & b.
the ichnography is thus

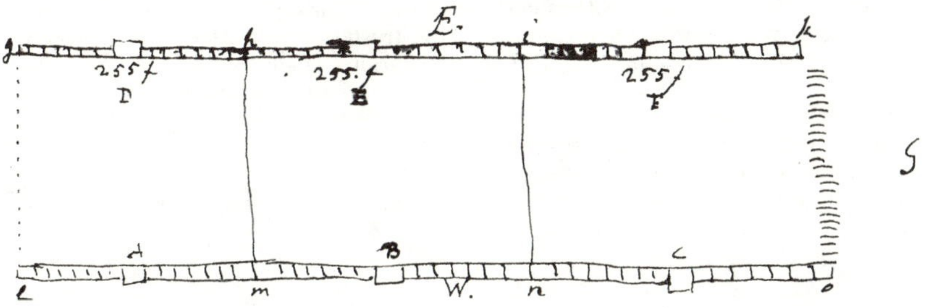

the square ghlm will be about 3. f higher than himn, & that as much higher than ikno. such is the law of the ground. we shall complete the pavilion B. this year, and A. & C.[1] the next with their dormitories, so that there will be a continued line of building from l. to o. the progress of the side ghik will depend on our funds. we leave open the end g.l. that if the state should establish there the University they contemplate, they may fill it up with something of the grand kind. on the probability that such of the professors as are married will want more than 2. rooms, we leave the back side of our pavilions without windows so that we can add 2. or [4.][2] rooms at will [. . .] the whole basement story with the dormitories will be Tuscan, with arches at the pavilions and columns in front of the dormitories. the p[avi]lion now begun is to be a regular Doric above with a portico of 5. columns (supported by the arches below) and a pediment of the whole breadth of the front. the columns 16 I. diam. the dormitories will be covered flat, as the offices of the President's house at Washington was, and will furnish a fine walk from the chambers of the professors. what we now want is a variety of sketches for the fronts of the pavilions; out of which we may chuse the handsomest. of the 2. to be erected the next year, one will have it's upper story Ionic, the other Corinthian. the succeeding ones may exhibit the best variations of the Doric, Ionic, and Corinthian. [. . .] sketches of designs for fronts which you will be so good as to furnish us, and [. . .] hints on any part of the subject will be thankfully recieved as your [cont]ribution to the establishment, and if the subscriptions proceed as liberal[ly] as they have begun, & especially, if the state adopt the site for their university I will promise that it shall be second to no place of education in the US. nor any more eligible for the education of your sons. I set out for my other home near Lynchburg in 4. or 5. days & shall not return till the latter part of September. I salute you with great friendship and respect TH: JEFFERSON

PoC (DLC); on reused address cover to TJ; damaged at seal and holes in manuscript; at foot of first page: "Mr Latrobe"; endorsed by TJ.

TJ's 5 Jan. 1805 letter to Littleton W. TAZEWELL on the subject of education included a description of an academical village (NjMoHP: Lloyd W. Smith Collection). Early plans that TJ DREW for the trustees of the Albemarle Academy are printed above at 18 Nov. 1814. An ICHNOGRAPHY is a ground plan or horizontal section of a building (*OED*).

[1] Manuscript: "B."
[2] Number illegible.

To John Love

DEAR SIR [M]ontic[ello] Aug. 3.[1] 17.

Your favor of July 16. came to hand yesterday evening only, and I feel much indebted to the President for having thought of me, & to yourself for giving me an opportunity of procuring a supply of the Lawler wheat for seed. I have heard much of it's superior security from the fly, and indeed known something of it from an example in my own neighborhood. how it may stand in comparison with our red bearded wheat in other important circumstances we do not know, and therefore I have concluded[2] to sow enough of it only to produce my stock of seed for another year. the little necessary for this I get in my own neighborhood and leave therefore the benefit you offer me for the supply of others who will want, with abundant thanks for the preference you have been so good as to offer me. of smut we have had but one example here. I think with you it proceeds from bad or infected grain. recollecting always with pleasure the scenes of our cooper[ation] in the public councils I pray you to accept assurances of my continu[ed] esteem & respect TH: JEFFERSON

PoC (CSmH: JF-BA); on verso of a reused address cover from Thomas Eston Randolph to TJ; dateline faint; torn at seal; at foot of text: "John Love esq."; endorsed by TJ.

[1] Reworked from "2."
[2] Manuscript: "cocluded."

From James Oldham

DEAR SIR Richmond August 3rd 1817.

The ½ dozen mortice doorlocks and edge bolte which you rote for, I have sent them by the stage on friday last directed to Sharlotsvill, Mr Watson Junr of milton promissed me to se them safe delivered,

In executing of these little commissions I do ashore you Sir it is not Troublesome to me, they will always be Gratefully performed with my best Judgement.

With Grate Respect I have the Honor to be Sir your Ob^{t} Sev^{t}

J; OLDHAM

P.S. the 2 plated Locks are the onley pattern[1] in richmond.

RC (MHi); endorsed by TJ as received 7 Aug. 1817 and so recorded in SJL. RC (DLC); address cover only; with PoC of TJ to Benjamin W. Crowninshield, 1 Nov. 1817, on verso; addressed: "Thos Jefferson Esqre Monticello"; stamp canceled; franked; postmarked Richmond, 4 Aug.

[1] Manuscript: "patron."

From Andrew Alexander

SIR

Lexington Augt 4th 1817

Your letter of the 11th June to Mr Caruther, (whose death we have to lament!) was rec^{d} after his death

Patrick Henry the free man of colour is very[1] willing to accept of your land at the Natural bridge on the terms you propose—but he does not know the boundery—and wishes you to send him a copy of the courses &c—as he supposes trespasses have been committed—

I enquired of the Sherif he informed me there are three[2] years taxes due on your land—$2.91

For future trespasses if they should be made—perhaps it might be well to direct Patrick Henry how to proceed—

Yours &c

AND^{W} ALEXANDER

RC (MHi); endorsed by TJ as received <*28*> 29 Aug. 1817 and so recorded in SJL. RC (DLC); address cover only; with PoC of TJ to Joseph C. Cabell, 19 Dec. 1817, on verso; addressed: "Thomas Jefferson Esqr near Milton Albemarl"; stamp canceled; franked; postmarked Lexington, 5 Aug.

Andrew Alexander (1768–1844), surveyor and public official, studied in the 1780s at Liberty Hall Academy (successively renamed the Washington Academy, Washington College, and Washington and Lee University). He represented Rockbridge County in the House of Delegates, 1798–99, and again from 1800 until he resigned in 1806 to become county surveyor. In 1801 TJ decided against making Alexander the federal marshal for the western district of Virginia. Along with John Marshall, Alexander served on the 1812 Virginia river commission, and he created the survey and map for the commission's report. Four years later he was elected a director of the state's Board of Public Works. In 1817 Alexander sought unsuccessfully to be named surveyor for Mississippi Territory. Beginning about 1819 he assisted John Wood in surveying and mapping the counties of Virginia. Alexander was elected to the House of Delegates again in 1818 and served until 1822. He was a longtime supporter of his alma mater, serving as a trustee from 1796 until his death and as secretary of the board during his last three years. After an 1802 fire at the school, Alexander traded property in the city of Lexington to the institution, and it moved there (*PTJ*, 32:359–60, 398–9, 33:643, 34:258; Marshall, *Papers*, 7:355–78; Oren F. Morton, *A History of Rockbridge County Virginia* [1920], 193, 564; Leonard, *General Assembly*; *CVSP*, 10:455–6, 501–2; E. M. Sanchez-Saavedra, *A Description of the Country: Virginia's Cartographers and Their Maps, 1607–1881* [1975], 61–2; Earl G. Swem, comp., *Maps Relating to Virginia in the Virginia State Library* [1989], 87, 89, 90, 92–3; *JHD* [1815–16 sess.], 184 [14 Feb. 1816]; Andrew Moore to James Monroe, 4 Mar. 1817 [DNA: RG 59, LAR, 1817–25]; *Catalogue of the Officers and Alumni of Washington and Lee University, Lexington, Virginia, 1749–1888* [1888], 37, 39, 50; Rockbridge Co. Will Book, 9:356–7, 358–63; gravestone inscription in Stonewall Jackson Memorial Cemetery, Lexington).

William Caruthers (CARUTHER) died on 11 June 1817 in Lexington (Norfolk *American Beacon and Commercial Diary*, 25 June 1817). While at Natural Bridge on 14 Aug. 1817, TJ gave Patrick Henry $5 to pay Rockbridge County sheriff John Leyburn past and future TAXES on the property (*MB*, 2:1337).

[1] Manuscript: "verrry."
[2] Word interlined in place of "two."

Circular to Prospective Donors to Central College

DEAR SIR Monticello Aug. 4. 17.

You have probably seen mentioned in the public papers that it is in contemplation to establish near Charlottesville a seminary of learning which shall embrace all the sciences deemed materially[1] useful in the present age. towards this object the legislature has passed[2] an act giving us a constitution nearly of our own choice, under the name of the Central College, making the Governor patron of the institution, and giving to him the appointment of the[3] Visitors. he has accordingly appointed mr Monroe the present President of the US. mr Madison the late President, Genl Cocke, mr Cabell, mr Watson, characters of eminence in the circumjacent counties, and myself in the immediate vicinity of the place as the President is also when at home. the subscriptions have so far proceeded[4] with great liberality, the county of Albemarle alone having already subscribed and otherwise contributed to the amount of about 27,000[5] Dollars to which a considerable addition is still expected from them. other counties have also commenced with very[6] favorable dispositions; the buildings are begun, those for one professorship, embracing several branches of learning, are expected to be compleated by the next spring, and a professor will be engaged to commence instruction at that time, and we hope to be enabled to erect in the ensuing summer two or three other professorships, which will take in the mass of the useful sciences. the plan of this institution has nothing local in view. it is calculated for the wants, and the use of the whole state, and it's centrality of situation, to the population of the state, salubrity of climate, and abundance and cheapness of the necessaries of life, present it certainly with advantage to the attention of parents and guardians throughout the state, & especially to those who have not in their immediate vicinity a satisfactory establishment for general science. whatever we do will have a permanent basis, established on a deposit of funds of perpetual revenue adequate to it's maintenance. the limit of contributions will only limit the number of sciences to be taught without affecting the continuance of those once established. the Visitors under whom the direction of the course of education is placed, as well as the selection of Professors for the different sciences[7] will do whatever their own zeal can effect aided by the talents of others whom they may be able to engage in the service of the institution.

Under these circumstances, dear[8] Sir, I have thought I might avail myself of the advantage of your friendship to sollicit[9] your aid in this undertaking. your sense of the importance of education to a country wishing to continue[10] free, of the present want of such an establishment in a healthy and central part of our country, and your readiness to lend your efforts to the promotion of what is publickly[11] useful, will, I think engage your cooperation, and induce you to present this subject to those of our fellow citizens within your reach who may be disposed to contribute towards it's advancement. subscriptions in this quarter have been from 1000. down[12] to 50. Dollars, & I may say that some of the latter amount have really been the most liberal. for the convenience of the contributors the sum given by each is divided at the will of the subscriber into four annual instalments, the 1st payable in April next; in which form the subscriptions have been generally entered. if you should be so kind as to undertake this, I will ask the favor of you to return to me the subscription paper now inclosed, when it shall have reached the term you deem probable,[13] and to accept the assurance of my great esteem and respect.

Th: Jefferson

RC (WHi); at foot of first page: "William B. Giles esq." RC (ViU: TJP); at foot of first page: "The honble Thomas Newton." RC or PoC for different addressee (CSmH); fragmentary and torn; consisting of top left quadrant of first page and matching section of verso. 1st FC (ViU: TJP); entirely in TJ's hand; at foot of first page: "James Pleasants. John W. Eppes. Wm B. Giles. Randolph Harrison. Thos Newton, Wm A. Burwell. Archibd Thweatt." 2d FC (ViU: TJP); entirely in TJ's hand. The two FCs may have been PoCs of RCs to others of the addressees. Recorded in SJL as seven separate letters. Reprinted from an unidentified issue of the Petersburg *Republican* in the Norfolk *American Beacon and Commercial*

Diary, 1 Sept. 1817; described as an "*Extract of a letter from Mr. Jefferson to a gentleman in this vicinity.*" Enclosed in TJ to John Wayles Eppes, 6 Aug. 1817.

For examples of the enclosed SUBSCRIPTION PAPER, see document 4 in a group of documents on The Founding of the University of Virginia: Central College, 1816–1819, printed above at 5 May 1817.

[1] Word not in 2d FC.
[2] CSmH text and both FCs: "past."
[3] Word not in 2d FC.
[4] Norfolk *American Beacon*: "subscription has so far succeeded."
[5] In 2d FC TJ used asterisks to key a note in left margin, reading "now 30,000," to this point in text.
[6] Word not in Norfolk *American Beacon*.
[7] Preceding eleven words not in 2d FC.
[8] Word not in 2d FC.
[9] Instead of preceding ten words, 2d FC reads "take the liberty of sollicitng."
[10] Word interlined in place of "be" in RC to Newton. Norfolk *American Beacon*: "be."
[11] RC to Newton, both FCs, and Norfolk *American Beacon*: "publicly."
[12] Word not in 2d FC.
[13] Norfolk *American Beacon* ends here.

From Fernagus De Gelone

SIR New York August 5th 1817.

I have the honour of informing you that in obedience to your orders, I have directed to you per mail, from New York, the two volumes (the Second on this day) of Cormon's and Manni's Italian and french Dictionary, and from Philadelphia where I have also an establishment, the little pocket Dictionary of Graglia, English and Italian. The whole is $8.50.

I am very anxious of knowing what is become of the bundle containing Aristophane's theatre.—

I take the liberty to inform you, Sir, that being called by my friends to Europe for family business, I will probably leave this Country in about three weeks, and that I will use of this opportunity to offer to this Country, a collection of books well chossen and Such as will please the Men of Taste.

Your most humble obedient Servant

J. LOUIS FERNAGUS DE GELONE

RC (MHi); endorsed by TJ as received <*18*> 19 Aug. 1817 and so recorded in SJL. RC (DLC); address cover only; with PoC of TJ to Benjamin Henry Latrobe, [25] Aug. 1817, on verso; addressed: "Thomas Jefferson Esqr Monticelo. Milton/ Va"; franked; postmarked New York, 5 Aug.

To Patrick Gibson

Dear Sir Monticello Aug. 5. 17.

Your favor of July 14. was duly recieved with my acc^{t} annexed, which I believe is all right except that to the balance of 662.19 should be added an error of 10.D. in the account of Dec. 31. 1816. where the proceeds of the sale of 175. Bar. flour for 1581.75 is mis-entered as 1571.75 this error of the copyist is easily rectified. I believe also I have not yet been credited the charge of 31.D. ordered to be pd to Dufief but not actually paid, debited to me Aug. 4. 16 (see explanation in my lres of Feb. 9. & 17th Dufief's letter inclosed to you, and yours of Feb. 13.) I was surprised to learn by a letter of July 15. from mr Yancey that 3. hhds of my tob^{o} remained still at Lynchbg by failure of the promise of the boatmen; which however he said would go off in a few days. we have also a hogshead here which Johnson will take down the first swell of the river. be so good as to sell these on their arrival for what they will bring. I shall be obliged shortly to count on their proceeds in my draughts; as on my arrival at Poplar Forest, (to which I set out the day after tomorrow) I must draw in favor of mr Robertson for 800.D. and before my departure in fav^{r} of Saml Carr or order for about 150. or 160.D. my general view of the present state of my account is about thus.

1817. July 1.	bal^{ce} by acc^{t} rendered	662.19	1817. June 27.	Ord^{r} fav^{r} Southall	990.
1816. Aug. 4.	payment to Dufief charged.	31.	July 7.	Note bk Virgi redeem^{d}	2000.
Dec. 31.	miscopying of article of 1581.75.	10.		Ord. to be drawn. Robertson	800
1817. July 9.	note in bk US.	3000.			3790.
	4 hhds tob^{o} to be yet sold suppose	400.		balance	333.19
	2. Barrels condemn^{d} flour. suppose	20.			4123.19
		4123.19			

on this will be the draught in fav^{r} of Sam Carr, am^{t} not exactly known. I must also request you to send me a small bale of cotton the first time Johnson goes down. he will call on you for it. I shall not be able to replenish my funds until by 50. Bar. rent[1] flour about 90. days hence, and perhaps some crop flour from hence. I expect to remain in Bedford till the middle of next month. consequently a blank stamp for my note in the bk US due Sep. 9. should be forwarded to me in Bedford, and the sooner the surer. I am affectionately & respectfully yours

TH: JEFFERSON

PoC (MHi); on verso of reused address cover to TJ; endorsed by TJ.

NO FAVOR OF JULY 14. has been found, but a missing letter of 11 July from Gibson, received 16 July 1817 from Richmond, is recorded in SJL. Two missing letters from Joel Yancey OF JULY 15., both received 2 Aug. 1817 from Lynchburg, are also recorded in SJL. On 7 Aug. 1817 TJ paid Samuel CARR for corn with an order on Gibson & Jefferson for $208 (*MB*, 2:1337).

[1]Word interlined.

From Hezekiah Niles

SIR Balt. Aug 5. 1817

Feeling myself so sensibly the labor of reading & drudgery of answering long letters, I had almost resolved to retain the enclosed—but really & honestly, I know not well how to dispense with it, if I would effect the design proposed.[1]

Very respectfully Yr obt St H NILES

opened after [being] sealed, by HN

RC (DLC); one word illegible; endorsed by TJ as received <*18*> 19 Aug. 1817 and so recorded in SJL. RC (ViU: TJP); address cover only; with PoC of TJ to John Wood, 26 Nov. 1817, on recto and verso; addressed: "Thomas Jefferson, esquire late President US. (near) Milton Va"; franked; postmarked Baltimore, 5 Aug.

[1]Manuscript: "poposed."

ENCLOSURE

Circular from Hezekiah Niles to Prominent Subscribers

SIR Baltimore July 31 1817

After revolving upon some suitable apology for intruding myself with the following statement and request, I have thought[1] it most respectful to decline offering any, except[2] to observe that if ought appears to your better judgement improper in either, that you will attribute it to any [thing][3] else than a willingness on my part to act so, in any respect towards you.

For six years ending with the next month, I shall have published the Weekly Register, in Baltimore. The weight of the accumulated debts due to the establishment with the great labor & vexation they give me, added to the general necessity that persons in our line have of now and then "winding up their business" as the phrase is, combined to make me resolve to give up the publication in reality, or at least apparently. This idea having gone abroad has caused many, whose good [opinion][4] is enough to flatter any one, to urge me to persevere, & keep up the work in its present manner, spirit, and form, altering only its conditions in any way that might give ease to myself, under an assurance of adequate support[5] from the people of the United States. Thus encouraged, I have determined, as the only possible means of my continuing it, to attempt to enforce absolute payment in advance, which would not only releive me of a heavy expence and secure me from great losses, but give me nearly one half more time for editorial duties or needful relaxation from business—of which last I may be said to have had none at all, for the period stated.

To effect these objects—to realize the fruits of past labors & make those of the future less burthensome, I have determined to make the present, or 12th volume, conclude a series, to be completed by a very copious and general index of the whole, and commence in Sep. next, as it were, de novo.

I am perfectly aware that this arrangement will give a great[6] shock to my establishment, but it is the only one on which I can consent to continue it & it requires that I should bolster it by all fair and honorable means—among which is the public opinion of honorable men.

I have been flattered with the beleif that the Weekly Register is not only[7] useful as a book of almost universal reference as to past things & facts connected with the history and circumstances of nations, & especially those of the United States; but that it has done a good deal to rouse a[8] national feeling and build up pride of character, hitherto too much neglected through the contentions of parties; & that while it has avoided all sorts of personalities, it has contributed to extend and encourage, as much as any other work, the principles of our constitution & to explain those laws of natural right & the reason of things on which it is founded. These assurances I frankly, confess, are very agreeable,—but I am conscious that they have rather grown out of my habits of thinking, and of industry, than of any talents, as a writer that belong to me.

This explanation and preamble is necessary to my request, offered with diffidence & submitted with entire respect to your decission whether, to grant it or not. You have had an opportunity of seeing the Weekly Register from its commencement, & I solicit your opinion of it to spread before the people—to extend its circulation through your particular countenance, to enable me to withstand any effect of the change that must be made in its pecuniary arrangements.

A letter exactly similar to this has been addressed to Presidents Adams and Madison to vice President Tompkins; to Generals[9] Brown and Jackson, & Com. Rodgers and capt Porter; and if it is deemed right in you to give your opinion & for the purposes stated, I will be thankful to recieve it by the 20th[10] of August.

RC (DLC); in a clerk's hand, with corrections by Niles; endorsed by TJ as a letter from "Niles H." received 18 Aug. 1817, but recorded in SJL as received <*18*> 19 Aug. 1817. RC (MHi: Adams Papers); copy sent to John Adams; in a clerk's hand, with closing and signature by Niles; dated July 1817; endorsed by Adams. RC (DLC: Madison Papers); copy sent to James Madison; in a clerk's hand, with closing and signature by Niles; dated July 1817; addressed: "President Madison"; endorsed by Madison as a letter of 17 July 1817. RC (DLC: Jackson Papers);

copy sent to Andrew Jackson; in a clerk's hand, with closing and signature by Niles; dated 31 July 1817; addressed: "Major general Andrew Jackson Nashville Ten." The texts contain minor variations, only the most significant of which are noted below.

Niles published his GENERAL INDEX the following year as *General Index to the First Twelve Volumes, or First Series, of Niles' Weekly Register being a Period of Six Years: from September, 1811, to September, 1817* (Baltimore, 1818). He started DE NOVO with the 30 Aug. 1817 issue of *Niles' Weekly Register*, which began volume 13 of the work and volume 1 of the new series.

[1] Word interlined by Niles.

[2] All RCs: "expect."

[3] Omitted word supplied from RCs to Adams, Madison, and Jackson.

[4] Omitted word supplied from RCs to Adams, Madison, and Jackson.

[5] Word interlined by Niles in place of "success."

[6] RCs to Adams, Madison, and Jackson: "considerable."

[7] RC to TJ here adds "a," absent from other RCs and editorially omitted.

[8] RC to TJ: "to rouse of a." RC to Adams: "to rouse up a." RC to Madison: "to the rouse of a." RC to Jackson: "to rouse a."

[9] Manuscript: "Genlerals."

[10] Reworked from "25th."

To John Wayles Eppes

DEAR SIR Monticello Aug. 6. 17.

I set out for Bedford tomorrow, and shall leave this at Flood's. you will know therefore by it's receipt that we are passed on, to wit Ellen, Cornelia and myself. very soon after our arrival at Poplar Forest, perhaps a week, we shall go to the Natl bridge and be a[b]sent 4. or 5. days: and shall hope to see you & Francis soon after as given us to hope in yours of June 28. which was near 3. weeks on the road. the inclosed letter which I write at the request of the Visitors of the Central college will inform you of the state and prospects of our college. you may be assured that we shall have in it by early spring a better professor of languages than you can expect to find for Francis any where else; and that within one year after, which will be soon enough for him, we shall have professors of other sciences, of the first order; for we are determined to employ none of mere mediocrity. our's shall be second to none on the continent. it will be impossible therefore for Francis to be any where so well disposed of as here. but this is a subject for conversation when we see you at Poplar forest. I wish you could inform mr Baker also of this prospect. but he must become a subscriber: for as we are certain of 2. or 3. times as many offering as we can at first recieve,[1] it is understood that the sons of subscribers will be recieved in preference to those of non-subscribers. the hurry of getting ready for my [jo]urney must make this to be considered as an acknolegement of Francis's letter as well as your own. with my respects to mrs accept for yourself & Francis the assurance of my constant affection TH: JEFFERSON

PoC (CSmH: JF); on verso of a reused address cover from Joseph Milligan to TJ; two words faint; at foot of text: "M[r] Eppes"; endorsed by TJ. Enclosure: TJ's Circular to Prospective Donors to Central College, 4 Aug. 1817, and enclosure.

Eppes's letter of JUNE 28., not found, is recorded in SJL as received 15 July 1817 from Mill Brook. A missing letter to TJ from Francis Eppes, partially dated July 1817 and received 2 Aug. 1817 from Mill Brook, is also recorded in SJL.

[1]Manuscript: "recieved."

From John Goodman, Joseph Reed, Isaac Boyer, and William J. Duane

SIR— Phil[a] August 6, 1817.

After having so long and so faithfully served your country,[1] it ought to have been the desire of its friends that you should enjoy the happiness and tranquillity, which you sought by a voluntary retirement from political life. We perceive, with regret, however, that persons, who profess to revere your character and to respect your wishes,[2] have on a late occasion done violence to both.

Enclosed we send to you, Sir, extracts from news-papers published in this state, in which great freedom is taken with your name and reputation: We transmit them, not because we place the least reliance in the assertions, which they contain, but, because, such is the estimation in which you are held, that even a doubt of what may be your sentiments is favorable to those who excite it, for their own purposes.

It is our desire, and we hope that we make no improper request when we ask, that you will have the goodness to say,[3] whether there is any foundation for the assertion which the enclosed extracts convey to the public.

With sincere respect and consideration Y[r] Ob[t] S[ts]

JN[O] GOODMAN
JOS: REED
I BOYER
W. J. DUANE.

RC (DLC); in Duane's hand, signed by Goodman, Reed, Boyer, and Duane; dateline adjacent to first signature; at head of text: "Thomas Jefferson esq."; endorsed by TJ as received <*18*> 19 Aug. 1817 and so recorded in SJL. Printed in *Kline's Weekly Carlisle Gazette*, 18 Sept. 1817. Enclosures: (1) "Extract of a letter from Virginia," with dateline of 13 July 1817, reprinted from Chambersburg, Pa., *Franklin Republican*, 29 July 1817, describing a fictional 11 July 1817 visit to Monticello during which the author reported hearing TJ "express [his] anxious wish for the success of the *democratic* [*re*]*publican* gubernatorial candidate in Pennsylvani[a] as he says he has *no opinion of tool or turnab*[*out*] *politicians just to serve their own aggrand*[*ise*]*ment*" (undated clipping from unidentified newspaper, in DLC: TJ Papers, 210:37555a; edge trimmed, with missing text supplied from TJ's response of [22] Aug. 1817). (2) Newspaper account of a 4 Aug. 1816 meeting in the New Market Ward of Philadelphia of the supporters of Pennsylvania Republican gubernatorial candidate William Findlay, condemning the caucus in Carlisle that nominated Findlay's opponent Joseph Hiester as "a most daring and impudent attempt to deceive the people and lead them astray from correct republican principles"; labeling Hiester a "*political deserter*" and "traitor to the cause of democracy"; expressing approval of "the sentiments of Thomas Jefferson, Esqr. late president of the U States—that firm and undeviating democrat who penn-ed the declaration of independence, relative to the election of Joseph Heister, *that he has no opinion of tools and turnabout politicians just to serve their own aggrandizement*"; and vowing to employ all honorable means to support Findlay's election (clipping, from unidentified issue of Philadelphia *Democratic Press*, in DLC: TJ Papers, 210:37555a).

John Goodman (1763–1851), public official, was born in Germantown, Pennsylvania, and educated at the Germantown Academy. He was present with the Continental army at the Battle of Trenton in 1776. From 1803–06 Goodman sat in the Pennsylvania House of Representatives. Governor Thomas McKean appointed him a justice of the peace for Philadelphia County on the termination of his term as representative, and he served in this position until about 1833. Goodman became a notary public for Philadelphia County in 1809, working in this capacity until about 1842, and he was appointed prothonotary of the district court in 1822. During the War of 1812 he served as a colonel commanding a militia unit and as secretary of Philadelphia's Committee of Defence. Between 1835–37 Goodman was an alderman. He retired from business about 1843, and he owned real estate valued at $22,000 seven years later. Goodman died in Philadelphia (Henry Simpson, *The Lives of Eminent Philadelphians* [1859], 428–31; Philadelphia city directories; Philadelphia *Poulson's American Daily Advertiser*, 29 Aug. 1814; DNA: RG 29, CS, Philadelphia, 1850; Philadelphia *North American and United States Gazette*, 25 Mar. 1851).

Joseph Reed (1772–1846), attorney and public official, was born in Philadelphia, studied briefly at the Moravian School in Bethlehem, Pennsylvania, and graduated in 1792 from the College of New Jersey (later Princeton University). Soon after that he began practicing law in Philadelphia, and he was appointed clerk of the city's court of quarter sessions in 1796. Reed served as prothonotary of the Supreme Court of Pennsylvania beginning about 1806, Philadelphia city solicitor in 1810, state attorney general, 1810–11, and city recorder, 1810–29. He retired from the law about 1829. Reed edited volumes 6–10 of *The Laws of the Commonwealth of Pennsylvania* (Philadelphia, 1822–44), covering the statutes of the legislative sessions between 1812–13 and 1829–30. He was elected to the American Philosophical Society in 1816. Reed died in Philadelphia (*Princetonians*, 1791–94, pp. 211–7; *Philadelphia Minerva*, 12 Nov. 1796; John Hill Martin, *Martin's Bench and Bar of Philadelphia* [1883], 83, 88, 97, 188–9, 305; APS, Minutes, 9 Jan. 1816 [MS in PPAmP]; Philadelphia *North American*, 6 Mar. 1846).

Isaac Boyer (ca. 1773–1821), merchant, was working as a grocer in Philadelphia by 1799 as a partner in the firm of Boyer & Morton. After this company dissolved in 1800, Boyer continued to operate a grocery business and in 1809 was a partner in the firm of Boyer & Wilt. He continued as a merchant for the remainder of his life. Boyer commanded a militia regiment in 1815–16, ran unsuccessfully for state senator in 1815, and served on Philadelphia's Select Council, 1819–20. He died in Philadelphia (Cornelius William Stafford, *The Philadelphia Directory, for 1799* [Philadelphia, 1799], 24; Philadelphia *Claypoole's American Daily Advertiser*, 29 Aug. 1800; Philadelphia *Poulson's American Daily Advertiser*, 11 Feb. 1806, 29 Aug. 1809, 2 Feb. 1811, 12 Oct. 1815; James Robinson, *The Philadelphia Directory for 1807* [Philadelphia, 1807]; Philadelphia *Tickler*, 18 Sept. 1811; Philadelphia *Weekly Aurora*, 10 Oct. 1815, 21 Sept. 1816; *Journal of the twenty fifth House of Representatives of the Commonwealth of Pennsylvania* [Harrisburg, 1814], 374 [13 Feb. 1815]; *Acts of the General Assembly of the Commonwealth of Pennsylvania* [Harrisburg, 1816], 221; John Bioren, *Bioren's Pennsylvania Pocket Remembrancer, for the year 1819* [Philadelphia, (1818)]; Bioren, *Bioren's Pennsylvania Pocket Remembrancer for the year 1820* [Philadelphia, (1819)]; *The Philadelphia Directory and Register, for 1821* [Philadelphia, 1821]; Robert Desilver, *The Philadelphia Index, or Directory, for 1823* [Philadelphia, 1823]; *Boston Commercial Gazette*, 28 June 1821).

William John Duane (1780–1865), attorney and public official, was the son of the publisher and TJ correspondent William Duane. The younger Duane was born in Clonmel, Ireland, and grew up there and in London. The Duane family moved to Philadelphia in 1796, where Duane worked in his father's various printing concerns there until 1806. He then became a paper merchant. Duane served in the Pennsylvania House of Representatives in 1809, 1812, and 1819. He began to study law in 1812 and was admitted to the bar three years later. From 1820–23 he served as prosecuting attorney for the mayor's court of Philadelphia, and in 1829 he was elected to the city's Select Council. In 1831 President Andrew Jackson appointed Duane a commissioner under a treaty with Denmark, and in 1833 he served briefly as secretary of the treasury before Jackson dismissed him for refusing to withdraw government deposits from the Second Bank of the United States without congressional consent. He died in Philadelphia (*DAB*; *Biographical Memoir of William J. Duane* [1868]; Martin, *Martin's Bench and Bar of Philadelphia*, 264; *JEP*, 4:170, 172 [2, 3 Mar. 1831]; Philadelphia *North American and United States Gazette*, 27 Sept. 1865; gravestone inscription in Laurel Hill Cemetery, Philadelphia).

An "Independent Republican Convention" in Carlisle nominated Hiester for governor of Pennsylvania on 4 Mar. 1817. Goodman, Reed, Boyer, Duane, and John W. Thompson were chosen to represent the city and county of Philadelphia on a statewide "grand committee of correspondence" to advance his cause (Philadelphia *Weekly Aurora*, 10 Mar. 1817).

[1] *Kline's Weekly Carlisle Gazette*: "the republic."

[2] *Kline's Weekly Carlisle Gazette*: "virtues."

[3] Preceding eight words not in *Kline's Weekly Carlisle Gazette*.

To Harrison Hall

SIR Monticello Aug. 6. 17.

I have duly recieved your favor of July 17. I really did not know that I was a subscriber to the Law Journal, or the supposed default should not have happened. I have no written memorandum of it nor does my memory supply it. however in that I have no confidence, and therefore I suppose you are right. I now inclose you 21.D. to wit 6.D for the Portfolio 10.D. for the 5th & 6th vols of the Law Journal & 5.D. for the 7th in advance. as to the Portfolio I shall be glad to be discontinued, as my time is so entirely engrossed by a most oppressive correspondence, that I have scarcely a moment in the day that I can find time to read any thing. I began for example 10. days ago to read the case of Hunter & Fairfax in your last law journal, and altho given every moment I had to spare from writing to the reading of that I am not half thro'. I have not had as much time as would permit me to read a portfolio for many months. it is quite useless therefore for me to engage for what I can never read. when your Digest shall be compleat, I shall wish it to be in a separate volume. I salute you with esteem & respect. TH: JEFFERSON

PoC (DLC); on verso of reused address cover to TJ; torn at seal, with missing words rewritten by TJ; at foot of text: "Mr Harrison Hall"; endorsed by TJ; notation by TJ above endorsement: "Newspapers."

The article on the CASE of *Fairfax's Devisee v. Hunter's Lessee* was published in the *American Law Journal* 6 (1817): 313–460. For more on this case, see Marshall, *Papers*, 5:228–63, 8:108–26; James Monroe to TJ, 23 Sept. 1815, and note; and TJ to Spencer Roane, 12 Oct. 1815.

From Quinette de Rochemont

MONSIEUR, new york. 6. aout 1817.

j'ai L'honneur de vous adresser 3 brochures que je ne crois pas indignes de votre attention la 1ere renferme des faits que L'amour-propre de L'auteur raconte avec une naïveté qui en garantit L'exactitude. la 2de fait assez bien connoitre L'état actuel des partis en france. la 3ieme prouve que la france possède des defenseurs éclairés[1] des droits des citoyens. la loi sur les élections dont j'ai eu l'avantage de vous entretenir fortifiera la representation nationale et donnera pour ainsi dire la Vie à la charte constitutionnelle. ainsi, monsieur, la gloire et les malheurs de la france n'ont point perdu la cause de la liberté, elle triomphera.

permettés-moi de déposer cette pensée consolante et qui a Sur moi toute la force d'un sentiment profond dans le sein d'un ami de L'humanite et de l'un des fondateurs les plus distingués de L'independance américaine.

Veuillez agréer, monsieur, L'expression de mon respect et de ma consideration. QUINETTE DE ROCHEMONT.
Jay-Street no 12

EDITORS' TRANSLATION

SIR, new york. 6. August 1817.

I have the honor of sending you three pamphlets that I believe are not unworthy of your attention. The first one contains facts that the author's amour propre relates with a naïveté that guarantees their exactness. The second makes well known the current state of the parties in France. The third proves that France possesses enlightened defenders of the rights of citizens. The law on elections, which I had the privilege to discuss with you, will strengthen national representation and will, so to speak, give life to the constitutional charter. So, sir, the glory and misfortunes of France have in no way defeated the cause of liberty, which will triumph.

Allow me to lay this consoling thought, which has deeply affected me, on the bosom of a friend of humanity and one of the most distinguished founders of American independence.

Please accept, sir, my respectful and considerate regards.

QUINETTE DE ROCHEMONT.
Jay-Street n° 12

RC (ViW: TC-JP); endorsed by TJ as received <*28*> 29 Aug. 1817 and so recorded in SJL. Translation by Dr. Genevieve Moene. Enclosure: Dominique Georges Frédéric de Pradt, *Récit Historique sur la Restauration de la Royauté en France, le 31 Mars 1814* (Paris, 1816). Other enclosures not found.

Nicolas Marie Quinette de Rochemont (1762–1821), French public official, was born in Soissons, where he was a notary public before the French Revolution. He was successively appointed an administrator of the department of Aisne and that department's deputy to the Legislative Assembly, where he strongly supported the revolution and advocated the confiscation of émigré property. Quinette de Rochemont was elected to the subsequent National Convention and voted for the execution of Louis XVI. During a mission to the French army he was taken prisoner by the Austrians and held for over two years. Quinette de Rochemont was released in a prisoner exchange in 1793 and served on the Council of Five Hundred, 1796–97. In 1799 he was named interior minister. Napoleon made him prefect of the department of Somme after taking power later that year. Quinette de Rochemont stayed in this position through Napoleon's 1815 downfall, when he became a member of the provisional government. In 1816 he was exiled as a regicide, arriving in New York in April of that year. Quinette de Rochemont traveled in the United States for several months in 1817 and paid a visit to TJ at Monticello that June. By early in 1818 he had resolved to return to Europe, and he settled in Brussels, where he died (*Biographie universelle*, 34:655–6; Hoefer, *Nouv. biog. générale*, 41:355; Bennington, Vt., *Green-Mountain Farmer*, 15 Apr. 1816; *New-York Columbian*, 19 July 1817; Washington *Daily National Intelligencer*, 11 Oct. 1817; *New-York Evening Post*, 27 July 1821).

One of the unidentified BROCHURES enclosed here was a work by Henri Benjamin Constant de Rebecque, possibly his pamphlet *De La Liberté des Brochures, des Pamphlets et des Journaux* (Paris, 1814).

[1]Manuscript: "éclairé."

To Benjamin Henry Latrobe

DEAR SIR Monticello Aug. 7. 17.

I wrote on the 3d in answer to your's of the 24th July. that of the 28th is delivered to me just as I am setting out for Bedford to be absent 6. weeks. after the date of mine to you on the subject of the Stone cutter, we had a meeting of our visitors who supposing you had full employment for all your hands desired me to write to Leghorn for a stone cutter, which I have done. the qualification I have required is the being able to cut an Ionic capital. we shall finish our Doric pavilion by the 1st April, and shall then begin the Ionic one, & after that the Corinthian. possibly our workmen may not be equal to this Capital, & if so and you can spare then mr Johnson, we may ask him of you to do the Corinthian work. the ornaments of the frize of all of them I propose to have of lead. I have been fortunately able to get a bricklayer who makes & lays the oil stock brick, a capital hand. I hope we shall recieve in time some sketches of fronts from you. a thousand preparatives for my journey oblige me to place here the renewal of my assurances of esteem & respect.

TH: JEFFERSON

PoC (DLC); on verso of reused address cover to TJ; torn at seal, with five words rewritten by TJ; at foot of text: "B. H. Latrobe esq."; endorsed by TJ.

The BRICKLAYER was probably David Knight.

To William Lee

DEAR SIR Monticello Aug. 7. 17.

We now send on a young man Michael Graham to be entered as an apprentice to the weaving of knit work according to the offer you were so kind as to make us. he has no funds of his own, but for his necessary expences they will be remitted from hence on his writing to mr James Leitch from time to time as they are wanting, & without any delay. and that he may be liable to no doubt as to them, I make myself personally responsible for them. recommending him to your patronage and good offices I renew to you the assurance of my great esteem and respect TH: JEFFERSON

PoC (DLC); on verso of reused address cover of George Ticknor to TJ, 22 Dec. 1816; at foot of text: "William Lee esq."; endorsed by TJ.

To Daniel Colclaser

Sir Monticello Aug. 8. 17.

You enquired the other day what number of barrels I should be able to furnish. we have barrel stuff enough in the woods ready cut off to serve two seasons. I have now set mr Goodman's force to riving and dressing ready to put up, and mean that they shall always get and dress the timber, so that Barnaby & the other two with him shall do nothing but set up. I count on their setting up ready for delivery from 90 to 100. a week, & that they will do this at least 40. weeks in the year, as nothing but harvest or sickness will ever take them a day out of their shop. I therefore count on delivering you 4000. barrels a year. they have 50. in the barn ready for delivery and will begin on Monday to prepare their 90. or 100. a week. I have instructed mr Bacon to give the hauling necessary in this business a preference over every other call. I tender you my best wishes.

Th: Jefferson

PoC (MHi); on verso of reused address cover to TJ; at foot of text: "Mr Colclaser"; endorsed by TJ.

Daniel Colclaser, miller, partnered with Thomas Eston Randolph as tenants of TJ's flour mill from 1816 until about 1822 (*MB*; DNA: RG 29, CS, Albemarle Co., 1820; Newton B. Jones, ed., "A List of Manufactures in Fredericksville Parish, Albemarle County, Virginia, in 1820," *MACH* 10 [1949/50]: 25; Edmund Bacon to TJ, 2 Aug. 1822).

From Hugh Chisholm

Dear Sir Charlottsville agst 10 1817

when you was hear Last you mentioned to me that mr Jerdon wished to helpe me in Doeing this work for the Cellorz—but on Reflecttion I will not have any thing to Doe with Jerdon in any Shape What Ever for a Bisness of the Sort I dislike and Mr Perry will make the Briks for me as fast as I Can use them and mak them as I woud wish made and that is all we want is to get the Bricks in tim—mr Perry Says he will use Every Step for the quikness of Bisness Going on I have now doubt but we Shall do it in good tim and Leave Jerdon at hom with Esteem

Hugh Chishm

RC (MHi); endorsed by TJ as received <*16*> 17 Aug. 1817 and so recorded in SJL.

Mr jerdon may have been the brickmason John Jordan, who had worked at Monticello in 1805 (*MB*, 2:1108, 1161).

From Victor du Pont and Eleuthère I. du Pont de Nemours

Sir — Brandywine. August 11th 1817

Knowing that you have honored with your friendship our excellent & much lamented father we think it our duty to inform you of his death, which took place on the 7th instant after a very severe and painfull illness of eleven days—

you will find in the national intelligencer in Niles Register and in the Aurora a short notice of his life; not much known in this Country which is the Country of his Children & Great Children we thought it was proper to publish a Sketch in order to point out his worth & his deeds, and hope it will meet with your approbation—

We inclose a pamphlet on education received by him few weeks ago with a request to forward you one.

With great Respect We have the honor to be Your obedient servants

V. du Pont
E. I. du Pont.

RC (DLC); in Victor du Pont's hand, signed by Victor du Pont and Eleuthère I. du Pont de Nemours; at head of text: "Thomas Jefferson Esqre Monticello"; endorsed by TJ as a letter from Eleuthère I. du Pont de Nemours received <*28*> 29 Aug. 1817 and so recorded in SJL. Enclosure: Marc Antoine Jullien, *Esquisse et Vues Préliminaires d'un Ouvrage sur l'Éducation Comparée . . . et Séries de Questions sur l'Éducation* (Paris, 1817; Poor, *Jefferson's Library*, 5 [no. 211]; TJ's copy in DLC: Rare Book and Special Collections, with handwritten, signed inscription by Jullien dated Paris, 1 Apr. 1817: "À Monsieur jefferson, Ancien président des Etats-Unis, Hommage d'estime respectueuse de la part de l'auteur, qui lui a déjà offert, il y a neuf ans, un Essai Général d'Education physique, morale et intellectuelle, et qui désire vivement qu'un citoyen aussi distingué veuille appuyer de son suffrage dans sa patrie l'entreprise philantropique dont on ébauche ici le plan" ["To Mr. Jefferson, former president of the United States, a tribute of respectful esteem on the part of the author, who has already sent him nine years ago his *Essai Général d'Éducation physique, morale, et intellectuelle*, and who has a lively hope that such a distinguished citizen would like to support by his commendation, in his country, the philanthropic enterprise outlined in this plan"]).

The notice of the life of Pierre Samuel Du Pont de Nemours is in the Washington *Daily National Intelligencer*, 15 Aug. 1817, and Baltimore *Niles' Weekly Register*, 16 Aug. 1817.

From John Le Tellier

Respected Sir — Richmond August 11. 1817

It is a Greate Gratification to me to find that I am held in such high esteem by Mr Jefferson as for him to take so lively an interest in my welfare as to recommend me in prefereance to all others to the Inhabitants of Charlottesville likewise with gratitude bearing in memory former favours, the description[1] which you give of the County of albemarle Charlottesville[2] & the Inhabitants are very enticing but my situation at present prevents my taking up with your kind interposition in my behalf, as I hold the place of keeper of the Poorhouse in this place and have held it for these four years last past also Keeper of the City Magazine for storage of Gun Powder, I believe there is not one silver smith in this City that I could recommend as a good workman & of Character that would be willing to[3] undertake it. the delay your kind letter met with is the accasion of my not answering it before I this day was put in possession of it

I remain your Esteemed friend JOHN LE TELLIER.

RC (MoSHi: TJC-BC); adjacent to closing: "Thomas Jefferson Esq[r] Monticello"; endorsed by TJ as received <*28*> 29 Aug. 1817 and so recorded in SJL.

[1] Manuscript: "decription."
[2] Manuscript: "Charlettesille."
[3] Manuscript: "to to."

From James Ligon (for Patrick Gibson)

SIR Richmond 11[h] Aug[t] 1817

your favor of the 5[h] Ins[t] is rec[d] & its contents noticed—the 31$ paid mr Fisher on account of mr Dufief has never been refunded by him, he having stopped payment—if you will examine the account Sales of the 175 Bbls flour you will find the nett proceed should be but $<u>1571.75</u> in the view you have taken of your account you have overlooked your dft of the 15. Ap[l] favor V W Southall for $250 which was paid with the one for $990—the Condemned flour was sold for but $6\frac{1}{2}$\$—I inclose you a note for your Signature as you direct

very respectfully your ob[t] serv[t] PATRICK GIBSON
℔ JA[S] LIGON

RC (ViU: TJP-ER); in Ligon's hand; endorsed by TJ as a letter from Gibson received <*16*> 17 Aug. 1817 and so recorded in SJL. RC (ViU: TJP); address cover only; with PoC of TJ to Hugh Chisholm, 31 Aug. 1817, on verso; addressed: "Thomas Jefferson Esq[r] Poplar Forest Care of mr S J Harrison Lynchburg"; stamp canceled; postmarked Richmond, 11 Aug. Enclosure not found.

From John Patterson

DEAR SIR Baltimore 11th Augt 17—

Mr Knox has retired with a competency from the business of instructing youth, & now occupies a small establishment, which he purchased, in the immediate vicinity of this place—His character as a teacher is high among those who are acquainted with him, & he is much esteemed as a man of good morals, & correct habits—He is however said to be a man of violent temper, & has, I learn, had a quarrel with Mr Glendy, to appease which, the interference of their mutual friends became necessary—It originated in some real or supposed maltreatment of a son of Glendy's who was in Knoxe's school, & I suppose that the one, was as likely to be wrong as the other—Knoxe's family consists of his wife & one daughter, his other children being separated from him by marriage &^{c}—

I am sorry to learn from a letter of Robt Nicholas, that your relation Dabney Terril, has been put to great inconvenience at Geneva, by the refusal of his banker to make him the usual advances of money, in consequence of the failure of Geo: P Stevenson, from whom his letters of credit were derived. He requested assistance of M^{r} N, but the amount required, $1500 per annum, being more than his own limited funds permitted him to furnish, he could only advise him to diminish his expences, & observe the strictest œconomy, until his friends could reestablish his credit—

There occurred yesterday in this part of the country, the most mischievous inundation, that has ever been known here; every milldam & bridge within the circuit, we have heard from, is destroyed, & the stream which passes through the City, has destroyed houses and other property to a very great amount, some lives were lost, & much disease[1] is apprehended, from the deposit of mud in the cellars & streets of the lower part of the town—I hope that we may not have had a Similar visitation, for the loss of our wheat crop, ought to redeem, us at least—

I remain with great respect Your Hble: serv^{t}

JN^{O} PATTERSON

RC (CSmH: JF); at foot of text: "Thomas Jefferson Esqr"; endorsed by TJ as received <22> 23 Aug. 1817 and so recorded in SJL.

An INUNDATION of heavy rain in Baltimore began on 8 Aug. 1817 and continued overnight, causing widespread flooding (*Baltimore Patriot & Mercantile Advertiser*, 9, 11–14 Aug. 1817).

[1] Word interlined.

From David Whitehead

REVERAND FATHER City of New York. August 11th 1817.

the 4th Instant i was at my Brothers 20 Miles From this City above Springfield New Jersey & he informed me that Bishop Hobert, in the time of this Last war he went twise to Canida and From the top of his hous thare Can be Segnal maid, to be Seen to Sandy Hook. that When Said B. Came Back he Always Sent a Black man off, On my Return home I had not been home 3 hours my Yongest Son of 10 years Old Brought me this Pamplelit. I Read the Contents. It is the Only one I have Seen it Plainly Discoverd what my Br told me the 4th. I have Lived In this ward about 20 years, Sinc then I have tryed to Discover the Revinew the Church of Engling Draws yearly of this Ward, which Said Church Seized in Time of the Old Revilution And by Corruption and Bribery, Still Hold Say 2000[1] Lotts on Lease Some at $160 per year, Some they have Sold to Upwards of $5000 Dollars, & by the Same Chanul of Corruption & Bribery they Same British Emiseries Doth Detain from My Brother and me to the vallue of $1000. Dollars.—

Sir 16 years ago I Derected N1 Federil Spye to you I Shold be Glad of a Line from you to know you had Receved it I Expect you In Decline of Life, but I hope kind Heavin Hath Prolonged your Sences & give you Wisdom to,[2] Aid and assist in this [verri] grait and Important Moment, to the Welfair of our Independanc And to the Glory of the Grait Omnipotant To Hurl Down, Those Monsters that is Feasting on the Spoil of the widow & the Fatherless at Salleriye of $6000 Dollars Per years I Expect you was one well Acquainted with my Grate Unkel A Clark

DAVID WHITEHEAD
56–2–26
19t. F I. — — d.
Grenwich Street No 343

RC (MHi); one word illegible; dateline adjacent to signature; addressed: "Thomas Jefferson Montecilla Virginna"; franked; postmarked New York, 12 Aug.; endorsed by TJ as received 29 Aug. 1817 and so recorded in SJL, which has the additional notation (brackets in original) "[insane]."

David Whitehead (b. 1761) was a native of Essex County, New Jersey. He volunteered as a private in the New Jersey militia in 1777 and served for a total of about fourteen months spread over a number of years. Whitehead lived in Vermont for several months in both 1786 and 1791, working as a planter and surveyor. He subsequently moved to New York City, where he was variously occupied from at least 1799 to 1829 as a currier, tanner, grocer, and gardener. By 1832 Whitehead was living in Woodbridge, New Jersey (Whitehead diary [photocopied excerpts in VtHi]; DNA: RG 15, SRRWPBLW; *Longworth's New York Directory* [1799]: 388; [1803]: 310; [1809]: 380; [1820]: 472; [1821]: 467; [1822]: 477; [1829]: 605; New York *Daily Advertiser*, 16 Nov.

1802; *New-York Evening Post*, 27 May 1819; Whitehead, *An Oration, Delivered at Potter's Field; on the Fourth of July, 1826 ... Also, An Oration Delivered on the Fourth of July, 1827 in the Park, in the City* [1827]).

BISHOP HOBERT: John Henry Hobart, third Episcopal bishop of New York. The enclosed pamphlet (PAMPLELIT) has not been found. The numbers 56–2–26 refer to the years, months, and days since Whitehead's birth on 16 May 1761.

[1] Reworked from "200."

[2] Page one ends here with "over" at foot of text.

ENCLOSURE

Abraham Clark's Recommendation of David Whitehead

Philedelphia December 30 1793

I hereby Certify that the Barer David Whitehead is a Native of the Town in which I Live he is of a reputable Famely who I was well acquainted with I have but a Slight personel Acquaintenc withe the barer but never heard any thing of him to his disadvantage and From his general Carector think him Deserving the Esteem of Such as he may Fall among he being about going to the Northard

ABRAHM CLARK.

Tr (MHi); entirely in Whitehead's hand; dateline adjacent to signature; at foot of text: "a Coppy"; on verso of an undated, canceled, printed form announcing a meeting at Tammany Hall of the Mount Vernon Masonic lodge.

Abraham Clark (1726–94), surveyor and public official, was a native of Elizabethtown (later Elizabeth), New Jersey. He held a series of overlapping political offices over several decades, including clerk of the New Jersey Assembly, 1752–66, and sheriff of Elizabethtown and Essex County beginning in the latter year. In 1774 Clark joined the New Jersey Committee of Safety, and he was selected for the colony's Provincial Congress in 1775. That body appointed him a delegate to the Second Continental Congress, 1776–78, 1780–83, and 1786–88, where he voted for independence and signed the Declaration of Independence. Clark represented Essex County in the Senate of New Jersey, 1778–79, sat on the state's Legislative Council in 1778, and was elected to the General Assembly in 1783, where he served until about 1785. He represented his state in the United States House of Representatives from 1791 until his death. Clark favored the interests of debtors and less restrictive policies concerning paper money in the 1780s, and he argued for a small and inexpensive army during his final years in Congress. He died at his farm near Elizabethtown (*ANB*; *DAB*; Ruth Bogin, *Abraham Clark and the Quest for Equality in the Revolutionary Era, 1774–1794* [1982], esp. 39, 42, 48, 51; Philadelphia *Dunlap and Claypoole's American Daily Advertiser*, 18 Sept. 1794; gravestone in Rahway Cemetery, Rahway, N.J.).

From George Flower

Princetown Indiana[1] 30 miles south of Vincennes
DEAR SIR Aug't 12. 1817

We have terminated a prosperous tho' laborious journey to this place. Since our families have been stationary Mr Birkbeck & myself have explored the southern part of the Illinois territory & have enter'd lands at the Shawnee Town office; in an agreable prarie country between the Big & Little Wabash. Well satisfied as we are with this new country, we lament the impossibility of our friends & countrymen settling around us from the daily entries that are made by americans to lands adjacent to our choice.

Among the numbers who are disposed to emigrate from Great Britain many respectable cultivators have express'd a wish to reside in the neighbourhood of our settlement if a sufficient scope of land could be obtained upon[2] favourable terms.

We wish to make a proposal to the Government to the following effect. That we may be allowed to purchase a tract of land in the Illinois Territory under favourable terms as to price & time of payment for the purpose of introducing a colony of English Farmers. For the advice which you may give us as to the mode of prosecuting our plan, or any assistance you may afford us that would not be attended with too much trouble to yourself, we should be particularly thankful.

The interest we take in the object I[3] have mentioned is my only apology for adding one letter to the pile of extranious correspondence which is heaped upon you so unmercifully.

With the best wishes for your health and that of the family at Monticello

I remain with the greatest respect & esteem Yrs &ct^r

GEORGE FLOWER

P. S. Our Letters are at present address'd to us at the Post Office Vincennes.

RC (MHi); postscript on verso of address leaf; addressed: "Thomas Jefferson Esqr Monticello Virginia"; address partially canceled and redirected in an unidentified hand to Lynchburg; stamp canceled; franked; postmarked Cincinnati, 23 Aug., and Charlottesville, 6 Sept.; endorsed by TJ as received <*12*> 11 Sept. 1817 and recorded under the earlier date in SJL.

On 20 Nov. 1817 Flower's partner Morris Birkbeck made an unsuccessful PROPOSAL to Congress to purchase a tract of land in Illinois Territory for their proposed English settlement (*Terr. Papers*, 17:545–6; *JHR*, 11:60 [18 Dec. 1817]; Flower, *History of the English Settlement in Edwards County Illinois, Founded in 1817 and 1818, by Morris Birkbeck and George Flower* [1882], 81–3).

[1] Word interlined.
[2] Flower here canceled "reasonable."
[3] Reworked from "we."

To David Knight

Sir — Poplar Forest Aug. 11. [12] 17.

I recieved your letter two or three days only before I sat out for this place, which occasioned my delaying the answer till I should arrive here. I shall be glad to have your aid in the brickwork, as well of the building we are now preparing to erect as in those to be erected the ensuing summer. they are going on well in making the brick, and will have them all ready by the middle of next month, & perhaps the cellar done. about that time I shall return there myself, and then also you will be wanting. I shall probably be at Lynchburg while in this neighborhood[1] and will then see you, and explain to you more particularly the work we have to do, and whatever else relating to it which you may wish to know. Accept my best wishes & respects

Th: Jefferson

PoC (DLC: TJ Papers, 210:37558); on verso of reused address cover of John Adams to TJ, 18 May 1817; misdated; at foot of text: "Mr Knight"; endorsed by TJ as a letter of <*11*> 12 Aug. 1817 and so recorded in SJL.

[1] Manuscript: "neighhood."

From Benjamin Henry Latrobe

Dear Sir — Washington Augt 12h 1817.

A slight indisposition having prevented my attendance at my office, I did not receive your favor of the 2d (post mark 4th) till the 9th when you would have left Monticello, and I therefore did not immediately answer it, and now direct this letter where I hope it will soon reach You. I now offer to you, with the utmost freedom, a freedom which your request, as well as your long friendship to me authorizes and invites, such remarks as occur to me on the general plan of your Academy;—and as I write without preparation, you must extend your indulgence to the desultory manner, as well as to the freedom of my observations.—

The drawings I have made are still by me, & I now beg you to inform me whether, as you remain so long near Lynchburg, I shall not send them to you thither.—My letter of the 25th July you do not appear to have received on the 2d of Augt. If you have since then obtained it,

I beg the favor of you to inform me, whether you will engage the Stone cutter whose terms I mentioned, & whom I can strongly recommend,—as he remains in suspense at present. I employ him now at the Capitol. The plan and description which your letter contains perfectly explains the situation, on which your Academy must be located,—and I cannot help beginning my remarks, by calling it a most unfortunate one.—For if the general design contained in your letter be carried into execution,—and at the first view, it is that, which appears to be unavoidably imposed upon you,—it necessarily follows, that all your apartments must face East & West.—Every one who has had the misfortune to reside in a house,—especially if it constituted part of a range of houses, facing East & West, has experienced, both in Summer and Winter the evils of such an Aspect. In Winter the accumulation of Snow on the East, & the severity of the cold on the West, together with the absence of the Sun during $\frac{3}{4}$th of the day,—and in Summer, the horizontal Rays of the morning Sun heating the East, & of the evening Sun burning the West side of the house,—render such a position highly exceptionable.—In a large Country house, surrounded with Trees, and in which the number of Apartments enables the Inhabitants to emigrate from one side of the house to the other, as the Abyssinian Shepherds, from the forests to the deserts,—in such a house the aspect is of less importance, and the house may be located with a regard to the View, to the range of a hill, or of the road leading to it. But where no recourse can be had to opposite apartments, and especially where a long extent of portico on one side only creates an eddy, for the wind to accumulate Snow, & for the Sun to heat the air confined under it,—I cannot help being of opinion that the utmost power of art ought to be employed to force the aspect of the house into a North & South position.—And from long experience in my profession, and from having witnessed the uniform regret of those whom I have been unable to persuade into my opinion on this head in the position of their houses,—I have learned to consider, the easy access to water to be the first, and the North & South position to be the second absolutely indispensible principle, on which a good position of a building depends. I could enumerate so many instances of these regrets, & on the other hand, so many proofs of advantage (especially in the position of new Streets recommended by me in Philadelphia) that they would fill my letter. But to you they are unnecessary & I will at present only ask, whether you are so far committed, as to render the adoption of the plan of arrangement irrevocable, and to make any respectful project which I might take the liberty to submit to You useless.

On the receipt of your letter of the I suspended my drawing. It contained a plan of the principal range of building (as I then supposed it) and seven or eight Elevations of pavilions, with a general Elevation of the long range of Pavilions & portico. In this state I will send it to you. If there is any thing in it which you think usefull, it is yours, & I particularly beg the favor of you to give me further opportunity of being useful to your establishment, & of testifying my respect for yourself.—I draw with great rapidity, & ease & pleasure to myself, & you must not be deterred by any idea that you give me trouble.—If therefore what I have said seems to you worthy of consideration, it will be a pleasure to me to suggest such a plan, as the principles I think so essential, may dictate.—

I have now at the Capitol Nine blocks of the Columbian Marble nearly finished for the Columns of the Hall of Representatives. I have never seen anything so beautifully magnificent. Even the most clamorous opposers of their introduction are now silenced. When the columns are in their places, they will be a lasting proof of the firmness of the character of the present President of the U. States; who in order to decide on the merits of the opposition of the introduction of this Marble, went himself, in the worst weather, to the quarry, and in person gave those orders, which, altho' they did not quell such opposition as could still be made, will ultimately be effectual, & not only render our public buildings rich in native magnificence, but make these useless rocks an article of considerable external commerce.

I have lately had a very interesting letter from Count Volney, who has sent me his last work, "Recherches nouvelles sur L'histoire ancienne," in three Volumes. It is principally confined to ancient Chronology, and exhibits a depth & ingenuity of research, far surpassing any thing I have yet read, on the subject. In fact, it leaves, in my opinion nothing more to be done in that barren field.—I presume that you have received the book; if not, I will use any opportunity you will point out to send it to You.—For my part, I have derived great & unexpected information from it; for tho' foreign to the profession which inclination as well as necessity has imposed upon me, the accidental bent of my early education, made me not entirely unacquainted with oriental learning My early acquirement of some knowledge of Greek & Hebrew, was afterwards suceeded by the desire (rendered easy of gratification)[1] to assist Mr Bruce in the publication of his Travels,—the whole first volume of which, with the drawings it contains was published from my manuscript. The following were (I believe) done into English by Fennel, the comedian.—Having apologized for the desultory character of this letter, I hope I have your permission to proceed to say,—that my uncle, John Antes, whose work on Egypt you have probably seen, resided 12 Years at Cairo, where he had the Character of a Jeweller & Watchmaker, as necessary to his allowed residence, but being a man of letters, great courage, & ingenuity, he brought with him to Europe, an inexhaustible source of information, and had he not also brought along with it a large fortune, and a somewhat indolent habit, he might have enriched our libraries, with a great store of Egyptian facts, now probably lost forever. He had been a favorite with Ali Bey before his fall, & was able to throw great light on the transactions of that singular Man.—He was connected with the Moravian Mission among the Cophts, and when Bruce came to Egypt, he became acquainted with my uncle through the introduction of a Cophtic Merchant. During Bruce's residence in Gondar, my uncle supplied him with money, & altho' in his original manuscript he had done my uncle great justice & acknowledged the obligations he owed to him, he has in his printed travels only slightly mentioned him, as a German watchmaker. He was no German, but the son of the well known Henry Antes, of Philadelphia, my Grandfather, formerly familiarly called, the King of the Germans. Mr Antes gave Bruce a letter to my father, who after the revolution resided constantly & died in England. His manuscript was written in as uncouth a style as can be well conceived, and like his conversation, was that of a Scotchman who had left his highlands late in life. The honble Daines Barrington, was the great patron of his publication, & as I was then more a man of pleasure & letters than of business in London, Mr Barrington half in earnest, half in play proposed to me the revision[2] of Mr Bruce's papers, which excepting as to style, were however remarkably well digested, and ordered.—I seized the proposition with avidity, and for two or three months devoted three hours every morning to this singular Man. His removal to Scotland put a stop to my agency, but left me an enthusiast in the pursuit of oriental litterature. The arrival of my uncle Mr Antes in England, afterwards, and the arrangement of the papers of Mr G. Livius, a cousin of ours (a Canadian) who had been many years Military Storekeeper General in the East indies, & was a man of considerable learning,—and afterwards of Quintin Craufurd, well known for his works on Indian subjects (both of which my zeal for that sort of knowledge induced me to undertake),—all this enabled me to store my memory with such facts,—as, (to return from my long ramble) have made Mr Volney's work exceedingly interesting to me.

I have seen in the papers a notice, that Mr Volney has published a new edition of his ruins, with correction of such opinions as he had formed hastily in his Youth. The evident bearing of the notice was to insinuate that he had changed his religious sentiments. I find nothing in the "Recherches nouvelles" to authorize such a supposition, but rather the contrary: if I were to pass any censure on his book, it would be, to remark, that he does not use language as temperate, respecting generally[3] received opinions on the divine origin of the Bible, as he might have done without weakening his arguments: and that his book is throughout written in a peevish style, unnecessary, & not conciliating the reader to the favorable admission of his deductions. The captatio benevolentiae, is perhaps out of the province of polemic writers, but the excitement of prejudice may be avoided.—

I dare add no more than that I am very sincerely & truly Y^{rs}

B HENRY LATROBE.

On saturday the 9th we had the most terrible & continued rain ever remembered here. 9$\frac{1}{2}$ inches fell from 8 to 1 o'clock. In Baltimore, Jones falls creek was so swelled as to carry Milldams, Mills, houses, cattle, & many persons along to destruction. The damage is estimated now by report[4] at 5 Millions. All the Bridges between this & Baltimore destroyed excepting one, & no mail since Saturday morning from thence.

RC (DLC); at head of text: "Thos Jefferson Esqr near Lynchburg V^{a}"; endorsed by TJ as received <22> 23 Aug. 1817 and so recorded in SJL; with notes by TJ for his [25] Aug. 1817 reply beneath endorsement:

"

his lres	rec^{d} by me	answered
June 28.	July 15	July 16
July 24	Aug 2	Aug. 3
July 18	Aug. 7	Aug. 7.
Aug. 12	Aug. 22	

."

TJ's FAVOR OF THE 2^{D} was actually dated 3 Aug. 1817. Latrobe's LETTER OF THE 25TH JULY was actually dated 28 July 1817, although incorrectly referred to by TJ in his notes on verso of this letter as one of 18 July. Late in March 1817 President James Monroe visited a QUARRY in Maryland opposite Leesburg, Virginia, to inspect the marble for the United States Capitol (Leesburg *Genius of Liberty*, 1 Apr. 1817).

Latrobe was one of several people who helped James BRUCE edit and publish his *Travels to discover the Source of the Nile, In the Years 1768, 1769, 1770, 1771, 1772, and 1773*, 5 vols. (Edinburgh, 1790; Sowerby, no. 3958). The actor James Fennell (FENNEL) was another such assistant (Latrobe, *Papers*, 3:308, 933; *ODNB*, 8:306, 19:297). In his work Bruce credited Latrobe's uncle JOHN ANTES with aiding him in making a brass measuring rod (Bruce, *Travels*, 3:702).

Numerous newspapers published A NOTICE that in the recent 5th edition of his 1791 publication, *The Ruins: or A Survey of the Revolutions of Empires*, Volney had updated the work by "suppressing opinions which experience has proved to be erroneous, and adding reflections which the events of a long life have suggested to him" (*New-York Columbian*, 28 July 1817; Sowerby, nos. 1277–8; Poor, *Jefferson's Library*, 9 [nos. 468–9]). CAPTATIO BENEVOLENTIAE: rhetorical strategies for garnering an audience's goodwill (*OCD*, 289).

[1]Preceding two words and closing parenthesis interlined.

[2]Word interlined in place of "arrangement."

[3]Word interlined.

[4]Preceding two words interlined.

From Maxfield Ludlow

Surveyor General's Office Town of Washington
State of Mississippi August 12th 1817.—

SIR,

I take the liberty of enclosing to you a Subscription, & also a Copy of a Certificate from Gideon Fitz; principal Dep. Surveyor of the South West District, State of Louisiana.—The Certificate is in the following words.

Being informed by Mr Maxfield Ludlow that he is about to publish a map embracing with other parts of the State of Louisiana, that of the Western Land District, lying South of Red River, the Surveying whereof has been under my Superintendance as Principal Deputy Surveyor, I am induced at the request of Mr Ludlow, to State, that he had the opportunity of taking any transcripts which he may have thought proper from the returns of Surveyors[1] made to my office prior to his leaving Opelousas to be employed as Chief Clerk in the Office of the Surveyor General South of Tennessee in the fall of the year 1813. at which time this part of the District had been surveyed generally into Townships, many of which were Surveyed into Sections.

In consequence of the opportunity which Mr Ludlow has had of obtaining information from Surveys made in the State of Louisiana & the Mississippi Terry I have no doubt that his map will be[2] the most accurate of any yet published of these countries.—

Opelousas July 10th 1817. (Signed) GIDEON FITZ
Principal Dep. Surveyor
S.W. District State of Louisiana

This Original Certificate of Mr Fitz's will hereafter be handed to you by Capt Richard Fletcher, my agent &c who is now at Philadilphia superentending the engraving of my map—He informs me that he is personally acquainted with you, & on his return with the maps he will call on you at Monticello. I wish not to intrude on your goodness, nor to give you any unnecessary trouble, you will do me a great favor by handing this Subscription to Some person that will get Subscribers,—and when Capt Fletcher calls, please to inform him where he may find it.

I, have been employed by Mr Fitz, & Thomas Freeman Esqr

Surveyor Gen[l] South of the State of Tennessee for 8. Years past, during which time, Occasionally I have been deleniating this usefull work,—This map will distinctly shew the Indian boundary lines from Actual Survey, and in particular the Alabama Country and every other part as set forth in the Prospectus.—

The engraving & paper &[c] will cost me five Thousand dollars—and without the aid of some Eastern Gentleman, I fear, whether I ever get my own money again—I do consider that a few of favorable words from you Sir, in my behalf of this work will in a measure releive me, I, wish this only to be done on the examination of the map Your self[3]—

In great haste Your friend MAXFIELD LUDLOW

(Our State Constitution is this day Signed)[4]

No doubt Sir but you have seen the map published by M[r] Darby. This gentleman (if such he be worthy to be called) informs the public, that his map is from actual Survey.

M[r] Darby I am well acquainted with, his private Surveys returned to M[r] Fitz's office, generally was condemned for their inacuracies. These Sir, are the men that generally destroy the works of honest good men,—his map is entirely Erroneous—in particular that part which lies East of the Mississippi River—I am not ashamed to assert this to the World, and can prove the facts, by the Records in this office.—You will Sir, take particular notice of M[r] Darby's Indian boundary line, from the Homochitto River to the Tombigby River—compare his map with mine,—my map is laid off in Townships & Ranges, These Townships & ranges, Join this Indian Boundary alluded too!!!—and the Correctness of my work may be seen with the Commis[er] of the Gen[l] Land Office—Which maps I also made.—

M. L.

RC (MoSHi: TJC-BC); entirely in Ludlow's hand; addressed: "Thomas Jefferson Esq[r] Late President of the U. S. Monticello," with "Virginia" added in an unidentified hand; franked; postmarked Washington, Mississippi Territory, 13 Aug.; endorsed by TJ as received 21 Sept. 1817 and so recorded in SJL. Fitz certificate of 10 July 1817 printed by Ludlow in Natchez *Mississippi State Gazette*, 7 Feb. 1818. Enclosure: Ludlow, *Prospectus for Publishing by Subscription, A Map of the State of Louisiana, with a part of the State of Mississippi and Alabama Territory*, indicating that the proposed map would measure six feet six inches by four feet, on a scale of eight miles to an inch; outlining its boundaries; adding that it would include in one corner a plat illustrating the campaign of the British at New Orleans in 1815; specifying that the map would be "engraved by the best artist in the United States," consist of four sheets, and be delivered "on or about the first day of December next"; advertising a price of $10 for subscribers or $14 if the map is mounted on rollers; and concluding with a blank subscription list (undated broadside in MoSHi: TJC-BC).

Maxfield Ludlow (d. by 1828) was employed as a surveyor in Ohio as early as 1795 and worked extensively laying out townships in Ohio in the first decade of the nineteenth century. In 1804 he was commissioned an ensign in the militia of Hamilton County, Ohio. He was living near Cincinnati by 1807, when he sought a position as a land registrar. Ludlow subsequently moved to Mississippi Territory and was employed between about 1809 and 1817 under the surveyor general for the area south of Tennessee. About 1817 he published *A Map of the State of Louisiana with Part of the State of Mississippi and Alabama Territory* (Ristow, *American Maps and Mapmakers*, 145; *Sketches of Springfield* [1852], 5, 6; *Quarterly Publication of the Historical and Philosophical Society of Ohio* 13 [1918]: 118; *The History of Clark County, Ohio* [1881], 234; George William Hill, *History of Ashland County, Ohio* [1880], 46–8; John E. Hopley, *History of Crawford County, Ohio* [1912], 179, 264, 299, 338; DNA: RG 59, LAR, 1801–09; *Petition and documents of Gabriel Winter* [(Washington, 1818)], 18; *Terr. Papers*, 6:452; *A Register of Officers and Agents, Civil, Military, and Naval* [Washington, 1816], 38; Ludlow, *To the Public* [(Natchez, 1817)] [broadside in MWA]; *Natchez Gazette*, 7 July 1830).

The STATE CONSTITUTION of Mississippi was signed on 15 Aug. 1817 (*Terr. Papers*, 6:798).

[1] *Mississippi State Gazette*: "surveys."

[2] *Mississippi State Gazette* here adds "much."

[3] Manuscript: "sef."

[4] Remainder of text on verso of address cover.

To Archibald Robertson

DEAR SIR Poplar [Fore]st Aug. 11. [12] 17.

I have been longer than I expected in getting the produce of the year to market which has occasioned the delay of sending you the inclosed order on mess^rs Gibson & Jefferson for 800. Dollars. I wish it were more, but the late calamitous season and this not much better, put it out of my power. I shall be glad to recieve by the bearer the articles underwritten.

I set out for the Natural bridge with two of my grandaughters the day after tomorrow, and shall be absent 4. or 5. days. should your business after that draw you into this quarter I shall always be happy to see you. Accept the assurance of my great esteem and respect.

TH: JEFFERSON

2. ℔ tea
10. ℔ of rice.
10. ℔ brown sugar
2. loaves white sugar
10 ℔ coffee. with respect to coffee I will observe generally that the Bourbon is best, next the Java, or E. India, then the ripe dry W. India, but never the green.
a box of candles.

PoC (MHi); on verso of reused address cover of Patrick Gibson to TJ, 26 June 1817; misdated; place of composition faint; at foot of text: "Mr Robertson"; endorsed by TJ as a letter of 11 Aug. 1817 but corrected to 12 Aug. in SJL. Enclosure not found.

The two GRANDAUGHTERS who accompanied TJ to Natural Bridge were Ellen W. Randolph (Coolidge) and Cornelia J. Randolph.

From Archibald Robertson

DEAR SIR Lynchburg 12 aug^t^ 1817

Your favor of the 11th enclosing a dft on Messrs Gibson & Jefferson for $800 was received in my absence, the amount will be placed to your credit, for which we are very much obliged to you—

The articles you requested were sent, which hope were pleasing—you will receive herewith the last papers

Very Respectfully Your Ob St A. ROBERTSON

RC (MHi); endorsed by TJ as received 13 Aug. 1817 but corrected to 14 Aug. in SJL. Enclosures not found.

For the misdated FAVOR OF THE 11TH, see TJ to Robertson, [12] Aug. 1817.

From David Bailie Warden

Rue Pot de Fer, 12— Paris, 6 June, [ca. 12–22 Aug.] 1817.

DEAR SIR,

a few days since I had the pleasure of receiving your letter of the 6th of June last, by duplicate, I am glad to know that you are pleased with the Books and the manner in which the De Bures' have executed the commission: they expect to forward those, which you lately ordered, in the course of a week. It appears that the trunk of Books and pamphlets left at ghent nearly two years ago, has been lately forwarded to philadelphia. I hope that you have received the volumes and brochures which it contained, addressed to you by the late mr. Rochon and myself. I send this by mrs. Patterson, who from motives of prudence refuses to take charge of any letter of a political nature. This prevents me from giving you some account of passing events. I have informed Baron Humboldt, and the Count De Tracy of your intention of writing to them soon. The latter though nearly deprived of sight, is still fond of literary pursuits; and I having informed him of the English Translation of one of his productions being advertised at georgetown, he expressed a great desire to have a copy—mr. Ticknor, with whom I am much pleased, has set out to visit Switzerland, Italy, and Spain. I beg leave to inclose a copy of the prospectus of my intended publication; and am, with great respect

your very obliged Servt D. B. WARDEN

RC (DLC: TJ Papers, 210:37457); misdated, with conjectural date of composition based on Warden's endorsement of TJ's letter of 6 June 1817; at foot of text: "Thomas Jefferson Esquire"; endorsed by TJ as a letter of 6 June 1817 received 29 Oct. 1817 and so recorded in SJL. FC (MdHi: Warden Letterbook); in Warden's hand; undated; followed in Lb by a letter dated 22 Aug.

MRS. PATTERSON: Elizabeth Patterson Bonaparte. Joseph Milligan, of Georgetown, had ADVERTISED his translated edition of Destutt de Tracy, *Treatise on Political Economy*, using TJ's Title and Prospectus for the work, printed above at [ca. 6 Apr. 1816] (Washington *Daily National Intelligencer*, 7 Feb. 1817). The enclosed PROSPECTUS may have been a version of Warden, *Prospectus of a Statistical and Historical Account of the United States of America, from the Period of the First Establishments to the Present Day; on a new plan*, proposing an edition in four octavo volumes, with a new map of the United States, to be priced at $9; advertising Warden's unique qualifications to write the book; and outlining in detail its intended subjects (undated pamphlet in PPAmP).

To A. F. De Laage

DEAR SIR Poplar Forest Aug. 12. [13] 17.

My intention of being soon at this place induced me to defer acknoleging your letter of Adieu until my arrival here

I am sorry that in the place in which you have fixed your new residence, my acquaintance is so limited as to enable me to be of but little use to you. I inclose you however letters to mr Johnson, mr Harrison and mr Robertson, the only gentlemen there of my particular acquaintance. their great worth & high standing in that place will enable them to present you favorably to it's society and business. I am about 10. miles from it, at a possession which I visit 3. or 4. times a year, where I can give you but very plain plantation fare, but with a sincere welcome, whenever you can do me the favor to come thus far, and to recieve in person the assurances of my great esteem and respect. TH: JEFFERSON

PoC (DLC: TJ Papers, 210:37560); on verso of a reused address cover from John Barnes to TJ; misdated; at foot of text: "M. de Laage"; endorsed by TJ as a letter of <*12*> 13 Aug. 1817 and so recorded in SJL. Enclosure: TJ to Samuel J. Harrison, Charles Johnston, and Archibald Robertson, [13] Aug. 1817.

From A. F. De Laage

MONSIEUR, Lynchburg 12 [13] Aout 1817

J'ai reçu la Lettre que vous m'avez fait l'honneur de m'écrire, ainsi que Celles qu'elle renfermait: je manque d'expression, Monsieur, pour vous temoigner toute ma reconnoissance: je ne manquerai certainement pas de me présenter Chez vous pour vous en assurer moi même, aussitot votre Retour du Natural Bridge, ou on m'a dit que vous alliez: Croyez, je vous prie, à la Sincerité de mes Sentiments et au profond respect avec lequel

J'ai l'honneur d'Etre, Monsieur, Votre très humble et très obeissant Serviteur A. F. DE LAAGE

EDITORS' TRANSLATION

SIR, Lynchburg 12 [13] August 1817

I have received the letter you did me the honor of writing me, as well as those enclosed in it. Words fail, Sir, to express my gratitude. I will certainly plan to present myself at your house to do so in person, as soon as you have returned from the Natural Bridge, where I was told you had gone. Please believe in the sincerity of my feelings and in the most profound respect with which

I have the honor to be, Sir, your very humble and very obedient servant

A. F. DE LAAGE

RC (DLC: TJ Papers, 210:37566); misdated, based on TJ's erroneous dating of the letter to which this one responds; at foot of text: "Mr Jefferson"; endorsed by TJ as received <*13*> 14 Aug. 1817 but recorded under the earlier date in SJL. Translation by Dr. Genevieve Moene.

To Samuel J. Harrison, Charles Johnston, and Archibald Robertson

DEAR SIR Poplar Forest Aug. 12. [13] 17.

Monsr de Laage, a gentleman from France, lately removed to Lynchburg, has lived some time in Charlottesville, where he became known to myself, and greatly[1] esteemed by all for his great worth, his correct and amiable manners. he was in the military line in France, of the most respectable connections & standing there; but by the chances of their various & calamitous revolutions, has been obliged to leave his country and fortunes, & to seek both under another sky. the firmness with which he accomodates himself to his new situation, his frank and friendly dispositions, his good sense and unassuming demeanor render him truly worthy of the esteem of those among whom he is settled. I ask leave to present him to your notice and civilities, and any good offices you can render him will be gratefully recieved by him, and acknoleged thankfully by myself. with Madame de Laage I had not the opportunity of becoming personally acquainted, but was the witness of her praise from every one who knew her, altho' her merits could not but be obscured by[2] her not speaking our language. I avail myself of the occasion which the making known to you these worthy emigrants furnishes of assuring you of my great & friendly esteem & respect. TH: JEFFERSON

RC (DLC: Burton Harrison Collection); misdated; addressed: "Samuel Harrison esq. Lynchburg favored by M. de Laage." PoC of RC to Johnston (MoSHi: TJC-BC); on verso of reused address cover of otherwise unlocated letter from Joseph Gales (1761–1841) to TJ, 23 May 1817 (addressed: "Hon. Thos Jefferson, Monticello. Albermarl County Va"; franked; postmarked Raleigh, N.C., 25 May; recorded in SJL as received 31 May 1817 from Raleigh); edge trimmed and stained; at foot of text: "Mr Charles Johnson Saml Harrison Archibd Robertson"; endorsed by TJ as a letter to Johnston of <*12*> 13 Aug. 1817 and so recorded in SJL, which lists the letters to Harrison and Robertson separately. Enclosed in TJ to A. F. De Laage, [13] Aug. 1817.

[1] PoC: "highly."

[2] PoC: "her merits were the less obvious from."

Trip to Natural Bridge

I. EXTRACT OF CORNELIA J. RANDOLPH TO VIRGINIA J. RANDOLPH (TRIST), 17 AUG. 1817

II. EXTRACT OF ELLEN W. RANDOLPH (COOLIDGE) TO MARTHA JEFFERSON RANDOLPH, 18 AUG. [1817]

III. EXTRACT OF ELLEN W. RANDOLPH (COOLIDGE) TO MARTHA JEFFERSON RANDOLPH, [AFTER 29 AUG. 1817]

IV. CORNELIA J. RANDOLPH TO VIRGINIA J. RANDOLPH (TRIST), 30 AUG. 1817

V. EXTRACT OF CORNELIA J. RANDOLPH TO VIRGINIA J. RANDOLPH (TRIST) AND MARY ELIZABETH RANDOLPH (EPPES), 24 SEPT. 1817

EDITORIAL NOTE

On or about 13 Aug. 1817 Jefferson set out from Poplar Forest to visit Natural Bridge with his granddaughters Ellen W. Randolph (Coolidge) and Cornelia J. Randolph. Jefferson had most recently visited his Rockbridge County possession in 1815 with his friends José Corrêa da Serra and Francis W. Gilmer. On that occasion Jefferson measured the latitude of Natural Bridge. About the time of the present visit he briefly revised his description of the rock formation in his personal copy of *Notes on the State of Virginia.* He added in a note dated 16 Aug. 1817 that his original description needed to be corrected because it was based on a faulty memory that mountains could be viewed in both directions from the nearby fissure rather than from the base of the arch itself. Jefferson otherwise left little written comment on this family trip. The letters of Ellen and Cornelia Randolph extracted and printed below are therefore an important source for details of the visit and the subsequent activities of Jefferson and his granddaughters after their return to Poplar Forest about 17 Aug. (*MB*, 1:liv, 2:1337; Jefferson, *Notes on the State of Virginia* [London, 1787; Sowerby, no. 4167; Poor, *Jefferson's Library*, 7 [no. 365]; TJ's copy in ViU, with small sheet containing TJ's revisions to his description of Natural Bridge and his 16 Aug. 1817 note explaining the changes tipped in between pp. 34 and 35]). An image of Natural Bridge is reproduced elsewhere in this volume.

I. Extract of Cornelia J. Randolph to Virginia J. Randolph (Trist)

My Dear Virginia August 17 1817

We are return'd from the natural bridge more anxious to see it again than we were at first, because in the first place it far surpass'd our expectations, & in the second we saw it under many disadvantages, which will be remov'd when we go again, & grandpapa has promis'd that we shall; our trip was attended with disasters & accidents from the time we set off untill we return'd again, the morning we were to go when we got up we found it was a damp cloudy day, but Grandpapa decided at breakfast that it would not rain & sister Ellen and myself rejoic'd that the sun did not shine & that we should have a cool day for our journey we set off accordingly after Gil & Israel had made us wait two hours but we had not proceeded many miles before it clear'd up the sun shone out & we had one of the hottest most disagreable days for traveling that could be, then came our first misfortune in going over a high bridge one of the wheel horses broke through & sank up nearly half way in the hole we all got out as quick as we could & found that the bridge was entirely gone to decay & not only several of the logs but one of the sleepers had broken down & that we had been in great danger of going down carriage & horses & all, the horses were all loosened & poor Bremo pull'd out by main strength, for he seem'd so overcome with fright that he was incapable assisting himself & lay quite passive & let them do what they would with him, he was hurt in no other way than being much skin'd & bruis'd, but as it was we were oblig'd now to walk up a long tedious red hill & then pursued our journey in the carriage without any other accident, over abominable roads; about one o clock we came to a very wild looking part of the country just at the foot of the ridge here we met a man with a gun on his shoulder and a squirrel which he had just kill'd, grandpapa ask'd him some questions and found out he was the man at whose house we were to leave the carriage and that we were a very little distance from it, it was a log house in the woods, which were clear'd away immediately around it, a large family liv'd in it tho it had but one room, these people were the first of that half civiliz'd race who live beyond the ridge that we had seen. the man who before had not deign'd to take any notice of us & not even to go out of the road that we might pass, as soon as he heard what we wanted, was very polite, promis'd to take care of the carriage & to have the horses fed imediately, for he was one of those who tho they do not keep a tavern will accomodate you with what ever they can & take pay for it, while the horses were eating he ask'd us in to his house, where were his wife two old men, one his father, & a large family of children all the young ones being in their shifts & shirts; none of the men wore coats tho' they none of them apparently had not been at work[1] & I do not think I saw more than one coat while we were gone & not more than two or three pair of shoes. the people in the house were as perfectly at their ease as if they had known us all their lives; the two old men enter'd into conversation with grandpapa at once, and one of them said he had been forty three years living there (within twelve miles of the bridge) & had never seen it; now he said he was too old to go being 84, he was the most savage looking man of the two[2] tho they both were uncivilis'd, both in manners and apearance the other going with his hairy breast expos'd & both speaking of us and our family before our faces just as if we had been absent the oldest scarcely waited for grandpapa to go out, before he wonder'd who that old genllman was & the other having great surprise answer'd it was Colonel Jefferson, "then" said the first "I know where lives, he lives near parson Clay's in Bedford" but the other one said no, he did not live there he liv'd away down in Albemarle & only visited his place in Bedford call'd poplar Forest, sometimes, that he had possessions in both these counties, & that Randal used to have land in Bedford too. they said a good deal more about grandpapa & a great deal to us the first not even honouring us with the title of ladies, but calling us <u>young women</u>. how they knew so much about grandpapa I cant concieve for he never had seen either of them before. we left this place on horseback after having refresh'd ourselves with ripe[3] apples which they gave us & began to ascend the mountain, we cross'd it at Petites gap which is near the place where James river passes the ridge, we rode three miles before we came to the top where we dined on cold bacon & chicken, & then descended three. three more we had to go before we got to the place where we spent that night & the succeeding, Greenlee's ferry. the mountain is the wildest most romantic looking place I ever saw the trees remarkably large & tall & no under wood so that you could see for a great distance around you. I saw there oaks chesnuts & poplars, & spruce pine, which I never saw before it is a beautiful tree. I wish we had it at Monticello, & we found a rasberry which is better even than the garden rasberry having a fine flavour & the seeds being so small that you scarcely percieve them, the bushes were quite full of fruit tho it was so late in the season, they are a bright scarlet & the bush has no thorns, the people in the neighbourhood call'd it the mountain rasberry, & grandpapa remember'd that they had had them at Shadwell for many years under the name of the mountain strawberry, but they had never born there.

August 19 Grandpapa means to hurry Johny off so soon that I have not time to say any thing more of our trip to the Natural bridge particularly as I have written down three pages & have not got to the end of our first days journey, but if you are not tir'd already I will go on with our travels in the next letter, & will try to get a little better pen ink & paper that the reading them may not be such a task, at present I must answer the principle articles of your letter. C.R.

RC (NcU: NPT); extract consisting of bulk of letter, but omitting text written on 19 Aug. between end of text printed above and signature. In the unextracted portion of this letter, Randolph says she has not wanted Gonezalo and finds Perico more difficult than she did at first; argues that drawing figures is "more agreable" than drawing flowers and says that she has been working on drawings of Ariadne and the Shakespearean characters Ferdinand and Miranda; assumes that her aunt Mary Randolph has not yet arrived at Monticello; expects Mary Elizabeth Randolph (Eppes) to "render a faithful account of every thing she sees in her travels"; says that "Uncle & Mrs Eppes were not with us when we went to the natural bridge but we expect the former & Francis every day"; promises to write to Mary J. Randolph and Harriet F. Randolph (Willis) by the next cart if she has the energy; passes on the regards of Ellen W. Randolph (Coolidge) to her aunts Anne Scott Marks and Harriet Hackley and the latter's family, especially her stepdaughter Jane E. C. Hackley (Taylor); expresses pleasure that her aunt Jane Cary Randolph is recovering; and asks her mother to kiss Septimia A. Randolph (Meikleham) for her.

[1] Preceding nine words interlined in place of an illegible phrase, with "not" interlined above the rest of the new text.

[2] Word interlined in place of "three."

[3] Word interlined in place of "fresh."

II. Extract of Ellen W. Randolph (Coolidge) to Martha Jefferson Randolph

My dear Mama Poplar Forest Aug. 18th

Cornelia will probably give Virginia a detail of our Journey to the Natural Bridge—for me it was a complete chapter of accidents—my misfortunes began the day I left home and have not yet ceased, for a cold caught I believe in crossing the blue ridge settled upon my face and has kept me in almost constant agonies—I have not been free of pain one moment[1] for the last eight and forty hours and although not acute enough to confine me to my room it is yet sufficiently so to keep me constantly restless uneasy and nervous—I cannot however regret my trip for the wonder and delight I experienced at the sight of the bridge, (which surely deserves the name[2] of the "most sublime of Nature's works") was greater than I can describe. the limestone cavern near it was also a great curiosity for us, it is a cave in the solid lime stone rock divided into accessible apartments by a curtain of stone. there is a passage large enough to admit the body of a man on all fours which probably communicates with other apartments never explored. the earth in it is so impregnated with salt pitre that a pound has been got from a bushel of dirt. under the bridge I lost your beautifull little purse with three or four dollars which I had arrived with and the little pocket telescope given me by Aunt Jane, and which I valued very highly—our trip independent of the bridge would have been a very pleasant one if the weather had been more favorable and the accomodations better—the manners and character of the people are so different from anything we are accustomed to and the scenery of the country so wild and picturesque, that we almost fancied ourselves in a new world. there is in the men a stern independence and a contempt for forms and appearances, in the women a bustling activity that we do not meet with lower down the country, that is, if it is fair to draw general conclusions from particular instances and if in a tour of three days it was possible to make any observations which can apply to more than the few individuals who came under our notice—

I brought so much work from home with me, and I have been so tortured by pain that I have not had time to commence my system of industry—as we shall be here for a month to come I hope to have it in my power to do something. if it is only to recover the latin I have lost—we have as yet seen no one but Mrs Yancey—Mrs Clark is at the springs and the situation of Mrs Radford's brother will probably prevent her from visiting us. Cornelia and myself are not comfortably fixed. our room has been pulled down and it will be some time before we get in it—probably a fortnight—in the mean time we are in that little close disagreable room to the right as you enter the dining room, where we are so crouded we can scarcely turn—the weather hot, and as Cornelia observes we are shut up from all breezes but those of the North east—Maria is the same untutored savage you formerly knew and plagues us to death with her stupidity and indifference—

RC (ViU: Coolidge Correspondence); extract, consisting of salutation, dateline, and middle portion of letter; unsigned; partially dated. In the unextracted sections of this letter, Randolph expresses concern for members of the Smith and Goodwin families of Baltimore due to the recent flooding there; asks that, if handkerchiefs have arrived, they be sent to Poplar Forest with John Hern; states that the towels previously sent were "a 'heartsome sight'" but worries that Maria will ruin them in the wash; sends greetings to her sisters and a message to Virginia J. Randolph (Trist) that the song "Duncan Grey" is "not difficult, but will require practise"; asks to be remembered to her aunts Jane Cary Randolph and Harriet Hackley and their families; sends love to her father, Thomas Mann Randolph, if he is at home; inquires about her mother's headache and hopes she has been well enough to visit Thomas Jefferson Randolph, Jane H. Nicholas Randolph, and their baby Pat (Martha Jefferson Randolph [Taylor]); and requests a toothbrush and tooth powder.

TJ called Natural Bridge the MOST SUBLIME OF NATURE'S WORKS in his *Notes on the State of Virginia* (*Notes*, ed. Peden, 24).

[1] Preceding two words interlined.
[2] Word interlined in place of "epithet."

III. Extract of Ellen W. Randolph (Coolidge) to Martha Jefferson Randolph

MY DEAR MAMA [after 29 Aug. 1817]

Johnny's arrival gave us great pleasure as we began to be very anxious to hear from you, and I thank you very much for having spared time to write such a long letter. the head of Christ is really a great curiosity, Grand-papa is almost as much pleased with it as we are, and considers it extremely ingenious & original. it is certainly a very fine face and the character is so decided that I believe I should have known without being told for whom it was intended. we have studied it with so much attention that I think we know exactly the proper distance from the candle and the wall:—

We have been entirely alone since our return from the Natural Bridge, but have not felt at all solitary—we are anxious to see you all, but too constantly employed to suffer from Ennui—I go on with my latin bravely—Cornelia has finished Cordery, and will make an end of Gillies before she returns home. we have seen no body but Mrs Yancey; and Mrs Clay. the last came very kindly and spent a whole day with us—from ten o clock untill near sunset. you may imagine how rapidly the hours passed and what a "feast of reason and a flow of soul" it was for us.—I must do the old woman the justice to say that I do not believe she intended to have paid so long a visit,[1] but her savage husband wholly unconscious of the ridicule and impropriety of the thing insisted upon staying all day.[2] he is much more uncivilized than any Indian I ever saw, and indeed I doubt whether the wild Hottentots described by Peron are as bad—they certainly cannot be more savage in voice and manners, or more entirely ignorant of the rules of good breeding; but I have (as[3] Larry would say) wasted too much ink on them who d'ont desarve it. De Laage dined here the same day and was full of apologies for the state of confusion in which we found his "menage"[4] the day we called on his wife—"Mde[5] de Laage is the most foolish little woman in this world" said he "would you believe it mademoiselle she cried all day long after you left her, and could not be comforted for having been found in such a situation by Mrs Randolph & the young ladies."[6] he seems pleased with Lynchburg and very gratefull to Grandpapa for letters of recommendation which he says have been of essentiel benefit to him.

Grandpapa had heard of Mr Du Pont's death and was much distressed at it. he has received a letter from Baron Quinette who has got back to New-York. he sent him a french pamphlet which had been directed to M. de Rochemont, by which we conclude that he is probably called by that name in France—. I believe it is common for the French to take the names of their places—is it not? perhaps Papa may know him in his public character as Mr de Rochemont

RC (ViU: Coolidge Correspondence); extract consisting of first half of letter; undated, but composed after TJ's receipt on 29 Aug. 1817 of letters from Quinette de Rochemont of 6 Aug. and Victor du Pont and Eleuthère I. du Pont de Nemours of 11 Aug. 1817; addressed: "Mrs Randolph. Monticello." In the unextracted portion of this letter, Ellen W. Randolph (Coolidge) describes her nieces Pat (Martha Jefferson Randolph [Taylor]) and Margaret S. Randolph (Randolph); mentions the birth of Mary Mansfield Smith (Nicholas), the daughter of Cary Ann Nicholas Smith and John Spear Smith; describes her letter as being full of nonsense; sends greetings to the whole family, including "both my Aunts and their daughters"; and in a postscript expresses her displeasure at her aunt Mary Randolph for not sending any pocket handkerchiefs; says that they have sent back their spare clothes and books in anticipation of returning home; requests that Sally Cottrell (Cole) unpack her trunk and that Martha Jefferson Randolph take charge of the books, as some are borrowed; and states that she found *La Eudoxia* dull despite the recommendation of Elizabeth Goodwin Stevenson and George P. Stevenson.

For the *Colloquia* of Mathurin Cordier (CORDERY), see Ellen W. Randolph (Coolidge) to Martha Jefferson Randolph, [ca. 10 Nov. 1816]. FEAST OF REASON AND A FLOW OF SOUL comes from Alexander Pope's works in imitation of Horace (Pope, *The First Satire of the Second Book of Horace* [London, 1733], 39). François Perón (PERON) described various African peoples in his *Voyage de découvertes aux terres Australes*, 4 vols. (Paris, 1807–16). The character LARRY Brady admonishes himself, as quoted above, in a letter to his brother Pat in Maria Edgeworth, *The Absentee* (New York, 1812; first published in London the same year as part of her *Tales of Fashionable Life*), 1:237, 239.

[1] Preceding three words interlined in place of "unconscionable."

[2] Reworked from what appears to be "making a day of it."

[3] Omitted opening parenthesis editorially supplied.

[4] Omitted closing quotation mark editorially supplied.

[5] Omitted opening quotation mark editorially supplied.

[6] Omitted closing quotation mark editorially supplied.

IV. Cornelia J. Randolph to Virginia J. Randolph (Trist)

poplar Forest Aug. 30 1817

I am very much oblig'd to you my Dear Virginia for your two letters & am quite outrageous at Elizabeth Harriet & Mary's neglecting me so, however I will write to Harriet if I have time because I promis'd her faithfully to do so, Johnny does not go untill day after to morrow but to morrow sister Ellen & myself have to paste numbers on all of grand papa's books & it will take us nearly the whole day which I am very sorry for because besides wishing to write another letter I should like very well to have copied a beautiful Desdemona from Shakespear which I am afraid I cant do now for I only draw on sundays, & after this we shall only be here one more sunday & there is more to do in it than I can do in a day but to go on with our journey to the Natural bridge after we had cross'd that delightful mountain where the[1] temperature of the air was the most charming that I ever felt & [. . .] [the richest,?][2] the streams the most clear & rapid & the prospect which we saw here & there through the openings of the trees the finest I ever saw, we came to a level part of the country that was entirely clear'd & in cultivation & surrounded every where by mountains, when we had gone a mile or two grandpapa call'd to us to look back & I never was more supris'd than to see the mountain we had cross'd so long that it seem'd from that distance to extend at least half way round the horizon, in one continu'd & unbroken ridge, the next day tho' we saw one still longer, the mountains here are of entirely a different shape from those in Albemarle they are not round & regular as ours are but some are these long ones & others are shap'd like sugar loaves, one that we saw the sides seem'd quite as perpendicular as those of a sugar loaf, I suppose it must be impossible to climb up it. when we got to Greenlee's the house was an excelent brick house as well built as the houses of Lynchburg & there were three others building in the same yard two of brick & one of stone the one we went into was well finish'd in the inside but the filthiest place, I could not help thinking of sister Ellens wondering when she was a little girl if the house in which she was had been sweep'd today & the people & the children look'd as if their cloths never had been taken off since they were put on new. I felt exactly as if the place was polluted. I could not bear to touch any thing, & at night they carried us into a very good little room but the sheets of our bed were dirty & we were oblig'd to sleep on the outside this night as sister Ellen had such a dreadful pain in the face that she walked up and down the room all night & did not sleep at all, grandpapa said he had a very nice comfortable bed but he slept in the room with two or three people. the next day it rain'd as hard as it could pour untill one oclock it held up then & we went to the bridge tho' it was showery all day, about two or three hundred yards from the bridge Patrick Henry a mulatto man lives, on the land of the widow Ochiltree he keeps the key of the shot tower & generally goes with persons who go to see the bridge he went with us, we knew the instant we were on the bridge & I cant concieve how any one can go on it without knowing, for you see the sides of the precipice; on looking down it has very much the effect on your head that looking down a well has, we stood on the edge & look'd down with perfect safety, & afterwards look'd out of the shot tower window, it is impossible to judge of the height from the top but when you go down & see how large objects are which you thought quite small you are astonish'd I thought I saw fern growing remarkably close to the ground & afterwards found out it was young walnut trees about 3 or four feet high we saw a barrel sunk almost entirely in to the ground which prov'd to be a thing made to protect some of the shot works about 8 feet high, the stream below look'd like a little branch & was in reality larger than Moores creek, what I took for stepping stones were large rocks large enough for us all to set on together with the greatest ease but above all what gave us the best idea of the heighth was a linen tube reaching from top to bottom, looking out of the window we thought it must be a great deal smaller at bottom than at top although it was so long but we found it was the same size all the way. There was only one steep difficult path to get down the hill & after we got there we found that a dam had been made which together with the rise of the water prevented us entirely from getting under the bridge & we should have been oblig'd to come away with scarcely an idea of the bridge if it had not been for the exertions of Patrick Henry who worked for nearly an hour to contrive us a way by which we might get along, which he did by laying planks & logs from one point of the rock to another with great difficulty we succeeded & then the scene was beyond any thing you can imagine possibly; I always thought the scene of the storm in the antiquary was unnatural but now I can easily believe it possible for had the water risen higher where we were the[re would?] have been no possibility of getting out of its way the least rise would have prevented us from returning the way we came & we could no more climb up the rock than we could up any other high wall but I believe it was at its highest for it did not rise while we were there tho' we staid untill 5 oclock in the evening, afterwards we walk'd about a quarter of a mile down a steep path to a cave the entrance into this cave would make a beautiful picture, the rocks rise to a great distance above your head, & before you is the stream which runs under the bridge & a little island but we were told that it was an island only when the water was very high, we could not stand upright in the cave but in two or three places because a great quantity of stones & dirt had been thrown into it which had been dug to make salt petre grandpapa said he would have them all taken out & have a path made to the cave from the bridge & the dam taken away, & several other improvements made, when we went in it was so cold that we did not stay there long enough to see what the temperature was by the thermometer being afraid of taking cold after heating ourselves by scrambling among the rocks. when we return'd we had to cross the river & found we had just got there in time to be able to get over it was rising so fast it rose six inches in the time that they came over in the boat & return'd with us, & it is not very wide here the people said they never remember'd to have seen it rise so fast. Adieu my Dear Virginia. I have neither time nor paper to write any more & I dare say this will more than satisfy you yours C.R.

RC (NcU: NPT); damaged at seal and holes in manuscript; addressed: "Miss Virginia Randolph Monticello."

In chapter seven of Sir Walter Scott's novel, THE ANTIQUARY (Edinburgh, 1816), several characters are trapped on a cliff when the tide rises quickly after a storm.

[1]Manuscript: "the the."
[2]Phrase illegible.

V. Extract of Cornelia J. Randolph to Virginia J. Randolph (Trist) and Mary Elizabeth Randolph (Eppes)

My Dear girls Monticello September 24 ..17

I wrote Virginia another very long letter from poplar forest giving her an account of our journey to the Natural bridge but it arriv'd after you had left this place, I dare say you have met with nothing wilder & more savage than we did traveling on horse back through a country where there was no carriage road. we made a great many enquiries about bears, wolves, panthers, & rattle snakes & found they were nearly exterminated which I was very much surprised at seeing the country look'd as if it had scarcely any other inhabitants, we heard tho that a bear had eaten a child sometime before we were there & that wolves were frequently[1] heard howling in the mountains. in the immediate neighbourhood of the bridge the people were more civiliz'd than they were just on this side of the ridge. When we were returning to poplar forest we came to a bridge which had been broken down & that a good many people were mending, they imediately brought logs & laid across from one bank to the other but these banks were very high & the bridge form'd in this hasty manner so dangerous that I could scarcely prevail on myself to follow sister Ellen whom grandpapa was leading on before, a man bare legg'd & without any coat on immediately came to my assistance & led me across in safety another instance of the gallantry of our countrymen on this side of the ridge, I do not know what it is on the other side, I dare say Virginia remembers our being help'd by some waggoners, in a very dangerous situation once before, & sister Ellen who has travel'd more than any of us, has more than once had occasion to remark the difference between Virginians & the people of the other states in this respect.

RC (NcU: NPT); extract, consisting of salutation, dateline, and middle portion of letter, which is signed "C.R." In the unextracted sections of this letter Randolph relates her initial dismay that the recipients left for the springs while she was away but consoles herself that she has been promised a trip there next year and a visit to Richmond in the current autumn; states that "Grandpapa has given his note for our trip to Richmond & if Elizabeth goes I shall like it very well, Sister Ellen & myself are anxious that Virginia should accompany us, but I am afraid there is very little probability of it"; comments that the Rivanna River was too high to cross in order to visit Ashton; mentions that Ann C. Bankhead had come the previous day with her son Thomas Mann Randolph Bankhead, who was recovering from an illness; remarks that as the younger Bankhead grows up he looks less like a Randolph, while he once resembled Martha Jefferson Randolph's children as well as Arthur M. Randolph; indicates that she and Ellen W. Randolph (Coolidge) have been studious while away, but that she is unable to settle down to a routine until they are all home and have discussed their travels; and sends greetings to her aunt Mary Randolph.

Mary Elizabeth Cleland Randolph (Eppes) (1801–35), known within the family as Elizabeth, was the daughter of TJ's cousin Thomas Eston Randolph and Thomas Mann Randolph's sister Jane Cary Randolph. She was born at Dungeness plantation in Goochland County, grew up in Albemarle County at the family estates of Glenmore and Ashton, and became intimate with the family at Monticello, particularly TJ's granddaughters. Late in 1822 she became the first wife of TJ's grandson Francis Eppes and moved with him to Poplar Forest soon afterwards. After the Eppes family sold Poplar Forest in 1828, Francis traveled to Florida Territory to purchase land. Elizabeth and their children joined him the following year in Leon County at property near Tallahassee. Her parents and several siblings also relocated in 1829 to Florida and settled nearby. Eppes died at her residence in Leon County several days after the birth of her sixth child (Shackelford, *Descendants*, 1:172–8; Randolph Whitfield and John Chipman, *The Florida Randolphs, 1829–1978* [2d ed., 1987], 22–8, 32–3, 58, 61; *Richmond Enquirer*, 1 May 1835; *Episcopal Recorder* 13 [16 May 1835]: 27; gravestone inscription in cemetery of Saint John's Episcopal Church, Tallahassee).

[1]Manuscript: "ferquently."

From George Ticknor

DEAR SIR, Paris Aug. 14.[1] 1817.

Your favour of June 6 reached me July 29 and contained—what I had long desired—the very welcome intelligence, that the Books Mr. Warden shipped from Havre and those I sent from Hamburg had reached you in good condition and met your approbation. Yesterday your duplicate of the same letter arrived, together with your order to the Messrs. De Bure. In this order I made but two alterations—one indicated by yourself, that of Schweigheuser's Herodotus, which was not published when I mentioned the other editions in my letter from Göttingen of Oct. 14. 1815—and one, of which I presume you had no knowledge—Durot de la Malle's translation of Livy in 10. 8vo which is much better than the translation of Guerin as well as more recent & in the form you prefer. On the whole[2] of the catalogue I consulted Mons. le Chevalier, whose Voyage de la Troade you had ordered; & who approved these changes but made no others. In this state, your order will be immediately executed and the books sent to America in the course of this month.

I have been in Paris about five months, & am now preparing to move slowly Southward, in the intention[3] of entering Italy in the first days of October and passing the winter there to finish my study of its language & literature.—In the Spring—extraordinary revolutions excepted—I purpose to pass into Spain with the same objects I have in Italy—spend a little time in Portugal & in the fall return to England, where I shall probably divide the winter between Edinboro' & London and, in May 1819 embark for America.—If, in the course of this series of Journies, I can be of any service to you, I hope it is not necessary for me to say, I am entirely at your disposal.—

In France, my expectations have been, in part exceeded—&, in part, disappointed, respecting the state of publick Instruction. After all the changes of the Revolution, you will recollect, that the System of national Education was fixed by Buonaparte in two decrees, one of 1808 & the other of 1811. By this System, all France was formed into one University as it was called, which was subdivided in Lycea, Colleges, Schools &c so that every Institution[4] in the Empire, of whatever kind, & whether publick or private was made a part of it & all depended on a Grand Master, who was endowed with extraordinary powers to keep the whole immense machine in just movement. It was, in fact, from what I can learn, & even what I see, an appalling system of military education and the whole University was a kind of grand military cloister, which, if it could have been made to operate in the spirit in which it was devised, would have blasted the whole land with the mildew of its influences. This, however, was not possible. It was in vain that severe laws were[5] enacted, & a kind of police introduced into the system of Education—it was in vain that the Professors & teachers were clothed with the power & took the tone of Officers rather than Instructers—and that their Disciples were dressed in uniform often and often marched to their exercises by the beat of the Drum—for here, as in his system of Government, Buonaparte seemed to think he could do the work of centuries in a single generation. But, though he could not anticipate the future in this, as he did in his conscriptions & taxes, he could obliterate the past & so faithfully has he done it, that no traces of the ancient style of instruction remain, and almost the means of restoration seem to be wanting. In the physical[6] & exact sciences, I presume there is nothing in Europe like Paris—; but in all that relates to what is commonly called Learning England & Germany vastly exceed her. Nothing, I imagine, in the world, can be brought to oppose the sixty four members of the Academy of Sciences;—but the three other Academies could ill meet the learned men of the North. The reason is, I suppose, that this has been the nature of the publick demand, which in all such matters always creates its own supply.—It is not, therefore, astonishing, that after an interval of thirty years of neglect, Learning does not come into the new order of things by Adhesion like wealth & power & rank. The Bourbons must reign, a long time in peace before they can have even an age of scholarship again, and, as to their Augustan age, I take it for granted from the principles of their language & the history of national talent, that this has gone by forever, and that futurity can have no Louis XIV for them.—In form, every thing rests now as it did, when Buonaparte left it—a desolate & inefficient University—except that there is no grand Master; but a commission of five with the Minister of the Interior at its head—& that the military tone & spirit no longer forces its defilement into the halls of Instruction. The lectures, in the mathematical & physical sciences, are, I am told, such as to leave nothing more to desire—on all the other subjects of publick Instruction they are bad. Solitary individuals give courses on History, Criticism, Belles-Lettres, Archeology &c &c that are much followed but a simple & severe style of teaching is not known. The Lecturer, to be popular, makes his lessons approach in a greater or less degree to that sort of spectacle wh. the genius of the French people requires in everything, so that when I go to hear Lacretelle, Villemain, Andrieux &c it is for the same reasons & with the same feelings, I go to y[e] Theatre. Excuse me for writing you so long a letter on a matter which you, no doubt, understand so well already, that I can tell you nothing new. Let me finish, then, by Saying to you, that I feel very grateful for your letters and for the kind expressions they contain of your regard & that of your family, which, I hope, I shall study to deserve.—

Your's respectfully GEO: TICKNOR.

P. S. Before closing my letter, it occurs to me, that it is probable you are acquainted with Mr. Irving our Minister at Madrid; & if you are, that you will perhaps do me the favour to give me your countenance in an introductio[n] to him, which you can forward through my father.—If this request be in the least inconvenient to you, I pray you, that it may be, as if it had never been made.— G. T.—

RC (DLC); torn at seal; addressed: "Thomas Jefferson, Esquire, Monticello, Albermarle County, Virginia"; stamped "Forwarded by your obedient servants Welles Williams & Greene Havre 18 " and "SHIP"; franked; postmarked Baltimore, 7 Nov.; endorsed by TJ as received 11 Nov. 1817 and so recorded in SJL.

For the TWO DECREES, see *Bulletin des Lois de l'Empire Français* 8 (1808): 145–71; 15 (1812): 425–56. The Académie des Sciences of the Institut de France was comprised of sixty-five members, not SIXTY FOUR. The THREE OTHER ACADEMIES were the Académie Française, the Académie des Inscriptions et Belles-Lettres, and the Académie des Beaux-Arts (Charles Franquet, comte de Franqueville, *Le Premier Siècle de l'Institut de France* [1895], 26–7).

[1] Reworked from "12."
[2] Word interlined in place of "rest."
[3] Manuscript: "intendion."
[4] Manuscript: "Instution."
[5] Ticknor here canceled "established."
[6] Word interlined in place of "mathematical."

From James Maury

DEAR SIR, Liverpool 15 Aug[t] 1817

In my letter of the 7th November last I mentioned the loss I was to sustain in my friend mr Gwathmey's being about to return to Virginia: this is intended to be delivered to you by that friend, whom I request you to favor with your civilities.

Tobacco is falling in price & so is Flour, which had been at 80/. but is now about 50/. ℔ barrel: Cotton, contrary to all expectation, is high: of 143.000 Bales imported into this place from all countries since the 1st Jany to the 30th June last, the United States furnish two thirds!

I am your old obliged friend JAMES MAURY

RC (DLC); at foot of text: "Thomas Jefferson Monticello"; endorsed by TJ as received 7 Nov. 1817 and so recorded in SJL.

Robert Gwathmey (1778–1855), merchant, was a native of Virginia. He partnered in a Richmond firm that was variously known as Robert & Temple Gwathmey and Temple & Robert Gwathmey. About 1810 Gwathmey moved to Liverpool, England, to represent the firm's interests there, and he stayed until 1817. He became a director of the Bank of Virginia in 1819 and worked as a tobacco and commission agent in Richmond until at least 1852 (*VMHB* 16 [1908]: 213; *MB*, 2:1233; Richmond *Enquirer*, 8 May 1810; *Liverpool Mercury, Or Commercial, Literary, and Political Herald*, 28 July 1815; Washington *Daily National Intelligencer*, 15 Aug. 1818; *American Beacon and Norfolk & Portsmouth Daily Advertiser*, 11 Jan. 1819; *Richmond Enquirer*, 26 Nov. 1830, 30 June 1835; DNA: RG 29, CS, Richmond, 1850; William L. Montague, *The Richmond Directory and Business Advertiser, For 1852* [(1852)], 62; *Richmond Whig and Public Advertiser*, 13 Mar. 1855; gravestone inscription in Shockoe Hill Cemetery, Richmond).

From Robert Walsh

August 15[t] 1817 M[t] Pleasant near Philadelphia

I have requested the Bookseller to transmit at once by Post to M[r] Jefferson his Copy of the 2[d] Vol: of the American Register & to Correct with a pen the errors of phrase which would have been avoided, if my position had allowed me to revise the proof-sheets more attentively. I trust that M[r] Jefferson will be pleased with my (too hasty) translation of M[r] de Marbois' work. I have the honor to be, his very ob[t] Servt ROBERT WALSH J[R]

RC (DLC); dateline at foot of text; addressed: "Thomas Jefferson Esqre"; endorsed by TJ as received 21 Sept. 1817 and so recorded in SJL.

Walsh's TRANSLATION of Barbé Marbois, *Complot d'Arnold et de Sir Henry Clinton contre Les États-Unis d'Amérique et contre le Général Washington. Septembre 1780* (Paris, 1816; Poor, *Jefferson's*

Library, 4 [no. 138]; TJ's copy in MoSW) appeared in the *American Register; or Summary Review of History, Politics, and Literature* (Poor, *Jefferson's Library*, 14 [no. 926]) 2 (1817): 3–63.

From Joseph C. Cabell

Dear Sir, Edgewood. 18 August. 1817.

I now do myself the pleasure to enclose you the list of English Books sold by Barrois at Paris, agreeably to my promise to you at Mr Madison's. Upon examination I find there are but few works, which you would probably wish to purchase. You would oblige me by the return of the catalogue[1] at some future day, as I shall wish to make use of it from time to time. But I shall not want it for a good while.

I have sent subscription papers enclosed in letters of explanation to the following persons in the following counties & places—Campbell, Col: Wm J. Lewis—Lynchburg, Doct: George Cabell. Amherst, Roderick M^c^Cullock, Edmund Winston, Robert Walker, John Camm, Thos Eubanks, Sterling Claiborne, Hill Carter, & David S. Garland (without a letter). Nelson, Robert Rives & Spottswood Garland. Powhatan, Wm Pope. Winchester, Henry St George Tucker. Stafford, William Brent. Lancaster, Ellyson Currie. It occurred to me, after we separated, that it was very doubtful whether the counties of the northern neck would contribute anything. It seemed to be the wish of yourself and Mr Madison, & the general understanding, that, except in the counties where a local interest would operate, the subscription papers should not be exhibited without a well grounded hope of success. The counties of the northern neck are not in my view locally connected with Albemarle in regard to the Central College, and having suffered excessively by the war, will probably have but little, if any money to spare. yet there are some liberal men in those counties, particularly towards Fredericksburg. I have, therefore, adopted a course somewhat different from the one I promised, and I hope it will be satisfactory to you and the other gentlemen: I wrote to Mr Currie of Lancaster, enclosing him a subscription paper, & requesting him to shew it to some of the most liberal men in the counties of Lancaster, Northumberland, Westmoreland & Richmond, to advise with them on the subject, and, if it should be their opinion that the measure would not meet with a decent support in that quarter, not to exhibit the paper publicly. In the opposite event, I desired him to give it currency and to procure subscribers. To Mr William Brent of Stafford, I wrote to the same effect, in regard to the counties of Stafford, Fairfax and King George. These are liberal, enlightened and active young men, with whom I am intimately acquainted, and are as suitable persons as any that could have been addressed on this occasion.

I fear the subscription in this county, Amherst, & Campbell will be very small. I shall attend Nelson Court on monday, with the view of doing every thing in my power to promote it.

It appeared to be the opinion of so many of my friends that the publication of the catalogue of subscribers would be attended with no advantage, that I have declined for the present to trouble Mr Ritchie with a request to that effect. Should it be the opinion of yourself & the other Visitors, when we meet in Septr, that such publication would be advantageous, I will then cause it to take place.

A genteel, sensible young man passed here yesterday on his way from the upper part of the northern neck. He had called at the Houses of many of the best informed people in the course of his journey: and heard every where the Central College spoken of in very high terms.

I am very happy to hear that the Albemarle subscription already amounts to nearly $30,000.

On my return from Mr Madison's, I found my mother had relapsed. The fever continued for four weeks, at the end of which, all remedies proving unsuccessful, we had the affliction to lose her.

I remain, Dr Sir, very sincerely yours JOSEPH C. CABELL

P. S. I have just copied your manuscript on meteorological subjects, in which you have condensed a vast variety of most instructive & amusing information. It is astonishing how you could find time, in the midst of your other engagements to make such a prodigious number of observations. I enclose the paper to Mr Madison by to-day's mail.

RC (ViU: TJP-PC); addressed: "Mr Jefferson Monticello"; endorsed by TJ as received <*28*> 29 Aug. 1817 and so recorded in SJL. Enclosure: an unidentified number of the *Catalogue des Livres Anglais qui se trouvent chez T. Barrois fils*, serially issued by the Paris bookseller Louis Théophile Barrois.

Cabell's MOTHER, Hannah Carrington Cabell, died on 7 Aug. 1817 after a thirty-six-day illness (*Richmond Enquirer*, 26 Aug. 1817). The MANUSCRIPT ON METEOROLOGICAL SUBJECTS was TJ's Analysis of his Weather Memorandum Book, printed above at the end of January 1817.

[1] Manuscript: "cataIougue."

To Patrick Gibson

DEAR SIR Poplar Forest Aug. 17. [18] 17.

Your's of Aug. 11. came to hand yesterday & I now inclose the note of 3000.D. for the bank of the US. signed. I note the observations on the articles of 250.D. which I recollect, that of the 31. D of which I had not before been ascertained, and the 10. respecting which I have not the papers here, but I presume your corrections are right as to that as well as the others. accept the renewal of assurances of my friendship & respect. TH: JEFFERSON

PoC (DLC: TJ Papers, ser. 10); on verso of reused address cover of Thomas Humphreys to TJ, 2 July 1817; misdated; at foot of text: "Mr Gibson"; endorsed by TJ as a letter of <*17*> 18 Aug. 1817 and so recorded in SJL. Enclosure not found.

From Francis W. Gilmer

DEAR SIR. Winchester. 18th August 1817.

I am penetrated with regret at the death of your illustrious friend, and I would fain call him mine—Mr. DuPont (de Nemours)—It is a consolation to me that I had redeemed before his death every promise which I ever made him.—His treatise on National Education was translated, of which I apprized him before I heard that he was indisposed. So long as he lived his own genius preserved the freshness, & lustre of his honors, and I was less solicitous about the translation—I knew that I could add nothing to his reputation; I was unwilling to borrow any thing from it. Now that he is no more, you owe it to friendship, and I to gratitude, to do what is best for the memory of a Patriot, a Philanthropist, and a Philosopher. .. Direct me, for it is properly your office, what to do with the translation. If the compliment could flatter the affection of his friends, I would willingly consent to violate the dictates of my own discretion in publishing it. But you know the jealousy of French Books in the U.S., especially of such as have appeared in the last 25 years, more particularly on moral subjects, & most of all on education. The essay certainly teems with the spirit of innovation which was the fashion of the day. Innovation at present, however necessary, is not popular; and while I admire the genius & eloquence of your departed friend—I fear that the publication of his work might not be successful. I never had a hope that his scheme would be adopted: the time has not yet arrived for so philosophical a system of education. I translated it as a compliment to him, for his many distinguished favors, and as due to my friendship for you—I have shewn him my gratitude, & you my esteem—so if you please, let the work remain with us. You have already superseded it by a more practical plan.

Before dismissing the subject however, permit me to ask your assistance in translating a single sentence. It is in a note on page 13 of Mr. DuPonts pamphlet, in case you should not have the book, I transcribe the whole paragraph.

"Ma brochure oubliée, j'ai vainement tenté d'en faire adopter les principes, a quelques amis; presque personne n'a voulu renouveller mon expérience. On s'en est constamment tenu, dans mon pays, aux diverses variétés du bureau typographique, qui depuis soixante-dix ans, sont encore des nouveautés, et n'ont pas même pénétré dans les petites écoles, ou la méthode de M. Choron n'a fait aussi que peu de progrés." The first sentence is obvious enough, but I do not understand to what the expressions 'aux diverses variétés du bureau typographique,' and 'sont encore des nouveautés.' refer.

I am also at a loss to know how to render the expression 'la chimie docimastique' in another part of the work,[1] we have no such word as 'docimastic,' and the french word docimastique is not in the dictionaries; I have supposed it to be one of the words of the French neology, and to be derived from Δοκιμαζω (exploro) meaning as applied to chemistry, analytic. I would not venture on my own conjecture—so please to instruct me.

I inclose for Mrs. Randolph a few seeds of the plant which has been dedicated to you, under the name Jeffersonia. It is not very beautiful but is curious, and its name will I am sure recommend it to her piety. It grows in deep, shady bottoms, like the May apple [podophyllum peltatum.]. The seeds came from Harpers Ferry, where all the regions of nature have conspired to do you honor.

accept the assurance of my admiration & esteem

F. W. GILMER.

P.S. I received letters from Ticknor lately, he always mentions his visit to Monticello with the most flattering recollections... Mr Corrêa is in the East, he & Walsh have promised to be in Virginia in September.

RC (MoSHi: Gilmer Papers); ellipses and brackets in original; postscript on verso of address cover; addressed: "Thomas Jefferson esquire Monticello," with "Charlottsville V^{a}" added in an unidentified hand, then redirected in another hand to "Lynchburg"; franked; postmarked Winchester, 20 Aug.; endorsed by TJ as received 11 Sept. 1817 and so recorded in SJL.

The passage in Pierre Samuel Du Pont de Nemours's work beginning MA BROCHURE OUBLIÉE can be translated thus: "My pamphlet having been forgotten, I tried in vain to persuade various friends to adopt my method. Almost no one wanted to repeat my experiment. In my country we continue to cling to the several varieties of typographic bureau, which after seventy years are still considered novelties and do not even extend to small schools, where Mr. Choron's method has likewise made little progress" (Du Pont de Nemours, *Sur l'éducation nationale dans les États-Unis d'Amérique* [2d ed., Paris, 1812; Poor, *Jefferson's Library*, 5 (nos. 207, 209–10)], 12–3). TJ supplied his own translation of this passage in his 14 Oct. 1817 reply to Gilmer.

The BUREAU TYPOGRAPHIQUE ("typographic desk") had compartments for each letter, number, and punctuation sign. Developed in 1732 by the French educator Louis Dumas to teach children to read and write, it was used like a case of printers' type to compose words and sentences (Dumas, *La Bibliothèque des enfans ou les Premiers Elemens des lettres contenant le système du bureau typographique* [Paris, 1732]; Marcel Grandière, "Louis Dumas et le système typographique, 1728–1744," *Histoire de l'éducation* 81 [1999]: 35–62). In 1802 the French mathematician and musicologist Alexandre Étienne CHORON introduced a new method to teach reading and writing based on his work in music composition (Choron, *Méthode Prompte et Facile Pour apprendre en même temps à lire, à écrire, à suivre l'orthographe et à bien prononcer* [Paris, 1801]; *Musical Library Monthly Supplement* 10 [1835]: 115).

Du Pont de Nemours argues that the United States needs a school of mines with a professor of LA CHIMIE DOCIMASTIQUE ("docimastic chemistry" or "the science of assaying minerals") (Du Pont de Nemours, *Sur l'éducation nationale*, 126, 137).

[1] Preceding six words interlined.

From Randolph Harrison

DEAR SIR, Clifton 18th Augt 1817

Yesterday's mail brought me your letter of the 4th instt, and I avail myself of its return, to assure you of the heartfelt pleasure I enjoy, at the prospect of seeing a seminary of learning established in our State, upon so enlarged and liberal a scale. The favourable auspices under which it has commenced, afford the most flattering views of a successful issue. It will be pleasing to me to yield my feeble support, to a plan so honourable to its founders, and promising so much benefit to our country. I fear however, as you recede from the scite destined for the central college, you will find a diminution of zeal, and liberality, greater than you anticipate. Particularly since it seems to be in the contemplation of our leading men, to disseminate learning through the state, by institutions of a similar kind in all the counties. Yet we must believe from the general character of our fellow citizens, that a number will be found possessing a sufficient stock of publick spirit, to call forth their pecuniary aid in this principal establishment.

The kind and friendly sentiments conveyed by your letter, are highly gratifying to me, as all your affectionate attentions have been. Be assured of my affection, and my earnest prayers, that this most laudable effort, may be crowned with a success, which will add largely to your claims upon the gratitude of the present, and succeeding generations.

Very respectfully Yours RANDOLPH HARRISON

RC (MHi); endorsed by TJ as received <*28*> 29 Aug. 1817 and so recorded in SJL.

To Chapman Johnson

[Dea]r Sir Poplar forest Aug. 17. [18] 17.

I now inclose you mr Divers's answer given without form or the ceremony of an oath. his health, and hurry to depart for the springs rendered it necessary to dispense with useless formalities. I furnished the def[s] with a copy of the bill some months ago, but I know nothing of the progress of their answers. as soon as they shall be given in, I will pray you to send me office copies as guides in examining witnesses. the same copies shall be returned to you for the use of counsel. I wish all unnecessary delay avoided, as the locks will soon be impassable and I can permit no fundamental repairs till my right is cleared. the passage of produce will of course be stopped to the great prejudice of the upper land holders on the river. I salute you with great esteem & respect

Th: Jefferson

PoC (MHi); on verso of a reused address cover from Christopher Clark to TJ; misdated; salutation faint; at foot of text: "M[r] Johnson"; endorsed by TJ as a letter of <*17*> 18 Aug. 1817 and so recorded in SJL. Enclosures: (1) George Divers's Answer to Interrogatories in *Jefferson v. Rivanna Company*, [ca. 23 July 1817]. (2) TJ's Notes on Divers's Answer to Interrogatories in *Jefferson v. Rivanna Company*, [after 23 July 1817]. Enclosed in TJ to Martha Jefferson Randolph, 18 Aug. 1817.

To Martha Jefferson Randolph

Poplar Forest Aug. 18. 17.

I inclose the within, to you, my dearest daughter & friend, because it is of great consequence, to be put into the post office at Charlottesville from which place it will go safer to Staunton than from hence. Ellen writes to you and of course will give the news of this place if she can muster up any. the history of our expedition to the Natural bridge she will write you of course. the sun, moon and stars move here so much like what they do at Monticello, and every thing else so much in the same order, not omitting even the floods of rain, that they afford nothing new for observation. it will not be new that we give all our love to young & old, male & female of the family, and our kisses to Septimia particularly, with gingerbread which she will prefer to them.

Th: Jefferson

RC (NNPM); addressed (torn): "M[rs] Mar[...]"; endorsed by Randolph. Not recorded in SJL. Enclosure: TJ to Chapman Johnson, [18] Aug. 1817, and enclosures.

Based on TJ's consistent misdating of letters written and received at Poplar Forest in August 1817, this letter may actually have been written on 19 Aug. 1817.

To Philip Thornton

Dear Sir Poplar Forest Aug. 17. [18] 17.

A visit to the Nat[l] bridge, from which I am just returned, presents me an occasion of saying what indeed I have for some time been intending to say to you; for it is some time since I was informed that you had discontinued the business of shot-making there. I suppose that of course you would rather be rid of your lease; & certainly I do not wish to recieve a rent for the use of a thing of which you make no use. the object of the present letter therefore is to propose that on your returning to me the lease, & naming the day of your abandonment of the manufacture, it shall be considered as having ceased from that day. in that case you will of course instruct some one to dispose of all your moveable utensils there. I think to fit up the little shot-house on the bridge, and the one at the dam, as sheltering houses for the company visiting the place, & to break up the dam, which reflows the water up under the bridge, so as to render it impracticable to get there. this was it's state, the other day, there being a small swell in the stream. I think also to have some other[1] work done there which may give a good walk from the bridge up to the cave. I shall remain at this place till the middle of Sep. till which time therefore a letter will find me here, and afterwards at Monticello. I salute you with assurances of great esteem & respect Th: Jefferson

PoC (MHi); misdated; at foot of text: "Doct[r] Philip Thornton"; endorsed by TJ as a letter of <*17*> 18 Aug. 1817 and so recorded in SJL. Enclosed in TJ to Thornton, 8 Jan. 1818.

[1] Word interlined.

To Thomas Appleton

D[r] Sir Aug. 19. [20]

On the 1st inst. I dispatched the Original of which the preced[g] is a dupl. thro' mr V.[1] and soon after the departure of the mail I rec[d] one from mr Carmigniani of Apr. 11. by this I found that he had not rec[d] mine of July 18. and on recurring to your diff[t] lres I found that none of them acknol[d] the rec[t] of the one of the same date written to you. I conclude with certainity therefore that that packet miscarried, altho' sent thro the Sec[y] of St's office with a request that it might go under the protection of his first consular dispatches for you. I regret this much, because I must have been suffering in the opn of the family from so long an apparent silence, when in truth those letters were full on the subject of their affairs in my hands, and I never doubted their being safely rec^{d}. this loss however will be now fully supplied by the preceding lre to you, and by the one of this date to mr Carmign. now enclosed. I leave it open for your perusal that as you have been our channel of confidence hitherto you may[2] know fully what passes. when you shall have read it, be so good as to stick a wafer in it & deliver it. mr Fancelli suffers also by this miscarriage as his money lies still in the bank [...] & unproductive.[3] this will be confided to the Sec. of St's office, in the[4] hope it will be more fortunate than the last, thro' the same channel & that should the original thro' mr V. miscarry this may supply it's loss. I repeat to you the assurance of my gr^{t} frdshp & esteem. TH:J.

Dft (DLC: TJ Papers, 211:37615); on verso of RC of Craven Peyton to TJ, 23 July 1817; misdated and partially dated; edge trimmed and under tape; at foot of text: "Mr Appleton"; illegible and probably unrelated notation adjacent to signature. Recorded in SJL as a letter of <*19*> 20 Aug. 1817. Enclosure: TJ to Giovanni Carmignani, [20] Aug. 1817. Enclosed in TJ to Daniel Brent, [23] Aug. 1817 (noted at TJ to Appleton, 1 Aug. 1817).

[1] Abbreviation for John Vaughan, here and below.

[2] TJ here canceled "possess."

[3] Sentence interlined.

[4] TJ here canceled "certain."

To Giovanni Carmignani

SIR August 19. [20] 1817.

Your letter of Apr. 11. came to hand just as I had dispatched one to mr Appleton, of the 1st inst. on the same subject, which he will probably recieve and communicate to you before this reaches you.

that which you wrote the preceding year, covering a copy of the last will of[1] my deceased friend Mazzei, and the attestations respecting it, had come to hand in due time; & on the 18th of July of the same year (1816) I wrote you an acknolegement of the reciept of these papers, with explanations as to the remittances of the effects of mr Mazzei in this country which might be expected. your letter,[2] last recieved convinces me of the miscarriage of mine which I extremely regret indeed, because the want of the information it contained must have left you so long in a state of anxiety & uncertainty as to a subject interesting to his family and to yourself. I sent the letter thro the office of the Secretary of state, with a request that he would give it the protection of his cover, with his first Consular dispatches to mr Appleton. I wrote to mr Appleton at the same time, on the same subject, and at the date of mine of the 1st inst. I did not yet doubt but that he had recieved it.

your's now at hand first proves to me that my whole packet has miscarried. you have seen, from my letters to mr Mazzei that his lots in Richmond after a long law suit for their recovery, had remained on hand unsold, & deemed unsaleable, until the refusal of our banks to pay their own notes producing a distrust of them, the holders were glad to exchange them for any thing else; and this produced us not only a sale, but at such a price as had never been thought of. all intercourse with Europe was at that time cut off, by the war & close blockade of our harbors, so that the money could not be remitted there, and to place it in our banks which had recently stopped payment, was not to be thought of. in this state of things, I was induced to employ the money myself, really more to save it for my friend than for any occasion I had for it. I wrote him this, at the time, and that, whenever intercourse should be re-opened,[3] I should not be able to withdraw the money from it's investment but by instalments. this appeared to have been thought advantageous by the family, as they requested me, through mr Appleton, to retain the money in my hands, which became in the end a convenience to me. the war & total cessation of commerce and of the sale of produce having left us in a state of entire exhaustion. this misfortune has since been highly aggravated by an unparalleled succession of unfruitful seasons. at the date of my letter to you of July 18. altho' the season till that date had been most inauspicious, yet the hope of a change for the better encoraged me to say to you that a commencement of remittance of principal and interest should be made in this present year (17.) and should be compleated in a 2^d^ & 3^d^ year, by equal portions. but the drought which was prevailing at the date of my letter continued thro' the whole season of the growth of our crops, & produced another almost total failure, insomuch that the price of bread (maize) has been lately at five times what is usual. the present year too has been equally afflicting to the crop of wheat, by such an inundation of the insect called the Hessian fly as has never before been known. a great part of my own crop particularly has not yielded seed; many fields not having produced an ear for every square foot: & many persons turned their cattle on their wheat, to make something from it as pasture. these are calamities to which farmers are liable, and I am a farmer, depending solely on the produce of my fields, & consequently on the caprice of the seasons. after such a disaster then the last year, and so gloomy a prospect for the present, I have not only been unable to make the remittance I had promised, of the 1st portion of principal and interest, but am really afraid to promise it for the next, such are the prospects of the present season: and unwilling, by renewed and precise engagements, to hazard renewed & mortifying breaches of them, I am constrained to sollicit the consent of the family to let the money lie awhile in my hands, & to recieve remittances of it in portions, as I can make them. they may be assured these shall be made as soon and as fast as would be in my power, were I to engage specific sums & dates. the interest I solemnly engage to send them annually, & about this season of the year. I am in hopes that the punctual reciept of the interest from hence will be the same to them, as if recieved from a depository there, while it will be a kind accomodation to me; and I hope this the more as this is really money which I recovered out of the fire for them, by lawsuits & persevering efforts, and which I am certain mr Mazzei, no more than myself, had never hoped to obtain. with respect to the ultimate safety of the principal in my hands, any person from this state can satisfy them that my landed property alone is of more than 50. times the amount of this sum. flattering myself then that, under these circumstances, and where the difference to them is only whether they shall recieve their interest from one person or from another, I shall be indulged with this accomodation, I have remitted to mr Vaughan, my correspondent in Philadelphia, a sum to be invested in a bill payable to mr Appleton, whom I have requested to pay to those authorised to recieve it, a year's interest, to wit, 380.D. 52 cents. altho' I suggest an indulgence indefinite in it's particular term, I have no idea of postponing the commencement of my remittances, by thirds, more than a year or two longer. if the seasons should, against the course of nature hitherto observed, continue constantly hostile to our agriculture, I will certainly relieve myself at once by a sale of property sufficient to refund this whole debt, however disagreeable to curtail the provision for my heirs, while the expectation is reasonable of doing it from the annual profits: and mr Mazzei's representatives will always be free to discontinue the indulgence, if the delay should be protracted unreasonably, and inconveniently to them. the nett proceeds of the sale of the ground in Richmond was 6342. say six thousand three hundred & forty two Dollars, recieved July 14. 1813. if the family consents to my proposal, I will, on being so informed, settle up the back-interest, add it to the principal, send them a specific obligation, & thenceforward remit annually the interest of 6. percent, with portions of the principal, as fast as I shall be able. I think there remains no other item of account between mr Mazzei & myself, except 50.D. paid to the lawyer employed in the recovery, & 20.D. to mr Derieux, by particular request of mr Mazzei.

I wrote all this to mr Appleton in my letter of the 1st instant because he had been the channel of communication with the family on this business, and on the supposition that the marriage of miss Mazzei with mr Pini had determined your agency, requesting mr Appleton at the same time, to pay the remittance of interest to whoever was entitled to recieve it. I shall now be uneasy until I learn that those interested are contented with the arrangement I have been obliged to propose, and therefore asked from mr Appleton, as I now do from yourself, the satisfaction of an early reply. in the meantime I pray you to accept the assurances of my high consideration, esteem & respect

Th: Jefferson

RC (ItPiAFM); misdated; at foot of first page: "M. Carmigniani." PoC (DLC: TJ Papers, 211:37616–7); misdated; edge trimmed; endorsed by TJ as a letter of <*19*> 20 Aug. 1817 and so recorded in SJL. Tr (ItPiAFM); misdated; in Italian. Enclosed in TJ to Thomas Appleton, [20] Aug. 1817, and TJ to Daniel Brent, [23] Aug. 1817 (noted at TJ to Appleton, 1 Aug. 1817).

[1] Manuscript: "of of."
[2] TJ here canceled "just."
[3] Prefix interlined.

To Fernagus De Gelone

Sir Poplar Forest near Lynchburg. Aug. 19. [20] 17.

I recieved yesterday evening, and at this place 80. miles South West from Monticello, your letter of the 5th inst. and lose no time in inclosing you the 8 D. 50 cents, the amount of the books last sent. I am in hopes that notwithstanding the increased distance, they may reach you before your departure. on your return with a new cargo of books I shall be glad to recieve your catalogue as early as possible that I may not be anticipa[ted] by others in my choice. the packet with the Aristophane had safely arrived at Monticello before I left that place. I tender you my best wishes for a safe & prosperous voyage and return.

Th: Jefferson

PoC (MHi); on verso of a reused address cover from Isaac Briggs to TJ; misdated; one word faint; at foot of text: "Mr Fernagus de Gelone"; endorsed by TJ as a letter of 19 Aug. 1817. Recorded in SJL as a letter of <*19*> 20 Aug. 1817.

To John Goodman, Joseph Reed, Isaac Boyer, and William J. Duane

MESSRS GOODMAN, REED, BOYER & DUANE | Poplar Forest near Lynchburg. Aug. 21. [22] 17

Your letter of the 6th inst. is delivered to me at this place with an extract from the Franklin Republican of July 29. in these words. 'Extract of a letter from Virginia. July 13.[1] 1817. the day before yesterday I was at Monticello, & had the gratification to hear the chief of the elevated group there [mr Jefferson][2] express his anxious wish for the success of the democratic republican gubernatorial candidate in Pensylvania—as he says he has no opinion of tool or turnabout politicians just to serve their own aggrandisement.' now I declare to you, gentlemen, on my honor, that I never expressed a sentiment, or uttered a syllable to any mortal living on the subject of the election referred to in this extract. it is one into which I have never permitted even my wishes to enter, entertaining as I do a high respect for both the characters in competition and not doubting that the state of Pensylvania will be happy under the government of either. if any further proof of the falsehood of this letter writer were required, it would be found in the fact that on the 11th of July, when he pretends to have seen me at Monticello, & to have been entrusted by me with expressions so highly condemnable, I was a[t] this place 90. miles South West of that, attending to my harvest here[.] I had left Monticello on the 29th of June, & did not return to it until the 15th of July. the facts of my absence from the one place, & presence at the other, at that date, are well known to many inhabitants of the town of Charlotte[s]ville near the one, & of Lynchburg near the other place.

I am duly sensible of the sentiments of respect with which you are pleas[ed] to honor me in your letter; as I am also of those concerning myself in the resolutions of the respectable Committee of the New market ward, who have been led into error by this very false letter writer. these, I trust, will not be lessen[ed] on either side by my assurance that, considering this as a family questio[n] I do not allow myself to take any part in it, and the less as the issue either w[ay] cannot be unfavorable to republican government. I tender to both parti[es] sincere sentiments of esteem & respect TH: JEFFERSON

PoC (DLC: TJ Papers, 211:37619); on verso of reused address cover to TJ; misdated; edge trimmed; endorsed by TJ as a letter of <*21*> 22 Aug. 1817 and so recorded in SJL. Printed in Philadelphia *Weekly Aurora*, 15 Sept. 1817, and elsewhere.

[1] *Weekly Aurora*: "23."
[2] Brackets in original.

From Hugh Chisholm

Dear sir, Charlottesville, Augt 23rd 17.

I have the satisfaction to inform you, that, in spite of the wet weather, we have completed about eighty thousand bricks; which shall be prepared for burning the last of next week.

I must beg you will not engage the workmen for the building 'till you again hear from me; which shall be before your deporture from Poplor Forest.

The objection which I made, in my letter to you, against the proposition offered by yourself before you left Albemarle, I must yet make, having, as yet, no reason to withdraw it.

I am, respectfully, Hugh Chisholm.

RC (MHi); letter and signature in the hand of Valentine W. Southall; endorsed by TJ as received <*28*> 29 Aug. 1817 and so recorded in SJL. RC (CSmH: JF); address cover only; with PoC of TJ to Matthew Pate, 16 Dec. 1817, on verso; addressed by Southall: "Mr Thomas Jefferson, Poplar Forest, near Lynchburg"; franked; postmarked (faint) Charlottesville, [2]4 Aug.

Notes on Newspaper Subscriptions

[ca. 23 Aug. 1817]

1817. Jan. 25. remitted him 70.D. of which 10.D. was for his paper to May 1. 1817.
June 19. sent him 5.D. to May 1. 18

Duane.

Nat^{l} Intellig^{r}
1813. Oct. 17. pd to Oct. 31. 12.
1817. pd by J.B. 21.D. to Oct. 31. 1[7]

Niles. Weekly register.
1815. Mar. 22. pd to Sep. 16.
1816. Sep. 7. pd to Sep. 1817.
1817. Aug. 23. pd 5.D. to Sep. 18.

Eldredge T. New Y. Sale report
1816. Dec. 23. 5.D. advance

MS (DLC: TJ Papers, 204:36296); on verso of Bill from William Duane to TJ, [before 24 Apr. 1815] (accounted for above at TJ to Nicolas G. Dufief, 24 Apr. 1815); entirely in TJ's hand; undated; edge trimmed.

Duane's paper was the triweekly "country" edition of the Philadelphia *Aurora* (Duane to TJ, 9 Jan. 1817; TJ to Duane, 24 Jan. 1817). j.b.: John Barnes.

To Hezekiah Niles

Poplar Forest near Lynchburg Aug. 22. [23] 17.

Your letter of July 31. came to hand on the 18th inst. at this place, very distant from Monticello. I learn from it with real concern that there is danger of a discontinuance of the Weekly Register, for want of due support. I have found it very valuable as a Repertory of documents, original papers & the facts of the day, and for the ease with which the Index enables us to turn to them. these things are lost as soon as read in a Newspaper. if payment for the paper in advance can save it, I think that no one should object to that. it is as reasonable and as safe for your readers to trust you, as you them. I inclose you a year's subscription to commence at the end of the current year; which was paid by the remittance of September last, and sincerely wish success and continuance to the undertaking, with assurances of my esteem and respect.

TH: JEFFERSON

PoC (DLC: TJ Papers, 211:37620); on recto of portion of a reused address cover from Archibald Robertson to TJ; misdated; at foot of text: "Mr Niles"; endorsed by TJ as a letter of 22 Aug. 1817 to "Niles Henry." Recorded in SJL as a letter of <22> 23 Aug. 1817 to "Niles Henry," with bracketed additional notation: "5.D."

TJ later corrected his SJL entry of the date of receipt of Niles's 31 July 1817 Circular to Prominent Subscribers (printed above at its 5 Aug. covering letter from Niles to TJ) from THE 18TH INST. to 19 Aug. 1817. On 23 Aug. 1817 TJ recorded paying Niles $5 for his subscription to the Baltimore *Niles' Weekly Register* through September 1818 (*MB*, 2:1337).

To Benjamin Henry Latrobe

DEAR SIR; Poplar Forest Aug. 24. [25] 17.

Our letters, crossing one another by the way, have produced some confusion. their dates are as follows, in the margin. I shall be glad to

your lres	when reced	when answd
June 28.	July 15.	July 16
July 24	Aug. 2	Aug. 3.
July 18	Aug. 7.	Aug. 7.
Aug. 12.	Aug. 22.	Aug. 24.

recieve your drawings; but not at this place, to which the mail is uncertain, and I shall be at Monticello nearly as soon as they will. the elevations of pavilions will be most acceptable. I inclose you a very ragged sketch of the one now in hand. I am well aware of all the importance of aspect, and have always laid it down as a rule that in drawing the plan of a house, it's aspect is first to be known, that you may decide whether to give it most front or flank, and also on which side to throw passages & staircases, in order to have the South, whether front or flank unembarrassed for windows. the range of our ground was a law of nature to which we were bound to conform. it is S. 20.° W. we therefore make our pavilions one room only in front, and 1. or 2. in flank as the family of the professor may require. in his apartments, or the best of them, his windows will open to the South. the lecturing room below has the same advantage, by substituting an open passage adjacent instead of a dormitory. the dormitories admit of no relief but Venetian blinds to their window & door, and to the last the shade of the covered way. this will be the less felt too, as the pupils will be in the schoolrooms most of the day.

Volney's Recherches I have no doubt are curious, & marked with the stamp of genius, & I thank you for the offer of their perusal. but they are too bulky to come by mail, & not to be trusted to the stages. I have never moreover paid any attention to Oriental literature, antient or modern, and am therefore not qualified to recieve much edification or perhaps amusement from them. I read with pleasure what you say of Bruce's travels. it strengthens their authority which has been so much impaired by doubt.—a stiffening wrist obliges me now to curtail my letters. with constant esteem and respect your's

TH: JEFFERSON

PoC (DLC: TJ Papers, 211:37621); on verso of reused address cover of Fernagus De Gelone to TJ, 5 Aug. 1817; misdated; at foot of text: "Mr Latrobe"; endorsed by TJ as a letter of <*24*> 25 Aug. 1817 and so recorded in SJL. Enclosure not found.

Latrobe's letter to TJ of JULY 18 was actually dated 28 July 1817. TJ's dates of receipt and response for Latrobe's letter of AUG. 12. do not reflect TJ's ultimate correction of them to 23 and 25 Aug. 1817.

From James Pleasants

DEAR SIR, Goochland 25th Augt 1817

Your letter covering a subscription paper to the Central college reached me at our last court. on that day also I received a letter from General Cocke on behalf of the visitors, directed to my self and several other citizens of this county, who were associated with me, empowering us to solicit subscriptions for the benefit of the institution. Five of us out of seven, were at court, and had a meeting on the subject of the letter, and agreed upon a mode of proceeding. We were strongly impressed with the benefits which would arise from an institution established in that part of the country, under such regulations as the one contemplated will no doubt be placed. The healthfulness & cheapness of the Country are also strong recommendations. Most of the old institutions are so high in the expences attending, that it amounts to a prohibition to parents of small property. I am much in hopes we shall be able to make a respectable collection, though do not anticipate any thing like what has been done in Albemarle. A Copy of the subscription list was sent us, and we were impressed with the opinion that it was very liberal indeed. The subscriptions here will I think be all payable in the 4 instalments, which plan has I think enhanced the amount considerably, & will continue to do so. With sentiments of highest respect, I am dear Sir y[r] ob[t] &c

JAMES PLEASANTS JR

RC (CSmH: JF); endorsed by TJ as received 11 Sept. 1817 and so recorded in SJL. RC (MHi); address cover only; with PoC of TJ to Edmund Bacon, 29 Nov. 1817, on verso; addressed: "Thomas Jefferson esq[r] Monticello Albemarle"; address partially canceled and redirected in an unidentified hand to Lynchburg; stamp canceled; franked; postmarked Goochland Court House, 2 Sept. 1817, and Charlottesville, 6 Sept.

On 5 Aug. 1817 John H. COCKE recorded in his diary that he had "Sent George to Carysbrook & to Carry a letter to Maj[rs] Pleasants Poindexter &c &c of Goochland with a Subscription paper for the Central College" (MS in ViU: JHC).

From James Rawlings

DEAR SIR, Richmond 25 Aug 1817.

Your favour of 31 Ult[o] has remained unanswered for some time, in consequence of an absence from home—

The Statement touching the mill formerly Insured by John Henderson for the legatees of Bennet Henderson, which you have given, is sufficient to shew that the Mutual Assurance Society can have no claim on you for the Insurance thereof—And as all of the demands of the society, now appearing on their Books have originated since the 16th Feb[y] 1809. subsequent to the destruction of the Insured premises, none ought to be required either from you or any other person.

The failure on the part of all persons interested, to give notice of the demolition of the Mill House, has caused the requisitions of the Society to be made, which otherwise would not have been, but the circumstance now being made known, the charges will be relinquished.

With great Respect Y[r] most Ob JAMES RAWLINGS
P Ag[t] M A Sy

RC (MHi); endorsed by TJ as received 21 Sept. 1817 and so recorded in SJL; with TJ's additional notation beneath endorsement: "Henderson's mill house." RC (DLC); address cover only; with PoC of TJ to Thomas Carstairs, 1 Nov. 1817, on verso; addressed: "Thomas Jefferson Esq[r] Monticello near Milton"; stamp canceled; franked; postmarked Richmond, 25 Aug.

From Stephen Cathalan

MY DEAR SIR— Marseilles the 27th August 1817—

I had the honor of adressing you a Long Letter on the 8th July ult^{o}, it's original & 2ta via Havre, with Inclosures;—in this last, was also my Letter to you of the 16th d^{to}, with your Acc^{t} Cur^{t} with me, bearing a Balance in your Favor for F 102–$\frac{98}{100}$^{cs} Brought on a new account;—The 2ta of this Last Letter, with a Packet, unsealed for your Perusal, to the Secretary of the Navy, I Sent it under Cover of D. Strobel Esqr at Bordeaux, who Informed me, on the 1st Ins^{t}, that he was forwarding it by the Ship George, Cap^{n} Funk, to Sail out from that Port, on the 4th & 5th Ins^{t} for new York;

your very kind & acceptable Favor, dated at the P.S. 6th June 17—Reached me under Cover of m^{r} J. Vaughan of Philadelphia, on the 5th Ins^{t} with his Remitance, by your order & for your Acc^{t}, Step^{n} Girard's Draft on Perregaux Lafitte & c^{e} of Paris, unto my order, P^{ble} at 60 Days Sight for F 1364–75–

which I Sent to them[1] to be accepted or vised by them, in order to fix the Day it will be due; they have returned it to me Since, Pay^{ble} on the 10th october next;—as I have observed that it's amount, by your Said Letter is viz—

D^{ars} 200–	for yourself at f 5–$\frac{15}{100}$^{cs} is	F 1030–
& 65–	for your Grandson Thos Jefferson Randolph at d^{to} ℔ D^{ar} is	334–75–
D^{ars} 265–	This Bill as above Calculated cost exactly at Phil^{a} D 265, making at f 5–$\frac{15}{100}$^{cs} on Paris	F 1364. 75

on which very triffling charges are to be Deducted.

The D 200– Mr J. vaughan Remited me for y^{r} Acc^{t} on that Same house of Paris, which they Paid me in their Draft on marseilles on the 1st october 1815 at the Rate or the Exch^{ge} of f 5–$\frac{28}{100}$ ℔ D^{ar} ℔ F 1056–turned out at a more favorable Exch^{ge} for you.

I have taken a due note of the Separate Employment & Invoices, you Request from me out of that amount, or thereabout, to which I will Conform myself; being very happy that you have been Satisfied with the qualities of what I Sent you, & that I am Still not only usefull to you, but to your Good & worthy Grandson and that I may be Soon also to the hh^{ble} Col^{el} James Monroe the Actual President and to a number of your Friends, were forming a Company to Import from this quarter, thro me, once in the year, for their usual Consumption;—They may Rely on my best Cares and attentions in Sending to them, only what will be of the Best choice and at the Lowest Prices;—but you are by the news Papers & Prices Curts already Informed, that on account of the Bad or Short Crops of wines & olive oil, Since Two years and of our apprehension of having a Shorter one this Season, the Prices have Risen, and I cannot flater you to obtain Such wines as you wish, even not So fine at the Prices, they were Invoiced in my Last Invoices.

but the most Important is to have allways the Best qualities tho' they will become dearer on acct of the above mentioned unfortunate Circumstances; as the Duties of Entry are very high with you, but Cost the Same for Good or Common wines; but not So much in Casks, as in Bottles;—I have on Receipt wrote to Mr Fois Durand at Perpignan, to Mr Tournezon at Lédenon & to Messrs Mages & ce of nice Spreafico & the young Sasserno, to these Three Last in a Single Letter; Sending them at Same time, Copies of the Paragraphs of your Said Letter, Relative to your Demands, & the hopes you & I have that the qualities of their wines proved to be Good, will Soon procure Larger ones and Spread "de proche en Proche" in the United States, le bon Gout des vins du Sud de La France et de nice; I have given also a Copy of the Same to Mr Bergasse; who has already prepared—

4 Cases Containing Each 24. Bles old Red wine 96 Bles
1 dto white Dry wine Cassis, facon de Grave 24
5 Cases together 120 Bles[2]

This Dry white wine is very Good to be Drunk with Fresh oisters—no Doubt that, except in Summer, you may Eat fresh ones at monticello from the Cheasapeack;—I have Shipped them on the Brig Eliza Reilly of norfolk Capn willm Small—Bound for norfolk; also—

1 Box Containing 18 Blles of 1 Litre Each Sup fine aix oil
1 Box Containing 12 Large Bottles or Pobans } anchovies
1 Basket Conting 66 lb—maccaroni—[3]

as ℔ Invoice herewith, amounting for your acct *f* 141–40–
The Invoice of the wine, with a Small Basket of Maccaroni for your Grandson Ths Jeffon Randolph as Inclosed in my Letter to him amounts to *f* 151–05—

I herein Inclose also the answers of Messrs Pre Magés & ce amant Spreafico & of the young victor adolphus Sasserno of Nice, this Last aged 24 years, for whom you have been So kind as to obtain the President's Consent or Promise of appointing him as Consul of the united States at nice; Reffering you to their Contents, also for the wine I asked them by your order & for your account; I have not Received Since any further advices or Invoices for it; nor yet any answer for the wines of Ledenon, and Perpignan but I hope to hear Soon about them;

when they will have reached me, I will Ship them with the Remainder of the maccaroni & the Raisins to Compleat your orders; This Brig Eliza Reilly being ready to Sail.

I Congratulate you very Sincerely on the Satisf^{on} you Experience from your Grandson Th^{s} Jefferson Randolph; I wish and I hope that you will for many years enjoy of all your worthy and numerous family in Good health and encreasing in numbers;—for my own Part, I have been & am Still not So fortunate! far from it, with my Deceased Son in Law, & my Daughter his widow; The reward of what I have done for them, was from their Part ungratitude towards me!—the details would be too Long & disagreable; fortunately we don't want any mutual assistance;—I have not been better rewarded by M^{r} J^{us} oliver, who has turned as ungratefull for all what I did for him; on peut Pardonner les Ecarts de Jeunesse, mais les vices du Cœur, C'est bien difficile!

very Gratefull for all your kind Expressions towards me; I am allways, Dear sir, with Great Respect your obedient & Devoted Servant

STEPHEN CATHALAN.

P.S I am remitting the Bills of Loadings to the Collector of the District of norfolk

RC (MHi); at foot of first page: "Thos. Jefferson Esqr &^{a} &^{a} &^{a} Monticello"; endorsed by TJ as received 23 Dec. 1817 and so recorded in SJL.

DE PROCHE EN PROCHE: "little by little." LE BON GOUT ... ET DE NICE: "the good taste of the wines of the south of France and of Nice." WHITE DRY WINE CASSIS, FACON DE GRAVE: a wine from Cassis, Provence, in the style of a white wine from the Graves region in Bordeaux (Jancis Robinson, ed., *The Oxford Companion to Wine* [1994], 196, 462–3).

POBANS: a Provençal name for square glass bottles used for anchovies (*Encyclopédie du Commerçant. Dictionnaire du Commerce et des Marchandises*, ed. Gilbert U. Guillaumin [1837–39], 1:87). The INVOICE HEREWITH enclosed has not been found. ON PEUT PARDONNER ... C'EST BIEN DIFFICILE: "one can forgive the mistakes of youth, but it is difficult to pardon defects of the heart."

1 Manuscript: "to them to them."

2 In the left-hand margin Cathalan indicated that these five cases of wine would be marked $\mathbf{T^{R}J}$ to show that they were for TJ's grandson Thomas Jefferson Randolph.

3 In the left-hand margin Cathalan indicated that these items would be marked **TJ** to show that they were for TJ, with the additional notation: "oil anchovies macaroni."

ENCLOSURES

I

Victor Adolphus Sasserno to Stephen Cathalan

SIR Nice the 14th august 1817

Seeing that you have the Kindness to be concerned in my favour I take the liberty to answer to your honoured and obliging letter which mr Spreafico has communicated me. You desire of him Some informations on the commercial relations of Nice With the Unite-States of America—, and on the quantity of ships, belonging to that country, that touch at our port; to this; I'll tell you, Sir, that its commercial business, till now, have been of little consequence and the arrivals not frequent; but the liberty of Seas will certainly render its rapports more important; besides we have every winter a great deal of foreigners, and among them, there are allways Some American families (Unite-States) We expect for many of them this year; they are often troubled for their pass-ports, and obliged to make Steps, that a consul will do them avoid. In Short, we have a consul of every nation; excepting Swedin and Denmark, (who will be Soon named) this does prove that Nice is to be considered as well for its port as for its position on the frontiers.

Excuse, Sir, the trouble I cause you, and be certain, that I shall ever retain the remembrance of your complaisance with the most lively and real Sentiments of gratitude, therefore I dare Say me

Sir! your most obedient and most humble Servant.

VICTOR ADOLPHUS SASSERNO

RC (ViW: TC-JP); in an unidentified hand; dateline adjacent to closing; addressed: "A Monsieur Monsieur Etienne Cathalan Consul Général des Etats unis d'amérique A Marseille"; endorsed by Cathalan: "1817 Nice the 14th August Victor Adolphus Sasserno aged 24 years Received the 18th dto answered the   on the appointment of a Consul of the U. states at Nice, for him Self"; endorsed by TJ: "Sasserno, Victor Adolphus." Enclosed in enclosure no. 3 below.

Joseph Victor Adolphus Sasserno (b. 1795), merchant and public official, was the son of TJ's acquaintance Victor Sasserno and a native of Nice. With TJ's assistance he was appointed United States consul at that city in 1818 and held the position until he was replaced in about 1850. Sasserno helped TJ acquire wine from Europe, 1818–19. He was appointed in 1844 to the honor guard of the king of Sardinia, who ruled Nice throughout Sasserno's consulship (Sasserno genealogical materials in FrNiADAM: Georges Blondeau Papers; Cathalan to TJ, 19 Mar. 1816, and first enclosure; TJ to John Quincy Adams, 26 Dec. 1817; *JEP*, 3:115–6, 8:112 [27, 28 Jan. 1818, 4 Jan. 1850]; TJ to Sasserno, 22 Feb., 5 Apr. 1818, 26 May 1819).

II

Amant Spreafico (for Pierre Mages & Compagnie) to Stephen Cathalan

Monsieur Le Consul. Nice 15 Août 1817.

Nous sommes honorés de votre chère lettre 9 c^{t} qui nous porte Copie de celle que Vous a écrit v/ respectable ami Monsieur Thomas Jefferson ancien Président des états unis d'Amérique, ce dont nous vous remercions sincèrement, cette Lettre nous a fait d'autant plus de plaisir que nous avons eû la satisfaction d'apprendre que les 4 C^{es} vin que nous vous Expédiames en février 1816. ont été trouvées de bonne qualité, il était de la Cave de n/ S. Spreafico qui regrette bien de ne pas en avoir encore d'aussi bon à vous envoyer, pour remplir la nouvelle Commission des 200 B^{lles} que vous demande votre ami, mais nous allons nous en procurer, et vous enverrons des meilleurs que nous pourrons nous procurer, il n'y aura qu'une difficulté, c'est que cette Liqueur a beaucoup augmentée par deux années de suite de mauvaise recolte, et par surcroit de malheur Les vignes de Bellet ont assés souffert d'un Coup de vent du nord très froid que nous avons eu en mai dernier, nous pensons que cette augmentation ne sera que de *f.* 8 à 10. par Caisse de 50 B^{lles} ce qui n'est pas absolument bien conséquent, au reste, Monsieur le Consul, nous n'y gagnerons rien autre que n/ simple Commission.

Dans le Courant de la semaine p^{ne} nous vous en remettrons facture, en attendant veuillé agréer les sentimens d'Estime et de Consideration avec Lesquels nous avons L'honneur de nous dire Monsieur Le Consul.

Vos dévoués Serviteurs PP^{on} de P^{e} Mages & Comp^{e}

Amant Spreafico

EDITORS' TRANSLATION

Mr. Consul. Nice 15 August 1817.

We are honored by your dear letter of the 9th of this month, which brings us a copy of the one written to you by your respectable friend Mr. Thomas Jefferson, former president of the United States of America, for which we sincerely thank you. That letter gave us all the more pleasure as we had the satisfaction of learning that the 4 cases of wine that we sent you in February 1816 were judged to be of good quality. The wine was from the cellar of Mr. Spreafico, who is very sorry to have none of equal quality left to send you, to fill the new order of 200 bottles requested by your friend, but we are going to get some and will send you the best we can obtain. The only difficulty is that the price of this liqueur has greatly increased due to two consecutive years of bad crops, and by a further misfortune, the vineyards of Bellet suffered last May from a very cold gust of northerly wind. We think that this increase in price will be only of 8 to 10 francs per case of 50 bottles, which is not of great consequence; in any case, Mr. Consul, we will earn nothing but our simple commission.

Sometime next week we will send you the invoice for this order. In the meantime please accept the sentiments of respect and consideration with which we have the honor of being, Mr. Consul.

Your devoted servants on behalf of Pierre Mages & Company

AMANT SPREAFICO

RC (MHi); dateline at foot of text; with following enclosure conjoined; addressed: "A Monsieur Monsieur Etienne Cathalan Consul Général des Etats-unis d'Amérique, A Marseille Bouches du Rhône"; postmarked Nice; endorsed by Cathalan: "1817 Nice Le 15e aoust P^{re} Mages & Ce & Amant Spreafico Reçûe Le 18 dit—Rep^{due} Le au Sujet du vin de Bellet Pour Monsr Thos Jefferson & du Consulat des Etats unis pour Mr Victor Adolphe Sasserno agé de 24 ans" ("Nice 15 August 1817 Pierre Mages & Company & Amant Spreafico received 18 ditto—responded on on the subject of Bellet wine for Mr. Thomas Jefferson and an American consulship for Mr. Victor Adolphus Sasserno, aged 24 years"). Translation by Dr. Genevieve Moene.

The firm of Pierre Mages & Compagnie was established in Nice by 1805 and dealt in fabrics and wine (*Almanach du Commerce de Paris, des Départemens de l'Empire Français et des Principales Villes de l'Europe* [1805]: 566).

III

Amant Spreafico to Stephen Cathalan

MONSIEUR LE CONSUL Nice 19 Août 1817.

Permetté moi de vous remercier bien sincèrement de tout L'intérêt que vous voulé bien prendre en faveur de M. Sassernó fils de L'ami de Monsieur Jefferson, c'est dans cette même qualité que je prends la Liberté de vous prier de vouloir bien continuer d'appuyer de votre crédit, et de v/ protection, auprès du Respectable M. Jefferson ce jeune homme pour lequel je m'interesse vivement parce qu'il le merite, ce serait une grande obligation qu'il vous aurait ainsi que moi Si par vos bons offices il obtenait la place de Consul des Etats unis dans n/ Ville, il est vrai qu'il n'aborde guerres dans n/ port des bâtiments de cette Nation, mais il peut en Venir, ayant Le port de Villefranche qui peut en Recevoir même de Guerre, d'ailleurs ce port dans un mauvais tems peut servir d'abri à tout Navire qui aurait Le malheur d'Eprouver un mauvais Tems, ou qui se Trouvant dans nos parages aurait besoin de réparation; outre cette raison que je crois bonne, il est venu pendant 2 hyvers de suite des Citoyens des états unis qui auraient été bien charmés de Trouver un agent de Leur Nation pour les représenter, et leur éviter La peine et L'Embarras qu'ils doivent éprouver Lorsqu'ils veulent quitter n/ V. par toutes Les démarches et Courses nécessaires pour le simple visa de Leur passeport.

Nous avons ici des Consuls de toutes Les Nations, savoir: france, Autriche, Russie, Espagne, Portugal, Toscane, Rome, Naples, Angleterre, Dannemarck, on assure que la Prusse vient d'en nommer un qui est un nég^{t} de n/ Ville, ainsi que presque tous Les autres Consuls, car Excepté la france, L'Espagne et L'angleterre Tous Les autres sont des Niçois qui sont dans le Commerce, comme vous voyez, Monsieur Le Consul, il ne manque plus que celui des Etats unis d'amérique, et certes cette Nation est Trop respectable, pour ne pas avoir dans n/ Ville un Consul, Veuillés donc je vous en prie vous intéresser en faveur de Victor Adolphe Sassernó pour lui faire obtenir c/ place honorable, il est dans sa 24me année, et remplira je peut vous L'assurer cette place avec Toute la dignité,[1] et le Zèle qu'elle Exige, et surément à La pleine

Satisfaction des americains qui viendront jouir du Beau Climat de n/ V. Je vous joins ici une Lettre qu'il vous écrit en anglais, je desire que vous la Trouviés écrite correctement, et qu'elle vous engage à Vouloir bien continuer à L'honnorer de votre crédit et protection.

j'ai L'honneur d'être avec la Consideration la plus distinguée
Monsieur Le Consul
Votre Très dévoué serviteur AMANT SPREAFICO

EDITORS' TRANSLATION

MR. CONSUL Nice 19 August 1817.

Allow me to thank you very sincerely for all the interest you are kind enough to show in Mr. Sasserno, the son of Mr. Jefferson's friend. In this same capacity I take the liberty of asking you to be so kind as to continue to support, with your protection and your influence with the respectable Mr. Jefferson, this young man in whom I take much interest because he deserves it. He and I would be much obliged to you if through your mediation he obtained the position of consul of the United States at our city. It is true that hardly any American ships arrive in our port, but it may happen. We have the port of Villefranche, which can receive even warships, and in any case this port, during bad weather, could shelter any ship unfortunate enough to be caught in a storm or need repairs while in the vicinity. Besides this reason, which I believe to be good, American citizens have come here 2 winters in a row, and they would have been delighted to find an agent of their nation to represent them and save them the effort and annoyance they must go through when they want to leave our city, due to all the steps and procedures necessary to obtain a simple visa on their passports.

We have consuls here from every nation, namely France, Austria, Russia, Spain, Portugal, Tuscany, Rome, Naples, England, and Denmark. We are told that Prussia has just appointed a consul who is a merchant in our city, as are almost all the others. Except for those from France, Spain, and England, the consuls are all businessmen from Nice. So you see, Mr. Consul, that only the United States of America is lacking one, and indeed that nation is too respectable to have no consul in our city. Therefore, I beg you please to exercise your influence to help Victor Adolphus Sasserno obtain this honorable position. He is in his twenty-fourth year, and I can assure you that he will fulfill this position with all the dignity and zeal that it requires, and surely to the complete satisfaction of the Americans who will come here to enjoy the beautiful climate of our city. Enclosed please find a letter he wrote to you in English. I hope you will find it correctly written and that it will encourage you to be so kind as to continue honoring him with your credit and protection.

I have the honor to be, with the most distinguished consideration
Mr. Consul
Your very devoted servant AMANT SPREAFICO

RC (MHi); dateline at foot of text; conjoined with preceding enclosure. Translation by Dr. Genevieve Moene. Enclosure: first enclosure printed above.

The AMI DE MONSIEUR JEFFERSON was Victor Sasserno, father of Victor Adolphus Sasserno.

[1]Manuscript: "dignités."

From Absalom Townsend

SIR, *Albany*, [ca. 28] *August*, 1817.

You will perceive, by the notice in the last Numbers of the AMERICAN MAGAZINE, edited by Mr. SPAFFORD, that the Subscription to that work, has been duly assigned to me.—I must therefore earnestly request you to send Three Dollars, the amount of your subscription, to my Office, No. 84, State-street, Albany, by Mail or otherwise, without delay.

ABSALOM TOWNSEND, JR.
Attorney at Law.

RC (MHi); printed circular; partially dated; addressed: "His Ex[y] Thomas Jefferson Monticello Virginia"; franked; postmarked Albany, 28 Aug.; endorsed by TJ as a letter of Aug. 1817 received 21 Sept. 1817 and so recorded in SJL.

Absalom Townsend (1786–1861), attorney, was born in Orange County, New York, and moved with his family to Albany in about 1795. He graduated from Williams College in 1805 and subsequently studied law in New York City. Townsend qualified at the bar of the New York Supreme Court in 1808 and afterwards practiced law in Albany, serving also as a master in chancery. Between 1811 and 1818 he was an officer in the New York militia, eventually becoming a brigade judge advocate. Townsend was also a leader in the Albany Sunday School Society. The 1860 census valued his real-estate holdings at $30,000 and his personal property at $50,000 (Calvin Durfee, *Williams Biographical Annals* [1871], 270; *New-York Commercial Advertiser*, 26 Nov. 1808; Joseph Fry, comp., *The Albany Directory* [Albany, 1813], 48; Fry, *The Albany Directory, for the year 1814* [Albany, 1814], 8, 57; *Anniversary Report of the Board of Managers of the Albany Bible Society* [Albany, 1818], 27, 32; *Military Minutes of the Council of Appointment of the State of New York, 1783–1821* [1901–02], 2:1242, 1281, 1410, 1414, 3:1963; Joel Munsell, *The Annals of Albany* [1850–59], 7:179–80; DNA: RG 29, CS, Albany, 1860; *Albany Evening Journal*, 5 Oct. 1861).

Horatio G. Spafford announced that his accounts had been ASSIGNED to Townsend in the *American Magazine, a monthly miscellany* 1 (1816): 441–2.

From John Martin Baker

SIR, Montpellier—near Orange Court House August 29th 1817.

I have had the Honor this day to see M[r] Madison, who is pleased to inform me, that you were not at Monti-cello: but at your Seat in Bedford, which unhappily deprives me the Honor of paying you my respects in person, as I had proposed on my leaving George-town. D.C. where my family now reside: and who beg Sir to be Respectfully presented to you— permit me sir, to add, that unfortunately for me, I cannot continue my journey to Bedford, owing to the incapacity of the Horse, I hired at Fredericksburg.

Being very lately assured, that the Consulate of Amsterdam, has the Salary of Two thousand Dollars per anum, as agent for Seamen, and claims: I had the Honor to apply for that office on the Eighteenth instant: and take the liberty Sir, to herewith enclose copy of my Letter to the Secretary of State, (praying your perusal.) Soliciting the President of the United States, pleasure and consideration in my favor for said appointment.

I take the liberty Sir, and pray you to be so good as to oblige me with your protection in a line to the President of the United States: who I am informed is expected to be in Washington on or before the tenth of September next.—I beg pardon Sir, for this importunity, urged by my peculiar Situation, for the Support of an Amiable Wife, five infant deserving Children, and their Aged Respectable Grand-mother. Sensible of your feeling and Humane Consideration. I Have the Honor to Be, with the Highest Respect,

Sir, Your most Grateful faithful, obedient, humble Servant.

JOHN MARTIN BAKER.

I pray you Sir, to have the goodness to address to me at George town. D[t] C[a] where I have taken a house, the Second Brick dwelling, from the high Bridge, coming in from Washington.
M[r] Diggs, requested me Sir, to present you his Respectful Compliments.

RC (DLC); postscript on verso of final page; beneath signature: "To The Honorable Thomas Jefferson. Virginia"; endorsed by TJ as received 11 Sept. 1817 and so recorded in SJL.

President James Monroe nominated Alexander McRae for the United States consulship at AMSTERDAM on 18 Apr. 1818, and the Senate confirmed his appointment two days later (*JEP*, 3:138, 140). The AGED RESPECTABLE GRANDMOTHER was Elizabeth Williams Bogart Weissenfels.

ENCLOSURE

John Martin Baker to Richard Rush

SIR, Washington, August 18th 1817.

The Consulship and Agency for Seamen, and claims, at Amsterdam; Having become vacant by the death of the late Consul of the United States, Sylvanus Bourne Esquire; I beg leave Sir, with Respect to Solicit, and pray of the President of the United States of America, His consideration and pleasure to be appointed to that office; And beg Sir, to be permitted to state: That on the first day of March 1803. I had the Honor to be appointed by the President of the United States; Consul for the Balearean Islands: on which Islands I continued on my duty until the twenty third day of April 1807.—When I embarked with my family on my return Home, Having Sacrificed considerably for my families Support while at the Consulate, consequence of no American Commerce whatsoever there. On the ninth day of December 1807. The President of the United States, was pleased to grant me the additional port and district of Tarragona, to my Consulate: which united Consulate, I have the Honor to hold Since the stated dates of my Commissions. The President of the United States, on His feeling consideration of my Sacrifices at my Consulate, was pleased on the first day of May 1808—To appoint me Bearer of dispatches to France, and United States, Agent on Board the St Michaels: my return to Washington, on that duty was on the Second day of October—And on the first day of January 1809. The Secretary of State of the United states of America, was pleased to appoint me Clerk in the department of State, where I had the Honor to continue under that officer, on that duty, until July Succeeding: when the expectation of a Squadron of the United States, or some Vessels of War, were contemplated to Sail for the Mediterranean, to make port-Mahon, Island of Minorca, the rendezvous—And having the promise from the Secretary of the Navy of the United States: That by the first Ship or Vessel of War, destined to port Mahon, I would receive my Commission, and instructions as Navy agent for that port: I embarked at Washington, with my family on the ninth day of October 1809. on Board the Brig Blanchy, chartered by the United States Government, to carry cordage and Timbers to Algiers: after Eighty days at Sea, we anchored in distress in the gulf of Palmas, Island of Sardinia, where on the first day of January 1810. I landed with my family, and performed quarantine at the castle of St Antioch; (where I obtained a practical affrican coast pilot for the Vessel, and dispatched her, with the United States maritime Stores on Board, which were duly received by the United States, consul general at that Regency.)[1] I continued on my duty at Majorca, Tarragona, and port Mahon, Island of Minorca until the Second day of October 1813. (then at the latter port, where I have had constant correspondence for the discharge of American Seamen, constrainedly detained on Board H:B:M. Ships: with Admirals Sir Charles Cotton; Sir, Edward Pellew; (Lord Exmuth) Freemantle; Pickmore; Hollowell; and Captains, and commanders in H,B:M. fleet, &c many Men have been delivered up to me, which I have had the satisfaction to Send Home to their Country, and Suffering families.) At that time under British influence, when necessitously impelled by my peculiar station, and my circumstances reduced and finally wholly expending, consequence of no american arrival, owing to our State of War with Gt Britain, and Algiers; I embarked once more to endeavour to return Home with my family, (Mrs Baker and five Children) by the way of Sardinia, where I was friendly treated by the Sovereign of that State; after experiencing every difficulty with eminent danger to avoid captivity with the Algerines, we arrived at Leghorn.

when I reached Paris, it was indispensible for me to have an interview with the Ministers Plenipotentiaries of the United States, at Ghent, to solicit a passage for myself and family to return Home in one of the United States, dispatch Vessels: on my way there, when arrived at Lille, I was Seized with a delirious brain fever, which continued with heated violence, Eight days and nights, and obliged me to return to my family at Paris; (under care of a sick-assistant) all which is well known to The Honorable William H: Crawford, then United States, Minister plenipotentiary at Paris—while convalescent at Paris, Peace being concluded between the United States and Great Britain, and informed that a Squadron of the United States, would Sail for the Mediterranean, I decided to return to my Station and duty, as Consul: and navy agent; for port Mahon, and left my family[2] at Montpellier. I joined the United States Squadron, at Malaga, and Embarked on Board the frigate United States, Commodore John Shaw, on the twenty Eighth day of October 1815, and arrived at port Mahon, on the fifth day of November, where jointly with the Commodore, I had the Satisfaction to obtain from the Governor, His assent for the admission and continuance in port of all the vessels of the United States Squadron, consisting of the frigates, United States, and Constellation; Corvette Ontario: Ships John Adams, and Alert, and the Schooner Hornet. (The standing orders of H:C:M—are, that no greater number than two or three Vessels of war of any friendly nation, shall be admitted at any one time to Enter and continue, for Repairs or Provission at port-Mahon.—)

I obtained permission from the Intendant, to land and deposit, until the pleasure of H,C:M be known: The naval, and provission Stores[3] on Board the Ships John Adams: Alert, and Schooner Hornet; possessed the Governors grant of a tract of inclosed Building, in good repair, (free of charge to the United States.) on a healthy Situation, (the entrance of the Harbour.) consisting of fifteen chambers, good water, and conveniences for our Naval Hospital, where I attended myself with the Director of the Lazaretto, to designate and limit the bounds, to the satisfaction of the Surgeon General, Doctor M^c^Renolds: where he established the United States, Navy Hospital. I had the promise of the port Admiral, that in the case of any of the United states, Ships of war, requiring repair, they would have a free use of the Kings Arsenal &c—

The Secretary of the Navy of the United States, Paul Hamilton Esqe having deceased Since my last departure from Washington—Richard McCall, Esqe Consul of the United States for Barcelona, joined us on Board the United States, at Sea, off Carthagena, vested with the character of Navy Agent, for the expedition to Algiers, &c My disappointment, and in consequence, Mine and families sufferings, I pray you Sir, and ask the favor of your goodness to lay before the feeling consideration of the President of the United States of America.

I am now returned to my Country, arrived and landed at Philadelphia, on the third day of June last, with my Wife, and five Children, to Support, and decently Educate; with my Mother in Law, now Seventy two Years of Age, The Widow of the late Colonel Comt Frederick Weissenfels, of the American Revolutionary army, deceased at New Orleans.

I humbly beg pardon for this intrusion, and Solicit Sir, your kind indulgence, praying your consideration in my favor for the appointment I now have the Honor to Solicit, Assuring you Sir, of that just Zeal, and every personal exertion in my duty, in which I have efforted every power to give proof of, Since I have the Honor to Serve the United States of America, now in the fifteenth Year. I have the Honor to Be—With the highest Respect Sir

Your most obedient humble Servant. JOHN MARTIN BAKER.[4]

I beg your kind indulgence and pray you Sir, to permit me to state, that on joining the United States Squadron at Malaga, on my duty, to Endeavour to obtain admission and depot, at my Consulate. I necessarily abandoned the concern of a Small cargo of Rice, a vessel of thirty Eight Tons, on Board of which I had arrived at Malaga, from Cette, with a Small cargo of wines, &

Liquors, which were Sold at Gibraltar: the returns thereof, a cargo of Carolina[5] Rice, I had to consign back to the said port of Cette, to the House concerned with me, Joseph Mercier & Co when, owing to the length of time in arriving, (proving a Boisterous Season) that article had fallen in price in the south of France, and was Sold at twenty four francs per hundred weight—At Tarragona, my destiny, had I continued with my concern, the said Rice, would have commanded forty pistreens per hundred: making a difference to my loss of Seven hundred D[o]ll[ars an]d upwards, on the close of my adventure, undertaken by me, at the moment when no Vessel of my nation, arrived at any port of my Consulate; and the necessary indispensible wants of my family, in a foreign Country, Urged, every honest exertion & invention to Honorably obtain a competence, & preserve them from want.

JOHN MARTIN BAKER

Tr (DLC); in Baker's hand; damaged at crease; at head of text: "Copy"; beneath first signature: "To The Honorable Richard Rush. Acting Secretary of State, of the United States of America. &c &c &c Washington"; postscript on a separate sheet, lacking in RC, and thus possibly added specifically for TJ; endorsed by Baker: "Copy of Letter To The Honorable Richard Rush.—acting Secretary of State. August 18th 1817." RC (DNA: RG 59, LAR, 1817–25); lacking postscript; at foot of text: "To The Honorable Richard Rush. Acting Secretary of State of the United States of America. &c &c &c Washington."

The consul general at the REGENCY of Algiers in 1810 was Tobias Lear. HOLLOWELL: Sir Benjamin Hallowell Carew. H:C:M: "His Catholic Majesty" and "His Most Catholic Majesty" are titles traditionally accorded to the kings of Spain.

[1] Omitted closing parenthesis editorially supplied.
[2] RC here adds "then."
[3] RC here adds "then."
[4] RC ends here.
[5] Word interlined.

To Samuel L. Osborn

SIR Aug. 28. [29] 17.

Your favor of July came to hand on the 18th instant. and I am very sensible of the favor with which you are pleased to express yourself towards me. if, in the course of my political term of service, my fellow citizens think I have effected any thing useful for our country, my reward is in their approbation. I am thankful that I have lived to see the sacrifices of the revolutionary generation, whatever they may have been, result in so great a share of happiness to their descendants, and that they may perpetuate and improve these blessings, will be my last prayer. to yourself I tender the assurance of my best wishes & respects

TH: JEFFERSON

PoC (DLC: TJ Papers, 211:37623); on verso of reused address cover of Isaac Briggs to TJ, 21 May 1817; misdated; endorsed by TJ as a letter of 28 Aug. 1817. RC (Heritage Collectors' Society, Doylestown, Pa., 1994); address cover only;

addressed: "Mr Samuel L. Osburn Kennebunk, Maine"; franked; postmarked Lynchburg, 31 Aug. Recorded in SJL as a letter of <*28*> 29 Aug. 1817.

TJ later corrected the date of receipt of Osborn's FAVOR OF JULY 28 from 18 to 19 Aug. 1817 in SJL.

Anonymous (Thomas Jefferson) to the *Richmond Enquirer*

DEAR SIR Warm springs Aug. [ca. 29] 1817.

In compliance with your desire on my departure for the springs I availed myself of a short stay in Charlottesville to enquire into the plan, the progress and prospects of the Central college, which has been sometimes spoken of in your paper. I will give you the result shortly, & so much only as I get from sources to be relied on.

A law, it seems, had been past, authorising a board of trustees in and about Charlottesville, to establish a seminary of learning in the ordinary way of voluntary subscription and lottery. the healthiness of the country, it's fertility, it's central position with respect to the population of the state, and other advantages inducing the trustees to believe that, divesting it of local character, and enlarging it's scope to that of an institution for general science, it might offer convenience to the whole state, they petitioned the legislature, & obtained a law dissolving their board, making the Governor of the Commonwealth ex officio[1] Patron of the institution, by the name of the Central college, investing him with the perpetual nomination of Visitors, six in number, giving the proceeds of the sales of two glebes in that county, and permission to raise money by a lottery & by voluntary subscription, with other provisions for their good government. the Governor named, as Visitors, mr Monroe, present President of the US. mr Madison the late president, mr Jefferson a former one, mr Cabell, Genl Cocke & mr Watson, all of that, and the circumjacent country. these gentlemen have had two or three meetings, have purchased a site a mile above the town of Charlottesville, high, healthy, & with good water, have agreed on the outlines of their plan as a College of general science, & are now proceeding on it's execution. the subscription papers have been recieved with uncommon favor and confidence, the contributions of the county of Albemarle alone amounting to upwards of 30,000.D. and other parts of the country distant as well as near considering it's location as offering them a healthy and convenient situation for their youth, and reposing confidence in it's direction under visitors named by the Governor, are giving liberal aids to it's establishment, which, for the greater convenience of the contributors, are recieved in four annual instalments, the 1st on the first of April next. the intention of the Visitors is, not to erect a single and expensive building, which would at once exhaust[2] their funds; but to make it rather an Academical village. a small box, or Pavilion, is to be erected for each school and it's professor separately, with chambers, or dormitories for the students, all united by a covered colonnade, and arranged on each side of a lawn of 200. feet wide. besides the security which this arrangement gives against fire and infection, it has the great convenience of admitting building after[3] building to be erected successively as their funds come in, and as their professorships are subdivided. one of these pavilions is now in progress, and will be ready, by the 1st of April next, to recieve a professor, whose department is to be languages, history, rhetoric, oratory & belles lettres. the funds are believed to be already further sufficient for the erection of two others the ensuing summer, which are expected to embrace Mathematics, physiology,[4] anatomy, zoology, botany, mineralogy & chemistry; and it is hoped that the progress of the public favor will, the year following that, enable them to provide a 4th professorship embracing the Ideological, ethical, jurisprudential & political sciences. these will compleat the circle of what are deemed principally useful at this day, medecine excepted, which requires the accessory of a great hospital, so as to unite example with precept. I learn too that the visitors propose to establish no professorship, until they shall have capital, not only for the building, but to constitute a deposit in the public funds the interest of which shall furnish a moderate, but perpetual salary for the professor; so that what is once done, will be permanently done, and will constitute a nucleus to which what is wanting may be afterwards aggregated, and ramified progressively, as the public shall see it's advantage and contribute to make it what their interest requires it should be. it is also understood that they will employ as professors men only of the first order of eminence in the different sciences, seeking them in the US. if there to be had, or otherwise inviting the most eminent to be obtained from Europe. These, Sir, are such of the outlines as I could collect on sound authority, and from what I see and learn, I have good confidence in their success. I rode to the grounds and was much pleased with their commanding position & prospect. a small mountain adjacent is included in their purchase, & is contemplated as a site for an astronomical observatory, and a very remarkable one it will certainly be. the whole purchase is of 200. as which, besides the Observatory and building grounds, will afford a garden for the school of botany, & an experimental farm for that of Agriculture. should I on my return learn any thing further, and interesting, I will communicate it to you, as the position, the plan, and the superintendence under which it will be, give me the hope that we are at length to have a seminary of general education, in a central and healthy part of the country, with the comfort of knowing that while we are husbanding our hard earnings and savings to give to our sons the benefits of education, altho' we may not ourselves be judges of the course they pursue, yet that will be under the guidance of those who are competent, and whose best attentions are ensured by the motives which induce them gratuitously to undertake a charge, on the faithful exercise of which they know that the future destinies of their country will depen[d.][5]

I have found here & at the hot spring much company, and the other springs I am told are much crouded. it would be money well bestowed would the public employ a well educated and experienced[6] physician to attend at each of the medicinal springs, to observe, record, and publish the cases which recieve benefit, those recieving none, and those rendered worse by the use of their respective waters; whose office too it should be to administer advice to the poorer sick gratis. the medical effects of the different springs are now so little known, that they are used at random; & all of them by most which is pretty much as if a patient should take something of every thing in his Apothecary's shop, by way of making sure of what will hit his case.

PoC (DLC: TJ Papers, 211:37627–8); partially dated; at head of text: "Central College A letter from a correspondent of the Editor of the Enquirer." Enclosed in TJ to Thomas Ritchie, [29] Aug. 1817. Printed in the *Richmond Enquirer*, 5 Sept. 1817, and elsewhere; at head of text (one word editorially corrected): "CENTRAL COLLEGE, A single glance at the following article is sufficient to show, that as no subject is *more* worthy of attention, none could be *better* explained. We look forward to the Central College with high hopes. We look forward to it as the future nursery of Science and of Liberty; the *Alma Mater* of our *sons* and *grand-sons*. Who is it[s] first founder? *Jefferson*; who in his youth contended for Liberty; in his old days, for the means of perpetuating it. Such an *object* is worthy of such a *man*! TO THE EDITOR OF THE ENQUIRER."

For the LAW outlining plans for Central College, see TJ's Draft Bill to Create Central College and Amend the 1796 Public Schools Act, [ca. 18 Nov. 1814], and note.

[1] Manuscript: "offico."
[2] Manuscript: "ex-haust."
[3] Manuscript: "afte."
[4] *Richmond Enquirer*: "philosophy."
[5] Word left incomplete due to polygraph misalignment.
[6] Preceding four words interlined, with "experienced" substituted for "practised."

To Thomas Ritchie

[DE]AR SIR Poplar forest Aug. 28. [29] 17.

You have sometimes made favorable mention of our Central college, and Genl Cocke, one of our visitors, gave me reason to believe you would still do so occasionally. many, supposing that a brief account of our views, if laid before the public, might have good effect, I have, in compliance with their requests, prepared the within, disguised however as to it's source, because I am unwilling to give to cavillers any hold to draw me personally into contest before the public. the favor with which the establishment of a college at Charlottesville has been recieved, has encoraged us to hope it might draw to it the legislative adoption, and induce the establishment of an University on a large scale, which at present is supposed to hang in suspense with them. with these hopes the present visitors are laying their shoulders heartily to the work, and trus[t that?] we shall not fail of your aid on proper occasions. if the inclosed is too long, curtail it, and adapt it as you please to the convenience of your paper. I salute you with great esteem & respect. TH: JEFFERSON

PoC (DLC: TJ Papers, 211:37622); on verso of reused address cover of James Gibbon to TJ, 22 May 1817; misdated; salutation faint; damaged at seal; at foot of text: "Mr Ritchie"; endorsed by TJ as a letter of <*28*> 29 Aug. 1817 and so recorded in SJL. Enclosure: Anonymous (TJ) to the *Richmond Enquirer*, [ca. 29] Aug. 1817.

From Daniel Brent

DEAR SIR, Washington, Dep^{t} of State, Aug 30. 1817.

I had the Honor to receive yesterday your favor of the 22nd of this month, enclosing a letter for Mr Appleton, our Consul at Leghorn, with a request that I would forward it to Mr Appleton by some safe, rather than early opportunity, with the Consular Despatches of this Department; and I have now the pleasure to inform you, that it will this day be sent, under an Envelope of this Office, to M^{r} McCulloch, the Collector of the Customs at Baltimore, with a particular request to him to transmit it by the first opportunity which may promise a safe & sure conveyance to Leghorn.

As we have abundant experience of M^{r} McCulloch's scrupulous attention to similar Commissions, I have the satisfaction to add, that I could not have given your letter a better direction. I have the Honor to be, with the highest Respect & Esteem, Dear Sir, your faithful, Obed[t] servt.

DANIEL BRENT.

RC (DLC); at foot of first page: "M[r] Jefferson"; endorsed by TJ as received 21 Sept. 1817 and so recorded in SJL.

TJ's FAVOR OF THE 22ND ([23]) Aug. 1817 is accounted for above at his 1 Aug. 1817 letter to Thomas Appleton.

From Chapman Johnson

DEAR SIR, Staunton, 30th August 1817.

Yesterday morning I received your letter from "Poplar forest,"—enclosing M[r] Divers's answer to your bill against The Rivanna company—together with your notes thereon—

I have filed the answer; and in pursuance of your request, will send you office copies of the answers, as soon as they are filed—None others have yet been filed—I will endeavour, too, to effectuate your wish, of preventing all unnecessary delays, in bringing the cause to a final hearing—

Since I communicated with you, on this subject, I have been apprised of a decision made by the judge of the Chancery court, here, which makes it necessary, that in suits against corporations, the answer should be a corporate act, filed under the common seal. In a cause depending against the trustees of an Academy in Lexington,—a corporate body—the court upon hearing the cause, refused to make a decree, upon the seperate answers of the individuals, although, in that case, there was an attempt to charge them personally—and although by every answer it appeared that the plaintiff was entitled to a decree against the corporate funds;—and this was done by the court, though no objection to the answers was taken by the counsel—The cause stands over for the answer of the corporation—

In your case, therefore, an answer from the corporation will be required, I presume; and the individuals' answers will not be acted on—

M[r] Minor, who is now in this neighbourhood at the Springs, is apprised of this decision of the court, and is procuring, I believe, an answer for the corporation, to be drawn by M[r] Sheffey—

Very respectfully Y[r] very Obt Sv[t] C JOHNSON

RC (MHi); endorsed by TJ as received 11 Sept. 1817 and so recorded in SJL. RC (MHi); address cover only; with PoC of TJ to Martha Jefferson Randolph, 29 Nov. 1817, on verso; addressed: "Thomas Jefferson Esquire Monticello"; address partially canceled and redirected in an unidentified hand to Lynchburg; stamp canceled; franked; postmarked Staunton, 1 Sept., and Charlottesville, 5 Sept.

To Hugh Chisholm

DEAR SIR Poplar Forest Aug. 31. 17.

I have duly recieved your letters of the 10th & 23^{d} and am glad to learn that the bricks are in such forwardness. I wish you would by every week's mail drop a line stating what the progress then is. I am anxious to know that the cellars are dug, and their walls commenced laying. but be careful to inform me in time and exactly by what day you will have got the walls up to the surface of the earth; because there mr Knight must begin, and by that day I will make it a point to be in Albemarle, and have him there.

I take no interest in the partnership I suggested to you[1] other than as I supposed it would be agreeable. however, in acting for myself I might indulge partialities, I have no right to do so in a public concern. to have the work done in the best manner, is the first object, and the second to have it done at a fair price for both parties. I have offers from some of the best workmen in Lynchburg. the finest plaisterer I have ever seen in this state is anxious to undertake with us. I consider it as the interest of the College the town and neighborhood to introduce a reform of the barbarous workmanship hitherto practised there, and to raise us to a level with the rest of the country. on a trip to the Natural bridge, I found such brickwork and stone-work as cannot be seen in Albemarle. I hope we shall take a higher stand, and do justice to the high advantages that particular portion of our state possesses.

Accept my respects & best wishes TH: JEFFERSON

PoC (ViU: TJP); on verso of reused address cover of James Ligon (for Patrick Gibson) to TJ, 11 Aug. 1817; at foot of text: "Mr Chisolm"; endorsed by TJ.

The FINEST PLAISTERER was probably Joseph Antrim, to whom TJ paid $12 for thirty-six yards of plastering work on 30 Aug. 1817 (*MB*, 2:1338).

[1] Preceding two words interlined.

To Martha Jefferson Randolph

MY EVER DEAR MARTHA Poplar Forest Aug. 31. 17.

Ellen tells me that a request is communicated thro' Mr Randolph & yourself from the Freemason societies of Charlottesville to be permitted to lay the first brick of the Central college. I do not know that I have authority to say either yea or nay to this proposition; but as far as I may be authorised, I consent to it freely. the inhabitants of Charlottesville deserve too well of that institution to meet with any difficulty in that request, and I see no possible objection on the part of the other visitors which exposes me to risk in consenting to it.

Ellen and Cornelia are the severest students I have ever met with. they never leave their room but to come to meals. about twilight of the evening, we sally out with the owls & bats, and take our evening exercise on the terras. an alteration in that part of the house, not yet finished, has deprived them of the use of their room longer than I had expected; but two or three days more will now restore it to them. present me affectionately to mr Randolph, the girls & family. I trust to Ellen & Cornelia to communicate our love to Septimia in the form of a cake. my tenderest love attends yourself. TH: JEFFERSON

RC (NNPM); at foot of text: "M[rs] Randolph"; endorsed by Randolph. PoC (MHi); on verso of a reused address cover from Archibald Robertson to TJ; endorsed by TJ.

Appendix

Supplemental List of Documents Not Found

JEFFERSON's epistolary record and other sources describe a number of documents for which no text is known to survive. The Editors generally account for such material at documents that mention them or at other relevant places. Exceptions are accounted for below.

From Anonymous, no date. Recorded in SJL as received 28 Apr. 1817, with the additional notation (brackets in original) "[Aurora] Post office."

From Josiah Ankrim, 18 Aug. 1817. Recorded in SJL as received 21 Sept. 1817 from Jennerville, Pennsylvania.

INDEX

Abercrombie, John: *The Gardener's Pocket Dictionary*, 165
Aboville, François Marie, chevalier (later comte) d': and opossums, 367–8, 370n
Abregé des dix livres d'architecture de Vitruve (Vitruvius; ed. C. Perrault), 335, 352, 396, 456
The Absentee (M. Edgeworth), 627, 628n
Académie des Beaux-Arts, 633, 634n
Académie des Inscriptions et Belles-Lettres, 633, 634n
Académie des Sciences, 633, 634n
Académie Française, 633, 634n
An Account of Expeditions to the Sources of the Mississippi (Z. M. Pike), 574
Acta Sanctorum (J. de Bolland and others), 527
An Act concerning the clearing of the North Fork of James River (*1794*), 103, 106–8, 109n
An Act concerning the navigation of the United States (*1817*), 122, 123n, 410
An Act declaring who shall be deemed Citizens of this Commonwealth, and pointing out the mode by which the Right of Citizenship may be acquired or relinquished (*1792*), 146–7
An Act for arranging the Counties into Districts for the election of Senators, and for equalizing the Land Tax (*1817*), 133
An Act for clearing the great Falls of James River, the River Chickahominy, and the north Branch of James River (*1764*), 106, 109n
An Act for establishing a College in the county of Albemarle (*1816*), 257, 258n
An Act for establishing an University (*1819*), 315
An Act for opening, improving and extending the Navigation of the River Rappahannock, and all its improveable Branches (*1811*), 84–5n, 93n
An Act for reducing into one, the several Acts concerning the Land-Office; ascertaining the Terms and manner of granting waste and unappropriated Lands; for settling the Titles and Bounds of Lands; directing the mode of Processioning, and prescribing the Duty of Surveyors (*1792*), 105, 109n
An Act Incorporating a Company for improving the Navigation of Rivanna River (*1811*), 108, 109n
An Act Incorporating a Company to open and improve the Navigation of the Rivanna river, from Milton to Moore's ford, opposite the town of Charlottesville, in the county of Albemarle (*1806*), 75, 78, 98n, 103–4, 106–8, 109n, 554n
An Act more effectually to preserve the neutral relations of the United States (*1817*), 410, 412n
An Act to amend an Act, entitled, "An Act, concerning the Clearing of the North Fork of James River" (*1805*), 103n, 106–8, 109n
An Act to amend and explain the act concerning Public Roads (*1802*), 173n
An Act to amend the Act, entitled, "an Act incorporating a Company to open and improve the navigation of the Rivanna River from Milton to Moore's Ford, opposite the town of Charlottesville, in the county of Albemarle, and for other purposes" (*1814*), 75, 78–9, 108, 109n, 552, 554n, 557–8
An Act to change the mode of compensation to the members of the Senate and House of Representatives, and the delegates from territories (*1816*), 410
An Act to establish an uniform rule of Naturalization, and to repeal the acts heretofore passed on that subject (*1802*), 147
An Act to establish two new banks within this Commonwealth (*1817*), 67
An Act to prevent obstructions in the navigable water courses within the Commonwealth (*1816*), 83–4, 104–6, 109n
An Act to reduce into one the several Acts directing the course of Descents (*1792*), 146–7
An Act to secure to the Publick certain Lands heretofore held as a Common (*1780*), 105–6, 109n
Adams, Abigail Smith (John Adams's wife): identified, 6:298n; letter from, 294; and letters of introduction for T. Lyman, 294, 357; letter to, 357;

Adams, Abigail Smith (*cont.*)
TJ sends greetings to, 313; and TJ's syllabus on Jesus's doctrines, 138, 139n, 231, 232n

Adams, John: on *Acta Sanctorum* (J. de Bolland and others), 527; and American Society for the Encouragement of Domestic Manufactures, 442n; on books, 46, 163n; circular sent to, 595; *A Collection of State-Papers*, 49n, 201; and Columbian Institute for the Promotion of Arts and Sciences, 144n; on Condorcet, 45, 527; on correspondence, 46; and Declaration of Independence, 202–3, 252; and J. Delaplaine's *Repository*, 203; and Destutt de Tracy's writings, 45; *A Dissertation on the Canon and the Feudal Law*, 48, 49n, 201; family of, 46; friendship with schoolmates, 217, 218n; friendship with F. A. Van der Kemp, 48, 230–1, 232n; on human progress, 45; identified, 4:390–1n; on Jesuits, 269; letters from, 45–7, 267–70, 362–4, 382–5, 527; and letters of introduction for T. Lyman, 46, 294, 355, 356, 357, 360, 362–3; letter to, 311–3; letter to, from G. W. Jeffreys, 130n; on Montesquieu, 527; on Napoleon, 383; portraits of, 203, 252; presidency of, 46, 267–8, 269, 570n; presidential election of, 412; reading habits of, 268; reflects on his life, 267–9; relationship with T. Pickering, 267–8, 312; on religion, 45, 268–9, 312, 363, 382–3; sends works to TJ, 527; on TJ's appeal to younger generation, 46; and TJ's syllabus on Jesus's doctrines, 139n; works sent to, 31, 363, 364, 382, 384n

Adams, John Quincy: administration of, xlvi; mentioned, 452; minister plenipotentiary to Great Britain, 138, 139n; as secretary of state, 145–6, 512, 513, 532, 533

An Address, delivered before the Columbian Institute, for the Promotion of Arts and Sciences, at the City of Washington, on the 11th January, 1817 (E. Cutbush), 143–4n

Address delivered by Charles W. Peale, to the Corporation and Citizens of Philadelphia, on The 18th Day of July, 1816 (C. W. Peale), 372, 374n

Address of the American Society for the encouragement of Domestic Manufactures (W. Sampson), 23–5, 136

Address of the Connecticut Society for the Encouragement of American Manufactures, 169–70

Adelung, Friedrich: *Catherinens der Grossen Verdienste um die Vergleichende Sprachenkunde*, 562

Advice to Shepherds (Daubenton; trans. J. Bowdoin), 164

Aeschyli Tragoediae Quae Supersunt ac Deperditarum Fragmenta (Aeschylus; ed. C. G. Schütz), 414

Aeschylus: *Aeschyli Tragoediae Quae Supersunt ac Deperditarum Fragmenta* (ed. C. G. Schütz), 414

Aesop's Fables: referenced by TJ, 23, 25n, 558; study of, 396

Africa: colonization of blacks to, 7–8, 8–12, 60–1, 501

African Americans: as TJ's tenants, 397, 428, 589. *See also* slavery; slaves

Agenoria (brig), 531

Aggy (TJ's slave; b. *1789*; daughter of Dinah): family of, 546

aging: R. Peters on, 483; TJ on his own, 13, 160, 215, 436; TJ on youth, 338

L'Agricoltore Sperimentato (C. Trinci), 164

Agricultural Enquiries on Plaister of Paris (R. Peters), 165

Agricultural Society of Albemarle: formation of, 319; members of, 319; TJ's involvement with, 319

agriculture: American Board of Agriculture, 338, 339n; beekeeping, 165, 503–4; Berkshire Agricultural Society, 277, 279n, 338; books on, 162, 245–6, 398; contour plowing, 129; field cultivation of vegetables, 271–3, 308–9; and hawthorn hedges, 228; Kentucky Society for Promoting Agriculture, 4; and manufacturing interests, 23, 287, 345–6; *Massachusetts Agricultural Journal*, 270–2, 308; national board of proposed, 277–9, 338; C. W. Peale on farming, 157–8; Philadelphia Society for Promoting Agriculture, 172; Red House Agricultural Society, 129, 162, 245–6, 347; regional, 130n, 270–1; schools teach, 263–4, 266n; threshing machines, 200; TJ lists works on,

129, 164–5; TJ on, 168n, 344–5. *See also* Agricultural Society of Albemarle; crops; Hessian fly; Philadelphia Society for Promoting Agriculture; plows
Αἰθιοπικῶν βιβλία δέκα (Heliodorus), 452
Alabama Territory: French settlement in, 404n, 542–3, 545; maps of, 615–7
Albany Argus, 279n
Albemarle Academy: Board of Trustees, members of, 314, 318n; creation of, 316; lottery for, 316–7, 318n; requests Literary Fund dividend, 319; and sale of glebe lands, 253, 316–7; TJ's Estimate and Plans for Albemarle Academy/Central College, 317, 318n, 586, 588n. *See also* Central College; Virginia, University of
Albemarle County Court, Va., 73–5, 101, 172, 172–3, 220, 243–4, 244–5, 257, 258, 262, 275, 301, 336, 337, 549
Albemarle County Superior Court of Law, Va., 275
Albemarle County, Va.: map of, xli (*illus.*); petitions to General Assembly, 59, 119; and road orders, 243–4; roads in, 59, 66, 119, 132, 133, 139, 172–3, 200, 243, 244–5; Statement of TJ's Taxable Property in Albemarle County, 44–5; TJ on, 413, 548–9. *See also* Agricultural Society of Albemarle; Central College; Nicholas, John: as Albemarle Co. clerk; Virginia, University of
alcohol: abstinence from, 293; brandy, 296, 300, 345; porter, 293; sent to Poplar Forest, 207; spirits, 293; whiskey, 272–3. *See also* wine
Alert, USS (sloop), 662
Alexander I, emperor of Russia: in France, 458; policies of praised, 6; TJ on, 585–6; TJ's relationship with, 562; and U.S., 122
Alexander, Andrew: identified, 589–90n; letter from, 589–90; and Natural Bridge, 589
Alexander, Eli: and Henderson lands, 42–3; identified, 1:137–8n
alfalfa, 308–9
Algiers: dey of, 9, 122, 123n; *1816* U.S. treaty with, 123n; D. Humphreys's mission to, 60; U.S. consulate at, 534n
Ali Bey (ruler of Egypt), 613
almanacs, nautical: TJ purchases, 13, 31. *See also* Blunt, Edmund March
almonds: at Monticello, 39
altitude: barometers used to calculate, 51–2
Ama, Italy. *See* Casanuova di Ama, Italy
American Academy of Arts and Sciences, 273n
American Antiquarian Society: collections of, 454
American Board of Agriculture: founding of, 279n, 338, 339n
American Colonization Society, 61
American Farmer: prints TJ's catalogue of books on agriculture, 165n; prints TJ's correspondence, 163–4n
The American Gardener (J. Gardiner and D. Hepburn), 165
The American Gardener's Calendar (B. McMahon), 165, 352
American Law Journal (J. E. Hall), 541, 599–600
American Magazine: edited by H. G. Spafford, 5–6, 278, 279n, 659n; TJ subscribes to, 659
American Medical and Philosophical Register: or, Annals of Medicine, Natural History, Agriculture, and the Arts, 4
American Philosophical Society: collections of, 21–2, 125–6, 206, 426, 477; and papers of Lewis and Clark Expedition, 454, 486–7, 574; *Transactions*, 376, 398, 427, 454, 486; works given to, 501, 574
American Philosophical Society, Historical and Literary Committee: and W. Byrd manuscripts, 21–2, 125–6, 206, 487; identified, 9:179n; TJ sends works to, 21–2
American Register, or General Repository of History, Politics and Science (ed. R. Walsh), 178n
American Register; or Summary Review of History, Politics, and Literature (ed. R. Walsh), 178, 215, 635–6
American Revolution: books on, 313, 364; and Lafayette, 283; R. Peters on, 483–4; relics of, 167, 168, 344; speeches delivered during, 5. *See also* Revolutionary War
American Society for the Encouragement of Domestic Manufactures: addresses of, 136; identified, 442n; members of, 442n; TJ's membership, 441, 442n, 478

Ammianus Marcellinus: quoted, 424, 425n
amphibians: study of, 191
Amsterdam: U.S. consulate at, 659–60, 660
Anabaptists: mentioned, 363
Anacreon (Greek poet), 126
Analyse Raisonnée de l'Origine de Tous les Cultes, ou Religion Universelle (Destutt de Tracy), 359
anatomy: study of, 191
Ancell, Edward: and Barboursville plantation, 227; identified, 227n; visits Monticello, 227
anchovies, 407, 653
Anderson, Mr.: and dispute of C. L. Lewis and C. Peyton, 514, 517
Anderson, Alexander: as engraver, 115n
Anderson, Benjamin: and Central College subscription, 332
Anderson, Edmund: and Central College subscription, 326, 334
Anderson, Nathaniel: and Central College subscription, 326, 328
Andrei, Giovanni: sculptor for U.S. Capitol, 571
Andrew (ship), 283
Andrieux, François Guillaume Jean Stanislas: lectures of, 634
Angelucci, Jean Baptiste: sculptor, 267
Anglo-Saxon language: TJ's study of, 252
Ankrim, Josiah: letter from accounted for, 671
Annals of Agriculture and Other Useful Arts (A. Young), 165
Ann Smith Academy (Lexington), 134n
anonymous correspondence: letter from accounted for, 671; TJ writes anonymously for newspaper, 664–6
Antelope (sloop), 204
Antes, Henry: family of, 613
Antes, John: relationship with J. Bruce, 613, 614n
Anthony, Christopher: as Va. legislator, 8
Anthony, Mark (Marcus Antonius): J. Adams on, 269
anthropology: study of human migration, 192–3
The Antiquary (W. Scott), 630
Antiquities from Asia, brought to New-York in Jan. 1817, by Capt. Henry Austin, and now at Dr. Mitchill's, 114–5, 136
Antrim, Joseph: and plastering for Central College, 669; TJ pays, 669n
Appleton, Thomas: and C. Bellini's estate, 580; consul at Leghorn, 120, 128, 239–40, 247, 667; identified, 8:162n; letter from, 170–1; letters to, 196, 577–81, 642–3; and P. Mazzei's estate, 171, 577–9, 585, 642–3, 643–6; and sculptures of G. Washington, 171; and seeds for TJ, 170–1, 171–2, 302, 336, 353; and stonecutters for Central College, 579; TJ introduces W. C. Preston to, 196, 200; and wine for TJ, 131, 131–2, 171, 579–80
Arator; being a series of Agricultural Essays, Practical & Political (J. Taylor), 129, 165
Archimedes: *Œuvres d'Archimède* (trans. F. Peyrard), 127, 152, 175, 193, 295, 297, 395
architecture: books on, 335, 352, 396, 456; Central College buildings as models of, 256; TJ advises J. Barbour on, xlvi, 223–7, 227. *See also* building materials
Argenson, Marc René Marie de Voyer de Paulmy, marquis d': family of, 283
Ariadne (mythological character), 624n
Aristophanes: *Théatre d'Aristophane, avec les fragmens de Ménandre et de Philémon* (trans. L. Poinsinet de Sivry), 352, 397, 456, 547, 592, 646
Aristotle: referenced, 192
Armistead, William (ca. *1773–1840*): identified, 10:427n; seeks federal appointment, 149
Armstrong, John: identified, 1:20n; TJ reimburses, 523
Arnold, Benedict: works on, 436, 438n, 503, 635–6
art. *See* drawing; paintings; prints; sculpture
artichokes, 39, 179, 308–9
Asclepias. *See* milkweed
Ashton (T. E. Randolph's Albemarle Co. estate): proposed visit to, 631n
Asia Minor: and agriculture, 162
Asiatick Society: discourses to, 383, 384n
asparagus, 39
Aspland, Robert: identified, 10:123–4n; publishes TJ's syllabus on Jesus's doctrines, 138, 139n, 201, 202n, 230, 307, 308n
Astley, Thomas: and journals of Lewis and Clark Expedition, 43–4n

Astrea (schooner), 193
astronomy: books on, 13, 31
Atlantic Ocean: internal navigation to, 280–1
Augusti, Johann Christian Wilhelm: *Die katholischen Briefe: Neu übersesst und erklärt und mit Excursen und einleitenden Abhandlungen*, 307; *System der christlichen Dogmatik nach dem Lehrbegriffe der luterischen Kirche im Grundrisse*, 307
Augustus (Gaius Octavius; 1st Roman emperor), 34, 269
Aurora (Philadelphia newspaper): prints P. S. Du Pont de Nemours's obituary, 604; TJ's subscription to, 13, 455, 456, 648
Austin, Mr. (of Charlottesville), 274
Austin, Archibald: as U.S. representative from Va., 292, 293n
Austin, Benjamin (of Boston): identified, 9:249n; on Republican committee, 569–70n
Austin, Benjamin (of Charlottesville): and Central College subscription, 323, 328
Austin, Henry: and Asian antiquities, 115n
Austria: and Congress of Vienna, 540, 541n

bacon, 298, 299, 623
Bacon, Edmund: buys corn for TJ, 214; describes TJ's siting of Central College, 544–5n; identified, 1:52n; letters from, 211–2, 421; Monticello overseer, 211–2, 421; plans to move west, 211–2; TJ borrows money from, 451–2n
Bacon, Francis: mentioned, 390
Bacon, Mary Anne Williamson: account with TJ, 421, 451–2; identified, 451n
Bacot, Thomas Wright: and Seventy-Six Association, 530n
Baker, Harriet Weissenfels (John Martin Baker's wife): mentioned, 660, 661, 662
Baker, James: and fish for TJ, 66, 274, 295; letter from, 274–5; letters to, 66, 295; as Richmond merchant, 386
Baker, Jerman (*1776–1828*): and J. W. Baker's education, 18–9, 49, 59; and Central College subscription, 331, 596; identified, 9:278n; letters from, 59, 132–3; letter to, 18–9; and petition of P. I. Barziza, 19, 59, 146; and proposed Albemarle Co. road, 59, 119, 132
Baker, John Martin: as consul, 660–3; family of, 660, 661, 662; identified, 1:346n; letter from, 659–60; letter from, to R. Rush, 660–3; seeks appointment, 659–60, 660–3; visits Montpellier (Madison family estate), 659
Baker, John Wayles (TJ's grandnephew): education of, 18–9, 59; identified, 6:65n
Baker, Sir Richard: *A Chronicle of the Kings of England*, 274, 447
Baldwin, Briscoe: as attorney, 538–9
Baltimore, Md.: flooding in, 606, 614, 626n; and J. Monroe's presidential tour, 568, 569n; newspapers, 5, 277, 279n, 594, 594–6, 604, 648, 649. *See also* McCulloch, James Hugh (father of James H. McCulloh): collector at Baltimore
Bankhead, Ann (Anne) Cary Randolph (TJ's granddaughter; Charles Lewis Bankhead's wife): health of, 172; identified, 2:104n; pregnancy of, 15; visits Monticello, 631n
Bankhead, Charles Lewis (Ann Cary Randolph Bankhead's husband): identified, 3:188n; letters from accounted for, 244n; and proposed Albemarle Co. road, 243, 244n
Bankhead, John: family of, 172; identified, 8:278n
Bankhead, Thomas Mann Randolph (TJ's great-grandson): appearance of, 631n; health of, 631n
Bank of Columbia, 57, 124, 155
Bank of Richmond. *See* Bank of Virginia (Richmond)
Bank of the United States, Second: creation of, 110, 380; currency of, 585; and internal improvements, 123n; Richmond branch of, 304, 426, 451; TJ's loan from, 464, 476, 496, 593, 594, 605, 638
Bank of Virginia (Richmond): and Albemarle Academy, 253; banknotes of, 486, 585; and C. Bellini estate, 580; and Central College, 317; TJ's loan from, 208, 236–7, 290–1, 362, 379–80, 395, 426, 464, 476, 496, 593
The Bankrupt Law of America compared with The Bankrupt Law of England (T. Cooper), 369, 370n

banks: currency issued by, 356, 523; in Georgetown, D.C., 57, 124, 155; in New York, 508, 539; proliferation of, 288; TJ on, 194, 346; in Va., 67

Barbé Marbois, François, comte de: *Complot d'Arnold et de Sir Henry Clinton contre les États-Unis d'Amérique et contre le Général Washington. Septembre 1780*, 436, 438n, 503, 635–6; exile of, 436, 438n; identified, 437–8n; letter to, 436–8; T. Lyman introduced to, 294

Barbour, James: and Agricultural Society of Albemarle, 319; as governor of Va., 182; identified, 4:415–6n; letter from, 227; letter to, 3; portrait of, xlvi, 232 (*illus.*); seeks plants, 227; and TJ's designs for Barboursville, xlvi, 223–7, 227, 232 (*illus.*); and J. Trumbull's historical paintings, 3

Barbour, Philip Pendleton: and Agricultural Society of Albemarle, 319; identified, 5:391–2n

Barboursville (J. Barbour's Orange Co. plantation), xlvi, 223–7, 227, 232 (*illus.*)

Barclay, Samuel (ship captain), 531

Baring Brothers & Company (London firm): identified, 7:440n; and remittances to T. Kosciuszko, 350, 362

Barksdale, Nelson: as Central College proctor, 467n, 570; and Central College subscription, 326, 328

Barlow, Joel: identified, 1:589–90n; proposed historical work by, 461n

Barnaby (TJ's slave; b. *1783*). *See* Gillette, Barnaby (TJ's slave; b. *1783*)

Barnes, John: account with T. Kosciuszko, 57, 58n, 125; family of, 350; handles financial transactions, 425, 507–8, 539, 648; identified, 1:32n; and T. Kosciuszko's American investments, 27, 57–8, 124–5, 155, 187, 350, 361, 362, 447–8, 522, 523; letters from, 57–8, 155, 217–8, 350–1, 385–6, 402, 507–8, 522, 523–4, 539; letters to, 27, 124–5, 187, 361–2, 425–6, 438–9; letter to accounted for, 539n; letter to, from J. Milligan, 523–4; and runaway slave, 438–9, 522; sends newspaper to TJ, 217; ships goods to TJ, 523; TJ pays, 426n; TJ's account with, 522, 522–3; TJ's power of attorney to, 27, 57, 124–5, 155, 187; visits Monticello, 350, 361–2, 385–6, 402, 413, 425, 522

Barnet, Isaac Cox: as consul, 473; identified, 5:463–4n

barometers: altitude calculated with, 51–2

Barr, Thomas Tilton: identified, 10:593n; and Kentucky Society for Promoting Agriculture, 4; letter to, 4

barrels, 603

Barrington, Daines: as literary patron, 613

Barrois, Louis Théophile: as bookseller, 636

Barton, Benjamin Smith: identified, 1:521n; Indian vocabularies of, 454; and journals of M. Lewis, 486–7; and opossums, 367–8, 370n

Barton, Mary Pennington (Benjamin Smith Barton's wife): and journals of M. Lewis, 486–7, 574

Barziza, Giovanni (John L.), Count: TJ conveys letter to, 580

Barziza, Lucy Paradise, Countess (Antonio Barziza's wife; John and Lucy L. Paradise's daughter): family of, 147

Barziza, Philip Ignatius: and books for TJ, 120; identified, 9:7–8n; letter from, 120; letter to, 146–7; and L. L. Paradise estate, 19, 59, 66, 120, 146–7; visits Monticello, 580

Bassus, Cassianus: *Γεωπονικά Geoponicorum sive de re rustica libri XX* (ed. T. Owen; *1805–06*), 164; *Γεωπονικά Geoponicorum sive de re rustica libri XX* (trans. P. Needham; ed. J. N. Niclas; *1781*), 164

Battle, Mr.: and sheep, 347

Batture Sainte Marie, controversy over: lawsuit brought against TJ, 70. *See also* Livingston, Edward; *Livingston v. Jefferson*; *The Proceedings of the Government of the United States, in maintaining the Public Right to the Beach of the Missisipi* (Thomas Jefferson)

Bear Creek plantation (part of TJ's Poplar Forest estate): overseer at, 285

bears: in Va., 631

Bedford County, Va. *See also* Poplar Forest (TJ's Bedford Co. estate)

beekeeping: methods of, 503–4; works on, 165

beer: porter, 293

beets, 308
Bekker, Balthasar: *De Betoverde Weereld*, 231, 232n, 308
Bell, Thomas: as justice of the peace, 419n
Bellet (wine), 246, 404, 405, 407, 656, 657n
Bellini, Charles (Carlo Maria Marchionne): estate of, 580
Beloe, William: translates *Herodotus, Translated From The Greek, With Notes*, 268
Belsham, Thomas: *Memoirs of the Late Reverend Theophilus Lindsey, M.A.* (T. Lindsey), 230
Bergasse, Henri Joachim, 405
Bergasse, Henry, 405, 407, 653
Berkeley, George: works of, 383
Berkshire Agricultural Society: TJ as honorary member of, 279n; E. Watson as member of, 277, 279n, 338
Bernard, Simon: identified, 10:392n; introduced to TJ, 139–40, 180; letter from, 139–40; letter to, 180
De Betoverde Weereld (B. Bekker), 231, 232n, 308
Beverley Town, Va. *See* Westham, Va.
Bézout, Étienne: *Cours De Mathématiques*, 409, 452
Bible: 1 Corinthians referenced, 424; Ecclesiastes referenced by TJ, 338, 339n; Luke referenced, 115; Luke referenced by TJ, 24, 25n, 346, 347n; Matthew referenced, 115, 484; New Testament, 335, 368; Old Testament, 368; prints of scenes from, 403; Psalms referenced by TJ, 339–40; Ten Commandments, 525; TJ orders copies of, 30, 31, 452; works on, 115–6
Bibliothèque Britannique (eds. F. G. Maurice, C. Pictet de Rochemont, and M. A. Pictet), 444, 446n
Bibliothèque Universelle (eds. F. G. Maurice, C. Pictet de Rochemont, and M. A. Pictet), 443, 444, 446n
Biddle, Nicholas: identified, 2:74–5n; and Lewis and Clark Expedition, 43–4, 486–7, 574
Bidet, Nicolas: *Traité sur la nature et sur la culture de la Vigne*, 164
A Bill for the More General Diffusion of Knowledge (*1778*), 415, 416n
Bill Requiring the Sheriffs of the different counties and corporations within this Commonwealth, to take the sense of the people upon the propriety of calling a Convention (*1815*), 119n
birds: house martins, 39; swallows, 404; whip-poor-wills, 39; wood robins, 39
Birkbeck, Morris: *Notes on a Journey through France*, 124, 300–1; and settlement in U.S., 222, 301, 609
Bishop, Joseph: and Central College subscription, 322, 328
Bizet, Charles: acquires seed from TJ, 183; delivers letter, 248
Black, Christopher L.: identified, 529n; letter from, 528–30; letter to, 582; and Seventy-Six Association, 528–9, 582
Blackstone, William: as legal authority, 368
Blagden, George: and reconstruction of U.S. Capitol, 480
Blanchy (brig), 661
blindness, 359
Blue Ridge Mountains: routes through, 628–9
Blumenbach, Johann Friedrich: and classification of animals, 367
Blunt, Edmund March: *Blunt's Edition of the Nautical Almanac, and Astronomical Ephemeris, for the year 1817*, 13, 31; *Blunt's Edition of the Nautical Almanac, and Astronomical Ephemeris, for the year 1818*, 13, 31; identified, 4:13n
boatmen: payment of, 459
boats: military vessels, 498; and river navigation, 104, 413; steamboats, 32, 65–6, 111, 255, 435, 448, 457, 497–9, 539, 565; transfer goods to and from Richmond, 260, 290, 303, 337, 378, 548, 593
Bolingbroke, Henry St. John, Viscount: works of, 383
Bolland, Jean de: *Acta Sanctorum*, 527
Bolling, John (*1737–1800*) (TJ's brother-in-law): and Shadwell cemetery, 566
Bolling, William: and Central College subscription, 332
bolts, 548, 588
Bonaparte, Elizabeth Patterson: conveys letter, 618, 619n; identified, 8:378–9n
Bonaparte, Napoleon. *See* Napoleon I, emperor of France
Bond, Nathaniel S. (ship captain), 531

Bondurant, George W.: and Central College subscription, 331
Bondurant, William: and Central College subscription, 331
books: and African colonization, 11; on agriculture, 129, 162, 164–5, 245–6, 398; on American Revolution, 313, 364; on architecture, 335, 352, 396, 456; on astronomy, 13, 31; atlases, 582–3; binding of, 233, 247; binding of for TJ, 26, 205, 352, 362, 386, 394–5, 523, 539; biographical, 148; classical, 414; dictionaries, 13, 31, 67, 233, 247, 248n, 335, 352, 396, 397, 547, 592; on Egypt, 650; on gardening, 352; on history, 274, 447, 612, 650; on mathematics, 409, 537; on medicine, 4; on milling, 352; on moral philosophy, 283; on natural history, 192; on natural philosophy, 30, 31; novels, 254, 266, 627, 628n, 630; price of, 234; sent by N. G. Dufief, 13, 30, 31, 31–2, 161, 247; sent by Fernagus De Gelone, 193; sent by J. Laval, 283; sent by D. B. Warden, 417, 454, 501, 618; of speeches, 5; TJ recommends to G. W. Jeffreys, 164–5; TJ recommends to F. A. Van der Kemp, 307, 422; on War of *1812*, 159, 364, 382
Borda, Jean Charles de: *Description Et Usage Du Cercle De Réflexion*, 179, 193
Borda's circle (surveying instrument), 40, 179, 193
Bordley, John Beale: *Essays and Notes on Husbandry and Rural Affairs*, 165
Boston, Mass.: glass from, 112, 137, 307; Republican party in, 569–70
Boswell, James: anecdote of, 492; *The Life of Samuel Johnson LL.D.*, 495n
Botetourt, Norborne Berkeley, baron de: colonial governor of Va., 252
Botta, Carlo Giuseppe Guglielmo: identified, 2:529–30n; *Storia della Guerra dell' Independenza degli Stati Uniti d'America*, 313, 364, 452; works of, 205
Boudinot, Elias: *A Star in the West; or, A Humble Attempt to Discover the long lost Ten Tribes of Israel, preparatory to their return to their beloved city, Jerusalem*, 49, 230
Boulton, Matthew: manifold writer of, 481
Bourne, Sylvanus: death of, 660; identified, 2:352n
Bowdoin, James (*1752–1811*): identified, 3:96n; translates *Advice to Shepherds*, 164
Boyer, Isaac: identified, 598–9n; letter from, 597–9; letter to, 647; and politics in Pa., 597, 599n, 647
Bracken, John: and C. Bellini estate, 580; identified, 4:69n
Bradford & Inskeep (Philadelphia firm): and history of Lewis and Clark Expedition, 43–4n; identified, 7:289–90n
Bradley, James: and Barboursville plantation, 227; visits Monticello, 227
Bramham, Nimrod: and Central College subscription, 322, 328; identified, 5:528n; and Rivanna Company, 64, 76, 91, 99, 101–2, 259–60, 557–8
brandy: as wine additive, 296, 300, 345
Brazer, John: on Republican committee, 569–70n
Brazil: monarchy in, 355; relations with Portugal, 355, 384
bread: rye, 271
Bremo (J. H. Cocke's Fluvanna Co. estate), 274n
Bremo (TJ's horse): and carriage accident, 622
Brent, Daniel: identified, 8:495–6n; letters from, 458, 667–8; letters to, 421–2, 462; letter to accounted for, 580n; TJ sends letters through, 421–2, 458, 462, 667
Brent, William (brother of Daniel Brent): letter misaddressed to, 458
Brent, William (of Stafford Co.): and Central College subscription, 334, 636–7
brewing: at Monticello, 189, 216
Briggs, Isaac: and American Board of Agriculture, 338, 339n; and Erie Canal, 339, 357, 358n, 364–5, 376–7; family of, 358n, 376; identified, 9:476–7n; letters from, 339–40, 357–8, 376–7; letter to, 364–5; map praised by, 429, 430n; proposed as surveyor of Va., 365; recommends T. Moore, 358, 360, 376–7; seeks employment, 339–40; surveyor of federal lands, 364–5
Briggs, Mary Brooke: identified, 9:541n; mentioned, 339–40

Brisson, Mathurin Jacques: and scientific classification, 367
Broadhead, Achilles. *See* Brodhead (Broadhead), Achilles
Brockenbrough, Arthur Spicer: as University of Virginia proctor, 467n
Brodhead (Broadhead), Achilles: and Central College subscription, 328
Broglie, Achille Léonce Victor Charles, duc de: sends greetings to TJ, 117
Broglie, Albertine Ida Gustavine de Staël Holstein, duchesse de: marriage of, 283; sends greetings to TJ, 117
Broglie, Victor François, duc de: family of, 283
Brooke, Mary Brooke Briggs. *See* Briggs, Mary Brooke
Brougham, Henry Peter, Baron Brougham and Vaux: quoted, 23, 24–5n
Brown, Brightberry: and proposed Albemarle Co. road, 243
Brown, Charles (of Albemarle Co.): and Central College subscription, 324, 328
Brown, Elijah: and Central College subscription, 326, 328
Brown, Jacob Jennings: circular sent to, 595; as major general, 494; and J. Monroe's presidential tour, 568
Brown, John (*1762–1826*): Va. superior court judge, 71, 72
Brown, Mather: and portrait of J. Adams, 252
Brown, Robert: *A Treatise on Agriculture and Rural Affairs*, 165, 228
Brown, William (first listed, of Albemarle Co.): and Central College subscription, 326, 328
Brown, William (second listed, of Albemarle Co.): and Central College subscription, 328
Brown & Robertson (Lynchburg firm). *See* Robertson, Archibald
Bruce, James: *Travels to discover the Source of the Nile, In the Years 1768, 1769, 1770, 1771, 1772, and 1773*, 612–4, 650
Brumley, Reuben (ship captain), 531
Brutus, Marcus Junius: J. Adams on, 269
Bryant, Jacob: works of, 363, 527
Bryant, Lemuel: and J. Adams, 268–9
Bryce, Archibald: and Central College subscription, 332
Brzozowski, Tadeusz, 363, 364n
Buchanan, Joseph: *The Philosophy of Human Nature*, 364, 382
Buckley & Abbott (New York firm): and remittances to T. Kosciuszko, 350
Buffon, Georges Louis Leclerc, comte de: and classification of animals, 367; and natural history, 367
building materials: artificial stone, 389, 391n; bricks, 223–4, 225, 534–5, 558–9, 602, 603, 610, 648; cement, 113, 114n; lime (mineral), 113, 349; lumber, 207; mahogany, 307, 548; marble, 480–1, 535, 563, 572, 612, 614n; mortar, 389; paint, 142, 197–8; plank, 225; plaster, 389; shingles, 225; stone, 349–50; timber, 80, 81, 169, 179, 213, 603; window glass, 112, 137, 225, 307
Burger, Samuel: identified, 530n; letter from, 528–30; letter to, 582; and Seventy-Six Association, 528–9, 582
Burgoyne, John: J. Trumbull's painting of, 145, 166
Burk, John Daly: *The History of Virginia*, 283
Burlamaqui, Jean Jacques: as legal authority, 368
Burnley, Mr.: agricultural report by, 385
Burton, Hutchins Gordon: identified, 51n; letters from, 50–1, 238; letters to, 156, 300; and wine for TJ, 50, 156, 175, 237, 238, 292, 295–6, 300, 302
Burwell, William Armistead: and Central College subscription, 327n, 590–1; forwards papers to TJ, 6, 56, 153; identified, 2:105–6n; letters from, 6–7, 153; letters to, 56, 590–2
Busby (Bushby), Richard: anecdote of, 491
Bushby, Dr. *See* Busby (Bushby), Richard
Bussolari, Jacopo: F. A. Van der Kemp studies, 231, 232n, 308
Butler, Henry (ship captain), 397n
Byrd, William (*1674–1744*): *The History of the Dividing Line*, 21, 22, 127n, 206, 426, 477, 487, 524; library of, 477; *The Secret History of the Line*, 21–2, 125–6, 206, 239, 426, 450–1, 477, 524, 574
Byrd, William (*1728–77*): family of, 477

cabbage: seed, 221
Cabell, George: boats of, 290, 337; and Central College subscription, 566n,

Cabell, George (*cont.*) 636; identified, 9:589n; letter to, 300–1; TJ introduces G. Flower to, 300–1
Cabell, Hannah Carrington: death of, 637
Cabell, Joseph Carrington: and Agricultural Society of Albemarle, 319; on banks, 67; and Central College subscription, 322, 327n, 333, 636–7; and Destutt de Tracy's writings, 67; on hedges, 228; identified, 2:489–90n; letters from, 66–7, 133–4, 228, 275–6, 636–7; and petition of P. I. Barziza, 66, 146; and proposed Albemarle Co. road, 66, 133; and Rivanna Company, 69; as Va. state senator, 133, 172, 275; visits Monticello, 258, 565. *See also* Central College, Board of Visitors
Cabell, Landon: and Central College subscription, 333
Cabell, William (*1759–1822*): and Central College subscription, 333
Caesar, Julius: J. Adams on, 269
cake, 670
Calhoun, John Caldwell: as secretary of war, 146n, 452n; as U.S. representative from Ky., 165–6
Callaway, George: and Central College subscription, 333; identified, 4:165n
Callis, Ann Price: and H. Marks's estate, 567
Callis, William Overton: and H. Marks's estate, 400
Camm, John (*1775–1818*): and Central College subscription, 636
Campbell, John (of Albemarle Co.): and Agricultural Society of Albemarle, 319
Campbell, S.: as keeper of Richmond library, 395–6
Campbell, Thomas: *The Pleasures of Hope*, 396
Campbell, W. (of Goochland Co.): and Central College subscription, 332
Campbell's Mill (Albemarle Co.), 186
Canada: agriculture in, 136
canals: Champlain, 218–9, 259, 280–1, 358n; Delaware and Raritan, 415; Erie, 218–9, 259, 280–1, 339, 357–8, 360, 364–5, 376–7, 415, 434–5, 448; on Potomac River, 563, 565n; proposed, 218–9, 259; on Rivanna River, 70, 72–98, 108; at Shadwell mills, 102, 348–50, 550–4; in U.S., 122. *See also* Rivanna Company
Canby, William: identified, 6:447–8n; letter from, 115–6; and C. Thomson's writings, 115–6
candles, 617
cannon, 53–4, 54–5
Canova, Antonio: Italian sculptor, 171
Capitol, U.S.: construction and repair of, 480, 571; corncob capitals for, xlv–xlvi, 232 (*illus.*), 481; B. H. Latrobe works on, 480–1; marble for, 480–1, 535, 563, 572, 612, 614n; tobacco-leaf capitals for, xlv–xlvi, 232 (*illus.*), 481, 535, 572; J. Trumbull's paintings for, 3, 145, 166; and War of *1812*, 480
Carew, Sir Benjamin Hallowell: as British naval officer, 661, 663n
Carmignani, Giovanni: identified, 9:645n; letter from, 249–50; letter to, 643–6; and P. Mazzei's estate, 249, 577–9, 642–3, 643–6
Carnation cherry, 464
Carolina allspice, 174
Carr, Dabney (*1773–1837*) (TJ's nephew): and Central College subscription, 334; identified, 2:152n
Carr, Daniel Ferrell: and Agricultural Society of Albemarle, 319; and Central College subscription, 325, 328; identified, 7:618–9n
Carr, Frank: and Agricultural Society of Albemarle, 319; and Albemarle Academy, 314; and Central College subscription, 324, 328; correspondence of, 540, 541n; family of, 340–1; identified, 6:230n; letter from, 340–1
Carr, James O.: and Central College subscription, 328
Carr, John F.: and Central College subscription, 328
Carr, Peter (*1816–1858*): birth of, 340n
Carr, Samuel (TJ's nephew): and Agricultural Society of Albemarle, 319; and Central College subscription, 322, 328; identified, 3:454n; TJ pays, 593, 594n
Carr, Virginia Terrell (TJ's sister Martha Jefferson Carr's granddaughter; Frank Carr's wife): death of, 340–1n, 443, 447n
carriages: accidents of, 622; gigs, 14; odometers for, 504, 506n; platting instruments for, 504–6, 581; stagecoaches, 303; taxes on, 44

carrots, 271–2, 273n
Carter, Hill: and Central College subscription, 636
Carter, William (of Richmond): and Central College subscription, 334
Carter, William F.: and Central College subscription, 332
Carter's Mountain (Albemarle Co.): mentioned, 318–9
Caruthers, William: death of, 589, 590n; identified, 1:367n; introduces P. Henry, 397; letter from, 397–8; letter to, 428; and Natural Bridge, 397, 428
Cary, Miles: and Central College subscription, 325, 332
Cary, Wilson Jefferson: and Agricultural Society of Albemarle, 319; and Central College subscription, 325, 332; identified, 4:58–9n
Casanuova di Ama, Italy: wine from, 171, 579–80
Cassius Dio: edition of by F. W. Sturz, 415
Catalogue of Latin, English, French, Spanish, and Italian Books, Maps, &c. for sale by J. L. Fernagus De Gelone, Agent, for the United States, Canada, New-Orleans, Spanish America, and Isles (J. L. Fernagus De Gelone), 152n, 295, 335
Cathalan, Stephen (Étienne) (*1757–1819*): account with TJ, 420, 454, 455, 531–2, 533, 652–4; as commercial agent in Marseille, 128, 246, 405–6, 407, 584, 652–3; as consul, 487–8, 508–13, 532–4; family of, 542, 543n, 584, 654; identified, 1:313n; letters from, 508–14, 531–4, 652–4; letters to, 196–7, 404–7, 584–5; letters to, from A. Spreafico, 656–7, 657–8; letter to, from Pierre Mages & Compagnie, 656–7; letter to, from J. V. A. Sasserno, 655; mentioned, 420; recommends J. Dodge, 508–13, 533; sends flowers to TJ, 406, 531; TJ introduces W. C. Preston to, 196–7, 200; and wine for TJ, 131–2, 404–6, 407, 531–2, 584, 652–4, 656
Catherine II ("the Great"), empress of Russia: as linguist, 562
Catherinens der Grossen Verdienste um die Vergleichende Sprachenkunde (F. Adelung), 562
Catholicism: and ecclesiastical authority, 27–8, 63–4
Catiline: J. Adams on, 269
Cato the Elder: mentioned, 162; *Rei rusticae*, 164
cattle: in agricultural shows, 277; feed for, 171–2; fodder for, 158, 199, 271, 272, 308–9; and milk, 271, 272
cedar, 566
Census, U.S.: of *1810*, 12
Central College: as academical village, 586, 588n; brickmasons for, 534–5, 558–9, 602, 603, 610, 648, 669; builders for, 256, 273, 274n, 400, 401, 463, 464n, 468–9, 471; cellars at, 603, 669; Central College Subscription List, 322–7; construction of, 317, 545–6, 610; designs for, 387–90, 393, 431–2, 453, 479–81, 535, 563–5, 610–2; dormitory rooms at, 317; Draft Bill to Create Central College and Amend the *1796* Public Schools Act, 664, 666n; establishment of, 314–5, 364, 384, 548; and Freemasons, 669–70; land purchased for, xlv, 232 (*illus.*), 253, 258, 301, 302n, 315–7, 318–9, 321, 344, 401, 463, 464n, 465–7, 468, 471; lottery for, 317, 321; Master List of Subscribers to Central College, 328–35; pavilions at, 342–3, 388–9, 393, 468, 570; plan for, 664–6, 667; plasterers for, 669; plat of lands, xlv, 232 (*illus.*); proctor of, 253, 570; professors at, 335–6, 396, 566, 570, 596, 665; siting of, 502, 544–5, 545–6, 547n, 565, 611; as state university of Va., 133–4n, 257, 258, 315, 415, 458, 502, 587; stonecutters for, 535, 570, 571, 579, 602, 610–1; subscription for, 314–5, 317, 322–7, 328–35, 467n, 471, 485, 486, 535, 545, 546, 559, 561, 565–6, 590–1, 592n, 596, 636, 640, 650–1, 664–5; TJ's architectural designs for, 342–3, 431–2, 535, 563, 564, 586–7, 649–50, 665. *See also* Albemarle Academy; Virginia, University of
Central College, Board of Visitors: Anonymous Description of Meeting, 320–1; J. H. Cocke's Descriptions of Meetings, 318–9, 565–6; meetings of planned, 62, 181, 183, 218, 220, 228, 229, 232, 242, 248, 257, 257–8, 262, 275, 276, 291, 301, 545–6; members of, 253, 256, 274n, 303, 312–3, 335–6,

Central College, Board of Visitors (*cont.*) 342–3, 364, 384, 387, 391n, 432, 502, 579, 664, 667, 670; Minutes of, 314–5, 316–8, 570; and subscription, 327n, 546–7, 559, 561, 590–1
Ceracchi, Giuseppe: bust of TJ by, 267, 342, 387
Cerberus (mythological creature), 346
Champlain Canal, 218–9, 259, 280–1, 358n
Chapman, Eunice: divorce of, 412n
Chapman, James: divorce of, 412n
Chaptal, Jean Antoine, comte de: *Traité théorique et pratique sur la Culture de la Vigne*, 164
Charleston, S.C.: cisterns in, 113; learned societies in, 168; Seventy-Six Association, 528–30, 582; Sons of Liberty, 167, 168n
Charlottesville, Va.: description of, 258, 449; Freemasons of, 669–70; roads in, 243, 244n, 244–5; silversmith needed in, 413, 548–9, 604–5; stagecoach to, from Washington, 413; watchmaker needed in, 157, 198–9, 374; weavers needed in, 413, 449–50, 463–4, 470, 471–2, 506–7, 602; Wells's Hotel, 545
Chase, Samuel: as legal authority, 369, 370n
Chastellux, Marquis de: *Travels in North America in the Years 1780, 1781 and 1782*, 370n
Chateaubriand, François Auguste René, vicomte de: J. Adams reads, 268
Chauncey, Charles: and journals of Lewis and Clark Expedition, 43–4n
Chauncey, Isaac: as U.S. Navy commodore, 122, 123n, 509–10, 513n, 534n
Chazal, John P. (ship captain), 263
Cheatwood, Alexander: and Central College subscription, 331
cherries: Carnation, 464; as crop, 39
Chesapeake Bay: defense of, 448
Chesterfield, Philip Stanhope, 2d Earl of: anecdote about, 491
chestnut: in Va., 624
chickens, 623
Chicoilet de Corbigny, Louis Antoine Ange: *Tableaux Historiques des Campagnes d'Italie, depuis l'an IV jusqu'a la bataille de Marengo*, 402
chicory (succory), 308–10
children: letter to: P. A. Clay, 525–6; and TJ's Canons of Conduct, 525. *See also* education; games; health: pregnancy and childbirth; Henderson case: claims by minor heirs; Jefferson, Thomas: Family & Friends: great grandchildren; Jefferson, Thomas: Family & Friends: relations with grandchildren; Monticello (TJ's estate): schooling at; schools and colleges; *specific entries for TJ's Eppes and Randolph descendants*
Childress, Benjamin: and proposed Albemarle Co. road, 243
Chiles, Henry: Albemarle Co. land of, 466, 467n; and Central College subscription, 324, 328
chinaberry (Pride of China), 179
Chippewa, Battle of (*1814*), 494
Chisholm, Hugh: and brickwork for Central College, 471, 603, 648, 669; and Central College subscription, 323, 328; identified, 3:67–8n; letters from, 603, 648; letter to, 669
Choron, Alexandre Étienne: educational system of, 639, 640n
Christianity: Inquisition, 383; TJ on, 29, 308; F. A. Van der Kemp on, 307–8; works on, 423–4
A Chronicle of the Kings of England (R. Baker), 274, 447
Church, Angelica Schuyler (John Barker Church's wife), 160, 166
Church, John Barker, 166
Cicero: J. Adams on, 269; *De Officiis*, 289–90n; as legal authority, 368; quoted, 286, 290n; *Somnium Scipionis*, 232n
Ciracchi. *See* Ceracchi, Giuseppe
circles (surveying instruments). *See* Borda's circle (surveying instrument)
cisterns: in Charleston, S.C., 113
Claiborne, Richard: and duck-foot paddle, 497–9; identified, 499–500n; letter from, 497–500
Claiborne, Sterling: and Central College subscription, 636
claret (wine), 405, 407
Clark, Aaron: identified, 394n; letter from, 393–4; *An Oration. A Project For the Civilization of the Indians of North America*, 393, 394n
Clark, Abraham: family of, 607; identified, 608n; recommendation of D. Whitehead by, 608
Clark, Christopher Henderson: identified, 2:323–4n; letter from, 280; and

New London Academy, 280; and proposed road, 280
Clark, Mary Norvell (Christopher Henderson Clark's second wife): visits springs, 625
Clark (Clarke), William: as governor of Missouri Territory, 43; identified, 1:511n; and journals of Lewis and Clark Expedition, 43–4, 454, 486–7, 574; and letter for L. Marks, 43, 44n, 198; letter from, 43–4
Clarke, Mr. (of Albemarle Co.): as political candidate, 172
Clarke, James (of Albemarle Co.): and Central College subscription, 328
Clarke, James (of Powhatan Co.): identified, 506n; letter from, 504–6; letter to, 581; odometer of, 504, 506n; platting instrument of, 504–6, 581; visits Monticello, 504, 506n
Clarke, James Henry: and S. Cathalan, 509
Clarke, Samuel: works of, 383
classics: collegiate education in, 336; German scholarship on, 408, 414–5
Clavis Homerica: sive Lexicon Vocabulorum Omnium, Quæ continentur in Homeri Iliade et potissimâ parte Odysseæ (ed. S. Patrick), 205
Clay, Charles: and artichoke roots, 179; family of, 525; identified, 2:78n; letter to, 524–5; mentioned, 623; TJ visits, 524; visits Poplar Forest, 627
Clay, Editha Landon Davies (Charles Clay's wife): visits Poplar Forest, 627
Clay, Henry: declines appointment, 146; identified, 10:378n
Clay, Paul Aurelius: identified, 525–6n; letter to, 525–6; TJ's Canons of Conduct sent to, 525
Cleopatra's Barge (yacht), 512–3
Clericus, Johannes. *See* Leclerc, Jean (Johannes Clericus)
Cleverley, Joseph: and J. Adams's education, 268–9
Clinton, DeWitt: and Champlain Canal, 218–9, 259, 280–1; and J. Delaplaine's *Repository*, 202; and Erie Canal, 218–9, 259, 280–1, 339, 377; identified, 8:348n; letters from, 218–9, 280–1; letter to, 259; as Masonic grand master, 493; *Remarks on the Proposed Canal, from Lake Erie to the Hudson River*, 218–9
clocks: at Monticello, 130; repairman needed for, 157, 198–9, 374. *See also* sundials
cloth. *See* textiles
clothing: drawers, 450; handkerchiefs, 626n, 627n; manufacture of, 413, 449–50, 463–4, 470, 471–2, 506–7, 602; pantaloons, 450; petticoats, 450; purses, 625; stockings, 450; under-vests, 450; walking sticks, 167, 168, 344
clover: as crop, 163, 309, 421; red, 39
coaches. *See* carriages
Coade, Eleanor: manufactory of, 389, 391n
coal: in Va., 25, 65
Coalter, John: and Central College subscription, 334
Cobbs, John P.: and Central College subscription, 333
Cockburn, George: as British admiral, 480
Cocke, Charles: and Agricultural Society of Albemarle, 319; and Central College subscription, 323, 328
Cocke, John Hartwell: and Agricultural Society of Albemarle, 319; and Bremo (house), 274n; and Central College subscription, 322, 327n, 332; descriptions of Central College Board of Visitors meetings by, 318–20, 565–6; identified, 3:136n; letters from, 218, 546–7; letters to, 181–2, 219–20, 301–2, 545–6; slaves of, 651n; TJ sends plants to, 219–20; visits Monticello, 218, 258, 327n, 337, 546, 565; and wine, 218, 219, 300. *See also* Central College, Board of Visitors
cod: New England, 66, 274, 295; tongues and sounds, 66, 295
The Code of Agriculture (J. Sinclair), 381–2
coffee: clarification of, 5; cultivation of, 345; TJ purchases, 617
Coffman, Joseph: and Central College subscription, 328
Coke, Sir Edward: as legal authority, 368
Colclaser, Daniel: identified, 603n; letter to, 603; as miller, 168, 185, 603
Cole, Sally Cottrell (TJ's slave): as maid, 627n
Coleman, Joseph: and proposed Albemarle Co. road, 243
Coleman, Robert L.: and Central College subscription, 326, 328

Coleman, William (New York editor), 490–1
Coles, Edward: identified, 2:225–6n; as J. Madison's secretary, 122, 123n
Coles, Isaac A.: and Agricultural Society of Albemarle, 319; and Central College subscription, 323, 328; family of, 336, 337; identified, 1:53–4n; letter from, 337; letter to, 336; and seeds, 336, 337
Coles, John: and Agricultural Society of Albemarle, 319; and Central College subscription, 323, 328
Coles, Tucker: and Agricultural Society of Albemarle, 319; and Central College subscription, 323, 328
Coles, Walter: and Central College subscription, 323, 328
Colle (Albemarle Co. estate): and proposed Albemarle Co. road, 243, 244n, 244
A Collection of State-Papers (J. Adams), 49n, 201
colleges. *See* schools and colleges
Colloquia (M. Cordier), 627–8
Colloquia, nunc emendatiora (D. Erasmus), 452
Columbian Institute for the Promotion of Arts and Sciences: *An Address, delivered before the Columbian Institute, for the Promotion of Arts and Sciences, at the City of Washington, on the 11th January, 1817* (E. Cutbush), 143–4n; circular of, 144n; honorary members of, 144n; TJ elected honorary member of, 143, 144n, 148–9
Columbus, Christopher: mentioned, 193
Columella: *Rei rusticae*, 164
Combs, Leslie: sends books to J. Adams, 382, 384n
Commentary and Review of Montesquieu's Spirit of Laws (Destutt de Tracy): J. Adams on, 45; sent to J. Adams, 31; TJ on, 359
Commerce, Report on (Thomas Jefferson), 65
commode, 307
common law: and jurisprudence, 369, 433; and TJ's revision of laws, 432–4
A Compleat Body of Husbandry (T. Hale), 164
Complot d'Arnold et de Sir Henry Clinton contre les États-Unis d'Amérique et contre le Général Washington. Septembre 1780 (Barbé Marbois), 436, 438n, 503, 635–6
Conciones et Orationes Ex Historicis Latinis excerptæ, 452
Condorcet, Marie Jean Antoine Nicolas de Caritat, marquis de: J. Adams on, 45, 527; *The Life of M. Turgot*, 527; *Vie de Monsieur Turgot*, 527
Condy, Thomas Doughty: identified, 530n; letter from, 528–30; letter to, 582; and Seventy-Six Association, 528–9, 582
Congress, U.S.: activities of, 122–3; compensation for members of, 122, 123n, 269, 270n, 410; elections to, 410; and federalism, 433; *The Memorial Of Frederick Jenkins, and Rensselaer Havens, in behalf of the owners, officers, and crew of the late private armed brig General Armstrong*, 25, 26n, 65; *The Memorial Of Ship-owners, and others, interested in foreign commerce, convened by public notice at the Tontine Coffee House, in the city of New-York, the 17th January, 1817*, 25, 26n; and paintings for U.S. Capitol, 145, 166, 167n; petitions to, 25, 26n, 60, 279n, 609n; and slavery, 61. *See also* Capitol, U.S.; House of Representatives, U.S.; Library of Congress; Senate, U.S.
Connaissance des Temps: ou, des Mouvements célestes à l'usage des astronomes et des navigateurs, 13
Connecticut: Connecticut Society for the Encouragement of American Manufactures, 169–70, 215; elections in, 269–70, 312; governor of, 270n, 354, 355n; legislature of, 354
Considérations sur les principaux évènemens de La Révolution Françoise (Staël Holstein), 116–8
Constant de Rebecque, Henri Benjamin: *De La Liberté des Brochures, des Pamphlets et des Journaux*, 601n
Constantius II, Roman emperor: religious beliefs of, 424, 425n
Constellation, USS (frigate), 509, 534n, 662
Constitution, U.S.: and federalism, 123n, 369, 410–1, 415; threats to, 177n; and Va. Ratification Convention, 503
Continental Congress, U.S.: and Declaration of Independence, 202

Coolidge, Ellen Wayles Randolph (TJ's granddaughter): books critiqued by, 627n; delivers message, 669; education of, 625, 626–7, 632n, 670; friends of, 181; greetings sent to, 289; health of, 625, 629; identified, 6:646–7n; letters from, to M. J. Randolph, 625–6, 626–8; sends greetings to relatives, 624n; TJ gives money to, 523; travels of, xlv, 631n; visits Natural Bridge, xlvii–xlviii, 596, 617, 618n, 621–4, 625, 628–30, 631, 641; visits Poplar Forest, 626, 626–7, 628, 641, 669–70

Cooper, Thomas: *The Bankrupt Law of America compared with The Bankrupt Law of England*, 369, 370n; Central College professorship proposed for, 566; identified, 2:377n; *The Institutes of Justinian. With Notes*, 369, 370n, 433–4; religious beliefs of, 367

Coray, Adamantios: edition of Hierocles by, 251; edition of Homer by, 251; edits *Πλουτάρχου Βίοι Παράλληλοι* (Plutarch), 251, 296; edits *Τὸ Περὶ Ἀέρων, Ὑδάτων, Τόπων* (Hippocrates), 251

Cordier, Mathurin: *Colloquia*, 627–8

corks: sent to TJ, 216; TJ orders, 189, 193; velvet, 204

Cormon, Jacques Louis Barthélemi: *Dictionnaire portatif et de prononciation, Espagnol-Français et Français-Espagnol*, 335, 352, 396, 397; *Dizionario Portatile e di Pronunzia, Francese-Italiano, ed Italiano-Francese*, 547, 592

corn: cob capitals, xlv–xlvi, 232 (*illus.*), 481; as crop, 39, 163, 197–8, 284, 426; effect of weather on, 111, 290; as fodder, 158, 199, 272; Indian, 39, 271, 309, 482; price of, 62, 207; for slaves, 547; TJ buys, 57, 179, 207, 214, 236, 594n; transportation of, 179

Cornwallis, Charles, 2d Earl Cornwallis: surrender of, 166; J. Trumbull's painting of, 145, 166

Corny, Marguérite Victoire de Palerne de: health of, 166; identified, 1:175n; letter to, 160–1; TJ inquires about, 160–1, 173–4; TJ introduces R. C. Derby and M. C. Derby to, 142, 160

Corrêa da Serra, José: and American Philosophical Society, 125; identified, 4:538–9n; introduces R. C. Derby to TJ, 141; and journals of M. Lewis, 454, 486–7; letters from, 141, 526; letter to, 439–40; proposed visit of, 439–40, 526; travels with TJ, xlvii–xlviii, 621–2; U.S. travels of, 526, 639; on Virginia, 502

Correspondance Choisie de Benjamin Franklin (ed. W. T. Franklin), 255

Correspondance de Fernand Cortès avec l'empereur Charles-Quint (trans. Flavigny), 127, 152

Corso di agricoltura (M. A. Lastri), 164

Cortés, Hernán: correspondence of, 127

Cosway, Maria Louisa Catherine Cecilia Hadfield: friendship with TJ, 160, 166

Cottom, Peter: identified, 7:561n; as subscription agent, 541

cotton: price of, in Great Britain, 635; purchased by TJ, 593; as textile, 11

Cotton, Sir Charles (*1753–1812*): British admiral, 661

Cottrell, Sally (TJ's slave). *See* Cole, Sally Cottrell (TJ's slave)

Coup-D'Oeil sur L'État Actuel de la Litterature Ancienne et de l'Histoire en Allemagne (C. F. D. de Villers), 414–5

Cours complet d'agriculture, théorique, practique, économique, et de médicine rurale et vétérinaire ... ou dictionnaire universel d'agriculture (F. Rozier), 164

Cours De Mathématiques (É. Bézout), 409, 452

Court de Gébelin, Antoine: works of, 363, 527

Courtois, Edme Bonaventure: *Rapport fait au nom de la commission chargée de l'examen des papiers trouvés Chez Robespierre et ses complices*, 127, 152

cows. *See* cattle

Craufurd, Quintin: papers of, 613

Craven, John H.: and Central College subscription, 324, 328; identified, 2:112–3n

Craven's Mill (Albemarle Co.), 186

Crawford, William Harris: and T. Appleton's consular ambitions, 239; identified, 7:425–6n; as minister plenipotentiary to France, 661; as secretary of war, 146; seeds sent to, 171; as U.S. senator, 165–6

cress: winter, 271, 273n

Crèvecoeur, J. Hector St. John de: in London, xlvii–xlviii

Cropper, Thomas, 221

crops: alfalfa, 308–9; clover, 163, 309, 421; failure of, 122, 465; hay, 172, 272; potatoes, 221, 272–3, 309; rye, 475; strawberries, 39. *See also* corn; cotton; tobacco; wheat
Crouch, John G.: and Central College subscription, 332
Crowninshield, Benjamin Williams: family of, 488, 489n; identified, 9:412n; as secretary of the navy, 146, 488, 509, 512, 513, 533–4, 652
Crowninshield, George: and *Cleopatra's Barge*, 512–3; family of, 488, 489n; identified, 488n; letter from, 487–9; recommends J. Dodge to TJ, 487–8, 512–3
Cruger, Catherine "Kitty" Church, 142, 166, 173
cucumbers, 39
Cudworth, Ralph: works of, 383
Cullen, William: and nosology, 367
Culloden, Battle of (*1746*), 494, 495n
Culture de la Grosse Asperge dite de Hollande (J. J. Fillassier), 165
cuneiform: characters reproduced in print, 115n, 136
Curd, Isaac: and Central College subscription, 328
Curran, John Philpot: anecdote of, 492–3
currants: sweet-scented, 174
currency: exchange of, 455, 585; metallic, 67, 111; paper, 67, 194, 346, 356, 486, 523; U.S. House of Representatives Committee on, 165–6; works on, 61, 62n
Currie, Ellyson: and Central College subscription, 636
Cushing, Charles: friendship with J. Adams, 217, 218n
Cutbush, Edward: *An Address, delivered before the Columbian Institute, for the Promotion of Arts and Sciences, at the City of Washington, on the 11th January, 1817*, 143–4n
Cutting, Nathaniel: as consul at Le Havre, 60; and D. Humphreys's mission to Algiers, 60; identified, 10:677–8n; letter to, 60; and rope manufactory, 60; seeks congressional land grant, 60
Cuvier, Georges: and classification of animals, 367; identified, 6:470n

Dacier, André: *Extrait de la Vie d'Hippocrate,* in *Traduction des œuvres médicales d'Hippocrate, sur le texte grec, d'après l'édition de Foës* (ed. D. J. Tournon; trans. J. B. Gardeil), 127, 152, 297
Daily National Intelligencer (Washington newspaper). *See* National Intelligencer (Washington newspaper)
Dallas, Alexander James: death of, 153, 180–1; identified, 8:127n; library of, 503; *Proposals for publishing, by subscription, The Works of Alexander James Dallas* (G. M. Dallas), 153–4, 180–1
Dallas, George Mifflin: family of, 153, 180–1; identified, 154n; letter from, 153–4; letter to, 180–1; *Proposals for publishing, by subscription, The Works of Alexander James Dallas*, 153–4, 180–1
Dallas, Matilda, 181
Dalton, Tristram: on field cultivation of vegetables, 271–3, 308–9; friendship with J. Adams, 217, 218n; identified, 8:678–9n; letters from, 270–3, 386; letter to, 308–10; and plowing, 386; sends pamphlets to TJ, 270, 308, 386
dams: on Rivanna River, 69, 72–98, 102, 104, 108, 200, 550–4
Dandridge, William: as boundary commissioner, 22, 23n
Daniel, William: and Central College subscription, 331
Darby, William: *A Geographical Description of the State of Louisiana*, 429, 459–60; identified, 429–30n; letter from, 429–30; letter to, 459–60; map of Louisiana by, 429, 430n, 616
Darmsdatt, Joseph: and fish for TJ, 336–7; identified, 2:423n; letter to, 336–7; TJ pays, 336–7
Darnell, Mr. *See* Darnil, Nimrod
Darnil (Darnell; Darniel; Darnold), Nimrod: identified, 5:593n; TJ pays, 285
Daubenton, Louis Jean Marie: *Advice to Shepherds* (trans. J. Bowdoin), 164
David, Jacques Louis: compared to J. Trumbull, 3
David Moffit (brig), 531
Davy, Sir Humphry: safety lamp of, 501
Dawson, Allen: and Central College subscription, 323, 328
Dawson, Henry: and Central College subscription, 333

Dawson, Martin: and Central College subscription, 328; identified, 2:281–2n; and Milton lands, 43n, 263
Day, Charles: and Central College subscription, 326, 329
Deane, F. B.: and Central College subscription, 331
Dearborn, Henry Alexander Scammell: identified, 4:197n; letter from, 302; on Republican committee, 569–70n; and seeds for TJ, 302, 353, 378
de Bure Frères (Paris firm): identified, 10:232n; letter to, 408–9; TJ purchases books from, 296, 408–9, 414–5, 417, 418n, 618, 632; TJ's account with, 408–9, 414, 420, 454
Declaration of Independence: TJ as author of, 202–3, 252, 286, 434n; J. Trumbull's painting of presentation of, 145, 166
The Declaration of Independence (J. Trumbull), 145, 166
De Distributione Geographica Plantarum (Humboldt), 395, 434
Dedman, Dixon: and Central College subscription, 326, 328
De Laage, Madame (A. F. De Laage's wife): introduced by TJ, 621; sends greetings to M. J. Randolph, 575; TJ's granddaughters visit, 627
De Laage, A. F.: L. H. Girardin introduces, 296; identified, 576n; introduced by TJ, 619, 620–1; letters from, 575–6, 620; letter to, 619; moves to Lynchburg, 575, 619, 620–1, 627; visits Monticello, 296, 575; visits Poplar Forest, 620, 627
De La Liberté des Brochures, des Pamphlets et des Journaux (H. B. Constant de Rebecque), 601n
Delaplaine, Joseph: and biography of TJ, 202–3, 251–2; *Delaplaine's Repository*, 148, 202–3, 251–2; identified, 3:51n; letters from, 148, 202–3; letter to, 251–2; and publication of TJ's letters, 29, 46; visits Monticello, 202–3
Delaware: Quakers in, 354
Delaware and Raritan Canal, 415
Della Rocca, Abbé: *Traité Complet sur les Abeilles*, 165
Democritus (ancient Greek philosopher), 527
Dennie, Joseph: and W. Byrd manuscript, 126
dental care: dentures made by C. W. Peale, 158
De Officiis (Cicero), 289–90n
de Pradt, Dominique Georges Frédéric: *Récit Historique sur la Restauration de la Royauté en France, le 31 Mars 1814*, 601n
Derby, Martha Coffin (Richard C. Derby's wife): proposed visit to Monticello of, 134–5, 173; TJ introduces, 160; travels of, 142–3, 173–4
Derby, Richard Crowninshield: identified, 143n; introduced to TJ, 114–5, 134–5, 141; letter from, 142–3; letter to, 173–4; proposed visit to Monticello of, 134–5, 142, 173; TJ introduces, 160; travels of, 142–3, 173–4
Derieux, Maria Margherita Martin (Peter Derieux's wife): stepdaughter of P. Mazzei, 21
Derieux, Peter (Justin Pierre Plumard): identified, 3:395–6n; letter from, 566–7; letter to, 21; and P. Mazzei, 21, 566, 579, 645; requests assistance from TJ, 566
Descaves, Mark L.: conveys letter to TJ, 528, 581; identified, 528n; introduced to TJ, 282; letter from, 528; letter to, 581
Description et Usage du Cercle de Réflexion (J. C. de Borda), 179, 193
Desdemona (Shakespearean character), 628
Destutt de Tracy, Antoine Louis Claude: *Analyse Raisonnée de l'Origine de Tous les Cultes, ou Religion Universelle*, 359; *Commentary and Review of Montesquieu's Spirit of Laws*, 31, 45, 359; health of, 283, 359, 618; identified, 1:262n; and Lafayette, 283; letter to, 359–60; T. Lyman introduced to, 357, 360; *Observations sur le Systême Actuel d'Instruction Publique*, 359; *Principes Logiques, ou Recueil de Faits relatifs a l'Intelligence Humaine*, 359; *Traité de la volonté et de ses effets*, 359; *A Treatise on Political Economy*, 13, 26, 67, 109–10, 140, 205, 248, 356, 359–60, 362, 573, 574n, 618, 619n
Dexter, Aaron: as president of Massachusetts Society for Promoting Agriculture, 386; sends pamphlet to TJ, 386

Dexter, Samuel: friendship with J. Adams, 267–8; identified, 10:173n
Dick (Yellow Dick) (TJ's slave; b. *1767*): family of, 546n; as laborer, 179, 207; as wagoner, 207
Dickson, Adam: *The Husbandry of the Ancients*, 164
Dictionnaire portatif et de prononciation, Espagnol-Français et Français-Espagnol (J. L. B. Cormon), 335, 352, 396, 397
A Digest of the Laws of the United States of America (T. Herty), 120n, 147n
Digges, John: and Central College subscription, 333
Diggs, Mr.: sends greetings to TJ, 660
Dinah (TJ's slave; b. *1766*): family of, 546n
Dinsmore, James: as builder for Central College, 256, 273, 274n, 471, 545n; and building plan for J. Monroe, 273–4; and Central College subscription, 328; identified, 1:136n; letter from, 273–4; letters to, 256, 471; transmits goods to TJ, 274, 447; and work at Bremo (J. H. Cocke's Fluvanna Co. estate), 274n; works at Montpellier (Madison family estate), 469
Dinwiddie, Robert: as lieutenant governor of Va., 83, 93n
Dio, Cassius. *See* Cassius Dio
A Dissertation on the Canon and the Feudal Law (J. Adams), 48, 49n, 201
Divers, George: Answer to Interrogatories in *Jefferson v. Rivanna Company*, 550–4; and Central College subscription, 322, 328; health of, 344, 440, 549, 641; identified, 1:157–8n; letters from, 221, 549; letters to, 220–1, 440–1; livestock of, 240; mill of, 185; and Rivanna Company, 64, 76, 81, 91–3, 220–1, 221, 259–60, 552; testimony in *Jefferson v. Rivanna Company*, 440–1, 549, 550–4, 555, 556–8, 641, 668
Dixon, Alexander: as ship captain, 531
Dizionario d'agricoltura o sia la coltivazione italiana (I. Ronconi), 164
Dizionario Portatile e di Pronunzia, Francese-Italiano, ed Italiano-Francese (J. L. B. Cormon and V. Manni), 547, 592
D. Iunii Iuvenalis Aquinatis Satirae XVI (Juvenal; ed. G. A. Ruperti), 205, 296, 414
Doane, Isaac (ship captain), 531
Dodge, Joshua: family of, 488, 489n, 512; identified, 488–9n; seeks appointment, 487–8, 510–3, 533
dogwood, 39
Dougherty, Joseph: identified, 1:3–4n; letter from, 182–3; letter to, 214; makes payment for TJ, 456, 457n; seeks Senate doorkeeper appointment, 182, 214
Draffen, Thomas: and Central College subscription, 325, 329
Dramata (Euripides; ed. E. Zimmermann), 415
drawers (clothing), 450
drawing: and natural history, 191; by C. J. Randolph, 624n, 628
Drayton, William: and olive cultivation, 168n
Duane, William: and Destutt de Tracy's works, 13; identified, 1:49n; letters to, 13, 455; TJ's account with, 13, 455, 648; and weavers, 507; and *The Works of Dr. Benjamin Franklin, in Philosophy, Politics, and Morals*, 289, 290n, 376n
Duane, William John: identified, 599n; letter from, 597–9; letter to, 647; and Pa. politics, 597, 599n, 647
Dubouchage, François Joseph de Gratet, vicomte de: French minister of Marine, 255
Du Cotonnier et de sa Culture (C. P. De Lasteyrie), 164
Dufief, Nicolas Gouin: account with TJ, 13–4, 30, 31, 31–2, 67, 67–8, 118–9, 128, 161, 284, 593, 605; and J. Adams, 45; bookseller, 30, 31–2; identified, 3:98n; letters from, 30, 31–2, 161–2, 241, 247–8; letters to, 13–4, 67, 233, 250–1; *A New Universal and Pronouncing Dictionary of the French and English Languages*, 67, 161, 233, 247, 248n; plans trip to Europe, 241, 247, 250; TJ orders books from, 250–1
Duhamel Du Monceau, Henri Louis: *A Practical Treatise of Husbandry*, 164; *Traité sur la nature et sur la culture de la Vigne*, 164
Duke, Archibald B.: and Central College subscription, 329
Duke, Richard: and Central College subscription, 329
Dumas, Louis: bureau typographique of, 639, 640n

dumb fish (dunfish). *See* cod: New England
Duméril, André Marie Constant: works of, 452
Dunbar, William: writings of, 574
Duncan Grey (song), 626n
Dunkum, John: and Central College subscription, 324, 329
Dunkum, William: and Central College subscription, 323, 329
Du Ponceau, Peter Stephen: and Historical and Literary Committee of the American Philosophical Society, 21–2, 125–7; identified, 9:179n; letter from, 125–7; letter to, 21–3
du Pont, Victor Marie: and father's death, 604; identified, 5:200–1n; letter from, 604
du Pont de Nemours, Eleuthère Irénée: and father's death, 604; identified, 3:414n; letter from, 604
Du Pont de Nemours, Pierre Samuel: arrives in U.S., 357; death of, 604, 627, 638; identified, 1:201–2n; *Sur l'éducation nationale dans les États-Unis d'Amérique*, 638–40
Dupuis, Charles François: J. Adams on, 45, 268, 363; works of, 383, 527
Durand, Mr.: and wine for TJ, 532
Durand, François: TJ recommends wine from, 246, 405; and wine for TJ, 404, 532, 653
Dureau de la Malle, Jean Baptiste: translates *Histoire Romaine de Tite-Live*, 632
Durot, Mr.: letter from, 402–4; sells artwork, 402–4
Duryee, Abraham Jacob: education of, 350, 351n
Duryee, Maria: health of, 350
Dussieux. *See* Ussieux, Louis d'
Dwight, Timothy: as president of Yale, 350
Dyer, Francis B.: and Central College subscription, 329
Dyer, John: and Central College subscription, 332
Dyer, Samuel (*1756–1840*): and Central College subscription, 329
Dyer, Samuel (*1790–1834*): and Central College subscription, 329

Eastburn, James: identified, 10:668n; letter from, 234–6; letter to, 27; and New-York Historical Society, 234–5; publication plans of, 27
Eaton, William: and broad-tailed sheep, 347, 430
Eckel, Charles E.: as watchmaker, 507, 508
Eddy, John Henry: as geographer, 582n
Eddy, Thomas: and canals, 357–8, 360, 377; identified, 361n; letter from, 360–1; recommends T. Moore, 360
Edgeworth, Maria: *The Absentee*, 627, 628n; *Tales of Fashionable Life*, 628n
Edinburgh Review, 205, 303, 335, 352, 395
education: and African colonization, 11; in Baltimore, 606; books on, 604, 638–40; elementary, 133–4n; in France, 633–4, 638–40; Latin, 112; at Monticello, 18–9, 112, 233, 261, 409; Pestalozzi system, 266n; Spanish language, 14, 18–9, 112, 175, 233, 261; in Switzerland, 263–4, 266n; textbooks, 11; W. Thornton's proposed system of, 390, 391n; in Va., 133–4n. *See also* schools and colleges; *specific entries for TJ's Eppes and Randolph descendants*
education, collegiate: reform of, 133–4n
Edy (TJ's slave; b. *1787*). *See* Fossett, Edith (Edy) Hern (TJ's slave; b. *1787*)
Egypt: works on, 612–4, 650
Eldredge, Nathaniel T.: identified, 10:600n; and *New-York Public Sale Report*, 648
Elegy Written in a Country Churchyard (T. Gray), 254n
Les Élémens de Géométrie d'Euclide (F. Peyrard), 295, 297, 338, 352, 395, 397
Eliza Reilly (brig), 653, 654
Elk Island, 502
Ἑλληνικῶν παθημάτων θεραπευτική (Theodoret), 452
Elliott, Benjamin: identified, 8:315–6n; *An Oration, delivered in St. Philip's Church, before the inhabitants of Charleston, South-Carolina; on Friday, the Fourth of July, 1817, in commemoration of American Independence*, 528, 529n, 582
Ellis, Charles: travels of, 305
Ellis, Richard S.: and Central College subscription, 331
Ellsworth, Oliver: as legal authority, 369

Elogio del Dr. D. Eusebio Valli (T. Romay y Chacón), 377, 378n, 428
Embargo Act (*1812*): effects of, 284
Embargo Act (*1813*): TJ on, 284
The Enchanted Throne, An Indian Story translated from the Persian Language (D. Lescallier), 351, 441
Encyclopaedia Britannica, 271–3
Enfield, William: *The History of Philosophy*, 30, 31, 283; *Institutes of Natural Philosophy, Theoretical and Practical*, 30
English language: TJ on study of, 252
Enquirer (Richmond newspaper). *See* Richmond Enquirer (newspaper)
Eppes, Francis (TJ's brother-in-law): and Eppington, 200
Eppes, Francis Wayles (TJ's grandson): education of, at Monticello, 233, 261; education of, in Richmond, 18–9, 49, 50, 59, 112–3, 175, 233–4, 261, 292, 396; education of, TJ on, 14, 303, 409, 596; health of, 233; identified, 4:115n; letter from accounted for, 597n; at Monticello, 14; and Poplar Forest, 596, 624n; relationship with father, 14
Eppes, John Wayles (TJ's son-in-law): and Central College, 303; and Central College subscription, 327n, 331, 590–1, 596; family of, 409; health of, 292–3; identified, 1:337–8n; letter from, 292–3; letters from accounted for, 15n, 597n; letters to, 14–5, 174–5, 233–4, 302–3, 409, 590–2, 596–7; relationship with son, 14, 18–9, 49, 112–3, 175, 233–4, 261, 292, 596–7; slaves of, 14, 174, 292; sundial for, 174; as U.S. senatorial candidate, 14; visits Poplar Forest, 596, 624n; and wine for TJ, 50, 175, 238, 292, 300, 302
Eppes, Maria (Mary) Jefferson (TJ's daughter; John Wayles Eppes's first wife): family of, 252; mentioned, 202
Eppes, Martha Burke Jones (John Wayles Eppes's second wife): identified, 2:127n; mentioned, 624n; sends plants to TJ, 292; TJ sends greetings to, 175, 303, 409, 596–7; TJ sends plants to, 14, 174–5; and wine for TJ, 50
Eppes, Mary Elizabeth Cleland Randolph (Francis Wayles Eppes's wife; Thomas Eston Randolph's daughter): correspondence of, 628; identified, 632n; letter to, from C. J. Randolph, 631–2; travels of, 624n, 631n
Eppington (Eppes's Chesterfield Co. estate): James River at, 200
Erasmus, Desiderius: *Colloquia, nunc emendatiora*, 452
Erie, USS, 509, 534n
Erie Canal, 218–9, 259, 280–1, 339, 357–8, 360, 364–5, 376–7, 415, 434–5, 448
Erving, George William: identified, 2:32n; as minister plenipotentiary to Spain, 634
Esprit des Lois (Montesquieu), 438n
Esquisse et Vues Préliminaires d'un Ouvrage sur l'Éducation Comparée ... et Séries de Questions sur l'Éducation (M. A. Jullien), 604
Essai Général d'Éducation physique, morale, et intellectuelle (M. A. Jullien), 604n
Essay on Sheep (R. R. Livingston), 165
Essays and Notes on Husbandry and Rural Affairs (J. B. Bordley), 165
Estrées, Gabrielle d': print of, 403
Eubanks, Thomas: and Central College subscription, 636
Euclid: *Les Élémens de Géométrie d'Euclide* (F. Peyrard), 295, 297, 338, 352, 395, 397
Euripides: *Dramata* (ed. E. Zimmermann), 415; *Les Tragédies d'Euripide* (trans. P. Prévost), 179, 193
Europe: climate of, 34
Eustace, John Chetwode: J. Adams on, 45, 268
Evans, Oliver: identified, 7:109n; *The Young Mill-wright & Miller's Guide*, 352
Evelyn, John: *Sylva, or a Discourse on Forest-Trees*, 165; *Terra: A Philosophical Discourse of Earth*, 164
Everett, Edward: identified, 8:49–50n; travels to Europe, 142
Everette, Charles: and Central College subscription, 329; identified, 3:196n
Every Man His Own Gardener (T. Mawe), 165
exercise, physical: at college, 390
Exmouth, Edward Pellew, 1st Viscount of: as British admiral, 661

Fabbroni, Adamo: identified, 8:322n; *Istruzioni elementari di agricoltura*, 164
Fagg, John: and Central College subscription, 324, 329
Fairfax's Devisee v. Hunter's Lessee. *See* Martin v. Hunter's Lessee
Fancelli, Giovanni Battista: and C. Bellini estate, 580, 643
The Farmer's Guide in Hiring and Stocking Farms (A. Young), 165
Federalist party. *See* Hartford, Conn.: Federalist convention at
Federal Spy (Springfield, Mass. newspaper), 607
Fellenberg, Philipp Emanuel von: educational theories of, 263–4, 266n
Fennell, James: assists J. Bruce, 612–4
Feodorovna, Maria, empress consort of Russia: on TJ, 562
Ferdinand (Shakespearean character), 624n
Fernagus De Gelone, Jean Louis: as bookseller, 127, 152; *Catalogue of Latin, English, French, Spanish, and Italian Books, Maps, &c. for sale by J. L. Fernagus De Gelone, Agent, for the United States, Canada, New-Orleans, Spanish America, and Isles*, 152, 295, 335; identified, 127–8n; imports books from Europe, 592, 646; letters from, 152, 193–4, 338, 396–7, 592; letters to, 127–8, 175–6, 179–80, 234, 295, 335, 352, 456, 547–8, 646; sends book catalogues, 152, 338; TJ orders books from, 175–6, 179–80, 295, 296–7, 335, 352, 547; TJ's account with, 234, 396–7, 456, 592, 646
fevers: inflammatory, 461
figs: Marseille, 175, 218, 219, 220n; TJ sends to M. B. J. Eppes, 175
Fillassier, Jean Jacques: *Culture de la Grosse Asperge dite De Hollande*, 165
Findlay, William: as Pa. gubernatorial candidate, 598n
firearms: cannon, 53–4, 54–5; and velocity of military projectiles, 51, 52n, 52–4, 54–5
fire engines: described, 374
fireflies, 39
fireplaces: at Barboursville, 223–4; Rumford, 225. *See also* stoves
firewood: and rent settlement with Henderson heirs, 20
fish: anchovies, 407; cod, 66, 274, 295; herring, 336–7; ichthyology, 191; in Rivanna River, 73; salted, 66, 274, 295; shad, 39, 337, 344; TJ purchases, 66, 295, 336–7; tongues and sounds, 66, 295
Fisher, Mr.: and payment made for TJ, 118–9, 605
Fitch, Asa: as merchant in Marseille, 509–10, 513n, 534n
Fitch, William D.: account with TJ, 451, 452n; identified, 9:483n
Fitz, Gideon: identified, 1:215n; as surveyor, 615–6
Fitzgerald, G. H.: and Central College subscription, 331
Fitzwhylsonn, William Henry. *See* Fitzwhylsonn & Potter (Richmond firm)
Fitzwhylsonn & Potter (Richmond firm): binds publications for TJ, 205, 303, 352, 394–5; and books for TJ, 303; and *Edinburgh Review*, 205, 303; identified, 3:599n; letters to, 205, 303–4, 352, 394–5
Fitzwilliam, Richard: as boundary commissioner, 22, 23n, 125
Flavigny, Gratien Jean Baptiste Louis, vicomte de: translates *Correspondance de Fernand Cortès avec l'empereur Charles-Quint*, 127, 152
flax: cloth, 11
Fletcher, Richard: as publishing agent, 615
Flood's ordinary (Buckingham Co.; proprietor Henry Flood), 596
Florence, Italy: wine of, 131, 131–2, 137, 247
flour: from Poplar Forest, 179, 207, 236; price of, 261, 298–9, 395, 635; as rent, 185–6, 194–5, 210–1, 213, 380, 459, 593; at Richmond, 142, 261, 362; sale of, 290, 304, 380, 464, 476, 593, 605; shipment of, 104. *See also* Monticello (TJ's estate): flour from
Flower, George: identified, 9:668–9n; letter from, 609–10; and settlement in U.S., 221–2, 609; TJ introduces, 124, 300–1; U.S. tour of, 124
Flower, Richard: and G. Flower's settlement in U.S., 221–2; identified, 222–3n; letter from, 221–3
flowers. *See* plants; *specific flower names*
fly. *See* Hessian fly

fodder: for cattle, 158, 199, 271, 308–9; for hogs, 272; for horses, 171–2, 272; for oxen, 171–2, 272; for sheep, 171–2
Fonblanque, John de Grenier: *A Treatise of Equity*, 70, 97n, 98n
Fontaine, Peter: as boundary commissioner, 22, 23n
food: almonds, 39; anchovies, 407, 653; apples, 623; artichokes, 39, 179; asparagus, 39; bacon, 298, 299, 623; bread, 271; cabbage, 221; cakes, 670; carrots, 271–2; cherries, 39, 464; chicken, 623; cod, 274, 295; cod tongues and sounds, 66, 295; cucumbers, 39; fish, 66, 336–7; gingerbread, 641; honey, 503; kale, sprout, 151, 174–5; macaroni, 404, 407, 531, 653, 654; molasses, 237, 493; mutton, 240; olive oil, 407, 653; oysters, 653; peaches, 39, 221; peas, 39, 379; pies, 493; pork, 493; potatoes, 221, 272; raisins, 407, 654; raspberries, 624; strawberries, 39; veal, 240. *See also* alcohol; coffee; corn; currants; flour; oil; rice; sesame (benne; benni); sugar; tea; wine
Forsyth, William: *A Treatise on the Culture and Management of Fruit Trees; in which A New Method of Pruning and Training is Fully Described*, 165
Fort Erie (Upper Canada), 494
Fort George (Upper Canada), 494
Fort Masonic (Brooklyn, N.Y.), 493, 495n
Fossett, Edith (Edy) Hern (TJ's slave; b. *1787*): family of, 438
fossils: and New-York Historical Society, 187, 188–9, 192
Fouché, Joseph, duc d'Otrante, 282, 501
Fourth of July: celebrations, 497; orations, 528–9, 530n; sentiments evoked by, 483–4
France: Bourbon dynasty restored, 281–2, 351, 633–4; Chambre des Députés, 282, 283n; climate of, 412; and colonization in West Africa, 255, 256n, 457, 501; and Congress of Vienna, 540, 541n; Directory, 160, 435, 436; education in, 633–4, 638–40; emigrants from, 255, 256n, 448, 457–8; Louis XVIII's constitutional charter for, 282, 283n; political situation in, 600; and Spanish colonies, 354; Staël Holstein on, 116–7; TJ on, 160, 435–6; trees from, 219. *See also* Crawford, William Harris: minister plenipotentiary to France; Gallatin, Albert: minister plenipotentiary to France; Institut de France; Napoleon I, emperor of France
Francis, John Wakefield: identified, 235–6n; letter from, 234–6; and New-York Historical Society, 234–5
Franklin, Benjamin: anecdotes about, 375; *Correspondance Choisie de Benjamin Franklin* (ed. W. T. Franklin), 255; correspondence of, 255, 289, 290n, 375, 376n, 426–7, 458, 502; and Declaration of Independence, 202–3, 252; inventions of, 342n; praised, 489–90, 572; *The Private Correspondence of Benjamin Franklin, LL.D. F.R.S. &c.* (ed. W. T. Franklin), 255; *The Works of Dr. Benjamin Franklin, in Philosophy, Politics, and Morals* (ed. W. Duane), 289, 290n, 376n
Franklin, William Temple: edits *Correspondance Choisie de Benjamin Franklin*, 255; edits *The Private Correspondence of Benjamin Franklin, LL.D. F.R.S. &c.*, 255; and publication of B. Franklin's papers, 255, 289, 290n, 376n
Franklin Republican (Chambersburg, Pa., newspaper), 597–8n, 647
Fraser, Donald: criticizes W. Coleman, 490–1; defends certain politicians against newspaper attacks, 490–1; identified, 4:305n; letter from, 489–95; poetry of, 493–4
Fraser, Donald, Jr.: military career of, 494; toast by, 494
Fraser, Thomas: and Battle of Culloden, 494
Frederick William III, king of Prussia: in France, 458
Freeborn, Thomas: identified, 462–3n; introduced to TJ, 454, 462; letter from, 462–3; and plows, 462
Freeman, Thomas: as surveyor, 615–6
Freemasonry: and Central College, 669–70; in New York City, 493, 495n
Freinsheim, Johann: edits *Titi Livii Historiarum quod exstat* (Livy), 414
Fremantle, Sir Thomas Francis: British naval officer, 661

French language: dictionaries, 67, 161, 233, 247, 248n, 335; letters in, from: S. Bernard, 139–40; A. F. De Laage, 575–6, 620; P. Derieux, 566–7; N. G. Dufief, 30, 31–2, 161–2, 241, 247–8; Durot, 402–4; T. Kosciuszko, 398–9; J. Mourer, 305–6; M. A. Pictet, 443–7; Pierre Mages & Compagnie to S. Cathalan, 656–7; P. Poinsot, 472–5; Quinette de Rochemont, 600–1; A. Spreafico to S. Cathalan, 656–7, 657–8; Madame de Staël Holstein, 116–8; A. Thoüin, 263–6; P. de Valltone, 542–3; study of, 233, 261; TJ on study of, 252; translation of, 638–9; works written in, 501

French Revolution: TJ on, 436–7; works on, 116–8

Fretwell, John: and Central College subscription, 326, 329

The Fright of Astyanax (B. West), 135, 266, 342, 387

fringe (tree), 39

Fulton, Robert: and J. Delaplaine's *Repository*, 202; identified, 2:250–1n; and steamboats, 499, 565

Funk, Mr. (ship captain), 652

Fuqua, John: and Central College subscription, 325, 332

furniture: bureau typographique, 639, 640n; chests of drawers, 307; commodes, 307

Gadsden, Christopher: organizes Sons of Liberty, 167, 168n

Gage, J. (schooner captain), 302

Gale, Christopher: as boundary commissioner, 22, 23n

Galen (Greek physician), 251n

Gales, Joseph (*1761–1841*): identified, 457n; letter from, 476; letter from accounted for, 621n; letter to, 456–7; and *Raleigh Register*, 456–7, 476

Gales, Joseph (*1786–1860*): identified, 6:506n; TJ pays, 456, 457n

Gales & Seaton (Washington, D.C., firm): identified, 6:505–6n; and *National Intelligencer*, 425, 523; receipt from, 523n

Gallatin, Albert: conveys letters and parcels to France, 357, 410, 412, 420, 421, 458, 463; on European politics, 540; identified, 1:599n; letter from, 539–41; letters to, 197, 410–2, 463; T. Lyman introduced to, 294; as minister plenipotentiary to France, 116, 118n, 122, 255, 408, 435, 444, 511; and recommendations for D. C. Terrell, 412; TJ introduces W. C. Preston to, 197, 199; TJ on, 436

Gallatin, Hannah Nicholson (Albert Gallatin's wife): greetings sent to, 412

Gamble, Thomas: as American naval commander, 534n

games: billiards, xlvi–xlvii; handball, 390, 391n

Gardeil, Jean Baptiste: translates *Traduction des œuvres médicales d'Hippocrate, sur le texte grec, d'après l'édition de Foës* (ed. D. J. Tournon), 127, 152, 175, 193, 297, 395

The Gardeners Dictionary (P. Miller), 165

The Gardeners Kalendar (P. Miller), 165

The Gardener's Pocket Dictionary (J. Abercrombie), 165

Gardenier, Barent, 312

gardening: books on, 352. *See also* McMahon, Bernard; seeds

gardens: proposed Washington botanical garden, 136, 143n, 144n. *See also* McMahon, Bernard; Thoüin, André

Gardiner, John: *The American Gardener*, 165

Garland, David Shepherd: and Central College subscription, 636

Garland, Edward (d. *1822*): and Central College subscription, 332

Garland, Spottswood: and Central College subscription, 333, 636

Garnett, James: and Central College subscription, 325, 329

Garrett, Alexander: as Albemarle Co. clerk, 243, 467n; and Agricultural Society of Albemarle, 319; as Central College proctor, 253, 316–8, 319, 327n, 344, 400, 463, 464n, 465–8, 468–9, 547n, 565, 570; and Central College subscription, 322, 329; and fish for TJ, 344; identified, 5:567–8n; letters from, 253, 344; letter to, 463–4; visits Monticello, 327n; and weaver for Charlottesville, 463–4, 470

Garrett, Ira: and Central College subscription, 323, 329

Garth, Garland: and Central College subscription, 324, 329

Garth, Jesse: and Central College subscription, 323, 329
Garth, Jesse Winston: Albemarle Co. land of, 466; and Central College subscription, 323, 329, 467n; sells land to Central College, xlv, 467n
Garth, Thomas: TJ's account with, 307n
Garth, William: and Central College subscription, 324, 329
Garth, Willis Dabney: and Central College subscription, 324, 329
Geddes, James: and Champlain Canal, 358n
Gelston, David: and books for TJ, 255; collector at New York, 531; identified, 1:282n
General Armstrong (brig), 25, 26n, 65
General Marion (brig), 531
Geneva, Switzerland: schools in, 443–4
The Gentleman Farmer (H. H. Kames), 164
Gentry, Robert: and Central College subscription, 323, 329
The Genuine Works of Flavius Josephus (Josephus; trans. W. Whiston), 303
A Geographical Description of the State of Louisiana (W. Darby), 429, 459–60
geography. *See* maps
geology: of Va., 535, 536n, 563. *See also* mineralogy
Γεωπονικά Geoponicorum sive de re rustica libri XX (C. Bassus): edited by T. Owen (*1805–06*), 164; translated by P. Needham; edited by J. N. Niclas (*1781*), 164
George (J. H. Cocke's slave): delivers letters, 651n
George (ship), 652
George III, king of Great Britain: artistic taste of, 3
George, Prince Regent (later George IV, king of Great Britain): addresses parliament, 242n; TJ on, 24
Georgetown, D.C.: banks in, 57, 124, 155; *Messenger*, 217, 218n; postmaster at, 110
Georgetown College (later Georgetown University), 390, 391n
Georgia: and trade with Indians, 125
Germany: emigrants from, 305; scholarship in, 408, 414–5, 422, 633
Ghent: peace negotiations at, 501
Gibbon, Edward: works of, 206
Gibbon, James: identified, 2:669n; letter from, 378; letter to, 353; and seeds for TJ, 302, 353, 378
Gibbs, George: identified, 187–8n; letter from, 187–8; and New-York Historical Society, 187, 188–9
Gibson, Patrick: account with TJ, 67–8, 236–7, 593–4, 638; and goods for TJ, 189, 274, 378; identified, 4:523n; letters from, 118–9, 208, 304, 362, 395, 476–7, 605; letters from accounted for, 237n, 594n; letters to, 67–8, 128, 236–7, 290–1, 379–80, 380–1, 464–5, 496, 593–4, 638; payments made for TJ, 14, 31, 66, 67, 67–8, 112, 118–9, 128, 137, 161, 193, 237, 290, 291, 304, 307, 337, 362, 366, 380, 381, 395, 398, 419, 420, 465, 548; and TJ's bank note from Bank of Virginia, 208, 236–7, 290–1, 362, 379–80, 395, 426, 464, 476, 496, 593; and TJ's bank note from Second Bank of the United States, 304, 464, 476, 496, 593, 594, 605, 638; and TJ's flour, 236–7, 290, 304, 362, 380, 395, 459, 464, 476, 593, 605; and TJ's tobacco, 362, 380, 593; and window glass for TJ, 112, 137; and wine acquired by TJ, 238, 292, 300, 302. *See also* Gibson & Jefferson (Richmond firm)
Gibson & Jefferson (Richmond firm): account with TJ, 14; and books acquired by TJ, 175, 193, 352, 397, 398; and craftsmen for TJ, 580; identified, 1:44n; payments made for TJ, 13, 43n, 237, 285, 353, 380n, 400, 453n, 522, 567, 594n, 617, 618; transports goods, 481n, 535; and wine acquired by TJ, 131, 131–2, 137, 137–8, 144, 156, 204. *See also* Gibson, Patrick; Ligon, James
gigs: travel in, 14
Giles, William Branch: and Central College subscription, 327n, 590–1; identified, 3:205n; letter to, 590–2
Gill (TJ's slave; b. *1792*). *See* Gillette, Gill (TJ's slave; b. *1792*)
Gill, Valentine: identified, 254n; letter from, 253–4; solicits patronage, 253–4; as surveyor, 253
Gillette, Barnaby (TJ's slave; b. *1783*): as cooper, 603
Gillette, Gill (TJ's slave; b. *1792*): as wagoner, 622

Gillies, John: *The History of Ancient Greece, its Colonies, and Conquests*, 26, 110; *The History of the World, from the reign of Alexander to that of Augustus*, 26, 110; works of, 627
Gilmer, Francis Walker: and Central College subscription, 334; identified, 8:59n; letter from, 638–40; plans visit to Monticello, 440, 526; as translator, 638–9; travels with TJ, xlvii–xlviii, 621–2
Gilmer, George (d. *1836*): and Agricultural Society of Albemarle, 319
Gilmer, John (*1782–1834*): and Agricultural Society of Albemarle, 319
Gilmore, Joseph: Milton boatman, 303; receipt to B. Peyton accounted for, 261n; and rice for TJ, 260
Gimbrede, Thomas: engraving of J. Monroe, xlv; identified, 1:23n
gingerbread, 641
Girard, Stephen: account with TJ, 455; identified, 8:587–8n; letter to, 418; and TJ's lines of credit, 418, 420, 454, 455, 533, 652
Girardin, Louis Hue: and J. D. Burk's *History of Virginia*, 283, 296; identified, 1:633–4n; introduces A. F. De Laage, 296; letters from accounted for, 297n, 452n; letters to, 296–7, 452; TJ purchases books from, 296–7, 452; TJ recommends books to, 296; visits Monticello, 365
Giround, Honoré: and land grant of P. Poinsot, 474n
glass, window: for Barboursville, 225; Boston, 307; sent to TJ, 137; TJ orders, 112
Glendy, John: family of, 606; identified, 9:48–9n
Gonçalves da Cruz, Antônio: visits J. Adams, 384
Goodman, Horsley: and proposed Albemarle Co. road, 243
Goodman, Jeremiah Augustus: agreement with TJ, 573; and Central College subscription, 324, 327n, 329; identified, 4:374n; letter from, 546; letters to, 465, 547; as Poplar Forest overseer, 603; purchases slave from TJ, 546, 547, 573; TJ pays, 465
Goodman, John: identified, 598n; letter from, 597–9; letter to, 647; and Pa. politics, 597, 599n, 647
Goodman, Sally (TJ's slave; b. *1812*): identified, 9:216n; sold by TJ, 546, 547, 573
Gordon, Hendrick W.: and cloth manufacture, 141; identified, 141–2n; letter from, 141–2
Gordon, William Fitzhugh: and Agricultural Society of Albemarle, 319; and Central College subscription, 324, 329; identified, 5:270n
Gordon's Tavern (Gordonsville), 559
Gorham, John: *Inaugural Address, delivered in the Chapel of the University at Cambridge, December 11, 1816*, 386
Goss, John: and Central College subscription, 329
government. *See* politics
Graglia, Giuspanio: Italian-English dictionary of, 13, 31, 547, 592
Graham, Mr.: steam engine of, 6, 56, 153
Graham, Michael: as apprentice weaver, 471–2, 506–7, 602
Granger, Gideon: identified, 2:179n; *Speech of Gideon Granger, Esq. delivered before a Convention of the People of Ontario County, N.Y. Jan. 8, 1817, on the subject of a Canal from Lake Erie to Hudson's River*, 219n, 259
grapes: scuppernong, 292; vine cuttings, 292. *See also* viticulture; wine
grass: orchard, 336
Gray, Thomas: *Elegy Written in a Country Churchyard*, 254n
Gray, William: J. Adams on, 267–8
Gray, William Fairfax: identified, 2:482–3n; and transmission of packages to and from TJ, 205, 523, 537, 539
Great Britain: agriculture in, 162; boundary negotiations with, 115; and common law, 369–70, 433; and Congress of Vienna, 540, 541n; economic distress in, 23–4; emigrants from, 448–9; House of Commons, 242n, 303n; House of Lords, 242n, 303n; land records in, 560–1; laws of, 104–5; navy of, 26n; parliament of, 242n, 302, 303n; peace with, 417, 661–2; political unrest in, 25, 242, 302, 303n; prices in, 635; scholarship in, 633; and slave trade, 61n; TJ on

Great Britain (*cont.*)
war with, 353–4, 435–6; and U.S., 122, 123n, 410. *See also* Adams, John Quincy; George III; George, Prince Regent; War of *1812*; Wellesley, Richard Wellesley, Marquess
Great Lakes, 192
Greece, ancient: TJ on, 162
Greek language: lexicons of, 335, 395–6; study of, 112, 175, 233, 261, 396, 409; TJ on, 252
Green & Peyton (Richmond firm). *See* Peyton, Bernard
Greenlee's Ferry (Rockbridge Co.): on route to Natural Bridge, 623; tavern at, 629
Griffin, Lucy B. Lewis (TJ's niece): dispute with C. Peyton, 520n; identified, 3:91n
Grimm, Friedrich Melchior, Baron von: J. Adams on, 45, 46, 268; opinion of J. Trumbull, 3
groceries: purchased by TJ, 617, 618. *See also* food
Grotius, Hugo: as legal authority, 368
Gulliver's Travels. See *Travels into several Remote Nations of the World … by Lemuel Gulliver* (J. Swift)
gunpowder: and construction of TJ's mill, 72–3; and projectile velocity, 52n, 53–4, 54–5; TJ orders, 237
Gwathmey, Robert: friendship with J. Maury, 635; identified, 635n
Gyllenborg, Gustav Adolph: *The Natural and Chemical Elements of Agriculture* (trans. J. Mills), 164
gypsum (plaster of paris): used as fertilizer, 163, 165, 309

Hackley, Harriet Randolph (Richard S. Hackley's wife): greetings sent to, 624n, 626n
Hackley, Jane Elizabeth Catherine. *See* Taylor, Jane Elizabeth Catherine Hackley
Haiti: and African Americans, 501
Hale, Sir Mathew: as legal authority, 368
Hale, Thomas: *A Compleat Body of Husbandry*, 164
Hales, Stephen: *Statical Essays: containing Vegetable Staticks*, 164
Halesia. See silver bells
Hall, Francis: and cement, 113, 114n; identified, 10:647–8n; letter from, 113–4; visits Monticello, 113, 114n
Hall, Harrison: and *American Law Journal*, 541, 599–600; identified, 541–2n; letter from, 541–2; letter to, 599–600; and *Port Folio*, 541, 599–600
"Hamilton." *See* Richards, George H.
Hamilton, Paul (*1762–1816*): identified, 2:175–6n; as secretary of the navy, 661, 662
Hamlet (schooner), 398
Hamner, William: and Central College subscription, 329
Hampden-Sydney College: and state university for Va., 134n
Hancock, John: and American Revolution, 312
handball, 390, 391n
Handbuch der ältesten Christlichen Dogmen-Geschichte (F. Münter), 307
Harden, Benjamin: and Central College subscription, 325, 329
Hardesty, Samuel: and Central College subscription, 333
Harding, Chester: portrait of J. Barbour by, xlvi, 232 (*illus.*)
Hare, William B.: and Central College subscription, 333
Harper, Charles: and Central College subscription, 325, 329
Harpers Ferry, Va.: plants from, 639
Harris, Clifton: and Central College subscription, 323, 329; identified, 7:708–9n
Harris, Frederick: and Agricultural Society of Albemarle, 319; and Central College subscription, 333
Harris, Ira: and Central College subscription, 324, 329
Harris, John (d. *1832*): and Central College subscription, 329; identified, 6:482n
Harris, Levett: as consul at Saint Petersburg, 123n, 562; identified, 1:379–80n; letter from, 562; letter to, 585–6; returns to U.S., 562, 585; sends book to TJ, 562; visits Monticello, 562, 586
Harrison, Benjamin (*1787–1842*): and W. Byrd manuscripts, 239, 450–1, 477; identified, 477n; letter from, 524; letter to, 477

Harrison, Carter E.: and Central College subscription, 331
Harrison, Evelyn Taylor Byrd: and W. Byrd manuscripts, 524
Harrison, Joseph: *The Practice of the Court of Chancery*, 97n
Harrison, Randolph: and Central College subscription, 327n, 331, 590–1, 640; identified, 9:49n; letter from, 640; letter to, 590–2
Harrison, Samuel Jordan: and Central College subscription, 333; identified, 1:348n; letter to, 620–1; TJ introduces A. F. De Laage to, 619, 620–1
Harrison, Thomas H.: and Central College subscription, 331
Hart, Andrew: and Central College subscription, 329; and proposed Albemarle Co. road, 243
Hart, Samuel L.: and Central College subscription, 329
Hartford, Conn.: Federalist convention at, 353, 355n
Harvard University: faculty at, 386; J. T. Kirkland as president of, 142, 143n
Harvie, Jacquelin Burwell: and Central College subscription, 334
Hatfield, George, 166
Haüy, René Just: and classification of minerals, 367
Havens, Rensselaer: *The Memorial Of Frederick Jenkins, and Rensselaer Havens, in behalf of the owners, officers, and crew of the late private armed brig General Armstrong*, 25, 26n, 65
Hawkins, John Isaac: and polygraph, 481
hawthorn, 228. *See also* thorn
hay, 172, 272
health: alcohol abstinence, 293; blindness, 359; cataracts, 283; colds, 625; dental, 158; fever, 461; measles, 460; pregnancy and childbirth, 15; rheumatism, 229, 292, 396; of slaves, 497; TJ describes correspondents as insane, 607n; of TJ's family, 172, 631n; and warm springs, 666. *See also* aging; medicine
Heard, Josiah: publishes Zanesville *Muskingum Messenger*, 177
Heliodorus: *Αἰθιοπικῶν βιβλία δέκα*, 452
Hemmings, John (TJ's slave; b. ca. *1776*): as woodworker, 179
Hemmings, Peter (TJ's slave; b. *1770*): and Monticello brewery, 189, 216
hemp: substitute for, 136
Henderson, Bennett: lands of, 15, 16–8, 263n; legatees of, 19–42, 42–3; mill of, 521, 576–7, 651
Henderson, Bennett Hillsborough: identified, 3:594–5n; and Milton lands, 57
Henderson, Elizabeth Lewis (Bennett Henderson's wife): identified, 7:119n; and sale of Henderson lands, 57
Henderson, Frances. *See* Hornsby, Frances Henderson (Bennett Henderson's daughter; Thomas Walker Hornsby's wife)
Henderson, James L.: and Henderson estate, 17–8, 19
Henderson, John: Deed of Milton Property to C. Peyton, 5, 16, 19; identified, 7:353n; and Milton mill, 521, 577n, 651; and sales by minor heirs, 17; and TJ's land dispute with D. Michie, 209
Henderson, Lucy. *See* Wood, Lucy Henderson (Bennett Henderson's daughter; John T. Wood's wife)
Henderson, Nancy Crawford. *See* Nelson, Nancy Crawford Henderson (Bennett Henderson's daughter; Matthew Nelson's wife)
Henderson, Sarah. *See* Kerr, Sarah Henderson (Bennett Henderson's daughter; John B. Kerr's wife)
Henderson case: chancery case of *1795*, 72, 93n; claims by minor heirs, 5, 15, 16–8, 19–20, 42, 56–7, 58, 263; deeds related to, 5; described, 70. *See also* Michie, David
Hening, Mr.: and dispute of C. L. Lewis and C. Peyton, 485, 486, 514, 515, 517, 518, 520
Henkel, Solomon: as beekeeper, 503–4; identified, 504n; letter from, 503–4
Henry IV, king of France: print of, 403
Henry, Patrick (*1736–99*): governor of Va., 399, 472, 475n; identified, 4:604–5n
Henry, Patrick (of Rockbridge Co.): identified, 397–8n; as tenant at Natural Bridge, 397, 428, 589, 590n, 629, 630
Hepburn, David: *The American Gardener*, 165

Heraclitus (ancient Greek philosopher), 527
Hermitage (wine): described, 246; sent to TJ, 531; TJ recommends, 405
Hern, John (TJ's slave; b. *1800*): as messenger, 624, 626n, 626, 628
Hern, Thruston (TJ's slave; b. *1795*): escapes slavery, 438–9, 522
Herodoti Musae sive Historiarum Libri IX (Herodotus; ed. J. Schweighaeuser), 414–5, 632
Ἡροδότου Ἁλικαρνησσῆος Ἱστοριῶν (Herodotus; eds. G. H. Schaefer and F. W. Reiz), 414–5
Herodotus: *Herodoti Musae sive Historiarum Libri IX* (ed. J. Schweighaeuser), 414–5, 632; *Ἡροδότου Ἁλικαρνησσῆος Ἱστοριῶν* (eds. G. H. Schaefer and F. W. Reiz), 414–5
Herodotus, Translated From The Greek, With Notes (Herodotus; trans. W. Beloe), 268
Heroine (ship), 170, 302
herring: TJ orders, 336–7
Herty, Thomas: *A Digest of the Laws of the United States of America*, 120n, 147n
Hessian fly, 345, 366, 385, 475, 482–3, 536, 537n, 588, 644
Heyne, Christian Gottlob: edits *The Iliad* (Homer), 205, 296, 414, 537; edits Virgil, 205, 296, 414
Hickes, George: J. Adams on, 268
Hickman, Mr. (of Albemarle Co.): and cedar trees, 566
Hierocles (Greek author of witticisms): A. Coray edition of, 251
Hiester, Joseph: as Pa. gubernatorial candidate, 597–8n, 599n, 647
Higginbotham, David: crops of, 385; identified, 4:154n; letter from accounted for, 470n; letters from, 142, 245, 366; letters to, 197–8, 385; as merchant, 142; and paint for TJ, 142, 197–8; plans to order wine, 584; and W. Short's land, 245, 457, 500–1; TJ's debt to, 385; and TJ's mill, 576–7; and TJ's Westham lots, 366, 385
Highland (J. Monroe's Albemarle Co. estate): J. Monroe plans to visit, 258, 439–40, 569
Hippocrates (Greek physician): *Τὸ Περὶ Ἀέρων, Ὑδάτων, Τόπων* (ed. A. Coray), 251; *Traduction des œuvres médicales d'Hippocrate, sur le texte grec, d'après l'édition de Foës* (ed. D. J. Tournon; trans. J. B. Gardeil), 152, 193, 297, 395; works of, 127
Hirzel, Hans Caspar: *The Rural Socrates*, 165
Histoire des Croisades pour la delivrance de la Terre Sainte (L. Maimbourg), 274n
Histoire des Républiques Italiennes du moyen âge (Sismondi), 308, 313, 409
Histoire Romaine de Tite-Live (Livy; ed. G. A. Ruperti; trans. J. B. Dureau de la Malle), 632
Historia de la Conquista de Mexico, poblacion, y progresos de la America Septentrional, conocida por el nombre de Nueva España (A. de Solís y Rivadeneira), 179, 193, 395
Historiæ Byzantinæ Scriptores Tres Graeco-Latini (G. Akropolites, L. Chalkokondyles, and N. Gregoras; ed. P. de la Rovière), 452
history: R. Peters on, 483–4; TJ asked to write, 346; works of proposed, 460–1. *See also* books: on history
The History of Ancient Greece, its Colonies, And Conquests (J. Gillies), 26, 110
The History of Persia (J. Malcolm), 363
The History of Philosophy (W. Enfield), 30, 31, 283
The History of the Crusade; or, the Expeditions of the Christian Princes for the Conquest of the Holy Land (L. Maimbourg; trans. J. Nalson), 274, 447
The History of the Dividing Line (W. Byrd [*1674–1744*]): manuscript of, 21, 22, 125–7, 206, 426, 477, 487, 524
The History of the Late War between the United States and Great Britain (G. J. Hunt), 493–4, 495n
History of the Late War in the Western Country (R. B. McAfee), 364, 382
The History of the World, from the reign of Alexander to that of Augustus (J. Gillies), 26, 110
The History of Virginia (J. D. Burk, S. Jones, and L. H. Girardin): publication of, 296; sources for, 283
Hobart, John Henry: as bishop of N.Y., 607, 608n
Hodgson, Portia: and L. L. Paradise estate, 59
hoes, 163

hogs. *See* pigs
Holeman, George: and Central College subscription, 325, 332
Holland. *See* The Netherlands
Holmes, Hugh: and Central College subscription, 334; identified, 6:114–5n
Holy Alliance: mentioned, 383, 384n
Home, Francis: *The Principles of Agriculture and Vegetation*, 164
Home, Henry, Lord Kames. *See* Kames (Kaim), Henry Home, Lord
home manufacturing. *See* manufacturing, household
Homer: blindness of, 359; *Clavis Homerica: sive Lexicon Vocabulorum Omnium, Quæ continentur in Homeri Iliade Et potissimâ parte Odysseæ* (ed. S. Patrick), 205; A. Coray edition of, 251; C. G. Heyne edition of *Iliad*, 205, 296, 414, 537; *Ὁμήρου Ἰλιὰς σὺν τοῖς σχολίοις* (ed. Villoison), 414; *Odyssey*, 414
Ὁμήρου Ἰλιὰς σὺν τοῖς σχολίοις (Homer; ed. Villoison), 414
Homo's Letters on a National Currency, addressed to the People of the United States (T. Law), 61, 62n
honey, 503
Hope (sloop), 216
Hopkins, Cornelia: and L. L. Paradise estate, 59
Hopkins, John (commissioner of loans): and L. L. Paradise estate, 59
Horace: J. Adams on, 269; allusions to, 270n; study of, 396; TJ quotes, 346–7, 417, 418n; works of, 205
Hornet, USS (schooner), 662
Hornsby, Frances Henderson (Bennett Henderson's daughter; Thomas Walker Hornsby's wife): and Milton lands, 18, 19, 20, 42–3, 56–7
Horse-Hoeing Husbandry: or, An Essay on the Principles of Vegetation and Tillage (J. Tull), 164
horses: and carriage accidents, 622; disabled, 475, 558, 659; fodder for, 171–2, 272; taxes on, 44; and threshing machines, 200
Hosack, David: identified, 8:467–8n; letter to, 4; as medical educator, 350, 351n; sends books to TJ, 4
Houdon, Jean Antoine: bust of TJ, 267
houseflies, 39
household articles: bolts, 548, 588; candles, 617; corks, 189, 193, 204, 216; lightning rods, 341–2, 469–70; locks, 548, 588, 589; toothbrushes, 626n; tooth powder, 626n; towels, 626n. *See also* building materials; clocks; clothing; furniture; tools
House of Representatives, U.S.: chamber of, 480, 571, 612; Currency Committee, 165–6; members subscribe to book, 110; petitions to, 8–12, 498–500. *See also* Congress, U.S.
Howard, Mr. (of Philadelphia): travels of, 305
Howell, Mr. (of Philadelphia): and payment made for TJ, 118–9
Hudson, John: and Central College subscription, 329
Hudson River, 219n, 259
Hughes, Jesse: and Central College subscription, 331
Hulbert, John: and proposed national board of agriculture, 279n
Hull, William: governor of Mich. Territory, 277
Humboldt, Friedrich Wilhelm Heinrich Alexander, Baron von: *De Distributione Geographica Plantarum*, 395, 434; identified, 1:24–5n; letter to, 434–5; mentioned, 463, 618; and South American independence, 434; TJ sends greetings to, 417
Hume, David: works of, 383
Humphreys, David: mission to Algiers of, 60
Humphreys, Richard: captain of *Saucy Jack*, 131, 171
Humphreys, Thomas: on emancipation of slaves, 7–8, 8–12, 60–1; identified, 8n; letters from, 7–8, 497; letter to, 60–1; as physician, 497; Plan for Emancipating and Colonizing American Slaves, 8–12
Hunt, Gilbert John: *The History of the Late War between the United States and Great Britain*, 493–4, 495n; identified, 9:414n
Hunter, George: expedition of, 574
Hunter v. Fairfax. *See* Martin v. Hunter's Lessee
The Husbandry of the Ancients (A. Dickson), 164
Hyde de Neuville, Anne Marguerite Joséphine Henriette Rouillé de Marigny (Jean Guillaume Hyde de Neuville's wife), 166, 167n

Hyde de Neuville, Jean Guillaume: family of, 166, 167n; as French ambassador to U.S., 267; identified, 4:374–5n

Iardella, Francisco: as sculptor, xlv–xlvi
Ignatius of Loyola, Saint, 363
Iliad (Homer): C. G. Heyne's edition of, 205, 296, 414, 537
Illinois Territory: immigration to, 609
Inaugural Address, delivered in the Chapel of the University at Cambridge, December 11, 1816 (J. Gorham), 386
inaugurations: J. Monroe's presidential, 14–5, 122
indentures, 99–101
Independence Day. *See* Fourth of July
The Independent Whig: or, a Defence of Primitive Christianity, and of our Ecclesiastical Establishment, against the exorbitant claims and encroachments of fanatical and disaffected clergymen, 269–70
India (Hindustan; Indostan): ancient philosophers of, 383
Indiana: senator from, 6
Indian Camp (W. Short's Albemarle Co. estate): sale of to D. Higginbotham, 245, 457, 500–1
Indians, American: ancestry of, 49n; Delaware, 126; languages, 126–7, 454; plans for civilizing, 393, 394n; trade with, 125
Ingalls, William: on Republican committee, 569–70n
insects: entomology, 190–1; fireflies, 39; houseflies, 39; sawyers (beetles), 39. *See also* beekeeping; Hessian fly
Institut de France: academies of, 633, 634n
The Institutes of Justinian. With Notes (T. Cooper), 369, 370n, 433–4
Institutes of Natural Philosophy, Theoretical and Practical (W. Enfield), 30
Istruzioni elementari di agricoltura (A. Fabbroni), 164
insurance. *See* Mutual Assurance Society
interest: rate limits in Va., 378, 379n, 385; TJ's calculations of, 378–9
inventions: clarification of liquids, 5; duck-foot paddle, 497–9; odometer, 504, 506n; for platting roads, 504–6, 581; of H. G. Spafford, 6, 496. *See also* machines; patents
iron: bar (Swedish), 11; and construction of TJ's canal, 73; manufacture of, 11; in Va., 65
Irvine, Capt., 280
Irvine, Alexander: as boundary commissioner, 22, 23n
Isaac (slave): with T. M. Randolph at Varina, 172
Isaacs, David: and Central College subscription, 322, 329; identified, 7:321–2n; merchant, 545n
Iselin, Isaak: *Über die Geschichte der Menschheit*, 422, 423–5
Israel (TJ's slave; b. *1800*). *See* Jefferson, Israel Gillette (TJ's slave; b. *1800*)
L'Italia avanti il dominio dei Romani (G. Micali), 313
Italian language: dictionaries of, 13, 31, 547, 592; letter in, from: G. Carmignani, 249–50; TJ on study of, 252
Italy: agriculture in, 171–2; climate of, 34; stonecutters from, 570, 579, 602; F. A. Van der Kemp studies history of, 231, 308

Jackson, Andrew: circular sent to, 595–6
James, Richard P.: and Central College subscription, 331
James River: and navigation, 84n, 106–7; survey of, 50; water level of, 200. *See also* boats: transfer goods to and from Richmond
James River Company, 108
Jane (TJ's slave; b. *1816*): at Poplar Forest, 178, 179n
Jardin des plantes et Muséum National d'Histoire Naturelle: prints of collections of, 402, 403
Jarvis, William Charles: and Berkshire Agricultural Society, 279n
Jay, John: and J. Delaplaine's *Repository*, 202; praised, 491
Jefferson, George (TJ's cousin). *See* Gibson & Jefferson (Richmond firm)
Jefferson, Israel Gillette (TJ's slave; b. *1800*): as postilion, 622
Jefferson, Martha Wayles Skelton (TJ's wife): death of, 202, 252
Jefferson, Peter (TJ's father): and Westham land, 385; will of, 69, 72

JEFFERSON, THOMAS

Books & Library

binding of books, 205, 233, 247, 303, 352, 394, 523, 537; catalogues from booksellers, 127, 152, 636; labels on books, 628; and newspaper subscriptions, 13, 425, 455, 456–7, 476, 523, 594, 594–6, 648, 649; orders books, 26, 67, 127, 175–6, 179–80, 250–1, 295, 296–7, 303, 335, 338, 352, 395–6, 408–9, 414–5, 417, 420, 452, 456, 547; purchases from de Bure Frères (Paris firm), 296, 408–9, 418n, 618, 632; receives works, 4, 13, 23–4, 63, 65, 67, 136, 215, 259, 260, 308, 352, 359, 414, 428, 434, 436, 438n, 441, 447, 582, 646; recommends books, 164–5, 245–6, 296, 347; subscriptions, 215, 398, 486, 541, 599–600, 659; works sent to, 25, 30, 31, 31–2, 61, 110, 114, 115n, 120, 135, 136, 153–4, 156, 157n, 159, 165–6, 168, 169, 177, 178, 193, 205n, 218–9, 254, 255, 270, 274, 283, 351, 356, 381–2, 386, 393, 394n, 395n, 396–7, 398, 454, 501, 527, 528–9n, 530n, 537, 539, 562, 573, 574n, 592, 600, 604, 618, 632, 635–6 (*See also* Library of Congress; Poplar Forest [TJ's Bedford Co. estate]: library at)

Business & Financial Affairs

account with M. A. W. Bacon, 421, 451–2; account with J. Barnes, 522, 522–3; account with S. Cathalan, 420, 454, 455, 531–2, 533, 652–4; account with de Bure Frères, 408–9, 420, 454; account with W. Duane, 13, 455, 648; account with N. G. Dufief, 14, 31, 31–2, 67, 67–8, 118–9, 161, 284, 593, 605; account with J. L. Fernagus De Gelone, 234, 338, 396–7, 456, 592, 646; account with W. D. Fitch, 451, 452n; account with S. Girard, 418, 420, 455; account with J. Milligan, 26; account with W. Mitchell, 298–9; Account with *National Intelligencer*, 456, 523, 648; account with C. Peyton, 56–7, 58, 263; account with T. E. Randolph, 459, 461; account with A. Robertson, 284–5; account with J. Vaughan, 380, 395, 398, 404, 408, 409n, 454, 574; Agreement with Jeremiah A. Goodman, 573; and C. Bellini estate, 580; bonds with van Staphorst & Hubbard, 293, 419; buys and sells slaves, 546, 547, 573; debt to J. A. Goodman, 465; debt to D. Higginbotham, 385; debt to P. Mazzei, 577–9, 585, 644–5; debt to V. W. Southall, 380, 421, 451, 453, 464–5, 593, 605; debt to N. & J. & R. van Staphorst, 290–1, 293, 362, 366, 379, 380n, 380, 381n, 381, 395, 419; dispute with D. Michie, 208–10, 212–3; and T. Kosciuszko's American investments, 27, 57–8, 124–5, 155, 187, 350, 447–8, 522, 523; and lease of Natural Bridge, 237, 397, 428, 589, 642; and lease of Shadwell mills, 168–9, 185–6, 194–5, 210–1, 213; lines of credit in Europe, 418, 420, 455; loan from Bank of Virginia, 208, 236–7, 290–1, 362, 379–80, 395, 426, 464, 476, 496, 593; loan from Second Bank of the United States, 464, 476, 496, 593, 594, 605, 638; and H. Marks's estate, 44, 400, 567; and P. Mazzei's property, 171, 249, 579, 644, 645; Notes by Thomas Jefferson Randolph and Thomas Jefferson on a Land Purchase, 42–3; Order on United States Treasury, 523; orders wine from T. Appleton, 579–80; orders wine from S. Cathalan, 404–6, 407, 531–2, 652–4, 656; payments to J. Darmsdatt, 336–7; payments to T. J. Randolph, 380; pays taxes, 44, 428, 589, 590n; rent due TJ, 185–6; Rent Settlement with Henderson Heirs, 19–20; sale of Westham lots proposed, 366, 378–9, 385; sells flour, 605; and W. Short's property, 245, 457, 500–1 (*See also* Barnes, John; Gibson, Patrick; Gibson & Jefferson [Richmond firm]; Henderson case; *Jefferson v. Rivanna Company*; Mutual Assurance Society; Peyton, Bernard; Rivanna Company)

Jefferson, Thomas (*cont.*)

Correspondence

anonymous letter to, 671; anonymous publication by, 664–6; fatiguing to, 46, 157, 159n, 199, 427; letter of application and recommendation from, 364–5; letter of condolence, 180–1; letters of application and recommendation to, 253–4, 339–40, 357–8, 360–1, 376–7, 487–9, 508–14, 608, 657–8, 659–60; letters of introduction from, 124, 160, 196, 196–7, 197, 300–1, 355–6, 359–60, 620–1; letters of introduction to, 46, 114–5, 134–5, 141, 151, 183–4, 217, 282, 454; publication of papers, 111, 148, 157, 159n, 199; TJ on, 311–2

Descriptions of

conversation, 319

Family & Friends

dining, 379; friendship with L. Pio, 435–6; great-grandchildren, 160; relations with grandchildren, 160, 409, 670

Health

aging, 13, 160, 436; good health of, 160

Literary Quotes

Horace, 346–7, 417, 418n; Montesquieu, 437, 438n (*See also* Bible)

Opinions on

agricultural and manufacturing interests, 23, 345–6; agriculture, 162; Albemarle Co., 413, 548–9; Alexander I, 585–6; banks, 194, 346; British versus American society, 23–4; Christianity, 29, 308; colonial independence, 354–5; commerce, 65; Destutt de Tracy's works, 359–60; domestic manufacturing, 472, 478; France, 160, 435–6; French Revolution, 436–7; George, Prince Regent (later George IV), 24; Great Britain, 23–4, 302, 417; internal commerce, 345–6; Jesus, 312; living in U.S., 160, 435; Napoleon, 436–7; New England politics, 353–4; C. W. Peale's machines, 158, 159n; Quakers, 354; reading, 199; religion, 29, 63, 312; Republican party, 353–4, 647; retirement, 56, 262; Richmond, 65; slavery, 60–1; Spanish colonial self-government, 434; Spanish language study, 14, 18–9, 112; G. Ticknor, 408; U.S. Constitution, 410–1, 415; U.S. future, 417, 437; Warm Springs (Bath Co.), 666; war with Great Britain, 353–4, 435–6; wine, 300, 345; writing less, 56

Portraits

G. Ceracchi's bust, 267, 342, 387; J. Houdon's bust, 267; G. Stuart's paintings, 135, 266, 267n, 342, 387; W. Thornton's profile bust, 135, 266, 267n

Public Service

and Central College subscription, 322, 327n, 329; as governor of Va., 72; as minister to France, 72, 75, 423, 511; praised for, 285–9, 345; as president, 46, 510, 660–1; and revision of Va. laws, 133; as secretary of state, 60, 65, 511, 513n; as Va. burgess, 72, 202, 252. *See also* Central College, Board of Visitors

Travels

to Lynchburg, 471; to Montpellier (Madison family estate), 460, 545–6, 546, 559, 561, 565, 577, 584; to Natural Bridge, xlvii–xlviii, 428, 439, 596, 617, 618n, 620, 621–4, 625, 628–30, 631, 641, 669 (*See also* Poplar Forest [TJ's Bedford Co. estate])

Writings

Act for establishing Religious Freedom, 411–2, 415–6; Analysis of Weather Memorandum Book, 33–41; Anonymous (Thomas Jefferson) to the *Richmond Enquirer*, 664–6; Bill for the More General Diffusion of Knowledge, 415, 416n; Bill of Complaint against the Directors of the Rivanna Company, 72–98, 232 (*illus.*); bill of complaint in *Jefferson v. Rivanna Company*, xlviii, 68, 70–1, 154, 220–1, 221, 228, 229, 259–60, 291, 440–1, 549, 550–4, 555, 556–8, 668; Canons of Conduct, 525, 526n; Catalogue of Books on Agriculture, 164–5; Central College Subscription

JEFFERSON, THOMAS (*cont.*)
List, 322–7, 485, 486, 546, 591, 592n, 636, 650–1; Conveyance of Lands for Central College from John M. Perry and Frances T. Perry to Alexander Garrett, 465–8; Draft Bill to Create Central College and Amend the *1796* Public Schools Act, 664, 666n; Instructions for Setting a Sundial, 176–7; List of Wine and Food Ordered from Stephen Cathalan by Thomas Jefferson and Thomas Jefferson Randolph, 407–8; Memorandum to James Monroe on Scuppernong Wine, 295–6; Note for Destutt de Tracy's *Treatise on Political Economy*, 109–10; Notes and Drawings for Barboursville, 223–7; Notes on a Proposed Albemarle County Road, 244–5; Notes on George Divers's Answer to Interrogatories in *Jefferson v. Rivanna Company*, 556–8, 668; Notes on Legal Processes, 70; Notes on Newspaper Subscriptions, 648; Notes on the Canal Locks and Manufacturing Mill at Shadwell, 348–50; Notes on the Rent Claims of the Heirs of Bennett Henderson, 16n; Notes on the Rent of the Henderson Lands, 16–8; Notes on the Siting of Central College, 544–5; *Notes on the State of Virginia*, 415, 416n, 503, 536n, 621–2, 625, 626n; Notes on Value of Lots in Beverley Town (Westham), 378–9; Notes on Virginia Statutes for Clearing the Rivanna River, 104–9; *The Proceedings of the Government of the United States, in maintaining the Public Right to the Beach of the Missisipi, Adjacent to New-Orleans, against the Intrusion of Edward Livingston*, 70; Report on Commerce, 65; solicitations for, 376, 398, 427, 486; syllabus of Jesus's doctrines, 138, 139n, 201, 230–1, 232n, 307; Title and Prospectus for Destutt de Tracy's *Treatise on Political Economy*, 619n

Jeffersonia Antivenena. See *Jeffersonia diphylla* (twinleaf)

Jeffersonia diphylla (twinleaf): seeds of, 639

Jefferson v. Michie: decisions appealed, 208–10, 212–3; and depositions, 209, 213. *See also* Michie, David

Jefferson v. Rivanna Company: Bill of Complaint against the Directors of the Rivanna Company, 72–98, 232 (*illus.*); case documents in, 102–3, 103–4, 104–8; TJ's bill of complaint in, xlviii, 68, 70–1, 121, 154, 220–1, 221, 228, 229, 259–60, 291, 440–1, 549, 550–4, 555, 556–8, 641, 668; TJ's counsel in, xlviii, 64, 68, 71, 121, 154, 259–60, 291, 641, 668

Jeffreys, George Washington: catalogue of agricultural books for, 162, 245–6, 347; identified, 130n; letters from, 129–30, 245–6, 347–8; letters to, 162–4, 430–1; and T. M. Randolph's hillside plow, 162–4; and Red House Agricultural Society, 129, 130n, 347; and sheep, 347, 430–1

Jenkins, Frederick: *The Memorial Of Frederick Jenkins, and Rensselaer Havens, in behalf of the owners, officers, and crew of the late private armed brig General Armstrong*, 25, 26n, 65

Jenkinson, Robert Banks, 2d Earl of Liverpool: as British prime minister, 303n

Jennings, James: and Central College subscription, 331

Jeremiah (Jerry) (TJ's slave; b. *1777*): travels of, 207

Jerry (TJ's slave; b. *1777*). *See* Jeremiah (Jerry) (TJ's slave; b. *1777*)

Jerusalem artichokes, 308–9

Jesse (J. H. Cocke's slave): travels of, 220n

Jesuits: accused of despotism, 27–8; J. Adams on, 269; mentioned, 363, 383

Jesus: genealogy of, 115–6; likenesses of, 626; TJ on, 138, 139n, 201, 312, 433; F. A. Van der Kemp on study of, 201, 202n, 422

Jews: and American Indian ancestry, 49n

John (TJ's slave; b. ca. *1776*). *See* Hemmings, John (TJ's slave; b. ca. *1776*)

John (TJ's slave; b. *1800*). *See* Hern, John (TJ's slave; b. *1800*)

John Adams, USS (frigate), 662
John Mutter & Company (Richmond firm): buys tobacco, 362
Johnson, Mr. (of Louisa Co.): and H. Marks's estate, 44
Johnson, Mr. (stonecutter): and Central College, 571, 602, 610–1
Johnson, Chapman: as attorney, 538; identified, 5:530n; and *Jefferson v. Rivanna Company*, xlviii, 68, 70, 71, 121, 154, 259–60, 291, 641, 668; letters from, 154, 291, 668; letters to, 68–9, 259–60, 641; as Va. state senator, 134n
Johnson, Michael: witnesses document, 573n
Johnson, Samuel: anecdotes about, 492
Johnson, William (*1771–1834*): gives walking stick to TJ, 167, 168, 344; identified, 1:555n; letter from, 167–8; letter to, 344–5; *Nugæ Georgicæ; An Essay, delivered to the Literary and Philosophical Society of Charleston, South-Carolina, October 14, 1815*, 168, 344–5
Johnson, William (waterman): carries flour to Richmond, 304; carries tobacco to Richmond, 593; identified, 3:310n; rents Milton lands, 16, 18; transports goods from Richmond, 237, 303, 337, 593
Johnson, William B.: and Central College subscription, 325, 332
Johnson & Warner (Philadelphia firm), 303
Johnston, Charles: and Central College subscription, 333; identified, 2:230n; letter to, 620–1; TJ introduces A. F. De Laage to, 619, 620–1
Jones, Calvin: on scuppernong grape, 292
Jones, John: and Central College subscription, 329
Jones, Martha Burke. *See* Eppes, Martha Burke Jones (John Wayles Eppes's second wife)
Jones, Sir William (*1746–94*): identified, 9:285–6n; *The Philosophy of the Asiaticks*, 383, 384n; works of, 363, 527
Jordan, John (brickmason): and Central College, 603
Joseph Mercier & Company (firm), 663
Josephus: cited by I. Iselin, 424, 425n; *The Genuine Works of Flavius Josephus* (trans. W. Whiston), 303
Jourdan, Mr. (French winemaker), 405, 406
Joyce, Jeremiah: and TJ's syllabus on Jesus's doctrines, 138, 139n, 230
Judaism: works on, 422, 424, 425n
Julien, Honoré: identified, 2:115n; trains chefs for TJ, 438
Jullien, Marc Antoine: *Esquisse et Vues Préliminaires d'un Ouvrage sur l'Éducation Comparée ... et Séries de Questions sur l'Éducation*, 604; *Essai Général d'Éducation physique, morale, et intellectuelle*, 604n; identified, 1:676n
Jussieu, Bernard de: and botanical classification, 367
Justinian: *The Institutes of Justinian. With Notes* (T. Cooper), 369, 370n, 433–4
Juvenal: *D. Iunii Iuvenalis Aquinatis Satirae XVI* (ed. G. A. Ruperti), 205, 296, 414; works of, 205n

kale: sprout, 151, 174–5
Kames, Henry Home, Lord: *The Gentleman Farmer*, 164
Karay. *See* Coray, Adamantios
Die Katholischen Briefe: Neu übersesst und erklärt und mit Excursen und einleitenden Abhandlungen (J. C. W. Augusti), 307
Kean, Andrew: and H. Marks's estate, 567
Kearny, Francis: identified, 583n. *See also* Tanner, Vallance, Kearny, & Company (Philadelphia firm)
Kelly, John: identified, 2:452n; and Rivanna Company, 64, 76, 81, 91, 99, 259–60, 552
Kentucky: land prices in, 151; literature from, 364; newspapers, 157n
Kentucky Society for Promoting Agriculture: TJ elected honorary member of, 4
Kerr, John: as U.S. representative from Va., 8
Kerr, Sarah Henderson (Bennett Henderson's daughter; John B. Kerr's wife), 42–3n
Key, Jesse B.: and Central College subscription, 334
Key, Joshua: and Central College subscription, 325, 332
Kincaid, Robert J.: and Central College subscription, 333

King, Rufus: and J. Delaplaine's *Repository*, 202
Kinsolving, George Washington: and Central College subscription, 329
Kinsolving, James: and Central College subscription, 329
Kirkland, John Thornton: as president of Harvard University, 142, 143n
Kirwan, Richard: *The Manures Most Advantageously Applicable to The various Sorts of Soils*, 164
Klein, Jacob Theodor: and classification of animals, 367
Knight, David: and brickwork for Central College, 558–9, 602, 610, 669; identified, 559n; letter from, 558–9; letter to, 610
Knight, Thomas Andrew: *A Treatise on the Culture of the Apple & Pear, and on the Manufacture of Cider & Perry*, 165
Knox, Samuel: as educator, 566, 570, 606; identified, 2:174n
Kosciuszko, Tadeusz (Thaddeus) Andrzej Bonawentura: account with J. Barnes, 57, 58n, 125; Bank of Columbia stock of, 57, 124, 155; and J. Barnes, 350, 362; identified, 1:207n; and investment in U.S. government loan, 27, 57, 58n, 124–5, 155, 187; letter from, 398–9; letter to, 447–9; and P. Poinsot's land grant, 398–9, 472, 473; power of attorney from, 57, 58n; remittances to, 361, 447–8, 522, 523; TJ invites to live at Monticello, 449
Kosloff, Nicholas: accused of rape, 123n

La Brousse, Mr. de: *Traité de la Culture du Figuier, suivi d'observations & d'expériences sur la meilleure maniere de cultiver*, 165
Lacretelle, Jean Charles Dominique: lectures of, 634
Lafayette, Marie Joseph Paul Yves Roch Gilbert du Motier, marquis de: and American Revolution, 283; and Destutt de Tracy, 283; on events in France, 281–2; identified, 1:270–1n; introduces S. Bernard, 139–40, 180; introduces M. L. Descaves, 282; introduces G. Flower, 124; letter from, 281–3; letters from mentioned, 528, 581; letter to, 353–5; T. Lyman introduced to, 294, 355, 357, 360; and South American independence, 354–5; Madame de Staël Holstein on, 117, 118n; G. Ticknor carries letter to, 281; TJ on, 174
La Harpe, Jean François de: J. Adams reads, 268
Lake Champlain: fort on, 568, 569n; proposed canal to, 219n, 259, 280–1
Lake Erie: proposed canal to, 219n, 259, 280–1, 339, 357–8, 360, 364–5, 376–7, 415, 434–5, 448
Lamarck, Jean Baptiste Pierre Antoine de Monet de: works of, 192
Lambert, John: as U.S. senator, 182
lamps: safety, 501
Lance, William: identified, 4:106n; *An Oration, delivered on the Fourth of July, 1816, In St. Michael's Church, S. C. by appointment of the '76 Association*, 530n
land conveyances. *See* indentures
Langley, Batty: *Pomona: or, The Fruit-Garden Illustrated*, 165
language: Indian (American), 126–7, 454; Persian, 351, 441. *See also* Anglo-Saxon language; English language; French language; Greek language; Italian language; Latin language; Spanish language
La Salle, René Robert Cavelier de: and settlement of La., 460n
Lasteyrie-Dusaillant, Charles Philibert, comte De: *Du Cotonnier et de sa Culture*, 164; identified, 3:115n; introduces G. Flower, 124; *Traité sur les Bêtes-à-Laine d'Espagne*, 164
Lastri, Marco Antonio: *Corso di agricoltura*, 164
Latin language: study of, 112, 233, 261, 409, 625, 626–7; TJ on, 252
latitude: calculations for Monticello, 40
Latrobe, Benjamin: J. Bruce introduced to, 613
Latrobe, Benjamin Henry: and capitals (architectural), xlv–xlvi, 232 (*illus.*), 481, 535, 572; and Central College craftsmen, 535, 571, 602, 610–1; and Central College design, 315, 431–2, 453, 479–81, 535, 563–5, 586–7, 610–2, 649–50; and Columbian Institute for the Promotion of Arts and Sciences, 144n; edits J. Bruce's work, 612–4; family of, 613, 614n; identified, 1:474–5n; letters from, 453,

Latrobe, Benjamin Henry (*cont.*) 479–81, 563–5, 571–2, 610–5; letters to, 431–2, 534–6, 586–8, 602, 649–50; proposed visit to Monticello, 535, 565; and steamboats, 565; and TJ's sundial, 432; works on U.S. Capitol, 480–1
Laurence, Mr. (sloop captain), 204
Laval, John: as bookseller, 283–4; and N. G. Dufief's business, 241, 247, 283–4; identified, 284n; letter from, 283–4
La Vallière, Françoise Louise de la Baume Le Blanc de: print of, 403
lavender: sent by S. Cathalan, 406, 531
law: books on, 352; British, 369–70, 433; common, 369–70, 433; jurisprudence, 368–70, 432–4; study of, 11; TJ provides legal advice, 146–7, 478, 479, 485, 486, 514–20, 538, 538–9, 542. *See also* Virginia: laws of
Law, Edmund: and Columbian Institute for the Promotion of Arts and Sciences, 144n
Law, Thomas: and Columbian Institute for the Promotion of Arts and Sciences, 143, 148–9; *Homo's Letters on a National Currency, addressed to the People of the United States*, 61, 62n; identified, 3:209n; letters from, 61–2, 143–4, 165–6; letter to, 148–9; sends works to TJ, 61, 165–6
Lawler, James: wheat of, 537n
Lawrence, David (sloop captain), 216
Laws of the State of New-York, respecting Navigable Communications between The Great Western and Northern Lakes and the Atlantic Ocean, 281n
lead: for sundials, 176
Lear, Tobias: as consul at Algiers, 661, 663n; identified, 6:159n
leather: shaving machines, 240
Lechevalier, Jean Baptiste: as librarian, 632; *Voyage de La Troade, Fait dans les années 1785 et 1786*, 632
Leclerc, Jean (Johannes Clericus): edits *Titi Livii Historiarum quod exstat* (Livy), 414
Lédenon, France: wine of, 246, 404, 405, 407, 531, 653
Lee, Henry (of Winchester): and Central College subscription, 334
Lee, Richard Henry: as member of Continental Congress, 202
Lee, William (*1739–95*): and L. L. Paradise estate, 59
Lee, William (*1772–1840*): identified, 2:672n; letters from, 449–50, 506–7; letters to, 413, 471–2, 602; weaving enterprise of, 413, 449–50, 463–4, 470, 471–2, 506–7, 602
Leghorn (Livorno), Italy. *See* Appleton, Thomas
Leibniz, Gottfried Wilhelm: philosophy of, 268, 270n; works of, 383
Leiper, Thomas: and J. Delaplaine's *Repository*, 203; identified, 7:37n
Leitch, James: account with TJ, 426n; agent for TJ, 452; and Central College subscription, 322, 329, 565; identified, 1:65n; letter from, 470–1; and weaver, 463–4, 470, 602
Leitch, William: and Central College subscription, 324, 329
LeRoy, Bayard & Company (New York firm): identified, 9:580n; letters from, 366–7, 419; letters to, 293, 381; and TJ's debt to N. & J. & R. van Staphorst, 290–1, 293, 304, 362, 366, 379, 380n, 381, 395, 419
Lescallier, Daniel: *The Enchanted Throne, An Indian Story translated from the Persian Language*, 351, 441; identified, 1:184n; introduces Quinette de Rochemont, 351, 352n; letter from, 351–2; letter to, 441; sends publication to TJ, 351; *Le Trône Enchanté, Conte Indien traduit du Persan*, 351n
Leschot, Louis A.: identified, 365–6n; letter to, 365–6; payment to, 539; as watchmaker, 198–9, 365, 374, 413, 507–8
Leschot, Sophie Montandon (Louis A. Leschot's wife): TJ sends greetings to, 365
Le Tellier, John: identified, 2:316n; letter from, 604–5; letter to, 548–9; and silversmith for Charlottesville, 548–9, 604–5
Letter, Addressed to the Most Reverend Leonard Neale, Arch Bishop of Baltimore (J. F. Oliveira Fernandes), 28, 63–4
Letter from the Secretary of State, transmitting A List of the Names of Persons to whom Patents have been Issued, . . . from January 1st, 1816, to January 1st, 1817, 135, 136n

Lewis, Ann Marks (TJ's niece): identified, 3:91n; property dispute with C. Peyton, 520n
Lewis, Charles (d. *1806*) (TJ's nephew): property dispute with C. Peyton, 478, 479n, 485, 486, 514–20, 521n, 538, 538–9, 542
Lewis, Charles Lilburne (TJ's brother-in-law): dispute with C. Peyton, 478, 479, 485, 486, 514–20, 521n, 538, 538–9, 542; family of, 520n, 538; identified, 3:92–3n
Lewis, David Jackson: attests document, 243n; identified, 5:281n
Lewis, Howell: and Central College subscription, 325, 329
Lewis, James: and Henderson lands, 209; identified, 5:197n
Lewis, Jesse Pitman: and Central College subscription, 330
Lewis, John (of Albemarle Co.): land grant to, 560–1
Lewis, John (Col.): land claims of, 560–1
Lewis, Lawrence: estate of, 389, 391n
Lewis, Lucy B. *See* Griffin, Lucy B. Lewis (TJ's niece)
Lewis, Lucy Jefferson (TJ's sister; Charles Lilburne Lewis's wife): family of, 520n, 538; and property conveyances, 479n
Lewis, Martha Amanda Carr. *See* Monroe, Martha Amanda Carr Lewis (TJ's niece; Daniel Monroe's wife)
Lewis, Meriwether: identified, 1:436n; Lewis and Clark Expedition, 43–4, 220; papers of, 454, 486–7, 574
Lewis, Nicholas Hunter: and Central College subscription, 323, 329; identified, 10:369n
Lewis, William J.: and Central College subscription, 636; as Va. legislator, 8
Lewis and Clark Expedition: and Indian vocabularies, 398n, 454; journals of, 43–4, 486–7, 574; plants from, 174–5, 220
Lewis's Ferry (Albemarle Co.), 119, 139, 243
Lexington, Va.: academy in, 668; Ann Smith Academy, 134n
Leyburn, John: as sheriff of Rockbridge Co., 589, 590n
libraries: in Richmond, 395–6. *See also* Library of Congress
Library of Congress: portrait of TJ displayed in, 135; TJ sells personal library to, 5, 201, 279n; works given to, 70
The Life and Power of True Godliness; described in a Series of Discourses (A. McLeod), 159
The Life of M. Turgot (Condorcet), 527
The Life of Samuel Johnson LL.D. (J. Boswell), 495n
lightning rods, 341–2, 469–70
Ligon, James: as clerk for Gibson & Jefferson, 605; letter from, 605
lilac, 39
Lily, William: admonition by, 525, 526n
lime (mineral): as building material, 113, 349
limestone: in Va., 535
Lincoln, Benjamin: and American Academy of Arts and Sciences, 273n
Lindsay, Col., 429
Lindsay, James: and Central College subscription, 324, 330
Lindsay, Reuben: and Central College subscription, 330; identified, 8:397n
Lindsey, Theophilus: *Memoirs of the Late Reverend Theophilus Lindsey, M.A.* (T. Belsham), 230
linen, 11
Linnaeus, Carolus (Carl von Linné): and nosology, 367; and scientific classification, 367; *Systema Naturæ*, 367
Lips, Joest: works of, 452
Little, William (*1692–1734*): as boundary commissioner, 22, 23n, 125
Little, William (of Boston): on Republican committee, 569–70n
Little William (schooner), 302
livestock: feed for, 207, 271–2; for Monticello, 240. *See also* cattle; horses; pigs; sheep
Livingston, Edward: bill of complaint against TJ, 70; identified, 2:549–50n. *See also* Batture Sainte Marie, controversy over; *Livingston v. Jefferson*; *The Proceedings of the Government of the United States, in maintaining the Public Right to the Beach of the Missisipi* (Thomas Jefferson)
Livingston, Robert R.: *Essay on Sheep*, 165; identified, 4:638n; and partisan politics, 490
Livingston v. Jefferson: U.S. Circuit Court dismisses, 70. *See also* Batture Sainte Marie, controversy over
Livius, George Peter: papers of, 613

Livy: *Histoire Romaine de Tite-Live* (trans. J. B. Dureau de la Malle), 632; *Titi Livii Historiarum quod exstat* (eds. J. Leclerc and J. Freinsheim), 414; *T. Livii Patavini Historiarum libri qui supersunt* (ed. G. A. Ruperti), 414
Locke, John: anecdote about, 490; as legal authority, 368
locks, 70, 72–98, 548, 588, 589
locks (canal), 69, 100, 102, 104, 108, 552, 563
locust: bristly, 174, 219–20; common, 39
Logan, Mr. (of Staunton): letter to, 130; as watchmaker, 130
looms, 449–50, 507
Lothair (ship), 531
lotteries: for Albemarle Academy, 316–7, 318n; for Central College, 316–7, 321
Louis XIV, king of France: print of, 403; reign of, 633–4
Louis XVIII, king of France: constitutional charter of, 282, 283n; restoration of, 282
Louisiana (Spanish and French colony). *See* Louisiana Territory
Louisiana (state): maps of, 429, 430n, 615–7; works on, 459–60
Louisiana Territory: boundaries of, 460. *See also* Lewis, Meriwether
Love, John: identified, 537n; letter from, 536–7; letter to, 588; and wheat, 536–7, 588
Lovick, John: as boundary commissioner, 22, 23n
Loving, Samuel: and Central College subscription, 333
lucerne. *See* alfalfa
Lucian: works of, 415
Ludlow, Maxfield: identified, 617n; letter from, 615–7; map by, 615–6; *Prospectus for Publishing by Subscription, A Map of the State of Louisiana, with a part of the State of Mississippi and Alabama Territory*, 615–7
Lullin de Châteauvieux, Jacob Frédéric: *Manuscrit venu de St. Hélène, d'une manière inconnue*, 383, 384n
lumber: used at Poplar Forest, 207
lupinella. *See* sainfoin
Luther, Martin: mentioned, 424
Lyman, Theodore (*1755–1839*): family of, 46, 294
Lyman, Theodore (*1792–1849*): identified, 47n; letters of introduction requested for, 46, 294, 311, 357, 362–3; TJ introduces, 355, 356, 360
Lynch, Dominick: and American Society for the Encouragement of Domestic Manufactures, 441–2, 478; identified, 442n; letter from, 441–2; letter to, 478
Lynchburg, Va.: craftsmen of, 534–5; fish shipped to, 337; schools in, 18–9, 49, 59, 112–3, 175, 233–4, 261, 292; TJ visits, 471; toll bridge at, 475n
Lynchburg Press (newspaper): advertisements in, 238n

McAfee, Robert Breckinridge: *History of the Late War in the Western Country*, 364, 382
macaroni: T. J. Randolph orders, 407; sent to TJ, 404, 531, 653, 654; TJ orders, 407
McCall, Richard: consul at Barcelona, 662
McCandlish, William: and L. L. Paradise estate, 120
McCleland, Thomas Stanhope: and Central College subscription, 333; identified, 2:303n
McCraw, Col.: as messenger, 480
McCraw, Samuel: and P. Mazzei's Richmond property, 579, 581n, 645; taxes paid to, 472–5
McCulloch, James Hugh (father of James H. McCulloh): collector at Baltimore, 667; identified, 10:407–8n
McCulloch, Robert: and proposed Albemarle Co. road, 243
McCulloch, Roderick: and Central College subscription, 636
McGehee, Francis: and Central College subscription, 330
machines: corn brake, 158, 199; fire engine, 374; and labor savings, 23; leather shavers, 240; polygraph, 481, 535, 571–2; sawing, 158, 159n; steam engine, 6, 56; stylograph, 535; threshing, 200
McIlhenney, Joseph E.: identified, 10:393n; as watchmaker, 157, 159n, 198–9
McKean, Thomas: death of, 483
McLeod, Alexander: *The Life and Power of True Godliness; described in a Series of Discourses*, 159; *A Scriptural View of the Character, Causes, and Ends of the Present War*, 159
Maclure, William: travels of, 305

McMahon, Bernard: *The American Gardener's Calendar*, 165, 352; identified, 2:91n
McRae, Alexander: as consul at Amsterdam, 660n; delivers letter, 480; identified, 1:355–6n
McReynolds, John D.: as naval surgeon, 662
Madison, Dolley Payne Todd (James Madison's wife): J. Adams on, 46; plans to visit Monticello, 262, 266; TJ sends greetings to, 262, 560; TJ's granddaughter visits, 523; visits Monticello, 336, 337, 342, 387
Madison, James (*1723–1801*): meteorological records of, 37, 460, 461n
Madison, James (*1751–1836*): J. Adams on, 46; and American Board of Agriculture, 279n, 338, 339n; and American Society for the Encouragement of Domestic Manufactures, 442n; and S. Cathalan's claim, 532; and Central College subscription, 327n, 334; circulars sent to, 595; and E. Coles, 122; and Columbian Institute for the Promotion of Arts and Sciences, 144n; criticized, 491; and J. Delaplaine's *Repository*, 148, 202; described, 319; and *1808* election, 412; employs carpenters, 469; family of, 37; identified, 1:7n; as legal authority, 369, 370n; letter from accounted for, 62n; letter of introduction to, 454n; letters from, 121–3, 248–9; letters to, 62, 124, 257, 262, 460–1, 559–60; mentioned, 344, 537n, 637; *Money* (essay), 460, 461n; and W. C. Nicholas, 149–50; and pensions, 494, 495n; plans to visit TJ, 135, 248, 262, 266; and portrait of J. Adams, 203; presidency of, 115, 122, 570n; proposed historical work by, 460–1; retirement from presidency, 46, 262, 312–3, 510; as secretary of state, 661; seeds sent to, 577, 581n; and H. G. Spafford, 6, 62, 121; TJ introduces G. Flower to, 124; TJ visits, 577; and J. Trumbull's historical paintings, 166; vetoes bills, 122, 123n, 410–1, 415; visits Monticello, 258, 327n, 336, 337, 342, 387, 439n. *See also* Central College, Board of Visitors
Mages, Pierre, & Compagnie. *See* Pierre Mages & Compagnie
Magruder, John Bowie: identified, 4:421n; milldam of, 108; as Rivanna River Company commissioner, 108; riverine locks of, 108
Maimbourg, Louis: *Histoire des Croisades pour la delivrance de la Terre Sainte*, 274n; *The History of the Crusade; or, the Expeditions of the Christian Princes for the Conquest of the Holy Land* (trans. J. Nalson), 274, 447
Main (Maine), Thomas: and hawthorn hedges, 228; identified, 2:132n
Maine: weather in, 40, 412
Malcolm, Sir John: *The History of Persia*, 363; works of, 383
Mallory, Charles King: as collector at Norfolk, 131, 204, 531; identified, 10:344n; letter from, 131; letter to, 144; and wine for TJ, 131, 144, 204
mammals: study of, 191, 368
Manilius, Marcus: J. Adams on, 383
Manners, John: and classification of animals, 367–8; identified, 7:153n; on jurisprudence, 368–70, 432–4; letter from, 367–70; letter to, 432–4; on natural history, 367–8; religious beliefs of, 367
Manni, Vincenzo: *Dizionario Portatile e di Pronunzia, Francese-Italiano, ed Italiano-Francese*, 547, 592
Mansfield, William Murray, 1st Earl of: S. Johnson on, 492
manufacturing: of clothing, 413, 449–50, 463–4, 470, 506–7, 602; encouragement of in U.S., 23–4, 169–70, 215, 287–8, 441, 472, 478; protection of U.S. interests in, 136; TJ on, 215, 472, 478
manufacturing, household: cloth, 141
The Manures Most Advantageously Applicable to The various Sorts of Soils (R. Kirwan), 164
Manuscrit venu de St. Hélène, d'une manière inconnue (J. F. Lullin de Châteauvieux), 383, 384n
Map of the United States with the contiguous British & Spanish Possessions (J. Melish), 375, 376n, 427
Mappa, Adam Gerard: meets TJ in France, 423; as translator, 423, 425n
maps: of Alabama Territory, 615–7; of Albemarle Co., xli (*illus.*), 59; of Louisiana, 429, 430n, 615–7; of

maps (*cont.*)
Mississippi Territory, 615–7; of TJ's Virginia, xlii–xliii (*illus.*); of U.S., 582–3; of Virginia, 396. *See also* Melish, John
marble: for U.S. Capitol, 480–1, 535, 563, 572, 612, 614n; in Va., 536n
Marbois. *See* Barbé Marbois, François de, marquis de
Marheinecke, Philipp Konrad: *Universalkirchenhistorie des Christenthums*, 307
Maria (Poplar Forest slave): criticized, 626
Marius, Gaius: J. Adams on, 269
Marks, Anne Scott Jefferson (TJ's sister; Hastings Marks's wife): greetings sent to, 624n; identified, 6:35n; and H. Marks's estate, 44, 400, 567
Marks, Hastings (TJ's brother-in-law; Anne Scott Jefferson Marks's husband): estate of, 44, 400, 567
Marks, John Hastings: and Central College subscription, 324, 330
Marks, Lucy Meriwether Lewis (Meriwether Lewis's mother): identified, 198n; and journals of Lewis and Clark Expedition, 43–4; letter to, 198; portrait of, xlvii, 232 (*illus.*); TJ forwards letter to, 44n, 198
Marseille: quarantine at, 509–10, 513n, 534n; U.S. consulship at, 246, 487–8, 508–13, 533. *See also* Cathalan, Stephen (Étienne) (*1757–1819*)
Marshall, John: and American Revolution, 283; identified, 4:302n
Martin (J. W. Eppes's slave): training of, 14, 174
Martin, Cyril: as ship captain, 531
Martin, James: identified, 2:6n; and TJ's timber, 179, 207
Martin, Maria Margherita. *See* Derieux, Maria Margherita Martin (Peter Derieux's wife)
Martin v. Hunter's Lessee, 600
Maryland: crops in, 483
Mason, Armistead Thomson: and Central College subscription, 333
Mason, John (of Georgetown): family of, 277; identified, 1:23n; and national board of agriculture, 277, 278, 279n; as president of Bank of Columbia, 57
Massachusetts: agriculture in, 130n; TJ on, 311–2, 354. *See also* newspapers
Massachusetts Agricultural Journal: sent to TJ, 270–2, 308
Massachusetts Society for Promoting Agriculture: and T. M. Randolph's hillside plow, 386
mathematics: books on, 409, 537; collegiate education in, 11; elementary education in, 409; logarithms, 378–9; study of, 233, 261
Maupin: *Nouvelle méthode non encore publiée pour planter et cultiver la vigne*, 164
Maurice, Frédéric Guillaume: edits *Bibliothèque Britannique*, 444, 446n; edits *Bibliothèque Universelle*, 443, 444, 446n; and D. C. Terrell, 443–4, 539–40
Maurice, Jean Frédéric Théodore: as master of requests in Paris, 443
Maurice, Pierre André Georges Pyrame: as student, 443
Maurice, Rose Vanière: and D. C. Terrell, 443
Maury, James: friendship with R. Gwathmey, 635; identified, 1:82n; letter from, 635
Maury, John W.: letter from, 156–7; letter to, 260; *An Oration In commemoration of the birth of General Washington*, 156, 157n, 260
Maury, Reuben: and Central College subscription, 324, 330
Maury, Thomas Walker: and Central College subscription, 330; identified, 4:500n; and proposed Albemarle Co. road, 59, 66; as Va. legislator, 172
Mawe, Thomas: *Every Man His Own Gardener*, 165
mayapple (*Podophyllum peltatum*), 639
Mayo, William: as surveyor, 22, 23n, 125
Mazzei, Antonia Antoni (Philip Mazzei's second wife): and P. Mazzei's estate, 21, 171; TJ sends greetings to, 580
Mazzei, Elisabetta. *See* Pini, Elisabetta Mazzei (Philip Mazzei's daughter; Andrea Pini's wife)
Mazzei, Philip: death of, 171, 249; and P. Derieux, 21, 566, 579; family of, 249; identified, 3:380–1n; Richmond property of, 579, 644, 645; TJ's debt to, 577–9, 585, 644–5; will of, 21, 249, 643
measles, 460
medals: from Europe, 402, 404n

medicine: books on, 4; and physicians, 251n; professional education in, 11; trusses, 497. *See also* health
Meigs, Henry: as publisher, 115n
Meikleham, Septimia Anne Randolph (TJ's granddaughter): greetings sent to, 624n, 641, 670
Melish, John: identified, 3:385–6n; *Map of the United States with the contiguous British & Spanish Possessions*, 375, 376n, 427; works of, 429
Melvill, Thomas: letter from accounted for, 279n; letter to accounted for, 279n; on Republican committee, 569–70n
Memoirs of My Own Times (J. Wilkinson), 364
Memoirs of the Late Reverend Theophilus Lindsey, M.A. (T. Lindsey; T. Belsham), 230
Memoirs of the Philadelphia Society for Promoting Agriculture, 165, 347, 348n, 484n
The Memorial Of Frederick Jenkins, and Rensselaer Havens, in behalf of the owners, officers, and crew of the late private armed brig General Armstrong, 25, 26n, 65
The Memorial Of Ship-owners, and others, interested in foreign commerce, convened by public notice at the Tontine Coffee House, in the city of New-York, the 17th January, 1817, 25, 26n
Memorial of the Citizens of New-York, in favour of a Canal Navigation between the Great Western Lakes and the Tide-Waters of the Hudson, 219n, 259
Mercier, Joseph, & Company. *See* Joseph Mercier & Company
Merewether, William H.: and Central College subscription, 323, 330
merino sheep: TJ raises, 430. *See also* sheep
Meriwether, William Douglas: and Henderson case, 19–20; identified, 1:74n; mill of, 186; and Rivanna Company, 64, 69n, 76, 80–1, 82, 85n, 91, 99, 101–2, 229, 259, 260n, 552; and Rivanna River Company, 108, 109n
Metastasio, Pietro: *Il Sogno di Scipione*, 229–32
meteorological observations: by J. Madison (*1723–1801*), 37, 460, 461n; at Montpellier, 39; by TJ, 33–41, 460, 637. *See also* weather
Methodists: mentioned, 363
Micali, Giuseppe: *L'Italia avanti il dominio dei Romani*, 313
Michie, David: identified, 5:140n; *Jefferson v. Michie*, 208–10, 212–3; letter from, 208–10; letter to, 212–3
military: and African colonization, 11; and collegiate curriculum, 390; and projectile velocity, 51, 52n, 52–4, 54–5
milkweed, 135–6
Miller, John (of Cumberland Co.): and Central College subscription, 331
Miller, Joseph: as brewer, 189; and corks for TJ, 189, 216; and craftsmen for TJ, 580; health of, 216; identified, 6:537n; letter from, 216; letter to, 189; plans to visit TJ, 216
Miller, Philip: *The Gardeners Dictionary*, 165; *The Gardeners Kalendar*, 165
Miller, Robert (overseer): TJ pays, 285
Miller, Thomas: and Central College subscription, 332
Miller, William (governor of N.C.): and statue of G. Washington, 171
Miller, William J. (overseer): TJ pays, 285
Milligan, Joseph: account with TJ, 26, 109, 110; binds books for TJ, 26, 205, 362, 386, 522, 523, 539; and Destutt de Tracy's *Treatise on Political Economy*, 26, 67, 109–10, 140, 205, 248, 362, 573, 574n, 619n; family of, 350; identified, 1:37–8n; letter from accounted for, 221n; letter from, to J. Barnes, 523–4; letters from, 109–10, 140, 248, 537, 573–4; letters to, 26, 205–6; sends books to TJ, 537; TJ orders books from, 26; and transmission of packages to and from TJ, 175
Milligan, Samuel: as J. Barnes's assistant, 350, 385–6
mills: advice on requested, 200; Campbell's, 186; construction costs of, 200; Craven's, 186; dam for, 200; G. Divers's, 185; Henderson family's, 521, 576–7, 651; manufacturing, 186; W. D. Meriwether's, 186; C. W. Peale's, 157–8; at Pen Park, 185; on Rivanna River, 185–6; stones for, 200, 521n, 576, 577n. *See also* Shadwell mills

Mills, John: translates *The Natural and Chemical Elements of Agriculture* (G. A. Gyllenborg), 164
Milly (TJ's slave; b. *1797*): family of, 178, 179n
Milton, John: blindness of, 359
Milton, Va.: boats traveling to and from, 303, 352, 548; Henderson mill at, 208, 521, 576–7, 651; postmaster at, 193, 204; and Rivanna Company, 69, 75, 76, 78, 100, 101, 107, 108, 552, 554n; and Rivanna River navigation, 74, 78, 103n, 106–7, 108, 553; road at, 243, 244n, 244; stagecoach to, from Richmond, 548; TJ orders fish shipped to, 337. *See also* Henderson case
mineralogy: and New-York Historical Society, 187, 188–9; study of, 640n. *See also* geology
Minor, Dabney: and Agricultural Society of Albemarle, 319; and Central College subscription, 324, 330; and Henderson case, 15, 19–20; identified, 15–6n; letter to, 15–6; and Rivanna Company, 76, 81, 91, 99, 101–2, 228, 229, 259–60, 552
Minor, James (of Albemarle Co.): and Central College subscription, 324, 330
Minor, James (of Louisa Co.): and Central College subscription, 333
Minor, John (of Albemarle Co.): and Central College subscription, 325, 327n
Minor, Lancelot: identified, 4:511n; letters from, 44, 567; letter to, 400; and H. Marks's estate, 44, 400, 567
Minor, Martha Jefferson Terrell (TJ's sister Martha Jefferson Carr's granddaughter; Dabney Minor's second wife): correspondence of, 340–1n, 540, 541n
Minor, Peter: and Agricultural Society of Albemarle, 319; and Central College, 228, 229; and Central College subscription, 326, 330; and Henderson case, 15, 19–20; identified, 3:146n; letters from, 99–101, 102–3, 229; letters to, 15–6, 228; and Rivanna Company, 71, 76–7, 93n, 94n, 95n, 99, 99–101, 101–2, 228, 229, 553, 668
Minor, William Tompkins: health of, 567; identified, 8:199n
Miranda (Shakespearean character), 624n
Mississippi (state): constitution of, 616, 617n
Mississippi River: Spanish claims to, 219n. *See also* Batture Sainte Marie, controversy over
Mississippi Territory: land claims in, 560–1; maps of, 615–7
Missouri Territory: W. Clark on, 43
Mitchell, William: account with TJ, 298–9; and Central College subscription, 333; identified, 4:86–7n
Mitchill, Samuel Latham: and geographical exploration, 115; identified, 8:604n; introduces R. C. Derby, 114–5; letters from, 114–5, 190; letter to, 136; and natural history, 367, 373–4; and New-York Historical Society, 190, 190–3; sends work to TJ, 114, 115n, 136
Mitford, John Freeman: *A Treatise on the Pleadings in Suits in the Court of Chancery, by English Bill*, 70
The Modern Practice of Physic (R. Thomas), 4
molasses: consumed, 493; provided to TJ, 237
Money (essay by J. Madison), 460
Monroe, James: and American Society for the Encouragement of Domestic Manufactures, 441, 442n; and appointments, 406–7, 653, 659–60, 662; and Central College subscription, 330; described, 319; identified, 1:349n; letters from, 145–6, 276–7, 291, 568–70; letters to, 183, 246–7, 257–8, 262; and W. C. Nicholas, 149–50; plans to visit Highland estate, 569; plans to visit TJ, 146, 276; portrait of, xlv, 232 (*illus.*); presidency of, 145–6, 165, 276, 354, 382, 510–3, 533; as presidential candidate, 412; presidential inauguration of, 14–5, 122; presidential tour, 276, 289, 439–40, 442n, 448, 502, 503n, 568–70; and proposed national agricultural board, 278, 279n; as secretary of state, 532; TJ congratulates, 246, 247; TJ pays, 421; and J. Trumbull's historical paintings, 145; and U.S. Capitol construction, 480, 481, 612, 614n; visits Highland estate, 258, 439–40; visits Monticello, 406–7; and wheat for TJ, 536, 588;

and wine, 246–7, 276, 295–6, 405–6, 652–3. *See also* Central College, Board of Visitors; Oak Hill (J. Monroe's Loudoun Co. estate)
Monroe, Martha Amanda Carr Lewis (TJ's niece; Daniel Monroe's wife): dispute with C. Peyton, 520n; identified, 3:91n
Monteagle (C. Peyton's Albemarle Co. estate): dispute over, 478, 479, 485, 486, 514–20, 521n, 538, 538–9, 542
Montepulciano (wine): TJ orders, 579–80; TJ recommends, 247
Montesquieu, Charles Louis de Secondat: J. Adams on, 527; *Esprit des Lois*, 438n; TJ quotes, 437, 438n. *See also* Destutt de Tracy, Antoine Louis Claude: *Commentary and Review of Montesquieu's Spirit of Laws*
Montgomery, Fitch & Company (Marseille firm), 509
Monthly Repository of Theology and General Literature: publishes TJ's syllabus of Jesus's doctrines, 138, 139n, 201, 202n, 230–1, 232n, 307, 308n; publishes F. A. Van der Kemp's writings, 138, 139n, 231, 232n

MONTICELLO (TJ's estate): approach to, 502; brewery at, 189, 216; climate at, 33–40; clocks at, 130; clover crop at, 421; corn crop at, 426; crops at, 465; described, 572n; dining at, 258, 379; dining room (breakfast room) at, xlvii–xlviii; dome room at, xlvi–xlvii, 232 (*illus.*), 407n; fig trees at, 219, 220n; fish for, 66; flour from, 236, 290, 593; grass at, 336; invitations to visit, 379; latitude of, 40; natural history observations at, 39; paint for, 142, 197–8; peas grown at, 39; poem about, 113–4; rye crop at, 475; schooling at, 18–9, 112, 233, 261, 409; slaves at, 14; stairs at, xlvi–xlvii, 232 (*illus.*); sundial at, 432; tea room at, 406; tobacco crop at, 236, 593; weather recorded at, 33–40; wheat crop at, 39, 385, 475, 588, 644

Visitors to

Ancell, Edward, 227; Bankhead, Ann C., 631n; Barnes, John, 350, 361–2, 385–6, 402, 413, 425, 522; Barziza, Philip I., 580; Bradley, James, 227; Cabell, Joseph C., 258, 565; Clarke, James, 504, 506n; Cocke, John H., 218, 258, 318, 320, 327n, 337, 546, 565; De Laage, A. F., 296, 575; Delaplaine, Joseph, 202–3; fictional visit, 597–8n, 647; Garrett, Alexander, 327n; Girardin, Louis H., 365; Hall, Francis, 113, 114n; Harris, Levett, 562, 586; Madison, Dolley and James, 258, 318, 327n, 336, 337, 342, 387, 439n; Monroe, James, 318, 406–7; Quinette de Rochemont, 441, 458, 501; Randolph, Mary, 624n; Southall, Valentine W., 327n; Stuart, Josephus B., 25, 375, 376n; Ticknor, George, 639; unidentified, 542, 560, 571, 572n; Valltone, P. de, 542–3; Walsh, Michael H., 251; Watson, David, 258

Montpellier (Montpelier; J. Madison's Orange Co. estate): meteorological observations at, 37, 460, 461n; natural history observations at, 39; TJ visits, 460, 545–6, 546, 559, 561, 565–6, 577, 584; visitors to, 545–6, 546, 559, 561, 565–6, 637, 659; work at, 469
Moore, Thomas (of Montgomery Co., Md.): as engineer, 358, 360, 376–7; identified, 1:173n
Moore's Ford (Albemarle Co.), 59, 75, 76, 107, 108, 132, 243, 244n
Moravians: mentioned, 363
Morgan, George: and beekeeping, 503, 504n
Morris, Anthony: travels of, 305
Morris, Robert (of Lynchburg): and Central College subscription, 333
Morris, William (of Albemarle Co.): and Central College subscription, 326, 330
Morris, William (of Louisa Co.): and Central College subscription, 333
Morse, Jedidiah: mentioned, 203
Morse, Samuel Finley Breese: and J. Delaplaine's *Repository*, 203
mortar, 389
Morton, John Archer: financial assistance by, 540; identified, 4:592n
Mosby, John: and Central College subscription, 333
Moseley, Edward: as boundary commissioner, 22, 23n, 125

The Mother-In-Law: or Memoirs of Madam de Morville (H. G. Spafford), 254, 266
Mounier, Jean Joseph: *Recherches sur les causes Qui ont empêché les François de devenir libres et sur les moyens qui leur restent pour acquérir la liberté*, 127, 152
Mourer, Jean: on indentured servitude, 305; letter from, 305–6
Mousley, Walter: account with TJ, 307n
Mozart, Wolfgang Amadeus: operas of, 232n
Muhammad (founder of Islam), 363
mulberry: paper, 218, 219
mules: as draft animals, 179; at Monticello, 207; TJ purchases, 421
Münter, Friedrich: *Handbuch der ältesten Christlichen Dogmen-Geschichte*, 307
Murray, William. *See* Mansfield, William Murray, 1st Earl of
Muséum National d'Histoire Naturelle. *See* Jardin des plantes et Muséum National d'Histoire Naturelle
museums: Philadelphia Museum, 371–4
music: *Duncan Grey* (song), 626n; opera, 232n
Mutter, John & Company (Richmond firm). *See* John Mutter & Company (Richmond firm)
mutton, 240
Mutual Assurance Society: and TJ's insurance, 521, 576–7, 651
Myers, Jacob: and Central College subscription, 325, 332

Nace (TJ's slave; b. *1773*): health of, 497; tasks for, 179
Nace (TJ's slave; b. *1796*): at Poplar Forest, 475
Nalson, John: translates *The History of the Crusade; or, the Expeditions of the Christian Princes for the Conquest of the Holy Land* (L. Maimbourg), 274, 447
Naples: U.S. minister to, 122, 123n
Napoleon I, emperor of France: abdicates, 282; campaigns of, 402, 404n; code of, 369; criticized, 117; defeated at Battle of Waterloo, 282; educational system of, 633–4; exiled to Saint Helena, 498, 500n; mentioned, 384; purported autobiography of, 383, 384n; returns to power, 256n, 281–2; TJ on, 160, 435–6, 436–7
National Advocate (New York newspaper), 490–1
National Institute of France. *See* Institut de France
National Intelligencer (Washington newspaper): prints British political reports, 302, 303n; prints P. S. Du Pont de Nemours's obituary, 604; prints B. H. Latrobe's article on marble for U.S. Capitol, 480–1, 563; prints prospectus for Destutt de Tracy's *Treatise on Political Economy*, 109–10; prints TJ's correspondence, 24n, 111; reports on manufacturing, 413; TJ's account with, 425, 523, 648; TJ subscribes to, 456
The Natural and Chemical Elements of Agriculture (G. A. Gyllenborg; trans. J. Mills), 164
Natural Bridge, Va.: lease of, 237, 238n, 397, 428, 589, 642; print of, xlvii–xlviii, 232 (*illus.*); saltpeter cave near, 625, 630; and shot manufactory, 629, 642; taxes on, 237, 238n, 428, 589, 590n; TJ's grandchildren visit, xlvii–xlviii, 596, 617, 618n, 622–4, 625, 628–30, 631, 641; TJ visits, xlvii–xlviii, 428, 439, 596, 617, 618n, 620, 621–4, 625, 628–30, 631, 641, 669; visitors to, xlvii–xlviii, 621–2
natural history: books on, 192; classification of animals, 367–8; and New-York Historical Society, 190–3; observations on, 39, 367–8, 370n
naturalization: An Act to establish an uniform rule of Naturalization, and to repeal the acts heretofore passed on that subject (*1802*), 147n; TJ on, 146–7
natural law: TJ on, 147
natural rights: TJ on, 432–4
The Nautical Almanac and Astronomical Ephemeris (E. M. Blunt): sent to TJ, 13, 31
navigation. *See* Rivanna River
Navy Department, U.S. *See* Crowninshield, Benjamin Williams; Hamilton, Paul (*1762–1816*)
Neale, Leonard: as archbishop of Baltimore, 28, 64n
Needham, Peter: translates *Γεωπονικά Geoponicorum sive de re rustica libri XX* (C. Bassus; *1781*), 164

Neilson, Hall: and Central College subscription, 334
Neilson (Nelson), John: as builder for Central College, 256, 273, 274n, 471; identified, 5:299–300n; sends greetings to TJ, 274; and work at Bremo (J. H. Cocke's Fluvanna Co. estate), 274n
Nelson, Mr. *See* Neilson (Nelson), John
Nelson, Hugh: conveys packages to TJ, 159; forwards letter, 32, 111; identified, 1:500n; letter from, 32; letter to, 111
Nelson, Nancy Crawford Henderson (Bennett Henderson's daughter; Matthew Nelson's wife): and Milton lands, 18, 19, 20, 42–3, 56–7
The Netherlands: government of, 48; and Spanish colonies, 354
nettle, wood, 135–6
Nevil, Zachariah: and Central College subscription, 333
New England: and J. Monroe's presidential tour, 568–9
New Jersey: canals in, 415; crops in, 482–3
New London, Va.: academy at, 280, 335
New Orleans. *See* Batture Sainte Marie, controversy over
newspapers: *Albany Argus*, 279n; Baltimore *Niles' Weekly Register*, 5, 277, 279n, 594, 594–6, 604, 648, 649; Chambersburg, Pa., *Franklin Republican*, 597–8n, 647; Frankfort, Ky., *Commentator*, 157n; Georgetown *Messenger*, 217, 218n; *Lynchburg Press*, 238n; New York *Commercial Advertiser*, 242n; *New-York Evening Post*, 490; New York *National Advocate*, 490–1; *New-York Public Sale Report*, 648; Philadelphia *Aurora*, 13, 455, 456, 604, 648; publish false TJ quotes, 597–8, 647; *Raleigh Register*, 456–7, 476; *Salem Mercury* (Mass.), 273n; Springfield, Mass., *Federal Spy*, 607; subscriptions to, by TJ, 13, 455, 456–7, 476, 523; *Winchester Gazette*, 503, 504n; Winchester *Republican Constellation*, 238n; Zanesville, Ohio, *Muskingum Messenger*, 177. *See also* National Intelligencer (Washington newspaper); *Richmond Enquirer* (newspaper)
Newton, Sir Isaac: mentioned, 383, 390
Newton, Thomas: and Central College subscription, 327n, 590–1; identified, 3:611n; letter to, 590–2
A New Universal and Pronouncing Dictionary of the French and English Languages (N. G. Dufief), 67, 161, 233, 247, 248n
New York (city): *Commercial Advertiser*, 242n; defenses of, 493; *National Advocate*, 490–1; newspapers, 648; *New-York Evening Post*, 490. *See also* Gelston, David: collector at New York
New York (state): and canals, 218–9, 259, 280–1, 339, 357–8, 360, 364–5, 376–7, 415, 448; crops in, 482–3; *Laws of the State of New-York, respecting Navigable Communications between The Great Western and Northern Lakes and the Atlantic Ocean*, 281n; legislature of, 411, 412n, 415–6; *Memorial of the Citizens of New-York, in favour of a Canal Navigation between the Great Western Lakes and the Tide-Waters of the Hudson*, 219n, 259; and J. Monroe's presidential tour, 568; *Remarks on the Proposed Canal, from Lake Erie to the Hudson River* (D. Clinton), 219n, 259; *Report of the Commissioners of the State of New-York, on the Canals from Lake Erie to the Hudson River, and from Lake Champlain to the Same. Presented to the Legislature, 17th February, 1817*, 219n, 259; *Report of the Joint Committee of the Legislature of New-York, on the Subject of the Canals, from Lake Erie to the Hudson River, and from Lake Champlain to the Same. In Assembly, March 19, 1817*, 219n, 259; *Speech of Gideon Granger, Esq. delivered before a Convention of the People of Ontario County, N.Y. Jan. 8, 1817, on the subject of a Canal from Lake Erie to Hudson's River* (G. Granger), 219n, 259; *Transactions of the Society, instituted in the State of New-York, for the promotion of Agriculture, Arts, and Manufactures*, 165
New-York Evening Post (newspaper), 490
New-York Historical Society: circulars of, 188–9, 190–3, 234–5; identified, 7:120n; manuscript and scarce book committee of, 234–5; mineralogical

New-York Historical Society (*cont.*) committee of, 187, 188–9; zoological committee of, 190, 190–3
New-York Public Sale Report (newspaper), 648
Nice: U.S. consul at, 246–7, 406–7, 655, 657n, 657–8; wine from, 246, 404, 405, 407, 531
Nicholas, Cary Ann. *See* Smith, Cary Ann Nicholas (John Spear Smith's wife; Wilson Cary Nicholas's daughter)
Nicholas, Jane Hollins. *See* Randolph, Jane Hollins Nicholas (Thomas Jefferson Randolph's wife; Wilson Cary Nicholas's daughter)
Nicholas, John: as Albemarle Co. clerk, 419n; identified, 7:267n
Nicholas, Mary Mansfield Smith: birth of, 627n
Nicholas, Robert Carter (ca. *1788–1856*): finances of, 606; identified, 5:646n; seeks consular appointment, 239–40
Nicholas, Wilson Cary (*1761–1820*): on T. Appleton, 239–40; and appointment for W. Armistead, 149; and Bank of the United States (Second), 304, 426, 451, 464; and W. Byrd's *The Secret History of the Line*, 206, 239, 426, 450–1, 477; and Central College, 181, 314, 590, 664; and Central College subscription, 324, 330; identified, 1:223n; letters from, 149–50, 239–40, 450–1; letters to, 206, 426; and J. Madison's presidency, 149–50; and J. Monroe, 149–50; requests letter of recommendation for R. C. Nicholas, 239–40
Niclas, Johann Nicolaus: edits *Γεωπονικά Geoponicorum sive de re rustica libri XX* (C. Bassus; *1781*), 164
Niles, Hezekiah: and clarification of liquids, 5; identified, 4:178n; letters from, 594, 594–6; letters to, 5, 649; and *Niles' Weekly Register*, 594, 594–6, 649; and speeches of the American Revolution, 5
Niles' Weekly Register (Baltimore newspaper), 5, 277, 279n, 594, 594–6, 604, 648, 649
Noailles family: acquaintances of, 402
Non-Intercourse Act (*1809*): TJ on, 284
Norris, Opie: and Central College subscription, 324, 330; identified, 3:465n
North Carolina: agriculture in, 129, 245–6; boundary with Va., 21–2, 125–6, 206, 477, 487, 524; newspapers in, 456–7, 476; statue for capitol of, 171; wine from, 156, 218, 237, 238, 295–6, 345
nosology, 367
Notes on a Journey through France (M. Birkbeck), 124, 300–1
Notes on the State of Virginia (Thomas Jefferson): description of Natural Bridge in, 621–2; and education, 415, 416n; and geology, 536n; R. T. Rawle's edition, 503; references to, 625, 626n; TJ's revisions to, 621–2
Nouvelle méthode non encore publiée pour planter et cultiver la vigne (Maupin), 164
Nugæ Georgicæ; An Essay, delivered to the Literary and Philosophical Society of Charleston, South-Carolina, October 14, 1815 (W. Johnson), 168, 344–5

oak: in Va., 624
Oak Hill (J. Monroe's Loudoun Co. estate): construction of, 273–4
oats: as fodder, 272
Oberlin, Jeremias Jakob: edition of Tacitus by, 205, 296, 414
Oberling. *See* Oberlin, Jeremias Jakob
Observations sur le Systême Actuel d'Instruction Publique (Destutt de Tracy), 359
Ocean (brig), 531
oceanography: observations of marine life, 190, 191
Ochiltree, Mrs.: Rockbridge Co. land of, 629
odometers, 504, 506n
Odyssey (Homer): mentioned, 414
Œuvres d'Archimède (trans. F. Peyrard), 127, 152, 175, 193, 295, 297, 395
Ohio: newspapers, 177
oil: olive, 407, 653
Oldham, James: and hardware for TJ, 548, 588–9; identified, 3:520n; letter from, 588–9; letters to, 307, 548; and window glass, 307; and wood, 307, 548
Oliveira Fernandes, John Francisco: on ecclesiastical authority, 27–8; identified, 9:263–4n; *Letter, Addressed to the Most Reverend Leonard Neale,*

Arch Bishop of Baltimore, 28, 63–4; letter from, 27–8; letter to, 63–4
Oliver, Julius, 654
olives: cultivation of, 168, 345; oil, 407, 653
O'Neal, John L.: as assignee, 573n
Onís y González Vara López y Gómez, Luis de: identified, 1:602n; letter from, 377–8; letter to, 428; negotiations with U.S. government, 122; sends pamphlet to TJ, 377, 428
Ontario, USS (sloop of war), 662
opossum, 367–8, 370n
An Oration. A Project For the Civilization of the Indians of North America (A. Clark), 393, 394n
An Oration, delivered in St. Philip's Church, before the inhabitants of Charleston, South-Carolina; on Friday, the Fourth of July, 1817, in commemoration of American Independence (B. Elliott), 528, 529n, 582
An Oration, delivered on the Fourth of July, 1816, In St. Michael's Church, S. C. by appointment of the '76 Association (W. Lance), 530n
An Oration, delivered on the 17th March, 1817, before the Shamrock Friendly Association of New-York (A. Pyke), 204–5n
orchard grass: seeds, 336
Orleans Territory. *See* Louisiana Territory
Osborn, Samuel L.: identified, 572n; letter from, 572; letter to, 663–4; praises TJ, 572, 663
Otis, Bass: and J. Delaplaine's *Repository*, 203; identified, 10:90–1n
overseers: attempt to capture runaway slaves, 438–9, 522. *See also* Bacon, Edmund; Darnil (Darnell; Darniel; Darnold), Nimrod; Goodman, Jeremiah Augustus; Yancey, Joel (d. *1833*)
Owen, Thomas: edits *Γεωπονικά Geoponicorum sive de re rustica libri XX* (C. Bassus; *1805–06*), 164
oxen: fodder for, 171–2, 272
oysters, 653

Pacific Ocean, 192
Packman, Mr.: travels of, 305
Page, John (of Cumberland Co.): and Central College subscription, 331
Page, Mann (*1791–1850*): and Agricultural Society of Albemarle, 319; and Central College subscription, 323, 330
Pailherols, France: wine from, 531
paint, 142, 197–8
paintings: lent by TJ, 266–7, 342, 387; by J. Trumbull, 3, 135, 145, 166
Palladius: *Rei rusticae*, 164
Palmer, Carl Christian: *Paulus und Gamaliel. Ein Beitrag zur aeltesten Christengeschichte*, 307
pantaloons, 450
panthers: in Va., 631
Paradise, Lucy Ludwell (John Paradise's wife): estate of, 19, 59, 66, 120, 146–7; identified, 9:285n; marriage settlement of, 146–7
Parker, Daniel (of War Department): sends manuscripts to American Philosophical Society, 574
Parmentier, Antoine Auguste: *Traité théorique et pratique sur la Culture de la Vigne*, 164
Parny, Évariste de Forges de: writings of, 48, 49n, 201
Partridge, Alden: and calculation of altitude, 51–2; identified, 9:10n; introduces B. O. Tyler, 217; letter from, to J. Williams, 52–4; letters from, 51–2, 217; and velocity of military projectiles, 51, 52–4, 54–5
Pasteur, William (*1768–1823*): and Central College subscription, 325, 332
Patent Office, U.S. *See* Thornton, William
patents: of R. Claiborne, 498–500; of N. Cutting, 60; lists of, 135, 136n; of J. Perkins, 374n; and reform of patent system, 6
Patrick, Samuel: edits *Clavis Homerica: sive Lexicon Vocabulorum Omnium, Quæ continentur in Homeri Iliade Et potissimâ parte Odysseæ* (Homer), 205
patronage: letter of application and recommendation from TJ, 364–5; letters of application and recommendation to TJ, 253–4, 339–40, 357–8, 360–1, 376–7, 487–9, 508–14, 608, 657–8, 659–60
Patterson, Elizabeth. *See* Bonaparte, Elizabeth Patterson
Patterson, John: and Agricultural Society of Albemarle, 319; and Central College subscription, 324, 330; friendship with J. H. Cocke,

Patterson, John (*cont.*)
320; identified, 10:559n; letter from, 606; sends news of Baltimore, 606
Paulus und Gamaliel. Ein Beitrag zur aeltesten Christengeschichte (C. C. Palmer), 307
Payne, Philip, 168
peaches: harvest of, 39; stones of, 221
Peaks of Otter, Va.: altitude of, 51; property near, 399
Peale, Charles Willson: *Address delivered by Charles W. Peale, to the Corporation and Citizens of Philadelphia, on The 18th Day of July, 1816*, 372, 374n; and farming, 157–8; health of, 157–8; identified, 1:45–6n; and improved saw, 158, 159n; letters from, 157–9, 371–4; letter to, 198–9; makes dentures, 158; and Philadelphia Museum, 158, 371–4; polygraph of, 481, 571–2; reflects on his life, 157–8; and watchmaker for Charlottesville, 157, 198–9
Peale, Elizabeth DePeyster (Charles Willson Peale's second wife): estate of, 373, 374n
Peale, Rubens: and Philadelphia Museum, 373
Pearson, Ephraim (ship captain), 398
peas: as crop, 39; dinner of, 379
Pelham, William: identified, 1:217n; letter from, 177; sends newspaper to TJ, 177; *A System of Notation; Representing the Sounds of Alphabetical Characters*, 177
Pemberton, Thomas: and Central College subscription, 332
Pendleton, Edmund (*1721–1803*): and revision of Va. laws, 133
Pendleton, William Garland: attests document, 474n; and Central College subscription, 332
pendulum: ballistic, 51, 52n, 52–4
Pennsylvania: crops in, 482–3; elections in, 597–8n, 647; legislature of, 411, 415–6
Perkins, Jacob: fire engine of, 374
Perkins, John R.: and Central College subscription, 325, 332
Pernambuco, Republic of: declares independence, 384
Péron, François: *Voyage de découvertes aux terres Australes*, 627, 628n
Perpignan wine. *See* Roussillon, France: wine from
Perrault, Claude: edits *Abregé des dix livres d'architecture de Vitruve* (Vitruvius), 335, 352, 396, 456
Perregaux, Laffitte & Compagnie (Paris firm): and TJ's lines of credit in France, 455, 533, 652
Perry, Frances T. (John M. Perry's wife): identified, 467n; sells land to Central College, xlv, 315, 465–8
Perry, John M.: as builder for Central College, 400, 401, 463, 464n, 468–9, 471, 603; and Central College subscription, 323, 330; identified, 1:192–3n; letter from, 400; letter to, 401–2; sells land to Central College, xlv, 253, 315, 316–7, 318–9, 344, 401, 463, 464n, 465–8, 468, 471
Perrygory, Moses: and Central College subscription, 330
Persia: history of, 363
Persian language: works translated from, 351, 441
Pestalozzi, Johann Heinrich: educational system of, 266n
Peter (TJ's slave; b. *1770*). *See* Hemmings, Peter (TJ's slave; b. *1770*)
Peters, Richard: *Agricultural Enquiries on Plaister of Paris*, 165; health of, 483; on history, 483–4; identified, 9:539–40n; as legal authority, 369; letter from, 482–4; letter from accounted for, 215n; and plows, 172, 482; as president of Philadelphia Society for Promoting Agriculture, 172, 482; on sheep, 347, 348n
Petit's Gap, Va.: on route to Natural Bridge, 623
petticoats, 450
Pettigrew, Ebenezer: and wine for TJ, 238, 295–6, 300
Peyrard, François: translates *Les Élémens de Géométrie d'Euclide* (Euclid), 295, 297, 338, 352, 395, 397; translates *Œuvres d'Archimède* (Archimedes), 127, 152, 175, 193, 295, 297, 395
Peyton, Bernard: and Central College subscription, 334; and correspondence for T. M. Randolph, 183, 204; and goods for TJ, 193, 204, 260; identified, 6:51–2n; and introductions for W. C. Preston, 183–4, 199–200, 204, 261; letters from, 183–4, 204, 260–1; letters to, 193, 199–200; letters to accounted for, 184n, 261n; payments made for TJ, 20, 573n

Peyton, Craven: account with TJ, 56–7, 58, 263; and Central College subscription, 327n, 485, 486; corn contract with TJ, 214; deed to from J. Henderson, 5; dispute with Lewis family, 478, 479, 485, 486, 514–20, 521n, 538, 538–9, 542; family of, 58, 478, 479; and Henderson case, 5, 15, 17, 19, 56–7, 58, 263; identified, 1:415n; *Jefferson v. Michie*, 209–10, 212–3; letters from, 5, 58, 214, 478, 479, 486, 538–9, 560; letters to, 56–7, 214, 263, 379, 485, 514–21, 538, 542; letter to accounted for, 5n; TJ invites to dine, 379; and visitors to Monticello, 560
Peyton, Jane Jefferson Lewis (TJ's niece; Craven Peyton's wife): dispute with Lewis family, 514, 516, 520n; identified, 1:463n
Peyton, John Howe: as attorney, 538–9; identified, 64n; and *Jefferson v. Rivanna Company*, xlviii, 64, 68, 71, 121; letter from, 121; letter to, 64
Phidias (ancient Greek sculptor), 114
Philadelphia: *Aurora*, 13, 455, 456, 604, 648; mayor's office, 500
Philadelphia Museum: relocation to New York considered, 373–4; rent for, 371–2. *See also* Peale, Charles Willson
Philadelphia Society for Promoting Agriculture: *Memoirs*, 165, 347, 348n, 484n; and T. M. Randolph's hillside plow, 172, 482, 484n
Philip (TJ's slave; b. *1796*): at Poplar Forest, 475
Philips, Naphtali (newspaper publisher), 491
The Philosophy of Human Nature (J. Buchanan), 364, 382
The Philosophy of the Asiaticks (W. Jones), 383, 384n
physics: velocity of military projectiles, 51–2, 52–4, 54–5
Pickering, Timothy: and J. Adams, 267–8, 270n, 312; and sheep, 347; as U.S. representative from Mass., 61n
Pickett, George C.: and Central College subscription, 332
Pickmore, Francis: British naval officer, 661
Pictet, Marc Auguste: correspondence of, 539; edits *Bibliothèque Britannique*, 444, 446n; edits *Bibliothèque Universelle*, 443, 444, 446n; identified, 8:322–3n; letter from, 443–7; TJ introduces D. C. Terrell to, 443–4
Pictet de Rochemont, Charles: edits *Bibliothèque Britannique*, 444, 446n; edits *Bibliothèque Universelle*, 443, 444, 446n
Pierre Mages & Compagnie: identified, 657n; letter from, to S. Cathalan, 656–7; and wine for TJ, 653–4, 656
Pierson, Mr. (of New York): travels of, 305
pies: pumpkin, 493
pigs: fodder for, 272; Guinea, 179
Pike, Zebulon Montgomery: *An Account of Expeditions to the Sources of the Mississippi*, 574; journal of, 574; and War of *1812*, 494
Pilot (brig), 531
"Pindar, Peter." *See* John Wolcot
Pini, Andrea (Elisabetta Mazzei Pini's husband): marriage of, 579, 646
Pini, Elisabetta Mazzei (Philip Mazzei's daughter; Andrea Pini's wife): marriage of, 579, 646; and P. Mazzei's estate, 21, 249; TJ sends greetings to, 580
Pinkney, William: identified, 1:414n; as minister plenipotentiary to Russia and Naples, 122, 123n
Pintard, John: identified, 7:120n; letter from accounted for, 189n; as recording secretary of New-York Historical Society, 189
Pio, Louis: identified, 10:355n; letter to, 435–6; TJ's friendship with, 435–6
planes, 176
plants: sent by TJ, 174–5, 219–20; sent to TJ, 292; specimens from Lewis and Clark Expedition, 174. *See also* seeds; *specific plant names*
plastering: of columns, 389
plaster (plaister) of paris. *See* gypsum (plaster of paris)
Plato: mentioned, 383
platypus, 368, 370n
Pleasants, James: and Central College subscription, 327n, 332, 590–1, 650–1; identified, 2:185n; letter from, 650–1; letter to, 590–2
The Pleasures of Hope (T. Campbell), 396
Pliny the Elder: J. Adams on, 269
Πλουτάρχου Βίοι Παράλληλοι (Plutarch; ed. A. Coray), 251, 296

plows: T. M. Randolph's hillside, 162–4, 172, 245, 309–10, 311 (*illus.*), 347, 386, 482, 484n; TJ's moldboard, 382; J. Wood's cast-iron, 216, 462
Plutarch: *Πλουτάρχου Βίοι Παράλληλοι* (ed. A. Coray), 251, 296
poetry: on Monticello, 113–4; sent to TJ, 113–4, 493–4
Poindexter, Maj.: and Central College subscription, 651n
Poinsinet de Sivry, Louis: translates *Théatre d'Aristophane, avec les Fragmens de Ménandre et de Philémon* (Aristophanes), 352, 397, 456, 547, 592, 646
Poinsot, Peter: identified, 475n; land grant to, 398–9, 472–5; letter from, 472–5
political economy: TJ's title and prospectus for Destutt de Tracy's *Treatise on Political Economy*, 109–10, 619n; works on, 136, 356, 359–60, 573, 574n
politics: elections, 412. *See also* Republican party
The Politics of Connecticut ("Hamilton" [G. H. Richards]), 527
Pollard, Richard: and Central College subscription, 333; identified, 9:146n
Pollock, John: and Central College subscription, 322, 330
polygraph: and M. Boulton, 481; and J. I. Hawkins, 481; B. H. Latrobe uses, 481, 571–2; at Monticello, 535; and C. W. Peale, 481, 571
Pomona: or, The Fruit-Garden Illustrated (B. Langley), 165
Pompey the Great, 269
Poor, Immanuel: as agent of the Rivanna Company, 551, 554n, 556, 558n
Pope, Alexander: quoted, 268, 270n, 627, 628n
Pope, John: identified, 185n; introduces T. G. Watkins to TJ, 184–5; letter from, 184–5
Pope, William: and Central College subscription, 636
poplar: Lombardy, 218, 219; in Va., 624
Poplar Forest (TJ's Bedford Co. estate): coopers at, 603; flour from, 179, 207, 236; groceries for, 617; gypsum used as fertilizer at, 163; harvest at, 475; hogs at, 179; invitations to visit, 619; library at, 628; lumber for, 207; main house at, 626, 670; medical care at, 497; paint for, 197–8; plowing at, 163, 164n; slaves at, 178, 179, 475, 546, 547, 573, 626; superintendent of, 178–9; TJ plans visit to, 179, 207, 237, 262, 361–2, 427, 428, 439, 452, 458, 459, 460, 465, 485, 500, 549, 585, 586, 587, 593–4; TJ returns from, 290, 534; TJ's grandchildren visit, 626, 626–7, 628, 641, 669–70; TJ visits, 296, 453, 524, 571, 572n, 596, 610, 619, 626–7, 628, 641, 642, 646, 647, 648, 649, 659, 669–70; tobacco grown at, 179, 207, 290, 380, 593; visitors to, 596, 620, 624n, 625, 627; weather at, 207; wheat grown at, 207. *See also* Bear Creek plantation; Tomahawk plantation
pork: consumed, 493
port (wine), 246
Porter, David: circular sent to, 595; identified, 1:444n
Porter, Peter: and Central College subscription, 330
Porter, Peter Buell: identified, 3:333n; and War of *1812*, 494
Port Folio: TJ subscribes to, 541, 599–600
Portugal: and Brazil, 355, 384n
potatoes, 221, 272–3, 309
Potomac River: locks on, 563, 565n; and navigation, 84n
Potter, Walter. *See* Fitzwhylsonn & Potter (Richmond firm)
A Practical Treatise of Husbandry (H. L. Duhamel du Monceau), 164
The Practice of the Court of Chancery (J. Harrison), 97n
Presbyterians: mentioned, 363
President's House: roof of, 432, 587
Preston, Francis: family of, 184; as U.S. representative from Va., 197n
Preston, James Patton: as governor of Va., 474n
Preston, William Campbell: identified, 184n; introduced to TJ, 183–4, 204; TJ introduces, 196, 196–7, 197, 199–200, 261
Prévost, Pierre: translates *Les Tragédies d'Euripide* (Euripides), 179, 193
Pride of China. *See* chinaberry (Pride of China)
Priestley, Joseph: on B. Franklin, 375; mentioned, 383; religious beliefs of, 367

Prince, John: seeds sent to, 171
Principes Logiques, ou Recueil de Faits relatifs a l'Intelligence Humaine (Destutt de Tracy), 359
The Principles of Agriculture and Vegetation (F. Home), 164
prints: collection of for sale, 402–4; of Natural Bridge, xlvii–xlviii, 232 (*illus.*). *See also* maps
The Private Correspondence of Benjamin Franklin, LL.D. F.R.S. &c. (ed. W. T. Franklin), 255
The Proceedings of the Government of the United States, in maintaining the Public Right to the Beach of the Missisipi, Adjacent to New-Orleans, against the Intrusion of Edward Livingston (Thomas Jefferson): published, 70
Proposals for publishing, by subscription, The Works of Alexander James Dallas (G. Dallas), 153–4, 180–1
Prospectus for Publishing by Subscription, A Map of the State of Louisiana, with a part of the State of Mississippi and Alabama Territory (M. Ludlow), 615–7
Prospectus of a Statistical and Historical Account of the United States of America (D. B. Warden), 619
Prosperity (ship), 531
Prussia: and Congress of Vienna, 540, 541n
Pufendorf, Samuel von: as legal authority, 368
purses, 625
Pyke, Alexander: *An Oration, delivered on the 17th March, 1817, before the Shamrock Friendly Association of New-York*, 204–5n
Pythagoras: mentioned, 383

Quakers: mentioned, 363; persecuted, 271; TJ on, 354
Quincy, Josiah: publishes article, 271–3
Quinette de Rochemont, Nicolas Marie: identified, 601n; introduced to TJ, 351, 352n; letter from, 600–1; sends pamphlets to TJ, 600, 601n, 627; visits Monticello, 441, 458, 501
Quintilian: J. Adams on, 269

Radford, Elizabeth Moseley: family of, 625–6
Ragland, John C.: and Central College subscription, 323, 330; identified, 7:502n
Ragland, William: and Central College subscription, 330
Railey, Daniel Mayo: and Central College subscription, 323, 330
raisins: TJ orders, 407, 654
Raleigh Register (newspaper), 456–7, 476
Ramirez, Alexandro: intendant general of Cuba, 377
Randolph, Ann (Anne) Cary. *See* Bankhead, Ann (Anne) Cary Randolph (TJ's granddaughter; Charles Lewis Bankhead's wife)
Randolph, Arthur Moray: appearance of, 631n
Randolph, Cornelia Jefferson (TJ's granddaughter): education of, 624n, 627, 632n, 670; identified, 3:635n; letter from, to M. E. C. R. Eppes, 631–2; letters from, to V. J. R. Trist, 622–4, 628–30, 631–2; sketches by, 624n, 628; travels of, 631n; visits Natural Bridge, xlvii–xlviii, 596, 617, 618n, 621–4, 625, 628–30, 631; visits Poplar Forest, 626, 626–7, 628, 670
Randolph, Ellen Wayles. *See* Coolidge, Ellen Wayles Randolph (TJ's granddaughter)
Randolph, Harriet Fluker. *See* Willis, Harriet Fluker Randolph
Randolph, Jane Cary (Thomas Eston Randolph's wife): gifts from, 625; greetings sent to, 626n; health of, 624n
Randolph, Jane Hollins Nicholas (Thomas Jefferson Randolph's wife; Wilson Cary Nicholas's daughter): family of, 626n; resides at Monticello, xlvi–xlvii; resides at Tufton, xlvi–xlvii, 404, 407n
Randolph, John (ca. *1727–84*): *A Treatise on Gardening*, 165
Randolph, John (of Roanoke): electoral defeat of, 292, 293n; as U.S. representative from Va., 61n
Randolph, Margaret Smith (TJ's great-granddaughter; Thomas Jefferson Randolph's daughter): birth of, xlvi–xlvii; described, 627n; resides at Tufton, 404, 407n
Randolph, Martha Jefferson (Patsy; TJ's daughter; Thomas Mann Randolph's wife): children of, 160,

Randolph, Martha Jefferson (*cont.*) 161n, 252, 436; forwards TJ's correspondence, 641; greetings sent to, 59, 132, 148, 166, 255, 289, 375; health of, 292, 626n; identified, 2:238n; letters to, 641, 669–70; letters to, from E. W. R. Coolidge, 625–6, 626–8; mentioned, 202; plans visit to Montpellier (Madison family estate), 460, 559–60; relations with A. C. R. Bankhead, 15; seeds sent to, 639; sends greetings to Eppes family, 409

Randolph, Martha Jefferson (TJ's great-granddaughter; Thomas Jefferson Randolph's daughter). *See* Taylor, Martha Jefferson Randolph (TJ's great-granddaughter; Thomas Jefferson Randolph's daughter)

Randolph, Mary (Thomas Mann Randolph's sister; David Meade Randolph's wife): greetings sent to, 632n; mentioned, 627n; visits Monticello, 624n

Randolph, Mary Elizabeth Cleland. *See* Eppes, Mary Elizabeth Cleland Randolph (Francis Eppes's wife; Thomas Eston Randolph's daughter)

Randolph, Mary Jefferson (TJ's granddaughter): mentioned, 624n, 628

Randolph, Peyton (ca. *1723–75*): and J. Delaplaine's *Repository*, 202; identified, 10:270–1n

Randolph, Sarah Nicholas (TJ's great-granddaughter; Thomas Jefferson Randolph's daughter): reminiscences of, xlvi–xlvii

Randolph, Septimia Anne. *See* Meikleham, Septimia Anne Randolph (TJ's granddaughter)

Randolph, Thomas Eston (TJ's cousin): account with TJ, 459, 461; and Central College subscription, 330; family of, 461; and Henderson case, 15, 16, 18; identified, 1:488n; letter from accounted for, 459n; letters from, 168–9, 185–6, 210–1, 459; letters to, 194–5, 213, 459, 461; and Shadwell mills, 168–9, 185–6, 194–5, 210–1, 213, 290, 380, 459

Randolph, Thomas Jefferson (TJ's grandson; Jane Hollins Nicholas Randolph's husband): and Agricultural Society of Albemarle, 319; and Central College subscription, 323, 330; family of, xlvi–xlvii, 626n; friendship with J. H. Cocke, 320; greetings sent to, 50; and Henderson case, 15, 16n, 20n, 42, 43n; identified, 1:190–1n; mentioned, 228, 654; Notes by Thomas Jefferson Randolph and Thomas Jefferson on a Land Purchase, 42–3; orders food and wine from Europe, 404–5, 407, 652–3, 654n; overseers of, 438–9; and proposed Albemarle Co. road, 173, 244n, 245; resides at Tufton, 404, 407n; slaves of, 438–9; TJ's payments to, 380; visits J. W. Eppes, 292

Randolph, Thomas Mann (*1768–1828*) (TJ's son-in-law; Martha Jefferson Randolph's husband): and Agricultural Society of Albemarle, 319; delivers goods, 394; delivers message, 395, 669; greetings sent to, 148, 255, 386, 626n, 670; hillside plow of, 162–4, 172, 245–6, 309–10, 311 (*illus.*), 347, 386, 482, 484n; as host at Monticello, 572n; identified, 1:420n; letter to, 172; mentioned, 183, 204; and navigation of Rivanna River, 78; Notes on George Divers's Answer to Interrogatories in *Jefferson v. Rivanna Company*, 555; and proposed Albemarle Co. road, 244n; and Rivanna Company, 553, 555; visits Richmond, 240

Randolph, Thomas Mann (*1792–1848*) (son of Thomas Mann Randolph [*1741–93*]; half-brother of Thomas Mann Randolph [*1768–1828*]): and Central College subscription, 332; identified, 1:524n

Randolph, Virginia Jefferson. *See* Trist, Virginia Jefferson Randolph (TJ's granddaughter)

Randolph, William Eston: death of, 461

Rappahannock River, 84n

Rapport fait au nom de la commission chargée de l'examen des papiers trouvés Chez Robespierre et ses complices (E. B. Courtois), 127, 152

raspberries: mountain, 624

rattlesnakes: in Va., 631

Rawle, Robert Turner: publishes *Notes on the State of Virginia*, 503

Rawlings, James: identified, 521n; letters from, 521, 651; letter to, 576–7; and Mutual Assurance Society, 521, 576–7, 651

Ray, John: and classification of animals, 367

Recherches Nouvelles sur L'Histoire Ancienne (Volney), 612–4, 650
Recherches sur les causes Qui ont empêché les François de devenir libres et sur les moyens qui leur restent pour acquérir la liberté (J. J. Mounier), 127, 152
Récit Historique sur la Restauration de la Royauté en France, le 31 Mars 1814 (D. G. F. de Pradt), 601n
redbud, 39
Red House Agricultural Society (North Carolina), 129, 162, 245–6, 347
Reed, Joseph (*1772–1846*): identified, 598n; letter from, 597–9; letter to, 647; and Pa. politics, 597, 599n, 647
Réflexions Succinctes sur l'état de l'Agriculture, et de quelques autres parties de l'administration, dans le Royaume de Naples, sous Ferdinand IV (D. Tupputi), 164
Rei rusticae (Cato; Columella; Palladius; Varro), 164
Reiz, Friedrich Wolfgang: edits *Ἡροδότου Ἁλικαρνησσῆος Ἱστοριῶν* (Herodotus), 414–5
religion: J. Adams on, 45, 268–9, 312, 363, 382–3; Anabaptists, 363; atheism, 383; Catholicism, 27–8, 63–4; and discrimination, 412n; education in, 11; Methodism, 363; Moravians, 363; and officeholding, 411, 415–6; Presbyterians, 363; Quakers, 271, 354, 363; Shakers, 411, 412n, 415–6; Swedenborgians, 363; TJ on, 29, 63, 308, 312; Unitarianism, 363; Virginia Act for Establishing Religious Freedom, 411–2, 415–6; works on, 115–6, 159, 422. *See also* Christianity
Remarks on the Proposed Canal, from Lake Erie to the Hudson River (D. Clinton), 219n, 259
rent: due from Henderson lands, 15, 16–8, 19–20, 42, 56–7, 58; due from T. E. Randolph, 380, 459; from Shadwell mills, 168–9, 185–6, 194–5, 210–1, 213, 593
Report of the Commissioners of the State of New-York, on the Canals from Lake Erie to the Hudson River, and from Lake Champlain to the Same. Presented to the Legislature, 17th February, 1817, 219n, 259
Report of the Joint Committee of the Legislature of New-York, on the Subject of the Canals, from Lake Erie to the Hudson River, and from Lake Champlain to the Same. In Assembly, March 19, 1817, 219n, 259
Repository of the Lives and Portraits of Distinguished Americans (J. Delaplaine), 148
Republican Constellation (Winchester newspaper), 238n
Republican party: of Boston, 569–70; electoral successes, 269–70, 312, 412; historical work proposed from perspective of, 460–1; in Pa., 597–8, 599n, 647; TJ on, 353–4
The Resignation of General Washington (J. Trumbull), 145, 166
Revolutionary War: battles of, 375; records destroyed or lost during, 560–1; J. Trumbull's paintings of, 3, 145, 166. *See also* American Revolution
rheumatism: M. J. Randolph's, 292; D. Watson's, 229; J. Wood's, 396
rheumatism root. See *Jeffersonia diphylla* (twinleaf)
Rhoades, Jacob: on Republican committee, 569–70n
rice: TJ orders, 260, 261n, 617
Richards, George H.: *The Politics of Connecticut*, 527
Richmond, Va.: banks in, 290–1, 304; boats transfer goods to and from, 260, 290, 303, 378, 413, 548, 593; British destroy public records in, 385; flour prices at, 142, 261, 362; flour shipped to, 290; library in, 395–6; P. Mazzei's property in, 579, 644; praised, 25, 65; schools in, 18–9, 49, 59, 112–3, 175, 233–4, 261, 292; tobacco prices at, 142, 240, 261; tobacco shipped to, 290. *See also* Bank of the United States, Second: Richmond branch of; Bank of Virginia (Richmond); Gibson, Patrick; Gibson & Jefferson (Richmond firm); Peyton, Bernard
Richmond Enquirer (newspaper): advertises sale of land for tax delinquencies, 237, 238n; prints descriptions of Central College Board of Visitors Meeting, 320–1; prints TJ's correspondence, 315, 664–6; T. Ritchie as editor of, 637, 667
Riddle, Joseph: as partner in Smith & Riddle, 112n
Rienzo, Cola di: F. A. Van der Kemp studies, 231, 232n, 308

Ritchie, Thomas: and anonymous letter by TJ, 667; as editor of Richmond *Enquirer*, 637, 667; identified, 1:214n; letter to, 667
Rivanna Company: act establishing, 69, 554n; agreement with, 70, 77, 99–101; directors of, xlviii, 64, 68, 69n, 69–71, 75–93, 95n, 99, 99–101, 101–2, 102–3, 121, 220–1, 221, 228, 229, 259–60, 440, 549, 550–4, 556–8, 641, 668; Extracts from Minutes of the Directors of, 99, 101–2; navigation rights of, 69–71, 99–101, 102–3, 106, 108, 229; Statement of the Dispute by the Directors of, 103–4. *See also* Jefferson v. Rivanna Company
Rivanna River: and Albemarle Co. roads, 243–4, 244–5; dams on, 200; inquest on TJ's mill (*1795*), 73, 90, 93n, 102, 103n, 104, 550, 554n; inquest on TJ's mill (*1805*), 73–5, 86–90, 92, 93n, 101, 102, 103n, 104, 220, 550, 554n; locks on, 100; milling on, 64; navigation of, 99, 101–2, 229, 550–4, 555, 556–8; navigation rights, 100–1; TJ's Notes on Virginia Statutes for Clearing, 104–8; water level of, 631n. *See also* Henderson case; Shadwell mills
Rivanna River Company: act establishing, 108; trustees of, 108, 109n
Rives, Robert: and Agricultural Society of Albemarle, 319; and Central College subscription, 333, 636; identified, 4:22n
Rives, William Cabell: and Agricultural Society of Albemarle, 319; and Central College subscription, 333; identified, 1:416n; visits J. C. Cabell, 67
Rivesaltes, France: wine from, 246, 532, 584
roads: in Albemarle Co., 59, 66, 119, 132, 133, 139, 172–3, 200, 243–4, 244–5; in U.S., 122; in Va., 59, 66, 119, 132, 139, 172–3, 280
Roanoke River, 168
Robbins, Benjamin: and velocity of military projectiles, 51, 52n
Roberts, William: painter, xlvii–xlviii, 232 (*illus.*)
Robertson, Archibald: account with TJ, 284–5; identified, 4:94–5n; letter from, 618; letters to, 284–5, 617–8, 620–1; and payments for TJ, 337; TJ introduces A. F. De Laage to, 619, 620–1; TJ orders groceries from, 617, 618; TJ pays, 290, 304, 593, 617, 618
Robertson, William J.: and Central College subscription, 326, 330
Robespierre, Maximilien François Marie Isidore de: as leader of French Revolution, 435; *Rapport fait au nom de la commission chargée de l'examen des papiers trouvés Chez Robespierre et ses complices* (E. B. Courtois), 127, 152; TJ on, 160
Robinia hispida. See locust: bristly
Rochon, Alexis Marie: death of, 255, 457, 501, 503n; identified, 5:302–3n; and safety lamps, 501; sends books and pamphlets to TJ, 501, 618; work on steamboats by, 457
Rockbridge County, Va.: taxes in, 237, 238n, 428, 589, 590n
Rockfish Gap, Va.: proposed road from, 59, 119, 132, 133, 139; University of Virginia commissioners meet at, 315
Roddy, B.: and Central College subscription, 334
Rodgers, John: circular sent to, 595; and sheep for TJ, 431n
Rogers, John (of Albemarle Co.): and Central College subscription, 330; TJ pays, 421
Romay y Chacón, Tomás: *Elogio del Dr. D. Eusebio Valli*, 377, 378n, 428
Ronconi, Ignazio: *Dizionario d'agricoltura o sia la coltivazione italiana*, 164
Ross, David: identified, 6:350n; and H. Marks's estate, 400
Ross, Robert: as British major general, 480
Rousseau, Jean Jacques: travels of, 305, 306n
Roussillon, France: wine from, 246, 404, 405, 407, 531, 532, 584, 653
Roxas, Joseph: and geology, 563
Rozier, François: *Cours complet d'agriculture, théorique, practique, économique, et de médicine rurale et vétérinaire ... ou dictionnaire universel d'agriculture*, 164; *Traité théorique et pratique sur la Culture de la Vigne*, 164
The Ruins: or A Survey of the Revolutions of Empires (Volney), 614
Rumford, Benjamin Thompson, Count: fireplace designed by, 225
Ruperti, Georg Alexander: edits *D. Iunii Iuvenalis Aquinatis Satirae XVI*

(Juvenal), 205, 296, 414; edits *T. Livii Patavini Historiarum libri qui supersunt* (Livy), 414
Rural Oeconomy: or, Essays on the Practical Parts of Husbandry (A. Young), 165
The Rural Socrates (H. C. Hirzel), 165
Rush, Benjamin: identified, 1:185–6n; and party politics, 490; TJ's confidential letters to, 139n
Rush, Richard: as acting secretary of state, 660–3; identified, 5:79n; introduces R. C. Derby to TJ, 134–5; letter from, 134–5; letter from accounted for, 118n; letter to, from J. M. Baker, 660–3
Russia: and Congress of Vienna, 540, 541n; and N. Kosloff affair, 123n; and Spanish colonies, 354; and U.S., 123n; U.S. minister to, 122, 123n. *See also* Alexander I, emperor of Russia; Harris, Levett
rye: bread, 271; as crop, 475

Saboureux de La Bonnetrie, Charles François: *Traduction d'Anciens Ouvrages Latins relatifs à l'Agriculture et à la Médicine Vétérinaire, avec des Notes*, 164
sainfoin, 170–1, 171–2, 302, 336, 337, 353, 378, 577, 581n
Sainte Marie, Batture. *See* Batture Sainte Marie, controversy over
St. Michaels (brig), 661
Salem Mercury (Mass. newspaper), 273n
Sallust: J. Adams on, 269
Sally (TJ's slave; b. *1812*). *See* Goodman, Sally (TJ's slave; b. *1812*)
Salmon, William (of Goochland Co.): and Central College subscription, 332
saltpeter, 625, 630
Sampson, Richard: and Central College subscription, 332; and proposed Albemarle Co. road, 243, 244n
Sampson, William: *Address of the American Society for the encouragement of Domestic Manufactures*, 23–5, 136; and American Society for the Encouragement of Domestic Manufactures, 136; identified, 10:557n; letter from, 111–2; letter to, 23–5; publishes letter from TJ, 111
Sander, Nicholas: J. Adams on, 268
Sanders, Daniel Clarke, 6
Sandy (TJ's slave; b. *1813*): at Poplar Forest, 178, 179n
Sasserno, Joseph Victor Adolphus: consulship for, 246–7, 406–7, 653–4, 655, 657n, 657–8; identified, 655n; letter from, to S. Cathalan, 655; and wine, 246, 405, 653
Sasserno, Victor: family of, 657, 658n; sends wine to TJ, 246
Saucy Jack (brig), 131, 171
Saunders, James W.: and Central College subscription, 324, 330
Saunders, Robert Hyde: identified, 342n; letter from, 341–2; letter to, 469–70; and lightning rods, 341–2, 469–70; property of, 341, 342n
Saunderson, Nicholas: blindness of, 359
Sauvages de Lacroix, François Boissier de: and nosology, 367
saws: C. W. Peale's sawing machine, 158, 159n
sawyers (beetles), 39
Say, Jean Baptiste: considers immigrating to U.S., 355–6; identified, 7:420n; letter to, 355–6; T. Lyman introduced to, 356, 357; *Traité d'Économie Politique*, 356
Schaefer, Gottfried Heinrich: edits *Ἡροδότου Ἁλικαρνησσῆος Ἱστοριῶν* (Herodotus), 414–5
schools and colleges: in Geneva, Switzerland, 443–4; Georgetown College (later Georgetown University), 390, 391n; in Lynchburg, 18–9, 49, 59, 112–3, 175, 233–4, 261, 292; national technology school proposed, 6; New London Academy, 280; and Pestalozzi educational system, 263–4, 266n; in Richmond, 18–9, 49, 59, 112–3, 175, 233–4, 261, 292. *See also* Albemarle Academy; Central College; Virginia, University of; William and Mary, College of
Schütz, Christian Gottfried: edits *Aeschyli Tragoediae Quae Supersunt ac Deperditarum Fragmenta* (Aeschylus), 414
Schweighaeuser, Johannes: edits *Herodoti Musae sive Historiarum Libri IX* (Herodotus), 414–5, 632
scientific instruments: ballistic pendulum, 51, 52n, 52–4; barometers, 51–2; sextants, 50, 112; spirit levels, 55; sundials, 174, 176, 432; telescopes, 50,

scientific instruments (*cont.*) 625; theodolites, 544; thermometers, 34. *See also* surveying
Scott, Charles A.: and Central College subscription, 325, 332; identified, 3:371n
Scott, John (of Albemarle Co.): and Central College subscription, 323, 330
Scott, Sir Walter: *The Antiquary*, 630
A Scriptural View of the Character, Causes, and Ends of the Present War (A. McLeod), 159
sculpture: of G. Washington, 171
scuppernong (wine), 50, 156, 175, 218, 219, 237, 238, 292, 295–6, 300, 302, 345
Sea Lion (schooner), 397n
Seaton, William Winston: and Columbian Institute for the Promotion of Arts and Sciences, 144n; identified, 6:506n
Secretary's Ford (Albemarle Co.): and Rivanna Company, 76, 78, 90, 93n, 550, 551; road at, 119, 243, 244n, 244, 245
The Secret History of the Line (W. Byrd [*1674–1744*]), 21–2, 125–6, 206, 239, 426, 450–1, 477, 524, 574
seeds: artichoke roots, 179; cabbage, 221; chicory (succory), 308–10; kale, sprout, 151, 174–5; orchard grass, 336; peach stones, 221; sainfoin, 170–1, 171–2, 302, 336, 337, 353, 378, 577, 581n; sent by TJ, 151, 183; sent to M. J. Randolph, 639; sent to TJ, 170–1, 263
Sellers, Coleman: and fire engines, 374
Senate, U.S.: and appointments, 146n; chamber of, 480; doorkeeper election, 182, 214; and inauguration of J. Monroe, 14–5; and public works, 122, 123n, 410–1. *See also* Congress, U.S.
Seneca, Lucius Annaeus, the younger: J. Adams on, 269
Senegal: and Société Coloniale Philanthropique de la Sénégambie, 255, 256n, 457, 501
sermons: sent to TJ, 159
Serres, Olivier de: mentioned, 162; *Le Théâtre d'Agriculture et Mesnage des Champs*, 164
servants, indentured: opinions on, 305
Serveto (Servetus), Miguel: F. A. Van der Kemp's work on, 138, 139n
sesame (benne; benni): cultivation of, 345
Seventy-Six Association (Charleston, S.C.): forwards orations, 528–9, 530n, 582; identified, 4:107n; letter from, 528–30; letter to, 582
sextant: for surveying, 50, 112
Shackleford, Zachariah: and Central College subscription, 326, 330
shad: given to TJ, 344; observations on, 39; TJ purchases, 337
Shadwell (TJ's estate): cemetery at, 566; raspberries at, 624; TJ inherits, 72
Shadwell mills: canal at, 102, 348–50; dam at, 102, 104; flour from, 290, 459; improvements to, 72–5; lease of, 185–6; manufacturing mill at, 348–50; and T. E. Randolph, 168–9, 185–6, 194–5, 210–1, 213, 459; rent for, 168–9, 185–6, 194–5, 210–1, 213, 380, 459; repairs to, 169; and Rivanna Company, 64, 69, 99, 100–1, 101–2, 550–4, 555, 556–8. *See also* Shoemaker, Jonathan
Shakers: civil status of, 411, 412n, 415–6
Shakespeare, William: characters of, 624n, 628; quoted, 483, 484n
Shaler, William: as consul general at Algiers, 122, 123n, 534n
Shaw, John (*1773–1823*): commands American squadron in Mediterranean, 509, 662
sheep: broadtail, 347, 348n, 430–1; fodder for, 171–2; mutton, 240; Spanish, 430–1. *See also* merino sheep
Sheffey, Daniel: as attorney, 538, 538–9; and *Jefferson v. Rivanna Company*, 668
Shelby, Isaac: declines appointment as secretary of war, 146
Shelton, Joseph: and Central College subscription, 333
Shelton, Nelson T.: and Central College subscription, 326, 330
Shelton, William A.: and Central College subscription, 326, 330
Shoemaker, Jonathan: identified, 1:109–10n; as Shadwell mill tenant, 551–2, 554n, 555, 556–7
Short, William: identified, 1:39n; and Indian Camp, 245, 457, 500–1; letter from, 500–3; letter to, 457–8; mentioned, 454; on J. Monroe, 502–3

shot manufacture, 177n, 642
Siau, Pierre: and P. Poinsot's land grant, 472
silver: smiths, 413, 548–9, 604–5
silver bells, 175
Simington, Robert: identified, 447n; letter to, 447; sends books to TJ, 274, 447
Simms, Charles: as collector at Alexandria, 406, 407n; identified, 4:221n
Simms, William Douglass: as deputy collector at Alexandria, 406, 407n, 531; identified, 10:194n
Sinclair, Sir John: *The Code of Agriculture*, 381–2; identified, 9:144n; letter from, 381–2; sends prospectus to TJ, 382
Singellton, William: identified, 529n; letter from, 528–30; letter to, 582; and Seventy-Six Association, 528–9, 582
Sismondi, Jean Charles Léonard Simonde de: J. Adams reads, 268, 313; *Histoire des Républiques Italiennes du moyen âge*, 308, 313, 409
Sketch of the Life of Servetus (F. A. Van der Kemp), 138, 139n
Skipwith, George N.: and Central College subscription, 331
Skipwith, William: and Central College subscription, 331
Slaughter, John: and Central College subscription, 325, 330; and proposed Albemarle Co. road, 243
slavery: and African colonization, 7–8, 8–12, 60–1, 501; effects on society of, 9–10; and emancipation proposals, 7–8, 8–12, 60–1; TJ on, 60–1
slaves: behavior of, 626; corn for, 547; as drivers, 559; of J. W. Eppes, 14, 174, 292; errands by, 337, 365, 617; fugitive, 438–9, 522; T. Humphreys's plan for emancipation of, 7–8, 8–12, 60–1; medical treatment for, 497; taxes on, 44; TJ sells, 546, 547, 573; travels of, 178, 207; valuation of, 194; and work plans for Poplar Forest, 179, 475. *See also* slavery
slave trade: and Great Britain, 61n
Small, William (ship captain), 653
Smith, Mr. (of Albemarle Co.): and proposed Albemarle Co. road, 244, 245
Smith, Andrew: as partner in Smith & Riddle (Richmond firm), 112n, 137n
Smith, C. H.: as artist, 115n
Smith, Cary Ann Nicholas (John Spear Smith's wife; Wilson Cary Nicholas's daughter): family of, 627n
Smith, Charles (ship captain), 170
Smith, George S.: and Central College subscription, 332
Smith, James (of New York): letter from, 234–6; and New-York Historical Society, 234–5
Smith, John Spear: family of, 627n
Smith, Mary Mansfield. *See* Nicholas, Mary Mansfield Smith
Smith, Richard: as cashier of office of discount and deposit, 539
Smith, Thomas Loughton: identified, 529–30n; letter from, 528–30; letter to, 582; and Seventy-Six Association, 528–9, 582
Smith & Riddle (Richmond firm): identified, 112n; letter from, 137; letter to, 112; TJ orders goods from, 112, 137
Smyth, John B.: as clerk for W. Duane, 13
snakes: rattle, 631
snowberry, 174, 220
Society of Friends. *See* Quakers
Socrates: anecdote about, 491n
Il Sogno di Scipione (P. Metastasio), 229–32
Solís y Rivadeneira, Antonio de: *Historia de la Conquista de Mexico, poblacion, y Progresos de la America Septentrional, conocida por el nombre de Nueva España*, 179, 193, 395
Somnium Scipionis (Cicero), 232n
Southall, Valentine Wood: and Central College subscription, 330; identified, 173n; letters from, 172–3, 453; and proposed Albemarle Co. road, 172–3; as secretary of Central College Board of Visitors, 316, 318n, 319, 565; TJ's debt to, 380, 421, 451, 453, 464–5, 593, 605; visits Monticello, 327n
South America: immigrants to, 255, 457–8; republics in, 135, 384, 410, 412n; TJ on independence movement in, 354–5, 434
Southey, Robert: *Wat Tyler*, 384
Southwest Mountains: described, 628; and Rivanna River, 83, 90, 550
Spafford, Horatio Gates: as editor of *American Magazine*, 5–6, 278, 279n, 659; identified, 1:106n; inventions of, 6, 496; letters from, 5–6, 254, 266,

Spafford, Horatio Gates (*cont.*) 495–6; and J. Madison, 6, 62, 121; *The Mother-In-Law: or Memoirs of Madam de Morville*, 254, 266; moves to Pa., 495–6; national technology school proposed by, 6; and patents and patent system, 6; proposed Va. gazetteer by, 5
Spain: colonies of, 354–5, 410, 412n, 434; and U.S., 122, 219n, 410, 412n. *See also* Onís y González Vara López y Gómez, Luis de; Spanish language
Spanish language: dictionaries of, 335; study of, 233, 261; TJ on study of, 14, 18–9, 112, 175, 252; works in, 179, 193, 395
Spark, USS (brig), 509, 534n
Speech of Gideon Granger, Esq. delivered before a Convention of the People of Ontario County, N.Y. Jan. 8, 1817, on the subject of a Canal from Lake Erie to Hudson's River (G. Granger), 219n, 259
spirit level: use of, 55
Spirit of Laws. See *Esprit des Lois* (Montesquieu)
spirits (alcohol), 293
Spreafico, Amant: and consulship for J. V. A. Sasserno, 406–7, 657n, 657–8; letters from, to S. Cathalan, 656–7, 657–8; and wine for TJ, 404, 653–4, 656
springs: temperature of as climate indicator, 39–40; therapeutic, 666; visitors to, 625, 631n. *See also* Warm Springs (Bath Co.)
spruce: in Va., 624
Stadler, Joseph Constantine: print by, xlvii–xlviii, 232 (*illus.*)
Staël Holstein, Anne Louise Germaine Necker, baronne de: *Considérations sur les principaux événemens de La Révolution Françoise*, 116–8; death of, 540, 541n; family of, 117, 282–3; on France, 116–7; health of, 282–3; identified, 5:452–3n; and Lafayette, 117, 118n; letter from, 116–8; T. Lyman introduced to, 294n; on U.S., 116–7
Staël Holstein, Auguste Louis, baron de: proposed U.S. visit of, 117
Staphorst, N. & J. & R. van: identified, 9:581n; TJ's debt to, 290–1, 293, 304, 362, 366, 379, 380n, 380, 381n, 381, 395, 419
A Star in the West; or, A Humble Attempt to Discover the long lost Ten Tribes of Israel, preparatory to their return to their beloved city, Jerusalem (E. Boudinot), 49, 230
Stark, Edwin: identified, 10:448–9n; letters from, 195–6, 204–5; letter to, 137; and wine for TJ, 137, 144, 195, 204
State Department, U.S.: forwards letters, 421–2, 458, 462, 486, 585, 642–3, 667; and presidential succession, 145–6. *See also* Adams, John Quincy; Brent, Daniel
statement on the batture case (Thomas Jefferson). *See* The Proceedings of the Government of the United States, in maintaining the Public Right to the Beach of the Missisipi (Thomas Jefferson)
Statical Essays: containing Vegetable Staticks (S. Hales), 164
Staunton, Va.: chancery court at, 71, 72, 554n, 668; as potential location for state university, 134n, 257, 258
steamboats: paddles for, 497–9; A. M. Rochon on history of, 255, 457; for U.S. river navigation, 32, 65–6, 111, 435, 448, 565; in Va., 539; *Washington*, 523
steam engine, 6, 56
steel: and construction of TJ's canal, 73
Steele, John: as collector at Philadelphia, 118–9, 128, 531; identified, 2:506–7n
Stevenson, Elizabeth Goodwin (George P. Stevenson's wife): books recommended by, 627n
Stevenson, George Pitt: bankruptcy of, 540, 541n, 606; books recommended by, 627n; correspondence of, 461; identified, 5:659n
Stevenson, John B.: identified, 151–2n; introduced to TJ, 151
Sthreshly, Amelia Magruder (Robert B. Sthreshly's wife), 151
Sthreshly, Robert B.: identified, 6:554n; introduces L. S. Towles to TJ, 151; letter from, 151; property of, 151
stockings, 450
Stone, John (ship captain), 531
Storia della Guerra dell' Independenza degli Stati Uniti d'America (C. G. G. Botta), 313, 364, 452

Storrs, Hiram: identified, 561n; and land claims, 560–1; letter from, 560–1
stoves: at Barboursville, 225
Stow, Joshua: and Connecticut Society for the Encouragement of American Manufactures, 215; identified, 170n; letter from, 169–70; letter to, 215
straw, 483
strawberries: as crop, 39
Strobel, Daniel: as acting consul at Bordeaux, 652
Stuart, Archibald: identified, 2:93–4n; and *Jefferson v. Michie*, 208–10
Stuart, Gilbert: identified, 7:526–7n; "Medallion" profile of TJ by, 135, 266, 267n, 342, 387
Stuart, Josephus Bradner: on American people, 285–9; identified, 10:611n; letters from, 25–6, 242, 285–90; letters to, 65, 345–7; and publication of B. Franklin's papers, 289, 290n; sends news to TJ, 242; and TJ's public service, 285–9, 345; travels of, 25; on U.S. trade policy, 25, 65; visits Monticello, 25, 375, 376n
Sturgis, Russell: on Republican committee, 569–70n
Sturz, Friedrich Wilhelm: edits works of Cassius Dio, 415
stylograph, 535
subscriptions, for publications: atlases, 582–3; journals, 215, 486, 541, 599–600, 659; maps, 615–7; newspapers, 13, 425, 455, 456–7, 476, 523, 594, 594–6, 648, 649. *See also* books
subscriptions, non-publication: for Central College, 314–5, 471, 485, 486, 535, 546, 559, 561, 565–6, 590–1, 596, 636–7, 640, 650–1, 664–5
Suburb Saint Mary. *See* Batture Sainte Marie, controversy over
succory. *See* chicory (succory)
sugar: cane, 345; TJ orders, 617
Sulla: J. Adams on, 269
Sullivan, James: family of, 32
Sullivan, John Langdon: identified, 10:675–6n; letter to, 65–6; promotes inland navigation, 32, 65–6, 111; steam towboat of, 32, 65–6, 111
sundials: at Monticello, 432; sent to J. W. Eppes, 174; TJ's Instructions for Setting, 176. *See also* clocks
Superior Court of Chancery for the Staunton District, 554n, 668
surgery: study of, 11
Sur l'éducation nationale dans les États-Unis d'Amérique (P. S. Du Pont de Nemours), 638–40
The Surrender of General Burgoyne at Saratoga (J. Trumbull), 145, 166
The Surrender of Lord Cornwallis at Yorktown (J. Trumbull), 145, 166
surveying: at Central College, 544; and new map of Va., 49–50, 112, 396, 409. *See also* scientific instruments
swallows: migration of, 404
Swann, Samuel: as boundary commissioner, 22, 23n
Swedenborg, Emanuel: followers of, 363
Swedish iron, 11
Swift, Jonathan: *Travels into several Remote Nations of the World ... by Lemuel Gulliver*, 269
Switzerland: education in, 263–4, 266n; emigrants from, 198–9, 305, 413, 448–9, 449, 506
Sydenham, Thomas: and nosology, 367
Sylla. *See* Cornelius Sulla Felix, Lucius
Sylva, or a Discourse on Forest-Trees (J. Evelyn), 165
A Synopsis of the Four Evangelists (C. Thomson), 115–6
Systema Naturæ (C. Linnaeus), 367
System der christlichen Dogmatik nach dem Lehrbegriffe der luterischen Kirche im Grundrisse (J. C. W. Augusti), 307
A System of Notation: Representing the Sounds of Alphabetical Characters (W. Pelham), 177

Tableaux Historiques des Campagnes d'Italie, depuis l'an IV jusqu'a la bataille de Marengo (L. A. A. Chicoilet de Corbigny), 402
Tacitus: J. Adams on, 269; J. J. Oberlin edition of, 205, 296, 414
Tales of Fashionable Life (M. Edgeworth), 628n
Taliaferro, Francis W.: and Central College subscription, 334
Tanner, Benjamin: identified, 583n. *See also* Tanner, Vallance, Kearny, & Company (Philadelphia firm)
Tanner, Henry Schenck: identified, 583n. *See also* Tanner, Vallance, Kearny, & Company (Philadelphia firm)

Tanner, Vallance, Kearny, & Company (Philadelphia firm): atlas by, 582–3; identified, 583n; letter from, 582–3
Tarragona, Spain: U.S. consul at, 661
Tausy, Thomas: delivers goods, 503
taxes: on carriages, 44; on free whites, 44; in Great Britain, 24; on horses, 44; on imports, 26n; on land, 17, 44, 237, 238n, 472–5; on Natural Bridge, 237, 238n, 428, 589, 590n; on slaves, 44; Statement of Taxable Property in Albemarle County, 44–5; TJ on, 24; TJ pays, 44, 237, 428, 589
Taylor, Jane Elizabeth Catherine Hackley: greetings sent to, 624n
Taylor, John (of Caroline): *Arator: being a series of Agricultural Essays, Practical & Political*, 129, 165; and books on agriculture, 163n; identified, 10:89–90n
Taylor, Martha Jefferson Randolph (TJ's great-granddaughter; Thomas Jefferson Randolph's daughter): birth of, xlvi–xlvii; described, 627n; family of, 626n
Taylor, Thomas: and W. Byrd manuscripts, 450–1; identified, 8:130n
Taylor, Waller: as U.S. senator, 6, 56, 153
Taylor, William D.: identified, 237–8n; letter from accounted for, 582n; letter to, 237–8; and TJ's taxes, 237, 238n
Tazewell, Littleton Waller: identified, 2:350n; as Va. state representative, 586, 588n
tea: for Poplar Forest, 617
Teel, Lewis: and Central College subscription, 330
telescopes: pocket, 625; for surveying, 50
Terra: A Philosophical Discourse of Earth (J. Evelyn), 164
Terrell, Dabney Carr (TJ's sister Martha Jefferson Carr's grandson): correspondence of, 340–1, 412; family of, 340–1n; finances of, 412, 417, 539–40, 606; identified, 9:482n; studies in Geneva, 443–4
Terrell, James H.: and Central College subscription, 324, 330
Terrell, Lucy Carr (TJ's niece): family of, 412
Terrell, Martha Jefferson. *See* Minor, Martha Jefferson Terrell (TJ's sister Martha Jefferson Carr's granddaughter; Dabney Minor's second wife)
textiles: cotton, 11; flax, 11; hemp, 136; home manufacture of, 141; linen, 11; milkweed, 135–6. *See also* manufacturing; manufacturing, household
Thacker, Martin: and Central College subscription, 324, 330
Le Théâtre d'Agriculture et Mesnage des Champs (O. de Serres), 164
Théatre d'Aristophane, avec les fragmens de Ménandre et de Philémon (Aristophanes; trans. L. Poinsinet de Sivry), 352, 397, 456, 547, 592, 646
theodolite, 544
Theodoret: *Ἑλληνικῶν παθημάτων θεραπευτική*, 452
thermometers: TJ uses, 34
Theus, Simeon: as collector at Charleston, 131–2, 137–8; identified, 132n; letter from accounted for, 138n; letters to, 131–2, 137–8; and wine for TJ, 131–2, 137, 137–8
Thomas, John: and Central College subscription, 325, 330
Thomas, John L.: and Central College subscription, 325, 330; identified, 4:52–3n
Thomas, Norborne K.: and Central College subscription, 325, 334; identified, 5:277n
Thomas, Robert: *The Modern Practice of Physic*, 4
Thomas M. Randolph & Company (Shadwell Mills, Va.). *See also* Randolph, Thomas Eston (TJ's cousin); Randolph, Thomas Mann (*1768–1828*) (TJ's son-in-law; Martha Jefferson Randolph's husband)
Thompson, Benjamin. *See* Rumford, Benjamin Thompson, Count
Thompson, George (of Albemarle Co.): and Rivanna River navigation, 106
Thompson, John W.: on Republican committee of correspondence, 599n
Thompson, Roger: and Rivanna River navigation, 106
Thomson, Charles: health of, 29; identified, 9:342n; letter to, 29; *A Synopsis of the Four Evangelists*, 115–6; and TJ's religious beliefs, 29
thorn: as agricultural fence, 228
Thornton, Philip: identified, 8:96n; leases Natural Bridge from TJ, 237, 238n, 428, 642; letter to, 642; and shot manufactory, 642

Thornton, William: borrows paintings from TJ, 135, 266–7, 342, 387; and design of Central College, 315, 342–3, 387–90, 393; educational system proposed by, 390, 391n; identified, 1:466n; introduces T. Freeborn to TJ, 454, 462; letters from, 135–6, 266–7, 387–92, 454; letter to, 342–3; as patent office superintendent, 6, 135; portrait of TJ by, 135, 266, 267n; and sculpture of TJ, 267; sends publications to TJ, 135; Sketches for a Corinthian Pavilion, 393
Thornton, William M.: and Central College subscription, 331
Thorp, Mr., 15
Thoüin, André: on education, 263–4; on European interest in U.S., 264; identified, 1:202n; letter from, 263–6; sends seeds to TJ, 263; on viticulture, 264
threshing machines, 200
Thruston (TJ's slave; b. *1795*). *See* Hern, Thruston (TJ's slave; b. *1795*)
Thweatt, Archibald: and Central College subscription, 327n, 590–1; identified, 2:85n; letters from accounted for, 132n, 201n, 233n; letters to, 200–1, 590–2; and mill construction, 200; and petition of P. I. Barziza, 146, 147n; and proposed Albemarle Co. road, 59, 66, 119, 132, 133, 200
Thweatt, Lucy Eppes (Archibald Thweatt's wife): TJ sends greetings to, 201
Tibullus (Roman poet), 126
Ticknor, Elisha: and books for TJ, 414; forwards letters to and from TJ, 419, 634; identified, 8:584n; letter to, 419–20
Ticknor, George: and books for TJ, 255, 296, 408, 414–5, 455, 632; carries TJ's letters to Europe, 281, 355–6; on education in Europe, 633–4; identified, 8:242n; letter from, 632–4; letter to, 414–6; TJ on, 408; TJ's letters of introduction for, 634; travels of, 142, 419, 618–9, 632–3; visits Monticello, 639
ticks, 39
Tims, Charles: as assistant U.S. Senate doorkeeper, 182
Titi Livii Historiarum quod exstat (Livy; eds. J. Leclerc and J. Freinsheim), 414
T. Livii Patavini Historiarum libri qui supersunt (Livy; ed. G. A. Ruperti), 414
tobacco: as cash crop, 285; grown at Monticello, 236, 593; grown at Poplar Forest, 179, 207, 290, 380, 593; grown in Va., 62; leaf capitals, xlv–xlvi, 232 (*illus.*), 481, 535, 572; price of in Great Britain, 635; price of in Richmond, 142, 240, 261; sale of, 290, 362, 593; shipment of, 104
Tobias, Morris: as watchmaker, 507
Todd, John Payne: identified, 4:188–9n; and W. Thornton, 267n; and walking stick for TJ, 167
Tomahawk plantation (part of TJ's Poplar Forest estate): overseer at, 285
Tompkins, Daniel D.: circular sent to, 595; identified, 7:370n; and party politics, 490–1
Toole, John: portrait of L. M. L. Marks, xlvii, 232 (*illus.*)
tools: and African colonization, 11; hoes, 163; levels, 176; planes, 176; rafter levels, 162–4; squares, 176
toothbrushes, 626n
tooth powder, 626n
Τὸ Περὶ Ἀέρων, Ὑδάτων, Τόπων (Hippocrates; ed. A. Coray), 251
A Tour in Holland, in MDCCLXXXIV (E. Watson), 277, 279n
Tourneyzon, Mr., 653
towels, 626n
Towles, Larkin Smith: identified, 151n; introduced to TJ, 151
Townsend, Absalom: and *American Magazine*, 659; identified, 659n; letter from, 659
Tracy. *See* Destutt de Tracy, Antoine Louis Claude
Traduction d'Anciens Ouvrages Latins relatifs à l'Agriculture et à la Médicine Vétérinaire, avec des Notes (Saboureux de La Bonnetrie), 164
Traduction des œuvres médicales d'Hippocrate, sur le texte grec, d'après l'édition de Foës (Hippocrates; ed. D. J. Tournon; trans. J. B. Gardeil), 127, 152, 175, 193, 297, 395
Les Tragédies d'Euripide (Euripides; trans. P. Prévost), 179, 193
Traité Complet sur les Abeilles (Della Rocca), 165
Traité d'Économie Politique (J. B. Say), 356

Traité de la Culture du Figuier, suivi d'observations & d'expériences sur la meilleure maniere de cultiver (La Brousse), 165
Traité de la volonté et de ses effets (Destutt de Tracy), 359
Traité sur la nature et sur la culture de la Vigne (N. Bidet and H. L. Duhamel Du Monceau), 164
Traité sur les Bêtes-à-Laine d'Espagne (C. P. De Lasteyrie), 164
Traité théorique et pratique sur la Culture de la Vigne (J. A. Chaptal, A. A. Parmentier, F. Rozier, and L. d'Ussieux), 164
Transactions of the Society, instituted in the State of New-York, for the promotion of Agriculture, Arts, and Manufactures, 165
Trattato di Piero Vettori delle lodi e della coltivazione degli ulivi (P. Vettori), 164
Travels during the years 1787, 1788 and 1789 (A. Young), 165, 308–9
Travels in North America in the Years 1780, 1781 and 1782 (Chastellux), 370n
Travels into several Remote Nations of the World . . . by Lemuel Gulliver (J. Swift), 269
Travels to discover the Source of the Nile, In the Years 1768, 1769, 1770, 1771, 1772, and 1773 (J. Bruce), 612–4, 650
Travis, Champion: and P. Poinsot's land grant, 474n
Treasury Department, U.S.: and government stock, 27, 57, 58n, 124–5, 155, 187. *See also* Dallas, Alexander James; Gallatin, Albert
A Treatise of Equity (Fonblanque), 70, 97n, 98n
A Treatise on Agriculture and Rural Affairs (R. Brown), 165, 228
A Treatise on Gardening (J. Randolph), 165
A Treatise on Political Economy (Destutt de Tracy), 13, 26, 67, 109–10, 140, 205, 248, 356, 359–60, 362, 573, 574n, 618, 619n
A Treatise on the Culture and Management of Fruit Trees: in which A New Method of Pruning and Training is Fully Described (W. Forsyth), 165
A Treatise on the Culture of the Apple & Pear, and on the Manufacture of Cider & Perry (T. A. Knight), 165
A Treatise on the Pleadings in Suits in the Court of Chancery, by English Bill (J. F. Mitford), 70
trees: almond, 39; cedar, 566; cherry, 39; chestnut, 624; chinaberry, 179; dogwood, 39; fig, 219, 220n; fringe, 39; locust, bristly, 174, 219–20; locust, common, 39; Lombardy poplar, 218, 219; maple, red, 39; mulberry, 218, 219; oak, 624; olive, 168; peach, 39; poplar, 624; redbud, 39; spruce, 624
Trent, Stephen Woodson: and Central College subscription, 331
Treutell and Würtz (publishers), 414
Trinci, Cosimo: *L'Agricoltore Sperimentato*, 164
Triplett, Hedgman: and P. Poinsot's land grant, 474n
Trist, Virginia Jefferson Randolph (TJ's granddaughter): identified, 10:492n; letters to, from C. J. Randolph, 622–4, 628–30, 631–2; and music, 626n; visits springs, 631n
Le Trône Enchanté, Conte Indien traduit du Persan (D. Lescallier), 351n
Trueheart, George W.: and Central College subscription, 333
Trumbull, John (artist): *The Declaration of Independence*, 145, 166; friendship with TJ, 160, 166; historical paintings of, 3, 135, 145, 166; identified, 10:616n; letter from, 166–7; *The Resignation of General Washington*, 145, 166; *The Surrender of General Burgoyne at Saratoga*, 145, 166; *The Surrender of Lord Cornwallis at York-town*, 145, 166
trusses, 497
Tucker, Abraham: J. Adams reads, 268
Tucker, Henry St. George: and Central College subscription, 334, 636
Tucker, St. George: and Central College subscription, 334; delivers message, 546; identified, 1:617n; as legal authority, 369
Tufton (TJ's Albemarle Co. estate): T. J. Randolph resides at, xlvi–xlvii, 404, 407n
Tull, Jethro: *Horse-Hoeing Husbandry: or, An Essay on the Principles of Vegetation and Tillage*, 164; TJ on, 308
Tupputi, Dominique: *Réflexions Succinctes sur l'état de l'Agriculture, et de*

quelques autres parties de l'administration, dans le Royaume de Naples, sous Ferdinand IV, 164
Turgot, Anne Robert Jacques: biography of, 527
Tuscany, Italy: wine from, 131
twinleaf. See *Jeffersonia diphylla* (twinleaf)
Tyler, Benjamin Owen: introduced to TJ, 217
Tyler, Walter (Wat) (leader of English peasant revolt): works on, 384

Über die Geschichte der Menschheit (I. Iselin), 422, 423–5
Unitarianism: mentioned, 363
United States: citizenship, 146–7; economy of, 287–8; elections in, 410, 412; future of considered, 437; and government stock, 27, 57, 58n, 124–5, 155, 187; and Great Britain, 417; history of proposed, 460–1; public works, 122, 123n, 410–1; reputation of, 540; state papers and public documents, 560–1; TJ on life in, 160, 435; trade of, 25, 26n, 65. *See also* Bank of the United States, Second; Congress, U.S.; Constitution, U.S.; *specific departments*
United States (ship), 255
United States, USS (frigate), 509, 534n, 662
Universalkirchenhistorie des Christenthums (P. K. Marheinecke), 307
Urtica Whitlowi. See nettle, wood
Ussieux, Louis d': *Traité théorique et pratique sur la Culture de la Vigne*, 164

Valck, Adriaan: Dutch consul at Baltimore, 472
Vallance, John: identified, 583n. *See also* Tanner, Vallance, Kearny, & Company (Philadelphia firm)
Valli, Eusebio Giacinto: funeral oration for, 377, 378n, 428; identified, 9:208n
Valltone, P. de: as S. Cathalan's alleged relation, 542, 543n, 584; identified, 543n; letters from, 542–3, 545; proposes to settle in Alabama Territory, 542–3, 545; visits Monticello, 542–3
Van der Kemp, Francis Adrian: friendship with J. Adams, 48, 230–1, 232n; health of, 47; identified, 4:501n; letters from, 47–9, 138–9, 229–32, 422–3; letters to, 201–2, 307–8; and proposed book, 47–8; proposed work on Jesus, 201, 307–8, 422; scholarship of, 230–1; sends work to TJ, 422, 423–5; *Sketch of the Life of Servetus*, 138, 139n; Synopsis of a Proposed Book, 422, 423n; and TJ's syllabus of Jesus's doctrines, 138, 139n, 201, 230, 307
Vanderlyn, John: portrait of J. Monroe, xlv, 232 (*illus.*)
Van der Marck, Frederik Adolf: as Dutch educator, 230, 232n
van Staphorst, N. & J. & R. *See* Staphorst, N. & J. & R. van
van Staphorst & Hubbard (Amsterdam firm): TJ's bonds to, 293, 419
Varnum, Joseph Bradley: as U.S. senator, 182, 183n, 214
Varro (Marcus Terentius Varro): mentioned, 162; *Rei rusticae*, 164
Vattel, Emmerich von: as legal authority, 368, 369
Vaughan, John: account with TJ, 291, 304, 380, 395, 398, 454, 574; and American Philosophical Society, 398, 454, 486–7, 501, 574; handles financial transactions, 585; identified, 1:453n; letters from, 398, 454–5, 574; letters to, 420, 486–7, 585; makes payments for TJ, 237, 578, 580, 645; TJ sends letters through, 420, 642–3; and TJ's lines of credit in Europe, 404, 406, 408, 409n, 418, 420, 652; transmits goods to TJ, 398, 501
veal, 240
venetian blinds, 650
Vernet, Antoine Charles Horace (Carle): prints after drawings of, 402
Vest, Charles: as postmaster at Milton, 110, 193, 204, 205
veterinary science: study of, 191–2
Vettori, Pietro: *Trattato di Piero Vettori delle lodi e della coltivazione degli ulivi*, 164
Vie de Monsieur Turgot (Condorcet), 527
Vienna, Congress of: negotiations at, 540, 541n
Villemain, Abel François: lectures of, 634
Villers, Charles François Dominique de: *Coup-D'Oeil sur L'État Actuel de la Litterature Ancienne et de l'Histoire en Allemagne*, 414–5

Villoison, Jean Baptiste Gaspard d'Ansse de: edits *Ὁμήρου Ἰλιὰς σὺν τοῖς σχολίοις* (Homer), 414
Virgil: J. Adams on, 269; *Aeneid*, 346; C. G. Heyne edition of, 205, 296, 414
Virginia: Act for establishing Religious Freedom, 411–2, 415–6; banks in, 67; boundary of with N.C., 21–2, 125–6, 206, 477, 487, 524; citizenship laws in, 146–7; climate of, 412; Council of State, 134n; crops in, 483; elections in, 292; and federal political positions, 145–6; General Assembly, 45n, 59, 69, 75, 103, 103–4, 104–9, 119, 120, 147n, 194, 256, 257, 258, 321, 411–2, 415–6; governor, 133n, 134n; House of Burgesses, 202; House of Delegates, 19, 66–7, 79, 119, 132, 134n, 139, 146; land grants in, 398–9, 472–5; laws of, 352, 517, 520n; Literary Fund, 134n, 315; maps of, xlii–xliii (*illus.*), 283; Ratification Convention of *1788*, 503; revision of laws, 133, 432–4; road proposed in, 133, 243–4; roads in, 132, 200, 244–5; Senate, 67, 79, 119n, 134n, 146, 275; Superior Courts of Chancery, 71, 72, 82–3, 102; surveys of, 49–50, 112, 396, 409. *See also* Bank of Virginia (Richmond); Barbour, James; Central College; *The History of Virginia* (J. D. Burk, S. Jones, and L. H. Girardin); Mutual Assurance Society; *Notes on the State of Virginia* (Thomas Jefferson); *Richmond Enquirer* (newspaper); Virginia, University of
Virginia, University of: founding of, 133–4n, 314–5; Pavilion VII, 315. *See also* Albemarle Academy; Central College
viticulture: in U.S., 264. *See also* grapes; wine
Vitruvius: *Abregé des dix livres d'architecture de Vitruve* (ed. C. Perrault), 335, 352, 396, 456
Volney, Constantin François Chasseboeuf, comte de: *Recherches Nouvelles sur L'Histoire Ancienne*, 612–4, 650; *The Ruins: or A Survey of the Revolutions of Empires*, 614
Voyage de découvertes aux terres Australes (F. Péron), 627, 628n
Voyage de La Troade, Fait dans les années 1785 et 1786 (J. B. Lechevalier), 632
Waddell, James Gordon: and Central College subscription, 331
Walker, Francis: and Rivanna River Company, 109n
Walker, John (of Albemarle Co.): and Central College subscription, 331
Walker, Robert: and Central College subscription, 636
Walker, Thomas (*1715–94*): as Va. legislator, 106
Walsh, Michael H.: letter from, 251; visits Monticello, 251
Walsh, Robert: editor of *American Register, or General Repository of History, Politics and Science*, 178n; editor of *American Register; or Summary Review of History, Politics, and Literature*, 178, 215, 635–6; identified, 178n; letters from, 178, 635–6; letter to, 215; translates *Complot d'Arnold* (Barbé Marbois), 635–6; travels with J. Corrêa da Serra, 639
Walton, Thomas N.: and Central College subscription, 331
Warden, David Bailie: and books for TJ, 255, 408, 414, 417, 418, 454, 501, 618, 632; as claims agent, 417, 418n; identified, 1:141n; letters from, 255–6, 618–9; letter to, 417–8; *Prospectus of a Statistical and Historical Account of the United States of America*, 619; sends publications to TJ, 444
War Department, U.S.: books for, 452; and papers of Lewis and Clark Expedition, 487. *See also* Calhoun, John Caldwell
Warm Springs (Bath Co.): TJ on, 666
War of *1812*: Battle of Chippewa, 494; British destruction in Washington, 480; compensation claims related to, 122, 123n; and economy, 284; and military preparations, 493; *A Scriptural View of the Character, Causes, and Ends of the Present War* (A. McLeod), 159; TJ on, 353–4; U.S. capture of Fort George, 494; U.S. capture of York, 494
Washington, D.C.: and Columbian Institute for the Promotion of Arts and Sciences, 143–4n, 148–9; proposed botanical garden in, 136, 143n, 144n; slaves run away to, 438–9, 522; stagecoach from, 413. *See also* Capitol,

U.S.; *National Intelligencer* (Washington newspaper)
Washington, Bushrod: and American Colonization Society, 61n; as legal authority, 369
Washington, George: J. Adams on, 46; on board of agriculture, 279n; bust of, at Monticello, 406; *An Oration In commemoration of the birth of General Washington* (J. W. Maury), 156, 157n, 260; portraits of, 145, 166; praised, 286–7, 290n, 489–90, 570n, 572; as president, 60, 502, 511; retirement from presidency, 510; statue of for N.C. state capitol, 171; and W. Thornton's educational system, 390, 391n; TJ on, 260
Washington (steamboat), 523
Washington, USS, 509, 534n
Washington Academy (later Washington and Lee University). *See* Washington College (later Washington and Lee University)
Washington and Lee University. *See* Washington College (later Washington and Lee University)
Washington College (later Washington and Lee University), 134n
watches: needing repair, 365; sold for L. A. Leschot, 507–8
Waterloo, Battle of (*1815*), 282
Watkins, Benjamin P.: and Central College subscription, 332
Watkins, Joseph S.: and Central College subscription, 332
Watkins, Thomas B.: and Central College subscription, 332
Watkins, Thomas G.: introduced to TJ, 184–5
Watkins, William H.: and Central College subscription, 331
Watson, Mr. (of Milton): delivers goods, 588
Watson, David: witnesses bond, 419n
Watson, David (*1773–1830*): and Agricultural Society of Albemarle, 319; and Central College subscription, 333; health of, 229, 242, 257, 258; identified, 181–2n; letter from, 242; letters to, 181–2, 232, 561; visits Monticello, 258. *See also* Central College, Board of Visitors
Watson, Elkanah: identified, 278–9n; letter from, 277–9; letter to, 338–9; national board of agriculture proposed by, 277–9, 338; *A Tour in Holland, in MDCCLXXXIV*, 277, 279n
Watson, Hugh: and Central College subscription, 331
Watson, James: and Central College subscription, 333
Watson, John (of Little Mountain): and Central College subscription, 326, 330
Watson, William: and Central College subscription, 323, 330; identified, 4:543n
Watts, William (of Bristol, England): and shot manufacture, 177n
Wat Tyler (R. Southey), 384
Wayt, Twyman: as assignee, 573n
Wayt & Winn (Charlottesville firm): as assignee, 573n
weather: clouds, 37; cold, 62, 111, 121–3, 135, 178–9, 412; drought, 179, 207, 236, 284, 290, 644; effect on crops, 121, 179, 236, 271, 290, 385; floods, 72, 606, 614, 626n; lightning rods, 341–2, 469–70; rain, 36–7, 38, 162–3, 207, 309; snow, 36–7, 38, 62; thermometer readings, 33–4; TJ on climate, 33–40; TJ's Analysis of Weather Memorandum Book, 33–40; in Va., 460; wind, 38. *See also* meteorological observations
weaving. *See* textiles
Wedgwood, Ralph: stylograph of, 535
Weekly Register. See *Niles' Weekly Register* (Baltimore newspaper)
Weissenfels, Elizabeth Williams Bogart: family of, 660, 662
Weissenfels, Frederick, baron de: family of, 662
Wellesley, Richard Wellesley, Marquess: as British foreign minister, 242n
Wellington, Arthur Wellesley, 1st Duke of (formerly Viscount): and Louis XVIII, 282
Wells, Thomas: and Central College subscription, 322, 333, 335n; forwards letters, 575; and goods for TJ, 452; identified, 240–1n; letter from, 240–1; and livestock for TJ, 240
Wells's Hotel (Charlottesville), 545
Wendover, Peter Hercules: identified, 8:229n; letter from, 159; on A. McLeod, 159; sends book to TJ, 159

Wertenbaker, Christian: and Central College subscription, 331
Wertenbaker, William: as Albemarle Co. clerk, 467n, 469
West, Benjamin: compared to J. Trumbull, 3; *The Fright of Astyanax*, 135, 266, 342, 387
Westham, Va.: plan and survey of, 385; TJ's lots in, 366, 378–9, 385
West Indies: U.S. trade with, 122
Whaler, Benjamin: witnesses document, 573n
wheat: as cash crop, 194, 195, 285, 298–9; as crop, 39, 172, 385; cultivated in northern states, 270–1; effect of weather on, 62, 111, 121, 236; ground at Shadwell mills, 185–6, 210–1; Lawler, 536–7, 588; at Monticello, 475, 644; at Poplar Forest, 207; red-bearded, 588; smut damages, 304, 536, 588
Wheat, Rezin: identified, 439n; and runaway slave, 438–9, 522
whip-poor-wills, 39
whiskey: potato, 272–3
Whiston, William: translates *The Genuine Works of Flavius Josephus* (Josephus), 303
Whitefield, George: mentioned, 363
Whitehead, David: on Episcopal Church, 607; identified, 607–8n; letter from, 607–8; recommendation of, by A. Clark, 608
White House. *See* President's House
Whitehurst, Arthur: and Central College subscription, 331
whites: taxes on, 44
Whitlow, Charles: identified, 4:427–8n; and proposed Washington botanical garden, 135–6; and wood nettle, 135–6
Wickham, John: gives legal opinion, 478, 479n, 486; identified, 2:395–6n
Wilberforce, William: TJ's beliefs compared to, 118n
Wilkinson, James: identified, 3:325n; *Memoirs of My Own Times*, 364
William and Mary, College of: and state university for Va., 134n; TJ attends, 252
Williams, Jonathan: identified, 3:94–5n; letter to, from A. Partridge, 52–4; and velocity of military projectiles, 51, 52–4
Williams, Samuel (of London): family of, 294
Willis, Harriet Fluker Randolph: mentioned, 624n, 628
Willis's Mountain: TJ takes latitude of, 174
Willoughby, Westel: as U.S. representative from N.Y., 48
Wills, Horatio: and Central College subscription, 325, 332
Wilson, D. A.: and Central College subscription, 332
Winchester Gazette (newspaper): sent to TJ, 503, 504n
Winchester, Va.: newspapers in, 503, 504n
wine: Bellet, 246, 404, 405, 407, 656, 657n; brandy added to, 296, 300, 345; Casanuova di Ama, 171, 579–80; claret, 405, 407; clarification of, 5; of Florence, 131–2, 137, 247; Hermitage, 246, 405, 531; of Lédenon, 246, 404, 405, 407, 531, 653; Montepulciano, 247, 579–80; of Nice, 246, 404, 405, 407, 531; of Pailherols, 531; port, 246; of Rivesaltes, 246, 532, 584; of Roussillon, 246, 404, 405, 407, 531, 532, 584, 653; scuppernong, 50, 156, 175, 218, 219, 237, 238, 292, 295–6, 300, 302, 345; sent to TJ, 131, 131–2, 137, 137–8, 144, 195, 204, 218, 238, 406, 656; tariff on, 246; TJ orders from H. G. Burton, 50, 156, 175, 238, 292, 300; TJ orders from S. Cathalan, 404–6, 407, 420, 531–2, 652–4, 656; TJ recommends to J. Monroe, 246–7, 276; of Tuscany, 131; white, 653, 654n. *See also* grapes; viticulture
Winn, John (d. *1837*): and Albemarle Academy, 253; and Central College subscription, 323, 331; identified, 2:201n
Winn, John (of Fluvanna Co.): and Central College subscription, 325, 332
Winston, Edmund: and Central College subscription, 636
Winston, John G.: and H. Marks's estate, 44, 567
Wirt, William: gives legal opinion, 478, 479n, 486; identified, 1:341–2n
Wistar, Caspar: and American Philosophical Society, 376, 427; and B. Franklin's correspondence, 375, 426–7; health of, 289; identified, 1:101n; introduces J. B. Stevenson, 151; letters from, 151–2, 375–6; letter

to, 426–7; proposed visit to Monticello of, 375, 427
witchcraft: alleged practitioners executed, 270–1
Wolcot, John: referenced, 507, 508n
Wolcott, Oliver (*1760–1833*): as governor of Conn., 270n, 354, 355n
wolves: in Va., 631
women: accounts with: M. A. W. Bacon, 421n, 451–2; education of, 134n, 670; letters from: A. S. Adams, 294; E. W. R. Coolidge to M. J. Randolph, 625–6, 626–8; C. J. Randolph to M. E. R. Eppes, 631–2; C. J. Randolph to V. J. R. Trist, 622–4, 628–30, 631–2; Madame de Staël Holstein, 116–8; letters to: A. S. Adams, 357; Madame de Corny, 160–1; M. E. R. Eppes from C. J. Randolph, 631–2; L. M. L. Marks, 198; M. J. Randolph, 641, 669–70; M. J. Randolph from E. W. R. Coolidge, 625–6, 626–8; V. J. R. Trist from C. J. Randolph, 622–4, 628–30, 631–2
wood: firewood, 20; for furniture, 307, 548. *See also* building materials
Wood, Drury: and Central College subscription, 324, 331
Wood, James (of Albemarle Co.): and Central College subscription, 331
Wood, Jethro: identified, 10:428n; letter to, 216; plow of, 216, 462
Wood, John (ca. *1775–1822*): and Central College, 303, 335–6, 396; and education of F. Eppes, 49, 50, 175, 233–4, 261, 292, 396, 409; health of, 396; identified, 2:96n; letters from, 49–50, 395–6; letters to, 112–3, 261, 335–6; and New London Academy, 280, 335; Richmond school of, 18–9, 49, 59, 112–3, 233–4, 261, 292; and surveying instruments, 50, 112; as Va. state surveyor, 396, 409
Wood, John T.: identified, 10:103n; and Milton lands, 42
Wood, Lucy Henderson (Bennett Henderson's daughter; John T. Wood's wife): and Milton lands, 18, 19, 20, 42–3, 56–7
Wood, Thomas (of Albemarle Co.): and Central College subscription, 331
Woodlawn (L. Lewis's Fairfax Co. estate): construction of, 389, 391n
Woods, George M.: and Central College subscription, 331
Woods, Micajah: and Central College subscription, 323, 331; as justice of Albemarle Co. court, 467n
Woods, Michael: and Central College subscription, 333
Woods, Richard: and Central College subscription, 331
Woods, William (ca. *1777–1849*): and Agricultural Society of Albemarle, 319; and Central College subscription, 331; identified, 9:662n; as justice of Albemarle Co. court, 467n
Woodson, Charles: and Central College subscription, 332
Woodson, J. B.: and Central College subscription, 332
Woodson, Tarlton: and Central College subscription, 332
The Works of Dr. Benjamin Franklin, in Philosophy, Politics, and Morals (ed. W. Duane), 289, 290n, 376n
worms: damage crops, 482
Wright, Benjamin: and Erie Canal, 358n
Wythe, George: and revision of Va. laws, 133

Yancey, Charles: identified, 2:405n; letters from, 119, 139; and proposed Albemarle Co. road, 59, 119, 133, 139, 200; as Va. legislator, 172
Yancey, Elizabeth Macon (wife of Joel Yancey [d. *1833*]): visits Poplar Forest, 625, 627
Yancey, Joel (d. *1833*): and builders for Central College, 558; and Central College subscription, 333; identified, 4:318n; letters from accounted for, 207n, 594n; letters to, 178–9, 207, 475; as superintendent of Poplar Forest, 178–9, 207, 236, 475, 593
Yellow Dick (TJ's slave; b. *1767*). *See* Dick (Yellow Dick) (TJ's slave; b. *1767*)
York, Mr.: as J. Monroe's farm manager, 421
York (now Toronto), Upper Canada: U.S. capture of, 494
Young, Arthur: *Annals of Agriculture and Other Useful Arts*, 165; *A Course of Experimental Agriculture*, 165; *The Farmer's Guide in Hiring and Stocking Farms*, 165; *Rural Oeconomy: or, Essays on the Practical Parts of Husbandry*, 165; TJ on, 308; *Travels*

Young, Arthur (*cont.*)
  during the years 1787, 1788 and 1789, 165, 308–9
The Young Mill-wright & Miller's Guide (O. Evans), 352

Zimmermann, Ernst: edits *Euripidis Dramata* (Euripides), 415
zoology: museum of, 190; and New-York Historical Society, 190–3
Zwingli, Huldrych: mentioned, 424

THE PAPERS OF THOMAS JEFFERSON are composed in Monticello, a font based on the "Pica No. 1" created in the early 1800s by Binny & Ronaldson, the first successful typefounding company in America. The face is considered historically appropriate for The Papers of Thomas Jefferson because it was used extensively in American printing during the last quarter-century of Jefferson's life, and because Jefferson himself expressed cordial approval of Binny & Ronaldson types. It was revived and rechristened Monticello in the late 1940s by the Mergenthaler Linotype Company, under the direction of C. H. Griffith and in close consultation with P. J. Conkwright, specifically for the publication of the Jefferson Papers. The font suffered some losses in its first translation to digital format in the 1980s to accommodate computerized typesetting. Matthew Carter's reinterpretation in 2002 restores the spirit and style of Binny & Ronaldson's original design of two centuries earlier.